Readings in Microeconomics

Readings in Microeconomics

WILLIAM BREIT, Ph.D.

Trinity University,
San Antonio, Texas

HAROLD M. HOCHMAN, Ph.D.

Baruch College and the Graduate School and
University Center, City University of New York,
New York, New York

EDWARD SAUERACKER, Ph.D.

Bernard Baruch College,
City University of New York,
New York, New York

with 100 *illustrations*

TIMES MIRROR/MOSBY
COLLEGE PUBLISHING

St. Louis   Toronto   Santa Clara   1986

Manuscript Editor: Connie Leinicke (Top Graphics)
Book Designer: Joanne Kluba (Top Graphics)
Cover Designer: Christine Leonard Raquepaw
Production: Billie Forshee (Top Graphics)

Library of Congress Cataloging in Publication Data

Main entry under title:

Readings in microeconomics.

   1. Microeconomics—Addresses, essays, lectures.
I. Breit, William. II. Hochman, Harold M.
III. Saueracker, Edward.
HB172.R33 1986   338.5   85-21398
ISBN 0-8016-0795-7

GW/VH/VH 9 8 7 6 5 4 3 2 1   02/C/251

Foreword

It is important that students be exposed to the writings of leading economists at the earliest possible stage in their specialization. There is a knowledge and wisdom in scholarly publications not reproducible in a textbook, no matter how high its quality. The text, indispensable as it is in basic courses, must by its nature be thorough in its coverage and cannot have the liveliness obtained by concentrating on a limited area. The value of a volume of readings is indeed confirmed by the fact that this book is currently undergoing this revision.

The readings to supplement a basic course in microeconomics should not, of course, deal with the finer points of theory or subtle empirical analyses appropriate to more advanced work. The aim is to show leading minds grappling with the fundamentals of the subject. What is economics all about? How does it assess evidence and come to conclusions? What do the basic concepts of the subject—demand, supply, and utility—mean? How does one identify them with empirically observed magnitudes? How can the applicability of these concepts be tested, and what uses can be made of them in interpreting economic phenomena? Not only must the general concepts be scrutinized, but also the ways in which they can be used for analyzing particular economic problems, especially the structure of markets.

The editors of this book have chosen a varied menu, which yet makes up a well-composed feast. Relatively old papers, going back even to the 1930s, mingle with papers of the last few years. Most of the essays are in the mainstream neoclassical tradition, but some, such as those of Leibenstein and Williamson, represent sharply varying views. Not all the economists listed are equally well known, but all the papers are of high quality. The student will learn that in a field with high standards, the reputation of the author is not necessary for the interest and intellectual power of the paper.

The student will indeed see a variety of insights into fundamentals, demand, supply, the meaning of economic welfare, and its institutional realization. Although these topics are at the foundations, our understanding is still evolving. But even at this stage in the student's career, he or she will learn about relatively new developments, about the economic problems of the allocation of time, and about rational economic responses to the problem of acquiring information and the presence of actors with differing degrees of knowledge. The field, as presented in this book, is seen as developing, not as a static body of received doctrine.

KENNETH J. ARROW

Acknowledgments

This revision of our previous edition, which was published in 1971, would never have reached the drawing board were it not for the encouragement of several colleagues and the effort put into the process of constructive suggestion by many of our friends. In the first category, special mention is due David Colander, Arnold Harberger, and the late Abba Lerner. In the latter we note, with but alphabetical distinction, Thomas Barthold, Thomas Borcherding, Edgar Browning, William Dougan, Kenneth Elzinga, and Ronald Warren. In addition, we wish to recognize our special debt to Kenneth Arrow, both for his suggestions, which were (as one would expect) first class and for agreeing, as the editorial advisor to The C.V. Mosby Company, to write the Foreword.

Needless to say, with a project of this kind, staff help with seemingly endless detail is critical. For such assistance we thank the support staff of the Center for the Study of Business and Government at Baruch College and, in particular, Jean Cracchiolo, Donna Lambert, Susan Massaro, and Eva Mattina. We hope that the current generation of economics students finds this edition of *Readings in Microeconomics* as useful as the earlier editions seem to have been to prior cohorts. Their comments, frequently registered in a passing comment at a professional meeting, have been a continuing source of gratification, and did much to rekindle our interest in this project.

WILLIAM BREIT
HAROLD M. HOCHMAN
EDWARD SAUERACKER

Contents

Part 1   Nature and Method of Economics

Social Economic Organization, 1
FRANK H. KNIGHT

The Methodology of Positive
Economics, 14
MILTON FRIEDMAN

Part 2   Demand and Supply

DEMAND AND UTILITY THEORY

The Marshallian Demand Curve, 35
MILTON FRIEDMAN

The Marshallian Demand Curve, 44
MARTIN J. BAILEY

Cardinal Utility, 51
ROBERT H. STROTZ

The Testability of the Law of
Demand, 60
YORAM BARZEL

Demand Curves for
Animal Consumers, 69
JOHN H. KAGEL, RAYMOND C. BATTALIO, HOWARD
C. RACHLIN, and LEONARD GREEN

De Gustibus Non Est Disputandum, 78
GEORGE J. STIGLER and GARY S. BECKER

Toward a Positive Theory of Consumer
Choice, 92
RICHARD THALER

A New Approach to Consumer
Theory, 105
KELVIN J. LANCASTER

SUPPLY AND THE THEORY OF
THE FIRM

The Basis of Some Recent Advances
in the Theory of Management of the
Firm, 124
ARMEN A. ALCHIAN

The Short Run Revisited, 131
LOUIS DE ALESSI

On the Economics of Transfer
Pricing, 139
JACK HIRSHLEIFER

Allocative Efficiency vs. "X-Efficiency,"
149
HARVEY LEIBENSTEIN

Hierarchical Control and Optimum
Firm Size, 164
OLIVER E. WILLIAMSON

**Part 3   Recent Advances in the Theory of
Resource Allocation**

INFORMATION AND TIME

The Economics of Information, 176
GEORGE J. STIGLER

A Theory of the Allocation of
Time, 186
GARY S. BECKER

Production, Information Costs, and
Economic Organization, 203
ARMEN A. ALCHIAN and HAROLD DEMSETZ

A Theory of Rationing by Waiting, 218
YORAM BARZEL

The Theory of Discrimination, 232
KENNETH J. ARROW

CONTRACTUAL ARRANGEMENTS
AND MARKET OUTCOMES

Transaction Costs, Risk Aversion, and
the Choice of Contractual
Arrangements, 246
STEVEN N.S. CHEUNG

A Neo-Classical Theory of Keynesian
Unemployment, 258
DONALD F. GORDON

CHOICE UNDER DIFFERENTIAL
INFORMATION

The Market for "Lemons": Quality
Uncertainty and the Market
Mechanism, 276
GEORGE A. AKERLOF

The Economics of Moral Hazard:
Comment, 284
MARK V. PAULY

Job Market Signaling, 289
A. MICHAEL SPENCE

Part 4   *Theory of Market Structures*
CONCEPTS OF MARKET
STRUCTURES

Economic Theory and the Meaning of
Competition, 302
PAUL J. McNULTY

The Concept of Monopoly and the
Measurement of Monopoly Power, 313
ABBA P. LERNER

Multiple-Plant Firms, Cartels, and
Imperfect Competition, 327
DON PATINKIN

APPLICATIONS OF THE THEORY
OF MARKET STRUCTURES

Why Regulate Utilities? 344
HAROLD DEMSETZ

Antitrust Penalties and Attitudes
Toward Risk: An Economic
Analysis, 351
WILLIAM BREIT and KENNETH G. ELZINGA

Contestable Markets: An Uprising in
the Theory of Industry Structure, 363
WILLIAM J. BAUMOL

Part 5   *General Equilibrium, Welfare,
and Allocation*

The Organization of Economic Activity:
Issues Pertinent to the Choice of
Market versus Nonmarket
Allocation, 377
KENNETH J. ARROW

The Simple Analytics of Welfare
Maximization, 389
FRANCIS M. BATOR

The Problem of Social Cost, 414
RONALD COASE

Diagrammatic Exposition of a Theory
of Public Expenditure, 441
PAUL A. SAMUELSON

An Economic Theory of Clubs, 449
JAMES M. BUCHANAN

Externality, 458
JAMES M. BUCHANAN and WILLIAM CRAIG
STUBBLEBINE

Pareto-Optimal Redistribution, 468
HAROLD M. HOCHMAN and JAMES D. RODGERS

Introduction

Price theory, unlike Picassos, chamber music, or giraffes, is not to be admired for its own sake. Rather, it is something utilitarian, like hammers, screwdrivers, and wrenches, that makes up, in Mrs. Joan Robinson's apposite phrase, "a box of tools." The purpose of this book is to familiarize the student with these tools as they are used by the professional economist. This has long held true for traditional policy issues, such as poverty and income distribution, or the explanation of such otherwise mysterious values as the price of caviar. In recent years, however, the instrumental power of microeconomics has been demonstrated through applications to such social problems as crime and environmental pollution, and to the provision of public goods and human resource development.

The excellent response to the first two editions, including their translation into Italian and Spanish, confirms our conviction that conventional textbooks, however clearly written and thorough, can satisfy but part of the needs of economic education. Seasoned students of economics must be thoroughly familiar with original articles in the professional literature, material which is all too often very limited in its availability. This book, therefore, tries to alleviate the need to oblige our students to spend countless hours in a reserve book room and restless nights under the threat of fine for failure to return reserve books by 9 AM—for most of us a depressing reminiscence. Moreover, to follow through on one of the major recent applications of pure theory, developed in one of the articles it reprints, the availability of this collection reduces, for students, the deadweight costs of travel time to and from libraries and time spent laboring over a photocopier, rather than reading in a comfortable easychair.

The papers reprinted in this book, as in the first two editions, focus on logic, methodology, and applications of microeconomics. We have, for the most part, selected articles that emphasize conceptual rather than empirical material, and articles that can be readily understood without significant formal training in any mathematics more advanced than geometry and, in a few cases, elementary calculus.

Microeconomics is that branch of economic theory concerned with the behavior of individual households and firms in the process of constrained choice. In working out the implications of this process, the theory explains how scarce resources are allocated among competing uses. There are two major subdivisions of microeconomics: one which explains the pricing of final products and another which explains the pricing of factors of production. The first deals with the division of output among consumers and the division of its production between firms and industries, while the second is concerned with the distribution of income. Taken together, they constitute the subject matter of microeconomics.

Microeconomics is sometimes called "price theory" because of its emphasis on how relative prices are determined and the crucial role such prices play in solving the problems of production and distribution. So important, in fact, are relative prices in organizing production and distribution that an economy primarily reliant on them to solve these problems is appropriately called a "price system."

The theory of price is one of the most challenging and rewarding subjects offered in a university curriculum. The student, in mastering its fundamentals, is enabled to sort out the considerations relevant to evaluation of the vast mass of policies that affect the allocation of resources. The papers collected in this volume were chosen on the basis of their ability to enable the student to learn and to apply the basic logic of this approach.

Part 1, "The Nature and Method of Economics," contains a classic paper by Frank Knight, in which the author defines the scope of economics and sets forth the five main functions of an economic system. He also provides an overview of the types of economic organizations that have attempted to perform these essential functions.

The second paper is an excursion into the domain of philosophy of social science. Milton Friedman's essay on methodology explains the important distinction between positive and normative economics. The author argues that undue emphasis on the descriptive "realism" of assumptions has caused economists to neglect the really crucial factor in the construction of good economic theory, namely, whether the theory enables us to accurately predict how consumers and producers will behave? To what extent are the implications of the theory borne out in practice? This, of course, implies that any adequate scientific theory must be put into the form of testable (conceivably refutable) hypotheses.

Part 2, "Demand and Supply," covers two major areas in the subject matter of price theory: (1) demand and utility theory and (2) supply and the theory of the firm.

The second paper by Friedman suggests that the usual conception of the demand curve does not meet the positivist test of conceivable refutability, inasmuch as the existence of the income effect allows the demand curve to have either a positive or a negative slope. Friedman, in seeking an operational tool, derives a hypothetical constant real income demand curve in which he eliminates the income effect of a change in price. Thus, with Friedman's characteristic skill and ingenuity, the law of demand becomes an operational proposition. Martin Bailey, however, points out that Friedman's construction does not take into account the overall fixity of resource supply. The various points along the constant real income demand curve may not represent available alternatives. Bailey, therefore, fixes the production possibilities of the community and derives a demand curve reflecting genuinely available alternatives.

Robert Strotz's essay analyzes the question of whether utility is subject to measure (the notion of "cardinal" utility) or simple ranking ("ordinal" utility). The publication of John von Neumann and Oskar Morgenstern's work on game theory in 1944 resurrected measurable utility in a way that bears little resemblance to the earlier notion of cardinal utility. But, as Strotz argues, the new notion of measurable utility rests on a superior understanding of the meaning of measurement in which the latter is not a property of things, but a predictive procedure. In so doing, Strotz clears up some of the confusion surrounding the debates of the cardinalists and ordinalists.

Yoram Barzel, in his contribution to the theory of demand, explains why the existence of an income effect on consumption impedes the empirical testing of the law of demand (the proposition that "demand curves are negatively sloped"). Barzel shows how one can identify a class of observations free of the income effect that enables the law of demand to be directly tested.

The testing of the law of demand is carried out under laboratory conditions in ingenious experiments constructed by John Kagel, Raymond Battalio, Howard Rachlin, and Leonard Green. They were able to demonstrate, using male albino rats as their laboratory animals, that demand curves are negatively sloped for nonhuman consumers, suggesting that for humans, along with other animals, evolutionary pressures have induced behavioral responses to stimuli that can be characterized as solutions to a constrained maximizing model. This essay is representative of the growing literature in the field of "experimental economics."

One of the central questions of demand theory is whether tastes are capricious and differ importantly between people or, on the contrary, are stable over time and similar among people. George Stigler and Gary Becker confront this question and argue that much of the behavior used to illustrate the instability of tastes (addiction, habitual behavior, advertising, and fashions) can be explained by a generalized calculus of utility-maximizing behavior consistent with the assumption of stable tastes. Thus the hypothesis of stable tastes yields more useful predictions about observable behavior than the alternative, which assumes that tastes are capricious. This permits Stigler and Becker to claim that differences in prices or incomes can explain any differences or changes in behavior. Richard Thaler, on the other hand, in developing a positive theory of consumer choice, argues that traditional consumer demand theory, in certain well-defined situations, predicts behavior that is inconsistent with actual behavior. Thaler shows that consumers often underweigh opportunity costs, fail to ignore sunk costs, choose not to choose, and engage in search behavior that is inconsistent with the predictions of orthodox theory. This does not mean that the rationality assumption must be jettisoned, but only that the orthodox economic model does a poor job of predicting the behavior of average, but rational, individual consumers. Kelvin Lancaster, in developing a new theory of consumer choice, breaks away from the traditional approach in which goods are the direct objects of utility, and assumes instead that the objects of utility are the characteristics of the goods from which utility is derived. The goods are inputs, and the output is a collection of characteristics. The Lancaster approach to consumer behavior is rich in heuristic and predictive power.

In the second section of Part 2 the theory of supply is analyzed. Armen Alchian explores some recent contributions to the theory of firm behavior in imperfectly competitive markets and argues that the utility-maximizing approach has implications consistent with the available evidence regarding managerial behavior. Louis De Alessi's paper relies heavily on Alchian's approach to firm behavior in showing that the use of a wealth-maximizing approach gives pertinent predictions regarding the short-run behavior of the firm. It also contains an examination of the "uneconomic" regions of the production function. Jack Hirshleifer goes deeper into the analysis of firm behavior by examining the problem of pricing commodities exchanged by the various divisional organizations within a single firm and indicates the pricing policies that would maximize the aggregate profits of the corporation. In an extremely influential paper, Harvey Leibenstein argues that the traditional concern of microeconomics with allocative efficiency is misplaced and that types of efficiency other than allocative efficiency (what Leibenstein calls "X-efficiency") are much more significant. The gains from increasing X-efficiency might be very large compared to gains that would be achieved by increasing allocative efficiency. Oliver Williamson takes up the important question of optimum firm size by looking at a bureaucratic theory under the "control-loss" phenomenon. Communication across successive hierarchical levels leads to an irreducible loss of control over an enterprise. Since this loss of control can be extensive, it puts a limit on firm size.

The papers in Part 3 are concerned with new developments in the theory of resource allocation. Stigler's essay in the area that has come to be called "search theory" shows that the determination of market price involves an important problem of information because sellers must be identified and their prices discovered. Stigler shows that price dispersion is the measure of ignorance in a market. Important aspects of economic organization are illuminated when considered from the viewpoint of the search for information. In particular, the theory has been shown to have significant implications for our understanding of investment markets and labor eco-

nomics. Just as Stigler introduced the costs of information into traditional economic analysis, Becker introduced the cost of time into the theoretical analysis of choice. In doing so, Becker assumes that households are producers as well as consumers, who produce goods by combining inputs of time and goods according to the cost-minimization rules of standard economic theory. Some of the intriguing implications of this way of looking at resource allocation are summarized in Becker's paper. Stigler's theory of information is utilized by Armen Alchian and Harold Demsetz to develop a new theory of the firm, in which it is a device for team use of input, to minimize the cost of collecting and collating information about heterogeneous resources. This paper enables us to interpret the firm as a special class of contracts among a group of joint inputs to a team production process. The contractual structure is a means of enhancing the efficient organization of team production, which economizes on costs of monitoring to reduce shirking. Barzel's second paper is related to Becker's treatment of the allocation of time. Waiting time is a cost of establishing property rights in a good, over and above the cost required to produce it. Barzel shows that waiting (such as queuing) provides an additional route whereby consumers can equate on the margin under disequilibrium conditions (when the price imposed is not at the intersection of demand and supply). In the next paper, Kenneth Arrow applies microeconomic theory to help us understand racial discrimination in labor markets. He shows how utility-maximizing theories provide a reasonable account of the effect of discriminatory tastes on wages and employment in the short run, but are unsatisfactory in the long run. Adjustments that would wipe out racial wage differentials in the long run do not occur when there are considerable costs of change. Arrow also suggests that discrimination in labor markets is not only a reflection of tastes but of employer perceptions of reality.

The next two papers in this book are concerned with the general topic of contractual arrangements and market outcomes. The first, by Steven Cheung, introduces the notion of transaction costs and risks to explain why different contractual arrangements are chosen under the same system of property rights. The second paper, by Donald Gordon, ventures into the area of macroeconomics. In so doing, however, it shows the microeconomic underpinnings of wage rigidity and involuntary unemployment. In Gordon's view, the typical auction market model (identified with Friedman and with Robert Lucas and Leonard Rapping) and the search model (identified with Edmund Phelps) entail both logical and empirical difficulties. Gordon, on the other hand, is able to explain rigidities in terms of implicit hiring contracts, which incorporate provisions relating to employee security and wages. This approach is an extension of neoclassical price theory and its maximizing postulates to labor markets.

The next three papers take up the problem of choice under uncertain information. George Akerlof's article deals with the problem consumers face when they are uncertain about product quality. Akerlof makes use of the market for used cars to illustrate the essence of his argument. Since sellers of used cars cannot capture the returns for good quality, which accrue to the entire group of sellers rather than to the individual seller, they have an incentive to market merchandise of poor quality. Because social and private returns differ in such markets, governmental interference may increase the welfare of all parties. The difficulty of distinguishing good from bad quality is inherent in many everyday business transactions, and Akerlof's analysis has extensions to those economic areas where trust is important.

The kind of market in which uncertainty is present is usually one in which insurance is common. But in the absence of private markets for insurance against uncertain events, should government provide insurance? Mark Pauly's paper argues in the negative. Pauly shows that insurance against some kinds of uncertain events may be suboptimal even if individuals are risk averse. Complete insurance may be inappropriate if its availability influences the demand for the services insurance policies provide.

In the third paper in this section, Michael Spence treats hiring in the job market as a type of investment under uncertainty, analogous to purchasing a ticket in a lottery. The wages the employer pays to enter the lottery depend on how he perceives it. The job applicant can affect that perception through observable characteristics, or signals, which the individual can manipulate. Education is one important form of signaling. Spence looks at the characteristics of a basic equilibrium signaling model. An equilibrium results when a set of expectations is confirmed by new data and tends to persist over time as new entrants come into the market. A considerable variety of mar-

ket phenomena can be viewed through the conceptual lens of market signaling this essay provides.

The papers in Part 4 are concerned with the concepts and applications of the theory of market structures. Paul McNulty provides a thorough rehearsal of the meaning of competition at the hands of major figures in the history of economic thought and distinguishes between the idea of competition and that of market structure. To McNulty, competition should be viewed as a disequilibrium behavioral concept. Perfect competition, on the other hand, involves an equilibrium situation, a market structure in which price is given and no market activity is possible.

The paper on monopoly by Abba Lerner shows that market power can be measured by the excess of price over marginal cost. Lerner's article does much more than its title indicates. Included is a discussion of the meaning of an "optimum" position (clarified with the device of production and consumption indifference curves) that provides an introduction to the subject of "welfare economics." An analysis of the behavior of multiple-plant firms, as contrasted with the more conventional one firm—one plant model, is provided by Don Patinkin. He suggests that a cartel model is the best approach to understanding the forces at work in imperfectly competitive markets. In addition to its substantive content, Patinkin's article provides a brisk exercise in the use of the geometry of price theory.

Harold Demsetz's paper is an application of the theory of competitive price to the problem of regulating public utilities. In the case where production is characterized by large economies of scale, the commodity will essentially be produced by only one firm. This has led some scholars to assert that effective public utility regulation by the state is necessary and desirable. Demsetz shows that the theory of natural monopoly provides no logical basis for this outcome. Since there can be many bidders for a utility franchise, market rivalry will lead to prices well below that of unregulated monopoly. The discipline of the open market place, through competitive bidding for the utility contract, will be greater than that provided by regulation. The paper by William Breit and Kenneth Elzinga utilizes indifference curves to analyze the risk attitudes of corporate management. This enables them to suggest reforms in penalties that would most effectively deter violations of the antitrust laws.

William Baumol's paper generalizes the concept of the perfectly competitive market to a "perfectly contestable market." A contestable market is one in which entry is absolutely free and exit is costless. It is the potential entrants into markets who exercise discipline over the incumbents. Entry can be prevented under perfect market contestability only if the incumbent firms (be they monopolists, oligopolists, or whatever) offer consumers the benefits of perfect competition.

The final selections in Part 5 are concerned with general equilibrium, welfare maximization, and public goods. Arrow's paper provides a convenient overview of the issues surrounding the choice of market versus nonmarket allocation. He provides a crisp exposition of the meaning of "externality" and distinguishes sharply between the notions of "increasing returns" and "market failure." Arrow shows that market failure is a more general category than externality and differs from increasing returns, which is a technological phenomenon unrelated to the mode of economic organization. Francis Bator's paper performs a veritable tour de force, because in a relatively few pages it summarizes most of welfare economics within the framework of the static and stationary neoclassical model. Its treatment of such theory is, moreover, nonmathematical. The reader will find this a most helpful review of almost all aspects of microeconomics.

The next paper in the book takes up the question of the nature of costs and explores the famous Pigouvian distinction between private and social costs. In this classic work on the nature of social cost, Ronald Coase comes to the rather surprising conclusion that private and social costs are equal under perfect competition. Since the manner in which our legal system assigns liability for damages does not affect private marginal costs of production, it has no effect on the composition of output. Paul Samuelson's classic paper treats private consumption goods and public consumption goods as extreme polar cases to provide a neat geometrical treatment of the theory of public expenditure. In the next paper, James Buchanan constructs a model to explain the optimal size of membership organizations or "clubs" in which exclusion is possible. Since such organizations involve aspects of "privateness" and "publicness," Buchanan's technique helps to bridge the gap between Samuelson's polar cases of private and public goods.

The paper by Buchanan and Craig Stubblebine rigorously defines the various forms of observed externality: marginal and inframarginal externalities; potentially relevant and irrelevant externalities. They show that the mere existence of external effects cannot support a judgment about the desirability of social intervention, because the benefits from a particular activity, net of costs, may exceed the external costs it imposes on others. In the final paper, Harold Hochman and James Rodgers demonstrate conceptually that progressive income taxation may be fully consistent with the Pareto criterion, by postulating the existence of benevolent interdependence among utility functions with such interdependence. They then attempt to use this apparatus, which describes a rudimentary theory of charity, to explain the observed pattern of redistribution through the fiscal process. It is entirely conceivable that some redistribution will make all parties to income transfers, not just the recipients, better off.

Part 1   Nature and Method of Economics

Social Economic Organization*

FRANK H. KNIGHT

Frank H. Knight (B.A., Milligan College, 1911; B.A./M.A., University of Tennessee, 1913; Ph.D., Cornell University, 1916) was born in McLean County, Illinois, in 1885 and died in 1972. Most of his academic career was spent at the University of Chicago, where he was the Morton D. Hall Distinguished Service Professor of Social Science and Philosophy. Throughout his long career, Knight was one of the world's leading economists, making significant contributions to many issues of both economic theory, including the theory of profit, and social philosophy. He is best known for *Risk, Uncertainty and Profit,* a monumental study of the role of the entrepreneur in economic life. In 1950 Knight served as president of the American Economic Association, and in 1957 was the recipient of its coveted Francis A. Walker Award, given "not more frequently than once every five years to the living [American] economist who in the judgment of the awarding body has during his career made the greatest contribution to economics."

SOCIAL ECONOMIC ORGANIZATION AND ITS FIVE PRIMARY FUNCTIONS

It is somewhat unusual to begin the treatment of a subject with a warning against attaching too much importance to it; but in the case of economics, such an injunction is quite as much needed as explanation and emphasis of the importance it really has. It is characteristic of the age in which we live to think too much in terms of economics, to see things too predominantly in their economic aspect; and this is especially true of the American people. There is no

more important prerequisite to clear thinking in regard to economics itself than is recognition of its limited place among human interests at large.

Common Definitions of Economics Much Too Broad, Though the Economic Conception of Life Is Too Narrow

In modern usage, the term economic has come to be used in a sense which is practically synonymous with intelligent or rational. This is the first and broadest conception of the term, within which we have to find by narrowing it down progressively, a definition which will describe the actual subject-matter of the science of political economy. It is in accord with good linguistic usage to think and speak

*Reprinted from *The Economic Organization* by Frank H. Knight by permission of Ethel Knight and George Stigler. Copyright 1933 by Harper and Row, Publishers, 1951 by Frank H. Knight, pp. 3–30.

of the whole problem of living as one of economy, the economical use of time, energy, etc.—*resource* of every sort. Many definitions of economics found in text books fall into this error of including virtually all intelligent behavior. One writer has actually given as his definition of economics the "science of rational activity." Others find its subject matter is "man's activity in making a living," or "the ordinary business of life." Such definitions come too near to saying that economics is the science of things generally, of everything that men are for practical reasons interested in. Such a definition is useless and misleading. It is necessary to devote a little time to making clear the restrictions which mark off the modestly limited domain of economic science within the inclusive sphere of knowledge as a whole.

In the first place, it should be understood that economizing, even in this broad sense of rational activity, or the intelligent use of given means in achieving given ends, does not include all human interests, and that the kind of knowledge on which such activity rests does not exhaust the field of human knowledge. It is, as we have said, one of the errors, not to say vices, of an age in which the progress of natural science and the triumphs of its application to life have engrossed men's attention, to look upon life too exclusively under this aspect of scientific rationality. It is requisite to a proper orientation to economic science itself as well as necessary to a sound philosophy of life, to see clearly that life must be more than economics, or rational conduct, or the intelligent accurate manipulation of materials and use of power in achieving results. Such a view is too narrow. It implies that the results to be achieved are to be taken for granted, whereas in fact the results themselves are often quite as much in question as the means and procedures for achieving results. Living intelligently includes more than the intelligent use of means in realizing ends; it is fully as important to select the ends intelligently, for intelligent action directed toward wrong ends only makes evil greater and more certain. One must have intelligent tastes, and intelligent opinions on many things which do not directly relate to conduct at all. Not only are the objectives of action in fact a practical problem, as well as the means of achievement, but intelligent discussion of the means cannot be separated from the discussion of the ends.

Living is an art: and art is more than a matter of

a scientific technique, and the richness and value of life are largely bound up in the "more." In its reaction from the futility of medievalism and mystical speculation, the modern Western world has gone far to the other extreme. It loses much of the value of life through neglect of the imponderables and incommensurables, and gets into a false conception of the character of social and individual problems. Our thinking about life-values runs too much in terms of material prerequisites and costs. It is an exaggeration which may be useful to say that economic goods as a class are predominantly "necessary" rather than truly valuable. The importance of economic provision is chiefly that of a prerequisite to the enjoyment of the free goods of the world, the beauty of the natural scene, the intercourse of friends in "aimless" camaraderie, the appreciation and creation of art, discovery of truth and communion with one's own inner being and the Nature of Things. Civilization should look forward to a day when the material product of industrial activity shall become rather its by-product, and its primary significance shall be that of a sphere for creative self-expression and the development of a higher type of individual and of human fellowship. It ought to be the first aim of economic policy to reduce the importance of economic policy in life as a whole. So it ought to be the highest objective in the study of economics to hasten the day when the study and the practice of economy will recede into the background of men's thoughts, when food and shelter, and all provision for physical needs, can be taken for granted without serious thought, when "production" and "consumption" and "distribution" shall cease from troubling and pass below the threshold of consciousness and the effort and planning of the mass of mankind may be mainly devoted to problems of beauty, truth, right human relations and cultural growth.

The Actual Subject Matter of Economics

What is discussed in the science of economics includes a relatively small fraction of the economic side of life taken in the broad sense. It has nothing to do with the concrete processes of producing or distributing goods, or using goods to satisfy wants. The study of these matters comes under the head of technology, including engineering, business management, and home economics. Economics deals with the *social organization* of economic activity. In practice its scope is much narrower still; there are many ways in which economic activity may be socially organized, but the predominant method in modern nations is the price system, or free enterprise. Consequently it is the structure and working of the system of free enterprise which constitutes the principal topic of discussion in a treatise on economics.

The Meaning of Organization

Everyone is familiar with the idea of division of labor—by which is really meant specialization of labor—and many economists have taken it as their point of departure in expounding the science of economics. This was the procedure of Adam Smith, for example, whose book, *The Wealth of Nations,* published in the year 1776, ranks as the first modern treatise on economics.

Modern economic society is often compared with a living body or "organism" and the comparison is certainly suggestive. The essential similarity and the fundamental idea for our purpose is precisely that of division of labor or specialization. But the expression "division" of labor, does not tell us enough. The idea is rather division into different *kinds* of labor. A number of men hoeing in a field or nailing shingles on a roof exemplify "division" of labor, but not organization. The problems of organization arise only when *different things are being done,* in the furtherance of a *common end,* and in definite relations to each other, i.e., in *coordination.* A single man in raising a crop or building a house shows division of labor in another sense, since he does many different things, but this is not yet organization in the sense with which we are concerned. The human body shows organization in the true sense, since the various "organs" not only perform different functions, but must all act in a substantially continuous manner and in proper adjustment to each other. Again, organization must be distinguished from cooperation; it involves cooperation, but more. If a group of men lift a stone which is too heavy for one to move alone, they cooperate, and increase their power by cooperation; their action is cooperative, but they are not organized, since they are all doing the same thing.

It is obvious enough that the economic or living-making activities of the modern world are very elaborately organized. We need not pause to comment on the number of persons who have contributed, and in what different ways, in supplying the wants of the humblest citizen today. The authorities of the federal census prepare a catalogue or classification of occupations which lists many thousands of these economic functions for the working population of the United States alone and which yet makes no pretense of distinguishing all specialized functions. For instance, farm laborers are classed together though different individuals work at the production of a wide variety of crops. It is evident also that the accomplishment of the ultimate purpose of it all, the provision for the needs and desires of the people, depends upon these various operations being carried on with a fair degree of continuity and tolerable coordination. The problem of organization, which sets the problem of economic science, deals with the concrete means or mechanism for dividing the general function of making a living for the people into parts and bringing about the performance of these parts in due proportion and harmony.

More specifically, it is a problem of the social machinery for accomplishing *five fairly distinct functions.* Every system of organization must perform these tasks, and it is its success or failure in discharging these functions which determines its value as a system. Back of the study of economics is the practical need of making the organization better, and we can hope for success in this task only if we proceed to it intelligently, which is to say on the basis of an understanding of the nature of the work which a system of organization has to perform, and of the alternatives open in the way of possible types of organization machinery.

THE FIVE MAIN FUNCTIONS OF AN ECONOMIC SYSTEM

The general task of organizing the economic activity of society may be divided into a number of fundamental functions. These are in fact very much inter-connected and overlapping, but the distinction is useful as an aid to discussing the existing economic order both descriptively and critically, its structure as well as its workings. These functions fall into a more or less logical sequence. The first is to decide what is to be done, that is, what goods and services are to be produced, and in what proportions. It is the function of setting standards, of establishing a social scale of values, or the function of social choice; the second is the function of organizing production, in the narrow sense, of getting done the things settled upon as most worth doing; third is distribution, the apportioning of the product among the members of society; the fourth is really a group of functions having to do with maintaining and improving the social structure, or promoting social progress.

1. The Function of Fixing Standards; The Notion of Efficiency

In a world where organizations were absent, where each individual carried on his life activities in isolation and independence of all others, the matter of standards would be simply a matter of individual choice. But when the production of wealth is socialized, there has to be a *social* decision as to the relative importance of different uses of productive power, as to which wants are to be satisfied and which left unsatisfied or to what extent any one is to be satisfied at the expense of any other. In the case of an individual, choice need be made only among his own wants; but in a social system, the wants of different individuals also come into conflict. As far as this is a quantitative question merely, of how far the wants of one are to be gratified at the expense of the wants of another, or left ungratified in favor of another, the problem is one of *distribution,* and will be noticed under another heading (the third function). But to a large and increasing extent, society finds it necessary or advisable further to regulate the individual's regulation of his own want-satisfaction, to enforce a community standard of living. As a matter of fact, these two problems are closely interlaced, the question of *whose* wants and that of *which* wants are to be given preference, and in what measure. It is important to observe that they are largely the same question. The difference in the "amount" consumed by different persons is not mainly a difference in the amounts of the same commodities; different persons consume different things, which are quantitatively compared only through the agency of the value scale itself. Nevertheless there seems to be ample justification for a logical separation of the questions of what is to be produced from that of who is to get the product, and for discussing separately the relations between the two phases of organization.

A point of fundamental importance in connection with the question of standards is that of the origin or ultimate source of wants. The system of social organization does more than reduce individual values to a common denominator or scale of equivalence.

In large part the individual wants themselves are *created* by social intercourse, and their character is also largely dependent upon the form of organization of the economic system upon which they are dependent for their gratification. The workings of the economic organization in this connection form a problem too large and complex to be discussed at any length in a small book like this one. Indeed, the subject of wants is not only vast in scope but apparently cannot be reduced to scientific terms, except within rather narrow limits, falling rather in the field of art. The scientific discussion of economics has to be restricted in the main to the analysis of the organization of want-satisfaction. In the science of economics the wants are largely taken for granted as facts of the time and place, and the discussion of their origin and formation is left for the most part to the distinct studies of social psychology and cultural anthropology.[1]

The problem of standards or values occupies a key position in Economics. The practical objective of economics, it must be kept in mind, is that of improving the social organization and increasing its efficiency. There is a common misconception that it is possible to measure or discuss efficiency in purely physical terms. The first principles of physics or engineering science teach that this is not true, that the term efficiency involves the idea of value, and some measure of value as well. It is perhaps the most important principle of physical science that neither matter nor energy can be created or destroyed, that whatever goes into any process must come out in some form, and hence as a mere matter of physical quantity, the efficiency of all operations would equal one hundred per cent. The correct definition of efficiency is the ratio, not between "output" and "input" but between *useful* output and total output or input. Hence efficiency, even in the simplest energy transformation, is meaningless without a measure of usefulness or value. In any attempt to understand economic efficiency, the notion of value is more obviously crucial since most economic problems are concerned with a number of kinds both of outlay and of return, and there is no conceivable way of making comparisons without first reducing all the

---

[1]The deliberate creation or changing of wants for specific commodities as by advertising, is to some extent an exception, but in the main such activities must be regarded as creating a *knowledge of* certain *means* of satisfying wants rather than as changing ultimate *wants.*

factors to terms of a common measure. It will appear in due course that the science of economics is largely taken up with description and analysis of the process by which this common denominator of things consumed and produced by the economic system is arrived at, that is, with the *problem of measuring values*.

2. The Function of Organizing Production

The second step, logically speaking, after the ranking and grading of the uses to which productive power may be put, is that of actually putting them to use in accordance with the scale of values thus established. From a social point of view, this process may be viewed under two aspects, (a) the assignment or *allocation* of the available productive forces and materials among the various lines of industry, and (b) the effective *coordination* of the various means of production in each industry into such groupings as will produce the greatest result. The second of these tasks properly belongs to technological rather than to economic science, and is treated in economics only with reference to the interrelations between the organization of society as a whole and the internal organization of the industries.

3. The Function of Distribution

This third function would not exist at all in an unorganized world. Each individual, acting independently of all others, would simply consume what he produced. But where production is socialized, the separate productive contribution of one participant in the process cannot be directly identified or separated. It is apparent that a modern factory operative, say one who spends all his time putting buttons on shoes or nailing the covers on packing cases, cannot live on his own product, physically interpreted. When we further consider that different individuals contribute to production in fundamentally different ways, many by furnishing land or other "natural resources" or material equipment or money or managerial or supervisory services, or by selling goods, and in other ways which make no identifiable physical change in any product, it is manifest that if everyone is to get a living out of the process some *social mechanism* of distribution is called for.

In this connection should be recalled the close relation between distribution and the control of production. The decision as to what to produce is closely bound up with the decision for whom to produce. There is also a close relation between the third function and the second. In our social system distribution is the chief agency relied upon to control production and stimulate efficiency. Ours is a system of "private property," "free competition" and "contract." This means that every productive resource or agent, including labor power, typically "belongs" to some person who is free within the legal conditions of marketing, to get what he can out of its use. It is assumed, and the course of the argument will show at length why it is true, that there is in some effective sense a real positive connection between the productive contribution made by any productive agent and the remuneration which its "owner" can secure for its use. Hence this remuneration (a distributive share) and the wish to make it as large as possible, constitute the chief reliance of society for an incentive to place the agency into use in the general productive system in such a way as to make it as productive as possible. The strongest argument in favor of such a system as ours is the contention that this direct, selfish motive is the only dependable method, or at least the best method, for guaranteeing that productive forces will be organized and worked efficiently. The argument assumes that in spite of the difficulty above referred to of identifying the particular contribution to the social product made by any person or piece of property, it is possible to separate it out, and measure it, in terms of value and that the distributive system does this with accuracy enough to make remunerations vary in accord with product. If this were not true in the main, remuneration could not really afford an incentive to productive efficiency, and an economic order based on individualism would not function.

4. Economic Maintenance and Progress

There is no moral connotation in the term progress; it refers to any persistent cumulative change, whether regarded as good or bad. The principal forms of economic progress include, (1) growth of population and any cumulative change in its composition or education which affects either its productive powers or its wants; (2) the accumulation of material aids to production or "capital" of all kinds, including such permanent sources of satisfaction as newly discovered natural resources and also works of art;[2] (3) improvements in technical processes or

---

[2]Destruction and exhaustion of resources not replaced is also a progressive change.

changes in the form of business organization. It is to be noted especially that progress has two sorts of significance for the economic organization. First, it is one of the products or values created by the latter, at a cost; i.e., it involves using productive power for this purpose and sacrificing its use for other purposes; and second, it affects and changes the character of the economic system itself and the conditions under which the system works.

This fourth function of organization, especially the provision for progress, cuts across all the other three. It is a matter of standards or values to decide how much progress society can afford or cares to have at the cost of sacrificing present values, and what forms it shall take; it is a matter of productive organization to utilize the determined share of available productive power to bring about progress in the amount and of the kinds decided upon, and it is a problem of distribution to apportion the burdens and benefits of progress among the members of society. We may be reminded also that it is true of progress as of all other lines of human action that it comes within the field of economics just in so far as it is related to the organized system of producing and distributing the means of want-satisfaction.

The first three of these functions (or four, since No. 2 is really double, involving two aspects) are relatively "short-time" in character. They are all aspects of the general problem of an economic society working under "given conditions," in contrast with the fourth function which relates to the problem of improving the given conditions through the course of time. The first three therefore make up the problems of what may be called the "stationary economy." If society either could not or did not try to grow and progress and make improvements, its economic problem would be entirely within this field. But since economic societies do in fact face problems of growth and improvement, and make some effort to solve them intelligently, we have to add the fourth function, or group of functions. Such problems are frequently referred to under the head of "dynamic" economics; for reasons which cannot be given in detail here, this is a seriously misleading use of language, and they should be called simply problems of progress or historical problems.

The "given conditions" of the stationary economy are included under the three heads of *resources, wants,* and *technology,* which may be subdivided and classified in more elaborate ways. The separation is based on the plain and simple fact that with reference to social calculations and plans which look ahead only a few years, these factors, resources, wants and the technological system will not change enough to affect the argument or plans seriously. But looking ahead over historical time they do change, to an indefinite extent, and the production and guidance of changes in them becomes the dominant character of the social economic problem. In the "short-run" (of a few years), however, the problem is to utilize in the best way the existing resources and technology in the satisfaction of existing wants.

A Fifth Function: To Adjust Consumption to Production Within Very Short Periods

For completeness, this survey of functions should point out that within *very short* periods society faces still another set of "given conditions," hence still another type of problem, and in consequence its economic organization has still another task or function to perform, though this fifth function is rarely distinguished sharply from those of the "stationary economy" point of view. From this latter point of view, the problem is to adjust production to consumption under the given conditions. But in many cases, production cannot be adjusted quickly, while demand conditions do change rapidly; and in addition, production in many fields is subject to fluctuations from causes beyond control. In consequence, the supply of many commodities is fixed for considerable periods of time, on a level more or less divergent from the best possible adjustment to existing conditions of demand. The supply on hand is of course the result of productive operations in the past, and has to suffice until it can be changed. In agriculture this is conspicuously true. The crop of a given year has to last until the next year's crop is produced (except in so far as other parts of the world having different crop seasons can be drawn upon). In the case of manufactured goods, production is not definitely periodic, but it is still true that the rate of production frequently cannot be changed in a short time, to meet changes in demand, at least not without enormous cost.

It follows that over short periods consumption has to be controlled and distributed with reference to an existing supply or current rate of production, at the same time that adjustment of production to consumption requirements is being made as rapidly as practicable. The existing supply of wheat or potatoes, for example, must be distributed (a) over the season for which it has to suffice and (b) among the different consumers and their different needs. Thus there is a fifth function of organization, the opposite in a sense, of number two in the four above discussed, namely the short-run adjustment of consumption to past or current production.[3]

ADVANTAGES AND DISADVANTAGES OF ORGANIZED ACTION
The Reasons for Organizing Activity

As previously remarked, a high degree of organization in human activity is a fairly recent development in the world's history, and is still restricted mainly to what we call the European peoples or cultures. The urge behind its development can be stated in the single word *efficiency*. The object of industrial activity is to utilize an available fund of productive agencies and resources in making the goods and services with which people satisfy their wants. Organized effort enables a social group to produce more of the means of want-satisfaction than it could by working as individuals. During the course of history, the possibility of increased efficiency has led to an ever greater degree of specialization, which in turn has constantly called for a more elaborate and effective mechanism of coordination and control, just as the higher animals require an enormously more complex nervous and circulatory system than the lower. It will be worth while to carry the analysis a little beyond the general notion of efficiency and see some of the reasons why specialized effort yields larger or better results. We must then turn to the other side of the picture and note some of the disadvantages of organization.

The Gains from Specialization[4]

The largest gain which the higher animals secure in comparison with lower, less organized forms, arises from the adaptation of structure to function.

In the most primitive animals the same kind of tissue has to perform all the divergent functions of locomotion, seizing and ingestion of food, digestion, assimilation, excretion of waste and reproduction, while in the mammalian body the specialization of tissues and organs for the various functions and the increased efficiency with which all are consequently performed, are too evident to need extended comment. Some social insects produce physically divergent types of individuals adapted by structure to perform different functions. In the familiar case of the bees, the bulk of the community is made up of "workers" and the reproductive function is specialized in the queens and drones. Certain species of ants and termites present a very complex social structure containing a dozen or more structurally specialized types of individuals. One of the most interesting facts in regard to human society is the absence of definite structural specialization of individuals. Human organization is an artificial thing, a culture product. Natural differences undoubtedly exist among human beings, and are taken advantage of, more or less, in fitting individuals to specialized functions; but the differences seem to be accidental, and unpredictable. Certainly human beings do not become fused into a super-organism in the manner of the cells in an animal body. It is in fact a matter of the greatest uncertainty and one of the most disputed questions in the whole field of knowledge, as to how far observed differences in kinds and degrees of capacity are innate and how far they are the result of "nurture" and the subtle influences of environment and social suggestion. The tendency of scientific study at the present time is to place more and more emphasis on the environment and less upon congenital structure. In any case, human differences are not so definitely transmitted by inheritance as to be predictable in advance; they have to be discovered and developed and the individual fitted to his place in the system by some artificial means. There is no mechanical solution of the human social problem, as in the case of the animal organism or even of insect societies; human beings have to form themselves into an organization as well as to control and operate it when constructed.

1. Utilization of Natural Aptitudes; Especially Those of Leaders and Followers. However, we are safe in asserting that there are some innate individual differences in human capacities and aptitudes, and the first in the list of gains from organization results

---

[3]It is rather typical of economic phenomena that cause and effect relations are apt to run in opposite directions in the short-run and the long-run. This is a common source of difficulty in the reasoning, as will appear more fully in the treatment of the forces which fix prices.
[4]It will be recalled that we are using the word "specialization" instead of the familiar "division of labor," not only is labor divided, but it is differentiated and co-ordinated, and the other elements or factors in production are likewise "specialized"—often more extensively and vitally than the human factor.

from taking advantage of them. One social problem is to discover such differences and utilize them as far as possible. They can never be predicted with any certainty before the birth of the individual, in fact they cannot usually be discerned at any time in life from clear external marks; and in the course of the development of the individual they become so largely overlaid with acquired traits that they can never be separated from the latter. The most important natural differences of which we can be reasonably sure are those of physical stature and dexterity and (with much less certainty) of general mental activity. The most important differentiation in function, or division of labor, between individuals is the separation between direction and execution, or the specialization of *leadership*. It may well be true that able leaders are in general also more competent workers or operatives, but the gain from superior direction is so much more important than that from superior concrete performance that undoubtedly the largest single source of the increased efficiency through organization results from having work planned and directed by the exceptionally capable individuals, while the mass of the people follow instructions.

2. Development and Utilization of Acquired Skill and Acquired Knowledge. The principal quality in man which gives him superiority over the animals is his ability to learn, including learning to know and learning to do. But even in man this capacity is exceedingly limited in scope in comparison with the whole of acquired human knowledge and activity, and a large part of the gain from organizing activity comes from the increase in the efficiency of learning which is connected with reducing the field in which an individual must exercise his learning ability. Even the specialization of leadership undoubtedly rests as much upon acquired as upon innate differences. In truth, the fundamental innate difference among men is in the capacity to learn itself. In other fields than leadership—fields of specialized knowledge and skill in the narrower sense—it is still more clearly impossible to separate the factor of innate capacity from that of acquired powers, and still more evident that the innate capacity itself is a capacity to learn rather than directly to perform. Even in the case of genius, what is inherited is an extraordinary capacity to learn, or learn to do, certain things, and the amount of actual specialization in the original bent is highly uncertain. In modern machine industry, where the operative is restricted to repetition of a few simple movements, an incredible increase of

speed as compared with that of an untrained worker may be achieved in a short space of time. The operations generally involve movements very different from any which are natural to man as an animal, movements such as setting type, playing a musical instrument, or sorting mail matter into boxes; but they can be learned by any normal person, and when mastered they make possible the employment of a technology vastly more efficient than that of primitive industry. (See No. 5 below.)

3. Changing Pieces of Work Cheaper, Within Limits, Than Changing Jobs. The saving of time and effort in changing from one operation to another is the third gain from specialization. It is true that if a man performs the same operation repeatedly, he must change from one object, or piece of work, to another. But by the use of mechanical conveyers, scientific routing and the like, it is found that, *within limits,* the process of bringing to the workman a procession of shoes, automobile cylinders, or hog carcasses is far less costly than having him make the changes in position, changes in tools used, etc., involved in performing successively on any one of them the various operations necessary to complete the making of a product, as was done under old handicraft conditions. This gain is evidently rather closely connected with that arising from specialized skill. It is to be especially emphasized, because so commonly overlooked, that in this connection there are offsetting costs, which only within limits are exceeded by the gains. Not only must the cost of changing jobs be compared with the cost of changing pieces of work as within a given factory. If each man completed a product, the workers would not have to be brought together into factories at all, a feature which also involves large costs, and neither would the materials have to be assembled from such a vast area or the product distributed back over a market perhaps nation-wide or even world-wide in extent. The costs of bringing together vast quantities of materials and of distributing the product tend in fact to offset very considerably the gains of large scale production. These costs include not merely actual transportation, but marketing costs in the form of profits, risks and losses from inaccurate forecasting of demand, idleness due to over-production, storage, insurance and the like. The public has been educated by apologists for monopoly to over-estimate seriously the real gains from large-scale factory methods; these offsetting losses are rarely appreciated to the full.

4. Natural Advantages in the Case of "Natural Resources." However uncertain we may be as to the innate differences in men, there can be no question that the natural resources of different regions are suited to widely divergent employments. In such extreme cases as mineral deposits, for example, specialization to regions is absolute, since minerals can only be extracted where they exist, and this is quite commonly in places where any other industry is virtually out of the question. Also, "geographical" or "territorial" specialization is almost a physical necessity as between different climatic zones. Other industries may be carried on in different regions, but usually some locations offer greater or lesser advantages over others, which may or may not be sufficient to offset transportation costs and other costs of specialization. The question of political interference with territorial specialization, through "tariffs," bounties, subsidies and the like, has formed an important political issue in all modern nations. Such measures practically always reduce the gains from specialization and the arguments used to support them are fallacious from a purely economic point of view. In some cases a political unit can profit at the expense of others, but this is rarely possible and still more rarely achieved by the policies adopted, and is always to the disadvantage of the world as a whole.

5. Artificial Specialization of Material Agents. Division of Operations Leads to Invention and Use of Machinery. Even natural resources are never used in their natural state. The process of developing and adapting them to particular uses is generally more or less of a specializing process and may be compared to the "education" of a human being. When we turn to the forms of productive equipment usually classed as artificial—tools, machines, buildings and the like, it is evident that specialization goes very far indeed. A tool or machine is usually much more specialized than a human being can ever be, and its efficiency in a particular task is connected with the degree of its specialization. Many things can be done, after a fashion, with a hammer; only one with an automatic printing-press or a watch-screw machine; but that one thing is done with wonderful precision and speed. Perhaps the very largest single source of gain from the specialization of labor is that it makes possible the development and use of machinery, the effectiveness of which is almost entirely a matter of its specialization to limited and relatively simple operations.

6. Minor Technical Gains. The gains from nat-

ural and artificial adaptation of men and things to tasks, plus that due to changing pieces of work instead of tasks (our No. 3 above) do not exhaust the economies of specialization. There is an economy in coordination due to the fact that a specialized worker need have access only to the tools used for the operations he continuously performs, and not to all those used in making the article. This is practically rather an incidental matter, subordinate to the specialization of equipment. In primitive industry little is invested in tools, and a large investment carries with it specialization of both workers and equipment. We may note also as a final consideration in connection with this whole subject, that in many cases any sort of effective work involves the performance of different operations simultaneously, which of course necessitates specialization.

Social Costs of Specialization

All the gains from specialization are summed up in the one word, *efficiency;* it enables us to get more goods, or better; its advantages are *instrumental.* On the other hand, specialization in itself, is an evil, measured by generally accepted human ideals. It gives us more products, but in its effects on human beings as such it is certainly bad in some respects and in others questionable. In the nature of the case[5] it means a narrowing of the personality; we like to see people of all-around, well-developed powers and capacities. In extreme instances, such as the monotonous work of machine-tending, or repetitive movements at a machine-forced pace, it may be ruinous to health and maddening to the spirit. In this connection it is especially significant that the most important source of gain also involves the most important human cost. The specialization of leadership means that the masses of the people work under conditions which tend to suppress initiative and independence, to develop servility as well as narrowness and in general to dehumanize them.

Technical Costs of Organization

We have already mentioned the fact that there is another side to the technical advantages of specialization, namely the costs of assembly and distribution. This aspect of the situation is hinted at in the

[5]Statements of this kind need a good deal of interpretation. In reality everything depends on the alternative system used as a basis of comparison. The idyllic system of universal craftsmanship certainly never existed historically; perhaps it could not exist; but we think we can imagine its existence.

famous saying of Adam Smith that the division of labor is limited by the extent of the market, that is, really, by distribution costs. To these we must add the broader category of costs of organization in general. The existing social organization is called an "automatic" system, and in some respects it is such. But any system of bringing large numbers of people into intercommunication and coordinating their activities must involve enormous costs in actual human and physical energy. Organizations are like water-drops, or snow-balls or stones, or any large mass; the larger they are the more easily they are broken into pieces, the larger *in proportion* is the amount of energy that must be consumed in merely holding them together. The larger the army the bigger the proportion of officers, and the more unwieldy the aggregate, even then. The losses from this source in the modern world are stupendous; the number of persons, and still more the amount of brain power, which must be entirely taken up with passing on directions and keeping track of what is being done and "oiling the machinery" in one way and another is truly appalling. And the opportunity for persons to secure private gain by dislocating the organization machinery leads to still greater waste and loss.

Interdependence

A final important disadvantage of organized production and distribution is the resulting interdependence of persons and groups. This interdependence is supposed to be mutual, in the long run; but for the time being, the persons who perform such functions as coal mining and transportation are very much more necessary to, say, school teachers or farmers than the latter are to them. Strikes or failures to function due to accidental causes produce a kind of suffering unknown in unorganized society, or even in small groups within which the pressure of public opinion is much more powerful. A phase of this interdependence manifests itself acutely in the ebb and flow of prosperity, particularly the recurrence of business crises bringing widespread distress.

TYPES OF SOCIAL ORGANIZATION
ECONOMICS AND POLITICS
Social Organization and Biological Organism: Analogy and Contrast

As an introduction to the survey and classification of forms of social organization it will be useful to revert briefly to the comparison between economic society and the human body—especially to emphasize the fundamental difference. In this comparison the human individual is said to correspond to the "cell," the ultimate unit of biological structure. Individuals, like the cells in an animal body, are aggregated into "tissues" and "organs," which carry on the elementary life functions, seizing nourishment, transforming it into a condition suitable for use or digestion, distribution, disposal of waste, etc. The analogy is indeed obvious, and no doubt useful within limits, if it is kept on the level of analogy and not pressed too far. However, reasoning from analogy is always dangerous, and the conception of the "social organism" has probably produced more confusion than enlightenment. The differences between society and an animal organism are practically more important than the similarities, for it is in connection with the differences that the social problems arise.

The division of labor between the organs of the body is based on an innate differentiation of physical structure, and the co-ordination of their activities is automatic and mechanical. The cells or tissues do not choose what positions they will take up or what functions they will perform, nor can they change from one position or function to another. They do not meet with any of the problems which make the study of human organization a practical concern; they have no separate interests which may conflict with each other or with those of the body as a whole, and there can be no competition among them in any but a figurative sense.

Human society is the opposite of all this. Definite machinery has to be deliberately designed to reconcile or compromise between the conflicting interests of its members, who are separate purposive units; the organization as a whole has no value in itself or purpose of its own, according to the dominant theory of democracy at least, but exists solely to promote the interests of its members. In the same way, as we have seen, planned provision must be made in human society for working out the division of labor, assigning the separate tasks to the various persons and apportioning productive equipment among them, for distributing the fruits of the activity, and even for determining the character of its own future life and growth.[6]

---

[6]See also the discussion of insect societies (above p. 7) to which the observations made in regard to the animal organism will largely apply though in a lesser degree.

Types of Organization

1. "Status" and Tradition, or the Caste System. The nearest approach to a mechanical division and coordination of activity which is reached or can be conceived of in human society would be a universal system of *status* or "caste." It is possible to imagine a social order in which elaborate specialization of activities is achieved on a purely customary basis, and some approximation to such an ideal is found in the caste system of India. We can suppose that rigid social custom might fix all the details of the division of occupations and technique of production, the assignment of individuals to their tasks being determined by birth, while tradition would also set the details of the standard of living for everyone. Such a society would have to be nearly unprogressive, though slow change in accordance with unconscious historical forces is compatible with the hypothesis.

There are two reasons for ascribing considerable theoretical importance to caste as a system of organization. It serves to bring out by contrast the characteristics of the modern Western system based on property and competition, a contrast made famous by Sir Henry Maine's theory that the transition from a régime of status to one of contract is a fundamental historical law. In the second place there is a large element of status in the freest society; social position, character of work and standard of living are determined even in America today, perhaps nearly as much by the "accident" of birth as by conscious or unconscious selection in accord with innate personal traits. Moreover, any society based on the natural family as a unit tends toward progressively greater rigidity of stratification. With the passing of the frontier and the special conditions of a new country, rapid change in this direction has come to be a conspicuous feature of American life, though political and social motives have led us to set up opposing forces such as free education.

2. The Autocratic or Militaristic System. The first step away from a caste system in the direction of increasing freedom is represented by a centralized, autocratic system most briefly described by comparing it with the organization of an army. In such a social order, worked out to logical completeness, the whole structure of society, the division of labor, determination of policies, and allocation of burdens and benefits, would be dictated by an absolute monarch. The individual need not be asked what he wants or thinks good for him in the way of either his consumption or his share in production. The idea of organization itself might be worked out to any degree of intricacy, and coordination might indeed be highly effective. In practice, such a system would have to contain a large element of caste, unless the family were abolished entirely, as in Plato's scheme for an ideal republic. The organizing principle in an autocratic system is personal authority resting upon "divine," or prescriptive, right.

It is to be observed that this principle, while theoretically reduced to a minimum in modern society, is actually, like that of tradition and caste, very much in evidence. The exercise of "authority," while limited in degree, is as real as either "free" exchange or persuasion, within the family, in the internal organization of business units and in the "democratic" system of government itself. In an autocratic system worked out to ideal perfection, the population as well as all material goods would be the *property* of the monarch; the political and economic systems, as we habitually understand the terms today, would be completely fused, the ideas of sovereignty and property identified. A picture of such a social order may be found in the story of Joseph in Egypt, in the book of Genesis, after first the chattels of the people and then their persons were turned over to Pharaoh in exchange for the grain stored up by Joseph against the lean years. The theory of medieval European feudalism may be regarded as a combination of the principles of caste and of autocracy. This means that under feudalism also, there is no separation between the economic and political aspects of the social organization. The contrast in meaning between the two in the modern world will presently be looked into.

3. Anarchism as a Possible System. In the third type of organization mechanism to be considered, we swing to the extreme opposite of the two preceding, from rigorous control by tradition or arbitrary authority to absolute freedom, or purely voluntary association. Whether such a system is possible, may well be doubted, as most of the world does doubt; but it is at least conceivable, and many cultivated and noble minds have, as is well known, advocated attempting it as a practical program. The idea is simple enough; it is contended that if inequality and all hope or thought of exploiting or exercising authority over other men were abolished, people might agree voluntarily as to what were best to be done in the various contingencies of social life and the best method for doing it, and proceed accordingly, without any giving or taking of orders, or any threat of compulsion or restraint by force. It is not necessary to suppose that everyone would have to be all-knowing in regard to every sort of question. It is fully consistent with the theory of anarchy to have recourse to expert opinion; it must be assumed only that the experts would be able to agree, or that the mass of people would agree on which expert to recognize and follow. The theorists of philosophic anarchism who have attracted serious attention assign a large rôle to custom and the force of social opinion. There is no doubt that custom has in fact played the leading part in both originating and enforcing laws, especially in early times. But the case for anarchism in the sense of voluntary agreement through rational deliberation—that is, for this system as opposed to a caste and custom organization—is much less plausible. Apparently insuperable difficulties stand in the way of the elimination of compulsion in an intricate machine civilization subject to the stresses of rapid material progress.

4. Democracy or Democratic Socialism. The two systems remaining to be considered represent combinations of or compromises between systems already named. The first, democratic socialism, is a compromise between the authoritarian and the anarchistic. The nearest approach to the freedom of anarchy which we even theoretically reach on any extended scale is the rule of the majority. In its main structural features a society organized entirely on this principle would resemble the autocratic, authoritarian system. The difference is that the controlling authority, instead of being an absolute autocrat, would itself be under the control of "public opinion," that is, the will of the majority of the citizens, expressed through some "political" apparatus. Again, the economic and political organizations would be fused and identified. This is the type of social structure advocated in the main by persons calling themselves "socialists" though by no means to the exclusion of other types of organization machinery, especially that of free bargaining. Custom could not of course be excluded in any case, and competitive characteristics would undoubtedly appear, since few socialists would absolutely prohibit market dealings. The exercise of personal authority—beyond that involved in the majority taking precedence over the minority in cases of disagreement as to policy—would be reduced to the minimum. It is hardly necessary to men-

tion the fact that the activities of modern societies are to a considerable and increasing extent organized "socialistically," that an increasing fraction of their activities are carried on under the mandatory direction of agencies selected by majorities and as far as practicable made subject to the will of the majority. Examples are the postal system, the schools, streets and highways, the central banks and an increasing proportion of public utility services.

5. The Exchange System. The last type of organization machinery to be distinguished is the one especially characteristic of modern Western nations, in which the whole system is worked out and controlled through exchange in an impersonal competitive market. It is variously referred to as the competitive system, the capitalistic system, the system of private property and free exchange, individual exchange cooperation, and so on. Its most interesting feature is that it is automatic and unconscious; no one plans or ever planned it out, no one assigns the participants their rôles or directs their functions. Each person in such a system seeks his own satisfaction without thought of the structure of society or its interests; and the mere mechanical interaction of such self-seeking units organizes them into an elaborate system and controls and coordinates their activities so that each is continuously supplied with the fruits of the labor of one vast and unknown multitude in return for performing some service for another multitude also large and unknown to him. Although the actuality diverges in many respects from such a simple idealized description, the results which are in fact achieved by this method are truly wonderful. Like the other systems described, it does not exist and can hardly be thought of as existing in a pure form. But so large a part of the ordinary work of the modern world is organized in this way that such expressions as "the present social system" or the "existing economic order," are commonly understood to refer to the organization of provision for the means of life through buying and selling.

Two Sub-Types of Exchange Organization

(A) Handicraft and (B) Free Enterprise. The first step in the description of the free exchange system must be to distinguish between two forms of it which differ in fundamental respects. That would be in the proper sense an exchange system or society, in which each individual produced a single commodity and exchanged his surplus of this, directly or through the medium of money, for the various other things required for his livelihood. Some approximation to this system existed in the handicraft organization of the medieval towns, and of course the farmers and a few city craftsmen of today typically produce concrete things to sell. We call this a "handicraft" system.

But such is by no means the characteristic form of modern economic organization. In modern industry in its most developed form no individual or small group can be said to "produce" anything. As it is sometimes put, we have gone beyond division of occupations to the division or subdivision of tasks. Typically, each individual merely performs some operative detail in the making of a commodity, or furnishes to some productive organization a part of the natural resources or capital it employs. But this difference in technology, as compared with a system where each person makes an entire article, is not so important as the difference in the personal relations, in the system of organization itself. In a handicraft system each one lives by producing and selling goods, and generally owns the material upon which he works and the article he makes when it is finished, as well as his shop or work place—most naturally in his home—and the tools or equipment used in performing his work.

In the modern free enterprise system, as exemplified in the large-scale industries, the relation of the individual to the system is of a quite different sort. As the worker produces nothing and owns nothing, he can exchange nothing, so far as want-satisfying goods are concerned. The individual in fact gets his living, not by selling and buying or exchanging *goods,* but by selling *productive services* for *money* and buying with the money the *goods* which he uses. And of course he does not carry out this exchange with other individuals, since they are in the same situation as himself, but typically with *business units.*

A business unit, or enterprise, is made up of individuals (among whom the man who sells to or buys from it may himself be included) but is distinct from these individuals and constitutes a fictitious person, company, a firm or typically a corporation. Production is now commonly carried on by such units. They are, of course, controlled by natural persons, but these "officers" act for the organization and not as individuals. Various separate persons (possibly with other business units as intermediaries) own and ultimately control any one business unit. The business unit itself partly owns but largely hires or leases from individuals (in some cases again indirectly) the productive power with which it operates, including the services of human beings and those of "property," natural and artificial.

It is a fact familiar to every reader of such a book as this that in the modern world economic activity has typically become organized in this form: *business units* buy productive services and sell products; *individuals or families* sell productive services and buy products. Hence the study of economics in our society is mainly the study of free enterprise.

The Methodology of Positive Economics*

MILTON FRIEDMAN[1]

Milton Friedman (A.B., Rutgers University, 1932; M.A., University of Chicago, 1933; Ph.D., Columbia University, 1946), the 1976 Nobel Laureate in Economics, was born in Rahway, New Jersey, in 1912. One of the most vigorous and able exponents of the free enterprise system and the author of such popular books as *Capitalism and Freedom* and *Free To Choose* (with his wife Rose Director Friedman), Friedman was on the faculty of the University of Chicago where he was the Paul Snowden Russell Distinguished Service Professor of Economics for more than thirty years, and is currently a Senior Research Fellow at the Hoover Institution. His distinguished academic record, spanning virtually all areas of economic theory, has included publication of such major books as *Essays in Positive Economics, A Theory of the Consumption Function, Price Theory, A Monetary History of the United States, 1867-1960* (with Anna J. Schwartz), *The Optimum Quantity of Money and Other Essays,* and *Dollars and Deficits.* In 1951 Friedman was awarded the John Bates Clark Medal by the American Economic Association, an award made "every two years to that American Economist under the age of 40 who is adjudged to have made a significant contribution to economic thought and knowledge." During 1967 he was president of the American Economic Association. The clarity of style and dialectic skill for which Milton Friedman is known are abundantly evident in the following selection, and his preeminence as a teacher attested to by his pervasive influence on young scholars.

*Reprinted from *Essays in Positive Economics* by Milton Friedman by permission of The University of Chicago Press. Copyright 1953, pp. 3–43.

[1] I have incorporated bodily in this article without special reference most of my brief "Comment" in *A Survey of Contemporary Economics,* Vol. II, B. F. Haley, ed. (Chicago: Richard D. Irwin, Inc., 1952), pp. 455–57.

I am indebted to Dorothy S. Brady, Arthur F. Burns, and George J. Stigler for helpful comments and criticism.

In his admirable book on *The Scope and Method of Political Economy,* John Neville Keynes distinguishes among "a *positive science* . . . [,] a body of systematized knowledge concerning what is; a *normative or regulative science* . . . [,] a body of systematized knowledge discussing criteria of what ought to be . . . ; an *art* . . . [,] a system of rules for the attainment of a given end"; comments that "confusion between them is common and has been the source of many mischievous errors"; and urges the importance of "recognizing a distinct positive science of political economy."[2]

This paper is concerned primarily with certain methodological problems that arise in constructing the "distinct positive science" Keynes called for—in particular, the problem how to decide whether a suggested hypothesis or theory should be tentatively accepted as part of the "body of systematized knowledge concerning what is." But the confusion Keynes laments is still so rife and so much of a hindrance to the recognition that economics can be, and in part is, a positive science that it seems well to preface the main body of the paper with a few remarks about the relation between positive and normative economics.

I. THE RELATION BETWEEN POSITIVE AND NORMATIVE ECONOMICS

Confusion between positive and normative economics is to some extent inevitable. The subject matter of economics is regarded by almost everyone as vitally important to himself and within the range of his own experience and competence; it is the source of continuous and extensive controversy and the occasion for frequent legislation. Self-proclaimed "experts" speak with many voices and can hardly all be regarded as disinterested; in any event, on questions that matter so much, "expert" opinion could hardly be accepted solely on faith even if the "experts" were nearly unanimous and clearly disinterested.[3] The conclusions of positive economics seem to be, and are, immediately relevant to important normative problems, to questions of what ought to be done and how any given goal can be attained. Laymen and experts alike are inevitably tempted to shape positive conclusions to fit strongly held normative preconceptions and to reject positive conclusions if their normative implications—or what are said to be their normative implications—are unpalatable.

Positive economics is in principle independent of any particular ethical position or normative judgments. As Keynes says, it deals with "what is," not with "what ought to be." Its task is to provide a system of generalizations that can be used to make correct predictions about the consequences of any change in circumstances. Its performance is to be judged by the precision, scope, and conformity with experience of the predictions it yields. In short, positive economics is, or can be, an "objective" science, in precisely the same sense as any of the physical sciences. Of course, the fact that economics deals with the interrelations of human beings, and that the investigator is himself part of the subject matter being investigated in a more intimate sense than in the physical sciences, raises special difficulties in achieving objectivity at the same time that it provides the social scientist with a class of data not available to the physical scientist. But neither the one nor the other is, in my view, a fundamental distinction between the two groups of sciences.[4]

Normative economics and the art of economics, on the other hand, cannot be independent of positive economics. Any policy conclusion necessarily rests on a prediction about the consequences of doing one thing rather than another, a prediction that must be based—implicitly or explicitly—on positive economics. There is not, of course, a one-to-one relation between policy conclusions and the conclusions of positive economics; if there were, there would be no separate normative science. Two individuals may agree on the consequences of a particular piece of legislation. One may regard them as desirable on balance and so favor the legislation; the other, as undesirable and so oppose the legislation.

I venture the judgment, however, that currently in the Western world, and especially in the United States, differences about economic policy among disinterested citizens derive predominantly from differ-

---

[2](London: Macmillan & Co., 1891), pp. 34–35 and 46.

[3]Social science or economics is by no means peculiar in this respect—witness the importance of personal beliefs and of "home" remedies in medicine wherever obviously convincing evidence for "expert" opinion is lacking. The current prestige and acceptance of the views of physical scientists in their fields of specialization—and, all too often, in other fields as well—derives, not from faith alone, but from the evidence of their works, the success of their predictions, and the dramatic achievements from applying their results. When economics seemed to provide such evidence of its worth, in Great Britain in the first half of the nineteenth century, the prestige and acceptance of "scientific economics" rivaled the current prestige of the physical sciences.

[4]The interaction between the observer and the process observed that is so prominent a feature of the social sciences, besides its more obvious parallel in the physical sciences, has a more subtle counterpart in the indeterminacy principle arising out of the interaction between the process of measurement and the phenomena being measured. And both have a counterpart in pure logic in Gödel's theorem, asserting the impossibility of a comprehensive self-contained logic. It is an open question whether all three can be regarded as different formulations of an even more general principle.

ent predictions about the economic consequences of taking action—differences that in principle can be eliminated by the progress of positive economics—rather than from fundamental differences in basic values, differences about which men can ultimately only fight. An obvious and not unimportant example is minimum-wage legislation. Underneath the welter of arguments offered for and against such legislation there is an underlying consensus on the objective of achieving a "living wage" for all, to use the ambiguous phrase so common in such discussions. The difference of opinion is largely grounded on an implicit or explicit difference in predictions about the efficacy of this particular means in furthering the agreed-on end. Proponents believe (predict) that legal minimum wages diminish poverty by raising the wages of those receiving less than the minimum wage as well as of some receiving more than the minimum wage without any counterbalancing increase in the number of people entirely unemployed or employed less advantageously than they otherwise would be. Opponents believe (predict) that legal minimum wages increase poverty by increasing the number of people who are unemployed or employed less advantageously and that this more than offsets any favorable effect on the wages of those who remain employed. Agreement about the economic consequences of the legislation might not produce complete agreement about its desirability, for differences might still remain about its political or social consequences; but, given agreement on objectives, it would certainly go a long way toward producing consensus.

Closely related differences in positive analysis underlie divergent views about the appropriate role and place of trade-unions and the desirability of direct price and wage controls and of tariffs. Different predictions about the importance of so-called "economies of scale" account very largely for divergent views about the desirability or necessity of detailed government regulation of industry and even of socialism rather than private enterprise. And this list could be extended indefinitely.[5] Of course, my judg-

ment that the major differences about economic policy in the Western world are of this kind is itself a "positive" statement to be accepted or rejected on the basis of empirical evidence.

If this judgment is valid, it means that a consensus on "correct" economic policy depends much less on the progress of normative economics proper than on the progress of a positive economics yielding conclusions that are, and deserve to be, widely accepted. It means also that a major reason for distinguishing positive economics sharply from normative economics is precisely the contribution that can thereby be made to agreement about policy.

II. POSITIVE ECONOMICS

The ultimate goal of a positive science is the development of a "theory" or "hypothesis" that yields valid and meaningful (i.e., not truistic) predictions about phenomena not yet observed. Such a theory is, in general, a complex intermixture of two elements. In part, it is a "language" designed to promote "systematic and organized methods of reasoning."[6] In part, it is a body of substantive hypotheses designed to abstract essential features of complex reality.

Viewed as a language, theory has no substantive content; it is a set of tautologies. Its function is to serve as a filing system for organizing empirical material and facilitating our understanding of it; and the criteria by which it is to be judged are those appropriate to a filing system. Are the categories clearly and precisely defined? Are they exhaustive? Do we know where to file each individual item, or is there considerable ambiguity? Is the system of headings and subheadings so designated that we can quickly find an item we want, or must we hunt from place to place? Are the items we shall want to consider jointly filed together? Does the filing system avoid elaborate cross-references?

The answers to these questions depend partly on logical, partly on factual, considerations. The canons of formal logic alone can show whether a particular language is complete and consistent, that is, whether

[5]One rather more complex example is stabilization policy. Superficially, divergent views on this question seem to reflect differences in objectives; but I believe that this impression is misleading and that at bottom the different views reflect primarily different judgments about the source of fluctuations in economic activity and the effect of alternative countercyclical action. For one major positive consideration that accounts for much of the divergence see "The Effects of a Full-Employment Policy on Economic Stability: A Formal Analysis," *infra*, pp. 117–32.

For a summary of the present state of professional views on this question see "The Problem of Economic Instability," a report of a subcommittee of the Committee on Public Issues of the American Economic Association, *American Economic Review*, XL (September, 1950), 501–38.
[6]Final quoted phrase from Alfred Marshall, "The Present Position of Economics" (1885), reprinted in *Memorials of Alfred Marshall*, ed. A. C. Pigou (London: Macmillan & Co., 1925), p. 164. See also "The Marshallian Demand Curve," *infra*, pp. 56–57, 90–91.

propositions in the language are "right" or "wrong." Factual evidence alone can show whether the categories of the "analytical filing system" have a meaningful empirical counterpart, that is, whether they are useful in analyzing a particular class of concrete problems.[7] The simple example of "supply" and "demand" illustrates both this point and the preceding list of analogical questions. Viewed as elements of the language of economic theory, these are the two major categories into which factors affecting the relative prices of products or factors of production are classified. The usefulness of the dichotomy depends on the "empirical generalization that an enumeration of the forces affecting demand in any problem and of the forces affecting supply will yield two lists that contain few items in common."[8] Now this generalization is valid for markets like the final market for a consumer good. In such a market there is a clear and sharp distinction between the economic units that can be regarded as demanding the product and those that can be regarded as supplying it. There is seldom much doubt whether a particular factor should be classified as affecting supply, on the one hand, or demand, on the other; and there is seldom much necessity for considering cross-effects (cross-references) between the two categories. In these cases the simple and even obvious step of filing the relevant factors under the headings of "supply" and "demand" effects a great simplification of the problem and is an effective safeguard against fallacies that otherwise tend to occur. But the generalization is not always valid. For example, it is not valid for the day-to-day fluctuations of prices in a primarily speculative market. Is a rumor of an increased excess-profits tax, for example, to be regarded as a factor operating primarily on today's supply of corporate equities in the stock market or on today's demand for them? In similar fashion, almost every factor can with about as much justification be classified under the heading "supply" as under the heading "demand." These concepts can still be used and may not be entirely pointless; they are still "right" but clearly less useful than in the first example because they have no meaningful empirical counterpart.

Viewed as a body of substantive hypotheses, theory is to be judged by its predictive power for the class of phenomena which it is intended to "explain."

Only factual evidence can show whether it is "right" or "wrong" or, better, tentatively "accepted" as valid or "rejected." As I shall argue at greater length below, the only relevant test of the *validity* of a hypothesis is comparison of its predictions with experience. The hypothesis is rejected if its predictions are contradicted ("frequently" or more often than predictions from an alternative hypothesis); it is accepted if its predictions are not contradicted; great confidence is attached to it if it has survived many opportunities for contradiction. Factual evidence can never "prove" a hypothesis; it can only fail to disprove it, which is what we generally mean when we say, somewhat inexactly, that the hypothesis has been "confirmed" by experience.

To avoid confusion, it should perhaps be noted explicitly that the "predictions" by which the validity of a hypothesis is tested need not be about phenomena that have not yet occurred, that is, need not be forecasts of future events; they may be about phenomena that have occurred but observations on which have not yet been made or are not known to the person making the prediction. For example, a hypothesis may imply that such and such must have happened in 1906, given some other known circumstances. If a search of the records reveals that such and such did happen, the prediction is confirmed; if it reveals that such and such did not happen, the prediction is contradicted.

The validity of a hypothesis in this sense is not by itself a sufficient criterion for choosing among alternative hypotheses. Observed facts are necessarily finite in number; possible hypotheses, infinite. If there is one hypothesis that is consistent with the available evidence, there are always an infinite number that are.[9] For example, suppose a specific excise tax on a particular commodity produces a rise in price equal to the amount of the tax. This is consistent with competitive conditions, a stable demand curve, and a horizontal and stable supply curve. But it is also consistent with competitive conditions and a positively or negatively sloping supply curve with the required compensating shift in the demand curve or the supply curve; with monopolistic conditions, constant marginal costs, and stable demand curve, of the particular shape required to produce this result; and so on indefinitely. Additional evidence with which

---

[7]See "Lange on Price Flexibility and Employment: A Methodological Criticism," *infra*, pp. 282–89.
[8]"The Marshallian Demand Curve," *infra*, p. 57.

[9]The qualification is necessary because the "evidence" may be internally contradictory, so there may be no hypothesis consistent with it. See also "Lange on Price Flexibility and Employment," *infra*, pp. 282–83.

the hypothesis is to be consistent may rule out some of these possibilities; it can never reduce them to a single possibility alone capable of being consistent with the finite evidence. The choice among alternative hypotheses equally consistent with the available evidence must to some extent be arbitrary, though there is general agreement that relevant considerations are suggested by the criteria "simplicity" and "fruitfulness," themselves notions that defy completely objective specification. A theory is "simpler" the less the initial knowledge needed to make a prediction within a given field of phenomena; it is more "fruitful" the more precise the resulting prediction, the wider the area within which the theory yields predictions, and the more additional lines for further research it suggests. Logical completeness and consistency are relevant but play a subsidiary role; their function is to assure that the hypothesis says what it is intended to say and does so alike for all users— they play the same role here as checks for arithmetical accuracy do in statistical computations.

Unfortunately, we can seldom test particular predictions in the social sciences by experiments explicitly designed to eliminate what are judged to be the most important disturbing influences. Generally, we must rely on evidence cast up by the "experiments" that happen to occur. The inability to conduct so-called "controlled experiments" does not, in my view, reflect a basic difference between the social and physical sciences both because it is not peculiar to the social sciences—witness astronomy—and because the distinction between a controlled experiment and uncontrolled experience is at best one of degree. No experiment can be completely controlled, and every experience is partly controlled, in the sense that some disturbing influences are relatively constant in the course of it.

Evidence cast up by experience is abundant and frequently as conclusive as that from contrived experiments; thus the inability to conduct experiments is not a fundamental obstacle to testing hypotheses by the success of their predictions. But such evidence is far more difficult to interpret. It is frequently complex and always indirect and incomplete. Its collection is often arduous, and its interpretation generally requires subtle analysis and involved chains of reasoning, which seldom carry real conviction. The denial to economics of the dramatic and direct evidence of the "crucial" experiment does hinder the adequate testing of hypotheses; but this is much less significant

than the difficulty it places in the way of achieving a reasonably prompt and wide consensus on the conclusions justified by the available evidence. It renders the weeding-out of unsuccessful hypotheses slow and difficult. They are seldom downed for good and are always cropping up again.

There is, of course, considerable variation in these respects. Occasionally, experience casts up evidence that is about as direct, dramatic, and convincing as any that could be provided by controlled experiments. Perhaps the most obviously important example is the evidence from inflations on the hypothesis that a substantial increase in the quantity of money within a relatively short period is accompanied by a substantial increase in prices. Here the evidence is dramatic, and the chain of reasoning required to interpret it is relatively short. Yet, despite numerous instances of substantial rises in prices, their essentially one-to-one correspondence with substantial rises in the stock of money, and the wide variation in other circumstances that might appear to be relevant, each new experience of inflation brings forth vigorous contentions, and not only by the lay public, that the rise in the stock of money is either an incidental effect of a rise in prices produced by other factors or a purely fortuitous and unnecessary concomitant of the price rise.

One effect of the difficulty of testing substantive economic hypotheses has been to foster a retreat into purely formal or tautological analysis.[10] As already noted, tautologies have an extremely important place in economics and other sciences as a specialized language or "analytical filing system." Beyond this, formal logic and mathematics, which are both tautologies, are essential aids in checking the correctness of reasoning, discovering the implications of hypotheses, and determining whether supposedly different hypotheses may not really be equivalent or wherein the differences lie.

But economic theory must be more than a structure of tautologies if it is to be able to predict and not merely describe the consequences of action; if it is to be something different from disguised mathematics.[11] And the usefulness of the tautologies themselves ultimately depends, as noted above, on the

[10]See "Lange on Price Flexibility and Employment" *infra, passim*.
[11]See also Milton Friedman and L. J. Savage, "The Expected-Utility Hypothesis and the Measurability of Utility," *Journal of Political Economy*, LX (December, 1952), 463–74, esp. pp. 465–67.

acceptability of the substantive hypotheses that suggest the particular categories into which they organize the refractory empirical phenomena.

A more serious effect of the difficulty of testing economic hypotheses by their predictions is to foster misunderstanding of the role of empirical evidence in theoretical work. Empirical evidence is vital at two different, though closely related, stages: in constructing hypotheses and in testing their validity. Full and comprehensive evidence on the phenomena to be generalized or "explained" by a hypothesis, besides its obvious value in suggesting new hypotheses, is needed to assure that a hypothesis explains what it sets out to explain—that its implications for such phenomena are not contradicted in advance by experience that has already been observed.[12] Given that the hypothesis is consistent with the evidence at hand, its further testing involves deducing from it new facts capable of being observed but not previously known and checking these deduced facts against additional empirical evidence. For this test to be relevant, the deduced facts must be about the class of phenomena the hypothesis is designed to explain; and they must be well enough defined so that observation can show them to be wrong.

The two stages of constructing hypotheses and testing their validity are related in two different respects. In the first place, the particular facts that enter at each stage are partly an accident of the collection of data and the knowledge of the particular investigator. The facts that serve as a test of the implications of a hypothesis might equally well have been among the raw material used to construct it, and conversely. In the second place, the process never begins from scratch; the so-called "initial stage" itself always involves comparison of the implications of an earlier set of hypotheses with observation; the contradiction of these implications is the stimulus to the construction of new hypotheses or revision of old ones. So the two methodologically distinct stages are always proceeding jointly.

Misunderstanding about this apparently straightforward process centers on the phrase "the class of phenomena the hypothesis is designed to explain." The difficulty in the social sciences of getting new evidence for this class of phenomena and of judging its conformity with the implications of the hypothesis makes it tempting to suppose that other, more readily available, evidence is equally relevant to the validity of the hypothesis—to suppose that hypotheses have not only "implications" but also "assumptions" and that the conformity of these "assumptions" to "reality" is a test of the validity of the hypothesis *different from* or *additional to* the test by implications. This

---

[12]In recent years some economists, particularly a group connected with the Cowles Commission for Research in Economics at the University of Chicago, have placed great emphasis on a division of this step of selecting a hypothesis consistent with known evidence into two substeps: first, the selection of a class of admissible hypotheses from all possible hypotheses (the choice of a "model" in their terminology); second, the selection of one hypothesis from this class (the choice of a "structure"). This subdivision may be heuristically valuable in some kinds of work, particularly in promoting a systematic use of available statistical evidence and theory. From a methodological point of view, however, it is an entirely arbitrary subdivision of the process of deciding on a particular hypothesis that is on a par with many other subdivisions that may be convenient for one purpose or another or that may suit the psychological needs of particular investigators.

One consequence of this particular subdivision has been to give rise to the so-called "identification" problem. As noted above, if one hypothesis is consistent with available evidence, an infinite number are. But, while this is true for the class of hypotheses as a whole, it may not be true of the subclass obtained in the first of the above two steps—the "model." It may be that the evidence to be used to select the final hypothesis from the subclass can be consistent with at most one hypothesis in it, in which case the "model" is said to be "identified"; otherwise is is said to be "unidentified." As is clear from this way of describing the concept of "identification," it is essentially a special case of the more general problem of selecting among the alternative hypotheses equally consistent with the evidence—a problem that must be decided by some such arbitrary principle as Occam's razor. The introduction of two substeps in selecting a hypothesis makes this problem arise at the two corresponding stages and gives it a special cast. While the class of all hypotheses is always unidentified, the subclass in a "model" need not be, so the problem arises of conditions that a "model" must satisfy to be identified. However useful the two substeps may be in some contexts, their introduction raises the danger that different criteria will unwittingly be used in making the same kind of choice among alternative hypotheses at two different stages.

On the general methodological approach discussed in this footnote see Tryvge Haavelmo, "The Probability Approach in Econometrics," *Econometrica*, Vol. XII (1944), Supplement; Jacob Marschak, "Economic Structure, Path, Policy, and Prediction," *American Economic Review*, XXXVII (May, 1947), 81–84, and "Statistical Inference in Economics: An Introduction," in T. C. Koopmans (ed.), *Statistical Inference in Dynamic Economic Models* (New York: John Wiley & Sons, 1950); T. C. Koopmans, "Statistical Estimation of Simultaneous Economic Relations," *Journal of the American Statistical Association*, XL (December, 1945), 448–66; Gershon Cooper, "The Role of Economic Theory in Econometric Models," *Journal of Farm Economics*, XXX (February, 1948), 101–16. On the identification problem see Koopmans, "Identification Problems in Econometric Model Construction," *Econometrica*, XVII (April, 1949), 125–44; Leonid Hurwicz, "Generalization of the Concept of Identification," in Koopmans (ed.), *Statistical Inference in Dynamic Economic Models*.

widely held view is fundamentally wrong and productive of much mischief. Far from providing an easier means for sifting valid from invalid hypotheses, it only confuses the issue, promotes misunderstanding about the significance of empirical evidence for economic theory, produces a misdirection of much intellectual effort devoted to the development of positive economics, and impedes the attainment of consensus on tentative hypotheses in positive economics.

In so far as a theory can be said to have "assumptions" at all, and in so far as their "realism" can be judged independently of the validity of predictions, the relation between the significance of a theory and the "realism" of its "assumptions" is almost the opposite of that suggested by the view under criticism. Truly important and significant hypotheses will be found to have "assumptions" that are wildly inaccurate descriptive representations of reality, and, in general, the more significant the theory, the more unrealistic the assumptions (in this sense).[13] The reason is simple. A hypothesis is important if it "explains" much by little, that is, if it abstracts the common and crucial elements from the mass of complex and detailed circumstances surrounding the phenomena to be explained and permits valid predictions on the basis of them alone. To be important, therefore, a hypothesis must be descriptively false in its assumptions; it takes account of, and accounts for, none of the many other attendant circumstances, since its very success shows them to be irrelevant for the phenomena to be explained.

To put this point less paradoxically, the relevant question to ask about the "assumptions" of a theory is not whether they are descriptively "realistic," for they never are, but whether they are sufficiently good approximations for the purpose in hand. And this question can be answered only by seeing whether the theory works, which means whether it yields sufficiently accurate predictions. The two supposedly independent tests thus reduce to one test.

The theory of monopolistic and imperfect competition is one example of the neglect in economic theory of these propositions. The development of this analysis was explicitly motivated, and its wide acceptance and approval largely explained, by the belief that the assumptions of "perfect competition" or "perfect monopoly" said to underlie neoclassical economic theory are a false image of reality. And this belief was itself based almost entirely on the directly perceived descriptive inaccuracy of the assumptions rather than on any recognized contradiction of predictions derived from neoclassical economic theory. The lengthy discussion on marginal analysis in the *American Economic Review* some years ago is an even clearer, though much less important, example. The articles on both sides of the controversy largely neglect what seems to me clearly the main issue—the conformity to experience of the implications of the marginal analysis—and concentrate on the largely irrelevant question whether businessmen do or do not in fact reach their decisions by consulting schedules, or curves, or multivariable functions showing marginal cost and marginal revenue.[14] Perhaps these two examples, and the many others they readily suggest, will serve to justify a more extensive discussion of the methodological principles involved than might otherwise seem appropriate.

III. CAN A HYPOTHESIS BE TESTED BY THE REALISM OF ITS ASSUMPTIONS?

We may start with a simple physical example, the law of falling bodies. It is an accepted hypothesis

---

[13]The converse of the proposition does not of course hold: assumptions that are unrealistic (in this sense) do not guarantee a significant theory.

[14]See R. A. Lester, "Shortcomings of Marginal Analysis for Wage-Employment Problems," *American Economic Review*, XXXVI (March, 1946), 62–82; Fritz Machlup, "Marginal Analysis and Empirical Research," *American Economic Review*, XXXVI (September, 1946), 519–54; R. A. Lester, "Marginalism, Minimum Wages, and Labor Markets," *American Economic Review*, XXXVII (March, 1947), 135–48; Fritz Machlup, "Rejoinder to an Antimarginalist," *American Economic Review*, XXXVII (March, 1947), 148–54; G. J. Stigler, "Professor Lester and the Marginalists," *American Economic Review*, XXXVII (March, 1947), 154–57; H. M. Oliver, Jr., "Marginal Theory and Business Behavior," *American Economic Review*, XXXVII (June, 1947), 375–83; R. A. Gordon, "Short-Period Price Determination in Theory and Practice," *American Economic Review*, XXXVIII (June, 1948), 265–88.

It should be noted that, along with much material purportedly bearing on the validity of the "assumptions" of marginal theory, Lester does refer to evidence on the conformity of experience with the implications of the theory, citing the reactions of employment in Germany to the Papen plan and in the United States to changes in minimum-wage legislation as examples of lack of conformity. However, Stigler's brief comment is the only one of the other papers that refers to this evidence. It should also be noted that Machlup's thorough and careful exposition of the logical structure and meaning of marginal analysis is called for by the misunderstandings on this score that mar Lester's paper and almost conceal the evidence he presents that is relevant to the key issue he raises. But, in Machlup's emphasis on the logical structure, he comes perilously close to presenting the theory as a pure tautology, though it is evident at a number of points that he is aware of this danger and anxious to avoid it. The papers by Oliver and Gordon are the most extreme in the exclusive concentration on the conformity of the behavior of businessmen with the "assumptions" of the theory.

that the acceleration of a body dropped in a vacuum is a constant—*g,* or approximately 32 feet per second per second on the earth—and is independent of the shape of the body, the manner of dropping it, etc. This implies that the distance traveled by a falling body in any specified time is given by the formula $s = \frac{1}{2}gt^2$, where s is the distance traveled in feet and t is time in seconds. The application of this formula to a compact ball dropped from the roof of a building is equivalent to saying that a ball so dropped behaves *as if* it were falling in a vacuum. Testing this hypothesis by its assumptions presumably means measuring the actual air pressure and deciding whether it is close enough to zero. At sea level the air pressure is about 15 pounds per square inch. Is 15 sufficiently close to zero for the difference to be judged insignificant? Apparently it is, since the actual time taken by a compact ball to fall from the roof of a building to the ground is very close to the time given by the formula. Suppose, however, that a feather is dropped instead of a compact ball. The formula then gives wildly inaccurate results. Apparently, 15 pounds per square inch is significantly different from zero for a feather but not for a ball. Or, again, suppose the formula is applied to a ball dropped from an airplane at an altitude of 30,000 feet. The air pressure at this altitude is decidedly less than 15 pounds per square inch. Yet, the actual time of fall from 30,000 feet to 20,000 feet, at which point the air pressure is still much less than at sea level, will differ noticeably from the time predicted by the formula—much more noticeably than the time taken by a compact ball to fall from the roof of a building to the ground. According to the formula, the velocity of the ball should be gt and should therefore increase steadily. In fact, a ball dropped at 30,000 feet will reach its top velocity well before it hits the ground. And similarly with other implications of the formula.

The initial question whether 15 is sufficiently close to zero for the difference to be judged insignificant is clearly a foolish question by itself. Fifteen pounds per square inch is 2,160 pounds per square foot, or 0.0075 ton per square inch. There is no possible basis for calling these numbers "small" or "large" without some external standard of comparison. And the only relevant standard of comparison is the air pressure for which the formula does or does not work under a given set of circumstances. But this raises the same problem at a second level. What is the meaning of "does or does not work"? Even if we could eliminate errors of measurement, the measured time of fall would seldom if ever be precisely equal to the computed time of fall. How large must the difference between the two be to justify saying that the theory "does not work"? Here there are two important external standards of comparison. One is the accuracy achievable by an alternative theory with which this theory is being compared and which is equally acceptable on all other grounds. The other arises when there exists a theory that is known to yield better predictions but only at a greater cost. The gains from greater accuracy, which depend on the purpose in mind, must then be balanced against the costs of achieving it.

This example illustrates both the impossibility of testing a theory by its assumptions and also the ambiguity of the concept "the assumptions of a theory." The formula $s = \frac{1}{2}gt^2$ is valid for bodies falling in a vacuum and can be derived by analyzing the behavior of such bodies. It can therefore be stated: under a wide range of circumstances, bodies that fall in the actual atmosphere behave *as if* they were falling in a vacuum. In the language so common in economics this would be rapidly translated into: the formula assumes a vacuum. Yet it clearly does no such thing. What it does say is that in many cases the existence of air pressure, the shape of the body, the name of the person dropping the body, the kind of mechanism used to drop the body, and a host of other attendant circumstances have no appreciable effect on the distance the body falls in a specified time. The hypothesis can readily be rephrased to omit all mention of a vacuum: under a wide range of circumstances, the distance a body falls in a specified time is given by the formula $s = \frac{1}{2}gt^2$. The history of this formula and its associated physical theory aside, is it meaningful to say that it assumes a vacuum? There may be other sets of assumptions that would yield the same formula. The formula is accepted because it works, not because we live in an approximate vacuum—whatever that means.

The important problem in connection with the hypothesis is to specify the circumstances under which the formula works or, more precisely, the general magnitude of the error in its predictions under various circumstances. Indeed, as is implicit in the above rephrasing of the hypothesis, such a specification is not one thing and the hypothesis another. The specification is itself an essential part of the hypothesis, and it is a part that is peculiarly likely to be revised and extended as experience accumulates.

In the particular case of falling bodies a more general, though still incomplete, theory is available, largely as a result of attempts to explain the errors of the simple theory, from which the influence of some of the possible disturbing factors can be calculated and of which the simple theory is a special case. However, it does not always pay to use the more general theory because the extra accuracy it yields may not justify the extra cost of using it, so the question under what circumstances the simpler theory works "well enough" remains important. Air pressure is one, but only one, of the variables that define these circumstances; the shape of the body, the velocity attained, and still other variables are relevant as well. One way of interpreting the variables other than air pressure is to regard them as determining whether a particular departure from the "assumption" of a vacuum is or is not significant. For example, the difference in shape of the body can be said to make 15 pounds per square inch significantly different from zero for a feather but not for a compact ball dropped a moderate distance. Such a statement must, however, be sharply distinguished from the very different statement that the theory does not work for a feather because its assumptions are false. The relevant relation runs the other way: the assumptions are false for a feather because the theory does not work. This point needs emphasis, because the entirely valid use of "assumptions" in *specifying* the circumstances for which a theory holds is frequently, and erroneously, interpreted to mean that the assumptions can be used to *determine* the circumstances for which a theory holds, and has, in this way, been an important source of the belief that a theory can be tested by its assumptions.

Let us turn now to another example, this time a constructed one designed to be an analogue of many hypotheses in the social sciences. Consider the density of leaves around a tree. I suggest the hypothesis that the leaves are positioned as if each leaf deliberately sought to maximize the amount of sunlight it receives, given the position of its neighbors, as if it knew the physical laws determining the amount of sunlight that would be received in various positions and could move rapidly or instantaneously from any one position to any other desired and unoccupied position.[15] Now some of the more obvious impli-

cations of this hypothesis are clearly consistent with experience: for example, leaves are in general denser on the south than on the north side of trees but, as the hypothesis implies, less so or not at all on the northern slope of a hill or when the south side of the trees is shaded in some other way. Is the hypothesis rendered unacceptable or invalid because, so far as we know, leaves do not "deliberate" or consciously "seek," have not been to school and learned the relevant laws of science or the mathematics required to calculate the "optimum" position, and cannot move from position to position? Clearly, none of these contradictions of the hypothesis is vitally relevant; the phenomena involved are not within the "class of phenomena the hypothesis is designed to explain"; the hypothesis does not assert that leaves do these things but only that their density is the same *as if* they did. Despite the apparent falsity of the "assumptions" of the hypothesis, it has great plausibility because of the conformity of its implications with observation. We are inclined to "explain" its validity on the ground that sunlight contributes to the growth of leaves and that hence leaves will grow denser or more putative leaves survive where there is more sun, so the result achieved by purely passive adaptation to external circumstances is the same as the result that would be achieved by deliberate accommodation to them. This alternative hypothesis is more attractive than the constructed hypothesis not because its "assumptions" are more "realistic" but rather because it is part of a more general theory that applies to a wider variety of phenomena, of which the position of leaves around a tree is a special case, has more implications capable of being contradicted, and has failed to be contradicted under a wider variety of circumstances. The direct evidence for the growth of leaves is in this way strengthened by the indirect evidence from the other phenomena to which the more general theory applies.

The constructed hypothesis is presumably valid, that is, yields "sufficiently" accurate predictions about the density of leaves, only for a particular class of circumstances. I do not know what these circumstances are or how to define them. It seems obvious, however, that in this example the "assumptions" of the theory will play no part in specifying them: the kind of tree, the character of the soil, etc., are the types of variables that are likely to define its range of validity, not the ability of the leaves to do complicated mathematics or to move from place to place.

A largely parallel example involving human be-

[15]This example, and some of the subsequent discussion, though independent in origin, is similar to and in much the same spirit as an example and the approach in an important paper by Armen A. Alchian, "Uncertainty, Evolution, and Economic Theory," *Journal of Political Economy,* LVIII (June, 1950), 211–21.

havior has been used elsewhere by Savage and me.[16] Consider the problem of predicting the shots made by an expert billiard player. It seems not at all unreasonable that excellent predictions would be yielded by the hypothesis that the billiard player made his shots *as if* he knew the complicated mathematical formulas that would give the optimum directions of travel, could estimate accurately by eye the angles, etc., describing the location of the balls, could make lightning calculations from the formulas, and could then make the balls travel in the direction indicated by the formulas. Our confidence in this hypothesis is not based on the belief that billiard players, even expert ones, can or do go through the process described; it derives rather from the belief that, unless in some way or other they were capable of reaching essentially the same result, they would not in fact be *expert* billiard players.

It is only a short step from these examples to the economic hypothesis that under a wide range of circumstances individual firms behave *as if* they were seeking rationally to maximize their expected returns (generally if misleadingly called "profits")[17] and had full knowledge of the data needed to succeed in this attempt; *as if,* that is, they knew the relevant cost and demand functions, calculated marginal cost and marginal revenue from all actions open to them, and pushed each line of action to the point at which the relevant marginal cost and marginal revenue were equal. Now, of course, businessmen do not actually

[16]Milton Friedman and L. J. Savage, "The Utility Analysis of Choices Involving Risk," *Journal of Political Economy,* LVI (August, 1948), 298. Reprinted in American Economic Association, *Readings in Price Theory* (Chicago: Richard D. Irwin, Inc., 1952), pp. 57–96.

[17]It seems better to use the term "profits" to refer to the difference between actual and "expected" results, between *ex post* and *ex ante* receipts. "Profits" are then a result of uncertainty and, as Alchian (*op. cit.,* p. 212), following Tintner, points out, cannot be deliberately maximized in advance. Given uncertainty, individuals or firms choose among alternative anticipated probability distributions of receipts or incomes. The specific content of a theory of choice among such distributions depends on the criteria by which they are supposed to be ranked. One hypothesis supposes them to be ranked by the mathematical expectation of utility corresponding to them (see Friedman and Savage, "The Expected-Utility Hypothesis and the Measurability of Utility," *op. cit.*). A special case of this hypothesis or an alternative to it ranks probability distributions by the mathematical expectation of the money receipts corresponding to them. The latter is perhaps more applicable, and more frequently applied, to firms than to individuals. The term "expected returns" is intended to be sufficiently broad to apply to any of these alternatives.

The issues alluded to in this note are not basic to the methodological issues being discussed, and so are largely by-passed in the discussion that follows.

and literally solve the system of simultaneous equations in terms of which the mathematical economist finds it convenient to express this hypothesis, any more than leaves or billiard players explicitly go through complicated mathematical calculations or falling bodies decide to create a vacuum. The billiard player, if asked how he decides where to hit the ball, may say that he "just figures it out" but then also rubs a rabbit's foot just to make sure; and the businessman may well say that he prices at average cost, with of course some minor deviations when the market makes it necessary. The one statement is about as helpful as the other, and neither is a relevant test of the associated hypothesis.

Confidence in the maximization-of-returns hypothesis is justified by evidence of a very different character. This evidence is in part similar to that adduced on behalf of the billiard-player hypothesis—unless the behavior of businessmen in some way or other approximated behavior consistent with the maximization of returns, it seems unlikely that they would remain in business for long. Let the apparent immediate determinant of business behavior be anything at all—habitual reaction, random chance, or whatnot. Whenever this determinant happens to lead to behavior consistent with rational and informed maximization of returns, the business will prosper and acquire resources with which to expand; whenever it does not, the business will tend to lose resources and can be kept in existence only by the addition of resources from outside. The process of "natural selection" thus helps to validate the hypothesis—or, rather, given natural selection, acceptance of the hypothesis can be based largely on the judgment that it summarizes appropriately the conditions for survival.

An even more important body of evidence for the maximization-of-returns hypothesis is experience from countless applications of the hypothesis to specific problems and the repeated failure of its implications to be contradicted. This evidence is extremely hard to document; it is scattered in numerous memorandums, articles, and monographs concerned primarily with specific concrete problems rather than with submitting the hypothesis to test. Yet the continued use and acceptance of the hypothesis over a long period, and the failure of any coherent, self-consistent alternative to be developed and be widely accepted, is strong indirect testimony to its worth. The evidence *for* a hypothesis always consists of its repeated failure to be contradicted, continues to accumulate so long as the hypothesis is used, and by its very nature is difficult to document at all comprehensively. It tends to become part of the tradition and folklore of a science revealed in the tenacity with which hypotheses are held rather than in any textbook list of instances in which the hypothesis has failed to be contradicted.

IV. THE SIGNIFICANCE AND ROLE OF THE "ASSUMPTIONS" OF A THEORY

Up to this point our conclusions about the significance of the "assumptions" of a theory have been almost entirely negative: we have seen that a theory cannot be tested by the "realism" of its "assumptions" and that the very concept of the "assumptions" of a theory is surrounded with ambiguity. But, if this were all there is to it, it would be hard to explain the extensive use of the concept and the strong tendency that we all have to speak of the assumptions of a theory and to compare the assumptions of alternative theories. There is too much smoke for there to be no fire.

In methodology, as in positive science, negative statements can generally be made with greater confidence than positive statements, so I have less confidence in the following remarks on the significance and role of "assumptions" than in the preceding remarks. So far as I can see, the "assumptions of a theory" play three different, though related, positive roles: *(a)* they are often an economical mode of describing or presenting a theory; *(b)* they sometimes facilitate an indirect test of the hypothesis by its implications; and *(c)*, as already noted, they are sometimes a convenient means of specifying the conditions under which the theory is expected to be valid. The first two require more extensive discussion.

A. The Use of "Assumptions" in Stating a Theory

The example of the leaves illustrates the first role of assumptions. Instead of saying that leaves seek to maximize the sunlight they receive, we could state the equivalent hypothesis, without any apparent assumptions, in the form of a list of rules for predicting the density of leaves: if a tree stands in a level field with no other trees or other bodies obstructing the rays of the sun, then the density of leaves will tend to be such and such; if a tree is on the northern slope of a hill in the midst of a forest of similar trees, then . . . ; etc. This is clearly a far less economical

presentation of the hypothesis than the statement that leaves seek to maximize the sunlight each receives. The latter statement is, in effect, a simple summary of the rules in the above list, even if the list were indefinitely extended, since it indicates both how to determine the features of the environment that are important for the particular problem and how to evaluate their effects. It is more compact and at the same time no less comprehensive.

More generally, a hypothesis or theory consists of an assertion that certain forces are, and by implication others are not, important for a particular class of phenomena and a specification of the manner of action of the forces it asserts to be important. We can regard the hypothesis as consisting of two parts: first, a conceptual world or abstract model simpler than the "real world" and containing only the forces that the hypothesis asserts to be important; second, a set of rules defining the class of phenomena for which the "model" can be taken to be an adequate representation of the "real world" and specifying the correspondence between the variables or entities in the model and observable phenomena.

These two parts are very different in character. The model is abstract and complete; it is an "algebra" or "logic." Mathematics and formal logic come into their own in checking its consistency and completeness and exploring its implications. There is no place in the model for, and no function to be served by, vagueness, maybe's, or approximations. The air pressure is zero, not "small," for a vacuum; the demand curve for the product of a competitive producer is horizontal (has a slope of zero), not "almost horizontal."

The rules for using the model, on the other hand, cannot possibly be abstract and complete. They must be concrete and in consequence incomplete—completeness is possible only in a conceptual world, not in the "real world," however that may be interpreted. The model is the logical embodiment of the half-truth, "There is nothing new under the sun"; the rules for applying it cannot neglect the equally significant half-truth, "History never repeats itself." To a considerable extent the rules can be formulated explicitly—most easily, though even then not completely, when the theory is part of an explicit more general theory as in the example of the vacuum theory for falling bodies. In seeking to make a science as "objective" as possible, our aim should be to formulate the rules explicitly in so far as possible and continually to widen the range of phenomena for which it is possible to do so. But, no matter how successful we may be in this attempt, there inevitably will remain room for judgment in applying the rules. Each occurrence has some features peculiarly its own, not covered by the explicit rules. The capacity to judge that these are or are not to be disregarded, that they should or should not affect what observable phenomena are to be identified with what entities in the model, is something that cannot be taught; it can be learned but only by experience and exposure in the "right" scientific atmosphere, not by rote. It is at this point that the "amateur" is separated from the "professional" in all sciences and that the thin line is drawn which distinguishes the "crackpot" from the scientist.

A simple example may perhaps clarify this point. Euclidean geometry is an abstract model, logically complete and consistent. Its entities are precisely defined—a line is not a geometrical figure "much" longer than it is wide or deep; it is a figure whose width and depth are zero. It is also obviously "unrealistic." There are no such things in "reality" as Euclidean points or lines or surfaces. Let us apply this abstract model to a mark made on a blackboard by a piece of chalk. Is the mark to be identified with a Euclidean line, a Euclidean surface, or a Euclidean solid? Clearly, it can appropriately be identified with a line if it is being used to represent, say, a demand curve. But it cannot be so identified if it is being used to color, say, countries on a map, for that would imply that the map would never be colored; for this purpose, the same mark must be identified with a surface. But it cannot be so identified by a manufacturer of chalk, for that would imply that no chalk would ever be used up; for his purposes, the same mark must be identified with a volume. In this simple example these judgments will command general agreement. Yet it seems obvious that, while general considerations can be formulated to guide such judgments, they can never be comprehensive and cover every possible instance; they cannot have the self-contained coherent character of Euclidean geometry itself.

In speaking of the "crucial assumptions" of a theory, we are, I believe, trying to state the key elements of the abstract model. There are generally many different ways of describing the model completely—many different sets of "postulates" which both imply and are implied by the model as a whole. These are all logically equivalent: what are regarded as axioms or postulates of a model from one point of view can be regarded as theorems from another, and conversely. The particular "assumptions" termed "crucial" are selected on grounds of their convenience in some such respects as simplicity or economy in describing the model, intuitive plausibility, or capacity to suggest, if only by implication, some of the considerations that are relevant in judging or applying the model.

B. The Use of "Assumptions" As an Indirect Test of a Theory

In presenting any hypothesis, it generally seems obvious which of the series of statements used to expound it refer to assumptions and which to implications; yet this distinction is not easy to define rigorously. It is not, I believe, a characteristic of the hypothesis as such but rather of the use to which the hypothesis is to be put. If this is so, the ease of classifying statements must reflect unambiguousness in the purpose the hypothesis is designed to serve. The possibility of interchanging theorems and axioms in an abstract model implies the possibility of interchanging "implications" and "assumptions" in the substantive hypothesis corresponding to the abstract model, which is not to say that any implication can be interchanged with any assumption but only that there may be more than one set of statements that imply the rest.

For example, consider a particular proposition in the theory of oligopolistic behavior. If we assume (a) that entrepreneurs seek to maximize their returns by any means including acquiring or extending monopoly power, this will imply (b) that, when demand for a "product" is geographically unstable, transportation costs are significant, explicit price agreements illegal, and the number of producers of the product relatively small, they will tend to establish basing-point pricing systems.[18] The assertion (a) is regarded as an assumption and (b) as an implication because we accept the prediction of market behavior as the purpose of the analysis. We shall regard the assumption as acceptable if we find that the conditions specified in (b) are generally associated with basing-point pricing, and conversely. Let us now change our purpose to deciding what cases to prosecute under the Sherman Antitrust Law's prohibition of a "conspir-

[18]See George J. Stigler, "A Theory of Delivered Price Systems," *American Economic Review*, XXXIX (December, 1949), 1143–57.

acy in restraint of trade." If we now assume (c) that basing-point pricing is a deliberate construction to facilitate collusion under the conditions specified in (b), this will imply (d) that entrepreneurs who participate in basing-point pricing are engaged in a "conspiracy in restraint of trade." What was formerly an assumption now becomes an implication, and conversely. We shall now regard the assumption (c) as valid if we find that, when entrepreneurs participate in basing-point pricing, there generally tends to be other evidence, in the form of letters, memorandums, or the like, of what courts regard as a "conspiracy in restraint of trade."

Suppose the hypothesis works for the first purpose, namely, the prediction of market behavior. It clearly does not follow that it will work for the second purpose, namely, predicting whether there is enough evidence of a "conspiracy in restraint of trade" to justify court action. And, conversely, if it works for the second purpose, it does not follow that it will work for the first. Yet, in the absence of other evidence, the success of the hypothesis for one purpose—in explaining one class of phenomena—will give us greater confidence than we would otherwise have that it may succeed for another purpose—in explaining another class of phenomena. It is much harder to say how much greater confidence it justifies. For this depends on how closely related we judge the two classes of phenomena to be, which itself depends in a complex way on similar kinds of indirect evidence, that is, on our experience in other connections in explaining by single theories phenomena that are in some sense similarly diverse.

To state the point more generally, what are called the assumptions of a hypothesis can be used to get some indirect evidence on the acceptability of the hypothesis in so far as the assumptions can themselves be regarded as implications of the hypothesis, and hence their conformity with reality as a failure of some implications to be contradicted, or in so far as the assumptions may call to mind other implications of the hypothesis susceptible to casual empirical observation.[19] The reason this evidence is indirect is that the assumptions or associated implications generally refer to a class of phenomena different from the class which the hypothesis is designed to explain;

indeed, as is implied above, this seems to be the chief criterion we use in deciding which statements to term "assumptions" and which to term "implications." The weight attached to this indirect evidence depends on how closely related we judge the classes of phenomena to be.

Another way in which the "assumptions" of a hypothesis can facilitate its indirect testing is by bringing out its kinship with other hypotheses and thereby making the evidence on their validity relevant to the validity of the hypothesis in question. For example, a hypothesis is formulated for a particular class of behavior. This hypothesis can, as usual, be stated without specifying any "assumptions." But suppose it can be shown that it is equivalent to a set of assumptions including the assumption that man seeks his own interest. The hypothesis then gains indirect plausibility from the success for other classes of phenomena of hypotheses that can also be said to make this assumption; at least, what is being done here is not completely unprecedented or unsuccessful in all other uses. In effect, the statement of assumptions so as to bring out a relationship between superficially different hypotheses is a step in the direction of a more general hypothesis.

This kind of indirect evidence from related hypotheses explains in large measure the difference in the confidence attached to a particular hypothesis by people with different backgrounds. Consider, for example, the hypothesis that the extent of racial or religious discrimination in employment in a particular area or industry is closely related to the degree of monopoly in the industry or area in question; that, if the industry is competitive, discrimination will be significant only if the race or religion of employees affects either the willingness of other employees to work with them or the acceptability of the product to customers and will be uncorrelated with the prejudices of employers.[20] This hypothesis is far more likely to appeal to an economist than to a sociologist. It can be said to "assume" single-minded pursuit of pecuniary self-interest by employers in competitive industries; and this "assumption" works well in a wide variety of hypotheses in economics bearing on many of the mass phenomena with which economics

[19]See Friedman and Savage, "The Expected-Utility Hypothesis and the Measurability of Utility," op. cit., pp. 466–67, for another specific example of this kind of indirect test.

[20]A rigorous statement of this hypothesis would of course have to specify how "extent of racial or religious discrimination" and "degree of monopoly" are to be judged. The loose statement in the text is sufficient, however, for present purposes.

deals. It is therefore likely to seem reasonable to the economist that it may work in this case as well. On the other hand, the hypotheses to which the sociologist is accustomed have a very different kind of model or ideal world, in which single-minded pursuit of pecuniary self-interest plays a much less important role. The indirect evidence available to the sociologist on this hypothesis is much less favorable to it than the indirect evidence available to the economist; he is therefore likely to view it with greater suspicion.

Of course, neither the evidence of the economist nor that of the sociologist is conclusive. The decisive test is whether the hypothesis works for the phenomena it purports to explain. But a judgment may be required before any satisfactory test of this kind has been made, and, perhaps, when it cannot be made in the near future, in which case, the judgment will have to be based on the inadequate evidence available. In addition, even when such a test can be made, the background of the scientists is not irrelevant to the judgments they reach. There is never certainty in science, and the weight of evidence for or against a hypothesis can never be assessed completely "objectively." The economist will be more tolerant than the sociologist in judging conformity of the implications of the hypothesis with experience, and he will be persuaded to accept the hypothesis tentatively by fewer instances of "conformity."

V. SOME IMPLICATIONS FOR ECONOMIC ISSUES

The abstract methodological issues we have been discussing have a direct bearing on the perennial criticism of "orthodox" economic theory as "unrealistic" as well as on the attempts that have been made to reformulate theory to meet this charge. Economics is a "dismal" science because it assumes man to be selfish and money-grubbing, "a lightning calculator of pleasures and pains, who oscillates like a homogeneous globule of desire of happiness under the impulse of stimuli that shift him about the area, but leave him intact";[21] it rests on outmoded psychology and must be reconstructed in line with each new development in psychology; it assumes men, or at least businessmen, to be "in a continuous state of 'alert,' ready to change prices and/or pricing

rules whenever their sensitive intuitions . . . detect a change in demand and supply conditions";[22] it assumes markets to be perfect, competition to be pure, and commodities, labor, and capital to be homogeneous.

As we have seen, criticism of this type is largely beside the point unless supplemented by evidence that a hypothesis differing in one or another of these respects from the theory being criticized yields better predictions for as wide a range of phenomena. Yet most such criticism is not so supplemented; it is based almost entirely on supposedly directly perceived discrepancies between the "assumptions" and the "real world." A particularly clear example is furnished by the recent criticisms of the maximization-of-returns hypothesis on the grounds that businessmen do not and indeed cannot behave as the theory "assumes" they do. The evidence cited to support this assertion is generally taken either from the answers given by businessmen to questions about the factors affecting their decisions—a procedure for testing economic theories that is about on a par with testing theories of longevity by asking octogenarians how they account for their long life—or from descriptive studies of the decision-making activities of individual firms.[23] Little if any evidence is ever cited on the conformity of businessmen's actual market behavior—what they do rather than what they say they do—with the implications of the hypothesis being criticized, on the one hand, and of an alternative hypothesis, on the other.

[22]Oliver, *op. cit.,* p. 381.

[23]See H. D. Henderson, "The Significance of the Rate of Interest," *Oxford Economic Papers,* No. 1 (October, 1938), pp. 1–13; J. E. Meade and P. W. S. Andrews, "Summary of Replies to Questions on Effects of Interest Rates," *Oxford Economic Papers,* No. 1 (October, 1938), pp. 14–31; R. F. Harrod, "Price and Cost in Entrepreneurs' Policy," *Oxford Economic Papers,* No. 2 (May, 1939), pp. 1–11; and R. J. Hall and C. J. Hitch, "Price Theory and Business Behavior," *Oxford Economic Papers,* No. 2 (May, 1939), pp. 12–45; Lester, "Shortcomings of Marginal Analysis for Wage-Employment Problems," *op. cit.;* Gordon, *op. cit.* See Fritz Machlup, "Marginal Analysis and Empirical Research," *op. cit.,* esp. Sec. II, for detailed criticisms of questionnaire methods.

I do not mean to imply that questionnaire studies of businessmen's or others' motives or beliefs about the forces affecting their behavior are useless for all purposes in economics. They may be extremely valuable in suggesting leads to follow in accounting for divergencies between predicted and observed results; that is, in constructing new hypotheses or revising old ones. Whatever their suggestive value in this respect, they seem to me almost entirely useless as a means of *testing* the validity of economic hypotheses. See my comment on Albert G. Hart's paper, "Liquidity and Uncertainty," *American Economic Review,* XXXIX (May, 1949), 198–99.

[21]Thorstein Veblen, "Why Is Economics Not an Evolutionary Science?" (1898), reprinted in *The Place of Science in Modern Civilization* (New York, 1919), p. 73.

A theory or its "assumptions" cannot possibly be thoroughly "realistic" in the immediate descriptive sense so often assigned to this term. A completely "realistic" theory of the wheat market would have to include not only the conditions directly underlying the supply and demand for wheat but also the kind of coins or credit instruments used to make exchanges; the personal characteristics of wheat-traders such as the color of each trader's hair and eyes, his antecedents and education, the number of members of his family, their characteristics, antecedents, and education, etc.; the kind of soil on which the wheat was grown, its physical and chemical characteristics, the weather prevailing during the growing season; the personal characteristics of the farmers growing the wheat and of the consumers who will ultimately use it; and so on indefinitely. Any attempt to move very far in achieving this kind of "realism" is certain to render a theory utterly useless.

Of course, the notion of a completely realistic theory is in part a straw man. No critic of a theory would accept this logical extreme as his objective; he would say that the "assumptions" of the theory being criticized were "too" unrealistic and that his objective was a set of assumptions that were "more" realistic though still not completely and slavishly so. But so long as the test of "realism" is the directly perceived descriptive accuracy of the "assumptions"—for example, the observation that "businessmen do not appear to be either as avaricious or as dynamic or as logical as marginal theory portrays them"[24] or that "it would be utterly impractical under present conditions for the manager of a multi-process plant to attempt . . . to work out and equate marginal costs and marginal revenues for each productive factor"[25]—there is no basis for making such a distinction, that is, for stopping short of the straw man depicted in the preceding paragraph. What is the criterion by which to judge whether a particular departure from realism is or is not acceptable? Why is it more "unrealistic" in analyzing business behavior to neglect the magnitude of businessmen's costs than the color of their eyes? The obvious answer is because the first makes more difference to business behavior than the second; but there is no way of knowing that this is so simply by observing that businessmen do

have costs of different magnitudes and eyes of different color. Clearly it can only be known by comparing the effect on the discrepancy between actual and predicted behavior of taking the one factor or the other into account. Even the most extreme proponents of realistic assumptions are thus necessarily driven to reject their own criterion and to accept the test by prediction when they classify alternative assumptions as more or less realistic.[26]

The basic confusion between descriptive accuracy and analytical relevance that underlies most criticisms of economic theory on the grounds that its assumptions are unrealistic as well as the plausibility of the views that lead to this confusion are both strikingly illustrated by a seemingly innocuous remark in an article on business-cycle theory that "economic phenomena are varied and complex, so any comprehensive theory of the business cycle that can apply closely to reality must be very complicated."[27] A fundamental hypothesis of science is that appearances are deceptive and that there is a way of looking at or interpreting or organizing the evidence that will reveal superficially disconnected and diverse phenomena to be manifestations of a more fundamental and relatively simple structure. And the test of this hypothesis, as of any other, is its fruits—a test that science has so far met with dramatic success. If a class of "economic phenomena" appears varied and complex, it is, we must suppose, because we have no adequate theory to explain them. Known facts cannot be set on one side; a theory to apply "closely to reality," on the other. A theory is the way we perceive "facts," and we cannot perceive "facts" without a theory. Any assertion that economic phenomena *are* varied and complex denies the tentative state of knowledge that alone makes scientific activity meaningful; it is in a

---

[24]Oliver, *op. cit.*, p. 382.

[25]Lester, "Shortcomings of Marginal Analysis for Wage-Employment Problems," *op. cit.*, p. 75.

[26]E.g., Gordon's direct examination of the "assumptions" leads him to formulate the alternative hypothesis generally favored by the critics of the maximization-of-returns hypothesis as follows: "There is an irresistible tendency to price on the basis of average total costs for some 'normal' level of output. This is the yardstick, the shortcut, that businessmen and accountants use, and their aim is more to earn satisfactory profits and play safe than to maximize profits" (*op. cit.*, p. 275). Yet he essentially abandons this hypothesis, or converts it into a tautology, and in the process implicitly accepts the test by prediction when he later remarks: "Full cost and satisfactory profits may continue to be the objectives even when total costs are shaded to meet competition or exceeded to take advantage of a sellers' market" (*ibid.*, p. 284). Where here is the "irresistible tendency"? What kind of evidence could contradict this assertion?

[27]Sidney S. Alexander, "Issues of Business Cycle Theory Raised by Mr. Hicks," *American Economic Review*, XLI (December, 1951), 872.

class with John Stuart Mill's justly ridiculed statement that "happily, there is nothing in the laws of value which remains [1848] for the present or any future writer to clear up; the theory of the subject is complete."[28]

The confusion between descriptive accuracy and analytical relevance has led not only to criticisms of economic theory on largely irrelevant grounds but also to misunderstanding of economic theory and misdirection of efforts to repair supposed defects. "Ideal types" in the abstract model developed by economic theorists have been regarded as strictly descriptive categories intended to correspond directly and fully to entities in the real world independently of the purpose for which the model is being used. The obvious discrepancies have led to necessarily unsuccessful attempts to construct theories on the basis of categories intended to be fully descriptive.

This tendency is perhaps most clearly illustrated by the interpretation given to the concepts of "perfect competition" and "monopoly" and the development of the theory of "monopolistic" or "imperfect competition." Marshall, it is said, assumed "perfect competition"; perhaps there once was such a thing. But clearly there is no longer, and we must therefore discard his theories. The reader will search long and hard—and I predict unsuccessfully—to find in Marshall any explicit assumption about perfect competition or any assertion that in a descriptive sense the world is composed of atomistic firms engaged in perfect competition. Rather, he will find Marshall saying: "At one extreme are world markets in which competition acts directly from all parts of the globe; and at the other those secluded markets in which all direct competition from afar is shut out, though indirect and transmitted competition may make itself felt even in these; and about midway between these extremes lie the great majority of the markets which the economist and the business man have to study."[29] Marshall took the world as it is; he sought to construct an "engine" to analyze it, not a photographic reproduction of it.

In analyzing the world as it is, Marshall constructed the hypothesis that, for many problems, firms could be grouped into "industries" such that the similarities among the firms in each group were more important than the differences among them. These are problems in which the important element is that a group of firms is affected alike by some stimulus—a common change in the demand for their products, say, or in the supply of factors. But this will not do for all problems: the important element for these may be the differential effect on particular firms.

The abstract model corresponding to this hypothesis contains two "ideal" types of firms: atomistically competitive firms, grouped into industries, and monopolistic firms. A firm is competitive if the demand curve for its output is infinitely elastic with respect to its own price for some price and all outputs, given the prices charged by all other firms; it belongs to an industry" defined as a group of firms producing a single "product." A "product" is defined as a collection of units that are perfect substitutes to purchasers so the elasticity of demand for the output of one firm with respect to the price of another firm in the same industry is infinite for some price and some outputs. A firm is monopolistic if the demand curve for its output is not infinitely elastic at some price for all outputs.[30] If it is a monopolist, the firm is the industry.[31]

As always, the hypothesis as a whole consists not only of this abstract model and its ideal types but also of a set of rules, mostly implicit and suggested by example, for identifying actual firms with one or the other ideal type and for classifying firms into industries. The ideal types are not intended to be descriptive; they are designed to isolate the features that are crucial for a particular problem. Even if we could estimate directly and accurately the demand curve for a firm's product, we could not proceed immediately to classify the firm as perfectly competitive or monopolistic according as the elasticity of the demand curve is or is not infinite. No observed demand curve will ever be precisely horizontal, so the estimated elasticity will always be finite. The relevant question always is whether the elasticity is "sufficiently" large to be regarded as infinite, but this is a question that cannot be answered, once for all, simply in terms of the numerical value of the elasticity

---

[28]*Principles of Political Economy* (Ashley ed.; Longmans, Green & Co., 1929), p. 436.
[29]*Principles*, p. 329; see also pp. 35, 100, 341, 347, 375, 546.

[30]This ideal type can be divided into two types: the oligopolistic firm, if the demand curve for its output is infinitely elastic at some price for some but not all outputs; the monopolistic firm proper, if the demand curve is nowhere infinitely elastic (except possibly at an output of zero).
[31]For the oligopolist of the preceding note an industry can be defined as a group of firms producing the same product.

itself, any more than we can say, once for all, whether an air pressure of 15 pounds per square inch is "sufficiently" close to zero to use the formula $s = \frac{1}{2}gt^2$. Similarly, we cannot compute cross-elasticities of demand and then classify firms into industries according as there is a "substantial gap in the cross-elasticities of demand." As Marshall says, "The question where the lines of division between different commodities [i.e., industries] should be drawn must be settled by convenience of the particular discussion."[32] Everything depends on the problem; there is no inconsistency in regarding the same firm as if it were a perfect competitor for one problem, and a monopolist for another, just as there is none in regarding the same chalk mark as a Euclidean line for one problem, a Euclidean surface for a second, and a Euclidean solid for a third. The size of the elasticity and cross-elasticity of demand, the number of firms producing physically similar products, etc., are all relevant because they are or may be among the variables used to define the correspondence between the ideal and real entities in a particular problem and to specify the circumstances under which the theory holds sufficiently well; but they do not provide, once for all, a classification of firms as competitive or monopolistic.

An example may help to clarify this point. Suppose the problem is to determine the effect on retail prices of cigarettes of an increase, expected to be permanent, in the federal cigarette tax. I venture to predict that broadly correct results will be obtained by treating cigarette firms as if they were producing an identical product and were in perfect competition. Of course, in such a case, "some convention must be made as to the" number of Chesterfield cigarettes "which are taken as equivalent" to a Marlborough.[33]

On the other hand, the hypothesis that cigarette firms would behave as if they were perfectly competitive would have been a false guide to their reactions to price control in World War II, and this would doubtless have been recognized before the event. Costs of the cigarette firms must have risen during the war. Under such circumstances perfect competitors would have reduced the quantity offered for sale at the previously existing price. But, at that price, the wartime rise in the income of the public presumably increased the quantity demanded. Under conditions of perfect competition strict adherence to the legal price would therefore imply not only a "shortage" in the sense that quantity demanded exceeded quantity supplied but also an absolute decline in the number of cigarettes produced. The facts contradict this particular implication: there was reasonably good adherence to maximum cigarette prices, yet the quantities produced increased substantially. The common force of increased costs presumably operated less strongly than the disruptive force of the desire by each firm to keep its share of the market, to maintain the value and prestige of its brand name, especially when the excess-profits tax shifted a large share of the costs of this kind of advertising to the government. For this problem the cigarette firms cannot be treated *as if* they were perfect competitors.

Wheat farming is frequently taken to exemplify perfect competition. Yet, while for some problems it is appropriate to treat cigarette producers as if they comprised a perfectly competitive industry, for some it is not appropriate to treat wheat producers as if they did. For example, it may not be if the problem is the differential in prices paid by local elevator operators for wheat.

Marshall's apparatus turned out to be most useful for problems in which a group of firms is affected by common stimuli, and in which the firms can be treated *as if* they were perfect competitors. This is the source of the misconception that Marshall "assumed" perfect competition in some descriptive sense. It would be highly desirable to have a more general theory than Marshall's, one that would cover at the same time both those cases in which differentiation of product or fewness of numbers makes an essential difference and those in which it does not. Such a theory would enable us to handle problems we now cannot and, in addition, facilitate determination of the range of circumstances under which the simpler theory can be regarded as a good enough approximation. To perform this function, the more general theory must have content and substance; it must have implications susceptible to empirical contradiction and of substantive interest and importance.

The theory of imperfect or monopolistic competition developed by Chamberlin and Robinson is an attempt to construct such a more general theory.[34] Unfortunately, it possesses none of the attributes that

---

[32]*Principles,* p. 100.

[33]Quoted parts from *ibid.*

[34]E. H. Chamberlin, *The Theory of Monopolistic Competition* (6th ed.; Cambridge: Harvard University Press, 1950); Joan Robinson, *The Economics of Imperfect Competition* (London: Macmillan & Co., 1933).

would make it a truly useful general theory. Its contribution has been limited largely to improving the exposition of the economics of the individual firm and thereby the derivation of implications of the Marshallian model, refining Marshall's monopoly analysis, and enriching the vocabulary available for describing industrial experience.

The deficiencies of the theory are revealed most clearly in its treatment of, or inability to treat, problems involving groups of firms—Marshallian "industries." So long as it is insisted that differentiation of product is essential—and it is the distinguishing feature of the theory that it does insist on this point—the definition of an industry in terms of firms producing an identical product cannot be used. By that definition each firm is a separate industry. Definition in terms of "close" substitutes or a "substantial" gap in cross-elasticities evades the issue, introduces fuzziness and undefinable terms into the abstract model where they have no place, and serves only to make the theory analytically meaningless—"close" and "substantial" are in the same category as a "small" air pressure.[35] In one connection Chamberlin implicitly defines an industry as a group of firms having identical cost and demand curves.[36] But this, too, is logically meaningless so long as differentiation of product is, as claimed, essential and not to be put aside. What does it mean to say that the cost and demand curves of a firm producing bulldozers are identical with those of a firm producing hairpins?[37] And if it is meaningless for bulldozers and hairpins, it is meaningless also for two brands of toothpaste—so long as it is insisted that the difference between the two brands is fundamentally important.

The theory of monopolistic competition offers no tools for the analysis of an industry and so no stopping place between the firm at one extreme and general equilibrium at the other.[38] It is therefore incompetent to contribute to the analysis of a host of important problems: the one extreme is too narrow to be of great interest; the other, too broad to permit meaningful generalizations.[39]

VI. CONCLUSION

Economics as a positive science is a body of tentatively accepted generalizations about economic phenomena that can be used to predict the consequences of changes in circumstances. Progress in expanding this body of generalizations, strengthening our confidence in their validity, and improving the accuracy of the predictions they yield is hindered not only by the limitations of human ability that impede all search for knowledge but also by obstacles that are especially important for the social sciences in general and economics in particular, though by no means peculiar to them. Familiarity with the subject matter of economics breeds contempt for special knowledge about it. The importance of its subject matter to everyday life and to major issues of public policy impedes objectivity and promotes confusion between scientific analysis and normative judgment. The necessity of relying on uncontrolled experience rather than on controlled experiment makes it difficult to produce dramatic and clear-cut evidence to justify the acceptance of tentative hypotheses. Reliance on uncontrolled experience does not affect the fundamental methodological principle that a hypothesis can be tested only by the conformity of its implications or predictions with observable phenomena; but it does render the task of testing hypotheses more difficult and gives greater scope for confusion about the methodological principles involved. More than other scientists, social scientists need to be self-conscious about their methodology.

One confusion that has been particularly rife and has done much damage is confusion about the role of "assumptions" in economic analysis. A meaningful scientific hypothesis or theory typically asserts that certain forces are, and other forces are not, important in understanding a particular class of phenomena. It is frequently convenient to present such a hypothesis by stating that the phenomena it is desired to predict

[35] See R. L. Bishop, "Elasticities, Cross-elasticities, and Market Relationships," *American Economic Review,* XLII (December, 1952), 779–803, for a recent attempt to construct a rigorous classification of market relationships along these lines. Despite its ingenuity and sophistication, the result seems to me thoroughly unsatisfactory. It rests basically on certain numbers being classified as "large" or "small," yet there is no discussion at all of how to decide whether a particular number is "large" or "small," as of course there cannot be on a purely abstract level.

[36] *Op. cit.,* p. 82.

[37] There always exists a transformation of quantities that will make either the cost curves or the demand curves identical; this transformation need not, however, be linear, in which case it will involve different-sized units of one product at different levels of output. There does not necessarily exist a transformation that will make both pairs of curves identical.

[38] See Robert Triffin, *Monopolistic Competition and General Equilibrium Theory* (Cambridge: Harvard University Press, 1940), esp. pp. 188–89.

[39] For a detailed critique see George J. Stigler, "Monopolistic Competition in Retrospect," in *Five Lectures on Economic Problems* (London: Macmillan & Co., 1949), pp. 12–24.

behave in the world of observation *as if* they occurred in a hypothetical and highly simplified world containing only the forces that the hypothesis asserts to be important. In general, there is more than one way to formulate such a description—more than one set of "assumptions" in terms of which the theory can be presented. The choice among such alternative assumptions is made on the grounds of the resulting economy, clarity, and precision in presenting the hypothesis; their capacity to bring indirect evidence to bear on the validity of the hypothesis by suggesting some of its implications that can be readily checked with observation or by bringing out its connection with other hypotheses dealing with related phenomena; and similar considerations.

Such a theory cannot be tested by comparing its "assumptions" directly with "reality." Indeed, there is no meaningful way in which this can be done. Complete "realism" is clearly unattainable, and the question whether a theory is realistic "enough" can be settled only by seeing whether it yields predictions that are good enough for the purpose in hand or that are better than predictions from alternative theories. Yet the belief that a theory can be tested by the realism of its assumptions independently of the accuracy of its predictions is widespread and the source of much of the perennial criticism of economic theory as unrealistic. Such criticism is largely irrelevant, and, in consequence, most attempts to reform economic theory that it has stimulated have been unsuccessful.

The irrelevance of so much criticism of economic theory does not of course imply that existing economic theory deserves any high degree of confidence. These criticisms may miss the target, yet there may be a target for criticism. In a trivial sense, of course, there obviously is. Any theory is necessarily provisional and subject to change with the advance of knowledge. To go beyond this platitude, it is necessary to be more specific about the content of "existing economic theory" and to distinguish among its different branches; some parts of economic theory clearly deserve more confidence than others. A comprehensive evaluation of the present state of positive economics, summary of the evidence bearing on its validity, and assessment of the relative confidence that each part deserves is clearly a task for a treatise or a set of treatises, if it be possible at all, not for a brief paper on methodology.

About all that is possible here is the cursory expres-

sion of a personal view. Existing relative price theory, which is designed to explain the allocation of resources among alternative ends and the division of the product among the co-operating resources and which reached almost its present form in Marshall's *Principles of Economics,* seems to me both extremely fruitful and deserving of much confidence for the kind of economic system that characterizes Western nations. Despite the appearance of considerable controversy, this is true equally of existing static monetary theory, which is designed to explain the structural or secular level of absolute prices, aggregate output, and other variables for the economy as a whole and which has had a form of the quantity theory of money as its basic core in all of its major variants from David Hume to the Cambridge School to Irving Fisher to John Maynard Keynes. The weakest and least satisfactory part of current economic theory seems to me to be in the field of monetary dynamics, which is concerned with the process of adaptation of the economy as a whole to changes in conditions and so with short-period fluctuations in aggregate activity. In this field we do not even have a theory that can appropriately be called "the" existing theory of monetary dynamics.

Of course, even in relative price and static monetary theory there is enormous room for extending the scope and improving the accuracy of existing theory. In particular, undue emphasis on the descriptive realism of "assumptions" has contributed to neglect of the critical problem of determining the limits of validity of the various hypotheses that together constitute the existing economic theory in these areas. The abstract models corresponding to these hypotheses have been elaborated in considerable detail and greatly improved in rigor and precision. Descriptive material on the characteristics of our economic system and its operations have been amassed on an unprecedented scale. This is all to the good. But, if we are to use effectively these abstract models and this descriptive material, we must have a comparable exploration of the criteria for determining what abstract model it is best to use for particular kinds of problems, what entities in the abstract model are to be identified with what observable entities, and what features of the problem or of the circumstances have the greatest effect on the accuracy of the predictions yielded by a particular model or theory.

Progress in positive economics will require not only the testing and elaboration of existing hypotheses but also the construction of new hypotheses. On this problem there is little to say on a formal level. The construction of hypotheses is a creative act of inspiration, intuition, invention; its essence is the vision of something new in familiar material. The process must be discussed in psychological, not logical, categories; studied in autobiographies and biographies, not treatises on scientific method; and promoted by maxim and example, not syllogism or theorem.

Part 2   Demand and Supply

DEMAND AND UTILITY THEORY

The Marshallian Demand Curve*

MILTON FRIEDMAN[1]

See "The Methodology of Positive Economics" for the author's biography.

Alfred Marshall's theory of demand strikingly exemplifies his "impatience with rigid definition and an excessive tendency to let the context explain his meaning."[2] The concept of the demand curve as a functional relation between the quantity and the price of a particular commodity is explained repeatedly and explicitly in the *Principles of Economics:* in words in the text, in plane curves in the footnotes, and in symbolic form in the Mathematical Appendix. A complete definition of the demand curve, including, in particular, a statement of the variables that are to be considered the same for all points on the curve and the variables that are to be allowed to vary, is nowhere given explicitly. The reader is left to infer the contents of *ceteris paribus* from general and vague statements, parenthetical remarks, examples that do not purport to be exhaustive, and concise mathematical notes in the Appendix.

In view of the importance of the demand curve in Marshallian analysis, it is natural that other economists should have constructed a rigorous definition to fill the gap that Marshall left. This occurred at an early date, apparently without controversy about the interpretation to be placed on Marshall's comments. The resulting definition of the demand curve is now so much an intrinsic part of current economic theory and is so widely accepted as Marshall's own that the assertion that Marshall himself gave no explicit rigorous definition may shock most readers.

Yet why this particular interpretation evolved and why it gained such unquestioned acceptance are a mystery that requires explanation. The currently accepted interpretation can be read into Marshall only by a liberal—and, I think, strained—reading of his remarks, and its acceptance implicitly convicts him of logical inconsistency and mathematical error at the very foundation of his theory of demand. More important, the alternative interpretation of the demand curve that is yielded by a literal reading of his remarks not only leaves his original work on the theory of demand free from both logical inconsis-

*Reprinted from the *Journal of Political Economy* (December 1949) by permission of The University of Chicago Press. Copyright 1949, pp. 463–74.
[1] I am deeply indebted for helpful criticism and suggestions to A. F. Burns, Aaron Director, C. W. Guillebaud, H. Gregg Lewis, A. R. Prest, D. H. Robertson, G. J. Stigler, and, especially, Jacob Viner, to whose penetrating discussion of the demand curve in his course in economic theory I can trace some of the central ideas and even details of this article. The standard comment that none is to be held responsible for the views expressed herein has particular relevance, since most disagreed with my interpretation of Marshall as presented in an earlier and much briefer draft of this article.
[2] C. W. Guillebaud, "The Evolution of Marshall's *Principles of Economics,*" *Economic Journal,* LII (December, 1942), 333.

tency and mathematical error but also is more useful for the analysis of most economic problems.

Section I presents the two interpretations of the demand curve and compares them in some detail; Section II argues that a demand curve constructed on my interpretation is the more useful for the analysis of practical problems, whatever may be the verdict about its validity as an interpretation of Marshall; . . .

I. ALTERNATIVE INTERPRETATIONS OF MARSHALL'S DEMAND CURVE

The demand curve of a particular group (which may, as a special case, consist of a single individual) for a particular commodity shows the quantity (strictly speaking, the maximum quantity) of the commodity that will be purchased by the group per unit of time at each price. So far, no question arises; this part of the definition is explicit in Marshall and is common to both alternatives to be discussed. The problem of interpretation relates to the phrase, "other things the same," ordinarily attached to this definition.

In the first place, it should be noted that "same" in this phrase does not mean "same over time." The points on a demand curve are alternative possibilities, not temporally ordered combinations of quantity and price. "Same" means "same for all points on the demand curve"; the different points are to differ in quantity and price and are not to differ with respect to "other things."[3] In the second place, "all" other things cannot be supposed to be the same without completely emasculating the concept. For example, if *(a)* total money expenditure on all commodities, *(b)* the price of every commodity other than the one in question, and *(c)* the quantity purchased of every other commodity were supposed to be the same, the amount of money spent on the commodity in question would necessarily be the same at all prices, simply as a matter of arithmetic, and the

demand curve would have unit elasticity everywhere.[4] Different specifications of the "other things" will yield different demand curves. For example, one demand curve will be obtained by excluding *b* from the list of "other things"; another, quite different one, by excluding *c*.

A. The Current Interpretation

The current interpretation of Marshall's demand curve explicitly includes in the list of "other things" (1) tastes and preferences of the group of purchasers considered, (2) their money income, and (3) the price of every other commodity. The quantities of other commodities are explicitly considered as different at different points on the demand curve, and still other variables are ignored.[5]

On this interpretation it is clear that, while money income is the same for different points on the demand curve, real income is not. At the lower of two prices for the commodity in question, more of some commodities can be purchased without reducing the amounts purchased of other commodities. The lower the price, therefore, the higher the real income.

B. An Alternative Interpretation

It seems to me more faithful to both the letter and the spirit of Marshall's writings to include in the list

---

[3]Of course, when correlations among statistical time series are regarded as estimates of demand curves, the hypothesis is that "other things" have been approximately constant over time or that appropriate allowance has been made for changes in them. Similarly, when correlations among cross-section data are regarded as estimates of demand curves, the hypothesis is that "other things" are approximately the same for the units distinguished or that appropriate allowance has been made for differences among them. In both cases the problem of estimation should be clearly distinguished from the theoretical construct to be estimated.

[4]Yet Sidney Weintraub not only suggests that Marshall intended to keep *a*, *b*, and *c* simultaneously the same but goes on to say: "Clearly Marshall's assumption means a unit elasticity of demand in the market reviewed and no ramifications elsewhere; that was why he adopted it" ("The Foundations of the Demand Curve," *American Economic Review,* XXXII [September, 1942], 538–52, quotation from n. 12, p. 541). Weintraub even adds the condition of constant tastes and preferences to *a*, *b*, and *c*, speaking of a change in tastes as shifting the demand curve. Obviously, *a*, *b*, and *c* together leave no room for tastes and preferences or, indeed, for anything except simple arithmetic.

[5]Explicit definition of the demand curve in this way by followers of Marshall dates back at least to 1894 (see F. Y. Edgeworth, "Demand Curves" [art.], *Palgrave's Dictionary of Political Economy,* ed. Henry Higgs [rev. ed.; London: Macmillan & Co., 1926]). Edgeworth's article apparently dates from the first edition, which was published in 1894. While Edgeworth does not explicitly attribute this interpretation to Marshall, it is clear from the context that he is talking about a Marshallian demand curve and that he does not regard his statements as inconsistent in any way with Marshall's *Principles.* Though no explicit listing of "other things" is given by J. R. Hicks, *Value and Capital* (Oxford, 1939), the list given above is implicit throughout chaps. i and ii, which are explicitly devoted to elaborating and extending Marshall's analysis of demand. For statements in modern textbooks on advanced economic theory see G. J. Stigler, *The Theory of Price* (New York: Macmillan Co., 1946), pp. 86–90, and Kenneth E. Boulding, *Economic Analysis* (rev. ed.; New York: Harper & Bros., 1948), pp. 134–35.

of "other things" (1) tastes and preferences of the group of purchasers considered, (2) their real income, and (3) the price of every closely related commodity.

Two variants of this interpretation can be distinguished, according to the device adopted for keeping real income the same at different points on the demand curve. One variant, which Marshall employed in the text of the *Principles,* is obtained by replacing "(2) their real income" by (2a) their money income and (2b) the "purchasing power of money." Constancy of the "purchasing power of money" for different prices of the commodity in question implies compensating variations in the prices of some or all other commodities. These variations will, indeed, be negligible if the commodity in question accounts for a negligible fraction of total expenditures; but they should not be disregarded, both because empirical considerations must be sharply separated from logical considerations and because the demand curve need not be limited in applicability to such commodities. On this variant all commodities are, in effect, divided into three groups: *(a)* the commodity in question, *(b)* closely related commodities, and *(c)* all other commodities. The absolute price of each commodity in group *b* is supposed to be the same for different points on the demand curve; only the "average" price, or an index number of prices, is considered for group *c*; and it is to be supposed to rise or fall with a fall or rise in the price of group *a,* so as to keep the "purchasing power of money" the same.

The other variant, which Marshall employed in the Mathematical Appendix of the *Principles,* is obtained by retaining "(2) their real income" and adding (4) the average price of all other commodities. Constancy of real income for different prices of the commodity in question then implies compensating variations in money income. As the price of the commodity in question rises or falls, money income is to be supposed to rise or fall so as to keep real income the same.

These two variants are essentially equivalent mathematically,[6] but the assumption of compensating variations in other prices is easier to explain verbally and can be justified as empirically relevant by considerations of monetary theory, which is presumably why Marshall used this variant in his text. On the other hand, the assumption of compensating variations in income is somewhat more convenient math-

ematically, which is presumably why Marshall used this variant in his Mathematical Appendix.

On my interpretation, Marshall's demand curve is identical with one of the constructions introduced

---

[6]Let x and y be the quantity and price, respectively, of the commodity in question; x' and y', the quantity and price of a composite commodity representing all other commodities; and m, money income. Let

$$x = g(y, y', m, u) \tag{1}$$

be the demand curve for the commodity in question, given a utility function,

$$U = U(x, x', u) \tag{2}$$

where u is a parameter to allow for changes in taste, and subject to the condition

$$xy + x'y' = m \tag{3}$$

From eq. (3) and the usual utility analysis, it follows that eq. (1), like eq. (3), is a homogeneous function of degree zero in y, y', and m; i.e., that

$$g(\lambda y, \lambda y', \lambda m, u) = g(y, y', m, u) \tag{4}$$

On the current interpretation, a two-dimensional demand curve is obtained from eq. (1) directly by giving y' (other prices), m (income), and u (tastes) fixed values. A given value of y then implies a given value of x from eq. (1), a given value of x' from eq. (3), and hence a given value of U (i.e., real income) from eq. (2). The value of U will vary with y, being higher, the lower y is.

On my alternative interpretation, u and U are given fixed values and x' is eliminated from eqs. (2) and (3). This gives a pair of equations,

$$x = g(y, y', m, u_0) \tag{5}$$

$$U_0 = U_0\left(x, \frac{m - xy}{y'}, u_0\right) \tag{6}$$

where the subscript 0 designates fixed values. The two-dimensional variant involving compensating variations in other prices is obtained by eliminating y' from eqs. (5) and (6) and giving m a fixed value; the variant involving compensating variations in income, by eliminating m from eqs. (5) and (6) and giving y' a fixed value.

The homogeneity of eqs. (5) and (6) in y, y', and m means that x is a function only of ratios among them. Thus eqs. (5) and (6) can be written:

$$x = g(y, y', m, u_0) = g\left(\frac{y}{m}, \frac{y'}{m}, 1, u_0\right)$$

$$= g\left(\frac{y}{y'}, 1, \frac{m}{y'}, u_0\right) \tag{5'}$$

$$U_0 = U_0\left(x, \frac{m - xy}{y'}, u_0\right)$$

$$= U_0\left(x, \frac{1 - x\frac{y}{m}}{\frac{y'}{m}}, u_0\right) \tag{6'}$$

$$= U_0\left(x, \frac{m}{y'} - x\frac{y}{y'}, u_0\right)$$

The choice of price-compensating variations is equivalent to selecting the forms of these two equations in the next to the last terms of eqs. (5') and (6'); of income-compensating variations, to selecting the forms in the last terms.

by Slutsky in his famous paper on the theory of choice, namely, the reaction of quantity demanded to a "compensated variation of price," that is, to a variation in price accompanied by a compensating change in money income.[7] Slutsky expressed the compensating change in money income in terms of observable phenomena, taking it as equal to the change in price *times* the quantity demanded at the initial price. Mosak has shown that, in the limit, the change in income so computed is identical with the change required to keep the individual on the same level of utility (on the same indifference curve).[8] It follows that a similar statement is valid for compensating changes in other prices. In the limit the change in other prices required to keep the individual on the same indifference curve when his money income is unchanged but the price of one commodity varies is identical with the change in other prices required to keep unchanged the total cost of the basket of commodities purchased at the initial prices, that is, to keep unchanged the usual type of cost-of-living index number.

C. Comparison of the Interpretations

The relation between demand curves constructed under the two interpretations is depicted in Fig. 1. Curve *Cc* represents a demand curve of an individual consumer for a commodity *X* drawn on the current interpretation. Money income and the prices of other commodities are supposed the same for all points on it; in consequence, real income is lower at *C* than at *P*, since, if the individual sought to buy *OM* of *X* at a price of *OC*, he would be forced to curtail his purchases of something else. As the curve is drawn, of course, he buys none of *X* at a price of *OC*, spending the sum of *OHPM* on other commodities that his action at a price of *OH* shows him to value less highly than he does *OM* units of *X*. The ordinate is described as the ratio of the price of *X* to the price of other commodities. For the demand curve *Cc* this is a question only of the unit of measure, since other

[7]Eugenio Slutsky, "Sulla teoria del bilancio del consumatore," *Giornale degli economisti*, LI (1915), 1–26, esp. sec. 8. [A translation of this article is now available in American Economic Association, *Readings in Price Theory* (Chicago: Richard D. Irwin, Inc., 1952), pp. 27–56.]
[8]Jacob L. Mosak, "On the Interpretation of the Fundamental Equation of Value Theory," in O. Lange, F. McIntyre, and T. O. Yntema (eds.), *Studies in Mathematical Economics and Econometrics* (Chicago: University of Chicago Press, 1942), pp. 69–74, esp. n. 5, pp. 73–74, which contains a rigorous proof of this statement by A. Wald.

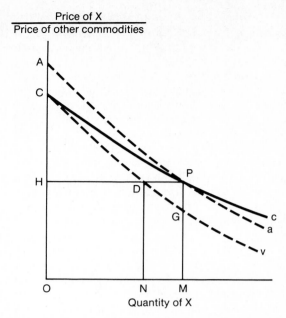

Fig. 1. Comparison of demand curves constructed under the two interpretations.

prices are supposed to be the same for all points on it.

From the definition of the demand curve *Cc*, *OC* is obviously the maximum price per unit that an individual would be willing to pay for an infinitesimal initial increment of *X* when his money income and the prices of other commodities have the values assumed in drawing *Cc*. Let us suppose him to purchase this amount at a price of *OC*, determine the maximum price per unit he would be willing to pay for an additional increment, and continue in this fashion, exacting the maximum possible amount for each additional increment. Let these successive maximum prices per unit define the curve *Cv*. The consumer obviously has the same real income at each point on *Cv* as at *C*, since the maximum price has been extracted from him for each successive unit, so that he has gained no utility in the process.

Cv is now a demand curve constructed according to my interpretation of Marshall. If other prices are supposed to be the same, the necessary compensating variations in money income as the price of *X* falls are given by triangular areas exemplified by *HCD* for a price of *OH*: *OH* is the maximum price per unit that the individual will give for an additional infinitesimal increment of X when he has spent $OCDN$ for ON of X out of his initial income of, say, m; but his situation is exactly the same if, when the price of X is OH, his income is $(m - HCD)$ and he spends $OHDN$ on X; he has the same amount left to spend on all other commodities, their prices are the same, and he has the same amount of X; accordingly, his demand price will be the same, and he will buy ON of X at a price of OH and an income of $(m - HCD)$.[9]

If compensating variations in other prices rather than in money income are used to keep real income the same, the absolute price of neither X nor other commodities can be read directly from Fig. 1, p. 38. For each ratio of the price of X to the price of other commodities, the quantity of X purchased will be that shown on Cv. But the prices of other goods will vary along Cv, rising as the relative price of X falls, so the absolute price of X can no longer be obtained by multiplying the ordinate by a single scale factor.

Fig. 1, p. 38 is drawn on the assumption that X is a "normal" commodity, that is, a commodity the consumption of which is higher, the higher the income. This is the reason Cv is drawn to the left of Cc—at every point on Cv other than C, real income is less than at the corresponding point on Cc; hence less X would be consumed.

[9]In the notation of n. 5, except that u is omitted for simplicity, the quantities of X and X' that will be purchased for any given values of y and y' and any given real income, U_0, are obtained by solving simultaneously:

$$\frac{U_x}{U_{x'}} = \frac{y}{y'} \tag{1}$$

and

$$U(x, x') = U_0 \tag{2}$$

where U_x and $U_{x'}$ stand for the partial derivatives of U with respect to x and x', respectively, i.e., for the marginal utility of X and X'. The solution of these equations gives the demand curve on my interpretation of Marshall, using compensating variations in money income.

$U_0 (0, m/y')$ is the utility at C in the diagram. For any given amount of X and given value of y', the amount of X' purchased is obtained by solving

$$U(x, x') = U_0 \left(0, \frac{m}{y'}\right) \tag{3}$$

which is identical with eq. (2). The amount paid for X (the area under Cv) is

$$m - x'y' \tag{4}$$

The maximum price that will be paid per unit of X is the derivative of eq. (4), or

$$y = -\frac{dx'}{dx} y' = \frac{U_x}{U_{x'}} y' \tag{5}$$

which is identical with eq. (1). It follows that Cv is a demand curve constructed on my interpretation of Marshall.

Curve Aa represents a demand curve on my interpretation of Marshall for a real income the same as at point P on Cc; it is like Cv but for a higher real income. Real income is higher on Aa than on Cc for prices above OH, lower for prices below OH, which is the reason Aa is to the right of Cc for prices above OH and to the left of Cc for prices below OH.

D. Why Two Interpretations Are Possible

The possibility of interpreting Marshall in these two quite different ways arises in part from the vagueness of Marshall's exposition, from his failure to give precise and rigorous definitions. A more fundamental reason, however, is the existence of inconsistency in the third and later editions of the *Principles*. In that edition Marshall introduced the celebrated passage bearing on the Giffen phenomenon. This passage and a related sentence added at the same time to the Mathematical Appendix fit the current interpretation better than they fit my interpretation. Although these are the only two items that I have been able to find in any edition of the *Principles* of which this is true, they provide some basis for the current interpretation. . . .

II. THE RELATIVE USEFULNESS OF THE TWO INTERPRETATIONS

The relative usefulness of the two interpretations of the demand curve can be evaluated only in terms of some general conception of the role of economic theory. I shall use the conception that underlies Marshall's work, in which the primary emphasis is on positive economic analysis, on the forging of tools that can be used fairly directly in analyzing practical problems. Economic theory was to him an "engine for the discovery of concrete truth."[10] "Man's powers are limited: almost every one of nature's riddles is complex. He breaks it up, studies one bit at a time, and at last combines his partial solutions with a supreme effort of his whole small strength into some sort of an attempt at a solution of the whole riddle."[11] The underlying justification for the central role of the concepts of demand and supply in Marshall's entire structure of analysis is the empirical general-

[10]Alfred Marshall, "The Present Position of Economics" (1885), reprinted in *Memorials of Alfred Marshall*, ed. A. C. Pigou (London: Macmillan & Co., 1925), p. 159.

[11]Alfred Marshall, "Mechanical and Biological Analogies in Economics" (1898), *Ibid.*, p. 314.

ization that an enumeration of the forces affecting demand in any problem and of the forces affecting supply will yield two lists that contain few items in common. Demand and supply are to him concepts for organizing materials, labels in an "analytical filing box." The "commodity" for which a demand curve is drawn is another label, not a word for a physical or technical entity to be defined once and for all independently of the problem at hand. Marshall writes:

> The question where the lines of division between different commodities should be drawn must be settled by convenience of the particular discussion. For some purposes it may be best to regard Chinese and Indian teas, or even Souchong and Pekoe teas, as different-commodities; and to have a separate demand schedule for each of them. While for other purposes it may be best to group together commodities as distinct as beef and mutton, or even as tea and coffee, and to have a single list to represent the demand for the two combined.[12]

A. The Distinction Between Closely Related and All Other Commodities

A demand function containing as separate variables the prices of a rigidly defined and exhaustive list of commodities, all on the same footing, seems largely foreign to this approach. It may be a useful expository device to bring home the mutual interdependence of economic phenomena; it cannot form part of Marshall's "engine for the discovery of concrete truth." The analyst who attacks a concrete problem can take explicit account of only a limited number of factors; he will inevitably separate commodities that are closely related to the one immediately under study from commodities that are more distantly related. He can pay some attention to each closely related commodity. He cannot handle the more distantly related commodities in this way; he will tend either to ignore them or to consider them as a group. The formally more general demand curve will, in actual use, become the kind of demand curve that is yielded by my interpretation of Marshall.

The part of the Marshallian filing box covered by *ceteris paribus* typically includes three quite different kinds of variables, distinguished by their relation to the variable whose adaptation to some change is di-

rectly under investigation (e.g., the price of a commodity): *(a)* variables that are expected both to be materially affected by the variable under study and, in turn, to affect it; *(b)* variables that are expected to be little, if at all, affected by the variable under study but to materially affect it; *(c)* the remaining variables, expected neither to affect significantly the variable under study nor to be significantly affected by it.

In demand analysis the prices of closely related commodities are the variables in group *a*. They are put individually into the pound of *ceteris paribus* to pave the way for further analysis. Holding their prices constant is a provisional step. They must inevitably be affected by anything that affects the commodity in question; and this indirect effect can be analyzed most conveniently by first isolating the direct effect, systematically tracing the repercussions of the direct effect on each closely related commodity, and then tracing the subsequent reflex influences on the commodity in question. Indeed, in many ways, the role of the demand curve itself is as much to provide an orderly means of analyzing these indirect effects as to isolate the direct effect on the commodity in question.

The average price of "all other commodities," income and wealth, and tastes and preferences are the variables in group *b*. These variables are likely to be affected only negligibly by factors affecting primarily the commodity in question. On the other hand, any changes in them would have a significant effect on that commodity. They are put into the pound in order to separate problems, to segregate the particular reactions under study. They are put in individually and explicitly because they are so important that account will have to be taken of them in any application of the analysis.

Price changes within the group of "all other commodities" and an indefinitely long list of other variables are contained in group *c*. These variables are to be ignored. They are too numerous and each too unimportant to permit separate account to be taken of them.

In keeping with the spirit of Marshallian analysis this classification of variables is to be taken as illustrative, not definitive. What particular variables are appropriate for each group is to be determined by the problem in hand, the amount of information available, the detail required in results, and the patience and resources of the analyst.

---

[12]Marshall, *Principles of Economics* (8th ed.; London: Macmillan & Co., 1920), p. 100 n. All subsequent page references to the *Principles*, unless otherwise stated, are to the eighth and final edition.

B. Constancy of Real Income

It has just been argued that any actual analysis of a concrete economic problem with the aid of demand curves will inevitably adopt one feature of my interpretation of Marshall—consideration of a residual list of commodities as a single group. For somewhat subtler reasons this is likely to be true also of the second feature of my interpretation of Marshall—holding real income constant along a demand curve. If an analysis, begun with a demand curve constructed on the current interpretation, is carried through and made internally consistent, it will be found that the demand curve has been subjected to shifts that, in effect, result from failure to keep real income constant along the demand curve.

An example will show how this occurs. Let us suppose that the government grants to producers of commodity X a subsidy of a fixed amount per unit of output, financed by a general income tax, so that money income available for expenditure (i.e., net of tax and gross of subsidy) is unchanged. For simplicity, suppose, first, that no commodities are closely related to X either as rivals or as complements, so that interrelations in consumption between X and particular other commodities can be neglected; second, that the tax is paid by individuals in about the same income class and with about the same consumption pattern as those who benefit from the subsidy, so that complications arising from changes in the distribution of income can be neglected; and, third, that there are no idle resources. Let DD in Fig. 2 be a demand curve for commodity X, and SS be the initial supply curve for X, and let the initial position at their intersection, point P, be a position of full equilibrium. The effect of the subsidy is to lower the supply curve to $S'S'$. Since we have ruled out repercussions through consumption relations with other markets and through changes in the level or distribution of money income, it is reasonable to expect that the intersection of this new supply curve and the initial demand curve, point P', will itself be a position of full equilibrium, involving a lower price and larger quantity of X. Yet, if the demand curve is constructed on the current interpretation and if the supply curve is not perfectly inelastic,[13] point P' is not a position of full equilibrium. This can be seen most easily by supposing DD to have unit elasticity, so that the same amount is spent on X at P' as at P. The same amount is then available to spend on all other commodities, and, since their prices are supposed to be the same for all points on DD under the current interpretation, the same quantity of each of them will be demanded. But then where do the resources come from to produce the extra MN units of X? Obviously, our assumptions are not internally consistent. The additional units of X can be produced only by bidding resources away from the production of other commodities, in the process raising their prices and reducing the amount of them produced. The final equilibrium position will therefore involve higher prices and lower quantities of other commodities. But, on the current interpretation, this means a shift in the demand curve for X—say, to $D'D'$—and a final equilibrium position of, say P'."[14]

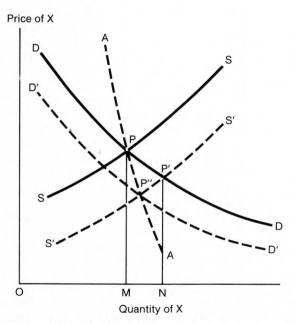

Price of X

Quantity of X

Fig. 2. Illustrative analysis of effect of subsidy.

[13]If it is perfectly inelastic, neither the price nor the quantity of X is changed, so the new position of equilibrium coincides with the old; but the demand curve will pass through the initial position of equilibrium whether constructed on the current interpretation or on mine; hence the two coincide at the one point on them that is relevant.

[14]$D'D'$ will not necessarily be to the left of DD even for a "normal" commodity. The reason is that the ordinate of Fig. 2 measures the absolute price of X, so that ordinates of the same height on DD and $D'D'$ represent different ratios of the price of X to the price of other commodities. If the ordinate measured the ratio of the price of X to the price of other commodities, $D'D'$ would always be to the left of DD for "normal" commodities, always to the right for "inferior" commodities.

The assumption that the elasticity of DD is unity is not, of course, essential for this argument. If the elasticity of DD is less than unity, a larger amount than formerly is available to spend on other commodities; at unchanged prices this means a larger quantity demanded. In consequence, while the additional amount of resources required to produce the increased amount of X demanded is smaller when DD is inelastic than when it has unit elasticity, this is counterbalanced by increased pressure for resources to produce other commodities. Similarly, when DD is elastic, the additional amount of resources required to produce the increased quantity of X demanded is larger than when DD has unit elasticity, but some resources are released in the first instance from the production of other commodities.

No such internal inconsistency as that just outlined arises if the demand curve is constructed by keeping real income the same. Curve AA is such a demand curve. At prices of X less than PM, prices of other commodities are supposed to be sufficiently higher than at P to keep real income the same, which involves the release of just enough resources so that the position of final equilibrium, P'', lies on the demand curve so constructed—at least for small changes in the price of X.[15]

---

[15]Let X' be a single composite commodity representing all commodities other than X; x and x', the quantities of X and X'; and y and y', their prices. Let the subscript 1 refer to values at the initial position of equilibrium, P; the subscript 2, to values at the final position, P''. The condition of constant total expenditures means that

$$x_1 y_1 + x'_1 y'_1 = x_2 y_2 + x'_2 y'_2 \qquad (1)$$

As was pointed out above (Sec. I, B), in the limit, holding real income constant is equivalent to holding constant the cost of a fixed basket of commodities. Thus, if P'' is considered close to P,

$$x_1 y_1 + x'_1 y'_1 = x_1 y_2 + x'_1 y'_2 \qquad (2)$$

In the neighborhood of P, y_1 can be regarded as the cost per unit of producing X; y'_1, as the cost per unit of producing X'. The condition that sufficient resources are released to permit the production of the requisite additional amount of X is therefore

$$(x_2 - x_1)y_1 = -(x'_2 - x'_1)y'_1 \qquad (3)$$

which is equivalent to

$$x_1 y_1 + x'_1 y'_1 = x_2 y_1 + x'_2 y'_1 \qquad (4)$$

But, in the limit, eqs. (1) and (2) imply eq. (4), as can be seen by subtracting eq. (2) from eq. (1) and replacing y_2 and y'_2 in the result by $(y_2 - y_1 + y_1)$ and $(y'_2 - y'_1 + y'_1)$, respectively.

More generally, constant real income [with constant total expenditures] involves keeping a price index unchanged; constant use of resources involves keeping a quantity index unchanged; and, in the limit, a constant price index and constant total expenditures imply a constant quantity index.

Note that AA need not be steeper than DD in a graph like Fig. 2. The point in question is that commented on in n. 14.

The fundamental principle illustrated by this example can be put more generally. The reason why a demand curve constructed under the current interpretation fails to give the correct solution even when all disturbing influences can be neglected is that each point on it implicitly refers to a different productive capacity of the community. A reduction in the price of the commodity in question is to be regarded as enabling the community, if it so wishes, to consume more of some commodities—this commodity or others—without consuming less of any commodity. But the particular change in supply whose consequences we sought to analyze—that arising from a subsidy—does not make available any additional resources to the community; any increase in the consumption of the commodity in question must be at the expense of other commodities. The conditions for which the demand curve is drawn are therefore inconsistent with the conditions postulated on the side of supply. On the other hand, if the demand curve is constructed by keeping "real income" the same, no such inconsistency need arise. True, constant "real income" in the sense of "utility" and constant "real income" in the sense of outputs attainable from a fixed total of resources are different concepts, but they converge and can be treated as the same in the neighborhood of a position of equilibrium.

Of course, not all shifts in supply that it is desired to analyze arise in ways that leave the productive capacity of the community unaltered. Many involve a change in productive capacity—for example, changes in supply arising from improvements in technology or the discovery of previously unknown resources. Even in these cases, however, a demand curve constructed on the current interpretation will not serve. There is no reason to expect the differences in productive capacity implicit in constant money income and constant prices of other goods to bear any consistent relation to the change in productive capacity arising on the side of supply.[16] The better plan, in these cases, is to allow separately and directly for the increase in productive capacity by redrawing the demand curves to correspond to an appropriately higher real income and then to use a demand curve on which all points refer to that higher real income.

---

[16]Note the difference from the previous case of constant productive capacity. As stated above, there is reason to expect constant real income along a demand curve to bear a consistent relation to constant productive capacity in the neighborhood of equilibrium. The reason, in effect, is provided by one of the conditions at equilibrium: the tangency of consumption and production indifference curves.

The main point under discussion can be put still more generally. The opportunities open to a consumer to satisfy his wants depend principally on two factors—the total resources at his disposal and the terms on which he can exchange one commodity for another, that is, on his real income and on relative prices. The form of analysis that is now fashionable distinguishes three effects of changes in his opportunities—the income effect arising from changes in his money income; the income effect arising from changes in the price of a commodity, with unchanged money income and prices of other commodities; and the substitution effect arising from a change in the relative price of a commodity, with unchanged real income.

The distinction between the so-called "substitution" and "income" effects of a change in price is a direct consequence of defining the demand curve according to the current interpretation of Marshall. Its basis is the arithmetic truism that at given prices for all commodities but one, a given money income corresponds to a higher real income, the lower the price of the remaining commodity—at a lower price for it, more of some commodities can be purchased without purchasing less of others. In consequence, a decline in the price of a commodity, all other prices constant, has, it is argued, two effects: first, with an unchanged real income, it would stimulate the substitution of that commodity for others—this is the substitution effect; second, if the money income of the consumers is supposed to be unchanged, the increase in their real income as a result of the decline in price causes a further change in the consumption of that commodity as well as of others—this is the income effect.[17]

The two different kinds of income effects distinguished in this analysis—one arising from a change in money income, the other from a change in the price of one commodity—are really the same thing, the effect of a change in real income with given relative prices, arising in different ways. It is hard to see any gain from combining the second income effect with the substitution effect; it seems preferable to combine the two income effects and thereby gain a sharp contrast with the substitution effect.

It has often been stated that Marshall "neglected the income effect."[18] On my interpretation of his demand curve, this statement is invalid. One must then say that Marshall recognized the desirability of separating two quite different effects and constructed his demand curve so that it encompassed solely the effect that he wished to isolate for study, namely, the substitution effect. Instead of neglecting the income effect, he "eliminated" it.

The conclusion to which the argument of this section leads is identical with that reached by Frank H. Knight in a recent article, in which he says:

> We have to choose in analysis between holding the prices of all other goods constant and maintaining constant the "real income" of the hypothetical consumer.... The treatment of the Slutzky school adopts the assumption that ... the prices of all other goods (and the consumer's money income) are constant. Hence, real income must change. Of the two alternatives, this seems to be definitely the wrong choice.... The simple and obvious alternative is to draw the demand curves in terms of a change in *relative* prices, i.e., to assume that the value of money is held constant, through compensating changes in the prices of other goods, and not that these other prices are held constant.[19]

[17]See Slutsky, *op. cit.*; Henry Schultz, *The Theory and Measurement of Demand* (Chicago: University of Chicago Press, 1938), pp. 40–46; J. R. Hicks and R. G. D. Allen, "A Reconsideration of the Theory of Value," *Economica*, XIV (1934), 52–76 and 196–219; Hicks, *op. cit.*, Part I.

[18]Hicks, *op. cit.*, p. 32.
[19]"Realism and Relevance in the Theory of Demand," *Journal of Political Economy*, LII (December, 1944), 289–318, esp. Sec. III, "The Meaning of a Demand Curve," pp. 298–301. Quotation from p. 299.

The Marshallian Demand Curve*

MARTIN J. BAILEY[1]

Martin J. Bailey (B.A., University of California at Los Angeles, 1951; M.A., The Johns Hopkins University, 1953; Ph.D., 1956) was born in Taft, California, in 1927. At present he serves as Economic Advisor to the Undersecretary for Economic Affairs at the U.S. Department of State. Bailey was previously on the faculties of the University of Maryland, the University of Rochester, where he was Associate Dean of the College of Business Administration, and the University of Chicago. In addition, he has been a member of the Economic and Political Studies Division of the Institute for Defense Analyses, Special Assistant to the Assistant Secretary of Defense for Systems Analysis for Southeast Asia Forces, and Deputy Assistant Secretary of the Treasury for Tax Analysis. His recent research interests are in economic theory, primarily the theory of money and public finance, and the economics of defense. He is the author of *National Income and the Price Level* and numerous articles in professional journals.

In an article with the above title, Professor Friedman[2] has urged that a constant-real-income demand curve is a more satisfactory tool for economic analysis than the customary constant-other-prices-and-money-incomes demand curve and that, at least in the first two editions of the *Principles,* this was the type of demand curve which Marshall really had in mind. On the latter, historical question nothing will be said here; but on the former, analytical question I shall contend that Friedman did not make the best choice of a curve as an improvement on the conventional one and that the constant-real-income curve, strictly interpreted, does not on balance possess the superiority he claims for it. Of the various interesting alternative types of demand curve which can be defined, one at least possesses most, if not all, of the advantages which Friedman can claim for any type of constant-real-income demand curve and none of its disadvantages.

In his argument in support of the constant-real-income demand curve Friedman demonstrated that the use of an ordinary demand curve in a demand-

*Reprinted from the *Journal of Political Economy* (June 1954) by permission of The University of Chicago Press. Copyright 1954, pp. 255–261.
[1] I wish to thank Mr. Amotz Morag and Professors Arnold C. Harberger and Carl F. Christ for their helpful advice and criticisms of early drafts of this note; and I wish to thank Professor Milton Friedman for his advice and criticism at a later stage. Specific acknowledgments to Professor Friedman appear at appropriate points in the text of this note. Responsibility for such errors as remain is, of course, my own.
[2] Milton Friedman, "The Marshallian Demand Curve," *Journal of Political Economy*, LVII (1949), 463–95.

supply diagram to show the effects of a subsidy on a given commodity fails to take account of the necessary withdrawal of resources from other uses; on the other hand, the constant-real-income demand curve, which in the limit is an approximation of what the community can actually have, allows for this withdrawal of resources and therefore presents a better picture of the final outcome.[3] While Friedman's analysis does not contain any errors, it is liable to serious misinterpretation if its assumptions and their relevance are overlooked; on the other hand, with a different type of demand curve which I shall propose the pitfalls can be avoided, and an analytically superior tool can be had in the bargain.

DEMAND CURVES AND PRODUCTION POSSIBILITIES

Suppose, for simplicity of arrangement, that a fully employed community has the production possibilities between its two competitively produced commodities X and Y as shown by the opportunity-cost curve ST in Fig. 1(a). Money, different from either commodity, is used as a unit of account only; money incomes are assumed to be spent in full, and the absolute price level to be determined arbitrarily.[4]

From the community indifference curves (for the moment assumed to be defined unambiguously) shown in Fig. 1(a), we may derive the two demand curves mentioned so far (the constant-real-income and the other-things-equal demand curves) in the customary manner. DD in Fig. 1(b) is defined by the price-consumption line PC in Fig. 1(b), and RR is obtained from the equilibrium indifference curve I_1 by noting the quantity of X at which I_1 has any given slope (i.e., marginal rate of substitution, interpreted as a price ratio, P_x/P_y).

Suppose now that the government pays a subsidy on production of X; the apparent effect after production adjusts itself to the new conditions will be to lower the price of X by some fraction of the amount of the subsidy, changing the price line from $S'T'$ to $S'L$ in Fig. 1(a), and to leave the price of Y and money income unchanged. Given this apparent opportunity, the community would like to consume to the point C in Fig. 1(a), that is, to the point W

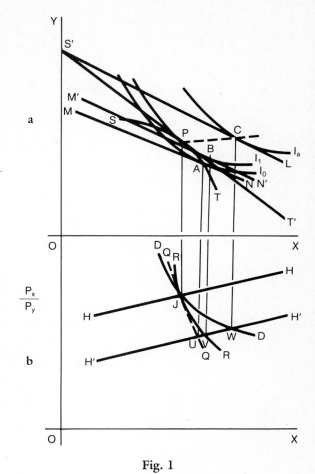

Fig. 1

[3]*Ibid.*, pp. 467–74.
[4]Friedman's assumption of a fixed supply of factor services is retained here, since its retention does not cause any loss of generality in the argument.

in Fig. 1(b). However, as Friedman pointed out, this is clearly impossible. Physical supplies are not available, and corresponding to this lack there is an inflationary gap equal to the going amount of the subsidy; also the relative price of Y must fall owing to the shift of production toward more X.

Hence we must further suppose that the government imposes an income tax always equal to the subsidy. The final equilibrium point is found where a price line which is tangent to an indifference curve where it crosses the production frontier differs in slope from the slope of the production frontier at that point by an amount corresponding to the subsidy. $S'L$ will "shift" to MN, where it is tangent to the indifference curve I_0, lower than I_1, at A. This equilibrium point is only slightly distant from B, the point at which $M'N'$ is tangent to I_1. ($S'L$, $M'N'$, and *MN* have it in common that each one's slope differs by the rate of subsidy from the slope of the production frontier beneath the point where each one is tangent to an indifference curve.)

It can be seen from this result that neither *DD* nor *RR*, in Fig. 1(*b*), shows the final outcome correctly. The correct outcome could be obtained only from another type of demand curve, the "production-frontier" demand curve, which would show, for each amount of *X*, the marginal rate of substitution of the indifference curve which crosses the production frontier at the point where that amount of *X* is produced. This demand curve is shown as *QQ* in Fig. 1(*b*); if *X* is not an inferior good, *QQ* must lie to the left of both *RR* and *DD* below *J* and must lie between them above *J* where *J* in Fig. 1(*b*) corresponds to *P* in Fig. 1(*a*). Its intersection with *H'H'* at *U*, corresponding to *A* in Fig. 1(*a*), shows the true outcome as the result of the imposition of the combination subsidy and income tax.

The production-frontier demand curve is clearly the one hypothetically most desirable for use in the comparative statics of demand analysis, since it shows what in fact the community will take when the repercussions on the production of other commodities are taken into account. Its weakness is that it is defined only for given production conditions. Presumably tastes are relatively constant, whereas real or apparent production conditions are always changing because of fluctuations in weather and crops, changes in government policy, and other factors. Data on market behavior may, to the extent that this is true, be supposed to tell us something about consumer preferences but to tell us little about production conditions. At any moment of time, however, production conditions are in some sense fixed; and for economic analysis it would be desirable to take these conditions into account in analyzing demand. Lacking knowledge of these conditions of the moment, we must adopt some more or less arbitrary method of approximating the effects of a change in policy or the like.

Friedman argues in effect that *RR* [in Fig. 1(*b*)] is a better approximation to *QQ* than is *DD*, since I_1 is tangent to *ST* at *P* and so approximates it in the limit, whereas *PC* has no such limiting property. That is to say, *RR* is tangent to *QQ*, but *DD* is not. This is correct, as long as the community preference field (the function represented by the indifference map) is innocent of any discontinuities in the first and all higher derivatives. Though I suppose there

is no reason to doubt its innocence for practical purposes, this qualification should be recognized as relevant. But other arguments developed below substantially weaken the case for the constant-real-income demand curve.

THE CONSTANT-REAL-INCOME CONCEPT

The argument so far has been greatly aided by the use of unexplained community indifference curves. It is now necessary to investigate the meaning of these curves of constant community real income and of the idea of a constant-real-income demand curve. The construction of community indifference curves will not be repeated here; suffice it to say that constant community real income means constant real income for *every individual* in the community.[5] The relevant construction necessarily implies the existence of different distributions of money incomes at different points along a given community indifference curve; the reason for this will become clear in the following discussion.

Consider, in Fig. 2, the indifference curves of two individuals whose money incomes are equal.[6] When the two indifference maps are superimposed on one another, their opportunity lines will coincide, as, for example, in *AB*. The individual *I* will be in equilibrium at *P*, and the individual *J* will be in equilibrium at *Q*, given the opportunity line *AB*. Now for an arbitrary change in the price of, say, commodity *Y*, what price change of *X* will keep both individuals on the same levels of real income *J* and *I*? It is at once apparent that there need not be *any* price change of *X* which will do the trick. If the price of *Y* should rise until the given money income of each individual could purchase only *OC* of *Y*, then a price of *X* corresponding to the opportunity line *CD* would do it, since *CD* happens to be tangent to both *I* and *J* at *R* and *S*, respectively. But the set of points *C* through which a line can be drawn tangent to both indifference curves is in general a finite set (the principal exception being the case where the two indif-

[5]William J. Baumol, "The Community Indifference Map: A Construction," *Review of Economic Studies,* XVII (1949–50), 189–97; and E. J. Mishan, "The Principle of Compensation Reconsidered," *Journal of Political Economy,* LX (1952), 514–17.
[6]For persons with different money incomes, the scales of *X* and *Y* quantities for the person with the larger income may be compressed (in the same proportion) until the two opportunity lines coincide when the indifference maps are superimposed. The argument in the text then applies without change to this case.

ference curves coincide) and may be empty, aside from the point A. A price compensating constant-real-income demand function for the two individuals must remain undefined except at points such as C—that is, we cannot, in general, have a constant-real-income demand "curve" at all, as long as money incomes are held constant.

On the other hand, if money income changes are used—in general, a different change for each individual—then it will always be possible to find an income change for each individual that will just offset any price change (or set of price changes) and permit him to achieve the same indifference curve as before. This, in effect, is what is done in defining community indifference curves.

But if the method of compensating price changes is used, there is no such thing as a constant-real-income demand curve for two individuals taken together. Such a curve can be defined for each one, but the curves cannot be aggregated because the price changes of Y offsetting a given price change of X would be different for the two individuals. This would be true a fortiori for a larger community; and it would continue to be true whatever the number of commodities.

It should be clear, then, that a constant-real-income demand curve for a community cannot be defined in terms solely of offsetting price movements for all possible price changes of a given commodity unless everybody's tastes are, in effect, identical. In fact, identity of tastes is not sufficient when money incomes are different. What is required is that the indifference curve on which each individual finds himself in equilibrium must be an exact projection of the corresponding indifference curve of every other individual. Unless all indifference systems were homogeneous, identity of tastes would guarantee this coincidence only for an equal distribution of income.

TWO APPROXIMATIONS: CONSTANT APPARENT REAL INCOME AND CONSTANT APPARENT PRODUCTION

The objections against a constant-real-income demand curve, as I have so far defined it, are for any practical purpose overwhelming; recourse may be had, however, to an approximating concept which

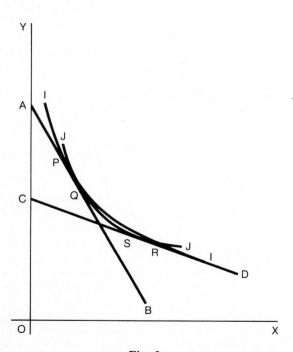

Fig. 2

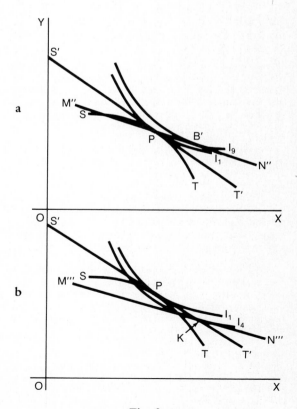

Fig. 3

avoids these objections.[7] This concept is that of the constant-*apparent*-real-income demand curve, which can be defined for constant-money incomes all around and with no particular knowledge of individual consumer preferences. In Fig. 3(a) the point P represents, as before, the initial equilibrium point, and S'T' is the equilibrium price line. If the price of X is lowered, the consumers' real income will "apparently" be the same if the price of Y is raised to the point where the consumers are just able to buy the same bill of goods they bought before; that is, the new price line M"N" should pass through P. This, to a first order of approximation, cancels out the income effect to consumers in the aggregate[8] but allows them a small gain in "real income" by substituting X for Y; the new bill of goods they would choose if they had this opportunity would be B', on the community indifference curve I_3, higher than I_1.

The demand curve derived in this way is not the same thing as the true constant-real-income demand curve as previously defined (which depended on the shape of I_1 only), but it can be proved to be a first-order approximation of it,[9] just as the true constant-real-income demand curve is a first-order approximation of the production-frontier demand curve. It follows that the constant-apparent-real-income demand curve is a first-order approximation of the production-frontier demand curve. Furthermore, it does not suffer from the difficulties of definition of the other curve, since it can unambiguously be defined in terms of constant-money incomes for every individual.

In practice, something in the nature of a constant-apparent-real-income demand curve could be derived statistically from ordinary total market data; whereas a true constant-real-income demand curve could not but would require data on every individual. With a statistically derived demand curve in our hands, we would not know what values of the price variables (if any) would give every consumer the same real income (for a constant-money income) as some other set of values of the price variables. However, it would be a simple matter to choose a set of price variables giving the same *apparent* real income (as here defined) to the community as some other set; all that has to be done is to choose a set of prices which keeps a base-weights price index unchanged in value.[10]

However, the possibilities for better practical approximation of the production-frontier demand curve are not yet exhausted. We may with comparable simplicity define a constant-apparent-*production* demand curve; and this will be the best approximation of the lot. In Fig. 3(b) the line S'T' represents the equilibrium price line as before, and, being tangent to the production frontier ST at P, it represents a local approximation of ST, just as does I_1. A useful demand concept is defined by moving along S'T': for any given price ratio for X and Y, we obtain from the community indifference map that bill of goods among those along S'T' which the community would prefer; that is, we find the community indifference curve I_4, which at its point of crossing of S'T' has the same slope as the given price line, M'''N'''.

We may now compare the different conceptions of demand set forth here; the curves are illustrated in Fig. 4, which is derived from Figs. 1(a), 3(a), and 3(b) in the same manner as Fig. 1(b) is derived from Fig. 1(a). The curves DD, RR, and QQ in Fig. 4 are the same as in Fig. 1(a); the new curves R'R' and Q'Q' are the approximations—constant *apparent* real income and production, respectively—discussed in this section.

[7]In his text Friedman uses the constant-apparent-real-income demand curve (*op. cit.*, pp. 466–67 [p. 92 of the present book]).

[8]If individual incomes are not adjusted, then "income effects" are not removed by this procedure even to a first order of approximation for individuals, since no individual need be consuming the two commodities in the same proportions as they are consumed by the whole community.

However, this consideration may be ignored for the constant-apparent-real-income demand curve, if we like, whereas in the nature of the case it cannot be ignored for the "true" constant-real-income demand curve. Furthermore, if we choose not to ignore it, we need only to know the original quantities bought by each consumer in order to define the constant-apparent-real-income demand curve, whereas for the constant-real-income demand curve one must know the shape and position of each consumer's relevant indifference curve. Similar remarks apply to the constant-apparent-production demand curve discussed below in the text.

So far as I can see, the production-frontier demand curve has the disadvantage that there is no logical way to define it for each individual in the community—it is a purely aggregate function, and any relative income distribution is consistent with its definition. This disadvantage is the antithesis of the disadvantage of the constant-real-income demand curve, which in effect is defined only for the individual.

My earlier omission of the points in this footnote was brought to my attention by Friedman.

[9]See Jacob L. Mosak, "On the Interpretation of the Fundamental Equation of Value Theory," in O. Lange *et al.* (eds.), *Studies in Mathematical Economics and Econometrics* (Chicago: University of Chicago Press, 1942), p. 73 n.

[10]Friedman, *op. cit.*, p. 467 [p. 92 of the present book].

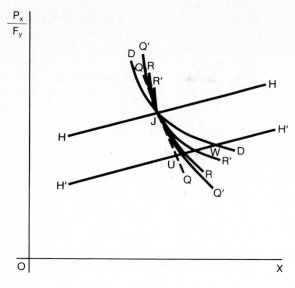

Fig. 4

volves keeping a base-weights quantity index constant. Such awkwardness of definition as exists in the constant-apparent-production demand curve disappears if the Continental procedure of expressing prices as a function of quantity is adopted.[11]

The constant-apparent-production curve has the advantage, however, that it represents the true possibilities closer than does the constant-real-income demand curve. *It utilizes information which the latter curve does not use, namely, that the equilibrium price ratio is itself an approximation of the alternative bills of goods which the community can in fact have.*

There is one other point on which the suggested "improvement" of the conventional demand curve might be rejected: the conventional demand curve is unambiguous about how "other prices" behave, whereas none of the other demand curves is. If there are several commodities, a given change in the price of commodity X may be offset by price changes in other goods in any of a number of different ways still meeting the specifications of the other four types of demand curves. It may make a good deal of difference to the demand for X whether the prices of closely competing or complementary goods are changed a little or a lot to compensate for the change in the price of X. If any demand curve other than the all-other-prices-and-incomes-equal demand curve is used, some arbitrary specification must be made as to how other prices are to change to offset changes in the price of X, such as that all other prices change in the same proportion. It should be recognized that such a solution *is* arbitrary, since whatever choice is made does not necessarily have any connection with the way these prices would really change if, say, a subsidy were imposed on commodity X. The conventional demand curve solves this problem (also arbitrarily, of course) by assuming that other prices do not change at all.

FINAL COMMENT

The conclusion of the above remarks finds me substantially in agreement with Friedman's argument in favor of revising the conventional notion of a demand curve when we desire to analyze the effects of an excise tax or subsidy, although I have come out in favor of even greater revision than he suggested. In the policy problem in question, the community's production opportunities are unaffected, but *appar-*

The curves $R'R'$, RR, and $Q'Q'$ are all tangent to QQ at J, a condition which will hold provided the necessary continuity obtains in preference and production; and it can also be seen that $R'R'$, RR, and $Q'Q'$ are successively better approximations in that order to QQ, which represents the demand derived from what the community can actually have. (The relative positions of the various curves depend on the assumption that commodity X is not inferior.) No importance should be attached to the absolute curvatures of the different curves, which depend on the conditions of preference and production; but under the assumed conditions it is necessarily true that QQ, $Q'Q'$, RR, and $R'R'$ are successively more concave upward and that $Q'Q'$ is the best approximation to the shape of QQ.

The constant-apparent-production demand curve can, like the constant-apparent-real-income demand curve, be derived from market data on quantities sold and prices. Just as the constant-apparent-real-income demand curve is obtained from the knowledge of the original equilibrium quantities and of the relevant part of the consumer preference field as revealed in market data, so the constant-apparent-production curve is obtained from a knowledge of the original equilibrium *prices* and of the relevant part of the consumer preference field. The first involves keeping a base-weights price index constant; the second in-

---

[11]I am indebted to Friedman for this point.

ent supply conditions are changed. Therefore, it is simplest to use a demand curve along which true supply conditions are (exactly or approximately) unchanged. The conventional demand curve does not meet this specification; consequently, in the problem under consideration one must show a shift in such a demand curve, as well as in the apparent supply curve, as the effect of the policy action.[12] If market data are sufficiently informative, both demand and supply conditions are hypothetically ascertainable, and the production-frontier demand curve may be used. If not, the approximations discussed here may be used, the better of which is the constant-apparent-production demand curve.

The situation is not the same if the problem under consideration involves changes in actual supply conditions such as *(a)* changes in technique, *(b)* crop variations and the like, and *(c)* changes in government activity, altering the availabilities to the private sector of the economy. In any such case the relevant demand curve would change, that is, would "shift." This is true of the production-frontier demand curve

[12]Friedman, *op. cit.*

and of all three of its approximations. It is possible that, by coincidence, the new equilibrium might be on the old price-consumption line (*PC* in Fig. 1(*a*)); and in this case the conventional demand curve would give the true result without shifting. No such coincidence is possible for the other four demand curves if the new production frontier lies entirely above or below the old one. Beyond this, however, nothing can be said as to whether the outcome of a change in conditions can or cannot be approximated with any single demand curve defined here.

It is therefore evident that the choice of a demand curve for purposes of analysis should depend on the problem in hand; and for some problems no demand curve will perform with the simplicity we might desire. It should therefore also be evident that the use of general equilibrium diagrams such as Fig. 1(*a*) is an important supplement to clear and accurate analysis. With such diagrams it is still necessary to state the relevant qualifications regarding income distribution, but subject to this the interrelationships between different types of changes in conditions can be shown.

Cardinal Utility*

ROBERT H. STROTZ

Robert H. Strotz (A.B., University of Chicago, 1942; Ph.D., 1951) is currently the Chancellor of Northwestern University, having served as its President from 1970 to 1985. Professor of Economics since 1958, Strotz began his career at Northwestern in 1947 as an Instructor, and was named Dean of the College of Arts and Sciences in 1966. Professor Strotz has made major contributions to our understanding of econometric methods and mathematical models. Currently a Fellow of the Econometric Society, he served as a council member from 1961-1967.

This paper is concerned with the recent revival of the proposition that utility is measurable. This is an old issue and one on which our opinion has been largely reversed during the past few years. Initially we accepted the concept of utility as measurable, then we rejected it, and now we are in the process of accepting it again.

Utility was originally conceived as a psychic quantity, which, while it may not have been easily measured, was regarded as measurable, at least in principle. The notion of the diminishing marginal rate of utility came quite naturally for it appears to have had considerable appeal to one's intuition. Although the acceptance of a cardinal utility of this sort had been questioned earlier, that doctrine was not effectively interred until 1934, largely as a consequence of the work of Allen and Hicks. ("A Reconsideration of the Theory of Value," *Economica,* February, May, 1934.) Utility then came to be regarded as an ordinal sort of thing, subject to ranking but not to measurement. The principle of Occam's Razor lent sanctity to the new approach because it was found that ordinal utility served very well for the treatment of the problems to which utility theory was conventionally applied. The assumption of the cardinal, quantitative character of utility, doubtful and unneeded, was largely abandoned. The word utility persisted in our literature, however, but only as an indicator enabling us to say that if a consumer prefers A to B to C he derives greater utility from A than from B or C and greater utility from B than from C. But we denied that any meaningful statements could be made about whether the difference in the utilities provided by A and B is greater or less than the difference in the utilities provided by B and C. Utilities could be compared but differences between utilities could not.

*Reprinted from *American Economic Review* (May 1953) by permission of the American Economic Association. Copyright 1953, pp. 384-397.

This paved the way for a behavioristic rather than a hedonistic interpretation of utility. Utility no longer had to be thought of as a psychological entity measurable in its own right. It could now be regarded as simply a convenient label for the explicit value of a function which described consumer behavior. The definition of a utility that consumers maximized had become tautologous. The utility function was simply any function that was maximized and the empirical significance of the theory of consumer behavior resided in the qualitative restrictions that were imposed on the form of the utility function itself, notably by the requirement of the diminishing marginal rate of substitution. Professor Stigler could write in his *Theory of Competitive Price:* "It does not affect the formal theory of demand in the least whether the individual maximizes wealth, religious piety, the annihilation of crooners, or his waistline." (Page 64.) This statement clearly requires that no judgment be made as to whether utility be measured in dollars or in days indulgence, in octaves or in inches, and there certainly is no presumption that utility is to be measured in some psychological unit.

In 1945, however, with the publication of the *Theory of Games and Economic Behavior,* by von Neumann and Morgenstern (second edition, Chapter III and Appendix), measurable utility was resurrected, but only as a result, it should be understood, of a quite different and superior understanding of the meaning of measurement. Measurable utility in the von Neumann-Morgenstern sense bears little resemblance to the measurable utility that was discarded during the past two decades. During the interregnum from Allen and Hicks to von Neumann and Morgenstern such debate as existed between the vanishing cardinalists and the ascendant ordinalists was concerned essentially with the philosophical question of whether cardinality or quantifiability could reasonably be regarded as an intrinsic property of the entity called utility.[1] From the modern point of view, we now realize that this philosophical question of whether utility is intrinsically measurable is a spurious one and that measurement has meaning, not

as a property of things, but as a predictive procedure. Crucial to an understanding of this entire subject is the realization that measurement is always invented and never discovered!

Consider for a moment the question of measuring length. Suppose that there are two carpenters each of whom has the task of placing two boards end to end and then sawing a third board that will exactly cover the combined length of the first two. The first carpenter proceeds as we would. He measures the length of a board by counting the number of times he can lay down on it, end to end, a rule of unit length, where the unit is arbitrarily defined. If the rule can be placed end to end three times on the first board, he declares that board to be three rule-lengths, or, let us say, 3 feet long. Now this statement is arbitrary. He might just as well have said that the length of the board is the-square-root-of-three feet long or the-square-of-three feet long or any-other-function-of-three feet long. But his convention is a useful one, especially for the problem at hand. Finding the first board to be 3 feet long and the second board to be 4 feet long, he knows that the board to be cut must be 3 + 4 or 7 feet long. He need only know how to add to make a good prediction.

The second carpenter, having been apprenticed in a strange land, measures the first board in a different manner. His measure is the square of our measure. When he lays the rule down again and again he counts "1, 4, 9" and declares the board to be 9 feet long. The second board is measured by counting "1, 4, 9, 16." To determine then how long a board he should cut, he calculates $(\sqrt{9} + \sqrt{16})^2 = 49$, and so measures off a length of 49 counting "1, 4, 9, 16, 25, 36, 49." Forty-nine being the square of 7, his answer is really the same as that of the first carpenter. The method of the second carpenter requires somewhat better knowledge of arithmetic than the method of the first, as he must square a sum of square roots rather than simply add. But his method is not incorrect; it is simply awkward.

Suppose now that these two carpenters were given another assignment. This time they are to place the first two boards at right angles and saw a third board to form the hypothenuse of a right triangle. The first carpenter performs the calculation $\sqrt{3^2 + 4^2} = 5$; the second carpenter, 9 + 16 = 25. Twenty-five being the square of 5, both methods are correct, but this time it is the method of the first carpenter which is awkward. In short, one method of measurement

[1]This appears to be the case, for example, in O. Lange, "The Determinateness of the Utility Function," *Review of Economic Studies,* June, 1934; W. E. Armstrong, "The Determinateness of the Utility Function," *Economic Journal,* September, 1939; F. H. Knight, "Realism and Relevance in the Theory of Demand," *Journal of Political Economy,* December, 1944; and, more recently, D. H. Robertson, "Utility and All That," *Manchester School,* May, 1951.

may be more convenient than another for some purposes and less convenient for other purposes. A vast variety of methods may, however, all be correct.

Why do we customarily use the measure of the first carpenter rather than that of the second? I suppose the answer is that we more commonly encounter problems of placing lengths end to end than problems of constructing right triangles. But the important point is this: our choice of a measure is largely a matter of convenience or manageability.

An equally important point, of course, is that a measure which makes computation convenient must also work. If, for example, we found that although a board 7 feet long exactly covers the combined length of one 3 feet long and one 4 feet long, a board 70 feet long exceeds the combined length of boards 30 and 40 feet long, then the particular formula we use, namely, simple addition, would be incorrect and unsatisfactory. In short, what we want is to invent some arbitrary method of measuring things which, coupled with a simple formula, will enable us to make correct predictions.

Now the very same thing is true of utility. We want to find an arbitrary measure of utility so that we can under frequently encountered conditions predict consumer behavior by use of a simple formula.

An early example of this approach is to be found in Samuelson's essay entitled, "Constancy of the Marginal Utility of Income" (in O. Lange *et al., Studies in Mathematical Economics and Econometrics*). Here the following problem was raised.

Marshall found that a good deal of the analysis of consumer behavior could be greatly simplified by assuming that the marginal utility of income is constant. Now, the marginal utility of income is clearly a measure. Could we then invent a measure of utility so that the marginal utility of income would in fact be constant?

If so, we should then want to determine whether this measure would imply anything about reality that we might put to test, and, if there are any empirically testable theorems implicit in our acceptance of this measure, we should then want to know whether these theorems correspond to reality. Before pursuing the question of whether we can invent an acceptable measure of utility for which the marginal utility of income is constant, we must note, as Samuelson has pointed out, that the phrase, "the constancy of the marginal utility of income," is subject to diverse interpretations. For our illustrative purpose here, we propose the following particular interpretation. By "the marginal utility of income" let us mean the common value of the ratios of the marginal utilities of commodities to their prices. By "constancy" let us mean constancy with respect to independent changes in the various prices of commodities and in income. Now, we may see clearly what our problem is. As is well known, there is an infinite number of utility functions that will serve equally well to describe the behavior of a given individual. This is so because for any one of these functions that will describe his behavior any other function that increases, decreases, or stays the same whenever the first one increases, decreases, or stays the same will describe the consumer's behavior just as well.

Two functions which are related in this way are called "monotonically increasing functions of each other." The reason why any member of this family of monotonically increasing functions may be selected as the utility function is because a consumer who may be said to maximize any one of them subject to his budget may be said to maximize any other for they all go up and down together. Can we find among this infinite number of acceptable utility functions one that has the property that the marginal utility of income will remain constant for a change in any price or for a change in income? If so, we can define a measure of utility (that is, we can select this particular utility function) so that it is permissible to assume that the marginal utility of income is constant. What Samuelson then proceeded to show is that no such function is available. (This is analogous to showing that for no measure of length will the third side of a triangle, which is not necessarily a right triangle, be equal to the sum of the other two sides.)

Let us next change the problem a bit by changing our definition of constant to mean constant with respect to a change in any commodity price, although not constant with respect to a change in income. In answer to this problem Samuelson showed that a total utility function might be specified so that the marginal utility of income is constant in this sense. But he found, moreover, that there is an empirically testable proposition implicit in the acceptance of such a total utility function; namely, that the income elasticity of the demand for each commodity is unitary. This, clearly, does not square with the facts. To summarize, the question was whether a measure of total utility could be devised so that the marginal utility of income would be constant with respect to price changes. What was shown was that any measure that would satisfy this condition would entail the empirical restriction that income elasticities be unitary. Since income elasticities are not all unitary, we conclude that no such measure can be defined.

Just as it suits the Marshallian demand analysis to assume a total utility function for which the marginal utility of income is constant, so von Neumann and Morgenstern also had a purpose in assuming the existence of a total utility function with a convenient property. Dealing to a considerable extent in their *Theory of Games* with choices in situations involving risk, they found that it would be quite helpful to have a utility function that would make possible the use of a simple formula to describe an individual's choices among various risks. How nice it would be to say that every gamble can be reduced to a certainty equivalent, where the certainty equivalent would be that certain income (increment of income) which provides a utility equal to a weighted average of the utilities resulting from different possible outcomes of the gamble, the weights being probabilities. For example, it would be convenient if we could say that an individual would evaluate a 1/5 to 4/5 chance of winning either $0 to $10 as follows: If he in fact wins nothing his utility will be, say, 0; if he in fact wins $10 his utility will be, say, 1. The weighted average utility will therefore be $1/5 \cdot 0 + 4/5 \cdot 1 = 4/5$.

Now, we should like to continue, the individual will be indifferent between this particular gamble and any other gamble that provides a weighted average utility of 4/5 and he will be indifferent between this class of gambles and any certain awards that provide the same utility. The weighted average is known as his mathematical expectation of utility or, in Bernoulli's terms, his moral expectation. It is to be distinguished from the utility of the mathematical expectation of his winnings which would be the utility of the weighted average of the possible winnings; that is, the utility of $1/5 \cdot \$0 + 4/5 \cdot \$10$ or the utility of $8. We can make this distinction in more familiar terms. The mathematical expectation of utility or moral expectation we might call simply the "average utility of the winnings" or just "average utility." The utility of the mathematical expectation of the winnings we shall call the "utility of the average winnings."

Suppose the individual prefers the certainty of $8 to the 1/5-4/5 chance of nothing or $10. The utility of the average winnings is then greater than the average utility of the winnings. Suppose, however, that he is indifferent between the gamble and the certainty of $6. The utility of $6 is then equal to his average utility from the gamble, which is 4/5.

By varying the probabilities in the gamble and setting the average utility which we can compute equal to the utility of the certain payment to which the individual is indifferent (the certainty equivalent), his entire utility curve can be constructed between 0 and 10, and by the same general method the curve can be extended still further. Such a curve is a Neumann-Morgenstern utility function. There are, of course, many such functions but they differ one from another only in the choice of a unit of measurement and the location of zero. They are all related to one another in the same way that the centigrade thermometer is related to the Fahrenheit thermometer.

This defines three points on a utility curve (Fig. 1): for zero income, zero utility; for $10 income, 1 unit of utility; and for $6 income, 4/5 of a unit of utility. The first two points are arbitrarily defined; the last is obtained by finding the certain income which is equivalent to the gamble, the utility of which has been computed to be the weighted average utility of the possible outcomes.

Once we have constructed a Neumann-Morgenstern utility function it should, to be useful, enable us to answer all possible questions we can put to it about the choice that an individual would make among various gambles offered to him. If, for example, an individual had a choice between a gamble in which he might win any one of the amounts x_1,

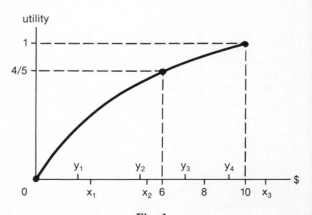

Fig. 1

x_2, x_3 with various probabilities and a gamble in which he might win any one of the amounts y_1, y_2, y_3, y_4 with various probabilities, it should follow that he will choose the gamble for which the average utility of the possible outcomes is the greater. Now, it is certainly conceivable that we might find someone whose behavior in situations involving risk could not be predicted from this function by use of the simple formula of average utility or moral expectation. But the possibility that we may not be able to make correct predictions indicates simply that the von Neumann-Morgenstern postulate has empirical content and is not an empty formalism. For the postulate to be significant, one must run the risk that it might be proved wrong.

What does our intuition tell us about this matter? Is it self-evident that people who are not pathological will order their preferences among gambles so that the existence of a Neumann-Morgenstern function will be assured? I am afraid my intuition tells me very little. It is not self-evident to me that this function either does exist or does not exist.

What then can be done to answer this question? We may move in either of two directions: First, we may replace the hypothesis that there exists a Neumann-Morgenstern utility function with an axiomatic system that implies this statement as a theorem. That is, we may seek a set of statements (axioms) which are logically equivalent to the statement that a Neumann-Morgenstern utility function exists. The existence of this function is then a theorem which can be logically derived from these axioms. The purpose of finding such axioms which really say the same thing as the theorem is that is may be easier for our rather opaque intuition to accept or reject the axioms than to accept or reject the theorem itself. A Supreme Being would have no need for axioms, but they are often found quite useful for mere men. Von Neumann and Morgenstern have provided us with an axiomatic system for their utility measure as have several other writers.[2] Let me sketch one of these systems, that of Professor Marschak, in a rather carefree fashion to indicate the main idea.

Marschak's axioms or postulates are as follows:

1. An individual's preferences are completely ordered. Any two "prospects," be they gambles or certainties, can be compared in the sense that one will be either preferred or indifferent to the other. Furthermore, the ranking of prospects is transitive, which means that if A is preferred to B and B preferred to C, A is preferred to C.

2. If A is preferred to B and B to C, then there exists a probability p between 0 and 1 such that the gamble A with probability p and C with probability $1 - p$, which we shall represent as $[pA + (1 - p)C]$, will be indifferent to B. This means that some probability combination of something better and something worse can be found to make such a gamble indifferent to something in between.

3. For any object of choice or "prospect" A and for any probability p (between 0 and 1) one can specify another prospect B such that A will not be indifferent to the probability combination $[pA + (1 - p)B]$. That is to say, for example, that if A is \$10 and p is $\frac{1}{2}$, one can find a sum of money such that a fifty-fifty chance of \$10 or that other sum is either better or worse than \$10. The real significance of this is that a gamble in which the probability of a given prospect of A is not 1, however close to 1 it may be, cannot always be regarded as equivalent to the certainty of A.

4. If A and B are indifferent and p is between 0 and 1, then for any prospect C, $[pA + (1 - p)C]$ is indifferent to $[pB + (1 - p)C]$. This has caused some confusion because of the possibility that B and C may be more complementary than are A and C so that one would prefer to have B and C to having A and C. This complementarity is irrelevant, however, because in a gamble of the sort considered one gets either one outcome or the other, but not both.

These axioms have strong intuitive appeal. It would seem that every normal person would clearly accept them as precepts of behavior. Now, Marschak shows that these axioms are just another way of saying that a Neumann-Morgenstern utility function exists. If you accept the axioms you are then logically required to accept the Neumann-Morgenstern theorem which can be derived from them.

Earlier I said that resort to the use of axioms is one of two methods of considering the validity of the Neumann-Morgenstern hypothesis. Another way is to find some concrete choice situations where the violation of the Neumann-Morgenstern hypothesis seems plausible or is actually revealed by observation. The following case will illustrate what I mean.

[2]Notably Jacob Marschak, "Rational Behavior, Uncertain Prospects, and Measurable Utility," *Econometrica*, April, 1950; I. N. Herstein and John Milnor, "An Axiomatic Approach to Measurable Utility," *Econometrica*, forthcoming.

Suppose an individual is confronted with choices among these alternatives:

$$A = (\$0, p = 1)$$
$$B = (\$5, p = 1)$$
$$C = (\$10, p = 1)$$
$$D = (\tfrac{1}{2} \cdot \$0 + \tfrac{1}{2} \cdot \$10)$$
$$E = (\tfrac{1}{2} \cdot \$0 + \tfrac{1}{2} \cdot \$20)$$
$$F = (\tfrac{2}{3} \cdot \$0 + \tfrac{1}{3} \cdot \$25)$$

and that he orders these alternatives as follows, where a letter higher on the page is preferred to one that is lower.

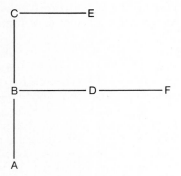

Is there anything preposterous or pathological about a person arranging his preferences in this way? Are we prepared to say that such a person would hardly be found walking the streets? I am not myself prepared to say this.

Suppose now we attempt to construct a Neumann-Morgenstern utility function for this person (Fig. 2). Let the utility of A be 0 and the utility of B be 1. Then the utility of $10 must be 2 because D is indifferent to B. The utility of $20 must be 4 because E is indifferent to C. The utility of $25 must then be 3 because F is indifferent to B. But this says that the utility of $25 is less than the utility of $20, which is an absurdity.

Is there something unbelievable about this person's preferences or is there something unrealistic about the Neumann-Morgenstern hypothesis? This much we can note. Because E is indifferent to C and because C enters into the probability combination D, we may substitute E for C ($10) in D. This describes a new prospect $D' = [\tfrac{1}{2} \cdot 0 + \tfrac{1}{2} (\tfrac{1}{2} \cdot \$0 + \tfrac{1}{2} \cdot \$20)]$ which is a fifty-fifty chance of winning nothing or of winning a lottery ticket which provides in turn a fifty-fifty chance of winning nothing or of winning $20. Using Marschak's fourth axiom, D' is then indifferent to D. Now D' may be

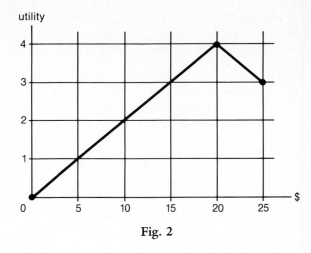

Fig. 2

written more simply as $[\tfrac{3}{4} \cdot \$0 + \tfrac{1}{4} \cdot \$20]$. Transitivity requires that since D' is indifferent to D and D is indifferent to F, D' must be indifferent to F. But this means that the individual does not prefer F to D' or does not prefer having the amount to be won increased from $20 to $25 simultaneously with an increase of the probability of winning from $\tfrac{1}{4}$ to $\tfrac{1}{3}$. In other words, F differs from D' only by offering a higher probability of winning more. F would, therefore, clearly be preferred to D'. The conclusion from the axioms that F and D' are indifferent therefore involves us in a contradiction.

Is there something irrational about a man's holding these preferences and contradicting the axioms of choice which we reviewed a bit ago? The rationality of these axioms seemed self-evident, but we ought now explain just what the meaning of rational is. A test for the propriety of using the word rational here is the following. Consider any person not deemed insane who holds contradictory preferences such as those illustrated here. Imagine that we explain to this person the nature of the contradiction, pointing out clearly how his preferences violate our axioms. Will he in consequence of understanding the nature of the contradiction decide that his preferences are ill-founded and proceed to change them, or will he persist in his original preferences even though it is entirely clear to him exactly what precepts his preferences violate. If for nearly every person holding contradictory preferences an understanding of the character of the contradiction induces him to straighten out his preferences, then the Neumann-Morgenstern axioms may properly be regarded as precepts of rational choice. My own feeling is that it would be a strange man indeed who would persist in violating these precepts once he understood clearly in what way he was violating them.

But to conclude that the Neumann-Morgenstern hypothesis provides a principle of rational behavior is not to conclude that it is empirically valid. My own casual impression of human nature does not permit me to deny a priori the existence of contradictory choice structures. Even after accepting the Neumann-Morgenstern principle as a rational one, choice among risks may not be an easy thing for an untutored man to keep straight and self-contradictory preferences like faulty arithmetic may not be uncommon. This is, of course, an empirical question and one might hope that future empirical work will shed some light on this subject. I should not want to prejudge the final answer. To emphasize the possibility that the Neumann-Morgenstern theory may be an incorrect generalization about reality is, of course, also to emphasize that it is a meaningful proposition that has something to say about reality.

Here is an interesting way to illustrate the fact that the Neumann-Morgenstern hypothesis has empirical content. Consider all possible risks which entail only some probability of winning some single amount of money. Any such risk may be represented by a point on the graph (Fig. 3) where the amount to be won is measured horizontally and the probability of winning that amount is measured vertically along a logarithmic axis. For example, A is a gamble offering a 1/10 chance of winning \$100. Consider now the indifference curves of an individual among these various gambles. (The probability of winning may be regarded as one commodity and the amount to be won as another). If the individual is rational according to the Neumann-Morgenstern axioms, these indifference curves will all be vertical displacements of one another, as drawn. This may be demonstrated as follows: Consider any two indifference curves such as those shown in Fig. 4 and lottery tickets $A = (p_a \cdot x_a)$ and $B = (1 \cdot x_a)$, and any $C = (p_c \cdot x_c)$ which is indifferent to B. To establish that the indifference curves are vertical displacements of one another we need only show line $DC = AB$. Since A is the probability p_a of winning x_a and B the certainty of x_a we may substitute the "sure" ticket B for x_a in ticket A. A can therefore be regarded as a lottery ticket offering the probability p_a of winning the "sure" ticket B; i.e., $A = [p_a \cdot (1 \cdot x_a)]$. Using the

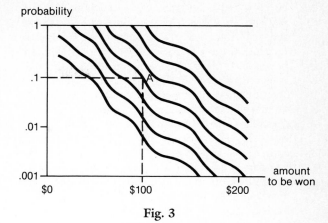

Fig. 3

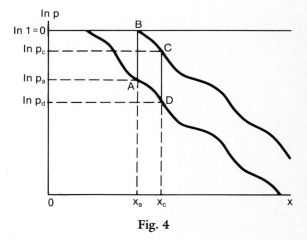

Fig. 4

fourth of Marschak's axioms we may substitute C for B in A because C and B are indifferent. This defines a new lottery ticket

$$D = [p_a \cdot (p_c \cdot x_c)] = (p_a p_c \cdot x_c) = (p_d \cdot x_c)$$

which is indifferent to A. We must now show ln $p_c - ln\ p_d = ln\ 1 - ln\ p_a$. Since $ln\ p_d = ln\ p_a + ln$ p_c and $ln\ 1 = 0$, this is straightforward. Therefore, $DC = AB$, as required. Another way of stating this is that the marginal rate of substitution between the logarithm of probability and the amount to be won must be independent of the probability.

There are several further aspects of the topic being discussed here and only a few of them can yet be considered even briefly.

One question concerns the extent to which the "love of gambling" has been ignored by the theory.

The "love of gambling" as a "love of danger" is clearly ruled out as behavior inconsistent with the theory (Marschak, *op. cit.*, pages 138, 139). Neumann-Morgenstern people do not play Russian Roulette. They may or may not commit suicide but they certainly do not prefer a 1/6 probability of death to either the impossibility or the certainty of death. The cylinders of their revolvers are either completely empty or fully loaded. The attraction of gambling which derives from the pleasure of the game, the spinning of the wheel, the bouncing of the dice, the party—these things are either abstracted from or included as part of the pay off. But the desire to gamble, even when gambling is dull, is not excluded. It is, as a matter of fact, one of the main things that the theory is about. The person who takes the dull gamble with a negative expected return is said to gamble because of increasing marginal utility which means that he finds the average utility of the possible outcomes to exceed the utility of the average outcome. It is a major contribution of the theory that it provides a hypothesis to explain this.

A related point refers to the fascinating psychological experiments conducted by Ward Edwards, of Johns Hopkins, in a paper entitled, "Experiments in Economic Decision-Making in Gambling Situations" (presented at the September, 1952, meetings of the Econometric Society). Edwards observed the preferences of subjects among various lottery tickets and found that he could explain their choices very neatly (in my opinion, more neatly than the von Neumann-Morgenstern utility function could explain them) in terms of assumed preferences for certain probabilities and dislikes of other probabilities. His subjects seem to have been attracted by certain probabilities and repelled by others independently of the winnings associated with them. Only small amounts of money were involved, however, and the probability preferences he found may well have been inconsequential and overpowered by Neumann-Morgenstern considerations had larger amounts been at stake.

Granted the existence of a Neumann-Morgenstern utility function, we have only found a particular measure of utility that proves to be highly manageable for dealing with problems of risk. We have in no way denied that other utility functions which are not Neumann-Morgenstern functions may just as correctly be defined. If U_1 in Fig. 5 is a Neumann-Morgenstern function in terms of which we can pre-

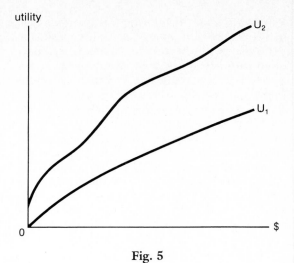

Fig. 5

dict a person's choices, then U_2, which is not a Neumann-Morgenstern function but which increases monotonically with U_1, will be equally correct. It will simply be more cumbersome in making the same predictions. This everyone has come to recognize, especially since William Baumol's note which insisted on the point ("The Neumann-Morgenstern Utility Index—An Ordinalist View," *Journal of Political Economy,* February, 1951). This means we have not reverted to the concept of a unique measure of utility in the sense in which cardinal utility was originally conceived. The behavioristic definition of utility as the value of any function the individual may be said to maximize has not been scuttled for the earlier, hedonistic concept of utility as a psychological quantity. The measure of utility provided by von Neumann and Morgenstern cannot therefore rehabilitate the utilitarian brand of welfare economics which requires the maximization of some scalar function of the cardinal utilities of the individuals in a society. For welfare economics there is no more reason to accept U_1 than to accept U_2.

Furthermore, the acceptance of the von Neumann-Morgenstern measure does not preclude the definition of still other measures. It is true that the von Neumann-Morgenstern measure is convenient and manageable for the class of problems involving risk, but it need not prove convenient for all classes of utility problems that may conceivably arise. Nothing rules out the usefulness of another measure for another purpose. And certainly no hypotheses about measurable utility can rebut the merits of the ordinal, indifference curve analysis of consumer behavior under certainty which seems to require the definition of no particular measure and which therefore does not impose unnecessary further restrictions on the nature of reality.

I should not want these final cautions concerning the use of the Neumann-Morgenstern measure to detract from the significance of this subject. Von Neumann and Morgenstern have given us an empirically meaningful and provocative hypothesis about economic behavior that may contribute substantially to a broad area of economic analysis. They have also straightened out the thinking of economists about the meaning of measurement and cleared aside the major misunderstanding that hampered the earlier disputations of cardinalists and ordinalists.[3]

[3]The reader who is interested in reading further on this subject is referred to the references already cited and in addition to J. Marschak, "Why 'Should' Statisticians and Businessmen Maximize Moral Expectation?" in J. Neyman, ed., *Proceedings of the Second Berkeley Symposium on Mathematical Statistics and Probability,* 1951; Milton Friedman and L. J. Savage, "The Utility Analysis of Choices Involving Risk," *Journal of Political Economy,* August, 1948; Frederick Mosteller and Philip Nogee, "An Experimental Measurement of Utility," *Journal of Political Economy,* October, 1951; and Milton Friedman and L. J. Savage, "The Expected-Utility Hypothesis and the Measurability of Utility," *Journal of Political Economy,* December, 1952.

The Testability of the Law of Demand*

YORAM BARZEL**

Yoram Barzel (B.A., The Hebrew University of Jerusalem, 1953; M.A., 1956; Ph.D., University of Chicago, 1961) was born in Jerusalem in 1931. Currently Professor of Economics at the University of Washington, Barzel has held visiting professor positions at University College in London, the Hoover Institution, and Washington University. Barzel is the author of *The Political Economy of the Oil Import Quota* (with C.D. Hall) and numerous articles.

Slutsky, in his magnificent article on demand, has attempted to formulate a law that would always hold true. Against such a formulation, contradictory empirical evidence would then be decisive. Slutsky's own statement is most eloquent: "One cannot call *law* any rule which admits of exceptions—it matters not whether they are few or many. . . ." Thus, the law can be "tested on the basis of scientifically arranged, empirical observations," (Slutsky, p. 45).

The law relates the price of a commodity to the quantity demanded by a person whose income is subject to "compensated variations." The Slutsky equation for an individual's purchase of commodity X is

$$\frac{\partial X^M}{\partial P} = \frac{\partial X^I}{\partial P} - X^M \frac{\partial X^M}{\partial M'} \qquad (1)$$

where P is the nominal price of X, and M is money income. The superscript M indicates that money income is held constant, and the superscript I indicates that (apparent) real income is held constant. The law of demand states that $\frac{\partial X^I}{\partial P} < 0$. To test the law, the compensating variations have to be effected. In Slutsky's own formulation the consumer is endowed with *money*, which he allocates among commodities. When a price rises, the value of the money declines, and a positive compensation is needed to restore its real value.

Two major problems impede empirical implementation: how to control for the second right-hand term in the equation; and how to perform the test, given that in reality consumers are endowed with resources, not with "money."

The term $\frac{\partial X^M}{\partial M}$ is the effect of income on consumption when relative prices are constant. To control for it, one needs data capable of yielding a satisfactory estimate of this magnitude. It is contended here that

*Reprinted from *Financial Economics: Essays in Honor of Paul Cootner*, edited by William F. Sharpe and Cathyrn M. Cootner, by permission of Prentice-Hall, Inc., Englewood Cliffs, N.J. Copyright 1982, pp. 233–245.

**I wish to thank M. Hashimoto, L. Kochin, K. Leffler, T. Ozenne, and W.F. Sharpe for their valuable comments.

the income measures commonly used in empirical studies are themselves the *result* of price changes and might, therefore, lead to apparent refutation of an otherwise valid law. This issue is discussed in the following section.

We next discuss the transition from a model in which the consumer holds money into one in which he holds resources. Armed with the proper account of these holdings, one can readily identify a class of observations free of any income effect. Since the effect of substitution is already isolated, the law can then be directly tested. The following section enumerates instances where the hypothesis might be tested. Finally, we identify an error in the accepted analysis of portfolio selection.

The analysis here is on the individual level; price changes are treated as exogenous. Thus, only seldom are the results applicable to the market as a whole. On the other hand, a more complete account than is usually the case is taken of the constraints of the individual's resources.

THE DEPENDENCE OF MEASURED INCOME ON PRICE

Consider a simplified version of a common demand-estimation equation:

$$X = b_0 + b_1 P + b_2 I \qquad (2)$$

where X is the quantity of a commodity purchased by a person, P is its relative price, and I is the person's real income.[1] It is said that the law of demand is refuted when $b_1 > 0$.

Data needed to estimate b_1 cannot vary in the nominal price of X alone, since then the income effect of the price change would not be isolated. Variability in I independently of P is essential to the estimation of b_2 to remove the effect of a change in nominal price on income. A more complete specification which separates the two income components is

$$X = b_0 + b_1 P + c_1 I_1 + c_2 I_2 \qquad (3)$$

where I_1 is income from changes in the nominal price of X, I_2 is other income, and $I_1 + I_2 \equiv I$. An as-

sumption implicit in the received approach, then, is that $c_1 = c_2 = b_2$. Now c_1, the coefficient of I_1, is what we wish to estimate so that the effect of I_1 can be netted out. Only if the effect of other income I_2 on X is the same as that of I_1 (that is, only if $c_1 = c_2$), can the effect on income of a price change be removed. By its definition, I_1 is a "pure" income change, maintaining relative prices constant. For the equality $c_1 = c_2$ to hold, variability in I_2 has to be free of changes in relative prices. It will now be shown that almost all components of income differences, as measured, are brought about by changes in relative prices.

In Slutsky's formulation, the individual can be viewed as receiving a cash endowment at the beginning of each period. However, as commonly used in empirical studies, income is a function of the individual's command over resources. It consists of earnings from assets, wages, and (sometimes) transfer payments. For the present we abstract from the latter. Income, then, depends on the quantities held by a person of each asset including human wealth (from which wages are the earned return) and the prices of those assets. The quantity of one asset held by a person can be increased only when he relinquishes a corresponding amount of another asset. Only a change in asset prices, then, can produce a change in personal income. Now asset prices depend ultimately on commodity prices; thus, personal income also depends, although indirectly, on commodity prices. The use of income in the estimation of demand for X, therefore, is inappropriate. When it is used, the coefficient c_2 would reflect both income and substitution effects, and the requirement that $c_1 = c_2$ would be violated.

The difficulties are compounded when the main, or only, source of income is wages. A wage change is equivalent to a change in the price of a particular commodity—leisure. Like any other price change, it will affect the quantity demanded of X through the (cross-) substitution effect and the income effect.[2] Moreover, as measured, the income effect is overstated. Wage income has to be "earned." At equilibrium in the labor market a person is indifferent about working or not working one more hour. The earnings from the last unit of time, therefore, contain no true income component; the "income" from the mar-

---

[1] The simplification consists of the use of a linear form and the omission of customary control variables, neither of which is relevant to our problem. Moreover, since we are concerned with an economic rather than an econometric problem, the error term is suppressed. Similarly, in terms of this paper's objective, there is no loss in considering only a single commodity out of a whole system.

[2] There is no a priori reason to expect the order of magnitude of this substitution effect to be smaller than that of the income effect.

ginal hour should be imputed wholly to the substitution effect.[3]

The problematic nature of income, as measured, is not confined to income variability experienced by a single person. Incomes will differ across persons with the levels of their asset holdings or their assets' prices. As with a wage change for a single person, differential wage earnings exert not only an income effect but also a substitution effect.[4] Thus, in this case c_1 also does not equal c_2, and in general, the estimate of b_1 is likely to be biased.

The difference in income from differential asset holdings across people provides the best opportunity to isolate the income effect; nevertheless difficulties abound here also. Income, as measured, may vary as a result of differences in human capital. Like income from work, human capital has to be earned. Two persons with different stocks of human capital will not necessarily differ in their "true" or "permanent" income—the larger holdings in one asset may well be at the expense of others. Consumption of X by the two may nevertheless differ because of differences in factors such as access to capital markets associated with varying levels of human capital. Obviously, such changes in consumption have little to do with income. We will return to this issue.

Nonhuman asset holdings which vary with the life cycle represent merely a change in the composition of permanent wealth rather than a change in its level. Such differences, then, would not yield the desired information. Additionally, the level of nonhuman assets a person holds will tend to affect both his borrowing rate and the value of his time. Therefore, a difference in income from that source is likely to be accompanied by (induced) differences in relative prices.[5]

Consider now transfers. To the extent that transfers are in the form of subsidies on commodities, as with food stamps or low-cost housing, these clearly are not "pure" income changes, and their lower price

will induce substitution towards them. It is necessary to *know* the substitution effect in order to obtain their net effect on income.

Other types of transfers may be more directly related to income. Nevertheless, unless they are unanticipated, they are not pure and have to be "earned."[6] In general, the gain in income is obtained only at a cost, as in the case of the requirement that some transfer recipients must meet certain criteria. To establish their claims, they have to expend resources, particularly in foregone leisure.[7]

The observed or measured change in income resulting from transfers, then, is higher than the real change; therefore, the income effect will be biased toward zero. Not only is the size of the bias unknown; it is likely to differ among individuals and types of transfer. Moreover, income and substitution effects are confounded in cases in which, because *measured* income must be low, some transfers will lead to a reduction in the implicit price of leisure.[8]

Indeed, it is exceedingly difficult even to conceive of an experiment which might isolate the pure income effect. People will spend resources to increase their chances of receiving the award (or its size), and such efforts annul the "purity" of the income.[9] Stated more generally, what are needed are observations of income changes accompanied neither by price changes nor by expenditure of resources to increase the income. Unacceptable by their very nature are those income changes generated by price changes, including that of leisure. Most other components of measured income are also unacceptable since, as objects of maximization, resources will be spent to acquire the income.

---

[3]For any asset, the quantity held is expected to change with a change in its price. Common methods of income accounting, however, are more likely to handle such a change correctly for nonhuman assets.

[4]Jacob Mincer recognizes that income differences arising from wage differences imply that the price of a consumption good is correspondingly affected. He limits his discussion, however, to the time cost of acquiring commodities.

[5]These differences may be controlled for, in part, by estimating the income effect of assets while holding age and education constant.

[6]Unanticipated transfers, including unexpected losses, are proper measures of income (or wealth). Data on such transfers, however, are hard to come by.

[7]These issues, while in different settings, are discussed in my paper on rationing by waiting.

[8]One other difficulty in obtaining the appropriate income correction is that since only nominal income is subject to income tax, changes in income induced by changes in consumption-basket prices are not taxed, whereas changes in earnings and other income are subject to tax and often at varying rates.

[9]It may appear that income differences generated by lotteries might be useful here. Even those, however, are subject to several, though perhaps unimportant, problems. If lotteries are unfair, or only just fair, only risk-seeking individuals will participate. If their expected value is positive, individuals will be willing to spend resources to participate. Random selection, then, would have to be strictly enforced for the experimental results to be valid.

DIRECT OBSERVATION OF THE SUBSTITUTION EFFECT

The difficulty in discovering income changes independent of price changes does not mean that the law of demand cannot be tested. On the contrary, such a test can be readily performed. In a wide variety of circumstances, a change in price simply will not affect income, thus dispensing altogether with the need for a correction.

Given the specification of the Slutsky equation, it is evident that an exogenous fall in price results in a positive income effect. When applied to leisure, however, the Slutsky equation is commonly written rather differently:

$$\frac{\partial X_e^M}{\partial P_e} = \frac{\partial X_e^I}{\partial P_e} + (24 - X_e) \frac{\partial X_e^M}{\partial M'} \qquad (4)$$

where X_e is the per-day amount of leisure and P_e is its price. A fall in price here—that of leisure—results in a negative income effect. The justification given for treating leisure differently than other commodities is that one can expend one's time as one wishes. In other words, people are assumed to be the owners not only of "money," but also of a stock of time whose value rises when its market price increases.

A person may own no asset other than himself, but in general, individuals must own other assets. Indeed, the *entire* stock of X (or of the resources used in producing it) has to be owned by somebody. To correctly analyze the demand for any commodity, such holdings have to be accounted for.[10] The Slutsky equation thus becomes

$$\frac{\partial X^M}{\partial P} = \frac{\partial X^I}{\partial P} + (X^0 - X) \frac{\partial X^M}{\partial M'} \qquad (5)$$

where X^0 is the initial endowment of X.[11] The received way of writing the equation, then, implicitly sets the endowments of commodities other than leisure at zero whereas the endowment of leisure is implicitly set larger than its consumption level. This, however, cannot hold for all individuals. People not only sell labor and buy commodities, they also buy labor and sell commodities. Slutsky's assumption that the individual is endowed with "money" rather than with real commodities (or factors) does not seem useful.[12]

The superior formulation immediately draws attention to the question whether, for any particular commodity, $X_0 - X$ is positive, negative, or zero; whether the individual is a net seller, a net buyer, or is "self-sufficient" with respect to X.[13] When $X_0 = X$, there is no income effect. The price line rotates through the consumption point, and actual income and "compensated income" are the same.

With respect to the bias in the Slutsky compensation, it is well known that for small price changes the bias can be ignored.[14] Note also that if $X_0 = X$ prior to the price change, the substitution effect always dominates in the Slutsky measure, no matter how large the change in price. That is, despite the presence of a nonvanishing income effect due to the Slutsky "overcompensation" (which is identical to the Laspyeres price index bias), the good can never become a Giffen good. The reason is that *only* by substituting toward the commodity with the lowered price can the increase in income be realized. The predictive capability, then is not impeded by overcompensation.

Two major forces may induce individuals to choose to be at the compensated point $X^0 = X$ before the change in market conditions occurs—a desire, first, to economize on transaction costs and, second, to insure against price fluctuations. One who acquires enough of a commodity to cover his consumption needs for several periods is reducing the number (hence, the cost) of transactions and is insulating himself from part of the risk associated with

---

[10]A. Alchian and W. R. Allen present a clear and satisfactory analysis of this point.

[11]George Stigler sets out this form, but he does not generalize the role of assets. Ronald Heiner also considers it, but he is mainly concerned with aggregate demand.

[12]Leon Walras, strictly concerned with excess demand, took proper account of initial holdings. Note, however, that since he assumed away inferior goods, the Giffen Paradox had no room in his model. On the other hand, he overlooked the possibility that demand might be positively sloped for a net seller of a commodity.

[13]Stigler's discussion of the Giffen Paradox makes it clear that Giffen was concerned only with *net* buyers of bread. (As Stigler pointed out to me, the price of bread in that period was set abroad, and Englishmen actually were net buyers.) Stigler's own analysis alternates between net buyers and the whole market, as does Marshall's in one of the citations in Stigler. Neither seems aware of the shift in the level of aggregation. See Stigler (1947).

[14]Jacob L. Mosak (with a proof he attributes to A. Wald) shows that the difference between the Slutsky compensation and a constant utility compensation tends to vanish.

a change in price.[15] He will still be expected to trade when the price changes. He is insured, however, since he will be hurt neither by a price increase nor by a price fall.[16] When these two forces are powerful enough, the consumer will place himself at the "compensated" position.

Compare the ownership of a condominium with the short-term lease of an apartment. Abstracting from life-cycle changes in demand, from depreciation, and from the differential costs of transacting, the quantity demanded at a given rental rate would then be the same whether it were obtained by short-term lease or by purchase. The two arrangements differ, however, in the predictability of the effect of a price change. The direction of the change in quantity is ambiguous in the first case but not in the second.

When rent increases, if apartment service is an inferior good a tenant may purchase more. On the other hand, if it is a "normal" good, the landlord may purchase more.[17] In either case, no prediction is possible. It is not even certain that the substitution effect will dominate when the effects on the landlord and his tenants are combined, although this seems likely.[18]

The owner of the condominium, however, rents from himself. Thus, he provides himself with an automatic adjustment of the rent component of the cost of living, and when rentals change he actually experiences a Slutsky compensation.[19] Because the in-

come term in his Slutsky equation has vanished, he is unambiguously predicted to demand less housing when rents increase.

We now wish to take into account the costs of transacting for different levels of service and to determine the effects of this factor on predictability. A person's pattern of demand for consumer durables (as for other commodities) changes with age. Moreover, the flow of services generated by a consumer durable will decline as the asset depreciates. Except for a brief moment, then, the quantity of service demanded will not be equal to that provided by a particular durable good. If transacting were costless, people would change their durables constantly; but as it is, the assets held in a particular moment are not, in general, "optimal."

To proceed with the analysis, we use automobiles rather than housing for illustration. Consider the allocation of the budget between automobile services and other goods. In Fig. 1, A is the flow of automobile service and B is other goods. The holdings[20] of an individual with a budget A_0B_0 are initially at point 0. Had a move been costless, it is possible that prior to any change in price he would have chosen to be at 1 or 2 rather than at 0. The individual purchased an automobile which, at the going price, he planned to hold, say, for 5 years. Only in the third year is his holding "optimal," in the sense that when the car was newer he obtained "too many" automobile services; when it is older, he will have too few. Given that point 0 represents his actual holding, if the car is still new, he is obtaining too much service. Point 2 may then be the point of tangency with an indifference curve. On the other hand, if the car is old, Point 1 may be preferred. However, he remains at 0 because to move away would be costly.

What will be his reaction to a fall in the price of A? The new price line (A_1B_1), which passes through Point 0 is steeper. Had the initial point of tangency been 0, the conventional incentive would now be to consume more A. There is an even stronger incentive

[15]There is no presumption that most people most of the time are averse to risk. But since the range in which risk is preferred is "inefficient," people would not be observed, except temporarily, in that range. See Bailey et. al. (1980).

[16]This analysis is incomplete, and it cannot be stated that a risk-averse person would, other things being equal, prefer ownership. A sufficient condition for preferring ownership is the homotheticity of the utility function. Since inferior goods are incompatible with a function, homotheticity cannot be assumed for the purpose of this paper. In its absence, the effect of price changes on income depends on, among other considerations, the income elasticity of demand for the commodity. The simple notion of risk-aversion seems not to apply here.

[17]This is a partial equilibrium analysis and *cannot* apply to the whole market. Rather, it is confined to those for whom the price change is exogenous and who are not substantially affected by other changes related to the initial change. If the change is due to the award of a major federal project, the only proper subjects of our study would be those whose income and other relevant prices are only negligibly affected.

[18]See Barzel and McDonald (1973) for an elaboration on the notion of cancellation.

[19]Owners of condominiums will benefit from either an increase or a decrease in rents, which they therefore prefer to stable rents! A risk-

averse person may wish to remove this source of income variability too, but the required contractual arrangement may become rather complicated. It should not be inferred that instability is to be preferred in general. In the aggregate, variability in prices is the consequence of change in endowment; thus, it is impossible for all individuals simultaneously to stay at their income-compensated points.

[20]The units in Fig. 1 are of flows of services. By "holdings" we refer here to those assets which generate the indicated flows in the current period.

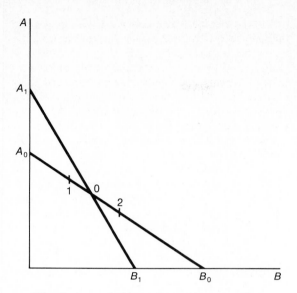

Fig. 1. Asset choice under costly transacting.

to increase A if 1 were the tangency point, since "too few" automobile services were consumed to start with. What if 2 were the initial point of tangency? Points superior to those on the segment $0B_1$ were available before but not chosen, so no point on $0B_1$ will be chosen now. No one, then, has the incentive to consume less of A than before, while some have an incentive to consume more. Thus, an unambiguous prediction is almost as fully warranted, in spite of the costs of making a change.

THE PREVALENCE OF ISOLATED SUBSTITUTION

It was pointed out in the previous section that, in principle, it should be possible to find situations of price change where an income effect is absent. We now show that such cases are common and that data for testing them should not be difficult to obtain. The ownership of consumer durables is but one instance where changes in some particular prices do not affect income. We now consider some other circumstances where individuals seem to find, or to place, themselves at the Slutsky-compensated position.

Take the case of a worker whose main source of income is wages and whose consumption basket resembles that underlying the consumer price index. If his wage is tied to the index, a change in price is

automatically subject to a Slutsky compensation. It is predicted then that he will purchase less of the commodity for which the price has increased. In the early 1970s the price of coffee rose sharply; it is not known whether, in general, the income effect of that increase dominated the substitution effect. But for those working under cost-of-living escalation clauses only the substitution effect was present. For them, the prediction would be clear cut.

Some workers, it seems, are implicitly guaranteed constant real wages (and hours) even when wages in their industry fluctuate. It is predicted that the supply of labor of such workers will never bend backwards. Since the level of their apparent real income is guaranteed a change in the market wage will not affect their wealth, but the prediction holds because they have an incentive to change their behavior on the margin.

For most individuals the life-cycle pattern is to borrow when young and to lend later in life. At the point in the cycle where net borrowing is zero, a change in the rate of interest will have no income effect. Substitution then is the only effect and a clear prediction follows.

Consider now advance purchase of commodities by consumers. The quantities contracted for are presumably at the expected consumption level given the price at the time of the agreement. The effect of a change in price is equivalent to a Slutsky-compensated change; thus, the quantity consumed is expected to move in a direction opposite to the change in price.

The household is often "self-sufficient" in some commodities. A farmer, for example, may keep a few hens so that he usually neither buys nor sells eggs. It is predicted that a fall in the price of eggs will result in some purchase of eggs whereas an increase in price will result in selling. Self-sufficiency precludes any price-induced wealth effect; the only effect is that of substitution.[21]

Some price changes are endogenous to the individual, and of these, that of leisure is the most notable. Education increases the value of time. Since this effect is fully anticipated, it takes place within the framework of a constant permanent income; only the substitution effect remains, and it is predictable that the demand for leisure will fall as education and

---

[21]Income may, however, increase because of the opportunity to adjust production; thus, some ambiguity is reintroduced.

its associated wage rate increase.[22] A complication appears, however, at this point. Individuals who are identical in every respect will obtain the same education; thus, when two people differ in education they must also differ in some other attribute. In particular, they have to face some nonidentical prices or costs—instance, their cost of capital or (due to diverse talents) their cost of acquiring education may differ. Spelling out the effects of such differences is beyond the scope of this paper. Nevertheless, prediction is possible since, being fully anticipated, the true income of the individual remains constant while the price of his time changes. A similar statement seems to apply to changes in costs that accompany aging and the associated accumulation of physical assets.

We now turn to a final example of price changes free of income effect. Sometimes a whole structure of prices changes simultaneously: Disneyland may raise the prices of all individual attractions while at the same time lowering the general admission fee. Suppose we can identify patrons for whom the two income effects cancel out at the level of past utilization. It is predicted that at the new price structure, these patrons will visit Disneyland more often and will buy fewer tickets not only per visit, but also per period. Similar predictions apply to a change in the rate structure of public utilities, to a change in medical insurance coverage accompanied by a change in premiums, and so on.

A remark on the income effect is now in order. It should by now be clear that in setting up a demand study it is not appropriate to allow automatically for the income effect of a given change in price. Since this effect may be lacking, its "correction" may introduce bias into an otherwise bias-free relationship.[23]

THE INCOME EFFECT
AND PORTFOLIO SELECTION

A central premise in the analysis of portfolio selection is that, other things equal, unexpected fluc-

tuation of income is to be avoided. It is clear from the foregoing discussion as well as from the literature that one can minimize price-induced fluctuations in income by purchasing in advance the commodity bundle he plans to consume.[24] Such a purchase may take the form of direct ownership of the commodities themselves (or of the assets which generate the consumption services). Alternatively one may hold corporate stocks whose prices vary with those in the consumer's consumption basket.

As already seen in comparing apartment rental to condominium ownership, a consumer is not indifferent to a choice of owning an asset or renting it. In discussing a firm's decision whether to buy or to lease, Merton H. Miller and Charles W. Upton (1976, p. 767) argue that under a lease arrangement the lower risk for a lessee is countered by a greater risk for the lessor. Competition will force the rental terms offered by a lessor to reflect the cost of this uncertainty; thus, the user bears the cost of the risk whether he buys or leases. Risk consideration is accordingly deemed irrelevant to the decision. This, however, ignores the asset holdings of individual lessees and lessors.

It has been pointed out above that price fluctuations generate income fluctuations for those whose endowments differ from their initial consumption— that is, when $X^0 = X$, and P fluctuates. When $X^0 = X$, the fluctuation in P does not introduce (first-order) income fluctuations. Thus, the risk of price fluctuations disappears for a consumer who owns the asset generating his consumption services but is present if he leases. The risk to the lessor does not cancel the risk to the lessee; on the contrary, the two coincide. Given risk-aversion, then, ownership is preferred.[25]

By a proper selection of assets, including corporate stocks, individuals can eliminate some otherwise inevitable price risks. The question whether a "firm" is subject to price risk is not meaningful—its individual stockholders are those to be considered. The purchaser of that firm's stock acquires insurance against price fluctuations of those commodities produced by the firm and correlated with the price of

---

[22]Lindsay emphasizes that since education has to be "earned," substitution is the dominant factor in the demand for leisure. The point here is that since a person plans his education, he is immediately incorporating in his permanent income whatever wealth effect may result.

[23]Once the constant-real-income price elasticity is obtained, the income elasticity of demand can be estimated by observing the behavior of those for whom real income is affected (in the received way) by price changes. Given the difficulty in discovering pure income changes, how-

ever, the knowledge of income elasticity does not seem useful in positive analysis.

[24]See, particularly, an analysis by Jack Hirshleifer (1975).

[25]This prediction, however, is subject to the same caveat stated in Footnote 16.

its shares. Such stockholders will not be indifferent as to whether the firm owns or leases.[26] As an example, take the case of mutual funds. Regardless of covariance considerations, some of these will hold in their total assets a fraction of residential properties expected to equal the fraction of total (uninsured) income represented by rents; other mutual funds will hold no residential properties. Apartment dwellers are expected to favor the former funds, home or condominium owners the latter. Such a prediction seems to be neither made nor implied by the received models of portfolio selection.[27] Consider, similarly, differences in the portfolios held by mutual funds as compared with pension funds. The latter are directed toward the needs of older people and are thus predicted to be heavily weighted toward commodities or services which loom large in senior budgets.

More generally, a person is protected against price fluctuations to the extent that his assets generate services matching his consumption pattern. One such asset is a long-term labor contract protecting against fluctuations in the relative price of leisure. If the contract is also tied to the cost of living, the person is protected against price fluctuations within the index as well. Assets such as consumer durables are often held directly. Protection against fluctuations in other prices can be provided by mutual funds with the appropriate asset composition.

People differ in their choice of directly owned assets or long-term commitments and thus their exposure to price risk is not uniform. It is predicted that mutual and pension funds will refrain from holding assets in which their clients are self-protected and will, instead, seek assets to protect them against remaining risks of price fluctuation.

CONCLUDING REMARKS

Discussion of the pure income effect is prominent in virtually any price theory text. An impression persists that income changes independently of relative price changes and that it need not be "earned." In reality, such instances are rare. Indeed, it is difficult even to conceive of an experiment to generate pure income changes. Since measured income changes are themselves the result of price changes, it is not appropriate to use them for testing the law of demand.

The law, however, *can* be tested readily without income corrections. This becomes evident when the Slutsky equation includes, as it should, the initial endowment of the commodity studied. When the endowment equals consumption, there is no income effect and substitution is the only effect of a change in price. Consumers have certain incentives to assume in advance a "compensated" position so that their real income is not affected by price changes. Identifying such situations, which is not difficult, allows for a direct test of the law.

Those wishing to avoid the risk of price fluctuations will hold assets whose streams of service match their consumption. To the extent that these assets are not held directly, a person's market portfolio is predicted to include such assets (thus, apartment dwellers will hold mutual funds heavy in residential properties whereas home owners will select mutual funds that shun such properties).

---

[26]If individuals could cheaply change their portfolios, they would simply realign their holdings toward the owner of the asset should the previous owner switch to a lease. Such a change presumably will have little effect on the values of the two stocks. Thus, firms may still be indifferent as to owning or leasing. Thanks are due to Harry DeAngelo for this point.

[27]David Mayers shows that the optimal market portfolio will vary across groups of individuals as they work for different firms and are subject to specific wage fluctuations within those firms. He does not, however, address the issue of avoiding the price risk by advance contracting.

REFERENCES

Alchian, A. A., and W. R. Allen, *Exchange and Production*. Belmont, Calif.: Wadsworth, 1977.

Bailey, M. J., M. Olson, and P. Wonnacott, "Marginal Utility of Income Does not Increase: Borrowing, Lending and Friedman-Savage Gambles," *American Economic Revue* (June 1980), 372–79.

Barzel, Y., "A Theory of Rationing by Waiting," *Journal of Law Economics* (April 1974), 73–95.

Barzel, Y., and R. J. McDonald, "Assets, Subsistence and the Supply Curve of Labor," *American Economic Revue* (September 1973), 621–33.

Heiner, R. A., "A Reformulation of the Law of Demand," *Economic Inquiry*, 2 (December 1974) 577–83.

Hirshleifer, J., "Speculation and Equilibrium: Information, Risk, and Markets," *Quarterly Journal of Economics* 79 (November 1975), 519–42.

Lindsay, C. M., "Measuring Human Capital Returns," *Journal of Political Economy*, 79 (November/December 1971), 1195–1255.

Mayers, D., "Portfolio Theory, Job Choice and the Equilibrium Structure of Expected Wages," *Journal of Financial Economics*, 1 (1974), 23–42.

Miller, M. H., and C. W. Upton, "Leasing, Buying, and the Cost of Capital Services," *Journal of Finance*, 31 (June 1976), 768–86.

Mincer, J., "Market Prices, Opportunity Costs, and Income Effects," in *Measurement in Mathematical Economics and Econometrics in Memory of Yehuda Grunfeld*. Berkeley, Calif.: Stanford University Press, 1963.

Mosak, J. L., "On the Interpretation of the Fundamental Equation of Value Theory," in *Studies in Mathematical Economics and Econometrics,* Oscar Lange, et al., eds., Chicago: Chicago University Press, 1943.

Slutsky, E. E., "On the Theory of the Budget of the Consumer," trans., reprinted in *Readings in Price Theory,* Homewood, Ill.: Richard D. Irwin, 1952.

Stigler, G. J., "Notes on the History of the Giffen Paradox, *Journal of Political Economy,* 55 (April 1947), 152–56.

_____, *The Theory of Price,* (3rd ed.), pp. 65–68. New York: Macmillan, 1966.

Walras, L., *Elements of Pure Economics,* pp. 116–18. London: Allen and Unwin, 1954.

Demand Curves for Animal Consumers*†

JOHN H. KAGEL
RAYMOND C. BATTALIO
HOWARD C. RACHLIN
LEONARD GREEN

John H. Kagel (B.A., Tufts University, 1964; M.P.I.A., University of Pittsburgh, 1966; M.S., Purdue University, 1968; Ph.D. 1970) was born in 1942 in New York City. Presently Professor of Economics at the University of Houston, he has served on the faculties of Texas A & M and Purdue Universities. From 1981 to 1982, Professor Kagel was a National Fellow at the Hoover Institution.

Raymond C. Battalio (B.S., University of California at Berkeley, 1966; M.S., Purdue University, 1968; Ph.D., 1970) was born in 1938 in Chicago, Illinois. An economist who has written papers dealing with experimental studies of consumer demand, he joined the faculty of Texas A & M University, where he currently is Professor of Economics, in 1969.

Howard C. Rachlin (B.M.E., Cooper Union, 1957; M.A., The New School for Social Research, 1962; Ph.D., Harvard University, 1965) was born in 1935 in New York City. Presently he is Professor of Psychology at SUNY at Stony Brook. Before joining Stony Brook in 1969, Rachlin was on the faculty of Harvard University.

Leonard Green (B.A., City College of CUNY, 1969; Ph.D., SUNY at Stony Brook, 1974) is currently Associate Professor of Psychology at Washington University. He has written many articles on a wide variety of topics, including experiments on animal demand.

*Reprinted from *The Quarterly Journal of Economics* (February 1981) by permission of John Wiley & Sons, Inc. Copyright 1981, pp. 1–14.

†An earlier version of this paper was presented at the Southern Economic Association Meetings, 1976. Helpful suggestions were provided by Gerald Dwyer, Jack Hirshleifer, and an anonymous referee. Research support from NSF Grants 32057, GS 27062, and BO 40540 is gratefully acknowledged.

Investigations and applications of formal theories of economic behavior have generally been limited to samples of human populations operating in "normal" economic environments. This decision to limit studies within economic science to humans stands in marked contrast to the comparative research programs in behavioral biology and psychology that have the investigation of behavioral processes across different species as a primary research aim. An important outcome of these comparative research programs has been to suggest that the principles of economic behavior would be virtually unique among behavioral principles if they did not apply, with some variation of course, to the behavior of nonhumans.

This paper reports the results of a series of experiments designed and carried out by economists (in collaboration with psychologists and biologists) to investigate the demand behavior of laboratory animals. Two types of demand curves are studied: *income-compensated* and *ordinary* or *uncompensated* demand curves. It is commonplace in economics that both types of demand curves are negatively sloped. In the first case the negative slope is a requirement for consistency with the Slutsky-Hicks theory, and in the second case, it is an observationally based law of human economic behavior. Consequently, finding negatively sloped demand curves for laboratory animals represents an important extension of economic principles to nonhumans that is of considerable interest in its own right.

The conformity of the behavior of laboratory animals to basic principles of consumer demand behavior also indicates a practical research method and a sample population for the experimental analysis of more complex aspects of economic behavior. The pragmatic value of such readily accessible and relatively inexpensive experimental methods for the development and verification of theories of economic behavior has been discussed elsewhere [Smith, 1976; Kagel and Winkler, 1972], and will not be repeated here. Understanding the economic behavior of nonhuman animals is also of growing practical value in its own right, given the increasing concerns that we, as humans, have in spillovers from our economic activities on animal populations. This follows from the fact that many of these ecological spillovers alter the animals' economic environments; e.g., alter the absolute and relative costs of food supplies. Consequently, increased understanding of animals' responses to these changes in economic conditions is

an important element in determining the costs and benefits of alternative human economic activities on the total environment.

In the following section the experimental procedures are outlined. We then present the results of income-compensated and income-constant price changes. The implications of the experiments for economic theory development in general, and consumer demand theory in particular, as well as some of the immediate practical implications of the research program, are discussed in the conclusions.

I. EXPERIMENTAL PROCEDURES

The theory of consumer demand is concerned with the structure of choices of commodity bundles made by a consumer when he is confronted with various prices and restrictions on the level of total expenditures. In a world with only two goods, the budget set is represented by the set of (x, y) values that satisfy equation (1):

$$p_x x + p_y y \leqq M, \qquad (1)$$

where p_x and p_y are the exchange rates or prices of the goods represented by x and y, respectively, and M is the consumer's income.

In the experiments reported, the budget constraint (1) was operationalized by placing male albino rats twenty-four hours a day in standard experimental chambers fitted with two levers.[1] In the essential commodity experiments, lever pressing resulted in the delivery of either standard laboratory food or fluid (water or a sodium saccharin solution) in premeasured amounts from an opening directly below each lever. No alternative food or liquid was available. In the other experiments, lever pressing resulted in the delivery of two alternative flavored fluids; root beer or cherry cola (allowed to go flat), Tom Collins mix (without alcohol) or sodium saccharin. The flavored fluid studies are referred to as nonessential commodity experiments, since food and water were continuously available in the chamber under this design and the subjects did not have to respond to changes in relative prices and incomes to satisfy any physiological needs.

Each rat had a limited total number of effective lever presses allotted each day that could be distrib-

[1]Standard experimental chambers and programming equipment (R. Gerbrands Co.) with a specially designed two-lever front panel were used. See Kagel, Battalio, Rachlin, Green, Basmann, and Klemm [1975] for a detailed description.

uted in any combination between the two levers. Each morning, after the cage was cleaned, the supply of commodities replenished, and the rat weighed, two sets of white lights, one pair over each lever, were lit. After the rat expended its allotted lever presses, the lights were automatically extinguished and not lit again until the next day. Lever presses were ineffective when the lights over the levers were out, something most rats learned quite quickly.

The number of lever presses required to deliver a commodity, the magnitude of the commodity delivered, and the effective number of lever presses allotted were all subject to experimental control, and established the budget set the animal faced. For example, fixing the number of lever presses per payoff at 1 for both levers, the food payoff at 5 (45 mg) pellets, the fluid payoff at 0.1cc, and the effective number of lever presses at 250 results in a budget set bounded by the straight line Z in Fig. 1. Increasing the total number of lever presses allotted, while holding payoff magnitudes and lever pressing requirements constant, results in a parallel outward shift in the boundary of the budget set; e.g., increasing allotted lever presses to 350, with other things equal, results in the budget line Z' in Fig. 1. Thus, the lever pressing allotment corresponds to the concept of income in the definition of the budget set and will be referred to as such.

Under the procedures adopted, changing the magnitude of the commodity delivered per payoff or al-

tering the number of lever presses required per payoff has the same effect on the budget set as a change in prices. For example, the rotation of the budget line from Z to Z'' in Fig. 1, corresponding to a doubling of the price of fluid, could be accomplished by either doubling the lever pressing requirements for fluid, while holding fluid cup size and everything else in the environment constant, or by halving the cup size to 0.05cc while holding lever pressing requirements and all else constant. Thus, the number of lever presses required per unit of commodity consumed corresponds to the concept of price in the definition of the budget set and will be referred to as such. In all but one of the experiments reported below, prices were changed by altering the magnitude of payoff delivered, holding lever pressing requirements per payoff constant. In all cases lever pressing requirements were small, relative to what rats can perform in experimental chambers [Collier, Hirsch, and Hamlin, 1972], and were not an effective constraint on total consumption, i.e., the animal expended all the allotted presses, generally well before the budget set was reconstituted.

The experimental procedures adopted can be compared to a consumer purchasing goods from a two-commodity vending machine. Since, for the particular consumers at hand, operating and handling money or tokens is a difficult behavior to learn, we do not require it to operate the machine. An effective budget constraint is maintained, however, by limiting the number of plunger pulls that deliver commodities. Further, as with many vending machine operations, prices were changed primarily through altering the magnitudes of commodities delivered per plunger pull.

The animal "knows" what the economic contingencies are that it faces in the same way that a human consumer in the vending machine analogy "knows" the economic contingencies that he faces: it experiences them. The subjects' responses to changes in economic contingencies has generally been quite fast, with major adjustments showing up in the data usually within three observation periods (days) or less.

Standard shaping procedures were used to train the rats to press the levers for the commodities. Each experimental condition (set of prices and income) was maintained for a minimum of fourteen days. Conditions were only changed after ten consecutive days of stable performance under each experimental condition. Unless noted otherwise, data reported re-

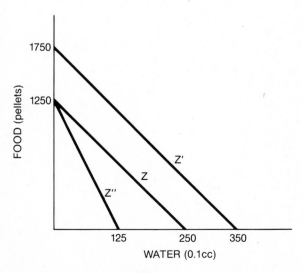

Fig. 1

fer to this final ten-day period of stable performance.[2]

The results of the price changes are reported through fitting log-linear functions to the data. Two functions are fit in each case; one for own-price effects:

$$\log q_i = \log \alpha_0 + \alpha_1 \log (p_i/p_j),$$

where

q_i = quantity of commodity i consumed, and

p_i = price of commodity i;

and a second function for cross-price effects:

$$\log q_j = \log \beta_0 + \beta_1 \log (p_i/p_j).$$

In cases of income-compensated price changes, since there are only two commodities, the choice of which one to employ in the own-price regression is arbitrary; we adopted the convention of always using food in the essential commodity experiments and root beer in the nonessential studies (see Tables 1 and 2). For cases of income-constant price changes, the commodity whose price changed served as the dependent variable in the own-price regression.

Functions were fit to the data using ordinary least squares on the daily observations from the final ten days of stable performance under the various experimental conditions.[3]

The log-linear regressions serve to provide convenient summary measures of price elasticity (the slopes of the least squares lines, α_1 and β_1, measuring own-price and cross-price elasticity, respectively) that are useful for comparing substitution effects between the different experiments. Alternative measures such as the average of the arc elasticities between pairs of points, or the entire set of arc elasticity values, yield the same conclusions regarding differences in price responsiveness between the different experiments. t-statistics reported along with the elasticity estimates provide a measure of the statistical significance of the experimental treatments on consumption. Function free tests, such as simple t-tests on mean consumption values between periods with different relative prices, yield the same conclusions regarding the statistical significance of the price changes on consumption.

[2]Occasional exceptions to this rule were made in cases where animals were rapidly changing weight following a change in conditions or in cases where a replication of experimental conditions showed no differences in response patterns after seven days.

[3]Thus, the number of different experimental conditions (price and income values) underlying each regression is obtained by dividing the number of observations N reported in the tables by 10 (except for E4 in Table I with changing cup sizes when six conditions were run, one of which was maintained for a shorter period of time than usual).

Table 1. Income-compensated price elasticities: Essential commodities

| Subject number | Own-price elasticity | | | Cross-price elasticity | | | N | Maximum | | Minimum | | Method of changing relative prices |
	Commodity	Elasticity (t-value)	R^2	Commodity	Elasticity (t-value)	R^2		P_F/P_L	Q_F/Q_L	P_F/P_L	Q_F/Q_L	
E2	Food	−0.04 (0.33)*	0.01	Water	0.03 (0.58)*	0.02	20	0.74	0.97	0.44	1.00	Pellets only
E4	Food	−0.17 (9.04)**	0.60	Water	0.13 (8.84)**	0.59	56	1.33	0.61	0.11	1.36	Cup sizes only
E4	Food	−0.05 (2.95)**	0.15	Water	0.09 (4.59)**	0.30	50	2.22	0.85	0.22	1.81	Pellets only
E5	Food	−0.18 (13.03)**	0.82	Saccharin	0.18 (6.26)**	0.51	40	6.67	0.26	0.37	0.82	Both pellets and cup sizes at same time
E5	Food	−0.10 (2.03)	0.13	Saccharin	0.06 (1.50)	0.07	30	2.22	0.61	0.44	0.82	Pellets only

*Significant at the 5 percent level.
**Significant at the 1 percent level.
P_F = price of food measured as presses per gram.
P_L = price of liquid measured as presses per milliliter.
Q_F = quantity of food consumption measured in grams.
Q_L = quantity of liquid consumption measured in milliliters.

II. INCOME-COMPENSATED DEMAND CURVES

The income-compensated demand curves reported are of the Slutsky type, where nominal income (effective number of lever presses) is simultaneously adjusted along with changes in relative prices, so that the consumer can continue to purchase the same commodity bundle as before the price change. In other words, starting from some initial price (p^0) and consumption (x^0) vectors, the demand curves are generated by introducing a new vector (p^1) and adjusting income so that (2) is satisfied:

$$p^0 x^0 = p^1 x^0, \text{ where } p^0 \neq p^1. \qquad (2)$$

Friedman [1976] has referred to these demand curves as apparent real income constant or Type III demand curves, to distinguish them from real income constant demand curves of the Hicks type, where income is adjusted to leave the consumer on the original indifference curve following a price change. Since the Slutsky measure of real income can be computed on the basis of directly observable data (namely, income, prices, and quantities purchased), whereas the Hicks measure cannot, its use is nonproblematical [Slutsky, 1915; Friedman, 1976].

Along any income-compensated demand curve (of the Slutsky type), the quantity demanded must always be inversely related to price if demand is to be characterized by a member of the class of Slutsky-Hicks systems of demand equations. Hicks [1956] and others have referred to this requirement as pro-

viding the basis for a direct consistency test of the theory. As such, this requirement has provided a focus for the original series of experiments.

Table 1 presents the results of the essential commodity experiments.[4] In all cases the own-price elasticity is negative, which is what it should be. In three cases the coefficient is significant at the 1 percent level, and for subject E5 the marginal significance level is 6 percent. The impact of the relative price changes for subjects E4 and E5 is clearly evidenced by the substantial differences in the food to liquid ratios obtained under the extreme values for the relative price ratios (columns 9–12). These significant changes in the subject's food to water consumption ratio, using a Slutsky-compensated price change, resulted in significant changes in the subject's weight under different experimental conditions. Since the animal always could obtain the original bundle, changes of this magnitude suggest that economic variables be added to the small, but growing, list of nonhomeostatic influences of basic consumatory behavior [Kissileff, 1973].

Separate price response functions are reported for subject E4 for the two different methods of altering the budget constraint, since preliminary tests on the data showed significant differences in consumption patterns depending on the method of changing rel-

[4]For a more detailed description of the experimental conditions and the results of these experiments, see Kagel, Battalio, Rachlin, and Green [1980].

Table 2. Income-compensated price elasticities: Nonessential commodities

| Subject number | Own-price elasticity | | | Cross-price elasticity | | | | Maximum | | Minimum | | Method of changing relative prices |
	Commodity	Elasticity (t-value)	R^2	Commodity	Elasticity (t-value)	R^2	N	P_{RB}/R_{OTH}	Q_{RB}/Q_{OTH}	P_{RB}/P_{OTH}	Q_{RB}/Q_{OTH}	
N1	Root beer	−0.31 (11.30)**	0.69	Collins mix	0.76 (9.42)**	0.60	60	4.00	0.48	0.25	9.23	Both cup sizes at same time
N2	Root beer	−0.59 (5.04)**	0.48	Collins mix	4.12 (9.20)**	0.75	30	4.00	0.27	1.00	39.82	Both cup sizes at same time
N3	Root beer	−2.22 (4.78)**	0.45	Cherry cola	0.72 (2.16)*	0.14	30	1.00	0.79	0.25	18.42	Both cup sizes at same time

*Significant at the 5 percent level.
**Significant at the 1 percent level.
P_{RB} = price of root beer measured as presses per milliliter.
P_{OTH} = price of other fluid measured as presses per milliliter.
Q_{RB} = quantity of root beer consumed in milliliters.
Q_{OTH} = quantity of other fluid consumed in milliliters.

ative prices.[5] This suggests that changing cup sizes, compared to changing the number of pellets per payoff, introduces an additional dimension to the choice situation not captured in the rudimentary form of the theory used here. This conclusion is supported by the fact that, in all three cases where relative prices were changed by changing the number of pellets while holding cup sizes fixed, the values of the *t*-statistics are less than for the cases where the cup sizes were changed. Although consumer theory typically ignores differences in the methods of achieving a given choice set, similar types of response differences to theoretically equivalent choice set changes have also been found using human subjects [Grether and Plott, 1979]. The separate price response functions for E5 correspond to two different real income levels, with income approximately 25 percent lower for the second series with the smaller elasticity value.

Table 2 presents the results for the nonessential commodity experiments. In all cases the own-price coefficient is negative and significant at the 1 percent level. The increased substitution between the two fluids, with food and water continuously available, is also apparent in the extremely large swings in the ratio of the two fluids consumed. This contrast with the results presented in Table 1 is not unexpected, in view of the physiological boundaries on substitution that underlie the essential commodity experiments.

III. ORDINARY (UNCOMPENSATED) DEMAND CURVES

> . . . the simple law of demand—the downward slope of the demand curve—turns out to be almost infallible in its working. Exceptions to it are rare and unimportant
> [Hicks, 1946, p. 35].

In this section we examine the "simple law of demand." The experimental changes in the budget constraint differ from the changes in the previous section, in that nominal income is no longer adjusted to force the new constraint through the original consumption bundle. Although the budget constraint was changed by changing a single price while holding the other price and nominal income constant, in comparing the results of this section with those in the previous section it is useful to view this change as having two component parts: (1) a rotation through the original consumption bundle, as in the previous

section, and (2) a parallel shift in the budget constraint. That is, we can view the single price change as a Slutsky-compensated change plus a change in nominal income. Viewed from this perspective, we can see that, if the good is normal (a result usually found for these subjects with these commodities), the own-price elasticity will be greater for the uncompensated demand curve than for the compensated curve. Also, since the demand curves are now derived with nominal income constant, we can examine whether the goods are *gross* complements or *gross* substitutes, the result of which depends upon the relative magnitudes of the price and income elasticities.[6]

Table 3 presents the data for the income-constant experiments. As is evident from the sign and significance of the own-price elasticity coefficients, these subjects satisfy the "simple law of demand" for both the essential and nonessential commodity experiments. For subjects N1 and N3, who experienced both income-compensated and income-constant price changes, the elasticities for the income-constant demand curves are larger, as they must be for normal goods. A similar result is observed comparing across subjects, since most of the values in Table 3 are larger than the values in Tables 1 and 2 above.

For the essential commodity subject E1, food and water are gross complements, and for subject N3, run under a nonessential design, the two commodities are gross substitutes.[7] For subjects N1 and N4 the two commodities are independent. The gross complementarity found for food and water under the essential commodity design is a result of the income effects overwhelming the substitution effects. This, in part, reflects the fact that there are physiological limits on the amount that animals can increase their food consumption without increasing their fluid intake.

It is also interesting to note that for subjects E1, N3, and N4, where we report demand curves for both goods depending upon which price changed and which was held constant, the classification of commodities as gross complements or gross substi-

---

[5]$F = 14.9$, *d.f.* = 2, 102, $p < 0.001$.

[6]Since nominal income is held constant, the income effect of the price change can overwhelm the substitution effect resulting in the two commodities being *gross* complements. This result is, of course, entirely consistent with the theorem which asserts that in a two-commodity world the goods must be *net* substitutes [Baumol, 1977].

[7]Subject E1 was not run under the income-compensated design.

Table 3. Nominal income constant price elasticities

| Subject number | Own-price elasticity | | | Cross-price elasticity | | | N | Maximum | | Minimum | | Method of changing relative prices |
	Commodity$_1$	Elasticity (t-value)	R^2	Commodity$_2$	Elasticity (t-value)	R^2		Pc_1/Pc_2	Qc_1/Qc_2	Pc_1/Pc_2	Qc_1/Qc_2	
E1	Food ($P_w = 20$)	−0.20 (2.66)*	0.20	Water	−0.55 (12.40)**	0.85	30	1.11	1.10	0.44	0.82	Pellets only
E1	Food ($P_w = 35$)	−0.12 (2.20)*	0.22	Water	−0.13 (11.95)**	0.89	20	0.25	1.13	0.06	1.11	Pellets & presses per pellet†
E1	Water	−0.90 (19.21)**	0.95	Food	−0.32 (2.10)*	0.20	20	3.94	0.88	2.25	1.22	Presses per water delivery only
N1	Root beer	−1.03 (8.93)**	0.82	Collins mix	0.15 (0.47)	0.01	20	0.25	9.23	0.13	20.40	Root beer cup size only
N3	Root beer	−6.39 (20.43)**	0.94	Cherry cola	2.27 (4.94)**	0.47	30	2.00	0.01	1.00	2.52	Root beer cup size only
N3	Cherry cola	−3.98 (13.0)**	0.82	Root beer	0.83 (8.74)**	0.67	40	2.00	0.01	0.50	4.10	Cherry cola cup size only
N4	Saccharin	−1.02 (6.41)**	0.52	Cherry cola	−0.01 (0.10)	0.00	40	0.50	0.91	0.17	2.63	Saccharin cup size only
N4	Cherry cola	−1.05 (7.55)**	0.67	Saccharin	0.01 (0.03)	0.00	30	2.00	1.01	1.00	2.15	Cherry cola cup size only

Pc_1 = price of commodity$_1$; Pc_1 = price of commodity$_2$.
Qc_1 = amount of commodity$_1$; Qc_2 = amount of commodity$_2$.
*Significant at the 5 percent level.
**Significant at the 1 percent level.
†At same time.

tutes does not change with the demand curve examined. This regularity in the observed data, which is not theoretically necessary [Samuelson, 1974], reflects an interesting degree of uniformity in the underlying behavior.

One further result that is extremely important for any attempts at understanding the behavioral processes at work is the change in the food to water ratios for subject E1. When the relative price of food was lowered for this subject, the actual food to water ratio *decreased*. (Consistency precludes this result for the income-compensated experiments.) This result suggests that the simple behavioral rule that animals consume relatively more of the good whose relative price has fallen will not organize the data. These subjects do not merely respond to the local contingencies of the relative price changes, but also obtain some feedback from the income constraint.

IV. CONCLUSIONS

The results reported explicate an experimental paradigm that facilitates the direct extension of the concepts underlying value theory to nonhumans. At the same time, the fact that the straightforward interpretation of the theory employed yields consistent results in a new domain of application provides renewed scientific evidence for the theoretical concepts in consumer demand theory. More importantly, the development of an experimental methodology under which the behavior of laboratory animals conforms to the basic principles of consumer demand theory provides a foundation for intensive experimental investigation of additional aspects of the theory. Consistent behavior, using pigeons as subjects, has also been obtained within the context of both labor supply and commodity choice behavior [Battalio, Kagel, and Green, 1979; Battalio, Kagel, Rachlin, and Green, 1981]. In addition, this experimental paradigm is ideally suited to studying adjustment behavior in response to changes in prices and incomes, and to testing between alternative theories concerning the effects of habit formation on dynamical adjustment processes. Conducting comparable studies using data for individual consumers from national economic systems, while technically feasible, is considerably more expensive than using laboratory methods.

The experiments reported here are directly related

to experiments in economics using human subjects that have been reported in this and other economic journals. For example, the convergence to equilibrium in auction experiments reported by V. Smith and his colleagues [Smith, 1964; Miller, Plott, and Smith, 1977] depends critically on the fact that subjects behave in a way which is consistent with utility-maximizing principles underlying consumer demand theory and that negatively sloped demand curves have been induced in the market [Smith, 1976]. The results of the present experiments provide rigorous independent support for both of these propositions. In this way the data provide independent experimental evidence for the generalizability of the auction experiment results.

The discovery that concepts from consumer demand theory can be applied to species other than humans in no way implies that economists must, or ever should, abandon concepts of rationality and utility maximization. What it may suggest is that evolutionary pressures have been such that humans, along with other animals, have behavioral repertoires that can be characterized as solutions to a constrained maximizing model.[8] Such inherited behavioral repertoires are of obvious value in the evolutionary struggle for survival. Further, whether or not animals (or humans for that matter) have consciously thought out their behavior is irrelevant to our characterization of that behavior as a solution to a constrained maximization problem. Economic theorists have long recognized this, as Samuelson notes:

> . . . it is possible to formulate our conditions of equilibrium as those of an extremum problem, even though it is admittedly not a case of an individual's behaving in a maximizing manner, just as it is often possible in classical dynamics to express the path of a particle as one which maximizes (minimizes) some quantity despite the fact that the particle is obviously not acting consciously or purposively [1947, p. 23].

The pragmatic value of writing theories as solutions to constrained maximization problems is well-known and, as such, is not affected by our results.

From a broader perspective, the data provide support for the fundamental concept of substitutability

that underlies so much of economic theory.[9] In this respect the data reported here are but one instance in a growing body of literature, to be found primarily in biology journals, showing that the composition of consumption can change, often quite dramatically, for individual animal consumers in response to changes in environmental conditions. Alterations in consumption patterns resulting from changes in environmental conditions that are readily characterizable in terms of changes in relative prices have been reported for a surprisingly large number of animal species, including protozoa [Rapport and Turner, 1977], social bumblebees [Heinrich, 1976], sunfish [Werner and Hall, 1976], and deer mice [Holling, 1965]. The relevance of consumer demand theory for understanding this behavior is indicated by the growing use by biologists and economists of these and related concepts to explain the behavior of animals [Rapport, 1971; Covich, 1972; Cody, 1974; and Tullock, 1970, 1971].

[9]We note that within biology these substitution effects correspond to what an economist might call the short run, as they involve changes within a fixed gene structure (an individual organism). A longer run response would involve genetic changes that take anywhere from 10 to 100 generations to occur, and its analysis requires a different theoretical structure. (See, for example, Wilson [1975].)

REFERENCES

Battalio, R. C., J. H. Kagel, and L. Green, "Labor Supply Behavior of Animal Workers: Towards an Experimental Analysis," *Research in Experimental Economics,* Vol. 1, V. L. Smith, ed. (Greenwich, CT: J.A.I., 1979).

Battalio, R. C., J. H. Kagel, H. Rachlin, and L. Green, "Commodity Choice Behavior with Pigeons as Subjects," *Journal of Political Economy,* LXXXIV (Feb. 1981), 116–151.

Baumol, W. J., *Economic Theory and Operations Analysis* (Englewood Cliffs: Prentice-Hall, Inc., 1977).

Cody, M. L., "Optimization in Ecology," *Science* CLXXXIII (March 22, 1974), 1156–64.

Collier, G., E. Hirsch, and P. H. Hamlin, "The Ecological Determinants of Reinforcement in the Rat," *Physiology and Behavior,* IX (1972), 705–16.

Covich, A., "Ecological Economics of Seed Consumption by *Peromyscus,*" *Transactions of Connecticut Academy of Arts and Sciences,* XLIV (Dec. 1972), 71–93.

Friedman, M., *Price Theory* (Chicago: Aldine Publishing Company, 1976).

Grether, D. M., and C. R. Plott, "Economic Theory of Choice and the Preference Reversal Phenomenon," *American Economic Review,* LXIX (Sept. 1979), 623–38.

Heinrich, B., "Bumblebee Foraging and the Economics of Sociality," *American Scientist,* LXIV (July–Aug. 1976), 384–95.

[8]Interestingly, biologists have also shown that individual plants respond to changes in environmental conditions (see Cody [1947] and Strong and Ray [1975]) and have, on occasion, found it useful to characterize such behavior as the solution to a maximization problem.

Hicks, J. R., *Value and Capital,* 2nd ed. (London: Oxford University Press, 1946).

—————, *A Revision of Demand Theory* (London: Oxford University Press, 1956).

Holling, C. S., "The Functional Response of Invertebrate Predators to Prey Density," *Memoirs of the Entomological Society of Canada,* XLVIII (1965), 1–86.

Kagel, J. H., and R. C. Winkler, "Behavioral Economics: Areas of Cooperative Research Between Economics and Applied Behavioral Analysis," *Journal of Applied Behavior Analysis,* V (Fall 1972), 335–42.

Kagel, H. J., R. C. Battalio, H. Rachlin, L. Green, R. L. Basmann, and W. R. Klemm, "Experimental Studies of Consumer Demand Behavior Using Laboratory Animals," *Economic Inquiry,* XIII (1975), 22–38.

Kagel, J. H., R. C. Battalio, H. Rachlin, and L. Green, "Consumer Demand Theory Applied to Choice Behavior of Rats," in *Limits to Action: The Allocation of Individual Behavior,* J. E. R. Staddon, ed. (New York: Academic Press, 1980).

Kissileff, H. R., "Nonhomeostatic Controls of Drinking," in A. M. Epstein, H. R. Kissileff, and E. Stellar, eds., *The Neuropsychology of Thirst* (Washington: Halsted Press, 1973).

Miller, R. M., C. R. Plott, and V. L. Smith, "Intertemporal Competitive Equilibrium: An Empirical Study of Speculation," this *Journal,* XCI (Nov. 1977), 599–624.

Rapport, D. J., "An Optimization Model of Food Selection," *The American Naturalist,* CV (Nov.–Dec. 1971), 575–87.

—————, and J. E. Turner, "Economic Models in Ecology," *Science,* CXCV (Jan. 28, 1977), 367–73.

Samuelson, P. A., *Foundations of Economic Analysis* (Cambridge: Harvard University Press, 1947).

—————, "Complementarity—An Essay on the 40th Anniversary of the Hicks-Allen Revolution in Demand Theory," *Journal of Economic Literature,* XII (Dec. 1974), 1255–89.

Slutsky, E., "On the Theory of the Budget of the Consumer," *Giornale Degli Economisti,* 1915 translation reprinted in *Readings in Price Theory* (Chicago: American Economic Association, 1952).

Smith, V. L., "Effect of Market Organization on Competitive Equilibrium," this *Journal,* LXXVIII (May 1964), 181–201.

—————, "Experimental Economics: Induced Value Theory," *American Economic Review,* LXVI (May 1976), 274–79.

Strong, D. R. Jr., and T. S. Ray, Jr., "Host Tree Location of a Tropical Vine (Monstora gigantea) by Skototropism," *Science,* LXL (Nov. 21, 1975), 804–06.

Tullock, G., "Switching in General Predators: A Comment," *Bulletin of the Ecological Society of America,* LI (Sept. 1970), 21–24.

—————, "The Coal Tit as a Careful Shopper," *The American Naturalist,* CV (Feb. 1971), 77–80.

Werner, E. E., and D. J. Hall, "Niche Shifts in Sunfishes: Experimental Evidence and Significance," *Science,* CXCI (Jan. 30, 1976), 404–06.

Wilson, E. O., *Sociobiology* (Cambridge: The Belknap Press, 1975).

De Gustibus Non Est Disputandum*

GEORGE J. STIGLER
GARY S. BECKER**

George J. Stigler (B.B.A., University of Washington, 1931; M.B.A., Northwestern University, 1932; Ph.D., University of Chicago, 1938), the Nobel Laureate in Economics in 1982, was born in Renton, Washington, in 1911. Currently, he is Charles R. Walgreen Distinguished Service Professor Emeritus and Director of the Center for the Study of the Economy and the State at the University of Chicago. Before joining the Chicago faculty in 1958, he taught at Iowa State University, the University of Minnesota, and Brown and Columbia Universities. He has been on the research staff of the National Bureau of Economic Research since 1947. Stigler is an outstanding authority in the theory of price and the history of economic thought, and has made seminal contributions to the theories of information and regulation. He is noted for the rigor of his thought and his insistence that conceptual hypotheses be supported by empirical evidence, as reflected in *The Journal of Political Economy,* which he edited for many years. Stigler's publications include his textbook, *The Theory of Price, Production and Distribution Theories,* and *The Organization of Industry*. He possesses the ability, rare among students of the "dismal science," to combine wit with wisdom, as exemplified by the essays published in his book, *The Intellectual and the Market Place*. His chief articles in doctrinal history have been collected in the volume *Essays in the History of Economics*. During 1964 Stigler was president of the American Economic Association.

Gary S. Becker (A.B., Princeton University, 1951; A.M., University of Chicago, 1953; Ph.D. 1955) was born in Pottsville, Pennsylvania, in 1930. Formerly in the Economics Department at Columbia University, he is now at the University of Chicago, where he is University Professor in the Departments of Economics and Sociology, and is also a Research Associate at the Economics Research Center, NORC. Perhaps the best

*Reprinted from *American Economic Review* (March 1977) by permission of the American Economic Association. Copyright 1977, pp. 76-90.

**University of Chicago. We have had helpful comments from Michael Bozdarich, Gilbert Ghez, James Heckman, Peter Pashigian, Sam Peltzman, Donald Wittman, and participants in the Workshop on Industrial Organization.

known of his numerous publications are *The Economics of Discrimination* and *Human Capital*. His brilliance as a research scholar was given formal recognition in 1966 when the American Economic Association awarded him its John Bates Clark medal, an honor given every other year "to that economist under the age of forty who is adjudged to have made a significant contribution to economic thought and knowledge." The citation conferring this honor upon him noted that "Gary Becker's versatility and imagination have enlarged the scope and power of our science. In his skillful hands, economic analysis illuminates basic aspects of human beings in society: the importance of investment to augment their productive capacity, the allocation of their time, the growth of their numbers, their crimes and punishments, their racial prejudices. Throughout his work he displays a rare combination of rigor and relevance." Becker, perhaps more than any other author, has clarified the role that price theory can play in understanding human behavior.

The venerable admonition not to quarrel over tastes is commonly interpreted as advice to terminate a dispute when it has been resolved into a difference of tastes, presumably because there is no further room for rational persuasion. Tastes are the unchallengeable axioms of a man's behavior: he may properly (usefully) be criticized for inefficiency in satisfying his desires, but the desires themselves are *data*. Deplorable tastes—say, for arson—may be countered by coercive and punitive action, but these deplorable tastes, at least when held by an adult, are not capable of being changed by persuasion.

Our title seems to us to be capable of another and preferable interpretation: that tastes neither change capriciously nor differ importantly between people. On this interpretation one does not argue over tastes for the same reason that one does not argue over the Rocky Mountains—both are there, will be there next year, too, and are the same to all men.

The difference between these two viewpoints of tastes is fundamental. On the traditional view, an explanation of economic phenomena that reaches a difference in tastes between people or times is the terminus of the argument: the problem is abandoned *at this point* to whoever studies and explains tastes (psychologists? anthropologists? phrenologists? sociobiologists?). On our preferred interpretation, one never reaches this impasse: the economist continues to search for differences in prices or incomes to explain any differences or changes in behavior.

The choice between these two views of the role of tastes in economic theory must ultimately be made on the basis of their comparative analytical produc-

tivities. On the conventional view of inscrutable, often capricious tastes, one drops the discussion as soon as the behavior of tastes becomes important—and turns his energies to other problems. On our view, one searches, often long and frustratingly, for the subtle forms that prices and incomes take in explaining differences among men and periods. If the latter approach yields more useful results, it is the proper choice. The establishment of the proposition that one may usefully treat tastes as stable over time and similar among people is the central task of this essay.

The ambitiousness of our agenda deserves emphasis: we are proposing the hypothesis that widespread and/or persistent human behavior can be explained by a generalized calculus of utility-maximizing behavior, without introducing the qualification "tastes remaining the same." It is a thesis that does not permit of direct proof because it is an assertion about the world, not a proposition in logic. Moreover, it is possible almost at random to throw up examples of phenomena that presently defy explanation by this hypothesis: Why do we have inflation? Why are there few Jews in farming?[1] Why are societies with polygynous families so rare in the modern era? Why aren't blood banks responsible for the quality of their product? If we could answer these ques-

[1] Our lamented friend Reuben Kessel offered an attractive explanation: since Jews have been persecuted so often and forced to flee to other countries, they have not invested in immobile land, but in mobile human capital—business skills, education, etc.—that would automatically go with them. Of course, someone might counter with the more basic query: but why are they Jews, and not Christians or Moslems?

tions to your satisfaction, you would quickly produce a dozen more.

What we assert is not that we are clever enough to make illuminating applications of utility-maximizing theory to all important phenomena—not even our entire generation of economists is clever enough to do that. Rather, we assert that this traditional approach of the economist offers guidance in tackling these problems—and that no other approach of remotely comparable generality and power is available.

To support our thesis we could offer samples of phenomena we believe to be usefully explained on the assumption of stable, well-behaved preference functions. Ultimately, this is indeed the only persuasive method of supporting the assumption, and it is legitimate to cite in support all of the existing corpus of successful economic theory. Here we shall undertake to give this proof by accomplishment a special and limited interpretation. We take categories of behavior commonly held to demonstrate changes in tastes or to be explicable only in terms of such changes, and show both that they are reconcilable with our assumption of stable preferences and that the reformulation is illuminating.

I. THE NEW THEORY OF CONSUMER CHOICE

The power of stable preferences and utility maximization in explaining a wide range of behavior has been significantly enhanced by a recent reformulation of consumer theory.[2] This reformulation transforms the family from a passive maximizer of the utility from market purchases into an active maximizer also engaged in extensive production and investment activities. In the traditional theory, households maximize a utility function of the goods and services bought in the marketplace, whereas in the reformulation they maximize a utility function of objects of choice, called commodities, that they produce with market goods, their own time, their skills, training and other human capital, and other inputs. Stated formally, a household seeks to maximize

$$U = U(Z_1, \ldots Z_m) \qquad (1)$$

with

$$Z_i = f_i(X_{1i}, \ldots X_{ki}, t_{1i}, \ldots t_{\ell i}, S_\ell, \ldots S_b, \Upsilon_i), \qquad (2)$$
$$i = 1 \ldots m$$

where Z_i are the commodity objects of choice entering the utility function, f_i is the production function for the ith commodity, X_{ji} is the quantity of the jth market good or service used in the production of the ith commodity, t_{ji} is the jth person's own time input, S_j the jth person's human capital, and Υ_i represents all other inputs.

The Z_i have no market prices since they are not purchased or sold, but do have "shadow" prices determined by their costs of production. If f_i were homogeneous of the first degree in the X_{ji} and t_{ji}, marginal and average costs would be the same and the shadow price of Z_i would be

$$\pi_i = \sum_{j=1}^k \alpha_{ji}\left(\frac{p}{w_1}, \frac{w}{w_1}, S, \Upsilon_i\right)p_j + \qquad (3)$$
$$\sum_{j=1}^l \beta_{ji}\left(\frac{p}{w_1}, \frac{w}{w_1}, S, \Upsilon_i\right)w_j$$

where p_j is the cost of X_j, w_j is the cost of t_j, and α_{ji} and β_{ji} are input-output coefficients that depend on the (relative) set of p and w, S, and Υ_i. The numerous and varied determinants of these shadow prices give concrete expression to our earlier statement about the subtle forms that prices take in explaining differences among men and periods.

The real income of a household does not simply equal its money income deflated by an index of the prices of market goods, but equals its full income (which includes the value of "time" to the household)[3] deflated by an index of the prices, π_i, of the produced commodities. Since full income and commodity prices depend on a variety of factors, incomes also take subtle forms. Our task in this paper is to spell out some of the forms prices and full income take.

II. STABILITY OF TASTES AND "ADDICTION"

Tastes are frequently said to change as a result of consuming certain "addictive" goods. For example, smoking of cigarettes, drinking of alcohol, injection of heroin, or close contact with some persons over

[2]An exposition of this reformulation can be found in Robert Michael and Becker. This exposition emphasizes the capacity of the reformulation to generate many implications about behavior that are consistent with stable tastes.

[3]Full income is the maximum money income that a household could achieve by an appropriate allocation of its time and other resources.

an appreciable period of time, often increases the desire (creates a craving) for these goods or persons, and thereby cause their consumption to grow over time. In utility language, their marginal utility is said to rise over time because tastes shift in their favor. This argument has been clearly stated by Alfred Marshall when discussing the taste for "good" music:

> There is however an implicit condition in this law [of diminishing marginal utility] which should be made clear. It is that we do not suppose time to be allowed for any alteration in the character or tastes of the man himself. It is therefore no exception to the law that the more good music a man hears, the stronger is his taste for it likely to become . . . [p. 94]

We believe that the phenomenon Marshall is trying to explain, namely that exposure to good music increases the subsequent demand for good music (for some persons!), can be explained with some gain in insight by assuming constant tastes, whereas to assume a change in tastes has been an unilluminating "explanation." The essence of our explanation lies in the accumulation of what might be termed "consumption capital" by the consumer, and we distinguish "beneficial" addiction like Marshall's good music from "harmful" addiction like heroin.

Consider first beneficial addiction, and an unchanging utility function that depends on two produced commodities:

$$U = U(M, Z) \qquad (4)$$

where M measures the amount of music "appreciation" produced and consumed, and Z the production and consumption of other commodities. Music appreciation is produced by a function that depends on the time allocated to music (t_m), and the training and other human capital conducive to music appreciation (S_m) (other inputs are ignored):

$$M = M_m(t_m, S_m) \qquad (5)$$

We assume that

$$\frac{\partial M_m}{\partial t_m} > 0, \frac{\partial M_m}{\partial S_m} > 0$$

and also that

$$\frac{\partial^2 M_m}{\partial t_m \partial S_m} > 0$$

An increase in this music capital increases the productivity of time spent listening to or devoted in other ways to music.

In order to analyze the consequences for its consumption of "the more good music a man hears," the production and consumption of music appreciation has to be dated. The amount of appreciation produced at any moment j, M_j, would depend on the time allocated to music and the music human capital at j: t_{mj} and S_{mj}, respectively. The latter in turn is produced partly through "on-the-job" training or "learning by doing" by accumulating the effects of earlier music appreciation:

$$S_{mj} = h(M_{j-1}, M_{j-2}. \ldots, E_j) \qquad (6)$$

By definition, the addiction is beneficial if

$$\frac{\partial S_{mj}}{\partial M_{j-v}} > 0, \text{ all } v \text{ in } (6)$$

The term E_j measures the effect of education and other human capital on music appreciation skill, where

$$\frac{\partial S_{mj}}{\partial E_j} > 0$$

and probably

$$\frac{\partial^2 S_{mj}}{\partial M_{j-}, \partial E_j} > 0$$

We assume for simplicity a utility function that is a discounted sum of functions like the one in equation (4), where the M and Z commodities are dated, and the discount rate determined by time preference.[4] The optimal allocation of consumption is determined from the equality between the ratio of their marginal utilities and the ratio of their shadow prices:

$$\frac{MU_{mj}}{MU_{zj}} = \frac{\partial U}{\partial M_j} \bigg/ \frac{\partial U}{\partial Z_j} = \frac{\pi_{mj}}{\pi_{zj}} \qquad (7)$$

The shadow price equals the marginal cost of adding a unit of commodity output. The marginal cost is complicated for music appreciation M by the positive effect on subsequent music human capital of the production of music appreciation at any moment j. This effect on subsequent capital is an investment

---

[4]A consistent application of the assumption of stable preferences implies that the discount rate is zero; that is, the absence of time preference (see the brief discussion in Section VI.)

return from producing appreciation at j that reduces the cost of production at j. It can be shown that the marginal cost at j equals[5]

$$\pi_{mj} = \frac{w\partial t_{mj}}{\partial M_j} - w \sum_{i=1}^{n-j} \frac{\partial M_{j+i}}{\partial S_{mj+i}} \bigg/ \frac{\partial M_{j+i}}{\partial t_{mj+i}} \cdot \frac{dS_{mj+i}}{dM_j} \cdot \qquad (8)$$

$$\frac{1}{(i+r)^i} = \frac{w\partial t_{mj}}{\partial M_j} - \dot{A}_j = \frac{w}{MP_{tmj}} - A_j$$

where w is the wage rate (assumed to be the same at all ages), r the interest rate, n the length of life, and A_j the effect of addiction, measures the value of the saving in future time inputs from the effect of the production of M in j on subsequent music capital.

With no addiction, $A_j = 0$ and equation (8) reduces to the familiar marginal cost formula. Moreover, A_j is positive as long as music is beneficially addictive, and tends to decline as j increases, approaching zero as j approaches n. The term w/MP_{tm} declines with age for a given time input as long as music capital grows with age. The term A_j may not change so much with age at young ages because the percentage decline in the number of remaining years is small at these ages. Therefore, π_m would tend to

decline with age at young ages because the effect on the marginal product of the time input would tend to dominate the effect on A. Although π_m might not always decline at other ages, for the present we assume that π_m declines continuously with age.

If π_z does not depend on age, the relative price of music appreciation would decline with age; then by equation (7), the relative consumption of music appreciation would rise with age. On this interpretation, the (relative) consumption of music appreciation rises with exposure not because tastes shift in favor of music, but because its shadow price falls as skill and experience in the appreciation of music are acquired with exposure.

An alternative way to state the same analysis is that the marginal utility of time allocated to music is increased by an increase in the stock of music capital.[6] Then the consumption of music appreciation could be said to rise with exposure because the marginal utility of the time spent on music rose with exposure, even though tastes were unchanged.

The effect of exposure on the accumulation of music capital might well depend on the level of education and other human capital, as indicated by equation (6). This would explain why educated persons consume more "good" music (i.e., music that educated people like!) than other persons do.

Addiction lowers the price of music appreciation at younger ages without any comparable effect on the productivity of the time spent on music at these ages. Therefore, addiction would increase the time spent on music at younger ages: some of the time would be considered an investment that increases future music capital. Although the price of music tends to fall with age, and the consumption of music tends to rise, the time spent on music need not rise with age because the growth in music capital means that the consumption of music could rise even when the time spent fell with age. The time spent would be more likely to rise, the more elastic the demand curve for music appreciation. We can express this result in a form that will strike many readers as surprising; namely, that the time (or other inputs) spent on music appreciation is more likely to be addictive—

---

[5]The utility function

$$V = \sum_{j=1}^{n} a^j U(M_j, Z_j)$$

is maximized subject to the constraints

$$M_j = M(t_{mj}, S_{mj}); \quad Z_j = Z(x_j, t_{zj})$$
$$S_{mj} = h(M_{j-1}, M_{j-2}, \ldots, E_j)$$

$$\sum \frac{px_j}{(1+r)^j} = \sum \frac{wt_{wj} + b_j}{(i+r)^j}$$

and $t_{wj} + t_{mj} + t_{zj} = t$,
where t_{wj} is hours worked in the jth period, and b_j is property income in that period. By substitution one derives the full wealth constraint:

$$\sum \frac{px_j + w(t_{mj} + t_{zj})}{(1+r)^j} = \sum \frac{wt + b_j}{(1+r)^j} = w$$

Maximization of V with respect to M_j and Z_j subject to the production functions and the full wealth constraint gives the first-order conditions

$$a^j \frac{\partial U}{\partial Z_j} = \frac{\lambda}{(1+r)^j} \left(\frac{p dx_j}{dZ_j} + \frac{w dt_{zj}}{dZ_j} \right) = \frac{\lambda}{(1+r)_j} \pi_{zj}$$

$$a^j \frac{\partial U}{\partial M_j} = \frac{\lambda}{(1+r)^j} \cdot \left(\frac{w\partial t_{mj}}{\partial M_j} + \sum_{i=1}^{n-j} \frac{w dt_{mj+i}}{dM_j} \cdot \frac{1}{(1+r)^i} \right) = \frac{\lambda}{(1+r)^j} \pi_{mj}$$

Since, however,

$$\frac{dM_{j+i}}{dM_j} = 0 = \frac{\partial M_{j+i}}{\partial S_{mj+i}} \frac{dS_{mj+i}}{dM_j} + \frac{\partial M_{j+i}}{\partial t_{mj+i}} \frac{dt_{mj+i}}{dM_j}$$

then

$$\frac{dt_{mj+1}}{dM_j} = -\frac{\partial M_{j+i}}{\partial S_{mj+1}} \bigg/ \frac{\partial M_{j+i}}{\partial t_{mj+i}} \cdot \frac{dS_{mj+i}}{dM_j}$$

By substitution into the definition of π_{mj}, equation (8) follows immediately.

[6]The marginal utility of time allocated to music at j includes the utility from the increase in the future stock of music capital that results from an increase in the time allocated at j. An argument similar to the one developed for the price of music appreciation shows that the marginal utility of time would tend to rise with age, at least at younger ages.

that is, to rise with exposure to music—the more, not less, elastic is the demand curve for music appreciation.

The stock of music capital might fall and the price of music appreciation rise at older ages because the incentive to invest in future capital would decline as the number of remaining years declined, whereas the investment required simply to maintain the capital stock intact would increase as the stock increased. If the price rose, the time spent on music would fall if the demand curve for music were elastic. Consequently, our analysis indicates that the observed addiction to music may be stronger at younger than at older ages.

These results for music also apply to other commodities that are beneficially addictive. Their prices fall at younger ages and their consumption rises because consumption capital is accumulated with exposure and age. The time and goods used to produce an addictive commodity need not rise with exposure, even though consumption of the commodity does; they are more likely to rise with exposure, the more elastic is the demand curve for the commodity. Even if they rose at younger ages, they might decline eventually as the stock of consumption capital fell at older ages.

Using the same arguments developed for beneficial addiction, we can show that all the results are reversed for harmful addiction,[7] which is defined by a negative sign of the derivatives in equation (6):

$$\frac{\partial S_j}{\partial H_{j-v}} < 0, \text{ all } v \text{ in (6)} \qquad (9)$$

where H is a harmfully addictive commodity. An increase in consumption at any age reduces the stock of consumption capital available subsequently, and this raises the shadow price at all ages.[8] The shadow price would rise with age and exposure, at least at younger ages, which would induce consumption to fall with age and exposure. The inputs of goods and time need not fall with exposure, however, because consumption capital falls with exposure; indeed, the

inputs are likely to rise with exposure if the commodity's demand curve were inelastic.

To illustrate these conclusions, consider the commodity "euphoria" produced with input of heroin (or alcohol or amphetamines.) An increase in the consumption of current euphoria raises the cost of producing euphoria in the future by reducing the future stock of "euphoric capital." The effect of exposure to euphoria on the cost of producing future euphoria reduces the consumption of euphoria as exposure continues. If the demand curve for euphoria were sufficiently inelastic, however, the use of heroin would grow with exposure at the same time that euphoria fell.

Note that the amount of heroin used at younger ages would be reduced because of the negative effect on later euphoric capital. Indeed, no heroin at all might be used only because the harmfully addictive effects are anticipated, and discourage any use. Note further that if heroin were used even though the subsequent adverse consequences were accurately anticipated, the utility of the user would be greater than it would be if he were prevented from using heroin. Of course, his utility would be still greater if technologies developed (methadone?) to reduce the harmfully addictive effects of euphoria.[9]

Most interestingly, note that the use of heroin would grow with exposure at the same time that the amount of euphoria fell, if the demand curve for euphoria and thus for heroin were sufficiently inelastic. That is, addiction to heroin—a growth in use with exposure—is the *result* of an inelastic demand for heroin, *not,* as commonly argued, the *cause* of an inelastic demand. In the same way, listening to music or playing tennis would be addictive if the demand curves for music or tennis appreciation were sufficiently elastic; the addiction again is the result, not the cause, of the particular elasticity. Put differently, if addiction were surmised (partly because the input of goods or time rose with age), but if it were not clear whether the addiction were harmful or beneficial, the elasticity of demand could be used to distinguish between them; a high elasticity suggests

---

[7] In some ways, our analysis of beneficial and harmful addiction is a special case of the analysis of beneficial and detrimental joint production in Michael Grossman.

[8] Instead of equation (8), one has

$$\pi_{bj} = \frac{w}{MP_{tj}} + A_j$$

where $A_j \geq 0$

[9] That is, if new technology reduced and perhaps even changed the sign of the derivatives in equation (9). We should state explicitly, to avoid any misunderstanding, that "harmful" means only that the derivatives in (9) are negative, and not that the addiction harms others, nor, as we have just indicated, that it is unwise for addicts to consume such commodities.

beneficial and a low elasticity suggests harmful addiction.[10]

We do not have to assume that exposure to euphoria changes tastes in order to understand why the use of heroin grows with exposure, or why the amount used is insensitive to changes in its price. Even with constant tastes, the amount used would grow with exposure, and heroin is addictive precisely *because* of the insensitivity to price changes.

An exogenous rise in the price of addictive goods or time, perhaps due to an excise tax, such as the tax on cigarettes and alcohol, or to restrictions on their sale, such as the imprisonment of dealers in heroin, would have a relatively small effect on their use by addicts if these are harmfully addictive goods, and a relatively large effect if they are beneficially addictive. That is, excise taxes and imprisonment mainly transfer resources away from addicts if the goods are harmfully addictive, and mainly reduce the consumption of addicts if the goods are beneficially addictive.

The extension of the capital concept to investment in the capacity to consume more efficiently has numerous other potential applications. For example, there is a fertile field in consumption capital for the application of the theory of division of labor among family members.

III. STABILITY OF TASTES AND CUSTOM AND TRADITION

A "traditional" qualification to the scope of economic theory is the alleged powerful hold over human behavior of custom and tradition. An excellent statement in the context of the behavior of rulers is that of John Stuart Mill:

> It is not true that the actions even of average rulers are wholly, or anything approaching to wholly, determined by their personal interest, or even by their own opinion of their personal interest. . . . I insist only on what is true of all rulers, viz., that the character and course of their actions is largely influenced (independently of personal calculations) by the ha-

bitual sentiments and feelings, the general modes of thinking and acting, which prevail throughout the community of which they are members; as well as by the feelings, habits, and modes of thought which characterize the particular class in that community to which they themselves belong. . . . They are also much influenced by the maxims and traditions which have descended to them from other rulers, their predecessors; which maxims and traditions have been known to retain an ascendancy during long periods, even in opposition to the private interests of the rulers for the time being. [p. 484]

The specific political behavior that contradicts "personal interest" theories is not clear from Mill's statement, nor is it much clearer in similar statements by others applied to firms or households. Obviously, stable behavior by (say) households faced with stable prices and incomes—or more generally a stable environment—is no contradiction since stability then is implied as much by personal interest theories as by custom and tradition. On the other hand, stable behavior in the face of changing prices and incomes might contradict the approach taken in this essay that assumes utility maximizing with stable tastes.

Nevertheless, we believe that our approach better explains when behavior is stable than do approaches based on custom and tradition, and can at the same time explain how and when behavior does change. Mill's "habits and modes of thought," or his "maxims and traditions which have descended," in our analysis result from investment of time and other resources in the accumulation of knowledge about the environment, and of skills with which to cope with it.

The making of decisions is costly, and not simply because it is an activity which some people find unpleasant. In order to make a decision one requires information, and the information must be analyzed. The costs of searching for information and of applying the information to a new situation are such that habit is often a more efficient way to deal with moderate or temporary changes in the environment than would be a full, apparently utility-maximizing decision. This is precisely the avoidance of what J.M. Clark termed the irrational passion for dispassionate rationality.

A simple example of economizing on information by the habitual purchase from one source will illustrate the logic. A consumer buys one unit of commodity X in each unit of time. He pays a price p_t at a time t. The choices he faces are:

1. To search at the time of an act of purchase to

---

[10] The elasticity of demand can be estimated from the effects of changes in the prices of inputs. For example, if a commodity's production function were homogeneous of degree one, and if all its future as well as present input prices rose by the same known percentage, the elasticity of demand for the commodity could be estimated from the decline in the inputs. Therefore the distinction between beneficial and harmful addiction is operational: these independently estimated commodity elasticities could be used, as in the text, to determine whether an addiction was harmful or beneficial.

obtain the lowest possible price $\hat{p}_t$ consistent with the cost of search. Then $\hat{p}_t$ is a function of the amount of search s (assumed to be the same at each act of purchase):

$$\hat{p}_t = f(s), f'(s) < 0 \qquad (10)$$

where the total cost of s is $C(s)$.

2. To search less frequently (but usually more intensively), relying between searches upon the outcome of the previous search in choosing a supplier. Then the price p_t will be higher (relative to the average market price), the longer the period since the previous search (at time t_0),

$$p_t = g(t - t_0), g' > 0$$

Ignoring interest, the latter method of purchase will have a total cost over period T determined by

1) K searches (all of equal intensity) at cost K $C(s)$.

2) Each search lasts for a period T/K, within which $r = T/K$ purchases are made, at cost $r\,\bar{p}$, where $\bar{p}$ is the average price. Assume that the results of search "depreciate" (prices appreciate) at rate δ. A consumer minimizes his combined cost of the commodity and search over the total time period; the minimizing condition is[11]

$$r = \sqrt{\frac{2C}{\delta\hat{p}}} \qquad (11)$$

In this simple model with r purchases between successive searches, r is larger the larger the amount spent on search per dollar spent on the commodity

---

[11]The price of the ith purchase within one of the K search periods is $p_i = \hat{p}(1 + \delta)^{i-1}$. Hence

$$\bar{p} = \frac{1}{r}\sum_{i=1}^{r}\hat{p}(1+\delta)^{i-1} = \hat{p}\frac{(1+\delta)^r - 1}{r\delta}$$

The total cost to be minimized is

$$TC = Kr\bar{p} + KC(s) = K\hat{p}\frac{(1+\delta)^r - 1}{\delta} + KC$$

By taking a second-order approximation to $(1 + \delta)^r$, we get

$$TC = T\left\{\hat{p}\left[1 + \frac{(r-1)\delta}{2}\right] + \frac{C}{r}\right\}$$

Minimizing with respect to r gives

$$\frac{\partial TC}{\partial r} = 0 = T\left(\frac{\hat{p}\delta}{2} - \frac{C}{r^2}\right)$$

or

$$r = \sqrt{\frac{2C}{\delta\hat{p}}}$$

$(C/\hat{p})$, and the lower the rate of appreciation of prices (δ). If there were full search on each individual act of purchase, the total cost could not be less than the cost when the optimal frequency of search was chosen, and might be much greater.

When a temporary change takes place in the environment, perhaps in prices or income, it generally would not pay to disinvest the capital embodied in knowledge or skills, or to accumulate different types of capital. As a result, behavior will be relatively stable in the face of temporary changes.

A related situation arises when an unexpected change in the environment does not induce a major response immediately because time is required to accumulate the appropriate knowledge and skills. Therefore, stable preferences combined with investment in "specific" knowledge and skills can explain the small or "inelastic" responses that figure so prominently in short-run demand and supply curves.

A permanent change in the environment, perhaps due to economic development, usually causes a greater change in the behavior of young than of old persons. The common interpretation is that young persons are more readily seduced away from their customs and traditions by the glitter of the new (Western?) environment. On our interpretation, young and old persons respond differently, even if they have the same preferences and motivation. To change their behavior drastically, older persons have to either disinvest their capital that was attuned to the old environment, or invest in capital attuned to the new environment. Their incentive to do so may be quite weak, however, because relatively few years remain for them to collect the returns on new investments, and much human capital can only be disinvested slowly.

Young persons, on the other hand, are not so encumbered by accumulations of capital attuned to the old environment. Consequently, they need not have different preferences or motivation or be intrinsically more flexible in order to be more affected by a change in the environment: they simply have greater incentive to invest in knowledge and skills attuned to the new environment.

Note that this analysis is similar to that used in the previous section to explain addictive behavior: utility maximization with stable preferences, conditioned by the accumulation of specific knowledge and skills. One does not need one kind of theory to explain addictive behavior and another kind to explain habitual or customary behavior. The same theory based on stable preferences can explain both types of behavior, and can accommodate both habitual behavior and the departures therefrom.

IV. STABILITY OF TASTES AND ADVERTISING

Perhaps the most important class of cases in which "change of tastes" is invoked as an explanation for economic phenomena is that involving advertising. The advertiser "persuades" the consumer to prefer his product, and often a distinction is drawn between "persuasive" and "informative" advertising.[12] John Kenneth Galbraith is the most famous of the economists who argue that advertising molds consumer tastes:

> These [institutions of modern advertising and salesmanship] cannot be reconciled with the notion of independently determined desires for their central function is to create desires—to bring into being wants that previously did not exist. This is accomplished by the producer of the goods or at his behest.—Outlays for the manufacturing of a product are not more important in the strategy of modern business enterprise than outlays for the manufacturing of demand for the product.
>   [pp. 155–56]

We shall argue, in direct opposition to this view, that it is neither necessary nor useful to attribute to advertising the function of changing tastes.

A consumer may indirectly receive utility from a market good, yet the utility depends not only on the quantity of the good but also the consumer's knowledge of its true or alleged properties. If he does not know whether the berries are poisonous, they are not food; if he does not know that they contain vitamin C, they are not consumed to prevent scurvy. The quantity of information is a complex notion: its degree of accuracy, its multidimensional properties, its variable obsolescence with time are all qualities that make direct measurement of information extremely difficult.

How can this elusive variable be incorporated into the theory of demand while preserving the stability

of tastes? Our approach is to continue to assume, as in the previous sections, that the ultimate objects of choice are commodities produced by each household with market goods, own time, *knowledge,* and perhaps other inputs. We now assume, in addition, that the knowledge, whether real or fancied, is produced by the advertising of producers and perhaps also the own search of households.

Our approach can be presented through a detailed analysis of the simple case where the output x of a particular firm and its advertising A are the inputs into a commodity produced and consumed by households; for a given household:

$$Z = f(x, A, E, y) \qquad (12)$$

where $\partial Z/\partial x > 0$, $\partial Z/\partial A > 0$, E is the human capital of the household that affects these marginal products, and y are other variables, possibly including advertising by other firms. Still more simply,

$$Z = g(A, E, y)x \qquad (13)$$

where $\partial g/\partial A = g' > 0$ and $\partial^2 g/\partial A^2 < 0$. With A, E, and y held constant, the amount of the commodity produced and consumed by any household is assumed to be proportional to the amount of the firm's output used by that household.[13] If the advertising reaching any household were independent of its behavior, the shadow price of Z, the marginal cost of x, would simply be the expenditure on x required to change Z by one unit. From equation (13), that equals

$$\pi_z = \frac{p_x}{g} \qquad (14)$$

where p_x is the price of x.

An increase in advertising may lower the commodity price to the household (by raising g), and thereby increase its demand for the commodity and change its demand for the firm's output, because the household is made to believe—correctly or incorrectly—that it gets a greater output of the commodity from a given input of the advertised product. Consequently, advertising affects consumption in this formulation not by changing tastes, but by changing prices. That is, a movement along a stable demand curve for commodities is seen as generating the apparently unstable demand curves of market goods and other inputs.

---

[12]The distinction, if in fact one exists, between persuasive and informative advertising must be one of purpose or effect, not of content. A simple, accurately stated fact ("I offer you this genuine $1 bill for 10 cents") can be highly persuasive; the most bizarre claim ("If Napoleon could have bought our machine gun, he would have defeated Wellington") contains some information (machine guns were not available in 1814).

[13]Stated differently, Z is homogeneous of the first degree in x alone.

More than a simple change in language is involved: our formulation has quite different implications from the conventional ones. To develop these implications, consider a firm that is determining its optimal advertising along with its optimal output. We assume initially that the commodity indirectly produced by this firm (equation (12)) is a perfect substitute to consumers for commodities indirectly produced by many other firms. Therefore, the firm is perfectly competitive in the commodity market, and could (indirectly) sell an unlimited amount of this commodity at a fixed commodity price. Observe that a firm can have many perfect substitutes in the commodity market even though few other firms produce the same physical product. For example, a firm may be the sole designer of jewelry that contributes to the social prestige of consumers, and yet compete fully with many other products that also contribute to prestige: large automobiles, expensive furs, fashionable clothing, elaborate parties, a respected occupation, etc.

If the level of advertising were fixed, there would be a one-to-one correspondence between the price of the commodity and the price of the firm's output (see equation (14)). If π_z were given by the competitive market, p_x would then also be given, and the firm would find its optimal output in the conventional way by equating marginal cost to the given product price. There is no longer such a one-to-one correspondence between π_z and p_x, however, when the level of advertising is also a variable, and even a firm faced with a fixed commodity price in a perfectly competitive commodity market could sell its product at different prices by varying the level of advertising. Since an increase in advertising would increase the commodity output that consumers receive from a given amount of this firm's product, the price of its product would then be increased relative to the fixed commodity price.

The optimal advertising, product price, and output of the firm can be found by maximizing its income

$$I = p_x X - TC(X) - A p_a \qquad (15)$$

where X is the firm's total output, TC its costs of production other than advertising, and p_a the (constant) cost of a unit of advertising. By substituting from equation (14), I can be written as

$$I = \pi_z^0 g(A)X - TC(X) - A p_a \qquad (15')$$

where π_z^0 is the given market commodity price, the advertising-effectiveness function (g) is assumed to be the same for all consumers,[14] and the variables E and y in g are suppressed. The first-order maximum conditions with respect to X and A are

$$p_x = \pi_z^0 g = MC(X) \qquad (16)$$

$$\frac{\partial p_x}{\partial A} X = \pi_z^0 X g' = p_a \qquad (17)$$

Equation (16) is the usual equality between price and marginal cost for a competitive firm, which continues to hold when advertising exists and is a decision variable. Not surprisingly, equation (17) says that marginal revenue and marginal cost of advertising are equal, where marginal revenue is determined by the level of output and the increase in product price "induced" by an increase in advertising. Although the commodity price is fixed, an increase in advertising increases the firm's product price by an amount that is proportional to the increased capacity (measured by g') of its product to contribute (at least in the minds of consumers) to commodity output.

In the conventional analysis, firms in perfectly competitive markets gain nothing from advertising and thus have no incentive to advertise because they are assumed to be unable to differentiate their products to consumers who have perfect knowledge. In our analysis, on the other hand, consumers have imperfect information, including misinformation, and a skilled advertiser might well be able to differentiate his product from other apparently similar products. Put differently, advertisers could increase the value of their output to consumers without increasing to the same extent the value of the output even of perfect competitors in the *commodity* market. To simplify, we assume that the value of competitors' output is unaffected, in the sense that the commodity price (more generally, the commodity demand curve) to any firm is not affected by its advertising. Note that when firms in perfectly competitive commodity markets differentiate their products by advertising, they still preserve the perfect competition in these markets. Note moreover, that if different firms were producing the same physical product in the same com-

[14] Therefore,

$$p_x X = \pi_z^0 g \sum_{i=1}^{n} x_i$$

where n is the number of households.

petitive commodity market, and had the same marginal cost and advertising-effectiveness functions, they would produce the same output, charge the same product price, and advertise at the same rate. If, however, either their marginal costs or advertising-effectiveness differed, they would charge different product prices, advertise at different rates, and yet still be perfect competitors (although not of one another)!

Not only can firms in perfectly competitive commodity markets—that is, firms faced with infinitely elastic commodity demand curves—have an incentive to advertise, but the incentive may actually be greater, the more competitive the commodity market is. Let us consider the case of a finite commodity demand elasticity.

The necessary conditions to maximize income given by equation (15′), if π_z varies as a function of Z, are

$$\frac{\partial I}{\partial X} = \pi_z\, g + X \frac{\partial \pi_z}{\partial Z} \frac{\partial Z}{\partial X} g - MC(X) = 0, \qquad (18)$$

or since $Z = gX$, and $\partial Z/\partial X = g$,

$$\pi_z\, g\left(1 + \frac{1}{\epsilon_{\pi_z}}\right) = p_x\left(1 + \frac{1}{\epsilon_{\pi_z}}\right) = MC(X) \qquad (18')$$

where ϵ_{π_z} is the elasticity of the firm's commodity demand curve. Also

$$\frac{\partial I}{\partial A} = X\frac{\partial p_x}{\partial A} - p_a =$$

$$\pi_z \frac{\partial Z}{\partial A} + \frac{\partial \pi_z}{\partial Z} \cdot \frac{\partial Z}{\partial A} \cdot Z - p_a = 0 \qquad (19)$$

or

$$X\frac{\partial p_x}{\partial A} = \pi_z\, g'X\left(1 + \frac{1}{\epsilon_{\pi_z}}\right) = p_a \qquad (19')$$

Equation (18′) is simply the usual maximizing condition for a monopolist that continues to hold when there is advertising.[15] Equation (19′) clearly shows that, given $\pi_z g'X$, the marginal revenue from additional advertising is greater, the greater is the elasticity of the commodity demand curve; therefore, the optimal level of advertising would be positively related to the commodity elasticity.

This important result can be made intuitive by considering Fig. 1. The curve DD gives the firm's

commodity demand curve, where π_z is measured along the vertical and commodity output Z along the horizontal axis. The firm's production of X is held fixed so that Z varies only because of variations in the level of advertising. At point e^0, the level of advertising is A_0, the product price is p_x^0, and commodity output and price are Z_0 and π_z^0, respectively. An increase in advertising to A_1 would increase Z to Z_1 (the increase in Z is determined by the given g' function). The decline in π_z induced by the increase in Z would be negatively related to the elasticity of the commodity demand curve: it would be less, for example, if the demand curve were $D'D'$ rather than DD. Since the increase in p_x is negatively related to the decline in π_z,[16] the increase in p_x, and thus the marginal revenue from the increase in A, is directly related to the elasticity of the commodity demand curve.[17]

The same result is illustrated with a more conventional diagram in Fig. 2: the firm's product output and price are shown along the horizontal and vertical axes. The demand curve for its product with a given level of advertising is given by dd. We proved earlier (fn. 15) that with advertising constant, the elasticity of the product demand curve is the same as the elasticity of its commodity demand curve. An increase in advertising "shifts" the product demand curve upward to $d'd'$, and the marginal revenue from additional advertising is directly related to the size of the shift; that is, to the increase in product price for any given product output. Our basic result is that the shift is itself directly related to the elasticity of the demand curve. For example, with the same increase in advertising, the shift is larger from dd to $d'd'$ than from ee to $e'e'$ because dd is more elastic than ee.

This role of information in consumer demand is capable of extension in various directions. For example, the demand for knowledge is affected by the

---

[15]If the level of advertising is held constant, Z is proportional to X, so

$$\epsilon_{\pi_z} = \frac{dZ}{Z}\bigg/\frac{d\pi_z}{\pi_z} = \epsilon_{p_x} = \frac{dX}{X}\bigg/\frac{dp_x}{p_x}$$

[16]Since $\pi_z g = p_x$,

$$\frac{\partial p_x}{\partial A} = \pi_z\, g' + g\frac{\partial \pi_z}{\partial A} > 0$$

The first term on the right is positive and the second term is negative. If g, g', and π_z are given, $\partial p_x/\partial A$ is linearly and negatively related to $\partial \pi_z/\partial A$.

[17]Recall again our assumption, however, that even firms in perfectly competitive markets can fully differentiate their products. If the capacity of a firm to differentiate itself were inversely related to the elasticity of its commodity demand curve, that is, to the amount of competition in the commodity market, the increase in its product price generated by its advertising might not be directly related to the elasticity of its commodity demand curve.

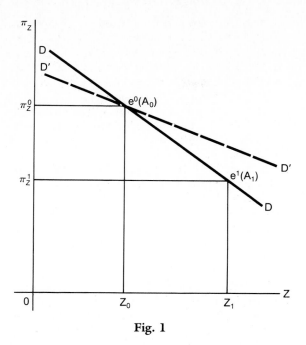

Fig. 1

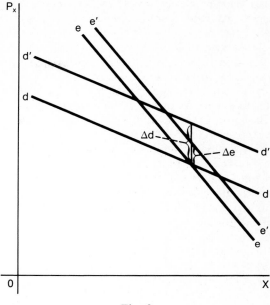

Fig. 2

formal education of a person, so systematic variations of demand for advertisements with formal education can be explored. The stock of information possessed by the individual is a function of his age, period of residence in a community, and other variables, so systematic patterns of purchase of heavily and lightly advertised goods are implied by the theory.

V. FASHIONS AND FADS

The existence of fashions and fads (short episodes or cycles in the consumption habits of people) seems an especially striking contradiction of our thesis of the stability of tastes. We find fashions in dress, food, automobiles, furniture, books, and even scientific doctrines.[18] Some are modest in amplitude, or few in their followers, but others are of violent amplitude: who now buys an ouija board, or a bustle? The rise and fall of fashions is often attributed to the fickleness of people's tastes. Herbert Blumer, the distinguished sociologist, gave a characteristic expression of this view:

> Tastes are themselves a product of experience, they usually develop from an initial state of vagueness to

a state of refinement and stability, but once formed they may decay and disintegrate. . . .

> The fashion process involves both a formation and an expression of collective taste in the given area of fashion. The taste is initially a loose fusion of vague inclinations and dissatisfactions that are aroused by new experience in the field of fashion and in the larger surrounding world. In this initial state, collective taste is amorphous, inarticulate, and awaiting specific direction. Through models and proposals, fashion innovators sketch possible lines along which the incipient taste may gain objective expression and take definite form. [p. 344]

The obvious method of reconciling fashion with our thesis is to resort again to the now familiar argument that people consume commodities, and only indirectly do they consume market goods, so fashions in market goods are compatible with stability in the utility function of commodities. The task here, as elsewhere, is to show that this formulation helps to illuminate our understanding of the phenomena under discussion; we have some tentative comments in this direction.

The commodity apparently produced by fashion goods is social distinction: the demonstration of alert leadership, or at least not lethargy, in recognizing and adopting that which will in due time be widely approved. This commodity—it might be termed *style*—sounds somewhat circular, because new things

[18]"Fashion" indeed, does not necessarily refer only to the shorter term preferences. Adam Smith says that the influence of fashion "over dress and furniture is not more absolute than over architecture, poetry, and music" (p. 283).

appear to be chosen simply because they are new. Such circularity is no more peculiar than that which is literally displayed in a race—the runners obviously do not run around a track in order to reach a new destination. Moreover, it is a commendation of a style good that it be superior to previous goods, and style will not be sought intentionally through less functional goods. Indeed, if the stylish soon becomes inferior to the unstylish, it would lose its attractiveness.

Style, moreover, is not achieved simply by change: the newness must be of a special sort that requires a subtle prediction of what will be approved novelty, and a trained person can make better predictions than an untrained person. Style is social rivalry, and it is, like all rivalry, both an incentive to individuality and a source of conformity.

The areas in which the rivalry of fashion takes place are characterized by public exposure and reasonably short life. An unexposed good (automobile pistons) cannot be judged as to its fashionableness, and fashions in a good whose efficient life is long would be expensive. Hence fashion generally concentrates on the cheaper classes of garments and reading matter, and there is more fashion in furniture than in housing.

Fashion can be pursued with the purse or with the expenditure of time. A person may be well-read (i.e., have read the recent books generally believed to be important), but if his time is valuable in the market place, it is much more likely that his spouse will be the well-read member of the family. (So the ratio of the literacy of wife to that of husband is positively related to the husband's earning power, and inversely related to her earning power.)

The demand for fashion can be formalized by assuming that the distinction available to any person depends on his social environment, and his own efforts: he can be fashionable, give to approved charities, choose prestigious occupations, and do other things that affect his distinction. Following recent work on social interactions, we can write the social distinction of the ith person as

$$R_i = D_i + h_i \qquad (20)$$

where D_i is the contribution to his distinction of his social environment, and h_i is his own contribution. Each person maximizes a utility function of R and other commodities subject to a budget constraint that depends on his own income and the exogenously

given social environment.[19] A number of general results have been developed with this approach (see Becker), and a few are mentioned here to indicate that the demand for fashion (and other determinants of social distinction) can be systematically analyzed without assuming that tastes shift.

An increase in i's own income, prices held constant, would increase his demand for social distinction and other commodities. If his social environment were unchanged, the whole increase in his distinction would be produced by an increase in his own contributions to fashion and other distinction-producing goods. Therefore, even an average income elasticity of demand for distinction would imply a high income elasticity of demand for fashion (and these other distinction-producing) goods, which is consistent with the common judgement that fashion is a luxury good.[20]

If other persons increase their contributions to their own distinction, this may lower i's distinction by reducing his social environment. For distinction is scarce and is to a large extent simply redistributed among persons: an increase in one person's distinction generally requires a reduction in that of other persons. This is why people are often "forced" to conform to new fashions. When some gain distinction by paying attention to (say) new fashions, they lower the social environment of others. The latter are induced to increase their own efforts to achieve distinction, including a demand for these new fashions, because an exogenous decline in their social environment induces them to increase their own contributions to their distinction.

Therefore, an increase in all incomes induces an even greater increase in i's contribution to his distinction than does an increase in his own income alone. For an increase in the income of others lowers i's social environment because they spend more on their own distinction; the reduction in his environment induces a further increase in i's contribution to his distinction. Consequently, we expect wealthy countries like the United States to pay more attention

---

[19] The budget constraint for i can be written as

$$\Pi_{R_i} R + \Pi_z Z = I_i + \Pi_{R_i} D_i = S_i$$

where Z are other commodities, Π_{R_i} is his marginal cost of changing R, I_i is his own full income, and S_i is his "social income."

[20] Marshall believed that the desire for distinction was the most powerful of passions and a major source of the demand for luxury expenditures (see pp. 87–88, 106).

to fashion than poor countries like India, even if tastes were the same in wealthy and poor countries.

VI. CONCLUSION

We have surveyed four classes of phenomena widely believed to be inconsistent with the stability of tastes: addiction, habitual behavior, advertising, and fashions, and in each case offered an alternative explanation. That alternative explanation did not simply reconcile the phenomena in question with the stability of tastes, but also sought to show that the hypothesis of stable tastes yielded more useful predictions about observable behavior.

Of course, this short list of categories is far from comprehensive: for example, we have not entered into the literature of risk aversion and risk preference, one of the richest sources of *ad hoc* assumptions concerning tastes. Nor have we considered the extensive literature on time preference, which often alleges that people "systematically undervalue . . . future wants".[21] The taste for consumption in say 1984 is alleged to continue to shift upward as 1984 gets closer to the present. In spite of the importance frequently attached to time preference, we do not know of any significant behavior that has been illuminated by this assumption. Indeed, given additional space, we would argue that the assumption of time preference impedes the explanation of life cycle variations in the allocation of resources, the secular growth in real incomes, and other phenomena.

Moreover, we have not considered systematic differences in tastes by wealth or other classifications. We also claim, however, that no significant behavior has been illuminated by assumptions of differences in tastes. Instead, they, along with assumptions of unstable tastes, have been a convenient crutch to lean on when the analysis has bogged down. They give the appearance of considered judgement, yet really have only been *ad hoc* arguments that disguise analytical failures.

We have partly translated "unstable tastes" into variables in the household production functions for commodities. The great advantage, however, of relying only on changes in the arguments entering household production functions is that *all* changes in behavior are explained by changes in prices and incomes, precisely the variables that organize and give power to economic analysis. Addiction, advertising, etc. affect not tastes with the endless degrees of freedom they provide, but prices and incomes, and are subject therefore to the constraints imposed by the theorem on negatively inclined demand curves, and other results. Needless to say, we would welcome explanations of why some people become addicted to alcohol and others to Mozart, whether the explanation was a development of our approach or a contribution from some other behavioral discipline.

As we remarked at the outset, no conceivable expenditure of effort on our part could begin to exhaust the possible tests of the hypothesis of stable and uniform preferences. Our task has been oddly two-sided. Our hypothesis is trivial, for it merely asserts that we should apply standard economic logic as extensively as possible. But the self-same hypothesis is also a demanding challenge, for it urges us not to abandon opaque and complicated problems with the easy suggestion that the further explanation will perhaps someday be produced by one of our sister behavioral sciences.

REFERENCES

G. S. Becker, "A Theory of Social Interaction," *J. Polit. Econ.*, Nov./Dec. 1974, *82*, 1063–93.

H. C. Blumer, "Fashion," in Vol. V, *Int. Encyclo. Soc. Sci.*, New York 1968.

Eugen von Böhm-Bawerk, *Capital and Interest*, vol. 2, South Holland, IL 1959.

John K. Galbraith, *The Affluent Society*, Boston 1958.

M. Grossman, "The Economics of Joint Production in the Household," rep. 7145, Center Math. Stud. Bus. Econ., Univ. Chicago 1971.

Alfred Marshall, *Principles of Economics*, 8th ed., London 1923.

R. T. Michael and G. S. Becker, "On the New Theory of Consumer Behavior," *Swedish J. Econ.*, Dec. 1973, *75*, 378–96.

John S. Mill, *A System of Logic*, 8th ed., London 1972.

Adam Smith, *Theory of Moral Sentiments*, New Rochelle 1969.

---

[21]This quote is taken from the following longer passage in Böhm-Bawerk:

We must now consider a *second* phenomenon of human experience—one that is heavily fraught with consequence. That is the fact that we feel less concerned about future sensations of joy and sorrow simply because they do lie in the future, and the lessening of our concern is in proportion to the remoteness of that future. Consequently we accord to goods which are intended to serve future ends a value which falls short of the true intensity of their future marginal utility. *We systematically undervalue our future wants and also the means which serve to satisfy them.* [p. 268]

Toward a Positive Theory of Consumer Choice*

RICHARD THALER**

Richard Thaler (B.A., Case Western Reserve University, 1967; M.A., University of Rochester, 1970; Ph.D, 1974) was born in 1945 in East Orange, New Jersey. Joining the faculty of Cornell University in 1978, Thaler currently holds the title of Associate Professor of Economics at the Graduate School of Management. Prior to his appointment at Cornell, he was on the faculty of the University of Rochester, a research economist at the Center for Naval Analyses, and held visiting appointments at the National Bureau of Economic Research (West) and the University of British Columbia. His research has focused on the area of psychology and economics.

1. INTRODUCTION

Economists rarely draw the distinction between normative models of consumer choice and descriptive or positive models. Although the theory is normatively based (it describes what rational consumers *should* do) economists argue that it also serves well

*Reprinted from *Journal of Economic Behavior and Organization* by permission of North-Holland Publishing Company, Amsterdam. Copyright 1980, pp. 39–60.

**The author wishes to acknowledge the many people who have made this paper possible. Colleagues, too numerous to name individually, at the Center for Naval Analyses, Cornell University, The National Bureau of Economic Research-West, Decision Research, and the University of Rochester have contributed importantly to the final product. Special thanks go to Daniel Kahneman, Amos Tversky, H.M. Shefrin, Thomas Russell, and particularly Victor Fuchs who has supported the research in every possible way. Of course, responsibility for remaining deficiencies is the author's. He also wishes to acknowledge financial support from the Kaiser Family Foundation, while he was a visiting scholar at NBER-West.

as a descriptive theory (it predicts what consumers in fact do). This paper argues that exclusive reliance on the normative theory leads economists to make systematic, predictable errors in describing or forecasting consumer choices.

In some situations the normative and positive theories coincide. If a consumer must add two (small) numbers together as part of a decision process then one would hope that the normative answer would be a good predictor. So if a problem is sufficiently simple the normative theory will be acceptable. Furthermore, the sign of the substitution effect, the most important prediction in economics, has been shown to be negative even if consumers choose at random [Becker (1962)]. Recent research has demonstrated that even rats obey the law of demand [Kagel and Battalio (1975)].

How does the normative theory hold up in more

complicated situations? Consider the famous birthday problem in statistics: if 25 people are in a room what is the probability that at least one pair will share a birthday? This problem is famous because everyone guesses wrong when he first hears it. Furthermore, the errors are systematic—nearly everyone guesses too low. (The correct answer is greater than 0.5.) For most people the problem is a form of mental illusion. Research on judgment and decision making under uncertainty, especially by Daniel Kahneman and Amos Tversky (1974, 1979), has shown that such mental illusions should be considered the rule rather than the exception.[1] Systematic, predictable differences between normative models of behavior and actual behavior occur because of what Herbert Simson (1957, p. 198) called 'bounded rationality':

> 'The capacity of the human mind for formulating and solving complex problems is very small compared with the size of the problems whose solution is required for objectively rational behavior in the real world—or even for a reasonable approximation to such objective rationality.'

This paper presents a group of economic mental illusions. These are classes of problems where consumers are particularly likely to deviate from the predictions of the normative model. By highlighting the specific instances in which the normative model fails to predict behavior, I hope to show the kinds of changes in the theory that will be necessary to make it more descriptive. Many of these changes are incorporated in a new descriptive model of choice under uncertainty called prospect theory [Kahneman and Tversky (1979)]. Therefore I begin this paper with a brief summary of prospect theory. Then several types of predicted errors in the normative theory are discussed. Each is first illustrated by an anecdotal example. These examples are intended to *illustrate* the behavior under discussion in a manner that appeals to the reader's intuition and experiences. I have discussed these examples with hundreds of friends, colleagues, and students. Many of the examples have also been used as questionnaires—I can informally report that a large majority of non-economists say they would act in the hypothesized manner. Yet I am keenly aware that more formal tests are necessary. I try to provide as many kinds of evidence as possible for each type of behavior. These kinds of evidence

range from questionnaires, to regressions using market data, to laboratory experiments, to market institutions that exist apparently to exploit these actions. I hope to gather more evidence in future experimental research. For readers who remain unconvinced, I suggest they try out the examples on some non-economist friends.

2. PROSPECT THEORY

Not very long after expected utility theory was formulated by von Neumann and Morgenstern (1944) questions were raised about its value as a descriptive model [Allais (1953)]. Recently Kahneman and Tversky (1979) have proposed an alternative descriptive model of economic behavior that they call 'prospect theory'. I believe that many of the elements of prospect theory can be used in developing descriptive choice models in deterministic settings. Therefore, I will present a very brief summary of prospect theory here.

Kahneman and Tversky begin by presenting the results of a series of survey questions designed to highlight discrepancies between behavior and expected utility theory. Some of these results are presented in Table 1. A prospect is a gamble (x, p, y, q) that pays x with probability p and y with probability q. If $q = 0$ that outcome is omitted. A certain outcome is denoted (z). N refers to number of subjects who responded, the percentage who chose each option is given in parentheses, and majority preference is denoted by *. Subjects were also given problems such as these:

Problem 11. In addition to whatever you own you have been given 1,000. You are now asked to choose between

A: (1,000, 0.5) and B: (500) $N = 70$.
(16)   (84)

Problem 12. In addition to whatever you own, you have been given 2,000. You are now asked to choose between

C: $(-1,000, 0.5)$ and D: (-500) $N = 68$.
(69)   (31)

The results of these questionnaires led to the following empirical generalizations.

(1) Gains are treated differently than losses. (Notice the reversal in signs of preference in the two columns in table 1.) Except for very small probabilities, risk seeking is observed for losses while risk aversion is observed for gains.

---

[1] Some of these studies have recently been replicated by economists. See Grether and Plott (1979) and Grether (1979).

Table 1. Preferences between positive and negative prospects[a]

	Positive prospects			Negative prospects	
Problem 3	(4,000, 0.80)	<(3,000)	Problem 3'	(−4,000, 0.80)	>(−3,000)
N = 95	(20)	(80)*	N = 95	(92)*	(8)
Problem 4	(4,000, 0.20)	>(3,000, 0.25)	Problem 4'	(−4,000, 0.20)	<(−3,000, 0.25)
N = 95	(65)*	(35)	N = 95	(42)	(58)
Problem 7	(3,000, 0.90)	>(6,000, 0.45)	Problem 7'	(−3,000, 0.90)	<(−6,000, 0.45)
N = 66	(86)*	(14)	N = 66	(8)	(92)*
Problem 8	(3,000, 0.002)	<(6,000, 0.001)	Problem 8'	(−3,000, 0.002)	>(−6,000, 0.001)
N = 66	(27)	(73)*	N = 66	(70)*	(30)

[a]*Source:* Kahneman and Tversky (1979).

(2) Outcomes received with certainty are over-weighted relative to uncertain outcomes. (Compare 3 and 3' with 4 and 4'.)

(3) The structure of the problem may affect choices. Problems 11 and 12 are identical if evaluated with respect to final asset positions but are treated differently by subjects.

Kahneman and Tversky then offer a theory that can predict individual choices, even in the cases in which expected utility theory is violated. In expected utility theory, an individual with initial wealth w will value a prospect $(x, p; y, q)$ as $EU = pU(w + x) + qU(w + y)$ if $p + q = 1$. In prospect theory the objective probabilities are replaced by subjective decision weights $\pi(p)$. The utility function is replaced by a value function, v, that is defined over changes in wealth rather than final asset position. For 'regular' prospects (i.e., $p + q < 1$ or $x \geq 0 \geq y$ or $x \leq 0 \leq y$) then the value of a prospect is given by

$$V(x, p; y, q) = \pi(p)v(x) + \pi(q)v(y). \quad (1)$$

If $p + q = 1$ and either $x > y > 0$ or $x < y < 0$ then

$$V(x, p; y, q) = v(y) + \pi(p)[v(x) - v(y)]. \quad (2)$$

The value function is of particular interest here since I will discuss only deterministic choice problems. The essential characteristics of the value function are:

(1) It is defined over gains and losses with respect to some natural reference point. Changes in the reference point can alter choices as in Problems 11 and 12.

(2) It is concave for gains and convex for losses. The shape of the value function is based on the psy-

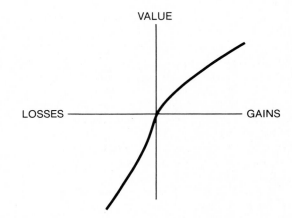

Fig. 1. A hypothetical value function.

chophysical principle that the difference between 0 and 100 seems greater than the difference between 1,000 and 1,100 irrespective of the sign of the magnitudes. This shape explains the observed risk-seeking choices for losses and risks averse choices for gains.[2]

(3) It is steeper for losses than for gains. 'The aggravation that one experiences in losing a sum of money appears to be greater than the pleasure associated with gaining the same amount.'[3]

A hypothetical value function with these properties is pictured in Fig. 1. Insurance purchasing and gambling are explained through the π function which is regressive with respect to objective probabilities and

[2]The loss function will be mitigated by the threat of ruin or other discontinuities. See Kahneman and Tversky (1979, p. 279).
[3]Kahneman and Tversky (1979, p. 279).

has discontinuities around 0 and 1. For details, of course, the reader is encouraged to read the original paper.

3. OPPORTUNITY COSTS AND THE ENDOWMENT EFFECT

Example 1. Mr. R bought a case of good wine in the late '50's for about $5 a bottle. A few years later his wine merchant offered to buy the wine back for $100 a bottle. He refused, although he has never paid more than $35 for a bottle of wine.

Example 2. Mr. H. mows his own lawn. His neighbor's son would mow it for $8. He wouldn't mow his neighbor's same-sized lawn for $20.

Example 3. Two survey questions: (a) Assume you have been exposed to a disease which if contracted leads to a quick and painless death within a week. The probability you have the disease is 0.001. What is the maximum you would be willing to pay for a cure? (b) Suppose volunteers were needed for research on the above disease. All that would be required is that you expose yourself to a 0.001 chance of contracting the disease. What is the minimum payment you would require to volunteer for this program? (You would not be allowed to purchase the cure.)

The results. Many people respond to questions (a) and (b) with answers which differ by an order of magnitude or more! (A typical response is $200 and $10,000.)

These examples have in common sharp differences between buying and selling prices. While such differences *can* be explained using income effects or transactions costs, I will argue that a more parsimonious explanation is available if one distinguishes between the opportunity costs and out-of-pocket costs.

The first lesson of economics is that all costs are (in some sense) opportunity costs. Therefore opportunity costs *should* be treated as equivalent to out-of-pocket costs. How good is this normative advice as a descriptive model? Consider Kahneman and Tversky's Problems 11 and 12. In Problem 11 the gamble is viewed as a chance to gain while in Problem 12 it is viewed as a chance to avert a loss. We know the problems are viewed differently since the majority responses are reversed. Kahneman and Tversky incorporate this in their model by focusing on gains and losses (rather than final asset positions which are

identical in these two problems) and by having the loss function steeper than the gains function, $v(x) < - v(x)$. This shape of the value function implies that if out-of-pocket costs are viewed as losses and opportunity costs are viewed as foregone gains, the former will be more heavily weighted. Furthermore, a certain degree of inertia is introduced into the consumer choice process since goods that are included in the individual's endowment will be more highly valued than those not held in the endowment, *ceteris paribus*. This follows because removing a good from the endowment creates a loss while adding the same good (to an endowment without it) generates a gain. Henceforth, I will refer to the underweighting of opportunity costs as the *endowment effect*.

Clearly the endowment effect can explain the behavior in Examples 1–3. In Example 1 it works in two ways. First, as just mentioned, giving up the wine will induce a loss while purchasing the same bottle would create a (less highly weighted) gain. Second, the money paid for a bottle purchased might be viewed as a loss[4] while the money received for the sale would be viewed as a gain.

The endowment effect is a hypothesis about behavior. What evidence exists (aside from Kahneman and Tversky's survey data) to support this hypothesis? Unfortunately, there is little in the way of formal tests. One recent study by SRI International does provide some supporting evidence. Weiss, Hall and Dong (1978) studied the schooling decision of participants in the Seattle-Denver Income Maintenance Experiment. They found that variation in the out-of-pocket costs of education had effects which were 'stronger and more systematic than that of a controlled change in opportunity costs'.[5]

An experimental test was conducted by Becker, Ronen and Sorter (1974). They asked MBA students to choose between two projects that differed only in that one had an opportunity cost component while the other had only out-of-pocket costs. The students systematically preferred the projects with the opportunity costs. However, some problems with their experimental design make this evidence inconclusive. [See Neumann and Friedman (1978).]

Other kinds of evidence in support of the endowment effect hypothesis are less direct but perhaps

---

[4]More about the psychology of spending appears in section 4.
[5]Weiss, Hall and Dong (1978).

more convincing. I refer to instances in which businesses have used the endowment effect to further their interests.

Credit cards provide a particularly clear example. Until recently, credit card companies banned their affiliated stores from charging higher prices to credit card users. A bill to outlaw such agreements was presented to Congress. When it appeared likely that some kind of bill would pass, the credit card lobby turned its attention to form rather than substance. Specifically, it preferred that any difference between cash and credit card customers take the form of a cash discount rather than a credit card surcharge. This preference makes sense if consumers would view the cash discount as an opportunity cost of using the credit card for the surcharge as an out-of-pocket cost.[6]

The film processing industry seems also to have understood the endowment effect. Some processing companies (notably Fotomat) have a policy whereby they process and print any photographs no matter how badly exposed they are. Customers can ask for refunds (on their next trip if they wish) for any pictures they don't want. The endowment effect helps explain why they are not beseiged by refund requests.

Other marketing strategies can be understood with the use of the endowment effect. Consider the case of a two week trial period with a money back guarantee. At the first decision point the consumer thinks he can lose at most the transactions costs of taking the good home and back. If the transactions costs are less than the value of the utilization of the good for two weeks, then the maximizing consumer pays for the good and takes it home. The second decision point comes two weeks later. If the consumer has fully adapted to the purchase, he views the cost of keeping the good as an opportunity cost. Once this happens the sale is more likely. Of course, it is entirely possible that were the good to be stolen

and the price of the good refunded by his insurance company he would fail to repurchase the good.[7]

A final application of the endowment effect comes from the field of sports economics. Harold Demsetz (1972) argues that the reserve clause (which ties a player to a team for life) does not affect the distribution of players among teams. His argument is as follows. Resources go to their highest valued use. Teams are free to sell or trade players to other teams. Thus if a player is owned by one team but valued more highly by another, a transaction will take place. Since the transaction costs appear to be low, the argument seems correct, but the facts clearly contradict the conclusion!

Consider first the free agent draft in football. Teams take turns selecting players who have finished their collegiate eligibility. The teams pick in a specified order. Demsetz (and economic theory) would suggest that teams should draft at their turn the player with the highest market value and then trade or sell him to the team that values him most. Thus we should expect to see a flurry of trades right after the draft. Instead, while drafting rights (i.e., turns to pick) are frequently traded, players drafted are virtually never traded during the period between the draft and the start of the season. Why? Before offering an answer, consider another empirical observation. In baseball over the last few years the reserve clause has been weakened and many players (starting with 'Catfish' Hunter) have become free agents, able to sign with any team. If players are already on the teams where their value is highest these free agents should all re-sign with their former teams (at new higher salaries that give the rents to the player rather than the owner). Yet this has not happened. Instead, virtually all of the players who have become free agents have signed with new teams.

I believe that the endowment effect can explain at

[6]In his testimony before the Senate Committee on Banking, Housing and Urban Affairs, Jeffrey Bucher of the Federal Reserve Board argued that surcharges and discounts should be treated the same way. However he reported that 'critics argued that a surcharge carries the connotation of a penalty on credit card users while a discount is viewed as a bonus to cash customers. They contended that this difference in psychological impact makes it more likely that surcharge systems will discourage customers from using credit cards. . . .' This passage and other details are in United States Senate (1975).

[7]Suppose your neighbors are going to have a garage sale. They offer to sell any of your household goods for you at one half of the original purchase price. You must only tell them which goods to sell and they will take care of everything else, including returning any unsold items. Try to imagine which goods you would decide to sell and which goods you would decide to keep. Now imagine that some of the goods you decided to keep are stolen, and that your insurance will pay you half the original price. If you could also replace them at half price how many would you replace? (Assume identical quantity.) Many people say that there would be some items which they would not sell in the first case *and* wouldn't buy in the second case, even though transactions costs have been made very low in this example.

least part of these puzzles. When a player is drafted he becomes part of the fans' endowment. If he is sold or traded this will be treated by the fans as a *loss*. However, when a player is declared a free agent he drops out of the endowment, and the fans will recognize that he can only be regained at substantial *out-of-pocket* expense. Similarly, trading the rights to draft a player will be preferred to trading the player since he will never enter the fans' endowment.

4. SUNK COSTS: MODELING PSYCHIC COSTS

Example 4. A family pays $40 for tickets to a basketball game to be played 60 miles from their home. On the day of the game there is a snowstorm. They decide to go anyway, but note in passing that had the tickets been given to them, they would have stayed home.

Example 5. A man joins a tennis club and pays a $300 yearly membership fee. After two weeks of playing he develops a tennis elbow. He continues to play (in pain) saying 'I don't want to waste the $300!'

Economic theory implies that only incremental costs and benefits *should* affect decisions. Historical costs should be irrelevant. But do (noneconomist) consumers ignore sunk costs in their everyday decisions? As Examples 4 and 5 suggest, I do not believe that they do. Rather, I suggest the alternative hypothesis that paying for the right to use a good or service will increase the rate at which the good will be utilized, *ceteris paribus*. This hypothesis will be referred to as the *sunk cost effect*.

Gathering evidence to test this hypothesis is complicated by problems of selectivity bias. People who have paid to join a tennis club are likely to enjoy tennis more than those who have not, and thus they are likely to use it more than another group who didn't have to pay the membership fee. This problem makes market tests difficult. Other evidence does exist, however, and it is generally supportive.

First, some of Kahneman and Tversky's survey questions indicate a sunk cost effect. For example, one set of subjects preferred (0) to ($-800, 0.2; 200, 0.8$), while a different set preferred ($-1,000, 0.2$) to (-200). This suggests that the 200 subtracted from the first problem to obtain the second is not viewed as sunk by the subjects. Kahneman and Tversky also cite the empirical finding that betting on longshots increases during the course of a racing

day, again implying that bettors have not adapted to their losses. Similar behavior is well known to anyone who plays poker.

Second, social psychologists have done experiments on a related concept. Aronson and Mills (1959) tested to see whether people who had to undertake considerable effort to obtain something would like it better. Their procedure was to advertise for students to participate in a discussion group. Subjects were then assigned to one of three groups: severe initiation, mild initiation and control. Those in the severe initiation group had to read aloud an embarrassing portion of some sexually oriented material. Those in the mild condition read aloud some more timid material. Those in the control group had no initiation. Basically, the results confirmed the hypothesis of the experimenters. Those in the severe initiation group reported enjoying the subsequent group discussion (which, in fact, was deadly dull) more than those in the other group. These results were later replicated by Gerard and Mathewson (1966).[8]

Third, there are many examples of the government failing to ignore sunk costs. A dramatic example of this was revealed in a Congressional investigation of the Teton Dam disaster.[9] One part of the hearings was devoted to an analysis of the *theory of momentum*—'that is, the inclination on the part of the Bureau of Reclamation to continue dam construction, once commenced, despite hazards which might emerge during the course of construction . . .'.[10] The commissioner of the Bureau of Reclamation denied that such a problem existed. However, when asked to 'give an example of any dam whose construction was halted or even paused or interrupted temporarily once the physical construction processes actually began on the dam itself',[11] the Commissioner came up empty handed.

Finally, perhaps the strongest support for the sunk cost hypothesis can be found in the classroom. Any-

---

[8]I also plan some experiments to test the sunk cost effect. In one pilot study undertaken by one of my students, Lewis Broad, customers at an all-you-can-eat pizza restaurant were randomly given free lunches. They, in fact, ate less than the control group who paid the $2.50 normal bill.

[9]This example was suggested by Paul Slovic.

[10]U.S. Government (1976, p. 14). This issue was raised because the Bureau had in fact received such warnings about the Teton Dam.

[11]*Ibid*, p. 14.

one who has ever tried to teach this concept knows that it is not intuitively obvious, even to some experienced businesspeople.

4.1. Modeling Sunk Costs

If the sunk cost effect does exist, it is interesting to speculate on the thought process that produces it. A reasonable explanation can be offered using prospect theory. First, however, we must consider the individual's psychic accounting system. To do this it is necessary to introduce a psychic equivalent to debits and credits which, for lack of better terms, I will call pleasure and pain. In terms of prospect theory, pleasure can be thought of as the value function in the domain of gains while pain corresponds to the value function in the domain of losses. (Henceforth, for expository purposes, I will refer to the value function for losses as $\bar{v}$.) When will a customer feel pain? Pain will *not* be felt when a purchase is made for immediate consumption (like buying a hamburger for lunch) as long as the price is 'reasonable'. If the value of the hamburger is g and the cost is c, then the net pleasure will be $v(g) + \bar{v}(-c)$.[12] Only in the event of a loss will there be actual net pain.

Now, however, consider the case described in Example 4. When the basketball tickets are purchased the consumer just exchanges cash for an asset (the tickets). At this point the consumer *could* experience $40 worth of pain with the expectation of feeling pleasure at the game as if the tickets had been free, but this seems unlikely. A much more plausible story is that no pain or pleasure is felt at this point except perhaps in anticipation of the game. Then when the game is attended the consumer feels net pleasure as in the case of the hamburger. The snowstorm, however, creates a problem. If the tickets aren't used then their value has become zero and the consumer should feel a $40 loss ($\bar{v}(-40)$). But, the economist would say, how does going to the game help? Let's assume that the cost of going to the game through the snow is c and the value of seeing the game is g. (I will ignore uncertainty about getting to the game as it would add nothing to the analysis.) Further, assume that had the tickets been free, the consumer would

have been indifferent about going, i.e., $v(g) = -\bar{v}(-c)$. In this case the $40 paid for the tickets will induce the consumer to go since $v(g) + \bar{v}(-(c + 40)) > \bar{v}(-40)$ due to the convexity of $\bar{v}$.

4.2. Sunk Costs and Multipart Pricing

Example 5 can be used to illustrate an application of the sunk cost effect in microeconomics. The tennis club uses a two-part pricing scheme. The membership fee is $300 and the court fees are $10 per hour. Suppose the membership fee is raised to $400 keeping the court fees fixed. The standard theory would predict the following effects: (i) some members will drop out, (ii) those who remain will use the club slightly less because of the income effect of the increased membership fee (assuming tennis playing is normal), and (iii) *average* utilization will rise if the change in the mix of members toward higher demanders outweighs the income effect, otherwise average utilization will fall. Total utilization will certainly fall.

If the sunk cost effect is valid then the analysis of effect (ii) must be changed. The sunk cost effect will increase utilization, which is in the opposite direction of the income effect. If the sunk cost effect is large enough in magnitude, then raising the membership fee could increase *total* utilization. Given the wide ranging uses of multipart pricing this analysis could have many important applications.

5. SEARCHING AND THE PSYCHOPHYSICS OF PRICES

Example 6. (a) You set off to buy a clock radio at what you believe to be the cheapest store in your area. When you arrive, you find that the radio costs $25, a price consistent with your priors (the suggested retail price is $35). As you are about to make the purchase, a reliable friend comes by and tells you that the same radio is selling for $20 at another store ten minutes away. Do you go to the other store? What is the minimum price differential which would induce you to go to the other store? (b) Now suppose that instead of a radio you are buying a color television for $500 and your friend tells you it is available at the other store for $495. Same questions.

On the second page of his price theory text, George Stigler (1970) states a traditional theory of consumer search behavior:

> 'To maximize his utility the buyer searches for additional prices until the expected saving from the

---

[12]What if the price is 'unreasonable'? In this case the consumer will feel pain that is a function of the difference between the price paid and some reference (or just) price. Similarly if the price is especially low there will be extra pleasure that is related to the difference between the reference price and the price paid. A complete analysis of these issues will be presented in a future paper.

purchase equals the cost of visiting one more dealer. Then he stops searching, and buys from the dealer who quotes the lowest price he has encountered.'

Example 6 suggests an alternative to Stigler's theory. The alternative theory states that search for any purchase will continue until the expected amount saved as a proportion of the total price equals some critical value.

This hypothesis is a simple application of the Weber-Fechner law of psychophysics.[13] The law states that the just noticeable difference in any stimulus is proportional to the stimulus. If the stimulus is price then the law implies that

$$\Delta p/p = k,$$

where Δp is the just noticeable difference, p is the mean price, and k is a constant.

Again this hypothesis is difficult to test empirically. However, a recent paper by Pratt, Wise, and Zeckhauser (1977) studied price dispersions of consumer goods and found nearly a linear relationship between the mean price of a good and its standard deviation. They interpret this result as inconsistent with the standard search theory: 'if search costs were constant, we might expect that the expected gains from searching would lead to ratios between standard deviation and price that declined rather rapidly with mean price'.[14] While these results are supportive, they are inconclusive because the observed price dispersions represent an equilibrium resulting from both buyer *and* seller behavior. Thus even if consumers searched optimally, firm behavior could produce this result. A cleaner test may only be possible experimentally.

Because of its psychophysical foundation, prospect theory can be used to model search behavior as observed in Example 6. To see how, reconsider eq. (2) (repeated here for convenience),

$$V(x,p;y,q) = v(y) + \pi(p)[v(x) - v(y)]. \quad (2)$$

Notice that the decision weight given to the chance of winning, $\pi(p)$, is multiplied by the difference in the variation of the alternative prizes $(v(x) - v(y))$ rather than the value of the monetary differences $(v(x - y))$. Because of the concavity of $v, v(x) - v(y) < v(x - y)$. Similarly, the value of obtaining the clock radio at $20 instead of $25 would be $\bar{v}(-25) - \bar{v}(-20)$ which is greater than $\bar{v}(-500) -$

$\bar{v}(-495)$ because of the convexity of $\bar{v}$. Put simply, $5 seems like a lot to save on a $25 radio but not much on a $500 TV. Needless to say, it would be virtually unnoticed on a $5,000 car.

Market behavior consistent with this hypothesis is easy to find. An old selling trick is to quote a low price for a stripped-down model and then coax the consumer into a more expensive version in a series of increments each of which seems small relative to the entire purchase. (One reason why new cars have whitewall tires and old cars do not is that $20 seems a small extra to equip a *car* with whitewalls but a large extra for a new set of *tires*.) Funeral parlors, as well as automobile dealers, are said to make a living off this idea.[15]

6. CHOOSING NOT TO CHOOSE: REGRET

Example 7.[16] Members of the Israeli Army display a resistance to trading patrol assignments, even when it would be convenient for both individuals to do so.

Example 8.[17] Mr. A is waiting in line at a movie theater. When he gets to the ticket window he is told that as the 100,000th customer of the theater he has just won $100.

Mr. B is waiting in line at a different theater. The man in front of him wins $1,000 for being the 1,000,000th customer of the theater. Mr. B wins $150.

Would you rather be Mr. A or Mr. B?

This and the following section discuss situations where individuals voluntarily restrict their choices. In section 5 the motive is self-control. Choices in the future are reduced because the current self doesn't trust the future self. In this section we consider a motive for reducing choice which is a special kind of decision-making cost. Here the act of choosing or even just the knowledge that choice exists induces costs, and these costs can be reduced or eliminated by restricting the choice set in advance. These costs

---

[13]For more on the Weber–Fechner Law see Stigler (1965).
[14]Pratt, Wise, and Zeckhauser (1977, p. 22).

[15]Madison Avenue also seems to understand this principle. An advertisement appeared on television recently for a variable month car loan (46 months, say, instead of the usual 48). The bank wanted to stress the amount of interest that could be saved by financing the car over two fewer months. In the advertisement an actor had about $5,000 in bills stacked up on a table to represent the total amount of money repaid. He then took $37 representing the interest saved, removed it from the pile, and said, 'It may not seem like a lot here . . .' (pointing to the pile) '. . . but it will feel like a lot here' (pointing to his wallet).
[16]This example is due to Daniel Kahneman and Amos Tversky.
[17]This example is due to Ronald Howard.

fall into the general category of *regret* which will be defined to include the related concepts of *guilt* and *responsibility*.

That responsibility can cause regret is well illustrated by Example 7. If two men trade assignments and one is killed, the other must live with the knowledge that it could (should?) have been he. By avoiding such trades these costs are reduced. Since the opportunity to exchange assignments must surely be a valued convenience, the observed resistance to trading suggests that the potential responsibility costs are non-trivial.

Sometimes just information can induce psychic costs. This is obvious, since it is always possible to make someone feel terrible just by relating a horror story of sufficient horror. Example 8 illustrates the point in a more interesting way. There seems little doubt that were the prizes won by Mr. A and Mr. B the same, Mr. A would be better off. The knowledge that he just missed winning causes regret to Mr. B, enough to cause some people to prefer Mr. A's position in the example as stated!

Whenever choice can induce regret consumers have an incentive to eliminate the choice. They will do so whenever the expected increase in utility (pleasure) derived from making their own choices is less than the expected psychic costs which the choices will induce.

Regret, in prospect theory, can be modeled through induced changes in the reference point. In Example 8, Mr. A simply gains $100 or $v(100)$. Mr. B however must deal with the near miss. If, for example, the person in front of him cut into the line he may feel he has gained $150 but lost $1,000 yielding $v(150) + \bar{v}(-1,000)$.

Two markets seem to have been strongly influenced by this preference for not choosing: the health care industry, and the vacation and recreation industry.

Choosing not to choose is apparent at many levels in the health care industry. It explains, I believe, two major institutional features of the health delivery system. A puzzle for many economists who have studied the industry is the popularity of shallow, first dollar (no deductible or low deductible) coverage which is precisely the opposite pattern which would be predicted by a theoretical analysis of the problem. Many economists have criticized the system because the insurance creates a zero marginal cost situation for most consumers and this, it is argued, helps create the massive inflation we have experienced in this sec-

tor in recent years. The analysis may be correct, but an important issue seems ignored. Why do consumers want the first dollar coverage? I believe the reasons involve regret. Most consumers find decisions involving tradeoffs between health care and money very distasteful. This is especially true when the decision is made for someone else like a child. A high deductible policy would force individuals to make many such decisions, at considerable psychic costs. The costs can occur no matter which way the decision is made. Consider a couple which must decide whether to spend X for a diagnostic test for their child. There is some small probability p that the child has a serious disease which could be treated if detected early enough. There will surely be regret if the decision is made not to get the test and the child later is found to have the disease. If the disease can be fatal, then the regret may loom so large that the test will be administered even for very large values of X or very small values of p. Yet once the test is ordered and the likely negative result is obtained, the couple may regret the expenditure, especially if it is large relative to their income. Obviously, these costs are avoided if all health care is prepaid, via either first dollar coverage or a prepaid health organization.

Though many individuals seem averse to explicit tradeoffs between money and health, money does not have to be at stake for regret to enter the picture. The health industry has frequently been criticized for failing to involve the patient in the decision-making process, even when no out-of-pocket expenses are involved. Again, regret seems to provide an attractive explanation for this characteristic of the system. Suppose that a patient must have an operation, but two different procedures are possible. Assume that only one of the procedures can ever be attempted on any individual, that each has the same probability of success and (to make the case as clean as possible) that physicians know that if one procedure doesn't work the other would have. Clearly in this situation a rational consumer would want the physician to make the choice and furthermore, he would not want to know that a choice existed! In less dramatic examples there will still be an incentive to let the physician choose, particularly if the physician knows the patient well (and thus can do a good job of reflecting the patient's preferences).

Of course the physician must then bear all the responsibility costs so there may be advantages to further delegation. One method is to obtain a second opinion, which at least divides the responsibility. Another is to utilize rules-of-thumb and standard-operating-procedures which may eliminate the costs altogether.[18]

The other major example of the market yielding to consumer preferences to not choose is the recreation industry. An excellent case in point is Club Med which is actually not a club but rather a worldwide chain of resort hotels.[19] One heavily promoted characteristic of the resorts is that they are virtually cashless. Almost all activities including food and drink are prepaid, and extra drinks are paid for via poppit beads which are worn necklace style.[20] This example presents an interesting contrast with the health example. Consumers may feel guilty about not buying health and guilty about spending on their vacation. Having everything prepaid avoids decisions about whether to *spend* to do something, and reduces the psychic costs of engaging in the costly activities. The reduction in psychic costs may be enough so that a consumer would prefer to spend $1,000 for a vacation than to spend $400 on plane fare and another $500 in $20 increments, especially given the hypothesis of the preceding section. Club Med has taken the prepaid concept furthest, but the basic idea is prevalent in the recreation industry. Other examples include ocean cruises, 'package travel tours', and one price amusement parks such as Marriot's Great America.

7. PRECOMMITMENT AND SELF-CONTROL[21]

Example 9. A group of hungry economists is awaiting dinner when a large can of cashews is opened and placed on the coffee table. After half the can is devoured in three minutes, everyone agrees to put the rest of the cashews into the pantry.

Example 10. Professor X agreed to give a paper at the AEA meetings 'to assure that the paper would get written by the end of the year'.

A basic axiom of economic theory is that additional choices can only make one better-off (and that an additional constraint can only make one worse-off). An exception is sometimes made due to decision-making costs, a concept that was expanded to include regret in the previous section. This section demonstrates that the axiom is also violated when self-control problems are present.

The question examined now is why individuals impose rules on themselves. This question was brought to economists' attention by Strotz (1955/56) in his now classic paper on dynamic inconsistency. Strotz begins his article with a famous quote from the Odyssey:

> '. . . but you must bind me hard and fast, so that I cannot stir from the spot where you will stand me . . . and if I beg you to release me, you must tighten and add to my bonds.'

Strotz described Ulysses' problem as one of *changing tastes*. He now would prefer not to steer his ship upon the rocks, but he knows that once he hears the Sirens he will want to get closer to their source and thus to the rocks. The solution Ulysses adopts is to have his crew tie him to the mast. Strotz refers to this type of solution as *precommitment*.

Strotz's formal model concerns savings behavior. How should an individual allocate a fixed exhaustible resource over his lifetime? The major finding in Strotz's paper is that unless the individual has an exponential discount function, he will not follow his own plan. That is, if at time t the individual reconsiders a plan formulated at time $t' < t$, he will change the plan. Thus people will be *inconsistent* over time. While changing tastes can explain inconsistency, they cannot explain precommitment. Why should the person with changing tastes bind himself to his *current* preferences, knowing that he will wish to break the binds in each succeeding period? Yet there is no denying the popularity of precommitment devices. One such device which has always been an enigma to economists is Christmas clubs which currently attract over one billion dollars a year in deposits from millions of depositors. Other examples of precommitment are discussed below.

The key to understanding precommitment is to recognize that it is a device used to solve problems

---

[18]I should add here that these comments about the health sector are strictly of a *positive* nature. I am simply offering an explanation of why the institutions are structured as they are. Policy implications must be drawn carefully.

[19]This example was suggested by Paul Joskow.

[20]'Cash is useless at Club Med. You prepay your vacation before leaving home. Included in the price are room accommodations, three fabulous meals each day, all the wine you can drink at lunch and dinner, scores of sports activities, plus expert instruction and use of rent-free sporting equipment. The only extras, if there are any, are totally up to you. Drinks at the bar, boutique purchases, optimal excursions, beauty salon visits—simply sign and then pay for them before leaving the village. And there's no tipping. So it couldn't be easier to stick to your vacation budget' (from a Club Med Brochure).

[21]The ideas in this section are explored in detail in Thaler and Shefrin (1979). Details on the formal model appear in Shefrin and Thaler (1979). Others who have written in this area are Ainslee (1975), Shelling (1978), Elster (1977) and Scitovsky (1976).

of *self-control*. While this seems obvious, it has not been incorporated in the formal models of dynamic choice behavior. Yet it is not difficult to do so. The concept of self-control suggests the existence of a controller and a controllee. To capture this, the individual can be modeled as an organization with a *planner* and a series of *doers*, one for every time period. Conflict arises because the current doer's preferences are always myopic relative to the planner's. This conflict creates a *control problem* of the same variety as those present in any organization. Since the planner's preferences are consistent over time it does make sense for him to adopt rules to govern the doers' behavior. These rules are adopted for the same reasons employees are not given complete discretion: the existence of a conflict of interest.

Since the full details of the model are available elsewhere I will limit my discussion here to the predictions of the model regarding market behavior. One immediate implication of the model is that self-control problems will be most important for those consumption activities which have a time dimension. Since the planner maximizes a function that depends on the doers' utilities, if all the costs and benefits of a particular activity occur in the present there will be no conflict. Of course, as long as there is a finite budget constraint, any current consumption will reduce future consumption, but the conflicts are likely to be greatest for saving *per se* and for those activities which have an explicit time dimension. For lack of a better term, I will refer to such activities as *investment goods*. Further, goods whose benefits accrue later than their costs (such as education and exercise) are termed *positive investment goods*, while those with the opposite time structure (such as tobacco and alcohol) are termed *negative investment goods*.

Since precommitment usually requires external help (Ulysses needed his crew to tie him to the mast), if it is an important phenomenon we should expect to see evidence of market provision of precommitment services in the investment goods industries. Indeed, such evidence is abundant.

Negative investment goods provide the most dramatic examples: Alcoholics Anonymous, drug abuse centers, diet clubs, 'fat farms', and smoking clinics. Note that addiction is not the only factor involved in these services. Calling food addictive is stretching the definition somewhat, so the diet clubs and fat farms can be considered pure self-control administrators. Even the drug examples such as Alcoholics

Anonymous perform most of their activities for individuals who are 'on the wagon'. The problem is not that they are addicted to alcohol, rather that they would quickly become readdicted. The problem is to avoid the first drink, and AA helps them do that. One extreme technique of precommitment used by alcoholics is taking the drug antabuse which makes the individual sick if he ingests any alcohol.

The most obvious positive investment good is saving itself, and here we find an industry dominated by precommitment devices. Christmas clubs, which have already been mentioned, were particularly noteworthy in previous years because they paid no interest and were thus a 'pure' self-control device.[22] Another curious savings institution is the passbook loan. A typical example would be of an individual who had $8,000 in a savings account and wanted to buy a $5,000 car. Rather than withdraw the $5,000 and lose the 5½% interest it was earning the individual uses the money in the account as collateral for a loan at 8%. These loans are reasonably popular, in spite of the obvious interest costs, because they guarantee that the money in the savings account will be replaced and not spent. A final example is whole life insurance which is often alleged to be a bad investment but again provides a specific savings *plan*.

Other investment goods such as education and exercise evidence self-control considerations in their pricing policies. Virtually all such services are sold via prepaid packages. This device lowers the cost to the doer of engaging in the investment activity on a day-to-day basis. If the sunk cost effect is also present then the membership fee will also act as an actual inducement to go.

8. CONCLUSION

Friedman and Savage (1948) defend economic theory as a positive science using an analogy to a billiard player:

> 'Consider the problem of predicting, before each shot, the direction of travel of a billiard ball hit by an expert billiard player. It would be possible to construct one or more mathematical formulas that would give the direction of travel that would score

[22]The vice president of one savings bank has reported to me the results of a survey his bank completed on Christmas club users. They found that the average savings account balance of Christmas club users was over $3,000. This suggests that Christmas clubs should not be considered as a device for people who can't save but as a tool of people who do!

points and, among these, would indicate the one (or more) that would leave the balls in the best positions. The formulas might, of course, be extremely complicated, since they would necessarily take account of the location of the balls in relationship to one another and to the cushions and of the complicated phenomena introduced by 'english'. Nonetheless, it seems not at all unreasonable that excellent predictions would be yielded by the hypothesis that the billiard player made his shots *as if* he knew the formulas, could estimate accurately by eye the angles etc., from the formulas, and could then make the ball travel in the direction indicated by the formulas. It would in no way disprove or contradict the hypothesis or weaken our confidence in it, if it should turn out that the billiard player had never studied any branch of mathematics and was utterly incapable of making the necessary calculations: unless he was capable in some way of reaching approximately the same result as that obtained from the formulas, he would not in fact be likely to be an expert billiard player.'[23]

I would like to make two points about this passage and the relationship between Friedman and Savage's position and mine. First, I do not base my critique of the economic theory of the consumer on an attack of the assumptions. I agree with Friedman and Savage that positive theories should be evaluated on the basis of their ability to predict behavior. In my judgment, for the classes of problems discussed in this paper, economic theory fails this test.

Second, Friedman and Savage only claim that their mathematical model would be a good predictor of the behavior of an *expert* billiard player. It is instructive to consider how one might build models of two non-experts.

A novice who has played only a few times will mainly be concerned with the choice of what ball to try to sink, which will depend primarily on the *perceived* degree of difficulty of the shot. (In contrast, an expert can make nearly any open shot and is likely to sink 50 or more in a row. Thus he will be concerned with planning several shots ahead.) The novice will use little or no 'english', will pay little attention to where the cue ball goes after the shot, and may be subject to some optical illusions that cause him to systematically mishit some other shots.

An intermediate player who has played an average of two hours a week for twenty years may only average 4 or 5 balls per turn (compared with expert's 50). He will have much less control of the cue ball

after it strikes another ball and will have some shots that he knows cause him trouble (perhaps long-bank shots or sharp angles). He will plan ahead, but rarely more than one or two shots.

Clearly, descriptive models for the novice or intermediate will have to be quite different than the model for the expert. If one wanted to model the behavior of the *average* billiard player, the model selected would be for some kind of intermediate player, and would probably resemble the model of the novice more than the model of the expert. Rules-of-thumb and heuristics would have important roles in this model.

It is important to stress that both the novice and intermediate players described above behave rationally. They choose different shots than the expert does because they have different technologies. Nonetheless, the expert model has a distinct normative flavor. The model chooses from all the shots available the *best* shot. Thus the novice and intermediate players choose rationally and yet violate a normative model. The reason, of course, is that the model is not an acceptable normative (or positive) model for *them*. The novice model (aim at the ball that seems easiest to sink—don't worry about much else) is also a normative model. It is the best the novice can do. Clearly the relationship between rationality and normative models is a delicate one.

How does consumer behavior relate to billiard behavior? Again there will be various classes of consumers. Some will be experts (Ph.D's in Economics?), others will be novices (children?). What I have argued in this paper is that the orthodox economic model of consumer behavior is, in essence, a model of robot-like experts. As such, it does a poor job of predicting the behavior of the average consumer.[24] This is not because the average consumer is dumb, but rather that he does not spend all of his time thinking about how to make decisions. A grocery shopper, like the intermediate billiard player, spends a couple of hours a week shopping and devotes a rational amount of (scarce) mental energy to that task. Sensible rules-of-thumb, such as don't waste, may lead to occasional deviations from the expert model, such as the failure to ignore sunk costs, but these shoppers are doing the best they can.

---

[23]Friedman and Savage (1948, p. 298).

[24]Some related issues have been discussed in the literature on the theory of the firm. See, for example, Winter (1975) and the references cited therein.

Prospect theory and the planner–doer model attempt to describe *human* decision-makers coping with a very complex and demanding world. Failure to develop positive theories such as these will leave economists wondering why people are frequently aiming at the balls lined up right in front of the pockets rather than at the three ball carom their computer model has identified as being optimal.

REFERENCES

Ainslie, George, 1975, Specious reward: A behavioral theory of impulsiveness and impulse control, Psychological Bulletin 82, no. 4, July, 463–496.

Allais, M., 1953, Le compartement de l'homme rationnel devant le risque, critique des postulats et axiomes de l'ecole Americaine, Econometrica 21, 503–546.

Aronson, Elliot and Judson Mills, 1959, The effects of severity of initiation on liking for a group, Journal of Abnormal and Social Psychology 59, 177–181.

Becker, Gary S., 1962, Irrational behavior and economic theory, Journal of Political Economy, Feb., 1–13.

Beeker, S., J. Ronen and G. Sorter, 1974, Opportunity costs—An experimental approach, Journal of Accounting Research, 317–329.

Demsetz, Harold, 1972, When does the rule of liability matter, Journal of Legal Studies, Jan., 13, 28.

Elster, Jon, 1977, Ulysses and the sirens: A theory of imperfect rationality, Social Science Information XVI, no. 5, 469–526.

Friedman, M. and L.J. Savage, 1948, The utility analysis of choices involving risks, Journal of Political Economy 56, 279–304.

Gerard, Harold B. and Groves C. Mathewson, 1966, The effects of severity of initiation on liking for a group: A replication, Journal of Experimental Social Psychology 2, 278–287.

Grether, David M., 1979, Bayes rule as a descriptive model: The representativeness heuristic, Social Science Working Paper no. 245 (California Institute of Technology) Jan.

Grether, D. and C. Plott, 1979, Economic theory of choice and the preference reversal phenomenon, American Economic Review, Sept., 623–638.

Kagel, John and Ramond Battalio, 1975, Experimental studies of consumer behavior using laboratory animals, Economic Inquiry, March, 22–38.

Kahneman, Daniel and Amos Tversky, 1979, Prospect theory, an analysis of decision under risk, Econometrica 47, March.

McGlothin, W.H., 1956, Stability of choices among uncertain alternatives, American Journal of Psychology 69, 604–615.

Neumann, B.R. and L.A. Friedman, 1978, Opportunity costs: Further evidence through an experimental replication, Journal of Accounting Research, Autumn, 400–410.

Pratt, John, David Wise and Richard Zeckhauser, 1977, Price variations in almost competitive markets (Harvard University, Kennedy School of Government, Cambridge, MA).

Schelling, T.C., 1978, Egonomics, or the art of self-management, The American Economic Review 63, no. 2, May, 290–294.

Scitovsky, Tibor, 1976, The joyless economy (Oxford University Press, New York).

Shefrin, H.M. and Richard Thaler, 1979, Rules and discretion in intertemporal choice (Cornell University, Ithaca, NY) June.

Simon, Herbert, 1957, Models of man (Wiley, New York).

Stigler, George, 1965, Essays in the history of economics (University of Chicago Press, Chicago, IL).

Stigler, George, 1970, The theory of price (Macmillan, New York).

Slovic, Paul, Baruch Fischhoff and Sarah Lichtenstein, 1977, Behavioral decision theory, Annual Review of Psychology 28, 1–39.

Strotz, Robert, 1955/56, Myopia and inconsistency in dynamic utility maximization, Review of Economic Studies 23, 165–180.

Thaler, Richard and H.M. Shefrin, 1979, An economic theory of self-control (Cornell University, Ithaca, NY) June.

Tversky, Amos and Daniel Kahneman, 1974, Judgment under uncertainty: Heuristics and biases, Science, 1124–1131.

United States Congress Committee on Government Operations, 1976, Teton dam disaster, Union Calendar no. 837, House Report no. 94–1667, Sept., 23.

United States Senate Hearings before the Subcommittee on Consumer Affairs of the Committee on Banking, Housing and Urban Affairs, 1975, Oct. 9.

Von Neumann, J. and O. Morgenstern, 1944, Theory of games and economic behavior (Princeton University Press, Princeton, NJ).

Weiss, Y., A. Hall and F. Dong, 1978, The effect of price and income in the investment in schooling: Evidence from the Seattle-Denver NIT experiment, SRI International.

Winter, Sidney, 1975, Optimization and evaluation in the theory of the firm, in: Richard Day and Theodore Groves, eds., Adaptive economic models (Academic Press, New York).

A New Approach to Consumer Theory*

KELVIN J. LANCASTER**

Kelvin J. Lancaster (B.Sc., University of Sydney, 1948; B.A., 1949; M.A., 1953; B.Sc., University of London, 1953; Ph.D., 1958) was born in 1924 in Sydney, Australia. Before joining the faculty of Columbia University in 1966, where he currently is the John Bates Clark Professor of Economics, Lancaster served on the faculties of the University of London and The Johns Hopkins University. His publications, which include development of the theory of second best (with R.G. Lipsey) and the "characteristics" approach to consumer theory, which emphasizes product variety and differentiation, have made significant contributions to our understanding of microeconomic phenomena. The author of several books, including *Consumer Demand: A New Approach* and *Variety, Equity and Efficiency,* Professor Lancaster is a Fellow of the Econometric Society.

I. THE CURRENT STATUS OF CONSUMER THEORY

The theory of consumer behavior in deterministic situations as set out by, say, Debreu (1959, 1960) or Uzawa (1960) is a thing of great aesthetic beauty, a jewel set in a glass case. The product of a long process of refinement from the nineteenth-century utility theorists through Slutsky and Hicks-Allen to the economists of the last twenty-five years,[1] it has been shorn of all irrelevant postulates so that it now stands as an example of how to extract the minimum of results from the minimum of assumptions.

To the process of slicing away with Occam's razor, the author made a small contribution (1957). This brought forth a reply by Johnson (1958) which suggested, somewhat tongue-in-cheek, that the determinateness of the sign of the substitution effect (the only substantive result of the theory of consumer behavior) could be derived from the proposition that goods are goods.

Johnson's comment, on reflection, would seem to be almost the best summary that can be given of the current state of the theory of consumer behavior. All

*Reprinted from *Journal of Political Economy* (April 1966) by permission of The University of Chicago Press. Copyright 1966, pp. 132–157.
**The author wishes to acknowledge helpful comments from various sources, including Gary Becker, Harry Johnson, and colleagues and students at Johns Hopkins University, especially Carl Christ, F. T. Sparrow, William Poole, C. Blackorby, T. Amemiya, and T. Tsushima.
[1]The American Economic Association *Index of Economic Journals* lists 151 entries under category 2.111 (utility, demand, theory of the household) over the period 1940 to 1963.

intrinsic properties of particular goods, those properties that make a diamond quite obviously something different from a loaf of bread, have been omitted from the theory, so that a consumer who consumes diamonds alone is as rational as a consumer who consumes bread alone, but one who sometimes consumes bread, sometimes diamonds (*ceteris paribus,* of course), is irrational. Thus, the only property which the theory can build on is the property shared by all goods, which is simply that they are goods.

Indeed, we can continue the argument further, since goods are simply what consumers would like more of; and we must be neutral with respect to differences in consumer tastes (some consumers might like more of something that other consumers do not want), that the ultimate proposition is that *goods are what are thought of as goods.*

In spite of the denial of the relevance of intrinsic properties to the pure theory, there has always been a subversive undercurrent suggesting that economists continue to take account of these properties. Elementary textbooks bristle with substitution examples about butter and margarine, rather than about shoes and ships, as though the authors believed that there was something intrinsic to butter and margarine that made them good substitutes and about automobiles and gasoline that made them somehow intrinsically complementary. Market researchers, advertisers, and manufacturers also act as though they believe that knowledge of (or belief in) the intrinsic properties of goods is relevant to the way consumers will react toward them.

The clearest case of conflict between a belief that goods do have intrinsic properties relevant to consumer theory but that they are not taken into account has been the long search for a definition of "intrinsic complementarity." The search was successful only where Morishima (1959) turned from traditional theory to an approach somewhat similar to that of the present paper.

Perhaps the most important aspects of consumer behavior relevant to an economy as complex as that of the United States are those of consumer reactions to new commodities and to quality variations. Traditional theory has nothing to say on these. In the case of new commodities, the theory is particularly helpless. We have to expand from a commodity space of dimension n to one of dimension $n + 1$, replacing the old utility function by a completely new one, and even a complete map of the consumer's preferences

among the n goods provides absolutely no information about the new preference map. A theory which can make no use of so much information is a remarkably empty one. Even the technique of supposing the existence of a utility function for all possible goods, including those not yet invented, and regarding the prices of nonexistent goods as infinite—an incredible stretching of the consumers' powers of imagination—has no predictive value.

Finally we can note the unsuitability of traditional theory for dealing with many of the manifestly important aspects of actual relationships between goods and consumers in I. F. Pearce's (1964) recent heroic but rather unsuccessful attempts to deal with complementarity, substitution, independence, and neutral want associations within the conventional framework.

II. A NEW APPROACH

Like many new approaches, the one set out in this paper draws upon several elements that have been utilized elsewhere. The chief technical novelty lies in breaking away from the traditional approach that goods are the direct objects of utility and, instead, supposing that it is the properties or characteristics of the goods from which utility is derived.

We assume that consumption is an activity in which goods, singly or in combination, are inputs and in which the output is a collection of characteristics. Utility or preference orderings are assumed to rank collections of characteristics and only to rank collections of goods indirectly through the characteristics that they possess. A meal (treated as a single good) possesses nutritional characteristics but it also possesses aesthetic characteristics, and different meals will possess these characteristics in different relative proportions. Furthermore, a dinner party, a combination of two goods, a meal and a social setting, may possess nutritional, aesthetic, and perhaps intellectual characteristics different from the combination obtainable from a meal and a social gathering consumed separately.

In general—and the richness of the approach springs more from this than from anything else— even a single good will possess more than one characteristic, so that the simplest consumption activity will be characterized by joint outputs. Furthermore, the same characteristic (for example, aesthetic properties) may be included among the joint outputs of many consumption activities so that goods which are apparently unrelated in certain of their characteristics may be related in others.

We shall assume that the structure we have interposed between the goods themselves and the consumer's preferences is, in principle, at least, of an objective kind. That is, the characteristics possessed by a good or a combination of goods are the same for all consumers and, given units of measurement, are in the same quantities,[2] so that the personal element in consumer choice arises in the choice between collections of characteristics only, not in the allocation of characteristics to the goods. The objective nature of the goods-characteristics relationship plays a crucial role in the analysis and enables us to distinguish between objective and private reactions to such things as changes in relative prices.

The essence of the new approach can be summarized as follows, each assumption representing a break with tradition:

1. The good, per se, does not give utility to the consumer; it possesses characteristics, and these characteristics give rise to utility.

2. In general, a good will possess more than one characteristic, and many characteristics will be shared by more than one good.

3. Goods in combination may possess characteristics different from those pertaining to the goods separately.

A move in the direction of the first assumption has already been made by various workers including Strotz (1957, 1959) and Gorman (1959), with the "utility tree" and other ideas associating a particular good with a particular type of utility. The theory set out here goes much further than these ideas. Multiple characteristics, structurally similar to those of the present paper but confined to a particular problem and a point utility function, are implicit in the classical "diet problem" of Stigler (1945), and multidimensioned utilities have been used by workers in other fields, for example, Thrall (1954). The third assumption, of activities involving complementary collections of goods, has been made by Morishima (1959) but in the context of single-dimensioned utility.

A variety of other approaches with similarities to that of the present paper occur scattered through the literature, for example, in Quandt (1956), or in Becker (1965), or in various discussions of investment-portfolio problems. These are typically set out as *ad hoc* approaches to particular problems. Perhaps the most important aspect of this paper is that the model is set out as a general replacement of the traditional analysis (which remains as a special case), rather than as a special solution to a special problem.

It is clear that only by moving to multiple characteristics can we incorporate many of the intrinsic qualities of individual goods. Consider the choice between a gray Chevrolet and a red Chevrolet. On ordinary theory these are either the same commodity (ignoring what may be a relevant aspect of the choice situation) or different commodities (in which case there is no a priori presumption that they are close substitutes). Here we regard them as goods associated with satisfaction vectors which differ in only one component, and we can proceed to look at the situation in much the same way as the consumer—or even the economist, in private life—would look at it.

Traditional theory is forever being forced to interpret quite common real-life happenings, such as the effects of advertising in terms of "change of taste," an entirely non-operational concept since there is no way of predicting the relationship between preference before and after the change. The theory outlined here, although extremely rich in useful ways of thinking about consumer behavior, may also be thought to run the danger of adding to the economist's extensive collection of non-operational concepts. If this were true, it need not, of course, inhibit the heuristic application of the theory. Even better, however, the theory implies predictions that differ from those of traditional theory, and the predictions of the new approach seem to fit better the realities of consumer behavior.

III. A MODEL OF CONSUMER BEHAVIOR

To obtain a working model from the ideas outlined above, we shall make some assumptions which are, on balance, neither more nor less heroic than those made elsewhere in our present economic theorizing and which are intended to be no more and no less permanent parts of the theory.

1. We shall regard an individual good or a col-

[2]Since the units in which the characteristics are measured are arbitrary, the objectivity criterion relating goods and characteristics reduces to the requirement that the *relative* quantities of a particular characteristic between unit quantities of any pair of goods should be the same for all consumers.

lection of goods as a consumption activity and associate a scalar (the level of the activity) with it. We shall assume that the relationship between the level of activity k, y_k, and the goods consumed in that activity to be both linear and objective, so that, if x_j is the jth commodity we have

$$x_j = \sum_k a_{jk}y_k, \tag{1}$$

and the vector of total goods required for a given activity vector is given by

$$x = Ay. \tag{2}$$

Since the relationships are assumed objective, the equations are assumed to hold for all individuals, the coefficients a_{jk} being determined by the intrinsic properties of the goods themselves and possibly the context of technological knowledge in the society.

2. More heroically, we shall assume that each consumption activity produces a fixed vector of characteristics[3] and that the relationship is again linear, so that, if z_i is the amount of the ith characteristic

$$z_i = \sum_k b_{ik}y_k, \tag{3}$$

or

$$z = By. \tag{4}$$

Again, we shall assume that the coefficients b_{ik} are objectively determined—in principle, at least—for some arbitrary choice of the units of z_i.

3. We shall assume that the individual possesses an ordinal utility function on characteristics $U(z)$ and that he will choose a situation which maximizes $U(z)$. $U(z)$ is provisionally assumed to possess the ordinary convexity properties of a standard utility function.

The chief purpose of making the assumption of linearity is to simplify the problem. A viable model could certainly be produced under the more general set of relationships

$$F_k(z, x) = 0, \quad k = 1 \ldots m. \tag{5}$$

The model could be analyzed in a similar way to that used by Samuelson (1953b) and others in analyzing production, although the existence of much jointness

among outputs in the present model presents difficulties.

In this model, the relationship between the collections of characteristics available to the consumer—the vectors z—which are the direct ingredients of his preferences and his welfare, and the collections of goods available to him—the vectors x—which represent his relationship with the rest of the economy, is not direct and one-to-one, as in the traditional model, but indirect, through the activity vector y.

Consider the relationships which link z and x. These are the equation systems: $x = Ay$ (2) and $z = By$ (4). Suppose that there are r characteristics, m activities, and n goods. Only if $r = m = n$ will there be a one-to-one relationship between z and x. In this case both the B and A matrixes are square (the number of variables equals the number of equations in both sets of equations) and we can solve for y in terms of x, $y = A^{-1}x$, giving $z = BA^{-1}x$. $U(z)$ can be written directly and unambiguously as a function $u(x)$. Otherwise the relations are between vectors in spaces of different dimensions. Consider some x^* in the case in which $m > n$: equation (2) places only n restrictions on the m-vector y, so that y can still be chosen with $m - n$ degrees of freedom. If $r < m$, then there are $m - r$ degrees of freedom in choosing y, given some z, but whether the ultimate relationship gives several choices of z for a given x, or several x for a given z, and whether all vectors z are attainable, depends on the relationships between r, m, and n and the structures of the matrixes A, B. In general, we will expect that the consumer may face a choice among many paths linking goods collections with characteristics collections. The simple question asked (in principle) in the traditional analysis—does a particular consumer prefer collection x_1 or collection x_2—no longer has a direct answer, although the question, does he prefer characteristics collection z_1 or z_2, does have such an answer.

If we take the standard choice situation facing the consumer in a free market, with a linear budget constraint, this situation, in our model, becomes:

> Maximize $U(z)$
> subject to $px \leqq k$
> with $\quad z = By$
> $\quad\quad x = Ay$
> $\quad x, y, z \geqq 0.$

This is a non-linear program of an intractable kind. The problem of solution need not worry us here,

---

[3]The assumption that the consumption technology A, B is fixed is a convenience for discussing those aspects of the model (primarily static) that are the chief concern of this paper. The consequences of relaxing this particular assumption is only one of many possible extensions and expansions of the ideas presented and are discussed by the author elsewhere (Lancaster, 1966).

since we are interested only in the properties of the solution.

IV. THE SIMPLIFIED MODEL

We shall simplify the model in the initial stages by supposing that there is a one-to-one correspondence between goods and activities so that we can write the consumer-choice program in the simpler form

$$\text{Maximize } U(z)$$
$$\text{subject to } px \leqq k$$
$$\text{with } z = Bx$$
$$z, x \geqq 0.$$

This is still, of course, a non-linear program, but we now have a single step between goods and characteristics.

The model consists of four parts. There is a maximand $U(z)$ operating on characteristics, that is, U is defined on characteristics-space (C-space). The budget constraint $px \leqq k$ is defined on goods-space (G-space). The equation system $z = Bx$ represents a transformation between G-space and C-space. Finally, there are non-negativity constraints $z, x \geqq 0$ which we shall assume to hold initially, although in some applications and with some sign conventions they may not always form part of the model.

In traditional consumer analysis, both the budget constraint and the utility function are defined on G-space, and we can immediately relate the two as in the ordinary textbook indifference-curve diagram. Here we can only relate the utility function to the budget constraint after both have been defined on the same space. We have two choices: (1) We can transform the utility function into G-space and relate it directly to the budget constraint; (2) we can transform the budget constraint into C-space and relate it directly to the utility function $U(z)$.

Each of these techniques is useful in different circumstances. In the case of the first, we can immediately write $U(z) = U(Bx) = u(x)$, so we have a new utility function directly in terms of goods, but the properties of the function $u(x)$ depend crucially on the structure of the matrix B and this, together with the constraints $x \geqq 0$ and $z = Bx \geqq 0$ give a situation much more complex than that of conventional utility maximization. The second technique again depends crucially on the structure of B and again will generally lead to a constraint of a more complex kind than in conventional analysis.

The central role in the model is, of course, played by the transformation equation $z = Bx$ and the structure and qualitative[4] properties of the matrix B. Most of the remainder of the paper will be concerned with the relationship between the properties of B, which we can call the *consumption technology*[5] of the economy, and the behavior of consumers.

Certain properties of the transformations between G- and C-space follow immediately from the fact that B is a matrix of constants, and the transformation $z = Bx$ is linear. These can be stated as follows, proof being obvious.

> *a)* A convex set in G-space will transform into a convex set in C-space, so that the budget constraint $px \leqq k$, $x \geqq 0$ will become a convex constraint on the z's.
>
> *b)* An inverse transformation will not necessarily exist, so that an arbitrary vector z in C-space may have no vector x in G-space corresponding to it.
>
> *c)* Where an inverse transformation does exist from C-space into G-space, it will transform convex sets into convex sets so that, for any set of z's which do have images in G-space, the convexity of the U function on the z's will be preserved in relation to the x's.

The properties are sufficient to imply that utility maximization subject to constraint will lead to determinate solutions for consumer behavior.

V. THE STRUCTURE OF CONSUMPTION TECHNOLOGY

The consumption technology, which is as important a determinant of consumer behavior as the particular shape of the utility function, is described fully only by the A and B matrixes together, but certain types of behavior can be related to more generalized descriptions of the technology. We shall distinguish broadly between structural properties of the technology, such as the relationship between the number of rows and columns of B and/or A and whether A, B are decomposable, and qualitative properties, such as the signs of the elements of A and B.

The leading structural property of the consumption technology is the relationship between the num-

---

[4] "Qualitative" is used here in a somewhat more general sense than in the author's work on the properties of qualitatively defined systems for which see Lancaster (1962, 1965).

[5] If the relationship between goods and activities is not one-to-one, the consumption technology consists of the two matrixes B, A, as in the technology of the Von Neumann growth model.

ber of characteristics (r) and the number of activities (m), that is, between the number of rows and columns of B. It will be assumed that B contains no linear dependence, so that its rank is the number of rows or columns, whichever is less. We shall assume, unless otherwise stated, a one-to-one relationship between goods and activities.

1. The number of characteristics is equal to the number of goods. In this case, there is a one-to-one relationship between activities vectors and characteristics vectors. We have $z = Bx$, $x = B^{-1}z$. If B is a permutation of a diagonal matrix then there is a one-to-one relationship between each component of z and each component of y, and the model becomes, by suitable choice of units, exactly the same as the traditional model. If B is not a diagonal permutation, the objects of utility are composite goods rather than individual goods, and the model has some important differences from the conventional analysis. Note how specialized is the traditional case in relation to our general model.

If B is a diagonal permutation but there is not a one-to-one relationship between activities and goods so that A is not a diagonal permutation, we have a model similar to that of Morishima (1959).

2. The number of characteristics is greater than the number of goods. In this case, the relationships $Bx = z$ contain more equations than variables x_1, so that we cannot, in general, find a goods vector x which gives rise to an arbitrarily specified characteristics vector z. We can take a basis of any arbitrarily chosen n characteristics and consider the reduced $n \times n$ system $\bar{B} = \bar{z}$, which gives a one-to-one relationship between n characteristics and the n goods, with the remaining $r - n$ characteristics being determined from the remaining $r - n$ equations and the goods vector x corresponding to $\bar{z}$. In this case, it is generally most useful to analyze consumer behavior by transforming the utility function into G-space, rather than the budget constraint into C-space. What does the transformed utility function look like?

As shown in the Appendix, the utility function transformed into G-space retains its essential convexity. An intuitive way of looking at the situation is to note that all characteristics collections which are actually available are contained in an n-dimensional slice through the r-dimensional utility function, and that all slices through a convex function are themselves convex. The transformation of this n-dimensional slice into G-space preserves this convexity.

For investigation of most aspects of consumer behavior, the case in which the number of characteristics exceeds the number of goods—a case we may often wish to associate with simple societies—can be treated along with the very special case (of which conventional analysis is a special subcase) in which the number of characteristics and goods is equal. In other words, given the consumption technology, we concern ourselves only with the particular n-dimensional slice of the r-dimensional utility function implied by that technology[6] and, since the slice of the utility function has the same general properties as any n-dimensional utility function, we can proceed as if the utility function was defined on only n characteristics.

3. In the third case, in which the number of goods exceeds the number of characteristics, a situation probably descriptive of a complex economy such as that of the United States, there are properties of the situation that are different from those of the two previous cases and from the conventional analysis.

Here, the consumption technology, $z = Bx$, has fewer equations than variables so that, for every characteristics vector there is more than one goods vector. For every point in his characteristics-space, the consumer has a choice between different goods vectors. Given a price vector, this choice is a pure efficiency choice, so that for every characteristics vector the consumer will choose the most efficient combination of goods to achieve that collection of characteristics, and the efficiency criterion will be minimum cost.

The efficiency choice for a characteristics vector z^* will be the solution of the canonical linear program

$$\text{Minimize} \quad px$$
$$\text{subject to } Bx = z^*$$
$$x \geqq 0.$$

Since this is a linear program, once we have the solution x^* for some z^*, with value k^*, we can apply a scalar multiple to fit the solution to any budget

[6]Assuming no decomposability or singularities in the consumption technology matrix B, then, if z_n is the vector of any n components of z and B_n, the corresponding square submatrix of B, the subspace of C-space to which the consumer is confined, is that defined by $z_{r-n} = B_{r-n}B_n^{-1} z_n$, where z_{r-n}, B_{r-n} are the vector and corresponding submatrix of B consisting of the components not included in z_n, B_n.

value k and characteristics vector $(k/k^*)z^*$. By varying z^*, the consumer, given a budget constraint $px = k$, can determine a characteristics frontier consisting of all z such that the value of the above program is just equal to k. There will be a determinate goods vector associated with each point of the characteristics frontier.

As in the previous case, it is easy to show that the set of characteristics vectors in C-space that are preferred or indifferent to z transforms into a convex set in G-space if it is a convex set in C-space; it is also easy to show that the set of z's that can be obtained from the set of x's satisfying the convex constraint $px \leqq k$ is also a convex set. The characteristics frontier is, therefore, concave to the origin, like a transformation curve. For a consumption technology with four goods and two characteristics, the frontier could have any of the three shapes shown in Fig. 1. Note that, in general, if B is a positive matrix, the positive orthant in G-space transforms into a cone which lies in the interior of the positive orthant in C-space, a point illustrated in the diagrams.

A consumer's complete choice subject to a budget constraint $px \leqq k$ can be considered as consisting of two parts:

a) An efficiency choice, determining the characteristics frontier and the associated efficient goods collections.

b) A private choice, determining which point on the characteristics frontier is preferred by him.

The efficiency choice is an objective not a subjective choice. On the assumption that the consumption technology is objective, the characteristics frontier is also objective, and it is the same for all consumers facing the same budget constraint. Furthermore the characteristics frontier is expanded or contracted linearly and proportionally to an increase or decrease in income, so that the frontier has the same *shape* for all consumers facing the same prices, income differences simply being reflected in homogeneous expansion or contraction.

We should note that, if the consumption technology matrix has certain special structural properties, we may obtain a mixture of the above cases. For example, a matrix with the structure

$$B \equiv \begin{bmatrix} B_1 0 \\ 0 B_2 \end{bmatrix},$$

where B_1 is an $(s \times k)$ matrix and B_2 is an $(r - s) \times (n - k)$ matrix, partitions the technology into two disconnected parts, one relating s of the characteristics to k of the goods, the other separately relating $r - s$ of the characteristics to $n - k$ of the goods. We can have $s \geqq k$ and $r - s < n - k$ giving a mixed case.

Dropping the assumption of a one-to-one relationship between goods and activities does not add greatly to the difficulties of the analysis. We have, as part of the technology, $x = Ay$, so that the budget constraint $px \leqq k$ can be written immediately as $pAy \leqq k$. The goods prices transform directly into implicit activity prices $q = pA$. Interesting cases arise, of course. If the number of goods is less than the number of activities, then not all q's are attainable from the set of p's; and if the number of goods exceeds the number of activities, different p vectors will correspond to the same q vector. This implies that certain changes in relative goods prices may leave activity prices, and the consumer's choice situation, unchanged.

In most of the succeeding analysis, we will be concerned with the B matrix and the relationship between activities and characteristics, since this represents the most distinctive part of the theory.

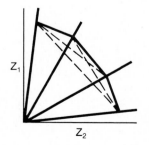 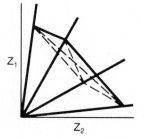 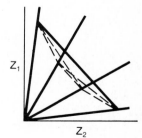

Fig. 1

VI. THE EFFICIENCY SUBSTITUTION EFFECT AND REVEALED PREFERENCE

At this stage, it is desirable to examine the nature of the efficiency choice so that we can appreciate the role it plays in the consumer behavior implied by our model. Consider a case in which there are two characteristics, a case that can be illustrated diagrammatically, and, say, four activities.

The activities-characteristics portion of the consumption technology is defined by the two equations

$$z_1 = b_{11}y_1 + b_{12}y_2 + b_{13}y_3 + b_{14}y_4; \qquad (6.1)$$
$$z_2 = b_{21}y_1 + b_{22}y_2 + b_{23}y_3 + b_{24}y_4.$$

With activity 1 only, the characteristics will be obtained in proportion, b_{14}/b_{21} (the ray labeled 1 in Fig. 2). Similarly with activities 2, 3, 4, one at a time, characteristics will be obtained in proportions b_{12}/b_{22}, b_{13}/b_{23}, b_{14}/b_{24}, respectively, corresponding to the rays 2, 3, 4 in the diagram.

We are given a budget constraint in goods space of the form $\Sigma_i p_i x_i \leq k$. If there is a one-to-one correspondence between goods and activities, the prices of the activities are given by p_i. If there is not a one-to-one relationship, but a goods-activities portion of the consumption technology

$$x_i = a_{i1}y_1 + a_{i2}y_2 + a_{i3}y_3 + a_{i4}y_4 \qquad (6.2)$$
$$i = 1 \ldots n,$$

then the budget constraint can be transformed immediately into characteristics space

$$\left(\sum_i p_i a_{i1} \right) y_1 + \left(\sum_i p_i a_{i2} \right) y_2 + \left(\sum_i p_i a_{i3} \right) y_3 + \qquad (6.3)$$

$$\left(\sum_i p_i a_{i4} \right) y_4 \leq k$$

where the composite prices $q_j = \Sigma_i p_i a_{ij}$, $j = 1 \ldots 4$ represent the prices of each activity. The number of goods in relation to the number of activities is irrelevant at this stage, since each activity has a unique and completely determined price q_j, given the prices of the goods.

Given q_1, q_2, q_3, q_4, and k, the maximum attainable level of each activity in isolation can be written down (corresponding to the points E_1, E_2, E_3, E_4, in Fig. 2) and the lines joining these points represent combinations attainable subject to the budget constraint. In the diagram it has been assumed that prices are such that combinations of 1 and 2, 2 and 3, 3 and 4 are efficient, giving the characteristics frontier, while combinations 1 and 3, 2 and 4, or 1 and 4 are inefficient.

Suppose that the consumer chooses characteristics in the combination represented by the ray z^*, giving a point E^* on the frontier. Now suppose that relative prices change: in particular, that the price of activity 2 rises so that, with income still at k, the point E_2 moves inward on ray 2. If the movement is small enough, the characteristics frontier continues to have a corner at E_2, and the consumer will continue to obtain characteristics in proportion z^* by a combination of activities 1 and 2. If income is adjusted so that the new frontier goes through E^*, the consumer will use the same activities in the same proportions as before.

If the price of activity 2 rises sufficiently, however, the point E_2 will move inward past the line joining E_1 and E_3 to E_2'. Combinations of 1 and 2 and of 2 and 3 are now inefficient combinations of activities, their place on the efficiency frontier being taken by a combination of 1 and 3. The consumer will switch from a combination of activities 1 and 2 to a combination of 1 and 3.

Thus there is an efficiency substitution effect which is essentially a switching effect. If price changes are too small to cause a switch, there is no efficiency substitution effect: If they are large enough, the effect comes from a complete switch from one activity to another.

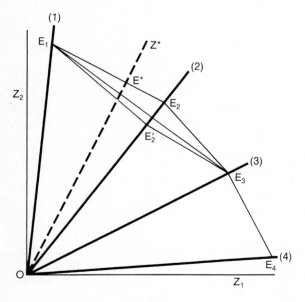

Fig. 2

The manifestation of the efficiency substitution effect in goods space depends on the structure of the A (goods-activities) matrix. There are two polar cases:

a) If there is a one-to-one relationship between goods and activities, the efficiency substitution effect will result in a complete switch from consumption of one good to consumption of another. This might be regarded as typical of situations involving similar but differentiated products, where a sufficiently large price change in one of the products will result in widespread switching to, or away from, the product.

b) If there is not a one-to-one relationship between goods and activities and, in particular, if all goods are used in all activities, the efficiency substitution effect will simply result in less consumption of a good whose price rises, not a complete disappearance of that good from consumption. If all cakes require eggs but in different proportions, a rise in the price of eggs will cause a switch from egg-intensive cakes to others, with a decline in the consumption of eggs, but not to zero.

The existence of an efficiency substitution effect depends, of course, on the number of activities exceeding the number of characteristics (otherwise switching of activities will not, in general, occur[7]) but does not require that the number of goods exceed the number of characteristics. In fact, with two goods, two characteristics, and three activities, the effect may occur. With two goods, two characteristics and one hundred activities (well spread over the spectrum), an almost smooth efficiency substitution effect would occur.

Since the efficiency substitution effect implies that consumers may change goods collections as a result of compensated relative price changes, simply in order to obtain the same characteristics collection in the most efficient manner, it is obvious that the existence of substitution does not of itself either require or imply convexity of the preference function on characteristics. In other words, the axiom of revealed preference may be satisfied even if the consumer always consumes characteristics in fixed proportions (and possibly even if the consumers had *concave* preferences), so that the "revelation" may be simply of efficient choice rather than convexity. A formal proof is given in the Appendix.

VII. OBJECTIVE AND SUBJECTIVE CHOICE AND DEMAND THEORY

In an economy or subeconomy with a complex consumption technology (many goods relative to characteristics), we have seen that there are two types of substitution effect:

1. Changes in relative prices may result in goods bundle I becoming an *inefficient* method of attaining a given bundle of characteristics and being replaced by goods bundle II even when the characteristics bundle is unchanged.

2. Changes in relative prices, with or without causing efficiency substitutions as in type 1, may alter the slope of the characteristics frontier in a segment relevant to a consumer's characteristics choice. The change in the slope of the frontier is analogous to the change in the budget line slope in the traditional case and, with a convex preference function, will result in a substitution of one characteristics bundle for another and, hence, of one goods bundle for another. Note that, even with smoothly convex preferences, this effect may not occur, since the consumer may be on a corner of the polyhedral characteristics frontier, and thus his characteristics choice could be insensitive to a certain range of slope changes on the facets.

The first effect, the efficiency substitution effect, is universal and objective. Subject to consumer ignorance or inefficiency,[8] this substitution effect is independent of the shapes of individual consumers' preference functions and hence of the effects of income distribution.

The second effect, the private substitution effect, has the same properties, in general, as the substitution effect in traditional theory. In particular, an aggregately compensated relative price change combined with a redistribution of income may result

---

[7]This is a somewhat imprecise statement in that, if the B matrix is partitionable into disconnected subtechnologies, for some of which the number of activities exceeds the number of characteristics and for others the reverse, an efficiency-substitution effect may exist over certain groups of activities, although the number of activities is less than number of characteristics over-all.

[8]One of the properties of this model is that it gives scope for the consumer to be more or less efficient in achieving his desired characteristics bundle, although we will usually assume he is completely efficient. This adds a realistic dimension to consumer behavior (traditional theory never permits him to be out of equilibrium) and gives a rationale for the Consumers' Union and similar institutions.

in no substitution effect in the aggregate, or a perverse one.

These two substitution effects are independent—either may occur without the other in certain circumstances—but in general we will expect them both to take place and hence that their effects will be reinforcing, if we are concerned with a complex economy. Thus, the consumer model presented here, in the context of an advanced economy, has, in a sense, more substitution than the traditional model. Furthermore, since part of the total substitution effect arises from objective, predictable, and income-distribution-free efficiency considerations, our confidence in the downward slope of demand curves is increased even when income redistribution takes place.

Since it is well known that satisfaction of the revealed preference axioms *in the aggregate* (never guaranteed by traditional theory) leads to global stability in multimarket models (see, for example, Karlin, 1959), the efficiency substitution effect increases confidence in this stability.

In a simple economy, with few goods or activities relative to characteristics, the efficiency substitution effect will be generally absent. Without this reinforcement of the private substitution effect, we would have some presumption that perverse consumer effects ("Giffen goods," backward-bending supply curves) and lower elasticities of demand would characterize simple economies as compared with complex economies. This seems to be in accord with at least the mythology of the subject, but it is certainly empirically verifiable. On this model, consumption technology as well as income levels differentiate consumers in different societies, and we would not necessarily expect a poor urban American to behave in his consumption like a person at the same real-income level in a simple economy.

VIII. COMMODITY GROUPS, SUBSTITUTES, COMPLEMENTS

In a complex economy, with a large number of activities and goods as well as characteristics, and with a two-matrix *(A, B)* consumption technology, it is obvious that taxonomy could be carried out almost without limit, an expression of the richness of the present approach. Although an elaborate taxonomy is not very useful, discussion of a few selected types of relationships between goods can be of use. One of the important features of this model is that

we can discuss relationships between goods, as revealed in the structure of the technology. In the conventional approach, there are, of course, no relationships between goods as such, only properties of individual's preferences.

The simplest taxonomy is that based on the zero entries in the technology matrixes. It may be that both matrixes *A, B* are almost "solid," in which case there is little to be gained from a taxonomic approach. If, however, the *B* matrix contains sufficient zeros to be decomposable as follows,

$$B \equiv \begin{bmatrix} B_1 0 \\ 0 B_2 \end{bmatrix}, \qquad (7.1)$$

so that there is some set of characteristics and some set of activities such that these characteristics are derived only from these activities and these activities give rise to no other characteristics, then we can separate that set of characteristics and activities from the remainder of the technology. If, further, the activities in question require a particular set of goods which are used in no other activities (implying a decomposition of the *A* matrix), then we can regard the goods as forming an *intrinsic commodity group*. Goods within the group have the property that efficiency substitution effects will occur only for relative price changes within the group and will be unaffected by changes in the prices of other goods. If the utility function on characteristics has the conventional properties, there may, of course, be *private* substitution effects for goods within the group when the prices of other goods changes. For an intrinsic commodity group, the whole of the objective analysis can be carried out without reference to goods outside the group.

Goods from different intrinsic commodity groups can be regarded as *intrinsically unrelated*, goods from the same group as *intrinsically related*.

If, within a group, there are two activities, each in a one-to-one relationship with a different good, and if the bundles of characteristics derived from the two goods differ only in a scalar (that is, have identical proportions), we can regard the two goods in question as *intrinsic perfect substitutes*. If the associated characteristics bundles are similar, the goods are *close substitutes*. We can give formal respectability to that traditional butter-margarine example of our texts by considering them as two goods giving very similar combinations of characteristics.

On the other hand, if a certain activity requires

more than one good and if these goods are used in no other activity we can consider them as *intrinsic total complements* and they will always be consumed in fixed proportions, if at all.

Many goods within a commodity group will have relationships to each other which are partly complementary and partly substitution. This will be true if two goods, for example, are used in different combinations in each of several activities, each activity giving rise to a similar combination of characteristics. The goods are complements within each activity, but the activities are substitutes.

IX. LABOR, LEISURE, AND OCCUPATIONAL CHOICE

Within the structure of the present theory, we can regard labor as a reversed activity, using characteristics as inputs and producing commodities or a commodity as output. This is similar to the standard approach of generalized conventional theory, as in Debreu (1959).

We can add to this approach in an important way within the context of the present model by noting that a work activity may produce characteristics, as well as the commodity labor, as outputs. This is structurally equivalent to permitting some of the columns of the B matrix to have both negative and positive elements, corresponding to activities that "use up" some characteristics (or produce them in negative quantities) and produce others. In a work activity, the corresponding column of the A matrix will contain a single negative coefficient for the commodity labor, or, more differentiated, for one or more types of labor. If a work activity corresponds to a column of mixed signs in the B matrix, it is a recognition of the obvious truth that some work activities give rise to valued characteristics directly from the work itself.

Consider a very simple model of two characteristics with two commodities, labor and consumption goods. Both labor and consumption goods correspond to separate activities giving rise to the two characteristics in different proportions—perhaps negative in the case of labor. With no income other than labor, and only one good available to exchange for labor, we can collapse work and consumption into a single work-consumption activity. Given the wage rate in terms of the consumption good, the characteristics resulting from the work-consumption activity are given by a linear combination of the char-

acteristics from work and consumption separately, the weights in the combination being given by the wage rate.

Add another activity, leisure, which gives rise to the two characteristics, and the constraint that the weighted sum of the levels of activity labor and activity leisure is a constant.

The model is illustrated in Fig. 3. W represents a work-consumption activity giving positive levels of both characteristics, l represents a leisure activity, also giving positive levels of both characteristics. The constraint on total time (so that a linear combination of w and l is a constant) is represented by some line joining w, l.

If the constraint line has, like AB in the diagram, a negative slope, then individual consumers' utility functions will be tangent to the constraint at different points (like m, m') and we will have a neoclassical type of labor-leisure choice in which the proportions depend on individual preferences. Some consumers' preferences may be such that they will choose A (maximum work) or B (maximum leisure), but it is a private choice.

In this model, however, for a certain level of the wage, given the coefficients of the technology, the constraint may have a positive slope as in $A'B$, or AB'. If the constraint is $A'B$ (corresponding, *ceteris paribus*, to a sufficiently low real wage), *all* individuals will choose B, the only efficient point on the constraint set $OA'B$. At a sufficiently high wage, giving constraint set OAB', A, the maximum labor

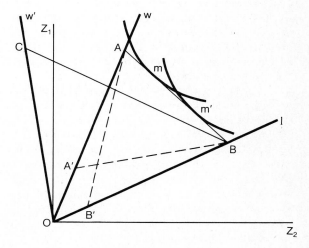

Fig. 3

choice, is the only efficient choice and will be chosen by *all* individuals.

The above effect, in which for some wage range there is a private labor-leisure choice between efficient points while outside the range all individuals will take maximum work or maximum leisure, can only occur if both the work-consumption and leisure activities give both characteristics in positive amounts. If the using up of characteristic 2 in labor exceeded the amount of that characteristic gained by consumption, then the work-consumption activity might lie outside the positive quadrant, like w'. In this case, a constraint like $A'B$ can exist, but not one like AB'. Furthermore, if the consumer will choose only positive characteristics vectors, no consumer will choose maximum work.

This model of the labor-leisure choice, which provides for objective and universal efficiency choices as well as private choices, may be the basis for a useful working model for an underdeveloped area. If the "leisure" be defined as "working one's own field," the work-consumption activity as entering the market economy, we see that there will be wages below which no peasant will offer himself as paid labor and that this is an *efficiency* choice and not a private choice.

We can use the same type of model also to analyze occupational choice. Suppose that we have two types of work (occupations) but otherwise the conditions are as above. If and only if the characteristics arising from the work itself are different in the two occupations, the two work-consumption activities will give rise to activities in different combinations. If the work characteristics are in the same proportion, the characteristics of the work-consumption activity will be in the same proportions and one or the other occupation will be the only efficient way to achieve this characteristics bundle.

Fig. 4 illustrates one possible set of relationships for such a model. In the diagram, w_1, w_2 represent the characteristics combinations from work-consumption activities in occupations 1 and 2, l the characteristics combinations from leisure. The frontier consists of the lines AC (combinations of w_1 and leisure) and AB (combinations of w_2 and leisure). We shall impose the realistic restriction that an individual can have only a single occupation so that AB is not a possible combination of activities.

The choice of occupation, given the relationships in the figure, depends on personal preferences, being

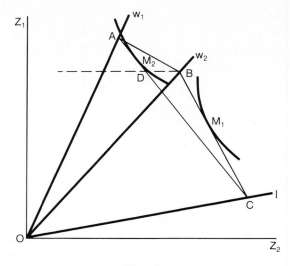

Fig. 4

M_1 (combination of w_2 and leisure) for an individual with preferences skewed towards z_2 and M_2 for an individual with preferences skewed towards z_1. But note a special effect. For some individuals whose indifference curves cannot touch BC but can touch AC, the efficient choice will be the corner solution M_3 ($= B$). There is, in fact, a segment of AC to the left of w_2 (the part of AC to the right of w_2 is dominated by BC), lying below the horizontal through B which is inefficient relative to B and will never be chosen.

In a configuration like the above we have the very interesting effect, where those who choose occupation 1 will work very hard at it; leisure-lovers will choose private combinations of occupation 2 and leisure—surely a good description of effects actually observed.

The loss to certain individuals from confinement to a single occupation is obvious. Could he choose a combination of occupations 1 and 2, the individual at M_2 would do so and be better off than with a combination of occupation 1 and leisure. In a two-characteristic, three-activity model, of course, two activities will be chosen at most, so that leisure plus both occupations will not appear.

The configuration in the diagram (Fig. 4) represents the situation for some set of technical coefficients and specific wages in the two occupations. A large number of other configurations is possible. In particular, if the wage rate in occupation 2 fell sufficiently, BC would lie inside AC and occupation 2 would cease to be chosen by any individual. All individuals, in this case, would choose their various personal combinations of occupation 1 and leisure.

Confinement to a single occupation need not result in a welfare loss, even when neither occupation dominates the other in an efficiency sense. If the technical coefficients were different, so that the characteristics vectors representing occupation 2 and leisure changed places, then the work-leisure combinations would be given by AB and BC, both efficient relative to any combination of occupations 1 and 2. In this case, all individuals would optimize by some combination of leisure and any one of the occupations.

Approaches similar to those outlined above seem to provide a better basis for analysis of occupational choice than the traditional, non-operational, catch-all "non-monetary advantages."

X. CONSUMER DURABLES, ASSETS, AND MONEY

Within the framework of the model, we have a scheme for dealing with durable goods and assets. A durable good can be regarded simply as giving rise to an activity in which the output consists of dated characteristics, the characteristics of different dates being regarded as different characteristics.

Given characteristics as joint outputs and two types of dimension in characteristics space—cross-section and time—any asset or durable good can be regarded as producing a combination of several characteristics at any one time, and that combination need not be regarded as continuing unchanged through time. In the decision to buy a new automobile, for example, the characteristic related to "fashion" or "style" may be present in relative strength in the first season, relatively less in later seasons, although the characteristics related to "transportation" may remain with constant coefficients over several seasons.

Elementary textbooks stress the multidimensional characteristics of money and other assets. The present model enables this multidimensionality to be appropriately incorporated. "Safety," "liquidity," and so forth become workable concepts that can be related to characteristics. We can use analysis similar to that of the preceding sections to show why efficiency effects will cause the universal disappearance of some assets (as in Gresham's Law) while other assets will

be held in combinations determined by personal preferences. It would seem that development along these lines, coupled with development of some of the recent approaches to consumer preferences over time as in Koopmans (1960), Lancaster (1963), or Koopmans, Diamond, and Williamson (1964) might eventually lead to a full-blooded theory of consumer behavior with respect to assets—saving and money—which we do not have at present.

In situations involving risk, we can use multiple characteristics better to analyze individual behavior. For example, we might consider a gamble to be an activity giving rise to three characteristics—a mathematical expectation, a maximum gain, and a maximum loss. One consumer's utility function may be such that he gives more weight to the maximum gain than to the maximum loss or the expected value, another's utility function may be biased in the opposite direction. All kinds of models can be developed along these lines, and they are surely more realistic than the models (Von Neumann and Morgenstern, 1944; Friedman and Savage, 1952) in which the expected value, alone, appears in the utility-maximizing decisions.

XI. NEW COMMODITIES, DIFFERENTIATED GOODS, AND ADVERTISING

Perhaps the most difficult thing to do with traditional consumer theory is to introduce a new commodity—an event that occurs thousands of times in the U.S. economy, even over a generation, without any real consumers being unduly disturbed. In the theory of production, where activity-analysis methods have become widely used, a new process or product can be fitted in well enough; but in consumer theory we have traditionally had to throw away our n-dimensional preference functions and replace them by totally new $(n + 1)$ dimensional functions, with no predictable consequences.

In this model, the whole process is extraordinarily simple. A new product simply means addition of one or more activities to the consumption technology. Given the technology (or the relevant portion of it) and given the intrinsic characteristic of the activity associated with the new good, we simply insert it in the appropriate place in the technology, *and we can predict the consequences.*

If a new good possesses characteristics in the same proportions as some existing good, it will simply fail to sell to anyone if its price is too high, or will completely replace the old good if its price is sufficiently low.

More usually, we can expect a new good to possess characteristics in somewhat different proportions to an existing good. If its price is too high, it may be dominated by some *combination* of existing goods and will fail to sell. If its price is sufficiently low, it will result in adding a new point to the efficiency frontier. In Fig. 5, *ABC* represents the old efficiency frontier, on which some individuals will consume combinations of goods g_1 and g_2 in various proportions, some combinations of g_2 and g_3. If the price of the new good, g_4, is such that it represents a point, D, on the old efficiency frontier, some persons (those using combinations of g_1 and g_2) will be indifferent between their old combinations and combinations of either g_1 and g_4 or g_2 and g_4. If the price of g_4 is a little lower, it will push the efficiency frontier out to D'. Individuals will now replace combinations of g_1 and g_2 with combinations of g_1 and g_4 or g_2 and g_4, depending on their preferences. The new good

will have taken away some of the sales from both g_1 and g_2, but completely replaced neither.

If the price of g_4 were lower, giving point D'', then combinations of g_4 and g_3 would dominate g_2, and g_2 would be replaced. At an even lower price, like D''', combinations of g_4 and g_3 would dominate g_2, and the corner solution g_4 only would dominate all combinations of g_1 and g_4 (since AD''' has a positive slope), so that g_4 would now replace both g_1 and g_2.

Differentiation of goods has presented almost as much of a problem to traditional theory as new commodities. In the present analysis, the difference is really one of degree only. We can regard a differentiated good typically as a new good within an existing intrinsic commodity group, and within that group analyze it as a new commodity. Sometimes there appear new commodities of a more fundamental kind whose characteristics cut across those of existing groups.

We may note that differentiation of goods, if successful (that is, if the differentiated goods are actually sold) represents a welfare improvement since it pushes the efficiency frontier outward and enables the consumer more efficiently to reach his preferred combination of characteristics.

Many economists take a puritanical view of commodity differentiation since their theory has induced them to believe that it is some single characteristic of a commodity that is relevant to consumer decisions (that is, automobiles are only for transportation), so that commodity variants are regarded as wicked tricks to trap the uninitiated into buying unwanted trimmings. This is not, of course, a correct deduction even from the conventional analysis, properly used, but is manifestly incorrect when account is taken of multiple characteristics.

A rather similar puritanism has also been apparent in the economist's approach to advertising. In the neoclassical analysis, advertising, if it does not represent simple information (and little information is called for in an analysis in which a good is simply a good), is an attempt to "change tastes" in the consumer. Since "tastes" are the ultimate datum in welfare judgments, the idea of changing them makes economists uncomfortable.

On the analysis presented here, there is much wider scope for informational advertising, especially as new goods appear constantly. Since the consumption technology of a modern economy is clearly very com-

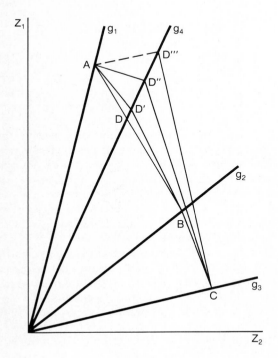

Fig. 5

plex, consumers require a great deal of information concerning that technology. When a new version of a dishwashing detergent is produced which contains hand lotion, we have a product with characteristics different from those of the old. The consumption technology is changed, and consumers are willing to pay to be told of the change. Whether the new product pushes out the efficiency frontier (compared, say, with a combination of dishwasher and hand lotion consumed separately) is, of course, another matter.

In any case, advertising, product design, and marketing specialists, who have a heavy commitment to understanding how consumers actually do behave, themselves act as though consumers regard a commodity as having multiple characteristics and as though consumers weigh the various combinations of characteristics contained in different commodities in reaching their decisions. At this preliminary stage of presenting the model set out here, this is strong evidence in its favor.

XII. GENERAL EQUILIBRIUM, WELFARE, AND OTHER MATTERS

Since the demand for goods depends on objective and universal efficiency effects as well as on private choices, we can draw some inferences relative to equilibrium in the economy.

A commodity, especially a commodity within an intrinsic commodity group, must have a price low enough relative to the prices of other commodities to be represented on the efficiency frontier, otherwise it will be purchased by no one and will not appear in the economy. This implies that if there are n viable commodities in a group, each in a one-to-one relation to an activity, the equilibrium prices will be such that the efficiency frontier has $n - 1$ facets in the two-characteristic case. In Fig. 6, for example, where the price of commodity 3 brings it to point A on the efficiency frontier, that price could not be allowed to rise to a level bringing it inside point B, or it would disappear from the market; and if its price fell below a level corresponding to C, commodities 2 and 4 would disappear from the market. Thus the limits on prices necessary for the existence of all commodities within a group can be established (in principle) from objective data. Only the demand within that price range depends on consumer preferences.

With a large number of activities relative to characteristics, equilibrium prices would give a many-

faceted efficiency frontier that would be approximated by a smooth curve having the general shape of a production possibility curve. For many purposes it may be mathematically simple to analyze the situation in terms of a smooth efficiency frontier. We can then draw on some of the analysis that exists, relating factor inputs to outputs of goods, as in Samuelson (1953b). Goods in our model correspond to factors in the production model, and characteristics in our model to commodities in the production model.

The welfare implications of the model set out here are quite complex and deserve a separate treatment. We might note several important aspects of the welfare problem, however, which arise directly from a many-faceted, many-cornered efficiency frontier:

1. Consumers whose choices represent a corner on the efficiency frontier are not, in general, *equating* marginal rates of substitution between characteristics to the ratio of any parameters of the situation or to marginal rates of substitution of other consumers.

2. Consumers whose choices represent points on different facets of the efficiency frontier are equating their marginal rates of substitution between characteristics to different implicit price ratios between characteristics. If there is a one-to-one relationship

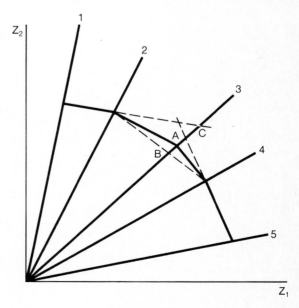

Fig. 6

between goods and activities, the consumers are reacting to relative prices between different sets of goods. The traditional marginal conditions for Paretian exchange optimum do not hold because the price ratio relevant to one consumer's decisions differs from the price ratio relevant to another's. In common-sense terms, the price ratio between a Cadillac and a Continental is irrelevant to my decisions, but the price ratio between two compact cars is relevant, while there are other individuals for whom the Cadillac/Continental ratio is the relevant datum. If the A matrix is strongly connected, however, the implicit price ratios between different activities can correspond to price ratios between the same sets of goods, and the Paretian conditions may be relevant.

Finally, we may note that the shape of the equilibrium efficiency frontier and the existence of the efficiency substitution effect can result in demand conditions with the traditionally assumed properties, even if the traditional, smooth, convex utility function does not exist. In particular, a simple utility function in which characteristics are consumed in constant proportions—the proportions perhaps changing with income—can be substituted for the conventional utility function.

XIII. OPERATIONAL AND PREDICTIVE CHARACTERISTICS OF THE MODEL

In principle, the model set out here can be made operational (that is, empirical coefficients can be assigned to the technology). In practice, the task will be more difficult than the equivalent task of determining the actual production technology of an economy.

To emphasize that the model is not simply heuristic, we can examine a simple scheme for sketching out the efficiency frontier for some commodity group. We shall assume that there is a one-to-one relationship between activities and goods, that at least one characteristic shared by the commodities is capable of independent determination, and that a great quantity of suitable market data is available.

In practice, we will attempt to operate with the minimum number of characteristics that give sufficient explanatory power. These may be combinations of fundamental characteristics (a factor-analysis situation) or fundamental characteristics themselves.

Consider some commodity group such as household detergents. We have a primary objective char-

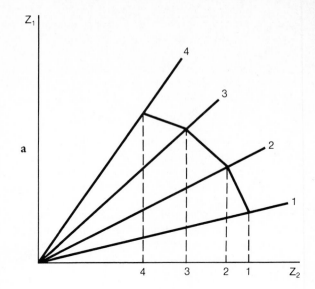

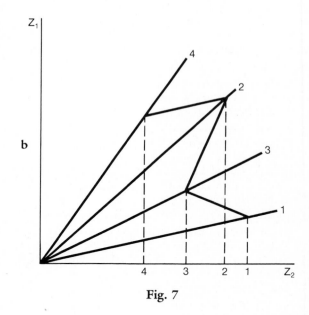

Fig. 7

acteristic, cleaning power, measured in some chosen way. We wish to test whether one or more other characteristics are necessary to describe the consumer-choice situation.

We take a two-dimensional diagram with characteristic "cleaning power" along one axis. Along the axis we mark the cleaning power per dollar outlay of all detergents observed to be sold at the same time. If this is the same for all detergents, this single char-

Chart 1

This Theory	*Conventional Theory*
Wood will not be a close substitute for bread, since characteristics are dissimilar	No reason except "tastes" why they should not be close substitutes
A red Buick will be a close substitute for a gray Buick	No reason why they should be any closer substitutes than wood and bread
Substitution (for example, butter and margarine) is frequently intrinsic and objective, will be observed in many societies under many market conditions	No reason why close substitutes in one context should be close substitutes in another
A good may be displaced from the market by new goods or by price changes	No presumption that goods will be completely displaced
The labor-leisure choice may have a marked occupational pattern	Labor-leisure choice determined solely by an individual preferences; no pattern, other than between individuals, would be predicted
(Gresham's Law) A monetary asset may cease to be on the efficiency frontier, and will disappear from the economy	No ex ante presumption that any good or asset will disappear from the economy.
An individual is completely unaffected by price changes that leave unchanged the portion of the efficiency frontier on which his choice rests	An individual is affected by changes in all prices
Some commodity groups may be intrinsic, and universally so	No presumption that commodities forming a group (defined by a break in spectrum of cross-elasticities) in one context will form a group in another context

acteristic describes the situation, and we do not seek further. However, we shall assume this is not so. From our observed market data, we obtain cross-price elasticities between all detergents, taken two at a time. From the model, we know that cross-price elasticities will be highest between detergents with adjacent characteristics vectors, so that the order of the characteristics vectors as we rotate from one axis to the other in the positive quadrant can be established.

The ordering of "cleaning power per dollar" along one axis can be compared with the ordering of the characteristics vectors. If the orderings are the same, an equilibrium efficiency frontier can be built up with two characteristics as in Fig. 7a. The slopes of the facets can be determined within limits by the limiting prices at which the various detergents go off the market. If the ordering in terms of cleaning power does not agree with the ordering in terms of cross-elasticity, as in Fig. 7b, two characteristics do not describe the market appropriately, since detergent with cleaning power 3 in the figure cannot be on the efficiency frontier. But with a third characteristic, detergent 3 could be adjacent to detergents 2 and 1

in an extra dimension, and we could build up an efficiency frontier in three characteristics.

Other evidence could, of course, be used to determine the efficiency frontier for a given market situation. Among this evidence is that arising from ordinary activity-analysis theory, that, with r characteristics we would expect to find some consumers who used r commodities at the same time, unless all consumers were on corners or edges of the efficiency frontier.

Last, but possibly not least, simply asking consumers about the characteristics associated with various commodities may be much more productive than attempts to extract information concerning preferences within the context of conventional theory.

In general, if consumer preferences are well dispersed (so that all facets of the efficiency frontier are represented in some consumer's choice pattern), a combination of information concerning interpersonal variances in the collections of goods chosen and of the effects of price changes on both aggregate and individual choices can, in principle, be used to ferret out the nature of the consumption technology. Some of the problems that arise are similar to those met by psychologists in measuring intelligence, personality, and other multidimensional traits, so that techniques similar to those used in psychology, such as factor analysis, might prove useful.

Even without specification of the consumption technology, the present theory makes many predictions of a structural kind which may be contrasted with the predictions of conventional theory. Some of these are set out in Chart 1.

XIV. CONCLUSION

In this model we have extended into consumption theory activity analysis, which has proved so penetrating in its application to production theory. The crucial assumption in making this application has been the assumption that goods possess, or give rise

to, multiple characteristics in fixed proportions and that it is these characteristics, not goods themselves, on which the consumer's preferences are exercised.

The result, as this brief survey of the possibilities has shown, is a model very many times richer in heuristic explanatory and predictive power than the conventional model of consumer behavior and one that deals easily with those many common-sense characteristics of actual behavior that have found no place in traditional exposition.

This paper is nothing more than a condensed presentation of some of the great number of possible ways in which the model can be used. It is hoped that a door has been opened to a new, rich treasure house of ideas for the future development of the most refined and least powerful branch of economic theory, the theory of the consumer himself.

APPENDIX

I. Transformation of the Utility Function into G-Space

Consider some characteristics vector z^* which does have an image x^* in G-space, and consider the set P of all vectors z preferred or indifferent to z^*. If U has the traditional properties, the set P is convex with an inner boundary which is the indifference surface through z^*. Now $z \geqq z^*$ implies z is in P so that every x such that $Bx \geqq z^*$, a set S, is preferred or indifferent to x^*. If we take some other z' in P, every x in S' such that $Bx \geqq z'$ is also preferred or indifferent to x'^*. Similarly for z'' in P and S'' such that that $Bx \geqq z''$, and so on. From the theory of inequalities, the sets S, S', S'' . . . are all convex, and since P is convex, a linear combination of z', z'' is in P, so that a linear combination of x's in S', S'' is also preferred or indifferent to x^*. Hence the set $\bar{P}$ of all x preferred or indifferent to x^* is the linear combination of all the sets S, S', S'', . . . and so is convex.

Thus the utility function transformed into G-space retains its essential convexity. A more intuitive way of looking at the situation is to note that all characteristics collections which are actually available are contained in an n-dimensional slice through the r-dimensional utility function and that all slices through a convex function are themselves convex. The transformation of this n-dimensional slice into G-space preserves this convexity.

II. "Revealed Preference" in a Complex Economy

We shall use the structural properties of the consumption technology A, B (dropping the assumption of a one-to-one relationship between goods and activities) to show that in a complex economy with more activities than characteristics the efficiency choice always satisfies the weak axiom of revealed preference and will satisfy the strong axiom for sufficiently large price changes, so that satisfaction of even the strong axiom does not "reveal" convexity of the preference function itself.

Consider an economy with a consumption technology defined by

$$z = By,$$
$$x = Ay,$$

and a consumer subject to a budget constraint of the form $p^*x \leqq k$ who has chosen goods x^* for activities y^*, giving characteristics z^*.

We know that if the consumer has made an efficient choice, y^* is the solution of the program (the value of which is k).

Minimize p^*Ay ($=p^*x$):

$$By = z^*, y \geqq 0, \tag{8.1a}$$

which has a dual (solution v^*).

$$\text{Maximize } vz^*: vB \leqq p^*A. \tag{8.1b}$$

The dual variables v can be interpreted as the implicit prices of the characteristics themselves. From the Kuh-Tucker Theorem, we can associate the vector v with the slope of the separating hyperplane between the set of attainable z's and the set of z's preferred or indifferent to z^*.

For the same satisfactions vector Z^* and a new price vector p^{**} the efficiency choice will be the solution y^{**} (giving x^{**}), v^{**}, of

$$\text{Min } p^{**}Ay: By = z^*, y \geq 0, \tag{8.2}$$
$$\text{Max } vz^*: vb \leqq p^{**}A.$$

Since z^* is the same in (8.1) and (8.2), y^{**} is a feasible solution of (8.1) and y^* of (8.2). From the fundamental theorem of linear programing we have

$$p^{**}Ay^* \geqq v^{**}z^* = p^{**}Ay^{**}, \tag{8.3}$$
$$p^*Ay^{**} \geqq v^*z^* = p^*Ay^*. \tag{8.4}$$

A program identical with (8.2) except that z^* is replaced by hz^* will have a solution hy^{**}, v^{**}. Choose h so that $hp^{**}Ay^{**} = p^{**}Ay^*$. From (8.3) $h \geqq 1$. From (8.4),

$$hp^*Ay^{**} \geqq p^*Ay^{**} \geqq p^*Ay^*. \tag{8.5}$$

If we now write p for p^*, p' for p^{**}; $x = Ay^*$, $x' = hAy^{**}$, we have

$$p'x' = p'x \text{ implies } px' \geqq px, \tag{8.6}$$

satisfying the *weak axiom of revealed preference*.

The equality will occur on the right in (8.6) only if equalities hold in *both* (8.3) and (8.4), and these will hold only if y^{**} is optimal as well as feasible in (8.1), and y^* is optimal as well as feasible in (8.2). In general, if the number of activities exceeds the number of characteristics, we can always find two prices p^*, p^{**} so related that neither of the solutions y^{**}, y^* is optimal in the other's program.

Hence, if the number of activities exceeds the number of characteristics (representing the number of primary constraints in the program), we can find prices so related that the strong axiom of revealed preference is satisfied, even though the consumer has obtained characteristics in unchanged proportions (z^*, hz^*) and has revealed nothing of his preference map.

The above effect represents an *efficiency substitution effect* which would occur even if characteristics were consumed in absolutely fixed proportions. If the consumer substitutes between different satisfactions bundles when his budget constraint changes, this private substitution effect is additional to the efficiency substitution effect.

Just as the conceptual experiment implicit in revealed preference implies "overcompensation" in the conventional analysis (see Samuelson 1948, 1953a), so the efficiency effect leads to "external overcompensation" additional to private overcompensation.

REFERENCES

Becker, Gary S. "A Theory of the Allocation of Time," *Econ. J.*, September, 1965.

Debreu, Gerald. *Theory of Value*. Cowles Foundation Monograph 17, 1959.

——————. "Topological Methods in Cardinal Utility Theory," in K. J. Arrow, S. Karlin, and P. Suppes (eds.). *Mathematical Methods in the Social Sciences, 1959*. Stanford, Calif.: Stanford Univ. Press, 1960.

Friedman, Milton, and Savage, L. J. "The Expected-Utility Hypothesis and the Measurability of Utility," *J.P.E.*, Vol. LX (December, 1952).

Gorman, W. M. "Separable Utility and Aggregation," *Econometrica*, Vol. XXVII (July, 1959).

Johnson, Harry G. "Demand Theory Further Revised or Goods Are Goods," *Economica*, N.S. 25 (May, 1958).

Karlin, S. *Mathematical Methods and Theory in Games, Programming and Economics*. New York: Pergamon Press, 1959.

Koopmans, T. C. "Stationary Ordinal Utility and Impatience," *Econometrica*, Vol. XXIII (April, 1960).

Koopmans, T. C., Diamond, P. A., and Williamson, R. E. "Stationary Utility and Time Perspective," *ibid.*, Vol. XXXII (January-April, 1964).

Lancaster, Kelvin J. "Revising Demand Theory," *Economica*, N.S. 24 (November, 1957).

——————. "The Scope of Qualitative Economics," *Rev. Econ. Studies*, Vol. XXIX (1962).

——————. "An Axiomatic Theory of Consumer Time Preference," *Internat. Econ. Rev.*, Vol. IV (May, 1963).

——————. "The Theory of Qualitative Linear Systems," *Econometrica*, Vol. XXXIII (April, 1965).

——————. "Change and Innovation in the Technology of Consumption," *A.E.R.*, Papers and Proceedings, May, 1966 (to be published).

Morishima, M. "The Problem of Intrinsic Complementarity and Separability of Goods," *Metroeconomica*, Vol. XI (December, 1959).

Pearce, I. F. *A Contribution to Demand Analysis*. New York: Oxford Univ. Press, 1964.

Quandt, R. E. "A Probabilistic Theory of Consumer Behaviour," *Q.J.E.*, Vol. LXX (November, 1956).

Samuelson, P. A. "Consumption Theory in Terms of Revealed Preference," *Economica*, N.S. 15 (November, 1948).

——————. "Consumption Theorems in Terms of Over-Compensation Rather than Indifference Comparisons," *ibid.*, N.S. 20 (February, 1953). *(a)*

——————. "Prices of Factors and Goods in General Equilibrium," *Rev. Econ. Studies*, Vol. XXI (1953). *(b)*

Stigler, G. J. "The Cost of Subsistence," *J. Farm Econ.*, Vol. XXVII (1945).

Strotz, Robert, "The Empirical Implications of a Utility Tree," *Econometrica*, Vol. XXV (April, 1957).

——————. "The Utility Tree: A Correction and Further Appraisal," *ibid.*, Vol. XXVII (July, 1959).

Thrall, Robert M., Coombs, C., and Davis, R. L. *Decision Processes*. New York: Wiley & Sons, 1954.

Uzawa, H. "Preference and Rational Choice in the Theory of Consumption," in K. J. Arrow, S. Karlin, and P. Suppes (eds.). *Mathematical Methods in the Social Sciences, 1959*. Stanford, Calif.: Stanford Univ. Press, 1960.

Von Neumann, J., and Morgenstern, O. *Theory of Games and Economic Behavior*. Princeton, N.J.: Princeton Univ. Press, 1944.

SUPPLY AND THE THEORY OF THE FIRM

The Basis of Some Recent Advances in the Theory of Management of the Firm*

ARMEN A. ALCHIAN

Armen A. Alchian (A.B., Stanford University, 1936; Ph.D., 1944) was born in Fresno, California, in 1914. Since 1946 he has served on the faculty of the University of California at Los Angeles, where he is now Professor Emeritus of Economics. From 1947–1964 he was a member of the Economics Division of the RAND Corporation. Alchian is famous for his work in price theory and for research on inflation, the economic theory of property rights, and the long-run effects of competitive processes. His textbook, *University Economics* (with William R. Allen), is noteworthy for the rigor and clarity of its exposition. He is a member of the Mont Pelerin Society and a past president of the Western Economic Association.

Attacks on the theory of the firm—or more accurately on the theory of behavior of individuals in the firm—have called attention to logical inconsistencies in the profit maximizing criterion and to empirical evidence refuting its implications in a wide class of firms. The empirical evidence seemed overwhelming that individuals working within a firm as managers or employees (and even as employers), pursued policies directed at, for example, increasing sales, gross assets, employees, expenditures for various equipment and facilities beyond those that yield a profit maximum.

Attempts to defend the profit maximizing theory

by rigorously treating profits as capital value increments, rather than as current transitory rates of net earnings—so as to avoid the short- and long-run pitfall—removed some conflicting evidence. Similarly a defense asserting that the aberrations are temporary deviations in a search process does eliminate some more of the embarrassing evidence. However, the defense is not adequate; a vast class of behavior conflicting with wealth maximizing remains to be explained.

The observations of behavior that refute the profit or wealth maximizing theory are the 'facts' that some managers incur expenditures apparently in excess of those that would maximize wealth or profits of the owners of the firm. Managers of corporations are observed to emphasize growth of total assets of the firm and of its sales as objectives of managerial ac-

*Reprinted from *Journal of Industrial Economics* (November 1965) by permission of Basil Blackwell Publisher Ltd. Copyright 1965, pp. 30–41.

tions. Also managers of firms undertake cost reducing, efficiency increasing campaigns when demand falls; under wealth maximization they would already have been doing this. Managerial actions not conducive to the greatest wealth to the stockholders are taken to be well-established facts—and with which there appears to be no quarrel. Baumol emphasizes the managerial objective of sales increases, even to the extent of postulating that sales maximization is an objective. Penrose emphasizes the growth of the asset size of the firms. None of these can be made consistent with stockholder wealth maximization. If one postulates asset growth or sales maximization he will explain some cases but reject a lot of others in which that simply does not hold. Similarly, attempts to posit asset or sales maximization subject to a minimum wealth or profit constraint also runs into the objection that it implies the firm will not make *any* sacrifice in sales no matter how large an increment in wealth would thereby be achievable. Observed behavior simply does not support that attempted revision of the theory. Thus the Baumol type of attempt to modify the theory flounders—which in no way diminishes the importance of the insistence on recognizing inadequacies in the then existing state of theory.

Attacking any theory is easy enough, since none is perfect. But the wide class of empirical observation that *is* explained by economic theory should caution one against sweeping that theory aside and setting up new *ad hoc* theories to explain *only* or *primarily* those events the standard theory will not explain. What is wanted is a generalization of economic theory to obtain an expanded scope of validity without eliminating any (or 'too much') of the class of events for which it already is valid. Too many new theories happen to be *ad hoc* theories, valid only for a smaller class of cases. And among recent attempts to increase the power of the theory of the firm one can find some sparkling examples. Though there is no point in our giving attention to those failures, credit is due them as reminders of the areas in which economic theory awaits valid generalization.

Deserving our attention here are those in which scientific progress toward a more generalized and valid theory is realized. Two recent works serve as good examples. Especially distinguished is the contribution in Oliver E. Williamson's *The Economics of Discretionary Behavior: Managerial Objective in a Theory of the Firm,* a doctoral thesis (which won a Ford

Foundation award) [11]. The other is Robin Marris, *The Economic Theory of Managerial Capitalism* [7]. Now that we have some advances we can look back and determine what prior works served as foundations for the advance. Especially noticeable as pathbreaker was Gary Becker's *Economics of Discrimination* [4], also a doctoral dissertation completed almost ten years ago. From Becker to Marris and Williamson there is worth noting here, the works of Downie [6], Baumol [3], Penrose [9], Simon [10], Averch and Johnson [2], Cyert and March [5].

Perhaps the nature of the advance can be characterized by asserting that the old schizophrenia between consumption and production behavior has been replaced by a consistent, more powerful criterion of utility maximizing. In a sense the utility theory underlying individual behavior in the consumption sphere has swallowed up producer or management theory—with, if we judge the recent literature aright, significant improvements in economic theory. Rather than concentrate on a detailed statement of who said what (and why he should or should not have said it), this paper is an attempt to indicate the nature of that advance—as a sort of survey review of the recent literature.

A means of advance was made explicit by Becker, who insisted that non-pecuniary sources of utility be included in the utility function of an income earner. An owner, manager or employee is prepared to sacrifice some pecuniary income as a source of utility if he is offered enough non-pecuniary goods, which also contribute to utility. Becker concentrated on race, religion and congeniality of colleagues or employees as a source of non-pecuniary utility. He emphasized the production trade-offs or transformation rates between money income and working conditions (including color of colleagues and other non-pecuniary goods) and he pointed out that changes in the trade-off rates would affect the extent to which a person chose non-pecuniary sources (goods) of utility relative to pecuniary income.

There is, of course, nothing novel in this proposition. One can find it in Adam Smith.[1] But with the growth of formalism and rigor of mathematical modes of analysis it seems to have dropped out of the theory. Becker's dissertation stimulated applications of the principle to see if different kinds of institutions implied different trade-off rates between

---

[1]Book V, Chapter 1, Article 2 and 3 of his *Wealth of Nations.*

pecuniary and non-pecuniary incomes to managers and employees. Thus, a paper by the present author and R. Kessel [1] applied the analysis to profit limited and regulated businesses—public utilities, for example, and derived the implication that discrimination against racial and religious groups is greater in profit controlled firms. Any firm already earning the maximum *allowable* profit found it almost costless (of profits) to 'buy' that kind of discrimination. Evidence was also presented to corroborate the analysis. Averch and Johnson applied the principle to investment activities of owners of public utilities and derived an implication about the extent to which investment in cost *increasing* activities would be induced.

Marris says the managers will be induced to sacrifice some increment of owner's profits for the sake of the increment of size of firm (and consequent increment of managerial salary). Manager's salaries are larger in larger firms. Therefore they will have an incentive to enlarge the firm beyond the owner's wealth, or profit, maximizing size. Marris makes explicit that stockholders are not blind to this; the costs of their detecting this effect and exerting controls are large enough to make it more economical for stockholders to tolerate the reduced wealth than to incur the costs required to keep the managers more strictly in line with the stockholder's wealth maximizing criterion.

Unfortunately Marris's analysis appears to be slightly marred by a logical confusion between rates of profit *per unit of investment* and absolute growth of wealth (profit)—in view of the fact that the investment is a discretionary *variable*.[2] If I am correct in my understanding, the implication derived by Marris, wherein the manager will seek a growth rate of assets beyond that which maximizes the above mentioned ratio, is completely consistent with simple wealth maximization *to the owners*. Diminishing marsetting that marginal rate of return equal to the rate of interest—maximizing neither the marginal nor the average rate of return per dollar of (variable) investment. However, it would be a simple task to set the analysis aright by formalizing into the manager's opportunity set of choices among wealth to stockholders versus wealth to managers the costs to stockholders of enforcing a stockholders' wealth maximizing criterion on the managers.

Marris says he uses a utility maximizing approach wherein the person has his utility increased not only by higher salaries but also by greater security in his continued incumbency. In a strict sense, this is a wealth maximizing rather than a utility maximizing, approach for the manager. It is that because a greater security is an increase in wealth. If risk of loss of future receipts is reduced, the present value is increased. Hence Marris uses a wealth function in which two components of greater wealth are made explicit—the projected future receipts and the probability of their being realized.

Competing with the utility maximizing approach is a wealth or growth of wealth maximizing criterion. Marris devotes most of his book to an exposition of a model in which the growth of the firm is constrained by internal saving out of its business generated income. As it turns out, a wealth growth maximizing criterion is a wealth maximizing criterion. Although Marris offers interesting observations it is his utility maximizing proposition that makes his approach most fruitful—in this reviewer's judgment.

As of the present moment, the best formulation of a theory that seems to be both more general and more valid than the wealth maximizing theory is the utility maximizing approach more fully presented by Williamson. He postulates that the manager can direct the firm's resources to increase his own utility in at least three ways. First, he can get a higher salary by obtaining greater profits for the owners, as in the older profit maximizing model. Second, he can direct the firm's resources so as to increase his salary at the expense of a decrease in profits. In particular, if the manager believes that a large firm is correlated with higher salaries (holding profits constant as a *ceteris paribus*), he will strive more to enlarge the gross asset size of the firm.

Third, the manager can sacrifice some increments to stockholder profits in order to increase expenditures for his own non-pecuniary emoluments within the firm. The extent to which these three avenues are used depends on the costs to the stockholders of detecting and policing the manager's behavior and effectiveness, *i.e.* on the costs, of enforcing contracts. In the modern, large corporation these costs are higher than in the single owner enterprise (and are absent in the owner-operated enterprise).

The third of the avenues listed above is formally admissible if one uses a utility maximizing theory rather than a pecuniary wealth maximizing postulate. By doing so, the manager's behavior is interpreted

[2]Pp. 254–60.

as choosing among opportunities to obtain increments of non-pecuniary goods in his utility function (*e.g.*, pretty secretaries, thick rugs, friendly colleagues, leisurely work load, executive washrooms, larger work staff, relaxed personnel policies involving job security, time off for statesmanlike community activities, gifts of company funds to colleges, out of town hotel suites, racial and religious discrimination in personnel policy, etc.). The utility maximizing theory is applicable and useful if, and only if, (1) we can identify some of its components (beside direct pecuniary wealth) *and* if (2) we can identify circumstances that involve differences in the costs of each of the various types of managerial non-pecuniary 'goods'. By satisfying these two conditions, we can deduce the relative extent of such activities in each of those circumstances.

One circumstance is the type of ownership of the firm, *e.g.*, corporate ownership, non-profit firm, public utility (with a restricted profit rate), and governmentally owned organizations. In this context, the contributions of the recent literature lie in the clues about the differences in relative costs among various types of organizations.

In conformity with the familiar fundamental theorem of demand, the lower the cost of a good or activity (whether it be a traditional type of economic good or one of a more general class of goods, like pleasant surroundings and those mentioned above) the more it will be demanded. This is all merely standard economic theory applied in a broader nexus of utility affecting components and is in no way an abandonment of the traditional basic theorems.

Williamson and Marris provide advances along the second and third avenues, indicate how to test the theory, and provide examples of tests. Williamson considers emoluments and staff preference as two ways of spending beyond the profit maximizing rate. The preference for larger staffs exists because salaries to a manager are correlated with a larger staff under a manager—a phenomenon best explained, to my knowledge, by Mayer [8].[3]

The approach used by Williamson is expressible as a maximization of the manager's utility, which is a function of several specified variables (*e.g.*, size of staff and profits of the firm). The utility is subject to

constraints on the choices he can make about staff and profit. Williamson postulates that profits are affected by the size of the staff (at first profits and staff size are positively related for increasing staff up to level and thereafter negatively related for larger staffs—given the demand environment of the firm). The owners of the firm, by detecting and policing their employees' actions, seek to induce them to select the maximum profit combination, which maximizes owners' utility. Unfortunately for the owners, there are costs of detecting and policing his actions so as to make sure he does select that point. Once these costs are recognized, it is obviously better to avoid some of these costs if the profits saved are less than the costs. Cash registers, sales books and accounting systems are in part devices to enable more efficient detecting and policing of employees' deviations from profit maximization. The greater the costs of this detection and policing, the greater will managers sacrifice profits for the sake of staff size and other means of increasing management utility.

Perhaps Williamson's analysis can be most easily illustrated without doing it too much violence, by his graphic technique. In Fig. 1, the vertical axis measures profit to the owner-stockholders. The horizontal axis measures staff (or emoluments) to the manager. Curve *AA* is the feasibility curve portraying the opportunity set of combinations of profits and 'staff' open to the manager. The initial positively sloped portion indicates joint increases in staff and

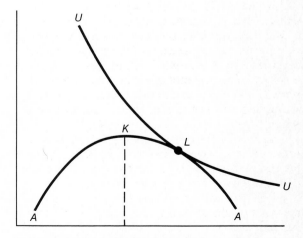

Fig. 1. Stockholder profits and staff size as sources of utility or pecuniary income to manager shift equilibrium beyond maximum profit size.

[3]Mayer's explanation, in terms of the dependence of marginal product of managers upon the size of assets affected by the managers' decisions, avoids many of the superficial, misleading or downright erroneous explanations relying on convention, prestige, privilege of rank, etc.

profits; the negative portion indicates staff can be larger than the profit maximizing level indicated at the point K. One typically shaped utility curve is drawn UU. Profits to stockholders enter the manager's utility function in so far as larger profits imply larger salaries to the manager. Similarly, staff enters as an argument in the manager's utility or wealth function in that this too is correlated with salary as well as with emoluments. The familiar conflict of interest between stockholders and manager or between owner and employee, or between taxpayer and government employee is portrayed by the utility curves of the employee-manager's utility function which contains the firm's staff or emolument component whereas only the profit or net value of the firm enters the stockholder's utility function. Point L is chosen by the manager. That point K is not chosen reflects the costs that must be borne by stockholders if he tried to detect and prevent *all* deviations from point K. The opportunity set bounded by AA would be vertically bounded on the right by the dotted line straight down from K if, and only if, detection of profit maximizing actions and the policing were costless.

Any events, circumstances or factors that affect the feasibility curve (taxes, changes in business conditions) can shift the optimum tangency point. (Similarly, anything that shifts the shapes of the utility map will shift the equilibrium position.) Williamson derives the implied effects of corporate tax changes on the position and shape of the opportunity set bounded by AA. He also analyses the effects of a decline in business conditions on the curve AA. Williamson shows that the decrease in demand (and profitability) implies an increased effort to achieve greater *efficiency* in staff size—such as presumably would already have been achieved if the managers were maximizing profits of the stockholder owners. Thus the results differ from those of profit maximization, and they are more like those that seem to be observed in reality.

The significant point is that the equilibrium or solution values involve staff size, corporate expenditures and emoluments beyond the maximum profit combination of profits and staff or emoluments. Thus the owner's profit maximizing hypothesis is apparently replaced with a more general utility maximizing postulate for the manager with the indicated resultant implications. A fixed total tax shifts the AA downward vertically; this leads to a solution with smaller gross size of firm, emoluments and staff. Williamson points out that a firm with several subdivisions could in effect impose a fixed tax on each subdivision—calling it an overhead cost—thereby inducing the subdivision managers to shift their actions more toward profits and less toward staff and gross asset size. The lower the profit to the subdivision the greater the marginal rate of substitution in consumption for managers between profit and other 'goods'. The tax does not change the feasible or opportunity rate of substitution between salary from larger profits and gains from the size and staff, because the slope of the AA curve is unchanged as it is shifted vertically downward. This leads to the leftward revision of the tangency point between the curve AA and the utility line. Marris, as we said, came close to the same result; in fact his book presents a diagram much like Williamson but the axes are different and no utility maximizing approach is involved.

The significance of the utility maximizing approach for the sales maximization approach is rather interesting. Sales maximization, advanced conjecturally by Baumol, is constrained by a 'minimum requisite' profit. Unfortunately, this minimum requisite profit squares neither with the rest of economic theory nor with the facts of life. Managers do not maximize sales regardless of how much they could increase profits if they sacrificed some increment of sales. While sales maximization subject to the postulated constraint gives *some* implications that agree with observed events, it also implies many other things that are refuted by all available evidence. The hypothesis cannot be held out as a serious proposition. Instead, Williamson's model seems to explain the facts that Baumol was seeing and emphasizing. He saw some firm's managers with their eyes on sales—even to the point of increasing sales beyond what everyone would have agreed was the profit maximizing level. Williamson makes this sensible, in that the incentive to increase sales is not treated as a single criterion for maximization, but rather as *a* means of the manager increasing his salary—in much the same fashion as a larger staff under the manager has the same effect. Substitution between these various components (salaries correlated with firm's profits, sales, assets, employees, etc.) affecting the manager's income or utility is the crucial factor, and Williamson emphasizes the factors making the substitution rate non-zero.

Without tarnishing the brilliance of Williamson's work, we can point out a bit of ambiguity. The derivation or basis of his profit-staff feasibility curve *AA* is not clear. In particular, he does not indicate exactly what is being held constant as a constraint defining the opportunity set. Furthermore, pecuniary and non-pecuniary benefits are mixed together on his emolument and staff division, thus making the utility isoquant an ambiguous concept. However, this can be easily corrected, formally, by adding a new dimension by which he can separate the pecuniary from the non-pecuniary goods to the manager. This would require at least a three dimensional graph and a more detailed mathematical formulation.

One could then include business expenditures designed to increase, not the manager's pecuniary salary, but rather the *non-pecuniary* benefits available within the firm, like those mentioned above in the 'third avenue'. If quantities of these non-pecuniary benefits were explicitly included in the utility function and also indicated along one of the axes of the graph, we could draw iso-utility curves, showing combinations of pecuniary and non-pecuniary goods that yield a constant *utility* to the manager. Then the tangencies of the utility function with the feasibility function (production function of wealth and non-pecuniary benefits) would yield the solution values of profits and types of non-pecuniary managerial benefits for the managers.

If one formulates his analyses in this way, the changes in taxes and especially of changes in ownership structures (which affect the costs for owners to detect and punish non-profit maximizing behavior by their employees) will be reflected in the feasibility set or production function on which the managers can operate. For example, the incentive to achieve maximum feasible profits for any given level of emoluments depends upon the costs of the owners detecting that full realizability and appropriately rewarding or punishing the manager. If a large corporation with many stockholders involves higher detection and policing costs, the inducement for managers to depart from the objective of their employers is increased. In effect the profit-emolument curve is lowered and made flatter, pushing the manager toward greater emolument and less profit to stockholders.

This model can, and has been, applied to profit-limited public utilities and to non-profit corporations. A lesson to be drawn from these applications

is that we can readily improve our analysis of managerial behavior if we first categorize firms according to whether the firm is a public utility (with constraints on the retainable profits) or is a non-profit organization (rather than according to size or simply to corporate versus non-corporate firms). Much loose talk and erroneous blanket generalizations about managerial behavior would be avoided if the differences among *types* of corporate ownership were recognized. Drawing inferences from the behavior of managers of *large* (public utility firms) and applying those inferences to managers of non-public utility firms is not generally justified. What is more viable in one firm is not so viable in another. A further temptation to compare the small manager's behavior with that of a large non-profit or public utility is to confound size with different forms of ownership. Improvements in this direction await merely the application of some routine intellectual toil.

This model certainly can be applied to government ownership, where it may serve to shock some people who think that more government ownership or regulation will solve the problem of making managers conform more to the criteria they are 'told' to seek.

The approach in the literature reviewed here is in stark contrast to that which attempts to use new types of utility functions, such as lexicographic or discrete utility functions. Lexicographic functions rank goods by some criterion and assert that those of a lower rank provide no utility until those of a higher rank achieve some critical amount. For example, there may be no utility of non-pecuniary goods (via prestige, leisure, emoluments, pretty secretaries, etc.) until profits or income achieve some minimum level. Furthermore, increments of the higher ranking goods beyond the critical level have zero utility, so that in effect, substitution among goods is denied. The analyses covered in this review retain the classic utility function but revise the types of constraints on the opportunity set of choices open to the utility maximizer (instead of revising the utility function). It is difficult for this reviewer to place much hope in this lexicographic type of utility function—in view of the clear cut refutation of its implications. The refutation of some of the implications derived with the classic utility functions seem (now that one examines these new analyses) to be the result of the postulated constraint system. By revising the constraints, rather than the utility function, new implications are being derived. Instead of postulating classic constraints of private property with zero costs of detecting and policing employee behavior, a more general theory can be derived from more general or varied types of property constraints. Perhaps unwittingly the literature of managerial behavior is enlarging the realm of formal economic theory to be applicable to more than conventional, individual private property systems.

Another apparent 'casualty' of the utility maximizing approach under the revised constraints is the 'satisficing' or 'aspiration' approaches. The discussion by Marris [10: pp. 266–77] is especially effective in bankrupting 'satisficing', perhaps even more than Marris intended. As he points out, in one sense it amounts to a statement of a constraint, rather than an objective. That is, certain conditions must be satisfied (*i.e.*, losses not incurred). In another sense it indicates a 'maximum'—given the costs of getting more information about the possibility and location of still superior positions. As Marris suggests, the subject faced with a problem involving effort in finding the solution, sets up a tentative solution or target as an aspiration or satisficing level. If he happily succeeds in exceeding that level, he raises his 'aspiration', target or 'satisficing' level. And conversely. In this sense the word is simply a name of the search process for maximizing some criterion—not a replacement or substitute.

There is no sense in trying to summarize a review. Instead a couple of personal impressions are offered. First, and least important, it is embarrassing that some economists feel compelled to preface or defend their work by an attack on the irrelevancy of existing economic theory. Even more embarrassing is their subsequent erroneous use of that theory.

Second, it is a genuine puzzle to me why economics has no 'field' or section (analogous to the 'fields' of money and banking, international trade, public finance, labor, etc.) devoted to 'property rights'. The closest thing to it is the field known as comparative economic systems; yet even there the fundamental role of the particular set of property right, as a specification of the opportunity set of choices about uses of resources, seems inadequately recognized. Especially puzzling is this in view of the fact that Adam Smith's *Wealth of Nations* is heavily concerned with exactly such questions. Perhaps the answer is that the whole of economics is the analysis of property rights in non-free goods. But if that is so, it is puzzling why it has taken so long to bring rigorous analytical techniques to bear on the implications about behavior under different forms of property rights. In any event, a substantial start has now been made—even if it has not been explicitly recognized. Hence one of the major points of this paper has been to try to make explicit and emphasize this basis which, I think, underlies the advances of analyses here reviewed.

REFERENCES

[1] Armen A. Alchian and Reuben A. Kessel, 'Competition, Monopoly and the Pursuit of Pecuniary Gain', *Aspects of Labor Economics*, Princeton: National Bureau of Economic Research 1962.

[2] H. Averch and L. L. Johnson, 'Behavior of the Firm Under Regulatory Constraint'. *American Economic Review*, December 1962, 52, 1052–69.

[3] William J. Baumol, *Business Behavior, Value and Growth*, Macmillan Co., New York, 1959.

[4] Gary Becker, *The Economics of Discrimination*, University of Chicago Press, Chicago, 1957.

[5] Richard M. Cyert and James G. March, editors, *A Behavioral Theory of the Firm*, Prentice-Hall, Englewood Cliffs, 1963.

[6] Jack Downie, *The Competitive Process*, Gerald Duckworth & Co., London, 1958.

[7] Robin Marris, *The Economic Theory of 'Managerial' Capitalism*, Free Press of Glencoe, 1964.

[8] Thomas Mayer, 'The Distribution of Ability and Earnings', *The Review of Economics and Statistics*, May 1960, pp. 189–95.

[9] Edith T. Penrose, *The Theory of the Growth of the Firm*, John Wiley and Sons, New York, 1959.

[10] J. G. March and H. A. Simon, *Organizations*, John Wiley and Sons, New York, 1958.

[11] Oliver E. Williamson, *The Economics of Discretionary Behavior: Managerial Objectives in a Theory of the Firm*, Prentice-Hall, Englewood Cliffs, 1964.

The Short Run Revisited*

LOUIS DE ALESSI[1]

Louis De Alessi (B.A. University of California at Los Angeles, 1954; M.A., 1955; Ph.D., 1961) was born in Turin, Italy, in 1932. Presently he is Professor of Economics and Director of the Products Liability Project at the University of Miami Law and Economics Center. De Alessi has also served on the faculties of Duke and George Washington Universities. His primary research interests have been in the fields of price theory, public choice, and the theory of property rights.

The theory of the firm has been the subject of voluminous literature. Nevertheless, some ambiguities and inconsistencies still persist. In particular, the traditional approach to the short run as a period in which the quantities of some inputs cannot be varied[2] requires clarification. The failure to recognize explicitly that the adjustment of a firm to a change in market conditions depends upon the costs and receipts associated with the adjustment leads to a number of ambiguities, including some confusion regarding the regions of the production function that are empirically relevant.

Section I contains a brief statement of the traditional short-run theory of the firm; then, as a first approximation, the main implications regarding the

paths of prices and of input proportions in the short run are derived from higher-level economic hypotheses. Section II indicates how the relevant predictions regarding the short-run behavior of the firm may be derived from the wealth-maximizing (stock) approach, avoiding some shortcomings of the traditional profit-maximizing (flow) approach. Section III extends the analysis to the "uneconomic" regions of the production function. Section IV contains a few concluding remarks.

Consider a competitive firm whose production function[3]

$$Z = f(a_1, a_2) \qquad (1)$$

is hypothesized to be a single-valued, continuous function with continuous first- and second-order partial derivatives; all variables represent flows per unit

*Reprinted from *American Economic Review* (June 1967) by permission of the American Economic Association. Copyright 1967, pp. 450–461.
[1]The author . . . acknowledges helpful comments by D. G. Davies, C. E. Ferguson, and J. S. McGee.
[2]For example, see [11, p. 41].

[3]The following exposition, equations (1) through (3), is standard in the literature. For example, see [6, Ch. 3].

time.[4] The parameter $Z°$ defines a particular output isoquant, conforming to the usual requirement, with slope at a point equal to $-f_1/f_2$.

Let the firm purchase inputs a_1 and a_2 in perfectly competitive markets at constant prices p_1 and p_2. Total costs of production are given by the linear equation:

$$C = p_1a_1 + p_2a_2, \qquad (2)$$

and the parameter $C°$ defines a particular isocost with constant slope equal to $-p_1/p_2$.

Well-known first-order conditions for cost minimization subject to an output constraint require that the input-output combination be on the locus of points (least cost path) where:

$$\frac{f_1}{f_2} = \frac{p_1}{p_2}, \qquad (3)$$

that is, where the ratio of the marginal products of the inputs is equal to the ratio of their prices.[5] Fig. 1, the least cost path is shown by OE.

Given the output demand function, the long-run equilibrium conditions for a profit-maximizing firm are easily obtained. Traditional statements of the theory then turn to the main problem at hand, the re-

---

[4] The traditional production function relates rates of input utilization to rates of output. As A. A. Alchian [1] has suggested, however, planned volume (V) of output may be a crucial variable; this point, together with some shortcomings of the flow relative to the stock approach in the analysis of the firm, will be examined in subsequent sections of this paper.

[5] Fulfillment of second-order conditions implies that output isoquants are concave from above over the relevant range [6, p. 51].

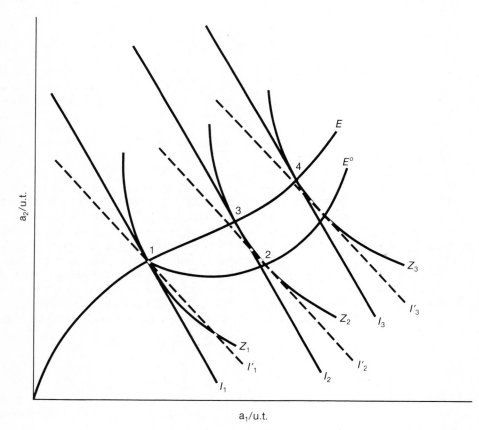

Fig. 1

sponse of the individual firm to changes in circumstances (e.g., an increase in the demand for the output of the firm) that disrupt the equilibrium.[6] Let T measure the period from the instant of time some disturbance occurs to the instant of time a given adjustment is completed, where the adjustment may involve a change in input proportions as well as a change in the absolute quantity and in the form of the inputs utilized. The usual procedure is to consider adjustment periods or runs of progressively longer duration, where the longer the run, the more inputs the firm "can" vary and the greater the variation permitted in the quantity of any given input. In the two-input case, one short run may thus be shown by holding a_2 fixed at the initial equilibrium level (e.g., point 1 in Fig. 1) and allowing a_1 to vary.

The purpose of distinguishing between runs of different length presumably is to explain the empirical observations that, the shorter the period T, the higher is the cost of the change in output and the fewer the inputs that are varied. It follows that economic theory, *inter alia,* must yield implications consistent with this evidence. By defining the short run as the time period in which some inputs cannot be varied, the desired implications regarding costs are obtained, e.g., [5, pp. 111–15]. This solution, however, avoids a crucial theoretical issue. Implications regarding the proportions in which factors are varied in a given market situation must also be derived from the theory. In particular, the statement that some inputs are held fixed during a given period must be interpreted as a falsifiable proposition implied by economic theory. The phenomenon in question may be identified (defined) as a short run, but the definition in no sense substitutes for the hypothesis.

All factors of production are variable over any given time interval greater than zero. The rate at which different inputs in fact are varied over time in response to some change in market conditions must depend upon the relative costs and receipts of all the alternative production strategies technologically available to the firm.

As a first approximation, hypothesize that the closer an output program is moved to the present (the shorter the period T) the greater are the costs [1]. Applied to the sellers of the inputs, this proposition implies that as shorter T's are considered the input supply curves decrease (shift to the left) and the greater is the cost to the buyer of varying any given input. That is,

$$p_i = p_i(T), \ p'_i < 0, \quad (i = 1, 2); \qquad (4)$$

substituting[7] into equation (3) yields:

$$\frac{f_1}{f_2} = \frac{p_1(T)}{p_2(T)}. \qquad (5)$$

Equation (4) does not deny that each firm purchases its inputs competitively. The input supply curve facing the individual firm is still hypothesized to be perfectly elastic at the price associated with a particular T; however, the shorter the period the higher is the price intercept.

As shorter periods T are considered, not only do supply functions decrease, but the rates of shifting differ among at least some of the inputs. The ratio $p_1(T)/p_2(T)$ increases, remains the same, or decreases depending upon whether the rate of change in p_1 with respect to T is greater than, equal to, or less than the rate of change in p_2 with respect to T (in all cases, all isocosts shift to the left as shorter T's are considered).

Each firm is thus hypothesized to consult a family of sets of budget constraints, where each set contains all possible alternative budget constraints of a given slope associated with the particular run contemplated by the firm for the (possibly partial) adjustment. Presumably one family of sets is applicable to expansion and another is applicable to contraction. Given the iso-product map derived from the traditional production function, a least cost path exists for each input price ratio associated with each adjustment period T. Each short-run least cost path is discontinuous at the original equilibrium point (e.g., $1E°$ in Fig. 1), since the firm presumably can continue to produce the current output at the current least cost.

---

[6]For the sake of brevity, the analysis in this paper is usually limited to the consequences associated with an increase in the demand for the output of the firm. The analysis, however, can be easily extended to include the consequences of a decrease in demand, of changes in the input supply function(s), and of changes in the firm's production function due to technological innovations.

[7]Although the analysis developed in this paper is not dependent upon the validity of the following conditions, it may be presumed that eventually $p_i' = 0$, and that $p_i'' > 0$ over at least part of the interval where $p_i' < 0$.

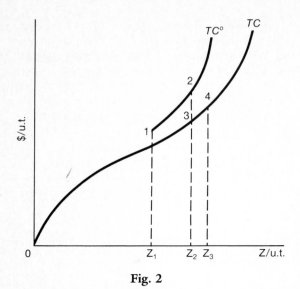

Fig. 2

Each short-run least cost path yields a short-run total cost curve. If diminishing returns prevail, the total cost curve *(TC)* for an increase in output during a particular short run $T°$ would be similar to $TC°$ in Fig. 2.[8] The longer the adjustment period T, the closer the short-run total cost curve approaches the long-run TC. Thus, the long-run TC (e.g., TC in Fig. 2) is the boundary of all the short-run TC curves.

Economic theory also asserts that the shorter the time interval, the smaller is the price elasticity of the market demand for a commodity. Thus, even in the case of a firm selling its output under purely competitive conditions, different output prices will prevail during at least some of the different adjustment periods considered by the firm. The form of the function relating the demand price per unit of output to T presumably has the same general properties attributed in equation (4) to the input price functions. It follows that a unique total revenue curve and a unique total cost curve may be associated with each

run,[9] and the usual criteria may be used to derive the profit-maximizing program for each period.

The analysis developed in this section implies that the firm is induced to seek full adjustment over time rather than instantaneously, and to vary inputs in different proportions as longer T's are considered. In particular, the firm may *choose* to hold one or more inputs fixed during periods of partial adjustment. For example, suppose that a firm initially is producing under conditions of long-run equilibrium (e.g., point 1 in Figs. 1 and 2), and that the demand for its output increases. Given the elasticity of this demand over time and the family of all short-run relative input prices, the profit-maximizing program during a particular short run may be that associated with the input price ratio shown by I'_2 (Fig. 1), and with point 2 (Figs. 1 and 2) in particular. In this event, the firm would choose to hold a_2 fixed for a time. The long-run equilibrium output, for an unchanged *schedule* of input prices, would still be along OE (e.g., point 4 in Figs. 1 and 2). It should be noted that, in the absence of any information regarding the relative costs of varying inputs in different proportions over different time periods, there is no a priori reason for predicting which factor, if any, will be held constant.[10]

It seems generally recognized that adjustment to a change in market conditions is not a free good. So far, the main assertion contained in this paper is that the extent of the adjustment depends upon the relevant costs and receipts. The traditional statement that the quantities of some inputs cannot be varied in the short run implies a denial of the higher-level economic hypotheses that demand curves are negatively sloped (the lower the cost of changing the input mix, *ceteris paribus*, the quicker the full adjustment) and that supply curves are positively sloped (the quicker the full adjustment sought, *ceteris paribus*, the higher the cost of changing the input mix).

Similarity with traditional analysis, however, has

---

[8]Note that the behavior of the individual firm is at issue. Thus, the *schedule* of input prices (where each price relates to a particular "run") is impounded in *ceteris paribus*. If expansion or contraction of all firms in the industry affects the schedules of input prices (input supply functions facing the industry are not perfectly elastic), then the firm's cost curves will shift accordingly.

The discontinuity in $TC°$ is associated with the approximation developed in this section and the two-dimensional nature of the diagram. A more complete statement of the appropriate cost surface is presented in Section II.

[9]This approach yields the familiar implication that firms will specialize in the speed (time elapsed) of their responses to changes in market conditions.

[10]This conclusion does not seem to be inconsistent with observation. Without allowing empirical evidence to intrude, it might be granted that in some cases the short-run cost of varying the quantity of some types of labor is greater than the cost of varying some types of plants or equipment, while in other cases the opposite cost relationship prevails. For an example of empirical evidence inconsistent with the classical treatment of labor as a purely variable factor, see [9].

been maintained by choosing the particular set of isocosts associated with a particular run, relating the short-run least cost path to the price per unit of output associated with that run, and identifying the profit-maximizing input-output combination.

The isoquant-based theory of the firm yields decision rules in terms of flows: under long-run competitive equilibrium, at the margin the rate of expenditures on all inputs is equal to the rate of receipts from the sale of the output, where presumably the rates in question remain constant indefinitely. When a disturbance occurs, *ceteris paribus*, the new long-run equilibrium flows may be derived and used to predict the long-run response of the firm. Under these circumstances, the present value of the constant rate of outlay given by each isocost and the present value of the constant rate of receipts associated with each output isoquant will yield present value total cost and total revenue curves with the same shape as the total cost and the total revenue curves given by the profit-maximizing model of traditional theory. Thus application of the usual marginal rules to the stock (wealth) and to the flow (profit) models would yield the same predictions regarding the long-run behavior of the firm. As Alchian and others have emphasized, however, the crucial concept is the *wealth* effect of the alternative strategies considered by the firm; this must be so, since the firm can always alter the time pattern of the flows by either lending or borrowing.

During the process of adjusting to a given disturbance, the pattern of flows for a given firm may be expected to vary from period to period. Predictions regarding the behavior of the firm in the (traditional) short run are usually obtained by examining progressively longer "representative" short runs of unspecified duration. Similarly, the short-run least cost paths derived in the preceding section may be useful pedagogically in deriving implications with respect to the nature of the short-run cost curves, and, in addition, to the short-run changes in input proportions. However, it must be recognized that the decision of the firm to adopt a particular input-output program during a particular time period can only be predicted by discounting to the present the flows associated with the alternative input-output programs for different periods, and then choosing the wealth-maximizing sequence of programs. That is, a rational firm must consider a multiperiod horizon in determining the input-output rates in a specific pe-

riod; in particular, a firm owning resources must decide the intertemporal allocation of such resources.

A firm responding to a change in market conditions may be viewed as producing the adjustment involved in addition to the other product (Z) under consideration. The present value cost, C_p, of the adjustment may be hypothesized to be a function of (1) x, the rate at which the adjustment is undertaken, (2) V, the total planned adjustment, (3) T^*, the length of the interval between the time when the disturbance occurs and the time when the adjustment is begun, and (4) m, the length of the interval between the time when the adjustment is begun and the time when the adjustment is completed:[11]

$$C_p = f(x, V, m, T^*), \ C_p \geq 0, \qquad (6)$$

where $f_x > 0, f_{xx} > 0, f_V > 0, f_{VV} < 0, f_x V < 0, f_T{}^* > 0$ [1]. The total quantity of the adjustment undertaken and its schedule over time would then be determined at the margin in conjunction with the present value of the receipts from the adjustment. In this construct, the long run may be defined as the time period in which deferred changes in the quantity (and form) of each input used by the firm would not lead to a lower input price to the firm in present-value terms.

That is, the individual firm is hypothesized to adjust the quantity and the form of each input it uses until the present value of the marginal stream of outlays is equal to the present value of the marginal stream of receipts for each input. The firm chooses the least-cost mesh of the alternative input adjustments subject to a set of output constraints related to the elasticity over time of the demand for the firm's output. The wealth-maximizing solution thus yields the total planned change in the quantity and form of each input, the rate at which the change is undertaken, the instant of time when the change is begun, and the time period taken to complete it.[12] *Inter alia*, this approach yields information regarding the time period during which a specific input is held fixed and the schedule at which each input adjustment is phased into the production process.

---

[11]The T^* used in this paper corresponds to the T used by Alchian [1]. Following Alchian, m is a dummy variable whose value is determined by the values assigned to x and to V, where $V = \int_{T^*}^{T^* + m} x(t) dt$ and x may vary over time.

[12]In the case of one type of labor, for example, the present value of the hiring and training costs would be related to the planned number of workers to be added to the labor force, the rate at which such individuals are to be hired and trained, and the instant of time when the hiring and training programs are to begin.

The procedure outlined in the preceding paragraph would yield one point on the (flow) iso-product map for each period. The input-output program presumably will vary from period to period as the firm completes its adjustment, and may involve holding the rate of utilization of one or more inputs fixed during a given time period.[13]

These comments suggest that a particular input-output combination may appear to be irrational in terms of the flows prevailing in that period, and yet be the rational choice in terms of the wealth-maximizing model. Put more strongly, the flows prevailing in one time period do not provide, by themselves, sufficient information to determine the choice of the output program for that period [1]. Economists have obtained propositions regarding the short-run behavior of the firm from a model designed to predict long-run behavior under constant flows, but they have done so only at the cost of ignoring some relevant portions of economic theory.

III

The production function of a firm, according to one definition, ". . . shows the (maximum) quantity of product it [the firm] can produce for given quantities of each of the various factors of production it uses" [5, p. 123]. This definition has been taken to imply that a firm would not use additional quantities of a given input[14] beyond the economic region;[15] that is, output isoquants outside the relevant ridge lines would be straight lines parallel to their respective axes [3, p. 304]. A second definition of the production function rests on the minimum factor quantities necessary for given outputs. On this definition, the segments of the output isoquants outside the ridge lines are taken to vanish [3, p. 304].

Recently, Borts and Mishan have argued for a reinterpretation of the first definition. If a factor is taken to be fixed (and indivisible) during a given time period, and if the firm sells its output under monopolistic conditions, then output isoquants supposedly have meaning in the uneconomic region for the fixed factor and are straight lines parallel to the axis in the uneconomic region for the variable factor.[16] Borts and Mishan conclude that ". . . it is logically inadmissible to construct a diagram in which in both uneconomic regions the iso-product curves are uniquely determined" [3, p. 307].

---

[13] J. Hirshleifer has suggested that a firm may choose to hold some inputs fixed in the short run because of uncertainty regarding the permanence of the initial disturbance [7, p. 250]. The argument developed in this paper, although reinforced by the introduction of uncertainty, suggests that some inputs may be held fixed under conditions of certainty.

[14] As M. Friedman has pointed out, however, this presumes that the cost of discarding some units of this input is zero [5, pp. 130–131].

[15] The economic region is frequently defined (Rule I) as the range over which the marginal products (MP) of all inputs are greater than zero (and, possibly, equal to zero for some inputs); G. H. Borts and E. J. Mishan do so initially [3, p. 300]. Friedman [5, p. 130] and others, including Borts and Mishan later in the same article [3, p. 305], have noted that the maxim of rational behavior for a firm (Rule II) is to use such a combination of factors that the average product (AP) to each input separately is falling (or at least remains constant).

As Friedman and others recognize, these two rules yield the same answer only if the production function is homogeneous of degree one; then the locus of points (ridge line) where the AP of one input is maximum and the ridge line where the MP of the other input is equal to zero coincide. If the production function is homogeneous of degree less than one, then the ridge lines for AP maximum are outside the ridge lines for MP = 0; if the production function is homogeneous of degree greater than one, the order of the ridge lines is reversed.

The two rules, of course, are not mutually exclusive. As Friedman concludes, "The point not to be exceeded is the point of vanishing (marginal) returns; the prudent man will seek to exceed the point of diminishing (average) returns" [5, p. 130].

If production functions are taken to be homogeneous of degree less than one, with degree one as the limit, satisfying the marginal conditions (operating in the range where the output isoquants are concave from above) is sufficient to insure that the AP of each input is either decreasing or constant.

Some economists, e.g., [10, p. 177], have suggested that the derivative of output, dZ (taken with respect to one of the inputs, when all inputs vary proportionately), first increases (increasing returns to scale) and then decreases (decreasing returns to scale). In the range of increasing returns to scale, application of rules I and II for rational behavior implies that the segments of the negatively sloped output isoquants outside the ridge lines for AP maximum would be in the "uneconomic" region of the production function.

Production functions yielding increasing returns to scale throughout are taken to be empirically irrelevant, since evidence purporting to support such functions has failed to allow for changes in the planned volume of output.

It may be useful to examine the form of the production function implied by Alchian's reformulation of the cost function. If planned volume (V) of output is held constant, the production surface with respect to the rate (x) of output exhibits decreasing returns to scale throughout. If the rate of output is held constant, the production surface with respect to V exhibits increasing returns to scale throughout. If V and x are taken to vary proportionately (the usual case, as suggested by Hirshleifer [7] and apparently accepted by Alchian [2, Ch. 21]), the production envelope at first exhibits increasing returns to scale and then decreasing returns to scale.

[16] Borts and Mishan [3, p. 307] argue that (i) if both factors are indivisible in the short period, the firm is restricted to a point within the economic region; (ii) if both factors are variable during the period in question, all choices must fall within the economic region.

If "uneconomic" regions exist,[17] the flow analysis developed in Section I of this paper implies that a firm would not operate within them.[18] Since it has been suggested that a noncompetitive firm using an "indivisible" factor may in fact operate in one of the uneconomic regions in the short run, the point deserves consideration.

The first issue to be examined is that of indivisibility.[19] Why should a factor be indivisible in the short run? To take a standard example, consider a firm using tractors as one of the inputs. Following Friedman [5, pp. 131–32], suppose that tractors come in two sizes, with the tractor of size II being in some relevant sense "twice" the tractor of size I. Tractors presumably come in these two sizes, given the demand function for tractors, due to the lower unit cost associated with producing a larger planned volume of output (V) of each of the fewer models relative to the cost of producing a smaller V of each of a broader range of models [1]. A firm using tractors of size I, following some change such as an increase in the demand for its output, may well prefer to shift to an intermediate-size tractor at an intermediate price.[20] If the cost of an intermediate-size tractor produced to order is sufficiently high, however, the firm may choose to acquire more of the standard sizes. That is, the choice to acquire some inputs in lumps can be predicted, at least in some relevant cases, by cost considerations alone. It may seem that this argument, if acceptable, applies to "indivisibility in acquisition" and not to "indivisibility in use" [8, pp. 231–33]. But "divisibility" of all inputs in acquisition implies "divisibility" of all inputs in use, since a firm, at some cost, may always

choose to modify the structure of its assets or change the form of its inputs.[21] The theory must be capable of predicting the revealed choice of a firm in the short run, under specified circumstances, to vary some inputs in discrete quantities rather than in infinitesimally small quantities; it is not helpful to cloak in the name of indivisibility what is really a plea of ignorance.[22]

The second issue is whether a firm would ever operate in the uneconomic region. The usual argument asserts that a competitive firm ". . . can never produce in the uneconomic region. For if the price falls below the lowest average variable cost (equals highest average return to the variable factor, given the factor price) it will incur negative quasi-rents"[23] [3, p. 305, fn. 2]. A firm facing a negatively sloped demand, however, apparently may do so: "All that is required in order to encompass the uneconomic region . . . is to regard some fixed amount of a factor . . . as being indivisible during the period in question" [3, p. 304].

If the concept of indivisibility is rejected as a short-run crutch, must output programs within the uneconomic region also be rejected? Given the argument developed in Section II, the answer seems to be negative. As the firm considers alternative adjustment periods, the present value cost of varying one input may be sufficiently greater than the present value cost of varying the other input(s) that the firm may choose to operate in one of the uneconomic regions during some limited time period. If wealth, rather than profit, is used as the relevant criterion, a competitive as well as a monopolistic firm may

---

[17]This paper is not concerned with the empirical question of whether "uneconomic" regions exist.

[18]As noted earlier, second-order conditions for profit maximization imply that the firm would operate in the range where iso-product curves are concave from above. Moreover, a firm (at least a competitive firm) would operate beyond the region of increasing returns to scale if such a region existed.

[19]The term "indivisibility" has been used to cover a variety of phenomena. For example some economists have used it to describe a factor which cannot be varied during a given interval of time, e.g., [3, p. 304]; some economists have also noted that ". . . indivisibility is necessary for economies of size or scale" [3, p. 305]. This paper is concerned with indivisibility as a short-run phenomenon.

[20]The "half-size man" to drive the "half-size tractor" [5, p. 132] apparently would not be a limit here. In any event I fail to see why, at some suitable price, the "half-size man" (in the technologically relevant sense) would not be forthcoming.

[21]The distinction between fixed and variable costs is also ambiguous. Whether a firm chooses to vary a particular cost depends upon the relative gains and losses of doing so. At some cost a contract can be broken (as any lawyer will gladly admit), a private radio network substituted for a telephone, and so on.

The only costs which legitimately (i.e., implied by economic theory) cannot be varied are "sunk" costs; such costs, of course, are irrelevant to the decision process.

[22]The preceding statements are not inconsistent with an alternative meaning of indivisibility. As Alchian suggests, the term may be interpreted to cover the phenomenon whereby more durable "dies" result in more than proportional increases in output potential [1, p. 29]. In this sense indivisibility is simply the name given to the sign of certain partial derivatives; it does not explain anything.

[23]It should be noted that Borts and Mishan are working with a linearly homogeneous production function. Their statements would not be necessarily correct, even in the context of flow analysis, if, for example, the production function in question were homogeneous of degree less than one.

choose to operate for a time in the uneconomic re-gion—particularly if it is granted that uncertainty may exist regarding the permanence of the change in circumstances inducing the adjustment in out-put.[24]

The preceding comments suggest that, for analyt-ical purposes, it is necessary to show the uniquely determined iso-product curves in each uneconomic region.[25] Whether the firm will operate within any such region during a particular short run can only be determined *after* allowing for the appropriate cost and revenue considerations. Furthermore, although at most one such region would be relevant in the two-input case, n-1 regions may be relevant in the n-inputs case.

The concept of a priori fixed, indivisible inputs is misleading. Among other things, such an approach masks the implication that a competitive firm may find it profitable to operate for a time within the uneconomic region.[26]

IV

The traditional approach to the short run as a period in which some inputs cannot be varied is the-oretically inadmissible. The substitution of a defini-tion for the corresponding falsifiable hypothesis im-plied by economic theory masks some empirically relevant issues. In what proportion are inputs to be varied in the short run? Which inputs, if any, are to be held constant? Which regions of the production function are empirically relevant? Why?

The production function must specify which in-put-output combinations are technologically rele-vant; cost and revenue information alone can deter-mine which combinations are economically relevant. If it is granted that variation in the input mix is not a free good, then the proportion in which inputs are varied in response to some change in market con-ditions will depend upon the relative costs and re-ceipts of all the alternative production strategies tech-nologically available to the firm. Moreover, tradi-tional flow analysis yields propositions regarding behavior of the firm in the short run only at the cost of some ambiguities. The wealth-maximizing model suggests that, if "uneconomic" regions exist, they are relevant for competitive as well as for monopolistic firms.

REFERENCES

1. A. A. Alchian, "Costs and Outputs," in M. Abramovitz and others, *The Allocation of Economic Resources: Essays in Honor of Bernard F. Haley.* Stanford, Calif. 1959.
2. _____ and W. R. Allen, *University Economics,* Bel-mont, Calif. 1964.
3. G. H. Borts and E. J. Mishan, "Exploring the 'Uneco-nomic Region' of the Production Function," *Rev. Econ. Stud.,* Oct. 1962, *9,* 300–12.
4. R. H. Coase, "The Problem of Social Cost," *Jour. Law and Econ.,* Oct. 1960, *3,* 1–44.
5. M. Friedman, *Price Theory,* Chicago 1962.
6. J. M. Henderson and R. E. Quandt, *Microeconomic Theory.* New York 1958.
7. J. Hirshleifer, "The Firm's Cost Function: A Successful Reconstruction?" *Jour. Bus.,* July 1962, *35,* 235–55.
8. F. Machlup, *The Economics of Sellers' Competition.* Balti-more 1952.
9. W. Y. Oi, "Labor as a Quasi-Fixed Factor," *Jour. Pol. Econ.,* Dec. 1962, *70,* 538–55.
10. W. S. Vickrey, *Microstatics.* New York 1964.
11. A. A. Walters, "Production and Cost Functions: An Econ-ometric Survey," *Econometrica,* Jan.–Apr. 1963, *31,* 1–66.

[24] R. H. Coase's suggestion that an input be considered ". . . as a right to perform certain (physical) actions" [4, pp. 43–44] is a promising point of departure for further investigations in this area.

[25] E.g., if the present-value cost of not using some resources is zero, the least cost path for these resources outside the relevant ridge lines would then be straight lines parallel to their respective axes.

[26] As Borts and Mishan point out, there is nothing necessarily uneco-nomic about operating in the uneconomic region.

On the Economics of Transfer Pricing*

JACK HIRSHLEIFER[1]

Jack Hirshleifer (A.B., Harvard University, 1945; A.M., 1948; Ph.D., 1950) was born in 1925 in New York City. Presently he is Professor of Economics at the University of California at Los Angeles. Prior to joining the UCLA faculty in 1958 he served on the faculty of the School of Business at the University of Chicago. Hirshleifer's major contributions have dealt with optimal investment decisions, the theory of equilibrium in speculative markets, and biological analogies in economics. Among his other publications are the widely used textbook *Price Theory and Applications*. Hirshleifer is a co-editor of the *Journal of Economic Literature* and the *Journal of Economic Behavior and Organization*.

In order to achieve the benefits of decentralization in decision-making, many corporations have developed divisional organizations in which some or all of the separate divisions are virtually autonomous "profit centers." This paper is concerned with the problem of pricing the goods and services that are exchanged between such divisions within a firm and with how these prices should be set in order to induce each division to act so as to maximize the profit of the firm as a whole. The problem is an important one, because the prices which are set on internal transfers affect the level of activity within divisions, the rate of return on investment by which each division is judged, and the total profit that is achieved by the firm as a whole.

Two recent papers which have drawn attention to the crucial importance of transfer-price policies have also discussed alternative approaches to the problem.[2] The paper by Cook recommends the use of market-based prices, at least as an ideal, while Dean favors "negotiated competitive prices." Such brief description does not, of course, do justice to either of the articles, both of which were more concerned with drawing attention to the importance of decentralization and transfer pricing than with rigorous determination of optimal transfer-price rules. The

*Reprinted from *Journal of Business* (July 1956) by permission of The University of Chicago Press. Copyright 1956, pp. 172–184.
[1]The author would like to thank Milton Friedman for his criticisms and suggestions.

[2]Paul W. Cook, Jr., "Decentralization and the Transfer-Price Problem," *Journal of Business*, XXVIII (April, 1955), 87–94; and Joel Dean, "Decentralization and Intra-company Pricing," *Harvard Business Review*, XXXIII (July–August, 1955), 65–74.

argument made in the present paper is that market price is the correct transfer price only where the commodity being transferred is produced in a competitive market, that is, competitive in the theoretical sense that no single producer considers himself large enough to influence price by his own output decision. If the market is imperfectly competitive, or where no market for the transferred commodity exists, the correct procedure is to transfer at marginal cost (given certain simplifying conditions) or at some price between marginal cost and market price in the most general case.[3]

A. CONDITIONS OF THE ANALYSIS

For the sake of precision, we shall somewhat more formally restate the problem under investigation. A firm sets up two or more internal profit centers. Each of these is to maximize its own separate profits, possibly subject to restraints or rules imposed by overall management. Exchanges of goods may take place between two such centers. At what price should the unit of commodity be valued for the purpose of computing the "profits" of the selling and buying centers? The goal, for the present theoretical analysis, will be to establish that mode of pricing which leads the autonomous profit centers to make decisions yielding the largest aggregate profit for the firm as a whole.

As a concrete case, let us take a firm with two such centers: a manufacturing unit (the seller division) and a distribution unit (the buyer division). The commodity exchanged—called the "intermediate product"—is the commodity as it leaves the manufacturing unit. There is also a final product to be sold by the distribution unit.

Unless stated otherwise, we shall assume that both *technological independence* and *demand independence* apply between the operations of the two divisions. Technological independence means that the operating costs of each division are independent of the level of operations being carried on by the other. Demand independence means that an additional external sale by either division does not reduce the external demand for the products of the other. Demand independence is a more special assumption than technological independence. The latter, we

might expect, would apply at least approximately to a wide variety of practical situations. In general, however, we would expect there to be at least some demand dependence—for example, additional sales of the final product by the distribution division would tend to reduce external demand for the intermediate product. This point will be discussed in more detail later.

B. TRANSFER PRICE FOR BEST JOINT LEVEL OF OUTPUT

Suppose that a single joint level of output is to be determined for the two divisions; the distribution division will handle exactly as much product as the manufacturing division will turn out. A common level of output might rationally be required by central management under either of two different sets of circumstances: (1) there might be no market for the intermediate product at all, in which case there is no way for the manufacturing division to dispose of a surplus or for the distribution division to make up a deficiency, or (2) there might be a strong relation of technological dependence between the operations of the two divisions, such that marginal costs for either division jump sharply in shifting to dealings with the outside market. For example, imagine an integrated steel mill, with two divisions exchanging molten iron. Shipping excess iron out of the mill could involve high handling costs to the selling division, and purchasing iron outside could involve high reheating costs to the buying division so that trading on the external market might rationally occur only under very unusual conditions. (This point will be alluded to again in Section F, which discusses technological dependence.)

The determination of the best joint level of output is shown in Fig. 1. In this diagram quantity of output is measured along the horizontal axis for both divisions, q_m representing output of the manufacturing division and q_d of the distribution division. (We assume that the units of the intermediate and the final commodities are commensurate. In some cases there will be an obvious natural unit: e.g., pairs of shoes exchanged between a shoe-manufacturing and a shoe-retailing division. Sometimes, as when the intermediate product is copper and the final product copper wire, it may be necessary to express the quantities of the latter in terms of some transformed unit like pounds of copper contained.) Prices and costs per unit of output are measured vertically. The curves

[3]This statement is itself an oversimplification, since pricing at marginal cost is a necessary but not a sufficient condition. What is involved is a whole mode of procedure, described below, for finding the optimum price from the point of view of the overall interests of the firm.

labeled *mmc* and *mdc* represent the marginal manufacturing cost and the marginal distribution cost, respectively, each as a function of output.

Assuming that there is a competitive market for the final product, the distribution division will face a ruling price P. The best solution for the firm as a whole is to set the joint level of q_m and q_d at the output such that $mmc + mdc = P$ —that is, where the over-all marginal cost equals the price of the final product. If P equals the vertical distance OM in Fig. 1, the optimum output is OL.

Such an output would be established by central management by adding the *mdc* and *mmc* curves of the separate divisions. It is simple, however, to devise a transfer-price rule which will lead the divisions autonomously to the same solution. Suppose that the distribution division calls for and secures from the manufacturing division a schedule showing how much the manufacturing division would produce (i.e., sell to the distribution division) at any transfer price p^* for the intermediate commodity. This schedule would, in fact, be the same as the *mmc* curve if the manufacturing division rationally determines its

output to set $mmc = p^*$.[4] With this information, the distribution division can then determine a curve showing the difference or "margin" $(P - p^*)$ between market price and transfer price for any level of output which it might set. The distribution division then finds its own output where $mdc = P - p^*$ at OL and establishes the transfer price $LD = ON$. Evidently, the manufacturing division will then also produce at OL, since that is where $mmc = p^*$. The upper shaded area in Fig. 1 represents the separate profit of the manufacturing division, and the lower shaded area that of the distribution division. One condition must be stipulated: the distribution division must not be permitted to increase its separate profit by finding a quasi-marginal revenue curve *marginal* to $P - p^*$ (the one labeled "*mr*") and establishing an output of OR and a transfer price of $RS = OU$. This would amount to the distribution division's exploiting the manufacturing division by acting as a monopolistic buyer of

[4]Technically, this statement is correct only over the range where *mmc* exceeds average variable cost.

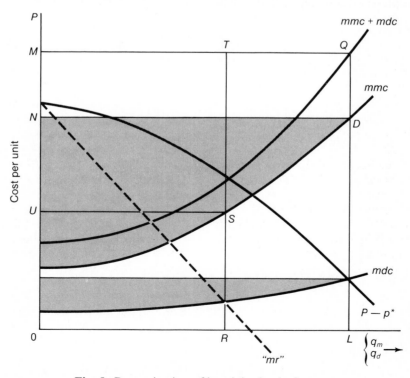

Fig. 1. Determination of best joint level of output.

the latter's product, in which case the gain to the former would be more than offset by the loss to the latter, and so the firm as a whole would lose thereby. The net loss is evident from the fact that firm output would be set at OR rather than at the optimal level of OL.

In the current discussion the distribution division has been given the dominant role in decision-making. This could be reversed without any essential change; instead of the distribution division working with the supply function of the manufacturing division, the latter could work with the demand function of the former. A parallel stipulation would also apply: the manufacturing division must be prevented from exploiting the distribution division as a monopolistic seller. Incidentally, bilateral bargaining might lead to a rather poor solution in these circumstances.

The solution remains essentially unchanged if the market for the final product is not perfectly competitive. In that case, a sloping demand curve and marginal revenue curve could be constructed instead of the horizontal demand curve MTQ used in Fig. 1. The process is exactly as before, except that what corresponds to the curve labeled $P - p^*$ in Fig. 1 would be $MR - p^*$, where MR is marginal revenue for the final product.

The result in this section may be considered marginal cost pricing for the intermediate product, since $p^* = mmc$. We shall find, in fact, that marginal cost pricing in this sense is a quite general answer for transfer pricing under conditions of demand independence. It is, however, marginal cost pricing only in a special sense, where the rules of procedure described above are set up. These rules are designed so as to correspond to the solution that a centralized management would arrive at with full information—namely, to set the sum of the divisional marginal costs equal to price (in the perfectly competitive case) or marginal revenue (in the imperfectly competitive case) in the final market.

C. TRANSFER PRICE WITH COMPETITIVE INTERMEDIATE MARKET

We shall now drop the assumption that a single joint level of output must be established for the two divisions together. Instead, each division is assumed to be free to determine its own output, with the manufacturing division selling its excess production, if any, on the intermediate market, and the distri-

bution division similarly calling on this market to supply any excess of the quantity it desires to handle over that available from the manufacturing division. For the present, we assume that the intermediate market is competitive, so that a price p for the intermediate commodity exists. The final market is also assumed to be competitive. It then follows from the assumption of technological independence that each of the divisions is indifferent between trading the intermediate commodity within or outside the firm.

In Fig. 2(a), manufacturing cost per unit is measured *upward* along the vertical axis, and distribution cost per unit is measured *downward*. If $p = OH = BC$, then the manufacturing division should produce the output OC. If $P - p = EF$, the distribution division should handle the output OE. If both are required to set a best joint level of output, however, that output is OL, which is where $mmc + mdc = P$. Here P is measured by the vertical distance AD, which is constructed so as to equal $BC + EF$ (i.e., $p + [P - p]$). Evidently, the requirement of a single joint level of output led to the manufacturing division's producing too much and the distribution division too little. The net increase in profit over that solution is measured by the excess of the area $JKFD$ over the area $BHGA$ in Fig. 2(a). Since $GH = JK$, it is evident from the geometry that the excess must be positive. This argument assumes technological independence.

If a transfer price p^* is to be established in this case, clearly it should be equal to p, because at any other p^* one of the two divisions will refuse to trade. Actually, under our assumptions there is no particular need for internal trading at all, since the divisions are effectively independent firms with common ownership. On the other hand, there is no objection to internal trading, and this can only take place if $p^* = p$.

The assumption of a competitive market for the *final* commodity is not essential for this result. If we assume that the distribution division faces a sloping demand curve as in Fig. 2(b),[5] we merely substitute marginal revenue MR for P in making our output decision. In Fig. 2(b) the distribution division produces at OE where $mdc = MR - p$. The correct transfer price remains $p^* = p$.

---

[5]The demand curve is labeled $D - p$, representing the quantity demanded in terms of the netback to the distribution division after subtracting the transfer outlay of p.

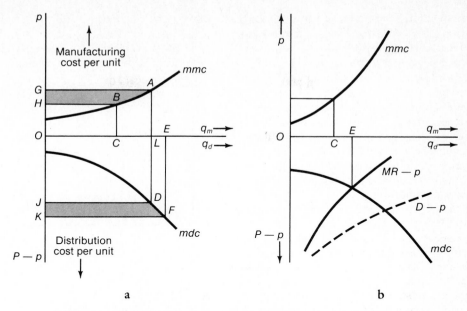

Fig. 2. Best divisional levels of output, competitive intermediate market.

In general, then, if the intermediate market is competitive, the transfer price should be the market price irrespective of the competitiveness of the market for the final product. For this case, however, p also equals *mmc*, so our earlier contention that marginal-cost pricing is the more general solution is not refuted by this result.

D. TRANSFER PRICE WITH IMPERFECTLY COMPETITIVE INTERMEDIATE MARKET

We now turn to the substantially more difficult case where the market for the intermediate product is not perfectly competitive, so that—setting aside the demand of the distribution division itself—the external market for the intermediate product facing the manufacturing division has a sloped demand curve. However, we assume demand independence, that is, sales made by the manufacturing division in the intermediate market do not reduce the demand for the final product sold by the distribution division, and, conversely, internal sales to the distribution division do not reduce external demand. In general, we would expect some demand dependence. For example, if the manufacturing division sells shoes both internally and externally, one would expect that each additional sale to the distribution division would re-

duce the final market demand for shoes sold to independent distributors, and this demand reduction would soon be reflected in the intermediate market demand for external sales of the manufacturing division. Nevertheless, we can imagine reasonable cases where the internal and external sales would have substantially independent demands. For example, our shoe firm could distribute its manufactured products solely through independent distributors in the domestic market, its own distribution division being limited to sales in the foreign market. Or a copper concern might use some of its copper internally only for a wire-fabricating division, while selling externally only to producers who make pots and pans or any copper products other than wire.

Under these conditions the firm is in a position akin to that of a discriminating monopolist; it sells the output of its manufacturing division in one market and of its distribution division in another.[6] We shall first derive the over-all solution for the firm and then find that mode of transfer pricing which will permit autonomous realization of this solution. The over-all solution is to equate the joint marginal cost

[6]The firm need only have the power to separate its markets and to face imperfect competition in the intermediate market. The final market may be perfectly competitive.

of production with the net marginal revenue in each separate market. The word "net" means that we must adjust the market marginal revenue by the incremental cost of delivering to the market concerned.[7] In this case, we assume no delivery cost to the market for the intermediate product, so the relevant marginal revenue is simply that derived from the external demand for the intermediate product. In the case of the distribution division, however, marginal distribution cost must be subtracted from market marginal revenue to derive net marginal revenue for the firm's output of the final commodity.

The solution is illustrated in Fig. 3. Fig. 3(a) shows the demand curve d and the marginal revenue curve mr for the intermediate product. Fig. 3(b) shows the demand curve D and the marginal revenue curve MR facing the distribution division in the final product market. The mdc curve is as before, and the net marginal revenue curve nMR is the vertical difference between MR and mdc. In Fig. 3(c) the two curves mr and nMR are plotted, together with their horizontal sum mr_t. The maximum profit solution is to establish the output q_m of the manufacturing division by the intersection of the mmc and mr_t curves at Q.[8] The amount sold on the intermediate market is OM (shown also in Fig. 3(a)), and the amount sold by the distribution division is OD (shown also in Fig. 3(b)).

The solution just discussed would be arrived at directly by a central decision agency with the appropriate information. We have not yet discussed the pattern of transfer pricing which would lead to the optimal result, given autonomous decision-making by one or both divisions. It can be seen immediately, however, that the correct transfer price to achieve the maximum-profit result is $p^* = OA = mmc$. In Fig. 3(b) setting p^* equal to OA would lead the distribution division to handle the correct amount OD. It would arrive at this by setting p^* equal to nMR, which is equivalent to setting $mmc + mdc$ equal to MR. This suggests the rule that marginal-cost pricing (i.e., setting the transfer price equal to mmc) be adopted for the conditions examined here. However, we do not know quite enough to assert this yet, because the level of mmc is a function of q_m,

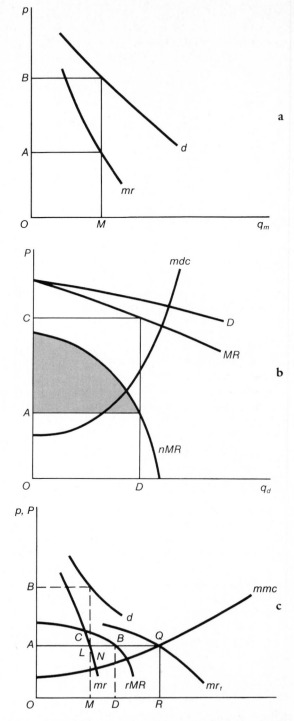

a

b

c

Fig. 3. Solution for imperfectly competitive intermediate market.

[7]This point is neglected in standard economic textbooks but usually is of great importance in applied economic problems.
[8]An explanation of this standard solution is given in economic texts (see, e.g., G. J. Stigler, *The Theory of Price* [rev. ed.; New York: Macmillan Co., 1952], p. 217).

and q_m itself is dependent upon q_d. This difficulty, however, is not hard to resolve. All that is required is that the distribution division indicate to the manufacturing division its demand for the intermediate product as a function of p^*—namely, the curve nMR. The manufacturing division, incidentally, must be instructed to accept this curve as a marginal revenue curve to be added to mr to get mr_t. This stipulation, analogous to those made in Section B, is necessary, because there might otherwise be an incentive for the manufacturing division to treat the demand curve of its affiliate on the same par as an external demand curve, which would lead to constructing a curve *marginal* to nMR for adding to mr to get mr_t, with a view to charging the affiliate a transfer price higher than mmc. This would be equivalent to using the monopoly power of the manufacturing division to exploit the internal as well as the external market for the intermediate commodity; the effect of doing so would be to increase the apparent profit of the manufacturing division separately but to depart from the over-all optimum for the firm by imposing a greater loss of profit upon the distribution division.

Our transfer-price rule, then, for the case where demand independence and technological independence apply, with the market for the intermediate commodity imperfectly competitive (the market for the final product may be perfectly or imperfectly competitive), is to establish the price at marginal manufacturing cost—or, more generally, at the marginal producing cost of the seller division. This is to be understood, however, as a shorthand statement for following the rules indicated in the previous paragraph, which we may state more formally as follows:

Distribution division:

1. Determine the nMR curve and convey the information to the manufacturing division.

2. Given the transfer price p^*, produce where $p^* = nMR$.

Manufacturing division:

1. Determine mr and sum mr and nMR to get mr_t.

2. Produce where $mmc = mr_t$.

3. Establish p^* at the mmc determined by (2)—OA in Fig. 3(c).

4. Establish p at the price along the demand curve d corresponding to the output reserved to outsiders—in Fig. 3(c) OM is sold to outsiders at the price OB. Evidently, p always exceeds p^*.

One defect of this analysis is that the divisional "profits" determined by the transfer price established

as here advocated do not provide an unequivocal answer as to whether or not to abandon a subsidiary. (This was also true in the analysis of Sec. B.) Turning again to Fig. 3(b), the shaded area represents the profit of the distribution division before allowing for any separable fixed costs of that division. Suppose that the separable distribution fixed costs are such as to exactly equal the shaded area and that it is possible to avoid these costs by abandoning the distribution operation. The implication, then, is that we are indifferent as to having the distribution subsidiary. In fact, however, we are not, because, with the mmc curve as drawn, the distribution division is being charged a transfer price p^* which is contributing to the "profit" of the manufacturing division. In Fig. 3(c) the quantity OM is sold directly by the manufacturing division, and the quantity $OD = CQ$ is transferred to the distribution division. The total manufacturing cost for the items transferred is $MLQR$, while the aggregate transfer payments are $MCQR$. The incremental advantage to the manufacturing division of the internal market is the area LCQ less the small triangular area CLN, the latter representing the additional profit on external sales of the intermediate commodity which would have been made had there been no transfers to the distribution division.

Unfortunately, the true profitability to the firm of having a distributing division is not always greater than the profitability of that division alone. A differently shaped mmc curve yielding the same marginal solution—in particular, a ∪-shaped curve with most of the area above OA—can lead to the distribution division's being, on balance, a negative contributor to the profits of the manufacturing division. We may summarize the present point by saying that the transfer-price policy indicated gives the correct solution for firm operations in terms of autonomous determination of marginal levels of operations. For non-marginal adjustments like abandoning a subsidiary, the autonomous calculations based on the transfer-price rule discussed will not generally be correct, and a correct decision requires an over-all examination of the cost and revenue functions of the firm as a whole.

E. DEMAND DEPENDENCE

The analysis to this point has assumed demand independence—that the markets for the intermediate commodity and for the final commodity are entirely independent. Generally speaking, the firm's two markets will be connected in that an additional internal sale to a distributing subsidiary would be expected to lead to some reduction of external demand on the part of purchasers of the intermediate commodity who compete with the distributing subsidiary in the market for the final good. However, demand dependence is a matter of degree. For the instance already cited of a firm making an internal transfer of copper to be used only for wire, and external sales of copper to be used only for pots and pans, our demand independence model of Section D would apply in all substantial respects. If, however, both the internal and the external demands were for copper to be used for wire, demand dependence would probably be too strong to be ignored.

For analytical purposes it is convenient to define a category of "perfect demand dependence," which is a situation in which customers in the final product market are perfectly indifferent between purchasing the product of the distributing subsidiary or of its competitors, perfect competition being assumed, and where all the competitors as well as the distributing subsidiary secure the intermediate product solely from the manufacturing subsidiary of the firm studied. For this case, the following points briefly summarize the results of a somewhat complex analysis which is not reproduced here.

1. In long-run equilibrium, as defined in economic theory, enough firms enter any industry so as to eliminate economic profit in that industry; that is, what is eliminated is any economic surplus over and beyond the normal return to factors employed in the industry, plus rents accruing to unique factors (such as unusually favorable location) responsible for reducing the cost functions of particular firms below the general level of the industry. Under these conditions, and assuming that there are no unusual features about the cost function of the distributing subsidiary which distinguish it from the outside competitors, there is no advantage to be gained by granting the distributing subsidiary any lower price for the transferred commodity than the price charged to outsiders. The manufacturing unit can, by its monopolistic situation, essentially secure all the surplus available to the industry, and so there is no point in attempting to get more by artificially expanding the output of the distributing subsidiary—in fact, this can lead only to a net loss for the firm as a whole.[9]

[9]This result was pointed out to the author by Milton Friedman.

2. In the short run, however, all the economic profit in the industry may not have been eliminated by changes of scale of plants or entry of new competitors. In these circumstances the monopolist of the intermediate product can capture some of this economic surplus by selling at a subsidized price to a subsidiary operating in the final product market. It follows from the above that, if a monopolist in the intermediate market does not have such a subsidiary, he will in general be able to gain by buying out an independent distributor at the value of the latter's economic surplus—which will be less than the net advantage of the subsidiary to the manufacturing unit.

The case for a subsidized price can be illustrated in terms of a numerical example. Suppose that there are a hundred firms in the final product market, that Q_e is the quantity being distributed by outsiders, q_d is the quantity distributed by the subsidiary in the final product market, and P is the price of the final product.

Let the demand for the product be given by the equation

$$P = 100 - \frac{1}{100}(Q_e + q_d),$$

let the marginal manufacturing cost be given by $mmc = 0$,[10] and let the marginal distribution cost be given by $mdc = 20 + 2q_d$ for each of the independent distributors as well as the distributing subsidiary.

Given these relations, it can be shown that the optimal market price p (assuming no subsidy) is equal to 40. However, if a subsidy is permitted, it can be shown that the optimal transfer price p^* is approximately 13⅓. Since mmc is zero throughout, this result for the optimal transfer price falls between the market pricing of Section C and the marginal-cost pricing of Sections B and D. While this is a special case, it reveals the nature of the general solution.

3. The analysis of this section has, up to this point, assumed perfect demand dependence. More generally speaking, a degree of demand dependence may

[10]This assumption is made only to simplify the analysis. It could occur in a real situation if, for example, the branch of the firm here called the "manufacturing division" (but actually simply the selling division in an internal exchange) was engaged solely in licensing use of a patent in exchange for a royalty on each unit of output produced by the licensee.

exist somewhere between perfect dependence and absolute independence. Perhaps the most likely situation is that in which the product of the distributing subsidiary is differentiated, to some degree, from that of its competitors. Still, there may be some demand dependence in that additional sales of the distributing subsidiary would have some adverse effect on outside sales. Partial demand dependence might also occur if the firm we are considering is not a sole monopolist in the intermediate market but shares the market as an oligopolist with one or a few other firms. In this case an additional sale of the distributing subsidiary might lead to losses of sales for all the oligopolists together, but the manufacturing branch of the firm subsidizing its subsidiary might not bear the full impact of the loss. (This argument assumes that the oligopolists in the intermediate market jointly establish the optimum monopoly price for the group, each taking a certain fraction of the market.) In general, the solution for partial demand dependence will lie somewhere between the solutions discussed in Section D and in the earlier paragraphs of this section.

F. TECHNOLOGICAL DEPENDENCE— SOME COMMENTS

Technological dependence may affect, in more or less complicated ways, the indicated optimum output for the firm as a whole and therefore the transfer-price rule which determines the optimum output for the divisions operating separately. The level of operations in Division A may raise or lower the marginal cost function of Division B, and vice versa.

We shall not attempt an analytical solution of the over-all problem here. A formal solution for optimum behavior of the firm would run in terms of the economic theory of multiple products, but this would only be a first step to the solution in terms of transfer price. We shall, instead, make only some general comments.

1. In the typical firm producing more than one product, it seems likely that additional production in any one line will tend to reduce the average and the marginal costs of producing the other. The existence of such complementarities in production (i.e., the ability to produce the products jointly more cheaply than if they were produced separately) is a common reason for producing a secondary product, and, even if a secondary product were produced for other reasons, it would be unlikely to be retained by

a firm if its adverse effect on the other products were serious.

2. It appears that a beginning approach to the problem of transfer pricing under conditions of technological dependence would involve establishment of an internal "tax" or "subsidy" to make the autonomous calculations of the separate division take into account the effects on the margin of impaired or enhanced productivity in the other divisions.

3. Fairly frequently, a vertically integrated firm will not trade outside the firm on an intermediate market at all but will instead establish a level of joint output at which the selling division and the buying division will both produce. Under technological independence, such behavior is difficult to explain (see Sec. C above). With technological dependence under conditions of complementarity, however, such behavior becomes more understandable. When any division produces beyond the level which keeps it in step with the other vertically integrated divisions, the excess units are more costly to produce than if all the divisions had increased output together.

G. CONCLUSIONS

1. If a single joint level of output is to be determined (because no market for the intermediate commodity exists, or for any other reason), this output should be such that the sum of the divisional marginal costs equals the marginal revenue in the final market. To achieve this result by internal pricing, the transfer price must equal the marginal costs of the seller division. This is only a necessary condition, however, and not a sufficient one. The full solution involves one of the divisions presenting to the other its supply schedule (or demand schedule, as the case may be) as a function of the transfer price. The second division then establishes its output and the transfer price by a rule which leads to the optimum solution specified above for the firm as a whole.

2. Given technological independence and demand independence, if a perfectly competitive market for the intermediate commodity exists, transfer price should be market price. If the market for the intermediate commodity is imperfectly competitive, transfer price should be at the marginal costs of the selling division. The latter is the more general solution. In the general case of imperfect competition, the price of the intermediate commodity will exceed the marginal cost of the seller division. Transfer pricing at the market will then lead to excessive output

by the seller division and insufficient output by the buyer division—in comparison with the optimum solution.

3. Where technological dependence exists, the situation is so complex that we have not been able to indicate even the nature of the general solution. We suspect that the prospects for divisional autonomy may be poor under these conditions.

4. Where demand dependence exists, the analysis is rather complex. Generally speaking, the solution falls between market price and marginal cost.

5. Even under the assumptions of demand independence and technological independence, the optimal rule for transfer price leads to correct output adjustments only on the margin. It does not follow that, if an autonomous division is apparently losing money at the established transfer price, the firm would really increase its profits by abandoning the operation concerned.

We may close with some remarks about the practical implications of the foregoing analysis. Most commonly, divisional autonomy is probably desired not so much to rationalize interdivisional trading as to create incentives for the separate "profit centers" which will lead to improved internal efficiency within each. Nevertheless, cases may arise in which the former objective is the dominant one, and even where the latter is dominant some of the potential gains may be lost by an improper transfer-price rule or policy. In practice, the rule of pricing at the market is apparently the one most frequently adopted, and there are circumstances in which that rule is appropriate. Where it is not, however, the consequences of adopting it may be serious. Perhaps even more serious are the possible consequences of the error warned of in paragraph 5 above—evaluating the over-all operations of a division (with a view toward either expanding or abandoning it) on the basis of its separate "profit" calculated from the established transfer price, whether correct or incorrect. When non-marginal decisions like abandoning a subsidiary are under consideration, a calculation of the incremental revenues and costs of the operation as a whole to the firm should be undertaken.

Allocative Efficiency vs. "X-Efficiency"*

HARVEY LEIBENSTEIN

Harvey Leibenstein (B.S., Northwestern University, 1945; M.A., 1946; Ph.D., Princeton University, 1951) joined the faculty of Harvard University in 1967 where he is the Andelot Professor of Economics. Previously Professor Leibenstein served on the faculty of the University of California at Berkeley. In 1963 he was named a Guggenheim Memorial Foundation Fellow. He has written widely in the fields of economic theory, economic development, and demography. He is the author of *Economic Backwardness and Economic Growth, The Theory of Economic-Demographic Development, Beyond Economic Man,* and numerous articles. He has also served as a consultant to the RAND Corporation.

At the core of economics is the concept of efficiency. Microeconomic theory is concerned with allocative efficiency. Empirical evidence has been accumulating that suggests that the problem of allocative efficiency is trivial. Yet it is hard to escape the notion that efficiency in some broad sense is significant. In this paper I want to review the empirical evidence briefly and to consider some of the possible implications of the findings, especially as they relate to the theory of the firm and to the explanation of economic growth. The essence of the argument is that microeconomic theory focuses on allocative efficiency to the exclusion of other types of efficiencies that, in fact, are much more significant in many instances. Furthermore, improvement in "nonalloca-

tive efficiency" is an important aspect of the process of growth.

In Section I the empirical evidence on allocative efficiency is presented. In this section we also consider the reasons why allocation inefficiency is frequently of small magnitude. Most of the evidence on allocative inefficiency deals with either monopoly or international trade. However, monopoly and trade are not the focus of this paper. Our primary concern is with the broader issue of allocative efficiency versus an initially undefined type of efficiency that we shall refer to as "X-efficiency." The magnitude and nature of this type of efficiency is examined in Sections II and III. Although a major element of "X-efficiency" is motivation, it is not the only element, and hence the terms "motivation efficiency" or "incentive efficiency" have not been employed.

As he proceeds, the reader is especially invited to

*Reprinted from *American Economic Review* (June 1966) by permission of the American Economic Association. Copyright 1966, pp. 392–415.

keep in mind the sharp contrast in the magnitudes involved between Tables 1 and 2.

I. ALLOCATIVE INEFFICIENCY: EMPIRICAL EVIDENCE

The studies that are of interest in assessing the importance of allocative efficiency are summarized in Table 1. These are of two types. On the one side we have the studies of Harberger and Schwartzman on the "social welfare cost" of monopoly. On the other side we have a number of studies, among them those by Johnson, Scitovsky, Wemelsfelder, Janssen, and others, on the benefits of reducing or eliminating restrictions to trade. In both cases the computed benefits attributed to the reallocation of resources turn out to be exceedingly small.

Let us look at some of the findings. In the original Harberger study [14] the benefits for eliminating monopoly in the United States would raise income no more than 1/13 of 1 per cent. Schwartzman's [28] study which recomputes the benefits of eliminating monopoly by comparing Canadian monopolized industries as against counterpart competitive U.S. industries, and vice versa in order to determine the excess price attributable to monopoly, ends up with a similar result. Similarly, the benefits attributed to superior resource allocation as a consequence of the Common Market or a European Free Trade Area are also minute—usually much less than 1 per cent.

The calculations made by Scitovsky of the benefits to the Common Market (based on Verdoorn's data) led him to the conclusion that ". . . the most striking feature of these estimates is their smallness."

The one that is really important (for reasons to appear presently), the gain from increased specialization . . . which is less than one-twentieth of one per cent of the gross social product of the countries involved. This is ridiculously small . . ." [29, p. 64]. J. Wemelsfelder [33, p. 100] has calculated that the welfare gain of reducing import duties and increasing imports and exports accordingly amounts to .18 of 1 per cent of national income. Harry Johnson in an article on England's gain in joining a Free Trade Area [17, pp. 247 ff.] calculates the net gain from trade at less than 1 per cent. That is, Johnson arrives at the conclusion that 1 per cent of the national income would be the absolute maximum gain for Britain from entering the European Free Trade Area.

A recent study by L. H. Janssen [16, p. 132] calculates that the gains from increased specialization for the different countries of the European Economic Community would be largest for Italy, but even here the amount is only 1/10 of 1 per cent of total production.[1] Janssen points out that, if the production gain for Italy due to specialization were calculated

[1] R. A. Mundell in a review of Janssen's book appears to reach a similar conclusion to the point made in this paper when he speculates that:

> . . . there have appeared in recent years studies purporting to demonstrate that the welfare loss due to monopoly is small, that the welfare importance of efficiency and production is exaggerated, and that gains from trade and the welfare gains from tariff reduction are almost negligible. Unless there is a thorough theoretical re-examination of the validity of the tools on which these studies are founded, and especially of the revitalized concepts of producers' and consumers' surplus, someone inevitably will draw the conclusion that economics has ceased to be important! [22, p. 622].

Table 1. Product attributed to misallocation of resources

Study	Source	Country	Cause	Loss
A. C. Harberger	*A.E.R.* 1954	U.S.A. 1929	Monopoly	.07 per cent
D. Schwartzman	*J.P.E.* 1960	U.S.A. 1954	Monopoly	.01 per cent
T. Scitovsky	(1)	Common Market 1952	Tariffs	.05 per cent
J. Wemelsfelder	*E.J.* 1960	Germany 1958	Tariffs	.18 per cent
L. H. Janssen	(2)	Italy 1960	Tariffs	max. .1 per cent
H. G. Johnson	*Manchester School* 1958	U.K. 1970	Tariffs	max. 1.0 per cent
A. Singh	(3)	Montevideo Treaty Countries	Tariffs	max. .0075 per cent

Sources:
(1) [29].
(2) [16].
(3) Unpublished calculation made by A. Singh based on data found in A. A. Faraq, *Economic Integration: A Theoretical, Empirical Study,* University of Michigan, Ph.D. Thesis, 1963.

by Scitovsky's method, which he believes involves an overestimation, "the production gain in the most extreme case is still less than .4 per cent." Janssen concludes, as have others, that the welfare effects of a customs union based on the superior allocation of resources are likely to be trivial. He does, however, point to the possibility "that the mere prospect of the frontiers opening would infuse fresh energy into entrepreneurs." He recognizes that certain qualitative factors may be highly important and that the consequences of growth are certainly more significant than those of allocative welfare.

My research assistant, A. Singh, has calculated the gains from trade (following the Scitovsky method) for the Montevideo Treaty Countries[2] (Argentina, Brazil, Chile, Mexico, Paraguay, Peru, and Uruguay) and found it to be less than 1/150 of 1 per cent of their combined GNP. Even if we double or triple this result to allow for such factors as the effect of failing to take account of quantitative restrictions in the analysis, the outcome is still trivial.

Harberger's study on Chile [14] which involves the reallocation of both labor and capital yields a relatively large estimate. Harberger intends to obtain as large an estimate as possible of the consequences of reallocating resources by using what I believe to be (and what he admits to be) rather extreme assumptions in order to obtain maximum outer bounds. Despite this he comes up with a number that is between 9 and 15 per cent. However, no actual data are employed. What are used are outer-bound estimates based on personal impressions. I expect that a careful study similar to the Verdoorn-Scitovsky study would probably come up with numbers that would be no larger than 1 or 2 per cent.

The empirical evidence, while far from exhaustive, certainly suggests that the welfare gains that can be achieved by increasing *only* allocative efficiency are usually exceedingly small, at least in capitalist economies. In all but one of the cases considered all of the gains are likely to be made up in one month's growth. They hardly seem worth worrying about.

Let us see briefly why these gains are usually small. We cannot prove that we would expect them to be small on purely theoretical grounds. If we combine our theory with what we could agree are probably reasonable estimates of some of the basic magni-

tudes, then it appears likely that in many cases (but certainly not all *possible* cases) the welfare loss of allocative inefficiency is of trivial significance. The idea could be developed with the aid of the diagram employed by Harberger. (See Fig. 1.) In Fig. 1 we assume that costs are constant within the relevant range. D is the demand function. Under competition price and quantity are determined at the intersection C. The monopoly price is above the competitive price equal to AB in the figure. The monopoly output is determined at the point A. The welfare loss due to monopoly, which is the same as the welfare gain if we shifted to competition, is equal to the triangle ABC. We obtain an approximation to this amount by multiplying the price differential AB by the quantity differential BC by one-half and multiplying this by the proportion of national income in industries involving the misallocation.

Let us play around with some numbers and see the kind of results we get as a consequence of this formulation. Suppose that half of the national output is produced in monopolized industries and that the price differential is 20 per cent and that the average elasticity of demand is 1.5. Now the outcome will turn out to be 1½ per cent. But we really used enormous figures for the misallocation. And yet the result is small. Monopoly prices, according to estimates, appear to be only about 8 per cent on the average above competitive prices. We can substitute some

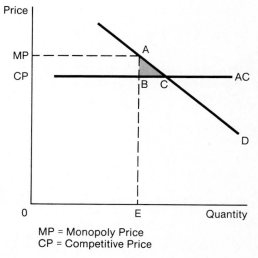

MP = Monopoly Price
CP = Competitive Price

Fig. 1

reason other than monopoly for the misallocation and still come out with similar results.[3]

Consider the cases of subsidized industries under some sort of governmental inducements to growth; and that of governmentally run industries. In the subsidy case the calculation would be similar. Suppose that as much as 50 per cent of the industries are subsidized to the extent of a 20 per cent difference in cost and that the output point on the demand function is where elasticity is unity. This last point may be reasonable since the operators of subsidized industries might want gross revenue to be as large as possible. If, on the other hand, we assume that they are profit maximizers and restrict output to a greater extent, then we might assume a price elasticity of two. This latter, however, is unlikely because monopoly profits are inconsistent with subsidized industries. Those who receive the subsidy would have the legitimate fear that the subsidy would be lowered if unusual profits were earned. Hence, behavior in the direction of revenue maximization appears reasonable and the calculated welfare loss is less than 2 per cent.

A similar result could be achieved in the case in which the government runs industries that affect 50 per cent of the national income of an economy. In all the cases we have considered, the magnitudes chosen appear to be on the large side and the outcome is on the small side.

Of course, it is possible that the magnitude of allocative inefficiency would be large if there are large discontinuities in productivity between those industries where inputs are located and those industries to which the same inputs could be moved. This, in effect, is the basic assumption that Harberger made in his study of Chile [14]. But if it turns out that there is a reasonable degree of continuity in productivity, and that the only way shifts could be made is by simultaneously increasing either social overhead capital or direct capital in order to make the shifts

involved, then, of course, a great deal of the presumed gains would be eaten up by the capital costs and the net marginal gains would turn out to be rather small. My general impression is that this is likely to be the case in a great many underdeveloped countries where differential productivities appear to exist between the agricultural sector and the industrial sector. One cannot go beyond stating vague impressions since there is a lack of hard statistical evidence on this matter.

Why are the welfare effects of reallocation so small? Allocational inefficiency involves only the net marginal effects. The basic assumption is that every firm *purchases and utilizes* all of its inputs "efficiently." Thus, what is left is simply the consequences of price and quantity distortions. While some specific price distortions might be large it seems unlikely that all relative price distortions are exceptionally large. This implies that most quantity distortions must also be relatively small since for a given aggregate output a significant distortion in one commodity will be counterbalanced by a large number of small distortions in the opposite direction in quantities elsewhere. While it is possible to *assume* relative price distortions and quantity distortions that would be exceedingly high, it would be difficult to believe that, without intent, the sum of such distortions should be high. However, it is not *necessarily* so on purely *a priori* grounds.

There is one important type of distortion that cannot easily be handled by existing microeconomic theory. This has to do with the allocation of managers. It is conceivable that in practice a situation would arise in which managers are exceedingly poor, that is, others are available who do not obtain management posts, and who would be very much superior. Managers determine not only their own productivity but the productivity of all cooperating units in the organization. It is therefore possible that the actual loss due to such a misallocation might be large. But the theory does not allow us to examine this matter because firms are presumed to exist as entities that make optimal input decisions, apart from the decisions of its managers. This is obviously a contradiction and therefore cannot be handled.

II. X-EFFICIENCY: THE EMPIRICAL EVIDENCE

We have seen that the welfare loss due to allocational inefficiency is frequently no more than 1/10 of 1 per cent. Is it conceivable that the value of X-

---

[3]For the sake of completeness we should take the income effect into account in our estimation of consumer surplus. It may readily be seen that this magnitude is likely to be exceedingly small. Suppose that the initial effect of a superior allocation is 1 per cent; then the income effect for a noninferior good will be to shift the demand function to the right by 1 per cent on the average. Thus, the addition to consumers' surplus will be 1 per cent, and the consumers' surplus foregone will be roughly 1 per cent of 1 per cent. If we consider all consequent effects in a similar vein, then the estimated welfare loss will be .010101 . . . < .0102. The actual magnitude will, of course, be smaller because the demand will shift to the left in the case of inferior goods. For an excellent discussion of these matters see A. P. Lerner [21].

inefficiency would be larger than that? One way of looking at it is to return to the problem of the welfare loss due to monopoly. Suppose that one-third of the industries are in the monopolized sector. Is it possible that the lack of competitive pressure of operating in monopolized industries would lead to cost 3/10 of a per cent higher than would be the case under competition? This magnitude seems to be very small, and hence it certainly seems to be a possibility. The question essentially, is whether we can visualize managers bestirring themselves sufficiently, if the environment forced them to do so, in order to reduce costs by more than 3/10 of 1 per cent. Some of the empirical evidence available suggests that not only is this a possibility, but that the magnitudes involved are very much larger. As we shall see, the spotty evidence on this subject does not prove the case but it does seem to be sufficiently persuasive to suggest the possibility that X-efficiency exists, and that it frequently is much more significant than allocational efficiency.

Professor Eric Lundberg in his studies of Swedish industries points to the case of the steel plant at Horndal that was left to operate without any new capital investment or *technological change,* and furthermore maintenance and replacement were kept at a minimum, and yet output per man hour rose by 2 per cent per annum. Professor Lundberg asserts that according to his interviews with industrialists and technicians "sub-optimal disequilibrium in regard to technology and utilization of existing capital stock is a profoundly important aspect of the situation at any time." (This according to Gorin Ohlin's summary of Lundberg's findings [24].) If a suboptimal disequilibrium exists at any time, then it would seem reasonable that under the proper motivations managers and workers could bestir themselves to produce closer to optimality, and that under other conditions they may be motivated to move farther away from optimality.

Frederick Harbison reports visiting two petroleum refineries in Egypt less than one-half mile apart. "The labor productivity of one had been nearly double that in the other for many years. But recently, under completely new management, the inefficient refinery was beginning to make quite spectacular improvements in efficiency with the same labor force" [15, p. 373]. We may inquire why the management was changed only recently whereas the difference in labor productivity existed for many years. It is quite possible that had the motivation

existed in sufficient strength, this change could have taken place earlier.

In a recent book on the firm, Neil Chamberlain [5, p. 341] visualizes his firms reacting to variances between forecasted revenues and expenditures and actual. He quotes from the president of a corporation: "Actual sales revenue for the fiscal year varied one per cent from the original forecast. Expenditures varied 30 per cent. The reasons were practically entirely due to manufacturing problems of inefficiency and quality. . . . The only actions specifically taken were in attempted changes in methods of production . . . [and] the use of an engineering consulting firm. . . . " One would have thought that the cost-reducing activities mentioned could be carried out irrespective of the variance. Nevertheless, the quotation clearly implies that, in fact, they would not have been motivated to attempt the changes were it not that they were stimulated by the variance.

Before proceeding to present more empirical evidence on the possible magnitude of X-efficiency it is of importance to say something about the nature of the data. The empirical evidence does not present many unambiguous cases. Most of the evidence has to do with specific firms or, at best, industries, and not for the economy as a whole. In the evidence presented on allocative efficiency the entire economy was considered. It is quite possible that the cases considered are entirely atypical and could not be duplicated in large segments of the economy. In addition, the cases do not always deal with X-efficiency in a pure sense. Some additional inputs or reallocations are sometimes involved. Also uncertainty elements and accidental variations play a role. Nevertheless, it seems that the magnitudes involved are so large that they suggest that the conjecture that X-efficiency is frequently more significant than allocative efficiency must be taken seriously.

Now let us turn to Tables 1 and 2. In contrast to Table 1 where the misallocation effects are small, we see in Table 2 that the X-efficiency effects, at least for specific firms, are usually large. Table 2 abstracts (in the interest of conserving space) from a much more comprehensive table developed by Kilby [19] that summarizes the results of a number of ILO productivity missions. (I usually picked for each country the first three and the last items contained in Kilby's table.) It is to be observed that the cost-reducing methods used do not involve additional capital nor, as far as one can tell, any increase in depreciation or obsolescence of existing capital. The methods usually

Table 2. ILO productivity mission results

Factory or operation	Method*	Increase in labor productivity %	Impact on the firm (unit cost reduction)	
			Labor savings %	Capital† savings %
India				
Seven textile mills	n.a.	5-to-250	5–71	5–71
Engineering firms				
All operations	F, B	102	50	50
One operation	F	385	79	79
One operation	F	500	83	83
Burma				
Molding railroad brake shoes	A, F, B	100	50	50
Smithy	A	40	29	29
Chair assembly	A, B	100	50	50
Match manufacture	A, F	24	19	—
Indonesia				
Knitting	A, B	15	13	—
Radio assembly	A, F	40	29	29
Printing	A, F	30	23	—
Enamel ware	F	30	23	—
Malaya				
Furniture	A, D	10	9	9
Engineering workshop	A, D	10	9	9
Pottery	A, B	20	17	17
Thailand				
Locomotive maintenance	A, F	44	31	31
Saucepan polishing	E, D	50	33	—
Saucepan assembly	B, F	42	30	—
Cigarettes	A, B	5	5	—
Pakistan				
Textile plants	C, H, G			
Weaving		50	33	33
Weaving		10	9	9
Bleaching		59	37	37
Weaving		141	29	29
Israel				
Locomotive repair	F, B, G	30	23	23
Diamond cutting and polishing	C, B, G	45	31	—
Refrigerator assembly	F, B, G	75	43	43
Orange picking	F	91	47	—

*A = plant layout reorganized
B = machine utilization and flow
C = simple technical alterations
D = materials handling
E = waste control
F = work method
G = payment by results
H = workers training and supervision
†Limited to plant and equipment, excluding increased depreciation costs.
Source: P. Kilby [19, p. 305].

involve some simple reorganizations of the production process, e.g., plant-layout reorganization, materials handling, waste controls, work methods, and payments by results. It is of interest that the cost reductions are frequently above 25 per cent and that this result is true for a technically advanced country such as Israel as well as for the developing countries considered in other parts of the table. If the firms and/or operations considered are representative, then it would appear that the contrast in significance between X-efficiency and allocative efficiency is indeed startling. Representativeness has not been established. However, the reports of the productivity missions do not suggest that they went out of their way to work only on cases where large savings in costs could be obtained. By comparative standards (with other productivity missions) some of the results were modest, and in some cases Kilby reports that when some members of the missions returned to some of the firms they had worked on previously (e.g., in Pakistan) they found a reversion to previous methods and productivities.

There are of course a number of other studies, in addition to those by Lundberg and Harbison just mentioned which present results similar to the ILO reports. L. Rostas in his study of comparative productivity in British and American industry [26] points to the finding that differences in amount and quality of machinery per worker and the rates of utilization and replacement do not account for the entire difference in output per worker in the two countries. He further states that ". . . in a number of industries (or firms) where the equipment is very largely identical in the U.S. and U.K., eggs, boots and shoes, tobacco, strip steel (or in firms producing both in the U.K. and U.S. . . .), there are still substantial differences in output per worker in the U.K. and the U.S." Clearly there is more to the determination of output than the obviously observable inputs. The nature of the management, the environment in which it operates, and the incentives employed are significant.

That changes in incentives will change productivity per man (and cost per unit of output) is demonstrated clearly by a wide variety of studies on the effects of introducing payments by results schemes. Davison, Florence, Gray, and Ross [7, p. 203] review the literature in this area for British industry, survey the results for a number of manufacturing operations, and present illustrative examples of their findings from a number of firms. The summary of their findings follows: "The change in output per worker was found to vary among the different operations all the way from an increase of 7.5 per cent to one of 291 per cent, about half the cases falling between 43 per cent and 76 per cent. Such increases in output, most of them large, from our 'first-line' case histories, and from additional evidence, were found not to be just a 'flash in the pan' but were sustained over the whole period of study."

Roughly similar findings were obtained for the consequences of introducing payments by results in Australia, Belgium, India, the Netherlands, and the United States [36]. In Victoria it was found that "soundly designed and properly operated incentive plans have in practice increased production rate in the reporting firms from 20 to 50 per cent." In the Netherlands labor efficiency increases of 36.5 per cent were reported. It seems clear that with the same type of equipment the working tempo varies considerably both between different workers and different departments. Appropriate incentives can obviously change such tempos considerably and reduce costs, without any changes in purchasable inputs per unit.

The now-famous Hawthorne Studies [25] suggest that the mere fact that management shows a special interest in a certain group of workers can increase output. That is, management's greater interest in the group on whom the experiments were tried, both when working conditions were improved and when they were worsened, created a positive motivation among the workers. (The magnitudes were from 13 to 30 per cent [20].) In one of the ILO missions to Pakistan an improvement in labor relations in a textile mill in Lyallpur resulted in a productivity increase of 30 per cent. Nothing else was changed except that labor turnover was reduced by one-fifth [37] [38].

Individual variations in worker proficiency are probably larger than plant differences. Frequently the variation between the best to poorest worker is as much as four to one. Certainly improved worker selection could improve productivity at the plant level. To the extent that people are not working at what they are most proficient at, productivity should rise as a consequence of superior selection methods [13, p. 147].

Although there is a large literature on the importance of psychological factors on productivity, it is usually quite difficult to assess this literature because many psychologists work on the basis of high- and low-productivity groups but do not report the actual numerical differences. In general, it seems that some of the psychological factors studied in terms of small-group theory can account for differences in productivity of from 7 to 18 per cent. The discoveries include such findings as (1) up to a point smaller working units are more productive than larger ones; (2) working units made up of friends are more productive than those made up of nonfriends; (3) units that are generally supervised are more efficient than those that are closely supervised [1]; and (4) units that are given more information about the importance of their work are more proficient than those given less information [32]. A partial reason for these observed differences is probably the likelihood that individual motivation towards work is differently affected under the different circumstances mentioned.

The shorter-hours movement in Western Europe and in the United States, especially up to World War I, has some interesting lessons for productivity differentials without capital changes. Economists frequently assume that for a given capital stock and quality of work force, output will be proportional to number of hours worked. Experiments during World War I and later showed that not only was the proportionality law untrue, but that frequently *absolute* output actually increased with reductions in hours— say from a ten-hour day to an eight-hour day.[4] It was also found that with longer hours a disproportionate amount of time was lost from increased absenteeism, industrial accidents, and so on. In many cases it would obviously have been to a firm's interest to reduce hours below that of the rest of the industry. Firms could have investigated these relations and taken advantage of the findings. For the most part, governments sponsored the necessary research on the economics of fatigue and unrest under the stimulus of the war effort, when productivity in some sectors of the economy was believed to be crucial. The actual reduction of hours that took place was a consequence of the pressure of labor unions and national legislation.

In this connection it is of interest to note that Carter and Williams [4, pp. 57ff.] in their study of investment in innovations found that a high proportion (over 40 per cent) was of a "passive" char-

acter—i.e., either in response to the "direct pressure of competition" or "force of example of firms (etc.) other than immediate rivals." Unfortunately it is difficult to find data that would represent the obverse side of the coin; namely, data that would suggest the degree to which firms do not innovate for lack of a sufficient motivating force, such as a lack of competitive pressure. However, there is a great deal of evidence that the delay time between invention and innovation is often exceedingly long (sometimes more than 50 years),[5] and the lag time between the use of new methods in the "best practice" firms in an industry and other firms is also often a matter of years. Salter in his study on *Productivity and Technical Change* [27, p. 98] points to the following striking example. "In the United States copper mines, electric locomotives allow a cost saving of 67 per cent yet although first used in the mid-twenties, by 1940 less than a third of locomotives in use were electric."[6] Other similar examples are mentioned by Salter and others. A survey of industrial research undertaken by 77 companies showed that one-third were carrying on research for "aggressive purposes," but that two-thirds were "forced into research for defensive purposes."[7]

The relation between the "cost" of advice or consulting services and the return obtained has not been worked out for the ILO productivity missions as a whole. In one case (in Pakistan) the savings affected in three textile mills as a consequence of the work of the mission during the year that the mission was there "represented about 20 times the entire cost of the mission in that year." While the study does not indicate how representative this result was, the impression one gets is that rates of return of rather large magnitudes are not entirely unusual.

J. Johnston studied the return to consulting ser-

---

[4]The empirical findings and experimental literature are reviewed in a number of places. For a brief review of the literature see [37]. See page 5 for bibliography of major works in the area.

[5]See the table in [9, pp. 305–6].

[6][27]. See especially Appendix to Chapter 7, "Evidence Relating to the Delay in the Utilization of New Techniques." It seems to me that Salter did not quite draw the only possible conclusion from his Table 11. Plants with no significant changes in equipment, method, and plant layout had quite startling changes in output per man-hour, especially if we consider the fact demonstrated in the table that output per man-hour frequently falls under such circumstances. The range of variation in the changes (24 per cent) is larger for the plants without significant changes in equipment, etc., than for those with significant improvements. This is not to argue against the thesis that changes in techniques are important, but to suggest that significant variations in production can and do occur without such changes.

[7]See [3] for source.

vices in Great Britain. For the class of jobs where it was possible to make a quantitative assessment of the results (600 jobs were involved), it was found that on the average the rate of return was about 200 per cent on consulting fees [18, p. 248]. Johnston's study is of special interest for our purposes because (a) it is a very careful study, and (b) the magnitudes of increases in productivity are of the same order (although the variations are less extreme) as those obtained in underdeveloped countries. The nature of the consulting work was not too dissimilar to that carried out by the ILO teams. On the whole they involved improvements in general management, plant layout, personnel, production procedures, selling organization, management and budgeting and accounting systems. For the consulting jobs whose consequences were quantitatively assessed, the average increase in productivity was 53 per cent, the lowest quartile showed an increase of 30 per cent, and the highest quartile 70 per cent [18, p. 273].

The studies mentioned deal with examples that are more or less of a microeconomic nature. In recent years we have had a number of studies that are their *macro*economic complements. The work of Solow, Aukrust, Denison, and others show that only a small proportion of increase in GNP is accounted for by increases in inputs of labor or capital. The "unexplained residual" covers about 50 per cent to 80 per cent of growth in advanced countries [2] [10] [23] [30] [31]. The residual comprehends a greater range of "noninput" growth factors (e.g., technological change, education of the labor force) than was covered in the examples we considered, but the motivational efficiency elements may account for some fraction of the residual. (E.g., Johnston estimates that one quarter of the annual increase in product is accounted for by consulting services.)

What conclusions can we draw from all of this? First, the data suggest that there is a great deal of possible variation in output for similar amounts of capital and labor and for similar techniques, in the broad sense, to the extent that technique is determined by similar types of equipment. However, in most of the studies the nature of the influences involved are mixed, and in some cases not all of them are clear to the analyst. In many instances there appears to have been an attempt to impart knowledge, at least of a managerial variety, which accounts for *some* of the increase in output. But should this knowledge be looked upon as an increase in inputs of pro-

duction in all instances? Although the first reaction might be that such attempts involve inputs similar to inputs of capital or labor, I will want to argue that in many instances this is not the case.

It is obvious that not every change in technique implies a change in knowledge. The knowledge may have been there already, and a change in circumstances induced the change in technique. In addition, knowledge may not be used to capacity just as capital or labor may be underutilized. More important, a good deal of our knowledge is vague. A man may have nothing more than a sense of its existence, and yet this may be the critical element. Given a sufficient inducement, he can then search out its nature in detail and get it to a stage where he can use it. People normally operate within the bounds of a great deal of intellectual slack. Unlike underutilized capital, this is an element that is very difficult to observe. As a result, occasions of genuine additions to knowledge become rather difficult to distinguish from those circumstances in which no new knowledge has been added, but in which existing knowledge is being utilized to greater capacity.

Experience in U.S. industry suggests that adversity frequently stimulates cost-reducing attempts, some of which are successful, within the bounds of existing knowledge [12]. In any event, some of the studies suggest that motivational aspects are involved entirely apart from additional knowledge. The difficulty of assessment arises because these elements are frequently so intertwined that it is difficult to separate them.

Let us now consider types of instances in which the motivational aspect appears fairly clearly to play a role. The ILO studies discuss a number of cases in which there had been a reversion to previous less efficient techniques when demonstration projects were revisited after a year or more. This seems to have occurred both in India and in Pakistan [38, p. 157]. Clearly, the new knowledge, if there were such knowledge, was given to the management by the productivity mission at the outset, and the new management methods were installed at least for the period during which the productivity mission was on hand, but there was not a sufficient motivational force for the management to maintain the new methods. The "Hawthorne Effects" are of a more clear-cut nature. Here an intentional reversion to previous methods still led to some increases in output simply because the motivational aspects were more important than the changes in the work methods. The ILO mission reports also mention with regret the fact that techniques applied in one portion of a plant, which led to fairly large increases in productivity, were not taken over by the management and applied to other aspects of the production process, although they could quite easily have done so [38, p. 157]. In a sense we may argue that the knowledge was available to the management, but that somehow it was not motivated to transfer techniques from one portion of a plant to another.

Studies which showed increases in output as a consequence of introducing payment by results clearly involve motivational elements. For the men subjected to the new payment scheme economic motivations are involved. For the management the situation is less clear. It is possible that in many instances the firms were not aware of the possible advantages of payment by results until they obtained the new knowledge that led to the introduction of the scheme. However, it seems most likely that this scheme is so well known that this is not the case in all, or in many instances. Management quite likely had to be motivated to introduce the scheme by some factors either within the firm or within the industry. In any event, these studies clearly suggest that for some aspects of production, motivational elements are significant.

Both the ILO studies and the Johnston study speak of the need to get the acceptance of top management for the idea of obtaining and implementing consulting advice. In addition, the ILO studies make the point that low productivity is frequently caused by top management's concern with the commercial and financial affairs of the firm rather than with the running of the factory. The latter was frequently treated as a very subordinate task. Whether this last aspect involves a lack of knowledge or a lack of motivation is difficult to determine. However, it seems hard to believe that if some top-management people in some of the firms in a given industry were to become concerned with factory management and achieve desirable results thereby, some of the others would not follow suit. Johnston makes the point that, "without the willing cooperation of management the consultant is unlikely to be called in the first instance or to stay for long if he does come in" [18, p. 237]. The ILO missions make similar remarks.

It is quite clear that consulting services are not only profitable to consultants but also highly profitable to many of the firms that employ them. But it is rather surprising that more of these services are not called for. Part of the answer may be that managements of firms are not motivated to hire consultants if things appear to be going "in any reasonably satisfactory rate." There are, of course, numerous personal resistances to calling for outside advice. If the motivation is strong enough, e.g., the threat of the failure of the firm, then it is likely that such resistances would be overcome. But these are simply different aspects of the motivational elements involved.

III. THE RESIDUAL AND X-EFFICIENCY: AN INTERPRETATION

The main burden of these findings is that X-inefficiency exists, and that improvement in X-efficiency is a significant source of increased output. In general, we may specify three elements as significant in determining what we have called X-efficiency: (1) intraplant motivational efficiency, (2) external motivational efficiency, and (3) nonmarket input efficiency.

The simple fact is that neither individuals nor firms work as hard, nor do they search for information as effectively, as they could. The importance of motivation and its association with degree of effort and search arises because the relation between inputs and outputs is *not* a determinate one. There are four reasons why given inputs cannot be transformed into predetermined outputs: (a) contracts for labor are incomplete, (b) not all factors of production are marketed, (c) the production function is not completely specified or known, and (d) interdependence and uncertainty lead competing firms to cooperate tacitly with each other in some respects, and to imitate each other with respect to technique, to some degree.

The conventional theoretical assumption, although it is rarely stated, is that inputs have a fixed specification and yield a fixed performance. This ignores other likely possibilities. Inputs may have a fixed specification that yields a variable performance, or they may be of a variable specification and yield a variable performance. Some types of complex machinery may have fixed specifications, but their performance may be variable depending on the exact nature of their employment. The most common case is that of labor services of various kinds that have variable specifications and variable performance—although markets sometimes operate as if much of the labor of a given class has a fixed specification. Moreover, it is exceedingly rare for all elements of performance in a labor contract to be spelled out. A good deal is left to custom, authority, and whatever motivational techniques are available to management as well as to individual discretion and judgment.

Similarly, the production function is neither completely specified nor known. There is always an experimental element involved so that something may be known about the current state; say the existing relation between inputs and outputs, but not what will happen given changes in the input ratios. In addition, important inputs are frequently not marketed or, if they are traded, they are not equally accessible (or accessible on equal terms) to all potential buyers. This is especially true of management knowledge. In many areas of the world managers may not be available in well-organized markets. But even when they are available, their capacities may not be known. One of the important capacities of management may be the degree to which managers can obtain factors of production that in fact are not marketed in well-organized markets or on a universalistic basis. In underdeveloped countries the capacity to obtain finance may depend on family connections. Trustworthiness may be similarly determined. Some types of market information may be available to some individuals but not purchasable in the market. For these and other reasons it seems clear that it is one thing to purchase or hire inputs in a given combination; it is something else to get a predetermined output out of them.

Another possible interpretation of the data presented is in connection with the "residual" in economic growth analysis. The residual manifests itself in three basic ways: (1) through cost reduction in the production of existing commodities without inventions or innovations; (2) the introduction of innovations in processes of production; and (3) the introduction of new commodities or, what is the same thing, quality improvements in consumer goods or inputs. We have ignored the introduction of new commodities, but the other two elements are pertinent here. The data suggest that cost reduction that is essentially a result of improvement in X-efficiency is likely to be an important component of the observed residual in economic growth. In addition, there is no doubt that, in some of the cases of reduced cost, new knowledge was conveyed to the firms involved, and this too is part of the residual. It is of

special interest that such new knowledge involves knowledge dissemination rather than invention. The detailed studies suggest that the magnitudes are large, and hence a significant part of the residual does not depend on the types of considerations that have been prominent in the literature in recent years, such as those that are *embodied* in capital accumulation or in invention. We have considered the problem in terms of decreasing real costs per unit of output. It is clear that for a given set of resources, if real costs per unit of output are decreased, then total output will grow, and output per unit of input will also rise. Such efforts to reduce cost are part of the contribution of the residual to economic growth.

Both competition and adversity create some pressure for change. Even if knowledge is vague, if the incentive is strong enough there will be an attempt to augment information so that it becomes less vague and possibly useful. Where consulting advice is available it is significant that relatively few firms buy it. Clearly, motivations play a role in determining the degree that consulting advice is sought. The other side of the coin is that, where the motivation is weak, firm managements will permit a considerable degree of slack in their operations and will not seek cost-improving methods. Cyert and March [6, pp. 37, 38, 242] point to cases in which costs per unit are allowed to rise when profits are high. In the previous sections we have cited cases in which there was a reversion to less efficient methods after the consultants left the scene. Thus we have instances where competitive pressures from other firms or adversity lead to efforts toward cost reduction, and the absence of such pressures tends to cause costs to rise.

Some of the essential points made in the previous paragraphs can be illustrated diagramatically, if (in the interest of simplicity) we allow for abstraction from some of the realities of the situation. The main ideas to be illustrated are as follows: (1) Some firms operate under conditions of nonminimum costs, and it is possible for an industry to have a nonminimal cost equilibrium. (2) Improvements in X-efficiency are part of the process of development, and probably a significant proportion of the "residual." In what follows we assume that there are many firms, and that each firm's output is sufficiently small so as not to affect the output, costs, or prices set by other firms. For simplicity we also assume that for each firm there is an average total unit cost (ATUC) curve that has a significant horizontal segment at its trough, and that the output selected will be on that segment. When we visualize a firm's costs reacting to competitive conditions in the industry we imply that the entire ATUC curve moves up or down. Some firms are presumed to react to changes in the unit cost of production of the industry as a whole, i.e., to the weighted average of the unit costs of all the firms, in which each firm's weight is in proportion to its contribution to the output of the industry. Here we posit a one-period lag relation. Each firm's expectations of current industry units costs depends on actual industry unit cost in the previous period. If we choose sufficiently small periods, then this seems to be reasonable relation.

In Fig. 2 each curve represents the "reaction cost line" of a firm. The ordinate shows the actual unit cost of any firm determined by that firm's reaction to what it believes or expects to be the unit cost performance of the industry as a whole. The alternate expected unit cost performance of the industry is shown on the abscissa. Thus each point on line C_t^i associates the unit cost of firm i in period t, given the average unit cost in the industry in period t-1. The lines are drawn in such a way that they reflect the idea that if the unit cost that is the average for the industry is higher, then the firm's unit cost will also be higher. As average industry unit costs fall, some firms are motivated to reduce their unit costs accordingly. The higher the industry unit cost, the easier it is for any firm to search and successfully *find* means for reducing its own cost. Therefore, for a given incentive toward cost reduction, the firm is likely to find more successful ways of reducing its cost when industry costs are high compared to what they might find when they are low. As a consequence the typical reaction unit cost lines are more steeply sloped where industry unit costs are high compared to when they are low. Indeed, at very low industry unit costs the firm reaction cost lines approach an asymptote. It is not necessary for our analysis to assume that all firms are nonminimizers. Therefore some firms may have reaction cost lines that are horizontal.

The curve C^A is the average of the unit costs of all the firms in question, where the weight for any firm's cost is the proportion of its output to the total industry output. C^A is the average reaction cost line for all the firms. The basic assumption is that a firm's costs will be higher if the average industry costs are expected to be higher, and vice versa. Beyond some

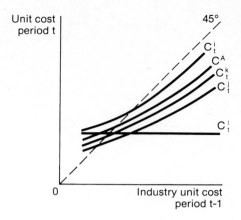

Fig. 2

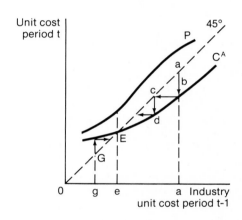

Fig. 3

point, where expected average industry costs are very low, every reaction cost line will be above the 45° line.

In Fig. 3 the line P is a locus of equilibrium prices. Each point on the line associates an equilibrium price with a level of industry unit cost in the previous period, which in turn determines the unit costs level of the various firms in the current period. Thus, given the industry unit cost in period t-1, this determines the unit cost level for each firm in period t. Each firm in turn will pick that output that maximizes its profits. The sum of all the outputs determines the industry output, and given the demand function for the product, the industry output determines the price. The price will be an equilibrium price if at that price no additional firms are induced to enter the industry or to withdraw from it. Thus the price for each industry unit cost is determined in accordance with conventional price theory considerations. If the price at the outset is above equilibrium price, then the entry of firms will bring that price down toward equilibrium, and if the price is below equilibrium, marginal firms will be forced to leave the industry, which in turn will cause the price to rise. Thus at every level of industry unit cost in period t-1 there is a determinate number of firms, that number consistent with the associated equilibrium price.

The point E in Fig. 3, the intersection between curve C^A and the 45° line, is an equilibrium point for all the firms. The process envisioned is that each firm sets its cost in period t in accordance with its expectation of the industry cost, which by assumption is what the industry cost was in period t-1. This is a one-period lag relation. Each firm finds out what all of its competitors were doing as a group in terms of cost and reacts accordingly in the next period. If the industry cost is equal to oe then in the subsequent period each firm would set its cost so that the weighted average unit cost of all the firms would be equal to oe. Hence E is an equilibrium point.[8]

But suppose that the initial industry costs were equal to oa. We want to show that this sets up a movement that leads eventually to the point E. The firms' unit costs will average out at ab, which generates a process shown by the set of arrows $abcd$, etc., toward the point E. In a similar fashion, if we start with an industry cost of og, a process is set in motion so that costs move from G toward the point E. Clearly E is a stable equilibrium point. It is to be noted that every point on curve C^A need not presume that the same number of firms exist in the industry. At higher costs more firms exist, but as costs decline, some firms

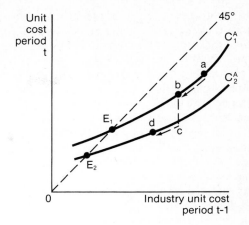

Fig. 4

are forced out and fewer firms exist. In terms of the weighted average indicated by the points on the curve C^A, this simply means that some of the outputs will be zero for some of the firms as we get to lower and lower industry costs.

Fig. 4 is intended to illustrate the cost reduction aspect of the residual in growth. When we begin the process the average reaction cost line is C_1^A. Firms start at point a and reduce costs along the arrow shown by ab. At this point additional information is introduced into the industry which is reflected in the diagram by the shift in the reaction cost line from C_1^A to C_2^A. Once firms are on C_2^A they then proceed with the cost reduction process as shown by the arrow cd. This illustrates two basic elements involved in the residual, the process of cost reduction in response to the motivation created by competitive pressures, as well as that part of cost reduction that is reflected in actual innovations, and is illustrated by downward shifts in the reaction cost lines.

IV. CONCLUSIONS

We have suggested three reasons for X-inefficiency connected with the possibility of variable performance for given units of the inputs. These are: (a) contracts for labor are incomplete, (b) the production function is not completely specified or known, and (c) not all inputs are marketed or, if marketed, are not available on equal terms to all buyers. These facts lead us to suggest an approach to the theory of the firm that does not depend on the assumption of cost-minimization by all firms. The level of unit cost

[8]In essence the existence of an equilibrium can be shown on the basis of Brouwer's fixed-point theorem. (Point E in Figure 3 can be interpreted as a fixed point.) It would be possible to develop a much more general theory along the same lines based on less restrictive assumptions and achieve essentially the same result. For instance the one-period lag in the reaction unit cost relation can readily be eliminated. Similarly, the unique relation between the firm's unit cost and the industry unit cost level can be relaxed. See G. Debreu [8, pp. 17–18 and p. 26]. However the essence of the theory would remain the same. To conserve space and in the interest of simplicity I present the more restrictive version.

depends in some measure on the degree of X-efficiency, which in turn depends on the degree of competitive pressure, as well as on other motivational factors. The responses to such pressures, whether in the nature of effort, search, or the utilization of new information, is a significant part of the residual in economic growth.

One idea that emerges from this study is that firms and economies do not operate on an outer-bound production possibility surface consistent with their resources. Rather they actually work on a production surface that is well within that outer bound. This means that for a variety of reasons people and organizations normally work neither as hard nor as effectively as they could. In situations where competitive pressure is light, many people will trade the disutility of greater effort, of search, and the control of other peoples' activities for the utility of feeling less pressure and of better interpersonal relations. But in situations where competitive pressures are high, and hence the costs of such trades are also high, they will exchange less of the disutility of effort for the utility of freedom from pressure, etc. Two general types of movements are possible. One is along a production surface towards greater allocative efficiency and the other is from a lower surface to a higher one that involves greater degrees of X-efficiency. The data suggest that in a great many instances the amount to be gained by increasing allocative efficiency is trivial while the amount to be gained by increasing X-efficiency is frequently significant.

REFERENCES

1. M. Argyle, G. Gardner, and F. Cioffi, "Supervisory Methods Related to Productivity, Absenteeism, and Labor Turnover," *Human Relations*, 1958, *10*, 23–29.
2. O. Aukrust, "Investment and Economic Growth," *Prod. Meas. Rev.*, Feb. 1959, *16*, 35–53.
3. Y. Brozen, "Research, Technology, and Productivity." *Industrial Productivity*, December 1951, Industrial Relations Research Association Paper 7, p. 30.
4. C. F. Carter and B. R. Williams, *Investment in Innovations*. London 1958.
5. N. Chamberlain, *The Firm: Micro Economic Planning and Action*. New York 1962.
6. R. M. Cyert and J. G. March, *A Behavioral Theory of the Firm*, Englewood Cliffs, N.J. 1963, pp. 36–38, and Ch. 9, by O. E. Williamson, pp. 237–52.
7. J. P. Davison, P. S. Florence, and B. Gray and N. Ross, *Productivity and Economic Incentives*. London 1958.
8. G. Debreu, *Theory of Value*, New York 1959.
9. J. L. Enos, "Invention and Innovation in the Petroleum Refining Industry," in *The Rate and Direction of Inventive Activity*, Princeton, NBER, 1962, pp. 305–6.
10. S. Fabricant, Basic Facts on Productivity. New York, NBER, 1959.
11. A. A. Faraq, *Economic Integration: A Theoretical Empirical Study*. Unpublished doctoral dissertation, Univ. Michigan, 1963.
12. J. J. Friedman, "Top Management Faces the Cost Challenge," *Dun's Rev. and Mod. Industry*, Jan. 1961, *77*, 34–36.
13. E. E. Ghiselli and C. W. Brown, *Personnel and Industrial Psychology*. New York 1948.
14. A. Harberger, "Using the Resources at Hand More Effectively," *Am. Econ. Rev. Proc.*, May 1959, *59*, 134–47.
15. F. Harbison, "Entrepreneurial Organization as a Factor in Economic Development," *Quart. Jour. Econ.*, Aug. 1956, *70*, 364–79.
16. L. H. Janssen, *Free Trade, Protection and Customs Union*, Leiden 1961, p. 132.
17. H. Johnson, "The Gains from Freer Trade with Europe: An Estimate," *Man. School Econ. Soc. Stud.*, Sept. 1958, *26*, 247–55.
18. J. Johnston, "The Productivity of Management Consultants," *Jour. Royal. Stat. Soc.*, Ser. A., 1963, *126*, Pt. 2, 237–49.
19. P. Kilby, "Organization and Productivity in Backward Economies," *Quart. Jour. Econ.*, May 1962, *76*, 303–10.
20. H. A. Landsberger, *Hawthorne Revisited*, Ithaca 1958, pp. 13 ff.
21. A. P. Lerner, "Consumer Surplus and Micro-Macro," *Jour. Pol. Econ.*, Feb. 1963, *71*, pp. 76 ff.
22. R. A. Mundell, review of L. H. Janssen, *Free Trade, Protection, and Customs Union*, in *Am. Econ. Rev.*, June 1962, *52*, pp. 621–22.
23. O. Niitamo, "Development of Productivity in Finnish Industry, 1925–1952," *Prod. Meas. Rev.*, Nov. 1958, *15*, 30–41.
24. G. Ohlin, review of E. Lundberg, *Productivity and Profitability: Studies of the Role of Capital in the Swedish Economy*, in *Am. Econ. Rev.*, Sept. 1962, *52*, 827–29.
25. F. T. Roethlisberger and W. J. Dickson, *Management and the Worker*. Cambridge 1939.
26. L. Rostas, *Comparative Productivity in British and American Industry*, Nat. Inst. Econ. Soc. Research Paper 13, Cambridge (England) 1964, pp. 64 ff.
27. W. E. G. Salter, *Productivity and Technical Change*. Cambridge (England) 1960.
28. D. Schwartzman, "The Burden of Monopoly," *Jour. Pol. Econ.*, Dec. 1960, *68*, 727–29.
29. T. Scitovsky, *Economic Theory and Western European Integration*. Stanford 1958.
30. R. Solow, "Technical Progress and the Aggregate Production Function," *Rev. Econ. Stat.*, Aug. 1957, *39*, 312–20.
31. ——————, "Investment and Economic Growth," *Prod. Meas. Rev.*, Nov. 1959, *16*, 62–68.

32. T. Tomekovic, "Levels of Knowledge of Requirements as a Motivational Factor in the Work Situation," *Human Relations,* 1962, *15,* 197–216.

33. J. Wemelsfelder, "The Short-Term Effect of Lowering Import Duties in Germany," *Econ. Jour.,* March 1960, *60,* 94–104.

34. S. G. Winter, Jr., *Economic Natural Selection and the Theory of the Firm.* Unpublished doctoral dissertation, mimeo, Yale Univ. 1963, pp. 83–85.

35. Anglo-American Council on Productivity, *Productivity Measurement in British Industry.* New York 1950.

36. International Labor Organization, "Payment by Results," *ILO Studies and Reports,* New Ser. No. 27. Geneva 1951.

37. —————, "ILO Productivity Missions to Underdeveloped Countries, Part 1," *Internat. Lab. Rev.,* July 1957, *76,* 1–29.

38. —————, "ILO Productivity Missions to Underdeveloped Countries, Part 2," *Internat. Lab. Rev.,* Aug. 1957, *76,* 139–66.

39. —————, "Repercussions of a Reduction in Hours of Work," *Internat. Lab. Rev.,* July 1956, *74,* 23–45.

Hierarchical Control and Optimum Firm Size*

OLIVER E. WILLIAMSON**

Oliver E. Williamson (S.B., Massachusetts Institute of Technology, 1955; M.B.A., Stanford University, 1960; Ph.D., Carnegie-Mellon University, 1963) was born in 1932 in Superior, Wisconsin. Currently he is the Gordon B. Tweedy Professor of Law and Organization at Yale University. In addition, he serves as Director of the American Law Institute's Corporate Governance Project. Before joining the Yale faculty in 1983, Williamson was the Charles and William L. Day Professor of Economics and Social Science and Director of the Center for the Study of Organizational Innovation at the University of Pennsylvania, and taught, in addition, at the University of California at Berkeley. Williamson is best known for his writings on managerial discretion in the large corporation, antitrust enforcement and regulation, and the implications of transactions costs for efficient organization. He currently serves on the editorial boards of the *Journal of Law, Economics, and Organization* (co-editor); *Journal of Economic Behavior and Organization* (associate editor); *MIT Press/Organization Studies, MIT Press/Regulation,* and *Cambridge Surveys of Economic Literature.*

There is a great deal of evidence that almost all organizational structures tend to produce false images in the decision-maker, and that the larger and more authoritarian the organization, the better the chance that its top decision-makers will be operating in purely imaginary worlds. This perhaps is the most fundamental reason for supposing that there are ultimately diminishing returns to scale.[1]

Although we are quite in agreement with Professor Boulding's judgment that problems of transmitting accurate images across successive levels in a hierarchical organization are fundamentally responsible for diminishing returns to scale, there is less than unanimity on this issue. Indeed, it has long been disputed whether or in what ways the management

*Reprinted from *The Journal of Political Economy* (April 1967) by permission of The University of Chicago Press. Copyright 1967, pp. 123–138.

**The author is on leave from the University of Pennsylvania as special economic assistant to the assistant attorney general for antitrust. The views expressed are not necessarily those of the Justice Department. Research on this paper was supported by a grant to the author from the National Science Foundation and from the Lilly Foundation grant to the University of California, Los Angeles, for the study of the economics of property rights.

[1] Kenneth E. Boulding, Richard T. Ely Lecture, 78th Annual Meeting of the American Economic Association.

factor is responsible for a limitation to firm size. Although descriptive treatments of this question have been numerous, these have generally been too imprecise to permit testable implications to be derived. The present analysis attempts a partial remedy for this condition by embedding in a formal model the control-loss features of hierarchical organization that have recently been advanced in the bureaucratic-theory literature. The background to this discussion of control loss as a limitation to firm size is reviewed in Section I. A simple model possessing basic control-loss attributes is developed and its properties derived in Section II. In Section III, we extend and elaborate the model, developing additional implications and indicating some of the problems to expect in empirical testing. The conclusions are given in Section IV.

I. BACKGROUND TO THE ANALYSIS

That the question of the optimum size firm presented a serious dilemma for the theory of the firm was noted by Knight in 1933. Thus, he observed:

> The relation between efficiency and size is one of the most serious problems of theory, being in contrast with the relation for a plant, largely a matter of personality and historical accident rather than of intelligible general principles. But this question is peculiarly vital because the possibility of monopoly gain offers a powerful incentive to *continuous and unlimited* expansion of the firm, which force must be offset by some equally powerful one making for decreased efficiency (in the production of money income) with growth in size, if even boundary competition is to exist [Knight, 1965, p. xxiii].

Within a year, Robinson (1934, 1962) proposed what we believe to be a substantially correct answer, namely, that problems of coordination imposed a static limitation to firm size; and Coase in his classic 1937 article on "The Nature of the Firm" generally supports this position (1952, pp. 340–41). Kaldor (1934), however, argued that problems of coordination vanished under truly static conditions, and hence only declining product-demand curves or rising factor-supply curves could be responsible for a static limitation to firm size. Only in the context of firm dynamics did coordination problems, in his view, constitute a genuine limitation to firm size. But as Robinson was quick to point out, Kaldor's argument rested on his peculiar specification of the static condition as one in which the control problem is defined to be absent. This approach to the eco-

nomics of the firm he found quite uninstructive for, as he pungently noted, "In Mr. Kaldor's long period we shall not only be dead but in Nirvana, and the economics of Nirvana . . . is surely the most fruitless of sciences" (Robinson, 1934, p. 250).

The argument remained there[2] until Ross (1952–53, p. 148), in a sweeping attack on the economic treatments of this question, took the position that this whole literature bordered on the irrelevant for its failure to incorporate "certain aspects of the theory of organization and management." Recasting the problem in what he regarded as suitable organizational terms, he concluded that "by appropriate measures of decentralization and control the firm may expand without incurring increasing costs of coordination over a range sufficiently wide to cover all possible cases within the limits imposed by scarcity of resources" (Ross, 1952–53, p. 154). Starbuck imputes similar views to Andrews, albeit incorrectly,[3] and, in apparent sympathy with Ross, likewise regards the treatment by economists of these issues as entirely too narrow and probably self-serving (Starbuck, 1964, p. 343).

Mrs. Penrose also finds this literature unsatisfactory, observing that "whether managerial diseconomies will cause long-run increasing costs [requires that] management . . . be treated as a 'fixed factor' and the nature of the 'fixity' must be identified with respect to the nature of the managerial task of 'coordination.' *This identification has never been satisfactorily accomplished*" (Penrose, 1959, p. 12; italics added). She continues to regard the issue as a vital one, however, but argues with Kaldor that it is the dynamics, not the statics of coordination, that give rise to a limitation to firm size. In their view, expansion is contingent on knowledgeable planning and skilful coordination where these are a function of internal experience. Since experience is available in restricted supply, the rate of growth is thereby necessarily restricted. Variations on this argument have since been developed, and some have come to

---

[2]Chamberlin (1948, pp. 249–50) objected to some aspects of the argument in his treatment of the divisibility question, but nevertheless acknowledged that problems of coordination arising from increasing complexity eventually were responsible for increasing unit costs.
[3]According to Starbuck, Andrews takes the position that "it is impossible to conceive of any human organization too vast for organized efficiency." Andrews (1949, pp. 134–35), however, is quite specific in stating otherwise.

regard the growth rate as the only limitation to firm size.[4]

It is unfortunate (although understandable) that the static limitation argument should continue to be misunderstood in this way. The difficulty is probably traceable to the distinction between truly static and quasi-static conditions. Those who reject the static-limitation argument tend to adopt the former position, while those who advocate it take the latter. This is implicit in the Kaldor-Robinson dispute cited above. Differences of this sort are especially difficult to resolve, but an effort to explicate the quasi-static position may nevertheless be useful.

The problem can be stated in terms of deterministic versus stochastic equilibrium. A steady state is reached in each. But whereas in the former the data are unchanging, in the latter the firm is required to adapt to circumstances which are predictable in the sense that although they occur with stochastic regularity, precise advance knowledge of them is unavailable. Although the deterministic condition provides circumstances in which the usual management functions can be progressively eliminated through the refinement of operations, this is the world of Kaldor's Nirvana and has limited relevance for an understanding of business behavior. Instead, customers come and go, manufacturing operations break down, distribution systems malfunction, labor and materials procurement are subject to the usual vagaries, all with stochastic regularity, not to mention minor shifts in demand and similar disturbing influences of a transitory nature. Throughout all of this, the management of the firm is required to adapt to the new circumstances: request the relevant data, process the information supplied, and provide the appropriate instructions. Coordination in these circumstances is thus essential. If, simultaneously, a general expansion of operations accompanies these quasi-static adjustments, additional direction would be required. But in no sense is growth a necessary condition for the coordinating function to exist. We,

therefore, take the position that bounded rationality[5] imposes a (quasi)-static limitation to firm size through the mechanism of control loss and that growth considerations act mainly to intensify this underlying condition.

In resorting to the notion of bounded rationality, we ally ourselves with Ross in his claim that economic arguments regarding a static limitation to firm size have not taken adequately into account the contributions which organization theory has made to this problem. But rather than resort to the normative literature of administrative management theory as Ross does, we turn instead to the positive theories of bureaucratic behavior. The former, as March and Simon (1958, pp. 22–32) have aptly observed, is a generally vacuous literature in which most of the interesting problems of organizational behavior are defined away. Although Ross' instincts were correct, his preference for a normative rather than a positive theory put him onto the wrong trail and inevitably led to untestable conclusions of the sort cited above.

The aspect of bureaucratic theory that we regard as particularly relevant for studying the question of a static limitation to firm size is what we will refer to as the "control-loss" phenomenon. It is illustrated daily in the rumor-transmission process and has been studied intensively by Bartlett in his experimental studies of serial reproduction. His experiments involved the oral transmission of descriptive and argumentative passages through a chain of serially linked individuals. Bartlett concludes from a number of such studies that:

> It is now perfectly clear that serial reproduction normally brings about startling and radical alterations in the material dealt with. Epithets are changed into their opposites; incidents and events are transposed; names and numbers rarely survive intact for more than a few reproductions; opinions and conclusions are reversed—nearly every possible variation seems as if it can take place, even in a relatively short series. At the same time the subjects may be very well

---

[4]Thus, John Williamson takes the position that: "One of the more discredited concepts in the theory of the firm is that of an 'optimum size' firm . . . [S]ince firms are not restricted to the sale of a single product or even a particular range of products, there is no more reason to expect profitability to decline with size than there is evidence to suggest that it does. This raises the question as to what does limit the size of a firm. The answer . . . is that there are important costs entailed in *expanding* the size of a firm, and that these expansion costs tend to increase with the firm's growth rate" [Williamson, 1966, p. 1].

[5]Robinson (1934, p. 254) came very close to stating it in these terms, but he failed to formalize the argument and lacked an explanation for the control-loss phenomenon. Hence, Mrs. Penrose's discontent with his argument as expressed above. For a modern discussion of the notion of bounded rationality, see March and Simon (1958, chap. vi). Simon (1957a, p. xxiv) observes that "it is precisely in the realm where human behavior is *intendedly* rational, but only *limitedly* so, that there is room for a genuine theory of organization and administration." The theory advanced here attempts to make explicit the way in which intended but limited rationality operates as a limitation to firm size.

satisfied with their efforts, believing themselves to have passed on all important features with little or no change, and merely, perhaps, to have omitted unessential matters [Bartlett, 1932, p. 175].

Bartlett (1932, pp. 180–81) illustrates this graphically with a line drawing of an owl which—when redrawn successively by eighteen individuals, each sketch based on its immediate predecessor—ended up as a recognizable cat; and the further from the initial drawing one moved, the greater the distortion experienced. The reliance of hierarchical organizations on serial reproduction for their functioning thus exposes them to what may become serious distortions in transmission.

Although this phenomenon is widely experienced, it was not generally regarded as having special theoretical significance until Tullock (1965, pp. 142–93) argued that not only was authority leakage possible in a large government bureau, but it was predictable and could be expressed as an increasing function of size. Downs has since elaborated the argument and summarized it in his "Law of Diminishing Control: *The larger any organization becomes, the weaker is the control over its actions exercised by those at the top*" (1966, p. 109). The cumulative loss of control as instructions and information are transmitted across successive hierarchical levels is responsible for this result.

Thus, assuming that economies of specialization have been exhausted and that superiors are normally more competent than subordinates, a quality-quantity trade-off necessarily exists in every decision to expand. It arises for two reasons, both of which are related to the distance of the top executive from the locus of productive activity. First, expansion of the organization (adding an additional hierarchical level) removes the superior further from the basic data that affect operating conditions; information regarding those conditions must now be transmitted across an additional hierarchical level which exposes the data to an additional serial reproduction operation with its attendant losses. Furthermore, the top executive or peak coordinator (to use Papandreou's term [1952, p. 204]) cannot have all the information that he had before the expansion plus the information now generated by the new parts (assuming that he was fully employed initially). Thus, he can acquire additional information only by sacrificing some of the detail provided to him previously. Put differently, he trades off breadth for depth in undertaking the

expansion; he has more resources under his control, but the quality (serial reproduction loss) and the quantity (bounded capacity constraint) of his information are both less with respect to the deployment of each resource unit. In a similar way, being further removed from the operating situation and having more subordinates means that his instructions to each are less detailed and are passed across an additional hierarchical level. For precisely the same reasons, therefore, the behavior of the operating units will scarcely correspond as closely to his objectives as it did prior to the expansion. Taken together, this loss in the quality of the data provided to the peak coordinator and in the quality of the instructions supplied to the operating units made necessary by the expansion will be referred to as "control loss." It will exist even if the objectives of the subordinates are perfectly consonant with those of their superiors and, a fortiori, when subordinate objectives are dissonant.

There are, of course, anti-distortion control devices that the leadership has access to, and Downs (1966, pp. 78–90) has examined a number of them. These include redundancy, external data checks, creation of overlapping areas of responsibility, counterbiases, reorganization so as to keep the hierarchy flat, coding, and so on. The problem with all of these is that they are rarely available at zero cost and invariably experience diminishing returns. Hence, eventually, increasing size encounters control loss. Our objective here is to show how this argument, initially developed in the context of the behavior of government bureaus, has relevance for the static limitation to firm size issue.[6]

II. THE BASIC MODEL

Consider a hierarchically organized business firm with the following characteristics: (1) only employees at the lowest hierarchical level do manual labor; the work done by employees at higher levels is entirely administrative (planning, forecasting, supervising, accounting, and so on); (2) output is a constant proportion of productive input; (3) the wage

[6]Monsen and Downs (1965) have used the argument that control loss varies directly with firm size to examine the self-interest seeking behavior of management in the large business firm. However, their analysis is entirely descriptive, and they pass over the optimum firm-size issue and focus instead on the implications of control loss for bureaucratic decision-making within the firm.

paid to employees at the lowest level is w_0; (4) each superior is paid β $(\beta > 1)$ times as much as each of his immediate subordinates; (5) the span of control (the number of employees a supervisor can handle effectively) is a constant s $(s > 1)$ across every hierarchical level; (6) product and factor prices are parameters; (7) all non-wage variable costs are a constant proportion of output; (8) only the fraction $\bar{\alpha}$ $(0 < \bar{\alpha} < 1)$ of the intentions of a superior are effectively satisfied by a subordinate; (9) control loss is strictly cumulative (there is no systematic compensation) across successive hierarchical levels.

The first assumption can be restated as: there are no working foremen.[7] This seems quite reasonable and permits us to simplify the analysis of the relation of output to input. Taken together with assumption (2) which assures that there are no economies of specialization in production (in the relevant range), we are able to express output as a constant proportion of productive input. The distinction between direct labor input and productive labor input should be emphasized. The former refers to the total labor input at the lowest hierarchical level. The latter is that part of the direct labor input which yields productive results. The latter is smaller than the former not by reason of labor inefficiencies but because of the cumulative control loss in the transmission of data and instructions across successive hierarchical levels.

Assumption (3) is innocuous; assumption (4) is plausible and appears to correspond with the facts. This is Simon's conclusion in his study (1957b) of the theory and practices of executive compensation. The constant β condition is also reported by a recent U.S. Department of Labor study (1964, p. 8) of salary structures in the large firm, which found that "the relationship maintained between salary rates for successive grades was more commonly *a uniform percentage spread* between grades than a widening percentage spread" (italics added). An independent check of this hypothesis is also possible from the data on executive compensation included in the Annual Reports of the General Motors Corporation from 1934 to 1942. This is developed in Appendix A.

Assumption (5), that the span of control is constant across levels, is also employed in the wage model tested in Appendix A, although the cumulative distribution relation tested does not uniquely imply

this relation.[8] Taken in conjunction with the Department of Labor findings on β, however, the fits reported in Appendix A also lend support to the constant span of control assumption. We nevertheless show in Section III where this assumption can be relaxed somewhat and the basic results preserved.

Assumption (6) permits us to treat prices in the product and factor markets as parameters. As we will show, this can also be relaxed without affecting the qualitative character of our results. Assumption (7) is not critical, but permits us a modest simplification. Assumptions (8) and (9) are merely restatements of the earlier argument. They are responsible for the control-loss attributes of the model. Since much of the exposition in subsequent parts of the paper will be explicitly concerned with them, we will say no more about them here.

For purposes of developing a model around these assumptions, let:

s = span of control
$\bar{\alpha}$ = fraction of work done by a subordinate that contributes to objectives of his superior $(0 < \bar{\alpha} < 1)$; it is thus a compliance parameter.
N_i = number of employees at the ith hierarchical level = s^{i-1}
n = number of hierarchical levels (the decision variable)
P = price of output
w_0 = wage of production workers
w_i = wage of employees at ith hierarchical level = $w_0 \beta^{n-i}$ $(\beta > 1)$
r = non-wage variable cost per unit output
Q = output = $\theta(\bar{\alpha}s)^{n-1}$
R = total revenue = PQ
C = total variable cost = $\Sigma_{i=1}^{n} w_i N_i + rQ$

Without loss of generality, we assume that $\theta = 1$. The objective is to find the value of n (the number of hierarchical levels, and hence the size of the firm) so as to maximize net revenue. This is given by:

---

[7]This assumption has been expressed in this way by Mayer (1960).

[8]Strictly speaking, the empirical results reported in Table A1 support the proposition that the ratio log s/log β is constant across successive hierarchical levels, not that s and β are identical across levels. Letting log s/log $\beta = \gamma$, where γ is a constant, implies that $\beta = s^{1/\gamma}$ at every level. Thus, changes in the span of control would be accompanied by changes in the wage multiple according to the relation $\beta_i = s_i^{1/\gamma}$. That β and s are related in this way seems at least as special as to assume that they are constant across levels. Moreover, in view of the Department of Labor report that β is indeed constant across levels, the constant s condition is implied by our results.

$$R - C = PQ - \Sigma_{i=1}^{n} w_i N_i - rQ$$
$$= P(\bar{\alpha}s)^{n-1} - \Sigma_{i=1}^{n} w_0 \beta^{n-i} s^{i-1} - r(\bar{\alpha}s)^{n-1} \qquad (1)$$

now

$$\Sigma_{i=1}^{n} w_0 \beta^{n-i} s^{i-1} = w_0 \left(\frac{\beta^n}{s}\right) \Sigma_{i=1}^{n} \left(\frac{s}{\beta}\right)^i$$

where

$$\Sigma_{i=1}^{n} \left(\frac{s}{\beta}\right)^i = \frac{\left(\frac{s}{\beta}\right)^{n+1} - \left(\frac{s}{\beta}\right)}{\frac{s}{\beta} - 1} \simeq \frac{s^{n+1}}{(s-\beta)\beta^n}.$$

Thus, we have

$$R - C = P(\bar{\alpha}s)^{n-1} - w_0 \frac{s^n}{s-\beta} - r(\bar{\alpha}s)^{n-1}. \qquad (1')$$

Differentiating this expression with respect to n and setting equal to zero (and letting ln denote natural logarithm), we obtain as the optimal value for n:

$$n^* = 1 + \frac{1}{ln\bar{\alpha}} \left[ln \frac{w_0}{P-r} + ln \frac{s}{s-\beta} + ln \left(\frac{lns}{ln(\bar{\alpha}s)}\right) \right]. \qquad (2)$$

The values of $\bar{\alpha}$ and $w_0/(P - r)$ in this expression are both between zero and unity, while $\beta < s$ and $\bar{\alpha}s > 1$. The condition $\beta < s$ must hold for the approximating relation to apply and is supported by the data.[9] The condition $\bar{\alpha}s > 1$ must hold if there is to be any incentive to hire employees. Not merely diminishing but negative returns would exist were $\bar{\alpha}s < 1$. Since $ln\bar{\alpha} < 0$, the expression in brackets must be negative, a condition which is virtually assured by the stipulation that the firm earn positive profits.[10] Assuming that the appropriate bounds and

inequality conditions are satisfied, the following *ceteris paribus* conditions are obtained from the model:

a) Optimal n increases as the degree of compliance with supervisor objectives ($\bar{\alpha}$) increases.
b) Optimal n is infinite if there is no loss of intention ($\bar{\alpha} = 1$) between successive hierarchical levels. Only a declining product-demand curve or rising labor-supply curve could impose a (static) limit on firm size in such circumstances.
c) Optimal n decreases as the ratio of the basic wage to the net price over non-wage variable costs ($w_0/P - r$) increases. Thus, the optimum size for an organization will be relatively small and the optimum shape relatively flat in labor intensive industries.
d) Optimal n increases as the span of control (s) increases. Intuition would have led us to expect that flatter organizations (fewer hierarchical levels) would be associated with wider spans of control, but obviously this is not the case.[11]
e) Optimal n decreases as the wage multiple between levels (β) increases.

Plausible values for $\bar{\alpha}$ can be obtained by substituting estimated values for each of the parameters into equation (2). This is done below. In addition, propositions (c), (d), and (e) can be tested empirically by observing that total employment is given by

$$N^* = \Sigma_{i=1}^{n^*} N_i = \Sigma_{i=1}^{n^*} s^{i-1}. \qquad (3)$$

The sum of this series is given by

$$N^* = \frac{s^{n^*} - 1}{s - 1} \simeq \frac{s^{n^*}}{s - 1}. \qquad (4)$$

Taking the natural logarithm and substituting the value of optimal n^* given by equation (2), we have:

$$ln\,N^* \simeq ln\left(\frac{1}{s-1}\right) + lns \left\{ 1 + \frac{1}{ln\bar{\alpha}} \left[ln \frac{w_0}{P-r} + \qquad (5) \right.\right.$$
$$\left.\left. ln \frac{s}{s-\beta} + ln\left(\frac{lns}{ln(\bar{\alpha}s)}\right) \right] \right\}.$$

Expressing the optimal size firm in this way avoids the necessity of collecting data by hierarchical levels.

Employment among the five hundred largest industrials in the United States runs generally between one thousand and one hundred thousand employees. For values of s between 5 and 10, which is the normal

---

[9] If $\beta > s$, then $(\log s/\log \beta) < 1$ and $a_1 = -(\log s/\log \beta) + 1 > 0$. But as the results in Table A1 show, a_1 is clearly negative, which requires that $s > \beta$, as assumed.

[10] The condition that the firm earn positive profits implies that

$$(P - r)(\bar{\alpha}s)^{n-1} - \frac{s^n}{s-\beta} w_0 > 0,$$

or

$$\frac{w_0}{P-r} \cdot \frac{s}{s-\beta} \cdot \frac{1}{\bar{\alpha}^{(n-1)}} < 1.$$

This requires that

$$\left[ln \frac{w_0}{P-r} + ln \frac{s}{s-\beta} + ln \frac{1}{\bar{\alpha}^{(n-1)}} \right] < 0.$$

Since $ln\,[1/\bar{\alpha}^{(n-1)}]$ is approximately of the same magnitude as $ln\,[ln\,s/ln(\bar{\alpha}s)]$, or if anything is likely to exceed it, the condition that the firm earn positive profits is tantamount to requiring the bracketed term in equation (2) to be negative.

[11] This result should be interpreted with some care. It assumes that $\bar{\alpha}$ is unaffected by increasing the span of control. Within any given firm, this is possible only if the increase in the span of control results from a management or technical innovation. Otherwise, increasing the span of control would lead to an increase in control loss. With this caveat in mind, the result indicated in the text is less counter-intuitive. See part 5, Section III.

range (Koontz and O'Donnell, 1955, p. 88), this implies an optimal n of between 4 and 7. If all of our assumptions were satisfied, if there were no additional factors (risk, growth, and so on) acting as limitations to firm size, and for values of β in the range 1.3 to 1.6 and $w_0/P - r$ in the range 1/3 to 2/3, the implied value of $\bar{\alpha}$ is in the neighborhood of 0.90. Since other factors are likely to act as limitations to some extent, the true value of $\bar{\alpha}$ may generally be higher than this. It is our contention, however, for the reasons given above, that values of $\bar{\alpha}$ less than unity are typical and that the cumulative effects of control loss are fundamentally responsible for limitations to firm size.

III. EXTENSIONS

Although the basic model developed in the preceding section makes evident the critical importance of control loss as a static limitation to firm size in a way which is more precise than was heretofore available and thus both clarifies the issues and expresses them in a potentially testable form, it is obviously a highly special model and may be properly regarded with scepticism for that reason. We attempt in this section to generalize the analysis in such a way as to make clear its wider applicability. First, the possibility of introducing economies of scale, either through the specialization of labor or in the non-labor inputs, to offset diseconomies due to control loss is examined. Second, we develop the properties of a model in which the utility function of the firm includes both profits and hierarchical expense. Next, imperfections in the product market are permitted. Fourth, we allow for the possibility of variations in the span of control at the production level. Finally, the compliance parameter $(\bar{\alpha})$ is expressed as a function of the span of control.

1. *Economies of scale.*—We assume above that economies of scale due to specialization of labor or in the non-labor inputs have been exhausted so that diseconomies of scale due to control loss give rise to increasing average cost conditions in the range of output under consideration. These assumptions can be made more precise here. For this purpose, we express the parameter θ which converts input to output as a function of n. Over the range where economies of specialization exist $\partial\theta/\partial n > 0$, whereas when these have been exhausted $\partial\theta/\partial n = 0$. Thus, average cost can be expressed as:

$$AC = w_0 \frac{s}{s - \beta} \cdot \frac{1}{\theta \bar{\alpha}^{n-1}} - r \qquad (6)$$

and AC will decrease so long as $\partial\theta/\partial n > \theta \ln \bar{\alpha}$. When these two are in balance, constant returns to the labor input will prevail, but as $\partial\theta/\partial n$ declines (and eventually goes to zero), diminishing returns due to control loss will set in.

In a similar way, the non-wage variable cost per unit output parameter, r, can be expressed as a function of output, where $\partial r/\partial Q < 0$ initially, but eventually $\partial r/\partial Q = 0$. Thus, average costs will at first decline for this reason as well, but the cumulative effects of control loss will ultimately dominate and the average cost curve will rise. Implicitly, the model in Section II assumes that both $\partial\theta/\partial n$ and $\partial r/\partial Q$ are zero, so that economies with respect to both labor and non-labor inputs are assumed to be exhausted in the relevant range. Actually, this is somewhat stronger than is necessary for control loss to impose a limitation to firm size; this result would obtain under the assumptions that $\partial^2\theta/\partial n^2 < 0$ and $\partial^2 r/\partial Q^2 > 0$. This latter, however, would lead only to changes in degree and not in kind from those derived above.

2. *A utility-maximizing version.*—As we have argued elsewhere, a shift from a profit-maximizing to a utility-maximizing assumption seems appropriate where large firm size is involved, since the characteristics of the opportunity set that the management has access to progressively favor non-profit objectives as size increases. In addition, the bureaucratic operations of a large firm may be less attractive to strictly profit-oriented managers than to managers who have broader objectives. Alternatively, if profit-directed managers are typically less adept politicians, they may simply be outmaneuvered and displaced in circumstances which encourage or permit the pursuit of non-profit goals. In any case, only modest changes in the above model are necessary to transform it to a utility-maximizing form of the sort that we have investigated previously (Williamson, 1964). For this purpose, we assume that the management has a utility function that includes both staff (or hierarchical expense) and profits as principal components. Designating staff expense as H and treating this as all wage expense above the operating level, we have

$$H = \sum_{i=1}^{n-1} w_0 \beta^{n-i} s^{i-1} \simeq w_0 \frac{\beta s^{n-1}}{s - \beta}. \qquad (7)$$

We represent the utility function by U and, given our assumption that staff and profits are the principal components, the objective becomes: maximize

$$U = U(H, R - C) = \qquad (8)$$
$$U\left[w_0 \frac{\beta s^{n-1}}{s - \beta}, P(\bar{\alpha}s)^{n-1} - w_0 \frac{s^n}{s - \beta} - r(\bar{\alpha}s)^{n-1}\right].$$

Treating n as the only decision variable and all other variables in this expression as parameters, optimal n is now given by:

$$n^* = 1 + \frac{1}{ln\bar{\alpha}}\left[ln\frac{w_0}{P - r} + ln\frac{s - (U_1/U_2)\beta}{s - \beta} + ln\left(\frac{lns}{ln\bar{\alpha}s}\right)\right]. \qquad (9)$$

Comparing this expression with that obtained in equation (2), we observe that the only difference is the presence of a $(U_1/U_2)\beta$ term in the brackets of equation (9), where U_1 is the first partial of the utility function with respect to staff, and U_2 is the first partial with respect to profits. Obviously, if staff is valued objectively only for the contribution that it makes to profits, U_1 is zero and (9) becomes identical with (2). If, however, the management displays a positive preference for hierarchical expense so that the ratio U_1/U_2 is not zero, the optimal value of n^* in the utility-maximizing organization will be larger than in the corresponding profit-maximizing organization with identical parameters.[12]

The response of n^* to an increase in each of the parameters is identical with that given previously with the exception of β. Whether n^* will increase or decrease in response to an increase in β depends on whether U_1/U_2 is greater than or less than unity respectively.

3. *Imperfection in the product market.*—If product price is not treated as a parameter but instead $P = P(Q)$, $\partial P/\partial Q < 0$, we obtain the following expression for optimal n:

$$n^* = 1 + \frac{1}{ln\bar{a}}\left\{ln\frac{w_0}{P\left(1 - \frac{1}{\eta}\right) - r} + \qquad (10)\right.$$
$$\left. ln\frac{s}{s - \beta} + ln\frac{lns}{ln(\bar{\alpha}s)}\right\},$$

where η is the elasticity of demand.

Obviously, in a perfect product market, where $\eta = \infty$, (10) is identical with (2). As is to be expected, the value of optimal n decreases as demand becomes more inelastic.

4. *Variation in the span of control over operators.*—It is assumed in the model developed in Section II that the span of control is uniform throughout the organization. Although variations in the span of control among the administrative levels of the organization are generally small, this is frequently untrue between the foremen and operatives. Typically, the span of control is larger here and the reasons are quite obvious: Tasks tend to be more highly routinized, and thus the need for supervision and coordination are correspondingly attenuated. Letting σ be the span of control between foremen and operatives, total employment of operatives is now given by the product of σ and the number of foremen, where this latter is s^{n-2}. Productive output is thus the product of control loss, $(\bar{\alpha})^{n-1}$, times σs^{n-2}, or $\bar{\alpha}\sigma(\bar{\alpha}s)^{n-2}$. The value of optimal n derived from this version of the model is:

$$n^* = 1 + \frac{1}{ln\bar{\alpha}}\left\{ln\frac{w_0}{P - r} + \qquad (11)\right.$$
$$\left. ln\left(\frac{\sigma + \beta s/s - \beta}{\sigma}\right) + ln\left[\frac{lns}{ln(\bar{\alpha}s)}\right]\right\}.$$

Again, it is obvious by comparing this expression with equation (2) that when $\sigma = s$ they are identical and that qualitatively the properties are the same. The additional implication that obtains from this model is that as σ increases, optimal n increases. That is, for $\bar{a}$ unchanged, increasing the span of control between the foremen and operatives leads to a general increase in the number of levels and, consequently, number of employees in the hierarchical organization, a result which is completely in accord with our intuition.

5. *Compliance and span of control interaction.*—The difficulties associated with the selection of an optimum span of control have been noted by Simon as follows:

> The dilemma is this: in a large organization with interrelations between members, a restricted span of control produces excessive red tape. . . . The alternative is to increase the number of persons who are under the command of an officer. . . . But this, too, leads to difficulty, for if an officer is required to supervise too many employees, his control over them is weakened.

---

[12] As we argue below, it seems plausible to suppose that $\bar{\alpha}$ will be larger in utility-maximizing organizations in which the goal of the firm represents a consensus among those managers whose preferences count.

Granted, then, that both the increase and the decrease in span of control have some undesirable consequences, what is the optimum point [Simon, 1957a, p. 28]?

More precisely, the dilemma can be stated in terms of compliance $(\bar{\alpha})$ and span of control (s) interaction. Whereas the preceding analysis treats the level of compliance $(\bar{\alpha})$ and the span of control (s) independently, in fact they are intimately related. Increasing the span of control means that while each supervisor has more productive capability responsive to him he has less time to devote to the supervision of each, and hence a loss of control results. For purposes of examining this behavior, we let

$$\bar{\alpha} = f(s), \quad \partial f/\partial s < 0. \tag{12}$$

Given that $\bar{\alpha}$ is a declining function of s as indicated, the question next arises: What is the optimum value of s and how is this related to size of firm? Now output is given by $Q = (\bar{\alpha}s)^{n-1}$, so that for any particular level of output, say $\overline{Q}$, choice of n implies a value for s (and, hence, through [12], $\bar{\alpha}$) and conversely.[13] To determine the relation between optimum s and $\overline{Q}$, we observe that since gross revenue is fixed given the level of output, the optimization problem can be expressed as one of minimizing labor costs subject to constraint. Thus, the objective is: minimize

$$C_L = w_0 \frac{s^n}{s - \beta}$$

subject to

$$
\begin{aligned}
&(i) \ (\bar{\alpha}s)^{n-1} = \overline{Q} \\
&(ii) \ \bar{\alpha} \quad\quad = f(s).
\end{aligned}
\tag{13}
$$

The standard technique for studying the behavior of this system is to formulate it as a Lagrangian and perturbate the first order conditions with respect to $\overline{Q}$.
Unfortunately, the resulting expressions cannot be signed on the basis of the general functional relation $\bar{\alpha} = f(s)$. Assuming, however, that the function is

Table 1. Comparative statics responses

Decision variable	Shift parameter	
	Output $(d\overline{Q})$	Goal inconsistency (dk)
Hierarchical level (dn)	+	+
Span of control (ds)	−	−
Control effectiveness $(d\bar{\alpha})$	+	?

bell-shaped on the right (which intuitively is the correct general configuration), we can replace (12) and, hence, the second constraint, by

$$\bar{\alpha} = e^{-ks^2}. \tag{12'}$$

The value of the exponent k in this expression can be interpreted as a goal-consistency parameter. As goal consistency increases, the value of k decreases and $\bar{\alpha}$ increases at every value of s.

The comparative statics responses of n and s (and hence $\bar{\alpha}$) to changes in firm size (as measured by output) and goal inconsistency (k) are shown in Table 1. The direction of adjustment of any particular decision variable to a displacement from equilibrium by an increase in either of those parameters is found by referring to the row and column entry corresponding to the decision variable-parameter pair.[14]

That the number of hierarchical levels should increase as output increases is not surprising. That the span of control should decrease, however, is less obvious. Moreover, it contradicts what little data there are on this question. Thus, Starbuck (1964, p. 375) concludes his systematic survey of the relevant literature bearing on this issue with the observation that the "administrative span of control . . . probably increases with organizational size." Unless our model can be somehow extended to explain this condition, it calls seriously into question the validity of the control-loss approach to organizational behavior. Thus, one of the merits of formalizing this argument as we have is that we can go beyond mere plausibility arguments to discover the less obvious properties of the model and address the relevant evidence to them. Appendix B concerns itself with this dilemma.

That an increase in k (goal inconsistency) leads to

---

[13]Actually, two values of s and $\bar{\alpha}$ are consistent with each feasible choice of n: a high $\bar{\alpha}$, low s pair and a low $\bar{\alpha}$, high s pair. Of these two, the high $\bar{\alpha}$, low s position is always preferred since, with output fixed, gross revenues are unaffected by choice of s (and the associated value of $\bar{\alpha}$), while increasing s for a given n leads to higher employment and hence increase. More precisely, costs vary roughly in proportion to s^{n-1}, and the lower the value of s the lower the associated labor costs.

[14]The responses to changes in k are unambiguous. Those for changes in $\overline{Q}$ hold over all relevant values of $\bar{\alpha}$ ($\geq .7$) and s (≥ 2).

a decrease in the span of control and hence increase in n for a fixed size organization is entirely in accord with our intuition. Indeed, given that control loss is cumulative across hierarchical levels, we would expect that consistency is relatively high (k is low) and thus the span of control large in large organizations. That organizations such as the Catholic Church successfully operate with relatively flat hierarchical structures is surely partly attributable to the high degree of goal consistency that the organization possesses. Selection and training procedures obviously contribute to this result.

High goal consistency is probably also more likely in business firms that are operated as utility-maximizing rather than profit-maximizing concerns, where the utility function of the former results from the goal consensus among the management, whereas the latter represents a constraint that is rarely identical with underlying managerial objectives (Williamson, 1964, pp. 32–37, 153–60). It does not follow, therefore, that requiring strict adherence to a profit goal necessarily leads to maximum profits. Contentious discord can be expected to develop in such circumstances which implies high k and may yield low profits. We thus have the paradox that (within limits) the permissive pursuit of nonprofit goals may actually lead to the realization of higher profits.

IV. CONCLUSIONS

The proposition that the management factor is responsible for a limitation to firm size has appeared recurrently in the literature. But the arguments have tended to be imprecise, lacked predictive content, and consequently failed to be convincing. The present paper attempts to overcome some of these shortcomings by developing a formal model in which the control-loss phenomenon is made central to the analysis. The importance of control loss to an understanding of bureaucratic behavior in non-market organizations has been noted previously. Our use of

this proposition here is based on one of the fundamental tenets of organization theory: namely, virtually all of the interesting bureaucratic behavior observed to exist in large government bureaucracies finds its counterpart in large nongovernment bureaucracies as well, and this is particularly true where the phenomenon in question is a result of the bounded rationality attributes of decision-makers. We, therefore, borrow from the bureaucracy literature the proposition that control loss occurs between successive hierarchical levels (and that this tends to be cumulative) and introduce it into a theory of the firm in which neither declining product-demand curves nor rising factor-supply curves are permitted to impose a static limit on firm size.

For any given span of control (together with a specification of the state of technology, internal experience, etc.) an irreducible minimum degree of control loss results from the simple serial reproduction distortion that occurs in communicating across successive hierarchical levels. If, in addition, goals differ between hierarchical levels, the loss in control can be more extensive.

The strategy of borrowing behavioral assumptions from the organization-theory literature and developing the implications of the behavior observed within the framework of economic analysis would seem to be one which might find application quite generally. Thus, the organization-theory approach to problems tends frequently to be rich in behavioral insights but weak analytically, while economics generally and the theory of the firm literature in particular has a highly developed modeling apparatus but has evidenced less resourcefulness in its use of interesting behavioral assumptions. Combining these two research areas so as to secure access to the strengths of each would thus appear to be quite promising. In any case, it is the strategy followed in this paper and, to the extent we have had any success, suggests itself for possible use elsewhere.

APPENDIX A

Test of the Wage Model

Our basic wage hypothesis is that $w_i = w_0 \beta^{n-i}$, where w_0 is the base level salary, n is the number of hierarchical levels, i is the particular level in question, and β is the wage multiple. Unfortunately, the General Motors data are reported by wage ranges of unequal size rather than by hierarchical levels. It can

nevertheless be used to test our hypothesis by developing the cumulative distribution counterpart of our model.

Taking logarithms of this wage relation, we have log $w_i = \log w_0 + (n - i) \log \beta$. By assumption (5), the total number of employees at level i is $N_i = s^{i-1}$, where s is the span

Table A1. Wage model fit to General Motors salary data, 1934–42*

	1934	1936	1938	1940	1942
No. Obs	10	11	6	6	6
$\bar{R}^2$	.940	.970	.956	.907	.944
Log $\bar{\alpha}_0$	10.022	10.828	10.688	11.859	10.822
	(0.733)	(0.523)	(0.882)	(1.400)	(1.077)
$\bar{\alpha}_1$	−1.904	−2.067	−2.037	−2.297	−2.045
	(0.160)	(0.116)	(0.193)	(0.306)	(0.236)

*Standard errors are shown in parentheses.

of control. Taking this logarithm, we obtain $\log N_i = (i - 1) \log s$. Solving for i in this second logarithmic expression and substituting into the first we obtain:[15]

$$\log N_i = \log b_0 - \left(\frac{\log s}{\log \beta}\right) \log w_i, \qquad (A1)$$

or

$$N_i = b_0 w_i^{-b_1}$$

where

$$\log b_0 = (\log s/\log \beta) \cdot [\log w_0 + (n - 1) \log \beta]$$

and

$$b_1 = (\log s/\log \beta).$$

We denote by $N(\overline{w})$ the total number of individuals having a wage greater than $\overline{w}$. This is given by

$$N(\overline{w}) = \int_{\overline{w}}^{\infty} b_0 w^{-b_1} dw = \left(\frac{b_0}{b_1}\right) \overline{w}^{(-b_1 + 1)} \qquad (A2)$$

[15]The derivation of equation (A1) is similar to Simon (1957*b*). Simon does not, however, go on to derive the cumulative relationship given by equation (A2), which is ordinarily the only testable version of the model. A similar derivation to ours can, however, be found in Davis (1941, chap. ix).

or

$$N(\overline{w}) = a_0 \overline{w}^{-a_1}$$

where

$$a_0 = b_0/b_1$$

and

$$a_1 = -b_1 + 1.$$

This cumulative form does not require either information about the hierarchical levels or uniform size classes and, hence, can be applied to the General Motors (or any similar class of) wage data. Being derived from our wage-employment hypotheses, it should produce a good fit to the data if these hypotheses are substantially close approximations. The results are reported in Table A1.

As is quickly apparent from inspecting the Table A1 results, the wage model given by (A2) provides an excellent fit to the data. The coefficients of determination adjusted for degrees of freedom all exceed .90, and the estimates of the coefficients are both stable over the entire interval and significantly different from zero in every year. Assuming that General Motors salary schedules are not atypical (and since General Motors is frequently regarded as a model of better management practices we might expect imitation from other firms in this respect), we have some confidence that the assumptions underlying our wage model are correct at least for the class of large corporations that we are principally concerned with.

APPENDIX B

A Digression on Dynamics

The analysis in the text has at least two disturbing implications. First, not only does control loss impose a limit to firm size, but once this limit is reached the firm will stabilize at this level. Since continuing expansion of large firms is common, the model appears to be at variance with reality in this aspect. Second, the model predicts that the span of control decreases with firm size, while the evidence points to the contrary. Either the control-loss argument must be fundamentally incorrect, or the model must be amended in one or more respects.

We propose an extension, one that mainly involves allow-

ance for dynamic conditions ignored in our static analysis. At least three factors are operative. First, increases in experience lead to refinements, shortcuts, and routinization, all of which permit increasing the span of control for a fixed level of control loss. And experience is obviously positively related to firm size. Second, although most of the economies of scale resulting from specialization and indivisibilities are ordinarily exhausted at a relatively modest firm size (Bain, 1956, chap. iii), the economies that result from a large data-processing capability may well extend considerably beyond this size. Since for a given level of control loss increases in information-processing capability permit the span of control to be expanded, the association of an increasing span of control and large firm size may be due in part to this information processing and firm size relation. Third, the rate of change of firm size may have an important influence. Penrose (1959, pp. 44–48) has argued persuasively that the dynamics of growth require additional hierarchical personnel than are needed when the expansion is completed. Presumably this is because problems of coordination and control are more serious during periods of expansion. Expressing this argument in span of control terms, an inverse relation is to be expected between span of control and the growth rate. The remaining question then is what, if any, association between growth rate and size is to be expected. The data here are scant, but the results from the stochastic, serial correlation, growth models of Ijiri and Simon (1964, pp. 86–87) are at least suggestive, namely, that "firms which grow large experience most of their growth [early in their history] . . ., then reach a plateau." Assuming that this is generally valid, growth rates will tend to be inversely related to firm size. Thus here again we have a dynamic, size-related condition that helps to explain the apparent contradiction between the data relating span of control to firm size and our static analysis.

Taking these dynamic or age-related characteristics into account suggests that, given the value of $\bar{\alpha}$, the optimum span of control be expressed as:

$$s = \varphi \ (Q, \ k, \ t, \ d, \ dQ/dt, \ . \ . \ .) \tag{B1}$$

where

Q = output: $\varphi_Q < 0$
k = goal inconsistency parameter; $\varphi_k < 0$
t = chronological age (a proxy for experience); $\varphi_t > 0$
d = data processing capability; $\varphi_d > 0$
dQ/dt = rate of change of output; $\varphi(dQ/dt) < 0$

Among the advantages of this formulation is that it permits us to accommodate parts of Mrs. Penrose's theory as a part of our own. Thus, if increases in dQ/dt reduce the span of control, additional hierarchical levels will be required to sustain the level of output. But for fixed $\bar{\alpha}$, cumulative control loss which is given by $(1 - \bar{\alpha}^n)$ now increases. Hence, costs increase as dQ/dt increases, and the optimum growth rate is therefore restricted. Although Mrs. Penrose's emphasis is on internal experience and no attention is given to notions such as the span of control, the existence of control loss is implicit in her discussion and our model helps make this clear. Similarly, she observes that "as plans are completed and put into operation, managerial services absorbed in the planning processes will be gradually released" (Penrose, 1959, p. 49). Plan realization here implies that dQ/dt decreases, hence the span of control increases and the release of managerial services follows necessarily.

The above formulation also points up the very real dangers of performing simple correlations between s and Q. For the reasons given above, Q is positively related to t and d and negatively related to dQ/dt. Inasmuch as φ_t and φ_d are positive while $\varphi dQ/dt$ is negative, the combined effect of these three factors could easily swamp the true effect of Q on s (as predicted by our static model) if simple bivariate analysis were attempted.

REFERENCES

Andrews, P. W. S. *Manufacturing Business*. New York: Macmillan Co., 1949.

Bain, J.S. *Barriers to New Competition*. Cambridge, Mass.: Harvard Univ. Press, 1956.

Bartlett, F. C. *Remembering*. New York: Cambridge Univ. Press, 1932.

Chamberlin, E. H. "Proportionality, Divisibility and Economies of Scale," *Q.J.E.*, LXII (February, 1948), 229–62.

Coase, R. H. "The Nature of the Firm," *Economica*, N.S., IV (1937), 386–405. Reprinted in George J. Stigler and Kenneth E. Boulding (eds.). *Readings in Price Theory*. Homewood, Ill.: Richard D. Irwin, Inc., 1952.

Davis, H. T. *The Analysis of Economic Time Series*. Granville, Ohio: Principia Press, 1941.

Downs, Anthony, *Bureaucratic Structure and Decisionmaking*. (RM- 4646- PR.) Santa Monica, Calif.: RAND, March, 1966.

Ijiri, Yuji, and Simon, H. A. "Business Firm Growth and Size," *A.E.R.*, LIV (March, 1964), 77–89.

Kaldor, Nicholas. "The Equilibrium of the Firm," *Econ. J.*, XLIV (March, 1934), 70–71.

Knight, F. H., *Risk, Uncertainty and Profit*. New York: Harper & Row, 1965.

Koontz, H., and O'Donnell, C. *Principles of Management*. New York: McGraw-Hill Book Co., 1955.

March, J. G., and Simon, H. A. *Organizations*. New York: John Wiley & Sons, Inc., 1958.

Mayer, Thomas. "The Distribution of Ability and Earnings," *Rev. Econ. and Statis.*, XLII (May, 1960), 189–98.

Monsen, R. J., Jr., and Downs, Anthony. "A Theory of Large Managerial Firms," *J.P.E.*, LXXIII (June, 1965), 221–36.

Papandreou, A. G. "Some Basic Issues in the Theory of the Firm," in B. F. Haley (ed.). *A Survey of Contemporary Economics*. Homewood, Ill.: Richard D. Irwin, Inc., 1952.

Penrose, Edith. *The Theory of the Growth of the Firm*. New York: John Wiley & Sons, 1959.

Robinson, E. A. G. "The Problem of Management and the Size of Firms," *Econ. J.*, XLIV (June, 1934), 240–54.

————. *The Structure of Competitive Industry*. Chicago: Univ. of Chicago Press, 1962.

Ross, N. S. "Management and the Size of the Firm," *Rev. Econ. Studies*, XIX (1952–53), 148–54.

Simon, H. A. *Administrative Behavior*. 2d ed. New York: Macmillan Co., 1957 *(a)*.

————. "The Compensation of Executives," *Sociometry* (March, 1957), pp. 32–35 *(b)*.

Starbuck, W. H. "Organizational Growth and Development," in J. G. March (ed.). *Handbook of Organizations*. Chicago: Rand McNally & Co., 1964.

Tullock, Gordon. *The Politics of Bureaucracy*. Washington: Public Affairs Press, 1965.

U.S. Department of Labor. *Salary Structure Characteristics in Large Firms* (1963). (Bull. No. 1417.) Washington, August, 1964.

Williamson, John. "Profit, Growth and Sales Maximization," *Economica*, XXXIII (February, 1966), 1–16.

Williamson, O. E. *The Economics of Discretionary Behavior: Managerial Objectives in a Theory of the Firm*. New York: Prentice-Hall, Inc., 1964.

Part 3 Recent Advances in the Theory of Resource Allocation

INFORMATION AND TIME

The Economics of Information*

GEORGE J. STIGLER[1]

See "De Gustibus Non Est Disputandam" for author's biography.

One should hardly have to tell academicians that information is a valuable resource: knowledge *is* power. And yet it occupies a slum dwelling in the town of economics. Mostly it is ignored: the best technology is assumed to be known; the relationship of commodities to consumer preferences is a datum. And one of the information-producing industries, advertising, is treated with a hostility that economists normally reserve for tariffs or monopolists.

There are a great many problems in economics for which this neglect of ignorance is no doubt permissible or even desirable. But there are some for which this is not true, and I hope to show that some important aspects of economic organization take on a new meaning when they are considered from the viewpoint of the search for information. In the present paper I shall attempt to analyze systematically one important problem of information—the ascertainment of market price.

I. THE NATURE OF SEARCH

Prices change with varying frequency in all markets, and, unless a market is completely centralized, no one will know all the prices which various sellers (or buyers) quote at any given time. A buyer (or seller) who wishes to ascertain the most favorable price must canvass various sellers (or buyers)—a phenomenon I shall term "search."

The amount of dispersion of asking prices of sellers is a problem to be discussed later, but it is important to emphasize immediately the fact that dispersion is ubiquitous even for homogeneous goods. Two examples of asking prices, of consumer and producer goods respectively, are displayed in Table 1. The automobile prices (for an identical model) were those quoted with an average amount of "higgling": their average was $2,436, their range from $2,350 to $2,515, and their standard deviation $42. The prices for anthracite coal were bids for federal government purchases and had a mean of $16.90 per ton, a range from $15.46 to $18.92, and a standard deviation of $1.15. In both cases the range of prices was significant on almost any criterion.

Price dispersion is a manifestation—and, indeed, it is the measure—of ignorance in the market. Dispersion is a biased measure of ignorance because there is never absolute homogeneity in the commodity if we include the terms of sale within the concept of the commodity. Thus, some automobile dealers might perform more service, or carry a larger

*Reprinted from *Journal of Political Economy* (June 1961) by permission of The University of Chicago Press. Copyright 1961, pp. 213–225.
[1]I have benefited from comments of Gary Becker, Milton Friedman, Zvi Griliches, Harry Johnson, Robert Solow, and Lester Telser.

range of varieties in stock, and a portion of the observed dispersion is presumably attributable to such differences. But it would be metaphysical, and fruitless, to assert that all dispersion is due to heterogeneity.

At any time, then, there will be a frequency distribution of the prices quoted by sellers. Any buyer seeking the commodity would pay whatever price is asked by the seller whom he happened to canvass, if he were content to buy from the first seller. But, if the dispersion of price quotations of sellers is at all

large (relative to the cost of search), it will pay, on average, to canvass several sellers. Consider the following primitive example: let sellers be equally divided between asking prices of $2 and $3. Then the distribution of minimum prices, as search is lengthened, is shown in Table 2. The buyer who canvasses two sellers instead of one has an expected saving of 25 cents per unit, etc.

The frequency distributions of asking (and offering) prices have not been studied sufficiently to support any hypothesis as to their nature. Asking prices are probably skewed to the right, as a rule, because the seller of reproducible goods will have some minimum but no maximum limit on the price he can accept. If the distribution of asking prices is normal, the distributions of minimum prices encountered in searches of one, two, and three sellers will be those displayed in Fig. 1. If the distribution is rectangular, the corresponding distributions would be those shown in Panel B. The latter assumption does not receive strong support from the evidence, but it will be used for a time because of its algebraic simplicity.

In fact, if sellers' asking prices (p) are uniformly

Table 1. Asking prices for two commodities

A. Chevrolets, Chicago, February, 1959*

Price (dollars)	No. of dealers
2,350–2,400	4
2,400–2,450	11
2,450–2,500	8
2,500–2,550	4

B. Anthracite coal, delivered (Washington, D.C.), April, 1953†

Price per ton (dollars)	No. of bids
15.00–15.50	2
15.50–16.00	2
16.00–16.50	2
16.50–17.00	3
17.00–18.00	1
18.00–19.00	4

*Allen F. Jung, "Price Variations Among Automobile Dealers in Metropolitan Chicago," *Journal of Business*, XXXIII (January, 1960), 31–42.
†Supplied by John Flueck

Table 2. Distribution of hypothetical minimum prices by numbers of bids canvassed

No. of prices canvassed	Probability of minimum price of		Expected minimum price
	$2.00	$3.00	
1	.5	.5	$2.50
2	.75	.25	2.25
3	.875	.125	2.125
4	.9375	.0625	2.0625
∞	1.0	0	2.00

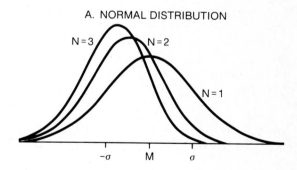

A. NORMAL DISTRIBUTION

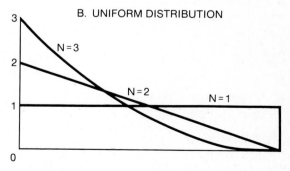

B. UNIFORM DISTRIBUTION

Fig. 1. Distribution of minimum prices with varying amounts of search.

distributed between zero and one, it can be shown that:[2] (1) The distribution of minimum prices with n searches is

$$n(1 - p)^{n-1}, \qquad (1)$$

(2) the average minimum price is

$$\frac{1}{n+1},$$

and (3) the variance of the average minimum price is

$$\frac{n}{(n+1)^2(n+2)}.$$

Whatever the precise distribution of prices, *it is certain that increased search will yield diminishing returns as measured by the expected reduction in the minimum asking price.* This is obviously true of the rectangular distribution, with an expected minimum price of $1/(n+1)$ with n searches, and also of the normal distributions.[3] In fact, if a distribution of asking prices did not display this property, it would be an unstable distribution for reasons that will soon be apparent.[4]

For any buyer the expected savings from an ad-

ditional unit of search will be approximately the quantity (q) he wishes to purchase times the expected reduction in price as a result of the search,[5] or

$$q \left| \frac{\partial P_{min}}{\partial_n} \right|. \qquad (2)$$

The expected saving from given search will be greater, the greater the dispersion of prices. The saving will also obviously be greater, the greater the expenditure on the commodity. Let us defer for a time the problem of the time period to which the expenditure refers, and hence the amount of expenditure, by considering the purchase of an indivisible, infrequently purchased good—say, a used automobile.

The cost of search, for a consumer, may be taken as approximately proportional to the number of (identified) sellers approached, for the chief cost is time. This cost need not be equal for all consumers, of course: aside from differences in tastes, time will be more valuable to a person with a larger income. If the cost of search is equated to its expected marginal return, the optimum amount of search will be found.[6]

Of course, the sellers can also engage in search and, in the case of unique items, will occasionally do so in the literal fashion that buyers do. In this—empirically unimportant—case, the optimum amount of search will be such that the marginal cost of search equals the expected increase in receipts, strictly parallel to the analysis for buyers.

With unique goods the efficiency of personal search for either buyers or sellers is extremely low, because the identity of potential sellers is not known—the cost of search must be divided by the fraction of potential buyers (or sellers) in the population which is being searched. If I plan to sell a used car and engage in personal search, less than one family in a random selection of one hundred families is a potential buyer of even a popular model within the next month. As a result, the cost of search is increased more than one hundredfold per price quotation.

The costs of search are so great under these con-

---

[2] If $F(p)$ is the cumulative-frequency function of p, the probability that the minimum of n observations will be greater than p is

$$[1 - F(p)]^n = [\textstyle\int^1 dx]^n.$$

[3] The expected minimum prices with a normal distribution of mean M and standard deviation σ are

Search	Expected minimum price
1	M
2	$M - .564\sigma$
3	$M - .846\sigma$
4	$M - 1.029\sigma$
5	$M - 1.163\sigma$
6	$M - 1.267\sigma$
7	$M - 1.352\sigma$
8	$M - 1.423\sigma$
9	$M - 1.485\sigma$
10	$M - 1.539\sigma$

[4] Robert Solow has pointed out that the expected value of the minimum of a random sample of n observations,

$$E(n) = n\textstyle\int_0^1 p(1 - F)^{n-1}F'dp,$$

is a decreasing function of n, and

$$[E(n+2) - E(n+1)] - [E(n+1) - E(n)]$$

is positive so the minimum decreases at a decreasing rate. The proofs involve the fact that the density function for the rth observation from the maximum in a sample of n is

$$n \binom{n-1}{r-1} F^{n-r}(1 - F)^{r-1}F'dp.$$

[5] The precise savings will be *(a)* the reduction in price times the quantity which would be purchased at the higher price—the expression in the text—*plus (b)* the average saving on the additional purchases induced by the lower price. I neglect this quantity, which will generally be of a smaller order of magnitude.

[6] Buyers often pool their knowledge and thus reduce the effective cost of search; a few remarks are made on this method below.

ditions that there is powerful inducement to localize transactions as a device for identifying potential buyers and sellers. The medieval markets commonly increased their efficiency in this respect by prohibiting the purchase or sale of the designated commodities within a given radius of the market or on nonmarket days. The market tolls that were frequently levied on sellers (even in the absence of effective restrictions on nonmarket transactions) were clear evidence of the value of access to the localized markets.

Advertising is, of course, the obvious modern method of identifying buyers and sellers: the *classified* advertisements in particular form a meeting place for potential buyers and sellers. The identification of buyers and sellers reduces drastically the cost of search. But advertising has its own limitations: advertising itself is an expense, and one essentially independent of the value of the item advertised. The advertising of goods which have few potential buyers relative to the circulation of the advertising medium is especially expensive. We shall temporarily put advertising aside and consider an alternative.

The alternative solution is the development of specialized traders whose chief service, indeed, is implicitly to provide a meeting place for potential buyers and sellers. A used-car dealer, turning over a thousand cars a year, and presumably encountering three or five thousand each of buying and selling bids, provides a substantial centralization of trading activity. Let us consider these dealer markets, which we shall assume to be competitive in the sense of there being many independent dealers.

Each dealer faces a distribution of (for example) buyers' bids and can vary his selling prices with a corresponding effect upon purchases. Even in the markets for divisible (and hence non-unique) goods there will be some scope for higgling (discrimination) in each individual transaction: the buyer has a *maximum price* given by the lowest price he encounters among the dealers he has searched (or plans to search), *but no minimum price.* But let us put this range of indeterminacy aside, perhaps by assuming that the dealer finds discrimination too expensive,[7] *and inquire how the demand curve facing a dealer is determined.*

Each dealer sets a selling price, p, and makes sales to all buyers for whom this is *the minimum price.*

[7]This is the typical state of affairs in retailing except for consumer durable goods.

With a uniform distribution of asking prices by dealers, the number of buyers of a total of N_b possible buyers who will purchase from him is

$$N_i = KN_b n(1 - p)^{n-1}, \qquad (3)$$

where K is a constant.[8] The number of buyers from a dealer increases as his price is reduced, and at an increasing rate.[9] Moreover, with the uniform distribution of asking prices, the number of buyers increases with increased search if the price is below the reciprocal of the amount of search.[10] We should generally expect the high-price sellers to be small-volume sellers.

The stability of any distribution of asking prices of dealers will depend upon the costs of dealers. If there are constant returns to scale, the condition of equal rates of return dictates that the difference between a dealer's buying and selling prices be a constant. This condition cannot in general be met: any dealer can buy low, and sell high, provided he is content with a small volume of transactions, and he will then be earning more than costs (including a competitive rate of return). No other dealer can eliminate this non-competitive rate of profit, although by making the same price bids he can share the volume of business, or by asking lower prices he can increase the rewards to search and hence increase the amount of search.

With economies of scale, the competition of dealers will eliminate the profitability of quoting very high selling and very low buying prices and will ren-

---

[8]Since $n(1 - p)^{n-1}$ is a density function, we must multiply it by a dp which represents the range of prices between adjacent price quotations. In addition, if two or more sellers quote an identical price, they will share the sales, so $K = dp/r$, where r is the number of firms quoting price p.

[9]For

$$\frac{\partial N_i}{\partial p} = -\frac{(n-1)\,N_i}{(1-p)} < 0,$$

and

$$\frac{\partial^2 N_i}{\partial p^2} = \frac{(n-1)(n-2)\,N_i}{(1-p)^2} > 0$$

if $n > 2$.

[10]Let

$$\log N_i = \log K + \log N_b + \log n + (n-1)\log(1-p).$$

Then

$$\frac{1}{N_i}\frac{\partial N_i}{\partial n} = \frac{1}{n} + \log(1-p) = \frac{1}{n} - p,$$

approximately.

prices.[11] Many distributions of prices will be inconsistent with any possible cost conditions of dealers,[12] and it is not evident that strict equalities of rates of return for dealers are generally possible.

If economies of scale in dealing lead to a smaller dispersion of asking prices than do constant costs of dealing, similarly greater amounts of search will lead to a smaller dispersion of observed selling prices by reducing the number of purchasers who will pay high prices. Let us consider more closely the determinants of search.

DETERMINANTS OF SEARCH

The equation defining optimum search is unambiguous only if a unique purchase is being made—a house, a particular used book, etc. If purchases are repetitive, the volume of purchases based upon the search must be considered.

If the correlation of asking prices of dealers in successive time periods is perfect (and positive!), the initial search is the only one that need be undertaken. In this case the expected savings of search will be the present value of the discounted savings on all future purchases, the future savings extending over the life of the buyer or seller (whichever is shorter).[13] On the other hand, if asking prices are uncorrelated in

successive time periods, the savings from search will pertain only to that period,[14] and search in each period is independent of previous experience. If the correlation of successive prices is positive, customer search will be larger in the initial period than in subsequent periods.[15]

The correlation of successive asking prices of sellers is usually positive in the handful of cases I have examined. The rank correlation of anthracite price bids (Table 1) in 1953 with those in 1954 was .68 for eight bidders; that for Chevrolet dealers in Chicago February and August of 1959 was .33 for twenty-nine dealers—but, on the other hand, it was zero for Ford dealers for the same dates. Most observed correlations will, of course, be positive because of stable differences in the products or services, but our analysis is restricted to conditions of homogeneity.

As a rule, positive correlations should exist with homogeneous products. The amount of search will vary among individuals because of differences in their expenditures on a commodity or differences in cost of search. A seller who wishes to obtain the continued patronage of those buyers who value the gains of search more highly or have lower costs of search must see to it that he is quoting relatively low prices. In fact, goodwill may be defined as continued patronage by customers without continued search (that is, no more than occasional verification).

A positive correlation of successive asking prices justifies the widely held view that inexperienced buyers (tourists) pay higher prices in a market than do experienced buyers.[16] The former have no accumulated knowledge of asking prices, and even with an optimum amount of search they will pay higher prices on average. Since the variance of the expected minimum price decreases with additional search, the prices paid by inexperienced buyers will also have a larger variance.

If a buyer enters a wholly new market, he will have no idea of the dispersion of prices and hence no idea of the rational amount of search he should make. In such cases the dispersion will presumably be estimated by some sort of sequential process, and this

---

[11]This argument assumes that dealers will discover unusually profitable bids, given the buyers' search, which is, of course, only partly true: there is also a problem of dealers' search with respect to prices.

[12]With the rectangular distribution of asking prices, if each buyer purchases the same number of units, the elasticity of demand falls continuously with price, so that, if average cost equaled price at every rate of sales (with one seller at each price), marginal costs would have to be negative at large outputs. But, of course, the number of sellers can be less at lower prices.

[13]Let the expected minimum price be $p_1 = f(n)_1$ in period 1 (with f' <0) and let the expected minimum price in period 2, with r a measure of the correlation between sellers' successive prices, be

$$p_2 = \left(\frac{p_1}{f(n_2)}\right)^r f(n_2).$$

If the cost of search is λ per unit, total expenditures for a fixed quantity of purchases (Q) per unit of time are, neglecting interest,

$$E = Q (p_1 + p_2) + \lambda (n_1 + n_2).$$

Expenditures are a minimum when

$$\frac{\partial E}{\partial n_1} = Qf'(n_1) + Qr [f(n_1)]^{r-1} \times [f(n_2)]^{1-r} f'(n_1) + \lambda = 0$$

and

$$\frac{\partial E}{\partial n_2} = (1 - r) Q [f(n_1)]^r \times [f(n_2)]^{-r} f'(n_2) + \lambda = 0.$$

If $r = 1$, $n_2 = 0$, and n_1 is determined by $Qf'(n_1) = -\lambda/2$, the cost of search is effectively halved.

[14]See n. 13; if $r = 0$, $n_1 = n_2$.

[15]Let $f(n) = e^{-n}$. Then, in the notation of our previous footnotes,

$$n_1 - n_2 = \frac{2r}{1 - r},$$

approximately.

[16]For that matter, a negative correlation would have the same effects.

approach would open up a set of problems I must leave for others to explore. But, in general, one approaches a market with some general knowledge of the amount of dispersion, for dispersion itself is a function of the average amount of search, and this in turn is a function of the nature of the commodity:

1. The larger the fraction of the buyer's expenditures on the commodity, the greater the savings from search and hence the greater the amount of search.
2. The larger the fraction of repetitive (experienced) buyers in the market, the greater the effective amount of search (with positive correlation of successive prices).
3. The larger the fraction of repetitive sellers, the higher the correlation between successive prices, and hence, by condition (2), the larger the amount of accumulated search.[17]
4. The cost of search will be larger, the larger the geographical size of the market.

An increase in the number of buyers has an uncertain effect upon the dispersion of asking prices. The sheer increase in numbers will lead to an increase in the number of dealers and, *ceteris paribus,* to a larger range of asking prices. But, quite aside from advertising, the phenomenon of pooling information will increase. Information is pooled when two buyers compare prices: if each buyer canvasses *s* sellers, by combining they effectively canvass 2*s* sellers, duplications aside.[18] Consumers compare prices of some commodities (for example, liquor) much more often than of others (for example, chewing gum)—in fact, pooling can be looked upon as a cheaper (and less reliable) form of search.

SOURCES OF DISPERSION

One source of dispersion is simply the cost to dealers of ascertaining rivals' asking prices, but even if this cost were zero the dispersion of prices would not vanish. The more important limitation is provided by buyers' search, *and, if the conditions and participants in the market were fixed in perpetuity, prices would immediately approach uniformity.* Only those differences could persist which did not remunerate additional search. The condition for optimum search

[17]If the number of sellers *(s)* and the asking-price distributions are the same in two periods, but *k* are new sellers, the average period-1 buyer will have lost proportion *k/s* of his period-1 search.

[18]Duplications will occur more often than random processes would suggest, because pooling is more likely between buyers of similar location, tastes, etc.

would be (with perfect correlation of successive prices):

$$q \left| \frac{\partial p}{\partial n} \right| = i \times \text{marginal cost of search},$$

where i is the interest rate. If an additional search costs \$1, and the interest rate is 5 per cent, the expected reduction in price with one more search would at equilibrium be equal to \$0.05/q—a quantity which would often be smaller than the smallest unit of currency. But, indivisibilities aside, it would normally be unprofitable for buyers or sellers to eliminate all dispersion.

The maintenance of appreciable dispersion of prices arises chiefly out of the fact that knowledge becomes obsolete. *The conditions of supply and demand, and therefore the distribution of asking prices, change over time.* There is no method by which buyers or sellers can ascertain the new average price in the market appropriate to the new conditions except by search. Sellers cannot maintain perfect correlation of successive prices, even if they wish to do so, because of the costs of search. Buyers accordingly cannot make the amount of investment in search that perfect correlation of prices would justify. *The greater the instability of supply and/or demand conditions, therefore, the greater the dispersion of prices will be.*

In addition, there is a component of ignorance due to the changing identity of buyers and sellers. There is a flow of new buyers and sellers in every market, and they are at least initially uninformed on prices and by their presence make the information of experienced buyers and sellers somewhat obsolete.

The amount of dispersion will also vary with one other characteristic which is of special interest: the size (in terms of both dollars and number of traders) of the market. As the market grows in these dimensions, there will appear a set of firms which specialize in collecting and selling information. They may take the form of trade journals or specialized brokers. Since the cost of collection of information is (approximately) independent of its use (although the cost of dissemination is not), there is a strong tendency toward monopoly in the provision of information: in general, there will be a "standard" source for trade information.

II. ADVERTISING

Advertising is, among other things, a method of providing potential buyers with knowledge of the identity of sellers. It is clearly an immensely powerful instrument for the elimination of ignorance—comparable in force to the use of the book instead of the oral discourse to communicate knowledge. A small $5 advertisement in a metropolitan newspaper reaches (in the sense of being read) perhaps 25,000 readers, or fifty readers per penny, and, even if only a tiny fraction are potential buyers (or sellers), the economy they achieve in search, as compared with uninstructed solicitation, may be overwhelming.

Let us begin with advertisements designed only to identify sellers; the identification of buyers will not be treated explicitly, and the advertising of price will be discussed later. The identification of sellers is necessary because the identity of sellers changes over time, but much more because of the turnover of buyers. In every consumer market there will be a stream of new buyers (resulting from immigration or the attainment of financial maturity) requiring knowledge of sellers, and, in addition, it will be necessary to refresh the knowledge of infrequent buyers.

Suppose, what is no doubt too simple, that a given advertisement of size a will inform c per cent of the potential buyers in a given period, so $c = g(a)$.[19] This contact function will presumably show diminishing returns, at least beyond a certain size of advertisement. A certain fraction, b, of potential customers will be "born" (and "die") in a stable population, where "death" includes not only departure from the market but forgetting the seller. The value of b will obviously vary with the nature of the commodity; for example, it will be large for commodities which are seldom purchased (like a house). In a first period of advertising (at a given rate) the number of potential customers reached will be cN, if N is the total number of potential customers. In the second period $cN(1 - b)$ of these potential customers will still be informed, cbN new potential customers will be informed, and

$$c\left[(1 - b)n - cN(1 - b)\right]$$

old potential customers will be reached for the first time, or a total of

$$cN\left[1 + (1 - b)(1 - c)\right].$$

This generalizes, for k periods, to

$$cN\left[1 + (1 - b)(1 - c) + \ldots + (1 - b)^{k-1}(1 - c)^{k-1}\right],$$

and, if k is large, this approaches

$$\frac{cN}{1 - (1 - c)(1 - b)} = \lambda N. \qquad (4)$$

The proportion (λ) of potential buyers informed of the advertiser's identity thus depends upon c and b.

If each of r sellers advertises the same amount, λ is the probability that any one seller will inform any buyer. The distribution of N potential buyers by the number of contacts achieved by r sellers is given by the binomial distribution:

$$N(\lambda + [1 - \lambda])^r,$$

with, for example,

$$\frac{Nr!}{m!(r - m)!}\lambda^m(1 - \lambda)^{r-m}$$

buyers being informed of exactly m sellers' identities. The number of sellers known to a buyer ranges from zero to r, with an average of $r\lambda$ sellers and a variance of $r\lambda(1 - \lambda)$.[20]

The amount of relevant information in the market, even in this simple model, is not easy to summarize in a single measure—a difficulty common to frequency distributions. If all buyers wished to search s sellers, all buyers knowing less than s sellers would have inadequate information, and all who knew more than s sellers would have redundant information, although the redundant information would not be worthless.[21] Since the value of information is the amount by which it reduces the expected cost to the buyer of his purchases, if these expected reductions are $\Delta C_1, \Delta C_2, \ldots$, for searches of $1, 2, \ldots$, the value of the information to buyers is approximately

$$\sum_{m=1}^{r} \frac{r!}{m!(r - m)!}\lambda^m(1 - \lambda)^{r-m}\Delta C_m.$$

The information possessed by buyers, however, is not simply a matter of chance; those buyers who spend more on the commodity, or who search more for a given expenditure, will also search more for advertisements. The buyers with more information will, on average, make more extensive searches, so the value of information will be greater than this last formula indicates.

---

[19] The effectiveness of the advertisement is also a function of the skill with which it is done and of the fraction of potential buyers who read the medium, but such elaborations are put aside.

[20] This approach has both similarities and contrasts to that published by S. A. Ozga, "Imperfect Markets through Lack of Knowledge," *Quarterly Journal of Economics*, LXXIV (February, 1960), 29–52.

[21] The larger the number of sellers known, the larger is the range of prices among the sellers and the lower the expected minimum price after s searches. But this effect will normally be small.

We may pause to discuss the fact that advertising in, say, a newspaper is normally "paid" for by the seller. On our analysis, the advertising is valuable to the buyer, and he would be willing to pay more for a paper with advertisements than for one without. The difficulty with having the sellers insert advertisements "free" and having the buyer pay for them directly is that it would be difficult to ration space on this basis: the seller would have an incentive to supply an amount of information (or information of a type) the buyer did not wish, and, since numerous advertisements are supplied jointly, the buyer could not register clearly his preferences regarding advertising. (Catalogues, however, are often sold to buyers.) Charging the seller for the advertisements creates an incentive for him to supply to the buyer only the information which is desired.

It is commonly complained that advertising is jointly supplied with the commodity in the sense that the buyer must pay for both even though he wishes only the latter. The alternative of selling the advertising separately from the commodity, however, would require that the advertising of various sellers (of various commodities) would be supplied jointly: the economies of disseminating information in a general-purpose periodical are so great that some form of jointness is inescapable. But the common complaint is much exaggerated: the buyer who wishes can search out the seller who advertises little (but, of course, enough to be discoverable), and the latter can sell at prices lower by the savings on advertising.

These remarks seem most appropriate to newspaper advertisements of the "classified" variety; what of the spectacular television show or the weekly comedian? We are not equipped to discuss advertising in general because the problem of quality has been (and will continue to be) evaded by the assumption of homogeneous goods. Even within our narrower framework, however, the use of entertainment to attract buyers to information is a comprehensible phenomenon. The assimilation of information is not an easy or pleasant task for most people, and they may well be willing to pay more for the information when supplied in an enjoyable form. In principle, this complementary demand for information and entertainment is exactly analogous to the complementary demand of consumers for commodities and delivery service or air-conditioned stores. One might find a paradox in the simultaneous complaints of some people that advertising is too elaborate and school *houses* too shoddy.

A monopolist will advertise (and price the product) so as to maximize his profits,

$$\pi = Npq\lambda - \phi(N\lambda q) - ap_a,$$

where $p = f(q)$ is the demand curve of the individual buyer, $\phi(Nq\lambda)$ is production costs other than advertising, and ap_a is advertising expenditures. The maximum profit conditions are

$$\frac{\partial \pi}{\partial q} = N\lambda \left(p + q \frac{\partial p}{\partial q} \right) - \phi' N\lambda = 0 \qquad (5)$$

and

$$\frac{\partial \pi}{\partial a} = Npq \frac{\partial \lambda}{\partial a} - \phi' Nq \frac{\partial \lambda}{\partial a} - p_a = 0. \qquad (6)$$

Equation (5) states the usual marginal cost–marginal revenue equality, and equation (6) states the equality of (price − marginal cost) with the marginal cost $[p_a/Nq(\partial\lambda/\partial a)]$ of advertising.[22]

With the Cournot spring (where production costs $\phi = 0$) the monopolist advertises up to the point where price equals the marginal cost of informing a buyer: the monopolist will not (cannot) exploit ignorance as he exploits desire. The monopolist will advertise more, the higher the "death" rate (b), unless it is very high relative to the "contact" rate (c).[23] The monopolistic situation does not invite comparison with competition because an essential feature—the value of search in the face of price dispersion—is absent.

A highly simplified analysis of advertising by the competitive firm is presented in the Appendix. On the assumption that all firms are identical and that all buyers have identical demand curves and search equal amounts, we obtain the maximum-profit equation:

$$\text{Production cost} = p\left(1 + \frac{1}{\eta_{qp} + \eta_{Kp}} \right), \qquad (7)$$

[22]The marginal revenue from advertising expenditure,

$$\frac{Npq}{p_a} \frac{\partial \lambda}{\partial a},$$

equals the absolute value of the elasticity of demand by equations (5) and (6); see R. Dorfman and P. O. Steiner, "Optimal Advertising and Optimal Quality," *American Economic Review*, XLIV (1954), 826.

[23]Differentiating equation (6) with respect to b, we find that $\partial a/\partial b$ is positive or negative according as

$$b \lessgtr \frac{c}{1-c}.$$

If $c \geq \frac{1}{2}$, the derivative must be positive.

where η_{qp} is the elasticity of a buyer's demand curve and η_{Kp} is the elasticity of the fraction of buyers purchasing from the seller with respect to his price. The latter elasticity will be of the order of magnitude of the number of searches made by a buyer. With a uniform distribution of asking prices, increased search will lead to increased advertising by low-price sellers and reduced advertising by high-price sellers. The amount of advertising by a firm decreases as the number of firms increases.

Price advertising has a decisive influence on the dispersion of prices. Search now becomes extremely economical, and the question arises why, in the absence of differences in quality of products, the dispersion does not vanish. And the answer is simply that, if prices are advertised by a large portion of the sellers, the price differences diminish sharply. That they do not wholly vanish (in a given market) is due simply to the fact that no combination of advertising media reaches all potential buyers within the available time.

Assuming, as we do, that all sellers are equally convenient in location, must we say that some buyers are perverse in not reading the advertisements? Obviously not, for the cost of keeping currently informed about all articles which an individual purchases would be prohibitive. A typical household probably buys several hundred different items a month, and, if, on average, their prices change (in some outlets) only once a month, the number of advertisements (by at least several sellers) which must be read is forbiddingly large.

The seller's problem is even greater: he may sell two thousand items (a modest number for a grocery or hardware store), and to advertise each on the occasion of a price change—and frequently enough thereafter to remind buyers of his price—would be impossibly expensive. To keep the buyers in a market informed on the current prices of all items of consumption would involve perhaps a thousandfold increase of newspaper advertising.

From the manufacturer's viewpoint, uncertainty concerning his price is clearly disadvantageous. The cost of search is a cost of purchase, and consumption will therefore be smaller, the greater the dispersion of prices and the greater the optimum amount of search. This is presumably one reason (but, I conjecture, a very minor one) why uniform prices are set by sellers of nationally advertised brands: if they have eliminated price variation, they have reduced

the cost of the commodity (including search) to the buyer, even if the dealers' margins average somewhat more than they otherwise would.

The effect of advertising prices, then, is equivalent to that of the introduction of a very large amount of search by a large portion of the potential buyers. It follows from our discussion in Section I that the dispersion of asking prices will be much reduced. Since advertising of prices will be devoted to products for which the marginal value of search is high, it will tend to reduce dispersion most in commodities with large aggregate expenditures.

III. CONCLUSIONS

The identification of sellers and the discovery of their prices are only one sample of the vast role of the search for information in economic life. Similar problems exist in the detection of profitable fields for investment and in the worker's choice of industry, location, and job. The search for knowledge on the quality of goods, which has been studiously avoided in this paper, is perhaps no more important but, certainly, analytically more difficult. Quality has not yet been successfully specified by economics, and this elusiveness extends to all problems in which it enters.

Some forms of economic organization may be explicable chiefly as devices for eliminating uncertainties in quality. The department store, as Milton Friedman has suggested to me, may be viewed as an institution which searches for the superior qualities of goods and guarantees that they are good quality. "Reputation" is a word which denotes the persistence of quality, and reputation commands a price (or exacts a penalty) because it economizes on search. When economists deplore the reliance of the consumer on reputation—although they choose the articles they read (and their colleagues) in good part on this basis—they implicitly assume that the consumer has a large laboratory, ready to deliver current information quickly and gratuitously.

Ignorance is like subzero weather: by a sufficient expenditure its effects upon people can be kept within tolerable or even comfortable bounds, but it would be wholly uneconomic entirely to eliminate all its effects. And, just as an analysis of man's shelter and apparel would be somewhat incomplete if cold weather is ignored, so also our understanding of economic life will be incomplete if we do not systematically take account of the cold winds of ignorance.

APPENDIX

Under competition, the amount of advertising by any one seller (*i*) can be determined as follows. Each buyer will engage in an amount *s* of search, which is determined by the factors discussed above (Sec. 1). He will on average know

$$(r - 1) \lambda + \lambda_i$$

sellers, where λ_i is defined by equation (4) for seller *i*. Hence,

$$\frac{\lambda_i}{(r - 1) \lambda + \lambda_i}$$

per cent of buyers who know seller *i* will canvass him on one search, and

$$\left(1 - \frac{\lambda_i}{(r - 1) \lambda + \lambda_i}\right)^s$$

per cent of the buyers who know *i* will not canvass him in *s* searches,

$$s \le (r - 1) \lambda + \lambda_i.$$

Therefore, of the buyers who know *i*, the proportion who will canvass him at least once is[24]

$$1 - \left(1 - \frac{\lambda_i}{(r - 1) \lambda + \lambda_i}\right)^s.$$

If we approximate

$$\frac{\lambda_i}{(r - 1) \lambda + \lambda_i}$$

by

$$\frac{\lambda_i}{r \lambda}$$

and take only the first two terms of the binomial expansion, this becomes

$$\frac{s \lambda_i}{r \lambda}.$$

The receipts of any seller then become the product of (1) The number of buyers canvassing him,

$$\frac{s \lambda_i}{r \lambda} \lambda_i N = T_i,$$

(2) the fraction *K* of those canvassing him who buy from him, where *K* depends upon his relative price (and the amount of search and the number of rivals), and (3) sales to each customer, *pq*. If $\phi(T_i Kq)$ is production costs and ap_a advertising costs, profits are

$$\pi = T_i Kpq - \phi(T_i Kq) - ap_a.$$

[24] The formula errs slightly in allowing the multiple canvass of one seller by a buyer.

The conditions for maximum profits are

$$\frac{\partial \pi}{\partial p} = T_i \left(K \frac{\partial pq}{\partial p} + pq \frac{\partial K}{\partial p}\right) - T_i \phi' \left(K \frac{\partial q}{\partial p} + q \frac{\partial K}{\partial p}\right) = 0 \quad (8)$$

and

$$\frac{\partial \pi}{\partial a} = Kpq \frac{\partial T_i}{\partial a} - \phi' Kq \frac{\partial T_i}{\partial a} - p_a = 0. \quad (9)$$

The former equation can be rewritten in elasticities as

$$\phi' = p \left(1 + \frac{1}{\eta_{qp} + \eta_{Kp}}\right) \quad (8a)$$

Price exceeds marginal cost, not simply by $(-p/\eta_{qp})$ as with monopoly, but by the smaller amount

$$\frac{-p}{\eta_{qp} + \eta_{Kp}},$$

where η_{Kp} will generally be of the order of magnitude of the number of searches made by a buyer.[25] Equation (2) states the equality of the marginal revenue of advertising with its marginal cost. By differentiating equation (2) with respect to *s* and taking ϕ' as constant, it can be shown that increased search by buyers will lead to increased advertising by low-price sellers and reduced advertising by high-price sellers (with a uniform distribution of prices).[26]

By the same method it may be shown that the amount of advertising by the firm will decrease as the number of rivals increases.[27] The aggregate amount of advertising by the industry may either increase or decrease with an increase in the number of firms, *s*, depending on the relationship between λ and *a*.

[25] In the case of the uniform distribution, η_{Kp} is

$$\frac{-(s - 1) p}{1 - p}.$$

[26] The derivative $\partial a/\partial s$ has the sign of $(1 + \eta_{Ks})$, and this elasticity equals

$$1 + s \log [1 - p]$$

with a uniform distribution of prices.

[27] By differentiation of equation (2) with respect to *r* one gets

$$r \frac{\partial a}{\partial r} \left\{\lambda_i \frac{\partial^2 \lambda_i}{\partial a^2} + \left(\frac{\partial \lambda_i}{\partial a}\right)^2\right\} = \lambda_i \frac{\partial \lambda_i}{\partial a} \left(1 - \frac{r}{K} \frac{\partial K}{\partial r}\right).$$

The term in brackets on the left side is negative by the stability condition; the right side is positive.

A Theory of the Allocation of Time*

GARY S. BECKER

See "De Gustibus Non Est Disputandum" for author's biography.

I. INTRODUCTION

Throughout history the amount of time spent at work has never consistently been much greater than that spent at other activities. Even a work week of fourteen hours a day for six days still leaves half the total time for sleeping, eating and other activities. Economic development has led to a large secular decline in the work week, so that whatever may have been true of the past, to-day it is below fifty hours in most countries, less than a third of the total time available. Consequently the allocation and efficiency of non-working time may now be more important to economic welfare than that of working time; yet the attention paid by economists to the latter dwarfs any paid to the former.

Fortunately, there is a movement under way to redress the balance. The time spent at work declined secularly, partly because young persons increasingly delayed entering the labour market by lengthening their period of schooling. In recent years many economists have stressed that the time of students is one of the inputs into the educational process, that this time could be used to participate more fully in the labour market and therefore that one of the costs of education is the forgone earnings of students. Indeed, various estimates clearly indicate that forgone earnings is the dominant private and an important social cost of both high-school and college education in the United States.[1] The increased awareness of the importance of forgone earnings has resulted in several attempts to economise on students' time, as manifested, say, by the spread of the quarterly and trimester systems.[2]

Most economists have now fully grasped the importance of forgone earnings in the educational process and, more generally, in all investments in human capital, and criticise educationalists and others for neglecting them. In the light of this it is perhaps surprising that economists have not been equally sophisticated about other non-working uses of time.

*Reprinted from *The Economic Journal* (September 1965) by permission of Cambridge University Press. Copyright 1965, pp. 493-517.

[1] See T. W. Schultz, "The Formation of Human Capital by Education," *Journal of Political Economy* (December 1960), and my *Human Capital* (Columbia University Press for the N.B.E.R., 1964), Chapter IV. I argue there that the importance of forgone earnings can be directly seen, *e.g.,* from the failure of free tuition to eliminate impediments to college attendance or the increased enrolments that sometimes occur in depressed areas or time periods.

[2] On the cause of the secular trend towards an increased school year see my comments, *ibid.,* p. 103.

For example, the cost of a service like the theatre or a good like meat is generally simply said to equal their market prices, yet everyone would agree that the theatre and even dining take time, just as schooling does, time that often could have been used productively. If so, the full costs of these activities would equal the sum of market prices and the forgone value of the time used up. In other words, indirect costs should be treated on the same footing when discussing all non-work uses of time, as they are now in discussions of schooling.

In the last few years a group of us at Columbia University have been occupied, perhaps initially independently but then increasingly less so, with introducing the cost of time systematically into decisions about non-work activities. J. Mincer has shown with several empirical examples how estimates of the income elasticity of demand for different commodities are biased when the cost of time is ignored;[3] J. Owen has analysed how the demand for leisure can be affected;[4] E. Dean has considered the allocation of time between subsistence work and market participation in some African economies;[5] while, as already mentioned, I have been concerned with the use of time in education, training and other kinds of human capital. Here I attempt to develop a general treatment of the allocation of time in all other non-work activities. Although under my name alone, much of any credit it merits belongs to the stimulus received from Mincer, Owen, Dean and other past and present participants in the Labor Workshop at Columbia.[6]

[3]See his "Market Prices, Opportunity Costs, and Income Effects," in *Measurement in Economics: Studies in Mathematical Economics and Econometrics in Memory of Yehuda Grunfeld* (Stanford University Press, 1963). In his well-known earlier study Mincer considered the allocation of married women between "housework" and labour force participation. (See his "Labor Force Participation of Married Women," in *Aspects of Labor Economics* (Princeton University Press, 1962).)
[4]See his *The Supply of Labor and the Demand for Recreation* (unpublished Ph.D. dissertation, Columbia University, 1964).
[5]See his *Economic Analysis and African Response to Price* (unpublished Ph.D. dissertation, Columbia University, 1963).
[6]Let me emphasise, however, that I alone am responsible for any errors.
   I would also like to express my appreciation for the comments received when presenting these ideas to seminars at the Universities of California (Los Angeles), Chicago, Pittsburgh, Rochester and Yale, and to a session at the 1963 Meetings of the Econometric Society. Extremely helpful comments on an earlier draft were provided by Milton Friedman and by Gregory C. Chow; the latter also assisted in the mathematical formulation. Linda Kee provided useful research assistance. My research was partially supported by the IBM Corporation.

The plan of the discussion is as follows. The first section sets out a basic theoretical analysis of choice that includes the cost of time on the same footing as the cost of market goods, while the remaining sections treat various empirical implications of the theory. These include a new approach to changes in hours of work and "leisure," the full integration of so-called "productive" consumption into economic analysis, a new analysis of the effect of income on the quantity and "quality" of commodities consumed, some suggestions on the measurement of productivity, an economic analysis of queues and a few others as well. Although I refer to relevant empirical work that has come to my attention, little systematic testing of the theory has been attempted.

II. A REVISED THEORY OF CHOICE

According to traditional theory, households maximise utility functions of the form

$$U = U(y_1, y_2, \ldots, y_n) \tag{1}$$

subject to the resource constraint

$$\sum p_i' y_i = I = W + V \tag{2}$$

where y_i are goods purchased on the market, p'_i are their prices, I is money income, W is earnings and V is other income. As the introduction suggests, the point of departure here is the systematic incorporation of non-working time. Households will be assumed to combine time and market goods to produce more basic commodities that directly enter their utility functions. One such commodity is the seeing of a play, which depends on the input of actors, script, theatre and the playgoer's time; another is sleeping, which depends on the input of a bed, house (pills?) and time. These commodities will be called Z_i and written as

$$Z_i = f_i(x_i, T_i) \tag{3}$$

where x_i is a vector of market goods and T_i a vector of time inputs used in producing the ith commodity.[7] Note that, when capital goods such as refrigerators or automobiles are used, x refers to the services yield-

[7]There are several empirical as well as conceptual advantages in assuming that households combine goods and time to produce commodities instead of simply assuming that the amount of time used at an activity is a direct function of the amount of goods consumed. For example, a change in the cost of goods relative to time could cause a significant substitution away from the one rising in relative cost. This, as well as other applications, are treated in the following sections.

ed by the goods. Also note that T_i is a vector because, e.g., the hours used during the day or on weekdays may be distinguished from those used at night or on week-ends. Each dimension of T_i refers to a different aspect of time. Generally, the partial derivatives of Z_i with respect to both x_i and T_i are non-negative.[8]

In this formulation households are both producing units and utility maximisers. They combine time and market goods via the "production functions" f_i to produce the basic commodities Z_i, and they choose the best combination of these commodities in the conventional way by maximising a utility function

$$U = U(Z_i, \ldots Z_m) \equiv U(f_1, \ldots f_m) \equiv \qquad (4)$$
$$U(x_1, \ldots x_m; T_1, \ldots T_m)$$

subject to a budget constraint

$$g(Z_i, \ldots Z_m) = Z \qquad (5)$$

where g is an expenditure function of Z_i and Z is the bound on resources. The integration of production and consumption is at odds with the tendency for economists to separate them sharply, production occurring in firms and consumption in households. It should be pointed out, however, that in recent years economists increasingly recognise that a household is truly a "small factory":[9] it combines capital goods, raw materials and labour to clean, feed, procreate and otherwise produce useful commodities. Undoubtedly the fundamental reason for the traditional separation is that firms are usually given control over working time in exchange for market goods, while "discretionary" control over market goods and consumption time is retained by households as they create their own utility. If (presumably different) firms were also given control over market goods and consumption time in exchange for providing utility the separation would quickly fade away in analysis as well as in fact.

The basic goal of the analysis is to find measures of g and Z which facilitate the development of empirical implications. The most direct approach is to assume that the utility function in equation (4) is maximised subject to separate constraints on the expenditure of market goods and time, and to the pro-

duction functions in equation (3). The goods constraint can be written as

$$\sum_1^m p_i x_i = I = V + T_w \bar{w} \qquad (6)$$

where p_i is a vector giving the unit prices of x_i, T_w is a vector giving the hours spent at work and $\bar{w}$ is a vector giving the earnings per unit of T_w. The time constraints can be written as

$$\sum_1^m T_i = T_c = T - T_w \qquad (7)$$

where T_c is a vector giving the total time spent at consumption and T is a vector giving the total time available. The production functions (3) can be written in the equivalent form

$$\left. \begin{array}{l} T_i \equiv t_i Z_i \\[1mm] x_i \equiv b_i Z_i \end{array} \right\} \qquad (8)$$

where t_i is a vector giving the input of time per unit of Z_i and b_i is a similar vector for market goods.

The problem would appear to be to maximise the utility function (4) subject to the multiple constraints (6) and (7) and to the production relations (8). There is, however, really only one basic constraint: (6) is not independent of (7) because time can be converted into goods by using less time at consumption and more at work. Thus, substituting for T_w in (6) its equivalent in (7) gives the single constraint[10]

$$\sum p_i x_i + \sum T_i \bar{w} = V + T \bar{w} \qquad (9)$$

By using (8), (9) can be written as

$$\sum (p_i b_i + t_i \bar{w}) Z_i = V + T \bar{w} \qquad (10)$$

with

$$\left. \begin{array}{l} \pi_i \equiv p_i b_i + t_i \bar{w} \\[1mm] S' \equiv V + T \bar{w} \end{array} \right\} \qquad (11)$$

The full price of a unit of Z_i (π_i) is the sum of the prices of the goods and of the time used per unit of Z_i. That is, the full price of consumption is the sum of direct and indirect prices in the same way that the full cost of investing in human capital is the sum of

---

[8] If a good or time period was used in producing several commodities I assume that these "joint costs" could be fully and uniquely allocated among the commodities. The problems here are no different from those usually arising in the analysis of multi-product firms.

[9] See, e.g., A. K. Cairncross, "Economic Schizophrenia," *Scottish Journal of Political Economy* (February 1958).

[10] The dependency among constraints distinguishes this problem from many other multiple-constraint situations in economic analysis, such as those arising in the usual theory of rationing (see J. Tobin, "A Survey of the Theory of Rationing," *Econometrica* (October, 1952)). Rationing would reduce to a formally identical single-constraint situation if rations were saleable and fully convertible into money income.

direct and indirect costs.[11] These direct and indirect prices are symmetrical determinants of total price, and there is no analytical reason to stress one rather than the other.

The resource constraint on the right side of equation (10), S', is easy to interpret if $\bar{w}$ were a constant, independent of the Z_i. For then S' gives the money income achieved if all the time available were devoted to work. This achievable income is "spent" on the commodities Z_i either directly through expenditures on goods, $\sum p_i b_i Z_i$, or indirectly through the forgoing of income, $\sum t_i \bar{w} Z_i$, i.e., by using time at consumption rather than at work. As long as $\bar{w}$ were constant, and if there were constant returns in producing Z_i so that b_i and t_i were fixed for given p_i and $\bar{w}$ the equilibrium condition resulting from maximising (4) subject to (10) takes a very simple form:

$$U_i = \frac{\partial U}{\partial Z_i} = \lambda \pi_i \quad i = 1, \ldots m \qquad (12)$$

where λ is the marginal utility of money income. If $\bar{w}$ were not constant the resource constraint in equation (10) would not have any particularly useful interpretation: $S' = V + T\bar{w}$ would overstate the money income achievable as long as marginal wagerates were below average ones. Moreover, the equilibrium conditions would become more complicated than (12) because marginal would have to replace average prices.

The total resource constraint could be given the sensible interpretation of the maximum money income achievable only in the special and unlikely case when average earnings were constant. This suggests dropping the approach based on explicitly considering separate goods and time constraints and substituting one in which the total resource constraint necessarily equalled the maximum money income achievable, which will be simply called "full income."[12] This income could in general be obtained by devoting all the time and other resources of a household to earning income, with no regard for consumption. Of course, all the time would not usually be spent "at" a job: sleep, food, even leisure are required for efficiency, and some time (and other resources) would have to be spent on these activities in order to maximise money income. The amount spent would, however, be determined solely by the

effect on income and not by any effect on utility. Slaves, for example, might be permitted time "off" from work only in so far as that maximised their output, or free persons in poor environments might have to maximise money income simply to survive.[13]

Households in richer countries do, however, forfeit money income in order to obtain additional utility, i.e., they exchange money income for a greater amount of psychic income. For example, they might increase their leisure time, take a pleasant job in preference to a better-paying unpleasant one, employ unproductive nephews or eat more than is warranted by considerations of productivity. In these and other situations the amount of money income forfeited measures the cost of obtaining additional utility.

Thus the full income approach provides a meaningful resource constraint and one firmly based on the fact that goods and time can be combined into a single overall constraint because time can be converted into goods through money income. It also incorporates a unified treatment of all substitutions of non-pecuniary for pecuniary income, regardless of their nature or whether they occur on the job or in the household. The advantages of this will become clear as the analysis proceeds.

If full income is denoted by S, and if the total earnings forgone or "lost" by the interest in utility is denoted by L, the identity relating L to S and I is simply

$$L(Z_1, \ldots, Z_m) \equiv S - I(Z_1, \ldots, Z_m) \qquad (13)$$

I and L are functions of the Z_i because how much is earned or forgone depends on the consumption set chosen; for example, up to a point, the less leisure chosen the larger the money income and the smaller the amount forgone.[14] Using equations (6) and (8), equation (13) can be written as

$$\sum p_i b_i Z_i + L(Z_1, \ldots, Z_m) \equiv S \qquad (14)$$

This basic resource constraint states that full income is spent either directly on market goods or indirectly through the forgoing of money income. Unfortunately, there is no simple expression for the average price of Z_i as there is in equation (10). How-

---

[11]See my *Human Capital, op. cit.*
[12]This term emerged from a conversation with Milton Friedman.

[13]Any utility received would only be an incidental by-product of the pursuit of money income. Perhaps this explains why utility analysis was not clearly formulated and accepted until economic development had raised incomes well above the subsistence level.
[14]Footnote on p. 190.

ever, marginal, not average, prices are relevant for behaviour, and these would be identical for the constraint in (10) only when average earnings, $\overline{w}$, was constant. But, if so, the expression for the loss function simplifies to

$$L = \overline{w}T_c = \overline{w}\sum t_i Z_i \qquad (15)$$

and (14) reduces to (10). Moreover, even in the general case the total marginal prices resulting from (14) can always be divided into direct and indirect components: the equilibrium conditions resulting from maximising the utility function subject to (14)[15] are

$$U_i = T(p_i b_i + L_i), \quad i = 1, \ldots, m \qquad (16)$$

where $p_i b_i$ is the direct and L_i the indirect component of the total marginal price $p_i b_i + L_i$.[16]

Behind the division into direct and indirect costs is the allocation of time and goods between work-orientated and consumption-orientated activities. This suggests an alternative division of costs; namely, into those resulting from the allocation of goods and those resulting from the allocation of time. Write $L_i = \partial L / \partial Z_i$ as

$$L_i = \frac{\partial L}{\partial T_i} \frac{\partial T_i}{\partial Z_i} + \frac{\partial L}{\partial x_i} \frac{\partial x_i}{\partial Z_i} \qquad (17)$$

[14]Full income is achieved by maximising the earnings function

$$W = W(Z_1 \ldots Z_m) \qquad (1')$$

subject to the expenditure constraint in equation (6), to the inequality

$$\sum_1^m T_1 \leq T \qquad (2')$$

and to the restrictions in (8). I assume for simplicity that the amount of each dimension of time used in producing commodities is less than the total available, so that (2') can be ignored; it is not difficult to incorporate this constraint. Maximising (1') subject to (6) and (8) yields the following conditions

$$\frac{\partial W}{\partial Z_i} = \frac{p_i b_i \sigma}{1 + \sigma} \qquad (3')$$

where σ is the marginal productivity of money income. Since the loss function $L = (S - V) - W$, the equilibrium conditions to minimise the loss is the same as (3') except for a change in sign.

[15]Households maximise their utility subject only to the single total resource constraint given by (14), for once the full income constraint is satisfied, there is no other restriction on the set of Z_i that can be chosen. By introducing the concept of full income the problem of maximising utility subject to the time and goods constraints is solved in two stages: first, full income is determined from the goods and time constraints, and then utility is maximised subject only to the constraint imposed by full income.

[16]It can easily be shown that the equilibrium conditions of (16) are in fact precisely the same as those following in general from equation (10).

$$= l_i t_i + c_i b_i \qquad (18)$$

where $l_i = \dfrac{\partial L}{\partial T_i}$ and $c_i = \dfrac{\partial L}{\partial x_i}$ are the marginal forgone earnings of using more time and goods respectively on Z_i. Equation (16) can then be written as

$$U_i = T[b_i(p_i + c_i) + t_i l_i] \qquad (19)$$

The total marginal cost of Z_i is the sum of $b_i(p_i + c_i)$, the marginal cost of using goods in producing Z_i, and $t_i l_i$, the marginal cost of using time. This division would be equivalent to that between direct and indirect costs only if $c_i = 0$ or if there were no indirect costs of using goods.

Fig. 1 shows the equilibrium given by equation (16) for a two-commodity world. In equilibrium the slope of the full income opportunity curve, which equals the ratio of marginal prices, would equal the slope of an indifference curve, which equals the ratio of marginal utilities. Equilibrium occurs at p and p' for the opportunity curves S and S' respectively.

The rest of the paper is concerned with developing numerous empirical implications of this theory, starting with determinants of hours worked and concluding with an economic interpretation of various queueing systems. To simplify the presentation, it is assumed that the distinction between direct and indirect costs is equivalent to that between goods and time costs; in other words, the marginal forgone cost of the use of goods, c_i, is set equal to zero. The discussion would not be much changed, but would be more cumbersome were this not assumed.[17] Finally, until Section IV goods and time are assumed to be used in fixed proportions in producing commodities; that is, the coefficients b_i and t_i in equation (8) are treated as constants.

III. APPLICATIONS
(a) Hours of Work

If the effects of various changes on the time used on consumption, T_c, could be determined their effects on hours worked, T_w, could be found residually from equation (7). This section considers, among other things, the effects of changes in income, earnings and market prices on T_c, and thus on T_w, using

[17]Elsewhere I have discussed some effects of the allocation of goods on productivity (see my "Investment in Human Capital: A Theoretical Analysis," *Journal of Political Economy*, special supplement (October 1962), Section 2); essentially the same discussion can be found in *Human Capital, op. cit.*, Chapter II.

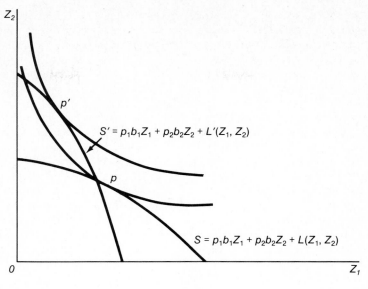

$$S' = p_1b_1Z_1 + p_2b_2Z_2 + L'(Z_1, Z_2)$$

$$S = p_1b_1Z_1 + p_2b_2Z_2 + L(Z_1, Z_2)$$

Fig. 1

as the major tool of analysis differences among commodities in the importance of forgone earnings.

The relative marginal importance of forgone earnings is defined as

$$a_i = \frac{l_i t_i}{p_i b_i + l_i t_i} \qquad (20)$$

The importance of forgone earnings would be greater the larger l_i and t_i, the forgone earnings per hour of time and the number of hours used per unit of Z_i respectively, while it would be smaller the larger p_i and b_i, the market price of goods and the number of goods used per unit of Z_i respectively. Similarly, the relative marginal importance of time is defined as

$$\gamma_i = \frac{t_i}{p_i b_i + l_i t_i} \qquad (21)$$

If full income increased solely because of an increase in V (other money income) there would simply be a parallel shift of the opportunity curve to the right with no change in relative commodity prices. The consumption of most commodities would have to increase; if all did, hours worked would decrease, for the total time spent on consumption must increase if the output of all commodities did, and by equation (7) the time spent at work is inversely related to that spent on consumption. Hours worked could increase only if relatively time intensive com-

modities, those with large γ, were sufficiently inferior.[18]

A uniform percentage increase in earnings for all allocations of time would increase the cost per hour used in consumption by the same percentage for all commodities.[19] The relative prices of different commodities would, however, change as long as forgone earnings were not equally important for all; in particular, the prices of commodities having relatively important forgone earnings would rise more. Now the fundamental theorem of demand theory states that a compensated change in relative prices would induce households to consume less of commodities rising in price. The figure shows the effect of a rise in earnings fully compensated by a decline in other income: the opportunity curve would be rotated

[18]The problem is: under what conditions would

$$\frac{-\partial T_w}{\partial V} = \frac{\partial T_c}{\partial V} = \sum t_i \frac{\partial Z_i}{\partial V} < 0 \qquad (1')$$

when

$$\sum (p_i b_i + l_i t_i) \frac{\partial Z_i}{\partial V} = 1 \qquad (2')$$

If the analysis were limited to a two-commodity world where Z_1 was more time intensive, then it can easily be shown that (1') would hold if, and only if,

$$\frac{\partial Z_1}{\partial V} < \frac{-\gamma_2}{(\gamma_1 - \gamma_2)(p_1 b_1 + l_1 t_1)} < 0 \qquad (3')$$

[19]Footnote on p. 192.

clockwise through the initial position p if Z_1 were the more earnings-intensive commodity. In the figure the new equilibrium p' must be to the left and above p, or less Z_1 and more Z_2 would be consumed.

Therefore a compensated uniform rise in earnings would lead to a shift away from earnings-intensive commodities and towards goods-intensive ones. Since earnings and time intensiveness tend to be positively correlated,[20] consumption would be shifted from time-intensive commodities. A shift away from such commodities would, however, result in a reduction in the total time spent in consumption, and thus an increase in the time spent at work.[21]

The effect of an uncompensated increase in earnings on hours worked would depend on the relative strength of the substitution and income effects. The former would increase hours, the latter reduce them; which dominates cannot be determined *a priori*.

The conclusion that a pure rise in earnings increases and a pure rise in income reduces hours of work must sound very familiar, for they are traditional results of the well-known labour-leisure analysis. What, then, is the relation between our analysis, which treats all commodities symmetrically and stresses only their differences in relative time and earning intensities, and the usual analysis, which distinguishes a commodity having special properties called "leisure" from other more commonplace commodities? It is easily shown that the usual labour-leisure analysis can be looked upon as a special case

of ours in which the cost of the commodity called leisure consists entirely of forgone earnings and the cost of other commodities entirely of goods.[22]

As a description of reality such an approach, of course, is not tenable, since virtually all activities use both time and goods. Perhaps it would be defended either as an analytically necessary or extremely insightful approximation to reality. Yet the usual substitution and income effects of a change in resources on hours worked have easily been derived from a more general analysis which stresses only that the relative importance of time varies among commodities. The rest of the paper tries to go further and demonstrate that the traditional approach, with its stress on the demand for "leisure," apparently has seriously impeded the development of insights about the economy, since the more direct and general approach presented here naturally leads to a variety of implications never yet obtained.

The two determinants of the importance of forgone earnings are the amount of time used per dollar of goods and the cost per unit of time. Reading a book, taking a haircut or commuting use more time per dollar of goods than eating dinner, frequenting a night-club or sending children to private summer camps. Other things the same, forgone earnings would be more important for the former set of commodities than the latter.

The importance of forgone earnings would be determined solely by time intensity only if the cost of time was the same for all commodities. Presumably, however, it varies considerably among commodities and at different periods. For example, the cost of time is often less on week-ends and in the evenings because many firms are closed then,[23] which explains why a famous liner intentionally includes a week-end

---

[19]By a uniform change of β is meant

$$W_1 = (1 + \beta)W_0(Z_1, \ldots Z_n)$$

where W_0 represents the earnings function before the change and W_1 represents it afterwards. Since the loss function is defined as

$$L = S - W - V$$
$$= W(\dot{Z}) - W(Z),$$

then

$$L_1 = W_1(\dot{Z}) - W_1(Z)$$
$$= (1 + \beta)[W_0(\dot{Z}) - W_0(Z)] = (1 + \beta)L_0$$

Consequently, all opportunities costs also change by β.

[20]According to the definitions of earning and time intensity in equations (20) and (21), they would be positively correlated unless l_i and t_i were sufficiently negatively correlated. See the further discussion later on.

[21]Let it be stressed that this conclusion usually holds, even when households are irrational; sophisticated calculations about the value of time at work or in consumption, or substantial knowledge about the amount of time used by different commodities is not required. Changes in the hours of work, even of non-maximising, impulsive, habitual, etc., households would tend to be positively related to compensated changes in earnings because demand curves tend to be negatively inclined even for such households (see G. S. Becker, "Irrational Behavior and Economic Theory," *Journal of Political Economy* (February 1962)).

[22]Suppose there were two commodities Z_1 and Z_2, where the cost of Z_1 depended only on the cost of market goods, while the cost of Z_2 depended only on the cost of time. The goods-budget constraint would then simply be

$$p_1b_1Z_1 = I = V + T_w\overline{w}$$

and the constraint on time would be

$$t_2Z_2 = T - T_w$$

This is essentially the algebra of the analysis presented by Henderson and Quandt, and their treatment is representative. They call Z_2 "leisure," and Z_1 an average of different commodities. Their equilibrium condition that the rate of substitution between goods and leisure equals the real wage-rate is just a special case of our equation (19) (see *Microeconomic Theory* (McGraw-Hill, 1958), p. 23).

[23]For workers receiving premium pay on the week-ends and in the evenings, however, the cost of time may be considerably greater then.

in each voyage between the United States and Europe.[24] The cost of time would also tend to be less for commodities that contribute to productive effort, traditionally called "productive consumption." A considerable amount of sleep, food and even "play" fall under this heading. The opportunity cost of the time is less because these commodities indirectly contribute to earnings. Productive consumption has had a long but bandit-like existence in economic thought; our analysis does systematically incorporate it into household decision-making.

Although the formal specification of leisure in economic models has ignored expenditures on goods, cannot one argue that a more correct specification would simply associate leisure with relatively important forgone earnings? Most conceptions of leisure do imply that it is time intensive and does not indirectly contribute to earnings,[25] two of the important characteristics of earnings-intensive commodities. On the other hand, not all of what are usually considered leisure activities do have relatively important forgone earnings: night-clubbing is generally considered leisure, and yet, at least in its more expensive forms, has a large expenditure component. Conversely, some activities have relatively large forgone earnings and are not considered leisure: haircuts or child care are examples. Consequently, the distinction between earnings-intensive and other commodities corresponds only partly to the usual distinction between leisure and other commodities. Since it has been shown that the relative importance of forgone earnings rather than any concept of leisure is more relevant for economic analysis, less attention should be paid to the latter. Indeed, although the social philosopher might have to define precisely the concept of leisure,[26] the economist can reach all his

traditional results as well as many more without introducing it at all!

Not only is it difficult to distinguish leisure from other non-work[27] but also even work from non-work. Is commuting work, non-work or both? How about a business lunch, a good diet or relaxation? Indeed, the notion of productive consumption was introduced precisely to cover those commodities that contribute to work as well as to consumption. Cannot pure work then be considered simply as a limiting commodity of such joint commodities in which the contribution to consumption was nil? Similarly, pure consumption would be a limiting commodity in the opposite direction in which the contribution to work was nil, and intermediate commodities would contribute to both consumption and work. The more important the contribution to work relative to consumption, the smaller would tend to be the relative importance of forgone earnings. Consequently, the effects of changes in earnings, other income, etc., on hours worked then become assimiliated to and essentially a special case of their effects on the consumption of less earnings-intensive commodities. For example, a pure rise in earnings would reduce the relative price, and thus increase the time spent on these commodities, *including the time spent at work;* similarly, for changes in income and other variables. The generalisation wrought by our approach is even greater than may have appeared at first.

Before concluding this section a few other relevant implications of our theory might be briefly mentioned. Just as a (compensated) rise in earnings would increase the prices of commodities with relatively large forgone earnings, induce a substitution away from them and increase the hours worked, so a (compensated) fall in market prices would also induce a substitution away from them and increase the hours worked: the effects of changes in direct and indirect costs are symmetrical. Indeed, Owen presents some evidence indicating that hours of work

---

[24]See the advertisement by United States Lines in various issues of the *New Yorker* magazine: "The S.S. *United States* regularly includes a weekend in its 5 days to Europe, saving [economic] time for businessmen" (my insertion).

[25]For example, *Webster's Collegiate Dictionary* defines leisurely as "characterized by leisure, taking *abundant time*" (my italics); or S. de Grazia, in his recent *Of Time, Work and Leisure*, says, "Leisure is a state of being in which activity is performed for its own sake or as its own end" (New York: The Twentieth Century Fund, 1962, p. 15).

[26]S. de Grazia has recently entertainingly shown the many difficulties in even reaching a reliable definition, and *a fortiori*, in quantitatively estimating the amount of leisure. See *ibid.*, Chapters III and IV; also see W. Moore, *Man, Time and Society* (New York: Wiley, 1963), Chapter II; J. N. Morgan, M. H. David, W. J. Cohen and H. E. Brazer, *Income and Welfare in the United States* (New York: McGraw-Hill, 1962), p. 322, and Owen, *op. cit.*, Chapter II.

[27]Sometimes true leisure is defined as the amount of discretionary time available (see Moore, *op. cit.*, p. 18). It is always difficult to attach a rigorous meaning to the word "discretionary" when referring to economic resources. One might say that in the short run consumption time is and working time is not discretionary, because the latter is partially subject to the authoritarian control of employers. (Even this distinction would vanish if households gave certain firms authoritarian control over their consumption time; see the discussion in Section II.) In the long run this definition of discretionary time is suspect too because the availability of alternative sources of employment would make working time also discretionary.

in the United States fell somewhat more in the first thirty years of this century than in the second thirty years, not because wages rose more during the first period, but because the market prices of recreation commodities fell more then.[28]

A well-known result of the traditional labour-leisure approach is that a rise in the income tax induces at least a substitution effect away from work and towards "leisure." Our approach reaches the same result only via a substitution towards time-intensive consumption rather than leisure. A simple additional implication of our approach, however, is that if a rise in the income tax were combined with an appropriate excise on the goods used in time-intensive commodities or subsidy to the goods used in other commodities there need be no change in full relative prices, and thus no substitution away from work. The traditional approach has recently reached the same conclusion, although in a much more involved way.[29]

There is no exception in the traditional approach to the rule that a pure rise in earnings would not induce a decrease in hours worked. An exception does occur in ours, for if the time and earnings intensities (i.e., $l_i t_i$ and t_i) were negatively correlated a pure rise in earnings would induce a substitution towards time-intensive commodities, and thus away from work.[30] Although this exception does illustrate the greater power of our approach, there is no reason to believe that it is any more important empirically than the exception to the rule on income effects.

(b) The Productivity of Time

Most of the large secular increase in earnings, which stimulated the development of the labour-leisure analysis, resulted from an increase in the productivity of working time due to the growth in human and physical capital, technological progress and other factors. Since a rise in earnings resulting from an increase in productivity has both income and substitution effects, the secular decline in hours worked appeared to be evidence that the income effect was sufficiently strong to swamp the substitution effect.

The secular growth in capital and technology also improved the productivity of consumption time: supermarkets, automobiles, sleeping pills, safety and electric razors, and telephones are a few familiar and important examples of such developments. An improvement in the productivity of consumption time would change relative commodity prices and increase full income, which in turn would produce substitution and income effects. The interesting point is that a very different interpretation of the observed decline in hours of work is suggested because these effects are precisely the opposite of those produced by improvements in the productivity of working time.

Assume a uniform increase only in the productivity of consumption time, which is taken to mean a decline in all t_i, time required to produce a unit of Z_i, by a common percentage. The relative prices of commodities with large forgone earnings would fall, and substitution would be induced towards these and away from other commodities, causing hours of work also to fall. Since the increase in productivity would also produce an income effect,[31] the demand for commodities would increase, which, in turn, would induce an increased demand for goods. But since the productivity of working time is assumed not to change, more goods could be obtained only by an increase in work. That is, the higher real income resulting from an advance in the productivity of consumption time would cause hours of work to *increase*.

Consequently, an emphasis on the secular increase in the productivity of consumption time would lead to a very different interpretation of the secular decline in hours worked. Instead of claiming that a powerful income effect swamped a weaker substitution effect, the claim would have to be that a powerful substitution effect swamped a weaker income effect.

---

[28]See *op. cit.,* Chapter VIII. Recreation commodities presumably have relatively large forgone earnings.

[29]See W. J. Corbett and D. C. Hague, "Complementarity and the Excess Burden of Taxation," *Review of Economic Studies,* Vol. XXI (1953–54); also A. C. Harberger, "Taxation, Resource Allocation and Welfare," in the *Role of Direct and Indirect Taxes in the Federal Revenue System* (Princeton University Press, 1964).

[30]The effect on earnings is more difficult to determine because, by assumption, time-intensive commodities have smaller costs per unit time than other commodities. A shift towards the former would, therefore, raise hourly earnings, which would partially and perhaps more than entirely offset the reduction in hours worked. Incidentally, this illustrates how the productivity of hours worked is influenced by the consumption set chosen.

[31]Full money income would be unaffected if it were achieved by using all time at pure work activities. If other uses of time were also required it would tend to increase. Even if full money income were unaffected, however, full real income would increase because prices of the Z_i would fall.

Of course, the productivity of both working and consumption time increased secularly, and the true interpretation is somewhere between these extremes. If both increased at the same rate there would be no change in relative prices, and thus no substitution effect, because the rise in l_i induced by one would exactly offset the decline in t_i induced by the other, marginal forgone earnings $(i_t t_i)$ remaining unchanged. Although the income effects would tend to offset each other too, they would do so comletely only if the income elasticity of demand for time-intensive commodities was equal to unity. Hours worked would decline if it was above and increase if it was below unity.[32] Since these commodities have probably on the whole been luxuries, such an increase in income would tend to reduce hours worked.

The productivity of working time has probably advanced more than that of consumption time, if only because of familiar reasons associated with the division of labour and economies of scale.[33] Consequently, there probably has been the traditional substitution effect towards and income effect away from work, as well as an income effect away from work because time-intensive commodities were luxuries. The secular decline in hours worked would only imply therefore that the combined income effects swamped the substitution effect, not that the income effect of an advance in the productivity of working time alone swamped its substitution effect.

Cross-sectionally, the hours worked of males have generally declined less as incomes increased than they have over time. Some of the difference between these relations is explained by the distinction between relevant and reported incomes, or by interdependencies among the hours worked by different employees;[34] some is probably also explained by the distinction between working and consumption productivity.

There is a presumption that persons distinguished cross-sectionally by money incomes or earnings differ more in working than consumption productivity because they are essentially distinguished by the former. This argument does not apply to time series because persons are distinguished there by calendar time, which in principle is neutral between these productivities. Consequently, the traditional substitution effect towards work is apt to be greater cross-sectionally, which would help to explain why the relation between the income and hours worked of men is less negatively sloped there, and be additional evidence that the substitution effect for men is not weak.[35]

Productivity in the service sector in the United States appears to have advanced more slowly, at least since 1929, than productivity in the goods sector.[36] Service industries like retailing, transportation, education and health, use a good deal of the time of households that never enter into input, output and price series, or therefore into measures of productivity. Incorporation of such time into the series and consideration of changes in its productivity would contribute, I believe, to an understanding of the apparent differences in productivity advance between these sectors.

An excellent example can be found in a recent study of productivity trends in the barbering industry in the United States.[37] Conventional productivity measures show relatively little advance in barbers' shops since 1929, yet a revolution has occurred in the activities performed by these shops. In the 1920s shaves still accounted for an important part of their sales, but declined to a negligible part by the 1950s because of the spread of home safety and electric razors. Instead of travelling to a shop, waiting in line, receiving a shave and continuing to another destination, men now shave themselves at home, saving travelling, waiting and even some shaving time. This considerable advance in the productivity of shaving nowhere enters measures for barbers' shops. If, however, a productivity measure for general bar-

[32]So the "Knight" view that an increase in income would increase "leisure" is not necessarily true, even if leisure were a superior good and even aside from Robbins' emphasis on the substitution effect (see L. Robbins, "On the Elasticity of Demand for Income in Terms of Effort," *Economica* (June 1930)).

[33]Wesley Mitchell's justly famous essay "The Backward Art of Spending Money" spells out some of these reasons (see the first essay in the collection, *The Backward Art of Spending Money and Other Essays* (New York: McGraw-Hill, 1932)).

[34]A. Finnegan does find steeper cross-sectional relations when the average incomes and hours of different occupations are used (*see* his "A Cross-Sectional Analysis of Hours of Work," *Journal of Political Economy* (October, 1962)).

[35]Note that Mincer has found a very strong substitution effect for women (see his "Labor Force Participation of Married Women," *op. cit.*).

[36]See the essay by Victor Fuchs, "Productivity Trends in the Goods and Service Sectors, 1929–61: A Preliminary Survey," N.B.E.R. Occasional Paper, October 1964.

[37]See J. Wilburn, "Productivity Trends in Barber and Beauty Shops," mimeographed report, N.B.E.R., September 1964.

bering activities, including shaving, was constructed, I suspect that it would show an advance since 1929 comparable to most goods.[38]

(c) Income Elasticities

Income elasticities of demand are often estimated cross-sectionally from the behaviour of families or other units with different incomes. When these units buy in the same market-place it is natural to assume that they face the same prices of goods. If, however, incomes differ because earnings do, and cross-sectional income differences are usually dominated by earnings differences, commodities prices would differ systematically. All commodities prices would be higher to higher-income units because their forgone earnings would be higher (which means, incidentally, that differences in real income would be less than those in money income), and the prices of earnings-intensive commodities would be unusually so.

Cross-sectional relations between consumption and income would not therefore measure the effect of income alone, because they would be affected by differences in relative prices as well as in incomes.[39] The effect of income would be underestimated for earnings-intensive and overestimated for other commodities, because the higher relative prices of the former would cause a substitution away from them and towards the latter. Accordingly, the income elasticities of demand for "leisure," unproductive and time-intensive commodities would be under-stated, and for "work," productive and other goods-intensive commodities over-stated by cross-sectional estimates. Low apparent income elasticities of earnings-intensive commodities and high apparent elasticities of other commodities may simply be illusions resulting from substitution effects.[40]

Moreover, according to our theory demand depends also on the importance of earnings as a source of income. For if total income were held constant an increase in earnings would create only substitution effects: away from earnings-intensive and towards goods-intensive commodities. So one unusual implication of the analysis that can and should be tested with available budget data is that the source of income may have a significant effect on consumption patterns. An important special case is found in comparisons of the consumption of employed and unemployed workers. Unemployed workers not only have lower incomes but also lower forgone costs, and thus lower relative prices of time and other earnings-intensive commodities. The propensity of unemployed workers to go fishing, watch television, attend school and so on are simply vivid illustrations of the incentives they have to substitute such commodities for others.

One interesting application of the analysis is to the relation between family size and income.[41] The traditional view, based usually on simple correlations, has been that an increase in income leads to a reduction in the number of children per family. If, however, birth-control knowledge and other variables were held constant economic theory suggests a positive relation between family size and income, and therefore that the traditional negative correlation resulted from positive correlations between income, knowledge and some other variables. The data I put together supported this interpretation, as did those found in several subsequent studies.[42]

Although positive, the elasticity of family size with respect to income is apparently quite low, even when birth-control knowledge is held constant. Some persons have interpreted this (and other evidence) to indicate that family-size formation cannot usefully be fitted into traditional economic analysis.[43] It was pointed out, however, that the small elasticity found

---

[38] The movement of shaving from barbers' shops to households illustrates how and why even in urban areas households have become "small factories." Under the impetus of a general growth in the value of time they have been encouraged to find ways of saving on travelling and waiting time by performing more activities themselves.

[39] More appropriate income elasticities for several commodities are estimated in Mincer, "Market Prices . . .," *op. cit.*

[40] In this connection note that cross-sectional data are often preferred to time-series data in estimating income elasticities precisely because they are supposed to be largely free of co-linearity between prices and incomes (see, *e.g.,* J. Tobin, "A Statistical Demand Function for Food in the U.S.A.", *Journal of the Royal Statistical Society,* Series A (1950)).

[41] Biases in cross-sectional estimates of the demand for work and leisure were considered in the last section.

[42] See G. S. Becker, "An Economic Analysis of Fertility," *Demographic and Economic Change in Developed Countries* (N.B.E.R. Conference Volume, 1960); R. A. Easterlin, "The American Baby Boom in Historical Perspective," *American Economic Review* (December 1961); I. Adelman, "An Econometric Analysis of Population Growth," *American Economic Review* (June 1963); R. Weintraub, "The Birth Rate and Economic Development: An Empirical Study," *Econometrica* (October 1962); Morris Silver, *Birth Rates, Marriages, and Business Cycles* (unpublished Ph.D. dissertation, Columbia University, 1964); and several other studies; for an apparent exception, see the note by D. Freedman, "The Relation of Economic Status to Fertility," *American Economic Review* (June 1963).

[43] See, for example, Duesenberry's comment on Becker, *op. cit.*

for children is not so inconsistent with what is found for goods as soon as quantity and quality income elasticities are distinguished.[44] Increased expenditures on many goods largely take the form of increased quality-expenditure per pound, per car, etc.—and the increase in quantity is modest. Similarly, increased expenditures on children largely take the form of increased expenditures per child, while the increase in number of children is very modest.

Nevertheless, the elasticity of demand for number of children does seem somewhat smaller than the quantity elasticities found for many goods. Perhaps the explanation is simply the shape of indifference curves; one other factor that may be more important, however, is the increase in forgone costs with income.[45] Child care would seem to be a time-intensive activity that is not "productive" (in terms of earnings) and uses many hours that could be used at work. Consequently, it would be an earnings-intensive activity, and our analysis predicts that its relative price would be higher to higher-income families.[46] There is already some evidence suggesting that the positive relation between forgone costs and income explains why the apparent quantity income elasticity of demand for children is relatively small. Mincer found that cross-sectional differences in the forgone price of children have an important effect on the number of children.[47]

(d) Transportation

Transportation is one of the few activities where the cost of time has been explicitly incorporated into economic discussions. In most benefit-cost evaluations of new transportation networks the value of the savings in transportation time has tended to overshadow other benefits.[48] The importance of the value placed on time has encouraged experiment with different methods of determination: from the simple

view that the value of an hour equals average hourly earnings to sophisticated considerations of the distinction between standard and overtime hours, the internal and external margins, etc.

The transport field offers considerable opportunity to estimate the marginal productivity or value of time from actual behaviour. One could, for example, relate the ratio of the number of persons travelling by aeroplane to those travelling by slower mediums to the distance travelled (and, of course, also to market prices and incomes). Since relatively more people use faster mediums for longer distances, presumably largely because of the greater importance of the saving in time, one should be able to estimate a marginal value of time from the relation between medium and distance travelled.[49]

Another transportation problem extensively studied is the length and mode of commuting to work.[50] It is usually assumed that direct commuting costs, such as train fare, vary positively and that living costs, such as space, vary negatively with the distance commuted. These assumptions alone would imply that a rise in incomes would result in longer commutes as long as space ("housing") were a superior good.[51]

A rise in income resulting at least in part from a rise in earnings would, however, increase the cost of commuting a given distance because the forgone value of the time involved would increase. This increase in commuting costs would discourage commuting in the same way that the increased demand for space would encourage it. The outcome depends on the relative strengths of these conflicting forces: one can show with a few assumptions that the distance commuted would increase as income increased if, and only if, space had an income elasticity greater than unity.

---

[44] See Becker, *op. cit.*

[45] In *Ibid.*, p. 214 fn. 8, the relation between forgone costs and income was mentioned but not elaborated.

[46] Other arguments suggesting that higher-income families face a higher price of children have generally confused price with quality (see *ibid.*, pp. 214–15).

[47] See Mincer, "Market Prices . . .," *op. cit.* He measures the price of children by the wife's potential wage-rate, and fits regressions to various cross-sectional data, where number of children is the dependent variable, and family income and the wife's potential wage-rate are among the independent variables.

[48] See, for example, H. Mohring, "Land Values and the Measurement of Highway Benefits," *Journal of Political Economy* (June 1961).

[49] The only quantitative estimate of the marginal value of time that I am familiar with uses the relation between the value of land and its commuting distance from employment (see *ibid.*). With many assumptions I have estimated the marginal value of time of those commuting at about 40% of their average hourly earnings. It is not clear whether this value is so low because of errors in these assumptions or because of severe kinks in the supply and demand functions for hours of work.

[50] See L. N. Moses and H. F. Williamson, "Value of Time, Choice of Mode, and the Subsidy Issue in Urban Transportation," *Journal of Political Economy* (June 1963), R. Muth, "Economic Change and Rural-Urban Conversion," *Econometrica* (January 1961), and J. F. Kain, *Commuting and the Residential Decisions of Chicago and Detroit Central Business District Workers* (April 1963).

[51] See Muth, *op. cit.*

For let Z_1 refer to the commuting commodity, Z_2 to other commodities, and let

$$Z_1 = f_1(x, t) \qquad (22)$$

where t is the time spent commuting and x is the quantity of space used. Commuting costs are assumed to have the simple form $a + l_1 t$, where a is a constant and l_1 is the marginal forgone cost per hour spent commuting. In other words, the cost of time is the only variable commuting cost. The cost per unit of space is $p(t)$, where by assumption $p' < 0$. The problem is to maximise the utility function

$$U = U(x, t, Z_2) \qquad (23)$$

subject to the resource constraint

$$a + l_1 t + px + h(Z_2) = S \qquad (24)$$

If it were assumed that $U_t = 0$—commuting was neither enjoyable nor irksome—the main equilibrium condition would reduce to

$$l_1 + p'x = 0 \qquad (25)$$[52]

which would be the equilibrium condition if households simply attempt to minimise the sum of transportation and space costs.[53] If $l_1 = kS$, where k is a constant, the effect of a change in full income on the time spent commuting can be found by differentiating equation (25) to be

$$\frac{\partial t}{\partial S} = \frac{k(\epsilon_x - 1)}{p''x} \qquad (26)$$

where ϵ_x is the income elasticity of demand for space. Since stability requires that $p'' > 0$, an increase in income increases the time spent commuting if, and only if, $\epsilon_x > 1$.

In metropolitan areas of the United States higher-income families tend to live further from the central city,[54] which contradicts our analysis if one accepts the traditional view that the income elasticity of demand for housing is less than unity. In a definitive

study of the demand for housing in the United States, however, Margaret Reid found income elasticities greater than unity.[55] Moreover, the analysis of distance commuted incorporates only a few dimensions of the demand for housing; principally the demand for outdoor space. The evidence on distances commuted would then only imply that outdoor space is a "luxury," which is rather plausible[56] and not even inconsistent with the traditional view about the total elasticity of demand for housing.

(e) The Division of Labour Within Families

Space is too limited to do more than summarise the main implications of the theory concerning the division of labour among members of the same household. Instead of simply allocating time efficiently among commodities, multi-person households also allocate the time of different members. Members who are relatively more efficient at market activities would use less of their time at consumption activities than would other members. Moreover, an increase in the relative market efficiency of any member would effect a reallocation of the time of all other members towards consumption activities in order to permit the former to spend more time at market activities. In short, the allocation of the time of any member is greatly influenced by the opportunities open to other members.

IV. SUBSTITUTION BETWEEN TIME AND GOODS

Although time and goods have been assumed to be used in fixed proportions in producing commodities, substitution could take place because different commodities used them in different proportions. The assumption of fixed proportions is now dropped in order to include many additional implications of the theory.

It is well known from the theory of variable proportions that households would minimise costs by setting the ratio of the marginal product of goods to that of time equal to the ratio of their marginal

[52]If $U_t \neq 0$, the main equilibrium condition would be

$$\frac{U_t}{U_x} = \frac{l_1 + p'x}{p}$$

Probably the most plausible assumption is that $U_t < 0$, which would imply that $l_1 + p'x < 0$.

[53]See Kain, op. cit., pp. 6–12.

[54]For a discussion, including many qualifications, of this proposition see L. F. Schnore, "The Socio-Economic Status of Cities and Suburbs," American Sociological Review (February 1963).

[55]See her Housing and Income (University of Chicago Press, 1962), p. 6 and passim.

[56]According to Reid, the elasticity of demand for indoor space is less than unity (ibid., Chapter 12). If her total elasticity is accepted this suggests that outdoor space has an elasticity exceeding unity.

costs.[57] A rise in the cost of time relative to goods would induce a reduction in the amount of time and an increase in the amount of goods used per unit of each commodity. Thus, not only would a rise in earnings induce a substitution away from earnings-intensive commodities but also a substitution away from time and towards goods in the production of each commodity. Only the first is (implicitly) recognised in the labour-leisure analysis, although the second may well be of considerable importance. It increases one's confidence that the substitution effect of a rise in earnings is more important than is commonly believed.

The change in the input coefficients of time and goods resulting from a change in their relative costs is defined by the elasticity of substitution between them, which presumably varies from commodity to commodity. The only empirical study of this elasticity assumes that recreation goods and "leisure" time are used to produce a recreation commodity.[58] Definite evidence of substitution is found, since the ratio of leisure time to recreation goods is negatively related to the ratio of their prices. The elasticity of substitution appears to be less than unity, however, since the share of leisure in total factor costs is apparently positively related to its relative price.

The incentive to economise on time as its relative cost increases goes a long way towards explaining certain broad aspects of behaviour that have puzzled and often disturbed observers of contemporary life. Since hours worked have declined secularly in most advanced countries, and so-called "leisure" has presumably increased, a natural expectation has been that "free" time would become more abundant, and

be used more "leisurely" and "luxuriously." Yet, if anything, time is used more carefully to-day than a century ago.[59] If there was a secular increase in the productivity of working time relative to consumption time (see Section III (b)) there would be an increasing incentive to economise on the latter because of its greater expense (our theory emphatically cautions against calling such time "free"). Not surprisingly, therefore, it is now kept track of and used more carefully than in the past.

Americans are supposed to be much more wasteful of food and other goods than persons in poorer countries, and much more conscious of time: they keep track of it continuously, make (and keep) appointments for specific minutes, rush about more, cook steaks and chops rather than time-consuming stews and so forth.[60] They are simultaneously supposed to be wasteful—of material goods—and overly economical—of immaterial time. Yet both allegations may be correct and not simply indicative of a strange American temperament because the market value of time is higher relative to the price of goods there than elsewhere. That is, the tendency to be economical about time and lavish about goods may be no paradox, but in part simply a reaction to a difference in relative costs.

The substitution towards goods induced by an increase in the relative cost of time would often include a substitution towards more expensive goods. For example, an increase in the value of a mother's time may induce her to enter the labour force and spend less time cooking by using pre-cooked foods and less time on child-care by using nurseries, camps or baby-sitters. Or barbers' shops in wealthier sections of town charge more and provide quicker service than those in poorer sections, because waiting by barbers is substituted for waiting by customers. These examples illustrate that a change in the quality of goods[61] resulting from a change in the relative cost of goods may simply reflect a change in the methods used to produce given commodities, and not any corresponding change in *their* quality.

---

[57]The cost of producing a given amount of commodity Z_i would be minimised if

$$\frac{\partial f_i / \partial x_i}{\partial f_i / \partial T_i} = \frac{P_i}{\partial L / \partial T_i}$$

If utility were considered an indirect function of goods and time rather than simply a direct function of commodities the following conditions, among others, would be required to maximise utility:

$$\frac{\partial U / \partial x_i}{\partial U / \partial T_i} \equiv \frac{\partial Z_i / \partial x_i}{\partial Z_i / \partial T_i} = \frac{p_i}{\partial L / \partial T}$$

which are exactly the same conditions as above. The ratio of the marginal utility of x_i to that of T_i depends only on f_i, x_i and T_i, and is thus independent of other production functions, goods and time. In other words, the indirect utility function is what has been called "weakly separable" (see R. Muth, "Household Production and Consumer Demand Functions," unpublished manuscript).

[58]See Owen, *op. cit.,* Chapter X.

[59]See, for example, de Grazia, *op. cit.,* Chapter IV.
[60]For a comparison of the American concept of time with others see Edward T. Hall, *The Silent Language* (New York: Doubleday, 1959), Chapter 9.
[61]Quality is usually defined empirically by the amount spent per physical unit, such as pound of food, car or child. See especially S. J. Prais and H. Houthakker, *The Analysis of Family Budgets* (Cambridge, 1955); also my "An Economic Analysis of Fertility," *op. cit.*

Consequently, a rise in income due to a rise in earnings would increase the quality of goods purchased not only because of the effect of income on quality but also because of a substitution of goods for time; a rise in income due to a rise in property income would not cause any substitution, and should have less effect on the quality of goods. Put more dramatically, with total income held constant, a rise in earnings should increase while a rise in property income should decrease the quality chosen. Once again, the composition of income is important and provides testable implications of the theory.

One analytically interesting application of these conclusions is to the recent study by Margaret Reid of the substitution between store-bought and home-delivered milk.[62] According to our approach, the cost of inputs into the commodity "milk consumption at home" is either the sum of the price of milk in the store and the forgone value of the time used to carry it home or simply the price of delivered milk. A reduction in the price of store relative to delivered milk, the value of time remaining constant, would reduce the cost of the first method relatively to the second, and shift production towards the first. For the same reason a reduction in the value of time, market prices of milk remaining constant, would also shift production towards the first method.

Reid's finding of a very large negative relation between the ratio of store to delivered milk and the ratio of their prices, income and some other variables held constant, would be evidence both that milk costs are a large part of total production costs and that there is easy substitution between these alternative methods of production. The large, but not quite as large, negative relation with income simply confirms the easy substitution between methods, and indicates that the cost of time is less important than the cost of milk. In other words, instead of conveying separate information, her price and income elasticities both measure substitution between the two methods of producing the same commodity, and are consistent and plausible.

The importance of forgone earnings and the substitution between time and goods may be quite relevant in interpreting observed price elasticities. A given percentage increase in the price of goods would be less of an increase in commodity prices the more important forgone earnings are. Consequently, even if all commodities had the same true price elasticity, those having relatively important forgone earnings would show lower apparent elasticities in the typical analysis that relates quantities and prices of goods alone.

The importance of forgone earnings differs not only among commodities but also among households for a given commodity because of differences in income. Its importance would change in the same or opposite direction as income, depending on whether the elasticity of substitution between time and goods was less or greater than unity. Thus, even when the true price elasticity of a commodity did not vary with income, the observed price elasticity of goods would be negatively or positively related to income as the elasticity of substitution was less or greater than unity.

The importance of substitution between time and goods can be illustrated in a still different way. Suppose, for simplicity, that only good x and no time was initially required to produce commodity Z. A price ceiling is placed on x, it nominally becomes a free good, and the production of x is subsidised sufficiently to maintain the same output. The increased quantity of x and Z demanded due to the decline in the price of x has to be rationed because the output of x has not increased. Suppose that the system of rationing made the quantity obtained a positive function of the time and effort expended. For example, the quantity of price-controlled bread or medical attention obtained might depend on the time spent in a queue outside a bakery or in a physician's office. Or if an appointment system were used a literal queue would be replaced by a figurative one, in which the waiting was done at "home," as in the Broadway theatre, admissions to hospitals or air travel during peak seasons. Again, even in depressed times the likelihood of obtaining a job is positively related to the time put into job hunting.

Although x became nominally a free good, Z would not be free, because the time now required as an input into Z is not free. The demand for Z would be greater than the supply (fixed by assumption) if the cost of this time was less than the equilibrium price of Z before the price control. The scrambling by households for the limited supply would increase the time required to get a unit of Z, and thus its cost.

[62] See her "Consumer Response to the Relative Price of Store versus Delivered Milk," *Journal of Political Economy* (April 1963).

Both would continue to increase until the average cost of time tended to the equilibrium price before price control. At that point equilibrium would be achieved because the supply and demand for Z would be equal.

Equilibrium would take different forms depending on the method of rationing. With a literal "first come first served" system the size of the queue (say outside the bakery or in the doctor's office) would grow until the expected cost of standing in line discouraged any excess demand;[63] with the figurative queues of appointment systems, the "waiting" time (say to see a play) would grow until demand was sufficiently curtailed. If the system of rationing was less formal, as in the labour market during recessions, the expected time required to ferret out a scarce job would grow until the demand for jobs was curtailed to the limited supply.

Therefore, price control of x combined with a subsidy that kept its amount constant would not change the average private equilibrium price of Z,[64] but would substitute indirect time costs for direct goods costs.[65] Since, however, indirect costs are positively related to income, the price of Z would be raised to higher-income persons and reduced to lower-income ones, thereby redistributing consumption from the former to the latter. That is, women, the poor, children, the unemployed, etc., would be more willing to spend their time in a queue or otherwise ferreting out rationed goods than would high-earning males.

V. SUMMARY AND CONCLUSIONS

This paper has presented a theory of the allocation of time between different activities. At the heart of the theory is an assumption that households are producers as well as consumers; they produce commodities by combining inputs of goods and time according to the cost-minimisation rules of the traditional theory of the firm. Commodities are produced in quantities determined by maximising a utility function of the commodity set subject to prices and a constraint on resources. Resources are measured by what is called full income, which is the sum of money income and that forgone or "lost" by the use of time and goods to obtain utility while commodity prices are measured by the sum of the costs of their goods and time inputs.

The effect of changes in earnings, other income, goods prices and the productivity of working and consumption time on the allocation of time and the commodity set produced has been analysed. For example, a rise in earnings, compensated by a decline in other income so that full income would be unchanged, would induce a decline in the amount of time used at consumption activities, because time would become more expensive. Partly goods would be substituted for the more expensive time in the production of each commodity, and partly goods-intensive commodities would be substituted for the more expensive time-intensive ones. Both substitutions require less time to be used at consumption, and permit more to be used at work. Since the reallocation of time involves simultaneously a reallocation of goods and commodities, all three decisions become intimately related.

The theory has many interesting and even novel interpretations of, and implications about, empirical phenomena. A few will be summarised here.

A traditional "economic" interpretation of the secular decline in hours worked has stressed the growth in productivity of working time and the resulting income and substitution effects, with the former supposedly dominating. Ours stresses that the substitution effects of the growth in productivity of working and consumption time tended to offset each other, and that hours worked declined secularly primarily because time-intensive commodities have been luxuries. A contributing influence has been the secular decline in the relative prices of goods used in time-intensive commodities.

Since an increase in income partly due to an increase in earnings would raise the relative cost of time and of time-intensive commodities, traditional cross-sectional estimates of income elasticities do not hold either factor or commodity prices constant. Consequently, they would, among other things, be biased downward for time-intensive commodities, and give a misleading impression of the effect of

---

[63] In queueing language the cost of waiting in line is a "discouragement" factor that stabilises the queueing scheme (see, for example, D. R. Cox and W. L. Smith, *Queues* (New York: Wiley 1961)).

[64] The social price, on the other hand, would double, for it is the sum of private indirect costs and subsidised direct costs.

[65] Time costs can be criticised from a Pareto optimality point of view because they often result in external diseconomies: *e.g.*, a person joining a queue would impose costs on subsequent joiners. The diseconomies are real, not simply pecuniary, because time is a cost to demanders, but is not revenue to suppliers.

income on the quality of commodities consumed. The composition of income also affects demand, for an increase in earnings, total income held constant, would shift demand away from time-intensive commodities and input combinations.

Rough estimates suggest that forgone earnings are quantitatively important and therefore that full income is substantially above money income. Since forgone earnings are primarily determined by the use of time, considerably more attention should be paid to its efficiency and allocation. In particular, agencies that collect information on the expenditure of money income might simultaneously collect information on the "expenditure" of time. The resulting time budgets, which have not been seriously investigated in most countries, including the United States and Great Britain, should be integrated with the money budgets in order to give a more accurate picture of the size and allocation of full income.

Production, Information Costs, and Economic Organization*

ARMEN A. ALCHIAN**
HAROLD DEMSETZ**

See "The Basis of Some Advances in the Theory of Management of the Firm" for Armen A. Alchian's biography.

Harold Demsetz (B.S., University of Illinois, 1953; M.B.A., Northwestern University, 1954; M.A., 1955; Ph.D., 1959) was born in 1930 in Chicago, Illinois. Currently he is Professor of Economics at the University of California at Los Angeles. Before joining the UCLA faculty, Demsetz was Professor of Economics at the University of Chicago and Director of the Economics/Business Program and taught as well at the University of Michigan. Professor Demsetz, whose major teaching and research interests are in the fields of microeconomic theory and market organization, has also been active in the research community, having served with both the RAND Corporation and the Center for Naval Analyses. He has published widely in professional journals, with articles on the nature of costs and equilibrium, and the emergence and implications of property rights, in alternative market contexts, particularly in monopolistic competition.

The mark of a capitalistic society is that resources are owned and allocated by such nongovernmental organizations as firms, households, and markets. Resource owners increase productivity through cooperative specialization and this leads to the demand for economic organizations which facilitate cooperation. When a lumber mill employs a cabinetmaker, cooperation between specialists is achieved within a firm, and when a cabinetmaker purchases wood from a lumberman, the cooperation takes place across markets (or between firms). Two important problems face a theory of economic organization—to explain the conditions that determine whether the gains from specialization and cooperative production can better be obtained within an organization like the firm, or

*Reprinted from *American Economic Review* (December 1972) by permission of the American Economic Association. Copyright 1972, pp. 777–795.

**Professors of economics at the University of California, Los Angeles. Acknowledgment is made for financial aid from the E. Lilly Endowment, Inc. grant to UCLA for research in the behavioral effects of property rights.

across markets, and to explain the structure of the organization.

It is common to see the firm characterized by the power to settle issues by fiat, by authority, or by disciplinary action superior to that available in the conventional market. This is delusion. The firm does not own all its inputs. It has no power of fiat, no authority, no disciplinary action any different in the slightest degree from ordinary market contracting between any two people. I can "punish" you only by withholding future business or by seeking redress in the courts for any failure to honor our exchange agreement. That is exactly all that any employer can do. He can fire or sue, just as I can fire my grocer by stopping purchases from him or sue him for delivering faulty products. What then is the content of the presumed power to manage and assign workers to various tasks? Exactly the same as one little consumer's power to manage and assign his grocer to various tasks. The single consumer can assign his grocer to the task of obtaining whatever the customer can induce the grocer to provide at a price acceptable to both parties. That is precisely all that an employer can do to an employee. To speak of managing, directing, or assigning workers to various tasks is a deceptive way of noting that the employer continually is involved in renegotiation of contracts on terms that must be acceptable to both parties. Telling an employee to type this letter rather than to file that document is like my telling a grocer to sell me this brand of tuna rather than that brand of bread. I have no contract to continue to purchase from the grocer and neither the employer nor the employee is bound by any contractual obligations to continue their relationship. Long-term contracts between employer and employee are not the essence of the organization we call a firm. My grocer can count on my returning day after day and purchasing his services and goods even with the prices not always marked on the goods—because I know what they are—and he adapts his activity to conform to my directions to him as to what I want each day . . . he is not my employee.

Wherein then is the relationship between a grocer and his employee different from that between a grocer and his customers? It is in a *team* use of inputs and a centralized position of some party in the contractual arrangements of *all* other inputs. It is the *centralized contractual agent in a team productive process*—not some superior authoritarian directive or disciplinary power. Exactly what is a team process

and why does it induce the contractual form, called the firm? These problems motivate the inquiry of this paper.

I. THE METERING PROBLEM

The economic organization through which input owners cooperate will make better use of their comparative advantages to the extent that it facilitates the payment of rewards in accord with productivity. If rewards were random, and without regard to productive effort, no incentive to productive effort would be provided by the organization; and if rewards were negatively correlated with productivity the organization would be subject to sabotage. Two key demands are placed on an economic organization—metering input productivity and metering rewards.[1]

Metering problems sometimes can be resolved well through the exchange of products across competitive markets, because in many situations markets yield a high correlation between rewards and productivity. If a farmer increases his output of wheat by 10 percent at the prevailing market price, his receipts also increase by 10 percent. This method of organizing economic activity meters the *output directly,* reveals the marginal product and apportions the *rewards* to resource owners in accord with that direct measurement of their outputs. The success of this decentralized, market exchange in promoting productive specialization requires that changes in market rewards fall on those responsible for changes in *output.*[2]

The classic relationship in economics that runs from marginal productivity to the distribution of income implicitly *assumes* the existence of an organi-

---

[1]Meter means to measure and also to apportion. One can meter (measure) output and one can also meter (control) the output. We use the word to denote both; the context should indicate which.

[2]A producer's wealth would be reduced by the present capitalized value of the future income lost by loss of reputation. Reputation, i.e., credibility, is an asset, which is another way of saying that reliable information about expected performance is both a costly and a valuable good. For acts of God that interfere with contract performance, both parties have incentives to reach a settlement akin to that which would have been reached if such events had been covered by specific contingency clauses. The reason, again, is that a reputation for "honest" dealings—i.e., for actions similar to those that would probably have been reached had the contract provided this contingency—is wealth.

Almost every contract is open-ended in that many contingencies are uncovered. For example, if a fire delays production of a promised product by A to B, and if B contends that A has not fulfilled the contract, how is the dispute settled and what recompense, if any, does A grant to B? A person uninitiated in such questions may be surprised by the

zation, be it the market or the firm, that allocates rewards to resources in accord with their productivity. The problem of economic organization, the economical means of metering productivity and rewards, is not confronted directly in the classical analysis of production and distribution. Instead, that analysis tends to assume sufficiently economic—or zero cost—means, as if productivity automatically created its reward. We conjecture the direction of causation is the reverse—the specific system of rewarding which is relied upon stimulates a particular productivity response. If the economic organization meters poorly, with rewards and productivity only loosely correlated, then productivity will be smaller; but if the economic organization meters well productivity will be greater. What makes metering difficult and hence induces means of economizing on metering costs?

II. TEAM PRODUCTION

Two men jointly lift heavy cargo into trucks. Solely by observing the total weight loaded per day, it is impossible to determine each person's marginal productivity. With team production it is difficult, solely by observing total output, to either define or determine *each* individual's contribution to this output of the cooperating inputs. The output is yielded by a team, by definition, and it is not a *sum* of separable outputs of each of its members. Team production of Z involves at least two inputs, X_i and X_j, with $\partial^2 Z / \partial X_i \partial X_j \neq 0$.[3] The production function is *not* separable into two functions each involving only inputs X_i or only inputs X_j. Consequently there is no *sum* of Z of two separable functions to treat as the Z of the team production function. (An example of a *sep-*

arable case is $Z = aX_i^2 + bX_j^2$ which is separable into $Z_i = aX_i^2$ and $Z_j = bX_j^2$, and $Z = Z_i + Z_j$. This is not team production.) There exist production techniques in which the Z obtained is greater than if X_i and X_j had produced separable Z. Team production will be used if it yields an output enough larger than the sum of separable production of Z to cover the costs of organizing and disciplining team members—the topics of this paper.[4]

Usual explanations of the gains from cooperative behavior rely on exchange and production in accord with the comparative advantage specialization principle with separable additive production. However, as suggested above there is a source of gain from cooperative activity involving working as a *team*, wherein individual cooperating inputs do not yield identifiable, separate products which can be *summed* to measure the total output. For this cooperative productive activity, here called "team" production, measuring *marginal* productivity and making payments in accord therewith is more expensive by an order of magnitude than for separable production functions.

Team production, to repeat, is production in which 1) several types of resources are used and 2) the product is not a sum of separable outputs of each cooperating resource. An additional factor creates a team organization problem—3) not all resources used in team production belong to one person.

We do not inquire into why all the jointly used resources are not owned by one person, but instead into the types of organization, contracts, and informational and payment procedures used among owners of teamed inputs. With respect to the one-owner case, perhaps it is sufficient merely to note that (a) slavery is prohibited, (b) one might assume risk aversion as a reason for one person's not borrowing enough to purchase all the assets or sources of services rather than renting them, and (c) the purchase-resale spread may be so large that costs of short-term ownership exceed rental costs. Our problem is viewed basically as one of organization among different people, not of the physical goods or services, however much there must be selection and choice of combination of the latter.

How can the members of a team be rewarded and

---

extent to which contracts permit either party to escape performance or to nullify the contract. In fact, it is hard to imagine any contract, which, when taken solely in terms of its stipulations, could not be evaded by one of the parties. Yet that is the ruling, viable type of contract. Why? Undoubtedly the best discussion that we have seen on this question is by Stewart Macaulay.

There are means not only of detecting or preventing cheating, but also for deciding how to allocate the losses or gains of unpredictable events or quality of items exchanged. Sales contracts contain warranties, guarantees, collateral, return privileges and penalty clauses for specific nonperformance. These are means of assignment of *risks* of losses of cheating. A lower price without warranty—an "as is" purchase—places more of the risk on the buyer while the seller buys insurance against losses of his "cheating." On the other hand, a warranty or return privilege or service contract places more risk on the seller with insurance being bought by the buyer.

[3] The function is separable into additive functions if the cross partial derivative is zero, i.e., if $\partial^2 Z / \partial X_i \partial X_j = 0$.

[4] With sufficient generality of notation and conception this team production function could be formulated as a case of the generalized production function interpretation given by our colleague, E. A. Thompson.

induced to work efficiently? In team production, marginal products of cooperative team members are not so directly and separably (i.e., cheaply) observable. What a team offers to the market can be taken as the marginal product of the team but not of the team members. The costs of metering or ascertaining the marginal products of the team's members is what calls forth new organizations and procedures. Clues to each input's productivity can be secured by observing *behavior* of individual inputs. When lifting cargo into the truck, how rapidly does a man move to the next piece to be loaded, how many cigarette breaks does he take, does the item being lifted tilt downward toward his side?

If detecting such behavior were costless, neither party would have an incentive to shirk, because neither could impose the cost of his shirking on the other (if their cooperation was agreed to voluntarily.) But since costs must be incurred to monitor each other, each input owner will have more incentive to shirk when he works as part of a team, than if his performance could be monitored easily or if he did not work as a team. If there is a net increase in productivity available by team production, net of the metering cost associated with disciplining the team, then team production will be relied upon rather than a multitude of bilateral exchange of separable individual outputs.

Both leisure and higher income enter a person's utility function.[5] Hence, each person should adjust his work and realized reward so as to equate the marginal rate of substitution between leisure and production of real output to his marginal rate of substitution in consumption. That is, he would adjust his rate of work to bring his demand prices of leisure and output to equality with their true costs. However, with detection, policing, monitoring, measuring or metering costs, each person will be induced to take more leisure, because the effect of relaxing on *his realized* (reward) rate of substitution between output and leisure will be less than the effect on the *true* rate of substitution. His realized cost of leisure will fall more than the true cost of leisure, so he "buys" more leisure (i.e., more nonpecuniary reward).

If his relaxation cannot be detected perfectly at zero cost, part of its effects will be borne by others

in the team, thus making *his* realized cost of relaxation less than the true total cost to the team. The difficulty of detecting such actions permits the private costs of his actions to be less than their full costs. Since each person responds to his private realizable rate of substitution (in production) rather than the true total (i.e., social) rate, and so long as there are costs for other people to detect his shift toward relaxation, it will not pay (them) to force him to readjust completely by making him realize the true cost. Only enough efforts will be made to equate the marginal gains of detection activity with the marginal costs of detection; and that implies a lower rate of productive effort and more shirking than in a costless monitoring, or measuring, world.

In a university, the faculty use office telephones, paper, and mail for personal uses beyond strict university productivity. The university administrators could stop such practices by identifying *the* responsible person in each case, but they can do so only at higher costs than administrators are willing to incur. The extra costs of identifying each party (rather than merely identifying the presence of such activity) would exceed the savings from diminished faculty "turpitudinal peccadilloes." So the faculty is allowed some degree of "privileges, perquisites, or fringe benefits." And the total of the pecuniary wages paid is lower because of the irreducible (at acceptable costs) degree of amenity-seizing activity. Pay is lower in pecuniary terms and higher in leisure, conveniences, and ease of work. But still every person would prefer to see detection made more effective (if it were somehow possible to monitor costlessly) so that he, as part of the now more effectively producing team, could thereby realize a higher pecuniary pay and less leisure. If everyone could, at zero cost, have his reward-realized rate brought to the true production possibility real rate, all could achieve a more preferred position. But detection of the responsible parties is costly; that cost acts like a tax on work rewards.[6] Viable shirking is the result.

What forms of organizing team production will

---

[5]More precisely: "if anything other than pecuniary income enters his utility function." Leisure stands for all nonpecuniary income for simplicity of exposition.

[6]Do not assume that the sole result of the cost of detecting shirking is one form of payment (more leisure and less take home money). With several members of the team, each has an incentive to cheat against each other by engaging in more than the average amount of such leisure if the employer can not tell at zero cost which employee is taking more than average. As a result the total productivity of the team is lowered. Shirking detection costs thus change the form of payment and also result in lower total rewards. Because the cross partial derivatives are positive, shirking reduces other people's marginal products.

lower the cost of detecting "performance" (i.e., marginal productivity) and bring personally realized rates of substitution closer to true rates of substitution? Market competition, in principle, could monitor some team production. (It already *organizes* teams.) Input owners who are not team members can offer, in return for a smaller share of the team's rewards, to replace excessively (i.e., overpaid) shirking members. Market competition among potential team members would determine team membership and individual rewards. There would be no team leader, manager, organizer, owner, or employer. For such decentralized organizational control to work, outsiders, possibly after observing each team's total output, can speculate about their capabilities as team members and, by a market competitive process, revised teams with greater productive ability will be formed and sustained. Incumbent members will be constrained by threats of replacement by outsiders offering services for lower reward shares or offering greater rewards to the other members of the team. Any team member who shirked in the expectation that the reduced output effect would not be attributed to him will be displaced if his activity is detected. Teams of productive inputs, like business units, would evolve in apparent spontaneity in the market—without any central organizing agent, team manager, or boss.

But completely effective control cannot be expected from individualized market competition for two reasons. First, for this competition to be completely effective, new challengers for team membership must know where, and to what extent, shirking is a serious problem, i.e., know they can increase net output as compared with the inputs they replace. To the extent that this is true it is probably possible for existing fellow team members to recognize the shirking. But, by definition, the detection of shirking by observing team output is costly for team production. Secondly, assume the presence of detection costs, and assume that in order to secure a place on the team a new input owner must accept a smaller share of rewards (or a promise to produce more). Then his incentive to shirk would still be at least as great as the incentives of the inputs replaced, because he still bears less than the entire reduction in team output for which he is responsible.

III. THE CLASSICAL FIRM

One method of reducing shirking is for someone to specialize as a monitor to check the input performance of team members.[7] But who will monitor the monitor? One constraint on the monitor is the aforesaid market competition offered by other monitors, but for reasons already given, that is not perfectly effective. Another constraint can be imposed on the monitor: give him title to the net earnings of the team, net of payments to other inputs. If owners of cooperating inputs agree with the monitor that he is to receive any residual product above prescribed amounts (hopefully, the marginal value products of the other inputs), the monitor will have an added incentive not to shirk as a monitor. Specialization in monitoring plus reliance on a residual claimant status will reduce shirking; but additional links are needed to forge the firm of classical economic theory. How will the residual claimant monitor the other inputs?

We use the term monitor to connote several activities in addition to its disciplinary connotation. It connotes measuring output performance, apportioning rewards, observing the input behavior of inputs as means of detecting or estimating their marginal productivity and giving assignments or instructions in what to do and how to do it.(It also includes, as we shall show later, authority to terminate or revise contracts.) Perhaps the contrast between a football coach and team captain is helpful. The coach selects strategies and tactics and sends in instructions about what plays to utilize. The captain is essentially an observer and reporter of the performance at close hand of the members. The latter is an inspector-steward and the former a supervisor manager. For the present all these activities are included in the rubric "monitoring." All these tasks are, in principle, negotiable across markets, but we are presuming that such market measurement of marginal productivities and job reassignments are not so cheaply performed for team production. And in particular our analysis suggests that it is not so much the costs of spontaneously negotiating contracts in the markets among groups for team production as it is the detection of

---

[7] What is meant by performance? Input energy, initiative, work attitude, perspiration, rate of exhaustion? Or output? It is the latter that is sought—the *effect* or output. But performance is nicely ambiguous because it suggests both input and output. It is *nicely* ambiguous because as we shall see, sometimes by inspecting a team member's input activity we can better judge his output effect, perhaps not with complete accuracy but better than by watching the output of the *team*. It is not always the case that watching input activity is the only or best means of detecting, measuring or monitoring output effects of each team member, but in some cases it is a useful way. For the moment the word performance glosses over these aspects and facilitates concentration on other issues.

the performance of individual members of the team that calls for the organization noted here.

The specialist *who receives the residual rewards* will be the monitor of the members of the team (i.e., will manage the use of cooperative inputs). The monitor earns his residual through the reduction in shirking that he brings about, not only by the prices that he agrees to pay the owners of the inputs, but also by observing and directing the actions or uses of these inputs. *Managing or examining the ways to which inputs are used in team production is a method of metering the marginal productivity of individual inputs to the team's output.*

To discipline team members and reduce shirking, the residual claimant must have power to revise the contract terms and incentives of *individual* members without having to terminate or alter every other input's contract. Hence, team members who seek to increase their productivity will assign to the monitor not only the residual claimant right but also the right to alter individual membership and performance on the team. Each team member, of course, can terminate his own membership (i.e., quit the team), but only the monitor may unilaterally terminate the membership of any of the other members without necessarily terminating the team itself or his association with the team; and he alone can expand or reduce membership, alter the mix of membership, or sell the right to be the residual claimant-monitor of the team. It is this entire bundle of rights: 1) to be a residual claimant; 2) to observe input behavior; 3) to be the central party common to all contracts with inputs; 4) to alter the membership of the team; and 5) to sell these rights, that defines the *ownership* (or the employer) of the *classical* (capitalist, free-enterprise) firm. The coalescing of these rights has arisen, our analysis asserts, because it resolves the shirking-information problem of team production better than does the noncentralized contractual arrangement.

The relationship of each team member to the *owner* of the firm (i.e., the party common to all input contracts *and* the residual claimant) is simply a "quid pro quo" contract. Each makes a purchase and sale. The employee "orders" the owner of the team to pay him money in the same sense that the employer directs the team member to perform certain acts. The employee can terminate the contract as readily as can the employer, and long-term contracts, therefore, are not an essential attribute of the firm. Nor are "au-thoritarian," "dictational," or "fiat" attributes relevant to the conception of the firm or its efficiency.

In summary, two necessary conditions exist for the emergence of the firm on the prior assumption that more than pecuniary wealth enter utility functions: 1) It is possible to increase productivity through team-oriented production, a production technique for which it is costly to directly measure the marginal outputs of the cooperating inputs. This makes it more difficult to restrict shirking through simple market exchange between cooperating inputs. 2) It is economical to estimate marginal productivity by observing or specifying input behavior. The simultaneous occurrence of both these preconditions leads to the contractual organization of inputs, known as the *classical capitalist firms* with (a) joint input production, (b) several input owners, (c) one party who is common to all the contracts of the joint inputs, (d) who has rights to renegotiate any input's contract independently of contracts with other input owners, (e) who holds the residual claim, and (f) who has the right to sell his central contractual residual status.[8]

Other Theories of the Firm

At this juncture, as an aside, we briefly place this theory of the firm in the contexts of those offered by Ronald Coase and Frank Knight.[9] Our view of the firm is not necessarily inconsistent with Coase's; we attempt to go further and identify refutable implications. Coase's penetrating insight is to make more of the fact that markets do not operate costlessly, and he relies on the cost of using markets to *form* contracts as his basic explanation for the existence of firms. We do not disagree with the proposition that, *ceteris paribus,* the higher is the cost of transacting across markets the greater will be the comparative advantage of organizing resources within the firm; it is a difficult proposition to disagree with or to refute. We could with equal ease subscribe to a theory of the firm based on the cost of managing, for surely it is true that, *ceteris paribus,* the lower is the cost of managing the greater will be the comparative advantage of organizing resources within the firm. To move the theory forward, it is necessary to know what is meant by a firm and to explain the

---

[8]Removal of (b) converts a capitalist proprietary firm to a socialist firm.
[9]Recognition must also be made to the seminal inquiries by Morris Silver and Richard Auster, and by H. B. Malmgren.

circumstances under which the cost of "managing" resources is low relative to the cost of allocating resources through market transaction. The conception of and rationale for the classical firm that we propose takes a step down the path pointed out by Coase toward that goal. Consideration of team production, team organization, difficulty in metering outputs, and the problem of shirking are important to our explanation but, so far as we can ascertain, not in Coase's. Coase's analysis insofar as it had heretofore been developed would suggest open-ended contracts but does not appear to imply anything more—neither the residual claimant status nor the distinction between employee and subcontractor status (nor any of the implications indicated below). And it is not true that employees are generally employed on the basis of long-term contractual arrangements any more than on a series of short-term or indefinite length contracts.

The importance of our proposed additional elements is revealed, for example, by the explanation of why the person to whom the control monitor is responsible receives the residual, and also by our later discussion of the implications about the corporation, partnerships, and profit sharing. These alternative forms for organization of the firm are difficult to resolve on the basis of market transaction costs only. Our exposition also suggests a definition of the classical firm—something crucial that was heretofore absent.

In addition, sometimes a technological development will lower the cost of market transactions while, at the same time, it expands the role of the firm. When the "putting out" system was used for weaving, inputs were organized largely through market negotiations. With the development of efficient central sources of power, it became economical to perform weaving in proximity to the power source and to engage in team production. The bringing in of weavers surely must have resulted in a reduction in the cost of negotiating (forming) contracts. Yet, what we observe is the beginning of the factory system in which inputs are organized within a firm. Why? The weavers did not simply move to a common source of power that they could tap like an electric line, purchasing power while they used their own equipment. Now team production in the joint use of equipment became more important. The measurement of marginal productivity, which now involved interactions between workers, especially

through their joint use of machines, became more difficult though contract negotiating cost was reduced, while managing the *behavior* of inputs became easier because of the increased centralization of activity. The firm as an organization expanded even though the cost of transactions were reduced by the advent of centralized power. The same could be said for modern assembly lines. Hence the emergence of central power sources expanded the scope of productive activity in which the firm enjoyed a comparative advantage as an organization form.

Some economists, following Knight, have identified the bearing of risks of wealth changes with the director or central employer without explaining why that is a viable arrangement. Presumably, the more risk-averse inputs become employees rather than owners of the classical firm. Risk averseness and uncertainty *with regard to the firm's fortunes* have little, if anything, to do with our explanation although it helps to explain why all resources in a team are not owned by one person. That is, the role of risk taken in the sense of absorbing the windfalls that buffet the firm because of unforeseen competition, technological change, or fluctuations in demand are not central to our theory, although it is true that imperfect knowledge and, therefore, risk, in *this* sense of risk, underlie the problem of monitoring team behavior. We deduce the system of paying the manager with a residual claim (the equity) from the desire to have efficient means to reduce shirking so as to make team production economical *and not from the smaller aversion to the risks of enterprise in a dynamic economy.* We conjecture that "distribution-of-risk" is not a valid rationale for the *existence* and organization of the *classical* firm.

Although we have emphasized team production as creating a costly metering task and have treated team production as an essential (necessary?) condition for the firm, would not other obstacles to cheap metering also call forth the same kind of contractual arrangement here denoted as a firm? For example, suppose a farmer produces wheat in an easily ascertained quantity but with subtle and difficult to detect quality variations determined by how the farmer grew the wheat. A vertical integration could allow a purchaser to control the farmer's behavior in order to more economically estimate productivity. But this is not a case of joint or team production, unless "information" can be considered part of the product. (While a good case could be made for that broader

conception of production, we shall ignore it here.)
Instead of forming a firm, a buyer can contract to
have his inspector on the site of production, just as
home builders contract with architects to supervise
building contracts; that arrangement is not a firm.
Still, a firm might be organized in the production of
many products wherein no team production or jointness of use of separately owned resources is involved.

This possibility rather clearly indicates a broader,
or complementary, approach to that which we have
chosen. 1) As we do in this paper, it can be argued
that the firm is the particular policing device utilized
when joint team production is present. If other
sources of high policing costs arise, as in the wheat
case just indicated, some other form of contractual
arrangement will be used. Thus to each source of
informational cost there may be a different type of
policing and contractual arrangement. 2) On the
other hand, one can say that where policing is difficult across markets, various forms of contractual
arrangements are devised, but there is no reason for
that known as the firm to be uniquely related or even
highly correlated with team production, as defined
here. It might be used equally probably and viably
for other sources of high policing cost. We have not
intensively analyzed other sources, and we can only
note that our current and readily revisable conjecture
is that 1) is valid, and has motivated us in our current
endeavor. In any event, the test of the theory advanced here is to see whether the conditions we have
identified are necessary for firms to have long-run
viability rather than merely births with high infant
mortality. Conglomerate firms or collections of separate production agencies into one owning organization can be interpreted as an investment trust or
investment diversification device—probably along
the lines that motivated Knight's interpretation. A
holding company can be called a firm, because of the
common association of the word firm with any ownership unit that owns income sources. The term firm
as commonly used is so turgid of meaning that we
can not hope to explain every entity to which the
name is attached in common or even technical literature. Instead, we seek to identify and explain a
particular contractual arrangement induced by the
cost of information factors analyzed in this paper.

IV. TYPES OF FIRMS
A. Profit-Sharing Firms

Explicit in our explanation of the capitalist firm is
the assumption that the cost of *managing* the team's

inputs by a central monitor, who disciplines himself
because he is a residual claimant, is low relative to
the cost of metering the marginal outputs of team
members.

If we look within a firm to see who monitors—
hires, fires, changes, promotes, and renegotiates—
we should find him being a residual claimant or, at
least, one whose pay or reward is more than any
others correlated with fluctuations in the residual
value of the firm. They more likely will have options
or rights or bonuses than will inputs with other
tasks.

An implicit "auxiliary" assumption of our explanation of the firm is that the cost of team production
is increased if the residual claim is not held entirely
by the central monitor. That is, we assume that if
profit sharing had to be relied upon for *all* team
members, losses from the resulting increase in central
monitor shirking would exceed the output gains
from the increased incentives of other team members
not to shirk. If the optimal team size is only two
owners of inputs, then an equal division of profits
and losses between them will leave each with stronger
incentives to reduce shirking than if the optimal team
size is large, for in the latter case only a smaller percentage of the losses occasioned by the shirker will
be borne by him. Incentives to shirk are positively
related to the optimal size of the team under an equal
profit-sharing scheme.[10]

The preceding does not imply that profit sharing
is never viable. Profit sharing to encourage self-po-
licing is more appropriate for small teams. And, indeed, where input owners are free to make whatever
contractual arrangements suit them, as generally is
true in capitalist economies, profit sharing seems
largely limited to partnerships with a relatively small
number of *active*[11] partners. Another advantage of
such arrangements for smaller teams is that it permits
more effective reciprocal monitoring among inputs.
Monitoring need not be entirely specialized.

Profit sharing is more viable if small team size is
associated with situations where the cost of specialized management of inputs is large relative to the

---

[10]While the degree to which residual claims are centralized will affect
the size of the team, this will be only one of many factors that determine
team size, so as an approximation, we can treat team size as exogenously
determined. Under certain assumptions about the shape of the "typical"
utility function, the incentive to avoid shirking with unequal profit
sharing can be measured by the Herfindahl index.

[11]The use of the word active will be clarified in our discussion of the
corporation, which follows below.

increased productivity potential in team effort. We conjecture that the cost of managing team inputs increases if the productivity of a team member is difficult to correlate with his behavior. In "artistic" or "professional" work, watching a man's activities is not a good clue to what he is actually thinking or doing with his mind. While it is relatively easy to manage or direct the loading of trucks by a team of dock workers where input activity is so highly related in an obvious way to output, it is more difficult to manage and direct a lawyer in the preparation and presentation of a case. Dock workers can be directed in detail without the monitor himself loading the truck, and assembly line workers can be monitored by varying the speed of the assembly line, but detailed direction in the preparation of a law case would require in much greater degree that the monitor prepare the case himself. As a result, artistic or professional inputs, such as lawyers, advertising specialists, and doctors, will be given relatively freer reign with regard to individual behavior. If the management of inputs is relatively costly, or ineffective, as it would seem to be in these cases, but, nonetheless if team effort is more productive than separable production with exchange across markets, then there will develop a tendency to use profit-sharing schemes to provide incentives to avoid shirking.[12]

B. Socialist Firms

We have analyzed the classical proprietorship and the profit-sharing firms in the context of free association and choice of economic organization. Such organizations need not be the most viable when political constraints limit the forms of organization that can be chosen. It is one thing to have profit sharing when professional or artistic talents are used by small teams. But if political or tax or subsidy considerations induce profit-sharing techniques when these are not otherwise economically justified, then additional management techniques will be developed to help reduce the degree of shirking.

For example, most, if not all, firms in Jugoslavia are owned by the employees in the restricted sense that all share in the residual. This is true for large firms and for firms which employ nonartistic, or non-

professional, workers as well. With a decay of political constraints, most of these firms could be expected to rely on paid wages rather than shares in the residual. This rests on our auxiliary assumption that general sharing in the residual results in losses from enhanced shirking by the monitor that exceed the gains from reduced shirking by residual-sharing employees. If this were not so, profit sharing with employees should have occurred more frequently in Western societies where such organizations are neither banned nor preferred politically. Where residual sharing by employees is politically imposed, as in Jugoslavia, we are led to expect that some management technique will arise to reduce the shirking by the central monitor, a technique that will not be found frequently in Western societies since the monitor retains all (or much) of the residual in the West and profit sharing is largely confined to small, professional-artistic team production situations. We do find in the larger scale residual-sharing firms in Jugoslavia that there are employee committees that can recommend (to the state) the termination of a manager's contract (veto his continuance) with the enterprise. We conjecture that the workers' committee is given the right to recommend the termination of the manager's contract precisely because the general sharing of the residual increases "excessively" the manager's incentive to shirk.[13]

C. The Corporation

All firms must initially acquire command over some resources. The corporation does so primarily by selling promises of future returns to those who (as creditors or owners) provide financial capital. In some situations resources can be acquired in advance from consumers by promises of future delivery (for example, advance sale of a proposed book). Or where the firm is a few artistic or professional persons, each can "chip in" with time and talent until the sale of services brings in revenues. For the most part, capital can be acquired more cheaply if many (risk-averse) investors contribute small portions to a large invest-

---

[12]Some sharing contracts, like crop sharing, or rental payments based on gross sales in retail stores, come close to profit sharing. However, it is gross output sharing rather than profit sharing. We are unable to specify the implications of the difference. We refer the reader to S. N. Cheung.

[13]Incidentally, investment activity will be changed. The inability to capitalize the investment value as "take-home" private property *wealth* of the members of the firm means that the benefits of the investment must be taken as annual income by those who are employed at the time of the income. Investment will be confined more to those with shorter life and with higher rates or pay-offs if the alternative of investing is paying out the firm's income to its employees to take home and use as private property. For a development of this proposition, see the papers by Eirik Furobotn and Svetozar Pejovich, and by Pejovich.

ment. The economies of raising large sums of equity capital in this way suggest that modifications in the relationship among corporate inputs are required to cope with the shirking problem that arises with profit sharing among large numbers of corporate stockholders. One modification is limited liability, especially for firms that are large relative to a stockholder's wealth. It serves to protect stockholders from large losses no matter how they are caused.

If every stock owner participated in each decision in a corporation, not only would large bureaucratic costs be incurred, but many would shirk the task of becoming well informed on the issue to be decided, since the losses associated with unexpectedly bad decisions will be borne in large part by the many other corporate shareholders. More effective control of corporate activity is achieved for most purposes by transferring decision authority to a smaller group, whose main function is to negotiate with and manage (renegotiate with) the other inputs of the team. The corporate stockholders retain the authority to revise the membership of the management group and over major decisions that affect the structure of the corporation or its dissolution.

As a result a new modification of partnerships is induced—the right to sale of corporate shares without approval of any other stockholders. Any shareholder can remove his wealth from control by those with whom he has differences of opinion. Rather than try to control the decisions of the management, which is harder to do with many stockholders than with only a few, unrestricted salability provides a more acceptable escape to each stockholder from continued policies with which he disagrees.

Indeed, the policing of managerial shirking relies on across-market competition from new groups of would-be managers as well as competition from members within the firm who seek to displace existing management. In addition to competition from outside and inside managers, control is facilitated by the temporary congealing of share votes into voting blocs owned by one or a few contenders. Proxy battles or stock-purchases concentrate the votes required to displace the existing management or modify managerial policies. But it is more than a change in policy that is sought by the newly formed financial interests, whether of new stockholders or not. It is the capitalization of expected future benefits into stock prices that concentrates on the innovators the wealth gains of their actions if they own large numbers of shares.

Without capitalization of future benefits, there would be less incentive to incur the costs required to exert informed decisive influence on the corporation's policies and managing personnel. Temporarily, the structure of ownership is reformed, moving away from diffused ownership into decisive power blocs, and this is a transient resurgence of the classical firm with power again concentrated in those who have title to the residual.

In assessing the significance of stockholders' power it is not the usual diffusion of voting power that is significant but instead the frequency with which voting congeals into decisive changes. Even a one-man owned company may have a long term with just one manager—continuously being approved by the owner. Similarly a dispersed voting power corporation may be also characterized by a long-lived management. The question is the probability of replacement of the management if it behaves in ways not acceptable to a majority of the stockholders. The unrestricted salability of stock and the transfer of proxies enhances the probability of decisive action in the event current stockholders or any outsider believes that management is not doing a good job with the corporation. We are not comparing the corporate responsiveness to that of a single proprietorship; instead, we are indicating features of the corporate structure that are induced by the problem of delegated authority to manager-monitors.[14]

---

[14]Instead of thinking of shareholders as joint *owners,* we can think of them as investors, like bondholders, except that the stockholders are more optimistic than bondholders about the enterprise prospects. Instead of buying bonds in the corporation, thus enjoying smaller risks, shareholders prefer to invest funds with a greater realizable return if the firm prospers as expected, but with smaller (possibly negative) returns if the firm performs in a manner closer to that expected by the more pessimistic investors. The pessimistic investors, in turn, regard only the bonds as likely to pay off.

If the entrepreneur-organizer is to raise capital on the best terms to him, it is to his advantage, as well as that of prospective investors, to recognize these differences in expectations. The residual claim on earnings enjoyed by shareholders does not serve the function of enhancing their efficiency as monitors in the general situation. The stockholders are "merely" the less risk-averse or the more optimistic member of the group that finances the firm. Being more optimistic than the average and seeing a higher mean value future return, they are willing to pay more for a certificate that allows them to realize gain on their expectations. One method of doing so is to buy claims to the distribution of returns that "they see" while bondholders, who are more pessimistic, purchase a claim to the distribution that they see as more likely to emerge. Stockholders are then comparable to warrant holders. They care not about the voting rights (usually not attached to warrants); they are in the same position in so far as voting rights are concerned

D. Mutual and Nonprofit Firms

The benefits obtained by the new management are greater if the stock can be purchased and sold, because this enables *capitalization* of anticipated future improvements into present *wealth* of new managers who bought stock and created a larger capital by their management changes. But in nonprofit corporations, colleges, churches, country clubs, mutual savings banks, mutual insurance companies, and "coops," the future consequences of improved management are not capitalized into present wealth of stockholders. (As if to make more difficult that competition by new would-be monitors, multiple shares of ownership in those enterprises cannot be bought by one person.) One should, therefore, find greater shirking in nonprofit, mutually owned enterprises. (This suggests that nonprofit enterprises are especially appropriate in realms of endeavor where more shirking is desired and where redirected uses of the enterprise in response to market-revealed values is less desired.)

E. Partnerships

Team production in artistic or professional intellectual skills will more likely be by partnerships than other types of team production. This amounts to market-organized team activity and to a nonemploy-er status. Self-monitoring partnerships, therefore, will be used rather than employer-employee contracts, and these organizations will be small to prevent an excessive dilution of efforts through shirking. Also, partnerships are more likely to occur among relatives or long-standing acquaintances, not necessarily because they share a common utility function, but also because each knows better the other's work characteristics and tendencies to shirk.

F. Employee Unions

Employee unions, whatever else they do, perform as monitors for employees. Employers monitor employees and similarly employees monitor an employer's performance. Are correct wages paid on time and in good currency? Usually, this is extremely easy to check. But some forms of employer performance are less easy to meter and are more subject to employer shirking. Fringe benefits often are in nonpecuniary, contingent form; medical, hospital, and accident insurance, and retirement pensions are contingent payments or performances partly in *kind* by employers to employees. Each employee cannot judge the character of such payments as easily as money wages. Insurance is a contingent payment—what the employee will get upon the contingent event may come

---

as are bondholders. The only difference is in the probability distribution of rewards and the terms on which they can place their bets.

If we treat bondholders, preferred and convertible preferred stockholders, and common stockholders and warrant holders as simply different classes of investors—differing not only in their risk averseness but in their beliefs about the probability distribution of the firm's future earnings, why should stockholders be regarded as "owners" in any sense distinct from the other financial investors? The entrepreneur-organizer, who let us assume is the chief operating officer and sole repository of control of the corporation, does not find his authority residing in common stockholders (except in the case of a take over). Does this type of control make any difference in the way the firm is conducted? Would it make any difference in the kinds of behavior that would be tolerated by competing managers and investors (and we here deliberately refrain from thinking of them as owner-stockholders in the traditional sense)?

Investment old timers recall a significant incidence of nonvoting common stock, now prohibited in corporations whose stock is traded on listed exchanges. (Why prohibited?) The entrepreneur in those days could hold voting shares while investors held nonvoting shares, which in every other respect were identical. Nonvoting share holders were simply investors devoid of ownership connotations. The control and behavior of inside owners in such corporations has never, so far as we have ascertained, been carefully studied. For example, at the simplest level of interest, does the evidence indicate that nonvoting shareholders fared any worse because of not having voting rights? Did owners permit the nonvoting holders the normal return available to voting shareholders? Though evidence is prohibitively expensive to obtain, it is remarkable that voting and nonvoting shares sold for essentially identical prices, even during some proxy battles. However, our casual evidence deserves no more than interest-initiating weight.

One more point. The facade is deceptive. Instead of nonvoting shares, today we have warrants, convertible preferred stocks all of which are solely or partly "equity" claims without voting rights, though they could be converted into voting shares.

In sum, is it the case that the stockholder-investor relationship is one emanating from the *division* of *ownership* among several people, or is it that the collection of investment funds from people of varying anticipations is the underlying factor? If the latter, why should any of them be thought of as the owners in whom voting rights, whatever they may signify or however exercisable, should reside in order to enhance efficiency? Why voting rights in any of the outside, participating investors?

Our initial perception of this possibly significant difference in interpretation was precipitated by Henry Manne. A reading of his paper makes it clear that it is hard to understand why an investor who wishes to back and "share" in the consequences of some new business should necessarily have to acquire voting power (i.e., power to change the manager-operator) in order to invest in the venture. In fact, we invest in some ventures in the hope that no other stockholders will be so "foolish" as to try to toss out the incumbent management. We want him to have the power to stay in office, and for the prospect of sharing in his fortunes we buy nonvoting common stock. Our willingness to invest is enhanced by the knowledge that we can act legally via fraud, embezzlement and other laws to help assure that we outside investors will not be "milked" beyond our initial discounted anticipations.

as a disappointment. If he could easily determine what other employees had gotten upon such contingent events he could judge more accurately the performance by the employer. He could "trust" the employer not to shirk in such fringe contingent payments, but he would prefer an effective and economic monitor of those payments. We see a specialist monitor—the union employees' agent—hired by them and monitoring those aspects of employer payment most difficult for the employees to monitor. Employees should be willing to employ a specialist monitor to administer such hard-to-detect employer performance, even though their monitor has incentives to use pension and retirement funds not entirely for the benefit of employees.

V. TEAM SPIRIT AND LOYALTY

Every team member would prefer a team in which no one, not even himself, shirked. Then the true marginal costs and values could be equated to achieve more preferred positions. If one could enhance a common interest in nonshirking in the guise of a team loyalty or team spirit, the team would be more efficient. In those sports where team activity is most clearly exemplified, the sense of loyalty and team spirit is most strongly urged. Obviously the team is better, with team spirit and loyalty, because of the reduced shirking—not because of some other feature inherent in loyalty or spirit as such.[15]

Corporations and business firms try to instill a spirit of loyalty. This should not be viewed simply as a device to increase profits by *over*-working or misleading the employees, nor as an adolescent urge for belonging. It promotes a closer approximation to the employees' potentially available true rates of substitution between production and leisure and enables each team member to achieve a more preferred situation. The difficulty, of course, is to create economically that team spirit and loyalty. It can be preached with an aura of moral code of conduct—a morality with literally the same basis as the ten commandments—to restrict our conduct toward what we would choose if we bore our full costs.

VI. KINDS OF INPUTS OWNED BY THE FIRM

To this point the discussion has examined why firms, as we have defined them, exist? That is, why is there an owner-employer who is the common party to contracts with other owners of inputs in team activity? The answer to that question should also indicate the kind of the jointly used resources likely to be owned by the central-owner-monitor and the kind likely to be hired from people who are not team-owners. Can we identify characteristics or features of various inputs that lead to their being hired or to their being owned by the firm?

How can residual-claimant, central-employer-owner demonstrate ability to pay the other hired inputs the promised amount in the event of a loss? He can pay in advance or he can commit wealth sufficient to cover negative residuals. The latter will

---

[15]*Sports Leagues:* Professional sports contests among teams is typically conducted by a *league* of teams. We assume that sports consumers are interested not only in absolute sporting skill but also in skills *relative* to other teams. Being slightly better than opposing teams enables one to claim a major portion of the receipts; the inferior team does not release resources and reduce costs, since they were expected in the play of contest. Hence, absolute skill is developed beyond the equality of marginal investment in sporting skill with its true social marginal value product. It follows there will be a tendency to overinvest in training athletes and developing teams. "Reverse shirking" arises, as budding players are induced to overpractice hyperactively relative to the social marginal value of their enhanced skills. To prevent overinvestment, the teams seek an agreement with each other to restrict practice, size of teams, and even pay of the team members (which reduces incentives of young people to overinvest in developing skills). Ideally, if all the contestant teams were owned by one owner, overinvestment in sports would be avoided, much as ownership of common fisheries or underground oil or water reserve would prevent overinvestment. This hyperactivity (to suggest the opposite of shirking) is controlled by the league of teams, wherein the league adopts a common set of constraints on each team's behavior. In effect, the teams are no longer really owned by the team owners but are supervised by them, much as the franchisers of some product. They are not full-fledged owners of their business, including the brand name, and can not "do what they wish" as franchises. Comparable to the franchiser, is the league commissioner or conference president, who seeks to restrain hyperactivity, as individual team supervisors compete with each other and cause external diseconomies. Such restraints are usually regarded as anticompetitive, antisocial, collusive-cartel devices to restrain free open competition, and reduce players' salaries. However, the interpretation presented here is premised on an attempt to avoid hyperinvestment in team sports production. Of course, the team operators have an incentive, once the league is formed and restraints are placed on hyperinvestment activity, to go further and obtain the private benefits of monopoly restriction. To what extent overinvestment is replaced by monopoly restriction is not yet determinable; nor have we seen an empirical test of these two competing, but mutually consistent interpretations. (This interpretation of league-sports activity was proposed by Earl Thompson and formulated by Michael Canes.) Again, athletic teams clearly exemplify the specialization of monitoring with captains and coaches; a captain detects shirkers while the coach trains and selects strategies and tactics. Both functions may be centralized in one person.

take the form of machines, land, buildings, or raw materials committed to the firm. Commitments of labor-wealth (i.e., human wealth) given the property rights in people, is less feasible. These considerations suggest that residual claimants—owners of the firm—will be investors of resalable capital equipment in the firm. The goods or inputs more likely to be invested, than rented, by the owners of the enterprise, will have higher resale values relative to the initial cost and will have longer expected use in a firm relative to the economic life of the good.

But beyond these factors are those developed above to explain the existence of the institution known as the firm—the costs of detecting output performance. When a durable resource is used it will have a marginal product and a depreciation. Its use requires payment to cover at least use-induced depreciation; unless that user cost is specifically detectable, payment for it will be demanded in accord with *expected* depreciation. And we can ascertain circumstances for each. An indestructible hammer with a readily detectable marginal product has zero user cost. But suppose the hammer were destructible and that careless (which is easier than careful) use is more abusive and causes greater depreciation of the hammer. Suppose in addition the abuse is easier to detect by observing the way it is used than by observing only the hammer after its use, or by measuring the output scored from a hammer by a laborer. If the hammer were rented and used in the absence of the owner, the depreciation would be greater than if the use were observed by the owner and the user charged in accord with the imposed depreciation. (Careless use is more likely than careful use—if one does not pay for the greater depreciation.) An absentee owner would therefore ask for a higher rental price because of the higher *expected* user cost than if the item were used by the owner. The expectation is higher because of the greater difficulty of observing specific user cost, by inspection of the hammer after use. Renting is therefore in this case more costly than owner use. This is the valid content of the misleading expressions about ownership being more economical than renting—ignoring all other factors that may work in the opposite direction, like tax provision, short-term occupancy and capital risk avoidance.

Better examples are tools of the trade. Watch repairers, engineers, and carpenters tend to own their own tools especially if they are portable. Trucks are more likely to be employee owned rather than other equally expensive team inputs because it is relatively cheap for the driver to police the care taken in using a truck. Policing the use of trucks by a nondriver owner is more likely to occur for trucks that are not specialized to one driver, like public transit buses.

The factor with which we are concerned here is one related to the costs of monitoring not only the gross product performance of an input but also the abuse or depreciation inflicted on the input in the course of its use. If depreciation or user cost is more cheaply detected when the owner can see its use than by only seeing the input before and after, there is a force toward owner use rather than renting. Resources whose user cost is harder to detect when used by someone else, tend on this count to be owner-used. Absentee ownership, in the lay language, will be less likely. Assume momentarily that labor service cannot be performed in the absence of its owner. The labor owner can more cheaply monitor any abuse of himself than if somehow labor-services could be provided without the labor owner observing its mode of use or knowing what was happening. Also his incentive to abuse himself is increased if he does not own himself.[16]

The similarity between the preceding analysis and the question of absentee landlordism and of share-

---

[16]Professional athletes in baseball, football, and basketball, where athletes having sold their source of service to the team owners upon entering into sports activity, are owned by team owners. Here the team owners must monitor the athletes' physical condition and behavior to protect the team owners' wealth. The athlete has *less* (not, *no*) incentive to protect or enhance his athletic prowess since capital value changes have less impact on his own wealth and more on the team owners. Thus, some athletes sign up for big initial bonuses (representing present capital value of future services). Future salaries are lower by the annuity value of the prepaid "bonus" and hence the athlete has *less* to lose by subsequent abuse of his athletic prowess. Any decline in his subsequent service value would in part be borne by the team owner who owns the players' future service. This does not say these losses of future salaries have no effect on preservation of athletic talent (we are not making a "sunk cost" error). Instead, we assert that the preservation is reduced, not eliminated, because the amount of loss of wealth suffered is smaller. The athlete will spend less to maintain or enhance his prowess thereafter. The effect of this revised incentive system is evidenced in comparisons of the kinds of attention and care imposed on the athletes at the "expense of the team owner" in the case where athletes' future services are owned by the team owner with that where future labor service values are owned by the athlete himself. Why athletes' future athletic services are owned by the team owners rather than being hired is a question we should be able to answer. One presumption is cartelization and monopsony gains to team owners. Another is exactly the theory being expounded in this paper—costs of monitoring production of athletes; we know not on which to rely.

cropping arrangements is no accident. The same factors which explain the contractual arrangements known as a firm help to explain the incidence of tenancy, labor hiring or sharecropping.[17]

VII. FIRMS AS A SPECIALIZED MARKET INSTITUTION FOR COLLECTING, COLLATING, AND SELLING INPUT INFORMATION

The firm serves as a highly specialized surrogate market. Any person contemplating a joint-input activity must search and detect the qualities of available joint inputs. He could contact an employment agency, but that agency in a small town would have little advantage over a large firm with many inputs. The employer, by virtue of monitoring many inputs, acquires special superior information about their productive talents. This aids his *directive* (i.e., market hiring) efficiency. He "sells" his information to employee-inputs as he aids them in ascertaining good input combinations for team activity. Those who work as employees or who rent services to him are using him to discern superior combinations of inputs. Not only does the director-employer "decide" what each input will produce, he also estimates which heterogeneous inputs will work together jointly more efficiently, and he does this in the context of a privately owned market for forming teams. The department store is a firm and is a superior private market. People who shop and work in one town can as well shop and work in a privately owned firm.

This marketing function is obscured in the theoretical literature by the assumption of homogeneous factors. Or it is tacitly left for individuals to do themselves via personal market search, much as if a person had to search without benefit of specialist retailers. Whether or not the firm arose because of this efficient information service, it gives the director-employer more knowledge about the productive talents of the team's inputs, and a basis for superior decisions about efficient or profitable combinations of those heterogeneous resources.

In other words, opportunities for profitable team production by inputs already within the firm may be

ascertained more economically and accurately than for resources outside the firm. Superior combinations of inputs can be more economically identified and formed from resources already used in the organization than by obtaining new resources (and knowledge of them) from the outside. Promotion and revision of employee assignments (contracts) will be preferred by a firm to the hiring of new inputs. To the extent that this occurs there is reason to expect the firm to be able to operate as a conglomerate rather than persist in producing a single product. Efficient production with heterogeneous resources is a result not of having *better* resources but in *knowing more accurately* the relative productive performances of those resources. Poorer resources can be paid less in accord with their inferiority; greater accuracy of knowledge of the potential and actual productive actions of inputs rather than having high productivity resources make a firm (or an assignment of inputs) profitable.[18]

VIII. SUMMARY

While ordinary contracts facilitate efficient specialization according to comparative advantage, a special class of contracts among a group of joint inputs to a team production process is commonly used for team production. Instead of multilateral contracts among all the joint inputs' owners, a central common party to a set of bilateral contracts facilitates efficient organization of the joint inputs in team production. The terms of the contracts form the basis

---

[17] The analysis used by Cheung in explaining the prevalence of share-cropping and land tenancy arrangements is built squarely on the same factors—the costs of detecting output performance of jointly used inputs in team production and the costs of detecting user costs imposed on the various inputs if owner used or if rented.

[18] According to our interpretation, the firm is a specialized surrogate for a market for team use of inputs; it provides superior (i.e., cheaper) collection and collation of knowledge about heterogeneous resources. The greater the set of inputs about which knowledge of performance is being collated within a firm the greater are the present costs of the collation activity. Then, the larger the firm (market) the greater the attenuation of monitor control. To counter this force, the firm will be divisionalized in ways that economize on those costs—just as will the market be specialized. So far as we can ascertain, other theories of the reasons for firms have no such implications.

In Japan, employees by custom work nearly their entire lives with one firm, and the firm agrees to that expectation. Firms will tend to be large and conglomerate to enable a broader scope of input revision. Each firm is, in effect, a small economy engaging in "intranational and international" trade. Analogously, Americans expect to spend their whole lives in the United States, and the bigger the country, in terms of variety of resources, the easier it is to adjust to changing tastes and circumstances. Japan, with its lifetime employees, should be characterized more by large, conglomerate firms. Presumably, at some size of the firm, specialized knowledge about inputs becomes as expensive to transmit across divisions of the firms as it does across markets to other firms.

of the entity called the firm—especially appropriate for organizing team production processes.

Team productive activity is that in which a union, or joint use, of inputs yields a larger output than the sum of the products of the separately used inputs. This team production requires—like all other production processes—an assessment of marginal productivities if efficient production is to be achieved. Nonseparability of the products of several differently owned joint inputs raises the cost of assessing the marginal productivities of those resources or services of each input owner. Monitoring or metering the productivities to match marginal productivities to costs of inputs and thereby to reduce shirking can be achieved more economically (than by across market bilateral negotiations among inputs) in a firm.

The essence of the classical firm is identified here as a contractual structure with: 1) joint input production; 2) several input owners; 3) one party who is common to all the contracts of the joint inputs; 4) who has rights to renegotiate any input's contract independently of contracts with other input owners; 5) who holds the residual claim; and 6) who has the right to sell his central contractual residual status. The central agent is called the firm's owner and the employer. No authoritarian control is involved; the arrangement is simply a contractual structure subject to continuous renegotiation with the central agent. The contractual structure arises as a means of enhancing efficient organization of team production. In particular, the ability to detect shirking among owners of jointly used inputs in team production is enhanced (detection costs are reduced) by this arrangement and the discipline (by revision of contracts) of input owners is made more economic.

Testable implications are suggested by the analysis of different types of organizations—nonprofit, proprietary for profit, unions, cooperatives, partnerships, and by the kinds of inputs that tend to be owned by the firm in contrast to those employed by the firm.

We conclude with a highly conjectural but possibly significant interpretation. As a consequence of the flow of information to the central party (employer), the firm takes on the characteristic of an efficient market in that information about the productive characteristics of a large set of specific inputs is now more cheaply available. Better recombinations or new uses of resources can be more efficiently ascertained than by the conventional search through the general market. In this sense inputs compete with each other within and via a firm rather than solely across markets as conventionally conceived. Emphasis on interfirm competition obscures intrafirm competition among inputs. Conceiving competition as the *revelation and exchange* of knowledge or information about qualities, potential uses of different inputs in different potential applications indicates that the firm is a device for enhancing competition among sets of input resources as well as a device for more efficiently rewarding the inputs. In contrast to markets and cities which can be viewed as publicly or nonowned market places, the firm can be considered a privately owned market; if so, we could consider the firm and the ordinary market as competing types of markets, competition between private proprietary markets and public or communal markets. Could it be that the market suffers from the defects of communal property rights in organizing and influencing uses of valuable resources?

REFERENCES

M. Canes, "A Model of a Sports League," unpublished doctoral dissertation, UCLA 1970.

S.N. Cheung, *The Theory of Share Tenancy*, Chicago 1969.

R. H. Coase, "The Nature of the Firm," *Economica*, Nov. 1937, 4, 386-405; reprinted in G. J. Stigler and K. Boulding, eds., *Readings in Price Theory*, Homewood 1952, 331-51.

E. Furobotn and S. Pejovich, "Property Rights and the Behavior of the Firm in a Socialist State," *Zeitschrift für Nationalökonomie*, 1970, 30, 431-454.

F. H. Knight, *Risk, Uncertainty and Profit*, New York 1965.

S. Macaulay, "Non-Contractual Relations in Business: A Preliminary Study," *Amer. Sociological Rev.*, 1963, 28, 55-69.

H. B. Malmgren, "Information, Expectations and the Theory of the Firm," *Quart J. Econ.*, Aug. 1961, 75, 399-421.

H. Manne, "Our Two Corporation Systems: Law and Economics," *Virginia Law Rev.*, Mar. 1967, 53, No. 2, 259-84.

S. Pejovich, "The Firm, Monetary Policy and Property Rights in a Planned Economy," *Western Econ. J.*, Sept. 1969, 7, 193-200.

M. Silver and R. Auster, "Entrepreneurship, Profit, and the Limits on Firm Size," *J. Bus. Univ. Chicago*, Apr. 1969, 42, 277-81.

E. A. Thompson, "Nonpecuniary Rewards and the Aggregate Production Function," *Rev. Econ. Statist.*, Nov. 1970, 52, 395-404.

A Theory of Rationing by Waiting*

YORAM BARZEL**

See "The Testability of the Law of Demand" for author's biography.

When limited quantities of commodities are provided free by the government, it is frequently asserted that not all demand is satisfied. Such commodities are often allocated on a first-come-first-served basis. It will be shown that rationing by waiting, which is the economic counterpart to first-come-first-served, is just another way to "satisfy all demand." The mechanics and the implications of such rationing are the subject matter here.[1]

Compared with the price mechanism, rationing by waiting generally entails a different resource cost—the time spent in the queue.[2] The extent of that cost, sometimes designated "dissipation of rent," will be examined and the conditions specified under which it equals the entire consumer's surplus. The cost arises because no well-defined property rights originally exist to the "free" good. To establish a claim to such rights, one must spend whatever time is necessary to gain priority in the queue.

The provision of goods free of charge is often justified on grounds that the action will benefit the poor. However, it will be shown that even when the poor actually have a lower time cost and therefore a lower cost of waiting, they may not benefit from such action. Indeed, in some empirically relevant cases the rich rather than the poor will stand in line to obtain such goods.

Assuming that every individual is costlessly informed of the waiting time necessary to acquire a subsidized good, what can we say about the length of the queue or, more precisely, about the length of waiting time for each individual in line? For this type

*Reprinted from *Journal of Law and Economics* (April 1974) by permission of The University of Chicago Press. Copyright 1974, pp. 73-95.

**I wish to thank Mary Eysenbach, Chris Hall, Reuben Kessel, John McGee, Mike Rahm, and particularly Steve Cheung for their valuable comments. I was first exposed to the notion of the real costs induced by price control in Harberger's price theory course in Chicago in 1957. Thanks for secretarial help are given to the National Science Foundation Grant to the University of Washington for the investigation of contracts.

[1] The literature on rationing is extensive, but with few exceptions the rationed quantities are assumed to be allocated by mechanisms such as a point system, for which this kind of waiting does not arise. Some queuing problems are discussed by D. Nichols, E. Smolensky, & T. N. Tideman, Discrimination by Waiting Time in Merit Goods, 61 Am. Econ. Rev. 312 (1971) [hereinafter cited as Nichols]. Gary S. Becker discusses briefly the cost associated with queues in A Theory of the Allocation of Time, 75 Econ. J. 493 (1965).

[2] Queues occur also in unregulated markets. While some of the analysis of this paper may apply to such situations, we concentrate here on queuing problems emerging from government actions.

of market to clear, the *marginal* individual is at a point where *total cost* (time plus money) is equal with his *total* valuation of the good to be obtained. In other words, to the marginal individual the consumer's surplus is zero.

A recent event, verging on a controlled experiment, confirms that allocation by waiting is not just an economist's fancy but is actually a market phenomenon. On June 14, 1972, the United States of America Bank (of Chicago) launched an anniversary sale.[3] The commodity on sale was money, and each of the first 35 persons could "buy" a $100 bill for $80 in cash. Those farther down the queue could each obtain similar but declining bonuses: the next 50 could gain $10 each; 75, $4 each; 100, $2 each, and the following 100, $1 each. Each of the next 100 persons could get a $2 bill for $1.60 and, finally, 800 (subsequently, it seems, expanded to 1800) persons could gain fifty cents each. The expected waiting time in such an unusual event was unpredictable; on the other hand, it was easy to assess the money value of the commodity being distributed.

First in line were four black brothers aged 16, 17, 19, and 24. Since the smallest was 6'2", their priority right was assured. "I figured," said Carl, the youngest brother, "that we spent 17 hours to make a $20 profit. That's about $1.20 an hour."

"You can make better than that washing dishes," added another of the brothers. Had they been better informed they could have waited less time. The 35th person to join the line arrived around midnight, had to wait just 9 hours, and was the last to earn $20—$2.22 per hour. To confirm her right, she made a list of all those ahead of her in the line.

"Why am I here?" she asked. "Well, that $20 is the same as a day's pay to me. And I don't even have to declare it on my income tax. It's a gift, isn't it?"

Information is sparse on how the rest of the queue evolved, but by opening time an estimated 500 persons were in line. Between then and the noon deadline, another 1800 or so joined the queue to get fifty cents apiece. What emerges most clearly from this experience is that the identity of those in the queue was not random and that waiting time fell as the bonus declined. The money value of the "free" good was largely matched by waiting time, viewed as a cost by those in the queue.[4]

TIME AS A MARKET CLEARING PRICE

The term "rationing" is traditionally identified with disequilibrium, a condition under which individuals are unable to equate costs and values on the margin, as seems apparent when the price imposed is not at the intersection of demand and supply. But since time is costly, waiting provides an additional route whereby individuals can again equate on the margin. Adding the time constraint allows us to apply "equilibrium" analysis to this form of rationing.

In Fig. 1 the horizontal axis measures the quantity of a commodity and the vertical axis its money price. The conventional demand curve of a single individual is represented by $d(t_0)$. (Implicit is the notion that the pecuniary price represents the full cost of purchase where waiting time is zero, that is, $t_0 = 0$.) For each of the other curves, waiting time is assumed to be positive and, at the higher time price, these curves have to lie below $d(t_0)$. At $d(t_2)$ waiting time per unit of the commodity is $t_2 > 0$; at $d(t_3)$ waiting time is $t_3 > t_2$.

When the money price is reduced to zero and per-unit waiting time is t_3, the quantity demanded is k. If k is the per-person quantity being distributed "free" by the government, the individual will be willing to stay in line up to k × t_3 minutes to obtain his share.[5] By letting t vary continuously, every point inside $d(t_0)$ is a point on a demand curve. In this space, for every combination of quantity and money price there is a time price at which the individual will be able to equate on the margin and be in equilibrium. In particular, all points on the horizontal axis to the left of the $d(t_0)$ horizontal intercept, combined with the appropriate amounts of waiting, are equilibrium points. Holding the pecuniary price constant, we can trace the relation between the quantity demanded and the minutes-per-unit waiting price to obtain a demand curve in terms of waiting, as we will do below for the special case where the monetary price is set at zero.

---

[3] The information is obtained from the Seattle Times, June 12, 1972, and from four Chicago daily newspapers, the Chicago Sun Times and Chicago Today, June 14, 1972, and the Chicago Tribune and Chicago Daily News, June 15, 1972.

[4] From the viewpoint of the bank, which apparently sought publicity, waiting time was simply a purchased input; indeed, it turned out to be most productive, as attested by the prominent newpapers' writeups.
[5] If it is impossible to get fewer than k units at a proportionately lower waiting time, all-or-nothing demand becomes relevant. Such a demand relation is introduced *infra*.

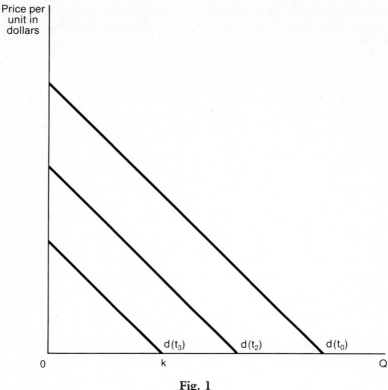

Fig. 1

It is important to recognize that when money price is zero, waiting time serves as a total price, and the analogy with pecuniary price is complete: demand with respect to this price will slope downwards. In the absence of discrimination among consumers only one time-price will prevail in the market.[6] The marginal valuation here is in terms of waiting time: as the quantity offered increases, the marginal valuation and, consequently, the per-unit waiting time will de-

cline, giving the curve its negative slope.[7]

Unless the individual allotment of the "free" good is restricted, one person may take the entire available supply. Thus the rules for distribution will fix quotas and may also stipulate whether each may join the queue only once per period or as many times as he wishes. The former arrangement prevails with the food stamp program and housing subsidies; the latter implicitly governs the utilization of public parks and roads. Both techniques are considered here.

The time-price an individual is willing to pay per unit of the good falls when the individual allotment increases. And, holding the per-person quantity con-

[6] The conclusion that waiting time is constant is derived under the assumption of certainty. P. Naor, The Regulation of Queue Size by Levying Tolls, 37 Econometrica 15 (1969) shows that with a random stream of customers the length of the queue will vary but will never exceed a given level equivalent to our uniform waiting time. He implicitly assumes there is no cost in ascertaining the length of the queue, so that at its maximum level there is no incentive to join. Symmetry would require, then, that when the queue is shorter than maximum, there is an incentive to join thereby lengthening the time in the queue towards the maximum. In any case, when the cost of information is taken into account, the decision whether to join will depend on the probability that the queue is shorter than the critical level. The higher this probability the stronger the incentive to explore, which in turn reduces the variability in the length of the queue.

[7] Given that a certain quantity of a commodity is distributed at a zero price, what can be said with respect to changes in the quantity? The cost of increasing the quantity is positive; but as the quantity increases, so does the rent to consumers since waiting time falls. If one is willing to add up dollar valuation of different individuals, a local maximum will occur when the rate of change in the sum of rents to consumers is equal to the rate of change in total cost of production. Second order as well as total conditions have to be also satisfied. In addition, it seems possible that several local maximum points may exist.

stant, the number of demanders will increase as the time-price falls. Just as with regular demand, so these two factors account for the negative slope of the aggregate demand curve when waiting time is the price. It might appear paradoxical that time decreases per unit of the good as more is made available for distribution and as the number waiting in line increases. The length of the queue may grow longer when the number of persons being served is larger. But regardless of the efficiency of distribution, for fixed individual allotments per-person waiting has to decline as the number of allotments is increased.

We will now demonstrate that per-person time in the queue is basically independent of the mechanics of distribution, first for a most efficient and speedy organization and then for a relatively slow one. Suppose that for a given amount of a commodity to be distributed free, one batch to a person, the per-person waiting time needed to clear the market is one hour. Now if the entire available amount can be dispensed instantaneously, the *whole* queue will have to form instantaneously one hour before distribution starts so that the time price is the same to all. If the line does not form instantaneously, the early joiner wastes his time, since he could still have obtained the commodity by coming later. He will do his best to join as late as possible, which is when the marginal man is indifferent between being in or out. Waiting cannot, however, be reduced to less than one hour, since positions will then be preempted by extramarginal individuals.

When the number of batches being distributed is increased, the number of individuals in the queue obviously will be larger, but, since the newcomers value a batch of the commodity less than they value one hour of their time, the market-clearing waiting time is shorter—say half an hour. Individuals will now line up only half an hour before distribution starts, or pressure will be exerted to bring it to that level. Thus the queue is longer, but per-person waiting time is less.

If the distribution arrangement is less efficient so that—say—six minutes are required to give out to one person the same amount as before, the first individual will arrive 54 minutes before distribution commences,[8] and from then on others will join the queue at six-minute intervals so that each spends one

hour waiting. No other spacing would persist, because if waiting takes more than one hour, some individuals will drop out; if less, some extra-marginal individuals will join. After the process is stabilized, the number in the line will be exactly 10, with accretions matching completers, and that level will hold until the last man appears one hour before closing time. For a larger quantity the waiting time required to clear the market is shorter. The total process will be stretched over a longer span (or over more distribution centers) so that the additional unit can be distributed; but at any point in time, except at the two ends, fewer individuals will be in the queue.

In the first situation it may seem that if the distribution were started one hour earlier, the line would disappear; but as the new opening time becomes known—instantaneously under the assumptions here—the queue would simply form yet one hour earlier. In the second situation, it may seem that if only the bureaucrats took fewer coffee breaks, less time would be wasted standing in line. But again the queue would eventually adjust to the new conditions and equilibrium waiting time would be restored to one hour.[9] An important corollary is that, given a fixed amount to be distributed free, attempts to improve efficiency will be wasted, since time in the queue will not change. Conversely, the lowest-cost method of distribution, no matter how cumbersome it may appear, is the most efficient in economic terms, since consumers' valuation is independent of such costs.

The speed of the distributing arrangements, however, may affect waiting time in two minor ways. First, under the terms of our numerical illustration, if the available quantity is so large that the equilibrium waiting time is less than six minutes, "technical" conditions then force the waiting price to six minutes. At that time-price some of the available amount will not be demanded and quicker handling is needed to reduce time below six minutes. Second, the dis-

---

[8]This is so because 54 minutes are spent in line before distribution starts and 6 minutes for actually getting the good.

[9]Gary S. Becker, *supra* note 1, at 516, n.3, states, "Time costs . . . often result in external diseconomies: for example, a person joining a queue would impose costs on subsequent joiners." This may appear contrary to our conclusion that the larger the number of batches to be distributed, the larger the number of waiters and the *lower* the waiting per person. Becker's statement, however, seems to apply to the process by which a queue evolves in the absence of adequate information rather than to differences among equilibria of distinct queuing situations for which a *larger* number of persons going through a queue results in a *shorter* per-person waiting time.

tributing organization may be so small that it can handle only part of the available amount. The analysis may now be carried on as before, with the quantity capable of distribution rather than the quantity available constituting the effective constraint.

Even when individuals are allowed to reenter the queue, the available supply may already have been exhausted by the time the first person is ready to step in line again. The quicker the distribution, the greater is the chance this will happen. Here, then, is a case where the distribution arrangement may significantly affect the market-clearing waiting time: speedier distribution shortens the waiting time, since there is less opportunity for multiple approaches.

Several major implications which, at least in principle, are testable emerge from the above discussion. We argue that time-price plays the same role as money price and that for a given stock of a "free" commodity a market-clearing time-price will be reached. Consequently, as the per-person allotment is increased with the number of persons served held constant, we predict that total per-person time in the queue will increase but that this increase will be less than proportionate to quantity, since time per unit is predicted to fall. In addition, holding the per-person allotment constant, per-person time in the queue will decline as the number of allotments is increased. And finally, since we argue that knowledge of the per-person quantity and of the number of persons served is sufficient to determine the market-clearing price, a testable implication is the invariance of waiting time in the queue with respect to the speed of the distribution.

THE RESOURCE COST OF THE QUEUE

In the main part of this section it is implicitly assumed that the only cost of getting a commodity to the final consumer is the cost of its production. Let us look briefly at some of the problems associated with this rather basic assumption. In the case of private markets, costs associated with selling are often considerable. On the other hand, freely disbursed commodities such as roads, elementary public schools, and parks, no resources are used in rationing the available quantity among consumers. The reduction in selling costs as compared with private markets is real enough. We cannot expect, however, that either the quantity supplied or the quality mix will be the same as those supplied by the market.

In any case, it is possible to avoid explicit rationing of roads, schools, and public parks because the rate at which consumers can acquire services is basically restricted to one unit per unit of time. Moreover, it is often prohibitively costly to resell such commodities. In the case of food, on the other hand, the first man in the queue may acquire the entire stock, either for his own consumption or to sell to others. The cost of a rationing organization to prevent this parallels the cost of selling in private markets. Adequate comparison between the two forms of providing commodities would require full assessment of the two types of rationing costs and would be beyond the scope of this paper, therefore we abstract from this problem, as follows.

What is the nature, and measure, of the cost associated with queuing? The mere presence of non-price rationing suggests that the quantity supplied differs from what would be offered in the absence of government intervention. The "misallocation" or "waste" associated with the government action may be measured, say, by the appropriate triangles. Time spent in the waiting line is an additional cost.[10] A pecuniary market price represents a transfer of resources from the buyer to the seller to the extent of the resource cost of producing the good. When a queue is the means of rationing, the time-resource spent to acquire the good is not captured by the producer. If the quantity provided free is equal to what the market would provide, no misallocation triangle appears, but the resource cost of the queue must still be accounted as additional to that of producing the good. Indeed, the two types of cost are basically the same for the marginal unit and are of the same order of magnitude for the entire quantity.

Suppose it were possible costlessly to identify in advance all those planning to be in the queue and to provide them with coupons to claim the good. The saving of time in the lineup would be a net gain, since no other resources were expended. In the absence of such arrangement, since the marginal man in the queue is indifferent between spending his time there or in some alternative use, the extent of the

---

[10]At a deeper level, "misallocation," "waste," and time in the queue may be viewed as costs similar in nature to those of selling and transacting. We might hypothesize that there are among the costs which the economy will attempt to minimize. Thus it is conceivable that the existing arrangement is the lowest in cost for achieving certain objectives, and we will touch on this notion later.

cost for that individual is identical with his total valuation of the "free" good.[11]

Consider a situation in which a large number of individuals have access to a good to be rationed at zero monetary price by means of a queue. In Fig. 2a the demand curve d_i of the ith individual is drawn with price in terms of waiting time. Points on this

demand curve are implicit in Fig. 1 and can be obtained by matching the quantity and the per unit time price at the intersection of each demand curve with the horizontal axis where pecuniary price is zero. For instance, as evident in Fig. 1, the time price the individual is willing to pay for k units is t_3 minutes per unit, which gives the point (t_3, k) on d_i in Fig. 2a.

If the individual is faced with an "all-or-nothing" decision to acquire k units, he will be willing to pay the entire area below the demand curve to quantity k, or an average price t_4, for the quantity.[12] D_i is the all-or-nothing demand curve corresponding to d_i.

In Fig. 2b, the all-or-nothing demand curves for several individuals are drawn, ordered (in the relevant range) from highest to lowest. While only a few individuals are represented in the drawing, we as-

[11]In popular discussion of conditions associated with consumption of free goods, the nature of the cost involved is usually (at best) only implicit. However, to cite one exception: "Of course, public [tennis] courts are free or relatively cheap but not always freely available for playing on. In Houston the public courts have become so overtaxed by the tennis boom that players must appear in person a full week before they want to play in order to sign up for their hour on the court. What the poor or parsimonious player may save in money, he can easily spend in time and inconvenience." Sophy Burnham, Tennis: A Whole New Ball Game, Saturday Review, July 29, 1972, at 44, 46.

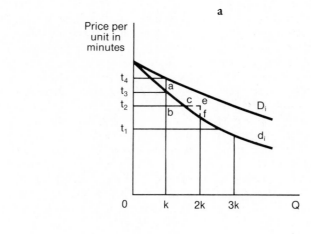

a

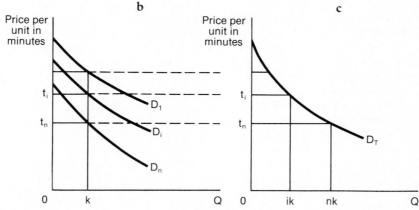

Fig. 2

sume that the total number is large and that at any quantity the distance between adjacent curves is small enough to be ignored. If the batch size is k, for any time-price we obtain the number of batches demanded by simply counting the number of individuals for whom the height of the all-or-nothing demand curve at quantity k is equal to or exceeds the specified time price. Given a fixed supply of n batches, price is market determined, and its equilibrium level is the height of the all-or-nothing curve of the nth individual. At that price, the $(n + 1)^{st}$ individual will not demand the good, since his total valuation of the batch is less than his cost. At any lower price, the $(n + 1)^{st}$ individual is better off with the good than without it; consequently, he will be in the line. The available quantity, however, will not provide the good to all those waiting, and this exerts upward pressure on the time-price, bringing it back to the height of the all-or-nothing demand of the nth individual. Thus the equilibrium, or market-clearing, price for n × k units is the all-or-nothing price for k units for the nth individual, who therefore earns no surplus since his total valuation is precisely exhausted by waiting.

The aggregate demand curve with batch size k and a single access to the queue is drawn in Fig. 2c. Notice that since the per unit market-clearing price for n batches is t_n, total waiting time is n × k × t_n which represents the total time spent in queuing.[13]

When more than one entry in the line is permitted, the demand curve becomes a mixture of the regular and the all-or-nothing curves. The all-or-nothing component applies to the last batch, while all previous ones are obtained at the going time-price.[14] At price t_2, the ith individuals will certainly join the queue and demand one batch, as shown in Fig. 2a. The height of t_2 determines that the area of the triangle abc equals that of cef, and so the valuation of the second batch equals its cost. When the price is t_2, the ith individual, then, would just be willing to join the queue a second time. Similarly, he will stand in line three times when the price falls to t_1, since t_1 is

his all-or-nothing price for the third batch.[15] For an individual obtaining just one batch, the conventional all-or-nothing demand holds. At each price, marginal consumers can be classified into two groups: those who have obtained at least one previous batch, and those just indifferent between getting or not getting one single batch.

Now n batches will be distributed among fewer than n individuals since at any time-price we would expect, in general, some consumers to obtain more than one. But some will enter the line only once and to the marginal individual in this group, the "free" good provides zero rent just as in the case of single access to the queue. Total time spent in queuing here is n × k × t'_n where t'_n is the market-clearing time-price for multiple access (which will be higher, in general, than t_n). We have shown, then, that whether the rule is single access or multiple access, the entire consumer's surplus that the marginal man in the queue derives from the good is exhausted by waiting.

If all individuals under consideration are identical in their utility functions, incomes, and time costs, then the marginal and the average individual are identical. Since the market-clearing waiting time is such that the marginal person in the line receives zero rent (or surplus), so too does the average person. Each is indifferent between having and not having the good, and the entire valuation of the good is lost in waiting.[16]

If those obtaining the good are not identical, the marginal individual is the only one for whom the entire economic rent is lost, and each of the intramarginal ones receives some rent. The rent is equal to the difference in valuation between the maximum amount of time that the particular individual is willing to wait and the actual waiting time. Given a quantity to be distributed free, the aggregate rent is larger the more diverse are those in the queue in terms of their willingness to wait. Homogeneity leads to highly elastic demand for a good whose price is in waiting time, to low returns to those in the queue, and to relatively high cost of waiting in terms

---

[12]We abstract from the difference between income underlying the all-or-nothing decision and that underlying the regular demand curve.

[13]In the above discussion, n, k (and their product nk) were treated as given. Provided that some quantity is distributed free, one may wish to explore why the particular values of n and k were selected.

[14]Again we abstract from differential income effects.

[15]This analysis differs from the common textbook analysis of demand in that the units of the commodity being distributed are assumed discrete rather than continuous. If the batch size goes to zero, a regular demand curve results. But in the real world the unit by which commodities are sold is seldom fully divisible, consequently the analysis here is more appropriate than that found in most textbooks.

[16]Instead of "There is no such thing as a free lunch," we have now "If there is a free lunch, it will come to have zero value."

of loss of alternative output. Thus the notion that the cost of the free good is low is not generally correct, and we might reject the statement that "to the low wage people, the money cost of the queue is *minimal* and they will receive a *substantial* benefit due to the lower money price."[17]

Turning the problem around, we gain added insight into the political process involved. Queuing uses resources the return from which, on the average, is larger the lower the demand elasticity of the subsidized commodity. If the demand is perfectly elastic, no consumer gains from the subsidy; consequently, little political support can be expected from consumers for the subsidization of such commodities, the less elastic the demand, the larger the gains on intramarginal units and the greater potential political support. We predict, then, that commodities provided free and distributed on a first-come-first-served basis will have, on the average, lower demand elasticities in terms of waiting time than the average for all commodities and we will show that such commodities are less likely to be obtained by the poor.[18]

Once the consequences of the first-come-first-served rule are recognized, one can readily analyze the effect of a strictly maintained price ceiling[19] on the demand for related goods. In panel a of Fig. 3,

[17]Nichols, *supra* note 1 at 316 (italics added).
[18]A similar argument applies on the supply side. The lower the supply elasticity, the larger the gain to suppliers from subsidized purchases.
[19]If lax maintenance of the ceiling permits development of a black market, the analysis becomes much more complex, but the basic qualitative results still hold.

Q_f^e and P_f^e are the initial equilibrium levels of quantity and price of a commodity f. A ceiling price is set at $P_f^c < P_f^e$, at which the quantity supplied is $Q_f^c < Q_f^e$. A queue will form to allocate the limited quantity among demanders, of such length that on the margin the price in money-plus-time must equal the valuation. While the money price is only P_f^c the waiting price is $P_f^v - P_f^c$ which brings the total price to P_f^v, a level *higher* than the initial equilibrium price.[20] At the higher total price the demand for substitutes will shift to the right and that for complements to the left. Since, however, the real price paid by buyers is higher than that received by sellers, the difference being the value of waiting time, we have here a net resource cost resulting in a negative income effect that for superior goods will shift demand to the left, enhancing the price effect on complements but reducing that on substitutes.[21]

[20]We abstract from the problem that the demand curve under the new conditions will not be identical with D_f since not all demanders convert time to money price at the same rate.
[21]This result differs from that obtained by J. R. Gould & S. G. B. Henry, The Effects of Price Control on a Related Market, 34 Economica 42 (1967). When they view the ceiling as the effective price paid by the "satisfied" consumers for whom the price fell while for "unsatisfied" consumers the price is infinite, they fail to recognize that the "unsatisfied" consumers can effectively bid up the price by waiting and thus can restore equilibrium. And, of course, they implicitly assume that the resource cost of waiting time is zero. Note also that, given their model, they make the hardly necessary distinction between gross and net substitutes, not realizing that if consumers gain by paying at the lower rate, producers lose the same amount and the income effects of the two groups combined tend to wash out. (If the slopes of the Engel curves of the two groups are identical, the income effect will cancel exactly).

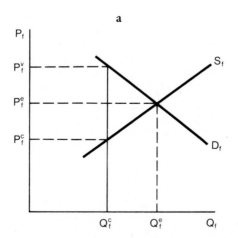

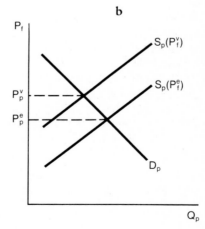

Fig. 3

Along the same lines, consider the effect of imposing a ceiling on the price of a factor of production. To the demander of such a factor, the control constitutes an effective increase (the cost of his time) in the price of that factor, which in turn will lead to an increase in the price of the final product. This is shown in panel b of Fig. 3 where, prior to the imposition of the price ceiling, the factor price underlying the supply of the product S_p was P_f^c. Since the price ceiling raised the effective factor price to P_f^y, the supply curve of the product shifted upwards to $S_p(P_f^y)$. The price ceiling in the factor market will, then, increase the price of the product from P_p^c to P_p^y. Thus, a refutable implication of our model is that fixing the price of a factor *below* its market price will *increase* the market price of the product. A price ceiling on food will result in an increase in restaurant meal prices; wage control on lumber workers will lead to higher lumber prices; and a "rollback" of steel prices will bring higher automobile prices.[22]

PROPERTY RIGHTS ON THE FREE GOOD

Many government goods are disbursed at lower than market price, mostly at zero price. Are they all allocated by queues subject to the associated costs? In the market process, goods are provided in exchange for other goods, whereas in the political process goods are transferred from one group to another. In the market, exchange will continue until on the margin the gain equals the cost. In the political arena the situation is more complex. The preceding discussion has evidenced that under certain circumstances individuals will spend resources to affect transfers to themselves to the point where on the margin, as in the market, the gain equals the cost. But is this unique to certain types of political transfers or is this the rule for all such transfers?[23]

A position in the queue implies a certain priority right to the good that was originally unassigned. But when property rights to the good, or to the transferred wealth, are once clearly assigned so that current or future action cannot further affect the transfer, there is no motive to spend resources on such

action.[24] Thus, point rationing precludes the costs of queuing by turning over property rights to those receiving points. Where such preassignment is not made resources will be spent to obtain the rights to the subsidy (or, by the same token, to avoid paying taxes). On the margin the value of these resources will equal the rate of the subsidy.[25]

Suppose, for illustration, that each of the poorest individuals in the community is to be provided free one unit of a commodity. If eligibility is determined by the level of income reported on a prior tax return which cannot be amended, then the right is clearly defined. But poverty may also be defined in terms of income to be shown on a future tax return. Whether an individual proves to be "poor" will then depend on his own action, and he may devote resources to qualifying himself—particularly by reducing any components which are measured as income for purposes of the subsidy but which do not entirely constitute real income. For instance, when he consumes more leisure and fewer market goods, his measured income declines more than his real income. To the marginal individual, the value of these resources (that is, the fall in real income) is exactly matched by the subsidy.[26]

If a subsidy is anticipated by some firm or individual as yet undesignated, resources may be spent in the present to assure future property rights. In this case, it may appear when the subsidy is eventually given that no resources were spent on acquiring the property rights, but they have simply been paid in advance.

In other cases, the property right can be obtained only when actual distribution takes place, as in queuing and the closely related phenomenon of crowding. In a classic article published half a century ago, Knight demonstrated the costs associated with crowding.[27] Where congestion occurs under condi-

---

[22]Note that the results are basically unaffected if the price ceiling P_f^y is replaced by a price floor P_f^y. When analyzing the behavior of sellers the effective price they receive, however, is not the price floor P_f^y but rather the lower P_f^c.

[23]Some transfers take place in the private sector, as with theft, with so-called "externalities," and to some extent within what is conventionally viewed as strictly market exchange.

[24]The property right to this idea is Steven N. S. Cheung's. See, A Theory of Price Control, 17 J. Law & Econ. 53 (1974).

[25]P. Naor, *supra* note 6, recognizes the inefficiency associated with the queue and suggests improvement either by charging tolls or by administratively limiting the length of the queue. The latter arrangement, however, implicitly assumes that individuals could not affect the decision whether they would be admitted; if they could do so, the administrative control would not yield the desired result.

[26]This last notion is discussed in detail by Gordon Tullock in a seminal article, The Welfare Costs of Tariffs, Monopolies and Theft, 5 Western Econ. J. 224 (1967).

[27]F. H. Knight, Some Fallacies in the Interpretation of Social Cost, 38 Q.J. Econ. 582 (1924), reprinted in Readings in Price Theory 217 (Amer. Econ. Ass'n, 1952).

tions of free entry, individuals who have the pertinent information will continue to crowd as long as the value of the service exceeds the time-and-money cost of acquiring it. In the case of crowding, the service is usually consumed during the waiting period, instead of later as with queuing.[28] Otherwise there is little difference between them.

Would the previous conclusion be altered if we consider the possibility of bribery? It may appear that bribery will eliminate, or at least reduce, the resource cost of obtaining the right to the subsidy, since waiting in the line will be replaced by a transfer from consumers to officials. Such an arrangement, however, may simply shift the cost from the final consumers to the officials. The value of a disbursing job will be increased by the valuation of the bribes; in the absence of property rights on such jobs, potential workers will then spend resources in queuing or whatever other activity may increase the chance of employment, to the point where the value of these resources equals the valuation of the bribes. The possibility of bribes, then, does not affect the conclusion that the resource cost of acquiring the good will be eliminated only if property rights to the disbursed goods are well defined. Note, however, that the cost of establishing property rights on the intramarginal units will differ in magnitude among different methods of allocation. With one important exception, only queuing as a means of distribution will be considered in the rest of the paper.

DISTRIBUTIVE EFFECTS OF FREE GOODS

Assuming temporarily that the free good will not be transferred, would the poor always get it? The lower the cost of time, the lower the cost of waiting—and the time cost of the poor is normally low. However, the question of benefits should not be overlooked. It is obvious that goods for which the income elasticity of demand is high would produce more benefits to the rich than to the poor. It is also clear that if the government-supplied good is available at the same time in the private market, the poor may be expected to pay by waiting while the rich will tend to pay the higher money price.

Consider the formal relation for a special case—

where the demand for the good by every individual is of the form $q = \alpha p^\beta y^\gamma$ where q is quantity, p is price, y is income, price elasticity is β and the income elasticity is γ. Individuals may differ in their incomes, but the quantities they receive are the same, and all pay the same time-price. Suppose also that time-costs (wages) are proportionate to income. Then only if $-\frac{\gamma}{\beta} < 1$ will the queue be composed of the poorest individuals. If $-\frac{\gamma}{\beta} > 1$ the richest individuals will be standing in line to obtain the good.[29] We find, then, that the higher the income elasticity and the lower the price elasticity the less is it likely that the poor will stand in line. This result is entirely general in that it holds, though not as a simple ratio, for other forms of demand.

In light of these findings, it seems evident that government giveaways aimed toward the poor should be commodities with low income elasticities and high price elasticities. This would suggest products for which close substitutes (or the identical goods) are available in private markets. Taking highways as an example: where private toll roads are allowed to operate side by side with free public roads, the latter become more attractive to the poor because their price elasticity is thus raised.

On the other hand, the subsidizing of opera is totally misdirected from the viewpoint of helping the poor. The apparently high income elasticity and low price elasticity of demand for opera results in a redistribution towards the rich since they, rather than the poor, will take advantage of the opportunity.

---

[28]Similarly utilities are often required to price their output at a level lower than the unregulated price and simultaneously meet the entire demand. When they fail, instead of queuing or crowding we experience "brownouts" and "blackouts."

[29]With $q = \alpha p^\beta y^\gamma$ we can write $p = \alpha^{-1/\beta} q^{1/\beta} y^{-\gamma/\beta}$ where p may be interpreted as the marginal valuation of the qth unit. To avoid infinite total utility, however, assume that the valuation of the entire first unit is, say, at the same rate as the valuation at $q = 1$. Given q, the relative valuation of the marginal unit by two individuals i and j with incomes y_i and y_j is $(y_i/y_j)^{-\gamma/\beta}$. Since this holds for any value of q common to the two individuals, it is also true of the total valuation. Given the assumption that across individuals time-costs, denoted by w are proportionate to income, the relative cost for the two individuals is $w_i/w_j = y_i/y_j$ and will exceed the relative valuation $(y_i/y_j)^{-\gamma/\beta}$ only if $-\gamma/\beta < 1$. For such values of γ/β, then, time-cost rises faster with income than does the valuation of the good. Consequently, if $-\gamma/\beta < 1$, as the number of units to be distributed increases, the order in which individuals will join the queue is from the poorest to the richest. If $-\alpha/\beta > 1$, the order is reversed. Both Becker and Nichols then, err in implying that queuing will necessarily result in a redistribution towards the poor. Finally, if $-\gamma/\beta = 1$, the time-cost rises at the same rate as income. At a low time-cost all individuals are indifferent whether they get the good or not, and for any individual in the queue the waiting cost equals the entire consumer surplus.

Another example is the municipal golf course where use is normally rationed not by money price but by waiting in lengthy lines, especially on weekends. Most private golf courses are not close substitutes, since they often restrict membership and sometimes are out of municipal limits. Thus, the price elasticity of demand for the municipal course is probably low while the income elasticity is in all likelihood high, and again the rich tend to benefit from this government service. A casual scrutiny of the set of goods freely supplied by the government and rationed by some form of queuing suggests that many of them fail to meet these two elasticity criteria and so are unlikely to end up in the hands of the poor.

It is often claimed that some of the goods provided free by the government are chosen on the ground that their actual consumption, especially by the poor, yields benefits to others. It is also claimed that the presence of such "public benefits" may explain why trading of the goods is frequently banned.[30] Still, abstracting from interdependence we might try to discover what would be the consequences of such trade. The time of the rich, as measured by the market, is usually more valuable than that of the poor. Would it not be more efficient to let the poor wait in line and then sell the good to the rich who value it more highly?[31] In analyzing this problem we assume that nobody wants to consume more than one unit of the commodity, as might be the case for a theater performance. With one important exception, at the (private) margin here, as elsewhere, rent is zero. But we will now show that when trading is allowed a greater rent accrues to *all* the previous intramarginal individuals in the queue and to some extramarginal ones.

To see this, suppose n units of the good are distributed, one unit per person. The analysis depends on whether the number of individuals in the community is less or more than 2n. We will commence with the case where this number is 2n or more. In the absence of trade, and assuming once more that incomes are proportionate to wages and that tastes are identical, the good will be obtained either by the n poorest individuals or by the n richest ones. We will first analyze the effects of permitting trade where

under prior restriction the good was obtained by the rich.

Suppose that H_R is the market-clearing price when trade is banned. The nth richest person, who is marginal in the queue, is indifferent between waiting H_R hours in the queue or paying a money price of $W_R H_R$ for the good where W_R is his wage rate. If trade is allowed, "waiting" is purchased in the market, and n units of this service will be demanded by the nth richest individuals. As to supply, we assume that each individual is willing to supply any number of hours at his alternative market wage, but that each may acquire only one unit of the good. Obviously, the poorest n individuals will supply the waiting service. Since the money price they will receive for selling the commodity is $W_R H_R$, the number of hours each will have to spend in waiting is $(W_R \cdot H_R)/W_P$ where W_P is the wage rate of the nth poorest individual. If waiting time needed to acquire the good is longer, the units of the good available will exceed the number of waiters, exerting a downward pressure on the time price; the converse will hold if the number of hours is less than $(W_R \cdot H_R)/W_P$. Since neither the marginal man performing the waiting services nor the marginal man buying the services earns any rent, for this unit, the valuation equals the cost of waiting.

But consider now the intramarginal individuals. Before trading was allowed, the poor ones obviously received no rent since they did not wait in line and did not get any of the commodity. To the extent that the supply price for waiting services of the intramarginal individuals is less than that of the marginal one, they receive some rent. With respect to the rich, all previously had to wait H_R hours, and now they all pay $H_R W_R$ dollars. The intramarginal man whose wage is $W_S > W_R$, previously had to pay $H_R W_S$ as the alternative cost of waiting in line; now he has to pay only $H_R W_R < H_R W_S$, and is better off. Both the rich and the poor, then, gain from the trade.[32]

What occurs in the case where the n poorest individuals would previously have obtained the good? When trade is initiated, since the rich value the good more, they eventually will get it at a price determined as above. All the intramarginal rich will now earn

[30] Nichols, *et al.*, designate these "merit goods," hence the title of their article. That characteristic seems to be the reason Nichols ignores the question of trading in these goods.
[31] If the good is not inferior, the rich always value it more highly.

[32] The above analysis fits rather well some theater experience. Queues sometimes form even though ticket price is not directly controlled, but while an incentive is thus created for additional trading, the law often bans resale at so-called scalping prices.

some rent. As to the poor, the same ones will be waiting in the queue, but they now wait longer. Those that previously earned rent will earn proportionately more. Again, both the rich and the poor are better off. Notice that in both cases the move is "Pareto optimal" in that the n-1 richest and the n-1 poorest are better off, while no other individual is worse off despite the fact that total time in the queue is larger.[33]

If the size of the eligible group is less than 2n and n units are being distributed, the set of the n richest partly overlaps that of the n poorest, which means that some of those in line will also consume the commodity. The money and waiting prices now have to satisfy the condition that those in the overlapping group feel sufficient incentive first to acquire the good by waiting in line and then to keep it rather than to sell it. Consequently, the money price of the commodity cannot exceed its valuation by the poorest in the middle group, otherwise he will not choose to retain it. Conversely, waiting time has to be short enough so that the richest in the middle group will choose to wait in line rather than to purchase the good. The simultaneous satisfaction of these two conditions guarantees no fewer than n waiters and no fewer than n consumers. The joint effect of the two conditions is that the poorest and the richest individuals in the middle as well as the rest in that group now earn some rent. All other individuals, as before, earn some positive rent and so it turns out that loss on the margin is not complete. In this case, then, every individual is better off when trade is permitted.

The importance of this case arises from a fact of political life: Majority voting is often the agent that generates the distribution of the free good. It seems likely, then, that a large fraction of the electorate expects to benefit from many of the approved government programs, so normally the number of units distributed free should be large relative to the population size in the electoral unit. Political considerations also suggest that individuals with low time costs relative to their incomes possess substantial political power. It is unfortunate then (or perhaps one should say "unaccountable") that trading of the good is not more widely permitted.[34]

We have seen that, given the assumption of proportionality between time costs and incomes, all the rich would be better off if permitted to purchase the freely distributed good from the poor who have substituted for them in the service of waiting. It is clear that they would pay a money-price identical with that which would prevail if the same quantity were directly offered under free enterprise. For that given quantity, then, none of the rich would be made better off when the good has been distributed free even when they have contributed nothing in taxes.[35]

This conclusion does not necessarily hold when a greater quantity is distributed free than the market equilibrium one. More importantly, since time-prices are not uniform within levels of income, those with the lower time-price benefit from waiting for the free good rather than paying the money-price in the market. Taking the case of state hunting areas as an example, we would expect that most hunters on these lands view the time-price they pay in crowding or in actual waiting in line as less costly than the money-price implicit in private hunting preserves. In fact, they will support the provision of public lands only if they consider their saving to be greater than their share of tax payments to maintain the public areas.

It is clear from the analysis of the last few sections that the relation between wages and incomes plays an important role in questions of distribution. Since some people who start life with a substantial amount of non-human wealth have little incentive to improve their own market skills, the wage rate for such individuals when they do join the labor force may be lower than the wage rate of many of those with a lower total income.[36] Obviously, the subsidizing of this high-asset and low-wage group is a curious way to help the poor, yet when the cost of time is an effective criterion for the subsidy, members of this group would be among those obtaining the free good. Similarly, we have been assuming that preferences are identical. Since in fact they differ widely, the provision of a free good benefits those who happen to have a taste for it at the expense of all others.

---

[33]Note that time in the queue here performs the function of transferring the good to those who value it more.

[34]If, however, the rationale for providing a free good is to benefit not the poor but rather, say, the producers of that good, it is not difficult to understand the restriction on trading.

[35]Note that the equivalence between waiting and money price does not hold when the poor are those that will be in line to obtain the free good. So, disregarding the question of taxes, the poor are better off with the free good.

[36]Similarly low might be the shadow price of their time when not in the labor market.

Within any income group, then, some are aided by the subsidy more than others.[37]

WAITING BY SUPPLIERS

Thus far the discussion has dealt only with prices set below the market-clearing level: paying particular attention to zero money-price allowed us to concentrate on the time-price. If the intended subsidy is for suppliers rather than demanders we have to deal with both money-price and time-price simultaneously, since the polar case to a zero demand-price is an infinite supply-price. Otherwise, little is changed in turning to a consideration of subsidies to suppliers. Thus when the government attempts to help the unemployed by fixing wages in some public works above the market-clearing level, we are likely to observe applicants for jobs standing in line; and the properties of the queue will be similar to those analyzed earlier. It is possible to find actual instances where sellers rather than buyers engage in lining up. Still, why is it that queues are predominantly manned by buyers, not sellers? The answer lies in the value of the good to be expected in each case.

Suppose the Chicago bank had offered to recipients amounts 1,000-fold larger than those actually given; that is, the first 35 claimants would have obtained $20,000 apiece, the next 50, $10,000 apiece, and so forth. Even with sufficent lead time it seems unlikely that sheer waiting would have determined the recipients. In the actual situation the gain to the 36th claimant from bumping the 35th would have been only $10. The first 35, however, had an incentive to provide some policing of the queue, and the bank itself had a similar incentive. The result was a sufficient policing to deter bumping—the cost of bumping exceeded $10—and the queue was "orderly." The hypothetical case changes that situation because the prizes now seem so valuable as to preclude counting on the "good behavior" of those farther back in the line or out of it altogether. A device

such as writing down the names of persons in order of priority would be totally inadequate. Rights to these amounts might have to be established by such forceful means as physical violence, full-fledged legal services, or what not. In such cases individuals would continue to spend resources to obtain the "free" good, but passive waiting would become subsidiary.

The prevalence of queuing when consumer goods are distributed free may be explained in terms of the low value of the individual allotments. When sellers rather than buyers are being subsidized, the value to each seller is usually high, and so we observe forms of rationing either added to that of waiting or replacing waiting altogether.[38]

Consider the supply of candidates to the restricted number of positions in medical schools. Let us assume that the rate of return in practicing medicine is higher than in alternative occupations. Would a loss of surplus take place here also? And if it would, in what form? It may appear that the selection process used by medical schools will avoid the resource costs associated with queuing. This, however, would be correct only to the extent that the selection is fully predetermined because some individuals hold property rights to the available positions (for example, by virtue of having an M.D. as a father). Many positions, however, are allocated by criteria such as grades and course contents in college. If it could be known in advance who would meet these criteria, the rent associated with acceptance to medical school would once more be appropriated. But since individuals can affect their ranking, they will spend resources to qualify. With perfect knowledge as to conditions in this market, when n positions were available, we would expect that exactly n individuals would attempt to qualify. To the marginal individual the expected return from resources invested to qualify to practice medicine would equal that in his best alternative occupation.[39] So here too, on the margin, the extra value of the good is exactly matched by the resource cost of acquiring it.

Relaxing the assumption of certainty does not change the results substantially although they may

---

[37]As mentioned earlier, restriction on the trading of "free" commodities is sometimes recommended on the ground that other members of society value the consumption of certain goods by the subsidized individual and that while the recipient might benefit from trading away his subsidized good, others would be made worse off. However, when trading is prohibited, the poor are thereby brought to the point which is optimal, not to them, but to the rest of society—their "benefactors." Thus the attempt at efficiency actually annuls the fundamental reason usually advanced for the distribution of goods free of charge—that is, to help the poor.

[38]Anne D. Krueger, The Political Economy of the Rent-Seeking Society, 64 Am. Econ. Rev. 291 (1974), considers some ways in which resources are spent to acquire the rights to import quotas.

[39]Better performance in college may lead to a higher return when practicing medicine. This higher return, however, would be incorporated in the student's calculations, and the equality of return on the margin is after this extra return is accounted for.

change greatly in appearance. Abstracting from the possibility of risk aversion, the marginal individual will be indifferent between medicine and his other alternative opportunities only in the expected sense. If he is "unlucky," his realized rate of return will be lower than normal. If he is "lucky" he will be practicing medicine, and his realized return will be above normal. But to the marginal individual among those contemplating going into medicine the rate of return cannot be higher than normal, otherwise "entry" will take place to drive down the return. The empirical observation of a high rate of return to those practicing medicine may be accurate enough; but these studies seldom, if ever, account for the resource cost of unsuccessful candidates to medical school.

In this situation, no literal queue exists but, as with congestion on highways, some waiting takes place side by side with other economic activities. Since admittance to medical schools is not first come first served but rather is based on other criteria, resources are spent which for the marginal individual bring the net present value from practicing medicine down to the level of the next best alternative.

Without elaborating, we again hypothesize (following Cheung) that since economic forces will tend to reduce to a minimum the cost associated with rationing, and since on the margin all the rent is used up, the best choice among a variety of devices for allocating the subsidized good is that which reduces cost with respect to the intramarginal units—that is, the most inelastic arrangement.

SUMMARY

When a good is available in limited quantity and below market price, in the absence of formal rationing individuals will achieve equilibrium by paying the pecuniary price and spending such additional resources on acquiring the good as will bring them to the point at which the marginal individual neither benefits nor loses from obtaining it. Queuing is a customary form of obtaining such goods. The main implications of this hypothesis are that the length of waiting time is basically independent of the speed with which the good is actually handed out and, rather, depends on the size and number of batches to be distributed. The larger each of these is, the shorter the time per unit of the good an individual must wait. An additional implication is that a price ceiling below market price imposed on a factor will result in an increase in the price of the product.

The resource cost of this form of allocation, time spent in the queue, represents a cost of establishing property rights in the good and is over and above the cost required to produce it. To individuals in the queue, the resource cost of producing the good is immaterial. For the marginal individual, his waiting time completely exhausts the benefit of obtaining the "free" good. Intramarginal individuals may benefit; and the less elastic their demand, the larger is their gain.

The attempt to redistribute income through the provision of free goods is costly because the time spent may be substantial compared with the distributive effect achieved. Moreover, not every good provided free necessarily helps the poor; the beneficiaries may often be among the rich. Within any income class the benefits are unevenly distributed: those with lower time cost as well as those with a "taste" for the free good benefit more. Finally, when the poor do obtain the commodity, they, as well as the buyers, could be made better off by being allowed to trade it. The ban on such action cannot benefit them.

The Theory of Discrimination*

KENNETH J. ARROW

Kenneth J. Arrow (B.S., City College of CUNY, 1940; M.A., Columbia University, 1941; Ph.D., 1951) was born in 1921 in New York City. The 1972 Nobel Laureate in Economics, he has been the Joan Kenney Professor of Economics and Professor of Operations Research at Stanford University since 1979, and since 1948, a consultant to the RAND Corporation. Professor Arrow previously served on the faculties of the University of Chicago and Harvard University, and has held Visiting appointments at Massachusetts Institute of Technology, Churchill College at Cambridge University, and the Institute for Advanced Studies in Vienna, Austria. Perhaps the most widely recognized of Professor Arrow's books is *Social Choice and Individual Values,* which related collective choices to individual preferences and traced out the logical difficulties of preference aggregation. He is justly renowned as well for his seminal writings on general equilibrium systems; the economics of information, uncertainty, production functions, and optimal inventory; and social investment policy. A scholar of international reputation, Professor Arrow's contributions to the understanding of economics have been recognized by many honors and awards, including the John Bates Clark Medal of the American Economic Association in 1957, the John R. Commons Lecture Award from Omicron Delta Epsilon in 1973, and honorary degrees from nine universities worldwide. Professor Arrow is the past president of The American Economic Association, the Econometric Society, The Institute of Management Sciences, the Western Economic Association, and the International Society of Inventory Research, and currently serves as president of the International Economic Association.

*Reprinted from *Discrimination in Labor Markets,* edited by O. Ashenfelter and A. Rees, by permission of Princeton University Press. Copyright 1973, pp. 3–33.

1. INTRODUCTION

The fact that different groups of workers, be they skilled or unskilled, black or white, male or female, receive different wages, invites the explanation that the different groups must differ according to some characteristic valued on the market. In standard economic theory, we think first of differences in productivity. The notion of discrimination involves the additional concept that personal characteristics of the worker unrelated to productivity are also valued on the market. Such personal characteristics as race, ethnic background, and sex have been frequently adduced in this context.

Discrimination in this paper is considered only as it appears on the market. Obviously, one can have discrimination in the same sense whenever decisions are made that concern other individuals, namely, when personal characteristics other than those properly relevant enter into the decision. Deliberate racial segregation and discrimination in entrance to schools and colleges, deprivation of the right to vote along social and sexual lines, and discriminatory taxation are all examples of nonmarket discrimination.

It may as well be admitted that the term "discrimination" has value implications that can never be completely eradicated, though they can be sterilized for specific empirical and descriptive analyses. I have spoken of personal characteristics that are "unrelated to productivity" and not "properly relevant." These terms imply definitions of product and of relevancy which are themselves value judgments or at any rate decisions by the scholar. The black steel worker may be thought of as producing blackness as well as steel, both evaluated in the market. We are singling out the former as a special subject for analysis because somehow we think it appropriate for the steel industry to produce steel and not for it to produce a black or white work force.

However, the value judgments are intrinsic only in determining which wage differences we regard as worth studying as an example of discrimination, *not* in the empirical or theoretical analysis of any form of discrimination once specified.

In the following, I will address myself specifically to racial discrimination in the labor market. For the most part, the analysis extends with no difficulty to sexual discrimination. The other markets in which discrimination has been most observed, especially housing but also insurance and capital, are analyzed by the same general methods, but the operation of these markets has led more often to simple exclusion and less to price differentials.

The basic aim here is to use as far as possible neoclassical tools in the analysis of discrimination.

As will be seen, even though the basic neoclassical assumptions of utility and profit-maximization are always retained, many of the usual assumptions will be relaxed at one point or another: convexity of indifference surfaces, costless adjustment, perfect information, perfect capital markets. As I will try to show, the abandonment of each of these assumptions is motivated by a clearly compelling reason in the theoretical structure of the subject. Personally, I believe there are many other economic phenomena whose explanation entails the abandonment of each of these assumptions, so the steps proposed here are not ad hoc analyses but should be important elements in a more general theory capable of analyzing the effects of social factors on economic behavior without either lumping them into an uninformative category of "imperfections" or jumping to a precipitate rejection of neoclassical theory with all its analytic power.

The first application of neoclassical theory to discrimination that I know of is that of Edgeworth, but the main study to date has been that of Becker.[1] The analysis to be presented here appears in a more technical form in an earlier paper.[2] It seeks to develop further Becker's models and to relate them more closely to the theory of general competitive equilibrium, though frequently by way of contrast rather than agreement.

Since I am presenting here the theory of discrimination in the labor market and not the entire theory of racial differences in income, I abstract from differences in productivity between the groups of workers. In an empirical study, it will be necessary to allow for this possibility. In the case of blacks and whites, some possible causes of productivity differences have been established (differences in educational quantity and quality, family size and socio-economic status, and household headed by woman); and others surmised (culturally varying attitudes toward work and future-orientation derived from the heritage of slav-

---

[1] See for example, F. Y. Edgeworth, "Equal Pay to Men and Women for Equal Work," *Economic Journal,* 31 (1922), 431–457; and Gary Becker, *The Economics of Discrimination* (Chicago: University of Chicago Press, 1959).

[2] For further analysis see Kenneth J. Arrow, "Models of Job Discrimination," Chapter 2 in A. H. Pascal (ed.) *Racial Discrimination in Economic Life* (Lexington, Mass.: D. C. Heath, 1972) pp. 83–102; and Arrow, "Some Models of Race in the Labor Market," Chapter 6 in A. H. Pascal, *ibid.*

ery and other historical factors).[3] These differences themselves may be the result of discrimination in other areas of life. But for theoretical analysis of discrimination in the labor market, it is legitimate to assume that there are two groups of workers, to be denoted by B and W, which are perfect substitutes in production.

For the simplest model, then, we have a large number of firms all producing the same product with the same production function. Discrimination means that some economic agent has some negative valuation for B or positive valuation for W, or both, a valuation for which the agent both is willing to pay and has the opportunity to pay. The agents who could possibly discriminate are the employer, who might sacrifice profits to reduce or eliminate B employment in his plant, or the W workers who might accept a lower wage to work in a plant with more W and less B workers. (It is also possible that, for products sold on a face-to-face basis, customers might discriminate by being willing to pay higher prices to buy from whites; this case could be studied along similar lines but will not be dealt with here.) Not all discriminatory feelings can find expression in the market; an entrepreneur who has a distaste for competing against firms with B workers has no way, within the economic system at least, of expressing his tastes and therefore of influencing wage levels.

I assume that, given the tastes, the markets work smoothly. General equilibrium requires full employment of both B and W workers; the wages of both will adjust to clear the market, and the discriminatory tastes will be reflected in wage differences.

Let us first consider the simplest case, that in which the employer discriminates. Then he accepts a trade-off between profits, π, and the numbers of B and W employees. That is, we suppose he seeks to maximize,

not profits, but a utility function, $U(\pi, B, W)$. We assume, to get the simplest case, that there is only one type of labor; in the short run, we also take capital as given, so that output is $f(W + B)$, since the two kinds of labor are perfect substitutes (at a one-to-one ratio). If we take output as numeraire, then profits are given by the expression

$$\pi = f(W + B) - w_W W - w_B B, \qquad (1)$$

where w_W and w_B are the wage rates, taken as given by the employers. If we proceed along conventional lines, the employer equates the marginal productivity of each hand of labor to the price to him. But here the "price" of B labor is the market price, w_B, *plus* the price the employer is willing to pay, in terms of profits, for reducing his B labor force by one. This second term is what Becker has termed the "discrimination coefficient," to be designated as d_B; it is the negative of the marginal rate of substitution of profits for B labor. If, as we usually suppose, the marginal utility of B labor is negative, then the discrimination coefficient, d_B, is positive.

In symbols,

$$MP_B = w_B + d_B, \qquad (2)$$

where $d_B = -MR\pi_{,B}$. Similarly,

$$MP_W = w_W + d_W, \qquad (3)$$

where d_W is negative (or zero if the employer has no positive liking for having W workers). But we are assuming that the two types of labor are interchangeable in production, so that $MP_W = MP_B = MP_L$, say. Then, from (2) and (3), $w_W + d_{aW} = w_B + d_B$, or

$$w_W - w_B = d_B - d_W > 0, \qquad (4)$$

so that equilibrium requires that W wages exceed B wages, as might be expected.

For the moment, assume that all firms have the same utility function, $U(\pi, B, W,)$. It then appears reasonable to assume that all hire the same amounts of B and W (but we will return to this point in the next section). Then each firm's labor force is the same, and the allocation of labor is efficient. The effects of discrimination are purely distributive. The most obvious implication then is that B workers are paid less than their marginal product, so that the W workers and employers together gain. Also, the W workers clearly gain, or at least do not lose, from (3), with $d_W \leqq 0$. The effect on profits, however, depends on the exact nature of the utility function.

[3] See for example, O. D. Duncan, "Inheritance of Poverty or Inheritance of Race?" in D. P. Moynihan (ed.) *On Understanding Poverty* (New York: Basic Books, 1969), Ch. 4, pp. 85–110. Although my concern here is with discrimination and not with productivity differences, I must note my skepticism about the frequently made argument that blacks have less future-orientation. For this disregards the well-known fact that at any given income level blacks save at least as much as whites. This remains essentially true even when "income" is understood to mean "permanent income"; see Milton Friedman, *The Theory of the Consumption Function* (Princeton, N.J.: Princeton University Press, 1957), pp. 79–85; and H. W. Mooney and L. R. Klein, "Negro-white Savings Differentials and the Consumption Function Problem," *Econometrica*, 21 (1953), 425–456.

Under the assumption made, it follows from (1-3) and the fact that $MP_W = MP_B = MP_L$ that,

$$\pi = f(L) - (MP_L) L + d_W W + d_B B, \qquad (5)$$

where $L = W + B$, the total labor force of the firm. If there were no discrimination, profits would be,

$$\pi_0 = f(L) - (MP_L) L,$$

and therefore the change in profits is simply,

$$\pi - \pi_0 = d_W W + d_B B. \qquad (6)$$

The right-hand term has a simple interpretation. If we consider an increase in the firm's labor force with the proportions of W and B workers constant, then the negative of the marginal rate of substitution of profits for this balanced increase is simply $d_W (W/L) + d_B (B/L)$; this is the firm's need for additional profits to compensate it for a balanced increase in size. This term may of course be positive or negative.

However, a plausible hypothesis which we shall maintain hereafter is that employers' satisfactions depend only on the ratio of B to W workers. In that case,

$$d_W W + d_B B = 0, \qquad (7)$$

and (6) tells us that employers neither gain nor lose by their discriminatory behavior. The entire effect is that of a transfer from B to W workers.

Let us now relax the assumption that utility functions are identical among firms. We continue to assume that for each firm, the utility depends only on the ratio of W to B workers, but some firms may be more discriminatory than others, in the sense that the marginal rate of substitution of profits for B workers will be more negative at any given ratio, B/W. Equations (4) and (7) hold for each firm, at least each firm that employs both types of workers. They can be regarded as a pair of linear equations in d_W and d_B, to yield,

$$d_B = W(w_W - w_B)/(W + B),$$
$$d_W = -B(w_W - w_B)/(W + B),$$

which can be rewritten,

$$W/L = d_B/(w_W - w_B);$$
$$B/L = -d_W/(w_W - w_B).$$

Since $d_B > 0$, if there are both B and W workers, it must be that $w_W > w_B$, as before. We will observe firms with different ratios of W to L. The firms that display the most discrimination at the margin, i.e. the highest values of d_B, have the highest ratios of

W to L. Thus an observation on all the firms in existence at equilibrium will reveal a dispersion of W-proportions in the labor force, and these ratios will measure the varying degrees of discrimination. Thus a partial degree of segregation appears; the B workers tend to be found in the less discriminatory firms, the W workers in the more discriminatory ones.

However, further analysis leads to implications which might raise some empirical questions. Specifically, equation (2) still holds, with $MP_B = MP_L$. Hence, according to the model, MP_L is higher for more discriminating firms. But then if we assume diminishing marginal productivity of labor, it follows that, the less discriminatory the firm, the larger it will be. This accords with common sense; discrimination is costly to the entrepreneur and acts as a tax on him, since it shifts his demand for labor to the more costly component. Hence, it restricts his scale.

Since MP_L is no longer the same from firm to firm, it follows that production is no longer efficient. The previous strong statements about the incidence of discrimination no longer hold exactly either. However, their general thrust is still probably correct. Efficiency losses are not apt to be great, and the main redistribution is still likely to be from B workers to W workers.

It has been seen that competition tends to reduce the degree of discrimination in the market, in the sense that the unweighted average of discrimination coefficients of the different firms exceeds the average weighted in proportion to the number of workers.

This result, which may or may not be empirically reasonable, appears more strongly and less likely when one pushes the analysis into the long run. Now we are assuming that capital, which has been hitherto held fixed, is adjusted optimally to the size of the labor force. Then capital will flow to the more profitable enterprises which, in this context, are the less discriminatory. In the long run, output is therefore simply proportional to labor (assuming the production function displays constant returns to capital and labor). The marginal product of labor is then constant. As a result, the competitive effect just studied assumes an exaggerated form. Only the least discriminatory firms survive. Indeed, if there were any firms which did not discriminate at all, these would be the only ones to survive the competitive struggle. Since in fact racial discrimination has survived for a long time, we must assume that the model just presented must have some limitation to which we will return in Section 4.

We have dealt extensively with the assumption of discrimination by employers. But, as we observed earlier, discrimination by co-workers is also a possibility. The most straightforward extension of the preceding analysis is to the case of complementary services. Suppose now there are two kinds of workers, say foremen and floor workers. It is the foremen who like working with W's and dislike working with B's. As before, we assume that the likes or dislikes are governed by the ratio of W to B floor workers. Each foreman then chooses among alternative employment opportunities on the basis of both wages and the W/B ratio. Assume that all foremen have the same utility function.

The equilibrium in this model is a trifle unorthodox. Instead of an equilibrium wage for foremen, there is an equilibrium relation between foremen's wages and W/B ratios in firms. Every firm must lie on this curve, and the equilibrium curve will be one of the foremen's indifference curves between wages and W/B.

Let F be the number of foremen, and w_F their wage. Then the firm faces fixed w_W and w_B for the floor workers and a fixed *relation*,

$$w_F = w_F(W/L) \qquad (8)$$

where $L = W + B$ is the total floor force. The firm's short-run profits are defined by,

$$\pi = f(L, F) - w_W W - w_B B - w_F F, \qquad (9)$$

where it is assumed, as before, that W and B floor workers are perfect substitutes.

Assume now that firms have no discriminatory tastes. They seek only to maximize profits. They will still not hire B workers at equal wages with W since an increase in W decreases the wages and therefore the cost of F, while an increase in B increases the cost of F. Hence, a W worker is worth more than his marginal product, while a B worker is worth less, exactly as in the case of employer discrimination. Further, the extent of the premiums over or deficits from marginal product depends only on the ratio of W to B. Hence, the previous analysis applies with suitable modifications. W workers are paid more than their marginal product, B workers less. If all firms wind up with the same levels of W and B, then the results are entirely parallel to those for employer discrimination: production remains efficient, and the

entire incidence of the foremen's discrimination falls negatively on the B workers and positively to an equal extent on the W workers.

As in the case of employer discrimination, the extent of the wage difference between B and W workers depends on the extent of discrimination. The precise formula is of some interest. Recall that, by (8), w_F is a function of the ratio, W/L. By w'_F, I will mean the derivative of w_F with respect to this ratio (this is negative). Then w'_F/w_F is the proportional rate of change of the demanded wage rate (along the equilibrium indifference curve between foremen's wages and W proportion in the floor force) and therefore is a measure of discriminatory tastes. Let S_F be total payments to foremen, S_L total payments to floor workers. Then the following has been shown:[4]

$$\frac{w_W - w_B}{MP_L} = -\frac{w'_F}{w_F}\frac{S_F}{S_L} \qquad (10)$$

The left-hand side is the market wage differential due to discriminatory tastes of foremen relative to the wage level in the absence of discrimination.

This formula has an interesting aspect. Given the degree of discrimination as measured by $-w'_F/w_F$, the observed wage differential depends on the ratio S_F/S_L. That is, the more important the share of foremen in the output of the firm relative to floor laborers, the greater the wage differential.

The language of the preceding analysis has assumed that it is the foremen or other supervisory employees who discriminate according to the composition of the floor workers. But the analysis itself is completely abstract. It may be illuminating to reverse the roles. Suppose that production workers have strong discriminatory feelings about their supervisors. Certainly the idea that white workers strongly resent being bossed by black supervisors or male workers by female foremen (foreladies? forepersons?) is a common one. Then if in (10) we understand by W and B those kinds of supervisory workers, by L the total number of such workers, and by F the floor workers, we have an excellent explanation of discrimination against B supervisory workers, for S_F then would be very large indeed compared with S_L.

Foremen may possibly differ in their tastes for discrimination. One might suppose that this will lead to a reduction in market wage differentials, analo-

[4]Arrow, "Some Models of Race in the Labor Market," Section B.

gous to the situation with employer discrimination. But a fuller analysis of this case remains to be done.

2. NONCONVEXITIES IN INDIFFERENCE SURFACES AND OPPORTUNITIES

I have gradually become convinced that the usual assumption that indifference surfaces are convex is inapplicable to the case of racial discrimination and indeed to many other problems in the economics of externalities. Pollution provides another example; Starrett has already pointed to the importance of nonconvexity in this context.[5] Assumptions which seem very reasonable in the contexts of discriminatory behavior *necessarily* imply a nonconvexity of the indifference surfaces of the firms in the case of employer discrimination or of the firm's profit function in the case of discrimination by complementary workers.

Actually, my view is that nonconvexity of indifference surfaces is in fact a widespread phenomenon. An excellent example in commodities with no externalities is residential location. One *could* after all live half the time in one place and half in the other. Convexity implies that such an arrangement would be at least as good as the least preferred of the two locations. If one is indifferent to the two, then one will prefer the mixture. In fact, taken literally, convexity would imply that individuals would be willing to spend half of any minute in one place and half in the other. But (except for a few "beautiful people") most individuals find it preferable to live in one place, even though there may be another to which they are indifferent.

Indeed, if one looks through the literature, it is hard to find a convincing intuitive explanation of convexity of indifference surfaces. The best argument is that convexity is a necessary and sufficient condition for the continuity of demand functions. But this argument applies only to individual demand functions. Since each individual is small on the scale of the entire market, even the largest discontinuity in an individual demand function implies a negligible discontinuity in the market demand function. Hence, observations which suggest approximate continuity in market demand functions in no way imply convexity of indifference surfaces. In particular, the ex-

istence of general competitive equilibrium remains unaffected, or, to be precise, the existence of an approximate equilibrium of supply and demand on all markets can be demonstrated. (This line of argument was suggested initially by Farrell and subsequently developed by Bator, Rothenberg, Aumann, and Starr; for one exposition, see Arrow and Hahn.)[6]

It is true that the market demand function, if it is effectively continuous, can be derived by adding up a new set of individual demand functions, each derived from a "convexified" indifference map obtained from the original by filling in all the holes in the indifference surfaces. From the point of view of prices and total market quantities, the newly formed indifference map predicts as well as does the original, and therefore one might be tempted to assume that one could act "as if" indifference surfaces were convex, though with some flat surfaces. But there is a loss of information, for the *distribution* of goods among individuals is quite different from what it would be if all individuals had convex indifference surfaces. Thus, in our residential location example, the market totals (how many people-hours are spent in each place) and the rents in the two places are well predicted by the convex approximation. But recognizing the underlying nonconvexities enables us to predict that half the people will be in one place all the time and half in the other, instead of each individual's spending half his time in one place and half in the other.

Let me give a brief diagrammatic illustration. Suppose every individual has the same indifference map, as given by Fig. 1, and the same initial endowment, represented by A. One's initial reaction, conditioned by years of working with convex indifference maps, is to assume that there is no trade; since all individuals are alike in every economic respect, they should wind up alike, which in this case means each with his own initial bundle. But this is clearly false. In fact the

---

[5]See D. Starrett, "Fundamental Non-convexities in the Theory of Externalities," *Journal of Economic Theory,* 4 (1972), 180–199.

[6]For further analysis, see M. J. Farrell, "The Convexity Assumption in the Theory of Competitive Markets," *Journal of Political Economy,* 67 (1969), 377–379; Francis Bator, "Convexity, Efficiency, and Markets," *Journal of Political Economy,* 69 (1961), 480–483; Jerome Rothenberg, "Non-convexity, Aggregation, and Pareto Optimality," *Journal of Political Economy,* 68 (1960), 435–468; R. J. Aumann, "Existence of Competitive Equilibria in Markets with a Continuum of Traders," *Econometrica,* 34 (1966), 1–17; R. Starr, "Quasi-equilibria in Markets with Nonconvex Preferences," *Econometrica,* 37 (1969), 25–38; and Kenneth J. Arrow and Frank Hahn, *General Competitive Analysis* (San Francisco: Holden-Day, 1971), Ch. 7.

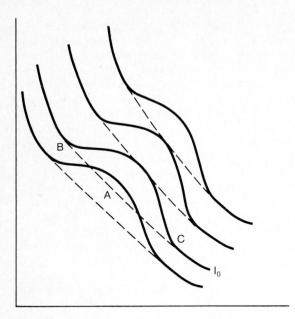

Fig. 1

equilibrium can be obtained as follows: convexify each indifference curve by filling in the hole with a straight line segment tangent to the curve at both ends, as, for example, the segment BC on curve I_0. Now we see that, if we pretend for the moment that the convexified map is the true indifference map for each individual, then each individual winds up on the convexified curve I_0. Since this curve is flat at the point A, the price ratio is determined by the slope of BC. Now return to the individual, who has the original indifference curve I_0. At these prices, he will maximize utility at two different points, B and C, but not at any point in between. If, for example, A is half-way between B and C, then market equilibrium is realized by having half the individuals at B and half at C. If A is two-thirds of the way from B to C, the market equilibrium is realized by having two-thirds of the individuals buy the bundle C and one-third the bundle B. Note that each individual is at a point of maximum utility for him subject to his budget constraint, so that this is truly a competitive equilibrium and therefore efficient. (The earlier reference to "approximate equilibrium" is relevant when there are not enough individuals to split them in the right proportions between B and C. Thus, if A is .71 of the way from B to C and there are only 50 indi-

viduals in the economy, there should be $35\frac{1}{2}$ individuals at C and $14\frac{1}{2}$ at B. Thus, at C or B the discrepancy between supply and demand cannot be reduced below half an individual. This is a relatively minor discrepancy between supply and demand.)

Thus nonconvexity implies the existence of distinct *niches* for economic agents in a sense of the work which I take to be close to that used in ecology. One observes agents, identical in their economic data, engaged in diverse consumption patterns or other economic activities. Any given agent may be indifferent between several of these niches, but equilibrium requires their coexistence. This argument underlies Adam Smith's discussion of specialization as opposed to Ricardo's, which was based on differences in the productivities of individuals or nations; it has been made explicit in an important but neglected paper of Houthakker.[7]

Let me now apply these abstract concepts to racial discrimination. We take up a model due to Becker and in a different form to Welch and not analyzed above.[8] Now we locate the discriminatory tastes in the W workers who are perfect substitutes for the B workers. To keep matters as simple as possible, assume there is only one kind of labor. Then, analogous to the assumption made about complementary forms of labor, we now assume that W workers have an indifference map between wages and the proportion W, so that at equilibrium, there is a relation,

$$w_W = w_W(W/L), \qquad (11)$$

where w_W decreases as W/L increases from 0 to 1. As part of profit maximization, the firm will certainly seek that combination of W and B which will minimize the cost of hiring whatever total number of workers, $W + B = L$, it does hire. This cost is

$$C(W, B) = w_W(W/L)\,W + w_B B. \qquad (12)$$

But it is easy to see that a firm will always achieve minimum cost with either an all-W or an all-B labor force. The two might be equally cheap, but certainly any combination with W and B both positive will be more costly than at least one extreme case and possibly more costly than both. To see this, consider two cases:

[7]See Hendrick S. Houthakker, "Economics and Biology: Specialization and Speciation," *Kyklos*, 9 (1956), 181–187.
[8]See for example, Gary Becker, *op. cit.*; and Finis Welch, "Labor Market Discrimination: An Interpretation of Income Differences in the Rural South," *Journal of Political Economy*, 75 (1967), 225–240.

(a) $w_W(1) \geqq w_B$: Recall that $W/L = 1$ means an all-W labor force. Then for any W, $0 < W < L$, $w_W(W/L) > w_W(1) \geqq w_B$ and therefore $w_W(W/L)$ $W + w_B B > w_B (W + B) = w_B L$; hence, an all-$B$ labor force, with cost $w_B L$, is cheaper than the mixture. An all-W labor force has a cost $w_W(1)L$ and then $w_W(1)L \geqq w_B L$, so the all-W labor force is at any rate no less costly; if $w_W(1) = w_B$, the two extreme cases are equally cheap.

(b) $w_W(1) < w_B$: Then if $W < L$, $w_W(W/L)W +$ $w_B B \geqq w_W(1)W + w_B B > w_W(1) (W + B) = w_W(1)$ L; the all-W labor force is cheaper than any other labor force.

Hence, if $w_W(1) > w_B$, every firm will find it cheapest to select an all-B labor force, and if $w_W(1) < w_B$, every firm will minimize cost by hiring an all-W labor force. But equilibrium requires full employment of both types of workers. The equilibrium then requires $w_W(1) = w_B$. But even then no firm will hire both W and B workers. At equilibrium every firm is segregated, but then the only observed wage for W workers is for those in all-W firms, i.e. $w_W(1)$, which is equal to w_B. Therefore, discrimination by W workers will not result in market wage differentials but instead does result in segregation.

In technical terms, the function, $C(W, B)$ is not a convex function, specifically, the isocost curves in W-B space are not concave to the origin. Convexity implies a tendency to the middle, to compromise; but here we have a rushing to extremes. We also have the characteristic implication of nonconvexity, a dispersion of firms with basically identical market opportunities into discrete niches.

Now, in going back over the analyses of Section 2, it can be observed that the case just discussed, of discriminatory tastes by a perfect substitute group of workers, is strikingly similar to that of discriminatory tastes by workers of a complementary type, the "foremen" of our example. Though a detailed analysis of the nonconvexities in this case has not yet been made, it is clear that the profit function defined by (9) is not in general a concave function. Rather, the surface defined by profits as a function of W and B has holes scattered through it. Hence, it is at least possible that for certain values of w_W and w_B and some equilibrium relation, $w_F(W/L)$, there are several distinct points of maximum profits. Equilibrium on the three labor markets (W, B, and F) may be achieved by different amounts of these, even though each firm has the same production function and each faces the same wages

for W and B and the same relation between w_F and W/L. Thus, there will be a partial segregation by firms.

The relation (10) stated earlier still holds for each firm, so the previous conclusions remain valid.

We can now reconsider the theory of employer discrimination. The utility function, $U(\pi, B, W)$, depends, it has been assumed, only on the ratio B/W. But it is shown in the Appendix that such a utility function cannot possibly have convex indifference surfaces everywhere.[9] Therefore it is possible and in fact likely that in the short run equilibrium will require the coexistence of firms of different sizes with different W/B ratios, even if all firms have the same utility function. Thus at least partial segregation is a likely outcome of the utility-maximization theory. All the firms will have to have the same utility, so that the larger firms will be those with the larger proportions of W workers since utility increases with π and with W/B.

In the long run, indeed, it can be seen that with constant returns to scale, there must be perfect segregation and equality of wages. For suppose there is not perfect segregation, i.e. there is at least one firm hiring both B and W workers. For that firm, $d_B > 0$ and $d_W < 0$. Since MP_L is constant in the long run, it follows from the preceding section that all B workers will be in firms with the smallest d_B and all W workers in firms with the (algebraically) smallest d_W. Then all firms have the same d_B and same d_W and therefore all have the same W/B ratio. The equilibrium values of w_W and w_B will be $MP_L - d_W$ and $MP_L - d_B$ respectively, where MP_L is the long-run marginal product of labor, a constant. But then any firm which increases its B/W ratio slightly can make positive profits; by increasing its scale, it can make indefinitely large profits with only a slightly altered W/B ratio. It would therefore have a higher utility, so we have a contradiction to the existence of equilibrium with at least one integrated firm. Hence, all firms are segregated. In an all-B firm, $d_B = 0$, for an increase in B does not change the W/B ratio and therefore leaves utility unchanged. Similarly, in an all-W firm, $d_W = 0$. It follows that, as in the case of discrimination by substitutes, the long-run equilibrium is one of perfect segregation and equal wages.

[9] The nonconvexity that arises when only ratios matter is of importance in the theory of pollution also. For the characteristic situation there is that the pollutee is faced with consuming air or water in which the proportion of pollutants is given to him.

The corresponding analysis for discrimination by complementary employees has not been worked out. It can be conjectured, though, that segregation plus possibly competition among foremen with varying discriminatory tastes will greatly weaken wage differentials.

3. COSTS OF ADJUSTMENT

Utility-maximization theories, then, provide a coherent and by no means unreasonable account of the effect of discriminatory tastes on the market in the short run. Yet they become unsatisfactory in the long run. I propose as a possible explanation that long-run adjustment processes do not work as perfectly as they are usually assumed to. When there are significant nonconvexities, the adjustment processes called for must be very rapid indeed; marginal adjustments are punished, not rewarded. In the case of discrimination by substitute workers, the firm would have to be willing to fire its entire all-W labor force and replace it by an all-B labor force or vice versa in response to a very small change in wages. It is not unreasonable to assume that there are costs, not ordinarily taken account of, which will restrain the firm from being quite so free in its adjustment behavior.

Now the idea that adjustment is costly has appeared in several diverse areas of economics. The costs of growth enter explicitly in some versions of the dynamic theory of the firm.[10] That is, the growth of the firm imposes a cost which depends on the rate of growth and which is additional to the purchase of capital goods.

The same principle, that capital costs of an unconventional kind play an important role in economic behavior and decisions, has been applied to the study of labor turnover, a problem more closely connected with ours. Operations researchers, in trying to draw up plans for hiring personnel, have incorporated in their models a fixed cost of hiring an individual. Sometimes it is also held that there is a cost attached to firing as well. These costs are partly in administration, partly in training. Even workers who have already been generally trained in the kind of work to be done must learn the ways of the par-

ticular firm. This approach, it has been argued by some, has important general economic implications; it implies that firms should not adjust their labor force to cyclical shifts in demand, since they then may incur both hiring and firing costs, costs that are avoided if the worker is retained during slack periods. Workers are being held in employment even though they contribute little to output to avoid the costs of rehiring them in the expected future boom. I do not know whether this explanation is in fact adequate but merely note that it is seriously considered.

A similar consideration may well explain why the adjustments which would wipe out racial wage differentials do not occur or at least are greatly retarded. We have only to assume that the employer makes an investment, let us call it a *personnel investment,* every time he hires a worker. He makes this investment with the expectation of making a competitive return on it; if he himself has no discriminatory feelings, the wage rate in full equilibrium will equal the marginal product of labor less the return on the personnel investment. Let us consider the simplest of the above models, that of discrimination by fellow employees who are perfect substitutes. If the firm starts with an all-W labor force, it will not find it profitable to fire that force, in which its personnel capital has already been sunk, and hire an all-B force, in which a new investment has to be made, simply because B wages are now slightly less than W wages. Of course, if the wage difference is large enough, it does pay to make the shift.

Obviously, in a situation like this, where there are costs to change, history matters a good deal. A fully dynamic analysis appears to be very difficult, but some insight can be obtained by study of a very special case. I here present only the results; the argument will be found in an earlier paper.[11] Suppose initially there are no B workers in the labor force. Then some enter; at the same time, there is an additional entry of W workers, and some new equilibrium emerges. Under the kinds of assumptions we have been making, a change, if it occurs at all, must be an extreme change, but there are now three kinds of extremes, or corner maxima. The typical firm may remain segregated W, though possibly adding more W workers; it may switch entirely to a segregated B state; or it may find it best to keep its present W workers while adding B workers. In the last case, of

[10]See Edith Penrose, *The Theory of the Growth of the Firm* (Oxford: Oxford University Press, 1959); and Robin Marris, *The Economic Theory of 'Managerial' Capitalism* (Cambridge: Cambridge University Press, 1964).

[11]Arrow, "Some Models of Race in the Labor Market," Section E.

course, it will have to increase the wages of the W workers to compensate for their feelings of dislike; but it may still find it profitable to do so because replacing the existing W workers by B workers means wasting a personnel investment. If we stick closely to the model with all of its artificial conditions, we note that only the all-W firms are absorbing the additional supply of W workers, so that there must be some of those in the new equilibrium situation. On the other hand, there must be some firms that are all-B or else some integrated firms whose new workers are B's in order to absorb the new B workers. It can be concluded in either case, however, that there will always remain a wage difference between B and W workers in this model. Further, there will be some segregated W firms. Whether the remaining firms will be segregated B or integrated depends on the degree of discriminatory feelings by W workers against mixing with B workers.

I have not worked out the corresponding analysis for the case where there are several types of workers with different degrees of discriminatory feelings against racial mixtures in the complementary types. Nevertheless, one surmises easily that similar conditions will prevail.

The generalization that may be hazarded on the basis of the discussion thus far can be stated as follows. If we start from a position where B workers enter an essentially all-W world, the discriminatory feelings by employers and by employees, both of the same and of complementary types, will lead to a difference in wages. The forces of competition and the tendency to profit-maximization operate to mitigate these differences. However, the basic fact of a personnel investment prevents these counteracting tendencies from working with full force. In the end, we remain with wage differences coupled with tendencies to segregation.[12]

4. IMPERFECT INFORMATION

There is an alternative interpretation of employer discrimination. It can be thought of as reflecting not tastes but perception of reality. That is, if employers have the preconceived idea that B workers have lower productivity than W workers, they may be expected to be willing to hire them only at lower wages. (Phelps has independently introduced a similar theory.)[13] One must examine in detail the conditions under which this argument can be maintained, that is, the conditions under which the effects of these preconceptions are the same as those of discrimination in the strict sense of tastes.

First, the employer must be able to distinguish W workers from B workers. More precisely, the cost of making the distinction should be reasonably low. An employer might derive from his reading the opinion that an employee with an unresolved Oedipus complex will be disloyal to him as a father-substitute; but if the only way of determining the existence of an unresolved Oedipus complex is a psychoanalysis of several years at the usual rates, he may well decide that it is not worthwhile for him to use this as a basis for hiring. Skin color and sex are cheap sources of information. Therefore prejudices (in the literal sense of pre-judgments, judgments made in advance of the evidence) about such differentia can be easily implemented. School diplomas undoubtedly play an excessive role in employer decisions for much the same reason.

Second, the employer must incur some cost before he can determine the employee's true productivity. If the productivity could be determined costlessly, there would be no reason to use surrogate information, necessarily less valid even under the most favorable conditions. I suppose, therefore, that the employer must hire the employee first and then incur a personnel investment cost, as discussed in the last section, before he can determine the worker's productivity. This personnel investment might, for example, include a period of training, only after which is it possible to ascertain the worker's productivity; or indeed it may be only a period of observation long enough for reliable determination of productivity. In the absence of a personnel investment cost, after all, the employer could simply hire everyone who applied and fire those unqualified, or pay them according to productivity.

Third, it must be assumed that the employer has some idea or at any rate preconception of the distribution of productivity within each of the two categories of workers.

The simplest model to bring out the implication of these assumptions seems to be the following. Suppose there are two kinds of jobs, complementary to

---

[12]The preceding five paragraphs have been quoted, with minor alterations, from Arrow, "Models of Job Discrimination," pp. 94–96.

[13]See Edwin S. Phelps, "The Statistical Theory of Racism and Sexism," *American Economic Review,* 62 (1972), 659–661.

each other, say unskilled and skilled. All workers are qualified to perform unskilled jobs, and this is known to all employers. Only some workers, however, are *qualified* to hold skilled jobs. The employers need make no personnel investment in hiring unskilled workers but must make such an investment for skilled workers. The employer cannot know whether any given worker is qualified; however, he does believe that the probability that a random W worker is qualified is p_W and that a random B worker is qualified is p_B. An employer will eventually know whether or not a worker hired for a skilled position is in fact qualified, but this information is not available to other employers. He thus can count on keeping the qualified workers he hires.

Let r be the necessary return per worker on the personnel investment for skilled jobs. If a W worker is hired, then with probability p_W he is qualified; his productivity is MP_S, the marginal productivity of skilled workers, but the employer must pay a wage, w_W, so that the net gain to the employer is $MP_S - w_W$. On the other hand, if the worker hired turns out to be unqualified, the employer receives nothing. Hence, the expected return to a W worker hired is $(MP_S - w_W) \ p_W$. If the employer is risk-neutral, this must be equal to r. Similarly,

$$r = (MP_S - w_B) \ p_B, \tag{13}$$

and therefore,

$$w_W = qw_B + (1 - q) \ MP_S, \tag{14}$$

where $q = p_B/p_W$. Thus, if, for any reason, $p_B < p_W$, w_W is a weighted average of w_B and MP_S and therefore lies between them; since from (13) we must have $w_B < MP_S$ (in order that the employer recoup his personnel investment), it follows that $w_{W > wB}$, i.e. the effect of the differential judgment as to the probability of being qualified is reflected in a wage differential.

If there are price rigidities which prevent w_B from falling much below w_W, the same forces may be reflected in a refusal to hire B workers at all for skilled jobs.

Once we shift the explanation of discriminatory behavior from unanalyzable (or at any rate unanalyzed) tastes to beliefs, we are led to seek to explain these beliefs. One possible explanation runs in terms of theories of psychological equilibrium, of which Festinger's theory of cognitive dissonance is one of the most developed.[14] The argument is that beliefs and actions should come into some sort of equilibrium; in particular, if individuals act in a discriminatory manner, they will tend to acquire or develop beliefs which justify such actions. Hence, discriminatory behavior and beliefs in differential abilities will tend to come into equilibrium. Indeed, the very fact that there are strong ethical beliefs which are in conflict with discriminatory behavior will, according to this theory, make the employer even more willing to accept subjective probabilities which will supply an appropriate justification for his conduct.

Finally, one can also seek explanations in which p_W and p_B differ in reality, even though the intrinsic abilities of W and B workers are identical. Such an explanation requires some further assumptions. Specifically, whether or not a worker is qualified is now taken to be the result of a decision by him, rather than some type of intrinsic ability. More specifically, a worker becomes qualified by making some type of investment in himself. In accordance with the previous assumptions, this investment must not be observable by the employer. Hence, the investments are not the usual types of education or experience, which are observable, but more subtle types of personal deprivation and deferment of gratification which lead to the habits of action and thought that favor good performance in skilled jobs, steadiness, punctuality, responsiveness, and initiative.

Finally, it must be assumed, as is reasonable, that the human capital needed to qualify cannot be acquired on a perfect capital market. It follows that the proportion of either group (W or B) who qualify is an increasing function of the gain from qualifying. In accordance with our basic assumption that there is no intrinsic productivity difference between W and B workers, we assume that the supply schedules for the two groups are the same. Specifically, let $v_W = w_W - w_U$ be the gain to a W worker from qualifying, where w_U is the wage rate for unskilled labor, and similarly let $v_B = w_B - w_U$. Then we postulate an increasing function, $S(v)$, such that,

$$p_W = S(v_W), \ p_B = S(v_B). \tag{15}$$

Let MP_U be the marginal productivity of unskilled labor, so that,

---

[14] For a more theoretical analysis see Leon Festinger, *A Theory of Cognitive Dissonance* (Evanston, Ill.: Row, Peterson, 1957).

$$MP_U = w_U. \tag{16}$$

Note that MP_S and MP_U are determined by the supplies of skilled and unskilled labor and these in turn are determined by the proportions p_W and p_B. Hence, the system consisting of the equations (13), (15), and (16) plus the equation obtained from (13) by replacing B with W constitute a system of equations in the unknowns w_W, w_B, w_U, p_W and p_U.

From the symmetric formulation of the system, it is clear that there can easily be a symmetric, nondiscriminatory equilibrium, i.e. one in which $p_W = p_B$ and $w_W = w_B$. Two questions can be raised: (1) can there be other, discriminatory, equilibria? (2) is the symmetric equilibrium stable? It can be shown that (1) in fact discriminatory equilibria are bound to exist, and (2) the stability of the symmetric equilibrium depends on the parameters of the problem.

(1) The multiplicity of equilibria can be seen most easily if we assume that the black labor force is small compared with the white, so that any variations in black response have only small effects on the marginal productivities of skilled and unskilled labor and therefore only small effects on the wages of white skilled and of unskilled labor and therefore on the proportion of whites who are qualified.

From (15), (13), (14), and the definition of v_B, the basic equilibrium relation for the black labor force is,

$$p_B = S(MP_S - MP_U - (r/p_B)) = S_B(p_B). \tag{17}$$

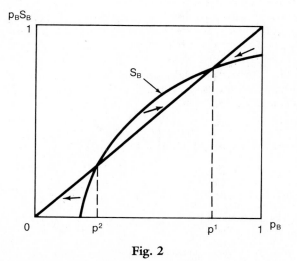

Fig. 2

This equation is to be solved for p_B; we shall argue it is reasonable that there will in general be more than one solution with $p_B = 0$, as well as an equilibrium at $p_B = 0$. Since we are assuming that the effect of the black choice of p_B on MP_S and MP_U is negligible, the right-hand side of (17) depends on p_B alone. The two sides of (17) are graphed in Fig. 2 below. The proportion qualifying can, of course, never exceed 1, and we may suppose that no wage difference within the range considered brings it up to 1; hence S_B, the proportion of blacks qualifying, is less than p_B for p_B close to 1. On the other hand, as p_B tends to zero, the wage differential between the skill levels,

$$v_B = MP_S - MP_U - (r/p_B),$$

tends to $-\infty$. There will surely be some wage differential which will cause a zero supply of qualified labor; even if skilled jobs are very attractive, so that there will be some supply even with a negative differential, the supply will surely disappear if the wage differential becomes a sufficiently large negative quantity, for example, if wages for skilled labor become close to zero. Hence, the S-curve in Fig. 2 has roughly the shape indicated. Equation (17) is satisfied when the S-curve intersects the 45° line; hence, from the diagram it is clear that if there are any intersections at all, there is more than one, so that multiple equilibria may be expected.

What happens when $p_B = 0$? Since $S_B = 0$ for p_B sufficiently small, as just argued, then $S_B = 0$ when $p_B = 0$. Hence, there must be at least three possible equilibria.

Notice that Fig. 2 could also be interpreted as the diagram for analyzing the qualifying propensities of white labor force, since we are assuming that the supply function is the same for both. Hence, we see it is perfectly compatible with equilibrium conditions that p_W is at the highest intersection of the S-curve with the 45° line, while p_B is at a lower level or even zero. Thus, discrimination due to differing performance is possible even though the underlying assumptions are symmetrical with respect to race.

To discuss the plausibility of this situation, we must look into the stability of the alternative equilibria. First, we confine our attention to the case already assumed, where the black labor force is small compared with the white, so that the marginal productivities of the two kinds of labor are independent of the behavior of the black labor force. To discuss stability, it is necessary to specify the dynamic model more precisely. We suppose that for given p_W and p_B, short-run equilibrium works itself out so quickly as to be instantaneously achieved. The basic dynamics then are Marshallian. That is, if the desired supply at any moment exceeds the current proportion qualified, the latter will increase and vice versa. In symbols,

$$dp_B/dt = k[S(v_B) - p_B]. \qquad (18)$$

Then the movements of p_B are those indicated by the arrows in Fig. 2; the highest possible equilibrium proportion qualified, p^1, is a stable equilibrium, and so is the value $p_B = 0$, but the intermediate value, p^2, is unstable.

If we venture a historical surmise, we may suppose that white workers started with a sufficiently large number of qualified individuals so that their proportion tended to p^1; but the black workers, starting from slavery with a low proportion qualified—a proportion correctly recognized by employers—drifted even lower toward zero or at least to some very low level. (It is unnecessary to caution the reader that this model is a gross simplification, intended to dramatize and make more extreme some existing tendencies, not to represent them literally.)

(2) We now argue that the nondiscriminatory equilibrium may be unstable. Here, we use the dynamic assumption (18) together with the same assumption for p_W; we no longer assume that the effects of black labor reactions on the whole labor market are negligible. Intuitively, we may consider a possible sequence of events, in which initially p_W slightly exceeds p_B for some reason. Then w_W slightly exceeds w_B and therefore, from (15), p_W tends to rise relative to p_B, therefore reinforcing the original disequilibrium. This verbal argument is certainly not conclusive nor very convincing, and in fact the conclusion is valid only for some values of the parameters. We have to investigate the stability of the system defined by the pair of differential equations, (18), and the corresponding equation with p_B replaced by p_W, in the neighborhood of the nondiscriminatory equilibrium. While the algebra involved is elementary enough, there seems to be no way of making the result intuitively obvious. Hence, we simply reproduce the stability condition here, referring the reader for proof to an earlier paper.[15]

Let w_S be the common value of w_W and w_B at the nondiscriminatory equilibrium, p the common value of p_W and p_B. Then $v = w_S - w_U$ is the common value of v_W and v_B. Let E be the elasticity of $S(v)$ with respect to v, computed at the symmetric equilibrium value of v. From (13), $MP_S - w_S = r/p$ at the symmetric equilibrium; it is the excess of marginal product over wages for skilled workers. Then the condition for stability turns out to be that,

$$E(MP_S - w_S)/(w_S - w_U) < 1.$$

As might be expected, the greater the elasticity of the supply schedule for qualified labor, the more likely is the system to be unstable. Similarly, the greater the difference between marginal product and wage for skilled workers, the more likely is instability; this difference would be zero if there were no personnel investment costs for skilled workers, and then the system would certainly be stable. Finally, and less intuitively, the larger the wage gap between the two types of labor, the less likely is instability.

I believe these results are only the barest fragment of what could be found with better and more detailed systems in which there is an interaction between reality and perceptions of it. One must consider still more precisely how individual employers acquire knowledge which will modify their initial estimates of distributions as differing between groups and in turn the effects of these perceptions on the market and therefore on any incentives to modify those abilities.

[15]Arrow, "Some Models of Race in the Labor Market," Section F.

APPENDIX

Nonconvexity of Indifference Maps Depending on Ratios

We suppose that employer discrimination is determined by a utility function, $U(\pi, B, W)$, where multiplying both B and W by the same positive constant leaves utility unchanged. We also assume that U is an increasing function of profits, π. It will be shown that the indifference map defined by U cannot have convex indifference surfaces; specifically, a convex combination of two indifferent points is not everywhere at least as good as either.

Choose any point (π_0, B_0, W_0). Then choose $\pi_1 < \pi_0$ (as close as needed) and B_1, W_1 so that

$$U(\pi_1, B_1, W_1) = U(\pi_0, B_0, W_0). \tag{1}$$

From the assumptions made, (1) will continue to hold if B_1 and W_1 are reduced in the same proportion. Hence, B_1 and W_1 can be chosen arbitrarily small.

If the indifference map defined by U has everywhere convex indifference surfaces, then the average of the two points must be at least as good as (π_0, B_0, W_0). That is,

$$U(\pi', B', W') \geqq U(\pi_0, B_0, W_0),$$

where $\pi' = \frac{1}{2}\pi_1 + \frac{1}{2}\pi_0$, $B' = \frac{1}{2}B_1 + \frac{1}{2}B_0$, $W' = \frac{1}{2}W_1 + \frac{1}{2}W_0$. But then, since,

$$U(\pi', 2B', 2W') = U(\pi', B', W'),$$

we have,

$$U(\pi', 2B', 2W') \geqq U(\pi_0, B_0, W_0),$$

or, by definition,

$$U(\pi', B_1 + B_0, W_1 + W_0) \geqq U(\pi_0, B_0, W_0).$$

But B_1 and W_1 can be chosen as small as desired. Let them approach 0; by continuity,

$$U(\pi', B_0, W_0) \geqq U(\pi_0, B_0, W_0),$$

which is a contradiction to the assumption that U is increasing in π, since $\pi' < \pi_0$.

CONTRACTUAL ARRANGEMENTS AND MARKET OUTCOMES

Transaction Costs, Risk Aversion, and the Choice of Contractual Arrangements*†

STEVEN N. S. CHEUNG

Steven N. S. Cheung (A.B., University of California at Los Angeles, 1961; M.A., 1962; Ph.D., 1967) was born in 1935 in Hong Kong. Professor of Economics at the University of Hong Kong since 1982, Cheung has served on the faculties of California State College at Long Beach, the University of Chicago, and from 1972 to 1984, the University of Washington. Because of his conviction that property rights affect economic behavior, Cheung's work has focused almost exclusively on various aspects of transactions costs. Professor Cheung's works apply the logic of microeconomics to topics as varied as sharecropping, beekeeping, ticket pricing, rent and price controls, and the licensing of patents and trade secrets. Cheung is the Editor of the *Asian Economic Journal* and a member of the Mont Pelerin Society.

*Reprinted from *Journal of Law and Economics* (April 1969) by permission of The University of Chicago Press. Copyright 1969, pp. 23-42.

†This article is an excerpt from my manuscript, The Theory of Share Tenancy—With Special Application to Asian Agriculture and the First Phase of Taiwan Land Reform (to be published by The University of Chicago Press). For their helpful comments I am indebted to Armen A. Alchian, R. H. Coase, Harold Demsetz, Jack Hirshleifer, D. Gale Johnson, Harry G. Johnson, John McManus, Theodore W. Schultz, and George J. Stigler. Thanks for financial support are given to the Lilly Endowment grant supporting the Study of Property Rights and Behavior at the University of California at Los Angeles, and to the Ford Foundation grant for International Studies including Agricultural Economics at the University of Chicago.

Every transaction involves a contract. The transactions conducted in the market place entail outright or partial transfers of property rights among individual contracting parties. The contractual arrangements through which these transfers are negotiated are several and varied.

It is common in land tenure literature to rank the relative efficiency of various lease contracts. For example, share tenancy (or sharecropping) has long been considered inefficient, as have leases with relatively short duration. These views are based on an inquiry into the resource use implied by the existing contractual arrangements. But the inquiry has been made without explicit consideration of the pertinent property right constraint and cannot account for the frequent choice of allegedly inefficient contracts. The wrong question has been asked.

Elsewhere[1] I have derived the theory of share tenancy on the condition that transaction costs, and in particular the costs of contractual negotiation and enforcement, are zero. It shows that economic efficiency is the same under various land tenure arrangements subject to the constraint of private property rights. Although transaction costs exist in the real world, the theory enables us to understand much of the farming behavior.[2] However, the presence of a variety of contractual arrangements under the *same* constraint of competition poses the question of the choice of these arrangements. In this article, I set out an approach based on non-zero transaction costs and risk aversion to explain the observed contractual behavior in agriculture. The observations used are largely drawn from the Chinese experience.

If a firm can increase efficiency in production by employing productive resources of more than one resource owner, a contract to combine the resources will obtain. The formation of the contract involves partial transfers of property rights in one form or another, such as leasing, hiring or mortgaging.[3] These transfers, and the associated coordination of inputs of various factors in production, are costly events.[4] There are costs of negotiating *and* of enforcing the stipulations of the contract.

Given the state of personal wealth distribution and the portfolios of assets held as private property by resource owners, some owners will seek contractual arrangements with others in combining resources for production.[5] There is a variety of arrangements under which this is done. At least two reasons may be offered for the existence of different types of contractual arrangements. First is the existence of *natural* risk, defined here as the contribution by nature or the state of the world to the variance (or standard deviation) of the product value.[6] Given a non-zero variance for the expected output yield (the total income for the contracting parties), different contractual arrangements allow different distributions of income variances among the contracting parties. Under the postulate of risk aversion, an individual will seek to avoid risk if the cost of doing so is less than the gain from the risk averted. He may avert risk either by searching for information about the future (which may not be attainable even at infinitely high cost), by choosing less risky options when investing (which options include portfolio diversification), or by choosing among arrangements with which his burden of risk can be dispersed to other individuals— such as insurance and various contractual arrangements. A second reason for the existence of different contractual arrangements lies in the different transaction costs that are associated with them. Transaction costs differ because the physical attributes of input and output differ, because institutional arrangements differ, and because different sets of stipulations require varying efforts in enforcement and negotiation.[7]

Let me advance the following hypothesis: the choice of contractual arrangement is made so as to maximize the gain from risk dispersion subject to the constraint of transaction costs. In the following three sections, I shall develop this hypothesis and apply it to some observations.

I. THE CHOICE OF CONTRACTS IN AGRICULTURE

Consider the three main forms of contracts in agriculture, namely, a fixed-rent contract (rent per acre stated in cash or in crop), a share contract and a wage contract. Under private property rights, the contracting parties are free to choose among these forms. The observed patterns of contractual choices vary from place to place. For example, share contracts were more frequent than fixed rents in Taiwan and

---

[1] Steven N. S. Cheung, Private Property Rights and Sharecropping, 76 J. Pol. Econ. 1107 (1968).

[2] See Steven N. S. Cheung, The Theory of Share Tenancy, chs. 3, 7 and 8.

[3] If only *outright* transfers exist for all resources, "owner" production will exist for all firms. Contracting for outright transfers does not concern us here.

[4] See R. H. Coase, The Nature of the Firm, N.S.4 Economica 386 (1937). Reprinted in Readings in Price Theory 331 (Kenneth E. Boulding & George J. Stigler, eds. 1952).

[5] Portfolio selection is a complicated subject. The two major theses that have been advanced center on anticipated changes in the general price level and on the aversion of risk. Transaction costs may imply a third.

[6] While this concept has the advantage of treating risk as a measurable quantity that can be conveniently applied to observations, it also has some theoretical difficulties. See for example, Jack Hirshleifer, Investment Decision under Uncertainty: Choice-Theoretic Approaches, 79 Q. J. Econ. 509 (1965).

[7] Transaction costs may also depend on other factors, such as the number of participants and transactions, which I shall not explore here. Changes in prices and innovations will also affect the costs of transactions. See for example, Theodore W. Schultz, Transforming Traditional Agriculture 162-174 (1964).

Southeast Asia before the agrarian reforms; in China fixed rents were more frequent than share rents in the 1930's; in Japan, fixed rents predominated; and in general, wage contracts (farm hands) have been infrequent, occurring in about one to five per cent of the farming households in various localities.[8] Why do the patterns of contractual choices differ? What determines the choice of contracts?

Any contract combining resources from different owners for production involves, in addition to negotiation costs, the enforcement costs of controlling inputs and distributing output, according to the terms of the contract. Contracting on a share basis appears to involve higher transaction costs as a whole (the sum of negotiation and enforcement costs) than a fixed-rent or a wage contract. The terms in a share contract, among other things, include the rental percentage, the ratio of non-land input to land, and the types of crops to be grown.[9] These are mutually decided by the landowner and the tenant. For fixed-rent and wage contracts, however, given the market prices, one party alone is sufficient to decide how much of the other party's resources he shall employ and what crops shall be grown. And since in a share contract the sharing of output is based on the *actual* yield, efforts must be made by the landowner to ascertain the harvest yield. Thus negotiation and enforcement are more complex for a share contract than for a fixed-rent or a wage contract.

The ranking of transaction costs of fixed-rent and wage contracts appears uncertain. The physical attributes of land are such that the cost of enforcing the contracted amount of input is lower than in the case of labor. That is, the "shirking" of labor input, which may exist in a wage contract (also in a share contract) without either enforcing the input or checking the output, is costly to prevent.[10] But while this "shirking" problem does not appear significant for land input in a fixed-rent contract, policing (or enforcing) the maintenance of soil and other assets owned by the landlord is more costly for a fixed-rent or a share contract than for a wage contract.[11]

If we accept the above reasoning, pending empirical confirmation, and if transaction cost is the only consideration, then the minimization of transaction cost implies that share contracts will never be chosen. Why, then, are share contracts chosen?

Suppose the transaction cost is zero or the same for all forms of contract. Let us employ a behavioral postulate of risk aversion, defined here to mean that an individual, given the same expected average income, prefers a lower to a higher variance. In agriculture, variables exogenous to the production function, such as weather conditions and pests, are risk factors which are difficult to forecast and which may significantly affect the variance of the value of output. Under a fixed-rent contract, the tenant bears most, if not all, of the risk; under a wage contract, the landowner bears most, if not all, of the risk. Share tenancy may then be regarded as a device for risk sharing (or risk dispersion); that is, the variance of the output yield is distributed among the contracting parties. Given the postulate of risk aversion, a share contract will be mutually preferred by the landowner and the tenant.[12] However, in varying degrees, risk

[8]For the case in China, see J. L. Buck, Land Utilization in China 198 (1938); for Japan, see R. P. Dore, Land Reform in Japan (1959); for other parts of Asia, see sources cited in Steven N. S. Cheung, The Theory of Share Tenancy, ch. 1 nn.10 & 14.

[9]These terms are implied by the theory in Cheung, Private Property Rights and Sharecropping, *supra* note 1. Samples of share contracts obtained from China (see next section) are consistent with this statement.

[10]For the tenant's incentive to use an amount of input less than that stipulated in a share contract, see Cheung, *supra* note 1. The adoption of different forms of contractual payment for *labor* alone due to "shirking" problems and enforcement costs appears to constitute an important subject which has not been explored. For example, a piece-rate contract will be preferred to a wage contract on an hourly basis if checking

output costs less than enforcing input. However, with piece rates the worker is inclined to be "sloppy" and produce products of lower quality. Thus, a piece-rate contract will be less preferable if the physical attributes of the product are such that it is relatively costly to police a specified standard. Similarly, commission payments (as in the case of insurance salesmen) are preferred to other forms when the value of output depends on the intensity of work per sale; "tipping" payments (as in the case of waitresses) are preferred to other forms when the quality of services is significant—in either case, the costs of enforcing "intensity" and "quality" of work appear to be relatively high.

[11]In horticulture, for example, the usual contracts other than owner cultivation are wage or piece-rate contracts. This may imply that in horticulture, owner management involves a lower cost of policing the orchard assets than fixed-rent contracts. On the other hand, one expects wage contracts would be infrequent when the land holding is large, for high costs of labor supervision would be incurred.

[12] This result is implied in William F. Sharpe, Capital Asset Prices: A Theory of Market Equilibrium Under Conditions of Risk, 19 J. Fin. 425 (1964); Jack Hirshleifer, *supra* note 6, and Investment Decision Under Uncertainty: Applications of the State-Preference Approach, 80 Q. J. Econ. 252 (1966). "Risk-exchange" models derived from the current state-preference and mean, variability approaches, with the aid of an Edgeworth-Bowley box, suggest that risk sharing is preferred—if we ignore transaction cost.

exists in any tenancy. Why, then, are fixed-rent and wage contracts chosen at all?

I suggest that the choice of contract should be analyzed by employing both the differences in transaction costs and the postulate of risk aversion. Given the state of risk associated with a particular output, a higher transaction cost will lead to lower returns to the productive assets. On the other hand, given the transaction cost, risk aversion implies that asset values and the variances of income are negatively related.[13] While in itself the dispersion of risk under a share contract will lead to higher values for the contracted resources, the higher associated transaction cost will lead to lower asset values. Wealth maximization (or utility maximization, depending on the relevant measurement problem) implies that the contractual arrangement chosen will be the one which yields the highest values for the contracted resources.

Given the variance of output value and the rental percentage, a share contract prescribes a specific distribution of income variances for the contracting parties. The associated state of risk dispersion may not conform to the most preferable state according to the parties' preference functions. However, since some dispersion of risk is preferred to no dispersion at all, a share contract will be chosen rather than a fixed rent or a wage contract if the higher transaction cost is at least compensated for by the gain from risk dispersion. There exist, of course, still other arrangements under which the dispersion of risk can be tailored to fit each case. But as we shall discuss in the next section, the transaction cost of an arrangement for risk dispersion more flexible than a share contract may be so high as to make it undesirable.

Evidence is available to support the applicability of this kind of analysis:

(1) Since transaction cost is assertedly higher for share than for fixed rents, there would be room for some third parties to insure the amount of crop yield. That is, if a third party (an insurance company) were to insure the expected mean yield, the contracting parties would choose a fixed-rent contract and would be willing to pay the insuring party an amount no higher than the saving from a lower transaction cost plus a premium for the virtually certain income now obtained as compared with the variable income in a share contract. Yet we seldom find the existence of

such a crop insurance without government taking an active role. The reason, perhaps, is that the cost of handling insurance transactions may be so high as to be prohibitive: the insuring agent would have to check not only the actual crop yields but also the amounts of inputs. For the French metayage (sharecropping), however, Constantia Maxwell observed:

> The usual procedure for French seigneurs was, while retaining the chateau and its immediate neighborhood for their own use, to let out their lands in *gros* to middlemen or *fermiers* (to be distinguished from *fermiers exploitants*), who paid a fixed sum to the proprietor and gathered the rents from *metayage* or from *censitaires* at their own risk for a personal profit. Some of these middlemen, like the landlords, were absentees and worked the estate through subagents.[14]

In this case we see the *fermiers,* a third party, interposing between landlords and tenants to provide a more certain income for the former.[15] To my knowledge, no similar arrangement existed in China, though another practice prevailed (see next section). In Japan, share tenancy has been rare; and, at the same time, a compulsory crop insurance system has been enforced.[16]

(2) In China, share tenancy is reportedly more frequent in the wheat region than in the rice region. Taking the hectare yield data of wheat and rice crops in Taiwan, we find significantly higher proportional variances for wheat than for rice. This is shown in Table 1. Due to the lack of price data, only the variances of physical output are computed, although

---

[13]For a theoretical treatment of asset prices and risk premiums as determined in the market place, see Sharpe, *supra* note 12.

[14]Arthur Young, Travels in France During the Years 1787, 1788 and 1789 at 395 ed. n. (C. Maxwell, ed. 1929).

[15]To interpret the existence of the *fermiers* on grounds of risk aversion alone seems inconclusive. R. H. Coase has pointed out to me that the *fermiers* resembled the "farmers" in England, who served to collect taxes and postal revenues for the Crown. Coase's explanation for the existence of the English "farmers" is as follows: a collecting agent who is allowed to take the difference between what he can collect and what he has to pay the Crown has a greater incentive to maximize receipts than if the same agent is paid a wage rate for his service. This argument, I believe, is correct, and can be expressed alternatively: transaction costs differ, among other things, because different sets of stipulations require varying efforts in enforcement and negotiation; and for collection a "farming" contract involves a lower cost of enforcement than a wage contract. The *fermier* of France may therefore be viewed as a "farming" agent as well as an "insuring" agent.

[16]See Agricultural Development in Modern Japan, ch. 13 (Takekayu Ogura ed. 1963). I have been unable to discover the frequency of share contracts in Japan before the introduction of the compulsory crop insurance.

Table 1. Mean Yield (μ) and Proportional Variance (σ_p^2) of Wheat and Rice Hectare Yield (kg.), Taiwan, 1901-1950

Value	Crop	1901-10	1911-20	Period 1921-30	1931-40	1941-50
μ	Wheat	880	710	759	1,058	625
	Rice	1,318	1,379	1,588	1,927	1,648
σ_p^2		291	118	357	1,180	1,158
	Rice	31	32	46	62	180

Source: Computed from data in Sino-American Joint Commission for Rural Reconstruction, Taiwan Agricultural Statistics 1901-1955 at 20, 24 (1956).

value of output would be a more appropriate measure.

In Table 1,

$$\sigma_p{}^2 = \frac{\sum\limits_{i=1}^{n} \left(\frac{X_i}{\mu} - 1\right)^2}{n},$$

where X_i is the hectare yield in kg., and n the number of years. The higher frequency of share contracts among wheat crops appears to be a universal phenomenon.[17]

(3) According to three independent surveys conducted in China (1930-1935), share rent is generally slightly higher than fixed (crop) rent,[18] and this premium may be regarded as a return for risk bearing to the landowner.

Let us summarize. The postulate of general risk aversion or the minimization of transaction costs, taken separately, do not explain well the observed coexistence of several forms of contracts. For this reason I use both, and the choice of contracts is determined by weighing the gains from risk dispersions and the costs of contracting associated with different contracts. Two factors appear to be important in explaining different patterns of contractual choices in different localities. First, different physical attributes of crops and types of climate often result in different variances of outputs in different agricultural areas. Second, different legal arrangements,

such as compulsory or subsidized crop insurance, affect the variances of incomes as well as affecting transaction costs for the contracting parties. An examination of some contractual details in the next section will suggest a third factor: different market arrangements also affect the choice of contractual forms.

II. CHARACTERISTICS OF FIXED AND SHARE CONTRACTS (CHINA, 1925-1940)

In this and the following section we analyze in some detail the observed stipulations of fixed and share contracts. This will serve not only to clarify the hypothesis that contractual arrangements are chosen to disperse risk bearing and minimize transaction cost, but also to illustrate that the contractual stipulations in sharecropping are consistent with efficient resource use.[19] I turn to some information from China, roughly from 1925 to 1940. This choice of data is based not only on the availability of information, but also on the fact that during this period in China, some 93 per cent of the farm land was held under private ownership.[20] Let me begin by translating a few sample contracts of fixed rent.

Sample (a)—fixed (crop) rent contract with definite lease duration (Shantung Province):

[17]See for example, J. L. Buck, *supra* note 8, at 198; and James O. Bray, Farm Tenancy and Productivity in Agriculture: The Case of the United States, 4 Food Research Institute Studies 25 (Stanford Univ. 1963).

[18]See Li Fa Yuan, Tung Chi Yueh Pao II, 5 (Legislative Yuan, Statistical Monthly, 1932); Nei Cheng Pu, Nei Cheng Kung Pao II (Dep't of Int. Affairs, Public Rep. of Inst. Affairs 1932); Shih Yeh Pu, Chung Kuo Ching Chi Nien Chien G62-83 (Dep't of Real Estates, China Econ. Yearbook, 1936). Some of these findings are reproduced in Steven N. S. Cheung, The Theory of Share Tenancy, App. B.

[19] The prevailing inefficiency argument against sharecropping can be briefly stated as follows. Since under sharecropping a portion of every output unit is taken as rent, it is similar to an *ad valorem* excise tax—where part of every unit produced is "taxed" by the landowner (government). The distribution of output is not the same as with fixed rent or owner cultivation—where the tiller obtains the *entire* incremental product. Sharecropping, therefore, is said to result in less intensive (and less efficient) farming because the tenant's incentive to work or invest in land is reduced. This thesis, however, ignores the terms in a share contract which the participating parties must *mutually* agree to abide by when the contract is formed.

[20]See J. L. Buck, Farm Ownership and Tenancy in China (1927).

Tenant A now leases from landowner B [so many acres] of land at location C. We hereby stipulate, with the presence of referee D, that the annual rent per acre includes [so many catties] of millet, soybean and Indian corn. The payment in wheat will be one month after the wheat harvest, and autumn crops two months after the autumn harvest. In a famine year, rental payments shall be adjusted [downward] according to local customs. The duration of the lease is [so many years].[21]

Sample (b)—fixed (crop) rent contract with indefinite lease duration (Kiangsi Province):

. . . we contractually establish an iron-sheet [firmly fixed] rent . . . . Regardless of good or bad years, not a fraction of rent can be reduced . . . . In the event that the rental payment is reduced or delayed, the landowner is free to take back the land, together with all existing crops, and [the right] to contract a new tenant for cultivation. . . . . Furthermore, the landowner shall pay the tenant 20 copper coins for the delivery of every 100 catties of grains.[22]

Sample (c)—fixed (crop) rent contract with landowner providing non-land farming inputs (Tsinghai Province):

. . . the landowner will furnish [so many catties] of seed, together with [so many pairs] of water buffalo, [so many head] of donkeys, and all essential farming equipment. The durable assets are for use purposes only, and shall not be damaged or lost [by the tenant], . . . and they must be returned to the landowner without delay at the termination of the lease. The [aforementioned] rental rate is subject to adjustment according to local customs in a famine year.[23]

The above samples of fixed (crop) rent contracts are about as representative as I could find. They are identical to cash rent contracts in all aspects except that in the latter rental payments are stated in monetary units.[24] According to observations collected by the Department of Real Estates, covering 22 provinces in China, cash rents are generally slightly lower than crop rents.[25] This differential can be explained by landowners' sharing in the product selling cost

undertaken by tenants. We may also note that with inflation occurring in 1938, due to the Sino-Japanese War beginning in 1937, 13.3 per cent of cash rents were converted into crop rents and 15.3 per cent were converted into share contracts.[26] This observation, of course, is consistent with minimizing transaction cost. Under inflation, renegotiation of cash rent contracts becomes more frequent and thus more costly.

The characteristics of fixed-rent contracts are not of special interest except for one feature. The one feature which we single out to elaborate on here is the frequent inclusion of the provision for rental reduction according to "local customs" in a "famine" year [see samples (a) and (c)], a provision which is absent under an "iron-sheet" rent [see sample (b)]. Let us call this provision an *escape clause* for the tenant, the inclusion of which in a fixed-rent contract imposes a risk burden on the landowner.

We may interpret "local customs" as a set of market prices for "famine" adjustments, even though the exact magnitude of the possible reduction of rent is not stated when the contract is signed. The escape clause comes into play only in a year so "bad" that the market considers it to be a "famine." Given a sufficiently large number of fixed-rent contracts which include the escape clause, competition among landowners to keep their tenants will yield certain market rates of rental reduction which each landowner will follow. Other things being equal, the increased risk burden on the landowner associated with the inclusion of the escape clause implies that a premium will be added to the "fixed" rent over the "iron-sheet."[27]

Although shifting the risk burden by including the escape clause in a fixed-rent contract is not quite the same as the risk dispersion in a share contract, we may imagine the formation of share contracts via the escape clause. Suppose "famine" is defined as occurring when the actual harvest is reduced to a certain per cent of the expected mean yield due to natural causes. The tenant under fixed rent has the option to choose between agreeing to an "iron-sheet" contract or buying an "escape" right by paying an "in-

[21]Kuo Min Cheng Fu, Tung Chi Chu, Chung Kuo Tsu Tien Chih Tu Chi Tung Chi Fen Hsi 52-53 (Nat'l Gov't, Statistics Dep't, Statistical Analysis of Tenancy System in China, 1942).

[22]Pe-Yu Chang & Yin-Yuen Wang, Chung Kuo Nung Tien Wen T'i 68 (Questions of Farm Tenancy in China, 1943).

[23]Nat'l Gov't, *supra* note 21, at 54-55.

[24]See Nat'l Gov't, *supra* note 21, at 53-54 and Chang & Wang, *supra* note 22, at 67-70.

[25]Shih Yeh Pu, Chung Kuo Ching Chi Nien Chien G62-83 (Dep't of Real Estates, China Econ. Yearbook, 1936).

[26]Hsing Cheng Yuan, Ti Chuan Pien Tung No. 2 (Executive Yuan, Changes in Land Rights 1942). The data were obtained from sample contracts in 14 provinces in 1938.

[27]Unfortunately, I have been unable to find data that would confirm or refute this statement.

surance" premium to the landowner—such that in the event of "famine," rental payment will be reduced by a certain percentage according to a market rule.

To further the argument: there could exist in the market place not just one escape clause as observed, but a wide range of similar clauses each associated with a different level of "famine," such that the tenant could obtain any or several of them by paying different premiums to the landowner. As such, the risk burden could be dispersed between the contracting parties in an infinite number of ways each with slightly different arrangements. This hypothetical world would perhaps exist if the costs of negotiating and marketing all of the different escape clauses were zero. But with increasing transaction cost associated with additional escape clauses—in particular the cost of defining different levels of "famine" in the market place and the cost of negotiating the rental reduction for each—the incremental gains of having them may be so small that no further "custom" is developed by the market. Instead, an alternative device chosen is a share contract, under which multiple "escape" provisions for the tenant will be implicit, and within which the rental payment is no longer fixed.[28]

From the above we may deduce two implications with respect to transaction cost and risk aversion. First, we have argued that the transaction cost is higher for share rent than for fixed rent, pending empirical confirmation. Observed contractual arrangements in China suggest that the transaction cost for a wide range of escape clauses is higher than for share rent. The reason is that a wide range of escape clauses would allow a greater variety of choice for risk dispersion than a share contract, and yet only one escape clause is observed as available. Thus, the range of contractual choices is constrained by transaction cost. Second, since, as noted earlier, evidence indicates that share rent is slightly higher than fixed rent due to the added risk burden imposed on the landowner, we conjecture that the landowner's income would be higher than with a share contract if an escape clause were adopted to the effect that the tenant's income variance is reduced to zero. Imaginative as it may seem, we find such an escape clause exists in the real world, disguised under the name of a wage contract.

Available data on the frequencies of escape clause adoptions under different contracts support my suggestions. A survey conducted by the University of Nanking, covering four provinces in China in 1935, reveals that the escape clause [as in contract samples (a) and (c)] was adopted in 83 per cent of the crop (fixed) rent contracts, 63 per cent of the cash (fixed) rent contract, and not at all in share contracts.[29] The higher frequency of adoption for crop rent than cash rent is what we would expect. In the event of a generally poor harvest, the market price of agricultural yield will rise, and with cash rent the tenant's income will be compensated by the rise in price more than with crop rent; hence, the escape clause will become less preferable to the tenant.

The existence of the escape clause in the market implies, other things being equal, a more frequent choice of fixed-rent contracts than of share contracts. Outside China in Southeast Asia, before the agrarian reforms, the escape clause was unpopular. However, there existed some guaranteed minimum rents or wages associated with share contracts. These guarantees could be similarly analyzed with the suggested choice-theoretic approach if more information were available. The different market practices explain, in part, the higher frequency of share contracts in Southeast Asia than in China. Indeed, the *fermiers* of the French metayage, the escape clause associated with fixed rents in China, and the minimum guarantees associated with share rents elsewhere are market practices that serve as intermediate arrangements between pure fixed rents and pure share rents. Each of them has different risk distributions and transaction costs, thus widening the range of contractual choices. Why these intermediate arrangements differ in different markets is a question which I do not seek to answer.

Turning to sample contracts of share rents in China, we find that their stipulations are more complex than those of fixed rents, due to the added stipulations on tenant inputs and crops to be grown.

Sample (d)—share contract with uniform sharing percentages for all crops (Shantung Province):

> . . . tenant A agrees to cultivate [so many mows] of land for landowner B. We hereby stipulate that tenant A provides [so many head] of water buffalo, [so many bodies] of men; and every year the tenant

---

[28]Note that with a share contract the landowner not only shares in the possible loss in a bad year, but also the gain of a good harvest which will reduce the risk premium by a fraction.

[29]See the University of Nanking, Ssu Hsing Chi Tsu Tien Chi Tu 65-67, Rental Systems in Four Provinces (1936).

must cultivate wheat once, Indian corn three times, and soybean twice. Fertilizer expenses are to be shared [in certain proportions]. The yields of all crops are to be shared [in certain proportions]. The lease may terminate only after the autumn harvest. . . .[30]

Sample (e)—share contract with varying sharing percentages (Honan Province):

[Stipulations of land size and nonland inputs]. . . . We hereby stipulate that wheat yield will be split 20-80; millet, yellow bean, sesame, green bean—all will be split 30-70; cotton and sweet potatoes split 50-50 . . .; millet straws, and bean and sesame stalks split 30-70. . . .[31]

Sample (f)—share contract with some products unshared (Honan Province):

. . . Tenant A . . . voluntarily agrees to furnish [so many] men, [so many head] of water buffalo and donkeys . . . and all plowing equipment. . . . We clearly stipulate that seeds of major crops are to be provided by the landowner, and seeds of minor crops by the tenant. All crop yields will be split equally, in dry and clean form. . . . But the straws go to the [tenant's] water buffalo entirely; the droppings go to the [landowner's] soil; . . . . and all fertilizer expenses are to be borne equally by both parties. All grinding equipment and living rooms are provided [by the landowner], which the tenant shall repair for his own use. These assets must be returned to the landowner at lease cancellation.[32]

In share contracts, several things should be noted. First, the explicit stipulations of tenant inputs and crop plantations are implied by economic theory. These stipulations are unnecessary for fixed rents. Evidence indicates, however, that only the actual yields are inspected, for by comparison with adjacent farms or past experience the landowner will be able to decide whether the contracted terms have been fulfilled:

. . . the absentee landlords send their agents, or go themselves, to the fields and estimate the yield of the crop and the share given by the tenant is based on this estimate. Such men are very expert in approximating the true yield . . . . [The tenant] commonly cheats by skillfully hiding some of the threshed grain before division takes place and also by giving the landlord inferior crops. On the other hand, the landlord or his agent often uses a large measure. When the agent collects rent the tenant

has to treat the agent very well and often has to bribe him in order to keep the land for cultivation another year.[33]

Exaggerated as this quotation might be, an intramarginal tenant with specific farming knowledge (hence, with higher yields than marginal tenants) can "hide" as much as the rent imputed to his special skill and still retain his tenancy; an agent can collect enforcement cost in "bribes" from both the landowner and the tenant as much as other competing agents allow. Nonetheless, this justifies our claim that transaction cost is higher for a share contract than for fixed rent.

A second characteristic of share contracts is that the precise and at times complex delineation of resource rights between the contracting parties suggests that the sharing of investment inputs can be adjusted together with the rental percentage so as to use resources efficiently. This is consistent with a conclusion I have reached elsewhere:[34] the landowner may either require the tenant to invest more in land and charge a lower rental percentage, or the landowner may invest in land himself and charge a higher rental percentage; the investment will be made in one way or the other if it leads to a higher rental annuity.

A third characteristic of share contracts is that the rental percentage may vary among different crops in one contract [see sample (e)]. As implied by the theory of share tenancy, the rental percentage is dependent upon the cost of tenant inputs and the relative fertility of land. Since different crops usually require different intensities of tenant inputs relative to land, the sharing percentages for different crops should be expected to differ within a single contract. However, any set of different rental percentages for different crops can also be expressed in terms of a single (weighted time average) rental percentage, uniform for all crops, to yield the same present value of the rental return. It appears that the latter option of a uniform rental percentage [see contract sample (d)] would be more convenient. However, if tenancy is subject to dismissal at any moment of time in the event of poor performance, the use of one rental percentage uniform for crops harvested at different seasons would be likely to lead to disputes or renegotiation should tenancy dismissal be in effect. We

[30]Nat'l Gov't, *supra* note 21 at 54.
[31]Chang & Wang, *supra* note 22 at 63.
[32]Chang & Wang, *supra* note 22 at 63-64.

[33]J. L. Buck, Chinese Farm Economy 149-150 (1930).
[34]Cheung, *supra* note 1.

usually find a uniform rental percentage being used in a share lease with specified duration, and that when multiple percentages are found in a lease with indefinite duration, a uniform percentage is usually used for different crops harvested in the same season [see contract sample (e)].

We may summarize the characteristics of share contracts by quoting the observation made by two writers—who were critical of tenant farming in China:

> Under the system of share rent, the yields after each harvest are to be shared according to certain mutually stipulated percentages between the landowner and the tenant. With the exception of some land used for farmstead purposes, the tenant is required to cultivate almost all the assigned fields for the production of crops. Sometimes, the tenant is even required to furnish farming equipment . . . and other expenses. The landowner and the tenant mutually decide the area to be used for each crop . . . . Besides the above, the only affair of management over which the landowner exercises control is confined to permanent improvements of land assets. This last characteristic is identical with fixed-rent contracts.[35]

III. THE DURATION OF LEASE CONTRACTS

An investigation conducted in China (1934), covering a total of 93 prefectures in 8 provinces, shows that the distribution of lease durations was as follows: 29 per cent of the tenant contracts were *indefinite* (that is, unspecified and usually terminable after every harvest), 25 per cent *annual* leases, 27 per cent from *3 to 10 years,* 8 per cent from *10 to 20 years,* and 11 per cent were *perpetual* leases.[36] Two things should be noted. First, a stipulated lease duration means only that tenancy may not be terminated as long as the contracted terms are fulfilled by each party. That the duration of the lease is specified does not prohibit mutual renegotiations within the

lease duration. Second, as the frequency of short-term leases has been used to illustrate the turnover rate of tenancy, it should be pointed out that lease termination is not the same as tenancy dismissal. Available data reveal that the frequency of tenancy dismissal was not high.[37]

In the literature of land tenure, two arguments have been commonly used in attacks upon the efficiency of lease durations of less than 10 years. One of these claims that short durations impose insecurity on the tenant and thus impair his incentive to farm. But insecurity, although undesirable to the tenant, may provide a stimulus to farming activity.[38] Another argument is that the short-term lease discourages investment in land. However, this is refuted by the fact that yields per acre on tenant farms are not lower than on owner farms; nor has any evidence been offered to show that, in China, productivity under tenancy varies with the duration of a leasing contract.[39]

The right to each privately owned resource is, by definition, transferable and exclusively delineated. Rights to resources invested in land and other assets are no exception. In the formation of a lease contract, the participating resource owners are free to accept or reject the contractual terms being negotiated. Again, the choice for the duration of the contract is no exception. Thus the relevant question here is not whether a "short-term" lease is inefficient; the relevant question is why different lease durations are chosen.

In a world uncomplicated by transaction costs and risks, in which the right to the income generated by

---

[35]Chang & Wang, *supra* note 22, at 49. For similar observations see Ching-Moh Chen, Chung Kuo Ko Hsing Te Ti Tsu (Land Rents of Various Provinces in China, 1936); Chi-Ming Chiao, Chung Kuo Nang Ch'un She Hui Ching Chi Hsueh ch. 9 (A Social and Economic Study of Farm Villages in China, 1938); and Chung Kuo Ke Hsueh Yan Ching Chi Yen Chiu So, Chung Kuo Ching Tai Nung Yeh Shih Tze Liao 1912-1927, at 89-95 (China Econ. Research Dep't, Source Materials of Recent Chinese Agricultural History, 1957).

[36] These percentages are computed from Shih Yeh Pu, Chung Kuo Ching Chi Nien Chien 101-104 (Dep't of Real Estates, China Econ. Yearbook, 1935). A similar investigation conducted in the same localities ten years earlier yielded a virtually identical distribution, *id.*

[37]According to a survey conducted by the Executive Yuan, *supra* note 26, covering 14 provinces in China (1937), 7.5% of the lease contracts were dismissed in that year. However, since inflation began in the same year, the cited percentage might be higher than that of preceding years. For the rise in prices due to the Sino-Japanese war, see Chang & Wang, *supra* note 22, at ch. 9.

[38]Armen A. Alchian has argued that the desire for security leads to "long-term" contracts. But his analysis is based on a property right system which is *not* private, where the private cost of acquiring security is relatively low. See his Private Property and the Relative Cost of Tenure, The Public Stake in Union Power 350-71 (Philip Bradley ed., 1959).

[39]During the period 1925-1937, surveys conducted by five organizations in China show no notable differences in acre yields or land prices that are attributable to different tenure arrangements. Among these surveys, two volumes are particularly comprehensive: Nat'l Gov't, *supra* note 21 and Land Utilization in China—Statistics—A Study of 16,786 Farms in 168 Localities and 38,256 Farm Families in Twenty-two Provinces in China, 1929-1933 (J. L. Buck ed., 1937).

private investment could be costlessly secured and transferred, and in which changes in contractual stipulations could be costlessly negotiated at any time, the duration of the lease becomes irrelevant and its explicit stipulation superfluous. With transaction costs included, I argue that the lease duration will be chosen so as to minimize these costs. To do so, it is convenient to separate the cost advantages for "long" and "short" lease durations.

1. The Choice of Relatively Long Lease Duration

A relatively long lease duration is chosen to reduce the cost of transferring (transacting) tenant assets attached to land. There exist differences in physical attributes of capital assets which involve different moving costs at lease dismissal. For example, a water buffalo owned by a tenant for grain grinding is easier to move at lease dismissal than an improvement in water irrigation made by him. Of course, the landowner could have invested in the water irrigation himself, or he could purchase the tenant's committed improvement outright.[40] But when assets attached to land are owned by the tenant, disputes may arise in the event of tenancy dismissal. A lease with a sufficiently long duration may become the preferred option.

However, the cost of moving the *physical* asset is not necessarily the relevant cost to consider. The tenant's property *right* to his committed investment may be transferred, either to a third party or to the landowner, at a market price. The problem is that such a price may not exist, or cannot be obtained in a short period of time, due to transaction costs. One need only point out that the depreciated value of a used asset is costly to evaluate; the landowner may choose to select his new tenant instead of allowing any party who purchases the asset to take over the lease. Also, other information problems exist in the market place. An appropriately long lease duration will thus reduce disputes and the anticipated cost of transferring the tenant's property right. This choice, however, can be made only at the expense of some

cost advantage which a shorter lease duration provides.

The foregoing discussion can be supported by observations on the perpetual lease in China:

> Under perpetual leases the landowner holds ownership right to the [bottom of] land, and the tenant owns the right to the soil . . . . These two rights are separate. The occurrences of perpetual leases are confined to the following: (1) The tenant exploited [privately owned] wasteland and developed it into farm land, thus gaining a perpetual [ownership] right to the soil from the landowner. (2) Permanent improvements in land made by the tenant . . . . such as building up water-conserving devices in otherwise sandy fields . . . . (3) . . . where labor is scarce and land plentiful, the landowners attracted tenants from afar by offering the perpetual right to till [the soil] . . . . (4) The tenant had paid a lump-sum payment to obtain the perpetual right to till . . . . And (5) the peasant, when in need of money, sold the ownership right to the land bottom but retained the right to till the soil. Since ownership rights to the bottom and surface of land are separate, both the landowner and the tenant can sell their rights freely, without the consent from each other . . . .[41]

In every case, the tenant's asset attached to land (for example, the right to the soil) is physically "permanent." With the perpetual lease and the contracted terms in effect, the landowner may not arbitrarily raise the "bottom" rent (or use other devices) to drive the tenant away. Yet such a lease duration would not be necessary if transaction costs were zero: If the "bottom" and "surface" rights were clearly delineated and costlessly enforced as private, and if these rights could be costlessly transferred, there would exist market prices for these rights at which transfers could be executed at any time.[42] Thus there would be no need for long lease durations to protect the "immobile" investments of the tenant. The same can be said for other assets attached to land.

2. The Choice of Relatively Short Lease Duration

The adoption of a relatively long lease duration involves forgoing some cost advantage which a shorter duration provides. When assets attached to land owned by the tenant are to be exhausted in a short

---

[40] Two independent surveys (China, 1921-1924 and 1935) reveal that, among tenant farms, landowners owned about 60 to 70% of the housing assets; tenants owned about 75% of the draft animals and 95% of the farming equipment. The total values of nonland assets on owner and tenant farms were roughly the same. See Nat'l Gov't, *supra* note 21, at 99-116.

[41] Chiao, *supra* note 35, at 261. For similar observations see Nat'l Gov't, *supra* note 21, at 56-58; and China Econ. Research Dep't, *supra* note 35 at 84-89.

[42] I apply here the thinking in R. H. Coase, The Problem of Social Cost, 3 J. Law & Econ. 1 (1960).

period of time, or when the landowner provides all the "permanent" assets, a relatively short lease duration reduces the cost of *enforcing* the contracted terms and of *renegotiating* these terms.

When a contract is formed, the contracting parties may lack sufficient information on each other's reliability. Within a specified lease duration, the violation of the contracted terms by either party may call for increasing enforcement efforts, or for revoking the contract before its termination date through court action or other means—all to be done at some cost. The choice of a shorter lease duration, which facilitates tenancy dismissal, will reduce these costs. As noted at the beginning of this section, however, the frequency of tenancy dismissals was far less than that of short-term leases, suggesting that most terminated leases were renewed. Available data show that the frequency of lease dismissals caused by rental disputes was low.[43] I conjecture, therefore, that in China short-term leases are chosen more as a device to facilitate contractual renegotiation rather than as a device to reduce the costs of enforcing the contracted terms.

It is useful to distinguish two types of contractual renegotiation (revision), though at times one relates to the other. The stipulated terms in any tenure contract in essence specify two things: (a) the state of resource use, or allocation, mutually agreed upon by the contracting parties, and (b) the contracted distribution of income for the parties. To revise (a) through renegotiation for more efficient resource use may benefit *all* parties to a contract, that is, all parties may gain or lose less. However, to revise (b) one party must lose.

Consider the contractual renegotiation which entails mainly a reallocation of resources, for example, changes in relative product prices which call for shifts to different crops, or innovations which call for the adoptions of new seeds or new methods of cultivation. Renegotiations of this type are largely confined to share contracts, since under fixed rents the tenants

are left to make their own decisions on resource use except improvements in land and maintenance of the landowner's assets. In principle, since all contracting parties expect to benefit from the revision, renegotiation can take place at any time and lease termination becomes unnecessary. However, different individual knowledge of the market may give rise to difference in opinions as to whether the revision is desirable. A relatively short lease duration is a convenient device which allows resource reallocation in the event of unsuccessful renegotiation.[44] This, together with the more complicated contractual enforcement required for share contracts, explains why durations for share leases are generally shorter than fixed rents.[45]

Consider further the contractual renegotiation which entails the revision of income distribution, when one party gains at the expense of the other. It applies to fixed and share contracts alike. Resource allocation may also be affected. For example, changes in relative asset prices of the contracted resources, a cash-rent contract with unanticipated inflation, or decision errors made in the initial contract—which call for a revision of the rental rates—are cases in point. Since some party must lose when revising the initial distributional terms, that is, the gainer either cannot or will not fully compensate the loser in making the revision, lease termination (hence, the choice of an appropriately short duration) is essential.[46] Again, this would not be necessary if transaction cost were zero (even if unanticipated events occur independently). In the absence of transaction cost, a contract would be designed to allow day to day changes in rental payments; within any lease duration, the distribution of income would not be held fixed throughout.

IV. CONCLUDING REMARKS

For generations economists and land tenure writers have sought to rank the relative efficiency of resource use under different leasing arrangements. But

[43]Legal records which cover 56 prefectures in 6 provinces (China, 1934-35) reveal a total of 124 tenancy disputes (mostly in rental payments) over a one year period. Even though the number of total tenant contracts is not available, the number of disputes brought to court appears to be so small that one suspects a substantial number of disputes were never brought to court. Over two-thirds of these recorded cases ended in tenancy dismissals, together with payment settlements. See Dep't of Real Estates, *supra* note 36, at G118-120; and *supra* note 25, at G143-144.

[44]With lease termination, for example, a share tenant who alone wants changes in production plan can request a fixed-rent contract, purchase the land outright, or seek tenancy with another landowner. Without lease termination, further negotiation may still take place if one party who wants the revision pays the reluctant party an amount to make the revision "convincing."

[45]Localities with higher frequencies of share leases (China, 1934) were associated with higher frequencies of short-term leases. See Nat'l Gov't, *supra* note 21, at 43, Tables 20 and 21; and at 59, Table 26.

their inquiries were undertaken without explicit reference to the property right constraint involved. And in many cases, the characteristics of various lease contracts had not been carefully examined. Different contractual arrangements do not imply different efficiencies of resource allocation as long as property rights are exclusive and transferable. The characteristics of lease contracts presented above also confirm this statement.

In this article I have asked: Why are different contractual arrangements chosen under the same system of private property rights? To answer this question I have introduced transaction costs and risks. The attempt to formulate a choice-theoretic approach to explain the observed contractual behavior in agriculture has perhaps raised more questions than it has answered.

Among some related problems that I have avoided explicitly, the following are significant. First, with respect to risk aversion, a more general analysis would include all risky choices, and not contractual choice alone. The analysis would be less difficult if transaction costs were not involved. Second, with respect to transaction costs, a more general analysis would derive some specific and well-behaved cost function of transactions. This step is essential to the development of a model of general equilibrium including transaction costs.

Still other problems I have avoided implicitly. In particular, some level of law enforcement by legal

authorities is taken for granted. We may well ask: What will happen to the choice of contracts if the government changes its enforcement efforts? To what extent will these efforts be consistent with the Pareto condition? What set of legal institutions is consistent with the operation of the market place? With these questions unanswered, the conditions defining efficiency with transaction costs are not all clear. Let me explain.

In production, cost minimization requires not only the fulfillment of the familiar set of marginal equalities, but also the choice of the lowest-cost production method available. In transactions, one relevant consideration is the cost of alternative *contractual* arrangements, which we have discussed at some length. One might think that, as a cost constraint, efficiency will be attained when, other things equal, the set of arrangements with the lowest transaction cost is chosen. However, transaction costs also depend on alternative *legal* arrangements. For example, the varying effectiveness of law enforcement, or the varying corruptibility of courts, will affect the costs of transactions in the market place. Given the existing legal institutions, I have attempted to explain the observed contractual arrangements. But insofar as I have ignored the choice and development of the legal institutions, the Pareto condition with transaction costs is ambiguous.

I have also not explored the contractual behavior associated with different property right constraints. Various restrictions on the transfer of property rights, or various methods of attenuating the right of a resource owner to obtain income from his resource, will affect the leasing arrangements as well as resource allocation.

---

[46]Given an unexpired lease which fixes the rental rate, changing economic conditions may lead to a redistribution of income. However, the efficiency of resource allocation may not thereby be hindered.

A Neo-Classical Theory of Keynesian Unemployment*†

DONALD F. GORDON

Donald F. Gordon (B.A., University of Saskatchewan, 1944; M.A., University of Toronto, 1946; Ph.D., Cornell University, 1949) was born in 1923 in Saskatchewan, Canada. Presently Professor of Economics and Finance at Baruch College and the Graduate School of The City University of New York (CUNY), Gordon has served on the faculties of the University of Washington, the University of Rochester, and Simon Frazer University. Professor Gordon, former director of Baruch's Center for the Study of Business and Government and Executive Officer of CUNY's Doctoral Program in Economics from 1974 to 1976, is a past president of the Western Economic Association. An economist of varied interests, Gordon is known for his writings on methodology and the history of economic thought, as well as his research on implicit contracts as an explanation for layoffs, job rationing, unemployment, and inflation.

This paper could be described as another effort to find a microeconomic rationale, or more simply and better, an economic rationale, for the Phillips curve.[1] The latter is defined for convenience as the negative relationship, which is here presumed to be a fact of observation for sufficiently short periods, between the level of unemployment and the rate of change of money wages. More accurately, however, the interest here is to find an economic rationale for wage rigidity and involuntary unemployment which, it will be ar-

*Reprinted from *Economic Inquiry* (December 1974) by permission of the Western Economic Association International. Copyright 1974, pp. 431-459.

†This paper, in essentially its present form, was originally given at the Rochester Conference on the Phillips Curve in April 1973 and is to appear together with other papers and comments at the conference in *The Phillips Curve and Labor Markets* (K. Brunner, ed.), to be published by North Holland Press. I would like to thank the North Holland Press for permission to publish here.

[1]The original stimulus for the paper I owe to John Young and George Freeman, Chairman and Commissioner, respectively, of the (Canadian) Prices and Incomes Commission, with whom I worked during the summer of 1971. Their skepticism regarding conventional explanations of unemployment persuaded me that a new approach was needed, and some aspects of the positive theory of this paper are contained in the Final Report of the Commission (1972). I have also benefited from conversations with and comments by many others, particularly, Armen Alchian, James Ferguson, John Floyd, Milton Friedman, Harry Gilman, J. Allen Hynes, Thomas Mayer, William Meckling, Ronald Schmidt, and the conferees at the Rochester conference on the Phillips curve, and my two critics.

gued, given the fluctuations in aggregate nominal demand that we typically observe, produce the sets of data that have been termed Phillips curves.

The introductory section contains a brief comment on the significance of an economic explanation of the Phillips curve and a discussion of its historical interpretation in a somewhat different fashion than appears to be customary. Section II contains a brief sketch of two recently developed classes of economic explanations for the Phillips curve and of what I believe are serious empirical and logical omissions in these accounts. In Section III an additional theory is offered together with some empirical implications.

I. BACKGROUND

At the risk of laboring the obvious I would enter a plea for wider recognition of the fact that without an economic explanation of the Phillips curve we have no theory of employment and unemployment and of movements of aggregate output and the price level in the short run. Certainly the "old" or pre-Keynesian quantity theory had no explanation since, to use the most common (if inaccurate) phrase, it "assumed" full employment. In other words, it postulated a vertical Phillips curve, thereby effectively denying the facts to be explained. The "new" quantity theory also has no explanation. It purports to be only a theory of the demand for money, and hence of aggregate nominal demand, and eschews any attempt to explain the division of a change in the nominal demand between changes in quantities (and hence employment and unemployment) and changes in prices.[2]

The "Keynesian model" as it has usually been interpreted is a simple right-angled Phillips curve with the horizontal branch at the zero rate of increase in money wages. (This is not inconsistent with the fact that at various points Keynes himself considered situations where the wage unit did in fact change.) While clearly accounting for short run fluctuations in output and employment in response to fluctuations in aggregate demand, it is not consistent with the fact that money wages rise substantially at levels of unemployment far in excess of some irreducible minimum, judged simply by past minima. And, of

course, many if not most economists have been troubled by Keynes' attempt to give an economic explanation of this wage rigidity.

Thus a first interpretation of the Phillips curve is that it arose, or more likely, that it became accepted, as a compromise between the right-angle and vertical versions, being compatible with both sets of facts that were inconsistent with one or the other of the previous models. But while the Phillips curve accounts for these facts, it does not explain them unless the curve itself can be shown to be explained by more fundamental forces (leaving aside the question of its stability). Indeed one could argue, and I believe correctly, that the Phillips curve is a contradiction of traditional price theory as it has developed over some two centuries. For that theory suggests that it is irrational for both workers and for employers to permit extended periods of non-equilibrium money wages, even for periods as brief and mild as, for example, the recession of 1969–71, let alone what we observe in major recessions.

Perhaps some economists would argue that there is no contradiction between Phillips curves and traditional price theory on the ground that the latter deals only with comparative statics and says nothing concerning rates of change to new equilibrium positions. They might contend that dynamic analysis of prices in disequilibrium arose only after the enunciation of Samuelson's (1947) fundamental postulate for competitive markets

$$dp/dt = F(D - S), F' = 0 \text{ and } F(0) = 0, \qquad (1)$$

where D and S are quantities demanded and supplied respectively. Thus a second interpretation of the Phillips curves is that it is merely the application of relationship (1) to labor markets in particular, with insignificant transformations of the variables to percentage changes.

However, this in itself simply transfers the need for an economic explanation of the special case of the Phillips curve to a need for an explanation of Samuelson's postulate. First, whether traditional price theory treats of dynamics or not, a relationship such as (1) would appear to be inconsistent with maximizing behavior, at least in markets for commodities which are in any degree storable or for labor which produces such commodities. If such relationships were to exist they would create opportunities for speculative buying and selling which would eliminate them. As the popular random walk theory of

---

[2]Cf. Friedman (1966). In a significant sense the new quantity theory is a retreat. The words "quantity theory" in the old sense were surely short for "the quantity theory of the value of money" or the price level; the new quantity theory should have a new name.

the stock market suggests, prices should *always* be in equilibrium, relative to current knowledge or belief, and these are already embodied in demand and supply curves.[3] Even apart from this logical difficulty, an economist, before accepting such an equation as an axiom, would naturally be curious concerning whose behavior is being described by the equation, particularly since it concerns competitive markets where buyers and sellers are usually assumed to regard price as parametric. He would be immediately inclined to search for a basis in maximizing behavior as in ordinary static demand, supply and cost schedules. The Phillips curve as an axiom is hardly a more satisfying explanation for unemployment than its predecessor, the rigid money wage.

Thus a future historian of economics might describe the rise of the Phillips curve as a natural theoretical advance growing out of the state of economic analysis and empirical evidence and produced by the logical requirements of two separate intellectual strands more or less simultaneously. One was the inconsistency between the facts and both the Keynesian and classical models; the other was Samuelson's development of disequilibrium price dynamics. *Such an historian would, I believe, be profoundly wrong.* Historically speaking, it would be more accurate to describe the Phillips curve as simply the embodiment in a differential equation of a loose set of impressionistic facts that have been observed by practical men for generations, if not centuries; that have been accepted and commented upon by many economists; and that were increasingly well known to be consistent with empirical evidence prior to the Keynesian era.

It would require a whole volume to track down and report on all the textual evidence bearing on this third interpretation; only a few examples will be given here. It has been a commonplace for centuries that "good times," i.e., rising output, have been associated with the opposite. The most plausible interpretations of the scores of economic writers of the mercantilist and pre-mercantilist periods would emphasize their recognition of the connection between the quantity of money and demand and in turn its favorable effects upon output. Many of these writers

likewise recognized the additional effect of money upon prices.

It is not clear, however, how many of the early writers saw that it was precisely because wages and prices were sticky that the demand created by money could stimulate output and employment. But Hume in the middle of the eighteenth century clearly saw the entire chain. An autonomous increase in the quantity of money enables employers "to employ more workmen than formerly, who never dream of demanding higher wages." (Hume, 1779, p. 304). Similarly, Henry Thornton, writing of recession rather than boom, contended that "A fall (in price) arising from temporary distress will be attended probably with no correspondent fall in the rate of wages" (Thornton, 1802, p. 82). In the late nineteenth and early twentieth centuries economists who studied the phenomenon of the "business cycle" found a correlation between rising output and wages, and their findings were later more thoroughly confirmed by the National Bureau of Economic Research. Even Irving Fisher in the twenties did a statistical study finding a negative correlation between unemployment and rising prices (Fisher, 1926). When the late Jacob Viner (1936) reviewed the *General Theory,* he suggested that most of Keynes' results were precisely the same as those of other economists who knew that sticky wages combined with fluctuations in velocity could create trouble.

A question might be raised whether it is proper to equate long held views about sticky wages with a belief in the Phillips curve. By "sticky" wages we presumably mean that they are slow moving relative to the movements of aggregate nominal demand. If, over a longish period, these fluctuations of nominal demand move back and forth around some average level, or rate of increase, we would observe a set of points which would be termed the Phillips curve for that period.

An economic explanation for the Phillips curve requires, therefore, no more (and no less) than an explanation for this long accepted relative rigidity of wages. Why are labor markets said to be so often in "disequilibrium"?[4] (This is a highly unfortunate expression since economic theory requires each employer or employee to be in equilibrium at all times,

---

[3]Note that this objection applies to purely *disequilibrium* price movements described by (1), which Samuelson was discussing. It is not applicable to any relationship describable by a differential or difference equation in which prices move over time but are always in equilibrium (where demand equals supply) relative to current output and beliefs.

[4]Aggregate Phillips curves can of course be derived by postulating individual labor markets in disequilibrium and their individual Phillips curves. But this is restating the problem rather than providing a solution.

relative to his beliefs, costs and obligations, or he would be doing something else). Even if monetarists and Keynesians resolve their conflicts over the determinants of aggregate demand, economists would still have no explanation for cyclical unemployment until the rigidities on the supply side cease to be loose empirical generalizations and yield to an explanation in terms of wealth maximizing behavior.

This sketch of a third interpretation of the historical place of the Phillips curve contrasts sharply with the view that it is the "only significant contribution to emerge from post-Keynesian theorizing" (Johnson and Croome, 1970, p. 110). In my view, it is neither theorizing, nor post-Keynesian, nor an advance. It is an ancient empirical generalization, superficially at odds with economic theory; the theoretical basis for it is unclear or at least not widely accepted, and it has only attracted attention during the last decade. It far pre-dates Keynes, and far from being an advance, it is a retreat—to reality, albeit common sense reality—from the formal classical or Keynesian models.

II. TWO KINDS OF EXPLANATION

While we have argued that the Phillips curve merely embodies an ancient piece of casual empiricism, it is likely that its explicit formulation has stimulated considerable thinking on the theoretical basis for such a relationship, and during the past decade two kinds of explanations have emerged.[5] In this section, we will briefly sketch both of them and indicate the respects in which they appear unsatisfactory or incomplete in their account. In the following section, a new explanation is offered. Both existing classes of explanation ignore the existence of labor unions and minimum wage laws and we will do the same. Most of the labor force is not unionized, and more important, the phenomena represented by the Phillips curve appear to have existed over long periods when labor unions were virtually nonexistent. Moreover, we will imagine that we are dealing with an economy which over a long period of time has exhibited a steady trend rate of increase in money wages, say 5 per cent. But while this is the trend over the long period, there have been shorter spans characterized by greater and lesser inflation. The basic question is: What are the fundamental forces that associate booms and depressions with these periods of greater and lesser inflation?

The Auction Market Model

The first explanation associated recently with Milton Friedman (1968) and Lucas and Rapping (1970) treats the labor market much as a commodity market in an ordinary commodity exchange. It could be termed the continuous auction market theory. Labor is presumed to be sufficiently homogeneous within classes so that "the" level of wages for a particular class of labor or skill can be observed by all participants. It is presumed, therefore, to fluctuate much as commodity prices fluctuate in response to demand and supply. Potential employees can always find employment at this "going" wage or at a wage that is a trivial amount below it. If there are fluctuations around the long run rate of increase in money wages and prices, workers will wish to work more at times when money wages and commodity prices are relatively high, or above the trend level. For money earned at such times can be spent (after it has been kept at the interest rate reflecting the inflationary trend) at times when commodity prices are relatively low. Thus to the extent that workers can vary over their lifetimes the periods in which they work more or less, varying their "vacations" or "overtime" accordingly, they will work more in relatively inflationary periods. This may be particularly true for part-time workers such as married females, the fairly young or the fairly old. Output as a consequence should be higher in relatively inflationary periods and lower in relatively deflationary periods, and such fluctuations in output would, of course, moderate the fluctuations in price.

The above effects may be strengthened if the worker believes that the transitory rise in his wage relative to trend is not part of a general increase in inflation but an increase in wage relative to other wages. This may be plausible, for he must only observe one price, his wage, to see the increased money demand for the item that he sells, while he must sample perhaps hundreds of prices before he can observe the general increase in inflation in the prices of the things that he buys. If this is the case, he may suspect that an increase has occurred not only in real wages measured in future (expected) prices, but in real wages measured in current prices.

[5]Space precludes dealing with all popular alternative explanations. "Market Power" has properly, I think, been rejected by many economists as incompatible with rational maximizing. Cf. for example, Tobin (1972) or Friedman (1966). The Keynesian allegation of concern over relative wages seems to require a very peculiar utility function in which putative money wages dominate actual money wages.

It is fairly clear that under the conditions that we have postulated, the commodity market theory of the labor market would give rise to what has been called the Phillips curve. Relatively inflationary periods will draw workers into the labor force while relatively deflationary conditions will induce them to retire temporarily. It is perhaps equally clear that should this long run 5 per cent trend be replaced by a long run 10 per cent trend, say, then the relationship will break down. To begin with, output will be stimulated by the thought that the increased inflation is temporary. But when it becomes clear that the continually higher rate of money wage increases are associated with continual commensurate increases in commodity price increases the short run stimulus to output will falter. Henceforth, if the long run trend rate of money increases remains at the new 10 per cent level, only temporary fluctuations of more than 10 per cent will induce greater output, and increases of less than 10 per cent will now be associated with depressions in output (or perhaps depressions in the rate of increase of output). The Phillips curve will have shifted upwards.[6]

For many purposes the auction market theory of the labor market is a useful abstraction. Relative to the lifetime of the individual there is a continuous market in lawyers, carpenters, doctors, and so forth. The young person can observe the going price—current incomes in these occupations—and use this in choosing a vocation. Even for shorter periods there is no doubt that it provides part of the explanation for the association of boom periods and increased employment for certain types of casual labor—for the young and the old, and possibly for married females who are frequently in and out of the

labor force—and for overtime and wartime increases in output.

Yet there are major respects in which it does not seem to coincide with widely known short period facts of employment and unemployment. It suggests that the downward phase of a recession is typically characterized by cuts in money wage increases and by workers quitting in response to such cuts. In fact, there is usually a decrease in quit rates during a recession. Secondly, while it explains unemployment of labor it is hard to see how it would explain the unemployment among non-human factors of production which does occur. In typical recessions, for example, rental residential housing suffers a significant increase in vacancies together with sticky prices. But the owners of such resources have no motive to withdraw them from the market, as with labor services, unless they cannot earn even their operating costs. They have no leisure alternative! Finally, a period of recession appears to be one in which laborers either search for jobs at "reasonable" wages, or in some cases, while they can observe the wage without search, they cannot get a job at that wage because of job rationing. They do not appear to observe an available job (in their usual occupation) and then decide to retire temporarily from the labor force.

The Search Model

The second explanation of the Phillips curve starts from the observed fact that when workers are unemployed, normally or abnormally, they are frequently looking for jobs. It may be called the search model and differs sharply from the previously sketched auction model.[7] Potential employees cannot observe a quoted price for their talents as on a commodity exchange. They do not know where the jobs are, at what price, and with what characteristics. The lack of an organized market in jobs can be attributed to the vast heterogeneity of workers on the one hand with respect to skill, temperament, and so forth, and the equally vast variety of job openings with respect to wages, working conditions, and skill requirements on the other. On securities and commodity exchanges there is also, of course, a vast heterogeneity. But presumably on those markets the essential characteristics can be much more accurately standardized, quantified and summarized, and hence prices are quoted. The labor market is more akin to the market for individual family residences.

[6]It might be reasonably argued that while this model produces a positive association between employment and the rate of change of money wages, it does not produce a negative association between measured unemployment and the rate of change of money wages. In a strict sense this is true since in an auction market all unemployment is obviously voluntary. Nevertheless, if we can imagine inserting current methods of measuring unemployment into such a highly abstract model, measured unemployment need not necessarily be zero. If an unemployed worker were asked if he had looked for a job he might plausibly answer in the affirmative, even if his looking had consisted of no more than eliciting an unsatisfactory wage quotation over the telephone from his job broker.

Milton Friedman has pointed out to me that these effects do not require that the employer and employee have systematically asymmetric price and wage expectations—since the real wage that is relevant for the employer, the "product wage," is different from the real wage that is relevant for the employee, his "basket-of-goods wage."

[7]Phelps *et. al.* (1970) provides a variety of search models.

The unemployed worker must formulate a search strategy. In one form of the search model, for example, he forms an estimate of the probabilities of finding a reasonable job at various wages, and chooses a wage to hold out for (and hence a probability of success in any one period) that balances the costs of continuing search against the costs of setting too low a wage. He would then continue to search until either he revises his estimate or finds a job at his chosen wage.

The employer is also searching the labor market. He likewise cannot observe a given wage or a given static supply curve which enables him to hire any desired quantity of labor "instantaneously." In a finite period of time, only a finite number of applicants will apply and a mutually satisfactory determination be made of the worker and of the job. He has, therefore, an estimate of a dynamic stochastic supply curve giving the probability distribution of achieving a net accession rate (hires minus quits) at different levels of the money wage. His supply curve

$$dN/dt = a = f(w, u) \tag{2}$$

where a is net acquisitions, w is the money wage, N is total employment and u is an error term, has the upward slope of a static monopsonistic supply curve even though in the long run he may be a purely competitive buyer.

There is an important difference between the imperfect information in the auction market model and in this search type model. In the auction market model the future is unknown, but the present is known.[8] In the search model the present as well as the future is unknown.

Unemployment would exist in search type labor markets even if there were no fluctuations in total demand tending to make wages rise and fall on the average. Unforeseen new tastes, new commodities, and new methods of production are continually appearing while older methods and older products fall into disuse. These forces created fluctuations in demand and supply for branches of the economy and for groups of workers even while overall demand is stable. These fluctuations require search on both sides of the labor market and this creates what might be called the normal or natural rate of unemployment. It might also be called frictional unemployment.

As in the case of the auction market model, the search model of the labor market gives rise, under the conditions that we have imagined, to a Phillips curve tradeoff between unemployment and rates of wage change. From a position of overall stability (in which employers are raising money wages at 5 per cent per year and are finding on average the desired change in the labor force) an increase in demand will first affect the employer's product. When he and all other employers raise their wage increases, workers who are searching for jobs will find higher wages available, and if they have previously formulated an optimum wage for which to search, unemployment will be reduced. The worker is "fooled" into taking more employment, since if he knew that there is a general increase in the rate of inflation proceeding he would revise upwards his acceptance wage (which already is rising, of course, at 5 per cent per year). Again, increases in employment will be associated with more rapidly rising wages and prices. The opposite will be true for decreases in the rate of increase of overall demand. (If the employer was not conscious that there was a general abnormal increase in demand he will be disappointed in the response to his wage increase, and after reformulating his estimate of the dynamic supply curve will raise his wage increase again).

It is likewise true that the Phillips curve associated with a long run trend of 5 per cent money wage increases is replaced if this trend is changed to one of increasing money wages at 10 per cent. Temporarily, wage increases and output will both increase. But the expectations of both sides will eventually change. The worker looking for a job will adjust his estimates of the wages he can expect to get, while the employer will likewise adjust his estimates of what he expects to pay. Only when fluctuations in the rate of increase in demand justify more than the expected 10 per cent will the employer be offering more than 10 per cent and the employee be fooled into accepting "too much" employment. Similarly, temporary recessions will occur even with rising money wages if demand is not increasing sufficiently to provide normal employment at wage estimates which will be rising at the expected rate of 10 per cent. In this case as in the commodity market model of the labor market, the Phillips curve will shift upward so that for each rate of unemployment the wage increase will be five per cent higher than before.

The search model no doubt accounts for a good deal of normal frictional unemployment and for some

[8]Save for the additional point elaborated on page 436 above, regarding the difficulty of knowing current consumer prices.

of the abnormal unemployment that appears in recessions. Contrary to the commodity market view, it is compatible with the impression that workers do search for jobs rather than simply make employment decisions on observed wages, and it predicts the unemployment of some forms of non-human capital such as residential housing.

But it has both logical and empirical difficulties.[9] A logical difficulty is the incompatibility between the decisions of prospective employees and the decisions of employers. A prospective employee can make an intelligent decision to accept or reject a job only if he has some idea, not only of the current wage, but of the future wage and employment at that wage. Most search models assume—sometimes implicitly—that the worker believes that each job being offered will continue indefinitely or that the wage will stay constant or both. (Some do allow for a constant probability of unemployment.) Otherwise he has a much more complicated decision problem involving presumably probability distributions of both future wages and unemployment periods. The assumption of stability, it will be argued in the following section, has a considerable element of validity, but until the reasons for this supposed stability are established the search model is both incomplete and contradictory. It is contradictory because such presumed stability is inconsistent with the presumed behavior of the employer. This latter is assumed to adjust more or less continually along a dynamic supply function which itself will be continually reformulated as he receives new data.

More important difficulties in the search model are empirical. It has no place for layoffs, it makes incorrect predictions about quits, and perhaps most vital it implies that all employers are always willing to hire in any job classification at any stage of the business cycle. With the onset of a recession an employer should gradually perceive the state of the labor market, lower money wage increases (perhaps making them negative) and experience decreased and very possibly negative accession rates. Symmetrical with boom conditions workers should be fooled into ac-

cepting too little employment by rejecting job offers and by increased quitting. In fact, quit rates decrease and presumably suitable job applicants rise. And surely it is true that a very large part of the time most firms are simply not hiring, or hiring only those quantities that they "need."

The facts concerning the quit rate, the fact of layoffs, and most important the fact that firms are frequently, or perhaps generally not hiring at their existing wage rates all point to the proposition that jobs are generally being rationed at existing money wages. The employer is typically off his dynamic supply curve (p. 438 above) setting a wage at which the supply of net accessions is greater than he wants to employ at that wage.[10] It is of some interest to note that if job rationing is prevalent, stickiness in money wages is produced by firms rather than workers. Keynes, his followers, and many of his critics have on the contrary supposed that rigid money wages are produced by the demands of the workers and their resistance to money wage cuts whether due to irrational money illusion or allegedly rational interest in relative wages. If jobs are rationed, workers do not get a chance to resist money wage cuts (except, of course, for the union sector).

Finally, some of the broad facts of economic history make the search model appear implausible. Even during the recent mild recession it seemed that unemployment was discussed *ad nauseam* in the media while money wages were rising substantially. Did employers really feel that such increases were necessary to maintain their employees?

If that recession is implausible on the basis of the search theory, the depression of the 1930's is incredible. Until 1933, money wages fell, although sluggishly. (They had fallen much more sharply in the recession of 1919-21 with substantially less stimulus from unemployment.) With about 24 per cent of the work force unemployed in 1933, real wages in manufacturing were higher than in 1929! After 1933, money wages rose annually despite massive unemployment.[11] The search theory requires us to believe that a degree of misinformation concerning

---

[9]The present author has been fully guilty of the incompleteness and errors ascribed in the text to the search theories. See Gordon and Hynes (1970). The housing and rental market models developed in that paper avoid the difficulties in the labor market which are here criticized. But we had no justification for extending that analysis to the labor market without further elaboration and such elaboration would have been incompatible with the sketch of the demand side. Cf. p. 382. I believe the theory developed in III below clears up these problems.

[10]In left wing literature, an important figure has been the heartless and avaricious employer who drives his workers to exhaustion by pointing out the window to the line of unemployed job applicants. What has to be explained is why such an employer is so generous.

[11]Unemployment, money wages and real wages for manufacturing in the thirties are cited in Kuh (1966); employment, real wages and money wages are cited for particular periods in Rees (1951) for separate manufacturing industries.

the state of the labor market that can only be described as fantastic persisted among employers for over a decade. It was not only during the 1970-71 recession that the "laws of economics" did not appear to work as expected.[12]

III. AN ECONOMIC RATIONALE FOR INVOLUNTARY UNEMPLOYMENT

In this section, a different model of the labor market is outlined, which attempts to account for rigidities in wages on the basis of a simple extension of neo-classical theory and its maximizing postulates. The discussion here is an informal first step in an attempt to develop the plausibility of the basic propositions and their empirical implications. No attempt will be made to derive formal general market solutions.

Two Basic Postulates

The basic idea is simply that job hirings can be typically viewed as implicit, and in some cases, explicit understandings—legally unenforceable contracts—promising that under reasonable and more or less understood conditions, employees have a certain security with respect to both wages and employment. We may term this model the quasi-contract model.[13] The quasi-contract model is suggested by fairly well-established economic propositions quite apart from the logical and empirical difficulties in the auction and search models which were discussed earlier. Some of the propositions are commonplaces of everyday life.

[12]It is frequently alleged and plausibly so, that certain actions of government depressed the demand for labor and retarded the recovery. This in no way resolves our question, however, which is why money wages did not respond to this unemployment.

[13]Since first formulating this "original" theory I have noticed a variety of forerunners. Hicks (1966, pp. 52, 55) hints at the desire for security on the part of employees and of the "social" aspects of labor markets as explaining rigidity of money wages. (But contrary to the theory of this paper he suggests that otherwise employees would leave during the recession.) Rees (1951) argues that it is employers rather than employees that hold wages rigid because, among other reasons, of a concern for future reputation as a "good employer." But he is skeptical of whether employers are optimistic enough during depressed periods to be much concerned for the future. Phelps (1970, p. 133) seizes upon the preference for security as a basis for rigidity but later appears to reject it (1972, p. 18). Finally, since this paper was completed I have learned that Martin Baily (1974) and Costas Azariadis (1973) have independently developed certain aspects of the same basic idea. The contribution of the present paper is primarily to provide a rationale for the asymmetric attitudes of employers and employees toward risk, and to draw some implications for rigid wages and other kinds of observed behavior.

The simplest version of the theory is based upon two fundamental but simple propositions. The first is that in a continuous auction labor market discrepancies would arise between the marginal rates of substitution of risk for income between sellers of the services of human as compared to sellers of non-human capital and that for legal reasons and for transactions cost reasons these discrepancies cannot be removed by voluntary exchanges which are legally enforceable.

For the vast majority of people, the bulk of their assets is in the form of prospective wage and salary income over a working life. Much of this human capital is fairly specialized and frequently cannot be transferred without loss in earnings to the production of a variety of commodities or services. Even if this were possible, it would be subject to cyclical variations. Thus, in a world of both micro and macro economic change and uncertainty, the owners of human capital might expect a considerable degree of risk.

Of course, the owners of non-human capital are also subject to risk, but this risk can be substantially reduced in two ways. In the first place, they can enter into long-term contracts or contingent contracts for the sale of the services or products of such assets at specified real or money prices. Such contracts, of course, can reduce risk to both seller and buyer. A particularly useful variant of this ability to commit the future services of non-human capital is the opportunity it creates for mortgaging those services, riding out downturns by borrowing, and hence diversifying over time. Secondly, holders of non-human capital can diversify by holding only a small fraction of their non-human wealth in any one asset.

It is widely recognized that human capital has important differences from other assets for institutional reasons. Because of the legal system, its services cannot be rented or sold under enforceable contracts for long periods of time, and even if they could, there would be important incentive costs since the productivity of human capital requires the cooperation of its owner in a manner that is not true of physical capital. It is likewise difficult to mortgage them. These forces create a second handicap in that one cannot diversify out of one form into many others. One cannot, for example, sell a piece of oneself if one is a lawyer in Cincinnati and buy a portion of a carpenter in San Diego. Thus, while human capital is not necessarily inherently more risky than physical capital, its owners cannot avoid risks in the same manner. At the same time, studies of financial markets suggest that the representative individual is risk averse, and so far as I know, where large portions of an individual's income and assets are concerned, there is general agreement that risk aversion is dominant. These forces, then, create the discrepancy in marginal rates of substitution between risk and return which is our first postulate.

The second fundamental proposition asserts the existence of quasi-contracts. A quasi-contract exists when an individual or firm, by behaving consistently in a particular manner, can induce another individual or firm to act to a large degree *as if* the former were legally constrained to act in that manner. This is no more than to say that people learn about the behavior of others, that they act upon that knowledge, and that such knowledge constrains the behavior of the first actors involved. Such constrained behavior covers the great mass of all "non-economic" behavior. But it also covers a wide variety of economic behavior.[14]

With these two postulates a mutual gain is available to employers and employees if we start from a world of purely auction labor markets. Employees will, to some degree, prefer a lower expected wage with a smaller variance to a larger more uncertain income. In the interest of getting cheaper labor, employers can enter into implicit long-term quasi-contracts with their employees by guaranteeing them some reasonable security.[15]

Since such guarantees will be unenforceable on the employer, he must somehow persuade the employee to accept the implied lower real wage. It seems clear that he can only do so by performance over a period of time which will create for him a reputation of being a "good employer." If, for example, wages fluctuate over a long period with a 5 per cent trend, such an employer will not take advantage of a slack market by lowering the rate of increase in money wages, or perhaps by not lowering real wages. On the other hand, the employee must be deterred from leaving to join other employers in boom times. He will be so constrained by the thought that his present employer will not be hiring during the next recession. His present employer will at that future time have redundant employees to whom he feels honor bound (or more accurately, profit bound) to maintain at reasonable (i.e., above market) wages.

Keynesian Unemployment

A first implication of this view of the labor market is that there will periodically be involuntary unemployment following the strict Keynesian definition. In a period of slump, the employer will have redundant labor because of a discrepancy between the current money wage and the current marginal revenue product, and hence he will be turning away new workers at that money wage. A general increase in demand will find a willing additional supply and a willing additional demand provided that the increase in demand is sufficient to eliminate redundancy among the previous employees. Since prices will rise, the employees will be working at a lower real wage. This is the Keynesian criterion:

> Men are involuntarily unemployed if, in the event of a small rise in the price of wage-goods relatively to the money wage, both the aggregate supply of labour willing to work for the current money-wage and the aggregate demand for it at that wage would be greater than the existing volume of employment (Keynes, 1936; p. 15).

But in contrast to Keynes and many of his followers, the rigidity in this model is created by employer job rationing.[16] We do not have to resort to worker resistance either because of money illusion or because of peculiar utility functions with respect to relative wages; nor must we imagine that during slumps employers are so amazingly uninformed on the state of the labor market.

This implication may sound paradoxical. Why, it may be asked, would a wage and employment system evolve which created unemployment in the interest of *security*? Surely an employee is more secure in a system of fluctuating wages than in a system characterized by high wages in the boom and zero wages during recessions.

---

[14]See Alchian, A. and Demsetz, H. (1972, p. 778, note 2) and the literature there cited.

[15]It should be noted that the insecurity which the worker avoids in this theory, to the extent that he avoids insecurity, does not simply consist of "set up" costs such as buying a home, making new associations, etc. It consists of all types of fluctuations in income whether cyclical or specific to a trade or occupation.

[16] The job rationing in this model is to be distinguished from the "hoarding" of labor in order to have a buffer stock against both fluctuations in demand for the final product and in accession to the labor force. Our model asserts that whatever the buffer stock there will be times when it will be paid more than sufficient to maintain it, even after allowing for all risks of stochastic fluctuations.

The resolution of this seeming paradox depends upon showing that these are not the relevant alternatives. First, we will show that a slightly formal but simple model will create Keynesian unemployment, but without the layoffs that are envisaged in the stated objection. Second, we will tackle the question of layoffs. Let Fig. 1 depict a specific labor market of the auction type in which demand fluctuates according to a rectangular distribution between D_1 and D_2. To simplify further, suppose there are no fluctuations in aggregate demand and that a fixed supply curve may be assumed. Finally, let long-term contracts for labor be strictly enforceable and negotiable without legal or incentive costs.

Without contracts, the wage would fluctuate between $4.00 and $2.00 and if employers and employees were risk neutral, they would be indifferent between this and a long-term fixed wage of $3.00. But if employees are risk averse while employers are risk neutral, any one employer can go to that class among all workers who are still in this labor market at the wage of $2.00 and who are most risk averse and find takers at something less than $3.00. Say this figure is $2.75 and that his demand at this figure is less than the amount supplied.

Assume that he is a "representative" competitive employer so that his demand at all prices is propor-

tional to total market demand, e.g. 1/1000 of total demand. Then, by change of scale, we may draw his demand curve as d. Notice that he hires OM rather than ON when he switches his employment policy for that is where his expected demand cuts the (to him) horizontal supply. Notice also, that at no demand below d would he be willing to hire "temporary" employees at the "going" market wage ($2.75) since his demand price, when he already has OM workers, is below that wage. (When the market wage is $2.00, his demand price for additional workers is $1.00.) Naturally in depressed periods, he also does not hire workers at his wage of $2.75. (This is not, of course, a market solution. Other employers will bid up the contractual wage so that the most risk averse employees will enjoy a rent.)

These simple numbers serve to illustrate the point. In this model what we may call the tenured employees do not choose between a system of high wages interspersed with periods of unemployment and a system of fluctuating wages. They have chosen "low" fixed wages and steady employment. This has created Keynesian unemployment for the non-tenured employees.[17] (No one in the academic field has surely ever imagined that academic tenure in a period of slow growth of demand is an advantage to those without it.)[18]

Layoffs

The model just discussed has no place for layoffs despite the possibility of involuntary unemployment. Using that model we might envisage a world where all employees had rigid tenure and all unemployment fell upon new entrants or re-entrants to the labor force; more plausibly perhaps we should imagine a group of fixed wage tenured employees plus a group of non-tenured employees with flexible wages. In this latter case there may still be substantial involuntary unemployment in the Keynesian sense. In either case there would be no layoffs, and while layoffs are among the most commonplace facts, they

[17]It should be noted that this theory is not the ancient proposition to the effect that workers will be paid more in occupations with much unemployment. That proposition deals with industries and occupations rather than firms, and does not itself explain the unemployment.

[18]Many readers will notice certain similarities between this model and the "lifetime security" said to be common in the Japanese economy. The argument of this paper is that the U.S. and other western economies are much more similar to the Japanese than is implied in auction models of the labor market.

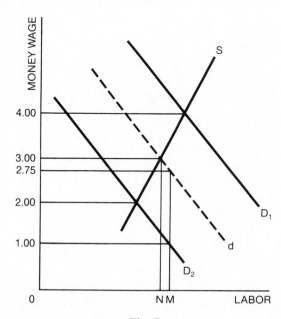

Fig. 1

pose awkward and obtrusive questions for economic theory which for the most part economists have somewhat shockingly managed to ignore.

The difficulties that economic theory has with the notorious fact of layoffs are illustrated in Fig. 2. The firm is observed to cut back its employment from L_j to L_i, and economists from Keynes (1936) to Alchian (1970), using essentially an auction market model, have interpreted this to mean a drop in demand from D_1 to D_2 combined with a horizontal supply curve S. The layoff simply short circuits wages cuts plus voluntary quits. (For the moment we ignore the other lines in Fig. 2.)

But this interpretation conflicts with the "common sense" belief that the short run supply curve at E typically has a positive finite slope. That this common sense impression can be consistent with rationality plus some information on the part of employees, is indicated by imagining the strained circumstances in which the short run supply curve would be perfectly elastic. If (a) there were no cyclical fluctuations of aggregate demands, (b) each drop in demand in a particular market were known to be permanent (or at least very long run) by all concerned, and (c) if each employer were small in the relevant labor market, then a completely elastic supply curve would indicate rational behavior (neglecting perhaps employees who are close to retirement). But if cyclical downturns are believed to be temporary on the basis

of common experience and if one has some knowledge of the general state of the labor market, it would be foolish to quit at a slight drop in wages. And the fact that quits decline rather than rise, at *given* money wages, at the onset of a recession indicates that the requisite information is available. Further, if declines in demand occurred in specific labor markets, if their duration were initially unknown, and if some job search were required, it would again seem irrational to quit immediately.

To refute the impression that employees typically have short run supply curves with finite slopes economists have had to resort to money illusion, to emphasis on relative (hypothetical) money wages as opposed to unemployment, or to an astonishing lack of information, and they have had to ignore the facts concerning quit rates. They resort to these devices because it would seem that if the short run supply curve were rising through E it would be mutually profitable for employers and some employees to move to lower wages, somewhat less employment, and some quits, rather than experience layoffs. If we accept the rising short run supply curve, why do layoffs occur?[19]

For some cases at least this dilemma can be resolved by another interpretation of the observed move from L_j to L_i even in the context of rigidly tenured and completely non-tenured employees. If L_i workers were tenured the supply curve of these workers to the firm would be the vertical line L_iS_T. The move from L_j to L_i would occur if the supply curve of non-tenured workers were S_N with corresponding marginal factor cost MFC_N and if the shift in the demand for labor had been from D_3 to D_4.[20] As in the conventional interpretation such layoffs are a substitute for wage cuts and subsequent quits. But in this case we do not have to assume a completely elastic supply curve. The layoffs occur because after the drop in demand it would require a very substantial, not a trivial drop in wages to make it worthwhile

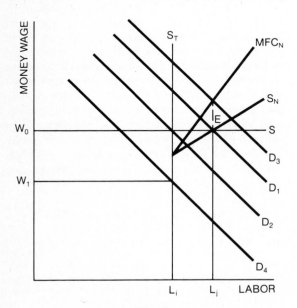

Fig. 2

---

[19]Of course we are speaking of involuntary layoffs where the individual suffers a finite loss of expected income and/or utility. This loss approaches zero presumably where layoffs are predictable, e.g., weekends off. (Ch. Alchian (1970) pp. 39–40). But from this point of view layoffs associated with a horizontal supply curve would also approach the voluntary, and these are not layoffs in which we are interested. If only the probability of a layoff is known the extent of its involuntary nature depends, it would seem, on its effect on the employees' risk, i.e., on his ability to diversify, and on his risk aversion.

[20]We are omitting the complexities arising from an employer's dynamic supply curve mentioned above.

to hire any of the non-tenured employees. And this is because the marginal revenue product of the tenured employees, W_1, is not an epsilon but far below the previous wage of the non-tenured employees. In this quasi-contract model the employer may know that the supply elasticity at the current wage for non-tenured workers is not infinite: but this is irrelevant because a mutually profitable exchange cannot take place at a slightly lower wage.

In this model, for any given horizontal change in demand, layoffs as opposed to wage cuts will be more frequent the smaller the elasticity of derived demand and the higher the proportion of tenured workers. What would make the demand very inelastic? We might first suppose—as Stigler suggested long ago and as more recent putty-clay capital models assume—that the short run variability of factor proportions is very low, or in the limit, zero. Then we would expect that layoffs, as opposed to wage cuts, would vary with the other Marshallian factors determining the elasticity of demand—the proportion of labor cost in variable cost, the elasticity of the supply of the other variable factors, and the elasticity of demand for the final product. We would hence predict that, holding other relevant variables constant, for a given change in demand there would be more layoffs and less wage cuts in concentrated industries (where the demand for the final product is more inelastic) and in those with a low proportion of wage costs in variable costs. These, of course, are testable propositions.

A Third Postulate: More Layoffs

The above analysis is not satisfactory in as much as it does not cover cases of "small" changes in demand, as a glance at Fig. 2 will show. In these instances conventional auction market models would expect the employer to slide down his marginal factor cost curve for non-tenured employees.[21] However, the principle involved—that layoffs will occur where the cut in wages required to employ profitably the workers involved is substantially rather than infinitesimally below the existing wage—can be more generally applied with the addition of a third postulate.

To this point, we have treated quasi-contracts in the labor market as if they shifted all risk from employee to employer, and we have envisaged only one type of quasi-contract which divides all employees into only two classes, tenured and non-tenured. But in some areas where the employer is subject to a great deal of "natural" risk, there may be more advantage to both parties in sharing this risk. Our third basic proposition, then, is that labor contracts will be similar to contracts in other markets in that they frequently exhibit risk sharing.

In security and other markets, there are virtually indefinite possibilities of varying the degree of riskiness of various instruments and providing for unforeseen contingencies, and as a consequence, there exists a bewildering variety of securities and other contracts. In the labor market we would expect, in addition to a necessary additional vagueness, at least as much variety. Some firms, with highly uncertain demands, will choose to offer very little security. Others will offer year to year security with expected seasonal variations. Still others may offer expected cyclical variations in their package. At the other extreme, even the most secure employee is not to be envisaged as having an implicit contract that guarantees his income in the face of threatened bankruptcy of the firm or even in the presence of long periods of sustained losses. In the face of uncertainty, a labor market contract must be thought of as being more in the nature of a preferred share rather than as a debenture or mortgage.

Another way of stating these facts is to say that in a plane with expected income and variance as axes few employers or employees will be in equilibrium at a corner solution. Employees will not typically sacrifice so much expected income so as to have zero risk, while employers will not absorb all risk in order to minimize wages. In a perfect market, between any two classes of employers and employees, contracts will be such that they make the marginal rates of substitution between risk and expected income the same for both.[22]

In many organizations, particularly in large organizations, we would suppose that the labor contract will take the form of a fairly clearly structured

---

[21]It could also be argued that it is unsatisfactory because it predicts behavior for other variables during a recession that we do not observe. If a very large portion of labor costs were fixed costs, the resulting low level of variable costs should produce sharper price fluctuations in final products, smaller decreases in output, and more bankruptcies than would otherwise be the case. It might, however, be difficult to translate these qualitative predictions into quantitative assertions with which to confront actual price changes, quantity changes and bankruptcies.

[22]We should probably require that employers as well as employees cannot buy and sell contracts in the labor market so that the results of portfolio theory and other aspects of the modern theory of finance are not applicable.

labor relations and wage policy administered by specialists in wage and personnel management. Employees and employers alike will work within a multitude of defined rules governing such items as pensions, seniority, overtime, job rules and privileges, job classifications and grades, steps within grade, and provisions for periodic wage and salary review. It seems reasonable to suppose that the more structured and formal such a wage and salary program is, the smaller the degree of subjective uncertainty the potential employee will feel. For that reason, he can be hired for less. (It would seem that one of the functions that unions provide for employers is to create a similar feeling of security.)

Thus, there is no reason why, within the firm, there should not be different risk sharing quasi-contracts with different employees, just as one may imagine different legal contracts with different customers or suppliers of non-labor inputs. In particular, there is no reason why a firm may not find it advantageous to offer all employees some security but with different groups, even among otherwise homogeneous employees, having different degrees of security.[23] If the firm were to experience a continuing decline in demand, or possibly if a given decline in demand were to continue for a long enough period, the continuing misfortunes would cause each class of employees to lose their security successively. Yet each time these undesirable outcomes triggered the loss of security for a particular group, that group may have a marginal revenue product far below (because of the number of still tenured employees) its contract wage and below its minimum supply price. If this were true, we would expect to see a succession of layoffs, of the nature analyzed earlier, rather than wage cuts.

Fig. 3, a modification of Fig. 2, illustrates some dimensions of a very simple risk-sharing contract which would produce rational layoffs and no wage flexibility. A group of employees, $(L_j - L_i)$, has been hired by this firm at wage W_0 with some degree of tenure, but with the least security of all employees.

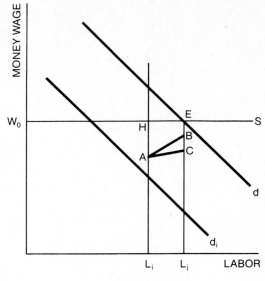

Fig. 3

They are guaranteed "full" employment at the wage W_0 until profits, P, have declined to a particular level, P_i, after which there are no further guarantees. Suppose that given this package, the long run supply curve, S, to the firm of such employees is horizontal, beginning at H. (It may, of course, require search time to move out along this curve.)

The short run supply curve, here labeled AC, (with marginal factor cost AB) is somewhat special in these circumstances, and does not bear the normal relationship to S. It shows the wage at which various numbers of these employees (or others outside the firm) could be employed if the quasi-contract were broken; that is, if it became known that the firm was henceforth going to hire them at the lowest possible wage, because in fact the firm had commenced to operate in this manner. Except coincidentally this short run curve will not go through the point E since the short run wage and the long run wage carry different non-wage provisions. In a boom market the short run curve should be above E, but in a depressed market, it would be below.[24]

Under these conditions if a fall in demand to some

[23]One criterion immediately suggests itself for choosing which employees to offer greater security—those with greater seniority. Security will be most valuable to those employees who are most risk averse and pay can be on average lower. Risk aversion cannot be directly observed, but one may guess that the class of employees who stayed through the last boom because of risk aversion ("loyalty to the firm"), are more likely to stay through the next boom than those who have just joined the firm and about whom one knows nothing. Therefore, if layoffs are necessary, the recent accessions would be the first to go.

[24]One cannot casually extend this supply curve to the right beyond C, even if there were an outside auction type labor market. These employees have hitherto opted for this particular arrangement and they cannot be considered homogeneous with employees in the outside market. Search costs in this and other employments will also be a factor.

level d_i reduces earnings of the firm to the level P_i the $(L_i - L_j)$ employees will be laid off. As before, the layoff occurs because a small cut in wages would be insufficient to permit mutually profitable employment despite the short run monopsonistic supply curve. If the demand were then to fall more, still more employees to the left of L_i would fall into a similar situation and we would observe a succession of layoffs. As in Fig. 2, layoffs would be more likely for any given horizontal change in demand the more inelastic that demand and the smaller the class of employees with the least security. But under the arrangements postulated there would be no short run wage flexibility; the contract precludes the employer from using the short run supply curve for any of his employees.

While this kind of contract resolves the puzzle of layoffs, that is, it explains why it is not mutually beneficial to employ some of the discharged workers at a lower wage, it is only illustrative, and is but one of an almost infinite variety that we could imagine. The theory does not require that wages be rigid, only that they do not fluctuate so as to clear the short run market. A complete analysis would require an extensive empirical investigation of actual wage and employment practices with the theoretical structure in mind, and would attempt to reconcile these practices with the tastes and opportunities of both employers and employees.[25]

Our discussion of layoffs should indicate that the paradox indicated earlier—a security system of quasi-contracts that creates insecurity in the form of layoffs—is a false one. For society as a whole, continuous full employment and perfectly flexible wages and prices will have a higher expected output and less variance than one with any layoffs. But no individual in our theory chooses less income with greater variance. The $(L_i - L_j)$ employees in our example do not necessarily have more variance in their income (the usual measure of risk) than if their wages fluctuated continuously. And if they do we would expect a higher expected income as compensation. Presumably they could have guaranteed themselves

against all unemployment but only at an unacceptable cost in terms of income. What is true in this risk sharing model as in the earlier rigid tenure model, and what is true in non-labor markets as in labor markets, is that for any given "objective" quantity of risk, the more security that is purchased by some individuals the less there is available for others. An employment system organized to create security for some at the expense of layoffs for others is no paradox; a similar phenomenon abounds in securities markets and creates the elementary distinction between stocks and bonds.

Naturally, when we allow employers and employees to share risk, we lay ourselves open to the charge that the model predicts that "anything can happen." Nevertheless, this third proposition makes specific predictions that diverge from received analysis. It predicts that among firms operating in the same labor market, those with higher profits at any point in time will grant larger wage increases. They are clearly not forced to do so by reason of scarcity; they do so because they are to some degree sharing the risk with their employees.

The Phillips Curve, or Why Wages Are Sticky

Like the auction and search theories of the labor market, this theory predicts that we should observe a Phillips curve. Like them, it also predicts that in the long run this curve will shift up or down due to the effects of expectations, whenever the unemployment rate is different from its long run equilibrium or "natural" value.[26] But the manner in which expectations operate are sharply different in this model than in the other two, and may be expected to operate with a much longer lag.

Dealing first with the short run, the Phillips curve is a combination of wage rigidity and flexibility. Naturally, the wage rigidity is a consequence of the quasi-contracts. Even short run wage flexibility follows from two factors. The first is the fact that the labor market contains some non-tenured employees who are in search type or auction type markets. The second is the degree to which employees share risk with employers.

Turning to the question of the long run shift in the Phillips curve, we must suppose that the quasi-contracts between employer and employee are free

[25]In our simple example we have avoided the question of the expected duration of the decline in demand which can be expected to play a role. In this connection it should be noted that if the employer has better information on the expected duration than the employee, he would be a "good employer" (giving up short run benefits for long run advantage) if, when he expected the decline in demand to be a long one, he laid off the employee rather than "exploit" him along the short run monopsonistic supply curve.

[26] The distinction between movements along and movements of the Phillips curve seems nonoperational; the data seem simply to suggest that wages are sticky but not wholly rigid.

from money illusion and are in terms of real wages. But the employer can hardly be expected to predict every wiggle in the business cycle, and it is the essence of the theory that he can and will avoid adjustments to short run supply and demand considerations—to the extent that he believes them to be transitory—even when he is fully aware of them. (Sharing current prosperity or losses, due to risk sharing provisions, is not inconsistent with this.)

On the other hand, we must suppose that his long run expectations are not perfectly rigid. A particularly lengthy boom, with higher prices and a tighter labor market than had been expected, will shift, to some degree, his subjective probability that the economy is entering a secular inflation, or a higher rate of secular inflation. Presumably, the amount of the shift will depend in a Bayesian manner upon the strength of his prior convictions and upon the degree of divergence from the expected. He will then change the money terms of his quasi-contracts by an appropriate amount, i.e., what we may call his personal Phillips curve will have shifted upward (for wealth maximizing reasons).

In the contract model, the Phillips curve shifts more slowly than, for example, in the search model, because of the nature of the prediction problem. In the search model, the employer changes his wage increase when he concludes from a *current* net accession rate that the labor market is such that the wage increase is not optimal for current conditions. His problem is to predict the current excess supply from his limited observation of a stochastic variable. Having concluded that the current labor market situation has changed, he would fully adapt to that change. In the quasi-contract model, the employer also adapts when he can form a conclusion as to the current state of the market; but in this case, *only to the extent that this conclusion affects his long-term prediction of future wages and prices.* He does not adjust optimally to meet the current situation.[27]

How long would a long run adjustment take? It

seems impossible to calculate a period of adjustment for a "rational" decision maker when that adjustment requires predicting the future. There is no "given" probability distribution with which to work, unless it be the whole of human history. There is no way to calculate a rational prior probability distribution, or a prior probability distribution of probability distributions, etc.

However, we would expect subjective prior judgments formed on past experience to be particularly resistant to events that are virtually historically unique, e.g., the collapse of aggregate demand during the thirties or the unprecedented secular inflation of the postwar period. It is not surprising that full adjustment may be slow. If the effects of inflation on money interest rates can be lagged by decades, one might expect similar adjustment periods for the full adaptation of employment practices.[28]

Involuntary Unemployment at Full Employment

It is of some interest to note that, according to this explanation, Keynesian unemployment will be widespread under conditions of "full employment." Full employment equilibrium has the property that the rate of increase in nominal demand cannot be increased without eventually raising the average rate of price and wage increase until unemployment returns to its previous level. It has always been recognized that full employment is consistent with a positive level of search or frictional unemployment. This would be the only kind of unemployment in a full employment equilibrium if aggregate demand were always distributed among separate labor markets in accordance with supplies in those markets. If, however, aggregate demand fluctuates over separate markets, and if supply cannot adjust instantaneously, some markets will be experiencing excess supply and involuntary unemployment with wage increases below the average. These will be offset by other markets with excess demand and higher than average wage increases.

Some economists might prefer the term "structural" for the additional unemployment created by fluctuating demands. Terms are of little consequence.

---

[27]Given the difficulty of the prediction problem, one might suppose that the individual firm or industry would look to other firms or industries for clues as to the future. If wage increases in one industry or firm provoke wage increases in other industries and firms, this is almost to be expected. It does not have to be looked upon as indicating the importance of relative wages in the employees' utility functions. Similarly one could almost predict that the circumstances discussed in the text would give rise to a variety of cost-push and other non-maximizing theories of inflation.

[28]With this qualification the contract theory predicts a vertical Phillips curve, absence of money illusion and no "inflationary biases." The long delayed effects of long run periods of secular inflation may, however, easily create the illusion of inflationary biases.

Yet it is important to notice that this is involuntary unemployment in the Keynesian sense and that it cannot be permanently lowered if the initial position is one of long run full employment equilibrium, i.e., it is one in which actual and expected wage and price increases are consistent with the rate of increase in nominal demand.

Certainly, an increase in the rate of growth of nominal demand will create additional employment at stable wage rates (or at least within stable individual wage and employment policies) since jobs were previously rationed in some industries, and this increased employment will be at lower real wage rates due to the more rapid rise in prices. But the increased pressure in the labor market and the higher rate of price increase will cause employers to revise (if only gradually) their long term expectations, and hence their quasi-contracts. The Phillips curves for all markets will rise until the level and rate of increase of wages again corresponds to nominal demand. Unemployment will rise to its original rate with its component of involuntary unemployment.

Other Implications

While the quasi-contract theory provides an alternative explanation for the Phillips curve, it also has a number of other testable implications. Perhaps its sharpest confrontation with the search and auction models arises from its prediction that quit-rates should fall in a recession and rise in a boom as they do. The other models predict the opposite. The contract model further predicts that hiring should be a lagging cyclical indicator and that (average) productivity should fluctuate pro-cyclically as it does.

Keynes, trained as a neo-classicist, predicted that real wages, and by implication productivity, should fluctuate contra-cyclically on the basis of diminishing marginal productivity. The quasi-contract theory cuts any necessary relationship between the *current* wage and *current* marginal productivity. If there is risk sharing between employer and employee, real wages will fluctuate pro-cyclically.

The theory also predicts that firms with relatively stable demands for their product over the cycle will have more stable and lower wages than do other firms. Such stable firms will find it cheaper to offer more security to more employees. This may not be a prediction which impresses the non-economist who will find it obvious that more stable firms "can afford" a reasonable wage increase even in recessions. But

for an economist it should be a puzzle despite its common sense sound. Do cyclically stable firms pay more for gasoline during a recession than others do? Presumably not, unless on the basis of this stable demand they have negotiated a long term contract; and this is precisely what the theory asserts about the labor market.

Finally, the theory predicts that returns to equity holders should fluctuate more than wages and salaries and that self-employed workers should have higher incomes with a greater variance than employed workers. These facts are commonplace, but their explanation is not clear outside of the contract theory.

Concluding Comments

(a) The contract theory is not a denial of the search theory insofar as the latter deals with optimal job search on the part of the potential employee. On the contrary, it complements that theory of the supply side, and removes its inconsistency, in some models, with the employer's behavior. It complements the search theory by specifying something about the things for which the worker is searching, and creates consistency between this and what the employer is offering.

(b) The contract theory is in the tradition of Knight and Say which finds the firm or employer as the principal risk bearer. But it is not simply that the more risk averse become employees rather than employers. This may be true, but the essential element is that being an employee, or owner of non-human capital, creates a greater degree of (marginal) risk aversion.

(c) It seems that a complete articulation of Becker's [3] well known theory of specific human capital requires something like a contract theory of the labor market. In that theory, the employer and employee split the cost of creating specific human capital skills that can be used with only one employer and later split the difference between the lower outside marginal product of the worker and his higher inside product. What is to prevent the employer from later cheating the employee by paying him merely an epsilon over his outside wage?

In a similar vein the existence of non-vested pension plans is difficult to understand without a contract theory of the labor market. Presumably, this is a risk sharing arrangement. But what is to prevent the employer from similarly cheating the employees by regularly laying them off a week, say, before their pensions become vested?

A sensible answer to these questions, which would occur to virtually anyone, is that of course the employer cannot so cheat without losing his reputation and experiencing later difficulties in hiring. But if this is so obvious, it should also apply to job and wage security where employees are risk averse, and this, as we have seen, has powerful implications for the question of wage rigidities.[29]

(d) Despite the teachings of many generations of neo-classical economists it is clear that people do in fact regard the price of labor as somehow different from the prices of commodities. Labor is not a commodity! Such attitudes have been the despair of many economists. While wages make up the livelihood of human beings, so do the prices of commodities. Why should attitudes about fairness dominate discussions of wages to a greater degree than discussions of prices? Any textbook on wage and salary administration will drive even a novitiate in economics to despair. Why can't personnel or human relations experts understand the simplest elements of demand and supply? Why is there a "social" element in wages in addition to an economic element, as J. R. Hicks (1966) argues? Is it all muddle-headedness?

This theory suggests an economic explanation for these attitudes. Even a tough-minded neo-classicist might admit that it is unfair to break negotiated and enforceable contracts (if one could get away with it) in the sense that it is a socially undesirable. By reducing the value of property rights, such behavior reduces the social gains from voluntary exchange.

But, in fact, there is only a continuum, not a sharp break between enforceable and non-enforceable contracts. The quasi-contract theory suggests that the same rationale lies behind non-contractual understandings.

The most frequent comment I have heard in discussing the rigidity of wages is the allegation that wage cuts would have a disastrous effect on morale and seriously damage productivity if not inducing outright sabotage. If this is true, it does not explain why sellers of farm commodities or corporate stock behave differently. Given that labor contracts do in fact exist, and that wage cuts are hence avoided save in drastic situations, it is very likely true that the effect on any one employer of an "unfair" wage cut might be as alleged. But this does not explain the original wage rigidity itself. It explains the serious consequences of deviating from the system once it is established and not the system itself.

(e) Wage controls have been defended on the grounds that they may be useful in breaking inflationary expectations, and the contract theory creates a much more powerful theoretical case for controls than does the search theory alone. According to both theories, a break in a long-term inflationary policy is going to produce an increase in unemployment until expectations are revised. But in the search theory, employers and employees must only correctly perceive the increased slack in the labor market in order to adjust their behavior. According to the contract theory, on the other hand, employers and employees must really believe that a new long-term era of price stability is at hand before wage increases are adjusted downward. Current excess supply is not sufficient. Thus wage and salary ceiling increases can, in principle, force the economy toward the long run equilibrium, given that the government is in fact going to maintain its rein on inflationary demand. Such controls on wage increases do not lower wages below an equilibrium and create shortages; they lower wages toward an equilibrium and eliminate surpluses. Naturally, with such wage controls there is no economic need for price controls.

I know of no instance in practice of such a control program, and it seems unlikely, if I may venture into a non-economic area, to be politically feasible.[30]

---

[29]Cf. also Oi (1962). Becker suggests that non-vesting may be a method of retaining the employee and the firm's investment in his specific human capital. As noted this would appear to admit the contract theory as part of the theory of specific human capital. Once, however, the employee's benefits are not tied closely to his current productivity there is no reason that these should be limited to pensions. In particular seniority pay raises with no precise connection with current productivity may be part of a contract. If this were true there would be more than specific human capital and its current productivity to account for the observed rising age-earnings profiles of typical employees.

A "pure" specific human capital theory devoid of all quasi-contract considerations is, however, distinct from the theory of this paper. It explains the relative incidence of layoffs for given wages. But if the short run supply curve is upward sloping this is not the relevant question, for both the wage and the level of employment must be explained jointly. Further it would appear that for given wages the specific human capital theory implies that employees approaching retirement, in whom the firm has little remaining capital to retain, will be particularly susceptible to layoffs (and of course without induced retirement benefits). The quasi-contract theory has no such implication.

[30]Another question of some interest is the extent to which employer provision of unemployment insurance has been reduced by public unemployment insurance. It would appear fairly obvious, because of adverse selection and moral hazard, that private insurance companies would find it difficult to enter this field.

REFERENCES

1. A. Alchian, "Information Costs, Pricing and Resource Unemployment," in Phelps, (1970).
2. _____ , and H. Demsetz, "Production, Information Costs, and Economic Organization," *American Economic Review,* December, 1972.
3. C. Azariadis, "On the Incidence of Unemployment," paper read at Econometric Society Meetings, December, 1973.
4. M. N. Baily, "Wages and Employment under Uncertain Demand," *Review of Economic Studies,* January, 1974.
5. G. Becker, *Human Capital.* New York, 1964.
6. Canada, Prices and Incomes Commission; *Final Report: Inflation, Unemployment and Incomes Policy.*
7. Irving Fisher, "A Statistical Relation between Unemployment and Price Changes," *International Labour Review,* June, 1926.
8. M. Friedman, "What Price Guidelines," in G. Schultz and R. Aliber, eds., *Guidelines: Informal Controls and the Market Place,* Chicago, 1966.
9. _____ , "The Role of Monetary Policy," *American Economic Review,* March, 1968.
10. _____ , "A Theoretical Framework for Monetary Analysis," *Journal of Political Economy,* March/April, 1970.
11. D. F. Gordon and J. A. Hynes, "On the Theory of Price Dynamics," in Phelps (1970).
12. J. R. Hicks, *The Theory of Wages.* 2nd ed., New York, 1966.
13. D. Hume, *Essays and Treatises on Several Subjects.* Dublin, 1779.
14. H. Johnson and D. Croome, *Money in Britain, 1959–1969.* London, 1970.
15. J. M. Keynes, *The General Theory of Employment, Interest and Money.* New York, 1936.
16. E. Kuh, "Unemployment, Production Functions, and Effective Demands," *Journal of Political Economy,* June, 1966.
17. R. Lucas and L. Rapping, "Real Wages, Employment, and Inflation," in Phelps (1970).
18. Walter Oi, "Labor as a Quasi-Fixed Factor," *Journal of Political Economy,* December, 1962.
19. E. Phelps, ed., *Microeconomic Foundations of Employment and Inflation Theory.* New York, 1970.
20. _____ , *Inflation Policy and Unemployment Theory.* New York, 1972.
21. A. Rees, "Wage Determination and Involuntary Unemployment," *Journal of Political Economy,* April, 1951.
22. P. Samuelson, *The Foundations of Economic Analysis.* Harvard, 1947.
23. H. Thornton, *An Enquiry into the Nature and Effects of the Paper Credit of Great Britain.* London, 1802.
24. J. Tobin, "Inflation and Unemployment," *American Economic Review,* March, 1972.
25. J. Viner, "Mr. Keynes on the Causes of Unemployment: A Review," *Quarterly Journal of Economics,* November, 1936.

CHOICE UNDER DIFFERENTIAL INFORMATION

The Market for "Lemons": Quality Uncertainty and the Market Mechanism*†

GEORGE A. AKERLOF

George A. Akerlof (B.A., Yale University, 1962; Ph.D., Massachusetts Institute of Technology, 1966) was born in 1940 in New Haven, Connecticut. Akerlof joined the faculty of the University of California at Berkeley in 1966 and is presently Professor of Economics. He has been a Visiting Professor at Harvard University; the Indian Statistical Institute, New Delhi; and the London School of Economics where he served as Cassel Professor of Money and Banking from 1978 to 1980. Professor Akerlof has authored numerous articles dealing with the demand for money, limited information, and unemployment. *An Economic Theorist's Book of Tales,* a recent collection of his papers, reflects his ability, unparalleled among his contemporaries, to spotlight an important argument with a catchy title.

I. INTRODUCTION

This paper relates quality and uncertainty. The existence of goods of many grades poses interesting and important problems for the theory of markets. On the one hand, the interaction of quality differences and uncertainty may explain important institutions of the labor market. On the other hand, this paper presents a struggling attempt to give structure to the statement: "Business in underdeveloped countries is difficult"; in particular, a structure is given for determining the economic costs of dishonesty. Additional applications of the theory include comments on the structure of money markets, on the notion of "insurability," on the liquidity of durables, and on brand-name goods.

There are many markets in which buyers use some market statistic to judge the quality of prospective purchases. In this case there is incentive for sellers to market poor quality merchandise, since the returns for good quality accrue mainly to the entire group whose statistic is affected rather than to the individual seller. As a result there tends to be a reduction

*Reprinted from *Quarterly Journal of Economics* (August 1970) by permission of John Wiley & Sons, Inc. Copyright 1970, pp. 488–500.
†The author would especially like to thank Thomas Rothenberg for invaluable comments and inspiration. In addition he is indebted to Roy Radner, Albert Fishlow, Bernard Saffran, William D. Nordhaus, Giorgio La Malfa, Charles C. Holt, John Letiche, and the referee for help and suggestions. He would also like to thank the Indian Statistical Institute and the Ford Foundation for financial support.

in the average quality of goods and also in the size of the market. It should also be perceived that in these markets social and private returns differ, and therefore, in some cases, governmental intervention may increase the welfare of all parties. Or private institutions may arise to take advantage of the potential increases in welfare which can accrue to all parties. By nature, however, these institutions are nonatomistic, and therefore concentrations of power—with ill consequences of their own—can develop.

The automobile market is used as a finger exercise to illustrate and develop these thoughts. It should be emphasized that this market is chosen for its concreteness and ease in understanding rather than for its importance or realism.

II. THE MODEL WITH AUTOMOBILES AS AN EXAMPLE
A. The Automobiles Market

The example of used cars captures the essence of the problem. From time to time one hears either mention of or surprise at the large price difference between new cars and those which have just left the showroom. The usual lunch table justification for this phenomenon is the pure joy of owning a "new" car. We offer a different explanation. Suppose (for the sake of clarity rather than reality) that there are just four kinds of cars. There are new cars and used cars. There are good cars and bad cars (which in America are known as "lemons"). A new car may be a good car or a lemon, and of course the same is true of used cars.

The individuals in this market buy a new automobile without knowing whether the car they buy will be good or a lemon. But they do know that with probability q it is a good car and with probability $(1 - q)$ it is a lemon; by assumption, q is the proportion of good cars produced and $(1 - q)$ is the proportion of lemons.

After owning a specific car, however, for a length of time, the car owner can form a good idea of the quality of this machine; i.e., the owner assigns a new probability to the event that his car is a lemon. This estimate is more accurate than the original estimate. An asymmetry in available information has developed: for the sellers now have more knowledge about the quality of a car than the buyers. But good cars and bad cars must still sell at the same price—since it is impossible for a buyer to tell the difference between a good car and a bad car. It is apparent that a used car cannot have the same valuation as a new car—if it did have the same valuation, it would clearly be advantageous to trade a lemon at the price of new car, and buy another new car, at a higher probability q of being good and a lower probability of being bad. Thus the owner of a good machine must be locked in. Not only is it true that he cannot receive the true value of his car, but he cannot even obtain the expected value of a new car.

Gresham's law has made a modified reappearance. For most cars traded will be the "lemons," and good cars may not be traded at all. The "bad" cars tend to drive out the good (in much the same way that bad money drives out the good). But the analogy with Gresham's law is not quite complete: bad cars drive out the good because they sell at the same price as good cars; similarly, bad money drives out good because the exchange rate is even. But the bad cars sell at the same price as good cars since it is impossible for a buyer to tell the difference between a good and a bad car; only the seller knows. In Gresham's law, however, presumably both buyer and seller can tell the difference between good and bad money. So the analogy is instructive, but not complete.

B. Asymmetrical Information

It has been seen that the good cars may be driven out of the market by the lemons. But in a more continuous case with different grades of goods, even worse pathologies can exist. For it is quite possible to have the bad driving out the not-so-bad driving out the medium driving out the not-so-good driving out the good in such a sequence of events that no market exists at all.

One can assume that the demand for used automobiles depends most strongly upon two variables—the price of the automobile p and the average quality of used cars traded, μ, or $Q^d = D(p, \mu)$. Both the supply of used cars and also the average quality μ will depend upon the price, or $\mu = \mu(p)$ and $S = S(p)$. And in equilibrium the supply must equal the demand for the given average quality, or $S(p) = D(p, \mu(p))$. As the price falls, normally the quality will also fall. And it is quite possible that no goods will be traded at any price level.

Such an example can be derived from utility theory. Assume that there are just two groups of traders: groups one and two. Give group one a utility function

$$U_1 = M + \sum_{i=1}^{n} x_i$$

where M is the consumption of goods other than automobiles, x_i is the quality of the ith automobile, and n is the number of automobiles.

Similarly, let

$$U_2 = M + \sum_{i=1}^{n} 3/2x_i$$

where M, x_i, and n are defined as before.

Three comments should be made about these utility functions: (1) without linear utility (say with logarithmic utility) one gets needlessly mired in algebraic complication. (2) The use of linear utility allows a focus on the effects of asymmetry of information; with a concave utility function we would have to deal jointly with the usual risk-variance effects of uncertainty and the special effects we wish to discuss here. (3) U_1 and U_2 have the odd characteristic that the addition of a second car, or indeed a kth car, adds the same amount of utility as the first. Again realism is sacrificed to avoid a diversion from the proper focus.

To continue, it is assumed (1) that both type one traders and type two traders are von Neumann-Morgenstern maximizers of expected utility; (2) that group one has N cars with uniformly distributed quality x, $0 \leq x \leq 2$, and group two has no cars; (3) that the price of "other goods" M is unity.

Denote the income (including that derived from the sale of automobiles) of all type one traders as Y_1 and the income of all type two traders as Y_2. The demand for used cars will be the sum of the demands by both groups. When one ignores indivisibilities, the demand for automobiles by type one traders will be

$$D_1 = Y_1/p \quad \mu/p > 1$$
$$D_1 = 0 \quad \mu/p < 1.$$

And the supply of cars offered by type one traders is

$$S_2 = pN/2 \quad p \leq 2 \tag{1}$$

with average quality

$$\mu = p/2. \tag{2}$$

(To derive (1) and (2), the uniform distribution of automobile quality is used.)

Similarly the demand of type two traders is

$$D_2 = Y_2/p \quad 3\mu/2 > p$$
$$D_2 = 0 \quad 3\mu/2 < p$$

and

$$S_2 = 0.$$

Thus total demand $D(p, \mu)$ is

$$D(p, \mu) = (Y_2 + Y_1)/p \quad \text{if } p < \mu$$
$$D(p, \mu) = Y_2/p \quad \text{if } \mu < p < 3\mu/2$$
$$D(p, \mu) = 0 \quad \text{if } p > 3\mu/2.$$

However, with price p, average quality is $p/2$ and therefore at no price will any trade take place at all: in spite of the fact that *at any given price* between 0 and 3 there are traders of type one who are willing to sell their automobiles at a price which traders of type two are willing to pay.

C. Symmetric Information

The foregoing is contrasted with the case of symmetric information. Suppose that the quality of all cars is uniformly distributed, $0 \leq x \leq 2$. Then the demand curves and supply curves can be written as follows:

Supply

$$S(p) = N \quad p > 1$$
$$S(p) = 0 \quad p < 1.$$

And the demand curves are

$$D(p) = (Y_2 + Y_1)/p \quad p < 1$$
$$D(p) = (Y_2/p) \quad 1 < p < 3/2$$
$$D(p) = 0 \quad p > 3/2.$$

In equilibrium

$$p = 1 \quad \text{if } Y_2 < N \tag{3}$$
$$p = Y_2/N \quad \text{if } 2Y_2/3 < N < Y_2 \tag{4}$$
$$p = 3/2 \quad \text{if } N < 2Y_2/3. \tag{5}$$

If $N < Y_2$ there is a gain in utility over the case of asymmetrical information of $N/2$. (If $N > Y_2$, in which case the income of type two traders is insufficient to buy all N automobiles, there is a gain in utility of $Y_2/2$ units.)

Finally, it should be mentioned that in this example, if traders of groups one and two have the same probabilistic estimates about the quality of individual automobiles—though these estimates may vary from automobile to automobile—(3), (4), and (5) will still describe equilibrium with one slight change: p will then represent the expected price of one quality unit.

III. EXAMPLES AND APPLICATIONS
A. Insurance

It is a well-known fact that people over 65 have great difficulty in buying medical insurance. The natural question arises: why doesn't the price rise to match the risk?

Our answer is that as the price level rises the people who insure themselves will be those who are increasingly certain that they will need the insurance; for error in medical check-ups, doctors' sympathy with older patients, and so on make it much easier for the applicant to assess the risks involved than the insurance company. The result is that the average medical condition of insurance applicants deteriorates as the price level rises—with the result that no insurance sales may take place at any price.[1] This is strictly analogous to our automobiles case, where the average quality of used cars supplied fell with a corresponding fall in the price level. This agrees with the explanation in insurance textbooks:

> Generally speaking policies are not available at ages materially greater than sixty-five. . . . The term premiums are too high for any but the most pessimistic (which is to say the least healthy) insureds to find attractive. Thus there is a severe problem of adverse selection at these ages.[2]

The statistics do not contradict this conclusion. While demands for health insurance rise with age, a 1956 national sample survey of 2,809 families with 8,898 persons shows that hospital insurance coverage drops from 63 per cent of those aged 45 to 54, to 31 per cent for those over 65. And surprisingly, this survey also finds average medical expenses for males aged 55 to 64 of $88, while males over 65 pay an average of $77.[3] While noninsured expenditure rises from $66 to $80 in these age groups, insured expenditure declines from $105 to $70. The conclusion is tempting that insurance companies are particularly wary of giving medical insurance to older people.

The principle of "adverse selection" is potentially present in all lines of insurance. The following statement appears in an insurance textbook written at the Wharton School:

> There is potential adverse selection in the fact that healthy term insurance policy holders may decide to terminate their coverage when they become older and premiums mount. This action could leave an insurer with an undue proportion of below average risks and claims might be higher than anticipated. Adverse selection "appears (or at least is possible) whenever the individual or group insured has freedom to buy or not to buy, to choose the amount or plan of insurance, and to persist or to discontinue as a policy holder."[4]

Group insurance, which is the most common form of medical insurance in the United States, picks out the healthy, for generally adequate health is a precondition for employment. At the same time this means that medical insurance is least available to those who need it most, for the insurance companies do their own "adverse selection."

This adds one major argument in favor of medicare.[5] On a cost benefit basis medicare may pay off: for it is quite possible that every individual in the market would be willing to pay the expected cost of his medicare and buy insurance, yet no insurance company can afford to sell him a policy—for at any price it will attract too many "lemons." The welfare economics of medicare, in this view, is *exactly* analogous to the usual classroom argument for public expenditure on roads.

B. The Employment of Minorities

The Lemons Principle also casts light on the employment of minorities. Employers may refuse to hire members of minority groups for certain types of jobs. This decision may not reflect irrationality or preju-

---

[1] Arrow's fine article, "Uncertainty and Medical Care" (*American Economic Review*, Vol. 53, 1963), does not make this point explicitly. He emphasizes "moral hazard" rather than "adverse selection." In its strict sense, the presence of "moral hazard" is equally disadvantageous for both governmental and private programs; in its broader sense, which includes "adverse selection," "moral hazard" gives a decided advantage to government insurance programs.

[2] O. D. Dickerson, *Health Insurance* (Homewood, Ill.: Irwin, 1959), p. 333.

[3] O. W. Anderson (with J. J. Feldman), *Family Medical Costs and Insurance* (New York: McGraw-Hill, 1956).

[4] H. S. Denenberg, R. D. Eilers, G. W. Hoffman, C. A. Kline, J. J. Melone, and H. W. Snider, *Risk and Insurance* (Englewood Cliffs, N. J.: Prentice Hall, 1964), p. 446.

[5] The following quote, again taken from an insurance textbook, shows how far the medical insurance market is from perfect competition:

". . . insurance companies must screen their applicants. Naturally it is true that many people will voluntarily seek adequate insurance on their own initiative. But in such lines as accident and health insurance, companies are likely to give a second look to persons who voluntarily seek insurance without being approached by an agent." (F. J. Angell, *Insurance, Principles and Practices,* New York: The Ronald Press, 1957, pp. 8–9.)

This shows that insurance is *not* a commodity for sale on the open market.

dice—but profit maximization. For race may serve as a good *statistic* for the applicant's social background, quality of schooling, and general job capabilities.

Good quality schooling could serve as a substitute for this statistic; by grading students the schooling system can give a better indicator of quality than other more superficial characteristics. As T. W. Schultz writes, "The educational establishment *discovers* and cultivates potential talent. The capabilities of children and mature students can never be known until *found* and cultivated."[6] (Italics added.) An untrained worker may have valuable natural talents, but these talents must be certified by "the educational establishment" before a company can afford to use them. The certifying establishment, however, must be credible; the unreliability of slum schools decreases the economic possibilities of their students.

This lack may be particularly disadvantageous to members of already disadvantaged minority groups. For an employer may make a rational decision not to hire any members of these groups in responsible positions—because it is difficult to distinguish those with good job qualifications from those with bad qualifications. This type of decision is clearly what George Stigler had in mind when he wrote, "in a regime of ignorance Enrico Fermi would have been a gardener, Von Neumann a checkout clerk at a drugstore."[7]

As a result, however, the rewards for work in slum schools tend to accrue to the group as a whole—in raising its average quality—rather than to the individual. Only insofar as information in addition to race is used is there any incentive for training.

An additional worry is that the Office of Economic Opportunity is going to use cost-benefit analysis to evaluate its programs. For many benefits may be external. The benefit from training minority groups may arise as much from raising the average quality of the group as from raising the quality of the individual trainee; and, likewise, the returns may be distributed over the whole group rather than to the individual.

C. The Costs of Dishonesty

The Lemons model can be used to make some comments on the costs of dishonesty. Consider a market in which goods are sold honestly or dishonestly; quality may be represented, or it may be misrepresented. The purchaser's problem, of course, is to identify quality. The presence of people in the market who are willing to offer inferior goods tends to drive the market out of existence—as in the case of our automobile "lemons." It is this possibility that represents the major costs of dishonesty—for dishonest dealings tend to drive honest dealings out of the market. There may be potential buyers of good quality products and there may be potential sellers of such products in the appropriate price range; however, the presence of people who wish to pawn bad wares as good wares tends to drive out the legitimate business. The cost of dishonesty, therefore, lies not only in the amount by which the purchaser is cheated; the cost also must include the loss incurred from driving legitimate business out of existence.

Dishonesty in business is a serious problem in underdeveloped countries. Our model gives a possible structure to this statement and delineates the nature of the "external" economies involved. In particular, in the model economy described, dishonesty, or the misrepresentation of the quality of automobiles, costs 1/2 unit of utility per automobile; furthermore, it reduces the size of the used car market from N to 0. We can, consequently, directly evaluate the costs of dishonesty—at least in theory.

There is considerable evidence that quality variation is greater in underdeveloped than in developed areas. For instance, the need for quality control of exports and State Trading Corporations can be taken as one indicator. In India, for example, under the Export Quality Control and Inspection Act of 1963, "about 85 per cent of Indian exports are covered under one or the other type of quality control."[8] Indian housewives must carefully glean the rice of the local bazaar to sort out stones of the same color and shape which have been intentionally added to the rice. Any comparison of the heterogeneity of quality in the street market and the canned qualities of the American supermarket suggests that quality variation is a greater problem in the East than in the West.

In our traditional pattern of development the mer-

---

[6] T. W. Schultz, *The Economic Value of Education* (New York: Columbia University Press, 1964), p. 42.

[7] G. J. Stigler, "Information and the Labor Market," *Journal of Political Economy*, Vol. 70 (Oct. 1962), Supplement, p. 104.

[8] *The Times of India*, Nov. 10, 1967, p. 1.

chants of the pre-industrial generation turn into the first entrepreneurs of the next. The best-documented case is Japan,[9] but this also may have been the pattern for Britain and America.[1] In *our* picture the important skill of the merchant is identifying the quality of merchandise; those who can identify used cars in our example and can guarantee the quality may profit by as much as the difference between type two traders' buying price and type one traders' selling price. These people are the merchants. In production these skills are equally necessary—both to be able to identify the quality of inputs and to certify the quality of outputs. And this is one (added) reason why the merchants may logically become the first entrepreneurs.

The problem, of course, is that entrepreneurship may be a scarce resource; no development text leaves entrepreneurship unemphasized. Some treat it as central.[2] Given, then, that entrepreneurship is scarce, there are two ways in which product variations impede development. First, the pay-off to trade is great for would-be entrepreneurs, and hence they are diverted from production; second, the amount of entrepreneurial time per unit output is greater, the greater are the quality variations.

D. Credit Markets in Underdeveloped Countries

(1) Credit markets in underdeveloped countries often strongly reflect the operation of the Lemons Principle. In India a major fraction of industrial enterprise is controlled by managing agencies (according to a recent survey, these "managing agencies" controlled 65.7 per cent of the net worth of public limited companies and 66 per cent of total assets).[3] Here is a historian's account of the function and genesis of the "managing agency system":

> The management of the South Asian commercial scene remained the function of merchant houses, and a type of organization peculiar to South Asia known as the Managing Agency. When a new venture was promoted (such as a manufacturing plant, a plantation, or a trading venture), the promoters would approach an established managing agency. The promoters might be Indian or British, and they might have technical or financial resources or merely a concession. In any case they would turn to the agency because of its reputation, which would encourage confidence in the venture and stimulate investment.[4]

In turn, a second major feature of the Indian industrial scene has been the dominance of these managing agencies by caste (or, more accurately, communal) groups. Thus firms can usually be classified according to communal origin.[5] In this environment, in which outside investors are likely to be bilked of their holdings, either (1) firms establish a reputation for "honest" dealing, which confers upon them a monopoly rent insofar as their services are limited in supply, or (2) the sources of finance are limited to local communal groups which can use communal—and possibly familial—ties to encourage honest dealing *within* the community. It is, in Indian economic history, extraordinarily difficult to discern whether the savings of rich landlords failed to be invested in the industrial sector (1) because of a fear to invest in ventures controlled by other communities, (2) because of inflated propensities to consume, or (3) because of low rates of return.[6] At the very least, however, it is clear that the British-owned managing

[4]H. Tinker, *South Asia: A Short History* (New York: Praeger, 1966), p. 134.
[5] The existence of the following table (and also the small per cent of firms under mixed control) indicates the communalization of the control of firms. *Source:* M. M. Mehta, *Structure of Indian Industries* (Bombay: Popular Book Depot, 1955), p. 314.

Distribution of Industrial Control by Community

	1911	1931 (number of firms)	1951
British	281	416	382
Parsis	15	25	19
Gujratis	3	11	17
Jews	5	9	3
Muslims	—	10	3
Bengalis	8	5	20
Marwaris	—	6	96
Mixed control	28	28	79
Total	341	510	619

Also, for the cotton industry see H. Fukuzawa, "Cotton Mill Industry," in V. B. Singh, editor, *Economic History of India, 1857–1956* (Bombay: Allied Publishers, 1965).
[6]For the mixed record of industrial profits, see D. H. Buchanan, *The Development of Capitalist Enterprise in India* (New York: Kelley, 1966, reprinted).

[9]See M. J. Levy, Jr., "Contrasting Factors in the Modernization of China and Japan," in *Economic Growth: Brazil, India, Japan,* ed. S. Kuznets, *et. al.* (Durham, N. C.: Duke University Press, 1955).
[1]C. P. Kindleberger, *Economic Development* (New York: McGraw-Hill, 1958), p. 86.
[2]For example, see W. Arthur Lewis, *The Theory of Economic Growth* (Homewood, Ill.: Irwin, 1955), p. 196.
[3]*Report of the Committee on the Distribution of Income and Levels of Living,* Part I, Government of India, Planning Commission, Feb. 1964, p. 44.

agencies tended to have an equity holding whose communal origin was more heterogeneous than the Indian-controlled agency houses, and would usually include both Indian and British investors.

(2) A second example of the workings of the Lemons Principle concerns the extortionate rates which the local moneylender charges his clients. In India these high rates of interest have been the leading factor in landlessness; the so-called "Cooperative Movement" was meant to counteract this growing landlessness by setting up banks to compete with the local moneylenders.[7] While the large banks in the central cities have prime interest rates of 6, 8, and 10 per cent, the local moneylender charges 15, 25, and even 50 per cent. The answer to this seeming paradox is that credit is granted only where the granter has (1) easy means of enforcing his contract or (2) personal knowledge of the character of the borrower. The middleman who tries to arbitrage between the rates of the moneylender and the central bank is apt to attract all the "lemons" and thereby make a loss.

This interpretation can be seen in Sir Malcolm Darling's interpretation of the village moneylender's power:

[7] The leading authority on this is Sir Malcolm Darling. See his *Punjabi Peasant in Prosperity and Debt*. The following table may also prove instructive:

	Secured loans (per cent)	Commonest rates for—Unsecured loans (per cent)	Grain loans (per cent)
Punjab	6 to 12	12 to 24 (18¾ commonest)	25
United Provinces	9 to 12	24 to 37½	25 (50 in Oudh)
Bihar		18¾	50
Orissa	12 to 18¾	25	25
Bengal	8 to 12	9 to 18 for "respectable clients" 18¾ to 37½ (the latter common to agriculturalists)	
Central Provinces	6 to 12	15 for proprietors 24 for occupancy tenants 37½ for ryots with no right of transfer	25
Bombay	9 to 12	12 to 25 (18 commonest)	
Sind		36	
Madras	12	15 to 18 (in insecure tracts 24 not uncommon)	20 to 50

Source: Punjabi Peasant in Prosperity and Debt, 3rd ed. (Oxford University Press, 1932), p. 190.

It is only fair to remember that in the Indian village the money-lender is often the one thrifty person amongst a generally thriftless people; and that his methods of business, though demoralizing under modern conditions, suit the happy-go-lucky ways of the peasant. He is always accessible, even at night; dispenses with troublesome formalities, asks no inconvenient questions, advances promptly, and if interest is paid, does not press for repayment of principal. He keeps in close personal touch with his clients, and in many villages shares their occasions of weal or woe. *With his intimate knowledge of those around him he is able, without serious risk, to finance those who would otherwise get no loan at all.* [Italics added.][8]

Or look at Barbara Ward's account:

A small shopkeeper in a Hong Kong fishing village told me: "I give credit to anyone who anchors regularly in our bay; but if it is someone I don't know well, then I think twice about it unless I can find out all about him."[9]

Or, a profitable sideline of cotton ginning in Iran is the loaning of money for the next season, since the ginning companies often have a line of credit from Teheran banks at the market rate of interest. But in the first years of operation large losses are expected from unpaid debts—due to poor knowledge of the local scene.[1]

IV. COUNTERACTING INSTITUTIONS

Numerous institutions arise to counteract the effects of quality uncertainty. One obvious institution is guarantees. Most consumer durables carry guarantees to ensure the buyer of some normal expected quality. One natural result of our model is that the risk is borne by the seller rather than by the buyer.

A second example of an institution which counteracts the effects of quality uncertainty is the brand-name good. Brand names not only indicate quality but also give the consumer a means of retaliation if the quality does not meet expectations. For the consumer will then curtail future purchases. Often too, new products are associated with old brand names.

[8] Darling, *op. cit.*, p. 204.
[9] B. Ward, "Cash or Credit Crops," *Economic Development and Cultural Change*, Vol. 8 (Jan. 1960), reprinted in *Peasant Society: A Reader*, ed. G. Foster *et al.* (Boston: Little Brown and Company, 1967). Quote on p. 142. In the same volume, see also G. W. Skinner, "Marketing and Social Structure in Rural China," and S. W. Mintz, "Pratik: Haitian Personal Economic Relations."
[1] Personal conversation with mill manager, April 1968.

This ensures the prospective consumer of the quality of the product.

Chains—such as hotel chains or restaurant chains—are similar to brand names. One observation consistent with our approach is the chain restaurant. These restaurants, at least in the United States, most often appear on interurban highways. The customers are seldom local. The reason is that these well-known chains offer a better hamburger than the *average* local restaurant; at the same time, the local customer, who knows his area, can usually choose a place he prefers.

Licensing practices also reduce quality uncertainty. For instance, there is the licensing of doctors, lawyers, and barbers. Most skilled labor carries some certification indicating the attainment of certain levels of proficiency. The high school diploma, the baccalaureate degree, the Ph.D., even the Nobel Prize, to some degree, serve this function of certification. And education and labor markets themselves have their own "brand names."

V. CONCLUSION

We have been discussing economic models in which "trust" is important. Informal unwritten guarantees are preconditions for trade and production. Where these guarantees are indefinite, business will suffer—as indicated by our generalized Gresham's law. This aspect of uncertainty has been explored by game theorists, as in the Prisoner's Dilemma, but usually it has not been incorporated in the more traditional Arrow-Debreu approach to uncertainty.[2] But the difficulty of distinguishing good quality from bad is inherent in the business world; this may indeed explain many economic institutions and may in fact be one of the more important aspects of uncertainty.

[2] R. Radner, "Équilibre de Marchés à Terme et au Comptant en Cas d'Incertitude," in *Cahiers d'Econometrie,* Vol. 12 (Nov. 1967), Centre National de la Recherche Scientifique, Paris.

The Economics of Moral Hazard: Comment*

MARK V. PAULY

Mark V. Pauly (A.B., Xavier University, 1963; M.A., University of Delaware, 1965; Ph.D., University of Virginia, 1967) is Professor of Health Care Systems and Public Management at the Wharton School and Professor of Economics in the School of Arts and Sciences of the University of Pennsylvania. He is also Executive Director of the Leonard Davis Institute of Health Economics and Robert D. Eilers Professor of Health Care Management and Economics. One of the nation's leading health economists, Professor Pauly has made significant contributions to the fields of medical economics and health insurance. He is widely published on such issues as physician-patient decisions, the operation of medical care markets, and national health policy, with a prevailing emphasis on the role of economics in the provision of medical care and health services. He is also noted for his research in public finance and insurance. Professor Pauly serves on the editorial boards of *Public Finance Quarterly* and the *Journal of Health Economics*. In addition, he is a Board member of the Association for Health Services Research; a member of the Health Advisory Board and adjunct scholar of the American Enterprise Institute; and consultant to the National Center for Health Services Research, the Health Insurance Association of America, the American Hospital Association, the Urban Institute, and the Michigan Hospital Association. Prior to joining Pennsylvania's faculty, he was a Visiting Research Fellow at the International Institute of Management in Berlin, West Germany, and Professor of Economics at Northwestern University. The article reprinted here was written while he was a graduate student at the University of Virginia.

When uncertainty is present in economic activity, insurance is commonly found. Indeed, Kenneth Arrow [1] has identified a kind of market failure with

the absence of markets to provide insurance against some uncertain events. Arrow stated that "the welfare case for insurance of all sorts is overwhelming. It follows that the government should undertake insurance where the market, for whatever reason, has failed to emerge" [1, pp. 945, 961]. This paper will

*Reprinted from *American Economic Review* (June 1968) by permission of the American Economic Association. Copyright 1968, pp. 531–538.

show, however, that even if all individuals are risk-averters, insurance against some types of uncertain events may be nonoptimal. Hence, the fact that certain kinds of insurance have failed to emerge in the private market may be no indication of nonoptimality, and compulsory government insurance against some uncertain events may lead to inefficiency. It will also be shown that the problem of "moral hazard" in insurance has, in fact, little to do with morality, but can be analyzed with orthodox economic tools.

The particular type of insurance for which the argument will be presented is that of insurance against medical care expenses, for it was in a discussion of medical expense insurance that Arrow framed the propositions cited above. However, the analysis is applicable as well to other types of insurance, such as automobile collision insurance.

I. THE WELFARE IMPLICATIONS OF INSURANCE

It is assumed that all individuals are expected utility maximizers and are risk-averters, and that the incidence of illness is a random event. This excludes preventive medicine from consideration, and it also ignores the effect that medical insurance might have on the purchase of preventive care. Bernoulli's theorem, as cited by Arrow [1, pp. 959–61], states that such individuals will prefer insurance with a premium m which indemnifies against all costs of medical care to facing without insurance a probability distribution of such expenditures with mean m.

There is a social gain obtained by purchase of this insurance (as long as the insurer suffers no social loss) since pooling of risks reduces the total risk, and therefore the risk per insured, because of the Law of Large Numbers. Of course, the existence of transactions costs means that the policy is not really offered at the actuarially fair premium m. However, since the individual preferred actuarially fair insurance to self-insurance, he will prefer some insurance with an actuarially unfair premium to self-insurance, so long as the premium is not too "unfair." His preference in this regard will depend on the intensity of his risk aversion and the strength of the Law of Large Numbers in reducing risk.

As indicated above, Arrow concluded from this analysis that the absence of commercial insurance against some uncertain medical-care expenses provides a case for government intervention to provide

such insurance. Dennis Lees and R. D. Rice [6] answered that this insurance was not offered because of selling and transactions costs. Arrow [2] replied, in effect, that such costs were dead-weight losses anyway, and indeed would be eliminated by compulsory social insurance. It seems clear, however, that there is another and better way to explain why some insurances are not offered commercially. It is to show that some, perhaps many, medical care expenses are not "insurable" in the standard sense.

In order for the welfare proposition given above to be valid, the costs of medical care must be random variables. But if such expenses are not completely random, the proposition no longer holds. The quantity of medical care an individual will demand depends on his income and tastes, how ill he is, and the price charged for it. The effect of an insurance which indemnifies against all medical care expenses is to reduce the price charged to the individual at the point of service from the market price to zero. Even if the incidence of illness is a random event, whether the presence of insurance will alter the randomness of medical *expenses* depends on the elasticity of demand for medical care. Only if this demand is perfectly inelastic with respect to price in the range from the market price to zero is an expense "insurable" in the strict sense envisioned by Arrow's welfare proposition.

Suppose, for example, that an individual faces the probability $p_1 = \frac{1}{2}$ that he will not be sick at all during a given time period (event I_1) and so will demand no medical care, probability $p_2 = \frac{1}{4}$ that he will contract sickness I_2, and probability $p_3 = \frac{1}{4}$ that he will contract "more serious" sickness I_3. The position of his demand curve for medical care depends on which illness, if any, he contracts. In Fig. 1, it is assumed that his demand curves D_2 and D_3 are perfectly inelastic, and that his demand curve for the "no illness" case is identical with the y-axis. Without insurance, the individual faces the probability p_1 that he will incur no medical expenses, the probability p_2 that he will need 50 units of medical care (which is assumed to be priced at marginal cost), and the probability p_3 that he will need 200 units of medical care at a cost of 200 MC. The mean of this probability distribution (or the expected values of the individual's medical care expenses) equals ($\frac{1}{2} \times 0 + \frac{1}{4} \times 50 \ MC + \frac{1}{4} \times 200 \ MC$) or 62.5 MC. Hence, an actuarially fair insurance which indemnifies the individual against all costs of medical care could be

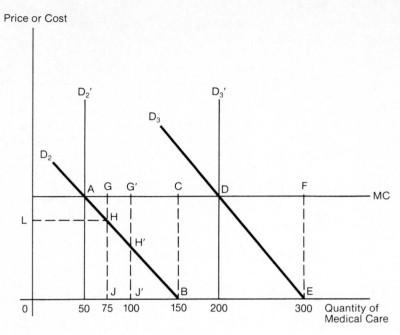

Fig. 1

offered at a premium P of 62.5 MC. Arrow's welfare proposition indicates that the individual would prefer paying a premium of 62.5 MC to risking the probability distribution with the mean $m = 62.5$ MC.

Suppose, however, that the individual's demand curves are not all perfectly inelastic, but are as D_2' and D_3'. Then the individual has to choose between facing, without insurance, the probability distribution ($\frac{1}{2} \times 0 + \frac{1}{4} \times 50\ MC + \frac{1}{4} \times 200\ MC$) with a mean m of 62.5 MC, and paying a premium of $P = (\frac{1}{2} \times 0 + \frac{1}{4} \times 150\ MC + \frac{1}{4} \times 300\ MC) = 112.5\ MC$ in order to obtain insurance. In such a case, he may well prefer the risk to the insurance.

The presence of elasticity in the demand curves implies therefore that the individual will alter his desired expenditures for medical care because of the fact of insurance. The individual who has insurance which covers all costs demands medical care as though it had a *zero* price, but when he purchases insurance, he must take account of the *positive* cost of that care, as "translated" to him through the actuarially necessary premium. Hence, he may well not wish to purchase such insurance at the premium his behavior as a purchaser of insurance and as a de-

mander of medical care under insurance makes necessary.[1]

The presence of a "prisoners' dilemma" motivation makes this inconsistency inevitable.[2] Each individual may well recognize that "excess" use of medical care makes the premium he must pay rise. No individual will be motivated to restrain his own use, however, since the incremental benefit to him for excess use is great, while the additional cost of his use is largely spread over other insurance holders, and so he bears only a tiny fraction of the cost of his use. It would be better for all insurance beneficiaries to restrain their use, but such a result is not forthcoming because the strategy of "restrain use" is dominated by that of "use excess care."

If the demand for medical care is of greater than zero elasticity, the existence of this "inconsistency" implies that inefficiency may well be created if individuals are forced, by taxation, to "purchase" in-

---

[1]This is exactly the same sort of "inconsistency" that Buchanan has noted in connection with the British National Health Service. Individuals demand medical care as though it were free but in voting decisions consider the positive cost of such care. Hence, they vote, through their representatives in the political process, to provide facilities for less medical care than they demand in the market. See [4].

[2]For a discussion of the prisoners' dilemma problem, see [7].

surance which indemnifies against some kinds of medical care expense. For an efficient solution, at least some price-rationing at the point of service may be necessary.

Suppose there are no significant income effects on the individual's demand for medical care resulting from his payment of a lump-sum premium for insurance. In Fig. 1, the inefficiency loss due to behavior under insurance, if that insurance were compulsory, would then be roughly measured by triangles ABC and DEF. These areas represent the excess that individuals do pay over what they would be willing to pay for the quantity of medical care demanded under insurance. Against this loss must be offset the utility gain from having these uncertain expenses insured, but the net change in utility from a compulsory purchase of this "insurance" could well be negative.

Moreover, if individual demands for medical care differ, it is possible that the loss due to "excess" use under insurance may exceed the welfare gain from insurance for one individual but fall short of it for another individual. It follows that it may not be optimal policy to provide compulsory insurance against particular events for all individuals. Some events may be "insurable" for some persons but not for others. It also follows that some events, though uncertain, may not be insurable for anyone. If persons differ (a) in the strength of their risk aversion or (b) in the extent to which insurances of various types alter the quantity of medical care they demand, an optimal state will be one in which various types of policies are purchased by various groups of people. There may be some persons who will purchase no insurance against some uncertain events.

Insurance is more likely to be provided against those events (a) for which the quantity demanded at a zero price does not greatly exceed that demanded at a positive price, (b) for which the extent of randomness is greater, so that risk-spreading reduces the risk significantly, and (c) against which individuals have a greater risk-aversion. There is uncertainty attached to "catastrophic" illness, but it appears that the elasticity of demand for treatment against such illness is not very great (in the sense that there is one and only one appropriate treatment). Furthermore, the "randomness" attached to such illnesses is relatively great, in the sense that they are unpredictable for any individual, and people's aversion to such risk is relatively great. Hence, one would expect to find, and does find, insurance offered against such events.

Similar statement might be made with respect to ordinary hospitalization insurance.

There is also some uncertainty attached to visits to a physician's office, but the extent of randomness and risk-aversion is probably relatively low for most persons. The increase in use in response to a zero price would be relatively great. One would not expect to find, and does not in general find, "insurance" against such events. Similar analysis applies to insurance against the cost of dental care, eyeglasses, or drugs.

II. MORAL HAZARD

It has been recognized in the insurance literature that medical insurance, by lowering the marginal cost of care to the individual, may increase usage; this characteristic has been termed "moral hazard." Moral hazard is defined as "the intangible loss-producing propensities of the individual assured" [4, p. 463] or as that which "comprehends all of the nonphysical hazards of risk" [5, p. 42]. Insurance writers have tended very strongly to look upon this phenomenon (of demanding more at a zero price than at a positive one) as a moral or ethical problem, using emotive words such as "malingering" and "hypochondria," lumping it together with outright fraud in the collection of benefits, and providing value-tinged definitions as "moral hazard reflects the hazard that arises from the failure of individuals who are or have been affected by insurance to uphold the accepted moral qualities" [5, p. 327], or "moral hazard is every deviation from correct human behavior that may pose a problem for an insurer" [3, p. 22]. It is surprising that very little economic analysis seems to have been applied here.[3]

The above analysis shows, however, that the response of seeking more medical care with insurance than in its absence is a result not of moral perfidy, but of rational economic behavior. Since the cost of the individual's excess usage is spread over all other

---

[3]In his original article, Arrow mentions moral hazard as a "practical limitation" on the use of insurance which does not "alter the case for creation of a much wider class of insurance policies than now exist." [1, p. 961]. However, Arrow appears to consider moral hazard as an imperfection, a defect in physician control, rather than as a simple response to price reduction. He does not consider the direct relationship which exists between the existence of moral hazard and the validity of the welfare proposition. More importantly, in the controversy that followed [2] [6], moral hazard seems to have been completely overlooked as an explanation of why certain types of expenses are not insured commercially.

purchasers of that insurance, the individual is not prompted to restrain his usage of care.

III. DEDUCTIBLES AND COINSURANCE

The only type of insurance so far considered has been an insurance which provides full coverage of the cost of medical care. However, various devices are written into insurance, in part to reduce the moral hazard, of which the most important are deductibles and coinsurance.[4] The individual may well prefer no insurance to full coverage of all expenses, but may at the same time prefer an insurance with these devices to no insurance.[5]

A. DEDUCTIBLES

Suppose the insurance contains a deductible. The individual will compare the position he would attain if he covered the deductible and received additional care free with the position he would attain if he paid the market price for all the medical care he consumed but did not cover the deductible. If income effects are absent in Fig. 1, the individual will cover a deductible and consume 150 units of medical care when event I_2 occurs as long as the "excess" amount he pays as a deductible (e.g., area AGH for a deductible of 75 MC) is less than the consumer's surplus he gets from the "free" units of care this coverage allows him to consume (e.g., area HJB). If the deductible exceeds 100 MC (at which point area $AG'H'$ equals area $H'J'B$), the individual will not cover the deductible and will purchase 50 units. Hence, the deductible either (a) has no effect on an individual's usage or (b) induces him to consume that amount of care he would have purchased if he had no insurance. If there are income effects on individual demands, because the deductible makes the individual poorer his usage will be restrained somewhat even if he covers the deductible.

B. COINSURANCE

Coinsurance is a scheme in which the individual is, in effect, charged a positive price for medical care, but a price less than the market price. The higher

the fraction paid by the individual, the more his usage will be curtailed. In Fig. 1, if he had to pay OL of each unit's cost, he would reduce his usage if event I_5 occurred from 150 units to 75 units. The smaller the price elasticity of demand for medical care, the less will be the effect of coinsurance on usage.

It is possible for the restraining effect of coinsurance to reduce moral hazard enough to make insurance attractive to an individual who would have preferred no insurance to full-coverage insurance. Indeed, there is an optimal extent of coinsurance for each individual. The optimal extent of coinsurance is the coverage of that percentage of the cost of each unit of medical care at which the utility gain to the individual from having an additional small fraction of the cost of each unit of care covered by insurance equals the utility loss to him upon having to pay for the "excess" units of care whose consumption the additional coverage encourages. If the marginal gain from the coverage of additional fractions of cost always exceeds the marginal inefficiency loss, he will purchase full coverage insurance; if the marginal loss exceeds the marginal gain for all extents of coinsurance, the individual will purchase no insurance. If individual demands differ, the optimal extent of coinsurance will differ for different individuals.

IV. CONCLUSION

It is possible to conclude that even if all individuals are risk-averters, some uncertain medical care expenses will not and should not be insured in an optimal situation. No single insurance policy is "best" or "most efficient" for a whole population of diverse tastes. Which expenses are insurable is not an objective fact, but depends on the tastes and behavior of the persons involved.

REFERENCES

1. K. J. Arrow, "Uncertainty and the Welfare Economics of Medical Care," *Am. Econ. Rev.*, Dec. 1963, 53, 941–73.
2. _____ , "Reply," *Am. Econ. Rev.*, March 1965, 55, 154–58.
3. J. M. Buchanan, *The Inconsistencies of the National Health Service*, Inst. of Econ. Affairs Occas. Paper 7. London 1964.
4. O. D. Dickerson, *Health Insurance*, rev. ed. Homewood, Ill. 1963.
5. E. J. Faulkner, *Health Insurance*. New York 1960.
6. D. S. Lees and R. G. Rice, "Uncertainty and the Welfare Economics of Medical Care: Comment," *Am. Econ. Rev.*, March 1965, 55, 140–54.
7. R. D. Luce and H. Raiffa, *Games and Decisions*. New York 1957.
8. G. F. Michelbacher, *Multiple-line Insurance*. New York 1957.

---

[4]A deductible is the exclusion of a certain amount of expenses from coverage; coinsurance requires the individual to pay some fraction of each dollar of cost.

[5]Arrow [1, pp. 969-73] gives some other arguments to explain why the individual will prefer insurance with deductibles or coinsurance to insurance without such devices.

Job Market Signaling*†

A. MICHAEL SPENCE

A. Michael Spence (B.A., Princeton University, 1966; B.A./M.A., Oxford University Rhodes Scholar, 1968; Ph.D., Harvard University, 1972) is presently at Harvard University where he is the Dean of the Faculty of Arts and Sciences and the George Gund Professor of Economics and Business Administration. Professor Spence, who has also taught at Stanford, also currently chairs the Project in Industry and Competitive Analysis. His Harvard dissertation earned the David A. Wells Prize in 1972; in 1981, in recognition of his contributions to economics, he was awarded the coveted John Bates Clark Medal by the American Economic Association. Professor Spence is the author of three books and almost 50 articles, many dealing with market structure, product differentiation, and the relationship of asymmetric and imperfect information to discrimination. He is currently a member of the editorial boards of *The American Economic Review, The Bell Journal of Economics, The Journal of Economic Theory,* and *Public Policy.*

*Reprinted from *Quarterly Journal of Economics* (August 1973) by permission of John Wiley & Sons, Inc. Copyright 1973, pp. 355–374.
†The essay is based on the author's doctoral dissertation ("Market Signalling: The Informational Structure of Job Markets and Related Phenomena," Ph.D. thesis, Harvard University, 1972), forthcoming as a book entitled *Market Signaling: Information Transfer in Hiring and Related Screening Processes* in the Harvard Economic Studies Series, Harvard University Press. The aim here is to present the outline of the signaling model and some of its conclusions. Generalizations of the numerical examples used for expositional purposes here are found in *ibid.* and elsewhere.

I owe many people thanks for help in the course of the current study, too many to mention all. However, I should acknowledge explicitly the magnitude of my debts to Kenneth Arrow and Thomas Schelling for persistently directing my attention to new and interesting problems.

1. INTRODUCTION

The term "market signaling" is not exactly a part of the well-defined, technical vocabulary of the economist. As a part of the preamble, therefore, I feel I owe the reader a word of explanation about the title. I find it difficult, however, to give a coherent and comprehensive explanation of the meaning of the term abstracted from the contents of the essay. In fact, it is part of my purpose to outline a model in which signaling is implicitly defined and to explain why one can, and perhaps should, be interested in it. One might accurately characterize my problem as a signaling one, and that of the reader, who is faced with an investment decision under uncertainty, as that of interpreting signals.

How the reader interprets my report of the content of this essay will depend upon his expectation concerning my stay in the market. If one believes I will be in the essay market repeatedly, then both the reader and I will contemplate the possibility that I might invest in my future ability to communicate by accurately reporting the content of this essay now. On the other hand, if I am to be in the market only once, or relatively infrequently, then the above-mentioned possibility deserves a low probability. This essay is about markets in which signaling takes place and in which the primary signalers are relatively numerous and in the market sufficiently infrequently that they are not expected to (and therefore do not) invest in acquiring signaling reputations.

I shall argue that the paradigm case of the market with this type of informational structure is the job market and will therefore focus upon it. By the end I hope it will be clear (although space limitations will not permit an extended argument) that a considerable variety of market and quasi-market phenomena like admissions procedures, promotion in organizations, loans and consumer credit, can be usefully viewed through the conceptual lens applied to the job market.

If the incentives for veracity in reporting anything by means of a conventional signaling code are weak, then one must look for other means by which information transfers take place. My aim is to outline a conceptual apparatus within which the signaling power of education, job experience, race, sex, and a host of other observable, personal characteristics can be determined. The question, put crudely, is what in the interactive structure of a market accounts for the informational content, if any, of these potential signals. I have placed primary emphasis upon (i) the definition and properties of signaling equilibria, (ii) the interaction of potential signals, and (iii) the allocative efficiency of the market.

2. HIRING AS INVESTMENT UNDER UNCERTAINTY

In most job markets the employer is not sure of the productive capabilities of an individual at the time he hires him.[1] Nor will this information nec-

essarily become available to the employer immediately after hiring. The job may take time to learn. Often specific training is required. And there may be a contract period within which no recontracting is allowed. The fact that it takes time to learn an individual's productive capabilities means that hiring is an investment decision. The fact that these capabilities are not known beforehand makes the decision one under uncertainty.

To hire someone, then, is frequently to purchase a lottery.[2] In what follows, I shall assume the employer pays the certain monetary equivalent of the lottery to the individual as wage.[3] If he is risk-neutral, the wage is taken to be the individual's marginal contribution to the hiring organization.

Primary interest attaches to how the employer perceives the lottery, for it is these perceptions that determine the wages he offers to pay. We have stipulated that the employer cannot directly observe the marginal product prior to hiring. What he does observe is a plethora of personal data in the form of observable characteristics and attributes of the individual, and it is these that must ultimately determine his assessment of the lottery he is buying. (The image that the individual presents includes education, previous work, race, sex, criminal and service records, and a host of other data.) This essay is about the endogenous market process whereby the employer requires (and the individual transmits) information about the potential employee, which ultimately determines the implicit lottery involved in hiring, the offered wages, and in the end the allocation of jobs to people and people to jobs in the market.

At this point, it is useful to introduce a distinction, the import of which will be clear shortly. Of those observable, personal attributes that collectively constitute the image the job applicant presents, some are immutably fixed, while others are alterable. For example, education is something that the individual can

[1]There are, of course, other informational gaps in the job market. Just as employers have less than perfect information about applicants, so also will applicants be imperfectly informed about the qualities of jobs and work environments. And in a different vein neither potential employees nor employers know all of the people in the market. The resulting activities are job search and recruiting. For the purpose of this essay I concentrate upon employer uncertainty and the signaling game that results.

[2]The term "lottery" is used in the technical sense, imparted to it by decision theory.

[3]The certain monetary equivalent of a lottery is the amount the individual would take, with certainty, in lieu of the lottery. It is generally thought to be less than the actuarial value of the lottery.

invest in at some cost in terms of time and money. On the other hand, race and sex are not generally thought to be alterable. I shall refer to observable, unalterable attributes as *indices,* reserving the term *signals* for those observable characteristics attached to the individual that are subject to manipulation by him.[4] Some attributes, like age, do change, but not at the discretion of the individual. In my terms, these are indices.

Sometime after hiring an individual, the employer will learn the individual's productive capabilities. On the basis of previous experience in the market, the employer will have conditional probability assessments over productive capacity given various combinations of signals and indices. At any point of time when confronted with an individual applicant with certain observable attributes, the employer's subjective assessment of the lottery with which he is confronted is defined by these conditional probability distributions over productivity given the new data.

From one point of view, then, signals and indices are to be regarded as parameters in shifting conditional probability distributions that define an employer's beliefs.[5]

3. APPLICANT SIGNALING

For simplicity I shall speak as if the employer were risk-neutral. For each set of signals and indices that the employer confronts, he will have an expected marginal product for an individual who has these observable attributes. This is taken to be the offered wage to applicants with those characteristics. Potential employees therefore confront an offered wage schedule whose arguments are signals and indices.

There is not much that the applicant can do about indices. Signals, on the other hand, are alterable and therefore potentially subject to manipulation by the job applicant. Of course, there may be costs of making these adjustments. Education, for example, is costly. We refer to these costs as *signaling costs.* Notice that the individual, in acquiring an education, need

not think of himself as signaling. He will invest in education if there is sufficient return as defined by the offered wage schedule.[6] Individuals, then, are assumed to select signals (for the most part, I shall talk in terms of education) so as to maximize the difference between offered wages and signaling costs. Signaling costs play a key role in this type of signaling situation, for they functionally replace the less direct costs and benefits associated with a reputation for signaling reliability acquired by those who are more prominent in their markets than job seekers are in theirs.

A Critical Assumption

It is not difficult to see that a signal will not effectively distinguish one applicant from another, unless the costs of signaling are negatively correlated with productive capability. For if this condition fails to hold, given the offered wage schedule, everyone will invest in the signal in exactly the same way, so that they cannot be distinguished on the basis of the signal. In what follows, we shall make the assumption that signaling costs are negatively correlated with productivity. It is, however, most appropriately viewed as a *prerequisite* for an observable, alterable characteristic to be a persistently informative signal in the market. This means, among other things, that a characteristic may be a signal with respect to some types of jobs but not with respect to others.[7]

Signaling costs are to be interpreted broadly to include psychic and other costs, as well as the direct monetary ones. One element of cost, for example, is time.

4. INFORMATION FEEDBACK AND THE DEFINITION OF EQUILIBRIUM

At this point it is perhaps clear that there is informational feedback to the employer over time. As new market information comes in to the employer through hiring and subsequent observation of productive capabilities as they relate to signals, the employer's conditional probabilistic beliefs are adjusted, and a new round starts. The wage schedule facing

---

[4] The terminological distinction is borrowed from Robert Jervis (*The Logic of Images in International Relations* (Princeton, N.J.: Princeton University Press, 1970)). My use of the terms follows that of Jervis sufficiently closely to warrant their transplantation.

[5] The shifting of the distributions occurs when new market data are received and conditional probabilities are revised or updated. Hiring in the market is to be regarded as sampling, and revising conditional probabilities as passing from prior to posterior. The whole process is a learning one.

[6] There may be other returns to education. It may be a consumption good or serve as a signal of things other than work potential (status for example). These returns should be added to the offered wage schedule.

[7] The reason is that signaling costs can be negatively correlated with one type of productive capability but not with another.

the new entrants in the market generally differs from that facing the previous group. The elements in the feedback loop are shown in Fig. 1.

It is desirable to find a way to study this feedback loop in the market over time. To avoid studying a system in a continual state of flux, it is useful to look for nontransitory configuration of the feedback system. The system will be stationary if the employer starts out with conditional probabilistic beliefs that after one round are not disconfirmed by the incoming data they generated. We shall refer to such beliefs as self-confirming. The sense in which they are self-confirming is defined by the feedback loop in Fig. 1.

A Signaling Equilibrium

As successive waves of new applicants come into the market, we can imagine repeated cycles around the loop. Employers' conditional probabilistic beliefs are modified, offered wage schedules are adjusted, applicant behavior with respect to signal choice changes, and after hiring, new data become available to the employer. Each cycle, then, generates the next one. In thinking about it, one can interrupt the cycle at any point. An equilibrium is a set of components in the cycle that regenerate themselves. Thus, we can think of employer beliefs being self-confirming, or offered wage schedules regenerating themselves, or

applicant behavior reproducing itself on the next round.[8]

I find it most useful to think in terms of the self-confirming aspect of the employer beliefs because of the continuity provided by the employer's persistent presence in the market.[9] Thus, in these terms an equilibrium can be thought of as a set of employer beliefs that generate offered wage schedules, applicant signaling decisions, hiring, and ultimately new market data over time that are consistent with the initial beliefs.

A further word about the definition of equilibrium is in order. Given an offered wage schedule, one can think of the market as generating, via individual optimizing decisions, an empirical distribution of productive capabilities given observable attributes or signals (and indices). On the other hand, the employer has subjectively held conditional probabilistic beliefs with respect to productivity, given signals. In an

[8]In pursuing the properties of signaling equilibria, we select as the object for regeneration whatever is analytically convenient, but usually employer beliefs or offered wage schedules.

[9] The mathematically oriented will realize that what is at issue here is a fixed point property. A mapping from the space of conditional distributions over productivity given signals into itself is defined by the market response mechanism. An equilibrium can be thought of as a fixed point of this mapping. A mathematical treatment of this subject is contained in Spence, *op. cit.*

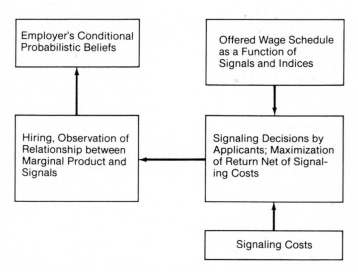

Fig. 1. Informational feedback in the job market.

equilibrium the subjective distribution and the one implicit in the market mechanism are identical, *over the range of signals that the employer actually observes.*[1] Any other subjective beliefs will eventually be disconfirmed in the market because of the employer's persistent presence there.

Indices continue to be relevant. But since they are not a matter of individual choice, they do not figure prominently in the feedback system just described. I shall return to them later.

5. PROPERTIES OF INFORMATIONAL EQUILIBRIA: AN EXAMPLE

I propose to discuss the existence and properties of market signaling equilibria via a specific numerical example.[2] For the time being, indices play no part. The properties of signaling equilibria that we shall encounter in the example are general.[3]

Let us suppose that there are just two productively distinct groups in a population facing one employer. Individuals in Group I have a productivity of 1, while those in Group II have a productivity of 2.[4] Group I is a proportion q_1 of the population; Group II is a proportion of $1 - q_1$. There is, in addition, a potential signal, say education, which is available at a cost. We shall assume that education is measured by an index y of level and achievement and is subject to individual choice. Education costs are both monetary and psychic. It is assumed that the cost to a member of Group I of y units of education is y, while the cost to a member of Group II is $y/2$.

We summarize the underlying data of our numerical example in Table 1.

To find an equilibrium in the market, we guess at a set of self-confirming conditional probabilistic beliefs for the employer and then determine whether

they are in fact confirmed by the feedback mechanisms described above. Suppose that the employer believes that there is some level of education, say y^* such that if $y < y^*$, then productivity is one with probability one, and that if $y \geq y^*$, then productivity will be two with probability one. If these are his conditional beliefs, then his offered wage schedule, $W(y)$, will be as shown in Fig. 2.

Given the offered wage schedule, members of each group will select optimal levels for education. Consider the person who will set $y < y^*$. If he does this, we know he will set $y = 0$ because education is costly, and until he reaches y^*, there are no benefits to increasing y, given the employer's hypothesized beliefs. Similarly, any individual who sets $y \geq y^*$ will in fact set $y = y^*$, since further increases would merely incur costs with no corresponding benefits. Everyone will therefore either set $y = 0$ or set $y = y^*$. Given the employer's initial beliefs and the fact just deduced, if the employer's beliefs are to be confirmed, then members of Group I must set $y = 0$, while members of Group II set $y = y^*$. Diagrams of the options facing the two groups are shown in Fig. 3.

Superimposed upon the wage schedule are the cost schedules for the two groups. Each group selects y to maximize the difference between the offered wages and the costs of education. Given the level of y^* in the diagram, it is easy to see that Group I selects

Table 1. Data of the model

Group	Marginal product	Proportion of population	Cost of education level y
I	1	q_1	y
II	2	$1 - q_1$	$y/2$

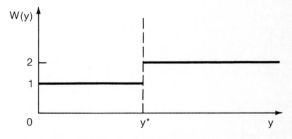

Fig. 2. Offered wages as a function of level of education.

---

[1] In a multi-market model one faces the possibility that certain types of potential applicants will rationally select themselves out of certain job markets, and hence certain signal configurations may never appear in these markets. When this happens, the beliefs of the employers in the relevant market are not disconfirmed in a degenerate way. No data are forthcoming. This raises the possibility of persistent informationally based discrimination against certain groups. The subject is pursued in detail in *ibid.*

[2] Obviously, an example does not prove generality. On the other hand, if the reader will take reasonable generality on faith, the example does illustrate some essential properties of signaling equilibria.

[3] See Spence, *op. cit.*

[4] For productivity the reader may read "what the individual is worth to the employer." There is no need to rely on marginal productivity here.

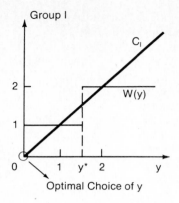
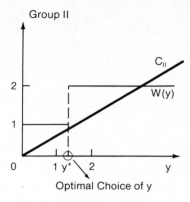

Fig. 3. Optimizing choice of education for both groups.

$y = 0$, and Group II sets $y = y^*$. Thus, in this case the employer's beliefs are confirmed, and we have a signaling equilibrium. We can state the conditions on behavior by the two groups, in order that the employer's beliefs be confirmed, in algebraic terms. Group I sets $y = 0$ if

$$1 > 2 - y^*.$$

Group II will set $y = y^*$ as required, provided that

$$2 - y^*/2 > 1.$$

Putting these two conditions together, we find that the employer's initial beliefs are confirmed by market experience, provided that the parameter y^* satisfies the inequality,

$$1 < y^* < 2.$$

It is worth pausing at this point to remark upon some striking features of this type of equilibrium. One is that within the class of employer expectations used above, there is an infinite number of possible equilibrium values for y^*. This means that there is an infinite number of equilibria. In any one of the equilibria the employer is able to make perfect point predictions concerning the productivity of any individual, having observed his level of education. The reader will realize that this property is special and depends, at least in part, upon the assumption that education costs are perfectly negatively correlated with productivity. However, even in this case, there are equilibria in which the employer is uncertain, as we shall shortly see.

The equilibria are not equivalent from the point

of view of welfare. Increases in the level of y^* hurt Group II, while, at the same time, members of Group I are unaffected. Group I is worse off than it was with no signaling at all. For if no signaling takes place, each person is paid his unconditional expected marginal product, which is just

$$q_1 + 2(1 - q_1) = 2 - q_1.$$

Group II may also be worse off than it was with no signaling. Assume that the proportion of people in Group I is 0.5. Since $y^* > 1$ and the net return to the member of Group II is $2 - y^*/2$, in equilibrium his net return must be below 1.5, the no-signaling wage. Thus, everyone would prefer a situation in which there is no signaling.

No one is acting irrationally as an individual. Coalitions might profitably form and upset the signaling equilibrium.[5] The initial proportions of people in the two groups q_1 and $1 - q_1$ have no effect upon the equilibrium. This conclusion depends upon this assumption that the marginal product of a person in a given group does not change with numbers hired.

Given the signaling equilibrium, the education level y^*, which defines the equilibrium, is an entrance requirement or prerequisite for the high-salary job— or so it would appear from the outside. From the point of view of the individual, it is a prerequisite that has its source in a signaling game. Looked at from the outside, education might appear to be pro-

[5]Coalitions to change the patterns of signaling are discussed in Spence, *op. cit.*

ductive. It is productive for the individual, but, in this example, it does not increase his real marginal product at all.[6]

A sophisticated objection to the assertion that private and social returns differ might be that, in the context of our example, the social return is not really zero. We have an information problem in the society and the problem of allocating the right people to the right jobs. Education, in its capacity as a signal in the model, is helping us to do this properly. The objection is well founded. To decide how efficient or inefficient this system is, one must consider the realistic alternatives to market sorting procedures in the society.[7] But notice that even within the confines of the market model, there are more or less efficient ways of getting the sorting accomplished. Increases in y^* improve the quality of the sorting not one bit. They simply use up real or psychic resources. This is just another way of saying that there are Pareto inferior signaling equilibria in the market.

It is not always the case that all groups lose due to the existence of signaling. For example, if, in the signaling equilibrium, $y^* < 2q_1$, then Group II would be better off when education is functioning effectively as a signal than it would be otherwise. Thus, in our example if $q_1 > \frac{1}{2}$ so that Group II is a minority, then there exists a signaling equilibrium in which the members of Group II improve their position over the no-signaling case. Recall that the wage in the no-signaling case was a uniform $2 - q_1$ over all groups.

We may generalize this bit of analysis slightly. Suppose that the signaling cost schedule for Group I was given by $a_1 y$ and that for Group II by $a_2 y$.[8] Then with a small amount of calculation, we can show that there is a signaling equilibrium in which Group II is better off than with no signaling,[9] provided that

$$q_1 > a_2/a_1.$$

How small a "minority" Group II has to be to have the possibility of benefiting from signaling depends upon the ratio of the marginal signaling costs of the two groups.[1]

Before leaving our education signaling model, it is worth noting that there are other equilibria in the system with quite different properties. Suppose that the employer's expectations are of the following form:

> If $y < y^*$: Group I with probability q_1,
>   Group II with probability $1 - q_1$;
> if $y \geq y^*$: Group II with probability 1.

As before, the only levels of y that could conceivably be selected are $y = 0$ and $y = y^*$. The wage for $y = 0$ is $2 - q_1$, while the wage for $y = y^*$ is simply 2. From Fig. 4 it is easy to see that both groups rationally set $y = 0$, provided that $y^* > 2q_1$. If they both do this, then the employer's beliefs are confirmed, and we have an equilibrium.

It should be noted that the employer's beliefs about the relationship between productivity and education for $y \geq y^*$ are confirmed in a somewhat degenerate, but perfectly acceptable, sense. There are no data relating to these levels of education and hence, by logic, no disconfirming data. This is an example of a phenomenon of much wider potential importance. The employer's beliefs may drive certain groups from the market and into another labor market. We cannot capture this situation in a simple one-employer, one-market model. But when it happens,

---

[6] I am ignoring external benefits to education here. The assertion is simply that in the example education does not contribute to productivity. One might still claim that the social product is not zero. The signal cost function does, in principle, capture education as a consumption good, an effect that simply reduces the cost of education.

[7] This question is pursued in Spence, *op. cit.*

[8] It is assumed that $a_2 < a_1$.

[9] Notice that the statement is that there exists a signaling equilibrium in which Group II is better off. It turns out that there always exists a signaling equilibrium in which Group II is worse off as well.

[1] The calculation is straightforward. Given these signaling costs groups will make the requisite choice to confirm the employer's beliefs provided that

$$1 > 2 - a_1 y^*$$

and

$$2 - a_2 y^* > 1.$$

These translate easily into the following condition on y^*:

$$\frac{1}{a_2} < y^* < \frac{1}{a_1}.$$

Now, if Group II is to be better off for some signaling equilibrium, then

$$2 - \frac{a_2}{a_1} > 2 - q_1,$$

or

$$q_1 > \frac{a_2}{a_1}.$$

This is what we set out to show.

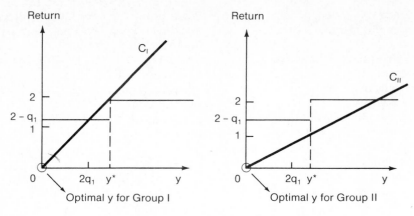

Fig. 4. Optimal signaling decisions for the two groups.

there is no experience forthcoming to the employer to cause him to alter his beliefs.[2]

Education conveys no information in this type of equilibrium. In fact, we have reproduced the wages and information state of the employer in the no-signaling model, as a signaling equilibrium.

Just as there exists a signaling equilibrium in which everyone sets $y = 0$, there is also an equilibrium in which everyone sets $y = y^*$ for some positive y^*. The requisite employer beliefs are as follows:

> If $y < y^*$: Group I with probability 1;
> if $y \geq y^*$: Group I with probability q_1,
>   Group II with probability $1 - q_1$.

Following our familiar mode of analysis, one finds that these beliefs are self-confirming in the market, provided that

$$y^* < 1 - q_1.$$

Again, the education level conveys no useful information, but in this instance individuals are rationally investing in education. If they as individuals did not invest, they would incur lower wages, and the loss would exceed the gain from not making the educational investment. The implication of this version of the signaling equilibrium is that there can be stable prerequisites for jobs that convey no information by virtue of their existence and hence serve no function.

It is interesting to note that this last possibility does not depend upon costs being correlated with productivity at all. Suppose that the signaling costs

for both groups were given by the one schedule y. And suppose further that employer beliefs were as described above. Then everyone will rationally select $y = y^*$, provided that

$$y^* < 1 - q_1.$$

The outcome is the same. But the interesting thing is that, because of the absence of any correlation between educational costs and productivity, education could *never* be an effective signal, in the sense of conveying useful information, in an equilibrium in this market.

We have dwelt enough upon the specifics of this model to have observed some of the effects the signaling game may have upon the allocational functioning of the market. The numerical example is not important. The potential effects and patterns of signaling are.

An alterable characteristic like education, which is a potential signal, becomes an actual signal if the signaling costs are negatively correlated with the individual's unknown productivity. Actually, the negative correlation is a necessary but not sufficient condition for signaling to take place. To see this in the context of our model, assume that the only values y can have are one and three. That is to say, one can only get units of education in lumps. If this is true, then there is no feasible value of y^* that will make it worthwhile for Group II to acquire an education. Three units is too much, and one unit will not distinguish Group II from Group I. Therefore, effective signaling depends not only upon the negative correlation of costs and productivities, but also upon

[2] This is discussed in detail in Spence, *op. cit.*

there being a "sufficient" number of signals within the appropriate cost range.[3]

An equilibrium is defined in the context of a feedback loop, in which employer expectations lead to offered wages to various levels of education, which in turn lead to investment in education by individuals. After hiring, the discovery of the actual relationships between education and productivity in the sample leads to revised expectations or beliefs. Here the cycle starts again. An equilibrium is best thought of as a set of beliefs that are confirmed or at least not contradicted by the new data at the end of the loop just described. Such beliefs will tend to persist over time as new entrants into the market flow through.

Multiple equilibria are a distinct possibility. Some may be Pareto inferior to others. Private and social returns to education diverge. Sometimes everyone loses as a result of the existence of signaling. In other situations some gain, while others lose. Systematic overinvestment in education is a distinct possibility because of the element of arbitrariness in the equilibrium configuration of the market. In the context of atomistic behavior (which we have assumed thus far) everyone is reacting rationally to the market situation. Information is passed to the employer through the educational signal. In some of our examples it was perfect information. In other cases this is not so. There will be random variation in signaling costs that prevent the employer from distinguishing perfectly among individuals of varying productive capabilities.

In our examples, education was measured by a scalar quantity. With no basic adjustment in the conceptual apparatus, we can think of education as a multidimensional quantity: years of education, institution attended, grades, recommendations and so on. Similarly, it is not necessary to think in terms of two groups of people. There may be many groups, or even a continuum of people: some suited to certain kinds of work, others suited to other kinds. Nor need education be strictly unproductive. However, if it is too productive relative to the costs, everyone will invest heavily in education, and education may cease to have a signaling function.

6. THE INFORMATIONAL IMPACT OF INDICES

In the educational signaling model we avoided considering any observable characteristics other than education. In that model education was a signal. Here we consider what role, if any, is played by indices. For concreteness I shall use sex as the example. But just as education can stand for any set of observable, alterable characteristics in the first model, sex can stand for observable, unalterable ones here. The reader may wish to think in terms of race, nationality, size, or in terms of criminal or police records and service records. The latter is potentially public information about a person's history and is, of course, unalterable when viewed retrospectively from the present.[4]

Let us assume that there are two groups, men and women. I shall refer to these groups as W and M. Within each group the distribution of productive capabilities and the incidence of signaling costs are the same. Thus, within M the proportion of people with productivity one and signaling (education) costs of y is q_1. The remainder have productivity two and signaling costs $y/2$. The same is true for group W. Here m is the proportion of men in the overall population of job applicants.

Data of the model

Race	Productivity	Education costs	Proportion within group	Proportion of total population
W	1	y	q_1	$q_1(1 - m)$
W	2	$y/2$	$1 - q_1$	$(1 - q_1)(1 - m)$
M	1	y	q_1	$q_1 m$
M	2	$y/2$	$1 - q_1$	$(1 - q_1)m$

Given the assumptions the central question is, "how could sex have an informational impact on the market?" The next few paragraphs are devoted to arguing that indices do have a potential impact and to explaining why this is true. We begin by noting that, under the assumptions, the conditional probability that a person drawn at random from the population has a productivity of two, given that he is a

[3] In *ibid.* it is argued that many potential signals in credit and loan markets effectively become indices because the "signaling" costs swamp the gains, so that characteristics that could be manipulated in fact are not. House ownership is an example of a potential signal that, in the context of the loan market, fails on this criterion and hence becomes an index.

[4]It is, or ought to be, the subject of policy decisions as well.

man (or she is a woman), is the same as the unconditional probability that his productivity is two. Sex
and productivity are uncorrelated in the population.
Therefore, *by itself,* sex could never tell the employer
anything about productivity.

We are forced to the conclusion that if sex is to
have any informational impact, it must be through
its interaction with the educational signaling mechanism. But here again we run up against an initially
puzzling symmetry. Under the assumptions, men
and women of equal productivity have the same signaling (education) costs. It is a general maxim in
economics that people with the same preferences and
opportunity sets will make similar decisions and end
up in similar situations. We may assume that people
maximize their income net of signaling costs so that
their preferences are the same. And since signaling
costs are the same, it would appear that their opportunity sets are the same. Hence, again we appear
to be driven to the conclusion that sex can have no
informational impact. But the conclusion is wrong,
for an interesting reason.

The opportunity sets of men and women of comparable productivity are *not* necessarily the same. To
see this, let us step back to the simple educational
signaling model. There are externalities in that model. One person's signaling strategy or decision affects
the market data obtained by the employer, which in
turn affect the employer's conditional probabilities.
These determine the offered wages to various levels
of education and hence of rates of return on education for the next group in the job market. The
same mechanism applies here, with a notable modification. If employers' distributions are conditional
on sex as well as education, then the external impacts
of a man's signaling decision are felt only by other
men. The same holds for women.

If at some point in time men and women are not
investing in education in the same ways, then the
returns to education for men and women will be
different in the next round. In short, their opportunity sets differ. In what follows, we demonstrate
rigorously that this sort of situation can persist in an
equilibrium. The important point, however, is that
there are externalities implicit in the fact that an individual is treated as the average member of the
group of people who look the same and that, as a
result, and in spite of an apparent sameness the opportunity sets facing two or more groups that are
visibly distinguishable may in fact be different.

The employer now has two potential signals to
consider: education and sex. At the start he does not
know whether either education or sex will be correlated with productivity. Uninformative potential
signals or indices are discarded in the course of reaching an equilibrium. As before we must guess at an
equilibrium form for the employer's expectations and
then verify that these beliefs can be self-confirming
via the market informational feedback mechanisms.
We will try beliefs on the following form.

If W and $y < y^*_W$, productivity = 1 with probability 1.
If W and $y \geq y^*_W$, productivity = 2 with probability 1.
If M and $y < y^*_M$, productivity = 1 with probability 1.
If M and $y \geq y^*_M$, productivity = 2 with probability 1.

These lead to offered wage schedules $W_W(y)$ and
$W_M(y)$ as shown in Fig. 5.

Because groups W and M are distinguishable to
the employer, their offered wages are not connected
at the level of employer expectations. Applying the
reasoning used in the straightforward educational
signaling model, we find that the required equilibrium conditions on y^*_W and y^*_M are

$$1 < y^*_W < 2$$

and

$$1 < y^*_M < 2.$$

No logical condition requires that y^*_W equals y^*_M in
an equilibrium.

Essentially we simply have the educational signaling model iterated twice. Because sex is observable, the employer can make his conditional probability assessments depend upon sex as well as education. This has the effect of making signaling
interdependencies between two groups, W and M,
nonexistent. They settle into signaling equilibrium
configurations in the market independently of each
other. But in the first model there was not one equilibrium, there were many. Therefore, there is at least
the logical possibility that men and women will settle
into *different* stable signaling equilibria in the market
and stay there.

As we noted earlier, the signaling equilibria are
not equivalent from the point of view of social welfare. The higher that y^*_W (or y^*_M) is, the worse off
is the relevant group or, more accurately, the high-
productivity portion of the group. One example of
an asymmetrical equilibrium would be given by
$y^*_M = 1.1$ and $y^*_M = 1.9$. In this case high-produc-

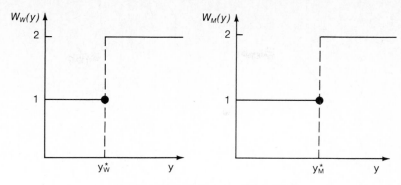

Fig. 5. Offered wages to W and M.

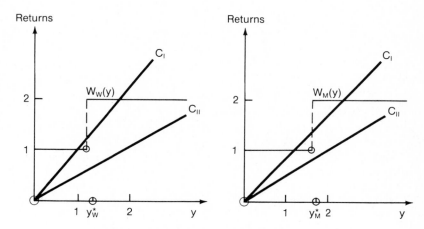

Fig. 6. Market equilibrium with sex as an index.

tivity women have to spend more on education and have less left over to consume in order to convince the employer that they are in the high-productivity group.

Notice that the proportions of high- and low-productivity people in each group do not affect the signaling equilibrium in the market. Hence, our initial assumption that the groups were identical with respect to the distribution of productive characteristics and the incidence of signaling costs was superfluous. More accurately, it was superfluous with respect to this type of equilibrium. As we saw in the educational signaling model, there are other types of equilibrium in which the proportions matter.

Since from an equilibrium point of view men and women really are independent, they might settle into different types of equilibrium. Thus, we might have men signaling $y = y^*_M = 1.1$ if they are also in the

higher productivity group, while other men set $y = 0$. On the other hand, we may find that all women set $y = 0$. In this case all women would be paid $2 - q_1$, and the upper signaling cutoff point y^*_M would have to be greater than $2q_1$. Notice that all women, including lower productivity women, would be paid more than low-productivity men in this situation.[5] High-productivity women would, of course, be hurt in terms of wages received. It is conceivable, however, that returns net of signaling would be higher for women with productivity of two. In other words, it is possible that

$$2 - q_1 > w - y^*_{M/2}.$$

---

[5] I have not assumed that employers are prejudiced. If they are, this differential could be wiped out. Perhaps more interestingly laws prohibiting wage discrimination, if enforced, would also wipe it out.

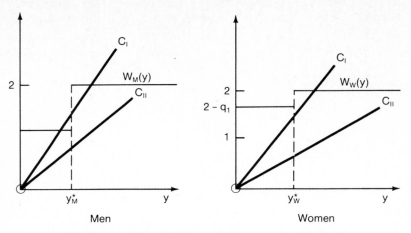

Fig. 7. Another equilibrium configuration in the market.

This will occur when

$$2q_1 < y^*_M.$$

Looking at this situation from outside, one might conclude that women receive lower wages than some men because of a lack of education, which keeps their productivity down. One might then go looking outside the job market for the explanation for the lack of education. In this model the analysis just suggested would be wrong. The source of the signaling and wage differentials is in the informational structure of the market itself.[6]

Because of the independence of the two groups, M and W, at the level of signaling, we can generate many different possible equilibrium configurations by taking any of the educational signaling equilibria in our first model and assigning it to W and then taking any education equilibrium and assigning it to M. However, an exhaustive listing of the possibilities seems pointless at this stage.

We have here the possibility of arbitrary differences in the equilibrium signaling configurations of two or more distinct groups. Some of them may be at a disadvantage relative to the others. Subsets of one may be at a disadvantage to comparable subsets of the others. Since the mechanism that generates the equilibrium is a feedback loop, we might, following Myrdal and others, wish to refer to the situation of the disadvantaged group as a vicious cycle,

albeit an informationally based one. I prefer to refer to the situation of the disadvantaged group as a lower level equilibrium trap, which conveys the notion of a situation that, once achieved, persists for reasons endogenous to the model. The multiple equilibria of the education model translate into arbitrary differences in the equilibrium configuration and status of two groups, as defined as observable, unalterable characteristics.

CONCLUSIONS

We have looked at the characteristics of a basic equilibrium signaling model and at one possible type of interaction of signals and indices. There remains a host of questions, which can be posed and partially answered within the conceptual framework outlined here. Among them are the following:

1. What is the effect of cooperative behavior on the signaling game?

2. What is the informational impact of randomness in signaling costs?

3. What is the effect of signaling costs that differ systematically with indices?

4. How general are the properties of the examples considered here?

5. In a multiple-market setting, does the indeterminateness of the equilibrium remain?

6. Do signaling equilibria exist in general?

7. What kinds of discriminatory mechanisms are implicit in, or interact with, the informational structure of the market, and what policies are effective or ineffective in dealing with them?

[6]Differential signaling costs over groups are an important possibility pursued in Spence, *op. cit.*

I would argue further that a range of phenomena from selective admissions procedures through promotion, loans and consumer credit, and signaling status via conspicuous consumption lends itself to analysis with the same basic conceptual apparatus. Moreover, it may be as important to explain the absence of effective signaling as its presence, and here the prerequisites for effective signaling are of some use.

On the other hand, it is well to remember that the property of relative infrequency of appearance by signalers in the market, which defines the class signaling phenomena under scrutiny here, is not characteristic of many markets, like those for consumer durables, and that, as a result, the informational structures of these latter are likely to be quite different.

Part 4   Theory of Market Structures

CONCEPTS OF MARKET STRUCTURES

Economic Theory and the Meaning of Competition*

PAUL J. McNULTY**

Paul J. McNulty (B.A., Hobart College, 1959; Ph.D., Cornell University, 1965) is Professor of Economics and Vice Dean for Academic Affairs at the Columbia University School of Business. Since joining the Columbia Business School faculty in 1965, he has specialized in business economics and public policy, the economics of energy, and business history. Since 1974 he has been Co-Director of Columbia's annual Energy Forum. Professor McNulty is the recipient of Woodrow Wilson, National Science Foundation, and Cornell Fellowships.

There is probably no concept in all of economics that is at once more fundamental and pervasive, yet less satisfactorily developed, than the concept of competition. Although the hesitancy and inconsistency which has characterized the history of American competitive policy is doubtless partly due, as is often emphasized, to the fact that competition is, in our system, a political and social *desideratum* no less than an economic one, with some possible resulting conflict between these various values,[1] surely it is due also to the failure of economists adequately to define competition. Not the least among the many achievements of economic science has been the ability to erect a rigorous analytical system on the principle of competition—a principle so basic to economic reasoning that not even such powerful yet diverse critics of orthodox theory as Marx and Keynes could avoid relying upon it—without ever clearly specifying what, exactly, competition is. The purpose of this paper is to examine some of the factors which ac-

*Reprinted from *Quarterly Journal of Economics* (November 1968) by permission of John Wiley & Sons, Inc. Copyright 1968, pp. 639–656.

**I am indebted to my colleague, Maurice Wilkinson, for a number of helpful suggestions and comments. Needless to say, I am solely responsible for the views expressed herein. I wish also to acknowledge the financial support provided by the faculty research fund of the Graduate School of Business, Columbia University.

[1]"It is possible, because of its indirect social or moral effect, to prefer a system of small producers, each dependent for his success upon his own skill and character, to one in which the great mass of those engaged must accept the direction of a few." *United States* v. *Aluminum Company of America*, 148 F. 2d 416 (1945). "Of course, some of the results of large integrated or chain operations are beneficial to consumers . . . But we cannot fail to recognize Congress' desire to promote competition through the protection of viable, small, locally owned businesses. Congress appreciated that occasional higher costs and prices might result from the maintenance of fragmented industries and markets. It resolved these competing considerations in favor of decentralization." *Brown Shoe Co.* v. *United States*, 370 U.S. 294 (1962).

count for this curious development, and to indicate some specific inadequacies of the economic concept of competition both for analysis and for policy.

I

Probably the most general tendency concerning the meaning of competition in economic theory is to regard it as the opposite of monopoly. An unfortunate result of this way of thinking has been no little confusion concerning the relationship between economic efficiency and business behavior. There is a striking contrast in economic literature between the analytical rigor and precision of competition when it is described as a market structure, and the ambiguity surrounding the idea of competition whenever it is discussed in behavioral terms. Since, as Hayek has rightly noted, "the law cannot effectively prohibit states of affairs but only kinds of action,"[2] a concept of economic competition, if it is to be significant for economic policy, ought to relate to patterns of business behavior such as might reasonably be associated with the verb "to compete." That was the case with the competition which Adam Smith made the central organizing principle of economic society in the *Wealth of Nations,* and with the competition whose effects Cournot, in the first formal statement of the idea of "perfect" competition, could accurately claim to be "realized, in social economy, for a multitude of products, and, among them, for the most important products."[3] Whether it was seen as price undercutting by sellers, the bidding up of prices by buyers, or the entry of new firms into profitable industries, the fact is that competition entered economics as a concept which had empirical relevance and operational meaning in terms of contemporary business behavior. Yet on the question of whether such common current practices as advertising, product variation, price undercutting, or other forms of business activity do or do not constitute competition, modern economic theory offers the clarification that they are "monopolistically" competitive. While this is a useful way of illustrating the truth that most markets are in some degree both controlled and controlling, it is less useful as a guide in implementing

a policy, such as our antitrust policy, which seeks at once to restrain monopoly and promote competition. It is too late in the history of economics, and it is surely not in any way here the purpose, to deemphasize the truly monumental character of E. H. Chamberlin's great achievement a generation ago[4] in reconciling economic theory with the undeniable fact that much of the business world was really a mixture of competition and monopoly, as those concepts were then defined in economics, which fitted neither of those traditional economic models of business enterprise. But it is not, perhaps, too late to suggest that the traditional distinction between competition and monopoly was, in a fundamental sense, inappropriate to begin with, and that the merging of the concepts in a theory of monopolistic competition, while representing a profound improvement over the simplicity of the older classification, and giving microeconomics a new vitality almost comparable to that which Keynes was at the same time bringing to employment theory, has, nonetheless, allowed us to avoid defining a concept of competition, *as distinct from the concept of a competitive market,* which is at once relevant and adequate both for economic analysis and for economic policy.

Clearly, the failure to distinguish between the idea of competition and the idea of market structure is at the root of much of the ambiguity concerning the meaning of competition. As far as market structure, conceived of in terms of the paucity or plethora of sellers (buyers), is the appropriate focus of analysis, consistency would suggest relying on terms such as monopoly (sony), duopoly, triopoly, oligopoly, polypoly, and, perhaps, a newly-coined term ending in "poly," the prefix of which means an indefinitely large number.[5] Such a classification, although it would add to an already cumbersome body of technical jargon, would nonetheless retain for market taxonomy the analytical usefulness it currently possesses, while having the further advantage of eliminating much of the confusion that now exists between competition and monopoly. As it is, it is one of the great paradoxes of economic science that every *act* of competition on

---

[2]F. A. Hayek, *The Constitution of Liberty* (Chicago: University of Chicago Press, 1960), p. 265.

[3]Augustin Cournot, *Researches into the Mathematical Principles of the Theory of Wealth,* trans. Nathaniel T. Bacon (New York: Macmillan, 1929), p. 90.

[4]Edward H. Chamberlin, *The Theory of Monopolistic Competition* (Cambridge, Mass.: Harvard University Press, 1956).

[5]Professor Machlup has employed a classification along these lines, adding the term "pliopoly" (more sellers) to cover the condition of free entry. Fritz Machlup, *The Economics of Sellers' Competition,* (Baltimore: The Johns Hopkins Press, 1952), Chap. 4.

the part of a businessman is evidence, in economic theory, of some degree of monopoly power, while the concepts of monopoly and perfect competition have this important common feature: both are situations in which the possibility of any competitive behavior has been ruled out by definition.

That perfect competition is an ideal state, incapable of actual realization, is a familiar theme of economic literature. That for various reasons it would be less than altogether desirable, even if it were attainable, is also widely acknowledged. But that perfect competition is a state of affairs quite incompatible with the idea of any and all competition has been insufficiently emphasized. It is this last feature of perfect competition, and not, as is sometimes incorrectly claimed, its high level of abstraction or the "unreality" of its assumptions, which limits its usefulness, especially for economic policy. What needs more stress than it has generally received is not the inescapably abstract and "unreal" nature of theory but, rather, the fact that while all other forms of competition represent, in economic theory, an *admixture* of monopoly and competition, perfect competition itself means the *absence* of competition in quite as complete a sense, although for different reasons, as does pure monopoly. Monopoly is a market situation in which intraindustry competition has been defined away by identifying the firm as the industry. Perfect competition, on the other hand, is a market situation which, although itself the *result* of the free entry of a large number of formerly competing firms, has evolved or progressed to the point (of equilibrium) where no *further* competition within the industry is possible, or, in the words of A. A. Cournot, its intellectual parent, to the point where "the effects of competition have reached their limit."[6] It is for this reason that Frank Knight can correctly stress, as he often has, that perfect competition involves "no presumption of psychological competition, emulation, or rivalry,"[7] and can rightly assert that "'atomism' is a better term for the idea."[8] Perfect competition, the only clearly and rigorously defined concept of competition to be found in the corpus of economic theory, which is free of all traces of business behavior associated with "monopolistic" elements, means simply the *existence* of an indefinitely

large number of noncompeting firms. Economists have sometimes criticized American competitive policy for its not infrequently manifested tendency over the years to identify the maintenance of competition with the maintenance of competitors. But economic theory offers no clear guide for distinguishing between them. To the extent that we look to economics for an answer to the question "What are the advantages of competition over monopoly?", we ought also to be able to look to economics for an answer to the question "How may a business firm be expected to compete without monopolizing?" And the critical reader will search economic literature in vain for a clear answer to that question.

An analysis of the ambiguities and weaknesses of the competitive concept confirms the correctness of Schumpeter's assertion (despite the apparently widely held contemporary view to the contrary) that in economics "modern problems, methods and results cannot be fully understood without some knowledge of how economists have come to reason as they do."[9] In order fully to understand how our thinking on competition has come to be what it is, it is necessary, then, to examine briefly the emergence and evolution of the concept within the larger framework of the historical development of economic science.

II

Although competition, as we noted earlier, has usually been conceived of as being in general the opposite of monopoly, the conception has taken two basic, and fundamentally different, forms. On the one hand, it has been the "force" which, by equating prices and marginal costs, assures allocative efficiency in the use of resources. Competition in this sense is somewhat analogous to the force of gravitation in physical science; through competition, resources "gravitate" toward their most productive uses, and, through competition, price is "forced" to the lowest level which is sustainable over the long run. Thus viewed, competition assures order and stability in the economic world much as does gravitation in the physical world. But competition has also been conceived of in a second way, as a descriptive term characterizing a particular (idealized) situation. The concept of perfect competition, for example, to continue the comparison with physical science, is analogous not to the principle of gravitation but rather to the

---

[6]Cournot, *op. cit.*, p. 90.
[7]Frank H. Knight, "Immutable Law in Economics: Its Reality and Limitations," *American Economic Review*, XXXVI (May 1946), 102.
[8]*Loc. cit.*

[9] Joseph A. Schumpeter, *History of Economic Analysis* (New York: Oxford University Press, 1954), p. 6.

idea of a perfect vacuum; it is not an "ordering force" but rather an assumed "state of affairs"—one which, although an "unrealistic,"—indeed, unrealizeable,—abstraction, is nonetheless a useful analytical device. That competition has been conceived of in these two quite different ways is of no small importance in explaining the ambiguity and confusion which has surrounded the concept.

It was the conception of competition as an ordering force which dominated classical economics. When Adam Smith spoke of competition, it was in connection with the forcing of market price to its "natural" level[1] or to the lowering of profits to a minimum.[2] It was not competition and monopoly per se, or as market models, which Adam Smith contrasted, but rather the level of prices resulting from the presence or absence of competition as a regulatory force.[3] Indeed, so unsystematic was any association between the idea of competition and that of market structure for Adam Smith that he applied the term to duopoly almost exactly as he did to a market in which a larger number of firms operated. If the capital sufficient to satisfy the demand for groceries in a particular town "is divided between two different grocers," he wrote, "their competition will tend to make both of them sell cheaper, than if it were in the hands of one only."[4] Although Smith and the classical economists generally acknowledged that competition was more effective with a larger number than with a smaller number of competitors, competition was viewed as a price-determining force operating in, but not itself identified as, a market. On this, Ricardo was explicit:

> In speaking, then, of commodities, of their exchangeable value, and of the laws which regulate their relative prices, we mean always such commodities . . . on the production of which *competition operates* without restraint.[5]

And John Stuart Mill wrote:

> So far as rents, profits, wages, prices, are determined by competition, laws may be assigned for them.

Assume competition to be their exclusive regulator and principles of broad generality and scientific precision may be laid down, according to which they will be regulated.[6]

The "perfection" of the concept of competition, that is, the emergence of the idea of competition as itself a market structure, was a distinguishing contribution of neoclassical economics. The groundwork for this development was laid by Cournot, whose interest was in specifying, as rigorously as possible, the *effects* of competition. According to him, the effects of competition had reached their limit when the output of each firm was "inappreciable" with respect to total industry output, and could be subtracted from the total output "without any appreciable variation resulting in the price of the commodity."[7] This implied a very large number of sellers, but Cournot was not much more explicit on the subject of market structure, and it was only with Jevons[8] and Edgeworth,[9] in the late nineteenth century, that the actual wedding of the concepts of competition and the market was effected, leading ultimately, after refinements by J. B. Clark[1] and Frank Knight,[2] to the concept of perfect competition as we know it today.[3] As Stigler has rightly stressed, "the merging of the concepts of competition and the market was unfortunate, for each deserved a full and separate treatment."

> A market is an institution for the consummation of transactions. It performs this function efficiently when every buyer who will pay more than the minimum realized price for any class of commodities succeeds in buying the commodity, and every seller who will sell it for less than the maximum realized price succeeds in selling the commodity. . . . A market may be perfect and monopolistic or imperfect and competitive. Jevons' mixture of the two has been widely imitated by successors, of course, so that even today a market is commonly treated as a concept subsidiary to competition.[4]

[6]John Stuart Mill, *Principles of Political Economy,* I (New York: D. Appleton, 1864), 306.

[7]*Op. cit.,* p. 90.

[8] W. Stanley Jevons, *The Theory of Political Economy* (4th ed.; London: Macmillan, 1911).

[9]F. Y. Edgeworth, *Mathematical Psychics* (London: C. Kegan Paul, 1881).

[1]J. B. Clark, *The Distribution of Wealth* (New York: Macmillan, 1900).

[2]Frank H. Knight, *Risk, Uncertainty and Profit* (London: London School of Economics and Political Science, Series of Reprints of Scarce Tracts, No. 16, 1933).

[3]George J. Stigler, "Perfect Competition, Historically Contemplated," *Journal of Political Economy,* LXV (Feb. 1957), 1–17.

[4]*Ibid.,* p. 6.

[1]Adam Smith, *The Wealth of Nations* (New York: Modern Library, 1937), pp. 56, 57.

[2]*Ibid.,* p. 87.

[3] "The price of monopoly is upon every occasion the highest which can be got. The natural price, or the price of free competition, on the contrary, is the lowest which can be taken . . . for any considerable time together." *Ibid.,* p. 61.

[4]*Ibid.,* p. 342.

[5]David Ricardo, *The Principles of Political Economy and Taxation* (London: J. M. Dent, 1955), p. 6, emphasis added.

Although we can agree that "the merging of the concepts of competition and the market was unfortunate," it is probably more accurate to say that competition has been conceived of as a concept subsidiary to that of the market rather than the other way around. In fact, Jevons' "mixture" of the concepts may be viewed as a development which was thoroughly in the tradition of, and, indeed, perhaps only a logical consequence of, the historical tendency on the part of economists to identify competition as entirely a phenomenon of exchange. For, if the classical economists did not, like their neoclassical successors, identify competition with a *particular* market structure, they did nonetheless conceive of it as taking place exclusively *in* the various markets in which the business firm was operating. Competition, that is, was never related in any systematic way to the technique of production within, or to the organizational form of, the business firm itself. The concept has thus been divorced, since the earliest days of scientific economic analysis, from a major area or facet of economic activity.

Economic goods and services possess, broadly speaking, two characteristics: quality and price. In a free enterprise economy, moreover, there are two primary institutions through which resources are organized, transformed, and channeled for ultimate consumption as goods or services: the private business firm and the market. These institutions correspond to the two characteristics possessed by economic goods. Production, or the determination of physical form, or quality, takes place within the business firm; exchange, or the determination of economic value, or price, within the various markets in which the firm operates. However, although economic activity encompasses both production and exchange, the concept of competition has been generally associated only with the latter. The operations of the business firm, except for the exchange relationships associated with its purchase or sale of a factor, product, or service, have not traditionally come within the meaning of competition nor, indeed, have they been a part of economic theory generally. In economic analysis, one firm is seen as differing from another only with respect to the kind of product or factor market in which it buys or sells, and the economic system as a whole is seen not as a complex set of varied and changing institutions but, rather, the process of buying and selling is isolated as the critical element of economic activity and the

economy is viewed as simply "a system of interrelated markets."[5] In short, as Allyn Young once put it, "for system's sake, the whole material equipment of human living is recast in molds fashioned after the notions of catallactics."[6]

Both the dominance of exchange, and hence of price, in economic theory generally, and the limitation of the concept of competition specifically to the firm's external relationships in the market, relate to the way in which competition entered economics and came to occupy the position of primacy which it has held in the science ever since the work of Adam Smith. In one sense Smith was, and in another sense he was not, the great "prophet of competition"[7] that historians of the subject have often made him appear to be. Smith was a prophet of competition in that he did for the concept what no others before him did so effectively: he made it literally a general organizing principle of economic society and of economic analysis. No writer before Smith presented so effectively the conception of competition as a force which, operating in an atmosphere of "perfect liberty," would lead self-seeking individuals unconsciously to serve the general welfare. In a sense, Smith did for economics, through the principle of competition, precisely what he himself credited Newton with having done for physics and astronomy through the principle of gravity; "the discovery of an immense chain of the most important and sublime truths, all closely connected together, by one capital fact, of the reality of which we have daily experience."[8] But while Smith gave to competition an intellectual and ideological significance it had never had before, neither its specific economic meaning, nor its particular analytical function, was original with him. On the contrary, he incorporated into the *Wealth of Nations* a concept of competition already well developed in the economic literature of his time. That concept was a behavioral one, the essence of which was the effort of the individual seller to undersell, or the individual buyer to outbid, his rivals in the marketplace, and

[5]Lloyd G. Reynolds, *The Structure of Labor Markets* (New York: Harper, 1951), p. 1.
[6]Allyn A. Young, "Some Limitations of the Value Concept," *Quarterly Journal of Economics,* XXV (May 1911), 424.
[7]John Maurice Clark, *Competition as a Dynamic Process* (Washington: The Brookings Institution, 1961), p. 24.
[8]Adam Smith, "The History of Astronomy," in *The Works of Adam Smith, LL.D.,* V, ed. Dugald Stewart (Aalen: Otto Zeller, 1963), pp. 189–90.

had earlier been employed and developed by a number of writers including Cantillon, Turgot, Hume, Steuart, and others, in their various efforts to explain how price was, in a free market, ultimately forced to a level which would just cover costs, that is, to the lowest level which would be sustainable over the long run.[9] Thus, although Smith played a major role in making the principle of competition quite literally the *sine qua non* of economic analysis, to the extent that Ricardo would later contemplate only cases in which "competition operates without restraint,"[1] and John Stuart Mill would go on to assert that "only through the principle of competition has political economy any pretension to the character of a science,"[2] he contributed little, if anything, to its economic meaning.

Had the concept of competition in fact been, as is often implied, a major contribution of Adam Smith, or had he added significantly to its economic meaning, there is some reason, indeed, to suppose that economic theory would have produced at an early date a concept of competition not unlike that later called for by Schumpeter, that is, competition associated with internal industrial efficiency and with the development of "the new technology, the new source of supply, [and] the new type of organization."[3] For Smith after all, writing in the environment of the English industrial revolution, was eminently aware of the importance of dynamic changes in productive technique and industrial organization, which he somewhat loosely termed "the division of labor." It was precisely the productive and organizational relationships within the business enterprise and not, as with the physiocrats, the natural fertility of the soil, or, as with the mercantilists, exchange in the market per se, which was for Adam Smith the ultimate source of economic surplus and the essential basis of economic activity. But having opened the *Wealth of Nations* with an uncommonly strong tribute to the idea of division of labor and the associated productive efficiency to be found within the contemporary business firm, Smith curiously failed to relate productive technique to the concept of competition, the central organizing principle upon which, according to him, society could safely in most cases depend. At one point, it is true, he did speak of "the competition of producers who, in order to undersell one another, have recourse to new divisions of labour, and new improvements of art, which might never otherwise have been thought of."[4] But this was little more than a passing comment, and came only in Book V, well after his extended, but separate, discussions of competition and division of labor in Book I. Moreover, the "recourse to new divisions of labour and new improvements of art" were clearly subsidiary aspects of his concept of competition, the essence of which was the effort to undersell in the market by lowering price. As division of labor was limited by the extent of the market, so its analysis in terms of the organization of production within the business firm came to be circumscribed, even for Adam Smith, by the analysis of the firm's external market relationships. Not the essence of the industrial revolution—the changing mode of production—but rather, the mercantilists' overriding concern with price, continued, with Smith, to be the central theme of economic analysis. The division of labor came, with his successors, to be "given" as "the state of the arts," changes in which were ruled out through the use of the "pound of *ceteris paribus*," and competition continued to be consistently viewed in terms of exchange relationships between existing and unchanging economic units.[5]

Although the classical economists thus viewed

[9]Paul J. McNulty, "A Note on the History of Perfect Competition," *Journal of Political Economy*, LXXV (Aug. 1967), Part I, 395–99.
[1]Ricardo, *op. cit.*, p. 6.
[2]Mill, *op. cit.*, p. 306.
[3]Joseph A. Schumpeter, *Capitalism, Socialism and Democracy* (New York: Harper and Row, 1962), p. 84.

[4]*Op. cit.*, p. 706.
[5] This is not to suggest that the leading neoclassical economists were unaware of the dynamic aspects of competition. Their failure was in their inability to integrate these aspects systematically into their economic theory. J. B. Clark, for example, in *The Essentials of Economic Theory—as Applied to Modern Problems of Industry and Public Policy* (New York: Macmillan, 1915), a volume on economic dynamics which followed his static analysis of *The Distribution of Wealth*, and which made it clear that he was eminently aware of the significance of the changing mode of production, spoke of "the competition which is active enough to change the standard shape of society rapidly—that, for example, which spurs on mechanical invention" (p. 198), and of those situations in which "competition has reduced the establishments in one subgroup to a half dozen or less" (p. 201). But it was Clark's static analysis of perfect competition, and not his observations on economic change, or on the dynamic aspects of competition, which had a permanent effect on the development of economic theory. Marshall, too, took a quite realistic view of competition. But (and perhaps for that very reason) Marshall's impact on the development of the concept of competition, in contrast to his impact on economics generally, was minimal. Indeed, as Stigler has noted (*op. cit.*, p. 9), Marshall's "treatment of competition was much closer to Adam Smith's than to that of his contemporaries, . . . [and was] almost as informal and unsystematic."

competition as exclusively a market process, the neo-classical development of the concept of perfect competition as itself a market structure nonetheless represented a sharp discontinuity in the development of social thought, for, although competition, according to the older view, took place exclusively within the market, the latter was always seen as allowing for individual initiative in buying and selling. That is, although the classical economists largely ignored the entrepreneurial function as far as it was concerned with operations within the business enterprise, their concept of competition was a disequilibrium one of market activity, with price a variable from the standpoint of the individual firm. Perfect competition, on the other hand, is an equilibrium situation in which price becomes a parameter from the standpoint of the individual firm and no market activity is possible. Thus the classical concept of competition as a guiding force, to which we earlier referred, is not only different from that of the neoclassical concept of competition as a state of affairs; the two are incompatible in a fundamental sense, reflecting precisely the difference between a condition of equilibrium and the behavioral pattern leading to it. As Hayek has rightly noted, the idea of perfect competition "throughout assumes that state of affairs already to exist which, according to the truer view of the older theory, the process of competition tends to bring about (or to approximate) . . . [and] if the state of affairs assumed by the theory of perfect competition ever existed, it would not only deprive of their scope all the activities which the verb 'to compete' describes but would make them virtually impossible."[6] Thus, the single activity which best characterized the meaning of competition in classical economics—price cutting by an individual firm in order to get rid of excess supplies—becomes the one activity impossible under perfect competition. And what for the classical economists was the single analytical function of the competitive process—the determination of market price—becomes, with perfect competition, the one thing unexplained and unaccounted for.[7] The per-

fection of competition thus drained the concept of all behavioral content, so that, using perfect competition as a standard, even price competition, the essence of the competitive process for Adam Smith, is imperfect or monopolistic. That perfect competition has come to be "a rigorously defined concept"[8] is not to be denied. But the result of that rigorous definition is that the verb "to compete" has no meaning in economic theory except in connection with activities which are also in some sense "monopolistic." Indeed, the perfectly competitive firm itself is but "a monopolist with a special environment."[9]

III

Some of the ambiguity concerning the relationship between the idea of perfect competition and business behavior might perhaps have been avoided if Cournot had not designated as "the hypothesis of unlimited competition" the very state of affairs which he had earlier characterized as that in which "the effects of competition have reached their limit."[1] But the classical, behavioral, "imperfect" concept of (price) competition itself possessed certain inherent weaknesses, which have persisted in economic theory to the present day. The remainder of this paper will be concerned with identifying what seem to be the most important of these, and with indicating their relevance for economic analysis and policy.

One fundamental deficiency of competition as the concept has been employed in economic theory is that it has never been related in a systematic way to costs of production. There has been a curious dichotomy in economic science in the assumption that self-interest alone will insure that the businessman will work optimally in the interests of society within the business enterprise, or in his *administration* of owned or hired resources and factors of production, while without the enterprise, in his *buying and selling* of factors or products in the market, either an "invisible hand" of competition, or a "visible hand" of public policy, is needed to insure efficiency. Although Adam Smith observed that monopoly "is a great enemy to good management, which can never be universally established but in consequence of that free and universal competition which forces everybody to have recourse to it for the sake of self-

---

[6] F. A. Hayek, *Individualism and Economic Order* (Chicago: University of Chicago Press, 1948), pp. 92, 96.

[7] As Arrow has pointed out, "there exists a logical gap in the usual formulation of the theory of the perfectly competitive economy, . . . [in that] there is no place for a rational decision with respect to prices as there is with respect to quantities." Kenneth J. Arrow, "Towards a Theory of Price Adjustment," in Moses Abramovitz and others, *The Allocation of Economic Resources* (Stanford, Calif.: Stanford University Press, 1959), p. 41.

[8] Stigler, *op. cit.*, p. 11.

[9] Arrow, *op. cit.*, p. 45.

[1] Cournot, *op. cit.*, pp. 90–91.

defence,"[2] his successors failed systematically to relate competition to the search for cost reduction or to "good management" generally. On the contrary, the competitive and monopolistic firms of economic theory differ only with respect to the *demand* curves they face, and the single analytical function of competition has been to get price down to the level of marginal cost. "Under free competition," as Senior wrote, "cost of production is the regulator of price."[3] But the question remains: what is the regulator of cost? Economic theory stresses the optimality of the equation of price and marginal cost. There is nothing optimal in this equation, however, if marginal cost is higher than need be due to internal inefficiencies, and there is reason, indeed, to suppose that the latter is not infrequently the case. Chandler's research in the history of American business administration points up the significance of the search for cost-reducing methods *within the company itself* as one of the significant forces shaping the reorganization of American industry around the turn of the century. The 1901 Annual Report of the National Biscuit Company, for example, highlighted the company's dissatisfaction with its earlier policies of price competition and acquisition of competitors.

> The first meant a ruinous war of prices and a great loss of profits; the second, constantly increased capitalization. ... We soon satisfied ourselves that within the company itself we must look for success.
> We turned our attention and bent our energies to improving the internal management of our business, to getting full benefit from purchasing our raw materials in large quantities, to economizing the expenses of manufacture, to systematizing the rendering more effective our selling department, and above all things and before all things to improving the quality of our goods and the conditions in which they should reach the customer.[4]

There is, of course, nothing in this list of undertakings which is inconsistent with the postulates of economic theory. On the contrary, the trouble is precisely that economic theory assumes the company should have been doing those things all along. To say that this company was not operating in a fully (or even moderately) competitive market is not to

eliminate the problem. The fact is that there is no explanation even in the theory of the perfectly competitive firm for the minimization of costs; the latter is merely assumed. If all firms are equally inefficient in internal administration, a perfectly competitive equilibrium could involve a welfare loss not less significant than any which might result from market imperfections.

That there may currently be considerable room for increased efficiency within business enterprises is suggested by the evidence Leibenstein has summarized concerning the existence of what he calls "X-inefficiencies,"—those which, unlike "allocative inefficiencies," stem not from imperfections in the structure of the market but rather from the fact that "for a variety of reasons people and organizations normally work neither as hard nor as effectively as they could."[5] If economic efficiency is truly a goal of competitive policy, and if Leibenstein is correct that "in a great many instances the amount to be gained by increasing allocative efficiency is trivial while the amount to be gained by increasing X-efficiency is frequently significant,"[6] the desirability of a new dimension in American competitive policy no less than in the economic concept of competition—one which will relate to principles of managerial science as well as to those of market taxonomy—is apparent.

Another fundamental weakness of the competitive concept, and one not unrelated to the above discussion, has been its consistent failure to relate to economic growth. In this respect, competition seems never to have fully recovered from the influence of Ricardo, who, in a letter to Malthus, once wrote:

> Political Economy you think is an enquiry into the nature and causes of wealth—I think it should rather be called an enquiry into the laws which determine the division of the produce of industry amongst the classes who concur in its formation. ... Every day I am more satisfied that the former enquiry is vain and delusive, and the latter only the true object of science.[7]

The analytical refinement of the concept of competition, from the work of Cournot to that of Frank Knight, is at one with this general point of view. Edgeworth's definition of a "perfect field of com-

[2] *Op. cit.,* p. 147.

[3] Nassau W. Senior, *An Outline of the Science of Political Economy* (New York: Augustus M. Kelly, 1951), p. 102.

[4] Alfred D. Chandler, Jr., *Strategy and Structure* (Cambridge, Mass.: The Massachusetts Institute of Technology Press, 1962), p. 33.

[5] Harvey Leibenstein, "Allocative Efficiency vs. 'X-Efficiency'," *American Economic Review,* LVI (June 1966), 413.

[6] *Ibid.*

[7] *Works and Correspondence,* Vol. 8, ed. Piero Sraffa (Cambridge, England: Cambridge University Press, 1958), p. 278.

petition," for example, ran entirely in terms of contracting and recontracting over the division of an existing and unchanging quantity of economic resources.[8] Although economic theory is no longer coterminous with price theory, and although the question of allocative efficiency now seems, indeed, to be of less urgency and relevance than that of economic growth (the precise relationship between the two being, apparently, a matter of considerable uncertainty), the concept of competition has been only partially transformed from one of pure catallactics to one more closely related to the question of economic change. It is true that the beginnings of such a transformation are to be found in Chamberlin's reformulation, especially in his analysis of the product as a variable, his attention to sales effort, and in his general emphasis on commodities as "the most volatile things in the economic system."[9] But the focus of the Chamberlinian analysis is still allocative efficiency, and much more needs to be done by way of systematically relating product and sales competition to economic change and growth. Moreover, Chamberlin's emphasis on variability of the product needs to be complemented by an increased emphasis on the variability of the form of the business firm itself and of the conditions under which commodities are produced and distributed—the latter being, perhaps, hardly less "volatile" than commodities themselves, and undoubtedly of no less significance for the overall growth process.

It was precisely during the years when the concept of competition was being analytically refined by becoming more and more closely identified with the atomistic market at the hands of Jevons, Edgeworth, J. B. Clark, and Knight,[1] that the industrial structures of the advanced economies of the world were taking shape, largely through changes in organizational forms which had little to do with price competition except in terms of the search for ways to avoid it. The analysis of these changes—indeed, the whole question of economic growth—was by that time largely becoming the province of the newly emerging discipline of economic history, which has necessarily had to give a broader meaning to competition than that traditionally associated with economic theory. The theorist cannot, for example, view the transfor-

mation of (say) the meat-packing industry in the United States during those years as a "competitive" development, for it was a movement which resulted in a market structure dominated by a "Big Four" or "Big Five"—results exactly opposite to those specified by Cournot. The historian, on the other hand, can—indeed, must—view this development as an adaptive response on the part of Armour, Morris, Cudahy, and Schwarzschild and Sulzberger, who, faced with the innovations in production and marketing introduced by Gustavus Swift, "had to build similarly integrated organizations" if they were "to compete effectively."[2] It is well known that the essence of industrialization and economic growth is a changing production function and the development of new products, techniques, and forms of business organization. What has been lacking is any systematic effort to relate these changes to the concept of competition. The separation of so central a concept of economic theory from much of the analysis of our most pressing economic problem is unfortunate. Clearly, the time has come to incorporate into *the mainstream of economic theory* (as distinct from monographs on "new" or "workable" competition recurrently emerging in the specialized literature of industrial organization) a concept of competition closer to that occasionally suggested by Adam Smith and strongly advocated by Schumpeter—competition associated with new "divisions of labor" within the business firm and in the industrial structure generally, and one that is more closely allied with concepts of "internal, especially technological, efficiency."[3] It is unfortunate that Schumpeter's defense of monopoly and big business has tended to overshadow his insights into the competitive process, insights which extended beyond those of even Chamberlin because they included an appreciation of the importance of changing methods of production and forms of industrial organization. Although Schumpeter was probably wrong, as recent evidence suggests,[4] in his assertion that "the large scale establishment . . . has come to be the most powerful engine of progress and in particular of the long run expansion of total output,"[5] he seems less likely to be mistaken in his

[8]*Op. cit.,* pp. 17–19.
[9]*Towards a More General Theory of Value* (New York: Oxford University Press, 1957), p. 114.
[1]Stigler, *op. cit.*

[2]Chandler, *op. cit.,* p. 26.
[3]Schumpeter, *op. cit.,* p. 106.
[4]F. M. Scherer, "Firm Size, Market Structure, Opportunity, and the Output of Patented Inventions," *American Economic Review,* LV (Part I, Dec. 1965), 1097–1125.
[5]Schumpeter, *op. cit.,* p. 106.

insistence that, at least from the standpoint of economic growth, "it is not . . . [price] competition which counts but the competition from the new commodity, the new technology, the new source of supply, the new type of organization . . . competition which commands a decisive cost or quality advantage and which strikes not at the margin of the profits and the outputs of the existing firms but at their foundations and their very lives."[6]

Finally, a persistent weakness of the concept of competition has been the tendency of economists to minimize, ignore, or deny, its externally interdependent nature, that is, the extent to which the competition of one economic unit tends to affect the economic position of others, and thus, the overall industrial structure. Despite the etymology of the verb (literally, "to seek together"), to compete, in economic theory, has generally meant to act independently. "The meaning of 'competition'," Frank Knight has written, is simply that the competing units "are numerous and act independently."[7] Even the literature of the so-called "new" or "workable" competition reflects the influence of this way of thinking.[8] This emphasis on independence has meant a close conceptual connection between competition, on the one hand, and both economic rationality and economic freedom, on the other. Thus Henry Moore, in his classic categorization of the various meanings given to competition in economic theory concluded that "the essential meaning of the term" is that "every economic factor seeks and obtains a maximum net income,"[9] and Knight, on another occasion, wrote: "What competition actually means is simply the freedom of the individual to 'deal' with any and all other individuals and to select the best terms as judged by himself, among those offered."[1]

The trouble with this view is that it fails to specify *how* the competing units act, either in terms of securing a "maximum net income" or in "dealing" with "any and all other individuals." Moreover, it ascribes to the competing unit altogether too passive a pattern of behavior. Rather than merely "selecting" the best terms among those offered, a competitor may well choose to try to twist the terms of trade to his own advantage. In this respect, as Morris Copeland has rightly noted, "competition frequently means discrimination."

> In fact a competitor that gets ahead in an industry may do so in substantial part by developing business connections, i.e., arrangements that give him preferential treatment in terms of financing, in terms of purchase, in access to market information, in the award of private contracts, even preferential treatment in the administration of a public office.[2]

Implicit in Professor Copeland's view of competition is the realistic notion that some competitors may be better *able* to compete than others. Such a difference in competitive ability would allow for differential growth and profit rates among the firms within an industry—variables to which the Jevonian "Law of Indifference" need not, apparently, apply even in an otherwise conceptually perfect market. Moreover, competition which involves the active effort to improve the terms on which one trades, rather than the merely passive selection of the best terms available, may well be, in fact, competition for a position of monopoly power—a not unrealistic view of the actual competitive process in the light of our industrial history. To compete for monopoly power is not, of course, necessarily to realize it. But to the extent that the result, not to say the purpose, of economic competition is a changed environment in which that competition proceeds, the case is strengthened for distinguishing between, rather than identifying, the idea of competition and that of market structure.

IV

A promising, if not yet altogether satisfying, new dimension has been suggested for microeconomics in recent years in the various efforts to develop a "behavioral theory of the firm," in which analysis would go beyond that of the traditional determinate equilibrium toward which the business firm is assumed to be perfectly adapting in a world of no uncertainty, to include also "at least some description

---

[6]*Ibid.*, p. 84.

[7]"Immutable Laws in Economics," *op. cit.*, p. 102.

[8]In his last major work, J. M. Clark shifted his emphasis from "workable" to "effective" competition, and then went on to say: "For the competition to be effective, *the crucial thing seems to be that prices be independently made* under conditions that give some competitors an incentive to aggressive action that others will have to meet, whenever prices are materially above the minimum necessary supply prices at which the industry would supply the amounts demanded of the various grades and types of products it produces." *Competition as a Dynamic Process, op. cit.*, p. 18, emphasis added.

[9]Henry L. Moore, "Paradoxes of Competition," this *Journal*, XX (Feb. 1906), 213.

[1] "The Meaning of Freedom," *Ethics*, LII (Oct. 1941), 103.

[2]M. A. Copeland, "Institutionalism and Welfare Economics," *American Economic Review*, XLVIII (Mar. 1958), 13.

of the processes and mechanisms through which the adaptation takes place."[3] The reformulation and expansion of the concept of competition would appear to be an important, if yet underemphasized, part of that general task. To the degree that that effort is successful, it seems reasonable to predict that the idea of the market and that of competition may increasingly come to be separately identified, and competition itself may be, once again, what it was at the hands of Adam Smith: a disequilibrium, behavioral concept which is meaningful and relevant in terms of the contemporary pattern of economic life.

[3] H. A. Simon, "Theories of Decision-Making in Economics," *American Economic Review*, XLIX (June 1959), 256.

The Concept of Monopoly and the Measurement of Monopoly Power*

ABBA P. LERNER[1]

Abba P. Lerner (B.Sc., University of London, 1932; Ph.D., 1943) was born in Bessarabia, Russia, in 1903 and grew up in London, England. Prior to his retirement, Lerner was Professor of Economics at Florida State University. During his long career he also taught at The City University of New York (Queens College and The Graduate School and University Center), the London School of Economics, the University of Virginia, the University of Kansas City, Amherst College, the New School for Social Research, Roosevelt University, Michigan State University, and the University of California at Berkeley. Lerner's major works include *The Economics of Control, The Economics of Employment, Essays in Economic Analysis, Everybody's Business,* and *MAP—a Market Anti-Inflation Plan* (with David Colander). He wrote widely in many areas of economic theory, including welfare economics, capital theory, the theory of employment and inflation, and the theory of socialistic economies. Early in his career Lerner was a founder of *The Review of Economic Studies* and was its managing editor from 1933 to 1937. From 1953 to 1956 he was Economic Advisor to the government of Israel. He was a Fellow of the Econometric Society, and in 1966 was made a Distinguished Fellow of the American Economic Association. Lerner's rare abilities as a teacher and scholar are attested to by Milton Friedman in his review of *The Economics of Control,* which refers to Lerner's skill and patience in exposition, his flexibility of mind, his profound interest in social welfare, and his willingness to accept and courage to state what seems to him proper social policy, regardless of precedent or accepted opinion. Professor Lerner died in 1983.

*Reprinted from the *Review of Economic Studies* (June 1943) by permission of The Society for Economic Analysis Ltd. Copyright 1943, pp. 157–175.

[1]The great advances made in the subject of this article since the major part of it was written—particularly in the work of Mr. Chamberlin and Mrs. Robinson—have rendered many parts of it out of date. In preparing it for publication, while cutting out some of these parts, I have been so much under the influence of this recent work that I cannot say how much of what is here published is really my own.

I

Monopoly, says the dictionary, is the exclusive right of a person, corporation or state to sell a particular commodity. Economic science, investigating the economic aspects of this legal right, found that they all resolved themselves into the implications of the power of the monopolist—as distinguished from a seller in a competitive market—arbitrarily to decide the price of the commodity, leaving it to the buyers to decide how much they will buy at that price, or, alternatively, to decide the quantity he will sell, by so fixing the price as to induce buyers to purchase just this quantity. Technically this is expressed by saying that the monopolist is confronted with a falling demand curve for his product or that the elasticity of demand for his product is less than infinity, while the seller in a purely[2] competitive market has a horizontal demand curve or the elasticity of demand for his product is equal to infinity.

The monopolist is normally assumed to tend to fix the price at the level at which he makes the greatest profit or "monopoly revenue." This monopoly revenue constitutes a levy upon the consumers that the monopolist is able to appropriate for himself purely in virtue of his restrictive powers *qua* monopolist, and it is the consumers' objection to paying this levy that lies at the base of popular feeling against the monopolist.

In addition to this it is claimed that monopoly is harmful in a more objective sense. A levy which involves a mere transference from buyer to monopolist cannot be said to be harmful from a social point of view unless it can be shown that the monopolist is less deserving of the levy than the people who have to pay it; either because he is in general a less deserving kind of person, or because the transference will increase the evils of inequality of incomes. But the levy is not a mere transference. The method of raising it, namely, by increasing the price of the monopolised commodity, causes buyers to divert their expenditure to other, less satisfactory, purchases. This constitutes a loss to the consumer which is not balanced by any gain reaped by the monopolist, so that there is a net social loss.

The nature of the loss here loosely expressed seems to have defied attempts at more exact exposition, the difficulties encountered on these attempts having even induced some to declare that this commonsense view of a social loss is an illusion, while more careful sceptics prefer to say that nothing "scientific" can be said about it. The account given above clearly will not do as a general and accurate description of the

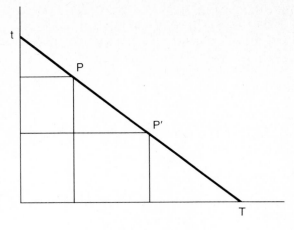

Fig. 1

nature of the social loss. Where a consumer spends as much as before on the monopolised commodity when the price is raised, he cannot be said to divert expenditure to other and less satisfactory channels, and where he spends more[3] upon the commodity than at the lower competitive price it might even be argued that there is a net social gain in so far as the consumer is induced to spend more on the commodity which is more urgently needed and less on other commodities! There seems little to choose be-

---

[2]"Pure" competition is different from "perfect" competition. The former implies perfection of competition only in respect of the complete absence of monopoly and abstracts from other aspects of perfection in competition. This useful distinction is suggested by Chamberlin. See his *Theory of Monopolistic Competition*, p. 6.

[3]Where as much or more is spent on a commodity when the price is raised the elasticity of demand is equal to or less than unity. This may appear incompatible with the condition of monopolistic equilibrium that elasticity of demand shall be greater than unity (as long as marginal cost is positive). There is, however, no incompatibility, for the two elasticities of demand are different things. The elasticity that has to be greater than unity for monopolistic equilibrium is the elasticity at the *point* on the demand curve corresponding to the position of monopolistic equilibrium. The elasticity that is equal to or less than unity when the amount spent on the commodity remains unchanged or increases as the price is raised, is the elasticity over the *arc* of the demand curve from the point of competitive equilibrium to the point of monopolistic equilibrium. The arc elasticity in this sense will normally be less than the point elasticity, as will appear from the diagram. If tT is the demand curve (here drawn a straight line), P' the point of competitive equilibrium, and P the point of monopolistic equilibrium, then the *point* elasticity at the monopoly equilibrium will be $\dfrac{P'T}{Pt}$ while the *arc* elasticity will be $\dfrac{P'T}{P't}$, which is smaller. The arc elasticity must be smaller unless the demand curve is so concave (upwards) that it shows a constant or increasing point elasticity as price is lowered. The point elasticity at the competitive position will, of course, be $\dfrac{PT}{P't}$. For the explanation of this definition of "arc elasticity," see my note on "The Diagrammatical Representation of Elasticity of Demand," in No. 1 of the REVIEW.

tween this argument and the counter-argument, that as long as the elasticity is greater than zero some consumer (or unit of consumption) is induced to change the direction of his expenditure so that he suffers the uncompensated inconvenience which constitutes the net social loss. Does this mean that if a man's demand is completely inelastic (so that the increased price brings no diminution in the amount of the monopolised commodity consumed and the whole of the levy is sacrificed ultimately in the form of other commodities) the expenditure of the income, as diminished by the amount of the levy, is not interfered with by the existence of the monopoly?—i.e. that if he had paid the levy in cash and prices were not affected he would have reduced his consumption of other commodities in the same way? Or is it more reasonable to suppose that a rise in a particular price will always tend to diminish purchases of the dearer commodity, where a cash levy (prices remaining unchanged) would diminish all expenditures in the same proportion so that if the same amount of the monopolised commodity is bought at the higher price, a cash diminution in income of the size of the levy would have *increased* the demand for that commodity? The problems do not seem to be amenable to treatment on these lines.[4]

The commonsense attitude is, however, not easily balked. Another attempt was made to deal with the problem by Marshall, by means of the apparatus of consumers' surplus. If it is assumed that the marginal utility of money is unchanged, or that the change is so small that it may legitimately be neglected, it can be shown that the money value of the consumers' surplus lost is greater than the monopoly revenue gained, so that we have a theoretical measure of the net social loss due to the monopoly. There are, of course, many important weaknesses in this treatment, and some ways of applying it are completely wrong. The marginal utility of money can be considered unchanged only if we are considering a small change in the price of only one commodity. This makes it impossible to add the consumers' surplus obtained by an individual from different goods. Quite wrong is any attempt to speak of the consumers' surplus of a community and to derive it from the communal demand curve. And there are other traps to be avoided in this connection which are quite well known. But the exclusive preoccupation of teachers of economics with putting their pupils on their guard against these insufficiencies and dangers has tended to make them deny the problem with which the concept of consumers' surplus was intended to deal—the net social loss and its nature. It is not intended here to deny or even to belittle the dangers and confusions attendant on the use of the concept of consumers' surplus, but it does seem that some light can be thrown on the problem by its use.

From the consumers' surplus approach there has emerged a clarification of the rent element in monopoly revenue. It is only in the case of constant or decreasing average cost that the amount of monopoly revenue is necessarily less than the loss of consumers' surplus. The monopoly revenue will be greater if the average cost curve rises steeply enough. This gave the impression that the monopolistic restriction brought about a net social gain so that the competitive output was too great and it would be beneficial to tax industries which were "subject to diminishing returns." In correcting this view it was shown that against the monopoly revenue was to be reckoned not only the loss of consumers' surplus, but also the reduction in rents as compared with those receivable under competition. If the reductions of rent is not allowed for, the diminution of costs of the marginal units, as output is restricted, is attributed to all the *infra*-marginal costs where there has been no reduction in social costs, but only a transference of income from the receivers of rent. In the accompanying Fig. 2 AR is the average revenue or demand curve (which, to avoid the quarrels over consumers' surplus, we can consider as the sum of a number of identical demand curves of similar individuals), MR is the marginal revenue curve, AC is average costs, and MC is marginal costs. P' will be the competitive point where output is OM' and price is $M'P'$, and P, which is perpendicularly above A, where MR and MC cut, will be the monopoly point where output is OM and price is MP. Consumers' surplus lost is equal to $SPP'T$, while monopoly revenue is $SPQR$, which may be greater. But against this must be reckoned the loss in rents, $RQP'T$, so that there is a net social loss of PQP'.

---

[4]In the last few months Dr. J. R. Hicks and Mr. R. G. D. Allen have been making investigations on these lines and have demonstrated by means of the indifference curve apparatus that, with continuous indifference curves, an absolutely inelastic demand curve must be accompanied by a negatively sloping expenditure curve. This means that a change in income (prices remain unchanged) would bring about a change *in inverse direction* of the amount of the commodity bought. They have not been interested, however, in the problems dealt with in this article.

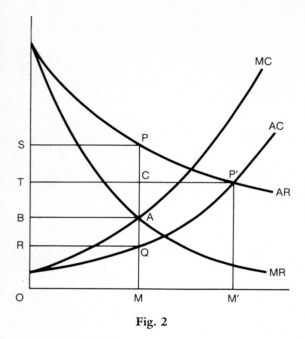

Fig. 2

One is tempted to divide the monopoly revenue *SPQR* into two parts, *SPCT* and *RQCT,* and to say that the former is the monopoly revenue extracted from consumers while the latter is the monopoly revenue extracted from receivers of rent or producers' surplus. It is exactly parallel to the extraction of monopoly revenue from the receivers of consumers' surplus, but is obtained in virtue of the monopolist being confronted with a rising supply curve instead of with a falling demand curve. It is a gain obtained by a "single" buyer instead of a gain obtained by a "single" seller. The appropriate parallel name for it would be *Monopsony Revenue.*[5] This dichotomy of the monopoly revenue is based on a comparison of the monopoly position with the competitive position.[6]

PC is the rise in price and *QC* is the fall in average cost, so that these quantities multiplied by the monopolistic output give the monopoly revenue and the monopsony revenue respectively.

It will, however, not do to compare the monopoly position with the competitive position for the purpose of making the dichotomy, for by this procedure it is made to depend upon the shape of the curves for outputs between the monopolistic output *OM* and the competitive output *OM',* which may be a long way from it. It does not seem reasonable that the degree of monopsony or monopoly at output *OM* should be dependent upon what happens to demand or cost curves in the vicinity of output *OM'.* And apart from this the taking of the competitive output and price as a base from which everything is to be measured leads to more concrete inconsistencies. Thus we may attempt to find the amount of monopoly revenue (in the more exact sense, that is, not including monopsony revenue), by considering what it would be if the average cost were constant at the competitive level so that there was no monopsony. *AC* and *MC* would then coincide with *TP',* and the monopoly revenue would not be *SPCT* but some other larger amount, for the output could not be *OM* but some other amount. If we reverse this process, assuming that the demand curve and the *MR* curve are horizontal, we again find that the monopsony revenue is not *RQCT* but some other larger amount, and the output is not *OM* but, again, some other amount.[7]

The direct comparison of monopolistic with competitive equilibrium further assumes that cost conditions are the same and that demand conditions are the same. Neither of these is likely, and the combination of both is much less likely.

A more reasonable procedure for the allocation of the gains as between monopoly and monopsony revenue is to take as a basis not the price which would

---

[5]Joan Robinson, in *The Economics of Imperfect Competition,* introduces the word Monopsony, but does not speak of Monopsony Revenue.
[6]By monopoly position is meant a position in which the demand curve does not appear horizontal to all the firms in the industry. The simplest case of this is when there is only one firm which coincides with the whole industry, and that is what is shown in Fig. 2 at the monopoly position *P.* Monopoly is essentially a property of *firms* and by a monopolistic industry is meant nothing more than an industry in which *firms* have downward sloping demand curves. And, of course, only a firm is interested in maximising monopoly revenue. If the demand curve for the whole industry is horizontal, the industry is in a competitive condition, but that is only because in this case every firm in the industry must also have a horizontal demand curve—even if there is only one firm.

[7]In Fig. 2, where both *AR* and *AC* are concave upwards, the output under monopoly without monopsony would be less than *OM,* and the output under monopsony without monopoly would be greater than *OM.* The outputs are given by the abscissae of the points where *TP'* is cut by *MR* and *MC* respectively. If *AR* and *AC* are convex, the outputs would move in the opposite direction. If they are straight lines, or if the convexity of one is just offset by the concavity of the other, the output will be the same as when the monopoly and monopsony are found in combination. If the elimination of monopsony changes the output in one direction, the elimination of monopoly would change output in the other direction, and *vice versa.*

obtain if there were neither monopoly nor monopsony, but instead of that the actual conditions of the monopoly-monopsony equilibrium. With the given demand curve pure[8] monopoly output could only be *OM* if the horizontal *AC* curve were coincident with *AB,* in which case the monopoly revenue would be equal to *SPAB.* With the given *AC* curve the pure monopsony output could only be *OM* if the horizontal demand curve is coincident with *AB,* in which case the monopsony revenue would be equal to *RQAB,* and *RQAB* and *SPAB* do add up to the monopoly-monopsony revenue *SPQR.*

From this it appears that the monopoly revenue per unit of output, *AP,* is the excess of price over marginal cost, so that the mark of the absence of monopoly is the equality of price or *average* receipts to *marginal* cost, and the mark of the absence of monopsony is the equality of *average* cost to *marginal* receipts.[9]

The test more usually accepted is the equality of average costs to price or average receipts. It is this equation which is regularly given as the definition of "competitive" position,[10] and a suggestion like the

one here given is likely to meet with a lecture on the impropriety of comparing averages with marginal values. It would seem, however, that the orthodox point of view is not only based upon too great a readiness to consider perfect competition as the ideal type of economic phenomena towards which all things tend, but are deterred more or less only by "frictions" (for in perfect competition all these equations become identical), but is in some measure induced by the habit of using straight lines in diagrams dealing with monopoly, and thus missing the problem. For in this case, *AB* of Fig. 2 would coincide with *P'T,* and the two dichotomies of the monopoly-cum-monopsony revenue are identical.

The point at issue is not merely a verbal one of definition—a quibble as to what it is better to call the "competitive" position. The importance of the competitive position lies in its implications of being a position which in some way or another is better than other positions. It is the position in which the "Invisible Hand" has exerted its beneficial influences to the utmost. It has become the symbol for the social optimum. Its importance for us here is in giving us a basis against which we can compare the effect of monopoly in order to see the social loss, if any, that the existence of a monopoly brings about. Is the social optimum that position at which prices are equal to average cost, or that at which price equals marginal cost and average cost equals marginal revenue?

The social optimum relative to any distribution of resources (or income) between different individuals (and we cannot here go into the problems connected with optimum distribution) will be reached only if the resources which are to be devoted to satisfying the wants of each individual are so allocated between the different things he wants, that his total satisfaction would not be increased by any transference of resources from the provision of any one of the things he gets to any other thing he wants. This would show itself in the impossibility of any individual being put in a preferred position without putting another individual in a worse position. We may adopt this as our criterion or test of the achievement of the relative optimum. If in any set of circumstances it is possible to move one individual into a preferred position without moving another individual into a worse position (i.e. such that the original position is preferred to it by the individual affected), we may say that the relative optimum is not reached; but if such a move-

---

[8]By *pure monopoly* is meant a case where one is confronted with a falling demand curve for the commodity one sells, but with a horizontal supply curve for the factors one has to buy for the production of the commodity; so that one sells as a monopolist but buys in a perfect market. Similarly, *pure monopsony* stands for perfect competition in the market where one sells, but monopsony in the market where one buys—being confronted with a horizontal demand curve but a rising supply curve. *Pure monopoly* is monopoly free from all elements of monopsony. *Pure monopsony* is monopsony free from all elements of monopoly. *Pure competition* stands for freedom from all elements of both monopoly and monopsony. The *purity* of monopoly or of monopsony has nothing to do with the *degree* of monopoly or monopsony.

[9]*Marginal* cost and *marginal* receipts are, of course, always equal to each other in any equilibrium, whether monopolistic or monopsonistic, or both or neither. It is, therefore, possible to express the same relationships in terms of the equality of price or average receipts to marginal receipts and the equality of average costs to marginal costs. But this procedure rules out conditions of disequilibrium together with monopoly or monopsony, so that to affirm this would be merely to say in other words that the demand or supply curve is horizontal, so that by definition there is no monopoly or monopsony. The relationships given in the text are not the merely mathematical relationships between an average and its corresponding marginal curve, but between real conditions of costs on the one hand and of receipts on the other. It will be seen below that these relationships will not always coincide with the tautologous alternatives suggested in this footnote.

[10]Even Mrs. Robinson defines "competitive output" and "competitive price" as that output or price at which *AC* = *AR* or price (*op. cit.,* p. 160), although she demonstrates most clearly in other parts of the book how this condition (*AC* = *AR*) is also reached in monopolistic or imperfectly competitive equilibrium.

ment is impossible, we may say that the relative optimum has been attained. The conditions which must be satisfied if the optimum is attained can be formulated quite simply.

Any change in the position of any individual means a change in the quantity of goods (and services) he consumes. For any such a change to take place it is necessary that there shall be either *(a)* a *similar* change in the total quantity of goods produced or *(b)* an *opposite* change in the total quantity of goods consumed by others, or *(c)* some combination of *(a)* and *(b)*. In the case of *(a)*, consumption by other people need not be interfered with by the change, the whole change in the consumption by one individual being covered by changes in production. In the case of *(b)*, there need be no change in production, any increase in the consumption of particular goods by one individual be provided by decreases in their consumption by others, and any decreases in the consumption of other goods by one individual being covered by increases in their consumption by others. In case *(c)* both kinds of compensating movements take place, but these can be separated and dealt with as cases of *(a)* and *(b)* so that no special treatment is necessary.

If a change in the consumption of various goods by one individual which improves his position is compensated solely by a movement of type *(a)*, consumption by all other individuals need not be affected. This means that the effect of the movement from the previous position was to make one individual better off without making any other individual worse off. The previous position could not, therefore, have been an optimum position. One condition, then, of the optimum position is that any change in the quantity of goods consumed by any individual which improves his position cannot be compensated by a movement of type *(a)*.

This is illustrated in Fig. 3,[11] *PP'* is a section of the displacement cost curve (or productive indifference curve) of the whole community. *I* and *II* are consumption indifference curves of one individual. The indifference curves are superimposed upon the displacement cost curve, so that the point on the indifference map which represents the quantities of the commodities *X* (measured horizontally) and *Y* (measured vertically), consumed by the individual in the initial position, coincides with the point on the

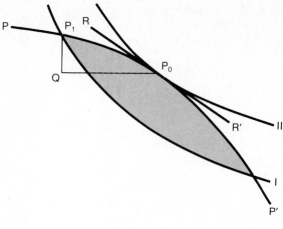

Fig. 3

communal displacement cost curve which represents the total amount of the commodities (*X* and *Y*) produced in the whole community in the initial position. If P_1 is this position, a movement from P_1 to any point above *I* represents a movement favourable to one individual. Compensating movements of type *(a)* from P_1 are, however, limited to points below *PP'*. The shaded area in the diagram represents positions to which movements from P_1 are favourable to one individual and can be compensated by movements of type *(a)*. Thus a movement from P_1 to P_0 represents a diminution in the production of *Y* by an amount P_1Q and an increase in the production of *X* by an amount QP_0,[12] accompanied by a similar change in one individual's consumption which moves him on to the higher indifference curve *II;* while the quantities of goods remaining to be consumed by other people are unaffected.

It is, of course, not necessary that any improve-

---

[11]I am indebted to Mr. V. Edelberg for the suggestion of the application of the indifference curve apparatus to the problem in this manner.

[12]It is not necessary that all or any of the identical units of factors set free from the production of *Y* should be used in the production of *X*. They, or a part of them, may go to the production of a third commodity *Z*, as substitutes for other factors which are released to produce the additional *X;* and there may be any number of such steps. This, of course, does not mean that every commodity is a *direct* displacement cost for every other commodity at the margin (in the sense that factors can move directly from one to the other without economic loss), as would be the case if each factor had the same marginal productivity in all uses—universal substitutability of factors at the margin. It only means that there is some path, however indirect, whereby a diminution in the production of one commodity permits an increase in the production of any other commodity, leaving the quantity of the rest of the commodities unaffected. That is what is meant by drawing a displacement cost curve for any two commodities.

ment should go up to the highest possible point—here P_0. A movement from P_1 to any other point in the shaded area indicates an improvement, but leaves room for still further improvement.

Such a movement is possible as long as the indifference curve cuts the displacement cost curve, giving an overlapping (shaded) area. Our first condition for the optimum position can be expressed by saying that these curves must not cut.

If the curves are smooth this will mean that they are tangential as at P_0, but our condition is satisfied without the tangency of the curves, if either (or both) of the curves changes directions suddenly at the point where the curves meet or that it forms an angle. What is necessary is merely that the curves shall meet at P_0 without cutting. This condition must be fulfilled for every individual in the community.

The movement of one individual to a preferred position, may, however, be covered by opposite changes in the consumption of others. This, too, can be examined in the same diagram. Let I and II represent the same indifference curves as before, but let PP' represent now not the displacement cost curve, but the indifference curve of any other individual, turned through 180° around the common point which shows the combinations of goods consumed by the individual. If the indifference curves cut, as they do in our diagram if P_1 is the common point, there is an overlapping area, shaded in the diagram, showing the possibility of improving the position of one without worsening the position of the other. A movement from P_1 to P_0 improves the position of *one* individual and leaves the other at another point on the same indifference curve PP', and, therefore, not worse off. Movements from P_1 to any intermediate point in the shaded area would make both individuals better off. In order to satisfy the condition of the optimum it is therefore again necessary that there should be no gap between the curves, i.e. that they should not cut. If they are smooth, it means that they are tangential, and that the slopes of the indifference curves of both individuals were parallel in the initial position, since the turning of a curve through 180° does not change any slopes.

The diagrammatical treatment restricts one to the consideration of only two commodities. This does not matter for the present purpose, since the relationships described have to obtain for every pair of all the commodities in the economy. This is because the failure of the conditions to be satisfied for *any* pair of commodities shows a possibility for improve-

ment which is incompatible with an optimum position.

If both of these conditions are satisfied, as between each individual's indifference curves and the communal displacement costs curve on the one hand, and as between each individual's indifference curves and every other individual's (inverted) indifference curves, on the other hand, it is impossible to improve the position of any individual without worsening the position of some other individual. The optimum position, relative to the distribution of income between individuals, is attained.

Can we make any use of such a complicated set of conditions? If it were necessary to investigate separately the slopes of the indifference curves of all individuals for all pairs of commodities in order to discover whether the conditions are satisfied, it would be most profitable to discontinue this analysis at once. But there is no need for all this. We need merely assume that some of the indifference curves are smooth at the positions representing the amounts consumed by the individuals, and that each individual, in buying goods for his own consumption, considers the price as given. Under these conditions the relative prices of each pair of goods in the market will accurately reflect the slopes of the indifference curves where these are smooth; and for those cases, where an indifference curve forms an angle, the ratio between the prices will give a line (RR' in Fig. 3) of such slope that the indifference curve will lie wholly *above* it, meeting it but not cutting it if it is superimposed on the consumption point P_0. The mere existence of a free market in consumption goods thus satisfies the second of our two conditions.

The first condition is satisfied if the price ratio on the market, represented by the slope of the line RR', is such that the displacement curve lies wholly *below* it, meeting it at the production-consumption point P_0, but not cutting it. If the displacement cost curve is smooth and, therefore, tangential to RR', this will mean that the price ratio is proportional to the marginal displacement costs, which condition is satisfied if *price is equal to marginal cost*.

From this analysis we see that the optimum is reached when the price reflects the alternatives given up at the margin, whether this alternative is considered in physical terms of some other commodity or whether we go direct to the satisfactions that the physical alternatives represent. The loss involved in monopoly can be seen in the divergence between price and this marginal cost. The loss involved in monopsony is of exactly the same nature, and a parallel analysis is rendered unnecessary if we translate the rising supply curve that is seen by the monopsonist into a falling demand curve by considering the purchase of A for B as the sale of B for A. This loss is avoided only if price to the consumer (AR) is equal to marginal cost (MC), and if the wages of labour (AC) are equal to its marginal product $(=MR)$. If we prefer we may put the latter statement in the form of demand. The price of leisure demanded by labourers (AR) (which is his wage) must be equal to the marginal cost of his leisure (MC) (which is equal to the marginal product of the labour withdrawn).

II

In considering the degree of monopoly in a particular field one's first inclination seems to be to hark back to the etymological meaning of the word and to see how close the situation is to the conditions which accompany a "single seller." On this line one would say that there is complete monopoly if there is actually only one seller, and that the monopoly element diminishes as the number of sellers increases. One could construct some kind of index of the degree of monopoly, such as the inverse of the number of sellers, which would give values ranging from unity in the case of this kind of "complete" monopoly to zero in the case of an infinite number of sellers.

The most obvious of the many reasons why this will not do is that there may be a very high degree of monopoly (in any sense other than that of the formula for such an index), even where there are many sellers, if one or two sellers control a sufficiently large proportion of the total supply. For this reason one turns instead to discover how great a proportion of the total supply is controlled by one or a few individuals or organisations. The same information may also be sought more indirectly by inquiries into the size of firms.

This procedure, however, is still quite inappropriate for measuring the degree of monopoly if we are interested in its economic and social implications of control over price and social loss as discussed in the first part of this paper. This is seen most clearly when we observe that control by a single firm of 100 per cent of the supply of a commodity for which the demand is infinitely elastic (which will always be the case if there is some equally satisfactory substitute available at a constant price) is absolutely unimportant and has no economic significance, while a "partial" monopoly of a commodity for which the demand is inelastic may be able to raise price by reducing output and is clearly a much more effective case of monopoly.

The statistical method of measuring monopoly, besides missing the main issue in this way, encounters enormous practical difficulties in which investigators can hardly hope to avoid getting entangled. The problems of allowing for changes in taste and technique, in transport and in business organisation, of dealing with firms making many products and of discovering the degree to which different firms compete with one another or mitigate the competition by Gentlemen's Agreements, trade conventions, business alliances, and so on, are just a few worth mentioning, but there is one that interests us particularly here, and that is the relatively simple one of defining the commodity.

A man may have a considerable degree of monopolistic power although he is in control of only a very small part of the supply of a commodity if he is afforded some protection from the competition of the rest of the supply by the cost of transporting other supplies to his market. Under these conditions the price of the commodity will be different in different places. The best way of dealing with this is to declare that objects having the same physical characteristics are not the same goods if they are at different places. Location is an essential and distinguishing characteristic of economic goods, and the only relationship between the prices of similar goods in different places is that which results from the possibilities of transforming the one good into the other by transporting it from the one place to the other.

And location is not the only variant of this kind, but rather the simplest species of a large genus, and is useful for a simplified exposition of the problems involved. Every specialised gradation of every particular quality of every "commodity" may be treated as "distance," and the cost of changing the quality to a particular grade as the cost of "transport." Some of these problems are dealt with by Hotelling in his article, "Stability in Competition," *Economic Journal*, 1929, p. 41, where he gives examples ranging from the sweetness of cider to the service of churches.

To these variants must be added also all fictitious variations, such as are successfully imposed upon the minds of buyers by skilful advertising, as well as the tendencies of customers to buy from one seller rather than from another by sheer force of habit. Here the "distance" is the fictitious difference in quality or the goodwill of the customer, while the "transport costs" are the costs involved in overcoming the "goodwill" whether by reducing price or by counter-advertisement.

This splitting up of the conception of a commodity of course multiplies the number of commodities indefinitely, and seems to create monopolies in the most unexpected places. Carried to its logical extreme, every firm now becomes a monopoly, since it is impossible for more than one unit of product to be in the same place. But even without going to such extremes it becomes impossible to apply the simple measures of monopoly that we are criticising. Further difficulties are yet to arise.

While the idea of considering the same things at different places as different goods seems to have spread considerably, the full revolutionary implications of this step forward in the picturing of the equilibrial forces do not seem to have been quite realised.

In calling the same thing at different places different commodities, we have rejected the criterion of physical similarity as a basis for the recognition or classification of commodities and have put in its place the principle of substitutability at the margin.

If the same thing at a different place is not the same commodity it is only because the difference in its location prevents it from being substituted for, or used in the same way as, the same thing here. But this principle can be applied in the converse form too. With substitutability as the principle it is no longer necessary for different units of the same commodity to have the same physical characteristics as long as they are substitutable at the margin for the purpose that the buyer wants them. This means that if one pound of coal gives me the same heating power as four pounds of wood, that both of these items cost the same on the market, and I am indifferent as to which I have, then one pound of coal and four pounds of wood represent the same number of units of the same commodity. It means, further, that if I am indifferent as to whether I have one hundred-weight of coal every week during the winter, or an overcoat to keep me warm, then a winter's coal and an overcoat are equal quantities of the same commodity. Further still, if I am indifferent as to whether I have a wireless set for £10 or whether I have the satisfaction of saving ten Chinese children from starvation, the wireless set in London is the same quantity of the same commodity as £10 worth of rice in China; while if I get the same satisfaction from a £100 motorcar here and now as I could from a Mediterranean cruise next year, which costs £100 plus the accumulated interest on the money, then the motor-car here and now and the Mediterranean cruise next year are equal quantities of the same commodity. Physical qualities, spacial and temporal position are irrelevant now that we have the ultimate criterion of substitutability at the margin. If any quantity or complex of goods and services can be substituted at the margin for any other quantity of goods and services (and therefore have the same market value), then they are both equal quantities of the same commodity. It would perhaps be best to give terminological recognition to such a break with traditional usage by speaking of "units of accommodation" instead of units of commodities.

If this way of looking at things seems paradoxical, it is only because we have not yet completely freed ourselves from the crudely materialistic conception of goods with which the Physiocrats and Adam Smith were the first to wrestle. The inadequacy of a purely physical criterion of commodities is obvious when we consider the enormous physical difference which we neglect if they do not affect the qualities in which we are interested (that is which affect our satisfactions), of which we are often completely unconscious, but which are of so much importance to Mr. Sherlock Holmes. Physically there are no two similar articles even apart from location. If two objects are considered to be items of the same good, it is only because they are "good for" the same purpose—always, ultimately, the satisfaction of a want. It is futile to say that the motor-car and the Mediterranean cruise satisfy different wants until we are able to define "similar" wants otherwise than as wants that are satisfied by physically similar objects. There is no *qualitative* criterion of wants. Wants can only be considered as similar when the person who feels them displays equal concern for their satisfaction and thus shows them to be equal in *quantity*. To follow any other course is to sacrifice the logic of the science to the irrelevant convenience of the shopkeeper.

It may be objected that this concept of commodity is so abstract and elusive as to be unusable. That is perfectly correct. But therein lies a great part of its advantages. It cannot be used like the more material conception to drown the theory in irrelevant statistics. It puts an end to attempts, here, to find a measure of monopoly in terms of the proportion of the supply of a commodity under single control and clears the way to a better understanding.

Another line of approach that suggests itself is to compare the amount of monopoly revenue with the total receipts, and to take this ratio as a measure of the degree of monopoly power. Allowance is thus made for the size of the industry or the firm. We will obtain values ranging from 0 in the case of perfect competition to 1 where the whole of receipts is monopoly revenue, and at first glance all seems well.

This procedure will, however, not do, for what we want in the measure of monopoly is not the amount of tribute individuals can obtain for themselves from the rest of the community, by being in an advantageous monopolistic position, but the divergence of the system from the social optimum that is reached in perfect competition. From this point of view the monopolist gains are not to be distinguished from rents of scarce property that he owns, or any other source of individual income. The independence of the monopolist gain from the social loss can perhaps most clearly be brought out by a consideration of how far they can vary independently. The limiting case is seen where the demand curve for the product of a monopolist coincides over considerable range with his average cost curve. Here the monopoly revenue is zero wherever the monopolist produces within this range, yet he has control over price, and the social loss will be different according to what output the monopolist decides to produce. It clearly will not do to say that the degree of monopoly power in such a case is zero.

If the average cost curve is horizontal such a divergence cannot occur. The firm can only change output while keeping monopoly revenue zero if the demand curve is also horizontal, and that means perfect competition in either case and no social loss. But in such a case we are comparing not merely monopoly revenue with total receipts, which is the same as the ratio between average receipts minus costs and average receipts (and which is also seen in the ratio between average costs and average receipts), but also *marginal costs* with *average receipts,* and it is in divergence between these, as we have seen above, that the essence of monopoly is to be found.

In such cases (where the cost curve is horizontal) the ratio of monopoly revenue to total receipts coincides exactly with the ratio of the divergence of price from marginal cost to price, and it is this latter formula that I wish to put forward as the measure of monopoly power. If P = price and C = marginal

cost, then the index of the degree of monopoly power is $\frac{P - C}{P}$.

It will be observed that this formula looks like the inverse of the formula for the elasticity of demand. It differs from it only in that the item marginal cost replaces the item marginal receipts. In equilibrium as normally conceived marginal costs coincide with marginal receipts so that our formula becomes identical with the inverse of the elasticity of demand. It will be best to consider this as a special case.

In this special case we can find the degree of monopoly power via the elasticity of demand. The determination of this elasticity of demand is not to be confused with that of Pigou and Schultz in finding the elasticity of demand (as part of the demand function) for a materially (physically) defined commodity on a market. What we want here is the elasticity of demand for the product of a particular firm. This is much easier to obtain, for it is only when he knows the shape of the demand curve for his product that any entrepreneur can obtain his maximum profit; and he is, therefore, always applying himself energetically to obtaining as accurate an estimate as possible of this elasticity. This does not mean that the entrepreneur will be able to fill in the elasticity of demand on a questionnaire form. He will rarely know what the term means. But his unfamiliarity with the technical jargon of economists must not be held to show an ignorance of so primary a principle for intelligent business management as the urgency of knowing the effect of price changes on sales. His behaviour in running the business for maximum profit will enable any student to deduce the (estimated) elasticity of demand from the firm's cost curve and the selling price. From the average cost curve the marginal cost curve can be derived. The marginal cost is equal to the marginal receipt, output being adjusted so as to make them equal if profit is maximised. The elasticity of demand is equal to the price divided by the difference between price and marginal cost—it is the inverse of our formula for the measurement of the degree of monopoly power.

In finding the degree of monopoly in this special case "via the elasticity of demand" we found that the easiest way of finding the elasticity of demand was via the degree of monopoly. We may, therefore, leave out the elasticity of demand altogether and just keep to our formula all the time. In the special case both come to the same thing, but we must use the new formula and not the inverse of the elasticity of demand whenever we consider cases where the maximum monopoly revenue is not obtained in practice.

This may be accidental, as when the monopolist does not know the shape of his demand curve and his estimate of the elasticity of demand at the actual output is erroneous; or it may be intentional. The price and output may intentionally be fixed in a manner which does not give the maximum monopoly revenue:

1. When the monopolist is not working on purely business principles, but for social, philanthropic or conventional reasons sells *below* this price commodities which it is considered socially desirable to cheapen—as when a public authority supplies cheap transport facilities—or sells *above* this price commodities which are considered socially harmful—as may be done by a State liquor monopoly.

2. When the monopolist is working on purely business principles, but keeps the price and his profits lower than they might be so as to avoid political opposition or the entry of new competitors. The second could, perhaps, better be considered as a case where the demand is more elastic in the long period, taking into account the contingent competition, than in the short period, and where the monopolist takes a long period view.

In all such cases our formula is not equal to the inverse of the elasticity of demand; but wherever there appears a divergence between the two it is our formula and not the inverse of the elasticity of demand which gives the measure of what we want. In the first case—where the monopolist's estimate of the elasticity of demand is erroneous—the consumers will in every way be in exactly the same position as if the elasticity were what the monopolist thinks it is. If he over-estimates the elasticity of demand he will sell a larger amount at a lower price. If he thinks the elasticity is infinite—i.e. that if he produced less he would not be able to get a better price—he will make price equal to marginal cost, and the effect on consumers will be the same as if there were perfect competition.[13] The unused monopoly power will be

there, but being unknown and unused it is, economically, as if it were not there. For practical purposes we must read monopoly power not as *potential* monopoly, but as monopoly *in force*.

If the monopolist underestimates the elasticity of demand he will sell a smaller quantity and at a higher price than at the point of maximum monopoly revenue. The only difference between this and the previous case is that the monopolist's error brings a loss to consumers instead of a gain. The monopolist himself, of course, loses by the error in either case. The consumer here has to pay a higher price or else do without. It is again just as if the elasticity of demand were what the monopolist thinks it is. This may sound as if the monopoly *in force* is here greater than the *potential* monopoly power, but the inverse of the elasticity of demand at the maximum revenue point does not really give the potential monopoly power. It gives just that degree of monopoly power which it is necessary to put into force in order to obtain the maximum revenue and which is in force where the maximum revenue is being obtained. The monopolist always has power in excess of this; but as the employment of it can only bring him a loss, he normally does not use it intentionally. If he chooses to use it he can, of course, for the exercise of this power consists of diminishing the amount he produces. Potential monopoly power is only used to its maximum when the monopolist stops all production. What our formula gives is the degree of monopoly power in force.

The same arguments apply to cases where the maximum monopoly revenue is not obtained for social, philanthropic or conventional reasons or for the purpose of avoiding political opposition or contingent competition. In the last case, our procedure saves us all further investigation into the complications involved in considering the length of the period upon which the demand curve is based. The appropriate costs to be reckoned are those of the present, or rather of the immediate future, so as to enable us to measure temporary monopolies. The degree of monopoly over a long period is perhaps best expressed in an average of the short-period monopolies over the period.

The primary unit to which our measure of monopoly applies is the firm in the very shortest period. In order to get a measure of monopoly over a period we had to take an average of such coefficients of monopoly. In order to get a measure of monopoly

---

[13]Mrs. Robinson has pointed out to me that the delusion that elasticity is infinite would persist only if MC happened to equal price already. This is the easiest case for the correction of a mistaken estimate in the process of adjustment to it. The same possibility exists with any estimated elasticity of demand as long as the marginal cost and the estimated marginal receipts do not coincide and so preclude any adjustments.

over an industry we have to follow the same procedure and find an average of monopoly of the separate firms included in the industry. The "industry"
is to be considered as a group of firms, chosen for
the purpose of the special investigation. It is quite
unnecessary, for this purpose, to say anything at all
about the "commodity" which the "industry" produces, nor is there any need to be able to draw demand or supply curves for the industry. All the difficulties of definition of "commodity" or "industry"
are completely avoided.

More strictly a simple average of the degrees of
monopoly in firms may be used to indicate the degree
of monopoly in an industry only in the very limited
sense of the degree of monopoly *at that stage*. It is
not a measure of the degree to which the application
of the resources of the community to the production
of the products of the "industry" diverges from the
social optimum. That depends upon two other sets
of conditions in addition to this *local* element of monopoly.

The first of these is the degree of monopoly in the
firms (or "industries") producing the raw materials
for all the previous stages in the production of the
products. The restriction of productions in any stage
has its effects in all the succeeding stages. The final
degree of reduction of product will depend upon the
degree of monopoly in all the preceding stages. These
have to be aggregated so as to give the tendency to
divergence from the social optimum in the whole
series of the production stages of the product; this
phenomenon may be called the transitiveness of monopoly.

Theoretically, this can be done quite simply. What
we want is the divergence between the price of the
product and its marginal *social* cost. If in all the previous stages price is equal to marginal cost, the marginal cost to the firm is also the marginal social cost.
If in any stage there is a divergence, price being above
marginal cost, that divergence is a gap in the social
cost. The social cost can then be calculated by multiplying the price by a factor for each stage in production, each factor being the ratio of the marginal
cost to the price in the corresponding stage. Thus,
if there are five stages and in each stage the degree
of monopoly is $\frac{1}{5}$, marginal cost over price in each
stage is $\frac{4}{5}$, the social cost is $(\frac{4}{5})^5$ of the price of the
final product, and by our formula the "social" degree
of monopoly is $I - (\frac{4}{5})^5$.

Practical difficulties that arise in attempts to measure the "social" degree of monopoly, or different
products may be attacked by any of the tricks of the
trade of mathematical statistics. It may be necessary
to assume average degrees of monopoly in separate
stages and to calculate "social" degree of monopoly
by the number of stages, and so on; but it is not
intended here to discuss anything but the simplest
theoretical implications.

The second set of complicating considerations
arise when we ask the even more ambitious question:
What is the (social) degree of monopoly in the society as a whole? From this general point of view the
conditions for that optimum distribution of resources between different commodities that we designate the absence of monopoly are satisfied if prices
are all *proportional* to social marginal cost. If the "social" degree of monopoly is the same for *all* final
products (including leisure) there is no monopolistic
alteration from the optimum at all. The absolute
height of "social" degrees of monopoly becomes
completely unimportant.

This is because if the "social" degree of monopoly
is the same for all products it *must* be equal to zero
in real terms. For from the social point of view, the
marginal cost of any product is always some other
product. If the "social" degree of monopoly for product A is positive, this means that the price of A is
greater than the price of some other product B which
is the alternative foregone. The price of B cannot
then be greater than the price of A. If both degrees
of monopoly are equal they must both be zero.

What is important is the deviations between the
degrees of monopoly; and it is this which must be
measured in order to answer our question. A suitable
measure for this is the standard deviation of the "social" degrees of monopoly of all final products in the
society.

Another complication arises in the growingly important cases where it is found to be profitable to
extend or maintain the amount sold, not by reducing
price but by expenditure on advertising, salesman-
ship, gifts, coupons and beautiful wrappings—all of
which can be subsumed under the heading of "marketing costs." In such cases what becomes of the
elasticity of demand?

In the recent cost controversy, "marketing costs"
were eagerly seized upon in attempts at a conciliation
between decreasing costs and competitive equilibri-

um.[14] Such arguments may be described with some justification as contriving to exhibit decreasing costs at peace with competitive equilibrium by the device of leaving out of account the marketing element in the costs which is increasing so rapidly that *total costs* are not decreasing at all; the contradiction being hidden by a separation of "productive" from "marketing" costs.

This solution of the problem cannot, however, be dismissed as mere word-jugglery. It does show the actual working of the forces involved, and it is only the terminology that is unfortunate. What we have here is not perfect competition but *monopolistic* or *imperfect* competition. Chamberlin and Robinson have developed a more satisfactory line of attack on these problems, but how are we to find the falling demand curve which will entitle us to put these cases into this category and enable us to deal with them in the same way?

In order to obtain this it is essential to separate productive from marketing costs. The marketing costs involved in selling a given quantity of product must be subtracted from the gross receipts, just as if they were all direct or indirect reductions in price, leaving a definite total and average net receipts. For each quantity produced different prices may be charged and different marketing costs incurred. For each output some combination of prices charged and marketing costs incurred will leave a maximum average (and total) residue after subtracting the average (or total) marketing costs, and this maximum is the relevant Average Net Receipts for that output. The locus of such points will be the Average Net Receipts curve for the firm, and this is the "demand curve" which we need. This average net receipts curve and the corresponding marginal net receipts curve have to be used in conjunction with the "productive" cost curves which we may call "net" cost curves.

If the average net receipts curve is negatively inclined, one proceeds just as in the simple analysis of imperfect competition where there are no selling costs. The firm equates its marginal net cost to its marginal net receipts, and the degree of monopoly is equal to average net receipts over average net receipts minus marginal net costs, and the divergence of the position from the social optimum is illustrated

by the fact that production is not carried on at the minimum average cost, but the firm produces less than this optimum output, stopping at a point where the average net cost curve is tangential to the average net receipts curve. The social loss, if any, due to the expenditure of resources on advertising is *not* taken into account in the measurement of monopoly. The measure will be the same whether the marketing costs are large or small, and whether they are given to the consumer in forms corresponding to cash, or whether they have important influences on his tastes for good or for bad. The social effects of different kinds of advertising constitute a quite separate problem.

If the average net receipts curve is horizontal where the marginal net costs curve cuts it, there is no monopoly. The existence of marketing costs is quite another matter.

But there is no reason why the average net receipts curve should not slope upwards! It may well be that a larger quantity can be sold at a higher price at the same or a smaller *average* cost of marketing, and there is no ground for considering such a combination of circumstances as in any way exceptional. We must apply the same analysis here and not be deterred if the results at first appear a little strange.

If the firm with a rising average net revenue curve has a constant cost curve, or can acquire more of the product from other firms without affecting its marketing possibilities, we have another form of the paradox of the incompatibility of equilibrium with a horizontal demand curve and a falling average cost curve below it. The marginal revenue and the marginal cost curves cannot meet until the conditions are changed. Either the receipts curves must begin to fall or the cost curves must rise.

The interesting case—the one which can remain in equilibrium in these conditions—is the case where the average costs of the firm rise after a time as output increases, and where it cannot obtain more from other firms at the same price, either because the other firms' costs rise or because to do this would interfere with the reputation of the firm and upset its marketing possibilities.

This is shown in Fig. 4, where the firm is in equilibrium producing an output *OM*.

Average net recepits *(ANR)* are equal to average net costs *(ANC)*, and marginal net receipts *(MNR)* are equal to marginal net costs *(MNC)*. The degree of monopoly is here *negative* since marginal cost is

[14]As by R. Harrod in his article on "The Law of Decreasing Costs," *Economic Journal*, Dec. 1931.

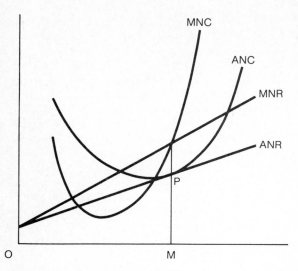

MNC

ANC

MNR

ANR

P

O   M

Fig. 4

greater than average receipts. This may appear sur-prising, but it merely means that the divergence from the social optimum is in the direction opposite to that usually brought about by monopolies. Instead of the firm producing *less* than it should, it is pro-ducing *more;* the same kind of social harm is done, and it is reflected in the same way by the excess of the average cost over the minimum.

In finding an average degree of monopoly in an "industry," positive and negative monopolies may cancel out in whole or in part. Does this harm our apparatus?

I do not think it does this at all. It rather brings out the true nature of our measure as an index of *divergence* from an optimum. In any group of firms taken together to make an "industry," divergences may, and should, be expected to some extent to can-cel out. For we are now considering the application of resources to this "industry" as against the rest of the economy. If of two firms within the "industry," one is producing too much and the other too little from the point of view of the economy as a whole; the industry may not be producing either too much or too little. The maladjustment becomes a local affair which we must neglect in this larger consideration.

When our "industry" becomes the whole society, there cannot be too much or too little resources used, and as we have seen above, all the individual positive and negative monopolies must cancel out. This does not mean that society as a whole must always be in an optimum position, nor does it take any meaning away from the concept. It only means that the larger the fraction of the whole society one wishes to ex-amine, the less legitimate is it to use particular anal-ysis. In applying the particular mechanism to the whole economy we get the appropriate *reductio ad absurdum*. What is relevant for general analysis is not the *sum* of individual degrees of monopoly but their *deviations*. The standard deviations as suggested above may perhaps be used one day to give an es-timate of the divergence of society from the social optimum of production relative to a given distri-bution of income.

Multiple-Plant Firms, Cartels, and Imperfect Competition*

DON PATINKIN[1]

Don Patinkin (B.A., University of Chicago, 1943; M.A., 1945; Ph.D., 1947) is President and Professor of Economics at The Hebrew University of Jerusalem. He was born in Chicago in 1922 and later emigrated to Israel after completing his formal education. Patinkin has also taught at the University of Chicago and the University of Illinois, and was on the staff of the Cowles Commission for Economic Research. From 1956–1972 Patinkin served as Director of Research at Maurice Falk Institute for Economic Research in Israel. His primary research has been in the microeconomic theory of money; he is, without question, among the most renowned of monetary theorists. Many recent students of economics have learned general equilibrium theory from his *Money, Interest and Prices,* and from his classic articles, "Price Flexibility and Full Employment," and "Keynesian Economics and the Quantity Theory," from which his recent research in Keynes' monetary thought derives. Patinkin is a Fellow of the Econometric Society and is a recipient of the Rothschild and Israel Prizes.

*Reprinted from *The Quarterly Journal of Economics* (February 1947) by permission of John Wiley & Sons, Inc. Copyright 1947, pp. 73–205.

[1]I cannot overemphasize my debt to Professor Henry C. Simons, on whose Economics 201 Syllabus (mimeographed, University of Chicago Bookstore) this article is so largely based. Although Professor Simons did not see the manuscript before his untimely death, I discussed with him several of the points involved. I am also indebted to Bert Hoselitz, H. Gregg Lewis, and William H. Nicholls (all of the University of Chicago), who read an earlier draft of this article and offered valuable criticisms and suggestions.

Although theories of imperfect competition have long since found a recognized place in textbooks, varying degrees of dissatisfaction with them have persisted due to their restrictive assumptions. To a very considerable extent this situation must continue until we have many more detailed studies of specific firms and industries and their methods of operation. The difficulty is, of course, the procuring of information. Even if many corporations overcame their reluctance to open their books to economists, those fundamental and intimate details of corporate policy formation which are not translatable into bookkeeping entries would still be lacking. To some extent, however, the empirical evidence already available to us provides a basis for significant improvement in the theory. Accordingly, I plan in this article (1) to extend the analysis to deal with multiple-plant firms[2] and (2) to present a generalized oligopoly solution which can be employed as a frame of reference in empirical studies.

I

To illustrate the problem of multiple-plant firms, I shall first consider a case of perfect monopoly. For simplicity assume a linear demand curve remaining constant throughout the discussion, completely unspecialized factors of production (precluding any monopsony power), and a single product. Assume that the monopoly firm consists of 100 individual (and identical) plants, each of the long-run optimum size and with cost curves indicated in Fig. 1, where *ac, mc,* and *avc* represent average, marginal, and average variable costs, respectively. For convenience we have assumed that the plant marginal cost curve is composed of two linear sections.

[2]The usual one-firm-one-plant analysis is completely unrealistic. Thus, in 1937 the 50 largest manufacturing corporations owned 2869 plants, or an average of 57.4 per firm. No firm owned less than seven plants, while one owned 497. (TNEC, Monograph No. 27, The Structure of Industry, pp. 675–714.)

We turn now to the problem of constructing the monopolist's short-run marginal cost curve (Fig. 2), noting that in the short-run (by definition) the monopolist cannot change the number of plants in existence. Consider a given output q_i;[3] the question is, how will the monopolist allocate this output among the different plants in order to minimize costs? The answer falls into two parts, according as q_i is greater or less than $q_2 = 100k_2$. In the former case the optimum allocation would be to have the output equally distributed among the plants. This readily follows from Fig. 1. If one plant is producing more than another, its marginal cost will be higher; consequently, a reduction in total cost can be effected by shifting the output from the former to the latter.[4] This process will continue until all plants are producing the same amount. We thus get the right-hand part of the marginal cost curve in Fig. 2. To construct the marginal cost curve for outputs less than q_2 we

[3]The units of the abscissa of Fig. 2 are related to those of Fig. 1 by the equation $k_j = q_j/100$ for any j.
[4]This holds for the cost curves usually dealt with, but is not general. Cf. Section II below.

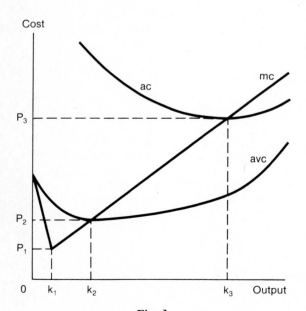

Fig. 1

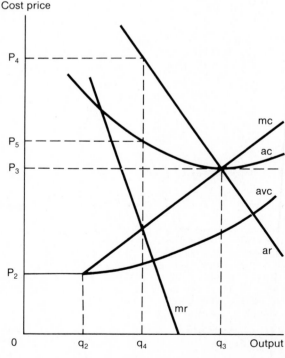

Fig. 2

note that no plant *in operation* will produce less than k_2; any desired output $q_i < q_2$ will be produced by having x plants produce k_2 units apiece (where k_2 is the output corresponding to minimum average variable costs for the plant—cf. Fig. 1), with the remaining $100-x$ plants left idle. (x is obviously determined by the relationship $xk_2 = q_i$.) This may be proved as follows. In the short run the monopolist must bear the fixed expenses of the 100 plants. Therefore he will minimize total expenses for any given output by minimizing total variable expenses. Consider now the given output $q_i < q_2$. If this output were equally allocated among all plants, each plant would produce $k_i < k_2$ at an average variable cost of $p_i > p_2$. Then the total variable costs would be $100k_ip_i$. However, the total variable costs, if x plants were to produce k_2 apiece, would be xk_2p_2. But $100k_ip_i > xk_2p_2$, since $100k_i = xk_2 = q_i$ and $p_i > p_2$. This is perfectly general and holds for any $q_i < q_2$ and $k_i < k_2$. In this range the monopolist would operate keeping some plants idle. The average variable cost would be $xk_2p_2/xk_2 = p_2$. Therefore, until q_2, the average variable cost curve is a horizontal line at a height p_2. By definition, the marginal cost curve, in this range, coincides with it.[5]

Strictly speaking the linear shape of the marginal cost curve is only an approximation which is ap-

proached as the number of plants increases. The actual shape is pictured in Fig. 3; this may be considered as a "blowup" of Fig. 2 (note the break in the vertical axis). For convenience, however, we have considered a firm consisting of only seven plants, each of the type described in Fig. 1. v_i is the average variable cost of the firm, if i plants (neither more nor *less*) are used to produce a given output in the cheapest way possible. The v_i have a common origin, since one unit of output will always be produced by one plant producing one unit, regardless of the number of plants. As i increases, v_i tends to flatten out, since any given increase in output will increase the output per plant less the more plants there are. From our previous discussion we know that v_i will reach its minimum at an output of ik_2 and a height of $p_2(i = 1, 2 \ldots 7)$; that is, the minimum points are equidistant and at the same height.[6] The intersection of v_i and v_{i+1} indicates where it would be profitable to employ an additional plant. The heavy kinked[7] curve is thus the relevant average variable cost curve of the firm. It is tangent to the horizontal line (p_2 units high) at the outputs $nk_2(n = 1, 2 \ldots 7)$. Similarly, we con-

---

[5]The position of the marginal cost curve in this range can also be established by noting that it can never be less than p_2, for the total expenses can always be reduced by at least p_2 per unit simply by closing down a plant.

[6]These results are given more generally with the aid of some very neat mathematics in M. F. W. Joseph, "A Discontinuous Cost Curve and the Tendency to Increasing Returns," *Economic Journal,* Vol. 43 (1933), pp. 390–393. However, the exposition there is impaired by the unwarranted assumption that any output is equally allocated among plants. Cf. Section II of this article.

[7]That is, a *continuous* curve with *discontinuous derivatives* at certain points. Curves of this type have been erroneously referred to in the literature as "discontinuous."

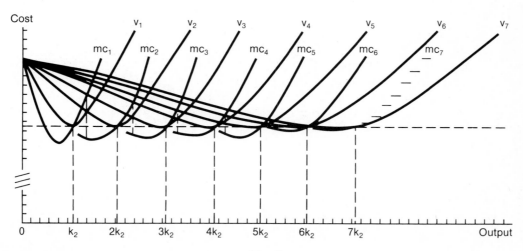

Fig. 3

struct a marginal cost curve mc_i for each v_i. For higher values of i, mc_i will approach closer to v_i since the latter tends to flatten out. It is possible that ranges may exist for which mc_i becomes a step function. This is especially true for the rising part, where the assumption that output will be equally allocated is more probable; mc_7 is drawn on this assumption. Then an output of $7k_2 + 1$ is produced, with six plants producing k_2 and one producing $k_2 + 1$; an output of $7k_2 + i$ ($i = 2, 3 \ldots 7$) is produced by having $7 - i$ plants produce k_2 apiece, and i produce $k_2 + 1$—so that the marginal cost for all these outputs is the same. Thus, for outputs greater than $7k_2$, mc_7 is a rising step function, with steps seven units wide. On corresponding assumptions, in Fig. 2 the marginal cost curve for outputs greater than q_2 is a step function with steps 100 units wide. As long as the width of the step is small relative to the scale of Fig. 2, we can approximate the rising part of the curve by a straight line.

In fact, due to the decreasing portions of the v_i and mc_i curves, we cannot construct these curves by allocating the output equally among the i plants. There do not seem to be any short-cut rules to follow, and the curves can be constructed only by trial and error allocations of the given output in different ways among the i plants and noting which way minimizes total variable cost. Similarly, it is impossible to determine by any simple rule when v_i and v_{i+1} will intersect—that is, when a new plant will be brought into operation. There might even be multiple intersection of v_i and v_{i+1}. For differently shaped plant cost curves we get entirely different results. Thus, for example, in the case of two plants we can construct cost curves such that the total variable cost is minimized by having one plant produce on the *rising* part of its marginal cost curve, and the other on the *falling* part (see Section II of this article).

Since the allocation of any given output is now determined, we can construct the other costs curves in Fig. 2 making use of the data in Fig. 1. For the demand curve *ar* the optimum output is at q_4, and the per-unit monopoly profit is $p_4 - p_5$. The usual textbook analysis stops at this point, with the implication that the monopolist is not producing at the point of minimum average cost (q_3) and should make no attempt to do so if he is to maximize profits. This certainly holds for the short run, but in the long run the monopolist can change his position by adjusting the number of plants through investment and disinvestment.

The problem is then one of determining the long-run cost curves of the monopolist (cf. Fig. 4). The fundamental fact which must be noted here is that even in the long run the monopoly will not proceed to build different sized plants; investment and disinvestment in the firm will take place only by changing the number of plants. This follows from our assumption that the existing plants are of the long-run optimum size.

The construction of the monopolist's long-run average cost curve is analogous to the construction of the short-run average variable cost curve for outputs less than q_2. The process is identical if we note that in the long run (by definition) all costs are variable costs. We need only to observe that in the argument p_2 is replaced by p_3 and q_2 becomes infinitely large. In the long run the monopolist will minimize the cost of producing any output q_j by arranging his investment and disinvestment policies so that he will have exactly y plants, each producing k_3 (cf. Fig. 1), where y is determined by the relation $y = q_j/k_3$. In

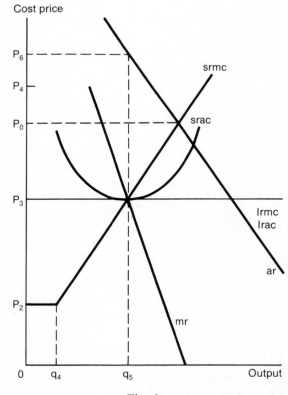

Fig. 4

other words, the optimum method of producing any given output is to have each plant producing at its minimum average cost point, and adjusting the number of plants (by investment and disinvestment) so that the desired output can be produced. The total cost of *any* output q_j will then be yk_3p_3 and the average cost p_3, so that the long-run average cost curve *(lrac)* will be a horizontal line at the height p_3; the long-run marginal cost curve *(lrmc)* will coincide with it.[8]

The long-run equilibrium price and output in Fig. 4 (assuming *ar* to remain constant) are p_6 and q_5, respectively. The long-run price and monopoly profits are each greater than in the short run. Once the optimum long-run output q_5 is determined, the optimum number of plants in the long run—$m = q_5/k_3$—is simultaneously determined. Thus, in the long run the monopolist will have m plants and the short-run average and marginal cost curves *srac* and *srmc* (Fig. 4). *srac* will obviously have its minimum point at the output q_5, since for that output each of the m plants will be producing at its own minimum point k_3. Since $m \leq 100$, the marginal cost curve for the firm with m plants remains horizontal at p_2 over a shorter interval than when the firm consists of 100 plants. Specifically, for the case of m plants, mc remains constant only until $q_6 = mk_2 < q_2 = 100k_2$. It is interesting to note that in the long run the monopolist will *of necessity* be producing at the minimum point of his short-run average cost curve. We must now determine what particular assumption we have made that has led to this unusual result.

First let us distinguish between intraplant and interplant economies and diseconomies. Intraplant economies are what we usually have in mind when we speak of economies of large-scale production. These are derived from increases in the size of plant which enable use of more specialized and efficient machinery, develops skills in performing specialized tasks, eliminates movements of workers, and so on. Interplant economies are reductions in (social) cost following from the fact that two or more plants operate under a common management, instead of being separately owned. These take the form of economies in purchases and sales of materials, research, flexibility, "scientific management," risk-bearing, financing, integration, etc. Diseconomies of both types are due to increasing difficulties of coordination, bureaucratic inefficiency, etc. That there are substantial and continuing intraplant economies has been shown to be true in many industries;[9] but on the question of interplant economies very little empirical evidence is available. Similarly, we have little information about the diseconomies.

Let us now consider the long-run average cost curve (Fig. 5).[10] The curve c_1 is the traditional Harrod-Viner envelope of the family of one-plant short-run cost curves, s_1. The specific s_1 (say s_{11}) which is tangent to c_1 at the latter's minimum point is (by assumption) our curve of Fig. 1. Consider now any specific curve of the s_2 family—say s_{21}. This curve is constructed by allocating a given output in the best way possible among two plants of *arbitrary size*. We construct an s_2 curve for every possible combination of different size plants. We then construct the c_2 curve by marking off for any given output an ordinate equal to that of the lowest point on any member of the family of curves s_2 for that given output. Strictly speaking, c_2 is not an envelope curve, since there can obviously be members of s_2 which do not touch it: for example, s_{22} in Fig. 5. From our previous exposition we know that the s_2 curve tangent to c_2 at the latter's minimum point is that formed from two identical plants each of the size indicated in Fig. 1. A similar interpretation holds for the other s_{jr} and c_i curves. The latter will tend to flatten out as i increases. We know from our preceding discussion that c_i will reach its minimum for an output of k_3i at a height of $p_3(i = 1, 2, \ldots \infty)$; that is, the minimum points are equidistant and at the same height.[11] The intersection of c_j and c_{j+1} indicates where it would be profitable for the monopolist to build a $(j + 1)$-st plant. The heavy kinked curve is therefore the long-run average cost curve. In the case of other indivisibilities, the c_i curves would also be kinked, resulting in the long-run average cost curve having still more kinks than pictured here. The long-run marginal cost curve is discontinuous and of the same general shape of that in Fig. 3 (for outputs less than $7k_1$), except that it extends indefinitely out, approaching more

---

[8] We must make reservations here analogous to those made above concerning the shape of the average variable cost curve for outputs less than q_2.

[9] J. M. Blair, "The Relation between Size and Efficiency of Business," *Review of Economic Statistics*, Vol. 24, pp. 125–135 (1942); Joseph Steindl, *Small and Big Business*, Oxford University Institute of Statistics, Monograph No. 1 (1945).

[10] Fig. 5 may be considered as a blowup of Fig. 4; note the break in the vertical axis.

[11] Cf. note 6 above.

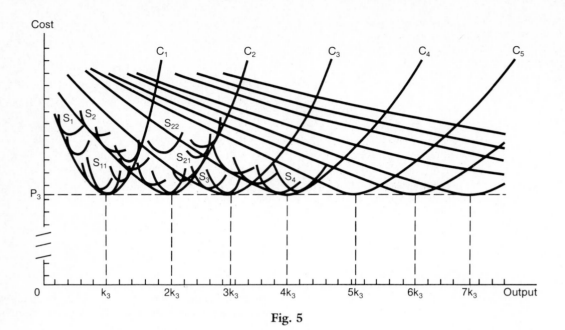

Fig. 5

and more to the horizontal line at p_3. In order not to make Fig. 5 too cumbersome, this curve has not been included.

The declining portion of c_1 measures the extent of intraplant economies: the greater k_3 the greater their importance. The importance of interplant economies is measured by the relative positions of the successive minimum points of the long-run average cost curve. There are four major possibilities. (1) They may lie on a horizontal line; this is the situation depicted in Fig. 5. It implies that there are no interplant economies or diseconomies, or that they offset each other identically for every output. (2) They may lie on a curve which remains a horizontal line for a significant distance and then begin to rise; here there are only interplant diseconomies. (3) The curve declines and then becomes horizontal; here there are only interplant economies. (4) The curve has the traditional U-shape pattern.

We see now that the previous unusual results for the monopoly case follow from our assuming situation (1) to hold; otherwise, there is no *necessity* for the monopolist to be operating at the minimum point of his short-run cost curve even in the long run. But it is essential to note that even in the traditional case (4), where from a purely probability viewpoint there is least likelihood that in the long

run he will operate at the minimum point, the *probability* is greater than usually realized that his cost will be close to the minimum cost. This follows from the construction of the cost curves, which makes it impossible for the long-run *multiple*-plant cost curve (even if U-shaped) to be less flat-bottomed than the long-run *single*-plant cost curve.[12]

Formulation of the problem in this way focuses attention on the central policy problem of monopoly: optimum size of firm. Dissolution as the answer to monopoly is subject to two fundamental criticisms. (a) If firms are to be of optimum size, there might not be enough independent firms resulting from the dissolution to make the operation of competition possible. In other words, we will replace monopoly with some oligopoly situation, and it is quite possible that we would be as badly off as under monopoly. We shall deal more fully with this in Section III. (b) Even if there are originally enough independent firms for competition to work, the situation might be unstable and develop into oligopoly.

Thus situation (1) is very favorable as far as (a) is concerned, depending only on the size of k_3 relative

---

[12]Though we have developed the theory of multiple-plant cost curves for monopoly only, it is clear that the construction of the cost curves is perfectly general and will hold in any of the cases of imperfect competition. These cases should be modified accordingly.

to market output. But the independent firms would then be in the familiar unstable situation of a long-run constant cost curve, and there would be no *economic* limit to their possible growth. The dissolution provisions would also have to define optimum firm and prevent firms from growing any larger.[13] Situation (2) is most favorable for a policy of dissolution, since it has the advantage over (1) that there is an economic limit to the growth of the independent firms. The case for dissolution is weakest under (3). Here again it depends on where the curve straightens out. Even if it is at a relatively small output (say $3k_3$, so that each competitive firm would consist of 3 plants), there would still be the problem of preventing indefinite growth. This problem would not be so bad under (4), but in either (3) or (4), if we insisted on making each plant a separate firm, we could do so only at the expense of efficiency in production. The cost would, of course, vary with the shape of the curve formed from the successive minimum points.

II

Our purpose in this section is to deal more mathematically with the short-run situation and show under what conditions equalization of marginal costs by equalizing outputs of the plants will not minimize costs to the firm.[14] We shall deal primarily with the case of a two-plant firm and offer (a) a geometric proof and then (b) a more general algebraic proof.

(a) Assume for convenience that each plant (A and B) has the same marginal cost curve reaching its min-

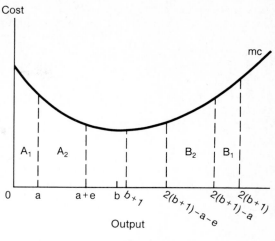

Fig. 6

imum at b. For total outputs $x < 2b$ it is well known that equalization of marginal cost does not minimize cost (cf. (b) below). It is also obvious that in the case of a symmetric marginal cost curve an output of $2b$ can be produced either with each plant producing b or with one producing $b + d$ and the other $b - d$, where d is any positive constant less than or equal to b. We shall ignore these more trivial cases and consider $x = 2(b + 1)$, which could be produced with each plant producing $b + 1$. In order that it should be produced, instead, with A producing a and B producing $2(b + 1) - a$, and *that this should be the only possible way of minimizing cost*, we have the following necessary and sufficient conditions (cf. Fig. 6):

1. $A_1 < B_1$—otherwise the entire output would be produced in B. This condition insures that *at least* a will be produced in A.

2. For any $0 < e \le b + 1 - a$ it is true that $A_2 > B_2$. The most important value of $e = b + 1 - a$; for this insures that, even though we equalize the marginal costs by equalizing outputs of the two operating plants, we are not minimizing costs. The statement must hold for the other values of e to insure that no other point on the falling part of the marginal cost curve is the minimizing one.

These two conditions are very general and impose no restrictions inconsistent with the generally accepted U-shaped marginal cost curve. In general the class of cost curves meeting these conditions will have the following characteristics: (a) sharply falling initial

[13]In the event that dissolution succeeded in placing each plant under separate ownership and making perfect competition work, in our preceding example we would have short-run equilibrium established at a price of p_0 (cf. Fig. 4). This follows from our assumption that the ingredients are completely unspecialized, so that the supply curve for the competitive industry coincides with the marginal cost curve of the monopolist. This supply curve intersects the industry demand curve at the price p_0, thus establishing the short-run price for the competitive industry. Since this price exceeds minimum average cost (p_3) the industry is not in long-run equilibrium: firms will flow into the industry and the supply curve will shift over to the right until a price p_3 is established (again employing the assumption of a constant costs industry). This will be the case when there are 100 firms (with one plant each) in the industry (cf. Fig. 2). Thus, in Cassels' terminology, for the monopoly we have no long-run excess capacity (in situation (1)), though there is underinvestment if we accept perfect competition as a criterion. (J. M. Cassels, "Excess Capacity and Monopolistic Competition," this JOURNAL, Vol. 51 (1936–37), pp. 440–443.) (Reprinted supra, pp. 224–234.)

[14]This section may be omitted without disturbing the continuity between Sections I and III.

stages, *(b)* flattening out for a short interval, then *(c)* rising even more sharply. *(c)* brings about condition (1); *(a)* and *(b)* together tend to bring about condition (2). To prove the first statement in this paragraph, we offer the following actual example.

Let A and B each have the cost curves described in Table 1. We must now construct the v_1 and v_2 curves (cf. Fig. 3). The v_1 curve is, of course, represented by Table 1. The v_2 curve is constructed in Table 2. From a comparison of Tables 1 and 2 we see that v_2 intersects v_1 between outputs 11 and 12, so that the v_2 curve for an output of 12 is the relevant

one. Yet this output, which could be produced by each plant producing at its minimum marginal cost output, is produced with one plant on the rising part of its marginal cost curve and the other on the falling.

(b) Consider again the case of a 2-plant firm.[15] Consider the plants as separate factors of production, and let $c(x_1)$ and $c(x_2)$ be the total variable cost curves of A and B, respectively, where x_1 is the output of A and x_2 of B. Then for any fixed output k the monopolist will seek to minimize

$$C = c(x_1) + c(x_2)$$

subject to the side condition

$$x_1 + x_2 = k$$

We employ the Lagrange multiplier and form

$$F = c(x_1) + c(x_2) - \lambda(x_1 + x_2 - k)$$

Minimizing F with respect to x_1 and then x_2 and eliminating λ we get as our first order conditions the familiar results

$$\partial c/\partial x_1 = \partial c/\partial x_2$$

In order that F should be a minimum, we need the second order conditions fulfilled.[16]

[15] I wish to express my appreciation to Trygve Haavelmo (University of Chicago) for his assistance in formulating the results of this paragraph.
[16] Cf. J. R. Hicks, *Value and Capital* (1939), pp. 305 ff.

Table 1

Output	avc	tvc	mc
1	15.0	15	15
2	14.0	28	13
3	13.0	39	11
4	12.0	48	9
5	11.0	55	7
6	10.0	60	5
7	9.4	66	6
8	9.1	73	7
9	9.0	81	8
10	9.0	90	9
11	9.1	100	10
12	9.8	117	17
13	11.1	144	27
14	13.1	184	40
15	15.9	239	55

Table 2

Output	Plant A		Plant B		TVC
	Output	tvc(A)	Output	tvc(B)	tvc(A) + tvc(B)
1	1	15	0	0	15
2	1	15	1	15	30
3	2	28	1	15	43
4	3	39	1	15	54
5	4	48	1	15	63
6	5	55	1	15	70
7	6	60	1	15	75
8	7	66	1	15	81
9	8	73	1	15	88
10	9	81	1	15	96
11	10	90	1	15	105
12	11	100	1	15	115
13	7	66	6	60	126
14	7	66	7	66	132
15	8	73	7	66	139

$$D = \begin{vmatrix} 0 & \dfrac{\partial c}{\partial x_1} & \dfrac{\partial c}{\partial x_2} \\[2ex] \dfrac{\partial c}{\partial x_1} & \dfrac{\partial^2 c}{\partial x_1^{\,2}} & 0 \\[2ex] \dfrac{\partial c}{\partial x_2} & 0 & \dfrac{\partial^2 c}{\partial x_2^{\,2}} \end{vmatrix}$$

$$= -\left(\frac{\partial c}{\partial x_1}\right)^2 \left(\frac{\partial^2 c}{\partial x_2^{\,2}}\right) - \left(\frac{\partial c}{\partial x_2}\right)^2 \left(\frac{\partial^2 c}{\partial x_1^{\,2}}\right) < 0$$

Noting that $\left(\dfrac{\partial c}{\partial x_i}\right)^2$ is identically > 0, and that $\dfrac{\partial^2 c}{\partial x_i^{\,2}} \substack{< \\ >} 0$ $(i = 1, 2)$ according as marginal cost is falling, at a minimum, or rising, we can formulate the following results:

1. For outputs $x = x_1 + x_2 < b$ (where b is the output for plant minimum marginal cost), each plant will of necessity be producing on the falling part of the curve. Therefore $D > 0$ and equalizing marginal cost by equalizing outputs will *maximize* total costs. Minimum costs are achieved by having one plant produce the entire output.

2. If $x_1 = x_2 = b$, then $D = 0$ and this allocation may be neither a minimum nor a maximum.

3. If $x = x_1 + x_2 > 2b$ and we equalize marginal costs by equalizing outputs, then each plant is producing on the rising part of the marginal cost curve and $D < 0$. This assures us that this allocation will minimize costs *relative to* all alternative allocations such that each plant is producing on the rising part of the marginal cost curve; that is, this allocation is the optimum one within a neighborhood such that every point is on the rising part of the curve. However, if we permit allocations such that one plant is producing on the falling part and one on its rising part, then for this allocation we may have $D > 0$; thus the allocation achieved by equalizing marginal costs may be neither a minimum nor a maximum relative to the whole extent of the marginal cost curve.

These results can be represented graphically with the aid of Fig. 7. From the shape of the marginal cost curve (which reaches its minimum as the output b) we know, for an output of $2(b + k)$, $C_1 > B_3$ as long as $d < k$. Therefore the total variable costs are less when the allocation is $b + k$ to each one than any other allocation $b + k + d$, $b + k - d$ (where $d < k$). Analogous results hold when total output is

less than b: then from the shape of the curve we see that equalizing marginal cost will bring about a greater total variable cost than any other allocation. When, however, we permit the possibility of the allocation being $b + k - e$, $b + k + e$ (where $e > k$) we are no longer sure that $b + k$, $b + k$ will yield a smaller total variable cost than the former allocation. Specifically, the former allocation will be less when

$$2A + B + C < 2(A + B)$$

where

$$B = B_1 + B_2 + B_3; \quad C = C_1 + C_2$$

This reduces to

$$C < B \text{ or } B_1 > C - (B_2 + B_3) > 0$$

Obviously by increasing the absolute value of the slope of the falling part of the marginal cost curve in the neighborhood of the minimum point, we can make B_1 as large as desired, while keeping the right side of this last inequality constant. Thus a marginal cost curve satisfying this inequality can easily be constructed.

These results can readily be generalized to the case of n plants, each with its own total variable cost curve $c_i(x_i)$, where the c_i are not necessarily the same. Our first and second order conditions are shown at the top of p. 336.

These results leave us with the conclusion that it is impossible to formulate any general rules to determine how many plants (in the short run) will be used to produce a given output, except the one proved in the section above, namely, with k plants, each with minimum average variable cost at $x_i = g$, outputs of $ng(n = 1, 2, \ldots k)$ will be produced by having n plants each produce g. Furthermore, it is theoretically possible that $x = x_1$ will be produced

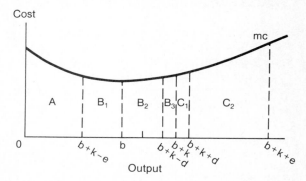

Fig. 7

$$\frac{\partial c_1}{\partial x_1} = \frac{\partial c_2}{\partial x_2} = \ldots = \frac{\partial c_n}{\partial x_n} \quad \begin{vmatrix} 0 & \dfrac{\partial c_1}{\partial x_1} & \dfrac{\partial c_2}{\partial x_2} \\[2ex] \dfrac{\partial c_1}{\partial x_1} & \dfrac{\partial^2 c_1}{\partial x_1^{\,2}} & 0 \\[2ex] \dfrac{\partial c_2}{\partial x_2} & 0 & \dfrac{\partial^2 c_2}{\partial x_2^{\,2}} \end{vmatrix} < 0 \quad \begin{vmatrix} 0 & \dfrac{\partial c_1}{\partial x_1} & \dfrac{\partial c_2}{\partial x_2} & \dfrac{\partial c_3}{\partial x_3} \\[2ex] \dfrac{\partial c_1}{\partial x_1} & \dfrac{\partial^2 c_1}{\partial x_1^{\,2}} & 0 & 0 \\[2ex] \dfrac{\partial c_2}{\partial x_2} & 0 & \dfrac{\partial^2 c_2}{\partial x_2^{\,2}} & 0 \\[2ex] \dfrac{\partial c_3}{\partial x_3} & 0 & 0 & \dfrac{\partial^2 c_3}{\partial x_3^{\,2}} \end{vmatrix} < 0$$

$$\ldots \quad \begin{vmatrix} 0 & \dfrac{\partial c_1}{\partial x_1} & \dfrac{\partial c_2}{\partial x_2} & \cdots & \dfrac{\partial c_n}{\partial x_n} \\[2ex] \dfrac{\partial c_1}{\partial x_1} & \dfrac{\partial^2 c_1}{\partial x_1^{\,2}} & 0 & \cdots & 0 \\[2ex] \dfrac{\partial c_2}{\partial x_2} & 0 & \dfrac{\partial^2 c_2}{\partial x_2^{\,2}} & \cdots & 0 \\ \cdot & \cdot & \cdot & & \cdot \\ \cdot & \cdot & \cdot & \cdots & \cdot \\ \cdot & \cdot & \cdot & & \cdot \\ \dfrac{\partial c_n}{\partial x_n} & 0 & 0 & \cdot & \dfrac{\partial^2 c_n}{\partial x_n^{\,2}} \end{vmatrix} < 0$$

with j plants, $x = x_1 + d$ with $j + 1$ plants, and $x = x_1 + d + e$ with j plants again. Consequently our Fig. 3 should allow for the possibility of multiple intersection of the v_i curves.[17]

Finally, we should note that these problems do not arise under perfect competition, which may well explain why they have so long been neglected. In imperfect competition there is only a demand curve for the firm as a whole, and not for any individual plant. Therefore, before we can discuss equilibrium for the firm we must construct the aggregate cost curve for the firm as a whole. However, under perfect competition there exists a separate demand curve for each plant, namely, an infinitely elastic curve at the level of the market price. Consequently we can de-

termine the equilibrium output of each plant independently of what takes place in other plants. In other words, the fact of the unlimited market which is present under perfect competition enables us to consider each plant separately.

Analytically this can be shown as follows. Consider a firm with n plants; the amount x_i is produced by the i-th plant, which has the total cost curve $g_i(x_i)$ $(i = 1, 2, \ldots n)$. Let p = price of the product sold by the firm. By our assumption of perfect competition p is considered by the firm as given. Then the firm maximizes its profit

$$\pi = px - \sum_{i=1}^{n} g_i(x_i)$$

subject to

$$x = \sum_{i=1}^{n} x_i.$$

Substituting we have

---

[17]In a comment on this article, Wassily Leontief showed that at most one plant would be operated on the decreasing part of its marginal cost curve. See W. W. Leontief, "Multiple-Plant Firms: Comment," *Quarterly Journal of Economics*, LXI (1947), pp. 650–651.—D. P.

$$\pi = p \sum_{i=1}^{n} x_i - \sum_{i=1}^{n} g_i(x_i)$$

from which follow our familiar maximizing conditions

$$\partial \pi / \partial x_i = p - \frac{\partial g_i(x_i)}{\partial x_i} = 0 \ (i = 1, 2, \ldots n)$$

that is, the marginal cost of each plant must equal the market price, our usual condition for equilibrium under perfect competition.

III

In this section I shall assume that the monopoly has been dissolved and replaced by one hundred independent firms, and then consider the arrangements that might grow up between them in the absence of perfect competition. This failure of competition to develop may be due either to active desire to achieve monopoly gains, or to passive acceptance of noncompetitive arrangements due to interdependence and indeterminacy which make it impossible to adopt the rules of perfect competition.

We must recognize at the outset that in any realistic approach to the problem of monopoly and oligopoly we cannot deal in purely economic terms, but must introduce concepts and motivations which more closely approximate international power politics. On the one hand, corporation leaders have "corporationistic" feelings, together with a desire for power that is inherent in large size. On the other, corporations frequently undertake expansion programs for defensive purposes as well as for aggressive: vertical integration must be undertaken to assure strategic raw materials and market outlets—the corporation cannot allow itself to become dependent on other firms for these essentials. (The analogy to protectionism and war is complete.) In democratic societies the freedom of individuals becomes the ultimate limit to this integrative process; these societies prevent the corporation from achieving complete security by restricting its control over the factor of production labor, with its right to strike, and freedom of contract. Similarly, horizontal integration must be adopted, if the firm is to retain its position in the industry. The firm must accumulate large reserves, for in the event of a price war, victory is not to the most efficient but to the one with the largest reserves. In each case, it is the fear of imperfect competition which makes the corporation adopt methods

of imperfect competition itself. This is what makes the oligopoly problem so difficult: it cannot be solved piecemeal. This vicious circle will continue until economists provide rules for the social control of oligopolies that will both protect the public and be workable: indeterminacy must be removed without leaving the door open to collusive exploitation. In brief, some criteria must be provided to distinguish "good" imperfect competition from "bad." It is quite likely that the controls devised will involve a much greater degree of direct government intervention than we have known heretofore.

Despite these qualifications, I now proceed to examine the workings of a market-sharing oligopoly arrangement among the newly independent firms. I shall attempt to show that this cartel arrangement (as we shall refer to it) should be used as a general model for practical studies of imperfect competition. This is not to say that as it stands it is realistic; in fact, its assumptions will prove to be quite arbitrary. However, it does provide a convenient "jumping-off" point from which modifications can be made to deal with actual cases.

Assume that the one hundred independent firms set up a central office which decides on a common price and output policy for the industry. The cartel allocates quotas among the different firms in such a way as to minimize the costs of any given output. We no longer continue with our unrealistic (monopoly) assumption that the cartel can control entry into the industry. In fact, and this is the distinguishing feature, we assume that, as a result of antimonopoly laws or the pressure of public opinion, there is free entry. Specifically, we assume that the antimonopoly laws prevent single ownership of the industry and restrictions on entry, but permit agreements (either tacit or explicit) among the supposedly competitive firms. The cartel must thus permit any firm which wishes to do so to enter the industry and become a member of the cartel. In order to determine the short-run and long-run equilibria of the cartel, we must first construct its cost curves.[18]

Let us first consider the short-run marginal cost curve. For outputs greater than q_2 (Figs. 8 and 2) the cartel will minimize costs by equalizing marginal

---

[18]The reader should make modifications to the shape and construction of these curves analogous to those pointed out for the curves in the preceding section. Since I have already dealt at length with this problem, it will be omitted here.

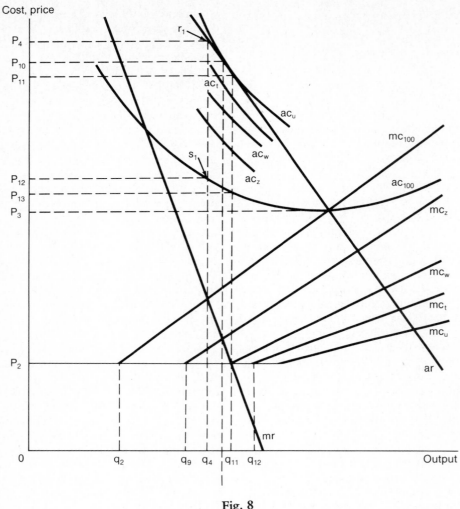

Fig. 8

costs among all firms and having each produce an equal amount. For outputs less than q_2 the cartel will follow exactly the same procedure as the monopoly in allocating production: x firms will produce k_2 units apiece, where x is determined by the equation $xq_2 = q_i$, where q_i is any output less than or equal to q_2. The short-run cartel situation is thus identical with short-run monopoly (Fig. 2). Each firm will produce k_4 to give a total output for the industry of q_4 and a price of p_4. The firms will share according to their quotas (and therefore equally) the cartel profits, which are equal to the area of the rectangle $p_4 r_1 s_1 p_{12}$.

In the long run the existence of these cartel profits

will attract new firms into the industry.[19] Assume that these too become part of the cartel. We must now consider what happens to the short-run cost curves of the cartel as new firms enter. By assumption the existing plant is the optimum one; therefore, assuming no changes in technology or prices of fac-

[19]New investment might of course also come from the old firms' expanding in order to increase their quotas and relative standing in the industry. Or they might wait until a new firm establishes itself, and then buy it up along with its quota. This last was the pattern of the German potash cartel and is also characteristic of the American meat packing industry. Cf. George W. Stocking, *The Potash Industry* (1931); Wm. H. Nicholls, "Market-Sharing in the Packing Industry," *Journal of Farm Economics,* Vol. 22 (1940), pp. 225–240.

tors, the new firms will build plants of exactly the same size. Assume also that one firm continues to operate only one plant.

As in the case of short-run monopoly, marginal cost can never fall below p_2. But in the long run, as new firms enter, the point corresponding to q_2 in Fig. 2 moves over further to the right (cf. Fig. 8). Specifically, for any number of plants $z > 100$, the marginal cost curve (mc_z) will be a horizontal line at the level p_2 until the point $q_9 = zk_2$. Outputs up to this point will be produced by keeping some plants idle and the remaining plants each producing k_2. For outputs greater than q_9 (with z firms), the cartel will allocate quotas equally among the firms and the marginal cost curve will rise. The marginal cost curve for z firms not only is horizontal for a longer stretch than that for 100 firms, but the slope of its rising part is smaller; therefore it will always lie below the marginal cost curve for 100 firms. This is true because for any given increase in output the increase in marginal cost for z firms is less than that for 100 firms, since the increased output can be shared among a greater number of firms. For example, for a given increase in the cartel output, with only 100 firms each one might have to increase output from k_1 to k_3; while for z firms, each one might only have to increase from k_1 to k_2, with a corresponding smaller increase in marginal costs (cf. Fig. 1). Another way of looking at this is to note that the "steps" in the rising part of the curve become wider as more firms enter (cf. above, p. 330).

So much for the marginal cost curve. As more firms enter, the total fixed cost, and therefore the average fixed cost curve, will rise uniformly. But the average variable cost for the cartel with any number of plants $z > 100$ will be less than, or equal to, the average variable costs with 100 firms. Until q_2 the curves will coincide as horizontal straight lines at the level p_2. For outputs from q_2 to q_9 the z curve will continue horizontally, while the other curve will begin to rise. For outputs greater than q_9 the average variable cost for z firms (avc_z) will also begin to rise, always remaining, of course, below its marginal cost curve. It will also lie below avc_{100}, since for any output $q_i > q_9$ each firm will produce a smaller output and will thus have lower average variable costs (cf. Fig. 1). Consequently there is no definite relationship between the average cost curve for z firms and that for 100 firms: it might be higher in some intervals and lower in others. For example, if the cartel output were such that with 100 firms each firm were pro-

ducing k_3 or less (Fig. 1), an increasing number of firms would reduce (for the fixed cartel output) the output per firm and drive each firm to the left and higher on its average cost curve. Therefore, the cartel average cost for this output would be greater with z firms than with 100. If, on the other hand, cartel output were such that with 100 firms each one were producing immediately to the right of k_3, then for a slight increase in the number of firms the cartel average cost for that output would be decreased, as each plant was pushed down to its minimum point k_3; while for larger increases in the number of plants each one would be pushed up on the falling part of the average cost curve until the cartel average cost was higher than with 100 firms. If, finally, with 100 firms the output is such that each plant is far to the right on its average cost curve, then even for large increases in the number of firms, cartel average cost would be reduced. However, for the output q_3 with 100 firms, each firm is producing at its minimum average cost. We have thus the first situation described here, and therefore for any given output $q_j < q_3$ the cartel average cost with a greater number of firms will be greater than with a smaller number. For outputs greater than q_3 the other two situations will hold.

From our previous discussion we see that, as new firms enter, the marginal cost curve is pushed uniformly to the right. Since we have assumed that the average revenue (and therefore the marginal revenue) curve remains constant, this means that in the long run cartel price will fall and output increase. Thus, for z firms we have equilibrium with output $q_{10} > q_4$ and price $p_{10} < p_4$.

Let us suppose that even with z firms there are still cartel profits; then new firms will continue to enter. Assume that the number of firms increases to w where $w = q_{11}/k_2$. The same relationships hold between the cost curves of the cartel with w firms and the cartel with z firms as between z firms and 100 firms. The equilibrium output will be $q_{11} > q_{10}$ and the price $p_{11} < p_{10}$. Assume, now, that even with w firms profits are still being made. Let the new number of firms be t, where $t = q_{12}/k_2$. Let us examine the effect of this new inflow of firms on the equilibrium situation.

The marginal cost curve (mc_t) is changed as indicated in Fig. 8. The first significant point is that *the equilibrium output has not changed* and is still at q_{11}. Furthermore, the output q_{11} will be produced in exactly the same way as with w firms: w plants will produce k_2 each to yield a total output of $k_2w = q_{11}$. The remaining $t - w$ plants will remain idle and be paid their fixed costs and aliquot share of the cartel profits.[20] The other significant point is that average costs for an output q_{11} with t firms *will definitely be greater* than for w firms. This follows because average variable cost is the same in both cases ($= p_2$), while average fixed cost is greater in the former due to the additional fixed costs of the $t - w$ new firms. Thus per-unit profit is definitely smaller. If there are still profits, new firms will continue to enter, driving up the average cost curve for the output q_{11} until it is tangent to the demand curve at that output. At this point price will equal average expense and there will be no profits and no further inducements to enter. The industry will then be in long-run equilibrium.[21] It can be shown, however, that both in theory and in practice this equilibrium is a very unstable one.

The long-run equilibrium number of firms in the industry, u, can be determined as follows. Total profits P, when there are w firms, are

$$P = p_{11}q_{11} - (q_{11}p_2 + wf)$$

where f is the total fixed cost per plant and p_2 the average variable cost. Then

$$u = w + \frac{P}{f}.$$

That is, the number of new firms above w is limited by the amount of cartel profits available to pay them their fixed expenses in order to keep them idle.[22]

The long-run equilibrium is thus one of both excess capacity (in the sense that the cartel is operating below its long-run minimum cost point) and over-investment.[23] If we measure excess capacity in terms of the output that could be yielded if output were

at a point where marginal cost equals price, the results are equally impressive. Although there are more plants in the cartel than under long-run competitive equilibrium, the industry output is less and the cost and price higher, with a very low (normal) rate of profit.[24]

Such long-run equilibria are highly unstable. This is clearly shown in our model by the discrepancy between the marginal revenue of the *firm* (which approximately equals price on the assumption of non-retaliation) and its own very low marginal cost. Each individual firm realizes the ease and profit with which it could sell additional units beyond its quota. Thus the temptation to "bootlegging," smuggling, and "chiseling" is strong. As cartel profits decrease with the influx of new firms, this pressure becomes irresistible, especially for the low-cost firms, and the eventual breakdown of cartel discipline is inevitable. The pernicious (for the cartel) fact remains that it is to the *maximum advantage* of each firm to stay out of the cartel and sell in unlimited quantities at the cartel price (or just below it), while all other firms remain members of the cartel and by their common restrictive policies hold up the price. This has been the pattern of breakdown of many cartels, with rubber (the Stevenson Plan) as the classic example.[25]

---

[24]Excess capacity is here presented as the outcome of cartel operations, and the cartel itself is depicted as beginning from a situation of perfect competition. As is well known, however, excess capacity frequently first arises through shifts in demand or technological changes, precipitates a disastrous period of "cutthroat competition," which is finally ended by setting up a cartel arrangement. This pattern has been especially important among products with low income elasticities of demand—the so-called primary products (e.g. the rubber, coffee, and wheat cartels). Thus excess capacity is itself a *cause* of the cartel. Cf. J. W. F. Rowe, *Markets and Men* (1936); Wallace and Edminster, op. cit., W. Y. Eliott et al., *International Control in the Non-Ferrous Metals* (1937).

[25]Cf. Rowe, op. cit.; K. E. Knorr, *World Rubber and Its Regulation* (1945); Rowe, "Studies in the Artificial Control of Raw Material Supplies: No. 2, Rubber," London and Cambridge Economic Service, Special Memorandum No. 34 (1931); C. R. Whittlesey, Governmental Control of Crude Rubber (1931). The last two are excellent critical studies of the Stevenson Plan.

That the same pattern was at work in the U. S. copper export cartel after the first World War is evident from the following testimony of C. F. Kelley (president of Anaconda Copper Mining Co.) before the TNEC (Hearings, Vol. 25, pp. 13164–13165):

"The Copper Export Association finally broke up due to two causes. One was the withdrawal of certain members, led by the Miami Copper Co. . . . There was an increase in competition from nonmembers abroad. There was a constant undercutting of price, and certain members felt *that they were holding the umbrella*, and it was more desirable to have freedom, and so gradually by withdrawals it lost its importance." (Italics mine.)

---

[20]Theoretically, at this point a new firm could obtain its share of cartel profits by merely *threatening* to build a new plant.

[21]The classic case of a cartel in such a long-run equilibrium is the German potash cartel, which in 1928 operated only 60 of 229 plants. B. R. Wallace and L. R. Edminster, *International Control of Raw Materials* (1930), Chap. 4.

[22]It is interesting to note that the graphic equilibrium obtained here is similar to that of the familiar Chamberlin product differentiation case. But here the curves refer to the *industry* as a whole, not to the individual firm. Also, here the equilibrium is obtained solely by shifts in the cost curves, while there the main shift takes place through the demand curve (for the individual firm).

[23]Whereas under monopoly there was no excess capacity and under-investment. This last pernicious and wasteful effect of the cartel is what makes many economists believe that a situation of out-and-out monopoly is preferable to a cartel. Cf. above, p. 268–269, note 13.

Another cause of instability lies in a fact from which our model abstracts by its assumption of uniform cost curves for all firms. There is a fundamental conflict of interest (within the cartel) between the low-cost and high-cost firms, with the latter insisting on high enough prices to cover their costs as the condition of their remaining in the cartel. There is also the very difficult problem of allocating quotas among the firms, which always creates much dissension and bickering. The forces described in this and the preceding paragraph go a long way in explaining the breakdown of many of our cartels. The cartel is in the unenviable position of having to satisfy everyone, for one dissatisfied producer can bring about the feared price competition and the disintegration of the cartel. Thus the successful cartel must follow a policy of continuous compromise.

In view of the difficulties of maintaining cartel discipline, it is not surprising that successful cartels have resorted to one or more of the following practices: *(a)* invoked government aid to compel membership and enforce cartel decisions (quotas and prices)—especially true of Europe; *(b)* controlled entry into, and operation within, the industry through patents—a frequent practice in the chemical industries; *(c)* controlled entry into, and operation within, the industry by ownership over the scarce raw material cartelized, e.g. tin, potash, lead; *(d)* compelled membership or prevented insubordination by dumping at (temporarily) greatly reduced prices in the market area of the non-coöperating producer. The cartel is frequently prevented from following this last practice by force of law (especially anti-dumping tariffs) or public opinion.

IV

In the United States open cartel arrangements of the type analyzed here are not frequent, since they are strongly discouraged by antitrust law—even more so than outright merger. Nevertheless, I shall show that many of the (tacit) arrangements which do evolve in our economy have striking similarities to our cartel model. An unfortunate result of the classification of imperfect competition into several types is the failure to recognize that in actual life these types are inextricably mixed. Insofar as our economy can be characterized by a single pattern, I think it is one in which the given industry produces differentiated products and consists of a few (say three or four) very large firms doing the bulk of the business, plus many smaller "independents." The

large firms act more or less as leaders for the industry in setting price policy, and so on. Some form of tacit or explicit market sharing arrangement (by percentages, market areas, recognized customers, etc.) exists to modify (if not remove) competition between the large firms. They might also proceed on the assumption that the other dominant firms will follow their prices both upwards and downwards. This gives results identical with our cartel model. The industry also has a trade association to help in maintaining discipline and implementing the price policies of the leading dominant firms.

The steel, petroleum, agricultural implements, anthracite coal, light bulb, cigarette, meat packing, and many other industries all fall within this general pattern.[26] In all these industries there has also been a decided tendency for the (original) dominant firms to decline in relative importance over the years. In some cases, this has been serious (steel, petroleum, meat packing); in others, relatively mild (anthracite coal, light bulb, cigarette). The decline has not taken place in absolute size; rather, the several industries have grown, but the dominant firms have grown at a slower rate. The dominant firms have apparently also attempted to pursue a policy of price stabilization, and have succeeded in varying degrees.

If we now interpret these facts in terms of our cartel model, we get very fruitful results. We must first consider the dominant firms as taking the place of the cartel "central office" and setting policies for the whole industry. They will discourage pricecutting by exhortation, "social" pressure, repeated stressing of the disaster which faces the industry as a result of price-cutting, and threats (explicit or implied) of underselling non-coöperating firms in their markets, if they persist. United States Steel and Standard Oil were, in their early years, notorious examples of this last practice. Through these methods the dominant firms are more or less able to maintain discipline within the industry and agreement on a common price. Even if the dominant firms are low-cost firms, they still may set a higher price than they themselves would prefer, in order to satisfy the other (high-cost) producers and prevent them from price cutting. As a rule, the dominant firms try to follow a policy of price stabilization. This may be due to the simplicity of the rule, or it may reflect the fear that arises every time the price is changed: whether

[26]Cf. A. R. Burns, *The Decline of Competition* (1936), especially Chap. 3 and pp. 140–145.

the lead will be followed. In brief, the relationship between leaders and followers may be so delicate that the leaders take every care to prevent subjecting it to stress.

The decline in the relative position of the leader is readily explained as the familiar cartel phenomenon of the inflow of new firms and the expansion of old ones. The dominant firms themselves may not expand at the same rate as the industry, since they tend to be near their maximum size, and further expansion might involve them in many of the inefficiencies of large-scale operation. It is also possible that the dominant firms are high-cost producers and that the price set by them, though yielding relatively small profits in their case, would enable the other (low-cost) firms to earn much higher profits, thus increasing their incentive to enter the industry and expand. Finally, it should be noted that the decline in relative position may be due to weakness in the control exercised by the dominant firms. During periods of declining demand the "independents" will indulge in much more price cutting in order to increase their sales. It is quite possible (and seems to have been the case in steel and copper, for example) that the dominant firm will continue with its stabilized higher price and not retaliate for a time; that is, it expects it will still profit by this policy, although it is in the position of "holding the umbrella" for the other firms and restricting its own output relatively more than theirs.[27]

Finally, it is very instructive to examine those industries in which the dominant firms have declined relatively little. The results are what we might have expected from our cartel model (cf. above, p. 341). General Electric has been able to maintain its position because it could control entry into the light bulb industry through ownership of vital patents. The dominant anthracite coal companies have control of most of the anthracite reserves. The "Big Four" in cigarettes have prevented entry by establishing monopoly through advertising. The depression, however, partly broke down this last monopoly by allowing the cheaper brands to establish themselves; and in recent years Philip Morris has established itself, in its turn, by a vigorous advertising campaign.[28]

The preceding paragraphs, though necessarily quite sketchy, provide a rough outline of the thesis I have tried to present in this section: that the cartel model is the most fruitful approach to economic analysis of our real world, focusing attention on the significant points of the problem. This general statement will now be amplified by applying the thesis to a specific industry and noting the particular ways in which the cartel features appear. The example I have chosen is the milk distributing industry, whose striking resemblance to our cartel model makes it truly a "textbook case."[29]

Due to the perishability and high transportation costs of their product, milkshed coöperatives, made up of thousands of members, are able to operate more or less within a closed market. The coöperative bargains collectively with the distributors and sets a price on fluid (Class I) milk. It cannot, however, control the output of its members, and therefore all milk not used in fluid form is sold as surplus (Class II) milk at prices near competitive levels. This is used for butter, cream, condensed milk, and other processed dairy products. The individual producer is either allotted a quota on which he can receive the Class I price (receiving the Class II price on everything above this quota) or he receives the Class I price on a percentage of his sales equal to the percentage of the total coöperative sales which was used for Class I purposes. Over a period of time expansion takes place as (1) new producers are attracted into the dairy industry within the existing milkshed, (2) the individual members expand their production, and (3) the higher price set by the coöperative itself extends the geographical area of the milkshed.

As the size and output of the milkshed increase, the proportion of surplus milk increases still faster. This brings down the average price received by the producer. If there were completely free entry, the *average* price would tend to fall to the competitive level, with two possible results.

1. At any time of the coöperative's existence, it is to the advantage of any individual producer to stay out of the coöperative and sell to non-participating dealers who sell primarily fluid milk. They will thus obtain a higher price than the average obtainable

---

[27]Cf. Burns, op. cit., pp. 140 ff.

[28]Cf. A. A. Bright and W. R. Maclaurin, "Economic Factors Influencing the Development and Introduction of the Fluorescent Lamp," *Journal of Political Economy*, Vol. 51 (1943), pp. 429–450; Burns, op. cit., p. 123.

[29]For the following account I have drawn heavily on John M. Cassels, *A Study of Fluid Milk Prices* (Harvard Economic Studies No. 54) (1937), Chaps. 5–6 and Appendix A; and Wm. H. Nicholls, Imperfect Competition within Agricultural Industries (1941), Chaps. 10–11.

within the coöperative, but lower than the bargained Class I price. Note that this is also to the advantage of the non-participating distributor, since it *(a)* enables him to obtain Class I milk at a lower price than his competitor (participating) distributors and *(b)* throws a greater burden of surplus milk on them. Thus it is to the common interest of producers' and distributors' organizations to prevent free entry at both levels. When increasing amounts of surplus milk continuously lower the average price and increase the discrepancy between it and the Class I price, this unremitting pressure becomes overwhelming and, if not counteracted, causes the disintegration of the cooperative long before the "competitive" price is reached.

2. But, of course, counter measures will be put into effect before this danger point is reached. Government assistance will be called in—health ordinances will be used to restrict the area of the milkshed and discipline recalcitrant producers. (The Rhode Island ordinance requiring milk from outside the state to be colored pink is classic.) Where this does not suffice, force can also be used (milk-dumping, for example). Action will also be directed at the non-participating distributors, for without these as an outlet the non-coöperating producer would be lost, unless he could do his own distributing. The producers' and distributors' organizations will thus try to eliminate them, either with government assistance (again via health ordinances) or pure coercion (their bottles broken or held back at the bottle-exchange, their workers beaten, and so on). Finally the government itself is called in to fix and enforce the price, usually by arbitrating or participating in the bargaining between coöperatives and distributors and giving these results legal sanction.[30]

V

In conclusion it should be noted that to a large extent the general imperfect competition case described above can be dealt with by a market-sharing

[30]Cf. TNEC Monograph No. 32, *Economic Standards of Government Price Control,* Part II, "Public Pricing of Milk" for government regulation of fluid milk marketing in Oregon, California, Indiana, Wisconsin, and New York. Federal price fixing is also discussed (pp. 57–229).

solution from the viewpoint of a single firm whose individual demand curve shifts to the left as new firms enter. For the following reasons, however, I believe that the cartel model is a more satisfactory analytical tool for revealing certain of the forces at work and should therefore be used in addition to the market-sharing analysis.

1. There are some cases for which the cartel model is an exact, and not merely an approximate, description, in the sense that there is an actual body making and enforcing decisions from the viewpoint of the industry as a whole. The market-sharing analysis, with its emphasis on the individual firm, is obviously inapplicable here. In our own economy we have the examples of the milk industry, bituminous coal (Guffey Coal Act), oil (state proration laws and the Connally Act), and industries with strong trade associations. When we extend our view to the international scene, the examples become much more numerous: rubber, tin, wheat, sugar, coffee, etc. None of these can be satisfactorily analyzed from a market-sharing point of view.

2. Even when the industry has not set up any official central office, our previous analysis has shown that through the interaction of dominant and independent firms we get approximate cartel results. Here, too, the dominant firms will make some decisions from the viewpoint of the industry. For example, they may not maximize short-run profits, in order not to attract new firms. But if we look at it from the viewpoint of each firm, the latter would not gain by foregoing its profit while the other firms retained theirs. The cartel model is necessary to bring out the nature of these industry decisions.

3. The cartel model shows with graphic clarity the development of long-run excess capacity and overinvestment.

4. Obviously, from a firm analysis we could not obtain the results of having new firms entering the industry and remaining idle.

5. The cartel model reveals more precisely the inner mechanisms, forces, and conflicts leading to the disintegration of industry agreements and explains the resort to extra-economic methods of maintaining them.

APPLICATIONS OF THE THEORY OF MARKET STRUCTURES

Why Regulate Utilities?*

HAROLD DEMSETZ**

See "Production, Information Costs and Economic Organization" for author's biography.

Current economic doctrine offers to its students a basic relationship between the number of firms that produce for a given market and the degree to which competitive results will prevail. Stated explicitly or suggested implicitly is the doctrine that price and output can be expected to diverge to a greater extent from their competitive levels the fewer the firms that produce the product for the market. This relationship has provided the logic that motivates much of the research devoted to studying industrial concentration, and it has given considerable support to utility regulation.[1]

In this paper, I shall argue that the asserted relationship between market concentration and com-

petition cannot be derived from existing theoretical considerations and that it is based largely on an incorrect understanding of the concept of competition or rivalry. The strongest application of the asserted relationship is in the area of utility regulation since, if we assume scale economies in production, it can be deduced that only one firm will produce the commodity. The logical validity or falsity of the asserted relationship should reveal itself most clearly in this case.

Although public utility regulation recently has been criticized because of its ineffectiveness or because of the undesirable indirect effects it produces,[2] the basic intellectual arguments for believing that truly effective regulation is desirable have not been challenged. Even those who are inclined to reject government regulation or ownership of public util-

*Reprinted from *Journal of Law and Economics* (April 1968) by permission of the University of Chicago Press. Copyright 1968, pp. 55–65.

**The author is indebted to R. H. Coase, who was unconvinced by the natural monopoly argument long before this paper was written, and to George J. Stigler and Joel Segall for helpful comments and criticisms.

[1] Antitrust legislation and judicial decision, to the extent that they have been motivated by a concern for bigness and concentration, *per se,* have also benefited from the asserted relationship between monopoly power and industry structure.

[2] Cf., George J. Stigler and Claire Friedland, What Can Regulators Regulate? The Case of Electricity, 5 J. Law & Econ. 1 (1962); H. Averch and L. Johnson, The Firm under Regulatory Constraint, 52 Am. Econ. Rev. 1052 (1962); Armen Alchian and Reuben Kessel, Competition, Monopoly, and the Pursuit of Pecuniary Gain, in Aspects of Labor Economics 157 (1962).

ities because they believe these alternatives are more undesirable than private monopoly, implicitly accept the intellectual arguments that underlie regulation.[3]

The economic theory of natural monopoly is exceedingly brief and, we shall see, exceedingly unclear. Current doctrine is reflected in two recent statements of the theory. Samuelson writes:

> Under persisting decreasing costs for the firm, one or a few of them will so expand their q's as to become a significant part of the market for the industry's total Q. We would then end up (1) with a single monopolist who dominates the industry; (2) with a few large sellers who together dominate the industry . . . or (3) with some kind of imperfection of competition that, in either a stable way or in connection with a series of intermittent price wars, represents an important departure from the economist's model of "perfect" competition wherein no firm has any control over industry price.[4]

Alchian and Allen view the problem as follows:

> If a product is produced under cost conditions such that larger rates . . . [would] mean lower average cost per unit, . . . only one firm could survive; if there were two firms, one could expand to reduce costs and selling price and thereby eliminate the other. In view of the impossibility of more than one firm's being profitable, two is too many. But if there is only one, that incumbent firm may be able to set prices above free-entry costs for a long time. Either resources are wasted because too many are in the industry, or there is just one firm, which will be able to charge monopoly prices.[5]

At this point it will be useful to state explicitly the interpretation of natural monopoly used in this paper. If, because of production scale economies, it is less costly for one firm to produce a commodity in a given market than it is for two or more firms, then one firm will survive; if left unregulated, that firm will set price and output at monopoly levels; the price-output decision of that firm will be determined

by profit maximizing behavior constrained only by the market demand for the commodity.

The theory of natural monopoly is deficient for it fails to reveal the logical steps that carry it from scale economies in production to monopoly price in the market place. To see this most clearly, let us consider the contracting process from its beginning.

Why must rivals share the market? Rival sellers can offer to enter into contracts with buyers. In this bidding competition, the rival who offers buyers the most favorable terms will obtain their patronage; there is no clear or necessary reason for *bidding* rivals to share in the *production* of the goods and, therefore, there is no clear reason for competition in bidding to result in an increase in per-unit *production* costs.

Why must the unregulated market outcome be monopoly price? The competitiveness of the bidding process depends very much on such things as the number of bidders, but there is no clear or necessary reason for *production* scale economies to decrease the number of *bidders*. Let prospective buyers call for bids to service their demands. Scale economies in servicing their demands in no way imply that there will be one bidder only. There can be many bidders and the bid that wins will be the lowest. The existence of scale economies in the production of the service is irrelevant to a determination of the number of rival bidders. If the number of bidders is large or if, for other reasons, collusion among them is impractical, the contracted price can be very close to per-unit production cost.[6]

The determinants of competition in market negotiations differ from and should not be confused with the determinants of the number of firms from which production will issue after contractual negotiations have been completed. The theory of natural monopoly is clearly unclear. Economies of scale in production imply that the bids submitted will offer increasing quantities at lower per-unit costs, but production scale economies imply nothing obvious about how competitive these prices will be. If one bidder can do the job at less cost than two or more, because each would then have a smaller output rate, then the bidder with the lowest bid price for the entire job will be awarded the contract, whether the good be cement, electricity, stamp vending machines,

[3]Thus, Milton Friedman, while stating his preference for private monopoly over public monopoly or public regulation, writes:

However, monopoly may also arise because it is technically efficient to have a single producer or enterprise. . . . When technical conditions make a monopoly the natural outcome of competitive market forces, there are only three alternatives that seem available: private monopoly, public monopoly, or public regulation. Capitalism and Freedom 28 (1962).

[4]Paul A. Samuelson, Economics 461 (6th rev. ed. 1964).

[5]Armen Alchian and William R. Allen, University Economics 412 (1st ed. 1964).

[6]I shall not consider in this paper the problem of marginal cost pricing and the various devices, such as multi-part tariffs, that can be used to approximate marginal cost pricing.

or whatever, but the lowest bid price need not be a monopoly price.[7]

The criticism made here of the theory of natural monopoly can be understood best by constructing an example that is free from irrelevant complications, such as durability of distributions systems, uncertainty, and irrational behavior, all of which may or may not justify the use of regulatory commissions but none of which is relevant to the theory of natural monopoly; for this theory depends on one belief only—price and output will be at monopoly levels if, due to scale economies, only one firm succeeds in producing the product.

Assume that owners of automobiles are required to own and display new license plates each year. The production of license plates is subject to scale economies.

The theory of natural monopoly asserts that under these conditions the owners of automobiles will purchase plates from one firm only and that firm, in the absence of regulation, will charge a monopoly price, a price that is constrained only by the demand for and the cost of producing license plates. The logic of the example does dictate that license plates will be purchased from one firm because this will allow that firm to offer the plates at a price based on the lowest possible per-unit cost. But why should that price be a monopoly price?

There can be many bidders for the annual contract. Each will submit a bid based on the assumption that if its bid is lowest it will sell to all residents, if it is not lowest it sells to none. Under these conditions there will exist enough independently acting bidders to assure that the winning price will differ insignificantly from the per-unit cost of producing license plates.

If only one firm submits the lowest price, the process ends, but if two or more firms submit the lowest price, one is selected according to some random selection device or one is allowed to sell or give his contracts to the other. There is no monopoly price although there may be rent to some factors if their supply is positively sloped. There is no regulation of firms in the industry. The price is determined in the bidding market. The only role played by the government or by a consumer's buying cooperative is some random device to select the winning bidder if more than one bidder bids the lowest price.

There are only two important assumptions: (1) The inputs required to enter production must be available to many potential bidders at prices determined in open markets. This lends credibility to numerous rival bids. (2) The cost of colluding by bidding rivals must be prohibitively high. The reader will recognize that these requirements are no different than those required to avoid monopoly price in any market, whether production in that market is or is not subject to scale economies.

Moreover, if we are willing to consider the possibility that collusion or merger of all potential bidding rivals is a reasonable prospect, then we must examine the other side of the coin. Why should collusion or merger of *buyers* be prohibitively costly if an infinite or large number of bidding rivals can collude successfully? If we allow buyers access to the same technology of collusion, the market will be characterized by bilateral negotiations between organized buyers and organized sellers. While the outcome of such negotiations is somewhat uncertain with respect to wealth distribution, there is no reason to expect inefficiency.

Just what is the supply elasticity of bidders and what are the costs of colluding are questions to be answered empirically since they cannot be deduced from production scale economies. There exist more than one firm in every public utility industry and many firms exist in some public utility industries. And this is true even though licensing restrictions have been severe; the assertion that the supply of potential *bidders* in any market would be very inelastic if licensing restrictions could be abolished would seem difficult to defend when producing competitors exist in nearby markets. The presence of active rivalry is clearly indicated in public utility history. In fact, producing competitors, not to mention unsuccessful bidders, were so plentiful that one begins to doubt that scale economies characterized the utility industry at the time when regulation replaced market competition. Complaints were common that the streets were too frequently in a state of disrepair for the purpose of accommodating competing companies. Behling writes:

> There is scarcely a city in the country that has not experienced competition in one or more of the utility industries. Six electric light companies were or-

---

[7]The competitive concept employed here is not new to economics although it has long been neglected. An early statement of the concept, which was known as "competition *for* the field" in distinction to "competition *within* the field" is given by Edwin Chadwick, Results of Different Principles of Legislation and Administration in Europe; of Competition for the Field, as compared with the Competition within the Field of Service, 22 J. Royal Statistical Soc'y. 381 (1859).

ganized in the one year of 1887 in New York City. Forty-five electric light enterprises had the legal right to operate in Chicago in 1907. Prior to 1895, Duluth, Minnesota, was served by five electric lighting companies, and Scranton, Pennsylvania, had four in 1906. . . . During the latter part of the nineteenth century, competition was the usual situation in the gas industry in this country. Before 1884, six competing companies were operating in New York City. . . . Competition was common and especially persistent in the telephone industry. According to a special report of the Census in 1902, out of 1051 incorporated cities in the United States with a population of more than 4,000 persons, 1002 were provided with telephone facilities. The independent companies had a monopoly in 137 of the cities, the Bell interests had exclusive control over communication by telephone in 414 cities, while the remaining 451, almost half, were receiving duplicated service. Baltimore, Chicago, Cleveland, Columbus, Detroit, Kansas City, Minneapolis, Philadelphia, Pittsburgh, and St. Louis, among the larger cities, had at least two telephone services in 1905.[8]

It would seem that the number of potential bidding rivals and the cost of their colluding in the public utility industries are likely to be at least as great as in several other industries for which we find that unregulated markets work tolerably well.

The natural monopoly theory provides no logical basis for monopoly prices. The theory is illogical. Moreover, for the general case of public utility industries, there seems no clear evidence that the cost of colluding is significantly lower than it is for industries for which unregulated market competition seems to work. To the extent that utility regulation is based on the fear of monopoly price, *merely because one firm will serve each market*, it is not based on any deducible economic theorem.

The important point that needs stressing is that *we have no theory that allows us to deduce from the observable degree of concentration in a particular market whether or not price and output are competitive*. We have as yet no general theory of collusion and certainly not one that allows us to associate observed concentration in a particular market with successful collusion.[9]

It is possible to make some statements about collusion that reveal the nature of the forces at work. These statements are largely intuitive and cannot be

pursued in detail here. But they may be useful in imparting to the reader a notion of what is meant by a theory of collusion. Let us suppose that there are no special costs to competing. That is, we assume that sellers do not need to keep track of the prices or other activities of their competitors. Secondly, assume that there are some costs of colluding that must be borne by members of a bidders' cartel. This condition is approximated least well where the government subsidizes the cost of colluding—for example, the U.S. Department of Agriculture. Finally, assume that there are no legal barriers to entry.

Under these conditions, new bidding rivals will be paid to join the collusion. In return for joining they will receive a pro rata share of monopoly profits. As more rivals appear the pro rata share must fall. The cartel will continue paying new rivals to join until the pro rata share falls to the cost of colluding. That is, until the cartel members receive a competitive rate of return for remaining in the cartel. The next rival bidder can refuse to join the cartel; instead he can enter the market at a price below the cartel price (as can any present member of the cartel who chooses to break away). If there is some friction in the system, this rival will choose this course of action in preference to joining the cartel, for if he joins the cartel he receives a competitive rate of return; whereas if he competes outside the cartel by selling at a price below that of the cartel he receives an above-competitive rate of return for some short-run period. Under the assumed conditions the cartel must eventually fail and price and output can be competitive even though only a few firms actually produce the product. Moreover, the essential ingredient to its eventual failure is only that the private per-firm cost of colluding exceeds the private per-firm cost of competing.

Under what conditions will the cost of colluding exceed the cost of competing? How will these costs be affected by allowing coercive tactics? What about buyer cartels? What factors affect how long is "eventually"? Such questions remain to be answered by a theory of collusion. Until such questions are answered, public policy prescriptions must be suspect. A market in which many firms produce may be competitive or it may be collusive; the large number of firms merely reflects production scale diseconomies; large numbers do not necessarily reflect high or low collusion costs. A market in which few firms produce may be competitive or it may be collusive; the small number of firms merely reflects production scale

---

[8]Burton N. Behling, Competition and Monopoly in Public Utility Industries 19–20 (1938).
[9]However, see George J. Stigler, A Theory of Oligopoly, 72 J. Pol. Econ. 44 (1964).

economies; fewness does not necessarily reflect high or low collusion costs. Thus, an economist may view the many retailers who sell on "fair trade" terms with suspicion and he may marvel at the ability of large numbers of workers to form effective unions, and, yet, he may look with admiration at the performance of the few firms who sell airplanes, cameras, or automobiles.

The subject of monopoly price is necessarily permeated with the subject of negotiating or contracting costs. A world in which negotiating costs are zero is a world in which no monopolistic inefficiencies will be present, simply because buyers and sellers both can profit from negotiations that result in a reduction and elimination of inefficiencies. In such a world it will be bargaining skills and not market structures that determine the distribution of wealth. If a monopolistic structure exists on one side of the market, the other side of the market will be organized to offset any power implied by the monopolistic structure. The organization of the other side of the market can be undertaken by members of that side or by rivals of the monopolistic structure that prevails on the first side. The co-existence of monopoly *power* and monopoly *structure* is possible only if the costs of negotiating are differentially positive, being lower for one set of sellers (or buyers) than it is for rival sellers (or buyers). If one set of sellers (or buyers) can organize those on the other side of the market more cheaply than can rivals, then price may be raised (or lowered) to the extent of the existing differential advantage in negotiating costs; this extent generally will be less than the simple monopoly price. In some cases the differential advantage in negotiating costs may be so great that price will settle at the monopoly (monopsony) level. This surely cannot be the general case, but the likelihood of it surely increases as the costs imposed on potential rivals increase; legally restricting entry is one way of raising the differential disadvantages to rivals; the economic meaning of restricting entry *is* increasing the cost of potential rivals of negotiating with and organizing buyers (or sellers).

The public policy question is which groups of market participants, *if any,* are to receive governmentally sponsored advantages and disadvantages, not only in the subsidization or taxation of production but, also, in the creation of advantages or disadvantages in conducting negotiations.

At this juncture, it should be emphasized that I have argued, not that regulatory commissions are

undesirable, but that economic theory does not, at present, provide a justification for commissions insofar as they are based on the belief that observed concentration and monopoly price bear any necessary relationship.

Indeed, in utility industries, regulation has often been sought because of the inconvenience of competition. The history of regulation is often written in terms of the desire to prohibit "excessive" duplication of utility distribution systems and the desire to prohibit the capture of *windfall* gains by utility companies. Neither of these aspects of the utility business are necessarily related to scale economies. Let us first consider the problem of excessive duplication of facilities.

Duplication of Facilities. Communities and not individuals own or control most of the ground and air rights-of-way used by public utility distribution systems. The problem of excessive duplication of distribution systems is attributable to the failure of communities to set a proper price on the use of these scarce resources. The right to use publicly owned thoroughfares is the right to use a scarce resource. The absence of a price for the use of these resources, a price high enough to reflect the opportunity costs of such alternative uses as the servicing of uninterrupted traffic and unmarred views, will lead to their overutilization. The setting of an appropriate fee for the use of these resources would reduce the degree of duplication to optimal levels.

Consider that portion of the ground controlled by an individual and under which a *utility's* distribution system runs. Confront that individual with the option of service at a lower price from a company that is a rival to the present seller. The individual will take into consideration the cost to him of running a trench through his garden and the benefit to him of receiving the service at lower cost. There is no need for excessive duplication. Indeed, there is no need for any duplication of facilities if he selects the new service, provided that one of the two conditions holds. If the *individual* owns that part of the distribution system running under his ground he could tie it in to whatever trunk line serves him best; alternatively, once the new company wins his patronage, a rational solution to the use of that part of the distribution system would be for the utility company owning it to sell it to the utility company now serving the buyer.

There may be good reasons for using community property rather than private property to house the main trunk lines of some utility distribution systems. The placement of such systems under or over streets, alleyways, and sidewalks, resources already publicly owned (a fact taken as datum here), may be less costly than routing them through private property. The failure of communities to charge fees for the use of public property, fees that tend to prevent excessive use of this property, can be explained in three ways.

(1) There was a failure to understand the prerequisites for efficient resource use. Some public officer must be given the incentives to act as a rational conservator of resources when these resources are scarce.

(2) The disruption of thoroughfares was not, in fact, costly enough to bother about.

(3) The setting of fees to curtail excessive use of thoroughfares by utility companies was too costly to be practical.

The first two explanations, if true, give no support to an argument for regulating utility companies. The third explanation may give support to some sort of regulation, for it asserts that the economic effects that are produced by the placing of distribution systems are such that it is too costly to economize through the use of a price system. The costs of taking account of these effects through some regulatory process must be compared with the benefits of realigning resource use, and if the benefits are worth the costs some regulation may be desirable. Note clearly: scale economies in serving a market are not at issue. To see this, imagine that electrical distribution systems are thin lines of a special conducting paint. The placing of such systems causes no difficulties. They are sprayed over either public or private property. Nonetheless, suppose that the use of each system is subject to scale economies. Clearly, the desire to regulate cannot now be justified by such problems as traffic disruption, even though scale economies are present. "Excess" duplication is a problem of externalities and not of scale economies.

Let us suppose that it is desirable to employ some sort of regulation because it is too costly to use the price system to take account of the disruptive effects of placing distribution systems. Regulation comes in all sizes and shapes, and it is by no means clear what type of regulation would be most desirable.

A franchise system that allows only a limited number of utility companies to serve a market area was employed frequently. A franchise system that awarded the franchise to that company which seemed to offer the best price-quality package would be one that allowed market competition between bidding rivals to determine that package. The restraint of the market would be substituted for that of the regulatory commission.

An alternative arrangement would be public ownership of the distribution system. This would involve the collection of competing bids for installing the distribution system. The system could then be installed by the bidder offering to do the specified job at the lowest price. This is the same process used by communities to build highways and it employs rival bidding and not commissions to determine that price. The community could then allow its distribution system to be used by that utility company offering to provide specified utility services at lowest cost to residents. Again the market is substituted for the regulatory commission. Public ownership of streets may make public ownership of distribution systems seem desirable, but this does not mean that the use of regulatory commissions is desirable.

The Problem of Windfalls. We must now consider a last difficulty that has sometimes been marshalled to support the regulation of utilities. This argument is based on the fact that events in life are uncertain. The application of this observation to the utility business goes like this. After a buyer enters into an agreement with a utility company for supplying utility service, there may be changes in technology and prices that make the agreed upon price obsolete. In such cases, it is asserted, the price should be changed to reflect the current cost of providing utility services. The regulation by commission of prices on the basis of current costs is needed in the utilities industries because of the durability of original investments in plant and distribution systems. This durability prohibits the use of recontracting in the market place as a method for bringing about appropriate changes in price.

Problems of uncertainty create a potential for positive or negative windfalls. If market negotiations have misjudged the development of a better technology and if there is some cost to rewarding contracts to other producers once they are agreed upon, then an unexpected improvement in the technology used by those who are awarded the contracts may generate a price that is higher than per-unit cost, but higher by an amount no greater than the cost of rewarding contracts. In such cases, the firms now holding the contracts may collect a positive windfall for a short-run period. Or, if input prices increase by more than is expected, these same firms may suffer from a negative windfall. But the same thing is true of all markets. If a customer buys eggs today for consumption tomorrow, he will enjoy a positive windfall if the price of eggs is higher tomorrow and a negative windfall if the price is lower. The difference in the two cases is that, where long-term contracts are desirable, the windfalls may continue for longer periods. In such cases it *may* be desirable to employ a cost-plus regulatory scheme or to enter a clause that reserves the right, for some fee, to renegotiate the contract.

The problem faced here is what is the best way to cope with uncertainty. Long-term contracts for the supply of commodities are concluded satisfactorily in the market place without the aid of regulation. These contracts may be between retailers and appliance producers, or between the air lines and aircraft companies, all of whom may use durable production facilities. The rental of office space for ninety-nine years is fraught with uncertainty. I presume that the parties to a contract hire experts to provide relevant guesses on these matters and that the contract concluded resolves these issues in a way that is satisfactory to both parties. Penalties for reopening negotiations at a later date can be included in the contract. I presume that buyers and sellers who agree to contract with each other have handled the problem of uncertainty in a mutually satisfactory way. The correct way to view the problem is one of selecting the best type of contract. A producer may say, "if you agree to buy from me for twenty-five years, I can use facilities that are expected to produce the service at lower costs; if you contract five years, I will not invest much in tooling-up, and, hence, I will need a higher price to cover higher per-unit costs; of course, the longer-run contract allows more time for the unexpected, so let us include an escape clause of some kind." The buyer and seller must then agree on a suitable contract; durability of equipment and longer-term commitments can be sacrificed at the cost of higher per-unit costs, but there is no reason to expect that the concluded contract will be biased as to outcome or nonoptimal in other respects.

Cost-plus rate regulation is one way of coping with these problems, but it has great uncertainties of its own. Will the commission be effective? Does a well defined cost-plus arrangement create an inappropriate system of incentives to guide the firm in its investment and operating policies? Do the continual uncertainties associated with the meaning of cost-plus lead to otherwise avoidable difficulties in formulating investment plans? Rate regulation by commissions rather than by market rivalry may be more appropriate for utility industries than for other industries, but the truth of this assertion cannot be established deductively from existing economic theory. We do not know whether regulation handles the uncertainty-rent problem better or worse than the market.

The problem of coping with windfalls must be distinguished from the problem of *forecastable* rents. Suppose that it is known that buyers will incur considerable recontracting cost if they decide to change sellers after they are part way through an awarded contract. It would appear that the seller who wins the initial contract will be able to collect a rent as large as this recontracting cost. But this is not true if this recontracting cost is forecastable, that is, if it is not a windfall. The bidding for the initial contract will take account of the forecastable rent, so that if the bidding is competitive the rent will be forfeited by the lower bid prices to which it gives rise.

To what degree should legislation and regulation replace the market in the utilities or in other industries and what forms should such legislation take? It is not the objective of this paper to provide answers to such questions. My purpose has been to question the conventional economic arguments for the existing legislation and regulation. An expanded role for government can be defended on the empirical grounds of a documented general superiority of public administration in these industries or by a philosophical preference for mild socialism. But I do not see how a defense can be based on the formal arguments considered here; these arguments do not allow us to deduce from their assumptions either the monopoly problem or the administrative superiority of regulation.

In the case of utility industries, resort to the rivalry of the market place would relieve companies of the discomforts of commission regulation. But it would also relieve them of the comfort of legally protected market areas. It is my belief that the rivalry of the open market place disciplines more effectively than do the regulatory processes of the commission. If the managements of utility companies doubt this belief, I suggest that they re-examine the history of their industry to discover just who it was that provided most of the force behind the regulatory movement.

Antitrust Penalties and Attitudes Toward Risk: An Economic Analysis*

WILLIAM BREIT**
KENNETH G. ELZINGA**

William Breit (B.A., University of Texas at Austin, 1955; M.A., 1956; Ph.D., Michigan State University, 1961) is the E.M. Stevens Distinguished Professor of Economics at Trinity University in San Antonio, Texas. Born in 1933 in New Orleans, Louisiana, Professor Breit has served on the faculties of Louisiana State University and the University of Virginia at Charlottesville and is an Adjunct Scholar of the American Enterprise Institute. The author of numerous articles and books in both law and economics and the history of economic thought, including *Academic Scribblers* (with R. L. Ransom) and *The Anti-Trust Penalties: A Study in Law and Economics* (with K. G. Elzinga), Breit is president of the Southern Economic Association. Under the pseudonym of Marshall Jevons, he is co-author of two murder mysteries, *Murder at the Margin* and *The Fatal Equilibrium*.

Kenneth G. Elzinga (B.A., Kalamazoo College, 1963; M.A., Michigan State University, 1966; Ph.D., 1967) was born in Coopersville, Michigan, in 1941. He is Professor of Economics at the University of Virginia, where he has been on the faculty since 1967, except for leaves as Fellow in Law and Economics at the University of Chicago and Special Assistant Attorney General for Antitrust in the U.S. Department of Justice. Professor Elzinga is noted for his teaching of introductory economics and has published widely on antitrust issues, in major law reviews, and economics literature. He is a past president of the Industrial Organization Society and serves as a member of the Board of Editors of the Antitrust Bulletin. In addition, he is the other personality of Marshall Jevons.

*Reprinted from *Harvard Law Review* (vol. 86, 1973) by permission of the Harvard Law Review Association. Copyright 1973, pp. 693–713.
**The authors wish to thank Edgar K. Browning, James M. Buchanan, W. P. Culbertson, Jr., Thomas F. Hogarty, Roger Sherman and Gordon Tullock for their helpful comments. The authors also received helpful suggestions from Warren Schwartz of the University of Virginia Law School and Joel Davidow and B. Barry Grossman of the Antitrust Division of the Department of Justice.

Within the past decade, the tools of economic analysis have been increasingly applied to areas outside the traditional focus of economic scrutiny. Such applications have been particularly useful in analyzing current methods of controlling and deterring criminal activities.[1] Thus far, however, no one has systematically applied modern economic theory to an analysis of the penalties for antitrust violations.[2] This article will attempt to remedy this deficiency by applying economic theory to an examination of the deterrent value of current federal antitrust policies and penalties;[3] as will be shown, this application is especially called for in light of the changing attitudes

toward risk of American corporate management. After identifying the currently used deterrent mechanisms and some of their costs, we shall demonstrate the importance of determining management's attitude toward risk to the development of efficient antitrust enforcement. Then, on the basis of some conclusions we shall draw as to the attitudes of present day corporate managers toward risk, we shall put forth specific proposals for reform consistent with the implications of our economic analysis.

I. ALTERNATIVE MEANS OF DETERRENCE

Under the current federal statutory framework, the judiciary can impose on antitrust violators four kinds of penalties, all of which have the potential to deter future monopolistic behavior:[4] 1) the payment of fines to the Government;[5] 2) the payment of treble damages to injured parties;[6] 3) imprisonment;[7] and 4) an order directing corporate dissolution.[8] By affecting the probability of violations being detected, a fifth factor, the intensity with which antitrust laws are enforced and with which violations are investigated, also has a potentially significant impact on the level of deterrence.

In our attempt to identify an optimum mix of deterrent mechanisms, we shall immediately eliminate from consideration the alternatives of heavy reliance on either imprisonment or dissolution. The provisions for imprisonment in the Sherman Act historically have been applied primarily to business racketeers, labor union leaders, and suspected spies.[9] The infrequency with which incarceration has been im-

---

[1]The work of Gary Becker in this area has been particularly outstanding. *See* Becker, *Crime and Punishment: An Economic Approach,* 76 J. Pol. Econ. 169 (1968). *See also* Schelling, *Economic Analysis and Organized Crime,* in The President's Commission on Law Enforcement and Administration of Justice, Task Force Report: Organized Crime 114 (1967). The earliest work relating economics to law is that of Cesare Beccaria in *Dei Delitti e Delle Pene,* published in 1764. Jeremy Bentham as well must be considered a precursor of those currently applying economic analysis to legal problems. *See* J. Bentham, The Theory of Legislation (1931 ed.).

[2]Until now, most studies of the operation of the antitrust laws have been more empirical than theoretical in nature. *See, e.g.,* Adams, *Dissolution, Divorcement, Divestiture: The Pyrrhic Victories of Antitrust,* 27 Ind. L.J. 1 (1951); Elzinga, *The Antimerger Law: Pyrrhic Victories?,* 12 J. Law & Econ. 43 (1969); Stigler, *The Economic Effects of the Antitrust Laws,* 9 J. Law & Econ. 225 (1966). Those few analyses that have been theoretical have not been directed at the issue of the comparative efficiency of the available antitrust deterrent mechanisms. Oliver Williamson's efforts to apply economic theory to the antitrust area have been restricted to the problems of economies of scale in antimerger cases, *see* Williamson, *Economies as an Antitrust Defense: The Welfare Tradeoffs,* 58 Am. Econ. Rev. 18 (1968), and of applying § 2 of the Sherman Act to cases of structural dominance. *See* Williamson, *Dominant Firms and the Monopoly Problem: Market Failure Considerations,* 85 Harv. L. Rev. 1512 (1972). Richard A. Posner's work has used economic analysis to argue that the Antitrust Division of the Department of Justice should direct its resources only at those practices that most clearly reduce economic output. *See* Posner, *A Program for the Antitrust Division,* 38 U. Chi. L. Rev. 500 (1971).

[3]Our focusing on the deterrent as opposed to the compensatory effect of antitrust penalties reflects our strong belief that it is largely from the deterrent viewpoint that these penalties should be evaluated. It is true that legal scholars have disagreed as to whether the primary legislative purpose in enacting the antitrust penalties was to deter future violations or to compensate injured parties. However, at least from the perspective of economics, the deterrent arguments seem much the more appealing. The party who is injured by monopolistic behavior is not just a given individual but rather society as a whole. By misallocating resources, monopoly causes too few goods to be produced and thereby directs scarce resources into the production of commodities that are less valuable. In this way the real income of all of society is reduced. Only to the extent that antitrust violations are deterred can such income losses be avoided.

[4]In our analysis, "monopolistic" or "anticompetitive" activity will refer to any behavior on the part of businessmen which causes price to diverge from marginal cost.

[5]*E.g.,* 15 U.S.C. §§ 1-2 (1970).

[6]15 U.S.C. § 15 (1970).

[7]*E.g.,* 15 U.S.C. §§ 1-2 (1970).

[8]The federal courts are authorized to "prevent and restrain" antitrust violations. 15 U.S.C. § 4 (1970). This power has for many years been interpreted broadly to allow the courts to "dissolve" illegal combinations. *See* Standard Oil Co. v. United States, 221 U.S. I, 78 (1911) (requiring the Standard Oil monopoly to divest itself of interests in numerous other companies).

[9]W. Hamilton & I. Till, Antitrust in Action 78–79 (TNEC Monograph No. 16, 1941). In the first five decades of the Sherman Act, only one "respectable man of business [went] to jail." *Id.* at 79. The first jail sentence for "pure" pricefixing was not imposed until the late 1950's. Even since then, only a small number of business conspirators have received nonsuspended jail sentences. Posner, *A Statistical Study of Antitrust Enforcement,* 13 J. Law & Econ. 365, 389–91 (1970).

posed on "simple" antitrust violators in itself may reflect a wholly appropriate judicial skepticism toward the efficacy of using imprisonment to deter monopolistic behavior.[10] The very high societal costs that would accompany an expanded use of the imprisonment alternative—costs in the form of guards, wardens, psychologists, probation officers, and violators' time—are excessive,[11] in view of the availability, discussed below, of a much more efficient deterrent alternative.

Several factors compel us to reject as well any expanded use of corporate dissolution orders as a means of deterring antitrust violations. First, empirically it appears that even when called for in court orders, comprehensive implementation of meaningful structural reorganization seldom occurs.[12] This enforcement failure can be traced to the dynamics of the enforcement bureaus themselves. The difficult task of physically unscrambling a business firm may be of peripheral institutional importance to an agency judged primarily by the number of cases it files and wins. In these bureaus the consummate goal is to win the antitrust case; after the victory, the trial lawyers—those people most familiar with the case—leave the implementation of relief to those who may see little gain to themselves from the use of the corporate scalpel. With little effective post-trial monitoring by the judiciary, the line of least resistance for bureau officials is to be conciliatory rather than aggressive toward those business managers with whom the detailed implementation of a court order must be negotiated.

A second reason for rejecting dissolution as an antitrust deterrent is simply that it is not so used in the present enforcement framework. Dissolution is generally employed only in civil antitrust suits involving mergers or single firm monopolies where, at least as a formal matter, it is seen as a remedy for an anticompetitive structural situation; its purpose is not deterrence. For example, in the recent ITT consent decree, most of the assets originally listed in the Government's complaint remained untouched by the settlement. One of the reasons given by former Antitrust Division chief Richard McLaren was the divestiture of those assets would adversely affect ITT's stock prices and therefore penalize its shareholders.[13]

Finally, as with incarceration, dissolution, if used extensively, would employ excessive amounts of scarce judicial and administrative resources. Although dissolution represents a deterrent in the sense that few potential cartelists would overlook the risk that monopolistic behavior might carry with it the penalty of breaking up their firms, the costs it imposes make other deterrent alternatives far more attractive. Only when highly significant remedial benefits (in addition to deterrent benefits) can be gained from corporate surgery should dissolution be used.

With imprisonment and dissolution being inappropriate deterrent tools, Congress can best deter anticompetitive behavior by manipulating the three remaining variables. For instance, heavier reliance could be placed on the enforcement budget: the probability of any given antitrust violator being apprehended and convicted could be raised by increasing the amount of resources devoted to the detection of such behavior. This would involve expanding the budgets of the Antitrust Division of the Department of Justice and the Federal Trade Commission. Such an approach has recently been recommended both by an antitrust study group led by Ralph Nader[14] and by a former director of the Federal Trade Commission's Bureau of Economics.[15]

A second option, one recommended by President Nixon's Task Force on Productivity and Competition,[16] would be to increase the fine for anticompetitive behavior and thereby place heavier reliance on that variable. Some members of Congress, too, have been attracted to this alternative. Senator Hart has recommended legislation which would raise the maximum fine for a Sherman Act violation from $50,000 per count to $500,000.[17]

Finally, the amount of reparations paid to injured private parties could be increased and could play a greater role in antitrust deterrence. This could be

---

[10]Of course, it also reflects a societal judgment that antitrust violators do not deserve the moral reprobation of the criminal law.

[11]These costs have moved Gary Becker to argue that institutionalization should seldom be used to penalize *any* criminal offenses. Becker, *supra* note 1, at 193–98.

[12]M. Goldberg, The Consent Decree: Its Formulation and Use (1962); Adams, *supra* note 2, at 33; Elzinga, *supra* note 2, at 46–53.

[13]S. Exec. Rep. No. 92-19, 92d Cong., 2d Sess., pt. 4, at 60 (1972).

[14]M. Green, The Closed Enterprise System 129-30 (Nader Study Group Report) (1972). The study group recommended an increase from the Division's "absurdly low" present budget of approximately $12 million to "at least $100 million." *Id.* at 122, 129–30.

[15]W. Mueller, A Primer on Monopoly and Competition 177 (1970).

[16]2 Antitrust L. & Econ. Rev. 13, 33 (1969) (statement of George Stigler).

[17]*See* M. Green, *supra* note 14, at 171.

done through a shift from treble to quadruple or quintuple damages.[18] The same effect could of course be achieved by easing the plaintiff's tasks in private antitrust suits in any of a number of ways: by further expanding the rules of standing;[19] by extending the statute of limitations on private actions;[20] by reducing standards of proof of damages;[21] or by further facilitating the initiation of class actions.[22]

From the point of view of the businessman, the choice between heavy reliance on fines and heavy reliance on reparations involves a distinction without a difference; the businessman is largely indifferent between paying a dollar to an individual in reparations and paying a dollar to the Government in fines. The *societal* costs of the two alternatives, however, are not the same. While the imposition of fines is not costless, as we shall see, still the costs of a fine-imposing procedure are considerably less than those associated with a private damage reparations action. In stark contrast to a deterrent system relying on fines, a reparations system demands the expenditure of real resources in the determination and allocation of the damages themselves. In addition, as now constituted, the reparations system involves resource consuming mechanisms of private pleadings and discovery, joinder, class actions, multidistrict litigation, and all the other paraphernalia of private damage actions.[23]

Moreover, only in a fine system will the Govern-

ment be able closely to control the degree to which costly resources are devoted to the enforcement of antitrust legislation. A governmental decision to increase or decrease society's expenditures on the detection of violations and the imposition of penalties against them can be most effectively implemented only when the Government actually controls the mechanisms which initiate enforcement. In a fine-oriented system, the Government initiates enforcement activity; in a reparations-oriented system, private parties, concerned not with efficient deterrence of violations but rather with their own individual welfare, initiate the expenditure of both their own and the Government's resources in enforcement activities. With dollar amounts of penalties held constant, then, it appears that a fine system is less costly and more efficient than a reparations system.[24]

From a more philosophical standpoint as well, we should note that private antitrust suits are undesirable. They have been seen as a type of vigilante justice wholly inappropriate for governing the business sector. Thurman Arnold, although himself an unquestionably staunch proponent of the regulation of anticompetitive behavior, nevertheless argued forcefully that private enforcement leads to a disrespect for the institution of law and "can only be justified as a transitory necessity to meet an emergency situation."[25]

We are left then with the question of whether heavy reliance on fines or heavy reliance on the enforcement budget would be likely to provide the more efficient means to effect antitrust deterrence. Of course, the answer to this question depends on the respective costs involved, costs which will be noted at a later point in our analysis. However, the answer obviously depends as well on the relative benefits from trying to deter monopolistic behavior by relying heavily on enforcement or by relying heavily on fines. This relation in turn is a function of the attitudes of the businessman toward risk. Consequently, it is now appropriate to examine the meaning of risk preference as it relates to managerial behavior.

[18] The treble damage action was made a part of the Sherman Act only in the late stages of its drafting. Senator Sherman's original bill called for double damages. It was Senator Hoar's revision that increased the multiple to three. H. Thorelli, The Federal Antitrust Policy 191, 213 (1954).

[19] *See* Comment, *Standing to Sue for Treble Damages Under Section 4 of the Clayton Act,* 64 Colum. L. Rev. 570 (1964); 82 Harv. L. Rev. 1374 (1969).

[20] *See* W. Erickson, Dissolution and Private Damages in Private Antitrust (no date), at 6 (unpublished paper on file at the *Harvard Law Review*). Erickson cites the present statute of limitations as one of the reasons for the ineffectiveness of private damage suits.

[21] *See* Rowley, *Proof of Damages in Antitrust Cases,* 32 Antitrust L.J. 75 (1966).

[22] *See* Comment, *Appealability of a Class Action Dismissal: The 'Death Knell' Doctrine,* 39 U. Chi. L. Rev. 403 (1972); 86 Harv. L. Rev. 438 (1972), *noting* Hackett v. General Host Corp., 455 F.2d 618 (3d Cir.), *cert. denied,* 407 U.S. 925 (1972).

[23] Private antitrust suits are at the heart of the recent increase in antitrust litigation; the number of these suits has more than tripled in the past decade. 1971 Annual Rep. of the Director of the Adm. Office of the U.S. Courts 185 (1972). More to the point, the disproportionate amount of judicial and litigative resources consumed by antitrust cases is evidenced by the high time study weight assigned them by the Administrative Office of the U.S. Courts. *See id.* at 174, 312.

[24] Of course, compensatory as well as deterrent benefits would be reaped from a reparations-oriented system. However, as indicated in note 3 *supra,* we feel that alternative antitrust enforcement systems should be evaluated far more on the basis of their deterrent than their compensatory impact.

[25] T. Arnold, The Bottlenecks of Business 166 (1940). Arnold felt that "[p]rivate enforcement of *any* public law will make of it an instrument detached from its real purpose." *Id.* (emphasis in original).

II. RISK PREFERENCE AND ANTITRUST POLICY

An illustration comparing a given large loss with a given smaller loss will prove instructive in clarifying the meaning of risk preference. Assume that the large loss is ten times the smaller loss. The expected value of these two losses is said to be equal if the probability of the occurrence of the small loss is ten times as great as that of the large loss. However, although the expected values are the same, individuals may have different expected disutilities from these losses depending upon their attitudes toward risk. The risk averse person will prefer the large probability of the small loss to the small probability of the large loss. The risk preferrer, on the other hand, will prefer the small probability of the large loss to the larger probability of the smaller loss. More technically, for the risk averse person the disutility of the larger loss is more than ten times as great as the disutility of the smaller loss. For the risk preferrer, the larger loss disutility is less than ten times that of the smaller loss.

Let us apply this risk attitude analysis to our antitrust policy problem of choosing between a primarily fine-oriented and a primarily detection-oriented deterrence system. Assume that the enforcement agencies are considering two alternative proposals. The first calls for both the imposition of a higher fine on convicted antitrust violators and a reduction in the amount of resources going into detection and conviction. The second calls for reducing the financial penalties, but also for increasing the resources devoted to enforcement, thereby causing an increase in the probability of detection and conviction. Let us assume further that the high financial penalty is ten times the lower penalty, but that because of the difference in the quantity of resources devoted to enforcement, the probability of being required to pay the lower penalty is ten times as great as the probability of being required to pay the high penalty. On these assumptions, the expected value of monopoly profits under either proposal is the same. The businessman's expected utility from antitrust violations, however, will vary depending upon his attitude toward risk. The risk averse manager's attitudes will lead him to collude more under the policy involving the larger probability of paying the smaller financial penalty. The risk preferrer, on the other hand, will collude more under the proposal involving the smaller probability of the large penalty.

The indifference maps of Fig. 1 provide graphic illustration of the attitudes of both a risk preferrer and a risk averter. On the horizontal axes of Panels A and B we measure the probability of detection and conviction of antitrust violations. On the vertical axes we measure fines paid when the firm is apprehended and convicted of restraints of trade.[26] In contrast to

[26] The magnitude of fines is independent of the probability of conviction and detection. Congress could increase the fines and not vote any additional resources to the enforcement agencies; furthermore, increased fines provide no significant inducement to private parties either to prosecute or to inform the Government of antitrust violations.

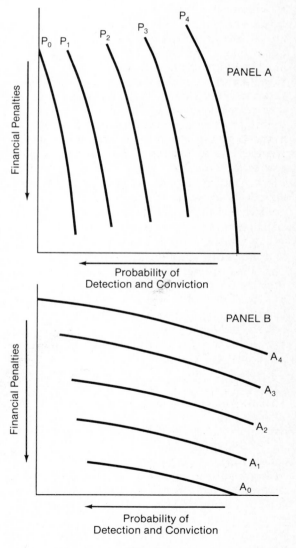

Fig. 1

relative magnitudes under the usual construction of such diagrams, the magnitudes measured on each axis become *smaller* as we move away from the origin. The indifference curves depicted shall be called "iso-expected utility" curves. They show for a given businessman combinations of antitrust policies associated with a particular expected utility from monopoly profits. A movement along any curve indicates the amount by which a decrease in the use of one policy instrument must be compensated by an increase in employment of the other instrument in order for a given businessman to maintain a given degree of utility from monopolistic activity. As the businessman moves out to higher iso-expected utility curves—that is, as he moves further away from the origin—the greater satisfaction which he can achieve from monopoly profits will encourage him to engage in more anticompetitive behavior.

In Panel A, we depict the case in which the manager is a risk preferrer. His indifference curves indicate that a relatively small reduction in the probability of apprehension and conviction must be compensated by a relatively large increase in financial penalties in order for him to maintain any given degree of expected utility from his monopolistic behavior. Precisely the opposite attitude is depicted in Panel B. There we see a case of a risk averse manager in which a relatively large reduction in the probability of detection and conviction needs to be compensated by only a relatively small increase in penalties in order to maintain any given expected utility.

The implications of attitudes toward risk for antitrust policy can be illustrated by superimposing the expected utility indifference curves of the risk preferrer (the curves depicted as P) on those of the risk averter (the curves depicted as A). This is done in Fig. 2. Let us assume that in terms of current expenditures of societal resources, antitrust policy places us at point Q, where the A_3 indifference curve of the risk averter cuts curve P_3 of the risk preferrer. The line KL passes through point Q and is drawn as an iso-expected value curve. By definition, any movement along KL leaves constant the expected value of the monopolist's profits, with any change in the financial penalty exactly compensated in terms of expected value by an opposite change in the probability of detection and conviction. The iso-expected value curve, a rectangular hyperbola, also represents the iso-expected utility curve of a risk-neutral businessman, a businessman who has no preference, say, between a ten percent probability of a \$10 loss and a

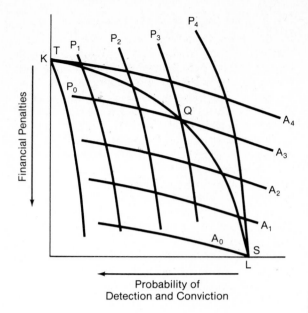

Fig. 2

100 percent probability of a \$1 loss. KL can thus be thought of as the line that divides risk preference from risk aversion. The slopes of iso-expected utility curves at each point of intersection with KL are greater or less than the slope of KL, depending upon whether they represent risk preferrers or risk averters.

If we were to start at point Q on KL and were to allow both P and A to design any antitrust policy they wished, with the only constraint being that the expected value of their monopoly profits would have to remain constant, we would expect each businessman to travel up or down the iso-expected value curve KL until he reached his highest iso-expected utility indifference curve. In our diagram, the risk averter reaches his highest indifference curve at point T, while the risk preferrer reaches his highest expected utility at point S. Point T represents relatively low monetary losses with a high likelihood of detection, while point S represents relatively high losses with a low probability of detection.

Of course, in reality both risk averse and risk loving managers must adjust their behavior to the same antitrust policy. We cannot allow them to choose the combination they each prefer under the constraint of a specific expected value of monopoly profits. With an initial policy placing them both at point Q, we can see that a new policy which would place them both at point S would move the risk preferrer to a higher indifference curve than he was on at point Q, but would move the risk averter to a lower curve than *he* was on at point Q. This means that by moving to point S the expected utility of the risk lover would rise relative to that of the risk averter. The risk preferrer would engage in or "demand" more anticompetitive collusion, boycotts, mergers, and the like while the risk averter would "demand" less. Put another way, the risk averter at point S will choose business practices and policies which involve less monopolistic activity because such activity offers him less expected utility. The risk preferrer, on the other hand, will engage in more monopolistic activity. He will receive more satisfaction from his monopoly profits when the probability of detection is low and the financial penalties high.

With any given antitrust enforcement policy, then, the degree of monopoly in the economy depends on whether managerial classes consist mainly of risk preferrers or risk averters. Changes in the risk attitudes of the managing classes may demand corresponding changes in antitrust policies. It is therefore highly pertinent to examine how risk attitudes of American business management have developed since the enactment of the Sherman Act in the late nineteenth century.[27]

III. THE PSYCHOLOGY OF MANAGERS AND ITS IMPLICATIONS FOR ANTITRUST POLICY

There is considerable evidence that today's business management is distinctly more cautious than its late nineteenth century counterpart; furthermore, this movement to risk aversion appears to be centered in the nation's oligopolies, those firms most subject to antitrust scrutiny. Joseph Schumpeter and Robert Aaron Gordon were among the earliest observers of this attitudinal change.[28] Schumpeter's sweeping description of the very success of capitalism smothering and making obsolete the entrepreneurial spirit dovetails with Gordon's careful investigation of large en-

terprise management. Gordon argued that the desire for security is "[v]ery probably . . . stronger among the leading executives of large and mature concerns that it was among an earlier generation of 'big' businessmen. . . ."[29]

Since Schumpeter's and Gordon's observations, other economists have also argued convincingly that the American economy has experienced a sharp increase in business prudence in recent decades. Both Robin Marris and John Kenneth Galbraith contend that control of large enterprises has passed from the individualistic entrepreneur to the organization-minded, group-oriented manager who is highly concerned with minimizing risk and uncertainty.[30] In the Galbraith-Marris corporate world, concern for individual and corporate security acts as an overriding constraint on desires for growth and profits:[31]

> Today, when one young executive describes another as a "good businessman," more often than not he does not mean . . . a man with a good nose for profits, but rather a man who keeps his records in order, his staff contented, his contacts active and his pipelines filled; . . . not rash, but not suffering from indecision; a good committee man who knows both when to open his mouth and when to keep it shut.

The use of complex decision theory and organization theory has led other economists similarly to conclude that contemporary management wishes to avoid risk and uncertainty.[32] These analysts portray a hired management interested not solely in maximizing profits but rather in pursuing a variety of goals; they describe a management geared to "homeostatic" business conduct rather than impetuous, swashbuckling strategies. According to many economists, then, the risk attitudes of contemporary man-

---

[27]In enacting the Sherman Act, Congress in all likelihood did not explicitly or implicitly consider the risk attitudes of American businessmen. The legislative history indicates that such matters were at best peripheral to the consideration of the legislation. *Cf.* H. Thorrelli, *supra* note 18. Nevertheless, as we have shown above, the ultimate effectiveness of the antitrust laws is in fact intimately related to management's attitudes toward risk.

[28]R. Gordon, Business Leadership in the Large Corporation 271–351 (1945); J. Schumpeter, Capitalism, Socialism, and Democracy 121–63 (3d ed. 1950).

[29]R. Gordon, *supra* note 28, at 283. *See also id.* at 310–11.

[30]J. Galbraith, The New Industrial State 11–178 (2d ed. 1971); R. Marris, The Economic Theory of "Managerial" Capitalism 1–109, 204–88 (1964).

[31]R. Marris, *supra* note 30, at 57–58. Galbraith's description is consistent: These characteristics [of individualistic entrepreneurial behavior] are not readily reconciled with the requirements of the technostructure. Not indifference but sensitivity to others, not individualism but accommodation to organization, not competition but intimate and continuing cooperation are the prime requirements for group action. . . . The assertion of competitive individualism . . . to the extent that it is still encountered, is ceremonial, traditional or a manifestation of personal vanity and . . . self delusion. J. Galbraith, *supra* note 30, at 92–93.

[32]*See, e.g.,* K. Boulding, A Reconstruction of Economics 26–38 (1950); R. Cyert & J. March, A Behavioral Theory of the Firm, 118–19 (1963); Simon, *Theories of Decision-Making in Economics and Behavioral Science,* 49 Am. Econ. Rev. 253 (1959).

agement are well summarized by Sir J. R. Hicks' early observation: "The best of all . . . profits is a quiet life."[33]

Economists have been joined by observers from other disciplines in noticing the changed risk attitude of contemporary management. William Whyte has argued that the displacement of the Protestant Ethic by the Social Ethic has led to the professionalization of management, strict pressures to conform, and constraints on individual expression.[34] Political scientist Antony Jay has compared the large corporation with the large state, arguing that both generate strong pressures to maintain the status quo. Jay believes that any risky moves that are made by today's management are aberrations, atypical phenomena having little connection with the risk attitudes of management at large.[35]

Observers find, then, that modern enterprise lacks the Carnegies, Fricks and Firestones of an earlier era. Such entrepreneurs have been displaced by a gradual evolution propelled by factors such as increasing education; changes in the social environment of business; the steady separation of ownership from control in large corporate enterprises; the "technique orientation" and conformity that seem to characterize business education; and perhaps the very nature of bureaucracy itself. In terms of our earlier analysis, these factors have caused the risk preferrers of the late nineteenth century to become the risk avoiders of the 1970's.

The implications of this attitudinal change for antitrust policy are clear. Policy designers should be highly sensitive to this change in risk attitude, realizing in line with our earlier analysis that a risk averse management is more likely to be deterred by high financial penalties than by a high probability of detection and conviction with accompanying penalties not severe. Thus, in the framework of current attitudes toward risk, the deterrent benefits of a policy of raised fines far outweigh the deterrent benefits of expending additional enforcement resources.

IV. POTENTIAL OBJECTIONS TO RAISING FINES

Even given the relative deterrent benefits of increasing fines as opposed to increasing enforcement

efforts, potential objections to a fine-oriented system still remain. First, it could be argued that judges and juries would be substantially less likely to convict a violator if such a conviction demanded a significantly higher fine. If this is true, a fine increase, even if enforcement efforts remained constant, would result in a decrease in the proportion of antitrust violators who are convicted. The decrease, the argument would assert, would result in the reduction of moral inhibitions against engaging in anticompetitive behavior and, as a consequence, would produce an increase in antitrust violations, even if management is risk averse and therefore initially inclined to avoid *any* flirtation with the increased penalties. This objection to a system based on higher fines rests on the belief that the moral, educative force of law is critical in influencing behavior and that to the extent that punishment occurs less frequently, that moral force is weakened.[36] Punishment, it is argued, greatly reinforces society's condemnation of inappropriate behavior. Hence, according to this argument, high fines which are seldom imposed would lead in the long run to more, rather than less, monopolistic behavior because the moral inhibitions against such behavior would be weakened.

However convincing this initial objection to a fine-oriented system appears at first glance, on closer examination it has two critical weaknesses. First, it is far from inevitable that statutory provisions for higher fines, even if mandatory, would impel judges and juries to punish fewer antitrust violators. Legislation which increased fines while eliminating private damage suits, for example, would clearly show that Congress intended the fine increase to be comprehensively implemented; this demonstrated intent could be expected to influence judges and even juries. Judges and juries would probably have a greater tendency to fine antitrust violations when assured that private treble damage actions would not follow. Furthermore, judges and perhaps juries could be expected to recognize that with relatively fewer investigative resources devoted to punishing anticompetitive behavior, fines would now carry a greater deterrent burden.

Second, even if one ignores the real possibility that the increased moral inhibitions accompanying heightened financial penalties may in themselves compensate for the moral inhibitions lost by a de-

---

[33]Hicks, *Annual Survey of Economic Theory: The Theory of Monopoly*, 3 Econometrica 1, 8 (1935).

[34]W. Whyte, The Organization Man 18–22 (1956).

[35]A. Jay, Management and Machiavelli (1967) (see especially 189–98).

[36]*See, e.g.,* Andenaes, *General Prevention—Illusion or Reality?*, 43 J. Crim. L. & Police Sci. 176 (1952).

crease in the frequency of enforcement, the moral force argument is not a persuasive one. It assumes that the decision to engage in unlawful behavior is made largely on the basis of an individual's personal moral code. We believe, on the contrary, that, at least in the area of antitrust deterrence, the attitude of managers toward risk is far more important than any of their moral attitudes, and that antitrust policy will be more effective in deterring illegal behavior if it takes more account of the former than the latter. In consequence, a fine-oriented system would produce less, rather than more, monopolistic behavior. Until attitudes of business management toward risk change, there is no reason to expect that these risk averse managers would ever return to their former monopolistic practices once fines were raised. With less monopolistic behavior prevalent in society, surely the moral inhibitions against such behavior—and perhaps against all illegal behavior—would be reinforced, rather than weakened.

A second potential objection to an increase in fines is that the costs of such an increase would be greater than the costs of an increase in enforcement efforts. The increased expenditure of scarce judicial and administrative resources which would inevitably accompany a system in which the enforcement of antitrust laws was intensified would of course be unnecessary in a system which relied simply on imposition of heavy fines once convictions were attained. However, other less tangible costs might accompany an increase in fines. First, such an increase might augment the sense of inequity fostered by a system which penalized some but not all violators. The equity in an after-the-fact sense (*ex post* equity) involved whenever some violators of a law are punished and others allowed to go free decreases as the potential punishment increases. However, to achieve complete *ex post* equity in antitrust enforcement would entail the apprehension and punishment of *all* lawbreakers, an employment of resources that would clearly be too costly from the point of view of economic efficiency. At some point a balance must be struck. The crucial question is: how much is society willing to give up to achieve *ex post* equity?

The answer to this question should be at least partially determined by the amount of equity in the before-the-fact sense (*ex ante* equity)[37] that exists in

the system under examination. Whatever the *ex post* equity in a fine-oriented system, the *ex ante* equity in such a system is potentially close to perfect. Each risk preferrer who cold-bloodedly decides to violate the law and enter a cartel could be made to have the same probability of being caught as anyone else. In terms of the Government's enforcement efforts, each individual violator could have an equal chance of actually paying the fine. So long as the chances of being detected are equalized at the start under a clear set of rules, perfect *ex ante* equity can prevail. The existence of this almost perfect *ex ante* equity combined with the high costs of achieving additional *ex post* equity would seem to indicate that a high fine system would not unduly disturb the society's general sense of relative equity.

Other costs of an increase in fines may, however, be more significant. First, wholly apart from notions of *relative* equity, it may be that a high fine, if it represents a sum far in excess of the amount of damage done by a given antitrust violation, will unduly infringe on society's sense of *absolute* equity. Furthermore, extremely high fines could cause the collapse of businesses which at least have the potential of making substantial contributions to the national economy.

Both of these costs, however, rather than demanding that fines not be raised at all, simply indicate that there is some ceiling above which fines should not go. At least as applied to many American businesses, the current fine structure certainly does not exceed that ceiling. The Sherman Act's maximum $50,000 fine is a pittance for many violators, threatening neither society's sense of absolute equity nor the violating company's existence. Nevertheless, the fact that there is a fine level beyond which marginal costs begin to be greater than marginal benefits should be kept in mind in designing a specific proposal for a fine-oriented system.

V. THE FINE: A SPECIFIC PROPOSAL

It should be clear from this discussion that the same absolute monetary exaction should not be set by statute for every antitrust violator.[38] An absolute fine level that might be an enormous deterrent for small firms might not deter larger firms from anticompetitive activity. What we are seeking is a fine

[37]The distinction between *ex ante* and *ex post* equity is that of Mark V. Pauly and Thomas D. Willett. *See* Pauly & Willett, *Two Concepts of Equity and Their Implications for Public Policy,* 53 Social Sci. Q. 8 (1972).

[38]As noted at p. 697 *supra,* Senator Hart has advocated that the maximum Sherman Act fine be raised from $50,000 per count to $500,000. His proposal, it should be noted, does not envision the elimination of private damage suits.

that is large enough in the case of each individual firm to make its management unlikely to violate the antitrust laws, but which is not so large as to cause a violator to go out of business or to offend our sense of absolute equity. Thus, we must think in terms of fines based on proportions rather than absolute amounts. These proportions should be of such a size, and applied in such a way, that the resultant fine would "hurt" each firm just enough to deter a risk averse manager.

Four possible measures of a firm's "ability to pay" come to mind. In the application of the first standard, managerial salaries, fines would be assessed against the managers themselves. With the other three alternative measures—sales, assets, and profits—the fines would be assessed against the violating firms.

Levying fines on managers themselves would not be without advantages. While economists are no longer highly prone to emphasize the separation of ownership and control in large corporations, it is still the case that some managers' actions may be insulated from stockholder control and reprisals. These managers may not be as much deterred by a potential fine on their companies' sales, assets, or profits as by the prospect of losing a percentage of their own salaries. Consequently, there is a great temptation to fine directly the businessman engaged in the illegal activity. Indeed, one of the proffered purposes of the Clayton Act was to enable punishment to be applied to the source of the violation.[39] If accomplished, this would seem not only to effectuate solid deterrence but also to constitute an equitable incidence of the fine. A manager willfully engaging in anticompetitive behavior should not be able to use a corporate shield to escape punishment.

Two factors, however, persuade us to reject levying a proportional fine upon managerial salaries. First, the task of clearly identifying those responsible for anticompetitive behavior, especially in large cor-

porations, might be excessively difficult to accomplish;[40] managers would be encouraged to develop very subtle methods of concealing the origins of anticompetitive behavior so that responsibility for the behavior could not be traced to them. A fine based on salaries could thus fall on those not responsible for the illegal activity. Indeed, judges, unsure that imposed fines would fall on the real violators, might be reluctant to impose fines high enough actually to deter; and convictions might be fewer if such fines were mandatory.

Second, the gains to be had from anticompetitive behavior are frequently so large relative to the salaries of the managers involved that boards of directors would find it tempting to arrange for hidden side payments as "bribes" to management to engage in violations of the antitrust laws. With potentially huge rewards for anticompetitive action, even a 100 percent fine on salaries would constitute a small amount relative to the potential monopoly gains to the firm; the existence of such potential "gains from trade" would clearly invite the development of means to circumvent the fine structure. Thus, although in an abstract sense levying fines on managers' salaries would unquestionably be an effective deterrent, practical problems of implementation would seem to dictate that the use of such a standard be rejected.

We turn, therefore, to the alternative standards which impose fines on the violating firms themselves. The sales figure standard has the advantage of being the least susceptible to illegal manipulation. This fact indeed may have led a recent study group to recommend that violations of the Sherman Act be punished by fines equal to a percentage of the violator's sales.[41] However, the benefits of using a sales standard are more than offset by the disproportionately

---

[39]In his message to Congress of January 20, 1914, in which he proposed new antitrust legislation, President Wilson said:
   . . . we ought to see to it . . . that penalties and punishments should fall not upon business itself, to its confusion and interruption, but upon the individuals who use the instrumentalities of business to do things which public policy and sound business practice condemn. Every act of business is done at the command or upon the initiative of some ascertainable person or group of persons. These should be held individually responsible, and the punishment should fall upon them, not upon the business organization of which they make illegal use.
   51 Cong. Rec. 1963 (1914).

[40]Reflecting on his hearings on the electrical equipment cartel of the late 1950's, Senator Estes Kefauver wrote:
   [I]t has been found that many times, top corporate executives "wink" at criminal antitrust violations going on right under their noses. Rather than assure that the antitrust laws were being obeyed by their subordinates, such executives take great pains to make certain they have no "knowledge" of any illegal activities. Press Release of Senator Estes Kefauver, July 13, 1961, quoted in Note, *Increasing Community Control over Corporate Crime—A Problem in the Law of Sanctions,* 71 Yale L.J. 280, 303 n.71 (1961). *See also id.* at 297, 302.
[41]M. Green, *supra* note 14, at 175. The basic proposal of this Nader study group was a fine ranging from 1% to 10% of the violating firm's sales (during the time of the violation) for the first offense and 5% to 10% of sales for a second violation with a five year period.

heavy impact that a fine on sales would have upon some firms. Firms with low profits/sales ratios would be hurt far more than those with high profits/sales ratios. In fact, a percentage fine in the 1 to 5 percent of sales range that could cause a retailing firm with a high inventory turnover to go out of business might be easily endured by many manufacturing firms. The deterrent value, equity, and destructive potential of a fine based on sales, then, would fluctuate so widely with the character of the violating firm that the sales standard should be rejected.

Basing the fine on assets would of course produce the same problem of widely varying impacts. On committing identical offenses, firms with low profits/assets ratios would in effect pay greater fines than firms with high ratios. Fines more than adequate to deter anticompetitive behavior in manufacturing firms (in which there is large investment in durable capital) might not dissuade the management of retailing or other merchandising enterprises with relatively few assets. In addition, the fact that varying depreciation methods in different industries exert a significant effect on the asset figure further reduces its usefulness as a peg upon which to hang the fine structure.[42]

A firm's profits constitute a far more desirable standard for the imposition of fines than either the standard of sales or that of assets. The profit standard would go further than either of the other two toward providing a constant impact, regardless of the sales-assets structures of the firms that are potential violators. Specifically, we recommend that antitrust violations be penalized exclusively by a mandatory fine of 25 percent of the firm's pre-tax profits for every year of anticompetitive activity.[43] Government tax returns would provide a very convenient measure by which to determine the relevant profit figure.

The 25 percent figure, we stress, is not to be taken as either an estimate of the firm's profits attributable to its antitrust violation or an estimate of the misallocative damage done to society by the firm's anticompetitive activity. Rather than being concerned with compensation, our proposal is directed solely toward deterrence; the 25 percent figure would seem

sufficient for this purpose. Even a management relatively isolated from its firm's owners still would feel the impact from a fine of this magnitude. The experience of lower stock prices, greater difficulties in attracting funds, and an increased probability of a takeover bid would be unpleasant consequences of such a fine. The 25 percent figure would, on the other hand, not seem so high as to cause violators to go out of business, and not so onerous as to offend the society's sense of absolute equity.

There are, of course, some problems in basing the fine on a percentage of company profits. Economists have long noted the inability of current accounting practices to reflect costs rationally and consistently; the vagaries of cost accounting are necessarily reflected in the profit residual. This results in two problems: (1) a fine on profits may have some disproportionate effects due to different accounting practices among firms and across industries, and (2) the malleability of cost figures, coupled with a potential fine on profits, gives management added incentive to hide profits. For example, a firm may have opportunities to engage in activities providing attractive tax shelters. Under our proposal of a 25 percent fine on profits, such tax shelters would benefit a firm not only with tax savings but also with lower anti-trust fines.[44] However, insofar as these problems are deemed substantial, they could be addressed by devising regulations which would use income tax profit figures not as a final base from which to compute antitrust penalties but rather as a starting point for computations.[45]

Our proposal might seem to impose an inappropriately heavy burden on multidivision firms, since the proposed fine is based on a given firm's aggregate profits while a particular antitrust violation might have been perpetrated by only one of the company's divisions. This "disproportion," however, is one of the strengths of the profits measure. Multidivision firms, because of their typically large size, are generally considered the firms most likely to inflict se-

---

[42]Moreover, during a time of inflation, a fine based on assets might impose greater hardships on new firms than on old ones since the older firms are more likely to have their assets undervalued.

[43]Under our proposed system corporate dissolution might still be used in some cases but only when its remedial benefits clearly warrant its use. See p. 696 supra.

[44]This problem should not be overstated. It is unlikely that our proposal would cause corporations to engage in much further tax-sheltered activity. Already existing inducements to minimize taxable income have probably exhausted concealment options.

[45]Incremental concealment of profits could if necessary be made less appealing by adjusting the profit figure for antitrust penalty purposes so as to take into account returns which are otherwise hidden through sheltering devices. Firms would then be fined on the basis of an adjusted profit figure.

rious welfare losses when they engage in anticompetitive behavior. More importantly, huge multidivision firms, with many sources of profit, would probably not be "hurt" or deterred by the threat of losing a portion of profits in only one division. Furthermore, imposing even relatively frequent but relatively low fines on the profits of single divisions of conglomerates would have particularly little deterrent effect if, as we earlier concluded, management is generally risk averse, and if the size and diversity of the enterprise makes the incidence of such fines more or less statistically predictable.

The benefits of determining antitrust fines by a profit standard, then, outweigh the costs of using that standard. Considerations of efficiency, ease of administration, and equity together compel the conclusion that the profit standard is the most desirable of the four options that have been analyzed here.

VI. CONCLUSION

We have shown that, given the general risk aversion of American management, it is more efficient to deter antitrust violations by heavy reliance on the level of financial penalties than by heavy reliance on the probability of detection and conviction. Furthermore, we have argued that penalties should be in the form of fines rather than in the form of private reparations. By eliminating the resource consuming processes involved in the determination and allocation of private damages, our proposal would, we feel, enable society to achieve the present degree of deterrence at lesser social cost or a much greater degree of deterrence at the same cost.

In advocating reliance on a single penalty instead of a host of weapons, and in recommending the elimination of private damage suits, a mechanism which has been called the "strongest pillar of antitrust,"[46] we are not, we stress, calling for a weakening of the antitrust laws. On the contrary, we are convinced that more discouragement of anticompetitive behavior is needed. However, an analysis of the benefits and the costs of any alternate antitrust policies moves us to reject the antitrust literature which simply recommends doing more of everything—more fines, longer jail terms, bigger government budgets, enlarged rules of standing, generally easier access to the courts—with little discussion of the relative efficiencies and costs of these several approaches.

[46]Loevinger, *Private Action—The Strongest Pillar of Antitrust*, 3 Antitrust Bull. 167 (1958).

Contestable Markets: An Uprising in the Theory of Industry Structure*

WILLIAM J. BAUMOL**

William Baumol (B.S.S., City College of CUNY, 1942; Ph.D., University of London, 1949) was born in New York City in 1922. He currently holds a joint appointment as Professor of Economics at Princeton and New York Universities. Baumol's contributions to the understanding of economics, which span virtually all of its fields, include the first comprehensive theory of the endogenous determination of industry structure, development of a model of unbalanced productivity growth in different economic sectors, and the first analytic model of behavior of firms with objectives other than profit maximization. The paper reprinted here reflects his current interest in market structure. Professor Baumol is the author of numerous books and articles, including *Welfare Economics and the Theory of the State, Performing Arts: The Economic Dilemma* (with W. G. Bowen), *The Theory of Environmental Policy* (with W. E. Oates) and two well-known textbooks, *Economic Dynamics* and *Economic Theory and Operations Analysis*. Currently a Fellow of the Econometric Society, he has served as a Guggenheim Memorial Foundation Fellow, a Ford Foundation Faculty Research Fellow, and an Honorary Fellow of the London School of Economics. Baumol is past president of the American Economic Association, the Eastern Economic Association, the Association of Environmental Resource Economists (Central New Jersey), and the American Statistical Association. His friends know him as well as an accomplished artist and patron of the arts.

*Reprinted from *American Economic Review* (March 1982) by permission of the American Economic Association. Copyright 1982, pp. 1–15.
**Presidential address delivered at the ninety-fourth meeting of the American Economic Association, December 29, 1981. I should like to express my deep appreciation to the many colleagues who have contributed to the formulation of the ideas reported here, and to the Economics Program of the Division of Social Sciences of the National Science Foundation, the Division of Information Science and Technology of the National Science Foundation, and the Sloan Foundation for their very generous support of the research that underlies it.

The address of the departing president is no place for modesty. Nevertheless, I must resist the temptation to describe the analysis I will report here as anything like a revolution. Perhaps terms such as "rebellion" or "uprising" are rather more apt. But, nevertheless, I shall seek to convince you that the work my colleagues, John Panzar and Robert Willig, and I have carried out and encapsulated in our new book enables us to look at industry structure and behavior in a way that is novel in a number of respects, that it provides a unifying analytical structure to the subject area, and that it offers useful insights for empirical work and for the formulation of policy.

Before getting into the substance of the analysis I admit that this presidential address is most unorthodox in at least one significant respect—that it is not the work of a single author. Here it is not even sufficient to refer to Panzar and Willig, the coauthors of both the substance and the exposition of the book in which the analysis is described in full. For others have made crucial contributions to the formulation of the theory—most notably Elizabeth Bailey, Dietrich Fischer, Herman Quirmbach, and Thijs ten Raa.

But there are many more than these. No uprising by a tiny band of rebels can hope to change an established order, and when the time for rebellion is ripe it seems to break out simultaneously and independently in a variety of disconnected centers each offering its own program for the future. Events here have been no different. I have recently received a proposal for a conference on new developments in the theory of industry structure formulated by my colleague, Joseph Stiglitz, which lists some forty participants, most of them widely known. Among those working on the subject are persons as well known as Caves, Dasgupta, Dixit, Friedlaender, Grossman, Hart, Levin, Ordover, Rosse, Salop, Schmalensee, Sonnenschein, Spence, Varian, von Weiszäcker, and Zeckhauser, among *many* others.[1] It is, of course, tempting to me to take the view that our book is the true gospel of the rebellion and that the doctrines promulgated by others must be combatted as heresy. But that could at best be excused as a manifestation of the excessive zeal one comes to expect on such occasions. In truth, the immediate authors of the work I will report tonight may perhaps be able to justify a claim to have offered some systematization and order to the new doctrines—to have built upon them a more comprehensive statement of the issues and the analysis, and to have made a number of

particular contributions. But, in the last analysis, we must look enthusiastically upon our fellow rebels as comrades in arms, each of whom has made a crucial contribution to the common cause.

Turning now to the substance of the theory, let me begin by contrasting our results with those of the standard theory. In offering this contrast, let me emphasize that much of the analysis rests on work that appeared considerably earlier in a variety of forms. We, no less than other writers, owe a heavy debt to predecessors from Bertrand to Bain, from Cournot to Demsetz. Nevertheless, it must surely be acknowledged that the following characterization of the general tenor of the literature as it appeared until fairly recently is essentially accurate.

First, in the received analysis perfect competition serves as the one standard of welfare-maximizing structure and behavior. There is no similar form corresponding to industries in which efficiency calls for a very limited number of firms (though the earlier writings on workable competition did move in that direction in a manner less formal than ours).

Our analysis, in contrast, provides a generalization of the concept of the perfectly competitive market, one which we call a "perfectly contestable market." It is, generally, characterized by optimal behavior and yet applies to the full range of industry structures including even monopoly and oligopoly. In saying this, it must be made clear that perfectly contestable markets do not populate the world of reality any more than perfectly competitive markets do, though there are a number of industries which undoubtedly approximate contestability even if they are far from perfectly competitive. In our analysis, perfect contestability, then, serves not primarily as a description of reality, but as a benchmark for desirable industrial organization which is far more flexible and is applicable far more widely than the one that was available to us before.

Second, in the standard analysis (including that of many of our fellow rebels), the properties of oligopoly models are heavily dependent on the assumed expectations and reaction patterns characterizing the firms that are involved. When there is a change in the assumed nature of these expectations or reactions, the implied behavior of the oligopolistic industry may change drastically.

In our analysis, in the limiting case of perfect contestability, oligopolistic structure and behavior are

---

[1] Such a list must inevitably have embarassing omissions—perhaps some of its author's closest friends. I can only say that it is intended just to be suggestive. The fact that it is so far from being complete also indicates how widespread an uprising I am discussing.

freed entirely from their previous dependence on the conjectural variations of *incumbents* and, instead, these are generally determined uniquely and, in a manner that is tractable analytically, by the pressures of *potential* competition to which Bain directed our attention so tellingly.

Third, the standard analysis leaves us with the impression that there is a rough continuum, in terms of desirability of industry performance, ranging from unregulated pure monopoly as the pessimal arrangement to perfect competition as the ideal, with relative efficiency in resource allocation increasing monotonically as the number of firms expands.

I will show that, in contrast, in perfectly contestable markets behavior is sharply discontinuous in its welfare attributes. A contestable monopoly offers us some presumption, but no guarantee, of behavior consistent with a second best optimum, subject to the constraint that the firm be viable financially despite the presence of scale economies which render marginal cost pricing financially infeasible. That is, a contestable monopoly has some reason to adopt the Ramsey optimal price-output vector, but it may have other choices open to it. (For the analysis of contestable monopoly, see my article with Elizabeth Bailey and Willig, Panzar and Willig's article, and my book with Panzar and Willig, chs. 7 and 8.)

But once each product obtains a second producer, that is, once we enter the domain of duopoly or oligopoly for each and every good, such choice disappears. The contestable oligopoly which achieves an equilibrium that immunizes it from the incursions of entrants has only one pricing option—it must set its price exactly *equal* to marginal cost and do *all* of the things required for a first best optimum! In short, once we leave the world of pure or partial monopoly, any contestable market must behave ideally in every respect. Optimality is *not* approached gradually as the number of firms supplying a commodity grows. As has long been suggested in Chicago, two firms can be enough to guarantee optimality (see, for example, Eugene Fama and Arthur Laffer).

Thus, the analysis extends enormously the domain in which the invisible hand holds sway. In a perfectly contestable world, it seems to rule almost everywhere. Lest this seem to be too Panglossian a view of reality, let me offer two observations which make it clear that we emphatically do not believe that all need be for the best in this best of all possible worlds.

First, let me recall the observation that real markets are rarely, if ever, perfectly contestable. Contestability is merely a broader ideal, a benchmark of wider applicability than is perfect competition. To say that contestable oligopolies behave ideally and that contestable monopolies have some incentives for doing so is not to imply that this is even nearly true of all oligopolies or of unregulated monopolies in reality.

Second, while the theory extends the domain of the invisible hand in some directions, it unexpectedly restricts it in others. This brings me to the penultimate contrast I wish to offer here between the earlier views and those that emerge from our analysis.

The older theoretical analysis seems to have considered the invisible hand to be a rather weak intratemporal allocator of resources, as we have seen. The mere presence of unregulated monopoly or oligopoly was taken to be sufficient per se to imply that resources are likely to be misallocated *within* a given time period. But *where the market structure is such as to yield a satisfactory allocation of resources within the period,* it may have seemed that it can, at least in theory, do a good job of intertemporal resource allocation. In the absence of any externalities, persistent and asymmetric information gaps, and of interference with the workings of capital markets, the amounts that will be invested for the future may appear to be consistent with Pareto optimality and efficiency in the supply of outputs to current and future generations.

However, our analysis shows that where there are economies of scale in the production of durable capital, intertemporal contestable monopoly, which may perform relatively well in the single period, cannot be depended upon to perform ideally as time passes. In particular, we will see that the least costly producer is in the long run vulnerable to entry or replacement by rivals whose appearance is inefficient because it wastes valuable social resources.

There is one last contrast between the newer analyses and the older theory which I am most anxious to emphasize. In the older theory, the nature of the industry structure was *not* normally explained by the analysis. It was, in effect, taken to be given exogenously, with the fates determining, apparently capriciously, that one industry will be organized as an oligopoly, another as a monopoly and a third as a set of monopolistic competitors. Assuming that this destiny had somehow been revealed, the older analyses proceeded to investigate the consequences of the exogenously given industry structure for pricing, outputs, and other decisions.[2]

The new analyses are radically different in this respect. In our analysis, among others, an industry's structure is determined explicitly, endogenously, and simultaneously with the pricing, output, advertising, and other decisions of the firms of which it is constituted. This, perhaps, is one of the prime contributions of the new theoretical analyses.

I. CHARACTERISTICS OF CONTESTABLE MARKETS

Perhaps a misplaced instinct for melodrama has led me to say so much about contestable markets without even hinting what makes a market contestable. But I can postpone the definition no longer. A contestable market is one into which entry is absolutely free, *and exit is absolutely costless*. We use "freedom of entry" in Stigler's sense, not to mean that it is costless or easy, but that the entrant suffers no disadvantage in terms of production technique or perceived product quality relative to the incumbent, and that potential entrants find it appropriate to evaluate the profitability of entry in terms of the incumbent firms' pre-entry prices. In short, it is a requirement of contestability that there be no cost discrimination against entrants. Absolute freedom of exit, to us, is one way to guarantee freedom of entry. By this we mean that any firm can leave without impediment, and in the process of departure can recoup any costs incurred in the entry process. If all capital is salable or reusable without loss other than that corresponding to normal user cost and depreciation, then any risk of entry is eliminated.

Thus, contestable markets may share at most one attribute with perfect competition. Their firms need not be small or numerous or independent in their decision making or produce homogeneous products.

In short, a perfectly competitive market is necessarily perfectly contestable, but not *vice versa*.

The crucial feature of a contestable market is its vulnerability to hit-and-run entry. Even a very transient profit opportunity need not be neglected by a potential entrant, for he can go in, and, before prices change, collect his gains and then depart without cost, should the climate grow hostile.

Shortage of time forces me to deal rather briefly with two of the most important properties of contestable markets—their welfare attributes and the way in which they determine industry structure. I deal with these briefly because an intuitive view of the logic of these parts of the analysis is not difficult to provide. Then I can devote a bit more time to some details of the oligopoly and the intertemporal models.

A. Perfect Contestability and Welfare

The welfare properties of contestable markets follow almost directly from their definition and their vulnerability to hit-and-run incursions. Let me list some of these properties and discuss them succinctly.

First, a contestable market never offers more than a normal rate of profit—its economic profits must be zero or negative, even if it is oligopolistic or monopolistic. The reason is simple. Any positive profit means that a transient entrant can set up business, replicate a profit-making incumbent's output at the same cost as his, undercut the incumbent's prices slightly and still earn a profit. That is, continuity and the opportunity for costless entry and exit guarantee that an entrant who is content to accept a slightly lower economic profit can do so by selecting prices a bit lower than the incumbent's.

In sum, in a perfectly contestable market any economic profit earned by an incumbent automatically constitutes an earnings opportunity for an entrant who will hit and, if necessary, run (counting his temporary but supernormal profits on the way to the bank). Consequently, in contestable markets, zero profits must characterize any equilibrium, even under monopoly and oligopoly.

The second welfare characteristic of a contestable market follows from the same argument as the first. This second attribute of any contestable market is the absence of any sort of inefficiency in production in industry equilibrium. This is true alike of inefficiency of allocation of inputs, X-inefficiency, ineffi-

---

[2]Of course, any analysis which considered the role of entry, whether it dealt with perfect competition or monopolistic competition, must implicitly have considered the determination of industry structure by the market. But in writings before the 1970's, such analyses usually did not consider how this process determined whether the industry would or would not turn out to be, for example, an oligopoly. The entry conditions were studied only to show how the *assumed* market structure could constitute an equilibrium state. Many recent writings have gone more explicitly into the determination of industry structure, though their approaches generally differ from ours.

cient operation of the firm, or inefficient organization of the industry. For any unnecessary cost, like any abnormal profit, constitutes an invitation to entry. Of course, in the short run, as is true under perfect competition, both profits and waste may be present. But in the long run, these simply cannot withstand the threat brandished by potential entrants who have nothing to lose by grabbing at any opportunity for profit, however transient it may be.

A third welfare attribute of any long-run equilibrium in a contestable market is that no product can be sold at a price, p, that is less than its marginal cost. For if some firm sells y units of output at such a price and makes a profit in the process, then it is possible for an entrant to offer to sell a slightly smaller quantity, $y - \epsilon$, at a price a shade lower than the incumbent's, and still make a profit. That is, if the price p is less than MC, then the sale of $y - \epsilon$ units at price p must yield a total profit $\pi + \Delta\pi$ which is greater than the profit, π, that can be earned by selling only y units of output at that price. Therefore, there must exist a price just slightly lower than p which enables the entrant to undercut the incumbent and yet to earn at least as much as the incumbent, by eliminating the unprofitable marginal unit.

This last attribute of contestable equilibria—the fact that price must always at least equal marginal cost—is important for the economics of antitrust and regulation. For it means that in a perfectly contestable market, no cross subsidy is possible, that is, no predatory pricing can be used as a weapon of unfair competition. But we will see it also has implications which are more profound theoretically and which are more germane to our purposes. For it constitutes half of the argument which shows that when there are two or more suppliers of any product, its price must, in equilibrium, be exactly equal to marginal cost, and so resource allocation must satisfy all the requirements of first best optimality.

Indeed, the argument here is similar to the one which has just been described. But there is a complication which is what introduces the two-firm requirement into this proposition. $p < MC$ constitutes an opportunity for profit to an entrant who drops the unprofitable marginal unit of output, as we have just seen. It would seem, symmetrically, that $p > MC$ also automatically constitutes an opportunity for profitable entry. Instead of selling the y-unit output of a profitable incumbent, the entrant can now offer

to sell the slightly larger output, $y + \epsilon$, using the profits generated by the marginal unit at a price greater than marginal cost to permit a reduction in price below the incumbent's. But on this side of the incumbent's output, there is a catch in the argument. Suppose the incumbent is a monopolist. Then output and price are constrained by the elasticity of demand. An attempt by an entrant to sell $y + \epsilon$ rather than y may conceivably cause a sharp reduction in price which eliminates the apparent profits of entry. In the extreme case where demand is perfectly inelastic, there will be no positive price at which the market will absorb the quantity $y + \epsilon$. This means that the profit opportunity represented by $p > MC$ can crumble into dust as soon as anyone seeks to take advantage of it.

But all this changes when the market contains two or more sellers. Now $p > MC$ does always constitute a real opportunity for profitable entry. The entrant who wishes to sell a bit more than some one of the profitable incumbents, call him incumbent A, need not press against the industry's total demand curve for the product. Rather, he can undercut A, steal away all of his customers, at least temporarily, and, in addition, steal away ϵ units of demand from any other incumbent, B. Thus, if A and B together sell $y_a + y_b > y_a$, then an entrant can lure away $y_a + \epsilon > y_a$ customers, for ϵ sufficiently small, and earn on this the incremental profit $\epsilon(p - MC) > 0$. This means that the entrant who sells $y_a + \epsilon$ can afford to undercut the prevailing prices somewhat and still make more profit than an incumbent who sells y_a at price p.

In sum, where a product is sold by two or more firms, any $p > MC$ constitutes an irresistible entry opportunity for hit-and-run entry in a perfectly contestable market, for it promises the entrant supernormal profits even if they accrue for a very short period of time.

Consequently, when a perfectly contestable market contains two or more sellers, neither $p < MC$ nor $p > MC$ is compatible with equilibrium. Thus we have our third and perhaps most crucial welfare attribute of such perfectly contestable markets—their prices, in equilibrium, must be equal to marginal costs, as is required for Pareto optimality of the "first best" variety. This, along with the conclusion that such markets permit no economic profits and no inefficiency in long-run equilibrium, constitutes their critical properties from the viewpoint of economic welfare. Certainly, since they do enjoy those three properties, the optimality of perfectly contestable equilibria (with the reservations already expressed about the case of pure monopoly) fully justifies our conclusion that perfect contestability constitutes a proper generalization of the concept of perfect competition so far as welfare implications are concerned.

B. On the Determination of Industry Structure

I shall be briefer and even less rigorous in describing how industry structure is determined endogenously by contestability analysis. Though this area encompasses one of its most crucial accomplishments, there is no way I can do justice to the details of the analysis in an oral presentation and within my allotted span of time. However, an intuitive view of the matter is not difficult.

The key to the analysis lies in the second welfare property of contestable equilibria—their incompatibility with inefficiency of any sort. In particular, they are incompatible with inefficiency in the *organization* of an industry. That is, suppose we consider whether a particular output quantity of an industry will be produced by two firms or by a thousand. Suppose it turns out that the two-firm arrangement can produce the given output at a cost 20 percent lower than it can be done by the 1,000 firms. Then one implication of our analysis is that the industry cannot be in long-run equilibrium if it encompasses 1,000 producers. Thus we already have some hint about the equilibrium industry structure of a contestable market.

We can go further with this example. Suppose that, with the given output vector for the industry, it turns out that *no* number of firms other than two can produce at as low a total cost as is possible under a two-firm arrangement. That is, suppose two firms can produce the output vector at a total cost lower than it can be done by one firm or three firms or sixty or six thousand. Then we say that for the given output vector the industry is a *natural duopoly*.

This now tells us how the industry's structure can be determined. We proceed, conceptually, in two steps. First we determine what structure happens to be most efficient for the production of a given output vector by a given industry. Next, we investigate when market pressures will lead the industry toward such an efficient structure in equilibrium.

Now, the first step, though it has many intriguing analytic attributes, is essentially a pure matter of computation. Given the cost function for a typical firm, it is ultimately a matter of calculation to determine how many firms will produce a given output most efficiently. For example, if economies of scale hold throughout the relevant range and there are sufficient complementarities in the production of the different commodities supplied by the firm, then it is an old and well-known conclusion that single firm production will be most economical—that we are dealing with a natural monopoly.

Similarly, in the single product case suppose the average cost curve is U shaped and attains its minimum point at an output of 10,000 units per year. Then it is obvious that if the industry happens to sell 50,000 units per year, this output can be produced most cheaply if it is composed of exactly five firms, each producing 10,000 units at its point of minimum average cost.

Things become far more complex and more interesting when the firm and the industry produce a multiplicity of commodities, as they always do in reality. But the logic is always the same. When the industry output vector is small compared to the output vectors the firm can produce at relatively low cost, then the efficient industry structure will be characterized by very few firms. The opposite will be true when the industry's output vector is relatively far from the origin. In the multiproduct case, since average cost cannot be defined, two complications beset the characterization of the output vectors which the firm can produce relatively efficiently. First, since here average cost cannot be defined, we cannot simply look for the point of minimum average costs. But we overcome this problem by dealing with output bundles having fixed proportions among commodity quantities—by moving along a ray in output space. Along any such ray the behavior of average cost *is* definable, and the point of minimum ray average cost (*RAC*) is our criterion of relatively efficient scale for the firm. Thus, in Fig. 1 we have a ray average cost curve for the production of boots and shoes when they are produced in the proportion given by ray *OR*. We see that for such bundles y^m is the point of minimum *RAC*. A second problem affecting the determination of the output vectors the firm can produce efficiently is the choice of output proportions—the location of the ray along which the firm will operate. This depends on the degree of complemen-

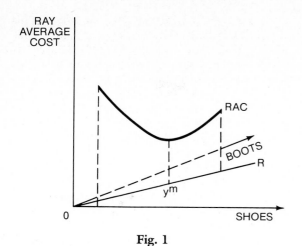

Fig. 1

tarity in production of the goods, and it also lends itself to formal analysis.

We note also that the most efficient number of firms will vary with the location of the industry's output vector. The industry may be a natural monopoly with one output vector, a natural duopoly with another, and efficiency may require seventy-three firms when some third output vector is provided by the industry.

This, then, completes the first of the two basic steps in the endogenous determination of industry structure. Here we have examined what industry structure is least costly for each given output vector of a given industry, and have found how the result depends on the magnitudes of the elements of that output vector and the shape of the cost function of the typical firm. So far the discussion may perhaps be considered normative rather than behavioral. It tells us what structure is most efficient under the circumstances, not which industry structure will emerge under the pressures of the market mechanism.

The transition toward the second, behavioral, stage of the analysis is provided by the observation that the optimal structure of an industry depends on its output vector, while that output vector in turn depends on the prices charged by its firms. But, since pricing depends on industry structure, we are brought full circle to the conclusion that pricing behavior and industry structure must, ultimately, be determined simultaneously and endogenously.

We are in no position to go much further than this for a market whose properties are unspecified. But, for a perfectly contestable market, we can go much further. Indeed, the properties of perfect contestability cut through every difficulty and tell us the equilibrium prices, outputs, and industry structure, all at once.

Where more than one firm supplies a product, we have already characterized these prices precisely. For we have concluded that each equilibrium price will equal the associated marginal cost. Then, given the industry's cost and demand relationships, this yields the industry's output quantities simultaneously with its prices, in the usual manner. Here there is absolutely nothing new in the analysis.

But what is new is the format of the analysis of the determination of industry structure. As I have already pointed out, structure is determined by the efficiency requirement of equilibrium in any contestable market. Since no such equilibrium is compatible with failure to minimize industry costs, it follows that the market forces under perfect contestability will bring us results consistent with those of our normative analysis. Whatever industry structures minimize total costs for the equilibrium output vector must turn out to be the only structures consistent with industry equilibrium in the long run.

Thus, for contestable markets, but for contestable markets *only,* the second stage of the analysis of industry structure turns out to be a sham. Whatever industry structure was shown by the first, normative, portion of the analysis to be least costly must also emerge as the industry structure selected by market behavior. No additional calculations are required by the behavioral analysis. It will all have been done in the normative cost-minimization analysis and the behavioral analysis is pure bonus.

Thus, as I promised, I have indicated how contestability theory departs from the older theory which implicitly took industry structure to be determined exogenously in a manner totally unspecified and, instead, along with other recent writings, embraces the determination of industry structure as an integral part of the theory to be dealt with simultaneously with the determination of prices and outputs.

At this point I can only conjecture about the determination of industry structure once we leave the limiting case of perfect contestability. But my guess is that there are no sharp discontinuities here, and that while the industry structures which emerge in reality are not always those which minimize costs, they will constitute reasonable approximations to the efficient structures. If this is not so it is difficult to account for the similarities in the patterns of industry structure that one observes in different countries. Why else do we not see agriculture organized as an oligopoly in any free market economy, or automobiles produced by 10,000 firms? Market pressures must surely make any very inefficient market structure vulnerable to entry, to displacement of incumbents by foreign competition, or to undermining in other ways. If that is so, the market structure that is called for by contestability theory may not prove to be too bad an approximation to what we encounter in reality.

II. ON OLIGOPOLY EQUILIBRIUM

I should like now to examine oligopoly equilibrium somewhat more extensively. We have seen that, except where a multiproduct oligopoly firm happens to sell some of its products in markets in which it has no competitors, an important partial monopoly case which I will ignore in what follows, all prices must equal the corresponding marginal costs in long-run equilibrium. But in an oligopoly market, this is a troublesome concept. Unless the industry output vector happens to fall at a point where the cost function is characterized by locally constant returns to scale, we know that zero profits are incompatible with marginal cost pricing. Particularly if there are scale economies at that point, so that marginal cost pricing precludes financial viability, we can hardly expect such a solution to constitute an equilibrium. Besides, we have seen that long-run equilibrium requires profit to be precisely zero. We would thus appear to have run into a major snag by concluding that perfect contestability always leads to marginal cost pricing under oligopoly.

This is particularly so if the (ray) average curve is U shaped, with its minimum occurring at a single point, y^m. For in this case that minimum point is the only output of the firm consistent with constant returns to scale and with zero profits under marginal cost pricing. Thus, dealing with the single product case to make the point, it would appear, say, that if the AC-minimizing output is 1,000, in a contestable market, equilibrium is possible if quantity demanded from the industry happens to be exactly 2,000 units (so two firms can produce 1,000 units each) or exactly 3,000 units or exactly 4,000 units, etc. But

suppose the demand curve happens to intersect the industry AC curve, say, at 4,030 units. That is, then, the only industry output satisfying the equilibrium requirement that price equals zero profit. But then, at least one of the four or five firms in the industry must produce either more or less than 1,000 units of output, and so the slope of its AC curve will not be zero at that point, precluding either MC pricing or zero profits and, consequently, violating one or the other of the requirements of equilibrium in a perfectly contestable market.

It would appear that equilibrium will be impossible in this perfectly contestable market unless by a great piece of luck the industry demand curve happens to intersect its AC curve at 2,000 or 3,000 units or some other integer multiple of 1,000 units of output.

There are a variety of ways in which one can grapple with this difficulty. In his dissertation at New York University, Thijs ten Raa has explored the issue with some care and has shown that the presence of entry costs of sufficient magnitude, that is, irreversible costs which must be borne by an entrant but not by an incumbent, can eliminate the existence problem. The minimum size of the entry cost required to permit an equilibrium will depend on the size of the deviation from zero profits under marginal cost pricing and ten Raa has given us rules for its determination. He has shown also that the existence problem, as measured by the required minimum size of entry cost, decreases rapidly as the equilibrium number of firms of the industry increases, typically attaining negligible proportions as that number reaches, say, ten enterprises. For, as is well known, when the firm's average cost curve is U shaped the industry's average cost curve will approach a horizontal line as the size of industry output increases. This is shown in Fig. 2 which is a standard diagram giving the firm's and the industry's AC curves when the former is U shaped. As a result, the deviations between average cost and marginal cost will decline as industry output increases and so the minimum size of the entry cost required to preserve equilibrium declines correspondingly.

However, here I want to describe another approach offered in our book to the problem of existence which I have just described—the difficulty of satisfying simultaneously the zero-profit requirement and the requirement of marginal cost pricing. This second avenue relies on the apparently unanimous

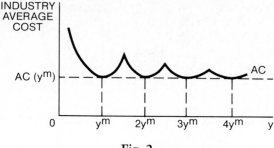

Fig. 2

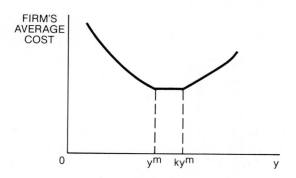

Fig. 3

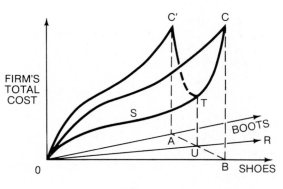

Fig. 4

conclusion of empirical investigators of the cost function of the firm, that AC curves are not, in fact, characterized by a unique minimum point as they would be if they had a smooth U shape. Rather, these investigators tell us, the AC curve of reality has a flat bottom—an interval along which it is horizontal. That is, average costs do tend to fall at first with size of output, then they reach a minimum and continue at that level for some range of outputs, after which they may begin to rise once more. An AC

curve of this variety is shown in Fig. 3. Obviously, such a flat segment of the AC curves *does* help matters because there is now a *range* of outputs over which MC pricing yields zero profits. Moreover, the longer the flat-bottomed segment the better matters are for existence of equilibrium. Indeed, it is easy to show that if the left-hand end of the flat segment occurs at output y^m and the right-hand end occurs at ky^m, then if k is greater than or equal to 2 the existence problem disappears altogether, because the industry's AC curves will be horizontal for any output greater than y^m. That is, in any contestable market in which two or more firms operate the industry AC curve will be horizontal and MC pricing will always yield zero profits. To confirm that this is so, note that if, for example, the flat segment for the firm extends from $y = 1,000$ to $y = 2,000$, then any industry output of, say, $9,000 + \Delta y$ where $0 \leqq \Delta y \leqq 9,000$ can be produced by nine firms, each of them turning out more than 1,000 but less than 2,000 units. Hence, each of them will operate along the horizontal portion of its AC curve, as equilibrium requires.

Thus, if the horizontal interval (y^m, ky^m) happens to satisfy $k \geqq 2$, there is no longer any problem for existence of equilibrium in a contestable market with two or more firms. But fate may not always be so kind. What if that horizontal interval is quite short, that is, k is quite close to unity? Such a case is shown in our diagram where for illustration I have taken $k = 4/3$.

I should like to take advantage of your patience by dealing here not with the simplest case—that of the single product industry—but with the multiproduct problem. I do this partly to offer you some feeling of the way in which the multiproduct analysis, which is one of the hallmarks of our study, works out in practice.

Because, as we have seen, there is no way one can measure average cost for all output combinations in the multiproduct case, I will deal exclusively with the total cost function. Fig. 4 shows such a total cost function for the single firm, which is taken to manufacture two products, boots and shoes.

Let us pause briefly to examine its shape. Along any ray such as *OR,* which keeps output proportions constant, we have an ordinary total cost curve, *OST.* With one exception, which I will note soon, I have drawn it to have the usual sort of shape, with marginal costs falling near the origin and rising at points much further from the origin. On the other hand,

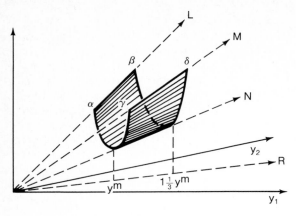

Fig. 5

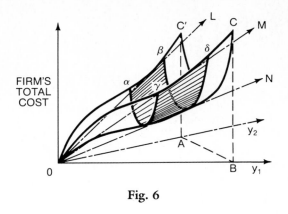

Fig. 6

the trans ray cut above *AB* yields a cross section *C'TC* which is more or less U shaped. This means that it is relatively cheaper to produce boots and shoes together (point *U*) than to produce them in isolation (point *A* or point *B*). That is, this convex trans ray shape is enough to offer us the complementarity which leads firms and industries to turn out a multiplicity of products rather than specializing in the production of a single good.

Now what, in such a case, corresponds to the flat bottom of an *AC* curve in a single product case? The answer is that the cost function in the neighborhood of the corresponding output must be linearly homogeneous. In Fig. 5 such a region, $\alpha\beta\gamma\delta$, is depicted. It is linearly homogeneous because it is generated by a set of rays such as *L, M,* and *N.* For simplicity in the discussion that follows, I have given this region a very regular shape—it is, approximately, a rectangle which has been moved into three-dimensional space and given a U-shaped cross section.

Now Fig. 6 combines the two preceding diagrams and we see that they have been drawn to mesh together, so that the linearly homogeneous region constitutes a portion of the firm's total cost surface. We see then that the firm's total cost does have a region in which constant returns to scale occur, and which corresponds to the flat-bottomed segment of the *AC* curve.

Moreover, as before, I have deliberately kept this segment quite narrow. Indeed, I have repeated the previous proportions, letting the segment extend from a distance y^m from the origin to the distance $1\frac{1}{3}y^m$ along any ray on the floor of the diagram.

Let us now see what happens in these circumstances when we turn to the total cost surface for the *industry.* This is depicted in Fig. 7 which shows a relationship that may at first seem surprising. In Fig. 7 I depict only the linearly homogeneous portions of the industry's cost surface. There we see that while for the firm linear homogeneity prevailed only in the interval from y^m to $1\frac{1}{3}y^m$, in the case of industry output linear homogeneity also holds in that same interval but, in addition, it holds for the interval $2y^m$ to $2\frac{2}{3}y^m$ and in the region extending from $3y^m$ to infinity. That is, everywhere beyond $3y^m$ the industry's total cost function is linearly homogeneous. In this case, then, we have three regions of local linear homogeneity in the industry's cost function, $\alpha\beta\gamma\delta$, which is identical with that of the individual firm, the larger region *abcd,* and the infinite region *aleph beth.* . . . .

Before showing why this is so we must pause to note the implications of the exercise. For it means that even a relatively small region of flatness in the *AC* curve of the individual firm, that is, of linear homogeneity in its total cost function, eliminates the bulk of the existence problem for oligopoly equilibrium in a contestable market. The problem does not arise for outputs nearer to the origin than y_m because such outputs are supplied most efficiently by a monopoly which is not required to price at marginal cost in a contestable market equilibrium. The problem also does not arise for any industry output greater than $3y^m$ in this case, because everywhere beyond that marginal cost pricing yields zero profits. There are two relatively narrow regions in which no equilibrium is, indeed, possible, but here we may conjecture that the vicissitudes of disequilibrium will

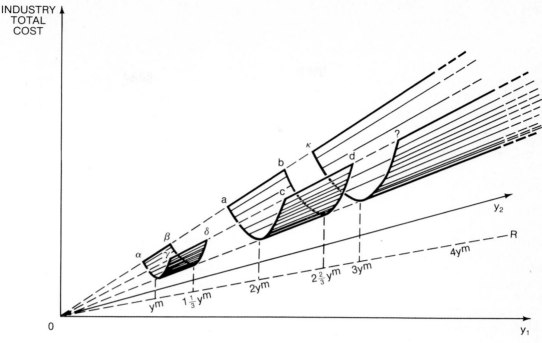

Fig. 7

cause shifts in the demand relationships as changing prices and changing consumption patterns affect tastes, and so the industry will ultimately happen upon an equilibrium position and remain there until exogenous disturbances move it away. Thus we end up with an oligopoly equilibrium whose prices, profits, and other attributes are determined without benefit of the conjectural variation, reaction functions, and the other paraphernalia of standard oligopoly analysis.

To complete this discussion of oligopoly equilibrium in a contestable market, it only remains for me to explain why the regions of linear homogeneity in the industry's cost function are as depicted in Fig. 7. The answer is straightforward. Let $C(y)$ be the firm's total cost function for which we have assumed for expository simplicity that in the interval from y^m to $1\frac{1}{3}y^m$ along each and every ray, total cost grows exactly proportionately with output. Then two firms can produce $2y^m$ at the same unit cost, and three firms can produce $3y^m$ at that same unit cost for the given output bundle, etc. But by exactly the same argument, the two firms together, each producing no more than $1\frac{1}{3}y^m$, can turn out anything up to

$2\frac{2}{3}y^m$ without affecting unit costs, and three firms can produce as much as $3\frac{3}{3}y^m$, that is, as much as $4y^m$. In sum, the intervals of linear homogeneity for the industry are the following:

Interval 1: from y^m to $1\frac{1}{3}y^m$
Interval 2: from $2y^m$ to $2\frac{2}{3}y^m$
Interval 3: from $3y^m$ to $4y^m$
Interval 4: from $4y^m$ to $5\frac{1}{3}y^m$
Interval 5: from $5y^m$ to $6\frac{2}{3}y^m$

. . . .

That is, each interval begins at an integer multiple of y^m and extends $1/3\ y^m$ further than its predecessor. Thus, beyond $3y^m$ successive intervals begin to touch or overlap and that is why linear homogeneity extends everywhere beyond $3y^m$ as I claimed.[3]

There is one complication in the multiproduct case which I have deliberately slid over, feeling the discussion was already complicated enough. The preceding argument assumes implicitly that the firms

[3]The reader can readily generalize this result. If the flat-bottomed segment for the firm extends from y^m to $y^m(1 + 1/w)$, where w is an integer, then there will be w regions of linear homogeneity in the industry cost function and it will be linearly homogeneous for any output $y \geqq wy^m$.

producing the industry output all employ the same output proportions as those in the industry output vector. For otherwise, it is not legitimate to move outward along a single ray as the number of firms is increased. But suppose increased industry output were to permit savings through increased specialization. Might there not be constant returns with fixed output proportions and yet economies of scale for the industry overall? This problem is avoided by our complementarity assumption used to account for the industry's multiproduct operation—our U-shaped trans-ray cross section. This, in effect, rules out such savings from specialization in the regions where linear homogeneity also rules out savings from increased scale.

This, then, completes my discussion of oligopoly equilibrium in perfectly contestable markets, which we have seen, yields a determinate set of prices and outputs that is not dependent upon assumptions about the nature of incumbent firm's expectations relating to entrants' behavior and offers us a concrete and favorable conclusion on the welfare implications of contestable oligopoly.

III. INTERTEMPORAL VULNERABILITY TO INEFFICIENT ENTRY

Having so far directed attention to areas in which the invisible hand manifests unexpected strength, I should like to end my story by dealing with an issue in relation to which it is weaker than some of us might have expected. As I indicated before, this is the issue of intertemporal production involving durable capital goods.

The analysis is far more general than the following story suggests, but even the case I describe is sufficiently general to make the point. We deal with an industry in which a product is offered by a single firm that provides it period after period. The equilibrium quantity of the commodity that is demanded grows steadily with the passage of time in a manner that is foreseen without uncertainty. Because of economies of scale in the production of capacity the firm deliberately builds some excess capacity to take care of anticipated growth in sales volume. But there is some point, let us say, $z = 45$ years in the future, such that it would be uneconomic to take further growth in sales volume into account in the initial choice of capacity. This is so because the opportunity (interest) cost of the capacity that remains idle for

45 or more years exceeds the savings made possible by the economies of scale of construction. Thus, after 45 years it will pay the firm to undertake a second construction project to build the added capacity needed to produce the goods demanded of it.

Suppose that in every particular period our producer is a natural monopolist, that is, he produces the industry's supply of its one commodity at a cost lower than it can be done by any two or more enterprises. Then considering that same product in different periods to be formally equivalent to different goods we may take our supplier to be an intertemporal natural monopolist in a multiproduct industry. That is, no combination of two or more firms can produce the industry's intertemporal output vector as cheaply as he. I will prove now under a set of remarkably unrestrictive assumptions that despite its cost advantages, there exists no intertemporal price vector consistent with equilibrium for this firm. That is, whatever his price vector, his market will at some time be vulnerable to partial or complete takeover by an entrant who has neither superior skills nor technological superiority and whose entrance increases the quantities of resources used up in production. In other words, here the invisible hand proves incapable of protecting the most efficient producing arrangement and leaves the incumbent producer vulnerable to displacement by an aggressive entrant. I leave to your imaginations what, if anything, this says about the successive displacements on the world market of the Dutch by the English, the English by the Germans and the Americans, and the Americans, perhaps, by the Japanese.

The proof of our proposition on the intertemporal vulnerability of incumbents to entry that is premature from the viewpoint of cost minimization does require just a little bit of algebra. To keep our analysis simple, I will divide time into two periods, each lasting $z = 45$ years so that capacity in the first period is, optimally, just sufficient to satisfy all demand, but in the second, it requires the construction of added capacity to meet demand growth because, by assumption, anticipatory construction to meet growth more than z years in the future simply is too costly. Also for simplicity, I will assume that there are no costs other than cost of construction. Of course, neither this nor the use of only two periods really affects the argument in any way. My only three substantive assumptions are that demand is growing with time, that there are economies of scale, that is, declining average costs in construction, and that there exists some length of time, z, so great that it does not pay in the initial construction to build capacity sufficient for the growth in quantity demanded that will occur beyond that date.

The argument, like the notation, is now straightforward. Let y_t be output in period t, p_t be price in period t, and $K(y)$ be the cost of construction of capacity sufficient to produce (a maximum of) y units per period. Here, both p_t and $K(y)$ are expressed in discounted present value.[4]

Then, by assumption, our firm will construct at the beginning of the first period capacity just sufficient to produce output y_1 at cost $K(y_1)$ and at the beginning of the second period it will produce the rest of the capacity it needs, $y_2 - y_1 > 0$, at the cost $K(y_2 - y_1)$.

The first requirement for the prices in question to be consistent with equilibrium is that they permit the incumbent to cover his costs, that is, that

$$p_1 y_1 + p_2 y_2 \geqq K(y_1) + K(y_2 - y_1). \qquad (1)$$

Second, for these prices to constitute an equilibrium they must protect the incumbent against any and all possible incursions by entrants. That is, suppose an entrant were to consider the possibility of constructing capacity y_1 and not expanding in the future, and, by undercutting the incumbent, selling the same output, y_1, in each period. Entry on these terms will in fact be profitable unless the prices are such that the sale of y_1 in each period does not bring in revenues sufficient to cover the cost, $K(y_1)$, of the entrant's once-and-for-all construction. That is, entry will be profitable unless

$$p_1 y_1 + p_2 y_1 \leqq K(y_1). \qquad (2)$$

Thus, the prices in question cannot constitute an equilibrium unless (2) as well as (1) are satisfied.

Now, subtracting (2) from (1) we obtain immediately

$$p_2(y_2 - y_1) \geqq K(y_2 - y_1)$$

or

$$p_2 \geqq K(y_2 - y_1)/(y_2 - y_1), \qquad (3)$$

but, by the assumption that average construction cost is declining, since $y_1 > 0$,

$$K(y_2 - y_1)/(y_2 - y_1) > K(y_2)/y_2. \qquad (4)$$

Substituting this into (3) we have at once

$$p_2 > K(y_2)/y_2$$

or

$$p_2 y_2 > K(y_2). \qquad (5)$$

Inequality (5) is our result. For it proves that any prices which satisfy equilibrium requirements (1) and (2) must permit a second-period entrant using the same techniques to build capacity y_2 from the ground up, at cost $K(y_2)$, to price slightly below anything the incumbent can charge and yet recover his costs; and that in doing so, the entrant can earn a profit.

Thus, our intertemporal natural monopolist cannot quote, *at time zero*, any prices capable of preventing the takeover of some or all of his market. Moreover, this is so despite the waste, in the form of replication of the incumbent's plant, that this entails. That, then, is the end of the formal argument, the proof that here the invisible hand manifests weakness that is, perhaps, unexpected.

You will all undoubtedly recognize that the story as told here in its barest outlines omits all sorts of nuances, such as entrants' fear of responsive pricing, the role of bankruptcy, depreciation of capital, and the like. This is not the place to go into these matters for it is neither possible nor appropriate here for me to go beyond illustration of the logic of the new analysis.

IV. CONCLUDING COMMENTS

Before closing let me add a word on policy implications, whose details must also be left to another place. In spirit, the policy conclusions are consistent with many of those economists have long been espousing. At least in the intratemporal analysis, the heroes are the (unidentified) potential entrants who exercise discipline over the incumbent, and who do so most effectively when entry is free. In the limit, when entry and exit are completely free, efficient incumbent monopolists and oligopolists may in fact be able to prevent entry. But they can do so only by behaving virtuously, that is, by offering to consumers the benefits which competition would otherwise bring. For every deviation from good behavior instantly makes them vulnerable to hit-and-run entry.

This immediately offers what may be a new insight on antitrust policy. It tells us that a history of absence

---

[4]That is, if p_1^*, p_2^*, represent the undiscounted prices, $p_1 = p_1^*$, $p_2 = p_2^*/(1 + r)$, where r is the rate of interest, etc.

of entry in an industry and a high concentration index may be signs of virtue, not of vice. This will be true when entry costs in our sense are negligible. And, then, efforts to change market structure must be regarded as mischievous and antisocial in their effects.

A second and more obvious conclusion is the questionable desirability of artificial impediments to entry, such as regulators were long inclined to impose. The new analysis merely reinforces the view that any proposed regulatory barrier to entry must start off with a heavy presumption against its adoption. Perhaps a bit newer is the emphasis on the importance of freedom of exit which is as crucial a requirement of contestability as is freedom of entry. Thus we must reject as perverse the propensity of regulators to resist the closing down of unprofitable lines of activity. This has even gone so far as a Congressional proposal (apparently supported by Ralph Nader) to require any plant with yearly sales exceeding $250,000 to provide fifty-two weeks of severance pay and to pay three years of taxes, before it will be permitted to close, and that only after giving two years notice!

There is much more to the policy implications of the new theory, but I will stop here, also leaving its results relating to empirical research for discussion elsewhere.

Let me only say in closing that I hope I have adequately justified my characterization of the new theory as a rebellion or an uprising. I believe it offers a host of new analytical methods, new tasks for empirical research, and new results. It permits reexamination of the domain of the invisible hand, yields

contributions to the theory of oligopoly, provides a standard for policy that is far broader and more widely applicable than that of perfect competition, and leads to a theory that analyzes the determination of industry structure endogenously and simultaneously with the analysis of the other variables more traditionally treated in the theory of the firm and the industry. It aspires to provide no less than a unifying theory as a foundation for the analysis of industrial organization. I will perhaps be excused for feeling that this was an ambitious undertaking.

REFERENCES

Bain, Joe S., *Barriers to New Competition*, Cambridge: Harvard University Press, 1956.

Baumol, William J., Bailey, Elizabeth E., and Willig, Robert D., "Weak Invisible Hand Theorems on the Sustainability of Multiproduct Natural Monopoly," *American Economic Review*, June 1977, *67*, 350–65.

——————, Panzar, John C., and Willig, Robert D., *Contestable Markets and the Theory of Industry Structure*, San Diego: Harcourt Brace Jovanovich, 1982.

Bertrand, Jules, Review of *Théorie Mathematique de la Richesse* and *Récherches sur les Principes Mathématiques de la théorie des Richesses*, *Journal des Savants*, 1883, 499–508.

Cournot, A. A., *Researches into the Mathematical Principles of the Theory of Wealth*, New York: A. M. Kelley, 1938; 1960.

Demsetz, Harold, "Why Regulate Utilities?," *Journal of Law and Economics*, April 1968, *11*, 55–65.

Fama, Eugene F. and Laffer, Arthur B., "The Number of Firms and Competition," *American Economic Review*, September 1972, *62*, 670–74.

Panzar, John C. and Willig, Robert D., "Free Entry and the Sustainability of Natural Monopoly," *Bell Journal of Economics*, Spring 1977, *8*, 1–22.

ten Raa, Thijs, "A Theory of Value and Industry Structure," unpublished doctoral dissertation, New York University, 1980.

Part 5   *General Equilibrium, Welfare, and Allocation*

The Organization of Economic Activity: Issues Pertinent to the Choice of Market versus Nonmarket Allocation*

KENNETH J. ARROW

See "The Theory of Discrimination" for author's biography.

The concept of public goods has been developed through successive refinement over a long period of time. Yet, surprisingly enough, nowhere in the literature does there appear to be a clear general definition of this concept or the more general one of "externality." The accounts given are usually either very general and discursive, difficult to interpret in specific contexts, or else they are rigorous accounts of very special situations. What exactly is the relation between externalities and such concepts as "appropriability" or "exclusion"?

Also, there is considerable ambiguity in the purpose of the analysis of externalities. The best-developed part of the theory relates to only a single problem: the statement of a set of conditions, as weak as possible, which ensure that a competitive equilibrium exists and is Pareto-efficient. Then the denial of any of these hypotheses is presumably a sufficient condition for considering resort to nonmarket channels of resource allocation—usually thought of

as government expenditures, taxes, and subsidies.

At a second level the analysis of externalities should lead to criteria for nonmarket allocation. It is tempting to set forth these criteria in terms analogous to the profit-and-loss statements of private business; in this form, we are led to benefit-cost analysis. There are, moreover, two possible aims for benefit-cost analysis. One, more ambitious but theoretically simpler, is specification of the nonmarket actions which will restore Pareto efficiency. The second involves the recognition that the instruments available to the government or other nonmarket forces are scarce resources for one reason or another, so that all that can be achieved is a "second best."

Other concepts that seem to cluster closely to the concept of public goods are those of "increasing returns" and "market failure." These are related to Pareto inefficiency on the one hand and to the existence and optimality of competitive equilibrium on the other; sometimes the discussions in the literature do not adequately distinguish these two aspects. I contend that market failure is a more general category than externality; and both differ from increasing returns in a basic sense, since market failures in general

*Reprinted from *Joint Economic Committee,* United States Congress, *The Analysis and Evaluation of Public Expenditures: The PPB System,* vol. 1 (Washington, D.C.: Government Printing Office, 1969), pp. 47–64.

and externalities in particular are relative to the mode of economic organization, while increasing returns are essentially a technological phenomenon.

Current writing has helped bring out the point that market failure is not absolute; it is better to consider a broader category, that of transaction costs, which in general impede and in particular cases completely block the formation of markets. It is usually though not always emphasized that transaction costs are costs of running the economic system. An incentive for vertical integration is the replacement of the costs of buying and selling on the market by the costs of intrafirm transfers; the existence of vertical integration may suggest that the costs of operating competitive markets are not zero, as is usually assumed in our theoretical analysis.

Monetary theory, unlike value theory, is heavily dependent on the assumption of positive transaction costs. The recurrent complaint about the difficulty of integrating these two branches of theory is certainly governed by the contradictory assumptions made about transaction costs. The creation of money is in many respects an example of a public good.

The identification of transaction costs in different contexts and under different systems of resource allocation should be a major item on the research agenda of the theory of public goods and indeed of the theory of resource allocation in general. Only the most rudimentary suggestions are made here. The "exclusion principle" is a limiting case of one kind of transaction cost, but the costliness of the information needed to enter and participate in any market, another type of cost, has received little attention. Information is closely related on the one hand to communication and on the other to uncertainty.

Given the existence of Pareto inefficiency in a free market equilibrium, there will be pressure in the system to overcome it by some sort of departure from the free market, that is, some form of collective action. This need not be undertaken by the government. I suggest that in fact there is a wide variety of social institutions—in particular, generally accepted social norms of behavior—which serve in some means as compensation for failure or limitation of the market, though each in turn involves transaction costs of its own. The question also arises of how the behavior of individual economic agents in a social institution (especially in voting) is related to their behavior on the market. A good deal of the theoretical literature of recent years seeks to describe political behavior as analogous to economic, and we may hope for a general theory of socioeconomic equilibrium. But it must always be kept in mind that the contexts of choice are radically different, particularly when the hypotheses of perfectly costless action and information are relaxed. It is not accidental that economic analysis has been successful only in certain limited areas.

COMPETITIVE EQUILIBRIUM AND PARETO EFFICIENCY

A quick review of the familiar theorems on the role of perfectly competitive equilibrium in the efficient allocation of resources will be useful at this point. Perfectly competitive equilibrium has its usual meaning: households, possessed of initial resources, including possibly claims to the profits of firms, choose consumption bundles to maximize utility at a given set of prices; firms choose production bundles so as to maximize profits at the same set of prices; the chosen production and consumption bundles must be consistent with each other in the sense that aggregate production plus initial resources must equal aggregate consumption.[1] The key points in the definition are the parametric role of the prices for each individual and the identity of prices for all individuals. Implicit are the assumptions that all prices can be known by all individuals and that the act of charging prices does not itself consume resources.

A number of additional assumptions are made at different points in the theory of equilibrium, but most clearly are factually valid in the usual contexts and need not be mentioned. The two hypotheses frequently not valid are C, the convexity of household indifference maps and firm production possibility sets, and M, the universality of markets. While the exact meaning of the last assumption will be explored later at some length, for the present purposes we mean that the consumption bundle which determines the utility of an individual is the same as that which he purchases at given prices subject to his budget constraint, and that the set of production bundles among which a firm chooses is a given range independent of decisions made by other agents in the economy.

---

[1] Sometimes this is stated to permit an excess of supply over demand, with a zero price for such free goods; but this can be included in the above formulation by postulating the existence of production processes (disposal processes) which have such surpluses as inputs and no outputs.

The relations between Pareto efficiency and competitive equilibrium are set forth in the following two theorems.

Proposition 1. If M holds, a competitive equilibrium is Pareto-efficient.

This theorem is true even if *C* does not hold.

Proposition 2. If C and M hold, then any Pareto-efficient allocation can be achieved as a competitive equilibrium by a suitable reallocation of initial resources.

When the assumptions of Proposition 2 are valid, then the case for the competitive price system is strongest. Any complaints about its operation can be reduced to complaints about the distribution of income, which should then be rectified by lump-sum transfers. Of course, as Pareto already emphasized, the proposition provides no basis for accepting the results of the market in the absence of accepted levels of income equality.

The central role of competitive equilibrium both as a normative guide and as at least partially descriptive of the real world raises an analytically difficult question: does a competitive equilibrium necessarily exist?

Proposition 3. If C holds, then there exists a competitive equilibrium.

This theorem is true even if *M* does not hold.

If both *C* and *M* hold, we have a fairly complete and simple picture of the achievement of desirable goals, subject always to the major qualification of the achievement of a desirable income distribution. The price system itself determines the income distribution only in the sense of preserving the status quo. Even if costless lump-sum transfers are possible, there is needed a collective mechanism reallocating income if the status quo is not regarded as satisfactory.

Of course *C* is not a necessary condition for the existence of a competitive equilibrium, only a sufficient one. From Proposition 1, it is possible to have an equilibrium and therefore efficient allocation without convexity (when *M* holds). However, in view of the central role of *C* in these theorems, the implications of relaxing this hypothesis have been examined intensively in recent years by Farrell (1959), Rothenberg (1960), Aumann (1966), and Starr (1969). Their conclusions may be summarized as follows: Let *C'* be the weakened convexity assumption that there are no indivisibilities large relative to the economy.

Proposition 4. Propositions 2 and 3 remain approximately true if C is replaced by C'.

Thus, the only nonconvexities that are important for the present purposes are increasing returns over a range large relative to the economy. In those circumstances, a competitive equilibrium cannot exist.

The price system, for all its virtues, is only one conceivable form of arranging trade, even in a system of private property. Bargaining can assume extremely general forms. Under the assumptions *C'* and *M*, we are assured that not everyone can be made better off by a bargain not derived from the price system; but the question arises whether some members of the economy will not find it in their interest and within their power to depart from the perfectly competitive price system. For example, both Knight (1921, pp. 190–194) and Samuelson (1967, p. 120) have noted that it would pay all the firms in a given industry to form a monopoly. But in fact it can be argued that unrestricted bargaining can only settle down to a resource allocation which could also be achieved as a perfectly competitive equilibrium, at least if the bargaining itself is costless and each agent is small compared to the entire economy. This line of argument originated with Edgeworth (1881, pp. 20–43) and has been developed recently by Shubik (1959), Debreu and Scarf (1963), and Aumann (1964).

More precisely, it is easy to show:

Proposition 5. If M holds and a competitive equilibrium prevails, then no set of economic agents will find any resource allocation which they can accomplish by themselves (without trade with the other agents) which they will all prefer to that prevailing under the equilibrium.

Proposition 5 holds for any number of agents. A deeper proposition is the following converse:

Proposition 6. If C' and M hold, and if the resources of any economic agent are small compared with the total of the economy, then, given any allocation not approximately achievable as a competitive equilibrium, there will be some set of agents and some resource allocation they can achieve without any trade with others which each one will prefer to the given allocation.

These two propositions, taken together, strongly suggest that when all the relevant hypotheses hold, (1) a competitive equilibrium, if achieved, will not be upset by bargaining even if permitted, and (2) for any bargain not achievable by a competitive equilibrium there is a set of agents who would benefit by change to another bargain which they have the full power to enforce.

The argument that a set of firms can form a monopoly overlooks the possibility that the consumers can also form a coalition, threaten not to buy, and seek mutually advantageous deals with a subset of the firms; such deals are possible since the monopoly allocation violates some marginal equivalences.

In real life, monopolizing cartels are possible for a reason not so far introduced into the analysis: bargaining costs between producers and consumers are high, those among producers low—a point made most emphatically by Adam Smith (1937, p. 128): "People of the same trade seldom meet together, even for merriment or diversion, but the conversation ends in a conspiracy against the public, or in some contrivance to raise prices." *It is not the presence of bargaining costs per se but their bias that is relevant.* If all bargaining costs are high, but competitive pricing and the markets are cheap, then we expect the perfectly competitive equilibrium to obtain, yielding an allocation identical with that under costless bargaining. But if bargaining costs are biased, then some bargains other than the competitive equilibrium can be arrived at which will not be upset by still other bargains if the latter but not the former are costly.

Finally, in this review of the elements of competitive equilibrium theory, let me repeat the obvious and well-known fact that in a world where time is relevant, the commodities which enter into the equilibrium system include those with future dates. In fact, the bulk of meaningful future transactions cannot be carried out on any existing present market, so that assumption *M,* the universality of markets, is not valid.

IMPERFECTLY COMPETITIVE EQUILIBRIUM

There is no accepted and well-worked-out theory corresponding to the title of this section. From the previous section it is clear that such a theory is needed perforce in the presence of increasing returns on a scale large relative to the economy (hereafter, the phrase "increasing returns" will always be understood to include the prepositional phrase just employed), and is superfluous in its absence.

There are two approaches to a theory of general equilibrium in an imperfectly competitive environment; most writers who touch on public policy questions implicitly accept one or the other of these prototheories without always recognizing that they have

made such a choice. One assumes that all transactions are made according to the price system, that is, the same price is charged for all units of the same commodity; this is the *monopolistic competition* approach. The alternative approach assumes unrestricted bargaining; this is the *game theory* approach. The first might be deemed appropriate if the costs of bargaining were high relative to the costs of ordinary pricing, while the second assumes costless bargaining.[2]

It cannot be too strongly emphasized that neither approach is, at the present stage, a fully developed theory, and it is misleading to state any implications about the working of these systems. Chamberlin's purpose (1933) was certainly the incorporation of monopoly into a general equilibrium system, together with a view that the commodity space should be considered infinite-dimensional, with the possibility of arbitrarily close substitutes in consumption; Triffin (1941) emphasized this aspect, but the only completely worked out model of general monopolistic equilibrium is that of Negishi (1960–61), who made the problem manageable by regarding the demand functions facing the monopolists as those perceived by them, with only loose relations to reality. Such a theory would have little in the way of deducible implications (unless there were a supplementary psychological theory to explain the perceptions of demand functions) and certainly no clear welfare implications.

Of course, whatever a monopolistic competitive equilibrium means, it must imply inefficiency in the Pareto sense if there are substantial increasing returns. For a firm can always make zero profits by not existing; hence, if it operates, price must at least equal average cost, which is greater than marginal cost. Kaldor (1935) and Demsetz (1964), however, have argued that in the "large numbers" case, the welfare loss may be supposed very small. I would conjecture that this conclusion is true, but it is not rigorously established, and indeed the model has never been

---

[2]Within the framework of each prototheory, attempts have been made to modify it in the direction of the other. Thus, price discrimination is a modification of the price system in the pure theory of monopoly, though I am aware of no attempt to study price discrimination in a competitive or otherwise general equilibrium context. Some game theorists (Luce, 1954, 1955a, 1955b; Aumann and Maschler, 1964) have attempted to introduce bargaining costs in some way by simply limiting the range of possible coalitions capable of making bargains.

formulated in adequate detail to discuss it properly.[3]

With unrestricted bargaining it is usual to conclude that the equilibrium, whatever it may be, must be Pareto-efficient, for, by definition, it is in the interest of all economic agents to switch from a Pareto-inefficient allocation to a suitably chosen Pareto-efficient one. This argument seems plausible, but it is not easy to evaluate in the absence of a generally accepted concept of solution for game theory. Edgeworth (1881) held the outcome of bargaining to be indeterminate within limits, and von Neumann and Morgenstern (1944) have generalized this conclusion. But when there is indeterminacy, there is no natural or compelling point on the Pareto frontier at which to arrive. It is certainly a matter of common observation, perhaps most especially in the field of international relations, that mutually advantageous agreements are not arrived at because each party is seeking to engross as much as possible of the common gain for itself. In economic affairs a frequently cited illustration is the assembly of land parcels for large industrial or residential enterprises whose value (net of complementary costs) exceeds the total value of the land in its present uses. Then the owner of each small parcel whose acquisition is essential to the execution of the enterprise can demand the entire net benefit. An agreement may never be reached or may be long delayed; at positive discount rates even the latter outcome is not Pareto-efficient. It is to avoid such losses that the coercive powers of the state are invoked by condemnation proceedings.

There is, however, another tradition within game theory which argues for the determinacy of the outcome of bargaining. Zeuthen (1930, chap. 4) had early propounded one such solution. After von Neumann and Morgenstern, Nash (1950, 1953) offered a solution, which Harsanyi (1956) later showed to be identical with that of Zeuthen. Nash's analysis of bargaining has been extended by Harsanyi (1959, 1963, 1966); variant but related approaches have been studied by Shapley (1953) and Selten (1964). The analysis has proceeded at a very general level, and its specific application to resource allocation has

yet to be spelled out. In the simplest situation, bargaining between two individuals who can cooperate but cannot injure each other except by withholding cooperation, and who can freely transfer benefits between them, the conclusion of the theories is the achievement of a joint optimum followed by equal splitting of the benefits of cooperation net of the amounts each bargainer could obtain without cooperation. Thus, in a land assembly, if the participation of all parcels is essential, each owner receives the value of his parcel in its present (or best alternative) use plus an equal share of the net benefits of the project. Without further analytic and empirical work it is not easy to judge the acceptability of this conclusion.

An elementary example may bring out the ambiguities of allocation with unrestricted bargaining. Since the perfectly competitive equilibrium theory is satisfactory (in the absence of marketing failures and costs) when increasing returns on a substantial scale are absent, the problem of imperfectly competitive equilibrium arises only when substantial increasing returns are present. In effect, then, there are small numbers of effective participants. Suppose there are only three agents. Production is assumed to take place in coalitions; the output of each coalition depends only on the number of members in it. If the average output of the members of a coalition does not increase with the number of members, then the equilibrium outcome is the perfectly competitive one, where each agent produces by himself and consumes his own product. If the average output of a coalition increases with the number of members, then clearly production will take place in the three-member coalition; but the allocation is not determined by the threats of individuals to leave the coalition and go on their own, nor by threats of pairs to form coalitions (for any one member can claim more than one-third of the total output and still leave the other two more than they could produce without him). But perhaps the most interesting case is that where the average output is higher for two individuals than for either one or three, that is, increasing returns followed by diminishing returns. For definiteness, suppose that one agent can produce one unit, two agents can produce four units, and all three agents together can produce five units. Clearly, Pareto efficiency requires the joint productive activity of all three. Since each pair can receive four units by

[3]Suppose that the degree of increasing returns is sufficient to prevent there being more than one producer of a given commodity narrowly defined, but not to prevent production of a close substitute. Is this degree of returns sufficiently substantial to upset the achievement of an approximately perfect competitive equilibrium, as discussed in the last section?

leaving the third agent out, it would appear that each pair must receive at least four units. But this implies that the total allocated to keep the three-man coalition together must be at least six, more than is available for distribution.[4]

(Theories of the Nash-Harsanyi type arrive at solutions in cases like this by assuming that the economic agents foresee these possible instabilities and recognize that any attempt by any pair to break away from the total coalition can itself be overturned. If each is rational and assumes the others are equally rational, then they recognize, in the completely symmetric situation of the example, that only a symmetric allocation is possible.)

The point of this discussion of possible game theory concepts of equilibrium is to suggest caution in accepting the proposition that bargaining costs alone prevent the achievement of Pareto efficiency in the presence of increasing returns, as Buchanan and Tullock (1962, p. 88) and Demsetz (1968, p. 61) assert.

RISK AND INFORMATION

The possible types of equilibria discussed in the previous two sections are not, in principle, altered in nature by the presence of risk. If an economic agent is uncertain as to which of several different states of the world will obtain, he can make contracts contingent on the occurrence of possible states. The real-world counterparts of these theoretical contingent contracts include insurance policies and common stocks. With these markets for contingent contracts, a competitive equilibrium will arise under the same general hypothesis as in the absence of uncertainty. It is not even necessary that the economic agents agree on the probability distribution for the unknown state of the world; each may have his own subjective probabilities. Further, the resulting allocation is Pareto-efficient if the utility of each individual is identified as his expected utility according to his own subjective probability distribution.

But, as Radner (1968) has pointed out, there is more to the story. Whenever we have uncertainty we have the possibility of information and, of course, also the possibility of its absence. No contingent contract can be made if, at the time of execution, either of the contracting parties does not know whether the specified contingency has occurred or not. This

principle eliminates a much larger number of opportunities for mutually favorable exchanges than might perhaps be supposed at first glance. A simple case is that known in insurance literature as "adverse selection." Suppose, for example, there are two types of individuals, A and B, with different life expectancies, but the insurance company has no way to distinguish the two; it cannot in fact identify the present state of the world in all its relevant aspects. The optimal allocation of resources under uncertainty would require separate insurance policies for the two types, but these are clearly impossible. Suppose further that each individual knows which type he belongs to. The company might charge a rate based on the probability of death in the two types together, but the insurance buyers in the two types will respond differently; those in the type with the more favorable experience, say A, will buy less insurance than those in type B, other things (income and risk aversion) being equal. The insurance company's experience will be less favorable than it intended, and it will have to raise its rates. An equilibrium rate will be reached which is, in general, between those corresponding to types A and B separately but closer to the latter. Such an insurance arrangement is, of course, not Pareto-efficient. It is not a priori obvious in general that this free market arrangement is superior to compulsory insurance, even though the latter is also not Pareto-efficient, because it typically disregards individual differences in risk aversion.

As the above example shows, the critical impact of information on the optimal allocation of risk bearing is not merely its presence or absence but its inequality among economic agents. If neither side knew which type the insured belonged to, then the final allocation would be Pareto-efficient if it were considered that the two types were indistinguishable; but in the above example the market allocation is Pareto-efficient neither with the types regarded as indistinguishable nor as distinguishable.

There is one particular case of the effect of differential information on the workings of the market economy (or indeed any complex economy) which is so important as to deserve special comment: one agent can observe the joint effects of the unknown state of the world and of decisions by another economic agent, but not the state or the decision separately. This case is known in the insurance literature as "moral hazard," but because the insurance examples are only a small fraction of all the illustrations

[4]The general principle illustrated by this example has been briefly alluded to by Shapley and Shubik (1967, p. 98, n. 5).

of this case and because, as Pauly (1968) has argued, the adjective "moral" is not always appropriate, the case will be referred to here as the "confounding of risks and decisions." An insurance company may easily observe that a fire has occurred but cannot, without special investigation, know whether the fire was due to causes exogenous to the insured or to decisions of his (arson, or at least carelessness). In general, any system which, in effect, insures against adverse final outcomes automatically reduces the incentives to good decision making.

In these circumstances there are two extreme possibilities (with all intermediate possibilities being present): full protection against uncertainty of final outcome (for example, cost-plus contracts for production or research) or absence of protection against uncertainty of final outcome (the one-person firm; the admiral who is shot for cowardice *pour encourager les autres*). Both policies produce inefficiency, though for different reasons. In the first, the incentive to good decision making is dulled for obvious reasons; in the second, the functions of control and risk bearing must be united, whereas specialization in these functions may be more efficient for the workings of the system.

The relations between principals and agents (for example, patients and physicians, owners and managers) further illustrate the confounding of risks and decisions. In the professions in particular they also illustrate the point to be emphasized later: that ethical standards may to a certain extent overcome the possible Pareto inefficiencies.

So far we have taken the information structure as given. But the fact that particular information structures give rise to Pareto inefficiency means that there is an economic value in transmitting information from one agent to another, as well as in the creation of new information. J. Marschak (1968), Hirshleifer (unpublished), and others have begun the study of the economics of information, but the whole subject is in its infancy. Only a few remarks relevant to the present purpose will be made here.

(1) As both communications engineering and psychology suggest, the transmission of information is not costless. Any professor who has tried to transmit some will be painfully aware of the resources he has expended and, perhaps more poignantly, of the difficulties students have in understanding. The physical costs of transmission may be low, though probably not negligible, as any book buyer knows; but the

"coding" of the information for transmission and the limited channel capacity of the recipients are major costs.

(2) The costs of transmitting information vary with both the type of information transmitted and the recipient and sender. The first point implies a preference for inexpensive information, a point stressed in oligopolistic contexts by Kaysen (1949, pp. 294–295) and in other bargaining contexts by Schelling (1957). The second point is relevant to the value of education and to difficulties of transmission across cultural boundaries (so that production functions can differ so much across countries).

(3) Because the costs of transmission are nonnegligible, even situations which are basically certain become uncertain for the individual; the typical economic agent simply cannot acquire in a meaningful sense the knowledge of all possible prices, even where they are each somewhere available. Markets are thus costly to use, and therefore the multiplication of markets, as for contingent claims as suggested above, becomes inhibited.

EXTERNALITIES ILLUSTRATED

After this long excursus into the present state of the theory of equilibrium and optimality, it is time to discuss some of the standard concepts of externality, market failure, and public goods generally. The clarification of these concepts is a long historical process, not yet concluded, in which the classic contributions of Knight (1924), Young (1913, pp. 676–684), and Robertson (1924) have in more recent times been enriched by those of Meade (1952), Scitovsky (1954), Coase (1960), Buchanan and Stubblebine (1962), and Demsetz (1966). The concept of externality and the extent to which it causes nonoptimal market behavior will be discussed here in terms of a simple model.

Consider a pure exchange economy. Let x_{ik} be the amount of the kth commodity consumed by the ith individual ($i = 1, \ldots, n; k = 1, \ldots, m$) and $\bar{x}_k$ be the amount of the kth commodity available. Suppose in general that the utility of the ith individual is a function of the consumption of all individuals (not all types of consumption for all individuals need actually enter into any given individual's utility function); the utility of the ith individual is $U_i(x_{11}, \ldots, x_{mn})$. We have the obvious constraints:

$$\sum_i x_{ik} \leq \bar{x}_k. \qquad (7\text{-}1)$$

Introduce the following definitions:

$$x_{jik} = x_{ik}. \qquad (7\text{-}2)$$

With this notation a Pareto-efficient allocation is a vector maximum of the utility functions $U_j(x_{j11}, \ldots, x_{jmn})$, subject to the constraints (7-1) and (7-2). Because of the notation used, the variables appearing in the utility function relating to the jth individual are proper to him alone and appear in no one else's utility function. If we understand now that there are n^2m commodities, indexed by the triple subscript jik, then the Pareto efficiency problem has a thoroughly classical form. There are n^2m prices, p_{jik}, attached to the constraints (7-2), plus m prices, q_k, corresponding to constraints (7-1). Following the maximization procedure formally, we see, much as in Samuelson (1954), that Pareto efficiency is characterized by the conditions

$$\lambda_j(\partial U_j/\partial x_{ik}) = p_{jik}, \qquad (7\text{-}3)$$

and

$$\sum_j \mathrm{p}_{jik} = q_k \qquad (7\text{-}4)$$

where λ_j is the reciprocal of the marginal utility of income for individual j. (These statements ignore corner conditions, which can easily be supplied.)

Condition (7-4) can be given the following economic interpretation: Imagine each individual i to be a producer with m production processes, indexed by the pair (i, k). Process (i, k) has one input, namely, commodity k, and n outputs, indexed by the triple (j, i, k). In other words, what we ordinarily call individual i's consumption is regarded as the production of joint outputs, one for each individual whose utility is affected by individual i's consumption.

The point of this exercise is to show that by suitable and indeed not unnatural reinterpretation of the commodity space, externalities can be regarded as ordinary commodities, and all the formal theory of competitive equilibrium is valid, including its optimality.

It is not the mere fact that one man's consumption enters into another man's utility that causes the failure of the market to achieve efficiency. There are two relevant factors which cannot be discovered by inspection of the utility structures of the individual. One, much explored in the literature, is the appropriability of the commodities which represent the external repercussions; the other, less stressed, is the

fact that markets for externalities usually involve small numbers of buyers and sellers.

The first point, Musgrave's "exclusion principle" (1959, p. 86), is so well known as to need little elaboration. Pricing demands the possibility of excluding nonbuyers from the use of the product, and this exclusion may be technically impossible or may require the use of considerable resources. Pollution is the key example; the supply of clean air or water to each individual would have to be treated as a separate commodity, and it would have to be possible in principle to supply it to some and not to others (though the final equilibrium would involve equal supply to all). But this is technically impossible.

The second point comes out clearly in our case. Each commodity (j, i, k) has precisely one buyer and one seller. Even if a competitive equilibrium could be defined, there would be no force driving the system to it; we are in the realm of imperfectly competitive equilibrium.

In my view, the standard lighthouse example is best analyzed as a problem of small numbers rather than of the difficulty of exclusion, though both elements are present. To simplify matters, I will abstract from uncertainty so that the lighthouse keeper knows exactly when each ship will need its services, and also abstract from indivisibility (since the light is either on or off). Assume further that only one ship will be within range of the lighthouse at any moment. Then exclusion is perfectly possible; the keeper need only shut off the light when a nonpaying ship is coming into range. But there would be only one buyer and one seller and no competitive forces to drive the two into a competitive equilibrium. If in addition the costs of bargaining are high, then it may be most efficient to offer the service free.

If, as is typical, markets for the externalities do not exist, then the allocation from the point of view of the "buyer" is determined by a rationing process. We can determine a shadow price for the buyer; this will differ from the price, zero, received by the seller. Hence, formally, the failure of markets for externalities to exist can also be described as a difference of prices between buyer and seller.

In the example analyzed, the externalities related to particular named individuals; individual i's utility function depended on what a particular individual, j, possessed. The case where it is only the total amount of some commodity (for example, handsome houses) in other people's hands that matters is a special case, which yields rather simpler results. In this case, $\partial U_j / \partial x_{ik}$ is independent of i for $i \neq j$, and hence, by condition (7-3), p_{jik} is independent of i for $i \neq j$. Let

$$p_{iik} = p_{ik}, \quad p_{jik} = \bar{p}_{jk} \quad \text{for } i \neq j.$$

Then condition (7-4) becomes

$$p_{ik} + \sum_{j \neq i} \bar{p}_{jk} = q_k$$

or

$$(p_{ik} - \bar{p}_{ik}) + \sum_j \bar{p}_{jk} = q_k,$$

from which it follows that the difference, $p_{ik} - \bar{p}_{ik}$, is independent of i. There are two kinds of shadow prices, a price $\bar{p}_{ik}$, the price that individual i is willing to pay for an increase in the stock of commodity k in any other individual's hands, and the premium, $p_{ik}, - \bar{p}_{ik}$, he is willing to pay to have the commodity in his possession rather than someone else's. At the optimum, this premium for private possession must be the same for all individuals.

Other types of externalities are associated with several commodities simultaneously and do not involve named individuals, as in the case of neighborhood effects, where an individual's utility depends both on others' behavior (for example, aesthetic, criminal) and on their location.

There is one deep problem in the interpretation of externalities which can only be signaled here. What aspects of others' behavior do we consider as affecting a utility function? If we take a hard-boiled revealed preference attitude, then if an individual expends resources in supporting legislation regulating another's behavior, it must be assumed that that behavior affects his utility. Yet in the cases that students of criminal law call "crimes without victims," such as homosexuality or drug taking, there is no direct relation between the parties. Do we have to extend the concept of externality to all matters that an individual cares about? Or, in the spirit of John Stuart Mill, is there a second-order value judgment which excludes some of these preferences from the formation of social policy as being illegitimate infringements of individual freedom?

MARKET FAILURE

The problem of externalities is thus a special case of a more general phenomenon, the failure of markets to exist. Not all examples of market failure can fruit-fully be described as externalities. Two very important examples have already been alluded to; markets for many forms of risk bearing and for most future transactions do not exist, and their absence is surely suggestive of inefficiency.

Previous discussion has suggested two possible causes for market failure: (1) inability to exclude; (2) lack of the necessary information to permit market transactions to be concluded.

The failure of futures markets cannot be directly explained in these terms. Exclusion is no more a problem in the future than in the present. Any contract to be executed in the future is necessarily contingent on some events (for example, that the two agents are still both in business), but there must be many cases where no informational difficulty is presented. The absence of futures markets may be ascribed to a third possibility: (3) supply and demand are equated at zero; the highest price at which anyone would buy is below the lowest price at which anyone would sell.

This third case of market failure, unlike the first two, is by itself in no way presumptive of inefficiency. However, it may usually be assumed that its occurrence is the result of failures of the first two types on complementary markets. Specifically, the demand for future steel may be low because of uncertainties of all types: sales and technological uncertainty for the buyer's firm, prices and existence of competing goods, and the quality specification of the steel. If, however, adequate markets for risk bearing existed, the uncertainties could be removed, and the demand for future steel would rise.

TRANSACTION COSTS

Market failure has been presented as absolute, but in fact the situation is more complex than this. A more general formulation is that of transaction costs, which are attached to any market and indeed to any mode of resource allocation. Market failure is the particular case where transaction costs are so high that the existence of the market is no longer worthwhile. The distinction between transaction costs and production costs is that the former can be varied by a change in the mode of resource allocation, while the latter depend only on the technology and tastes, and would be the same in all economic systems.

The discussions in the preceding sections suggest two sources of transaction costs: (1) exclusion costs and (2) costs of communication and information, including both the supplying and the learning of the terms on which transactions can be carried out. An additional source is (3) the costs of disequilibrium; in any complex system, the market or authoritative allocation, even under perfect information, it takes time to compute the optimal allocation, and either transactions take place which are inconsistent with the final equilibrium or they are delayed until the computations are completed (see T. Marschak, 1959).

These costs vary from system to system; thus, one of the advantages of a price system over either bargaining or some form of authoritative allocation is usually stated to be the economy in costs of information and communication. But the costs of transmitting and especially of receiving a large number of price signals may be high; thus, there is a tendency not to differentiate prices as much as would be desirable from the efficiency viewpoint. For example, the same price is charged for peak and off-peak usage of transportation or electricity.

In a price system, transaction costs drive a wedge between buyers' and sellers' prices and thereby give rise to welfare losses as in the usual analysis. Removal of these welfare losses by changing to another system (for example, governmental allocation on benefit-cost criteria) must be weighed against any possible increase in transaction costs (for example, the need for elaborate and perhaps impossible studies to determine demand functions without the benefit of observing a market).

The welfare implications of transaction costs would exist even if they were proportional to the size of the transaction, but in fact they typically exhibit increasing returns. The cost of acquiring a piece of information, for example, a price, is independent of the scale of use to which it will be put.

COLLECTIVE ACTION: THE POLITICAL PROCESS

The state may frequently have a special role to play in resource allocation because, by its nature, it has a monopoly of coercive power, and coercive power can be used to economize on transaction costs. The most important use of coercion in the economic context is the collection of taxes; others are regulatory legislation and eminent domain proceedings.

The state is not an entity but rather a system of individual agents, a widely extensive system in the case of democracy. It is appealing and fruitful to analyze its behavior in resource allocation in a manner analogous to that of the price system. Since the same agents appear in the two systems, it becomes equally natural to assume that they have the same motives. Hotelling (1929, pp. 54–55) and Schumpeter (1942, chap. 22) had sketched such politico-economic models, and von Neumann and Morgenstern's monumental work is certainly based on the idea that all social phenomena are governed by essentially the same motives as economics. The elaboration of more or less complete models of the political process along the lines of economic theory is more recent, the most prominent contributors being Black (1958), Downs (1957), Buchanan and Tullock (1962), and Rothenberg (1965).

I confine myself here to a few critical remarks on the possibilities of such theories. These are not intended to be negative but to suggest problems that have to be faced and are raised by some points in the preceding discussion.

1. If we take the allocative process to be governed by majority voting, then, as we well know, there are considerable possibilities of paradox. The possible intransitivity of majority voting was already pointed out by Condorcet (1785). If, instead of assuming that each individual votes according to his preferences, it is assumed that all bargain freely before voting (vote-selling), the paradox appears in another form, a variant of the bargaining problems already noted in the section on imperfectly competitive equilibrium. If a majority could do what it wanted, then it would be optimal to win with a bare majority and take everything; but any such bargain can always be broken up by another proposed majority.

Tullock (1967, chap. 3) has recently argued convincingly that if the distribution of opinions on social issues is fairly uniform and if the dimensionality of the space of social issues is much less than the number of individuals, then majority voting on a sincere basis will be transitive. The argument is not, however, applicable to income distribution, for such a policy has as many dimensions as there are individuals, so that the dimensionality of the issue space is equal to the number of individuals.

This last observation raises an interesting question. Why, in fact, in democratic systems has there been so little demand for income redistribution? The current discussion of a negative income tax is the first serious attempt at a purely redistributive policy. Hagström (1938) presented a mathematical model predicting on the basis of a self-interest model for voters that democracy would inevitably lead to radical egalitarianism.

2. Political policy is not made by voters, not even in the sense that they choose the vector of political actions which best suits them. It is in fact made by representatives in one form or another. Political representation is an outstanding example of the principal-agent relation. This means that the link between individual utility functions and social action is tenuous, though by no means completely absent. Representatives are no more a random sample of their constituents than physicians are of their patients.

Indeed, the question can be raised: to what extent is the voter, when acting in that capacity, a principal or an agent? To some extent, certainly, the voter is cast in a role in which he feels some obligation to consider the social good, not just his own. It is in fact somewhat hard to explain otherwise why an individual votes at all in a large election, since the probability that his vote will be decisive is so negligible.

COLLECTIVE ACTION: SOCIAL NORMS

It is a mistake to limit collective action to state action; many other departures from the anonymous atomism of the price system are observed regularly. Indeed, firms of any complexity are illustrations of collective action, the internal allocation of their resources being directed by authoritative and hierarchical controls.

I want, however, to conclude by calling attention to a less visible form of social action: norms of social behavior, including ethical and moral codes. I suggest as one possible interpretation that they are reactions of society to compensate for market failures. It is useful for individuals to have some trust in each other's word. In the absence of trust, it would become very costly to arrange for alternative sanctions and guarantees, and many opportunities for mutually beneficial cooperation would have to be forgone. Banfield (1958) has argued that lack of trust is indeed one of the causes of economic underdevelopment.

It is difficult to conceive of buying trust in any direct way (though it can happen indirectly, for example, a trusted employee will be paid more as being more valuable); indeed, there seems to be some inconsistency in the very concept. Nonmarket action might take the form of a mutual agreement. But the

arrangement of these agreements and especially their continued extension to new individuals entering the social fabric can be costly. As an alternative, society may proceed by internalization of these norms to the achievement of the desired agreement on an unconscious level.

There is a whole set of customs and norms which might be similarly interpreted as agreements to improve the efficiency of the economic system (in the broad sense of satisfaction of individual values) by providing commodities to which the price system is inapplicable.

These social conventions may be adaptive in their origins, but they can become retrogressive. An agreement is costly to reach and therefore costly to modify; and the costs of modification may be especially large for unconscious agreements. Thus, codes of professional ethics, which arise out of the principal-agent relation and afford protection to the principals, can serve also as a cloak for monopoly by the agents.

REFERENCES

Aumann, R. J., 1964. "Markets with a Continuum of Traders," *Econometrica*, vol. 32, pp. 39–50.

Aumann, R. J., 1966. "The Existence of Competitive Equilibria in Markets with a Continuum of Traders," *Econometrica*, vol. 34, pp. 1–17.

Aumann, R. J., and Maschler, M., 1964. "The Bargaining Set for Cooperative Games," in Dresher, M., Shapley, L. S., and Tucker, A. W. (eds.), *Advances in Game Theory. Annals of Mathematics Study*, Princeton, vol. 52, pp. 443–476.

Banfield, E. C., 1958. *The Moral Basis of a Backward Society*, Glencoe, Ill.

Black, D., 1958. *The Theory of Committees and Elections*, Cambridge, U.K.

Buchanan, J., and Stubblebine, W. C., 1962. "Externality," *Economica*, vol. 29, pp. 371–384.

Buchanan, J., and Tullock, G., 1962. *The Calculus of Consent*, Ann Arbor, Michigan.

Chamberlin, E. H., 1933. *The Theory of Monopolistic Competition*, 8th ed., Cambridge, Mass.

Coase, R. H., 1960. "The Problem of Social Cost," *Journal of Law and Economics*, vol. 3, pp. 1–44.

Condorcet, Marquis de, 1785. *Essai sur l'application de l'analyse à la probabilité des décisions rendues à la pluralité des voix*, Paris.

Debreu, G., and Scarf, H., 1963. "A Limit Theorem on the Core of an Economy," *International Economic Review*, vol. 4, pp. 236–246.

Demsetz, H., 1964. "The Welfare and Empirical Implications of Monopolistic Competition," *Economic Journal*, vol. 74, pp. 623–691.

Demsetz, H., 1966. "Some Aspects of Property Rights," *Journal of Law and Economics*, vol. 9, pp. 61–70.

Demsetz, H., 1968. "Why Regulate Utilities," *Journal of Law and Economics*, vol. 11, pp. 55–66.

Downs, A., 1957. *An Economic Theory of Democracy*, New York.

Edgeworth, F. Y., 1881. *Mathematical Psychics: An Essay on the Application of Mathematics to the Moral Sciences*, London.

Farrell, M. J., 1959. "The Convexity Assumption in the Theory of Competitive Markets," *Journal of Political Economy*, vol. 67, pp. 377–391.

Hagström, K. G., 1938. "A Mathematical Note on Democracy," *Econometrica*, vol. 6, pp. 381–383.

Harsanyi, J. C., 1956. "Approaches to the Bargaining Problem before and after the Theory of Games: A Critical Discussion of Zeuthen's, Hicks', and Nash's Theories," *Econometrica*, vol. 24, pp. 144–157.

Harsanyi, J. C., 1959. "A Bargaining Model for the Cooperative N-Person Game," in Tucker, A. W., and Luce, R. D. (eds.), *Contributions to the Theory of Games IV. Annals of Mathematics Study*, Princeton, pp. 325–355.

Harsanyi, J. C., 1963. "A Simplified Bargaining Model for the N-Person Cooperative Game," *International Economic Review*, vol. 4, pp. 194–220.

Harsanyi, J. C., 1966. "A General Theory of Rational Behavior in Game Situations," *Econometrica*, vol. 34, pp. 613–634.

Hotelling, H., 1929. "Stability in Competition," *Economic Journal*, vol. 39, pp. 41–57.

Kaldor, N., 1935. "Market Imperfection and Excess Capacity," *Economica*, vol. 2, pp. 33–50.

Kaysen, Carl, 1949. "Basing Point Pricing and Public Policy," *Quarterly Journal of Economics*, vol. 63, pp. 289–314.

Knight, F. H., 1921. *Risk, Uncertainty, and Profit*, Boston and New York.

Knight, F. H., 1924. "Some Fallacies in the Interpretation of Social Cost," *Quarterly Journal of Economics*, vol. 38, pp. 582–606.

Luce, R. D., 1954. "A Definition of Stability for N-Person Games," *Annals of Mathematics*, vol. 59, pp. 357–366.

Luce, R. D., 1955a. "Ψ-Stability: A New Equilibrium Concept for N-Person Game Theory," in *Mathematical Models of Human Behavior*, Stamford, Conn., pp. 32–44.

Luce, R. D., 1955b. "K-Stability of Symmetric and Quota Games," *Annals of Mathematics*, vol. 62, pp. 517–555.

Marschak, J., 1968. "Economics of Inquiring, Communicating, Deciding," *American Economic Review Papers and Proceedings*, vol. 58, pp. 1–18.

Marschak, T., 1959. "Centralization and Decentralization in Economic Organizations," *Econometrica*, vol. 27, pp. 399–430.

Meade, J. E., 1952. "External Economies and Diseconomies in a Competitive Situation," *Economic Journal*, vol. 62, pp. 59–67.

Musgrave, R. A., 1959. *The Theory of Public Finance: A Study in Public Economy*, New York.

Nash, J. F., Jr., 1950. "The Bargaining Problem," *Econometrica*, vol. 18, pp. 155–162.

Nash, J. F., Jr., 1953. "Two Person Cooperative Games," *Econometrica*, vol. 21, pp. 128–140.

Negishi, T., 1960–61. "Monopolistic Competition and General Equilibrium," *Review of Economic Studies*, vol. 28, pp. 196–201.

von Neumann, J., and Morgenstern, O., 1944. *Theory of Games and Economic Behavior*, Princeton, 2nd ed.

Pauly, M. V., 1968. "The Economics of Moral Hazard: Comment," *American Economic Review*, vol. 58, pp. 531–537.

Radner, R., 1968. "Competitive Equilibrium under Uncertainty," *Econometrica*, vol. 36, pp. 31–58.

Robertson, D. H., 1924. "Those Empty Boxes," *Economic Journal*, vol. 34, pp. 16–30.

Rothenberg, J., 1960. "Non-Convexity, Aggregation, and Pareto Optimality," *Journal of Political Economy*, vol. 68, pp. 435–468.

Rothenberg, J., 1965. "A Model of Economic and Political Decision-Making," in Margolis, J. (ed.), *The Public Economy of Urban Communities*, Washington, D. C.

Samuelson, P. A., 1954. "The Pure Theory of Public Expenditures," *Review of Economic Statistics*, vol. 36, pp. 387–389.

Samuelson, P. A., 1967. "The Monopolistic Competition Revolution," in Kuenne, R. E. (ed.), *Monopolistic Competition Theory: Studies in Impact*, New York, London, and Sydney, pp. 105–138.

Schelling, T., 1957. "Bargaining, Communication, and Limited War," *Journal of Conflict Resolution*, vol. 1, pp. 19–36.

Schumpeter, J., 1942. *Capitalism, Socialism, and Democracy*, 3rd ed., New York.

Scitovsky, T., 1954. "Two Concepts of External Economies," *Journal of Political Economy*, vol. 62, pp. 143–151.

Selten, R., 1964. "Valuation of N-Person Games," in Dresher, M., Shapley, L. S., and Tucker, A. W. (eds.), *Advances in Game Theory. Annals of Mathematics Study*, Princeton, vol. 52, pp. 577–626.

Shapley, L. S., 1953. "A Value for N-Person Games," in Kuhn, H. W., and Tucker, A. W. (eds.), *Contributions to the Theory of Games II. Annals of Mathematics Study*, Princeton, vol. 28, pp. 307–317.

Shapley, L. S., and Shubik, M., 1967. "Ownership and the Production Function," *Quarterly Journal of Economics*, vol. 81, pp. 88–111.

Shubik, M., 1959. "Edgeworth Market Games," in Tucker, A. W., and Luce, R. D. (eds.), *Contributions to the Theory of Games IV. Annals of Mathematics Study*, Princeton, vol. 40, pp. 267–278.

Smith, A., 1937. *An Enquiry Concerning the Causes of the Wealth of Nations*, New York.

Starr, R., 1969. "Quasi-Equilibria in Markets with Nonconvex Preferences," *Econometrica*, vol. 37, pp. 25–38.

Triffin, R., 1941. *Monopolistic Competition and General Equilibrium Theory*, Cambridge, Mass.

Tullock, G., 1967. *Toward a Mathematics of Politics*, Ann Arbor, Mich.

Young, A. A., 1913. "Pigou's Wealth and Welfare," *Quarterly Journal of Economics*, vol. 27, pp. 672–686.

Zeuthen, F., 1930. *Problems of Monopoly and Economic Warfare*, London.

The Simple Analytics of Welfare Maximization*

FRANCIS M. BATOR**

Francis M. Bator (B.S., Massachusetts Institute of Technology, 1949; Ph.D., 1956) was born in Budapest, Hungary, in 1925. He is, at present, Professor of Political Economy at the John F. Kennedy School of Government at Harvard University. Formerly he was Deputy Special Assistant to the President for National Security Affairs and, prior to this, a member of the faculty of MIT, where he served as a senior member of the Center for International Studies. Bator has made signal contributions to economics in many areas, including welfare economics, the theory of externalities and market failure, development, international economics, and the economics of national security. Outside the profession he is best known for his book, *The Question of Government Spending*.

It appears, curiously enough, that there is nowhere in the literature a complete and concise nonmathematical treatment of the problem of welfare maximization in its "new welfare economics" aspects. It is the purpose of this exposition to fill this gap for the simplest statical and stationary situation.

Part I consists in a rigorous diagrammatic determination of the "best" configuration of inputs, outputs, and commodity distribution for a two-input, two-output, two-person situation, where furthermore all functions are of smooth curvature and where

neoclassical generalized diminishing returns obtain in all but one dimension—returns to scale are assumed constant. Part II identifies the "price-wage-rent" configuration embedded in the maximum problem which would ensure that decentralized profit- and preference-maximizing behavior by atomistic competitors would sustain the maximum-welfare position. Part III explores the requirements on initial factor ownership if market-imputed (or "as if" market-imputed) income distribution is to be consistent with the commodity distribution required by the maximum-welfare solution. Part IV consists in brief comments on some technical ambiguities, *e.g.*, the presumption that all tangencies are internal; also on a number of feasible (and not so feasible) extensions: more inputs, outputs and households; elasticity in input supplies; joint and intermediate products; di-

*Reprinted from *American Economic Review* (March 1957) by permission of the American Economic Association. Copyright 1957, pp. 22–59.

**The author, a member of the senior staff of the Center for International Studies, Massachusetts Institute of Technology, is indebted to R. S. Eckaus and R. M. Solow for suggestive comment.

minishing returns to scale; external interactions. The discussion is still stationary and neoclassical in spirit. Then, in Part V, the consequences of violating some of the neoclassical curvature assumptions are examined. Attention is given to the meaning, in a geometric context, of the "convexity" requirements of mathematical economics and to the significance of an important variety of nonconvexity—increasing returns to scale—for "real" market allocation, for Lange-Lerner type "as if" market allocation, and for the solubility of a maximum-of-welfare problem. Finally, Part VI contains some brief remarks on possible dynamical extensions. A note on the seminal literature concludes the paper.[1]

I. INPUTS, OUTPUTS AND COMMODITY DISTRIBUTION

Take, as given:

(1) Two inelastically supplied, homogeneous and perfectly divisible inputs, labor-services (L) and land (D). This "Austrian" assumption does violate the full generality of the neoclassical model; elasticity in input supplies would make simple diagrammatic treatment impossible.

(2) Two production functions, $A = F_A(L_A, D_A)$, $N = F_N(L_N, D_N)$, one for each of the two homogeneous goods: apples (A) and nuts (N). The functions are of smooth curvature, exhibit constant returns to scale and diminishing marginal rates of substitution along any isoquant (*i.e.*, the isoquants are "convex" to the origin).

(3) Two ordinal preference functions, $U_X = f_X$ (A_X, N_X) and $U_Y = f_Y(A_Y, N_Y)$—sets of smooth indifference curves convex to the origin—one for X and one for Y. These reflect unambiguous and consistent preference orderings for each of the two individuals (X and Y) of all conceivable combinations of own-consumption of apples and nuts. For convenience we adopt for each function an arbitrary numerical index, U_X and U_Y, to identify the indifference curves. But the functions have no interpersonal implications whatever and for any one individual they only permit of statements to the effect that one situation is worse, indifferent or better than another. We do require consistency: if X prefers situation α to situation β and β to γ, then he must prefer α to γ; indifference curves must not cross. Also, satiation-type phenomena and Veblenesque or other "external" effects are ruled out.

(4) A social welfare function, $W = W(U_X, U_Y)$, that permits a unique preference-ordering of all possible states based only on the positions of both individuals in their own preference fields. It is this function that incorporates an ethical valuation of the relative "deservingness" of X and Y.

The problem is to determine the maximum-welfare values of labor input into apples (L_A), labor input into nuts (L_N), land input into apples (D_A), land input into nuts (D_N), of total production of apples (A) and nuts (N), and, last, of the distribution of apples and nuts between X and Y (A_X, N_X, A_Y, N_Y).

A. From Endowments and Production Functions to the Production-Possibility Curve

Construct an Edgeworth-Bowley box diagram, as in Fig. 1, with horizontal and vertical dimensions just equal to the given supplies, respectively, of D and L, and plot the isoquants for apples with the southwest corner as origin and those for nuts with origin at the northeast corner. Every point in the box represents six variables, L_A, L_N, D_A, D_N, A, N. The problem of production efficiency consists in finding the locus of points where any increase in the production of apples implies a necessary reduction in the output of nuts (and vice versa). The diagram shows that locus to consist in the points of tangency between the nut and apple isoquants (FF).

From this efficiency locus we can read off the maximal obtainable combinations of apples and nuts and plot these in the output (AN) space. Given our curvature assumptions we get the smooth concave-to-the-origin Pareto-efficient production-possibility curve $F'F'$ of Fig. 2.[2] This curve, a consolidation of FF in Fig. 1, represents input-output configurations such that the marginal rate of substitution (MRS) of labor for land in the production of any given quantity of apples—the absolute value of the slope of the apple

---

[1] Anyone familiar with the modern literature will recognize my debt to the writings of Professor Samuelson. Reference is to be made, especially, to Chapter 8 of *Foundations of Economic Analysis* (Cambridge, 1947); to "Evaluation of Real National Income," *Oxford Econ. Papers*, Jan. 1950, II, 1–29; and to "Social Indifference Curves," *Quart. Jour. Econ.*, Feb. 1956, LXX, 1–22.

[2] This presumes, also, that the intrinsic factor intensities of A and N differ. If they did not, $F'F'$ would be a straight line—a harmless special case. (See V-3-c below.)

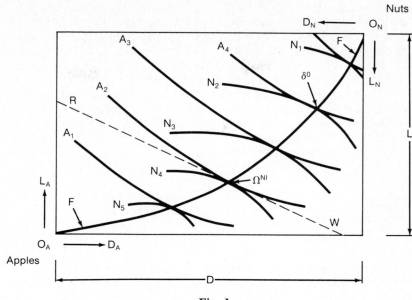

Fig. 1

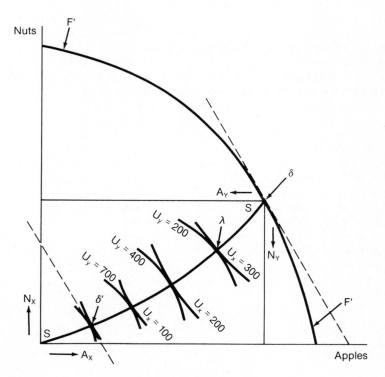

Fig. 2

isoquant—just equals the marginal rate of substitution of labor for land in the production of nuts.[3]

The slope (again neglecting sign) at any point on the production-possibility curve of Fig. 2, in turn, reflects the marginal rate of transformation (MRT) at that point of apples into nuts. It indicates precisely how many nuts can be produced by transferring land and labor from apple to nut production (at the margin), with optimal reallocation of inputs in the production of both goods so as to maintain the MRS-equality requirement of Fig. 1. It is the marginal nut-cost of an "extra" apple—or the reciprocal of the marginal apple-cost of nuts.

B. From the Production-Possibility Curve to the Utility-Possibility Frontier

Pick any point, δ, on the production-possibility curve of Fig. 2: it denotes a specific quantity of apples and nuts. Construct an Edgeworth-Bowley (trading) box with these precise dimensions by dropping from δ lines parallel to the axes as in Fig. 2. Then draw in X's and Y's indifference maps, one with the southwest, the other with the northeast corner for origin. Every point in the box again fixes six variables: apples to X (A_X) and to Y (A_Y), nuts to X (N_X) and to Y (N_Y), and the "levels" of satisfaction of X and Y as measured by the ordinal indices U_X and U_Y which characterize the position of the point with respect to the two preference fields. For example, at λ in Fig. 2, $U_X = 300$, $U_Y = 200$. Note again, however, that this 200 is incommensurate with the 300: it does not imply that at λ X is in some sense better off than is Y (or indifferent, or worse off).

The problem of "exchange-efficiency" consists in finding that locus of feasible points within the trading box where any increase in X's satisfaction (U_X) implies a necessary reduction in the satisfaction of Y, (U_Y). Feasible in what sense? In the sense that we just exhaust the fixed apple-nut totals as denoted by δ. Again, the locus turns out to consist of the points of tangency, SS, and for precisely the same analytical

reasons. Only now it is the marginal subjective rate of substitution of nuts for apples in providing a fixed level of satisfaction for X—the absolute slope of X's indifference curve—that is to be equated to the nut-apple MRS of Y, to the slope, that is, of *his* indifference curve.

From this exchange-efficiency locus,[4] SS, which is associated with the single production point δ, we can now read off the maximal combinations of U_X and U_Y obtainable from δ and plot these in utility $(U_X U_Y)$ space (S'S', Fig. 3). Each such *point* δ in output space "maps" into a *line* in utility space—the $U_X U_Y$ mix is sensitive to how the fixed totals of apples and nuts are distributed between X and Y.[5]

There is a possible short-cut, however. Given our curvature assumptions, we can trace out the grand utility-possibility frontier—the envelope—by using an efficiency relationship to pick just one point from each trading box contract curve SS associated with every output point δ. Go back to Fig. 2. The slope of the production-possibility curve at δ has already been revealed as the marginal rate of transformation, via production, of apples into nuts. The (equalized) slopes of the two sets of indifference contours along the exchange-efficiency curve SS, in turn, represent the marginal rates of substitution of nuts for apples for psychic indifference (the same for X as for Y). The grand criterion for efficiency is that it be impossible by any shift in production *cum* exchange to increase U_X without reducing U_Y. Careful thought will suggest that this criterion is violated unless the marginal rate of transformation between apples and nuts as outputs—the slope at δ—just equals the common marginal rate of substitution of apples and nuts, as consumption "inputs," in providing psychic satisfaction.

If, for example, at δ one can get two apples by

---

[3] In marginal productivity terms, MRS, at any point, of labor for land in, *e.g.* apple production—the absolute value (drop all minus signs) of the slope of the apple isoquant (Fig. 1)—is equal to

$$\left[\frac{\text{Marginal Physical Product of Land}}{\text{Marginal Physical Product of Labor}} \right]$$

in apple production at that point. In the symbolism of the calculus

$$\left| \frac{\partial L_A}{\partial D_A} \right|_{\Delta A = 0} = \left(\frac{\partial A}{\partial D_A} \right) \div \left(\frac{\partial A}{\partial L_A} \right).$$

[4] This is Edgeworth's contract curve, or what Boulding has aptly called the "conflict" curve—once on it, mutually advantageous trading is not possible and any move reflecting a gain to X implies a loss to Y.

[5] Each *point* in utility space, in turn, maps into a line in output-space. Not just one but many possible apple-nut combinations can satisfy a specified $U_X U_Y$ requirement. It is this reciprocal point-line phenomenon that lies at the heart of Samuelson's proof of the nonexistence of community indifference curves such as would permit the derivation of demand curves for apples and nuts. The subjective "community" MRS between A and N for given fixed A and N, *e.g.*, at δ in Fig. 2, would surely depend on how the A and N are distributed, *i.e.*, on which $U_X U_Y$ point on SS is chosen. Hence the slope of a "joint" XY indifference curve at δ is not uniquely fixed by AN. (See citation [11] in bibliography.)

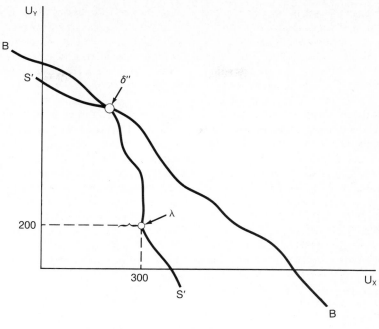

Fig. 3

diverting resources and reducing nut-output by one, a point on *SS* where the (equalized) marginal rate of substitution of apples for nuts along indifference curves is, *e.g.*, one to one, permits the following "arbitrage" operation. Shift land and labor so as to produce two more apples and one less nut. Then, leaving X undisturbed take away one nut from Y and replace it by one apple. By our assumption that MRS = 1 both X and Y are left indifferent: U_X and U_Y remain unaltered. But we have an extra apple left over; since this permits raising U_X and/or U_Y, the initial situation was not on the $U_X U_Y$ frontier.[6]

To be on the grand utility-possibility frontier (*BB* of Fig. 3), then, MRT_δ must equal the (equalized) MRS of the indifference contours along the *SS* associated with δ. This requirement fixes the single $U_X U_Y$ point on *SS* that lies on the "envelope" utility-possibility frontier, given the output point δ. Pick that point on *SS*, in fact, where the joint slope of the indifference curves is exactly parallel to the slope at δ of the production-possibility curve. In Fig. 2 this point is at δ′, which gives the one "efficient" $U_X U_Y$

combination associated with the *AN* mix denoted by δ. This $U_X U_Y$ combination can then be plotted as δ″ in Fig. 3.[7]

Repetition of this process for each point on the production-possibility curve—note that each such point requires a new trading box—will yield the grand utility-possibility frontier of Pareto-efficient input-output combinations, *BB*. Each point of this frontier gives the maximum of U_X for any given feasible level of U_Y and vice versa.

C. From the Utility-Possibility Frontier to the "Constrained Bliss Point"

But *BB*, the grand utility-possibility function, is a curve and not a point. Even after eliminating all combinations of inputs and outputs that are nonefficient in a Paretian sense, there remains a single-dimen-

---

[6]The above argument can be made perfectly rigorous in terms of the infinitesimal movements of the differential calculus.

[7]Never mind, here, about multiple optima. These could occur even with our special curvature assumptions. If, for example, both sets of indifference curves show paths of equal MRS that coincide with straight lines from the origin and, further, if the two preference functions are so symmetrical as to give an SS_δ that hugs the diagonal of the trading box, then either every point on SS_δ will satisfy the MRS = MRT criterion, or none will. For discussion of these and related fine points see Parts IV and V.

sional infinity of "efficient" combinations: one for every point on *BB*. To designate a single *best* configuration we must be given a Bergson-Samuelson social welfare function that denotes the ethic that is to "count" or whose implications we wish to study. Such a function—it could be yours, or mine, or Mossadegh's, though his is likely to be nontransitive—is intrinsically ascientific.[8] There are no considerations of *economic efficiency* that permit us to designate Crusoe's function, which calls for many apples and nuts for Crusoe and just a few for Friday, as economically superior to Friday's. Ultimate ethical valuations are involved.

Once given such a welfare function, in the form of a family of indifference contours in utility space, as in Fig. 4, the problem becomes fully determinate.[9] "Welfare" is at a maximum where the utility-possibility envelope frontier *BB* touches the highest con-

tour of the *W*-function.[10] In Fig. 4, this occurs at Ω.

Note the unique quality of that point Ω. It is the only point, of all the points on the utility frontier *BB*, that has unambiguous normative or prescriptive significance. Pareto-efficient production and commodity-distribution—being on *F'F'* and also on *BB*—is a necessary condition for a maximum of our kind of welfare function, but is not a sufficient condition.[11] The claim that any "efficient" point is better than "inefficient" configurations that lie inside *BB* is indefensible. It is true that given an "inefficient" point, there will exist *some* point or points on *BB* that represent an improvement; but there may well be many points on *BB* that would be worse rather than better. For example, in terms of the ethic denoted by the specific *W*-function of Fig. 4, Ω on *BB* is better than any other feasible point. But the efficient point ξ is distinctly inferior to any inefficient

---

[8]Though it may provide the anthropologist or psychologist with interesting material for scientific study.

[9]In the absence of implicit income redistribution these curves cannot be transposed into output-space. They are not community indifference curves which would permit the derivation of demand schedules. See fn. 5 and 12, also IV-3.

[10]If there are several such points, never mind. If the "ethic" at hand is really indifferent, pick any one. If it doesn't matter, it doesn't matter.

[11]Note, however, that Pareto-efficiency is not even a necessary condition for a maximum of just any conceivable *W*-function. The form of our type function reflects a number of ethically loaded restrictions, *e.g.*, that individuals' preference functions are to "count," and count positively.

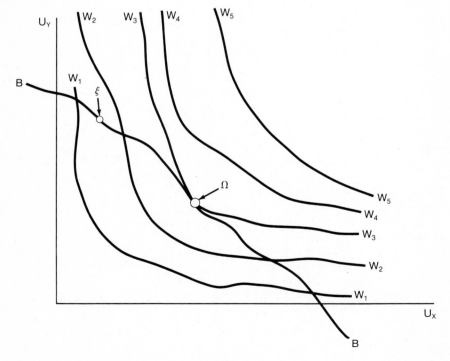

Fig. 4

point on or northeast of W_2. If I am X, and if my W-function, which reflects the usual dose of self-interest, is the test, "efficient" BB points that give a high U_Y and a very low U_X are clearly less desirable than lots of inefficient points of higher U_X.[12]

[12]Note, however, that no consistency requirements link my set of in-difference curves with "my" W-function. The former reflects a personal preference ordering based only on own-consumption (and, in the more general case, own services supplied). The latter denotes also values which I hold as "citizen," and these need not be consistent with max-imizing my satisfaction "*qua* consumer." X as citizen may prefer a state of less U_X and some U_Y to more U_X and zero U_Y. There is also an important analytical distinction. X's preference function is conceptually "observable": confronted by various relative price and income config-urations his consumption responses will reveal its contours. His W-function, on the other hand, is not revealed by behavior, unless he be dictator, subjected by "nature" to binding constraints. In a sense only a society, considered as exhibiting a political consensus, has a W-func-tion subject to empirical inference (*cf.* IV-3). The distinction—it has a Rousseauvian flavor—while useful, is of course arbitrary. Try it for a masochist; a Puritan. . . .

D. From "Bliss Point" to "Best" Inputs, Outputs and Commodity-Distribution

We can now retrace our steps. To Ω on BB in Fig. 4, there corresponds just one point, Ω', on the pro-duction-possibility curve $F'F'$ in Fig. 5. (We derived BB, point by point, from $F'F'$ of Fig. 2: and the $F'F'$ of Fig. 5 is copied from that of Fig. 2.) Ω' fixes the output mix: A and N. Then, by examining the trading-box contract curve $S_\Omega S_\Omega$ associated with Ω' of $F'F'$, we can locate the one point where U_X and U_Y correspond to the coordinates of Ω in utility space. The equalized slope of the indifference curves will at that point, Ω'', just equal the slope of $F'F'$ at Ω'. Ω'' fixes the apple-nut distribution implied by the maximum of W: A_X, A_Y, N_X, and N_Y. Further, we can now locate the point Ω''' on the Pareto-efficient input locus, FF of Fig. 1, that corresponds to Ω' of $F'F'$. It fixes the remaining variables, the factor allocations: L_A, D_A, L_N, and D_N. The maxi-

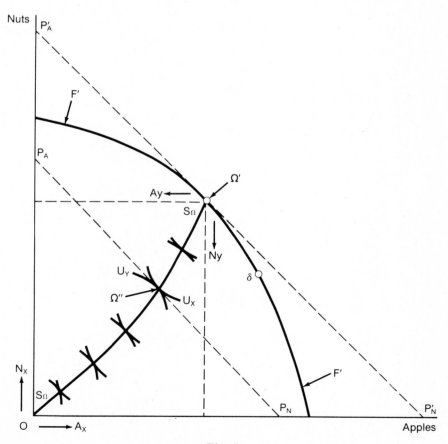

Fig. 5

mum-welfare configuration is determinate. We have solved for the land and labor to be used in apple and nut production, for the total output of apples and nuts, and for their distribution between X and Y.

II. PRICES, WAGES AND RENTS

The above is antiseptically independent of institutional context, notably of competitive market institutions. It could constitute an intellectual exercise for the often invoked man from Mars, in how "best" to make do with given resources. Yet implicit in the logic of this purely "technocratic" formulation, embedded in the problem as it were, is a set of constants which the economist will catch himself thinking of as prices. And wisely so. Because it happens—and this "duality" theorem is the kernel of modern welfare economics—that decentralized decisions in response to these "prices" by, or "as if" by, atomistic profit and satisfaction maximizers will result in just that constellation of inputs, outputs and commodity-distribution that our maximum of W requires.[13]

Can these constants—prices, wages, rents—be identified in our diagrammatic representations?[14] Only partially so. Two-dimensionality is partly at fault, but, as we shall see, a final indeterminacy is implied by the usual curvature assumptions themselves.[15] The diagrams will, however, take us part way, and a little algebra will do for the rest.

The exercise consists in finding a set of four constants associated with the solution values of the maximum problem that have meaning as the price of apples (p_A), the price of nuts (p_N), the wage rate of labor (w), and the rental rate of land (r).[16]

First, what can be said about w and r? Profit maximization by the individual producer implies that whatever output he may choose as most lucrative must be produced at a minimum total cost.[17] The elementary theory of the firm tells us that, for this condition to hold, the producer facing fixed input-prices—horizontal supply curves—must adjust his input mix until the marginal rate of substitution (MRS) of labor for land just equals the rent-to-wage ratio. It is easy to see the "arbitrage" possibilities if this condition is violated. If one can substitute one unit of L for two units of D, and maintain output constant, with $w = \$10$ and $r = \$10$, it surely reduces total cost to do so and keep doing so until any further reduction in D by one unit has to be matched, if output is not to fall, by adding no less than one unit of L. In the usual diagrammatic terms, then, the producer will cling to points of tangency between the isoquants and (iso-expenditure) lines whose absolute slope equals r/w.

Reversing the train of thought, the input blend denoted by the point Ω''' in Fig. 1 implies a shadow r/w ratio that just equals the MRS of labor for land in the production of both apples and nuts at that point Ω'''. $MRS_{\Omega'''}$ is given by the (equalized) slopes of the isoquants at Ω'''. The implicit r/w, therefore, must equal the slope of the line RW that is tangent to (both) the isoquants at Ω'''.[18]

The slope of RW identifies the rent:wage ratio implied by the maximal configuration. Essentially analogous reasoning will establish the equalized slope of the indifference curves through Ω'', in Fig. 5, as denoting the p_A/p_N ratio implied by the solution. X, as also Y, to maximize his own satisfaction as measured by U_x, must achieve whatever level of satisfaction his income will permit at a minimum expenditure. This requires that he choose an apple-nut mix such that the psychic marginal-rate-of-substitution between nuts and apples for indifference just equal p_A/p_N. He, and Y, will pick Ω'' only if p_A/p_N is equal to the absolute slope of the tangent $(P_A P_N)$ at

---

[13]Note that this statement is neutral with respect to (1) genuine profit maximizers acting in "real" but perfectly competitive markets; (2) Lange-Lerner-type bureaucrats ("take prices as given and maximize or Siberia"); or (3) technicians using electronic machines and trying to devise efficient computing routines.

[14] To avoid institutional overtones, the theory literature usually attempts verbal disembodiment and refers to them as shadow-prices. The mathematically oriented, in turn, like to think of them as Lagrangean multipliers.

[15] These very assumptions render this last indeterminacy, that of the absolute price level, wholly inconsequential.

[16] Since we are still assuming that all the functions have neoclassical curvature properties, hence that, *e.g.*, the production-possibility curve, as derived, has to be concave to the origin, we can impose the *strong* condition on the constants that they exhibit optimality characteristics for genuine, though perfect, markets. It will turn out, however, that two progressively weaker conditions are possible, which permit of some nonconvexities (*e.g.*, increasing returns to scale), yet maintain for the constants some essentially price-like qualities. More on this in Part V.

[17] In our flow model, unencumbered by capital, this is equivalent to producing the chosen output with minimum expenditure on inputs.

[18]Again, absolute values of these slopes are implied throughout the argument. Recall from footnote 3 that the labor-for-land MRS, the absolute slope of the isoquants at Ω''' as given by RO_A/WO_A, is equal to the

$$\left[\frac{\text{Marginal Physical Product of Land}}{\text{Marginal Physical Product of Labor}} \right] \text{ ratio.}$$

Our shadow r/w, then, turns out to be just equal to that ratio.

Ω''. This slope, therefore, fixes the Ω-value of p_A/p_N.[19]

Note that this makes p_A/p_N equal to the slope also of the production-possibility curve $F'F'$ at Ω'.[20] This is as it should be. If $p_A/p_N = 10$, i.e., if one apple is "worth" ten nuts on the market, it would be odd indeed, in our frictionlessly efficient world of perfect knowledge, if the marginal rate of transformation of nuts into apples, via production, were different from ten-to-one. Producers would not in fact produce the apple-nut combination of Ω' if p_A/p_N differed from MRT at Ω'.

We have identified the r/w and p_A/p_N implied by the maximum of W. These two constancies provide two equations to solve for the four unknown prices. Unfortunately this is as far as the two-dimensional diagrammatics will take us. None of the diagrams permit easy identification of the relationship between the input prices and the output prices. Yet such a relationship is surely implied. By the theory of the firm we know that the profit-maximizing producer facing a constant price for his product—the horizontal demand curve of the perfectly competitive firm—will expand output up to where his extra revenue for an additional unit of output, i.e., the price, just equals the marginal cost of producing that output.[21] And marginal cost, in turn, is sensitive to r and w.

It would be easy to show the implied price-wage or price-rent relationships by introducing marginal productivity notions. Profit maximization requires that the quantity of each input hired be increased up to the point where its marginal physical product times the price of the extra output, just equals the price of the added input. Since these marginal physical productivities are determinate curvature properties of the production functions, this rule provides a third relationship, one between an output price and an input price.

Alternatively, given our assumption that produc-

tion functions show constant returns to scale, we can make use of Euler's "product exhaustion" theorem. Its economic content is that if constant returns to scale prevails, the total as-if-market-imputed income of the factors of production just "exhausts" the total value of the product. This means, simply, that $wL + rD = p_A A + p_N N$, and it provides a third relationship between w, r, p_A and p_N for the Ω-values of L, D, A and N.[22]

At any rate, the maximal solution implies a third price-equation, hence we can express three of the prices in terms of the fourth. But what of the fourth? This is indeterminate, given the characteristics of the model. In a frictionless world of perfect certainty, where, for example, nobody would think of holding such a thing as money, only *relative* prices matter. The three equations establish the proportions among them implied by the maximum position, and the absolute values are of no import. If the $p_A:p_N:w:r$ proportions implied by Ω are $20:15:50:75$, profit and satisfaction maximizers will make the input-output-consumption decisions required for the maximum-of-W irrespective of whether the absolute levels of these prices happen to be just $20:15:50:75$, or twice, or one-half, or 50 times this set of numbers. This is the implication of the fact that for the maximum problem only the various transformation and substitution *ratios* matter. In all that follows we shall simply posit that nuts are established as the unit of account, hence that $p_N = 1$. This then makes p_A, w and r fully determinate constants.[23]

Summarizing: we have identified diagrammatically two of the three shadow-price relationships implied by the solution to the welfare-maximum problem and have established, in a slightly more roundabout way, the existence of the third. The purpose was to demonstrate the existence, at least in our idealized neoclassical model, of a set of constants embedded in the "technocratic" maximum-of-welfare problem, that can be viewed as competitive market

[19] The price-ratio relates reciprocally to the axes: $p_A/p_N = P_A O/P_N O$ in Fig. 5. Along, e.g., X's indifference curve (U_X at Ω'') a rise in p_A/p_N, i.e., a steepening of $P_A P_N$, results in a substitution by X of nuts for apples; ditto for Y.

[20] Remember, in choosing the one point on $S_\Omega S_\Omega$ that would lie on the envelope in utility space, we chose the point where the indifference curve slopes just equaled the marginal rate of transformation (see p. 393 above).

[21] Never mind here the "total" requirement—that this price exceed unit cost—if the real-life profit-seeking producer is to produce at all. More on this in Part V.

[22] The condition also holds for each firm. In a competitive and constant-returns-to-scale world the profit-maximum position is one of zero profit: total revenue will just equal total cost. It should be said, however, that use of the Euler theorem to gain a relationship between input price and output price involves a measure of sleight of hand. It is only as a consequence of the relationships between price and marginal productivity (cf. the preceding paragraph) that the theorem assures equality of income with value of product.

[23] For the possibility of inessential indeterminacies, however, see Part IV-2.

prices.[24] In what sense? In the sense that decentralized decisions in response to these constants, by, or "as if" by, atomistic profit and satisfaction maximizers will result in just that configuration of inputs, outputs and commodity-distribution that the maximum of our W requires.

III. FACTOR OWNERSHIP AND INCOME DISTRIBUTION

We have said nothing, so far, of how X and Y "pay" for their apples and nuts, or of who "owns" and supplies the labor and the land. As was indicated above, the assumption of constant returns to scale assures that at the maximum welfare position total income will equal total value of output, and that total revenue from the sale of apples (nuts) will just equal total expenditures for inputs by the producers of apples (nuts). Also, the "solution" implies definite "purchase" of apples and of nuts both by X and by Y. But nothing ensures that the initial "ownership" of labor-hours and of land is such that w times the labor-hours supplied by X, wL_X, plus r times the land supplied by X, rD_X—X's income—will suffice to cover his purchases as required by Ω'', i.e., $p_A A_X + p_N N_X$; similarly for Y. There does exist some Pareto-efficient solution of inputs, outputs and distribution that satisfies the "income = outgo" condition for both individuals for any arbitrary pattern of ownership of the "means of production"—a solution, that is, that will place the system somewhere on the grand utility-possibility envelope frontier (BB in Fig. 4). But only by the sheerest accident will that point on BB be better in terms of my W-function, or Thomas Jefferson's, or that of a "political consensus," than a multidimensional infinity of other points *on or off BB*. As emphasized above, only one point on BB can have ultimate normative, prescriptive significance: Ω; and only some special ownership patterns of land and of labor-services will place a market system with an "as imputed" distribution of income at that special point.[25]

The above is of especial interest in evaluating the optimality characteristics of market institutions in an environment of private property ownership. But the problem is not irrelevant even where all nonhuman means of production are vested in the community, hence where the proceeds of nonwage income are distributed independently of marginal productivity, marginal-rate-of-substitution considerations. If labor-services are not absolutely homogeneous—if some people are brawny and dumb and others skinny and clever, not to speak of "educated"—income distribution will be sensitive to the initial endowment of these qualities of mind and body and skill relative to the need for them. And again, only a very low probability accident would give a configuration consistent with any particular W-function's Ω.[26]

Even our homogeneous-labor world cannot entirely beg this issue. It is not enough to assume that producers are indifferent between an hour of X's as against an hour of Y's labor-services. It is also required that the total supply of labor-hours per accounting period be so divided between X and Y as to split total wage payments in a particular way, depending on land ownership and on the income distribution called for by Ω. This may require that X supply, *e.g.*, 75 per cent of total L; each man working $\frac{1}{2}L$ hours may well not do.[27]

But all this is diversion. For our noninstitutional purposes it is sufficient to determine the particular L_X, D_X, L_Y and D_Y that are consistent with Ω, given market-imputed, or "as if" market-imputed, distribution. Unfortunately the diagrams used in Part I again fail, but the algebra is simple. It is required that:

$$wL_X + rD_X = p_A A_X + p_N N_X,$$

and

$$wL_Y + rD_Y = p_A A_Y + p_N N_Y,$$

for the already-solved-for maximal Ω-values of

---

[24]On the existence of such a set of shadow prices in the kinky and flat-surfaced world of linear programming, see Part V, below.

[25]It is of course possible to break the link between factor ownership and "final" income distribution by means of interpersonal transfers. Moreover, if such transfers are effected by means of costless lump-sum devices—never mind how feasible—then it is possible, in concept, to attain the Ω-implied distribution irrespective of market-imputations. But no decentralized price-market-type "game" can reveal the pattern of taxes and transfers that would maximize a particular W-function. "Central" calculation—implicit or explicit—is unavoidable.

[26]If slavery were the rule and I could sell the capitalized value of my expected lifetime services, the distinction between ownership of labor and that of land would blur. Except in an "Austrian" world, however, it would not vanish. As long as men retain a measure of control over the quality and time-shape of their own services, there will always remain an incentive problem.

[27]All this is based on the "Austrian" assumption that labor is supplied inelastically; further, that such inelasticity is due not to external compulsion, but rather to sharp "corners" in the preference-fields of X and Y in relation to work-leisure choices. More than this, the W-function must not be sensitive to variations in the $L_X L_Y$ mix except as these influence income distribution.

A_X, N_X, A_Y, N_Y, p_A, p_N, w and r. Together with $L_X + L_Y = L$ and $D_X + D_Y = D$, we appear to have four equations to solve for the four unknowns: L_X, L_Y, D_X and D_Y. It turns out, however, that one of these is not independent. The sum of the first two, that *total* incomes equal *total* value of product, is implied by Euler's theorem taken jointly with the marginal productivity conditions that give the solution for the eight variables, A_X, N_X, A_Y, . . . which are here taken as known. Hence, we have only three independent equations. This is as it should be. It means only that with our curvature assumptions we can, within limits, fix one of the four endowments more or less arbitrarily and still so allocate the rest as to satisfy the household budget equations.

So much for the income-distribution aspects of the problem. These have relevance primarily for market-imputed income distribution; but such relevance does not depend on "private" ownership of nonlabor means of production. Note, incidentally, that only with the arbitrary "Austrian" assumption of fixed supplies of total inputs can one first solve "simultaneously" for inputs, outputs and commodity-distribution, and only subsequently superimpose on this solution the ownership and money-income distribution problem. If L_X, D_X, L_Y, D_Y, hence L and D were assumed sensitive to w, r, the p's and household income levels, the dimensions of the production-box of Fig. 1, hence the position of the production-possibility curve of Figs. 2 and 5, etc., would interdepend with the final solution values of L_X, D_X, L_Y and D_Y. We would then have to solve the full problem as a set of simultaneous equations from the raw data: production functions, tastes (this time with an axis for leisure, or many axes for many differently irksome kinds of labor), and the W-function. Three (or more) dimensional diagrams would be needed for a geometrical solution.

IV. SOME EXTENSIONS

We have demonstrated the solution of the maximum problem of modern welfare economics in context of the simplest statical and stationary neoclassical model. Many generalizations and elaborations suggest themselves, even if one remains strictly neoclassical and restricts oneself to a steady-state situation where none of the data change and no questions about "how the system gets there" are permitted to intrude. To comment on just a few:

1. The problem could well be solved for many households, many goods, and many factors: it has received complete and rigorous treatment in the literature. Of course the diagrammatics would not do; elementary calculus becomes essential. But the qualitative characteristics of the solution of the m by n by q case are precisely those of the 2 by 2 by 2. The same marginal rate of transformation and substitution conditions characterize the solution, only now in many directions. Nothing new or surprising happens.[28]

2. The solution did skirt one set of difficulties that were not explicitly ruled out by assumption. We tacitly assumed that the two sets of isoquants would provide a smooth locus of "internal" tangencies, FF, in the production box of Fig. 1; similarly, that we would get such an "internal" SS in the trading boxes of Figs. 2 and 5. Nothing in our assumptions guarantees that this should be so. What if the locus of maximum A's for given feasible N's, should occur not at points of strict tangency *inside* the box, but at what the mathematician would call corner-tangencies along the edges of the box? Fig. 6 illustrates this possibility. The maximum feasible output of A, for $N = 6000$, occurs at σ, where $A = 400$; but at σ the two isoquants are not strictly tangent (they touch but have different slopes). The economic meaning of this is simple. With endowments as indicated by the dimensions of the production box in Fig. 6, and with technology as denoted by the isoquants, it is not possible to reallocate inputs until the MRS of labor for land is the same in apple as in nut production. This is because apple technology (as depicted) is so land-using relative to nut production that the

$$\left[\frac{\text{marginal productivity of land}}{\text{marginal productivity of labor}}\right] \text{ratio}$$

in apple production exceeds that in nut production even when, as at σ, *all* land is devoted to apples.

Space precludes further analysis of such corner-tangency phenomena. They reflect the possibility that the maximum-welfare solution may require that not every input be used in producing every output (*e.g.*, no land in nut production or no brain surgeons in coal mining), and may even render one of the

---

[28]Rigorous general treatment of the $m \times n \times q$ situation does highlight a number of analytical fine points that are of interest to the pure theorist, *e.g.*, the difficulties encountered if the number of factors exceeds the number of goods. But the qualitative economics is the same. For a full treatment from a nonnormative point of view, see P. A. Samuelson, "Prices of Factors and Goods in General Equilibrium," *Rev. Econ. Stud.*, 1953–1954, XXI (1), No. 54, 1–20.

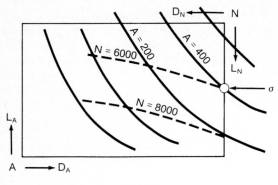

Fig. 6

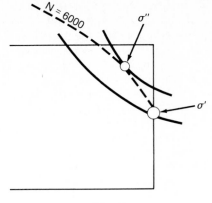

Fig. 7

inputs a "free good," so that its total use will not add up to the total available supply. Let it suffice to assert that by formulating the maximum conditions, not in terms of *equalities* of various slopes, but rather in terms of *inequalities;* by explicit statement of the proper second-order "rate-of-change-of-slope" conditions; and by allowing inequalities in the factor-balance conditions (*e.g.*, $L_A + L_N \leqq L$), such phenomena of bumping into the axes can be handled; further, that only inessential indeterminacies occur in the implied shadow-price configuration.[29]

3. We stressed, above, the nonexistence of *community* indifference contours such as would provide a unique ranking, for the community as a whole, of various output combinations.[30] Individual marginal

rates of substitution between, *e.g.*, apples and silk shirts, equalized along a trading-box contract curve to give a "community" MRS, are likely to be sensitive to the distribution of income[31] between gourmets and dandies; accordingly, community MRS at a given point in commodity space, *i.e.*, the slope of a curve of community indifference, will vary with movements along the associated utility-possibility curve. However, once the most desirable $U_X U_Y$ combination for a given package of A and N is fixed, MRS at that AN-point becomes determinate. It follows, as recently pointed out and proved by Samuelson,[32] that if the observed community continuously redistributes "incomes" in utopian lump-sum fashion so as to maximize, in utility space, over the W-function implied by a political consensus, then there does exist, in output space, a determinate *social* indifference function which provides a ranking for the community as a whole of all conceivable output combinations. This function, which yields conventionally convex social indifference contours, can be treated as though a single mind were engaged in maximizing it. Moreover, in concept and if granted the premise of continuous redistribution, its contours are subject to empirical inference from observed price-market data.

This existence theorem justifies the use of *social* indifference maps—maps "corrected" for distribution—in handling problems of production efficiency, international trade, etc.—a substantial analytical con-

---

[29]All this can perhaps be made clearer by two examples. The essential requirement for A_σ to be at a maximum for $N = 6000$ is that the intersection at the boundary be as in Fig. 6 rather than as in Fig. 7. In the latter, σ' gives a minimum of A for $N = 6000$; the true maximum is at σ''. The distinction between σ in 6 and σ' in 7 is between the relative rates of change of the two MRS's. The price indeterminacy implied by the maximum, *i.e.*, the fact that σ is consistent with an r/w that lies anywhere between the two isoquants, turns out to be inessential. A second example concerns the theory of the firm. It has been argued that if the marginal cost curve has vertical gaps and the price-line hits one of these gaps, then the $MC = p$ condition is indeterminate, hence that the theory is no good. As has been pointed out in the advanced literature (*e.g.*, by R. L. Bishop, in "Cost Discontinuities . . ." *Am. Econ. Rev.*, Sept. 1948, XXXVIII, 607–17) this is incorrect: What is important is that at smaller than equilibrium output MC be less than price and at higher outputs MC exceed price. It is true, but quite harmless to the theory, that such a situation does leave a range of indeterminacy in the price that will elicit *that* level of output. Such phenomena do change the mathematics of computation. Inequalities cannot in general be used to eliminate unknowns by simple substitution. On all this, see the literature of linear programming (*e.g.*, citations [10] and [13]).

[30]See fn. 5.

[31]In terms of abstract purchasing power.

[32]See citation [11].

venience.[33] More important, it provides a conceptual foundation, however abstract, for prescription based not on just any arbitrary ethic, but rather on the particular ethic revealed by a society as reflecting its own political consensus.[34]

4. It is useful, and in a mathematical treatment not difficult, to drop the "Austrian" assumption of inelastically supplied inputs, and introduce leisure-work choices.[35] The analytical effect is to sensitize the production-possibility curve to the psychic sensibilities—the preference functions—of individuals. Note that the empirical sense of doing so is not confined to an institutional or ethical context of non-imposed choice. A dictator, too, has to take account of such choices, if only because of feasibility limitations on coercion.

5. We assumed away joint-product situations. This is convenient for manipulation but hardly essential; the results can be generalized to cover most kinds of jointness. It turns out, in fact, that in dynamical models with capital stocks, one means for taking account of the durability of such stocks is to allow for joint products. A process requiring a hydraulic press "produces" both stamped metal parts and a "one-year-older" hydraulic press.

6. In our system the distinction between inputs (L, D) and outputs (A, N) could be taken for granted. But the distinction is clear only in a world of completely vertically-integrated producers, all hiring "primary" nonproduced inputs and producing "final" consumable goods and services. In a Leontief-like system that allows for interproducer transactions and intermediate products, many outputs: electricity, steel, corn, beef, trucks, etc., are simultaneously inputs. It is of interest, and also feasible, to generalize the analysis to take account of, e.g., coal being used not only to heat houses, but to produce steel required

in the production of mining machines designed for the production of coal. Moreover, none of the essential qualitative characteristics of our maximum problem is violated by such generalization.[36]

7. What if instead of assuming that production functions show constant returns to scale, we permit diminishing returns to proportional expansion of inputs? This could be due either to inherent nonlinearities in the physics and topography of the universe, or to the existence of some unaccounted-for but significant input in limited, finite-elastic supply.[37]

Diminishing returns to scale, as distinct from increasing returns, does not give rise to serious trouble, either for the analytical solubility of the system, or for the market-significance of the intrinsic price-wage-rent constants. It does introduce some ambiguities, however. For one thing, the "value" of output will exceed the total of market-imputed income. This makes intuitive sense in terms of the "unaccounted-scarce-factor" explanation of decreasing returns; the residual unimputed value of output reflects the income "due" the "hidden" factor. If that factor were treated explicitly and given an axis in the production-function diagram, returns would no longer diminish—since, on this view, the relative inexpansibility of that input gave rise to decreasing returns to scale to begin with—and the difficulty would vanish.[38]

---

[33]Note, however, that none of this eliminates the need for a W-function: social indifference contours are a convex function of individual taste patterns of the usual ordinal variety taken jointly with an implicit or explicit W-function of "regular" content and curvature. Further, no ultimate superiority attaches to the W-function implied by a particular political consensus. One may disapprove of the power relationships on which such consensus rests, etc.

[34]Needless to say, feasibility is not here at issue. Even on this level of abstraction, however, matters become much more difficult once account is taken of the fact that the world is not stationary.

[35]If we assume only one commodity, say apples, and replace the second good by leisure (or by negative labor input); and if we let the second-good production function be a simple linear relation, our previous geometry will portray the simplest goods-leisure situation.

[36]Analytically, this is done by designating all produced goods as X_1, $X_2, X_3 \ldots$. The gross production of, e.g., X_1 has two kinds of uses: It is partly used up as an input in the production of $X_2, X_3 \ldots$ and perhaps of X_1 (the automobile industry is a major user of automobiles). What remains is available for household consumption. The production functions have X's on the right- as well as the left-hand side.

[37]If "output" varies as the surface area of some solid body and "input" as its cubic-volume, a doubling of input will less than double output—this is an example of the first kind. A typical example of the second is the instance where the production function for fishing does not include an axis for the "amount" of lake, hence where beyond a certain point doubling of man-hours, boats, etc. less than doubles the output. There is a slightly futile literature on whether the first kind could or could not exist without some element of the second. If *every* input is really doubled, so say the proponents of one view, output *must* double. The very vehemence of the assertion suggests the truth, to wit, that it is conceptually impossible to disprove it by reference to empirical evidence. Luckily, the distinction is not only arbitrary—it depends on what one puts on the axes of the production-function diagram and what is built into the curvature of the production surface; it is also quite unimportant. One can think of the phenomenon as one will—nothing will change.

[38]The fact that the "hidden scarce factor" view is heuristically useful does not, however, strengthen its pretension to status as a hypothesis about reality.

In a market context, this suggests the explicit introduction of firms as distinct from industries. In our constant-returns-to-scale world the number of apple- or nut-producing firms could be assumed indeterminate. Every firm could be assumed able to produce any output up to A_Ω (or N_Ω) at constant unit cost. In fact, if we had a convenient way of handling incipient monopoly behavior, such as by positing frictionless entry of new firms, we could simply think of one giant firm as producing all the required apples (nuts). Such a firm would be compelled, nevertheless, to behave as though it were an "atomistic" competitor, *i.e.*, prevented from exploiting the tilt in the demand curve, by incipient competitors ready instantaneously to jump into the fray at the slightest sign of profit.

It is, however, natural, at least in a context of market institutions, to think of decreasing returns to scale, as associated with the qualitatively and quantitatively scarce entrepreneurial entity that defines the firm but is not explicitly treated as an input. Then, as apple production expands, relatively less efficient entrepreneurs are pulled into production—the total cost curve of the "last" producer and the associated shadow price of apples become progressively higher—and the intramarginal firms make "profits" due directly to the scarcity value of the entrepreneurial qualities of their "entrepreneurs." The number of firms, their inputs and outputs, are determinate. The last firm just breaks even at the solution-value of the shadow-price.[39]

At any rate, no serious damage is done to the statical system by decreasing returns to scale. When it is a matter of actually computing a maximum problem the loss of linearity is painful, but the trouble is in the mathematics.[40]

8. There is one kind of complication that does vitiate the results. We have assumed throughout that there exists no *direct* interaction among producers, among households, and between producers and households—that there are no (nonpecuniary) external economies or diseconomies of production and consumption. The assumption is reflected in four characteristics of the production functions and the preference functions:

a. The output of apples was assumed uniquely determined by the quantities of land and labor applied to apple production—A was assumed insensitive to the inputs and outputs of the nut industry; similarly for nuts. This voids the possibility that the apple production function might shift as a consequence of movements along the nut production function, *i.e.*, that for given D_A and L_A, A may vary with N, L_N and D_N. The stock example of such a "technological external economy" (or diseconomy) is the beekeeper whose honey output will increase, other things equal, if the neighboring apple producer expands *his* output (hence his apple blossom "supply").[41] The very pastoral quality of the example suggests that in a statical context such direct interaction among producers—interaction that is not reflected by prices—is probably rare. To the extent that it does exist, it reflects some "hidden" inputs or outputs (*e.g.*, apple blossoms), the benefits or costs of which are not (easily) appropriated by market institutions.

It should be emphasized that the assertion that such phenomena are empirically unimportant is defensible only if we rule out nonreversible dynamical phenomena. Once we introduce changes in knowledge, for example, or investment in changing the quality of the labor force via training, "external" effects become very important indeed.[42] But on our stratospheric level of abstraction such considerations are out of order.

---

[39]More precisely, the "next" firm in line could not break even. This takes care of discontinuity.

[40]It should perhaps be repeated, however, that there remains considerable ambiguity about how the imbalance between income and outlay in decreasing-returns-to-scale situations is best treated in a general equilibrium setup.

[41]The other type of externality treated in the neoclassical literature, the type Jacob Viner labeled "pecuniary," does not in itself affect the results. It consists in sensitivity of input prices to industry output, though not to the output of single firms. External pecuniary economies (as distinct from diseconomies) do, however, signal the existence of either *technological* external economies of the sort discussed here, or of internal economies among supplier firms. These last reflect increasing returns to scale along production functions—a most troublesome state discussed at length in Part V.

[42]The full "benefits" of most changes in "knowledge," of most "ideas," are not easily captured by the originator, even with strong patent and copyright protection. If, then, the energy and resources devoted to "creating new knowledge" are sensitive to private cost-benefit calculation, some potential for social gain may well be lost because such calculation will not correctly account for cost and benefit to society at large. All this is complicated by the peculiarity of "knowledge" as a scarce resource: unlike most other scarcities, just because there is more for you there is not necessarily less for me. As for training of labor: the social benefit accrues over the lifetime services of the trainee; the private benefit to the producer accrues until the man quits to go to work for a competitor.

b. The "happiness" of X, as measured by U_X, was assumed uniquely determined by his own consumption of apples and nuts. He was permitted no sensitivity to his neighbor's (Y's) consumption, and vice versa. This rules out not only Veblenesque "keeping up with . . ." effects, but such phenomena as Y tossing in sleepless fury due to X's "consumption" of midnight television shows; or X's temperance sensibilities being outraged by Y's quiet and solitary consumption of Scotch. Nobody with experience of a "neighborhood" will argue that such things are illusory, but it is not very fruitful to take account of them in a formal maximizing setup.[43]

c. X and Y were assumed insensitive, also, to the input-output configuration of producers, except as this affected consumption choices. Insensitivity to the allocation of their own working time is subsumed in the "Austrian" assumption, but more is required. Y's wife must not be driven frantic by factory soot, nor X irritated by an "efficiently" located factory spoiling his view.

d. There is still a fourth kind of externality: X's satisfaction may be influenced not only by his own job, but by Y's as well. Many values associated with job-satisfaction—status, power, and the like—are sensitive to one's *relative* position, not only as consumer, but as supplier of one's services in production. The "Austrian" assumption whereby U_X and U_Y are functions only of consumption possibilities, voids this type of interaction also.

Could direct interaction phenomena be introduced into a formal maximizing system, and if so, at what cost? As regards the analytical solubility of some maximum-of-W problem, there is no necessary reason why not. The mathematics of proving the existence or nonexistence of a "solution," or of a unique and stable "solution," or the task of devising a computational routine that will track down such a solution should one exist, may become unmanageable. But the problem need not be rendered meaningless by such phenomena.

Unfortunately that is saying very little indeed, except on the level of metaphysics. Those qualities of the system that are of particular interest to the economist—(i) that the solution implies a series of "efficiency conditions," the Pareto marginal-rate-of-substitution conditions, which are necessary for the maximum of a wide variety of W-functions, and (ii) that there exists a correspondence between the optimal values of the variables and those generated by a system of (perfect) market institutions *cum* redistribution—those qualities are apt either to blur or vanish with "direct interaction." Most varieties of such interaction destroy the "duality" of the system: the constants embedded in the maximum problem, if any, lose significance as prices, wages, rents. They will not correctly account for all the "costs" and "benefits" to which the welfare function in hand is sensitive.[44]

In general, then, most formal models rule out such phenomena. There is no doubt that by so doing they abstract from some important aspects of reality. But theorizing consists in just such abstraction; no theory attempts to exhaust all of reality. The question of what kinds of very real complications to introduce into a formal maximizing setup has answers only in terms of the strategy of theorizing or in terms of the requirements of particular and concrete problems. For many purposes it is useful and interesting to explore the implications of maximizing in a "world" where no such direct interactions exist.

V. RELAXING THE CURVATURE ASSUMPTIONS: KINKS AND NONCONVEXITIES

None of the above qualifications and generalizations violate the fundamentally neoclassical character of the model. What happens if we relinquish some of the nice curvature properties of the functions?

1. We required that the production functions and the indifference curves have well-defined and continuous curvatures—no sharp corners or kinks such as cause indeterminacy in marginal rates of substitution. Such smooth curvatures permit the use of the calculus, hence are mathematically convenient for larger

---

[43]For an important exception, however, see fn. 44 below.

[44]It should not be concluded, however, that the different types of direct interaction are all equally damaging. All will spoil market performance, almost by definition; but some, at least, permit of formal maximizing treatment such as will yield efficiency conditions analogous to those of Part I—conditions that properly account for full social costs and benefits. So-called "public goods," *e.g.*, national defense, which give rise to direct interaction since by definition their consumption is joint—more for X means not less but more for Y—are an important example. Maximizing yields MRS conditions that bear intriguing correspondence to those which characterize ordinary private-good situations. But these very MRS conditions serve to reveal the failure of duality. (Samuelson's is again the original and definitive treatment. See citation [12].)

than 2 by 2 by 2 models. They are, however, not essential to the economic content of the results. The analysis has been translated—and in part independently re-invented—for a world of flat-faced, sharp-cornered, production functions: Linear programming, more formally known as activity analysis, is the resulting body of theory.[45] All the efficiency conditions have their counterparts in such a system, and the existence of implicit "prices" embedded in the maximum problem is, if anything, even more striking.[46]

2. Easing of the neoclassical requirement that functions be smooth is not only painless; in the development of analytical economics it has resulted in exciting new insights. Unfortunately, however, the next step is very painful indeed. In our original assumptions we required that returns to scale for proportional expansion of inputs be constant (or at least nonincreasing) and that isoquants and indifference curves be "convex to the origin." These requirements guarantee a condition that the mathematicians call *convexity*. The violation of this condition, as by allowing increasing returns to scale in production— due, if you wish, to the inherent physics and topography of the universe or to lumpiness and indivisibilities—makes for serious difficulties.

The essence of convexity, a concept that plays a crucial role in mathematical economics, is rather simple. Take a single isoquant such as MM in Fig. 8a. It denotes the minimum inputs of L and D for the production of 100 apples, hence it is just the boundary of all technologically feasible input combinations that can produce 100 apples. Only points on MM are both feasible and technologically *efficient*, but any point within the shaded region is *feasible*: nobody can prevent me from wasting L or D. On the other hand, no point on the origin side of MM is feasible for an output of 100 apples: given the laws of physics, etc., it is impossible to do better. *Mathematical convexity obtains if a straight line connecting any two feasible points does not anywhere pass outside the set of feasible points.* A little experimentation will show that such is the case in Fig. 8a. In Fig. 8b, however, where the isoquant is of "queer" curvature—MRS of L for D increases—the line connecting, *e.g.*, the feasible points γ and ϕ does pass outside the "feasible" shaded area. Note, incidentally, that an isoquant of the linear programming variety, as in Fig. 8c, is "convex"—this is why the generalization of (1) above was painless.[47]

What kind of trouble does nonconvexity create? In the case of concave-to-the-origin isoquants, *i.e.*,

---

[45]Isoquants in such a setup consist of linearly additive combinations of processes, each process being defined as requiring absolutely fixed input and output proportions. This gives isoquants that look like that in Fig. 8c.

[46]A little diagrammatic experimentation will show that the geometric techniques of Part I remain fully adequate.

[47]It is important not to confuse mathematical convexity with curvature that appears "convex to the origin." Mathematical convexity is a property of *sets* of points, and the set of feasible output points bounded by a production-possibility curve, for instance, is convex if and only if the production-possibility curve itself is "*concave* to the origin" (or a straight line). Test this by the rule which defines convexity.

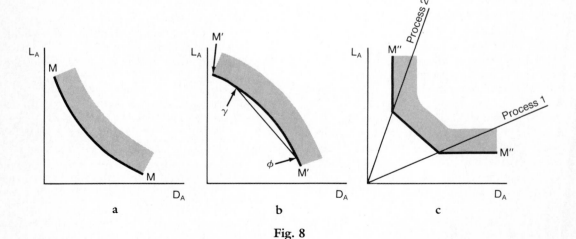

a   b   c

Fig. 8

nonconvex isoquants, the difficulty is easy to see. Look back at Fig. 1 and imagine that the old nut-isoquants are really those of apple producers, hence oriented to the southwest, and vice versa for nuts. Examination of the diagram will show that the locus of tangencies, *FF,* is now a locus of minimum combinations of *A* and *N.* Hence the rule that MRS's be equalized will result in input combinations that give a minimum of *N* for specified *A.*[48]

3. This is not the occasion for extensive analysis of convexity problems. It might be useful, however, to examine one very important variety of nonconvexity: increasing returns to scale in production. Geometrically, increasing returns to scale is denoted by isoquants that are closer and closer together for outward movement along any ray from the origin: to double output, you less than double the inputs. Note that the isoquants still bound convex sets in the *LD* plane (they are still as in Fig. 8a). But in the third or output dimension of a two-input, one-output production surface, slices by vertical planes through the origin perpendicular to *LD* will cut the production surface in such a way as to give a boundary such as *VV* in Fig. 9. It is evident that *VV* bounds a nonconvex set of feasible points, so the full three-dimensional set of feasible input-output points is not convex.

The effect of such nonconvexity in input-output

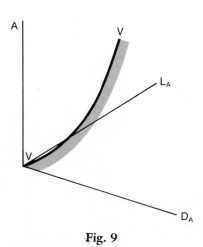

Fig. 9

space can be classified with respect to its possible implications for (a) the slopes of producers' average cost *(AC)* curves; (b) for the slopes of marginal cost *(MC)* curves; (c) for the curvature of the production-possibility curve.

a. *Increasing returns to scale and* AC *curves.* It is a necessary consequence of increasing returns to scale that at the maximal configuration of inputs, outputs and input prices, producers' *AC* curves decline with increasing output. By the definition of increasing returns to scale at a given point τ of a production function, successive isoquants in the neighborhood of τ lie closer and closer together for movement "northeast" along the ray from the origin through τ (*Z* in Fig. 10). As Fig. 10 is drawn, the ray *Z* happens also to correspond to an expansion path for the particular *r/w* ratio denoted by the family of isocost lines *R'W':* each *R'W'* is tangent to an isoquant along *Z.* Given *r/w* = | *tangent* θ |, a profit-maximizing apple producer will calculate his minimum total cost for various levels of output from input-output points along *Z.* But along *Z* the equal cost *R'W'* tangents in the neighborhood of τ lie closer and closer together for increasing output, as do the isoquants. This implies that the increase in total cost for equal successive increments in output declines. *Ergo,* the *AC* curve at τ for *r/w* = | tangent θ | must be falling.

Suppose the expansion path for *r/w* = | tangent θ | happened not to correspond to the ray *Z,* but only to cross it at τ. The intersection of A_4 with *Z* would not then mark the minimum-cost input-mix for an output of A_4, hence the increase in minimized total cost between A_3 and A_4 would be even less than in Fig. 10: the negative effect on *AC* would be reinforced. The point is, simply, that if for movement along a ray from the origin cost per unit of output declines, *AC* will decline even more should production at minimized total cost call for changes in the input-mix, *i.e.,* departure from the ray *Z.*

What, then, if the maximum-of-*W* input-output combination required of this particular producer is denoted by the point τ? It has just been shown that *AC* at τ is falling. A falling *AC* implies a marginal cost curve *(MC)* that lies *below* the average. But if τ is the Ω'''-point, the shadow-p_A will just equal *MC* of τ. It follows that the maximum-of-*W* configuration requires $p_A < AC$, *i.e.,* perpetual losses. Losses, however, are incompatible with real life (perfect) markets; hence where increasing returns to scale prevails correspondence between market-directed and

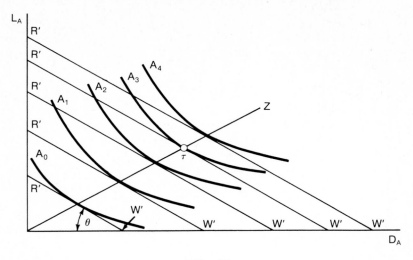

Fig. 10

W-maximizing allocation fails. In an institutional context where producers go out of business if profits are negative, markets will not do.[49]

Increasing returns to scale has also a "macro" consequence that is associated with $p < AC$. For constant returns to scale, we cited Euler's theorem as assuring that total factor incomes will just equal total value of output. In increasing-returns-to-scale situations, total imputed factor incomes will exceed the total value of output: $rD + wL > p_A A + p_N N$.[50]

b. *Increasing returns to scale and* MC *curves.* Where nonconvexity of the increasing-returns-to-scale variety results in falling AC curves, real-life (perfect) markets will fail. What of a Lange-Lerner socialist bureaucracy, where each civil-servant plant-manager is instructed to maximize his algebraic profits in terms of centrally quoted "shadow" prices regardless of losses? Will such a system find itself at the maximum-of-W configuration?

It may or may not. If AC is to fall, MC must lie below AC, but at the requisite Ω-output, MC's may nevertheless be rising, as for example at ϵ in Fig. 11.

If so, a Lange-Lerner bureaucracy making input and output decisions as atomistic "profit-maximizing" competitors but ignoring losses will make the "right" decisions, *i.e.,* will "place" the system at the maximum-of-W. Each manager equating his marginal cost to the centrally quoted shadow price given out by the maximum-of-W solution, will produce precisely the output required by the Ω-configuration. By the assumption of falling AC's due to increasing returns to scale either one or both industries will show losses, but these are irrelevant to optimal allocation.[51]

What if for a maximum-of-W producers are required to produce at points such as ϵ', where $p = MC$ but MC is declining?[52] The fact that ϵ' shows $AC > MC = p$, hence losses, has been dealt with above. But more is involved. By the assumption

---

[49]Needless to say, comments on market effectiveness, throughout this paper, bear only on the analogue-computer aspects of price-market systems. This is a little like talking about sexless men, yet it is surely of interest to examine such systems viewed as mechanisms pure and simple.
[50]The calculus-trained reader can test this for, say, a Cobb-Douglas type function: $A = L_A^{\alpha} D_A^{\beta}$, with $(\alpha + \beta) > 1$ to give increasing returns to scale.

[51]There is an ambiguity of language in the above formulation. If at the maximum-of-W configuration losses prevail, the maximum profit position "in the large" will be not at $p = MC$ but at zero output. Strictly speaking, a Lange-Lerner bureaucracy must be instructed to equate marginal cost to price or profit-maximize "in the small" without regard to the absolute value of profit. "Make any continuous sequence of small moves that increase algebraic profits, but do not jump to the origin." It is precisely the ruling-out of the zero-output position, unless called for by $MC > p$ everywhere, that distinguishes Lange-Lerner systems from "real-life" perfect markets, both viewed as "analogue computers."
[52]This would necessarily be the case, for instance, with Cobb-Douglas type increasing-returns-to-scale functions. Such functions imply ever-falling MC curves, for whatever r/w ratio.

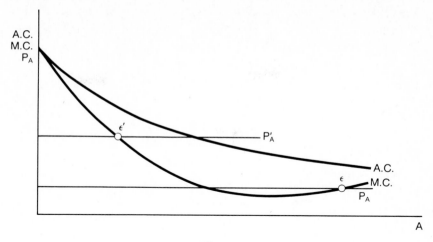

Fig. 11

of a falling *MC*-curve, the horizontal price line at ϵ' cuts the *MC* curve from below, hence profit at ϵ' is not only negative: it is at a *minimum*. A "real-life" profit maximizer would certainly not remain there: he would be losing money by the minute. But neither would a Lange-Lerner bureaucrat under instruction to maximize algebraic profits. He would try to increase his output: "extra" revenue (p_A) would exceed his *MC* by more and more for every additional apple produced. In this case, then, not only would real-life markets break down; so would simple-minded decentralized maximizing of profits by socialist civil servants.[53]

Paradoxically enough, the correct rule for all industries whose *MC* is falling at the Ω-point is: "minimize your algebraic profits." But no such rule can save the decentralized character of the Lange-Lerner scheme. In a "convex" world the simple injunction to maximize profits in response to centrally quoted prices, together with raising (lowering) of prices by the responsible "Ministries" according to whether supply falls short of (exceeds) demand, is all that is needed.[54] Nobody has to know *ex ante, e.g.,* the prices

associated with the Ω-point. In fact the scheme was devised in part as a counter to the view that efficient allocation in a collectivized economy is impossible due simply to the sheer administrative burden of calculation. With increasing returns to scale, however, the central authority must evidently know where *MC*'s will be falling, where rising: it must know, before issuing any instructions, all about the solution.

c. *Increasing returns to scale and the production-possibility curve.* What is left of "duality"? Real-life markets and unsophisticated Lange-Lerner systems have both failed. Yet it is entirely possible, even in situations where the Ω-constellation implies $AC > MC$ with declining *MC*, that the maximizing procedure of Part I remains inviolate, and that the constants embedded in the maximum problem retain their price-like significance. To see this we must examine the effect of increasing returns to scale on the production-possibility curve. There are two possible cases:

i. It is possible for both the apple and the nut production functions to exhibit increasing returns to scale, yet for the implied production-possibility curve to be concave to the origin, *i.e.,* mathematically convex (as in Fig. 2). While a proportional expansion of L_A and D_A by a factor of two would more than double apple output, an increase in A at the expense of N will, in general, not take place by means of such proportional expansion of inputs. Examination of *FF*

[53]Note that a falling *MC* curve is simply a reflection of nonconvexity in the total cost curve.

[54]Not quite all. Even in a statical context, the lump-sum income transfers called for by Ω require central calculation. And if adjustment paths are explicitly considered, complex questions about the stability of equilibrium arise. (*E.g.,* will excess demand always be corrected by raising price?)

in Fig. 1 makes this clear for the constant-returns-to-scale case. As we move from any initial point on FF toward more A and less N, the L_A/D_A and L_N/D_N proportions change.[55]

The point is that if, as in Fig. 1, land is important relative to labor in producing apples, and vice versa for nuts, expansion of apple production will result in apple producers having to use more and more of the relatively nut-prone input, labor, in proportion to land. Input proportions in apple production become less "favorable." The opposite is true of the input proportions used in nuts as nut production declines. This phenomenon explains why with constant returns to scale in both functions the production-possibility curve shows concave-to-the-origin curvature. Only if FF in Fig. 1 coincides with the diagonal: *i.e.*, if the intrinsic "usefulness" of L and D is the same in apple production as in nut production, will $F'F'$ for constant returns to scale be a straight line.

The above argument by proportions remains valid if we now introduce a little increasing returns to scale in both functions by "telescoping" each isoquant successively farther towards the origin. In fact, as long as the FF curve has shape and curvature as in Fig. 1, the production-possibility curve, $F'F'$ in Figs. 2 and 5, will retain its convexity.

In this "mild" case of increasing returns to scale, with a still convex production-possibility curve, the previous maximizing rules give the correct result for a maximum-of-W. Further, the constants embedded in the maximum problem retain their meaning. This is true in two senses: (1) They still reflect marginal rates of substitution and transformation. Any package of L, D, A and N worth \$1 will, *at the margin*, be just convertible by production and exchange into any other package worth \$1, no more, no less: a dollar is a dollar is a dollar. . . .[56] (2) The total value of maximum-welfare "national" output: $p_A A + p_N N$, valued at these shadow-price constants, will itself be at a maximum. A glance at Fig. 5 makes this clear: at the price-ratio denoted by the line $P'_A P'_N$, Ω' is the point of highest output-value. As we shall see, this correspondence between the maximum welfare

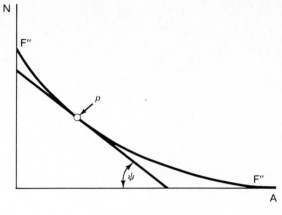

Fig. 12

and "maximum national product" solutions is an accident of convexity.

ii. It is of course entirely possible that both production functions exhibit sufficiently increasing returns to scale to give, for specified totals of L and D, a production-possibility curve such as $F''F''$ in Fig. 12.[57] This exhibits nonconvexity in output space. What now happens to the results?

If the curvature of $F''F''$ is not "too sharp," the constants given out by the maximum-of-W problem retain their "dollar is a dollar" meaning. They still reflect marginal rates of substitution in all directions. But maximum W is no longer associated with maximum shadow-value of output. A glance at Fig. 12 confirms our geometric intuition that in situations of nonconvex production possibilities the bliss point coincides with a minimized value-of-output. At the prices implied, as denoted by $|\tan \psi|$, the assumed Ω-point ρ is a point of minimum $p_A A + p_N N$.[58]

But with nonconvexity in output space, matters could get much more complicated. If the production-possibility curve is *sharply* concave outward, relative to the indifference curves, it may be that the "minimize profits" rule would badly mislead, even if both industries show declining MC's. Take a one-person situation such as in Fig. 13. The production-possibility curve $F'''F'''$ is more inward-bending than the

---

[55]Only if FF should coincide with the diagonal of the box will proportions not change. Then increasing returns to scale would necessarily imply an inward-bending production-possibility curve.
[56]For the infinitesimal movements of the calculus.

[57]Try two functions which are not too dissimilar in "factor intensity."
[58]For $p_A/p_N = |$ tangent $\Psi |$, $(p_A A + p_N N)$ is at its maximum at the intersection of $F''F''$ with the A-axis. Recall, incidentally, that in situations of falling MC producers were required to *minimize* profits.

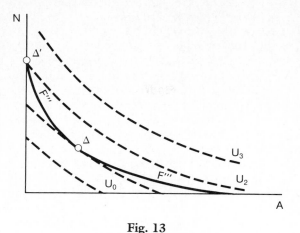

Fig. 13

indifference curves *(U)*, and the point of tangency Δ is a point of *minimum* satisfaction. Here, unlike above, you should rush away from Δ. The maximum welfare position is at Δ'—a "corner tangency" is involved. The point is that in nonconvex situations *relative* curvatures are crucial: tangency points may as well be minima as maxima.[59]

So much for nonconvexity. In its mildest form, if

isoquants and indifference curves retain their normal curvature and only returns to scale "increase," nonconvexity need not violate the qualitative characteristics of the maximum-of-*W* problem. The marginal-rate-of-substitution conditions may well retain their validity, and the solution still could give out a set of shadow prices, decentralized responses to which result in the maximal configuration of inputs, outputs and commodity distribution. But certain nonmarginal *total* conditions for effective real-life market functioning, *e.g.*, that all producers have at least to break even, are necessarily violated. The shortcoming is in market institutions: the maximum-of-*W* solution requires such "losses." The important moral is that where increasing returns to scale obtains, an idealized price system is not an effective way to raise money to cover costs. It may, however, still be an effective device for the rationing of scarcities.[60]

VI. DYNAMICS

We have examined in some detail what conditions on the allocation and distribution of inputs and outputs can be derived from the maximization of a social welfare function which obeys certain restrictions.[61] We have done so, however, using a statical mode of analysis and have ignored all the "dynamical" aspects of the problem. To charge that such statical treatment is "unrealistic" is to miss, I think, the essential meaning and uses of theorizing. It is true, however, that such treatment buries many interesting problems—problems, moreover, some of which yield illuminating insight when subjected to rigorous analysis. Full dynamical extension is not possible here, but some indication of the directions which such extension might take is perhaps warranted:

1. The perceptive reader will have noticed that very little was said about the dimensions of *A*, *N*, L_A, D_A, L_N, and D_N. The static theory of production treats outputs and inputs as instantaneous time rates,

---

[59]Recall that in our discussion of Part IV corner-tangencies were important in situations where no feasible internal tangencies existed. Here there exist perfectly good and feasible internal tangencies—but they are loci of minima rather than maxima. The second-order conditions, expressed as inequalities, constitute the crucial test of optimal allocation.

It is tempting, but a mistake, to think that there is a unique correspondence between the curvature of the production-possibility curve, and the relative slopes of the nut and apple *MC* curves. It is true that the $[MC_A/MC_N]$ ratio associated with a point such as Ω' in Fig. 5 must be smaller than $[MC_A/MC_N]$ at any point of *more A* and *less N* on *F'F'* (*e.g.*, δ): the absolute slope of *F'F'* has been shown to equal $pA/p_N = [MC_A/MC_N]$, and at Ω' the slope is less steep than at δ. It is also true that along a nonconvex production-possibility curve, such as that of Fig. 12, an increase in *A* and a decrease in *N* are associated with a *decline* in $[MC_A/MC_N]$. But it does not follow, *e.g.*, in the first case of Fig. 5, that at Ω' MC_A must be rising for an increase in *A* sufficiently to offset a possibly falling MC_N. (Remember, in moving from Ω' to δ we move to the right along the *A*-axis but to the left along the *N*-axis.) For any departure from Ω' will, in general, involve a change in input shadow-prices, hence *shifts* in the *MC* curves, while the slopes of the curves at Ω' were derived from a total cost curve calculated on the basis of the given, constant, Ω-values of *w* and *r*. The point is that cost curves are partial-equilibrium creatures, evaluated at *fixed* prices, while movement along a production-possibility curve involves a general-equilibrium adjustment that will *change* input prices. Hence it is entirely possible that at say Ω', in Fig. 5, both MC_N and MC_A are falling, though *F'F'* is convex.

[60]No mention has been made of the case that is perhaps most interesting from an institutional point of view: production functions that show increasing returns to scale initially, then decreasing returns as output expands further. No profit-seeking firm will produce in the first stage, where *AC* is falling, and A_Ω and N_Ω may only require one or a few firms producing in the second stage. If so, the institutional conditions for perfect competition, very many firms, will not exist. One or a few firms of "efficient" scale will exhaust the market. This phenomenon lies at the heart of the monopoly-oligopoly problem.

[61]See fn. 11.

"flows"—apples per day, labor-hours per week, etc. This ignores the elementary fact that in most production processes outputs and the associated inputs, and the various inputs themselves, are not simultaneous. Coffee plants take five years to grow, ten-year-old brandy has to age ten years, inputs in automobile manufacture have to follow a certain sequence, it takes time to build a power station and a refinery (no matter how abundantly "labor and land" are applied). One dynamical refinement of the analysis, then, consists in "dating" the inputs and resultant outputs of the production functions, relative to each other. In some instances only the ordinal sequence is of interest; in others, absolute elapsed time, too, matters—plaster has to dry seven days before the first coat of paint is applied.

2. Another characteristic of production, on this planet at least, is that service flows are generated by stocks of physical things which yield their services only through time. Turret-lathe operations can be generated only by turret-lathes and these have congealed in them service flows which cannot be exhausted instantaneously but only over time. In a descriptive sense, a turret-lathe's services of today are "joint" and indivisible from some turret-lathe's services of tomorrow. Strictly speaking, this is true of most service flows. But some things, like food, or coal for heating, or gasoline, exhaust their services much faster than, *e.g.,* steamrollers, drill presses, buildings, etc. The stock dimension of the former can be ignored in many problems; this is not true of the latter set of things, which are usually labeled as fixed capital.[62] A second dynamical extension, then, consists in introducing stock-flow relationships into the production functions.

3. Lags and stock-flow relations are implied also by the goods-in-process phenomenon. Production takes place over space, and transport takes time, hence seed cannot be produced at the instant at which it is planted, nor cylinder heads the moment they are required on the assembly line. They have to be in existence for some finite time before they are used.

4. One of the crucial intertemporal interrelations in allocation and distribution in a world where stocks matter and where production takes time, is due to the unpleasant (or pleasant) fact that the inputs of any instant are not manna from heaven. Their supply depends on past output decisions. Next year's production possibilities will depend, in part, on the supply of machine tools; this, in turn, partly depends on the resources devoted this year to the construction of new machine tools. This is the problem of investment. From today's point of view investment concerns choice of *outputs;* but choice of what kinds and amounts of machines to build, plants to construct, etc., today, makes sense only in terms of the *input-uses* of these things tomorrow. Input endowments, L and D, become unknowns as well as data.

5. Tomorrow's input availabilities are also affected by how inputs are used today. The nature and intensity of use to which machines are subjected, the way in which soil is used, oil wells operated, the rate at which inventories are run down, etc., partly determine what will be left tomorrow. This is the problem of physical capital consumption, wear and tear, etc.—the problem of what to subtract from gross investment to get "net" capital formation, hence the net change in input supplies.

How do these five dynamical phenomena fit into the maximum-of-welfare problem? Recall that our W-function was assumed sensitive to, and only to, X's and Y's consumption. Nothing was said, however, about the timing of such consumption. Surely not only consumption of this instant matters. In a dynamic context, meaningful welfare and preference functions have to provide a ranking not only with respect to all possible current consumption mixes but also for future time. They must provide some means for weighing apples next week against nuts and apples today. Such functions will *date* each unit of A and N, and the choice to be made will be between alternative time-paths of consumption.[63]

Given such a context, the above five dynamical phenomena are amenable to a formal maximizing treatment entirely akin to that of Parts I, II and III.

---

[62]Much depends on arbitrary or special institutional assumptions about how much optimization we leave in the background for the "engineer." For example, machines of widely varying design could very likely yield a given kind of service. "A lathe is not a lathe is. . . ." Further, no law of nature precludes the rather speedy using-up of a lathe—by using it, *e.g.,* as scrap metal. In some situations it could even be economic to do so.

[63]Note how little weight is likely to be given to current consumption relative to future consumption if we pick short unit-periods. This year certainly matters, but what of this afternoon versus all future, or this second? Yet what of the man who knows he'll die tomorrow? Note also the intrinsic philosophical dilemmas: *e.g.,* is John Jones today the "same" person he was yesterday?

They are, with one qualification,[64] consistent with the convexity assumptions required for solubility and duality. The results, which are the fruit of some very recent and pathbreaking work by R. M. Solow and P. A. Samuelson (soon to be published), define intertemporal production efficiency in terms of time-paths along which no increase in the consumption of any good of any period is possible without a decrease in some other consumption. Such paths are characterized by the superimposition, on top of the statical, one-period or instantaneous efficiency conditions, of certain intertemporal marginal-rate-of-substitution requirements. But the statical efficiency requirements retain their validity: for full-fledged dynamical Pareto-efficiency it is necessary that at any moment in time the system be on its one-period efficiency frontier.[65]

Incidentally, the geometric techniques of Part I are fully adequate to the task of handling a Solow-Samuelson dynamical setup for a 2 by 2 by 2 world. Only now the dimensions of the production box and hence the position of the production-possibility curve will keeep shifting, and the solution gives values not only for inputs, outputs and prices but also for their period-to-period changes.

There are many dynamical phenomena less prone to analysis by a formal maximizing system than the five listed above. The qualitative and quantitative supply of labor-input in the future is influenced by the current use made of the services of people.[66] There are, also, important intertemporal interdependences relating to the fact of space—space matters because it takes time and resources to span it. Moreover, we have not even mentioned the really "difficult" phenomena of "grand dynamics." Production functions, preference functions, and even my or your welfare function shift over time. Such shifts are compounded by what in a sense is the central problem of nonstationary dynamics: the intrinsic uncertainty

that attaches to the notion of future.[67] Last, the very boundaries of economics, as of any discipline, are intrinsically arbitrary. Allocation and distribution interact in countless ways with the politics and sociology of a society . . . "everything depends on everything." But we are way beyond simple analytics.

A HISTORICAL NOTE ON THE LITERATURE

Note: For a short but substantive history of the development of thought in this field, the reader is referred to Samuelson's synthesis (nonmathematical), pp. 203–19 of *Foundations* [1].

See also Bergson, "Socialist Economics," *Survey of Contemporary Economics,* Vol. I [2] and Boulding, "Welfare Economics," *Survey,* Vol. II [3].

The foundations of modern welfare theory are well embedded in the soil of classical economics, and the structure, too, bears the imprint of the line of thought represented by Smith, Ricardo, Mill, and Marshall. But in classical writing prescription and analysis are inseparably intertwined, the underlying philosophy is unabashedly utilitarian, and the central normative concern is with the efficacy of market institutions. In contrast, the development of modern welfare economics can best be understood as an attempt to sort out ethics from science, and allocative efficiency from particular modes of social organization.

The classical tradition reached its culmination in Professor Pigou's *Wealth and Welfare* [4]. Pigou, the last of the great premoderns was also, as witness the *Economics of Welfare* [5], among the first of the moderns. But he was not the first. Vilfredo Pareto, writing during the first years of the century, has a pre-eminent claim [6]. It is his work, and Enrico Barone's after him [7]—with their focus on the analytical implications of maximization—that constitute the foundations of the modern structure. Many writers contributed to the construction, but A. P. Lerner, Abram Bergson, and Paul Samuelson come especially to mind [8]. Bergson, in particular, in a single article in 1938, was the first to make us see the structure whole. More recently, Kenneth Arrow has explored the logical underpinnings of the notion of a social welfare function in relation to social choice [9]; T. C. Koopmans, Gerard Debreu and others

---

[64]Capital is characterized not only by the fact of durability, but also by lumpiness or indivisibility "in scale." Such lumpiness results in non-convexity, hence causes serious analytical troubles.

[65]For possible exception to this, due to sensitivity of the volume of saving, hence of investment, to "as imputed" income distribution, *cf.* my "On Capital Productivity, Input Allocation and Growth," *Quart. Jour. Econ.,* Feb. 1957, LXXI, 86–106.

[66]Although labor is in many respects analytically akin to other kinds of physical capital—resources can and need be invested to expand the stock of engineers, as to expand that of cows and machines. Machines, however, are not subject to certain costless "learning" effects.

[67]While formal welfare theory becomes very silent when uncertainty intrudes, much of economic analysis—*e.g.,* monetary theory, trade fluctuations—would have little meaning except for the fact of uncertainty.

have tested more complicated systems for duality [10]; Samuelson has developed a meaningful species of social indifference function [11] and derived efficiency conditions for "public goods" [12]; and Robert Solow and Samuelson, in work soon to be published, have provided a dynamical extension [13, 14].

There is, also, an important modern literature devoted to the possible uses of the structure of analysis for policy prescription. Three separate sets of writings are more or less distinguishable. There was first, in the 'twenties and 'thirties, a prolonged controversy on markets versus government. L. von Mises [15] and later F. A. Hayek [16] were the principal proponents of unadulterated *laissez faire,* while H. D. Dickinson, Oscar Lange, Lerner and Maurice Dobb stand out on the other side [17]. The decentralized socialist pricing idea, originally suggested by Barone and later by F. M. Taylor, was elaborated by Lange to counter the Mises view that efficient allocation is impossible in a collectivized economy due simply to the sheer scale of the administrative burden of calculation and control.

Second, in the late 1930's, Nicholas Kaldor [18] and J. R. Hicks [19] took up Lionel Robbins' [20] challenge to economists not to mix ethics and science and suggested a series of tests for choosing some input-output configurations over others independently of value.[68] Tibor Scitovsky pointed out an important asymmetry in the Kaldor-Hicks test [21] and Samuelson in the end demonstrated that a "welfare-function" denoting an ethic was needed after all [22]. I. M. D. Little tried, but I think failed, to shake this conclusion [23].[69] The Pareto conditions are necessary, but never sufficient.

Third, there is a body of writing, some of it in a partial-equilibrium mode, which is concerned with policy at a lower level of abstraction. Writings by Harold Hotelling, Ragnar Frisch, J. E. Meade, W. A. Lewis, are devoted to the question of optimal pricing, marginal-cost or otherwise, in public utility

(M.C. < A.C.) situations [24]. Hotelling, H. P. Wald, M. F. W. Joseph, E. R. Rolph and G. F. Break, Little, and more recently Lionel McKenzie, have, in turn, analyzed alternative fiscal devices for covering public deficits [25]. Last, a number of the above, notably Lerner, Kaldor, Samuelson, Scitovsky, Little, McKenzie and, most exhaustively, Meade, as well as R. F. Kahn, Lloyd Metzler, J. de V. Graaf, H. G. Johnson and others have applied the apparatus to questions of gains from international trade, optimal tariffs, etc. [26].

BIBLIOGRAPHY

[1] P. A. Samuelson, *Foundations of Economic Analysis* (Cambridge, 1947).

[2] A. Bergson, "Socialist Economics," in H. S. Ellis, ed., *A Survey of Contemporary Economics,* Vol. I (Philadelphia, 1948).

[3] K. E. Boulding, "Welfare Economics," in B. F. Haley, ed., *A Survey of Contemporary Economics,* Vol. II (Homewood, Ill., 1952).

[4] A. C. Pigou, *Wealth and Welfare* (London, 1912).

[5] ———— , *The Economics of Welfare,* 4th ed. (London, 1932).

[6] V. Pareto, *Manuel d'économie politique* (Paris, 1909).

[7] E. Barone, "The Ministry of Production in the Collectivist State," transl. in F. A. Hayek, *Collectivist Economic Planning* (London, 1935).

[8] See A. P. Lerner, *The Economics of Control* (London, 1944); A. Bergson (Burk), "A Reformulation of Certain Aspects of Welfare Economics," *Quart. Jour. Econ.,* Feb. 1938, LII, 310–14, reprinted in R. V. Clemence, ed., *Readings in Economic Analysis,* Vol. I (Cambridge, 1952); P. A. Samuelson, *op. cit.,* Ch. 8.
For other works, see references in Samuelson, *op. cit.,* p. 219, and in Bergson's and Boulding's *Survey* articles [2, 3].

[9] See K. J. Arrow, *Social Choice and Individual Values* (New York, 1951).

[10] P. A. Samuelson, *Market Mechanisms and Maximization* (unpublished, RAND Corporation Research Memo., 1949).
T. C. Koopmans, *Activity Analysis of Production and Allocation* (New York, 1951); also R. Dorfman, "Mathematical or 'Linear' Programming," *Am. Econ. Rev.,* Dec. 1953, XLIII, 797–825.

[11] P. A. Samuelson, "Social Indifference Curves," *Quart. Jour. Econ.,* Feb. 1956, LXX, 1–22.

[12] ———— , "The Pure Theory of Public Expenditure," *Rev. Econ. Stat.,* Nov. 1954, XXXVI, 387–89.
———— , "Diagrammatic Exposition of a Theory of Public Expenditure," *Rev. Econ. Stat.,* Nov. 1955, XXXVII, 350–56.

[13] R. Dorfman, R. M. Solow and P. A. Samuelson, *Linear Programming and Economic Analysis* (RAND Corporation, forthcoming), esp. Ch. 11, 12. Ch. 14 contains a most elegant exposition by R. M. Solow of modern welfare theory in linear programming terms.

---

[68]The Hicks-Kaldor line of thought has some ties to an earlier literature by Marshall, Pigou, Fisher, etc., on "what is income."

[69]While I find Little's alternative to a welfare function ("an economic change is desirable if it does not cause a bad redistribution of income, and if the potential losers could not profitably bribe the potential gainers to oppose it" [p. 105]) no alternative at all, his is a provocative evaluation of modern welfare theory. For an evaluation, in turn, of Little, see K. J. Arrow, "Little's Critique of Welfare Economics," *Am. Econ. Rev.,* Dec. 1951, XLI, 923–34.

[14] Four other works should be mentioned: M. W. Reder, *Studies in the Theory of Welfare Economics* (New York, 1947), is a book-length exposition of modern welfare theory; Hla Mynt's *Theories of Welfare Economics* (London, 1948), treats classical and neoclassical writings; W. J. Baumol in *Welfare Economics and the Theory of the State* (London, 1952), attempts an extension to political theory; in a different vein, Gunnar Myrdal's *Political Elements in the Development of Economic Theory,* transl. by Paul Streeten (London, 1953), with Streeten's appendix on modern developments, is a broad-based critique of the premises of welfare economics.

[15] For the translation of the original 1920 article by Mises which triggered the controversy, see F. A. Hayek, ed., *Collectivist Economic Planning* (London, 1935).

[16] See esp. F. A. Hayek, "Socialist Calculation: The Competitive Solution," *Economica,* May 1940, VII, 125–49; for a broad-front attack on deviations from *laissez faire* see Hayek's polemic, *The Road to Serfdom* (Chicago, 1944).

[17] H. D. Dickinson, "Price Formation in a Socialist Economy," *Econ. Jour.,* Dec. 1933, XLIII, 237–50; O. Lange, "On the Economic Theory of Socialism" in Lange and Taylor, *The Economic Theory of Socialism,* B. E. Lippincott, ed. (Minneapolis, 1938); A. P. Lerner, *op. cit.;* M. Dobb, "Economic Theory and the Problem of the Socialist Economy," *Econ. Jour.* Dec. 1933, XLIII, 588–98.

[18] N. Kaldor, "Welfare Propositions in Economics and Interpersonal Comparisons of Utility," *Econ. Jour.,* Sept. 1939, LXIX, 549–52.

[19] J. R. Hicks, "The Foundations of Welfare Economics," *Econ. Jour.,* Dec. 1939, LXIX, 696–712 and "The Valuation of the Social Income," *Economica,* Feb. 1940, VII, 105–23.

[20] L. Robbins, *The Nature and Significance of Economic Science* (London, 1932).

[21] T. Scitovsky, "A Note on Welfare Propositions in Economics," *Rev. Econ. Stud.,* 1941–1942, IX, 77–78. ———— , "A Reconsideration of the Theory of Tariffs," *Rev. Econ. Stud.,* 1941–1942, IX, 89–110.

[22] P. A. Samuelson, "Evaluation of Real National Income," *Oxford Econ. Papers,* Jan. 1950, II, 1–29.

[23] I. M. D. Little, *A Critique of Welfare Economics* (Oxford, 1950).

[24] H. Hotelling, "The General Welfare in Relation to Problems of Taxation and of Railway and Utility Rates," *Econometrica,* July 1938, VI, 242–69, is the first modern formulation of the problem that was posed, in 1844, by Jules Dupuit ("On the Measurement of Utility of Public Works," to be found in *International Economic Papers,* No. 2, ed. Alan T. Peacock *et al.*).

[25] See esp. Little, "Direct versus Indirect Taxes," *Econ. Jour.,* Sept. 1951, LXI, 577–84.

[26] For a comprehensive treatment of the issues, as well as for references, see J. E. Meade, *The Theory of International Economic Policy,* Vol. II: *Trade and Welfare* and *Mathematical Supplement* (New York, 1955).

The Problem of Social Cost*

RONALD COASE[1]

Ronald Harry Coase (B.Com., University of London, 1932; D.Sc., 1951), born in Middlesex, England, in 1910, is Professor Emeritus and Senior Fellow in Law and Economics at the University of Chicago Law School. Before assuming his post at Chicago in 1964, he was on the faculties of the London School of Economics, the University of Buffalo, and the University of Virginia. Coase, whose research interests are in law and economics, price theory, the history of economic thought, and the economics of public utilities and industrial organization, is one of the most careful and rigorous scholars in the profession. "The Nature of the Firm" and "The Marginal Cost Controversy," two of his most famous articles, have become acknowledged classics, and much of the new field of law and economics can be traced to the article reprinted here.

I. THE PROBLEM TO BE EXAMINED

This paper is concerned with those actions of business firms which have harmful effects on others. The standard example is that of a factory the smoke from which has harmful effects on those occupying neighbouring properties. The economic analysis of such a situation has usually proceeded in terms of a divergence between the private and social product of the factory, in which economists have largely followed the treatment of Pigou in *The Economics of Welfare*. The conclusions to which this kind of analysis seems to have led most economists is that it would be desirable to make the owner of a factory liable for the damage caused to those injured by the smoke, or alternatively, to place a tax on the factory owner varying with the amount of smoke produced and equivalent in money terms to the damage it would cause, or finally, to exclude the factory from residential districts (and presumably from other areas in which the emission of smoke would have harmful effects on others). It is my contention that the suggested courses of action are inappropriate, in that they lead to results which are not necessarily, or even usually, desirable.

*Reprinted from the *Journal of Law and Economics* (October 1960) by permission of the University of Chicago Press. Copyright 1960, pp. 1–44.

[1]This article, although concerned with a technical problem of economic analysis, arose out of the study of the Political Economy of Broadcasting which I am now conducting. The argument of the present article was implicit in a previous article dealing with the problem of allocating radio and television frequencies ("The Federal Communications Commission," 2. *J. Law & Econ.* [1959]) but comments which I have received seemed to suggest that it would be desirable to deal with the question in a more explicit way and without reference to the original problem for the solution of which the analysis was developed.

II. THE RECIPROCAL NATURE OF THE PROBLEM

The traditional approach has tended to obscure the nature of the choice that has to be made. The question is commonly thought of as one in which A inflicts harm on B and what has to be decided is: how should we restrain A? But this is wrong. We are dealing with a problem of a reciprocal nature. To avoid the harm to B would inflict harm on A. The real question that has to be decided is: should A be allowed to harm B or should B be allowed to harm A? The problem is to avoid the more serious harm. I instanced in my previous article[2] the case of a confectioner the noise and vibrations from whose machinery disturbed a doctor in his work. To avoid harming the doctor would inflict harm on the confectioner. The problem posed by this case was essentially whether it was worth while, as a result of restricting the methods of production which could be used by the confectioner, to secure more doctoring at the cost of a reduced supply of confectionery products. Another example is afforded by the problem of straying cattle which destroy crops on neighbouring land. If it is inevitable that some cattle will stray, an increase in the supply of meat can only be obtained at the expense of a decrease in the supply of crops. The nature of the choice is clear: meat or crops. What answer should be given is, of course, not clear unless we know the value of what is obtained as well as the value of what is sacrificed to obtain it. To give another example, Professor George J. Stigler instances the contamination of a stream.[3] If we assume that the harmful effect of the pollution is that it kills the fish, the question to be decided is: is the value of the fish lost greater or less than the value of the product which the contamination of the stream makes possible. It goes almost without saying that this problem has to be looked at in total *and* at the margin.

III. THE PRICING SYSTEM WITH LIABILITY FOR DAMAGE

I propose to start my analysis by examining a case in which most economists would presumably agree that the problem would be solved in a completely satisfactory manner: when the damaging business has

[2]Coase, "The Federal Communications Commission," 2 J. Law & Econ. 26–27 (1959).
[3]G. J. Stigler, *The Theory of Price*, 105 (1952).

to pay for all damage caused *and* the pricing system works smoothly (strictly this means that the operation of a pricing system is without cost).

A good example of the problem under discussion is afforded by the case of straying cattle which destroy crops growing on neighbouring land. Let us suppose that a farmer and cattle-raiser are operating on neighbouring properties. Let us further suppose that, without any fencing between the properties, an increase in the size of the cattle-raiser's herd increases the total damage to the farmer's crops. What happens to the marginal damage as the size of the herd increases is another matter. This depends on whether the cattle tend to follow one another or to roam side by side, on whether they tend to be more or less restless as the size of the herd increases and on other similar factors. For my immediate purpose, it is immaterial what assumption is made about marginal damage as the size of the herd increases.

To simplify the argument, I propose to use an arithmetical example. I shall assume that the annual cost of fencing the farmer's property is $9 and that the price of the crop is $1 per ton. Also, I assume that the relation between the number of cattle in the herd and the annual crop loss is as follows:

Number in herd (steers)	Annual crop loss (tons)	Crop loss per additional steer (tons)
1	1	1
2	3	2
3	6	3
4	10	4

Given that the cattle-raiser is liable for the damage caused, the additional annual cost imposed on the cattle-raiser if he increased his herd from, say, 2 to 3 steers is $3 and in deciding on the size of the herd, he will take this into account along with his other costs. That is, he will not increase the size of the herd unless the value of the additional meat produced (assuming that the cattle-raiser slaughters the cattle), is greater than the additional costs that this will entail, including the value of the additional crops destroyed. Of course, if, by the employment of dogs, herdsmen, aeroplanes, mobile radio and other means, the amount of damage can be reduced, these means will be adopted when their cost is less than the value of the crop which they prevent being lost. Given that the annual cost of fencing is $9, the cattle-raiser who wished to have a herd with 4 steers or more would pay for fencing to be erected and maintained, assuming that other means of attaining the same end would not do so more cheaply. When the fence is erected, the marginal cost due to the liability for damage becomes zero, except to the extent that an increase in the size of the herd necessitates a stronger and therefore more expensive fence because more steers are liable to lean against it at the same time. But, of course, it may be cheaper for the cattle-raiser not to fence and to pay for the damaged crops, as in my arithmetical example, with 3 or fewer steers.

It might be thought that the fact that the cattle-raiser would pay for all crops damaged would lead the farmer to increase his planting if a cattle-raiser came to occupy the neighbouring property. But this is not so. If the crop was previously sold in conditions of perfect competition, marginal cost was equal to price for the amount of planting undertaken and any expansion would have reduced the profits of the farmer. In the new situation, the existence of crop damage would mean that the farmer would sell less on the open market but his receipts for a given production would remain the same, since the cattle-raiser would pay the market price for any crop damaged. Of course, if cattle-raising commonly involved the destruction of crops, the coming into existence of a cattle-raising industry might raise the price of the crops involved and farmers would then extend their planting. But I wish to confine my attention to the individual farmer.

I have said that the occupation of a neighbouring property by a cattle-raiser would not cause the amount of production, or perhaps more exactly the amount of planting, by the farmer to increase. In fact, if the cattle-raising has any effect, it will be to decrease the amount of planting. The reason for this is that, for any given tract of land, if the value of the crop damaged is so great that the receipts from the sale of the undamaged crop are less than the total costs of cultivating that tract of land, it will be profitable for the farmer and the cattle-raiser to make a bargain whereby that tract of land is left uncultivated. This can be made clear by means of an arithmetical example. Assume initially that the value of the crop obtained from cultivating a given tract of land is $12 and that the cost incurred in cultivating this tract of land is $10, the net gain from cultivating the land being $2. I assume for purposes of simplicity that the farmer owns the land. Now assume that the cattle-raiser starts operations on the neighbouring property and that the value of the crops damaged is

$1. In this case $11 is obtained by the farmer from sale on the market and $1 is obtained from the cattle-raiser for damage suffered and the net gain remains $2. Now suppose that the cattle-raiser finds it profitable to increase the size of his herd, even though the amount of damage rises to $3; which means that the value of the additional meat production is greater than the additional costs, including the additional $2 payment for damage. But the total payment for damage is now $3. The net gain to the farmer from cultivating the land is still $2. The cattle-raiser would be better off if the farmer would agree not to cultivate his land for any payment less than $3. The farmer would be agreeable to not cultivating the land for any payment greater than $2. There is clearly room for a mutually satisfactory bargain which would lead to the abandonment of cultivation.[4] But the same argument applies not only to the whole tract cultivated by the farmer but also to any subdivision of it. Suppose, for example, that the cattle have a well-defined route, say, to a brook or to a shady area. In these circumstances, the amount of damage to the crop along the route may well be great and if so, it could be that the farmer and the cattle-raiser would find it profitable to make a bargain whereby the farmer would agree not to cultivate this strip of land.

But this raises a further possibility. Suppose that there is such a well-defined route. Suppose further that the value of the crop that would be obtained by cultivating this strip of land is $10 but that the cost of cultivation is $11. In the absence of the cattle-raiser, the land would not be cultivated. However, given the presence of the cattle-raiser, it could well be that if the strip was cultivated, the whole crop

---

[4]The argument in the text has proceeded on the assumption that the alternative to cultivation of the crop is abandonment of cultivation altogether. But this need not be so. There may be crops which are less liable to damage by cattle but which would not be as profitable as the crop grown in the absence of damage. Thus, if the cultivation of a new crop would yield a return to the farmer of $1 instead of $2, and the size of the herd which would cause $3 damage with the old crop would cause $1 damage with the new crop, it would be profitable to the cattle-raiser to pay any sum less than $2 to induce the farmer to change his crop (since this would reduce damage liability from $3 to $1) and it would be profitable for the farmer to do so if the amount received was more than $1 (the reduction in his return caused by switching crops). In fact, there would be room for a mutually satisfactory bargain in all cases in which a change of crop would reduce the amount of damage by more than it reduces the value of the crop (excluding damage)—in all cases, that is, in which a change in the crop cultivated would lead to an increase in the value of production.

would be destroyed by the cattle. In which case, the cattle-raiser would be forced to pay $10 to the farmer. It is true that the farmer would lose $1. But the cattle-raiser would lose $10. Clearly this is a situation which is not likely to last indefinitely since neither party would want this to happen. The aim of the farmer would be to induce the cattle-raiser to make a payment in return for an agreement to leave this land uncultivated. The farmer would not be able to obtain a payment greater than the cost of fencing off this piece of land nor so high as to lead the cattle-raiser to abandon the use of the neighbouring property. What payment would in fact be made would depend on the shrewdness of the farmer and the cattle-raiser as bargainers. But as the payment would not be so high as to cause the cattle-raiser to abandon this location and as it would not vary with the size of the herd, such an agreement would not affect the allocation of resources but would merely alter the distribution of income and wealth as between the cattle-raiser and the farmer.

I think it is clear that if the cattle-raiser is liable for damage caused and the pricing system works smoothly, the reduction in the value of production elsewhere will be taken into account in computing the additional cost involved in increasing the size of the herd. This cost will be weighed against the value of the additional meat production and, given perfect competition in the cattle industry, the allocation of resources in cattle-raising will be optimal. What needs to be emphasized is that the fall in the value of production elsewhere which would be taken into account in the costs of the cattle-raiser may well be less than the damage which the cattle would cause to the crops in the ordinary course of events. This is because it is possible, as a result of market transactions, to discontinue cultivation of the land. This is desirable in all cases in which the damage that the cattle would cause, and for which the cattle-raiser would be willing to pay, exceeds the amount which the farmer would pay for use of the land. In conditions of perfect competition, the amount which the farmer would pay for the use of the land is equal to the difference between the value of the total production when the factors are employed on this land and the value of the additional product yielded in their next best use (which would be what the farmer would have to pay for the factors). If damage exceeds the amount the farmer would pay for the use of the land, the value of the additional product of the factors

employed elsewhere would exceed the value of the total product in this use after damage is taken into account. It follows that it would be desirable to abandon cultivation of the land and to release the factors employed for production elsewhere. A procedure which merely provided for payment for damage to the crop caused by the cattle but which did not allow for the possibility of cultivation being discontinued would result in too small an employment of factors of production in cattle-raising and too large an employment of factors in cultivation of the crop. But given the possibility of market transactions, a situation in which damage to crops exceeded the rent of the land would not endure. Whether the cattle-raiser pays the farmer to leave the land uncultivated or himself rents the land by paying the land-owner an amount slightly greater than the farmer would pay (if the farmer was himself renting the land), the final result would be the same and would maximise the value of production. Even when the farmer is induced to plant crops which it would not be profitable to cultivate for sale on the market, this will be a purely short-term phenomenon and may be expected to lead to an agreement under which the planting will cease. The cattle-raiser will remain in that location and the marginal cost of meat production will be the same as before, thus having no long-run effect on the allocation of resources.

IV. THE PRICING SYSTEM WITH NO LIABILITY FOR DAMAGE

I now turn to the case in which, although the pricing system is assumed to work smoothly (that is, costlessly), the damaging business is not liable for any of the damage which it causes. This business does not have to make a payment to those damaged by its actions. I propose to show that the allocation of resources will be the same in this case as it was when the damaging business was liable for damage caused. As I showed in the previous case that the allocation of resources was optimal, it will not be necessary to repeat this part of the argument.

I return to the case of the farmer and the cattle-raiser. The farmer would suffer increased damage to his crop as the size of the herd increased. Suppose that the size of the cattle-raiser's herd is 3 steers (and that this is the size of the herd that would be maintained if crop damage was not taken into account). Then the farmer would be willing to pay up to $3 if the cattle-raiser would reduce his herd to 2 steers, up to $5 if the herd were reduced to 1 steer and would pay up to $6 if cattle-raising was abandoned. The cattle-raiser would therefore receive $3 from the farmer if he kept 2 steers instead of 3. This $3 foregone is therefore part of the cost incurred in keeping the third steer. Whether the $3 is a payment which the cattle-raiser has to make if he adds the third steer to his herd (which it would be if the cattle-raiser was liable to the farmer for damage caused to the crop) or whether it is a sum of money which he would have received if he did not keep a third steer (which it would be if the cattle-raiser was not liable to the farmer for damage caused to the crop) does not affect the final result. In both cases $3 is part of the cost of adding a third steer, to be included along with the other costs. If the increase in the value of production in cattle-raising through increasing the size of the herd from 2 to 3 is greater than the additional costs that have to be incurred (including the $3 damage to crops), the size of the herd will be increased. Otherwise, it will not. The size of the herd will be the same whether the cattle-raiser is liable for damage caused to the crop or not.

It may be argued that the assumed starting point— a herd of 3 steers—was arbitrary. And this is true. But the farmer would not wish to pay to avoid crop damage which the cattle-raiser would not be able to cause. For example, the maximum annual payment which the farmer could be induced to pay could not exceed $9, the annual cost of fencing. And the farmer would only be willing to pay this sum if it did not reduce his earnings to a level that would cause him to abandon cultivation of this particular tract of land. Furthermore, the farmer would only be willing to pay this amount if he believed that, in the absence of any payment by him, the size of the herd maintained by the cattle-raiser would be 4 or more steers. Let us assume that this is the case. Then the farmer would be willing to pay up to $3 if the cattle-raiser would reduce his herd to 3 steers, up to $6 if the herd were reduced to 2 steers, up to $8 if one steer only were kept and up to $9 if cattle-raising were abandoned. It will be noticed that the change in the starting point has not altered the amount which would accrue to the cattle-raiser if he reduced the size of his herd by any given amount. It is still true that the cattle-raiser could receive an additional $3 from the farmer if he agreed to reduce his herd from 3 steers to 2 and that the $3 represents the value of the crop that would be destroyed by adding the third

steer to the herd. Although a different belief on the part of the farmer (whether justified or not) about the size of the herd that the cattle-raiser would maintain in the absence of payments from him may affect the total payment he can be induced to pay, it is not true that this different belief would have any effect on the size of the herd that the cattle-raiser will actually keep. This will be the same as it would be if the cattle-raiser had to pay for damage caused by his cattle, since a receipt foregone of a given amount is the equivalent of a payment of the same amount.

It might be thought that it would pay the cattle-raiser to increase his herd above the size that he would wish to maintain once a bargain had been made, in order to induce the farmer to make a larger total payment. And this may be true. It is similar in nature to the action of the farmer (when the cattle-raiser was liable for damage) in cultivating land on which, as a result of an agreement with the cattle-raiser, planting would subsequently be abandoned (including land which would not be cultivated at all in the absence of cattle-raising). But such manoeuvres are preliminaries to an agreement and do not affect the long-run equilibrium position, which is the same whether or not the cattle-raiser is held responsible for the crop damage brought about by his cattle.

It is necessary to know whether the damaging business is liable or not for damage caused since without the establishment of this initial delimitation of rights there can be no market transactions to transfer and recombine them. But the ultimate result (which maximises the value of production) is independent of the legal position if the pricing system is assumed to work without cost.

V. THE PROBLEM ILLUSTRATED ANEW

The harmful effects of the activities of a business can assume a wide variety of forms. An early English case concerned a building which, by obstructing currents of air, hindered the operation of a windmill.[5] A recent case in Florida concerned a building which cast a shadow on the cabana, swimming pool and sunbathing areas of a neighbouring hotel.[6] The problem of straying cattle and the damaging of crops which was the subject of detailed examination in the

---

[5]See Gale on *Easements* 237–39 (13th ed. M. Bowles 1959).
[6]See *Fontainebleu Hotel Corp. v. Forty-Five Twenty-Five, Inc.*, 114 So. 2d 357 (1959).

two preceding sections, although it may have appeared to be rather a special case, is in fact but one example of a problem which arises in many different guises. To clarify the nature of my argument and to demonstrate its general applicability, I propose to illustrate it anew by reference to four actual cases.

Let us first reconsider the case of *Sturges v. Bridgman*[7] which I used as an illustration of the general problem in my article on "The Federal Communications Commission." In this case, a confectioner (in Wigmore Street) used two mortars and pestles in connection with his business (one had been in operation in the same position for more than 60 years and the other for more than 26 years). A doctor then came to occupy neighbouring premises (in Wimpole Street). The confectioner's machinery caused the doctor no harm until, eight years after he had first occupied the premises, he built a consulting room at the end of his garden right against the confectioner's kitchen. It was then found that the noise and vibration caused by the confectioner's machinery made it difficult for the doctor to use his new consulting room. "In particular . . . the noise prevented him from examining his patients by auscultation[8] for diseases of the chest. He also found it impossible to engage with effect in any occupation which required thought and attention." The doctor therefore brought a legal action to force the confectioner to stop using his machinery. The courts had little difficulty in granting the doctor the injunction he sought. "Individual cases of hardship may occur in the strict carrying out of the principle upon which we found our judgment, but the negation of the principle would lead even more to individual hardship, and would at the same time produce a prejudicial effect upon the development of land for residential purposes."

The court's decision established that the doctor had the right to prevent the confectioner from using his machinery. But, of course, it would have been possible to modify the arrangements envisaged in the legal ruling by means of a bargain between the parties. The doctor would have been willing to waive his right and allow the machinery to continue in operation if the confectioner would have paid him a sum of money which was greater than the loss of income which he would suffer from having to move to a more costly or less convenient location or from having to curtail his activities at this location or, as was suggested as a possibility, from having to build a separate wall which would deaden the noise and vibration. The confectioner would have been willing to do this if the amount he would have to pay the doctor was less than the fall in income he would suffer if he had to change his mode of operation at this location, abandon his operation or move his confectionery business to some other location. The solution of the problem depends essentially on whether the continued use of the machinery adds more to the confectioner's income than it subtracts from the doctor's.[9] But now consider the situation if the confectioner had won the case. The confectioner would then have had the right to continue operating his noise and vibration-generating machinery without having to pay anything to the doctor. The boot would have been on the other foot: the doctor would have had to pay the confectioner to induce him to stop using the machinery. If the doctor's income would have fallen more through continuance of the use of this machinery than it added to the income of the confectioner, there would clearly be room for a bargain whereby the doctor paid the confectioner to stop using the machinery. That is to say, the circumstances in which it would not pay the confectioner to continue to use the machinery and to compensate the doctor for the losses that this would bring (if the doctor had the right to prevent the confectioner's using his machinery) would be those in which it would be in the interest of the doctor to make a payment to the confectioner which would induce him to discontinue the use of the machinery (if the confectioner had the right to operate the machinery). The basic conditions are exactly the same in this case as they were in the example of the cattle which destroyed crops. With costless market transactions, the decision of the courts concerning liability for damage would be without effect on the allocation of resources. It was of course the view of the judges that they were affecting the working of the economic system—and in a desirable direction. Any other decision would have had "a prejudicial effect upon the development of land for

---

[7]11 Ch. D. 852 (1879).

[8]Auscultation is the act of listening by ear or stethoscope in order to judge by sound the condition of the body.

[9]Note that what is taken into account is the change in income after allowing for alterations in methods of production, location, character of product, etc.

residential purposes," an argument which was elaborated by examining the example of a forge operating on a barren moor, which was later developed for residual purposes. The judges' view that they were settling how the land was to be used would be true only in the case in which the costs of carrying out the necessary market transactions exceeded the gain which might be achieved by any rearrangement of rights. And it would be desirable to preserve the areas (Wimpole Street or the moor) for residential or professional use (by giving non-industrial users the right to stop the noise, vibration, smoke, etc., by injunction) only if the value of the additional residential facilities obtained was greater than the value of cakes or iron lost. But of this the judges seem to have been unaware.

Another example of the same problem is furnished by the case of *Cooke v. Forbes*.[10] One process in the weaving of cocoa-nut fibre matting was to immerse it in bleaching liquids after which it was hung out to dry. Fumes from a manufacturer of sulphate of ammonia had the effect of turning the matting from a bright to a dull and blackish colour. The reason for this was that the bleaching liquid contained chloride of tin, which, when affected by sulphuretted hydrogen, is turned to a darker colour. An injunction was sought to stop the manufacturer from emitting the fumes. The lawyers for the defendant argued that if the plaintiff "were not to use . . . a particular bleaching liquid, their fibre would not be affected; that their process is unusual, not according to the custom of the trade, and even damaging to their own fabrics." The judge commented: ". . . it appears to me quite plain that a person has a right to carry on upon his own property a manufacturing process in which he uses chloride of tin, or any sort of metallic dye, and that his neighbour is not at liberty to pour in gas which will interfere with his manufacture. If it can be traced to the neighbour, then, I apprehend, clearly he will have a right to come here and ask for relief." But in view of the fact that the damage was accidental and occasional, that careful precautions were taken and that there was no exceptional risk, an injunction was refused, leaving the plaintiff to bring an action for damages if he wished. What the subsequent developments were I do not know. But it is clear that the situation is essentially the same as that found in *Sturges v. Bridgman*, except that the

cocoa-nut fibre matting manufacturer could not secure an injunction but would have to seek damages from the sulphate of ammonia manufacturer. The economic analysis of the situation is exactly the same as with the cattle which destroyed crops. To avoid the damage, the sulphate of ammonia manufacturer could increase his precautions or move to another location. Either course would presumably increase his costs. Alternatively he could pay for the damage. This he would do if the payments for damage were less than the additional costs that would have to be incurred to avoid the damage. The payments for damage would then become part of the cost of production of sulphate of ammonia. Of course, if, as was suggested in the legal proceedings, the amount of damage could be eliminated by changing the bleaching agent (which would presumably increase the costs of the matting manufacturer) and if the additional cost was less than the damage that would otherwise occur, it should be possible for the two manufacturers to make a mutually satisfactory bargain whereby the new bleaching agent was used. Had the court decided against the matting manufacturer, as a consequence of which he would have had to suffer the damage without compensation, the allocation of resources would not have been affected. It would pay the matting manufacturer to change his bleaching agent if the additional cost involved was less than the reduction in damage. And since the matting manufacturer would be willing to pay the sulphate of ammonia manufacturer an amount up to his loss of income (the increase in costs or the damage suffered) if he would cease his activities, this loss of income would remain a cost of production for the manufacturer of sulphate of ammonia. This case is indeed analytically exactly the same as the cattle example.

Bryant v. Lefever[11] raised the problem of the smoke nuisance in a novel form. The plaintiff and the defendants were occupiers of adjoining houses, which were of about the same height.

> Before 1876 the plaintiff was able to light a fire in any room of his house without the chimneys smoking; the two houses had remained in the same condition some thirty or forty years. In 1876 the defendants took down their house, and began to rebuild it. They carried up a wall by the side of the plaintiff's chimneys much beyond its original height, and stacked timber on the roof of their

[10]L. R. 5 Eq. 166 (1867–1868).

[11]4 C.P.D. 172 (1878–1879).

house, and thereby caused the plaintiff's chimneys to smoke whenever he lighted fires.

The reason, of course, why the chimneys smoked was that the erection of the wall and the stacking of the timber prevented the free circulation of air. In a trial before a jury, the plaintiff was awarded damages of £40. The case then went to the Court of Appeals where the judgment was reversed. Bramwell, L.J., argued:

> . . . it is said, and the jury have found, that the defendants have done that which caused a nuisance to the plaintiff's house. We think there is no evidence of this. No doubt there is a nuisance, but it is not of the defendant's causing. They have done nothing in causing the nuisance. Their house and their timber are harmless enough. It is the plaintiff who causes the nuisance by lighting a coal fire in a place the chimney of which is placed so near the defendants' wall, that the smoke does not escape, but comes into the house. Let the plaintiff cease to light his fire, let him move his chimney, let him carry it higher, and there would be no nuisance. Who then, causes it? It would be very clear that the plaintiff did, if he had built his house or chimney after the defendants had put up the timber on theirs, and it is really the same though he did so before the timber was there. But (what is in truth the same answer), if the defendants cause the nuisance, they have a right to do so. If the plaintiff has not the right to the passage of air, except subject to the defendants' right to build or put timber on their house, then his right is subject to their right, and though a nuisance follows from the exercise of their right, they are not liable.

And Cotton, L. J., said:

> Here it is found that the erection of the defendants' wall has sensibly and materially interfered with the comfort of human existence in the plaintiff's house, and it is said this is a nuisance for which the defendants are liable. Ordinarily this is so, but the defendants have done so, not by sending on to the plaintiff's property any smoke or noxious vapour, but by interrupting the egress of smoke from the plaintiff's house in a way to which . . . the plaintiff has no legal right. The plaintiff creates the smoke, which interferes with his comfort. Unless he has . . . a right to get rid of this in a particular way which has been interfered with by the defendants, he cannot sue the defendants, because the smoke made by himself, for which he has not provided any effectual means of escape, causes him annoyance. It is as if a man tried to get rid of liquid filth arising on his own land by a drain into his neighbour's land. Until a right had been acquired by user, the neighbour might stop the drain without incurring liability by so doing. No doubt great inconvenience would be caused to the owner of the property on which the liquid filth arises. But the act of his neighbour would be a lawful act, and he would not be liable for the consequences attributable to the fact that the man had accumulated filth without providing any effectual means of getting rid of it.

I do not propose to show that any subsequent modification of the situation, as a result of bargains between the parties (conditioned by the cost of stacking the timber elsewhere, the cost of extending the chimney higher, etc.), would have exactly the same result whatever decision the courts had come to since this point has already been adequately dealt with in the discussion of the cattle example and the two previous cases. What I shall discuss is the argument of the judges in the Court of Appeals that the smoke nuisance was not caused by the man who erected the wall but by the man who lit the fires. The novelty of the situation is that the smoke nuisance was suffered by the man who lit the fires and not by some third person. The question is not a trivial one since it lies at the heart of the problem under discussion. Who caused the smoke nuisance? The answer seems fairly clear. The smoke nuisance was caused both by the man who built the wall *and* by the man who lit the fires. Given the fires, there would have been no smoke nuisance without the wall; given the wall, there would have been no smoke nuisance without the fires. Eliminate the wall *or* the fires and the smoke nuisance would disappear. On the marginal principle it is clear that *both* were responsible and *both* should be forced to include the loss of amenity due to the smoke as a cost in deciding whether to continue the activity which gives rise to the smoke. And given the possibility of market transactions, this is what would in fact happen. Although the wall-builder was not liable legally for the nuisance, as the man with the smoking chimneys would presumably be willing to pay a sum equal to the monetary worth to him of eliminating the smoke, this sum would therefore become for the wall-builder, a cost of continuing to have the high wall with the timber stacked on the roof.

The judges' contention that it was the man who lit the fires who alone caused the smoke nuisance is true only if we assume that the wall is the given factor. This is what the judges did by deciding that the man who erected the higher wall had a legal right to do so. The case would have been even more interesting if the smoke from the chimneys had injured the timber. Then it would have been the wall-builder who suffered the damage. The case would then have closely paralleled *Sturges v. Bridgman* and there can be little doubt that the man who lit the fires would have been liable for the ensuing damage to the timber, in spite of the fact that no damage had occurred until the high wall was built by the man who owned the timber.

Judges have to decide on legal liability but this should not confuse economists about the nature of the economic problem involved. In the case of the cattle and the crops, it is true that there would be no crop damage without the cattle. It is equally true that there would be no crop damage without the crops. The doctor's work would not have been disturbed if the confectioner had not worked his machinery; but the machinery would have disturbed no one if the doctor had not set up his consulting room in that particular place. The matting was blackened by the fumes from the sulphate of ammonia manufacturer; but no damage would have occurred if the matting manufacturer had not chosen to hang out his matting in a particular place and to use a particular bleaching agent. If we are to discuss the problem in terms of causation, both parties cause the damage. If we are to attain an optimum allocation of resources, it is therefore desirable that both parties should take the harmful effect (the nuisance) into account in deciding on their course of action. It is one of the beauties of a smoothly operating pricing system that, as has already been explained, the fall in the value of production due to the harmful effect would be a cost for both parties.

Bass v. Gregory[12] will serve as an excellent final illustration of the problem. The plaintiffs were the owners and tenant of a public house called the Jolly Anglers. The defendant was the owner of some cottages and a yard adjoining the Jolly Anglers. Under the public house was a cellar excavated in the rock. From the cellar, a hole or shaft had been cut into an old well situated in the defendant's yard. The well therefore became the ventilating shaft for the cellar. The cellar "had been used for a particular purpose in the process of brewing, which, without ventilation, could not be carried on." The cause of the action was that the defendant removed a grating from the mouth of the well, "so as to stop or prevent the free passage of air from [the] cellar upwards through the well. . . ." What caused the defendant to take this step is not clear from the report of the case. Perhaps

"the air . . . impregnated by the brewing operations" which "passed up the well and out into the open air" was offensive to him. At any rate, he preferred to have the well in his yard stopped up. The court had first to determine whether the owners of the public house could have a legal right to a current of air. If they were to have such a right, this case would have to be distinguished from *Bryant v. Lefever* (already considered). This, however, presented no difficulty. In this case, the current of air was confined to "a strictly defined channel." In the case of *Bryant v. Lefever,* what was involved was "the general current of air common to all mankind." The judge therefore held that the owners of the public house could have the right to a current of air whereas the owner of the private house in *Bryant v. Lefever* could not. An economist might be tempted to add "but the air moved all the same." However, all that had been decided at this stage of the argument was that there could be a legal right, not that the owners of the public house possessed it. But evidence showed that the shaft from the cellar to the well had existed for over forty years and that the use of the well as a ventilating shaft must have been known to the owners of the yard since the air, when it emerged, smelt of the brewing operations. The judge therefore held that the public house had such a right by the "doctrine of lost grant." This doctrine states "that if a legal right is proved to have existed and been exercised for a number of years the law ought to presume that it had a legal origin."[13] So the owner of the cottages and yard had to unstop the well and endure the smell.

The reasoning employed by the courts in determining legal rights will often seem strange to an economist because many of the factors on which the

---

[12]25 Q.B.D. 481 (1890).

[13]It may be asked why a lost grant could not also be presumed in the case of the confectioner who had operated one mortar for more than 60 years. The answer is that until the doctor built the consulting room at the end of his garden there was no nuisance. So the nuisance had not continued for many years. It is true that the confectioner in his affidavit referred to "an invalid lady who occupied the house upon one occasion, about thirty years before" who "requested him if possible to discontinue the use of the mortars before eight o'clock in the morning" and that there was some evidence that the garden wall had been subjected to vibration. But the court had little difficulty in disposing of this line of argument: ". . . this vibration, even if it existed at all, was so slight, and the complaint, if it can be called a complaint, of the invalid lady . . . was of so trifling a character, that . . . the Defendant's acts would not have given rise to any proceeding either at law or in equity" (11 Ch.D. 863). That is, the confectioner had not committed a nuisance until the doctor built his consulting room.

decision turns are, to an economist, irrelevant. Because of this, situations which are, from an economic point of view, identical will be treated quite differently by the courts. The economic problem in all cases of harmful effects is how to maximise the value of production. In the case of *Bass v. Gregory* fresh air was drawn in through the well which facilitated the production of beer but foul air was expelled through the well which made life in the adjoining houses less pleasant. The economic problem was to decide which to choose: a lower cost of beer and worsened amenities in adjoining houses or a higher cost of beer and improved amenities. In deciding this question, the "doctrine of lost grant" is about as relevant as the colour of the judge's eyes. But it has to be remembered that the immediate question faced by the courts is *not* what shall be done by whom *but* who has the legal right to do what. It is always possible to modify by transactions on the market the initial legal delimitation of rights. And, of course, if such market transactions are costless, such a rearrangement of rights will always take place if it would lead to an increase in the value of production.

VI. THE COST OF MARKET TRANSACTIONS TAKEN INTO ACCOUNT

The argument has proceeded up to this point on the assumption (explicit in Sections III and IV and tacit in Section V) that there were no costs involved in carrying out market transactions. This is, of course, a very unrealistic assumption. In order to carry out a market transaction it is necessary to discover who it is that one wishes to deal with, to inform people that one wishes to deal and on what terms, to conduct negotiations leading up to a bargain, to draw up the contract, to undertake the inspection needed to make sure that the terms of the contract are being observed, and so on. These operations are often extremely costly, sufficiently costly at any rate to prevent many transactions that would be carried out in a world in which the pricing system worked without cost.

In earlier sections, when dealing with the problem of the rearrangement of legal rights through the market, it was argued that such a rearrangement would be made through the market whenever this would lead to an increase in the value of production. But this assumed costless market transactions. Once the costs of carrying out market transactions are taken into account it is clear that such a rearrangement of rights will only be undertaken when the increase in the value of production consequent upon the rearrangement is greater than the costs which would be involved in bringing it about. When it is less, the granting of an injunction (or the knowledge that it would be granted) or the liability to pay damages may result in an activity being discontinued (or may prevent its being started) which would be undertaken if market transactions were costless. In these conditions the initial delimitation of legal rights does have an effect on the efficiency with which the economic system operates. One arrangement of rights may bring about a greater value of production than any other. But unless this is the arrangement of rights established by the legal system, the costs of reaching the same result by altering and combining rights through the market may be so great that this optimal arrangement of rights, and the greater value of production which it would bring, may never be achieved. The part played by economic considerations in the process of delimiting legal rights will be discussed in the next section. In this section, I will take the initial delimitation of rights and the costs of carrying out market transactions as given.

It is clear that an alternative form of economic organisation which could achieve the same result at less cost than would be incurred by using the market would enable the value of production to be raised. As I explained many years ago, the firm represents such an alternative to organising production through market transactions.[14] Within the firm individual bargains between the various cooperating factors of production are eliminated and for a market transaction is substituted an administrative decision. The rearrangement of production then takes place without the need for bargains between the owners of the factors of production. A landowner who has control of a large tract of land may devote his land to various uses taking into account the effect that the interrelations of the various activities will have on the net return of the land, thus rendering unnecessary bargains between those undertaking the various activities. Owners of a large building or of several adjoining properties in a given area may act in much the same way. In effect, using our earlier terminology, the firm would acquire the legal rights of all the parties and the rearrangement of activities would not follow on a rearrangement of rights by contract, but

---

[14]See Coase, "The Nature of the Firm," 4 *Economica*, New Series, 386 (1937). Reprinted in *Readings in Price Theory*, 331 (1952).

as a result of an administrative decision as to how the rights should be used.

It does not, of course, follow that the administrative costs of organising a transaction through a firm are inevitably less than the costs of the market transactions which are superseded. But where contracts are peculiarly difficult to draw up and an attempt to describe what the parties have agreed to do or not to do (e.g. the amount and kind of a smell or noise that they may make or will not make) would necessitate a lengthy and highly involved document, and, where, as is probable, a long-term contract would be desirable;[15] it would be hardly surprising if the emergence of a firm or the extension of the activities of an existing firm was not the solution adopted on many occasions to deal with the problem of harmful effects. This solution would be adopted whenever the administrative costs of the firm were less than the costs of the market transactions that it supersedes and the gains which would result from the rearrangement of activities greater than the firm's costs of organising them. I do not need to examine in great detail the character of this solution since I have explained what is involved in my earlier article.

But the firm is not the only possible answer to this problem. The administrative costs of organising transactions within the firm may also be high, and particularly so when many diverse activities are brought within the control of a single organisation. In the standard case of a smoke nuisance, which may affect a vast number of people engaged in a wide variety of activities, the administrative costs might well be so high as to make any attempt to deal with the problem within the confines of a single firm impossible. An alternative solution is direct government regulation. Instead of instituting a legal system of rights which can be modified by transactions on the market, the government may impose regulations which state what people must or must not do and which have to be obeyed. Thus, the government (by statute or perhaps more likely through an administrative agency) may, to deal with the problem of smoke nuisance, decree that certain methods of production should or should not be used (e.g., that smoke preventing devices should be installed or that coal or oil should not be burned) or may confine certain types of business to certain districts (zoning regulations).

The government is, in a sense, a superfirm (but of a very special kind) since it is able to influence the use of factors of production by administrative decision. But the ordinary firm is subject to checks in its operations because of the competition of other firms, which might administer the same activities at lower cost and also because there is always the alternative of market transactions as against organisation within the firm if the administrative costs become too great. The government is able, if it wishes, to avoid the market altogether, which a firm can never do. The firm has to make market agreements with the owners of the factors of production that it uses. Just as the government can conscript or seize property, so it can decree that factors of production should only be used in such-and-such a way. Such authoritarian methods save a lot of trouble (for those doing the organising). Furthermore, the government has at its disposal the police and the other law enforcement agencies to make sure that its regulations are carried out.

It is clear that the government has powers which might enable it to get some things done at a lower cost than could a private organisation (or at any rate one without special governmental powers). But the governmental administrative machine is not itself costless. It can, in fact, on occasion be extremely costly. Furthermore, there is no reason to suppose that the restrictive and zoning regulations, made by a fallible administration subject to political pressures and operating without any competitive check, will necessarily always be those which increase the efficiency with which the economic system operates. Furthermore, such general regulations which must apply to a wide variety of cases will be enforced in some cases in which they are clearly inappropriate. From these considerations it follows that direct governmental regulation will not necessarily give better results than leaving the problem to be solved by the market or the firm. But equally there is no reason why, on occasion, such governmental administrative regulation should not lead to an improvement in economic efficiency. This would seem particularly likely when, as is normally the case with the smoke nuisance, a large number of people are involved and in which therefore the costs of handling the problem through the market or the firm may be high.

There is, of course, a further alternative, which is to do nothing about the problem at all. And given that the costs involved in solving the problem by regulations issued by the governmental administrative machine will often by heavy (particularly if the

[15]For reasons explained in my earlier article, see *Readings in Price Theory*, n. 14 at 337.

costs are interpreted to include all the consequences which follow from the Government engaging in this kind of activity), it will no doubt be commonly the case that the gain which would come from regulating the actions which give rise to the harmful effects will be less than the costs involved in Government regulation.

The discussion of the problem of harmful effects in this section (when the costs of market transactions are taken into account) is extremely inadequate. But at least it has made clear that the problem is one of choosing the appropriate social arrangement for dealing with the harmful effects. All solutions have costs and there is no reason to suppose that government regulation is called for simply because the problem is not well handled by the market or the firm. Satisfactory views on policy can only come from a patient study of how, in practice, the market, firms and governments handle the problem of harmful effects. Economists need to study the work of the broker in bringing parties together, the effectiveness of restrictive covenants, the problems of the large-scale real-estate development company, the operation of Government zoning and other regulating activities. It is my belief that economists, and policy-makers generally, have tended to over-estimate the advantages which come from governmental regulation. But this belief, even if justified, does not do more than suggest that government regulation should be curtailed. It does not tell us where the boundary line should be drawn. This, it seems to me, has to come from a detailed investigation of the actual results of handling the problem in different ways. But it would be unfortunate if this investigation were undertaken with the aid of a faulty economic analysis. The aim of this article is to indicate what the economic approach to the problem should be.

VII. THE LEGAL DELIMITATION OF RIGHTS AND THE ECONOMIC PROBLEM

The discussion in Section V not only served to illustrate the argument but also afforded a glimpse at the legal approach to the problem of harmful effects. The cases considered were all English but a similar selection of American cases could easily be made and the character of the reasoning would have been the same. Of course, if market transactions were costless, all that matters (questions of equity apart) is that the rights of the various parties should be well-defined and the results of legal actions easy to forecast. But as we have seen, the situation is quite different when market transactions are so costly as to make it difficult to change the arrangement of rights established by the law. In such cases, the courts directly influence economic activity. It would therefore seem desirable that the courts should understand the economic consequences of their decisions and should, insofar as this is possible without creating too much uncertainty about the legal position itself, take these consequences into account when making their decisions. Even when it is possible to change the legal delimitation of rights through market transactions, it is obviously desirable to reduce the need for such transactions and thus reduce the employment of resources in carrying them out.

A thorough examination of the presuppositions of the courts in trying such cases would be of great interest but I have not been able to attempt it. Nevertheless it is clear from a cursory study that the courts have often recognized the economic implications of their decisions and are aware (as many economists are not) of the reciprocal nature of the problem. Furthermore, from time to time, they take these economic implications into account, along with other factors, in arriving at their decisions. The American writers on this subject refer to the question in a more explicit fashion than do the British. Thus, to quote Prosser on Torts, a person may

> make use of his own property or . . . conduct his own affairs at the expense of some harm to his neighbors. He may operate a factory whose noise and smoke cause some discomfort to others, so long as he keeps within reasonable bounds. It is only when his conduct is unreasonable, *in the light of its utility and the harm which results* [italics added], that it becomes a nuisance. . . . As it was said in an ancient case in regard to candle-making in a town, "Le utility del chose excusera le noisomeness del stink."
> The world must have factories, smelters, oil refineries, noisy machinery and blasting, even at the expense of some inconvenience to those in the vicinity and the plaintiff may be required to accept some not unreasonable discomfort for the general good.[16]

The standard British writers do not state as explicitly as this that a comparison between the utility

[16]See W. L. Prosser, *The Law of Torts* 398–99, 412 (2d ed. 1955). The quotation about the ancient case concerning candle-making is taken from Sir James Fitzjames Stephen, *A General View of the Criminal Law of England* 106 (1890). Sir James Stephen gives no reference. He perhaps had in mind *Rex. v. Ronkett*, included in Seavey, Keeton and Thurston, *Cases on Torts* 604 (1950). A similar view to that expressed by Prosser is to be found in F. V. Harper and F. James, *The Law of Torts* 67–74 (1956); *Restatement, Torts §§ 826, 827 and 828.*

and harm produced is an element in deciding whether a harmful effect should be considered a nuisance. But similar views, if less strongly expressed, are to be found.[17] The doctrine that the harmful effect must be substantial before the court will act is, no doubt, in part a reflection of the fact that there will almost always be some gain to offset the harm. And in the reports of individual cases, it is clear that the judges have had in mind what would be lost as well as what would be gained in deciding whether to grant an injunction or award damages. Thus, in refusing to prevent the destruction of a prospect by a new building, the judge stated:

> I know no general rule of common law, which . . . says, that building so as to stop another's prospect is a nuisance. Was that the case, there could be no great towns; and I must grant injunctions to all the new buildings in this town. . . .[18]

In *Webb v. Bird*[19] it was decided that it was not a nuisance to build a schoolhouse so near a windmill as to obstruct currents of air and hinder the working of the mill. An early case seems to have been decided in an opposite direction. Gale commented:

> In old maps of London a row of windmills appears on the heights to the north of London. Probably in the time of King James it was thought an alarming circumstance, as affecting the supply of food to the city, that anyone should build so near them as to take the wind out from their sails.[20]

In one of the cases discussed in section V, *Sturges v. Bridgman,* it seems clear that the judges were thinking of the economic consequences of alternative decisions. To the argument that if the principle that they seemed to be following:

> were carried out to its logical consequences, it would result in the most serious practical inconveniences, for a man might go—say into the midst of the tanneries of *Bermondsey,* or into any other locality devoted to any particular trade or manufacture of a noisy or unsavoury character, and by building a pri-

vate residence upon a vacant piece of land put a stop to such trade or manufacture altogether,

the judges answered that

> whether anything is a nuisance or not is a question to be determined, not merely by an abstract consideration of the thing itself, but in reference to its circumstances; What would be a nuisance in *Belgrave Square* would not necessarily be so in *Bermondsey;* and where a locality is devoted to a particular trade or manufacture carried on by the traders or manufacturers in a particular and established manner not constituting a public nuisance, Judges and juries would be justified in finding, and may be trusted to find, that the trade or manufacture so carried on in that locality is not a private or actionable wrong.[21]

That the character of the neighborhood is relevant in deciding whether something is, or is not, a nuisance, is definitely established.

> He who dislikes the noise of traffic must not set up his abode in the heart of a great city. He who loves peace and quiet must not live in a locality devoted to the business of making boilers or steamships.[22]

What has emerged has been described as "planning and zoning by the judiciary."[23] Of course there are sometimes considerable difficulties in applying the criteria.[24]

An interesting example of the problem is found in *Adams v. Ursell*[25] in which a fried fish shop in a predominantly working-class district was set up near houses of "a much better character." England without fish-and-chips is a contradiction in terms and the case was clearly one of high importance. The judge commented:

> It was urged that an injunction would cause great hardship to the defendant and to the poor people who get food at his shop. The answer to that is that it does not follow that the defendant cannot carry on his business in another more suitable place somewhere in the neighbourhood. It by no means follows that because a fried fish shop is a nuisance in one place it is a nuisance in another.

In fact, the injunction which restrained Mr. Ursell from running his shop did not even extend to the

---

[17] See Winfield on *Torts* 541–48 (6th ed. T. E. Lewis 1954); Salmond on the *Law of Torts* 181–90 (12th ed. R.F.V. Heuston 1957); H. Street, *The Law of Torts* 221–29 (1959).

[18] *Attorney General v. Doughty,* 2 Ves. Sen. 453, 28 Eng. Rep. 290 (Ch. 1752). Compare in this connection the statement of an American judge, quoted in Prosser, *op. cit. supra* n. 16 at 413 n. 54: "Without smoke, Pittsburgh would have remained a very pretty village," Musmanno, J., in *Versailles Borough v. McKeesport Coal & Coke Co.,* 1935, 83 Pitts, Leg. J. 379, 385.

[19] 10 C.B. (N.S.) 268, 142 Eng. Rep. 445 (1861); 13 C.B. (N.S.) 841, 143 Eng. Rep. 332 (1863).

[20] See Gale on *Easements* 238, n. 6 (13th ed. M. Bowles 1959).

[21] 11 Ch.D. 865 (1879).

[22] Salmond on the *Law of Torts* 182 (12th ed. R.F.V. Heuston 1957).

[23] C. M. Haar, *Land-Use Planning; A Casebook on the Use, Misuse, and Re-use of Urban Land* 95 (1959).

[24] See, for example, *Rushmer v. Polsue and Alfieri, Ltd.* [1906] 1 Ch. 234, which deals with the case of a house in a quiet situation in a noisy district.

[25] [1913] 1 Ch. 269.

whole street. So he was presumably able to move to other premises near houses of "a much worse character," the inhabitants of which would no doubt consider the availability of fish-and-chips to outweigh the pervading odour and "fog or mist" so graphically described by the plaintiff. Had there been no other "more suitable place in the neighbourhood," the case would have been more difficult and the decision might have been different. What would "the poor people" have had for food? No English judge would have said: "Let them eat cake."

The courts do not always refer very clearly to the economic problem posed by the cases brought before them but it seems probable that in the interpretation of words and phrases like "reasonable" or "common or ordinary use" there is some recognition, perhaps largely unconscious and certainly not very explicit, of the economic aspects of the questions at issue. A good example of this would seem to be the judgment in the Court of Appeals in *Andreae v. Selfridge and Company Ltd.*[26] In this case, a hotel (in Wigmore Street) was situated on part of an island site. The remainder of the site was acquired by Selfridges which demolished the existing buildings in order to erect another in their place. The hotel suffered a loss of custom in consequence of the noise and dust caused by the demolition. The owner of the hotel brought an action against Selfridges for damages. In the lower court, the hotel was awarded £4,500 damages. The case was then taken on appeal.

The judge who had found for the hotel proprietor in the lower court said:

> I cannot regard what the defendants did on the site of the first operation as having been commonly done in the ordinary use and occupation of land or houses. It is neither usual nor common, in this country, for people to excavate a site to a depth of 60 feet and then to erect upon that site a steel framework and fasten the steel frames together with rivets. . . . Nor is it, I think, a common or ordinary use of land, in this country, to act as the defendants did when they were dealing with the site of their second operation—namely, to demolish all the houses that they had to demolish, five or six of them I think, if not more, and to use for the purpose of demolishing them pneumatic hammers.

Sir Wilfred Greene, M.R., speaking for the Court of Appeals, first noted

> that when one is dealing with temporary operations, such as demolition and re-building, everybody has

to put up with a certain amount of discomfort, because operations of that kind cannot be carried on at all without a certain amount of noise and a certain amount of dust. Therefore, the rule with regard to interference must be read subject to this qualification. . . .

He then referred to the previous judgment:

> With great respect to the learned judge, I take the view that he has not approached this matter from the correct angle. It seems to me that it is not possible to say . . . that the type of demolition, excavation and construction in which the defendant company was engaged in the course of these operations was of such an abnormal and unusual nature as to prevent the qualification to which I have referred coming into operation. It seems to me that, when the rule speaks of the common or ordinary use of land, it does not mean that the methods of using land and building on it are in some way to be stabilised for ever. As time goes on new inventions or new methods enable land to be more profitably used, either by digging down into the earth or by mounting up into the skies. Whether, from other points of view, that is a matter which is desirable for humanity is neither here nor there; but it is part of the normal use of land, to make use upon your land, in the matter of construction, of what particular type and what particular depth of foundations and particular height of building may be reasonable, in the circumstances, and in view of the developments of the day. . . . Guests at hotels are very easily upset. People coming to this hotel, who were accustomed to a quiet outlook at the back, coming back and finding demolition and building going on, may very well have taken the view that the particular merit of this hotel no longer existed. That would be a misfortune for the plaintiff; but assuming that there was nothing wrong in the defendant company's works, assuming the defendant company was carrying on the demolition and its building, productive of noise though it might be, with all reasonable skill, and taking all reasonable precautions not to cause annoyance to its neighbors, then the plaintiff might lose all her clients in the hotel because they have lost the amenities of an open and quiet place behind, but she would have no cause of complaint. . . . [But those] who say that their interference with the comfort of their neighbors is justified because their operations are normal and usual and conducted with proper care and skill are under a specific duty . . . to use that reasonable and proper care and skill. It is not a correct attitude to take to say: 'We will go on and do what we like until somebody complains!' . . . Their duty is to take proper precautions and to see that the nuisance is reduced to a minimum. It is no answer for them to say: 'But this would mean that we should have to do the work more slowly than we would like to do it, or it would involve putting us to some extra expense.' All these questions are matters of common sense and degree, and quite clearly it would be un-

[26][1938] 1 Ch. 1.

reasonable to expect people to conduct their work so slowly or so expensively, for the purpose of preventing a transient inconvenience, that the cost and trouble would be prohibitive. . . . In this case, the defendant company's attitude seems to have been to go on until somebody complained, and, further, that its desire to hurry its work and conduct it according to its own ideas and its own convenience was to prevail if there was a real conflict between it and the comfort of its neighbors. That . . . is not carrying out the obligation of using reasonable care and skill. . . . The effect comes to this . . . the plaintiff suffered an actionable nuisance; . . . she is entitled, not to a nominal sum, but to a substantial sum, based upon those principles . . . but in arriving at the sum . . . I have discounted any loss of custom . . . which might be due to the general loss of amenities owing to what was going on at the back. . . .

The upshot was that the damages awarded were reduced from £4,500 to £1,000.

The discussion in this section has, up to this point, been concerned with court decisions arising out of the common law relating to nuisance. Delimitation of rights in this area also comes about because of statutory enactments. Most economists would appear to assume that the aim of governmental action in this field is to extend the scope of the law of nuisance by designating as nuisances activities which would not be recognized as such by the common law. And there can be no doubt that some statutes, for example, the Public Health Acts, have had this effect. But not all Government enactments are of this kind. The effect of much of the legislation in this area is to protect businesses from the claims of those they have harmed by their actions. There is a long list of legalized nuisances.

The position has been summarized in *Halsbury's Laws of England* as follows:

> Where the legislature directs that a thing shall in all events be done or authorises certain works at a particular place for a specific purpose or grants powers with the intention that they shall be exercised, although leaving some discretion as to the mode of exercise, no action will lie at common law for nuisance or damage which is the inevitable result of carrying out the statutory powers so conferred. This is so whether the act causing the damage is authorised for public purposes or private profit. Acts done under powers granted by persons to whom Parliament has delegated authority to grant such powers, for example, under provisional orders of the Board of Trade, are regarded as having been done under statutory authority. In the absence of negligence it seems that a body exercising statutory powers will not be liable to an action merely because

it might, by acting in a different way, have minimised an injury.

Instances are next given of freedom from liability for acts authorized:

> An action has been held not to be against a body exercising its statutory powers without negligence in respect of the flooding of land by water escaping from watercourses, from water pipes, from drains, or from a canal; the escape of fumes from sewers; the escape of sewage: the subsidence of a road over a sewer; vibration or noise caused by a railway; fires caused by authorised acts; the pollution of a stream where statutory requirements to use the best known method of purifying before discharging the effluent have been satisfied; interference with a telephone or telegraph system by an electric tramway; the insertion of poles for tramways in the subsoil; annoyance caused by things reasonably necessary for the excavation of authorised works; accidental damage caused by the placing of a grating in a roadway; the escape of tar acid; or interference with the access of a frontager by a street shelter or safety railings on the edge of a pavement.[27]

The legal position in the United States would seem to be essentially the same as in England, except that the power of the legislatures to authorize what would otherwise be nuisances under the common law, at least without giving compensation to the person harmed, is somewhat more limited, as it is subject to constitutional restrictions.[28] Nonetheless, the power is there and cases more or less identical with the English cases can be found. The question has arisen in an acute form in connection with airports and the operation of aeroplanes. The case of *Delta Air Corporation v. Kersey, Kersey v. City of Atlanta*[29] is a good example. Mr. Kersey bought land and built a house on it. Some years later the City of Atlanta constructed an airport on land immediately adjoining that of Mr. Kersey. It was explained that his property was "a quiet, peaceful and proper location for a home before the airport was built, but dust, noises and low flying of airplanes caused by the operation of the airport have rendered his property unsuitable as a home," a state of affairs which was described in the report of the case with a wealth of distressing detail. The judge first referred to an earlier case, *Thrasher v. City of Atlanta*[30] in which it was noted that the

---

[27]See 30 Halsbury, *Law of England* 690–91 (3d ed. 1960), Article on Public Authorities and Public Officers.
[28]See Prosser, *op. cit. supra* n. 16 at 421; Harper and James, *op. cit. supra* n. 16 at 86–87.
[29]Supreme Court of Georgia 193 Ga. 862, 20 S.E. 2d 245 (1942).
[30]178 Ga. 514, 173 S.E. 817 (1934).

City of Atlanta had been expressly authorized to operate an airport.

> By this franchise aviation was recognised as a lawful business and also as an enterprise affected with a public interest . . . all persons using [the airport] in the manner contemplated by law are within the protection and immunity of the franchise granted by the municipality. An airport is not a nuisance per se, although it might become such from the manner of its construction or operation.

Since aviation was a lawful business affected with a public interest and the construction of the airport was authorized by statute, the judge next referred to *Georgia Railroad and Banking Co. v. Maddox*[31] in which it was said:

> Where a railroad terminal yard is located and its construction authorized, under statutory powers, if it be constructed and operated in a proper manner, it cannot be adjudged a nuisance. Accordingly, injuries and inconveniences to persons residing near such a yard, from noises of locomotives, rumbling of cars, vibrations produced thereby, and smoke, cinders, soot and the like, which result from the ordinary and necessary, therefore proper, use and operation of such a yard, are not nuisances, but are the necessary concomitants of the franchise granted.

In view of this, the judge decided that the noise and dust complained of by Mr. Kersey "may be deemed to be incidental to the proper operation of an airport, and as such they cannot be said to constitute a nuisance." But the complaint against low flying was different:

> . . . can it be said that flights . . . at such a low height [25 to 50 feet above Mr. Kersey's house] as to be imminently dangerous to . . . life and health . . . are a necessary concomitant of an airport? We do not think this question can be answered in the affirmative. No reason appears why the city could not obtain lands of an area [sufficiently large] . . . as not to require such low flights. . . . For the sake of public convenience adjoining-property owners must suffer such inconvenience from noise and dust as result from the usual and proper operation of an airport, but their private rights are entitled to preference in the eyes of the law where the inconvenience is not one demanded by a properly constructed and operated airport.

Of course this assumed that the City of Atlanta could prevent the low flying and continue to operate the airport. The judge therefore added:

> From all that appears, the conditions causing the low flying may be remedied; but if on the trial it

should appear that it is indispensable to the public interest that the airport should continue to be operated in its present condition, it may be said that the petitioner should be denied injunctive relief.

In the course of another aviation case, *Smith v. New England Aircraft Co.*,[32] the court surveyed the law in the United States regarding the legalizing of nuisances and it is apparent that, in the broad, it is very similar to that found in England:

> It is the proper function of the legislative department of government in the exercise of the police power to consider the problems and risks that arise from the use of new inventions and endeavor to adjust private rights and harmonize conflicting interests by comprehensive statutes for the public welfare. . . . There are . . . analogies where the invasion of the airspace over underlying land by noise, smoke, vibration, dust and disagreeable odors, having been authorized by the legislative department of government and not being in effect a condemnation of the property although in some measure depreciating its market value, must be borne by the landowner without compensation or remedy. Legislative sanction makes that lawful which otherwise might be a nuisance. Examples of this are damages to adjacent land arising from smoke, vibration and noise in the operation of a railroad . . . ; the noise of ringing factory bells . . . ; the abatement of nuisances . . . ; the erection of steam engines and furnaces . . . ; unpleasant odors connected with sewers, oil refining and storage of naphtha. . . .

Most economists seem to be unaware of all this. When they are prevented from sleeping at night by the roar of jet planes overhead (publicly authorized and perhaps publicly operated), are unable to think (or rest) in the day because of the noise and vibration from passing trains (publicly authorized and perhaps publicly operated), find it difficult to breathe because of the odour from a local sewage farm (publicly authorized and perhaps publicly operated) and are unable to escape because their driveways are blocked by a road obstruction (without any doubt, publicly devised), their nerves frayed and mental balance disturbed, they proceed to declaim about the disadvantages of private enterprise and the need for Government regulation.

While most economists seem to be under a misapprehension concerning the character of the situation with which they are dealing, it is also the case that the activities which they would like to see stopped or curtailed may well be socially justified. It is all a question of weighing up the gains that would

---

[31]116 Ga. 64, 42 S.E. 315 (1902).

[32]270 Mass. 511, 523, 170 N.E. 385, 390 (1930).

accrue from eliminating these harmful effects against the gains that accrue from allowing them to continue. Of course, it is likely that an extension of Government economic activity will often lead to this protection against action for nuisance being pushed further than is desirable. For one thing, the Government is likely to look with a benevolent eye on enterprises which it is itself promoting. For another, it is possible to describe the committing of a nuisance by public enterprise in a much more pleasant way than when the same thing is done by private enterprise. In the words of Lord Justice Sir Alfred Denning:

> ... the significance of the social revolution of today is that, whereas in the past the balance was much too heavily in favor of the rights of property and freedom of contract, Parliament has repeatedly intervened so as to give the public good its proper place.[33]

There can be little doubt that the Welfare State is likely to bring an extension of that immunity from liability for damage, which economists have been in the habit of condemning (although they have tended to assume that this immunity was a sign of too little Government intervention in the economic system). For example, in Britain, the powers of local authorities are regarded as being either absolute or conditional. In the first category, the local authority has no discretion in exercising the power conferred on it. "The absolute power may be said to cover all the necessary consequences of its direct operation even if such consequences amount to nuisance." On the other hand, a conditional power may only be exercised in such a way that the consequences do not constitute a nuisance.

> It is the intention of the legislature which determines whether a power is absolute or conditional. . . . [As] there is the possibility that the social policy of the legislature may change from time to time, a power which in one era would be construed as being conditional, might in another era be interpreted as being absolute in order to further the policy of the Welfare State. This point is one which should be borne in mind when considering some of the older cases upon this aspect of the law of nuisance.[34]

It would seem desirable to summarize the burden of this long section. The problem which we face in dealing with actions which have harmful effects is not simply one of restraining those responsible for

them. What has to be decided is whether the gain from preventing the harm is greater than the loss which would be suffered elsewhere as a result of stopping the action which produces the harm. In a world in which there are costs of rearranging the rights established by the legal system, the courts, in cases relating to nuisance, are, in effect, making a decision on the economic problem and determining how resources are to be employed. It was argued that the courts are conscious of this and that they often make, although not always in a very explicit fashion, a comparison between what would be gained and what lost by preventing actions which have harmful effects. But the delimitation of rights is also the result of statutory enactments. Here we also find evidence of an appreciation of the reciprocal nature of the problem. While statutory enactments add to the list of nuisances, action is also taken to legalize what would otherwise be nuisances under the common law. The kind of situation which economists are prone to consider as requiring corrective Government action is, in fact, often the result of Government action. Such action is not necessarily unwise. But there is a real danger that extensive Government intervention in the economic system may lead to the protection of those responsible for harmful effects being carried too far.

VIII. PIGOU'S TREATMENT IN "THE ECONOMICS OF WELFARE"

The fountainhead for the modern economic analysis of the problem discussed in this article is Pigou's *Economics of Welfare* and, in particular, that section of Part II which deals with divergences between social and private net products which come about because

> one person A, in the course of rendering some service, for which payment is made, to a second person B, incidentally also renders services or disservices to other persons (not producers of like services), of such a sort that payment cannot be exacted from the benefited parties or compensation enforced on behalf of the injured parties.[35]

Pigou tells us that his aim in Part II of *The Economics of Welfare* is

---

[33] See Sir Alfred Denning, *Freedom Under the Law* 71 (1949).
[34] M. B. Cairns, *The Law of Tort in Local Government* 28–32 (1954).

[35] A. C. Pigou, *The Economics of Welfare* 183 (4th ed. 1932). My references will all be to the fourth edition but the argument and examples examined in this article remained substantially unchanged from the first edition in 1920 to the fourth in 1932. A large part (but not all) of this analysis had appeared previously in *Wealth and Welfare* (1912).

to ascertain how far the free play of self-interest, acting under the existing legal system, tends to distribute the country's resources in the way most favorable to the production of a large national dividend, and how far it is feasible for State action to improve upon 'natural' tendencies.[36]

To judge from the first part of this statement, Pigou's purpose is to discover whether any improvements could be made in the existing arrangements which determine the use of resources. Since Pigou's conclusion is that improvements could be made, one might have expected him to continue by saying that he proposed to set out the changes required to bring them about. Instead, Pigou adds a phrase which contrasts "natural" tendencies with State action, which seems in some sense to equate the present arrangements with "natural" tendencies and to imply that what is required to bring about these improvements is State action (if feasible). That this is more or less Pigou's position is evident from Chapter I of Part II.[37] Pigou starts by referring to "optimistic followers of the classical economists"[38] who have argued that the value of production would be maximised if the Government refrained from any interference in the economic system and the economic arrangements were those which came about "naturally." Pigou goes on to say that if self-interest does promote economic welfare, it is because human institutions have been devised to make it so. (This part of Pigou's argument, which he develops with the aid of a quotation from Cannan, seems to me to be essentially correct.) Pigou concludes:

> But even in the most advanced States there are failures and imperfections. . . . there are many obstacles that prevent a community's resources from being distributed . . . in the most efficient way. The study of these constitutes our present problem. . . . its purposes is essentially practical. It seeks to bring into clearer light some of the ways in which it now is, or eventually may become, feasible for governments to control the play of economic forces in such wise as to promote the economic welfare, and through that, the total welfare, of their citizens as a whole.[39]

[36]*Id.* at xii.
[37]*Id.* at 127–30.
[38]In *Wealth and Welfare,* Pigou attributes the "optimism" to Adam Smith himself and not to his followers. He there refers to the "highly optimistic theory of Adam Smith that the national dividend, in given circumstances of demand and supply, tends 'naturally' to a maximum" (p. 104).
[39]Pigou, *op. cit. supra* n. 35 at 129–30.

Pigou's underlying thought would appear to be: Some have argued that no State action is needed. But the system has performed as well as it has because of State action. Nonetheless, there are still imperfections. What additional State action is required?

If this is a correct summary of Pigou's position, its inadequacy can be demonstrated by examining the first example he gives of a divergence between private and social products.

> It might happen . . . that costs are thrown upon people not directly concerned, through, say, uncompensated damage done to surrounding woods by sparks from railway engines. All such effects must be included—some of them will be positive, others negative elements—in reckoning up the social net product of the marginal increment of any volume of resources turned into any use or place.[40]

The example used by Pigou refers to a real situation. In Britain, a railway does not normally have to compensate those who suffer damage by fire caused by sparks from an engine. Taken in conjunction with what he says in Chapter 9 of Part II, I take Pigou's policy recommendations to be, first, that there should be State action to correct this "natural" situation and, second, that the railways should be forced to compensate those whose woods are burnt. If this is a correct interpretation of Pigou's position, I would argue that the first recommendation is based on a misapprehension of the facts and that the second is not necessarily desirable.

Let us consider the legal position. Under the heading "Sparks from engines," we find the following in Halsbury's Laws of England:

> If railway undertakers use steam engines on their railway without express statutory authority to do so, they are liable, irrespective of any negligence on their part, for fires caused by sparks from engines. Railway undertakers are, however, generally given statutory authority to use steam engines on their railway; accordingly, if an engine is constructed with the precautions which science suggests against fire and is used without negligence, they are not responsible at common law for any damage which may be done by sparks. . . . In the construction of an engine the undertaker is bound to use all the discoveries which science has put within its reach in order to avoid doing harm, provided they are such as it is a reasonable for the company to adopt, having proper regard to the likelihood of the damage and to the cost and convenience of the remedy; but it is not negligence on the part of an undertaker if it refuses to use an apparatus the efficiency of which is open to bona fide doubt.

[40]*Id.* at 134.

To this general rule, there is a statutory exception arising from the Railway (Fires) Act, 1905, as amended in 1923. This concerns agricultural land or agricultural crops.

> In such a case the fact that the engine was used under statutory powers does not affect the liability of the company in an action for the damage. . . . These provisions, however, only apply where the claim for damage . . . does not exceed £200, [£100 in the 1905 Act] and where written notice of the occurrence of the fire and the intention to claim has been sent to the company within seven days of the occurrence of the damage and particulars of the damage in writing showing the amount of the claim in money not exceeding £200 have been sent to the company within twenty-one days.

Agricultural land does not include moorland or buildings and agricultural crops do not include those led away or stacked.[41] I have not made a close study of the parliamentary history of this statutory exception, but to judge from debates in the House of Commons in 1922 and 1923, this exception was probably designed to help the smallholder.[42]

Let us return to Pigou's example of uncompensated damage to surrounding woods caused by sparks from railway engines. This is presumably intended to show how it is possible "for State action to improve on 'natural' tendencies." If we treat Pigou's example as referring to the position before 1905, or as being an arbitrary example (in that he might just as well have written "surrounding buildings" instead of "surrounding woods"), then it is clear that the reason why compensation was not paid must have been that the railway had statutory authority to run steam engines (which relieved it of liability for fires caused by sparks). That this was the legal position was established in 1860, in a case, oddly enough, which concerned the burning of surrounding woods by a railway,[43] and the law on this point has not been changed (apart from the one exception) by a century of railway legislation, including nationalisation. If we treat Pigou's example of "uncompensated damage done to surrounding woods by sparks from railway engines" literally, and assume that it refers to the

period after 1905, then it is clear that the reason why compensation was not paid must have been that the damage was more than £100 (in the first edition of *The Economics of Welfare*) or more than £200 (in later editions) or that the owner of the wood failed to notify the railway in writing within seven days of the fire or did not send particulars of the damage, in writing, within twenty-one days. In the real world, Pigou's example could only exist as a result of a deliberate choice of the legislature. It is not, of course, easy to imagine the construction of a railway in a state of nature. The nearest one can get to this is presumably a railway which uses steam engines "without express statutory authority." However, in this case the railway would be obliged to compensate those whose woods it burnt down. That is to say, compensation would be paid in the absence of Government action. The only circumstances in which compensation would not be paid would be those in which there had been Government action. It is strange that Pigou, who clearly thought it desirable that compensation should be paid, should have chosen this particular example to demonstrate how it is possible "for State action to improve on 'natural' tendencies."

Pigou seems to have had a faulty view of the facts of the situation. But it also seems likely that he was mistaken in his economic analysis. It is not necessarily desirable that the railway should be required to compensate those who suffer damage by fires caused by railway engines. I need not show here that, if the railway could make a bargain with everyone having property adjoining the railway line and there were no costs involved in making such bargains, it would not matter whether the railway was liable for damage caused by fires or not. This question has been treated at length in earlier sections. The problem is whether it would be desirable to make the railway liable in conditions in which it is too expensive for such bargains to be made. Pigou clearly thought it was desirable to force the railway to pay compensation and it is easy to see the kind of argument that would have led him to this conclusion. Suppose a railway is considering whether to run an additional train or to increase the speed of an existing train or to install spark-preventing devices on its engines. If the railway were not liable for fire damage, then, when making these decisions, it would not take into account as a cost the increase in damage resulting from the additional train or the faster train or the failure to install

[41]See 31 Halsbury, *Laws of England* 474–75 (3d ed. 1960), Article on Railways and Canals, from which this summary of the legal position, and all quotations, are taken.
[42]See 152 H.C. Deb. 2622–63 (1922); 161 H.C. Deb. 2935–55 (1923).
[43]*Vaughan v. Taff Vale Railway Co.*, 3 H. and N. 743 (Ex. 1858) and 5 H. and N. 679 (Ex. 1860).

spark-preventing devices. This is the source of the divergence between private and social net products. It results in the railway performing acts which will lower the value of total production—and which it would not do if it were liable for the damage. This can be shown by means of an arithmetical example.

Consider a railway, which is *not* liable for damage by fires caused by sparks from its engines, which runs two trains per day on a certain line. Suppose that running one train per day would enable the railway to perform services worth $150 per annum and running two trains a day would enable the railway to perform services worth $250 per annum. Suppose further that the cost of running one train is $50 per annum and two trains $100 per annum. Assuming perfect competition, the cost equals the fall in the value of production elsewhere due to the employment of additional factors of production by the railway. Clearly the railway would find it profitable to run two trains per day. But suppose that running one train per day would destroy by fire crops worth (on an average over the year) $60 and two trains a day would result in the destruction of crops worth $120. In these circumstances running one train per day would raise the value of total production but the running of a second train would reduce the value of total production. The second train would enable additional railway services worth $100 per annum to be performed. But the fall in the value of production elsewhere would be $110 per annum; $50 as a result of the employment of additional factors of production and $60 as a result of the destruction of crops. Since it would be better if the second train were not run and since it would not run if the railway were liable for damage caused to crops, the conclusion that the railway should be made liable for the damage seems irresistible. Undoubtedly it is this kind of reasoning which underlies the Pigovian position.

The conclusion that it would be better if the second train did not run is correct. The conclusion that it is desirable that the railway should be made liable for the damage it causes is wrong. Let us change our assumption concerning the rule of liability. Suppose that the railway is liable for damage from fires caused by sparks from the engine. A farmer on lands adjoining the railway is then in the position that, if his crop is destroyed by fires caused by the railway, he will receive the market price from the railway; but if his crop is not damaged, he will receive the market price by sale. It therefore becomes a matter of in-

difference to him whether his crop is damaged by fire or not. The position is very different when the railway is *not* liable. Any crop destruction through railway-caused fires would then reduce the receipts of the farmer. He would therefore take out of cultivation any land for which the damage is likely to be greater than the net return of the land (for reasons explained at length in Section III). A change from a regime in which the railway is *not* liable for damage to one in which it *is* liable is likely therefore to lead to an increase in the amount of cultivation on lands adjoining the railway. It will also, of course, lead to an increase in the amount of crop destruction due to railway-caused fires.

Let us return to our arithmetical example. Assume that, with the changed rule of liability, there is a doubling in the amount of crop destruction due to railway-caused fires. With one train per day, crops worth $120 would be destroyed each year and two trains per day would lead to the destruction of crops worth $240. We saw previously that it would not be profitable to run the second train if the railway had to pay $60 per annum as compensation for damage. With damage at $120 per annum the loss from running the second train would be $60 greater. But now let us consider the first train. The value of the transport services furnished by the first train is $150. The cost of running the train is $50. The amount that the railway would have to pay out as compensation for damage is $120. It follows that it would not be profitable to run any trains. With the figures in our example we reach the following result: if the railway is not liable for fire-damage, two trains per day would be run; if the railway is liable for fire-damage, it would cease operations altogether. Does this mean that it is better that there should be no railway? This question can be resolved by considering what would happen to the value of total production if it were decided to exempt the railway from liability for fire-damage, thus bringing it into operation (with two trains per day).

The operation of the railway would enable transport services worth $250 to be performed. It would also mean the employment of factors of production which would reduce the value of production elsewhere by $100. Furthermore it would mean the destruction of crops worth $120. The coming of the railway will also have led to the abandonment of cultivation of some land. Since we know that, had this land been cultivated, the value of the crops destroyed by fire would have been $120, and since it is unlikely that the total crop on this land would have been destroyed, it seems reasonable to suppose that the value of the crop yield on this land would have been higher than this. Assume it would have been $160. But the abandonment of cultivation would have released factors of production for employment elsewhere. All we know is that the amount by which the value of production elsewhere will increase will be less than $160. Suppose that it is $150. Then the gain from operating the railway would be $250 (the value of the transport services) minus $100 (the cost of the factors of production) minus $120 (the value of crops destroyed by fire) minus $160 (the fall in the value of crop production due to the abandonment of cultivation) plus $150 (the value of production elsewhere of the released factors of production). Overall, operating the railway will increase the value of total production by $20. With these figures it is clear that it is better that the railway should not be liable for the damage it causes, thus enabling it to operate profitably. Of course, by altering the figures, it could be shown that there are other cases in which it would be desirable that the railway should be liable for the damage it causes. It is enough for my purpose to show that, from an economic point of view, a situation in which there is "uncompensated damage done to surrounding woods by sparks from railway engines" is not necessarily undesirable. Whether it is desirable or not depends on the particular circumstances.

How is it that the Pigovian analysis seems to give the wrong answer? The reason is that Pigou does not seem to have noticed that his analysis is dealing with an entirely different question. The analysis as such is correct. But it is quite illegitimate for Pigou to draw the particular conclusion he does. The question at issue is not whether it is desirable to run an additional train or a faster train or to install smoke-preventing devices; the question at issue is whether it is desirable to have a system in which the railway has to compensate those who suffer damage from the fires which it causes or one in which the railway does not have to compensate them. When an economist is comparing alternative social arrangements, the proper procedure is to compare the total social product yielded by these different arrangements. The comparison of private and social products is neither here nor there. A simple example will demonstrate

this. Imagine a town in which there are traffic lights. A motorist approaches an intersection and stops because the light is red. There are no cars approaching the intersection on the other street. If the motorist ignored the red signal, no accident would occur and the total product would increase because the motorist would arrive earlier at his destination. Why does he not do this? The reason is that if he ignored the light he would be fined. The private product from crossing the street is less than the social product. Should we conclude from this that the total product would be greater if there were no fines for failing to obey traffic signals? The Pigovian analysis shows us that it is possible to conceive of better worlds than the one in which we live. But the problem is to devise practical arrangements which will correct defects in one part of the system without causing more serious harm in other parts.

I have examined in considerable detail one example of a divergence between private and social products and I do not propose to make any further examination of Pigou's analytical system. But the main discussion of the problem considered in this article is to be found in that part of Chapter 9 in Part II which deals with Pigou's second class of divergence and it is of interest to see how Pigou develops his argument. Pigou's own description of this second class of divergence was quoted at the beginning of this section. Pigou distinguishes between the case in which a person renders services for which he receives no payment and the case in which a person renders disservices and compensation is not given to the injured parties. Our main attention has, of course, centred on this second case. It is therefore rather astonishing to find, as was pointed out to me by Professor Francesco Forte, that the problem of the smoking chimney—the "stock instance"[44] or "classroom example"[45] of the second case—is used by Pigou as an example of the first case (services rendered without payment) and is never mentioned, at any rate explicitly, in connection with the second case.[46] Pigou points out that factory owners who devote resources to preventing their chimneys from smoking render services for which they receive no payment.

---

[44]Sir Dennis Robertson, I *Lectures on Economic Principles* 162 (1957).
[45]E. J. Mishan, "The Meaning of Efficiency in Economics," 189, *The Bankers' Magazine* 482 (June 1960).
[46]Pigou, *op. cit. supra* n. 35 at 184.

The implication, in the light of Pigou's discussion later in the chapter, is that a factory owner with a smokey chimney should be given a bounty to induce him to install smoke-preventing devices. Most modern economists would suggest that the owner of the factory with the smokey chimney should be taxed. It seems a pity that economists (apart from Professor Forte) do not seem to have noticed this feature of Pigou's treatment since a realisation that the problem could be tackled in either of these two ways would probably have led to an explicit recognition of its reciprocal nature.

In discussing the second case (disservices without compensation to those damaged), Pigou says that they are rendered "when the owner of a site in a residential quarter of a city builds a factory there and so destroys a great part of the amenities of neighbouring sites; or, in a less degree, when he uses his site in such a way as to spoil the lighting of the house opposite; or when he invests resources in erecting buildings in a crowded centre, which by contracting the air-space and the playing room of the neighbourhood, tend to injure the health and efficiency of the families living there."[47] Pigou is, of course, quite right to describe such actions as "uncharged disservices." But he is wrong when he describes these actions as "anti-social."[48] They may or may not be. It is necessary to weigh the harm against the good that will result. Nothing could be more "anti-social" than to oppose any action which causes any harm to anyone.

The example with which Pigou opens his discussion of "uncharged disservices" is not, as I have indicated, the case of the smokey chimney but the case of the overrunning rabbits: ". . . incidental uncharged disservices are rendered to third parties when the game-preserving activities of one occupier involve the overrunning of a neighboring occupier's land by rabbits. . . ." This example is of extraordinary interest, not so much because the economic analysis of the case is essentially any different from that of the other examples, but because of the peculiarities of the legal position and the light it throws on the part which economics can play in what is apparently the purely legal question of the delimitation of rights.

The problem of legal liability for the actions of rabbits is part of the general subject of liability for animals.[49] I will, although with reluctance, confine my discussion to rabbits. The early cases relating to rabbits concerned the relations between the lord of the manor and commoners, since, from the thirteenth century on, it became usual for the lord of the manor to stock the commons with conies (rabbits), both for the sake of the meat and the fur. But in 1597, in *Boulston's* case, an action was brought by one landowner against a neighbouring landowner, alleging that the defendant had made coney-burrows and that the conies had increased and had destroyed the plaintiff's corn. The action failed for the reason that

> . . . so soon as the coneys come on his neighbor's land he may kill them, for they are ferae naturae, and he who makes the coney-boroughs has no property in them, and he shall not be punished for the damage which the coneys do in which he has no property, and which the other may lawfully kill.[50]

As *Boulston's* case has been treated as binding—Bray, J., in 1919, said that he was not aware that *Boulston's* case has ever been overruled or questioned[51]—Pigou's rabbit example undoubtedly represented the legal position at the time *The Economics of Welfare* was written.[52] And in this case, it is not far from the truth to say that the state of affairs which Pigou describes came about because of an absence of Government action (at any rate in the form of

---

[47]*Id.* at 185–86.

[48]*Id.* at 186 n.1. For similar unqualified statements see Pigou's lecture "Some Aspects of the Housing Problem" in B. S. Rowntree and A. C. Pigou, "Lectures on Housing," in 18 *Manchester Univ. Lectures* (1914).

[49]See G. L. Williams, *Liability for Animals—An Account of the Development and Present Law of Tortious Liability for Animals. Distress Damage Feasant and the Duty to Fence, in Great Britain, Northern Ireland and the Common Law Dominions* (1939). Part Four, "The Action of Nuisance, in Relation to Liability for Animals," 236–62, is especially relevant to our discussion. The problem of liability for rabbits is discussed in this part, 238–47. I do not know how far the common law in the United States regarding liability for animals has diverged from that in Britain. In some Western States of the United States, the English common law regarding the duty to fence has not been followed, in part because "the considerable amount of open, uncleared land made it a matter of public policy to allow cattle to run at large" (Williams, *op. cit. supra* 227). This affords a good example of how a different set of circumstances may make it economically desirable to change the legal rule regarding the delimitation of rights.

[50]5 Coke (Vol. 3) 104 b. 77 Eng. Rep., 216, 217.

[51]See *Stearn v. Prentice Bros. Ltd.* (1919), 1 K.B., 395, 397.

[52]I have not looked into recent cases. The legal position has also been modified by statutory enactments.

statutory enactments) and was the result of "natural" tendencies.

Nonetheless, *Boulston's* case is something of a legal curiosity and Professor Williams makes no secret of his distaste for this decision:

> The conception of liability in nuisance as being based upon ownership is the result, apparently, of a confusion with the action of cattle-trespass, and runs counter both to principle and to the medieval authorities on the escape of water, smoke and filth. . . . The prerequisite of any satisfactory treatment of the subject is the final abandonment of the pernicious doctrine in *Boulston's* case. . . . Once *Boulston's* case disappears, the way will be clear for a rational restatement of the whole subject, on lines that will harmonize with the principles prevailing in the rest of the law of nuisance.[53]

The judges in *Boulston's* case were, of course, aware that their view of the matter depended on distinguishing this case from one involving nuisance:

> This cause is not like to the cases put, on the other side, of erecting a lime-kiln, dyehouse, or the like; for there the annoyance is by the act of the parties who make them; but is is not so here, for the conies of themselves went into the plaintiff's land, and he might take them when they came upon his land, and make profit of them.[54]

Professor Williams comments:

> Once more the atavistic idea is emerging that the animals are guilty and not the landowner. It is not, of course, a satisfactory principle to introduce into a modern law of nuisance. If A. erects a house or plants a tree so that the rain runs or drops from it on to B.'s land, this is A.'s act for which he is liable; but if A. introduces rabbits into his land so that they escape from it into B.'s, this is the act of the rabbits for which A. is not liable—such is the specious distinction resulting from *Boulston's* case.[55]

It has to be admitted that the decision in *Boulston's* case seems a little odd. A man may be liable for damage caused by smoke or unpleasant smells, without it being necessary to determine whether he owns the smoke or the smell. And the rule in *Boulston's* case has not always been followed in cases dealing with other animals. For example, in *Bland v. Yates,*[56] it was decided that an injunction could be granted to prevent someone from keeping an *unusual and*

excessive collection of manure in which flies bred and which infested a neighbour's house. The question of who owned the flies was not raised. An economist would not wish to object because legal reasoning sometimes appears a little odd. But there is a sound economic reason for supporting Professor Williams' view that the problem of liability for animals (and particularly rabbits) should be brought within the ordinary law of nuisance. The reason is not that the man who harbours rabbits is solely responsible for the damage; the man whose crops are eaten is equally responsible. And given that the costs of market transactions make a rearrangement of rights impossible, unless we know the particular circumstances, we cannot say whether it is desirable or not to make the man who harbours rabbits responsible for the damage committed by the rabbits on neighbouring properties. The objection to the rule in *Boulston's* case is that, under it, the harbourer of rabbits can *never* be liable. It fixes the rule of liability at one pole: and this is as undesirable, from an economic point of view, as fixing the rule at the other pole and making the harbourer of rabbits always liable. But, as we saw in Section VII, the law of nuisance, as it is in fact handled by the courts, is flexible and allows for a comparison of the utility of an act with the harm it produces. As Professor Williams says: "The whole law of nuisance is an attempt to reconcile and compromise between conflicting interests. . . ."[57] To bring the problem of rabbits within the ordinary law of nuisance would not mean *inevitably* making the harbourer of rabbits liable for damage committed by the rabbits. This is not to say that the sole task of the courts in such cases is to make a comparison between the harm and the utility of an act. Nor is it to be expected that the courts will always decide correctly after making such a comparison. But unless the courts act very foolishly, the ordinary law of nuisance would seem likely to give economically more satisfactory results than adopting a rigid rule. Pigou's case of the overrunning rabbits affords an excellent example of how problems of law and economics are interrelated, even though the correct policy to follow would seem to be different from that envisioned by Pigou.

Pigou allows one exception to his conclusion that there is a divergence between private and social products in the rabbit example. He adds: ". . . un-

---

[53]Williams, *op. cit. supra* n. 49 at 242, 258.
[54]*Boulston v. Hardy,* Cro. Eliz., 547, 548, 77 Eng. Rep. 216
[55]Williams, *op. cit. supra* n. 49 at 243.
[56]58 Sol.J. 612 (1913–1914).

[57]Williams, *op. cit. supra* n. 49 at 259.

less . . . the two occupiers stand in the relation of landlord and tenant, so that compensation is given in an adjustment of the rent."[58] This qualification is rather surprising since Pigou's first class of divergence is largely concerned with the difficulties of drawing up satisfactory contracts between landlords and tenants. In fact, all the recent cases on the problem of rabbits cited by Professor Williams involved disputes between landlords and tenants concerning sporting rights.[59] Pigou seems to make a distinction between the case in which no contract is possible (the second class) and that in which the contract is unsatisfactory (the first class). Thus he says that the second class of divergences between private and social net product

> cannot, like divergences due to tenancy laws, be mitigated by a modification of the contractual relation between any two contracting parties, because the divergence arises out of a service or disservice rendered to persons other than the contracting parties.[60]

But the reason why some activities are not the subject of contracts is exactly the same as the reason why some contracts are commonly unsatisfactory—it would cost too much to put the matter right. Indeed, the two cases are really the same since the contracts are unsatisfactory because they do not cover certain activities. The exact bearing of the discussion of the first class of divergence on Pigou's main argument is difficult to discover. He shows that in some circumstances contractual relations between landlord and tenant may result in a divergence between private and social products.[61] But he also goes on to show that Government-enforced compensation schemes and rent-controls will also produce divergences.[62] Furthermore, he shows that, when the Government is in a similar position to a private landlord, e.g. when granting a franchise to a public utility, exactly the same difficulties arise as when private individuals are involved.[63] The discussion is interesting but I have been unable to discover what general conclusions about economic policy, if any, Pigou expects us to draw from it.

Indeed, Pigou's treatment of the problems considered in this article is extremely elusive and the discussion of his views raises almost insuperable difficulties of interpretation. Consequently it is impossible to be sure that one has understood what Pigou really meant. Nevertheless, it is difficult to resist the conclusion, extraordinary though this may be in an economist of Pigou's stature, that the main source of this obscurity is that Pigou had not thought his position through.

IX. THE PIGOVIAN TRADITION

It is strange that a doctrine as faulty as that developed by Pigou should have been so influential, although part of its success has probably been due to the lack of clarity in the exposition. Not being clear, it was never clearly wrong. Curiously enough, this obscurity in the source has not prevented the emergence of a fairly well-defined oral tradition. What economists think they learn from Pigou, and what they tell their students, which I term the Pigovian tradition, is reasonably clear. I propose to show the inadequacy of this Pigovian tradition by demonstrating that both the analysis and the policy conclusions which it supports are incorrect.

I do not propose to justify my view as to the prevailing opinion by copious references to the literature. I do this partly because the treatment in the literature is usually so fragmentary, often involving little more than a reference to Pigou plus some explanatory comment, that detailed examination would be inappropriate. But the main reason for this lack of reference is that the doctrine, although based on Pigou, must have been largely the product of an oral tradition. Certainly economists with whom I have discussed these problems have shown a unanimity of opinion which is quite remarkable considering the meagre treatment accorded this subject in the literature. No doubt there are some economists who do not share the usual view but they must represent a small minority of the profession.

The approach to the problems under discussion is through an examination of the value of physical production. The private product is the value of the additional product resulting from a particular activity of a business. The social product equals the private product minus the fall in the value of production elsewhere for which no compensation is paid by the business. Thus, if 10 units of a factor (and no other factors) are used by a business to make a certain product with a value of $105; and the owner of this

[58]Pigou, *op. cit. supra* n. 35 at 185.
[59]Williams, *op. cit. supra* n. 49 at 244–47.
[60]Pigou, *op. cit. supra* n. 35 at 192.
[61]*Id.* 174–75.
[62]*Id.* 177–83.
[63]*Id.* 175–77.

factor is not compensated for their use, which he is unable to prevent; and these 10 units of the factor would yield products in their best alternative use worth $100; then, the social product is $105 minus $100 or $5. If the business now pays for one unit of the factor and its price equals the value of its marginal product, then the social product rises to $15. If two units are paid for, the social product rises to $25 and so on until it reaches $105 when all units of the factor are paid for. It is not difficult to see why economists have so readily accepted this rather odd procedure. The analysis focusses on the individual business decision and since the use of certain resources is not allowed for in costs, receipts are reduced by the same amount. But, of course, this means that the value of the social product has no social significance whatsoever. It seems to me preferable to use the opportunity cost concept and to approach these problems by comparing the value of the product yielded by factors in alternative uses or by alternative arrangements. The main advantage of a pricing system is that it leads to the employment of factors in places where the value of the product yielded is greatest and does so at less cost than alternative systems (I leave aside that a pricing system also eases the problem of the redistribution of income). But if through some God-given natural harmony factors flowed to the places where the value of the product yielded was greatest without any use of the pricing system and consequently there was no compensation, I would find it a source of surprise rather than a cause for dismay.

The definition of the social product is queer but this does not mean that the conclusions for policy drawn from the analysis are necessarily wrong. However, there are bound to be dangers in an approach which diverts attention from the basic issues and there can be little doubt that it has been responsible for some of the errors in current doctrine. The belief that it is desirable that the business which causes harmful effects should be forced to compensate those who suffer damage (which was exhaustively discussed in section VIII in connection with Pigou's railway sparks example) is undoubtedly the result of not comparing the total product obtainable with alternative social arrangements.

The same fault is to be found in proposals for solving the problem of harmful effects by the use of taxes or bounties. Pigou lays considerable stress on this solution although he is, as usual, lacking in detail

and qualified in his support.[64] Modern economists tend to think exclusively in terms of taxes and in a very precise way. The tax should be equal to the damage done and should therefore vary with the amount of the harmful effect. As it is not proposed that the proceeds of the tax should be paid to those suffering the damage, this solution is not the same as that which would force a business to pay compensation to those damaged by its actions, although economists generally do not seem to have noticed this and tend to treat the two solutions as being identical.

Assume that a factory which emits smoke is set up in a district previously free from smoke pollution, causing damage valued at $100 per annum. Assume that the taxation solution is adopted and that the factory owner is taxed $100 per annum as long as the factory emits the smoke. Assume further that a smoke-preventing device costing $90 per annum to run is available. In these circumstances, the smoke-preventing device would be installed. Damage of $100 would have been avoided at an expenditure of $90 and the factory-owner would be better off by $10 per annum. Yet the position achieved may not be optimal. Suppose that those who suffer the damage could avoid it by moving to other locations or by taking various precautions which would cost them, or be equivalent to a loss in income of, $40 per annum. Then there would be a gain in the value of production of $50 if the factory continued to emit its smoke and those now in the district moved elsewhere or made other adjustments to avoid the damage. If the factory owner is to be made to pay a tax equal to the damage caused, it would clearly be desirable to institute a double tax system and to make residents of the district pay an amount equal to the additional cost incurred by the factory owner (or the consumers of his products) in order to avoid the damage. In these conditions, people would not stay in the district or would take other measures to prevent the damage from occurring, when the costs of doing so were less than the costs that would be incurred by the producer to reduce the damage (the producer's object, of course, being not so much to reduce the damage as to reduce the tax payments). A tax system which was confined to a tax on the producer for damage caused would tend to lead to unduly high costs being incurred for the prevention

[64]*Id.* 192–4, 381 and *Public Finance* 94–100 (3d ed. 1947).

of damage. Of course this could be avoided if it were possible to base the tax, not on the damage caused, but on the fall in the value of production (in its widest sense) resulting from the emission of smoke. But to do so would require a detailed knowledge of individual preferences and I am unable to imagine how the data needed for such a taxation system could be assembled. Indeed, the proposal to solve the smoke-pollution and similar problems by the use of taxes bristles with difficulties: the problem of calculation, the difference between average and marginal damage, the interrelations between the damage suffered on different properties, etc. But it is unnecessary to examine these problems here. It is enough for my purpose to show that, even if the tax is exactly adjusted to equal the damage that would be done to neighboring properties as a result of the emission of each additional puff of smoke, the tax would not necessarily bring about optimal conditions. An increase in the number of people living or of business operating in the vicinity of the smoke-emitting factory will increase the amount of harm produced by a given emission of smoke. The tax that would be imposed would therefore increase with an increase in the number of those in the vicinity. This will tend to lead to a decrease in the value of production of the factors employed by the factory, either because a reduction in production due to the tax will result in factors being used elsewhere in ways which are less valuable, or because factors will be diverted to produce means for reducing the amount of smoke emitted. But people deciding to establish themselves in the vicinity of the factory will not take into account this fall in the value of production which results from their presence. This failure to take into account costs imposed on others is comparable to the action of a factory-owner in not taking into account the harm resulting from his emission of smoke. Without the tax, there may be too much smoke and too few people in the vicinity of the factory; but with the tax there may be too little smoke and too many people in the vicinity of the factory. There is no reason to suppose that one of these results is necessarily preferable.

I need not devote much space to discussing the similar error involved in the suggestion that smoke producing factories should, by means of zoning regulations, be removed from the districts in which the smoke causes harmful effects. When the change in the location of the factory results in a reduction in production, this obviously needs to be taken into account and weighed against the harm which would result from the factory remaining in that location. The aim of such regulation should not be to eliminate smoke pollution but rather to secure the optimum amount of smoke pollution, this being the amount which will maximise the value of production.

X. A CHANGE OF APPROACH

It is my belief that the failure of economists to reach correct conclusions about the treatment of harmful effects cannot be ascribed simply to a few slips in analysis. It stems from basic defects in the current approach to problems of welfare economics. What is needed is a change of approach.

Analysis in terms of divergencies between private and social products concentrates attention on particular deficiencies in the system and tends to nourish the belief that any measure which will remove the deficiency is necessarily desirable. It diverts attention from those other changes in the system which are inevitably associated with the corrective measure, changes which may well produce more harm than the original deficiency. In the preceding sections of this article, we have seen many examples of this. But it is not necessary to approach the problem in this way. Economists who study problems of the firm habitually use an opportunity cost approach and compare the receipts obtained from a given combination of factors with alternative business arrangements. It would seem desirable to use a similar approach when dealing with questions of economic policy and to compare the total product yielded by alternative social arrangements. In this article, the analysis has been confined, as is usual in this part of economics, to comparisons of the value of production, as measured by the market. But it is, of course, desirable that the choice between different social arrangements for the solution of economic problems should be carried out in broader terms than this and that the total effect of these arrangements in all spheres of life should be taken into account. As Frank H. Knight has so often emphasized, problems of welfare economics must ultimately dissolve into a study of aesthetics and morals.

A second feature of the usual treatment of the problems discussed in this article is that the analysis proceeds in terms of a comparison between a state of laissez faire and some kind of ideal world. This approach inevitably leads to a looseness of thought since the nature of the alternatives being compared is never clear. In a state of laissez faire, is there a monetary, a legal or a political system and if so, what are they? In an ideal world, would there be a monetary, a legal or a political system and if so, what would they be? The answers to all these questions are shrouded in mystery and every man is free to draw whatever conclusions he likes. Actually very little analysis is required to show that an ideal world is better than a state of laissez faire, unless the definitions of a state of laissez faire and an ideal world happen to be the same. But the whole discussion is largely irrelevant for questions of economic policy since whatever we may have in mind as our ideal world, it is clear that we have not yet discovered how to get to it from where we are. A better approach would seem to be to start our analysis with a situation approximating that which actually exists, to examine the effects of a proposed policy change and to attempt to decide whether the new situation would be, in total, better or worse than the original one. In this way, conclusions for policy would have some relevance to the actual situation.

A final reason for the failure to develop a theory adequate to handle the problem of harmful effects stems from a faulty concept of a factor of production. This is usually thought of as a physical entity which the businessman acquires and uses (an acre of land, a ton of fertiliser) instead of as a right to perform certain (physical) actions. We may speak of a person owning land and using it as a factor of production but what the land-owner in fact possesses is the right to carry out a circumscribed list of actions. The rights of a land-owner are not unlimited. It is not even always possible for him to remove the land to another place, for instance, by quarrying it. And although it may be possible for him to exclude some people from using "his" land, this may not be true of others. For example, some people may have the right to cross the land. Furthermore, it may or may not be possible

to erect certain types of buildings or to grow certain crops or to use particular drainage systems on the land. This does not come about simply because of Government regulation. It would be equally true under the common law. In fact it would be true under any system of law. A system in which the rights of individuals were unlimited would be one in which there were no rights to acquire.

If factors of production are thought of as rights, it becomes easier to understand that the right to do something which has a harmful effect (such as the creation of smoke, noise, smells, etc.) is also a factor of production. Just as we may use a piece of land in such a way as to prevent someone else from crossing it, or parking his car, or building his house upon it, so we may use it in such a way as to deny him a view or quiet or unpolluted air. The cost of exercising a right (of using a factor of production) is always the loss which is suffered elsewhere in consequence of the exercise of that right—the inability to cross land, to park a car, to build a house, to enjoy a view, to have peace and quiet or to breathe clean air.

It would clearly be desirable if the only actions performed were those in which what was gained was worth more than what was lost. But in choosing between social arrangements within the context of which individual decisions are made, we have to bear in mind that a change in the existing system which will lead to an improvement in some decisions may well lead to a worsening of others. Furthermore we have to take into account the costs involved in operating the various social arrangements (whether it be the working of a market or of a government department), as well as the costs involved in moving to a new system. In devising and choosing between social arrangements we should have regard for the total effect. This, above all, is the change in approach which I am advocating.

Diagrammatic Exposition of a Theory of Public Expenditure*

PAUL A. SAMUELSON

Paul A. Samuelson (B.A., University of Chicago, 1935; M.A., Harvard University, 1936; Ph.D., 1941) was born in Gary, Indiana, in 1915. Samuelson is one of the world's most distinguished economists, having made outstanding contributions both at the most advanced and abstruse levels, and at the level of the economic novice. The 1970 Nobel Memorial Prize citation lauded his efforts "to raise the level of scientific analysis in economic theory." His book, *Foundations of Economic Analysis,* is a highly mathematical and sophisticated treatment of dynamic theory and general equilibrium economics. For a quarter of a century his introductory textbook, *Economics,* which has gone through twelve editions since it was first published in 1948, was the most widely used "principles" book in America. Samuelson's professional writings, covering an incredibly wide sweep of economic research, have been reprinted in the two-volume work, *The Collected Scientific Papers of Paul A. Samuelson.* Since 1940, Professor Samuelson has been on the faculty of the Massachusetts Institute of Technology.

In the November 1954 issue of this REVIEW my paper on "The Pure Theory of Public Expenditure" presented a mathematical exposition of a public expenditure theory that goes back to Italian, Austrian, and Scandinavian writers of the last 75 years. After providing that theory with its needed logically-complete optimal conditions, I went on to demonstrate the fatal inability of any decentralized market or voting mechanism to attain or compute this optimum.

The present note presents in terms of two-dimensional diagrams an essentially equivalent formulation of the theory's optimum conditions and briefly discusses some criticisms.

A POLAR-CASE MODEL OF GOVERNMENT

Doctrinal history shows that theoretical insight often comes from considering strong or extreme cases. The grand Walrasian model of competitive general equilibrium is one such extreme polar case. We can formulate it so stringently as to leave no economic role for government. What strong polar

*Reprinted from *Review of Economics and Statistics* (November 1955) by permission of Associated Scientific Publishers. Copyright 1955 by the President and Fellows of Harvard College, pp. 550–556.

case shall the student of public expenditure set alongside this pure private economy?

One possibility is the model of a group-mind. Such a model, which has been extensively used by nationalists and by Romantic critics of classical economics, can justify any, and every, configuration of government. So there is perhaps little that an economic theorist can usefully say about it.

My alternative is a slightly more sophisticated one, but still—intentionally—an extreme polar case. It is consistent with individualism, yet at the same time it explicitly introduces the vital external interdependencies that no theory of government can do without. Its basic assumption is an oversharp distinction between the following two kinds of goods:

(i) A *private* consumption good, like bread, whose total can be parcelled out among two or more persons, with one man having a loaf less if another gets a loaf more. Thus if X_1 is total bread, and X_1^1 and X_1^2 are the respective private consumptions of Man 1 and Man 2, we can say that the total equals the sum of the separate consumptions—or $X_1 = X_1^1 + X_1^2$.

(ii) A *public* consumption good, like an outdoor circus or national defense, which is provided for each person to enjoy or not, according to his tastes. I assume the public good can be varied in total quantity, and write X_2 for its magnitude. It differs from a private consumption good in that each man's consumption of it, X_2^1 and X_2^2 respectively, is related to the total X_2 by a condition of *equality* rather than of summation. Thus, by definition, $X_2^1 = X_2$, and $X_2^2 = X_2$.

Obviously, I am introducing a strong polar case. We could easily lighten the stringency of our assumptions. But on reflection, I think most economists will see that this is a natural antipodal case to the admittedly extreme polar case of traditional individualistic general equilibrium. The careful empiricist will recognize that many—though not all—of the realistic cases of government activity can be fruitfully analyzed as some kind of a blend of these two extreme polar cases.

GRAPHICAL DEPICTION OF TASTES AND TECHNOLOGY

The first three charts summarize our assumptions about tastes and technology. Each diagram has a private good, such as bread, on its vertical axis; each

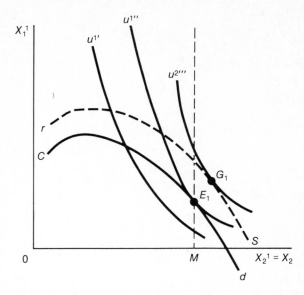

Fig. 1. Indifference contours relating Man 1's consumption of public and private goods.

has a public good on its horizontal axis. The heavy indifference curves of Fig. 1 summarize Man 1's preferences between public and private goods. Fig. 2's indifference curves do the same for Man 2; and the relative flatness of the contour shows that, in a sense, he has less liking for the public good.

The heavy production-possibility or opportunity-cost curve AB in Fig. 3 relates the total productions of public and private goods in the usual familiar manner: the curve is convex from above to reflect the usual assumption of increasing relative marginal costs (or generalized diminishing returns).[1]

Because of our special definition of a public good, the three diagrams are not independent. Each must be lined up with *exactly the same horizontal scale*. Because increasing a public good for society simultaneously increases it for each and every man, we must

---

[1]Even though a public good is being compared with a private good, the indifference curves are drawn with the usual convexity to the origin. This assumption, as well as the one about diminishing returns, could be relaxed without hurting the theory. Indeed, we could recognize the possible case where one man's circus is another man's poison, by permitting indifference curves to bend forward. This would not affect the analysis but would answer a critic's minor objection. Mathematically, we could without loss of generality set X_2^i = any function of X_2, relaxing strict equality.

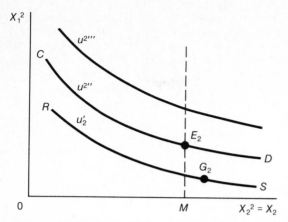

Fig. 2. Indifference contours relating Man 2's consumption of public and private goods.

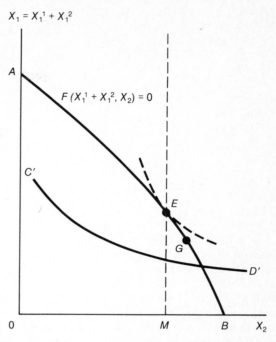

Fig. 3. Transformation schedule relating totals of public and private goods.

always be simultaneously at exactly the same longitude in all three figures. Moving an inch east in one diagram moves us the same amount east in all.

The private good on the vertical axis is subject to no new and unusual restrictions. Each man can be moved north or south on his indifference diagram independently. But, of course, the third diagram does list the total of bread summed over the private individuals; so it must have a larger vertical axis, and our momentary northward position on it must correspond to the sum of the independent northward positions of the separate individuals.

TANGENCY CONDITIONS FOR PARETO OPTIMA

What is the best or ideal state of the world for such a simple system? That is, what three vertically-aligned points corresponding to a determination of a given total of both goods and a determinate parcelling out of them among all separate individuals will be the ethically preferred final configuration?

To answer this ethical, normative question we must be given a set of norms in the form of a *social welfare function* that renders interpersonal judgments. For expository convenience, let us suppose that this will be supplied later and that we know in advance it will have the following special individualistic property: leaving each person on his same indifference level will leave social welfare unchanged; at any point, a move of each man to a higher indifference curve can be found that will increase social welfare.

Given this rather weak assurance about the forthcoming social welfare function, we can proceed to determine tangency conditions of an "efficiency" type that are at least necessary, though definitely not sufficient. We do this by setting up a preliminary maximum problem which will eventually necessarily have to be satisfied.

Holding all but one man at specified levels of indifference, how can we be sure that the remaining man reaches his highest indifference level?

Concretely, this is how we define such a tangency optimum: Set Man 2 on a specified indifference curve, say his middle one CD. Paying attention to Mother Nature's scarcity, as summarized in Fig. 3's AB curve, and following Man 1's tastes as given by Fig. 1 indifference curves, how high on those indifference curves can we move Man 1?

The answer is given by the tangency point E_1, and the corresponding aligned points E_2 and E.

How is this derived? Copy CD on Fig. 3 and call it $C'D'$. The distance between $C'D'$ and AB represents the amounts of the two goods that are physically available to Man 1. So subtract $C'D'$ vertically from *AB* and plot the algebraic result as *cd* in Fig. 1. Now where on *cd* would Man 1 be best off? Obviously at the tangency point E_1 where *cd* touches (but does not cross) his highest attainable indifference contour.[2]

How many such Pareto-optimal points are there? Obviously, for each of the infinite possible initial indifference curves to put Man 2 on, we can derive a new highest attainable tangency level for Man 1. So there are an infinity of such optimal points—as many in number as there are points on the usual contract curve. All of these Pareto-optimal points have the property that from them there exists no

[2]The reader can easily derive *rs* and the tangency point G_1 corresponding to an original specification of Man 2's indifference level at the lower level *RS* rather than at *AB*. He can also interchange the roles of the two men, thereby deriving the point E_2 by a tangency condition. As a third approach, he can *vertically add* Man 2's specified indifference curve to each and every indifference curve of Man 1; the resulting family of contours can be conveniently plotted on Fig. 3, and the final optimum can be read off from the tangency of *AB* to that family at the point *E*—as shown by the short broken-line indifference curve at *E*. It is easy to show that any of these tangencies are, in the two-good case, equivalent to Equation (2) of my cited paper; with a single private good my Equation (1) becomes redundant.

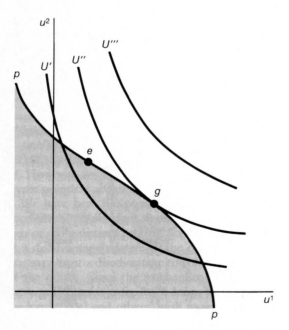

Fig. 4. Utility frontier of pareto-optimal efficiency and its tangency to highest attainable social welfare contour.

physically-feasible movement that will make every man better off. Of course we cannot compare two different Pareto points until we are given a social welfare function. For a move from one Pareto point to another must always hurt one man while it is helping another, and an interpersonal way of comparing these changes must be supplied.

Fig. 4 indicates these utility possibilities on an ordinal diagram. Each axis provides an indicator of the two men's respective indifference curve levels. The utility frontier of Pareto-optimal points is given by *pp:* the double fold infinity of "inefficient," non-Pareto-optimal points is given by the shaded area; the *pp* frontier passes from northwest to southeast to reflect the inevitable conflict of interests characterizing any contract locus; the curvature of the *pp* locus is of no particular type since we have no need to put unique cardinal numbers along the indifference contours and can content ourselves with east-west and north-south relationships in Fig. 4 without regard to numerical degree and to uneven stretchings of either utility axis.

THE OPTIMUM OF ALL THE PARETO OPTIMA

Now we can answer the fundamental question: what is the best configuration for this society?

Use of the word "best" indicates we are in the ascientific area of "welfare economics" and must be provided with a set of norms. Economic science cannot deduce a social welfare function; what it can do is neutrally interpret any arbitrarily specified welfare function.

The heavy contours labelled U', U'', and U''' summarize all that is relevant in the provided social welfare function (they provide the needed ordinal scoring of every state of the world, involving different levels of indifference for the separate individuals).[3]

[3]These social welfare or social indifference contours are given no particular curvature. Why? Again because we are permitting any arbitrary ordinal indicator of utility to be used on the axes of Fig. 4.

An ethical postulate ruling out all "dog-in-the-manger phenomena" will make all partial derivatives of the social welfare function $U(u^1, u^2, \dots)$ always positive. This will assure the usual negative slopes to the U contours of Fig. 4. However, without hurting the Pareto part of the new welfare economics, we can relax this assumption a little and let the contours bend forward. If, at every point there can be found at least one positive partial derivative, this will be sufficient to rule out satiation points and will imply the necessity of the Pareto-optimal tangency condition of the earlier diagrams.

Obviously society cannot be best off inside the utility frontier. Where then on the utility frontier will the "best obtainable bliss point" be? We will move along the utility frontier pp until we touch the highest social indifference curve: this will be at g where pp tangentially touches, without crossing, the highest obtainable social welfare level U''. In words, we can interpret this final tangency condition[4] in the following terms:

(i) The social welfare significance of a unit of any private good allocated to private individuals must at the margin be the same for each and every person.

(ii) The Pareto-optimal condition, which makes

---

[4]This tangency condition would have to be expressed mathematically in terms of numerical indicators of utility that are not invariant under a monotonic renumbering. However, it is easy to combine this tangency with the earlier Pareto-type tangency to get the formulation (3) of my cited paper, which is independent of the choice of numerical indicators of U, u^1, or u^2.

relative marginal social cost equal to the sum of all persons' marginal rates of substitution, is already assured by virtue of the fact that bliss lies on the utility frontier.[5]

RELATIONS WITH EARLIER THEORIES

This completes the graphical interpretation of my mathematical model. There remains the pleasant task of relating this graphical treatment to earlier work of Bowen[6] and others.

To do this, look at Fig. 5, which gives an alternative depiction of the optimal tangency condition at a point like E. I use the private good X_1 as numeraire, measuring all values in terms of it. The MC curve is derived from the AB curve of Fig. 3: it is nothing but the absolute slope of that production-possibility schedule plotted against varying amounts of the public good; it is therefore a marginal cost curve, with MC measured in terms of the numeraire good.

The marginal rate of substitution curves MRS^1 and MRS^2 are derived in a similar fashion from the respective indifference curves of Man 1 and Man 2: thus, MRS^1 is the absolute slope of the $u^{1''}$ indifference curve plotted against varying amounts of the public good; MRS^2 is the similar slope function derived from Man 2's indifference curve CD. (All three are "marginal" curves, bearing the usual relationship to their respective "total" curves.)

These schedules look like demand curves. We are accustomed to adding horizontally or laterally the separate demand curves of individuals to arrive at total market demand. But this is valid only for private goods. As Bowen rightly says, *we must in the case of public goods add different individuals' curves vertically.*

This gives us the heavy ΣMRS curve for the whole community. Where is equilibrium? It is at E, where the community MC curve intersects the community

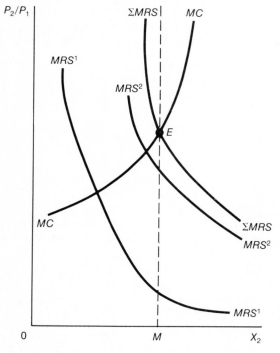

Fig. 5. Intersection of public good's marginal cost schedule and the vertically summed individual's marginal rates of substitution, as envisaged by Lindahl and Bowen.

---

[5]A remarkable duality property of private and public goods should be noted. Private goods whose totals add—such as $X_1 = X_1{}^1 + X_1{}^2$—lead ultimately to marginal conditions of simultaneous equality—such as $MC = MRS^1 = MRS^2$. Public goods whose totals satisfy a relation of simultaneous equality—such as $X_1 = X_2{}^1 = X_2{}^2$—lead ultimately to marginal conditions that add—such as $MC = MRS^1 + MRS^2$.

[6]Howard R. Bowen, "The Interpretation of Voting in the Allocation of Economic Resources," *Quarterly Journal of Economics*, LVIII (November 1943), 27–49. Much of this is also in Bowen's *Toward Social Economy* (New York, 1948), ch. 18.

ΣMRS curve. Upon reflection the reader will realize that the equality $MC = \Sigma MRS = MRS^1 + MRS^2$ is the precise equivalent of my mathematical equation (2) and of our Pareto-type tangency condition at E_1, E_2, or E. Why? Because of the stipulated requirement that Fig. 5's curves are to depict the absolute slopes of the curves of Figs. 1–3.

Except for minor details of notation and assumption, Fig. 5 is identical with the figure shown on page 31 of the first Bowen reference, and duplicated on page 177 of the second reference. I am happy to acknowledge this priority. Indeed anyone familiar with Musgrave's valuable summary of the literature bearing on this area[7] will be struck with the similarity between this Bowen type of diagram and the Lindahl 100-per-cent diagram reproduced by Musgrave.[8]

Once the economic theorist has related my graphical and mathematical analysis to the Lindahl and Bowen diagrams, he is in a position, I believe, to discern the logical advantage of the present formulation. For there is something circular and unsatisfactory about both the Bowen and Lindahl constructions: they show what the final equilibrium looks like, but by themselves they are not generally able to find the desired equilibrium. To see this, note that whereas we might know MC in Fig. 5, we would not know the appropriate MRS schedules for *all* men until we already were familiar with the final E intersection point. (We might know MRS^2 from the specification that Man 2 is to be on the AB level; but then we wouldn't know MRS^1 until Fig. 1's tangency had given us Man 1's highest attainable level, $u^{1'''}$.) Under conditions of general equilibrium, Figs. 1–3 logically contain Fig. 5 inside them, but not vice versa. Moreover, Figs. 1–3 explicitly call attention to the fact that there is an infinite number of different diagrams of the Lindahl-Bowen type, one for each specified level of relative interpersonal well-being.[9]

CONCLUDING REFLECTIONS

I hope that the analytic model outlined here may help make a small and modest step toward understanding the complicated realities of political economy. Much remains to be done. This is not the place to discuss the wider implications and difficulties of the presented economic theory.[10] However, I should like to comment briefly on some of the questions about this theory that have been raised in [the *Review of Economics and Statistics*].[11]

(i) On the deductive side, the theory presented here is, I believe, a logically coherent one. This is true whether expressed in my original mathematical notation or in the present diagrammatic form. Admittedly, the latter widens the circle of economists who can understand and follow what is being said. The present version, with its tangencies of methodologically the same type as characterize Cournot-Marshall marginal theory and Bergson-Pigou welfare theory, should from its easily recognized equivalence with the mathematical version make clear my refusal to agree with Dr. Enke's view that my use of mathematics was limited "to notation."

(ii) In terms of the history of similar theories, I hope the present paper will make clear relationships to earlier writers. (In particular, see the above discussion relating my early diagrams and equations to the Bowen-Lindahl formulation.) I shall not bore

[7]Richard A. Musgrave, "The Voluntary Exchange Theory of Public Economy," *Quarterly Journal of Economics*, LIII (February 1939), 213–17. This gives citations to the relevant works of Sax, De Viti de Marco, Wicksell, and Lindahl. I have greatly benefited from preliminary study of Professor Musgrave's forthcoming treatise on public finance, which I am sure will constitute a landmark in this area.

[8]Musgrave, *op. cit.*, 216, which is an acknowledged adaption from Erik Lindahl, *Die Gerechtigkeit in der Besteuerung* (Lund, 1919), 89. I have not had access to this important work. This diagram plots instead of the functions of Fig. 5 the exact same functions after each has been divided by the MC function. The equilibrium intersection corresponding to E now shows up as the point at which all persons will together voluntarily provide 100 per cent of the full (unit? marginal?) cost of the public service. (If MC is not constant, some modifications in the Musgrave diagram may be required.)

[9]The earlier writers from Wicksell on were well aware of this. They explicitly introduce the assumption that there is to have been a *prior* optimal interpersonal distribution of income, so what I have labelled E might better be labelled G. But the general equilibrium analyst asks: how can the appropriate distribution of income be decided on a prior basis *before* the significant problems of public consumptions have been determined? A satisfactory general analysis can resist the temptation to assume (i) the level of government expenditure must be so small as not to affect appreciably the marginal social significance of money to the different individuals; (ii) each man's indifference curves run parallel to each other in a vertical direction so that every and all indifference curves in Fig. 1 (or in Fig. 2) give rise to the same MRS^1 (or MRS^2) curve in Fig. 5. The modern theorist is anxious to free his analysis from the incubus of unnecessarily restrictive partial equilibrium assumptions.

[10]At the 1955 Christmas Meetings of the American Economic Association and Econometric Society, I hope to present some further developments and qualifications of this approach.

[11]Stephen Enke, "More on the Misuse of Mathematics in Economics: A Rejoinder," [*Review of Economics and Statistics*], XXXVII (May 1955), 131–33; Julius Margolis, "On Samuelson on the Pure Theory of Public Expenditure," this issue, p. 347.

the reader with irrelevant details of independent re-discoveries of doctrine that my ignorance of the available literature may have made necessary. Yet is it presumptuous to suggest that there does not exist in the present economic literature very much in the way of "conclusions and reasoning" that are, in Dr. Margolis' words, "familiar"? Except for the writers I have cited, and the important unpublished thoughts of Dr. Musgrave, there is much opaqueness in the literature. Much of what goes by the name of the "voluntary exchange theory of public finance" seems pure obfuscation.[12]

(iii) Far from my formulation's being, as some correspondents have thought, a revival of the voluntary exchange theory—it is in fact an attempt to demonstrate how right Wicksell was to worry about the inherent political difficulty of ever getting men to reveal their tastes so as to attain the definable optimum. This intrinsic "game theory" problem has been sufficiently stressed in my early paper so that it has not been emphasized here. I may put the point most clearly in terms of the familiar tools of modern literary economics as follows:

Government supplies products jointly to many people. In ordinary market economics as you increase the number of sellers of a homogeneous product indefinitely, you pass from monopoly through indeterminate oligopoly and can hope to reach a determinate competitive equilibrium in the limit. It is sometimes thought that increasing the number of citizens who are jointly supplied public goods leads to a similar determinate result. This is reasoning from an incorrect analogy. A truer analogy in private economics would be the case of a bilateral-monopoly supplier of joint products whose number of joint products—meat, horn, hide, and so on—is allowed to increase without number: such a process does not lead to a determinate equilibrium of the harmonistic type praised in the literature. My simple model is able to demonstrate this point—which does have "policy implications."

(iv) I regret using "the" in the title of my earlier paper and have accordingly changed the present title. Admittedly, public expenditure and regulation proceed from considerations other than those emphasized in my models. Here are a few:

a. Taxes and expenditure aim at redistributing incomes. I am anxious to clear myself from Dr. Margolis' understandable suspicion that I am the type of liberal who would insist that all redistributions take place through tax policies and transfer expenditures: much public expenditure on education, hospitals, and so on, can be justified by the feasibility consideration that, even if these are not 100 per cent efficient in avoiding avoidable dead-weight loss, they may be better than the attainable imperfect tax alternatives.[13]

b. Paternalistic policies are voted upon themselves by a democratic people because they do not regard the results from spontaneous market action as optimal. Education and forced paces of economic development are good examples of this.

c. Governments provide or regulate services that are incapable of being produced under the strict conditions of constant returns that go to characterize optimal self-regulating atomistic competition.

d. Myriad "generalized external economy and diseconomy" situations, where private pecuniary interest can be expected to deviate from social interests, provide obvious needs for government activity.

I am sure this list of basic considerations underlying government expenditure could be extended farther, including even areas where government probably ought not to operate from almost anyone's viewpoint.

(v) This brief list can end with the most important criticism that the various commentators on my paper have put forth. They all ask: "Is it factually true that most—or any!—of the functions of government can be properly fitted into your extreme category of a public good? Can education, the courts, public defense, highway programs, police and fire protection be put into this rigid category of a 'public good available to all'? In practically every one of these cases isn't there an element of variability in the benefit that can go to one citizen *at the expense* of some other citizens?"

---

[12]See Gerhard Colm, "The Theory of Public Expenditure," *Annals of the American Academy of Political and Social Sciences*, CLXXXIII (January 1936), 1–11, reprinted in his *Essays in Public Finance and Fiscal Policy* (New York, 1955), 27–43 for an admirable criticism of the Graziani statement, "We know that the tax tends to take away from each and all that quantity of wealth which they would each have voluntarily yielded to the state for the satisfaction of their purely collective wants" (page 32).

[13]See my "Evaluation of Real National Income," *Oxford Economic Papers*, N.S. II (January 1950), 18 ff. for analytic discussion of this important truth.

To this criticism, I fully agree. And that is why in the present formulation I have insisted upon the polar nature of my category. However, to say that a thing is not located at the South Pole does not logically place it at the North Pole. To deny that most public functions fit into my extreme definition of a public good is not to grant that they satisfy the logically equally-extreme category of a private good. To say that your absence at a concert may contribute to my enjoyment is not to say that the elements of public services can be put into homogeneous additive packages capable of being optimally handled by the ordinary market calculus.

Indeed, I am rash enough to think that in almost every one of the legitimate functions of government that critics put forward there is to be found a blending of the extreme antipodal models. One might even venture the tentative suspicion that any function of government not possessing any trace of the defined public good (and no one of the related earlier described characteristics) ought to be carefully scrutinized to see whether it is truly a legitimate function of government.

(vi) Whether or not I have overstated the applicability of this one theoretical model to actual governmental functions, I believe I did not go far enough in claiming for it relevance to the vast area of decreasing costs that constitutes an important part of economic reality and of the welfare economics of monopolistic competition. I must leave to future research discussions of these vital issues.

Economic theory should add what it can to our understanding of governmental activity. I join with critics in hoping that its pretentious claims will not discourage other economic approaches, other contributions from neighboring disciplines, and concrete empirical investigations.

An Economic Theory of Clubs*

JAMES M. BUCHANAN[1]

James M. Buchanan (B.S., Middle Tennessee State College, 1940; M.A., University of Tennessee, 1941; Ph.D., University of Chicago, 1948) was born in Murfreesboro, Tennessee, in 1919. Since 1973 Professor Buchanan has been the Harris University Professor of Economics and General Director of the Center for the Study of Public Choice at George Mason University in Fairfax, Virginia. He previously held the positions of University Distinguished Professor at Virginia Polytechnic Institute and McIntire Professor of Economics at the University of Virginia, and served on the faculties of the University of Tennessee, Florida State University, and the University of California at Los Angeles. Professor Buchanan, whose primary research has been in the fields of public finance and collective decision making, has contributed significantly to the profession's understanding of the relationship between individual preferences and political decision making and the constitutional choices among social and political rules and institutions, and is one of the founding fathers of the field of public choice. His many publications include *Public Principles of Public Debt, The Public Finances, Fiscal Theory and Political Economy, The Calculus of Consent* (with Gordon Tullock), *Public Finance in Democratic Process, The Demand and Supply of Public Goods, Cost and Choice, The Power to Tax: Analytical Foundations of a Fiscal Constitution* (with Geoffrey Brennan), *The Reason of Rules: Constitutional Political Economy* (with Geoffrey Brennan) and *Liberty, Market, and State*. Professor Buchanan, president of the Mont Pelerin Society, is a past president of the Southern Economic and Western Economic Associations, a past vice-president and Distinguished Fellow of the American Economic Association, and co-founder (with Gordon Tullock) of the Public Choice Society.

*Reprinted from *Economica* (February 1965) by permission of Tieto Ltd. Copyright 1965, pp. 1–14.
[1] I am indebted to graduate students and colleagues for many helpful suggestions. Specific acknowledgement should be made for the critical assistance of Emilio Giardina of the University of Catania and W. Craig Stubblebine of the University of Delaware.

The implied institutional setting for neoclassical economic theory, including theoretical welfare economics, is a régime of private property, in which all goods and services are privately (individually) utilized or consumed. Only within the last two decades have serious attempts been made to extend formal theoretical structure to include communal collective ownership-consumption arrangements.[2] The "pure theory of public goods" remains in its infancy, and the few models that have been most rigorously developed apply only to polar or extreme cases. For example, in the fundamental papers by Paul A. Samuelson, a sharp conceptual distinction is made between those goods and services that are "purely private" and those that are "purely public."[3] No general theory has been developed which covers the whole spectrum of ownership-consumption possibilities, ranging from the purely private or individualized activity on the one hand to purely public or collectivized activity on the other. One of the missing links here is "a theory of clubs," a theory of co-operative membership, a theory that will include as a variable to be determined the extension of ownership-consumption rights over differing numbers of persons.

Everyday experience reveals that there exists some most preferred or "optimal" membership for almost any activity in which we engage, and that this membership varies in some relation to economic factors. European hotels have more communally shared bathrooms than their American counterparts. Middle and low income communities organize swimming-bathing facilities; high income communities are observed to enjoy privately owned swimming pools.

In this paper I shall develop a general theory of clubs, or consumption ownership-membership arrangements. This construction allows us to move one step forward in closing the awesome Samuelson gap between the purely private and the purely public good. For the former, the optimal sharing arrangement, the preferred club membership, is clearly one person (or one family unit), whereas the optimal sharing group for the purely public good, as defined in the polar sense, includes an infinitely large number of members. That is to say, for any genuinely collective good defined in the Samuelson way, a club that has an infinitely large membership is preferred

to all arrangements of finite size. While it is evident that some goods and services may be reasonably classified as purely private, even in the extreme sense, it is clear that few, if any, goods satisfy the conditions of extreme collectiveness. The interesting cases are those goods and services, the consumption of which involves some "publicness," where the optimal sharing group is more than one person or family but smaller than an infinitely large number. The range of "publicness" is finite. The central question in a theory of clubs is that of determining the membership margin, so to speak, the size of the most desirable cost and consumption sharing arrangement.[4]

I

In traditional neo-classical models that assume the existence of purely private goods and services only, the utility function of an individual is written,

$$U^i = U^i(X_1^i, X_2^i, \ldots, X_n^i), \qquad (1)$$

where each of the X's represents the amount of a purely private good available during a specified time period, to the reference individual designated by the superscript.

Samuelson extended this function to include purely collective or public goods, which he denoted by the subscripts, $n + 1, \ldots, n + m$, so that (1) is changed to read,

$$U^i = U^i(X_1^i, X_2^i, \ldots, X_n^i; X_{n+1}^i, X_{n+2}^i, \ldots, X_{n+m}^i). \qquad (2)$$

This approach requires that all goods be initially classified into the two sets, private and public. Private goods, defined to be wholly divisible among the persons, $i = 1, 2, \ldots, s$, satisfy the relation

$$X_j = \sum_{i=1}^{s} X_j^i,$$

while public goods, defined to be wholly indivisible as among persons, satisfy the relation,

$$X_{n+j} = X_{n+j}^i.$$

I propose to drop any attempt at an initial classification or differentiation of goods into fully divisible and fully indivisible sets, and to incorporate in the

---

[2]It is interesting that none of the theories of Socialist economic organization seems to be based on explicit co-operation among individuals. These theories have conceived the economy either in the Lange-Lerner sense as an analogue to a purely private, individually oriented social order or, alternatively, as one that is centrally directed.

[3]See Paul A. Samuelson, "The Pure Theory of Public Expenditure," *Review of Economics and Statistics*, vol. XXXVI (1954), pp. 387–89; "Diagrammatic Exposition of a Theory of Public Expenditure," *Review of Economics and Statistics*, vol. XXXVII (1955), pp. 350–55.

[4]Note that an economic theory of clubs can strictly apply only to the extent that the motivation for joining in sharing arrangements is itself economic; that is, only if choices are made on the basis of costs and benefits of particular goods and services as these are confronted by the individual. In so far as individuals join clubs for camaraderie, as such, the theory does not apply.

utility function goods falling between these two extremes. What the theory of clubs provides is, in one sense, a "theory of classification," but this emerges as an output of the analysis. The first step is that of modifying the utility function.

Note that, in neither (1) nor (2) is it necessary to make a distinction between "goods available to the ownership unit of which the reference individual is a member" and "goods finally available to the individual for consumption." With purely private goods, consumption by one individual automatically reduces potential consumption of other individuals by an equal amount. With purely public goods, consumption by any one individual implies equal consumption by all others. For goods falling between such extremes, such a distinction must be made. This is because for such goods there is no unique translation possible between the "goods available to the membership unit" and "goods finally consumed." In the construction which follows, therefore, the "goods" entering the individual's utility function, the X_j's, should be interpreted as "goods available for consumption to the whole membership unit of which the reference individual is a member."

Arguments that represent the size of the sharing group must be included in the utility function along with arguments representing goods and services. For any good or service, regardless of its ultimate place along the conceptual public-private spectrum, the utility that an individual receives from its consumption depends upon *the number of other persons with whom he must share its benefits*. This is obvious, but its acceptance does require breaking out of the private property straitjacket within which most of economic theory has developed. As an extreme example, take a good normally considered to be purely private, say, a pair of shoes. Clearly your own utility from a single pair of shoes, per unit of time, depends on the number of other persons who share them with you. Simultaneous physical sharing may not, of course, be possible; only one person can wear the shoes at each particular moment. However, for any finite period of time, sharing is possible, even for such evidently private goods. For pure services that are consumed in the moment of acquisition the extension is somewhat more difficult, but it can be made none the less. Sharing here simply means that the individual receives a smaller quantity of the service. Sharing a "haircut per month" with a second person is the same as consuming "one-half haircut per month."

Given any quantity of final good, as defined in terms of the physical units of some standard quality, the utility that the individual receives from this quantity will be related functionally to the number of others with whom he shares.[5]

Variables for club size are not normally included in the utility function of an individual since, in the private-goods world, the optimal club size is unity. However, for our purposes, these variables must be explicitly included, and, for completeness, a club-size variable should be included for each and every good. Alongside each X_j there must be placed an N_j, which we define as the number of persons who are to participate as "members" in the sharing of good, X_j, including the ith person whose utility function is examined. That is to say, the club-size variable, N_j, measures the number of persons who are to join in the consumption-utilization arrangements for good, X_j, over the relevant time period. The sharing arrangements may or may not call for equal consumption on the part of each member, and the peculiar manner of sharing will clearly affect the way in which the variable enters the utility function. For simplicity we may assume equal sharing, although this is not necessary for the analysis. The rewritten utility function now becomes,

$$U^i = U^i[(X_1{}^i, N_1{}^i), (X_2{}^i, N_2{}^i), \ldots, (X_{n+m}{}^i, N_{n+m}{}^i)].^6 \quad (3)$$

We may designate a numeraire good, X_r, which can simply be thought of as money, possessing value only as a medium of exchange. By employing the convention whereby the lower case u's represent the partial derivatives, we get $u_j{}^i/u_r{}^i$, defined as the marginal rate of substitution in consumption between X and X_r for the jth individual. Since, in our construction, the size of the group is also a variable, we must also examine, $u_{Nj}{}^i/u_r{}^i$, defined as the marginal rate of

---

[5]Physical attributes of a good or service may, of course, affect the structure of the sharing arrangements that are preferred. Although the analysis below assumes symmetrical sharing, this assumption is not necessary, and the analysis in its general form can be extended to cover all possible schemes.

[6]Note that this construction of the individual's utility function differs from that introduced in an earlier paper, where "activities" rather than "goods" were included as the basic arguments. (See James M. Buchanan and Wm. Craig Stubblebine, "Externality," *Economica*, vol. XXXI (1962), pp. 371–84.) In the alternative construction, the "activities" of other persons enter directly into the utility function of the reference individual with respect to the consumption of all other than purely private goods. The construction here incorporates the same interdependence through the inclusion of the N_j's although in a more general manner.

substitution "in consumption" between the size of the sharing group and the numeraire. That is to say, this ratio represents the rate (which may be negative) at which the individual is willing to give up (accept) money in exchange for additional members in the sharing group.

We now define a cost or production function as this confronts the individual, and this will include the same set of variables,

$$F = F^i[(X_1^i, N_1^i), (X_2^i, N_2^i), \ldots, (X_{n+m}^i, N_{n+m}^i)]. \quad (4)$$

Why do the club-size variables, the N_j's, appear in this cost function? The addition of members to a sharing group may, and normally will, affect the cost of the good to any one member. The larger is the membership of the golf club the lower the dues to any single member, given a specific quantity of club facilities available per unit time.

It now becomes possible to derive, from the utility and cost functions, statements for the necessary marginal conditions for Pareto optimality in respect to consumption of each good. In the usual manner we get,

$$u_j^i/u_r^i = f_j^i/f_r^i. \quad (5)$$

Condition (5) states that, for the ith individual, the marginal rate of substitution between goods X_j and X_r, in consumption, must be equal to the marginal rate of substitution between these same two goods in "production" or exchange. To this acknowledged necessary condition, we now add,

$$u_{Nj}^i/u_r^i = f_{Nj}^i/f_r^i. \quad (6)$$

Condition (6) is not normally stated, since the variables relating to club size are not normally included in utility functions. Implicitly, the size for sharing arrangements is assumed to be determined exogenously to individual choices. Club size is presumed to be a part of the environment. Condition (6) states that the marginal rate of substitution "in consumption" between the size of the group sharing in the use of good X_j, and the numeraire good, X_r, must be equal to the marginal rate of substitution "in production." In other words, the individual attains full equilibrium in club size only when the marginal benefits that he secures from having an additional member (which may, and probably will normally be, negative) are just equal to the marginal costs that he incurs from adding a member (which will also normally be negative).

Combining (5) and (6) we get,

$$u_j^i/f_j^i = u_r^i/f_r^i = u_{Nj}^i/f_{Nj}^i. \quad (7)$$

Only when (7) is satisfied will the necessary marginal conditions with respect to the consumption-utilization of X_j be met. The individual will have available to his membership unit an optimal quantity of X_j, measured in physical units and, also, he will be sharing this quantity "optimally" over a group of determined size.

The necessary condition for club size may not, of course, be met. Since for many goods there is a major change in utility between the one-person and the two-person club, and since discrete changes in membership may be all that is possible, we may get,

$$\frac{u_j^i}{f_j^i} = \frac{u_r^i}{f_r^i} > \frac{u_{Nj}^i}{f_{Nj}^i}\bigg|_{Nj=1}; \frac{u_j^i}{f_j^i} = \frac{u_r^i}{f^r} < \frac{u_{Nj}^i}{f_{Nj}^i}\bigg|_{Nj=2} \quad (7A)$$

which incorporates the recognition that, with a club size of unity, the right-hand term may be relatively too small, whereas, with a club size of two, it may be too large. If partial sharing arrangements can be worked out, this qualification need not, of course, be made.

If, on the other hand, the size of a cooperative or collective sharing group is exogenously determined, we may get,

$$\frac{u_j^i}{f_j^i} = \frac{u_r^i}{f_r^i} > \frac{u_{Nj}^i}{f_{Nj}^i}\bigg|_{Nj=k} \quad (7B)$$

Note that (7B) actually characterizes the situation of an individual with respect to the consumption of any purely public good of the type defined in the Samuelson polar model. Any group of finite size, k, is smaller than optimal here, and the full set of necessary marginal conditions cannot possibly be met. Since additional persons can, by definition, be added to the group without in any way reducing the availability of the good to other members, and since additional members could they be found, would presumably place some positive value on the good and hence be willing to share in its costs, the group always remains below optimal size. The all-inclusive club remains too small.

Consider, now, the relation between the set of necessary marginal conditions defined in (7) and those presented by Samuelson in application to goods that were exogenously defined to be purely public. In the latter case, these conditions are,

$$\sum_{i=1}^{s} (u_{n+j}^i/u_r^i) = f_{n+j}/f_r, \quad (8)$$

where the marginal rates of substitution in consumption between the purely public good, X_{n+j}, and the numeraire good, X_r, summed over all individuals in the group of determined size, s, equals the marginal cost of X_{n+j} also defined in terms of units of X_r. Note that when (7) is satisfied, (8) is necessarily satisfied, provided only that the collectivity is making neither profit nor loss on providing the marginal unit of the public good. That is to say, provided that,

$$f_{n+j}/f_r = \sum_{i=1}^{s} (f_{n+j}{}^i/f_r{}^i). \qquad (9)$$

The reverse does not necessarily hold, however, since the satisfaction of (8) does not require that each and every individual in the group be in a position where his own marginal benefits are equal to his marginal costs (taxes).[7] And, of course, (8) says nothing at all about group size.

The necessary marginal conditions in (7) allow us to classify all goods only after the solution is attained. Whether or not a particular good is purely private, purely public, or somewhere between these extremes is determined only after the equilibrium values for the N_j's are known. A good for which the equilibrium value for N_j is large can be classified as containing much "publicness." By contrast, a good for which the equilibrium value of N_j is small can be classified as largely private.

II

The formal statement of the theory of clubs presented in Section I can be supplemented and clarified by geometrical analysis, although the nature of the construction implies somewhat more restrictive models.

Consider a good that is known to contain, under some conditions, a degree of "publicness." For simplicity, think of a swimming pool. We want to examine the choice calculus of a single person, and we shall assume that other persons about him, with whom he may or may not choose to join in some club-like arrangement, are identical in all respects with him. As a first step, take a facility of one-unit size, which we define in terms of physical output supplied.

On the ordinate of Fig. 1, we measure total cost

and total benefit per person, the latter derived from the individual's own evaluation of the facility in terms of the numeraire, dollars. On the abscissa, we measure the number of persons in possible sharing arrangements. Define the full cost of the one-unit facility to by Y_1, and the reference individual's evaluation of this facility as a purely private consumption good to be E_1. As is clear from the construction as drawn, he will not choose to purchase the good. If the single person is required to meet the full cost, he will not be able to enjoy the benefits of the good. Any enjoyment of the facility requires the organization of some co-operative-collective sharing arrangement.[8]

Two functions may now traced in Fig. 1, remaining within the one-unit restriction on the size of the facility. A total benefit function and a total cost function confronting the single individual may be derived. As more persons are allowed to share in the

[8] The sharing arrangement need not be either co-operative or governmental in form. Since profit opportunities exist in all such situations, the emergence of profit-seeking firms can be predicted in those settings where legal structures permit, and where this organizational form possesses relative advantages (Cf. R. H. Coase, "The Nature of the Firm," *Economica*, vol. IV (1937), pp. 386–405.) For purposes of this paper, such firms are one form of club organization, with co-operatives and public arrangements representing other forms. Generally speaking, of course, the choice among these forms should be largely determined by efficiency considerations.

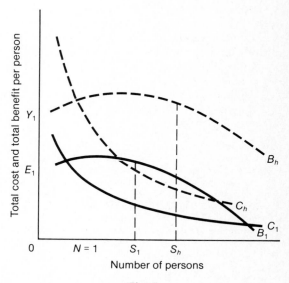

Fig. 1

[7] In Samuelson's diagrammatic presentation, these individual marginal conditions are satisfied, but the diagrammatic construction is more restricted than that contained in his earlier more general model.

enjoyment of the facility, of given size, the benefit evaluation that the individual places on the good will, after some point, decline. There may, of course, be both an increasing and a constant range of the total benefit function, but at some point congestion will set in, and his evaluation of the good will fall. There seems little doubt that the total benefit curve, shown as B_1, will exhibit the concavity property as drawn for goods that involve some commonality in consumption.[9]

The bringing of additional members into the club also serves to reduce the cost that the single person will face. Since, by our initial simplifying assumption, all persons here are identical, symmetrical cost sharing is suggested. In any case, the total cost per person will fall as additional persons join the group, under any cost-sharing scheme. As drawn in Fig. 1, symmetrical sharing is assumed and the curve, C_1, traces the total cost function, given the one-unit restriction on the size of the facility.[10]

For the given size of the facility, there will exist some optimal size of club. This is determined at the point where the derivatives of the total cost and total benefit functions are equal, shown as S_1 in Fig. 1, for the one-unit facility. Consider now an increase in the size of the facility. As before, a total cost curve and a total benefit curve may be derived, and an optimal club size determined. One other such optimum is shown as S_h, for a quantity of goods upon which the curves C_h and B_h are based. Similar constructions can be carried out for every possible size of facility; that is, for each possible quantity of good.

A similar construction may be used to determine optimal goods quantity for each possible size of club;

this is illustrated in Fig. 2. On the ordinate, we measure here total costs and total benefits confronting the individual, as in Fig. 1. On the abscissa, we measure physical size of the facility, quantity of good, and for each assumed size of club membership we may trace total cost and total benefit functions. If we first examine the single-member club, we may well find that the optimal goods quantity is zero; the total cost function may increase more rapidly than the total benefit function from the outset. However, as more persons are added, the total costs to the single person fall; under our symmetrical sharing assumption, they will fall proportionately. The total benefit functions here will slope upward to the right but after some initial range they will be concave downward and at some point will reach a maximum. As club size is increased, benefit functions will shift generally downward beyond the initial non-congestion range, and the point of maximum benefit will move to the right. The construction of Fig. 2 allows us to derive an optimal goods quantity for each size of club; Q_k is one such quantity for club size $N = K$.

The results derived from Figs. 1 and 2 are combined in Fig. 3. Here the two variables to be chosen, goods quantity and club size, are measured on the ordinate and the abscissa respectively. The values for optimal club size for each goods quantity, derived from Fig. 1, allow us to plot the curve N_{opt}, in Fig. 3. Similarly, the values for optimal goods quantity,

[9] The geometrical model here applies only to such goods. Essentially the same analysis may, however, be extended to apply to cases where "congestion," as such, does not appear. For example, goods that are produced at decreasing costs, even if their consumption is purely private, may be shown to require some sharing arrangements in an equilibrium or optimal organization.

[10] For simplicity, we assume that an additional "membership" in the club involves the addition of one separate person. The model applies equally well, however, for those cases where cost shares are allocated proportionately with predicted usage. In this extension, an additional "membership" would really amount to an additional consumption unit. Membership in the swimming club could, for example, be defined as the right to visit the pool one time each week. Hence, the person who plans to make two visits per week would, in this modification, hold two memberships. This qualification is not, of course, relevant under the strict world-of-equals assumption, but it indicates that the theory need not be so restrictive as it might appear.

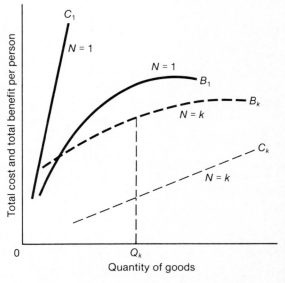

Fig. 2

for each club size, derived from Fig. 2, allow us to plot the curve, Q_{opt}.

The intersection of these two curves, N_{opt} and Q_{opt}, determines the position of full equilibrium, G. The individual is in equilibrium both with respect to goods quantity and to group size, for the good under consideration. Suppose, for example, that the sharing group is limited to size, N_k. The attainment of equilibrium with respect to goods quantity, shown by Q_k, would still leave the individual desirous of shifting the size of the membership so as to attain position L. However, once the group increases to this size, the individual prefers a larger quantity of the good, and so on, until G is attained.

Fig. 3 may be interpreted as a standard preference map depicting the tastes of the individual for the two components, goods quantity and club size for the sharing of that good. The curves, N_{opt} and Q_{opt}, are lines of optima, and G is the highest attainable level for the individual, the top of his ordinal utility mountain. Since these curves are lines of optima within an individual preference system, successive choices must converge in G.

It should be noted that income-price constraints have already been incorporated in the preference map through the specific sharing assumptions that are made. The tastes of the individual depicted in Fig. 3 reflect the post-payment or net relative evaluations of the two components of consumption at all levels. Unless additional constraints are imposed on the model, he must move to the satiety point in this construction.

It seems clear that under normal conditions both of the curves in Fig. 3 will slope upward to the right, and that they will lie in approximately the relation to each other as therein depicted. This reflects the fact that, normally for the type of good considered in this example, there will exist a complementary rather than a substitute relationship between increasing the quantity of the good and increasing the size of the sharing group.

This geometrical model can be extended to cover goods falling at any point along the private-public spectrum. Take the purely public good as the first extreme case. Since, by definition, congestion does not occur, each total benefit curve, in Fig. 1, becomes horizontal. Thus, optimal club size, regardless of goods quantity is infinite. Hence, full equilibrium is impossible of attainment; equilibrium only with respect to goods quantity can be reached, defined with respect to the all-inclusive finite group. In the construction of Fig. 3, the N curve cannot be drawn. A more realistic model may be that in which, at goods quantity equilibrium, the limitations on group size

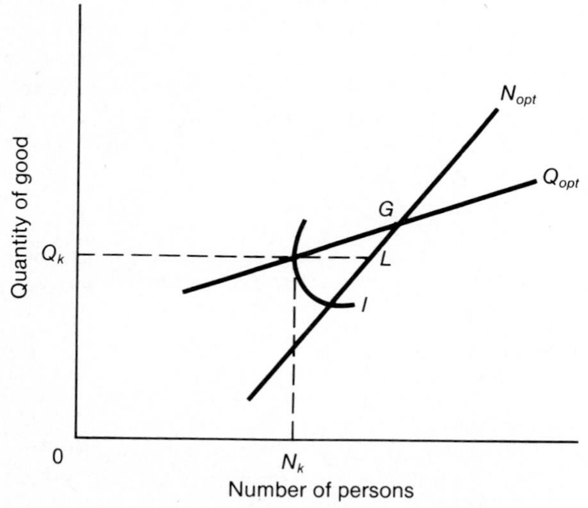

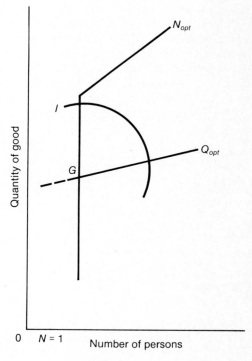

Fig. 4

Fig. 3

impose an inequality. For example, in Fig. 3, suppose that the all-inclusive group is of size, N_k. Congestion is indicated as being possible over small sizes of facility, but, if an equilibrium quantity is provided, there is no congestion, and, in fact, there remain economies to scale in club size. The situation at the most favourable attainable position is, therefore, in all respects equivalent to that confronted in the case of the good that is purely public under the more restricted definition.

Consider now the purely private good. The appropriate curves here may be shown in Fig. 4. The individual, with his income-price constraints is able to attain the peak of his ordinal preference mountain without the necessity of calling upon his fellows to join him in sharing arrangements. Also, the benefits that he receives from the good may be so exclusively his own that these would largely disappear if others were brought in to share them. Hence, the full equilibrium position, G, lies along the vertical from the $N = 1$ member point. Any attempt to expand the club beyond this point will reduce the utility of the individual.[11]

III

The geometrical construction implies that the necessary marginal conditions are satisfied at unique equilibrium values for both goods quantity and club size. This involves an oversimplification that is made possible only through the assumptions of specific cost-sharing schemes and identity among individuals. In order to generalize the results, these restrictions must be dropped. We know that, given any group of individuals who are able to evaluate both consumption shares and the costs of congestion, there exists some set of marginal prices, goods quantity, and club size that will satisfy (7) above. However, the quantity of the good, the size of the club sharing in its consumption, and the cost-sharing arrangements must be determined simultaneously. And, since there are always "gains from trade" to be realized in moving from non-optimal to optimal positions, distributional considerations must be introduced. Once these are allowed to be present, the final "solution" can be located at any one of a sub-infinity of points on the Pareto welfare surface. Only through some quite arbitrarily chosen conventions can standard geometrical constructions be made to apply.

The approach used above has been to impose at the outset a set of marginal prices (tax-prices, if the good is supplied publicly), translated here into shares or potential shares in the costs of providing separate quantities of a specific good for groups of varying sizes. Hence, the individual confronts a predictable set of marginal prices for each quantity of the good at every possible club size, independently of his own choices on these variables. With this convention, and the world-of-equals assumption, the geometrical solution becomes one that is relevant for any individual in the group. If we drop the world-of-equals assumption, the construction continues to hold without change for the choice calculus of any particular individual in the group. The results cannot, of course, be generalized for the group in this case, since different individuals will evaluate any given result differently. The model remains helpful even here, however, in that it suggests the process through which individual decisions may be made, and it tends to clarify some of the implicit content in the more formal statements of the necessary marginal conditions for optimality.[12]

---

[11]The construction suggests clearly that the optimal club size, for any quantity of good, will tend to become smaller as the real income of an individual is increased. Goods that exhibit some "publicness" at low income levels will, therefore, tend to become "private" as income levels advance. This suggests that the number of activities that are organized optimally under co-operative collective sharing arrangements will tend to be somewhat larger in low-income communities than in high-income communities, other things equal. There is, of course, ample empirical support for this rather obvious conclusion drawn from the model. For example, in American agricultural communities thirty years ago heavy equipment was communally shared among many farms, normally on some single owner-lease-rental arrangement. Today, substantially the same equipment will be found on each farm, even though it remains idle for much of its potential working time.

The implication of the analysis for the size of governmental units is perhaps less evident. In so far as governments are organized to provide communal facilities, the size of such units measured by the number of citizens, should decline as income increases. Thus, in the affluent society, the local school district may, optimally, be smaller than in the poor society.

[12]A note concerning one implicit assumption of the whole analysis is in order at this point. The possibility for the individual to choose among the various scales of consumption sharing arrangements has been incorporated into an orthodox model of individual behaviour. The procedure implies that the individual remains indifferent as to which of his neighbours or fellow citizens join him in such arrangements. In other words, no attempt has been made to allow for personal selectivity or discrimination in the models. To incorporate this element, which is no doubt important in many instances, would introduce a wholly new dimension into the analysis, and additional tools to those employed here would be required.

IV

The theory of clubs developed in this paper applies in the strict sense only to the organization of membership or sharing arrangements where "exclusion" is possible. In so far as non-exclusion is a characteristic of public goods supply, as Musgrave has suggested,[13] the theory of clubs is of limited relevance. Nevertheless, some implications of the theory for the whole excludability question may be indicated. If the structure of property rights is variable, there would seem to be few goods the services of which are non-excludable, solely due to some physical attributes. Hence, the theory of clubs is, in one sense, a theory of optimal exclusion, as well as one of inclusion. Consider the classic lighthouse case. Variations in property rights, broadly conceived, could prohibit boat operators without "light licenses" from approaching the channel guarded by the light. Physical exclusion is possible, given sufficient flexibility in property law, in almost all imaginable cases, including those in which the interdependence lies in the act of consuming itself. Take the single person who gets an inoculation, providing immunization against a communicable disease. In so far as this action exerts external benefits on his fellows, the person taking the action could be authorized to collect charges from all beneficiaries under sanction of the collectivity.

This is not, of course, to suggest that property rights will, in practice, always be adjusted to allow for optimal exclusion. If they are not, the "free rider" problem arises. This prospect suggests one issue of major importance that the analysis of this paper has neglected, the question of costs that may be involved in securing agreements among members of sharing groups. If individuals think that exclusion will not be fully possible, that they can expect to secure benefits as free riders without really becoming full-fledged contributing members of the club, they may be reluctant to enter voluntarily into cost-sharing arrangements. This suggests that one important means of reducing the costs of securing voluntary co-operative agreements is that of allowing for more flexible property arrangements and for introducing excluding devices. If the owner of a hunting preserve is allowed to prosecute poachers, then prospective poachers are much more likely to be willing to pay for the hunting permits in advance.

[13]See R.A. Musgrave, *The Theory of Public Finance*, New York, 1959.

Externality*

JAMES M. BUCHANAN
WILLIAM CRAIG STUBBLEBINE

See "An Economic Theory of Clubs" for James M. Buchanan's biography.

William Craig Stubblebine (B.S., University of Delaware, 1958; Ph.D., University of Virginia, 1963) was born in West Point, New York, in 1936. Currently he is the Von Tobel Professor of Political Economy, Research Professor in the Center for the Study of Law Structures, Chairman of the Department of Economics at the Claremont McKenna College, and a member of the Graduate Faculty at the Claremont Graduate School. He previously served on the faculties of the University of Virginia and the University of Delaware; as a National Science Foundation Faculty Fellow at the Massachusetts Institute of Technology; as a Visiting Professor at the University of Turin, Italy; Southern Methodist University; and Virginia Polytechnic Institute and State University. Stubblebine has participated in the formulation of theories of externalities, public goods, and property rights, and has been a major contributor in the development of constitutional limits on government taxing and spending. He is a past vice-president of the Western Tax Association.

Externality has been, and is, central to the neoclassical critique of market organisation. In its various forms—external economies and diseconomies, divergencies between marginal social and marginal private cost or product, spillover and neighbourhood effects, collective or public goods—externality dominates theoretical welfare economics, and, in one sense, the theory of economic policy generally. Despite this importance and emphasis, rigorous definitions of the concept itself are not readily available in the literature. As Scitovosky has noted, "definitions of external economies are few and unsatisfactory."[1] The following seems typical:

> External effects exist in consumption whenever the shape or position of a man's indifference curve depends on the consumption of other men.

[1] Tibor Scitovosky, "Two Concepts of External Economies," *Journal of Political Economy,* vol. LXII (1954), p. 143.

[External effects] are present whenever a firm's production function depends in some way on the amounts of the inputs or outputs of another firm.[2]

It seems clear that operational and usable definitions are required.

In this paper, we propose to clarify the notion of externality by defining it rigorously and precisely. When this is done, several important, and often overlooked, conceptual distinctions follow more or less automatically. Specifically, we shall distinguish marginal and inframarginal externalities, potentially relevant and irrelevant externalities, and Pareto-relevant and Pareto-irrelevant externalities. These distinctions are formally developed in Section I. As we shall demonstrate, the term, "externality," as generally used by economists, corresponds only to our definition of Pareto-relevant externality. There follows, in Section II, an illustration of the basic points described in terms of a simple descriptive example. In Section III, some of the implications of our approach are discussed.

It is useful to limit the scope of the analysis at the outset. Much of the discussion in the literature has been concerned with the distinction between *technological* and *pecuniary* external effects. We do not propose to enter this discussion since it is not relevant for our purposes. We note only that, if desired, the whole analysis can be taken to apply only to technological externalities. Secondly, we shall find no cause for discussing production and consumption externalities separately. Essentially the same analysis applies in either case. In what follows, "firms" may be substituted for "individuals" and "production functions" for "utility functions" without modifying the central conclusions. For expositional simplicity only, we limit the explicit discussion to consumption externalities.

I

We define an external effect, *an externality*, to be present when,

$$u^A = u^A (X_1, X_2, \ldots, X_m, Y_1) \tag{1}$$

This states that the utility of an individual, *A,* is dependent upon the "activities," $(X_1, X_2, \ldots, X_m)$, that are exclusively under his own control or authority, but also upon another single activity, Y_1,

which is, by definition, under the control of a second individual, *B*, who is presumed to be a member of the same social group. We define an *activity* here as any distinguishable human action that may be measured, such as eating bread, drinking milk, spewing smoke into the air, dumping litter on the highways, giving to the poor, etc. Note that *A*'s utility may, and will in the normal case, depend on other activities of *B* in addition to Y_1, and also upon the activities of other parties. That is, *A*'s utility function may, in more general terms, include such variables as $(Y_2, Y_3, \ldots, Y_m; Z_1, Z_2, \ldots, Z_m)$. For analytical simplicity, however, we shall confine our attention to the effects of one particular activity, Y_1, as it affects the utility of *A*.

We assume that *A* will behave so as to maximise utility in the ordinary way, subject to the externally determined values for Y_1, and that he will modify the values for the X's, as Y_1 changes, so as to maintain a state of "equilibrium."

A marginal externality exists when,

$$u^A_{Y_1} \neq 0 \tag{2}$$

Here, small u's are employed to represent the "partial derivatives" of the utility function of the individual designated by the super-script with respect to the variables designated by the subscript. Hence, $u^A_{Y_1} = \partial u^A / \partial Y_1$, assuming that the variation in Y_1 is evaluated with respect to a set of "equilibrium" values for the X's, adjusted to the given value for Y_1.

An infra-marginal externality holds at those points where,

$$u^A_{Y_1} = 0 \tag{3}$$

and (1) holds.

These classifications can be broken down into economies and diseconomies: a marginal external economy existing when,

$$u^A_{Y_1} > 0 \tag{2A}$$

that is, a small change in the activity undertaken by *B* will change the utility of *A* in the same direction; a marginal external diseconomy existing when,

$$u^A_{Y_1} < 0 \tag{2B}$$

An infra-marginal external economy exists when for any given set of values for $(X_1, X_2, \ldots, X_m)$, say, $(C_1, C_2, \ldots, C_m)$,

$$u^A_{Y_1} = 0, \text{ and } \int_0^{Y_1} u^A_{Y_1} \, d_{Y_1} > 0 \tag{3A}$$

---

[2]J. de V. Graaf, *Theoretical Welfare Economics*, Cambridge, 1957, p. 43 and p. 18.

This condition states that, while incremental changes in the extent of B's activity, Υ_1, have no effect on A's utility, the total effect of B's action has increased A's utility. An infra-marginal diseconomy exists when (1) holds, and, for any given set of values for $(X_1, X_2, \ldots, X_m)$, say, $(C_1, C_2, \ldots, C_m)$, then,

$$u^A_{\Upsilon_1} = 0, \text{ and } \int_0^{\Upsilon_1} u^A_{\Upsilon_1} \, d_{\Upsilon_1} < 0 \qquad (3\text{B})$$

Thus, small changes in B's activity do not change A's level of satisfaction, but the total effect of B's undertaking the activity in question is harmful to A.

We are able to classify the effects of B's action, or potential action, on A's utility by evaluating the "partial derivative" of A's utility function with respect to Υ_1 over all possible values for Υ_1. In order to introduce the further distinctions between *relevant* and *irrelevant* externalities, however, it is necessary to go beyond consideration of A's utility function. Whether or not a relevant externality exists depends upon the extent to which the activity involving the externality is carried out by the person empowered to take action, to make decisions. Since we wish to consider a single externality in isolation, we shall assume that B's utility function includes only variables (activities) that are within his control, including Υ_1. Hence, B's utility function takes the form,

$$u^B = u^B (\Upsilon_1, \Upsilon_2, \ldots, \Upsilon_m) \qquad (4)$$

Necessary conditions for utility maximisation by B are,

$$u^B_{\Upsilon_1}/u^B_{\Upsilon_j} = f^B_{\Upsilon_1}/f^B_{\Upsilon_j} \qquad (5)$$

where Υ_j is used to designate the activity of B in consuming or utilising some numeraire commodity or service which is, by hypothesis, available on equal terms to A. The right-hand term represents the marginal rate of substitution in "production" or "exchange" confronted by B, the party taking action on Υ_1, his production function being defined as,

$$f^B = f^B(\Upsilon_1, \Upsilon_2, \ldots, \Upsilon_m) \qquad (6)$$

where inputs are included as activities along with outputs. In other words, the right-hand term represents the marginal cost of the activity, Υ_1, to B. The equilibrium values for the Υ_i's will be designated as $\overline{\Upsilon}_i$'s.

An externality is defined as *potentially relevant* when the activity, to the extent that it is actually performed, generates *any* desire on the part of the externally benefited (damaged) party *(A)* to modify the behavior of the party empowered to take action *(B)* through trade, persuasion, compromise, agreement, convention, collective action, etc. An externality which, to the extent that it is performed, exerts no such influence is defined as *irrelevant*. Note that, so long as (1) holds, an externality remains; utility functions remain interdependent.

A potentially relevant marginal externality exists when,

$$u^A_{\Upsilon_1}\Big|_{\Upsilon_1 = \overline{\Upsilon}_1} \neq 0 \qquad (7)$$

This is a potentially relevant marginal external economy when (7) is greater than zero, a diseconomy when (7) is less than zero. In either case, A is motivated, by B's performance of the activity, to make some effort to modify this performance, to increase the resources devoted to the activity when (7) is positive, to decrease the quantity of resources devoted to the activity when (7) is negative.

Infra-marginal externalities are, by definition, irrelevant for small changes in the scope of B's activity, Υ_1. However, when large or discrete changes are considered, A is motivated to change B's behaviour with respect to Υ_1 in all cases *except* that for which,

$$u^A_{\Upsilon_1}\Big|_{\Upsilon_1 = \overline{\Upsilon}_1} = 0 \qquad (8)$$

and

$$u^A(C_1, C_2, \ldots C_m, \overline{\Upsilon}_1) \geqq u^A(C_1, C_2, \ldots C_m, \Upsilon_1)$$

for all $\Upsilon_1 \neq \overline{\Upsilon}_1$.

When (8) holds, A has achieved an absolute maximum of utility with respect to changes over Υ_1, given any set of values for the X's. In more prosaic terms, A is satiated with respect to Υ_1.[3] In all other cases, where infra-marginal external economies or diseconomies exist, A will have some desire to modify B's performance; the externality is potentially relevant. Whether or not this motivation will lead A to seek an expansion or contraction in the extent of B's performance of the activity will depend on the location of the infra-marginal region relative to the absolute maximum for any given values of the X's.[4]

---

[3]Note that $u^A_{\Upsilon_1}\Big|_{\Upsilon_1 = \overline{\Upsilon}_1} = 0$ is a necessary, but not a sufficient, condition for irrelevance.

[4]In this analysis of the relevance of externalities, we have assumed that B will act in such a manner as to maximise his own utility subject to the constraints within which he must operate. If, for any reason, B does not attain the equilibrium position defined in (5) above, the classification of his activity for A may, of course, be modified. A potentially relevant externality may become irrelevant and *vice versa*.

Pareto relevance and irrelevance may now be introduced. The existence of a simple desire to modify the behaviour of another, defined as potential relevance, need not imply the ability to implement this desire. An externality is defined to be Pareto-relevant when the extent of the activity may be modified in such a way that the externally affected party, A, can be made better off without the acting party, B, being made worse off. That is to say, "gains from trade" characterise the Pareto-relevant externality, trade that takes the form of some change in the activity of B as his part of the bargain.

A marginal externality is Pareto-relevant when[5]

$$(-)u^A_{\Upsilon_1}/u^A_{X_j} > [u^B_{\Upsilon_1}/u^B_{\Upsilon_j} - f^B_{\Upsilon_1}/f^B_{\Upsilon_j}]_{\Upsilon_1 = \bar{\tau}_1} \qquad (9)$$

and when $u^A_{\Upsilon_1}/u^A_{X_j} < 0$ and

$$u^A_{\Upsilon_1}/u^A_{X_j} > (-)[u^B_{\Upsilon_1}/u^B_{\Upsilon_j} - f^B_{\Upsilon_1}/f^B_{\Upsilon_j}]_{\Upsilon_1 = \bar{\tau}_1}$$

when $u^A_{\Upsilon_1}/u^A_{X_j} > 0$

In (9), X_j and Υ_j are used to designate, respectively, the activities of A and B in consuming or in utilising some numeraire commodity or service that, by hypothesis, is available on identical terms to each of them. As is indicated by the transposition of signs in (9), the conditions for Pareto relevance differ as between external diseconomies and economies. This is because the "direction" of change desired by A on the part of B is different in the two cases. In stating the conditions for Pareto relevance under ordinary two-person trade, this point is of no significance since trade in one good flows only in one direction. Hence, absolute values can be used.

The condition, (9), states that A's marginal rate of substitution between the activity, Υ_1, and the numeraire activity must be greater than the "net" marginal rate of substitution between the activity and the numeraire activity for B. Otherwise, "gains from trade" would not exist between A and B.

Note, however, that when B has achieved utility-maximising equilibrium,

$$u^B_{\Upsilon_1}/u^B_{\Upsilon_j} = f^B_{\Upsilon_1}/f^B_{\Upsilon_j} \qquad (10)$$

That is to say, the marginal rate of substitution in consumption or utilisation is equated to the marginal rate of substitution in production or exchange, i.e., to marginal cost. When (10) holds, the terms in the brackets in (9) mutually cancel. Thus, potentially rel-

evant marginal externalities are also Pareto-relevant when B is in utility-maximising equilibrium. Some trade is possible.

Pareto equilibrium is defined to be present when,

$$(-)u^A_{\Upsilon_1}/u^A_{X_j} = [u^B_{\Upsilon_1}/u^B_{\Upsilon_j} - f^B_{\Upsilon_1}/f^B_{\Upsilon_j}] \qquad (11)$$

and when $u^A_{\Upsilon_1}/u^A_{X_j} < 0$ and

$$u^A_{\Upsilon_1}/u^A_{X_j} = (-)[u^B_{\Upsilon_1}/u^B_{\Upsilon_j} - f^B_{\Upsilon_1}/f^B_{\Upsilon_j}]$$

when $u^A_{\Upsilon_1}/u^A_{X_j} > 0$

Condition (11) demonstrates that marginal externalities may continue to exist, even in Pareto equilibrium, as here defined. This point may be shown by reference to the special case in which the activity in question may be undertaken at zero costs. Here Pareto equilibrium is attained when the marginal rates of substitution in consumption or utilisation for the two persons are precisely offsetting, that is, where their interests are strictly opposed, and *not* where the left-hand term vanishes.

What vanishes in Pareto equilibrium are the Pareto-relevant externalities. It seems clear that, normally, economists have been referring only to what we have here called Pareto-relevant externalities when they have, implicitly or explicitly, stated that external effects are not present when a position on the Pareto optimality surface is attained.[6]

For completeness, we must also consider those potentially relevant infra-marginal externalities. Refer to the discussion of these as summarised in (8) above. The question is now to determine whether or not, A, the externally affected party, can reach some mutually satisfactory agreement with B, the acting party, that will involve some discrete (non-marginal) change in the scope of the activity, Υ_1. If, over some range, any range, of the activity, which we shall designate by $\Delta\Upsilon_1$, the rate of substitution between Υ_1 and X_j for A exceeds the "net" rate of substitution for B, the externality is Pareto-relevant. The associated changes in the utilisation of the numeraire commodity must be equal for the two parties. Thus, for external economies, we have

$$\frac{\Delta u^A}{\Delta\Upsilon_1}\Big/\frac{\Delta u^A}{\Delta X_j} > (-)\left[\frac{\Delta u^B}{\Delta\Upsilon_1}\Big/\frac{\Delta u^B}{\Delta\Upsilon_j} - \frac{\Delta f^B}{\Delta\Upsilon_1}\Big/\frac{\Delta f^B}{\Delta\Upsilon_j}\right]_{\Upsilon_1 = \bar{\tau}_1} \qquad (12)$$

---

[5]We are indebted to Mr. M. McManus of the University of Birmingham for pointing out to us an error in an earlier formulation of this and the following similar conditions.

[6]This applies to the authors of this paper. For recent discussion of external effects when we have clearly intended only what we here designate as Pareto-relevant, see James M. Buchanan, "Politics, Policy, and the Pigovian Margins," *Economica*, vol. XXVIX (1962), pp. 17–28, and, also, James M. Buchanan and Gordon Tullock, *The Calculus of Consent*, Ann Arbor, 1962.

and the same with the sign in parenthesis transposed for external diseconomies. The difference to be noted between (12) and (9) is that, with infra-marginal externalities, potential relevance need not imply Pareto relevance. The bracketed terms in (12) need not sum to zero when B is in his private utility-maximising equilibrium.

We have remained in a two-person world, with one person affected by the single activity of a second. However, the analysis can readily be modified to incorporate the effects of this activity on a multi-person group. That is to say, B's activity, Y_1, may be allowed to affect several parties simultaneously, several A's, so to speak. In each case, the activity can then be evaluated in terms of its effects on the utility of each person. Nothing in the construction need be changed. The only stage in the analysis requiring modification explicitly to take account of the possibilities of multi-person groups being externally affected is that which involves the condition for Pareto relevance and Pareto equilibrium.

For a multi-person group $(A_1, A_2, \ldots, A_n)$, any one or all of whom may be externally affected by the activity, Y_1, of the single person, B, the condition for Pareto relevance is,

$$(-) \sum_{i=1}^{n} u_{Y_1}^{Ai}/u_{Yj}^{Ai} > [u_{Y_1}^{B}/u_{Yj}^{B} - f_{Y_1}^{B}/f_{Y_i}^{B}]_{Y_1 = \bar{Y}_1} \quad (9A)$$

when $u_{Y_1}^{Ai}/u_{X_j}^{Ai} < 0$ and

$$\sum_{i=1}^{n} u_{Y_1}^{Ai}/u_{X_j}^{Ai} > (-)[u_{Y_1}^{B}/u_{Yj}^{B} - f_{Y_1}^{B}/f_{Y_i}^{B}]_{Y_1 = \bar{Y}_1}$$

when $u_{Y_1}^{Ai}/u_{X_j}^{Ai} > 0$

That is, the summed marginal rates of substitution over the members of the externally affected group exceed the offsetting "net" marginal evaluation of the activity by B. Again, in private equilibrium for B, marginal externalities are Pareto-relevant, provided that we neglect the important element involved in the costs of organising group decisions. In the real world, these costs of organising group decisions (together with uncertainty and ignorance) will prevent realisation of some "gains from trade"—just as they do in organised markets. This is as true for two-person groups as it is for larger groups. But this does not invalidate the point that potential "gains from trade" are available. The condition for Pareto equilibrium and for the inframarginal case summarised in (11) and (12) for the two-person model can readily be modified to allow for the externally affected multi-person group.

II

The distinctions developed formally in Section I may be illustrated diagrammatically and discussed in terms of a simple descriptive example. Consider two persons, A and B, who own adjoining units of residential property. Within limits to be noted, each person values privacy, which may be measured quantitatively in terms of a single criterion, the height of a fence that can be constructed along the common boundary line. We shall assume that B's desire for privacy holds over rather wide limits. His utility increases with the height of the fence up to a reasonably high level. Up to a certain minimum height, A's utility also is increased as the fence is made higher. Once this minimum height is attained, however, A's desire for privacy is assumed to be fully satiated. Thus, over a second range, A's total utility does not change with a change in the height of the fence. However, beyond a certain limit, A's view of a mountain behind B's property is progressively obscured as the fence goes higher. Over this third range, therefore, A's utility is reduced as the fence is constructed to higher levels. Finally, A will once again become wholly indifferent to marginal changes in the

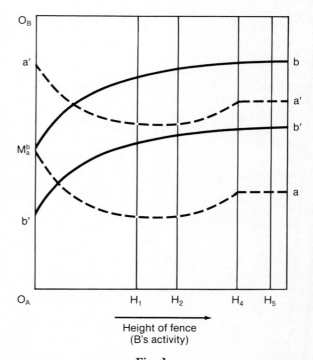

Height of fence
(B's activity)

Fig. 1

fence's height when his view is totally blocked out.

We specify that B possesses the sole authority, the only legal right, to construct the fence between the two properties.

The preference patterns for A and for B are shown in Fig. 1, which is drawn in the form of an Edgeworth-like box diagram. Note, however, that the origin for B is shown at the upper left rather than the upper right corner of the diagram as in the more normal usage. This modification is necessary here because only the numeraire good, measured along the ordinate, is strictly divisible between A and B. Both must adjust to the same height of fence, that is, to the same level of the activity creating the externality.

As described above, the indifference contours for A take the general shape shown by the curves aa,

$a'a'$, while those for B assume the shapes, bb, $b'b'$. Note that these contours reflect the relative evaluations, for A and B, between money and the activity, Y_1. Since the costs of undertaking the activity, for B, are not incorporated in the diagram, the "contract locus" that might be derived from tangency points will have little relevance except in the special case where the activity can be undertaken at zero costs.

Fig. 2 depicts the marginal evaluation curves for A and B, as derived from the preference fields shown in Fig. 1, along with some incorporation of costs. These curves are derived as follows: Assume an initial distribution of "money" between A and B, say, that shown at M on Fig. 1. The marginal evaluation of the activity for A is then derived by plotting the negatives (i.e., the mirror image) of the slopes of successive indifference curves attained by A as B is

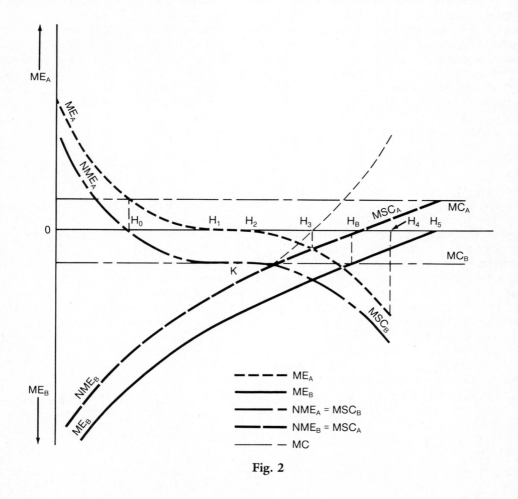

Fig. 2

assumed to increase the height of the fence from zero. These values remain positive for a range, become zero over a second range, become negative for a third, and, finally, return to zero again.[7]

B's curves of marginal evaluation are measured downward from the upper horizontal axis or base line, for reasons that will become apparent. The derivation of *B*'s marginal evaluation curve is somewhat more complex than that for *A*. This is because *B*, who is the person authorised to undertake the action, in this case the building of the fence, must also bear the full costs. Thus, as *B* increases the scope of the activity, his real income, measured in terms of his remaining goods and services, is reduced. This change in the amount of remaining goods and services will, of course, affect his marginal evaluation of the activity in question. Thus, the marginal cost of building the fence will determine, to some degree, the marginal evaluation of the fence. This necessary interdependence between marginal evaluation and marginal cost complicates the use of simple diagrammatic models in finding or locating a solution. It need not, however, deter us from presenting the solution diagrammatically, if we postulate that the marginal evaluation curve, as drawn, is based on a single presumed cost relationship. This done, we may plot *B*'s marginal evaluation of the activity from the negatives of the slopes of his indifference contours attained as he constructs the fence to higher and higher levels. *B*'s marginal evaluation, shown in Fig. 2, remains positive throughout the range to the point H_5, where it becomes zero.

The distinctions noted in Section I are easily related to the construction in Fig. 2. To *A*, the party externally affected, *B*'s potential activity in constructing the fence can be assessed independently of any prediction of *B*'s actual behaviour. Thus, the activity of *B* would,

1. Exert marginal external economies which are potentially relevant over the range OH_1

2. Exert infra-marginal external economies over the range $H_1 H_2$, which are clearly irrelevant since no change in *B*'s behaviour with respect to the extent of the activity would increase *A*'s utility

3. Exert marginal external diseconomies over the range $H_2 H_4$ which are potentially relevant to *A*

4. Exert infra-marginal external economies or dis-

economies beyond H_4, the direction of the effect being dependent on the ratio between the total utility derived from privacy and the total reduction in utility derived from the obstructed view. In any case, the externality is potentially relevant.

To determine Pareto relevance, the extent of *B*'s predicted performance must be determined. The necessary condition for *B*'s attainment of "private" utility-maximising equilibrium is that marginal costs, which he must incur, be equal to his own marginal evaluation. For simplicity in Fig. 2, we assume that marginal costs are constant, as shown by the curve, *MC*. Thus, *B*'s position of equilibrium is shown at H_B, within the range of marginal external diseconomies for *A*. Here the externality imposed by *B*'s behaviour is clearly Pareto-relevant: *A* can surely work out some means of compensating *B* in exchange for *B*'s agreement to reduce the scope of the activity—in this example, to reduce the height of the fence between the two properties. Diagrammatically, the position of Pareto equilibrium is shown at H_3 where the marginal evaluation of *A* is equal in absolute value, but negatively, to the "net" marginal evaluation of *B*, drawn as the curve NME_B. Only in this position are the conditions specified in (11), above, satisfied.[8]

III

Aside from the general classification of externalities that is developed, the approach here allows certain implications to be drawn, implications that have not, perhaps, been sufficiently recognised by some welfare economists.

The analysis makes it quite clear that externalities, external effects, may remain even in full Pareto equilibrium. That is to say, a position may be classified as Pareto-optimal or efficient despite the fact that, at the marginal, the activity of one individual externally affects the utility of another individual. Fig. 2 demonstrates this point clearly. Pareto equilibrium is attained at H_3, yet *B* is imposing marginal external diseconomies on *A*.

---

[7]For an early use of marginal evaluation curves, see J. R. Hicks, "The Four Consumer's Surpluses," *Review of Economic Studies*, vol. XI (1943), pp. 31–41.

[8]This diagrammatic analysis is necessarily oversimplified in the sense that the Pareto equilibrium position is represented as a unique point. Over the range between the "private" equilibrium for *B* and the point of Pareto equilibrium, the sort of bargains struck between *A* and *B* will affect the marginal evaluation curves of both individuals within this range. Thus, the more accurate analysis would suggest a "contract locus" of equilibrium points. At Pareto equilibrium, however, the condition shown in the diagrammatic presentation holds, and the demonstration of this fact rather than the location of the solution is the aim of this diagrammatics.

This point has significant policy implications for it suggests that the observation of external effects, taken alone, cannot provide a basis for judgment concerning the desirability of some modification in an existing state of affairs. There is not a *prima facie* case for intervention in all cases where an externality is observed to exist.[9] The internal benefits from carrying out the activity, net of costs, may be greater than the external damage that is imposed on other parties.

In full Pareto equilibrium, of course, these internal benefits, measured in terms of some numeraire good, net of costs, must be just equal, at the margin, to the external damage that is imposed on other parties. This equilibrium will always be characterised by the strict opposition of interests of the two parties, one of which may be a multi-person group.

In the general case, we may say that, at full Pareto equilibrium, the presence of a marginal external diseconomy implies an offsetting marginal *internal* economy, whereas the presence of a marginal external economy implies an offsetting marginal *internal* diseconomy. In "private" equilibrium, as opposed to Pareto equilibrium, these net internal economies and diseconomies would, of course, be eliminated by the utility-maximizing acting party. In Pareto equilibrium, these remain because the acting party is being compensated for "suffering" internal economies and diseconomies would, of course, be eliminated by the utility-maximising acting party. In Pareto equilibrium, these remain because the acting party is being

As a second point, it is useful to relate the whole analysis here to the more familiar Pigovian discussion concerning the divergence between marginal social cost (product) and marginal private cost (product). By saying that such a divergence exists, we are, in the terms of this paper, saying that a marginal externality exists. The Pigovian terminology tends to be misleading, however, in that it deals with the acting party to the exclusion of the externally affected party. It fails to take into account the fact that there are always two parties involved in a single externality relationship.[10] As we have suggested, a marginal externality is Pareto-relevant except in the position of Pareto equilibrium; gains from trade can arise. But

there must be two parties to any trading arrangement. The externally affected party must compensate the acting party for modifying his behaviour. The Pigovian terminology, through its concentration on the decision-making of the acting party alone, tends to obscure the two-sidedness of the bargain that must be made.

To illustrate this point, assume that A, the externally affected party in our model, successfully secures, through the auspices of the "state," the levy of a marginal tax on B's performance of the activity, Y_1. Assume further that A is able to secure this change without cost to himself. The tax will increase the marginal cost of performing the activity for B, and, hence, will reduce the extent of the activity attained in B's "private" equilibrium. Let us now presume that this marginal tax is levied "correctly" on the basis of a Pigovian calculus; the rate of tax at the margin is made equal to the negative marginal evaluation of the activity to A. Under these modified conditions, the effective marginal cost, as confronted by B, may be shown by the curve designated as MSC_B in Fig. 2. A new "private" equilibrium for B is shown at the quantity, H_3, the same level designated as Pareto equilibrium in our earlier discussion, if we neglect the disturbing interdependence between marginal evaluation and marginal costs. Attention solely to the decision calculus of B here would suggest, perhaps, that this position remains Pareto-optimal under these revised circumstances, and that it continues to qualify as a position of Pareto equilibrium. There is no divergence between marginal private cost and marginal social cost in the usual sense. However, the position, if attained in this manner, is clearly neither one of Pareto optimality, nor one that may be classified as Pareto equilibrium.

In this new "private" equilibrium for B,

$$u^B_{Y_1}/u^B_{Y_i} = f^B_{Y_1}/f^B_{Y_j} - u^A_{Y_1}/u^A_{X_i}, \qquad (13)$$

where $u^A_{Y_1}/u^A_{X_j}$ represents the marginal tax imposed on B as he performs the activity, Y_1. Recall the necessary condition for Pareto relevance defined in (9) above, which can now be modified to read,

$$(-)u^A_{Y_1}/u^A_{X_i} > [u^B_{Y_1}/u^B_{Y_i} - f^B_{Y_1}/f^B_{Y_i} + u^A_{Y_1}/u^A_{X_i}]_{Y_1 = \bar{Y}_1} \quad (9\text{B})$$

when $u^A_{Y_1}/u^A_{X_i} < 0$ and

$$u^A_{Y_1}/u^A_{X_i} > (-)[u^B_{Y_1}/u^B_{Y_i} - f^B_{Y_1}/f^B_{Y_j} + u^A_{Y_1}/u^A_{X_i}]_{Y_1 = \bar{Y}_1}$$

when $u^A_{Y_1}/u^A_{X_i} > 0$

In (9B), $\bar{Y}_1$ represents the "private" equilibrium value for Y_1, determined by B, after the ideal Pigovian

[9] Cf. Paul A. Samuelson, *Foundations of Economic Analysis*, Cambridge, Mass., 1948, p. 208, for a discussion of the views of various writers.
[10] This criticism of the Pigovian analysis has recently been developed by R. H. Coase; see his "The Problem of Social Cost," *Journal of Law and Economics*, vol. III (1960), pp. 1–44.

tax is imposed. As before, the bracketed terms represent the "net" marginal evaluation of the activity for the acting party, B, and these sum to zero when equilibrium is reached. So long as the left-hand term in the inequality remains non-zero, a Pareto-relevant marginal externality remains, despite the fact that the full "Pigovian solution" is attained.

The apparent paradox here is not difficult to explain. Since, as postulated, A is not incurring any cost in securing the change in B's behaviour, and, since there remains, by hypothesis, a marginal diseconomy, further "trade" can be worked out between the two parties. Specifically, Pareto equilibrium is reached when,

$$(-)u^A_{Ti}/u^A_{Xi} = [u^B_{Ti}/u^B_{Yi} - f^B_{Ti}/f^B_{Yi} + u^A_{Ti}/u^A_{Xi}] \quad (11\text{A})$$

when $u^A_{Ti}/u^A_{Xi} < 0$ and

$$u^A_{Ti}/u^A_{Xi} = (-)[u^B_{Ti}/u^B_{Yi} - f^B_{Ti}/f^B_{Yi} + u^A_{Ti}/u^A_{Xi}]$$

when $u^A_{Ti}/u^A_{Xi} > 0$.

Diagrammatically, this point may be made with reference to Fig. 2. If a unilaterally imposed tax, corresponding to the marginal evaluation of A, is placed on B's performance of the activity, the new position of Pareto equilibrium may be shown by first subtracting the new marginal cost curve, drawn as MSC_B, from B's marginal evaluation curve. Where this new "net" marginal evaluation curve, shown as the dotted curve between points H_3 and K, cuts the marginal evaluation curve for A, a new position of Pareto equilibrium falling between H_2 and H_3 is located, neglecting the qualifying point discussed in Footnote 8, page 464.

The important implication to be drawn is that full Pareto equilibrium can never be attained via the imposition of unilaterally imposed taxes and subsidies until all marginal externalities are eliminated. If a tax-subsidy method, rather than "trade," is to be introduced, it should involve bi-lateral taxes (subsidies). Not only must B's behaviour be modified so as to insure that he will take the costs externally imposed on A into account, but A's behaviour must be modified so as to insure that he will take the costs "internally" imposed on B into account. In such a double tax-subsidy scheme, the necessary Pareto conditions would be readily satisfied.[11]

In summary, Pareto equilibrium in the case of mar-

ginal externalities cannot be attained so long as marginal externalities remain, until and unless those benefiting from changes are required to pay some "price" for securing the benefits.

A third point worthy of brief note is that our analysis allows the whole treatment of externalities to encompass the consideration of purely collective goods. As students of public finance theory will have recognised, the Pareto equilibrium solution discussed in this paper is similar, indeed is identical, with that which was presented by Paul Samuelson in his theory of public expenditures.[12] The summed marginal rates of substitution (marginal evaluation) must be equal to marginal costs. Note, however, that marginal costs may include the negative marginal evaluation of other parties, if viewed in one way. Note, also, that there is nothing in the analysis which suggests its limitations to purely collective goods or even to goods that are characterised by significant externalities in their use.

Our analysis also lends itself to the more explicit point developed in Coase's recent paper.[13] He argues that the same "solution" will tend to emerge out of any externality relationship, regardless of the structure of property rights, provided only that the market process works smoothly. Strictly speaking, Coase's analysis is applicable only to inter-firm externality relationships, and the identical solution emerges only because firms adjust to prices that are competitively determined. In our terms of reference, this identity of solution cannot apply because of the incomparability of utility functions. It remains true, however, that the basic characteristics of the Pareto equilibrium position remain unchanged regardless of the authority undertaking the action. This point can be readily demonstrated, again with reference to Fig. 2. Let us assume that Fig. 2 is now redrawn on the basis of a different legal relationship in which A now possesses full authority to construct the fence, whereas B can no longer take any action in this respect. A will, under these conditions, "privately" construct a fence only to the height H_0, where the activity clearly exerts a Pareto-relevant marginal external economy on B. Pareto equilibrium will be reached, as before, at H_3, determined, in this case, by the intersection of the "net" marginal evaluation curve for A (which

---

[11]Although developed in rather different terminology, this seems to be closely in accord with Coase's analysis. Cf. R. H. Coase, *loc. cit.*

[12]Paul A. Samuelson, "The Pure Theory of Public Expenditure," *Review of Economics and Statistics*, vol. XXXVI (1954), pp. 386–9.
[13]R. H. Coase, *loc. cit.*

is identical to the previously defined marginal social cost curve, *MSC,* when *B* is the acting party) and the marginal evaluation curve for *B.*[14] Note that, in this model, *A* will allow himself to suffer an internal marginal diseconomy, at equilibrium, provided that he is compensated by *B,* who continues, in Pareto equilibrium, to enjoy a marginal *external* economy.

Throughout this paper, we have deliberately chosen to introduce and to discuss only a single externality. Much of the confusion in the literature seems to have arisen because two or more externalities have been handled simultaneously. The standard example is that in which the output of one firm affects the production function of the second firm while, at the same time, the output of the second firm affects the production function of the first. Clearly, there are two externalities to be analysed in such cases. In many instances, these can be treated as separate and handled independently. In other situations, this step cannot be taken and additional tools become necessary.[15]

---

[14]The H_3 position, in this presumably redrawn figure, should not be precisely compared with the same position in the other model. We are using here the same diagram for two models, and, especially over wide ranges, the dependence of the marginal evaluation curves on income effects cannot be left out of account.

[15]For a treatment of the dual externality problem that clearly shows the important difference between the separable and the non-separable cases, see Otto Davis and Andrew Whinston, "Externalities, Welfare, and the Theory of Games," *Journal of Political Economy,* vol. LXX (1962), pp. 241–62. As the title suggests, Davis and Whinston utilise the tools of game theory for the inseparable case.

Pareto-Optimal Redistribution*

HAROLD M. HOCHMAN**
JAMES D. RODGERS**

Harold M. Hochman (B.A., Yale University, 1957; M.A., 1959; Ph.D., 1965), Professor of Economics and Finance at Baruch College and The Graduate School of The City University of New York, was born in 1936 in New Haven, Connecticut. Currently Director of Baruch's Center for the Study of Business and Government, Hochman has also served on the faculty of the University of Virginia, and in research positions at the U.S. Treasury, the Institute for Defense Analyses, and The Urban Institute. He has held visiting appointments at the University of Turin, the London School of Economics and Centre for Environmental Studies, the University of California at Berkeley, and The Hebrew University of Jerusalem. Professor Hochman is primarily known for his work on theories of income redistribution and urban public finance.

James D. Rodgers (B.A., East Texas State University, 1966; Ph.D., University of Virginia, 1970) is Professor and Head of the Department of Economics at Pennsylvania State University where he has taught since 1969. During the academic year 1972–73 Professor Rodgers held a visiting appointment at the University of York in England. He has published numerous articles in leading journals, including papers on the theory of income transfers and the tax treatment of private charity (with Harold Hochman).

The neoclassical approach to public finance identified with Richard Musgrave [10, Ch. 1] divides the process of budget determination and the functions of government into three parts or branches.[1] The allocation branch, justified by the failure of the market to satisfy the demand for public goods, engages

*Reprinted from *American Economic Review* (September 1969) by permission of the American Economic Association. Copyright 1969, pp. 542–557.
**Among the many to whom we are indebted, we wish without implicating to give special acknowledgment to Gary S. Becker, James M. Buchanan, Alberto di Pierro, John R. Haring, and Edgar O. Olsen.

[1]It is, of course, an oversimplification to associate the sharp separation of allocation and distribution problems with Musgrave alone. This treatment is characteristic in neoclassical economics generally, and in particular in the "new welfare economics." See, for example, [1] and [9]. We cite Musgrave because his treatise is a core part of virtually every graduate course in public finance.

in explicit reallocative measures required to rectify this failure and achieve allocative efficiency. The distribution branch is charged with the purely normative responsibility of bringing about the desired size distribution of income, or optimal Lorenz curve, through taxation and transfer payments. The stabilization branch performs the conventional macroeconomic fiscal functions of attaining full employment, price stability, and a satisfactory rate of economic growth.

Though the interdependence of these three branches is generally recognized, their conceptual separation serves both a methodological and heuristic purpose. The distinction between actions designed to promote efficient use of resources and actions designed to make the distribution of income more equitable avoids the ". . . confusion of the underlying issues at the planning stage" that would result if the budget were viewed ". . . in consolidated terms from the outset" [10, p. 38] and helps the analyst to sort out the diverse issues with which public finance deals.[1] However, the neoclassical approach adopts the tripartite separation not only because it offers the analyst a useful intellectual framework, but because it also serves as a foundation on which a normative theory of the budget based on the value postulate of consumer sovereignty can be constructed. This, as argued elsewhere [4], raises logical difficulties. This normative theory permits only allocation activities, and even here only the provision of public goods that are not merit wants, to be judged in terms of the Pareto criterion. Its implication is that redistribution and stabilization cannot (or should not?) be consistent with consumer sovereignty.

We believe that this line of reasoning is misleading. It implies that redistribution yields no benefits to the parties who finance it, so that from this viewpoint it imposes a simple deadweight loss. The implication is rather unappealing, to say the least. If accepted, redistribution carried out by government institutions can only be explained as legalized Robin Hood activity, and redistribution through private institutions would seem to imply individual irrationality. While it is plausible to assume that some portion of governmental redistribution simply reflects the political power of the recipients, it is also plausible that part of this redistribution is beneficial to the taxpayers as well as to the recipients. The benefit to the former group would appear to stem from two sources, which

need not be mutually exclusive. One is the preference for security against drastic future income fluctuations, and the second is interdependence among individual utility functions. In the analysis which follows, a model is developed to explain redistribution in terms of this latter source of benefit—interdependent preferences.

Given interdependence among individual utility functions, it is possible that some redistribution will make everyone better off.[2] Efficiency criteria can be applied, therefore, to redistribution of income through the fiscal process.[3] If, for example, the utility of individuals with higher incomes depends upon and is positively related to the incomes of persons lower in the distributive scale, tax-transfer schemes which raise the disposable incomes of those in the poorer group may improve everyone's utility level. Where this is true, as we shall assume, Pareto optimality, contrary to the orthodox approach to public finance, is not only consistent with but requires redistribution. Both allocation and redistribution can be dealt with in terms of the same methodology and the same criterion—efficiency. Then it can be argued that the distributive goal of vertical equity is contained within the Paretian concept of efficiency.

A simple example, involving two persons, will clarify this approach to redistribution. Suppose that Mutt, the taller, has an annual income of $10,000 and Jeff, the shorter, an annual income of $3,000. Suppose, further, that Mutt's utility level varies directly with Jeff's income (i.e., $\partial U_M / \partial Y_J > 0$ where U_M is Mutt's utility and Y_J is Jeff's income). In determining the appropriate extent of redistribution between Mutt and Jeff, the neoclassical approach, as we interpret it, would not focus on this externality. Instead, it would refer to a social welfare function with a capacity for making interpersonal comparisons. This function would be either a social ordering of the Bergson type or a Benthamite cardinal utility calculus that permits judgments about the equity of distributional adjustments to be couched in terms of objective measures of sacrifice. Indeed, this is inherent in its strictly normative interpretation of redistribution. Our approach, in contrast, implies that

[2]Provided this interdependence takes the form of an external economy.
[3]Similar logic can be applied to the stabilization function. Aggregate targets, too, are public goods, and government action can be justified in terms of the "paradox of isolation." We shall, however, say nothing more about stabilization in this paper.

redistributive activities can be justified without a social welfare function that makes interpersonal comparisons, provided that utility interdependence is recognized and taken into account in formulating social policy. If, because increases in Jeff's income affect Mutt's utility favorably, gains from trade through redistribution are possible, and if there is no appropriate private vehicle through which Mutt will donate a portion of his income to Jeff,[4] the establishment of collective institutions through which such an income transfer can be processed may increase the welfare of both parties. Redistribution through the fiscal process is just as necessary for the attainment of Pareto optimality in these circumstances, as the collective provision of conventional public goods.[5]

So much for our rationale.[6] Section I examines the possible patterns of utility interdependence in the two-person case and, for one of these, devises a simple model of Pareto-optimal redistribution. Section II generalizes this model to the N-person case and discusses it in the context of two alternative representations of the size distribution of income. Section III examines the actual pattern of fiscal incidence in the United States, speculates about the conditions under which this pattern might be Pareto optimal, and offers some conjectures as to why actual incidence departs from the hypothetical patterns derived in Section II. Section IV contains some concluding remarks.

---

[4]Voluntary transfers, as within families, would likely occur in the two-person case. In the N-person case, however, individuals, unless coerced, may choose to be "free-riders" and it is the incentive to behave in this way that may be viewed as the raison d'etre of government. Since we are interested, ultimately, in the N-person case, we rule out voluntary transfers in the present two-person example. And when we turn to the N-person case, we assume that the possibility of voluntary redistribution through private charity has been exhausted, thus focusing attention on the incremental redistributive activities carried out under public auspices. For a thorough discussion and analysis of the conditions under which private charity can or will internalize Pareto-relevant interdependence, see David B. Johnson [8].

[5]An alternative way of viewing the problem posed in this paper is in terms of the utility possibility function, a construction frequently employed in welfare economics. The existence of external economies can result in this function having upward sloping portions, positions which cannot be efficient in the Pareto sense. The problem we analyze is one of moving, by means of redistributive transfers, from such an inefficient point to a point where the function no longer slopes upward. See [7, p. 59 ff.] or [13, p. 73 ff].

[6]Since the initial writing of this paper, other research by Becker [2] and Olsen [12] which makes much the same point has come to our attention. Becker's paper, in particular, develops a theoretical apparatus in which the model we use is, in effect, a special case. It deals briefly, in a similar vein, with the fiscal issues on which we focus.

I. PATTERNS OF UTILITY INTERDEPENDENCE AND PARETO OPTIMAL ADJUSTMENTS IN THE TWO-PERSON CASE

It is a fairly simple matter to identify the possible patterns of utility interdependence between two persons with unequal incomes and to select, for further analysis, those which are consistent with realistic distributional adjustments. Consider the utility functions of the two individuals, Mutt and Jeff, who are the only members of our hypothetical community:

$$U_M^0 = f_M(\Upsilon_M^0, \Upsilon_J^0) \tag{1}$$

$$U_J^0 = f_J(\Upsilon_M^0, \Upsilon_J^0), \tag{2}$$

where U_M^0 and Υ_M^0 are the initial values of Mutt's utility index and income, respectively, prior to any redistribution, and U_J^0 and Υ_J^0 are the corresponding values for Jeff. As before, we assume that Mutt has the higher income, i.e., $\Upsilon_M^0 > \Upsilon_J^0$. Interdependence is present because U_M depends on Υ_J and because U_J depends on Υ_M.[7]

Nine possible pairs of marginal interrelationships between the two utility functions can be identified,[8] and these are given by the cells in Table 1.

Most of these cases can be ruled out, so far as rationalizing distributive adjustments is concerned, by making a relatively weak assumption and by imposing certain reasonable restrictions. We assume (a) that both Mutt and Jeff, given prevailing prices of goods and services and the prevailing interest rate, have marginal utilities of income for own-consumption greater than zero (i.e., $\partial U_M/\partial \Upsilon_M$, $\partial U_J/\partial \Upsilon_J > 0$).

---

[7]Of course, variables other than income, e.g., wealth, consumption level, or consumption of particular commodities, could be the source of the interdependence. Income is employed here because it simplifies the analysis.

[8]Situations in which externalities are inframarginal are excluded from our consideration. An inframarginal externality exists when

$$\frac{\partial U^i}{\partial \Upsilon_j} = 0 \text{ and } \int_0^{\Upsilon_i} [\partial U^i/\partial \Upsilon_j] d\Upsilon_i \gtrless 0.$$

In such cases no transfer is appropriate, though one would be if, given the ith person's income and the assumption that the externality is an external economy, the jth person's income were sufficiently smaller than Υ_j. In our two-person example, utility interdependence might not be marginally relevant because Mutt's income is too low for his demand for Jeff's income to have become effective or because the initial difference between Mutt's and Jeff's incomes $(\Upsilon_M^0 - \Upsilon_J^0)$, on which we focus, is less than some critical minimum. In this paper, however, we shall apply no restrictions on either Υ_M^0 or $\Upsilon_M^0 - \Upsilon_J^0$, save the requirement that $\Upsilon_M^0 - \Upsilon_J^0$ exceed zero, in ascertaining whether interdependence is marginally relevant and, therefore, calls for a redistributive transfer. For rigorous definitions of the various types of externalities and their conceptual significance, see J. M. Buchanan and W. C. Stubblebine [5].

We require, in addition, that (b) all transfers be Pareto optimal (i.e., harm neither Mutt nor Jeff) and that (c) all transfers flow from the person with the higher income to the person with the lower income. Therefore, since Y_M exceeds Y_J, only one-way transfers from Mutt to Jeff are permitted. Furthermore, transfers large enough to reverse the initial distributional ordering are not allowed. For the two-person case, therefore, the transfer can be no greater than $(Y_M^0 - Y_J^0)/2$.

Using assumption (a) and restrictions (b) and (c), all interdependence patterns except those in the top row of Table 1 can immediately be eliminated. Cases IV and VII would require a transfer from Jeff to Mutt, violating restriction (c). Case V represents the situation of utility independence, the orthodox neoclassical assumption; a transfer in either direction, given (c), would harm one of the parties, violating (b). This same conclusion holds also for Cases VI, VIII, and IX. There is no possible transfer, in either direction, that would harm neither Mutt nor Jeff.

Hence only Cases I, II and III remain. The externality patterns of Cases II and III are, for purposes of indicating the Pareto optimal pattern of redistribution, one-way patterns, which imply that only Mutt's preferences need be consulted. So long as Jeff's utility is either independent of Mutt's income (Case II) or varies inversely with it (Case III), his utility function can be ignored; in either case, a transfer to Jeff, given (b), is certain to improve his welfare. In Case I, on the other hand, it is not certain that a transfer from Mutt to Jeff will increase Jeff's utility because the reduction in Mutt's disposable income that it implies makes Jeff feel worse. However, for Jeff to be harmed by a transfer from Mutt, his marginal utility of own-consumption $(\partial U_J/\partial Y_J)$ must be more than offset by the external diseconomy generated by the reduction of Mutt's income $(\partial U_J/\partial Y_M)$. Obviously, this is most unlikely, and in the analysis that follows, we assume that $(\partial U_J/\partial Y_J > \partial U_J/\partial Y_M)$, so that any transfer that Jeff receives, benefits him. It makes no difference, therefore, which of the three interdependence patterns in the top row of Table 1 is assumed. In all of them, transfers, given consumer sovereignty, are entirely a matter of Mutt's volition, and the process of determining a Pareto optimal redistributive transfer can concentrate on his preferences alone.

Hypothetical Patterns of Pareto Optimal Transfers

Suppose, now, that an increase in Y_J (as in Case II) augments Mutt's utility. How large a transfer will Mutt desire to make to Jeff? To answer this question, consider Fig. 1, which is concerned with Mutt's choice of how much of his income to retain for himself and how much to transfer to Jeff. This choice will obviously depend both on Y_M^0 and Y_J^0. We assume, largely because it facilitates our examination

Table 1. Possible patterns of utility interdependence

$\partial U_M/\partial Y_J$ (Evaluated at Y_M^0, Y_J^0)	Jeff / Mutt	>0	$=0$	<0
	>0	I	II	III
	$=0$	IV	V	VI
	<0	VII	VIII	IX

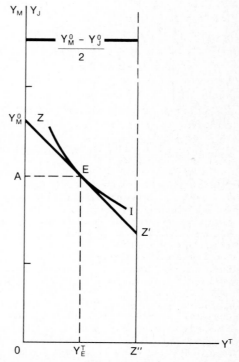

0Z: INITIAL INCOME DIFFERENTIAL, $Y_M^0 - Y_J^0$
Y^T: TRANSFER TO JEFF

Fig. 1

of redistribution in the N-person case, that the size of the transfer depends upon the differential $\Upsilon_M^0 - \Upsilon_J^0$, rather than, among other specifications, either the absolute levels of Υ_M^0 and Υ_J^0 or the initial ratio, $\Upsilon_M^0/\Upsilon_J^0$. Thus the ordinate of Fig. 1 measures the excess of Υ_M^0 over Υ_J^0, and the abscissa measures transfers from Mutt to Jeff, Υ^T. The situation in which $\Upsilon_M^0 = \Upsilon_J^0$ is represented by the origin of Fig. 1. (It is labeled "0" because this is where the differential is zero and where the transfer size is zero, not because Jeff's initial income Υ_J^0 is 0.) The terms on which Mutt is able to exchange own-consumption for increments in Jeff's income is given by the slope of $ZZ'Z''$, Mutt's opportunity locus or "budget line." The budget line becomes vertical at Z' because of the restriction that Υ^T must not be so large as to reverse the distributional ordering. The slope of the ZZ' segment is -1, since a given size transfer to Jeff reduces the amount of income that Mutt retains for his own use by the same amount. I is one of Mutt's (convex) indifference curves containing points which indicate the terms at which Mutt is willing to exchange own-consumption for increments in Υ_J.[9] The positive dependence of U_M on Υ_J is reflected by the negative slope; if U_M did not depend on Υ_J, Mutt's indifference map would simply consist of a set of horizontal lines. If the initial incomes are given by Υ_M^0 and Υ_J^0, so that the initial differential is equal to $0Z$, transfers to Jeff of any amount up to Υ_E^T raise Mutt's utility level and a transfer of Υ_E^T allows Mutt to attain equilibrium at E, where the marginal utility of a dollar of own-consumption equals the marginal utility of a one dollar increment in Jeff's income. Thus, point E, by definition, is a Pareto optimum.[10],[11]

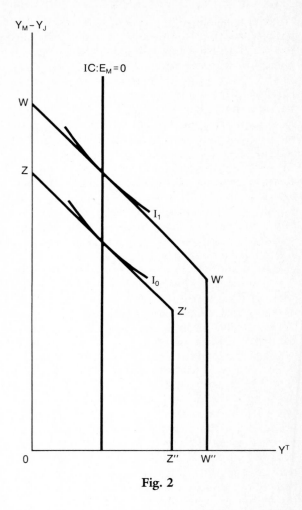

Fig. 2

[9]Because both axes in Fig. 1 are measured in terms of units of the numeraire, the only feasible points for Mutt lie on the budget line itself. With no transactions or administration cost and no charitable deductions to reduce Mutt's tax obligations, a dollar increase in Υ^T implies a dollar decrease in Mutt's income for own-use.

[10]There are transfers greater than Υ_E^T that would reduce Mutt's utility relative to the level implied by I but would leave him better off than he would have been in the absence of any transfer at all, i.e., on the indifference curve (not represented in Fig. 1) that cuts the ordinate at Z.

[11]Note, however, that although the presence of an external economy is a necessary condition for Pareto-optimal transfers, it is not a sufficient condition. If the slope of Mutt's indifference curves were everywhere less than unity in absolute value, he would regard the price of any income transfer, in terms of own-consumption foregone, as excessive. In this situation, there is no transfer to Jeff, either voluntary or coerced, that would be Pareto-optimal.

Similarly, concave indifference curves (not represented in Fig. 1) would also imply a corner solution at Z or an equilibrium at Z', the

Having provided an analysis to determine the size of the transfer that Mutt desires to make to Jeff for a given income differential, the next step is to determine how this amount varies with the differential, so that the structure of a Pareto optimal, explicitly redistributive tax-transfer system can be ascertained.

How should the tax on Mutt vary with the income differential? (1) Should it be a constant amount or fixed sum, or should it vary as the initial income differential $\Upsilon_M^0 - \Upsilon_J^0$ $(=0Z)$ varies? If the latter, should it increase (2) in proportion to $0Z$ or (3) less than proportionately? Or should it vary (4) inversely

kink in the budget line. Whether the equilibrium, in this case, would be at Z (implying that no transfer is Pareto optimal) or at Z' (implying that income equality is required for Pareto optimality) would depend on the precise shapes of the concave indifference loci.

with the differential? The answer, in the two-person model, depends on the elasticity, with respect to $Y_M - Y_J$, of Mutt's demand for increments in Jeff's income, which we shall refer to as Mutt's transfer-elasticity and denote as E_M.[12] Figs. 2 through 5 illustrate these four cases. Changes in the size of the initial differential, $0Z$, produce parallel shifts of the budget line, which generate a locus of equilibrium positions. E_M, in these diagrams, is the elasticity of this locus, the income-differential consumption (IC) line.[13] The IC lines in Figs. 2 through 5 require the particular tax-transfer patterns indicated in the four questions posed above, assuming that the equilibria are always to the left of Z'. If, for example, $E_M = 0$, a fixed sum transfer is Pareto optimal; if $E_M = 1$, the optimal transfer increases in proportion to $0Z$.

II. PARETO OPTIMAL ADJUSTMENTS IN THE N-PERSON CASE
The N-Person Model

Must a Pareto-optimal structure of redistributive taxes be progressive, proportional, or regressive?

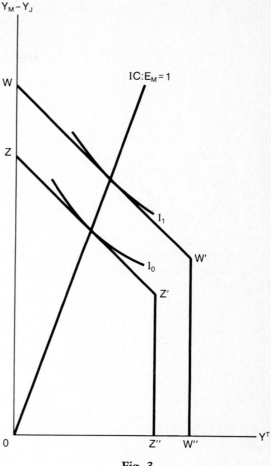

Fig. 3

[12]Transfer-elasticity differs only slightly from the more familiar income-elasticity of demand. Income-elasticity would measure the responsiveness of Mutt's demand for transfers to Jeff to changes in Y_M itself. Transfer-elasticity, on the other hand, measures its responsiveness to changes in $0Z = Y_M^0 - Y_J^0$, the initial differential, regardless of whether these are due to a change in Y_M^0 with Y_J^0 constant, a change in Y_J^0 with Y_M^0 constant, or changes in both Y_M^0 and Y_J^0.

The transfer-elasticity concept, indeed our use of $Y_M^0 - Y_J^0$ as the key variable, is clearly a simplification of reality. Our choice of the specific form that this formulation implies to attach to the utility functions specified earlier in general terms is based on intuition and convenience. To look at Fig. 1 as a subset of Y_M, Y_J space with the axes shifted by the amount of Y_J^0 would yield a more general analysis, but one which would be much less manageable than ours, which is general enough to enable us to make the points in which we are interested. Our argument is illustrative rather than definitive, and adoption of the differential as the crucial variable simplifies the illustrations in the N-person case of Section II, by allowing us to abstract from absolute levels of income in our calculations.

However, the implications of this simplification should be pointed out. Under our assumption, equal absolute increases in Mutt's and Jeff's incomes would leave the optimal transfer to Jeff unchanged. Nor does the response to a change in the differential depend on the starting income levels. If, instead, the optimal transfer were an increasing function of, say, the ratio of Y_M to Y_J, rather than the difference between them, it would decrease if Y_M and Y_J increased by the same absolute amount.

[13]The IC line is analogous to the income-consumption line. The difference is that $Y_M^0 - Y_J^0$ is variable here, whereas Y_M varies in the case of the income-consumption line. Because of the choice of axes on which to measure the transfer and initial differential, E_M varies inversely with the absolute slope of IC.

What pattern of fiscal residuals does such a tax structure imply? Answers to such questions require that our analysis be extended to the N-Person case.

We assume an institutional setting in which free-riding, i.e., strategic behavior, is precluded so that the political mechanism through which interdependence is internalized accurately reflects the distributional preferences of individuals in this regard. To secure the gains from trade that are possible because of interdependence, individuals choose to compel themselves to make redistributive transfers, just as they compel themselves to pay taxes to finance the provision of other collective goods. As in the two-person case, it is assumed that the tax transfer process does not change the initial distributional ordering, so that relative positions in the income scale are unaffected. It is assumed, further, that individuals have

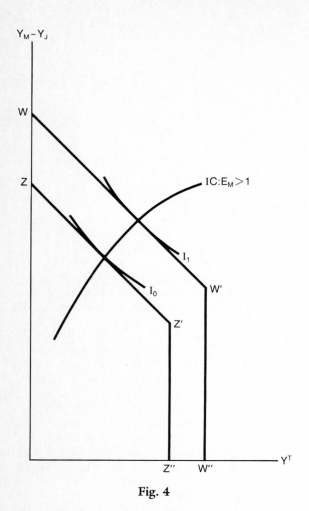

Fig. 4

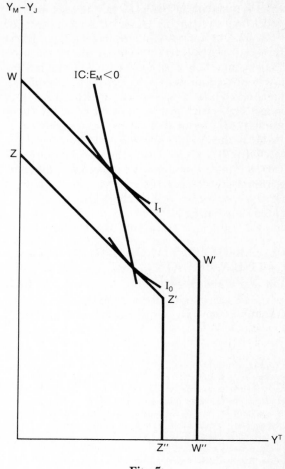

Fig. 5

identical tastes[14] (so that all would exhibit the same consumption patterns at any given income level), and that income taxation produces no incentive effects or excess burden (i.e., the supply of labor or demand for leisure are perfectly inelastic).

[14]Obviously, this assumption is unrealistic. Any real-world blanket redistributive tax would, of course, deviate from Pareto optimality not only because of differing transfer elasticities on the part of different individuals (Mutts) whose preferences exhibit row 1, Table 1 interdependence, but also because the preferences of some Mutts are characterized by row 2 or row 3. It does not follow from this, however, that interpersonal utility comparisons, in terms of a crude cardinal utility calculus or a more refined social welfare function, are needed to justify all redistribution. But it does raise the question of what governmental unit should intermediate redistributive transfers, and more broadly, of the optimal redistributive areas in a fiscal federalism, a question analogous in some respects to that of determining optimum currency areas in the theory of international trade.

Only two of the *IC* configurations are considered, the cases in which $E_M = 0$ (implying that Pareto optimality requires fixed-sum transfers) and $E_M = 1$ (implying that transfers proportional to $(Y_M^0 - Y_J^0)$ are optimal). It is assumed that each individual (1) makes a transfer to (permits himself to be taxed on behalf of) every person with a lower income (in a lower income bracket) and (2) receives a transfer from each individual with a higher income. Except for those in the lowest and highest income brackets, then, all individuals pay some redistributive taxes (are in Mutt's status relative to some persons) and receive some redistributive transfers (are in Jeff's status relative to others). Each individual's net outcome is the algebraic sum of the outcomes in the pairwise equilibrium relationships that emerge with all persons who have initial incomes different from his. Thus, in the N-Person model, Pareto optimal tax payments and transfers received depend on both E_M's (one's own and others) *and* the shape of the size distribution of income. E_M and $(\Upsilon_M^0 - \Upsilon_J^0)$ determine the Pareto-optimal transfer between each pair of individuals. One's position in the income scale determines the number of persons to whom he will make transfers and the number from whom he will receive them. Each individual's aggregate tax payments (summed over all Jeffs), transfer receipts (summed over all Mutts), and fiscal residual (receipts minus payments) depend, therefore, on both considerations.[15,16]

Pareto-Optimal Patterns of Redistribution

Pareto-optimal distributional adjustments are derived for two distributional settings, a rectangular distribution *(D_r)* and a summary representation of the actual income distribution in the U.S. in 1960 *(D_a)*. This is done twice for each distribution; once on the assumption that the E_M's of all N individuals are zero and once assuming that the E_M's are unity. Results in the four cases examined are summarized in the tables indicated in Table 2.

D_r, which is a useful benchmark case, is described numerically in the first two columns of Tables 3 and 4. It is a simple rectangular distribution for a community of five persons and contains five income classes of identical width. Each class contains one

Table 2. Pareto optimal redistributions classified by transfer elasticity and income distribution

Transfer-Elasticity	E_M	D / D_r	D_a
	$E_M = 0$	Table 3	Table 5
	$E_M = 1$	Table 4	Table 6

Income distributions

individual having an income equal to the mean of the class limits.

D_a, the second distribution, is described in the first two columns of Tables 5 and 6. It is the summary distribution, for the U.S. in 1960, which Gillespie [6] used in reporting his estimates of fiscal incidence in the U.S. (discussed in Section III). In using D_a, we assume, for convenience, that the community contains one hundred individuals or families, an assumption that permits us to use relative frequencies instead of the absolute distribution in our analysis. D_a contains seven income classes of varying width, with an open-ended class ($10,000 and over) at the top. Within income classes, families are treated as if they were identical in size. All incomes in the five intermediate classes are assumed to be equal to the mean of the class limits, referred to in the tables as the "representative class income."[17] To specify representative class incomes for the "under $2,000" and "$10,000 and over" classes, a linkage procedure was used, producing estimates of $800 for the first bracket (under $2,000) and $15,000 for the top bracket ($10,000 and over).[18]

Let us consider D_r. If E_M is zero for all individuals making transfers, the Pareto optimal tax structure is

---

[15]Our efforts to identify the incidence of Pareto optimal redistributive adjustments under different assumptions about E_M should not be confused with the problem of determining the appropriate incidence of the overall tax structure. We assume that the costs of allocative activities are distributed on a benefit basis, before redistribution is contemplated at all, and, therefore, deal only with the marginal incidence of distributional adjustments, ignoring the feedbacks of redistribution that might confound this prior application of the benefit principle. An overall Pareto optimum is, obviously, a matter of transfer-elasticity (or some analogous measure of distributional preferences) and these income-elasticities. Hence, we are implicitly assuming away any changes in evaluations of conventional public goods that the Pareto optimal transfers might bring about. Another way of putting the matter is to say that we are assuming that individuals, in choosing their consumption mixes, fully anticipate the transfers they are to receive.

[16]N, the absolute size of the community, is of no significance in our calculations. We can either assume that N is constant or that the fiscal residuals of individuals are unaltered, if it changes. This assumption requires that (1) changes in N are spread proportionately among all income classes, preserving the relative distribution; (2) the levies on individual Mutts are varied in inverse proportion to the number of Jeffs concerned; and (3) administration of the tax-transfer process is subject to constant returns to scale.

[17]This simplifies our calculations and assures that modest redistributive adjustments cannot reverse the distributional ordering.
[18]We calculated the total income received by each unit of one percent of all families in the two bottom and two top income brackets in D_a from Gillespie's distribution of aggregate income by size class [6, p. 174, Table 13, line 1]. We then computed the ratios of these figures for the two bottom brackets (.32) and the two top brackets (1.77). Our estimate of average income in the bottom bracket ($800) was derived by multiplying the representative class income of $2,500 in the second ($2,000 to $2,999) bracket by .32 and rounding the product to the nearest $100. Our estimate of average income in the top bracket ($15,000) was obtained by multiplying the representative class income of $8,750 in the $7,500 to $9,999 bracket by 1.77 and rounding.

Table 3. Pareto optimal redistributions
Rectangular income distribution (D_r) : Transfer-elasticity $(E_M) = 0$

		Fixed-sum transfers of $100			Tax structure	
Income	Number of individuals	Tax paid ($)	Transfer received ($)	Pareto optimal fiscal incidence ($)	Marginal rate	Average rate
1,000	1	—	400	$\div 400$	—	—
2,000	1	100	300	$\div 200$	.10	.050
3,000	1	200	200	0	.10	.067
4,000	1	300	100	-200	.10	.075
5,000	1	400	—	-400	.10	.080

Table 4. Pareto optimal redistributions
Rectangular income distribution (D_r) : Transfer-elasticity $(E_M) = 1$

		Transfer 5 percent of income differential			Tax structure	
Income	Number of individuals	Tax paid ($)	Differential transfer received ($)	Pareto optimal fiscal incidence ($)	Marginal rate	Average rate
1,000	1	—	500	$\div 500$	—	—
2,000	1	50	300	$\div 250$	.05	.025
3,000	1	150	150	0	.10	.050
4,000	1	300	50	-250	.15	.075
5,000	1	500	—	-500	.20	.100

Table 5. Pareto optimal redistributions
Accrual income distribution (D_a) : Transfer-elasticity $(E_M) = 0$

		Fixed-sum transfer of $5			Tax structure	
Representative class income[a]	Percent of families[b]	Tax paid ($)	Transfer received ($)	Pareto optimal fiscal incidence ($)	Marginal rate	Average rate
800	14	—	430	$\div 430$	—	—
2,500	9	70	385	$\div 315$	.042	.028
3,500	9	115	340	$\div 225$	.045	.033
4,500	11	160	285	$\div 125$	.045	.036
6,250	28	215	145	-70	.032	.034
8,750	15	355	70	-285	.056	.040
15,500	14	430	—	-430	.011	.028

[a]Class mid-points for all but bottom and top brackets. Procedure for obtaining "representative class incomes" for bottom and top brackets is discussed in fn. 18.
[b]Implies a community consisting of 100 families or individuals.

Table 6. Pareto optimal redistributions
Actual income distribution (D_a) : Transfer-elasticity $(E_M) = 1$

Representative class income	Percent of families	Transfer 0.1 percent of income differential (k = .001)			Tax structure	
		Tax paid ($)	Transfer received ($)	Pareto optimal fiscal incidence ($)	Marginal rate	Average rate
800	14	—	553	÷558	—	—
2,500	9	24	412	÷388	.014	.010
3,500	9	47	335	÷288	.023	.013
4,500	11	79	267	÷188	.032	.018
6,250	28	154	167	÷ 13	.043	.025
8,750	15	333	94	−239	.072	.038
15,500	14	914	—	−913	.086	.059

degressive, as Table 3 indicates. In our example, each of the five persons in the community, one at each income level, transfers $100 to each individual in a lower bracket. Thus, the individual with an income of $1,000 is exempt, while those with higher incomes are taxed at a constant marginal rate of 10 percent. The average rate increases, monotonically, from zero to 8 percent, and the Pareto-optimal fiscal residuals (distributional transfers received less taxes paid, after accounting for conventional public goods on a benefit basis) are symmetrical, by virtue of D_r's symmetry.

This outcome suggests that Pareto optimality requires more progressivity if, with a rectangular distribution, $E_M > 0$. This conclusion, with its implication that progressive taxation can be justified without interpersonal utility comparisons, is illustrated by Table 4, which summarizes the outcomes for the case in which all E_M's are unity. In this case the implied marginal rates of tax rise from zero to 20 percent. In our example, the factor of proportionality, k, is assumed to be .05, making the implied transfer between any pair of individuals in different income brackets .05 $(\Upsilon_M^0 - \Upsilon_J^0)$.

The results can be recast in terms of the IC lines of Figs. 2 and 3. In Fig. 2, $E_M = 0$ and Pareto optimality requires a degressive tax (degressivity). In Fig. 3, $E_M = 1$, and the IC line has a zero intercept and a slope equal to the reciprocal of k. In this case, the Pareto-optimal tax structure is clearly more progressive than it is with a vertical IC line; and, in

general, implied progressivity is greater, the smaller the slope of the IC line.

The outcomes with D_r tell us something about the incidence of Pareto optimal redistributive adjustments in the context of any distribution in which frequencies vary monotonically with income. With declining frequencies, the ratio of Jeffs (to whom transfers must be made) to Mutts (from whom transfers are received) increases more rapidly with income than it does with a rectangular distribution. Thus, if E_M is the same for all individuals, the Pareto optimal tax structure is necessarily more progressive than it is with D_r. In the unlikely case in which frequencies increase with income, the converse would hold true.

We turn now to D_a. (See Tables 5 and 6.)[19] Unlike D_r, which is symmetrical, D_a is skewed to the right.[20] Where $E_M = 0$, the implication of this asymmetry is that the structure of Pareto-optimal taxes is not uniformly progressive throughout the distribution. With "fixed-sum" transfers of $5 (Table 5) this tax structure is progressive up to, but not including, the modal income bracket ($5,000–$7,499); in this

[19]The size of the fixed-sum transfer (for Table 5) and the value of k (for the computations underlying Table 6) make no difference in the shape of the pattern of residuals and are thus analytically irrelevant. The values used in our computations were chosen for their convenience, to facilitate subsequent comparisons of our hypothetical residuals and the actual residuals reported by Gillespie.

[20]Columns (1) and (2) of Tables 5 and 6 show 71 percent of all families with incomes under $7,499, which is less than half the assumed midpoint of the top bracket, $15,500.

bracket the marginal tax rate decreases from 4.5 to 3.2 percent. This decline in the marginal rate occurs because the percentage change in "representative class income" between the fourth and fifth income brackets exceeds the percentage change in the number of individuals entitled to receive transfers. After this decline, the marginal rate increases to 5.6 percent in the sixth bracket ($7,500–$9,999) and then declines again to 1.1 percent in the "$10,000 and over" class.

When optimal incidence patterns are derived for D_a under the assumption that $E_M = 1$ (see Table 6) this complex rate structure is not obtained. The Pareto optimal tax structure is, rather, uniformly progressive. With k, the factor of proportionality, equal to .001, marginal rates of tax rise from 1.4 percent in the first bracket ($2,000–$2,999) to 8.6 percent for families with incomes of "$10,000 and over."

These examples have demonstrated a means of determining Pareto optimal redistributive adjustments, albeit under highly restrictive assumptions and only for certain special cases.[21] The structure of the Pareto optimal redistributive taxes, whether progressive, proportional, regressive, or lacking uniformity, depends on the values of the transfer-elasticities and the shape of the initially existing distribution of income, as determined by initial endowments and the operation of the market economy.

[21]We have considered only two values of the transfer-elasticities and two income distributions, and have assumed identical utility maps. While the analysis could be generalized by a mathematical formulation, there seemed to us to be virtue in simplicity.

III. ACTUAL INCIDENCE AND PARETO OPTIMAL REDISTRIBUTION

Granting all of the other assumptions we have made, under what assumptions about utility interdependence would the actual fiscal structure be Pareto optimal? To answer this question, among others, Table 7 compares the Pareto optimal fiscal residuals computed in Section II, for D_r, with one of the sets of residuals estimated by Gillespie [6, p. 162, Table 11]. Columns (1) and (2) of Table 7 describe D_a. Column (3), which reports the actual residuals, is derived from Gillespie's estimates of the consolidated fiscal incidence of federal, state, and local taxes and expenditures in the U.S. for 1960.[22] To obtain the figures in Column (3), we multiplied Gillespie's estimates of fiscal incidence in each income bracket,

[22]Needless to say, Gillespie faced many difficult problems, requiring essentially arbitrary choices, in compiling these estimates. One such problem was that of choosing an income base. The base for which the estimates in Column (3) of Table 5 are derived is adjusted broad income, money income adjusted for transfers, government expenditures, and taxes. Other problems included (1) distribution of the burdens of specific taxes, (2) imputation of the benefits of specific expenditures to beneficiary groups, and (3) distribution of these beneficiary groups among income classes. For taxes, Gillespie could use published material, e.g., Musgrave's study [11]. For expenditures, he had less to go on in the way of prior research. Since demand prices for public goods are not revealed, the only practicable alternative was to allocate benefits on the basis of some measure of cost undertaken on behalf of individuals. Perhaps the most intractable problem was the distribution of general (nonallocable) expenditures, e.g., national defense, among individuals and income groups. In Table 11 [6, p. 126], which we used as our source of Column (3), such expenditures are distributed on an income (rather than, say, on a per capita) basis.

Table 7. Comparison of fiscal incidence under alternative tax-transfer assumptions

(1) Representative class income ($)	(2) Percent of families	(3) U.S. fiscal structure, 1960 [a]	(4) $E_M = 0$ Fixed-sum transfers of $5 [b]	(5) $E_M = 1$ Transfer 0.1 percent of income differential ($) [a]
800	14	+ 441	+430	+558
2,500	9	+1,110	+315	+388
3,500	9	+ 648	+225	+288
4,500	11	− 58	+125	+188
6,250	28	− 131	− 70	− 13
8,750	15	+ 148	−285	−239
15,500	14	−2,046	−430	−913

[a]U.S. Fiscal Structure, 1960: Gillespie [6, p. 162, Table 11, line 11]. Reported figures are the product of "representative class incomes" and effective rate (expenditure benefits and transfers received minus taxes paid) of fiscal incidence.
[b]Table 5.
[c]Table 6.

which he reported in proportional terms, by the "representative class income." Thus Column (3) indicates, in absolute terms, the fiscal residuals (benefits of expenditures and transfers received, less taxes paid) which accrued to average individuals in each bracket. For comparison we report, in Columns (4) and (5), the Pareto optimal fiscal residuals with D_a in the "fixed-sum" ($E_M = 0$) and "proportional transfer" ($E_M = 1$) cases of Tables 5 and 6, respectively.[23]

Both of the hypothetical patterns of residuals, Columns (4) and (5), vary inversely with income. The real-world residuals in Column (3), however, do not fully conform with this pattern. The most obvious differences between the actual and hypothetical residuals occur in the first, second, and sixth income brackets. Instead of decreasing between the first and second brackets, the fiscal residual actually increases, almost in proportion to income, i.e., from \$441 to \$1,110. Furthermore, in the "\$7,500–\$9,999" bracket, the fiscal residual is positive, not negative. In terms of the absolute deviation from either of the hypothetical residuals (for $E_M = 0$ or 1), the first of these aberrations is more significant,[24] especially when compared to the level of income in the bracket in which it occurs. We choose, consequently, to ignore the aberration in the sixth bracket and discuss only the one in the second.

The fact that the fiscal process seems to subsidize the 14 percent of all families in the "under \$2,000" bracket less heavily than the 9 percent in the \$2,000–\$2,999 bracket does not coincide with our hypothetical computations in which the Pareto optimal residuals decrease monotonically as income increases.

It is worthwhile to explore alternative explanations of this outcome.

One possibility is that the first bracket may well consist, to a greater extent than those just above it, of rural poor. In rural areas, communities are smaller and social pressure to interact is consequently greater. Payment of income in kind is likely to be more common, and simple bilateral or multilateral transfers through private charity are more likely to be feasible, reducing dependence on the fiscal process as a redistributive mechanism. In urban areas social conditions may not fit this model as well. Urban poverty, moreover, is readily apparent to more individuals with relatively high incomes, and general interdependence among individuals in different income groups is by virtue of proximity even more pronounced. Fiscal machinery is more likely to enjoy a clear advantage as the mechanism of redistribution, because the social group is large and private arrangements that can overcome "free rider" behavior to the degree required are more difficult to devise.

A second, less benign, explanation is that those who are really poor, i.e., families with incomes under \$2,000, may be almost devoid of political power. Their welfare counts for less than that of individuals with higher incomes in the calculations of politicians, just as their preferences count for less in the market sector. This argument, implying that political power and effective demand go hand in hand, may be extended to a hypothesis that the actual fiscal structure reflects a coalition among middle income groups, that is, among families whose incomes lie between the bottom and top brackets. It should be noted, however, that this hypothesis is diametrically opposed to the notion that the actual fiscal structure comes at all close to being Pareto optimal; for, if it were Pareto optimal, families in the top bracket would, by definition, prefer the disproportionate tax burden they now bear, according to Gillespie's estimates, at least to a situation without redistribution, so no such coalition would be necessary.

A third, less provocative, though possibly more realistic explanation might attribute the apparent plight of the "under \$2,000" group to quirks in the statistical procedures underlying Gillespie's estimates and our own calculations. Many difficulties are encountered in imputing the burdens of taxation and the benefits of expenditures. Thus, the increase in residuals between the first and second brackets might, at least to some degree, be attributed to such

[23]The appropriate interpretation of Column (3) differs slightly from that of Columns (4) and (5). The latter indicate the net gain or loss, in strictly monetary (i.e., not welfare) terms, that would accrue to each individual from a Pareto optimal redistributive process. In addition to redistributive adjustments, the figures in Column (3) include imputations of the aggregate benefits accruing to individuals from public goods, minus the taxes paid to obtain these benefits. From our viewpoint, however, this difference in interpretation is of little importance. This may be seen by assuming (as we have) that the political mechanism, in providing public goods, accurately reflects individual preferences, and that both redistribution in kind and in money terms are consistent with such preferences, in the same sense in which monetary transfers alone internalize the general externalities taken into account in our simpler model.

[24]For example, in the second bracket the deviation of the actual residual from the computed residual in Column (5) is \$1,110–\$388; relating this deviation to income in the second bracket, we obtain (\$1,110–\$388)/\$2,500 = .31. This proportional deviation is much greater than that in the sixth bracket: (\$148–\$239)/\$8,750 = 0.04.

factors as the imputation of the benefits of general expenditures, e.g., national defense, on an income-related rather than per capita basis.

Despite aberrations and ambiguity, it is interesting to ask, "If the actual residuals in Table 7 are Pareto optimal, what are the implied patterns of utility interdependence?" If we suppose that the actual residuals reflect the exact amount of redistribution required to internalize such interdependence, so that the actual fiscal structure is by implication, Pareto optimal, we can infer something about the values of transfer-elasticities at various income levels and the shapes of individuals' IC lines. In general, the residuals with $E_M = 1$, the "proportional transfer case," seem to be better correlated with the actual pattern of incidence than the residuals in the "fixed-sum" case ($E_M = 0$). This is particularly clear in the top income bracket, which seem, according to Column (3), to finance the lion's share of any redistribution that actually occurs.[25] Residuals in the second through the seventh brackets, taken as a group, suggest that individuals in high brackets have larger transfer-elasticities than those in lower brackets; thus, instead of remaining constant, as Column (5) assumes, E_M appears to increase with income.[26] Furthermore, since the middle income groups (brackets four through six) seem, more or less, to break even in the fiscal process, it would appear that utility interdependence increases in significance as income increases and becomes really significant only when income reaches a level of $10,000 or more.[27] In terms of the diagrams, this suggests that the IC line coincides with the ordinate (and has a slope equal to or only slightly different from infinity) until the income differential begins to exceed, say, $6,000–$8,000. At this point its slope becomes finite (E_M begins to exceed zero). Thereafter, as $0Z = (\Upsilon_M^0 - \Upsilon_J^0)$ increases, E_M increases and the IC line, as in Fig. 4, bends downward to the right. Thus, to return to our general example,

where individuals are in Mutt's status, the income or consumption levels of those with Jeff's status appear to be normal goods. Stated a bit differently, the general implication is that the ratio of the marginal utility of own-consumption to the marginal utility of others' consumption declines over the income range considered.

IV. CONCLUSION

In trying to reconcile income redistribution (e.g., through a negative income tax) with consumer sovereignty and an individualistic interpretation of the fiscal and political processes, we have experimented with alternative hypotheses about utility interdependence. In the presence of such interdependence, Pareto optimality may not only be consistent with redistribution, but may require it. If so, the necessary fiscal adjustments depend on the implicit transfer-elasticities and the shape of the size distribution of income.

Pursuing this line of thought, we have calculated, for several situations, the patterns of tax burdens, transfers, and fiscal incidence that would be Pareto optimal. We have also tried to determine the type of utility interdependence that is implied by the actual fiscal residuals prevailing in the U.S. in 1960, on the assumption that those residuals were Pareto optimal.

An important implication of our analysis is the finding that the case for progressive taxation, aimed at redistributing income, may be far less "uneasy"[28] than most of us have come to believe. Quite to the contrary, progressive taxation, for explicit redistributive purposes, may be fully consistent with the Pareto criterion under quite reasonable conceptual assumptions. Progressivity, given such assumptions, may be interpreted as a matter of revealed preference, which does not require interpersonal utility comparisons for its justification. Whether these assumptions are empirically valid is, of course, another question, but one that should yield to empirical investigation.

All this does not pretend to claim that fiscal reality does not deviate from the requirements of Pareto optimality. It does. But the fact that it does may be

---

[25]Thus, so far as vertical equity is concerned, our observations suggest that typical discussions of the U.S. fiscal structure might overstate the normative significance of erosion of the tax base.

[26]Except for the minor lapse in the $7,500–$9,999 class.

[27]If, however, the actual residuals are not Pareto optimal, an alternative explanation of the disproportionate fiscal burden on the $10,000 and over group is required. The obvious alternative, that this burden reflects political weakness, controverts the generally held belief in the correlation of political and economic power. Our analysis, unfortunately, provides neither an answer to this riddle nor a criterion for choosing between such polar explanations of observed fiscal incidence.

[28]Blum and Kalven [3] is the classic discussion of progression. Their treatment, which examines progression as traditionally justified in terms of sacrifice and interpersonal comparisons, reinforced the pre-existing skepticism of the profession.

a technical matter and not a conceptual necessity. Departures of the actual fiscal structure from the Pareto ideal may simply reflect an operational inability to correctly juxtapose individual preferences and fiscal incidence. We are suggesting, therefore, that if more could be learned about utility interdependence through empirical investigation of private and public choice patterns and processes, it might turn out to be possible to utilize this information to achieve a fiscal structure more in accord with the individualist ethic that underlies the economist's model of resource allocation.

Of course, one might personally feel that the amount of redistribution dictated by the Pareto criterion will not be "enough." We are not saying that society should necessarily follow only the Pareto rule. It is possible, however, to develop a theory of redistribution based on such a rule, and considerable redistribution might be indicated if it were operationally possible to devise a fiscal structure consistent with this criterion.

REFERENCES

1. F. M. Bator, "The Simple Analytics of Welfare Maximization," *Amer. Econ. Rev.*, Mar. 1957. *47*, 22–59.
2. G. S. Becker, "Independent Preferences: Charity, Externalities and Income Taxation." Unpublished manuscript, Mar. 1968.
3. W. J. Blum and H. Kalven, Jr., *The Uneasy Case for Progressive Taxation*. Chicago 1953.
4. J. M. Buchanan, "The Theory of Public Finance," *Southern Econ. J.* Jan. 1960, *26*, 234–38.
5. —————, and W. C. Stubblebine, "Externality," *Economica*, Nov. 1962, *29*, 371–84.
6. W. I. Gillespie, "Effect of Public Expenditures on the Distribution of Income," in R. A. Musgrave, ed., *Essays in Fiscal Federalism*, Washington 1965, pp. 122–86.
7. J. de V. Graaff, *Theoretical Welfare Economics*, New York 1957.
8. D. B. Johnson, "The Fundamental Economics of the Charity Market." Unpublished doctoral dissertation, Univ. Virginia, 1968.
9. E. J. Mishan, "A Survey of Welfare Economics, 1939–59," *Econ. J.*, June 1960, *70*, 197–256.
10. R. A. Musgrave, *The Theory of Public Finance*. New York 1959.
11. —————— et al, "Distribution of Tax Payments by Income Groups: A Case Study for 1948," *Nat. Tax J.*, Mar. 1951, *4*, 1–53.
12. E. O. Olsen, "A Normative Theory of Transfers," *Public Choice*, spring 1969, *6*, 39–58.
13. J. Rothenberg, *The Measurement of Social Welfare*. Englewood Cliffs, 1961.